The
LESBIAN AND GAY
STUDIES READER

The LESBIAN AND GAY STUDIES READER

EDITED BY
HENRY ABELOVE
MICHÈLE AINA BARALE
DAVID M. HALPERIN

Routledge
New York London

Published in 1993 by

Routledge
29 West 35 Street
New York, NY 10001

Published in Great Britain by

Routledge
11 New Fetter Lane
London EC4P 4EE

Library of Congress Cataloging-in-Publication Data

The Lesbian and gay studies reader / edited by Henry Abelove, Michèle
  Aina Barale, David M. Halperin.
      p. cm.
    Includes bibliographical references.
    ISBN 0-415-90518-4(HB) — ISBN 0-415-90519-2(PB)
    1. Gays. 2. Homosexuality. I. Abelove, Henry. II. Barale,
  Michèle Aina. III. Halperin, David M., 1952–
  HQ76.25.L48   1993
  305.9′0664—dc20   93-16231
                                                                 CIP

British Library Cataloging-in-Publication Data also available.

Contents

Acknowledgments

Many friends and colleagues have helped us in our work on *The Lesbian and Gay Studies Reader*, and we are grateful to them all. We hope that the following list, inevitably incomplete because of the shortcomings of the editors' collective memory, includes most of them: Janaki Bakhle, Karen Bock, David A. Braaten, George Chauncey, Jr., Jason Dewees, Carolyn Dinshaw, Ann duCille, Lowell Durham and the staff and fellows of the University of Utah Humanities Center, Jeffrey Escoffier, Judith Frank, The Gay/Lesbian/Bisexual Alliance of Wesleyan University, William P. Germano, Herbert Green, Jr., Anne Ha, Gilbert Herdt, Margaret Hunt, Earl Jackson, Jr., Wayne Koestenbaum, the Lesbian/Gay Studies Faculty Discussion Group at the University of Utah, Joseph Litvak, Mel McCombie, Paul Morrison, Alfredo Monferré, Andrew Parker, Gregory M. Pflugfelder, Joe Powers, Queer Nation/Salt Lake City, Lisa B. Rofel, David Román, Dean Ronald C. Rosbottom of Amherst College, Ben. Sifuentes Jáuregui, Robert Schwartzwald, Nikhil Pal Singh, Rachel Toor, Clarence Walker, Julia Willis, and above all the authors who have agreed to our gathering and publishing their work here.

Copyright Information

Introduction

The forty-two essays gathered here constitute what we take to be some of the best and most significant recent English-language work in the field of lesbian/gay studies. They are derived from a wide variety of disciplines—philosophy, classics, history, anthropology, sociology, African-American studies, ethnic studies, literary studies, and cultural studies. They produce and engage many different kinds of knowledge and meaning; they suggest many different topics and subjects for further inquiry; they demonstrate the cogency of many different methods, theories, styles, and approaches; and taken together, they transform our view of our cultures and our world.

The history of the field to which these essays all contribute, lesbian/gay studies, has yet to be written. When such a history comes to be written, it is likely to be contested: like any institutional history, the history of lesbian/gay studies will doubtless constitute an act of definition, an exercise in legitimation and delegitimation, and an attempt at political intervention. This is not the time or the place to begin to specify the intellectual roots of the field, to describe the conditions that made its emergence possible, or to fix its theoretical, methodological, political, thematic, or disciplinary contours. It will be sufficient merely to point out that what now looks like work in lesbian/gay studies has been going on for well over two decades,[1] and that its pace and intensity have quickened enormously in the last dozen years.

As the essays collected here show, lesbian/gay studies is not limited to the study of lesbians, bisexuals, and gay men. Nor does it refer simply to studies undertaken by, or in the name of, lesbians, bisexuals, and gay men. Not all research into the lives of lesbians, bisexuals, and gay men necessarily qualifies as lesbian/gay studies. Lesbian/gay studies, in short, cannot be defined exclusively by its subject, its practitioners, its methods, or its themes. An analogy with women's studies may help to clarify this point. As the feminist historian Joan Kelly-Gadol wrote nearly twenty years ago, women's history is not intended to be merely additive; its effect is not to introduce another sub-department of history into the traditional panoply of historical fields—such as political history, economic history, social history, military history, diplomatic history, and intellectual history. Rather, women's history seeks to establish the centrality of *gender* as a fundamental category of historical analysis and understanding—a category central, in other words, to each of those previously existing sub-departments of history.[2] Thus, women's studies is not limited to the study of women's lives and contributions: it includes any research that treats gender (whether female or male) as a central category of analysis and that operates within the broad horizons of that diverse political and intellectual movement known as feminism.

Lesbian/gay studies does for *sex* and *sexuality* approximately what women's studies does for gender. That does not mean that sexuality and gender must be strictly partitioned. On the contrary, the problem of how to understand the connections between sexuality and gender continues to furnish an illuminating topic of discussion in both women's studies and lesbian/gay studies;[3] hence, the degree of overlap or of distinctness between the fields of lesbian/gay studies and women's studies is a matter of lively debate and ongoing negotiation. Without attempting to anticipate the outcome of that process, we can still describe lesbian/gay studies by saying that it intends to establish the analytical centrality of sex and sexuality within many different fields of inquiry, to express and advance the interests of lesbians, bisexuals, and gay men, and to contribute culturally and intellectually to the contemporary lesbian/gay movement. In particular, lesbian/gay studies focuses intense scrutiny on the cultural production, dissemination, and vicissitudes of sexual meanings. Lesbian/gay studies attempts to decipher the sexual meanings inscribed in many different forms of cultural expression while also attempting to decipher the cultural meanings inscribed in the discourses and practices of sex.

Like women's studies, lesbian/gay studies has an oppositional design. It is informed by the social struggle for the sexual liberation, the personal freedom, dignity, equality, and human rights of lesbians, bisexuals, and gay men; it is also informed by resistance to homophobia and heterosexism—by political and cultural opposition to the ideological and institutional practices of heterosexual privilege. Lesbian/gay studies necessarily straddles scholarship and politics, but it is more than a means of breaking down divisions between the two. It is also a field of scholarly inquiry and critical exploration whose intellectual distinction has been repeatedly demonstrated and whose influence is changing the shape of every branch of learning in the humanities and social sciences.

The emergence of lesbian/gay studies has not been an easy, smooth, or uninterrupted process, nor is its mere existence proof that it is securely established, even now. Each step in the institutional growth of the field has required a struggle. With the increasing prominence of lesbian/gay studies have also come increasingly virulent attacks on the field and its practitioners.[4] Funding remains hard to come by, especially since the United States Congress has in effect forbidden the National Endowments for the Humanities and the Arts to provide grants for research in lesbian/gay studies. Students entering the field must struggle against adverse pressure and discouragement, to say nothing of outright discrimination.[5] Despite these obstacles, however, lesbian/gay studies seems to be making good headway in academe—to be growing, diversifying, and consolidating itself on campuses throughout the United States.

That is at least partly because the rapid growth in the rate of scholarly and critical production in the field has stimulated curricular development across a broad spectrum of disciplines. Graduate and undergraduate classes in lesbian/gay studies have multiplied exponentially. When one adds to their number other classes in other fields that also address lesbian/gay concerns, the total represents a significant innovation in the curriculum of higher education in the United States. An already vast archive of syllabi is housed at the Center for Lesbian and Gay Studies at the City University of New York. And programs in lesbian/gay studies at U.S. colleges and universities are estimated by The National Gay and Lesbian Task Force to number close to fifty.

The Lesbian and Gay Studies Reader is the largest and most nearly comprehensive collection yet undertaken in the field. It is designed in part to meet the curricular needs created by the proliferation of undergraduate and graduate courses in lesbian/gay studies. Until now there has been no single, inclusive, cross-disciplinary anthology of scholarly and critical essays in lesbian/gay studies—no "Reader"—that students and teachers might use as a resource or as a textbook.[6] While this collection cannot pretend to provide complete coverage, it does represent a very wide range of distinguished work currently being done in the field as a whole. Because much of the important work in lesbian/gay studies is published in relatively obscure or specialized journals, it is often difficult for students and teachers who approach the field from one discipline to keep up with the insights emanating from other disciplines. So in preparing this collection, we have explored extensively in those specialized journals and gathered from them essays of many disparate kinds.

Despite all our efforts at comprehensiveness, we have had to omit some areas and subjects and even entire genres of writing. Sometimes such omissions have not been the result of considered decisions on our part but have simply reflected a certain unevenness in the disciplinary growth of lesbian/gay studies. For example, although current work in lesbian/gay history, literary criticism, and cultural theory can now claim a long and distinguished heritage, work in lesbian/gay economics has only recently begun to emerge.

Sometimes, however, we have deliberately omitted highly developed genres of lesbian/gay writing. For instance, we decided against including works of personal testimony in this anthology. Missing also from this *Reader* are examples of poetry, fiction, art, cartoons, and photographic essays—the kinds of cultural activism and analysis that have contributed so crucially to the growth and sophistication of lesbian and gay consciousness. We knew that other collections of fiction, poetry, personal testimony, graphic and photographic art are available at many bookstores throughout the United States and abroad, as well. What is missing from their shelves, and what in our opinion is needed, is a collection of scholarly and critical essays that conveys the intellectual intricacy and cohesiveness of current work on the academic side of lesbian/gay studies.

To that end, we have attempted to feature essays that reflect contemporary trends and tendencies in lesbian/gay studies, in preference to older work, even when it is still notable and influential. For example, we have had to exclude, with considerable regret, the writings of Karl Heinrich Ulrichs, Edward Carpenter, Jeannette Foster, Sigmund Freud, Joan Riviere, Alfred Kinsey, Frantz Fanon, Erving Goffman, Mary McIntosh, Kenneth Plummer, John Boswell, and Michel Foucault. Even of excellent recent work, we have had to omit much. There was not enough space to include everything we admired. We urge our readers to use the bibliographical essay, which appears at the end of the book, as a guide to the field as a whole.

It was difficult to decide what to title this anthology. We have reluctantly chosen not to speak here and in our title of "queer studies," despite our own attachment to the term, because we wish to acknowledge the force of current usage. The forms of study whose institutionalization we seek to further have tended, so far at least, to go by the names of "lesbian" and "gay." The field designated by them has become a site for inquiry into many kinds of sexual non-conformity, including, for instance, bisexuality, trans-sexualism, and sadomasochism. Moreover, the names "lesbian" and "gay" are probably more widely preferred than is the name "queer." And the names "lesbian" and "gay" are not assimilationist. Just as the project of seeking legitimate institutional and intellectual space for lesbian/gay studies need not render less forceful its challenge to the scholarly and critical *status quo*, so our choice of "lesbian/gay" indicates no wish on our part to make lesbian/gay studies look less assertive, less unsettling, and less queer than it already does.

We trust that this collection of essays not only takes stock of the present but also looks to the future. We dedicate it to our students, who we fully expect will remake the field of lesbian/gay studies—perhaps beyond recognition—in the years ahead.

H.A.

M.A.B.

D.M.H.

August 1992

NOTES

1. See, for example, Mary McIntosh, "The Homosexual Role," *Social Problems*, 16 (1968/69), 182–92.

2. Joan Kelly, "The Social Relation of the Sexes: Methodological Implications of Women's History," *Signs*, 1 (1975/76), 809–23, reprinted in *Women, History, and Theory: The Essays of Joan Kelly* (Chicago, 1984), 1–18; see, now, Joan Wallach Scott, *Gender and the Politics of History* (New York, 1988).

3. See, for example, the essays by Gayle S. Rubin, Adrienne Rich, Marjorie Garber, and John J. Winkler collected in this *Reader*.

4. See Martha Nussbaum, "The Softness of Reason," *New Republic*, 207:3–4 (July 13 and 20, 1992), 26–27, 30, 32, 34–35.

5. See, for example, John D'Emilio, "Not a Simple Matter: Gay History and Gay Historians," *Journal of American History*, 76 (1989), 435–42; reprinted in John D'Emilio, *Making Trouble: Essays on Gay History, Politics, and the University* (New York: Routledge, 1992), 138–47.

6. Recent anthologies include *Feminisms: An Anthology of Literary Theory*, ed. Robyn R. Warhol and Diane Price Herndle (New Brunswick, NJ: Rutgers University Press, 1991), and *Cultural Studies*, ed. Lawrence Grossberg, Cary Nelson, and Paula A. Treichler (New York: Routledge, 1992).

User's Guide

This guide is meant to offer another way, besides that of the Table of Contents, to organize the essays in the *Reader*. The Table of Contents is structured to suggest the mutual concerns shared by essays whose specific interests at times diverge.[1]

But the essays might also be rearranged so as to emphasize their disciplinarity, thereby highlighting the ways in which they cut across their respective fields as well as the ways in which they participate in them. Such a reorganization enables an overview of how the traditional disciplines have been enlarged and also enriched by the advent of lesbian/gay studies. If Deborah E. McDowell's analysis of Nella Larsen proceeds with the kinds of close reading that we have come to expect from literary-critical approaches, her insistence that we not read Larsen apart from her concerns with the political and social ramifications of representations of Black women's sexuality suggests how the focus of literary studies has widened its gaze to include the sexual as well as the textual. John J. Winkler's use of current lesbian-feminist analysis in his reading of the ancient Greek poet Sappho, as someone who wrote with an understanding of herself as within one culture and outside another; Lee Edelman's interest in uniting the private space of the men's bathroom with the public space of North American political history; Teresa de Lauretis's supreme comfort in discussing both the ancient Greek philosophers *and* contemporary film; Harriet Whitehead's demand that we attend to the ways that current political agendas shape our interpretations of Native American sexuality—all are examples of the ways that lesbian/gay studies has brought new approaches to existing areas and methods of scholarship.

Our alternative organization of the essays should not be taken as undermining the cross-disciplinary links and interconnections that our collection has worked hard to demonstrate as descriptive of the field of lesbian/gay studies. A number of our essays could not be categorized within a single disciplinary heading—no matter how broadly we conceived it. Thus, while Esther Newton's study of the three decades of lesbians who summered and lived in Cherry Grove can be placed quite rightly under *History*, as an example of the methods and concerns involved in writing women's history, Newton's own disciplinary perspective—her concern with the social structures and identifications within which these lesbian communities defined themselves—gives her a place in the *Anthropology* heading as well. Phillip Brian Harper's examination of the conflicting cultural imperatives that surrounded the Black TV anchorman Max Robinson, who died of AIDS in 1988, is an example of an essay that can be equally well situated under *African-American Studies*, *Sociology*, and *Cultural Studies*. His analysis of the demands made on Robinson because of his high-profile presence as a member of a racial minority in a position of visible authority is broader than any one of these disciplines' boundaries and yet draws on all three.

There are doubtless still other ways of organizing this material than the two most evident in our Table of Contents and this alternative ordering. One might take a single concern—sexual pedagogy, for instance, the ways in which sexuality is a social script both taught and learned—and trace it through a number of essays: Gayle S. Rubin, Barbara Smith, and Audre Lorde all offer essays clearly although variously focused on that topic, while essays by Simon Watney, Sasha Torres, D.A. Miller, Kobena Mercer, Cindy Patton, and Richard Meyer make pedagogy an aspect of slightly different concerns.

Or one could, for example, rearrange the essays to form a chronological map of the field's development, or, to put it in more colloquial terms, one could trace out who is talking to whom. By beginning with the earliest published essays we've collected, it would be possible to establish a kind of baseline of focus and approach and then trace out the branchings, seeing how quickly a particular area of inquiry developed, changed, and in turn gave rise to new branchings. The essays by Adrienne Rich and Stuart Hall, for instance, are both early in the academic development of lesbian/gay studies; each can be seen as enabling, possibly even influencing the appearance of other essays, just as Rich and Hall were themselves impelled by still earlier writings. While such a restructuring would seem to call for close attention to our authors' footnotes and end-notes, to their and this collection's bibliographical entries, the attempt to form a chronological map of the development of the field might be a most useful one.

Philosophy

Judith Butler, "Imitation and Gender Subordination"
Teresa de Lauretis, "Sexual Indifference and Lesbian Representation"
Marilyn Frye, "Some Reflections on Separatism and Power"
Monique Witting, "One Is Not Born a Woman"

History

Henry Abelove, "Freud, Male Homosexuality, and the Americans"
John D'Emilio, "Capitalism and Gay Identity"
Charlotte Furth, "Androgynous Males and Deficient Females: Biology and Gender Boundaries in Sixteenth- and Seventeenth-Century China"
David M. Halperin, "Is There a History of Sexuality?"
Esther Newton, "Just One of the Boys: Lesbians in Cherry Grove, 1960–1988"
Joan W. Scott, "The Evidence of Experience"
Martha Vicinus, " 'They Wonder to Which Sex I Belong': The Historical Roots of the Modern Lesbian Identity"

Anthropology

Ana Maria Alonso and Maria Teresa Koreck, "Silences: 'Hispanics,' AIDS, and Sexual Practices"
Serena Nanda, "Hijras as Neither Man nor Woman"
Esther Newton, "Just One of the Boys: Lesbians in Cherry Grove, 1960–1988"
Gayle S. Rubin: "Thinking Sex: Notes for a Radical Theory of the Politics of Sexuality"
Harriet Whitehead, "The Bow and the Burden Strap: A New Look at Institutionalized Homosexuality in Native North America"

Sociology and Psychology

Henry Abelove, "Freud, Male Homosexuality, and the Americans"
Tomás Almaguer, "Chicano Men: A Cartography of Homosexual Identity and Behavior"
Stuart Hall, "Deviance, Politics, and the Media"

Phillip Brian Harper, "Eloquence and Epitaph: Black Nationalism and the Homophobic Impulse in Responses to the Death of Max Robinson"

Gayle S. Rubin, "Thinking Sex: Notes for a Radical Theory of the Politics of Sexuality"

African-American Studies

Phillip Brian Harper, "Eloquence and Epitaph: Black Nationalism and the Homophobic Impulse in Responses to the Death of Max Robinson"

Gloria T. Hull, " 'Lines She Did Not Dare': Angelina Weld Grimké, Harlem Renaissance Poet"

Biddy Martin, "Lesbian Identity and Autobiographical Difference[s]"

Deborah E. McDowell, " 'It's Not Safe. Not Safe At All': Sexuality in Nella Larsen's *Passing*"

Kobena Mercer, "Looking for Trouble"

Cindy Patton, "From Nation to Family: Containing African AIDS"

Ethnic Studies

Tomás Almaguer, "Chicano Men: A Cartography of Homosexual Identity and Behavior"

Ana Maria Alonso and Maria Teresa Koreck, "Silences: 'Hispanics,' AIDS, and Sexual Practices"

Phillip Brian Harper, "Eloquence and Epitaph: Black Nationalism and the Homophobic Impulse in Responses to the Death of Max Robinson"

Gloria T. Hull, " 'Lines She Did Not Dare': Angelina Weld Grimké, Harlem Renaissance Poet"

Biddy Martin, "Lesbian Identity and Autobiographical Difference[s]"

Deborah E. McDowell, " 'It's Not Safe. Not Safe At All': Sexuality in Nella Larsen's *Passing*"

Kobena Mercer, "Looking for Trouble"

Yvonne Yarbro-Bejarano, "De-constructing the Lesbian Body: Cherríe Moraga's *Loving in the War Years*"

Politics

Jonathan Dollimore, "Different Desires: Subjectivity and Transgression in Wilde and Gide"

Lee Edelman, "Tearooms and Sympathy, or, The Epistemology of the Water Closet"

Marilyn Frye, "Some Reflections on Separatism and Power"

Stuart Hall, "Deviance, Politics, and the Media"

Audre Lorde, "The Uses of the Erotic: The Erotic as Power"

Cindy Patton, "From Nation to Family: Containing African AIDS"

Adrienne Rich, "Compulsory Heterosexuality and Lesbian Existence"

Gayle S. Rubin, "Thinking Sex: Notes for a Radical Theory of the Politics of Sexuality"

Barbara Smith, "Homophobia: Why Bring It Up?"

Simon Watney, "The Spectacle of AIDS"

Yvonne Yarbro-Bejarano, "De-constructing the Lesbian Body: Cherríe Moraga's *Loving in the War Years*"

Cultural Studies

Michèle Aina Barale, "When Jack Blinks: Si(gh)ting Gay Desire in Ann Bannon's *Beebo Brinker*"

Sue-Ellen Case, "Toward a Butch-Femme Aesthetic"

Danae Clark, "Commodity Lesbianism"

Douglas Crimp, "The Boys in My Bedroom"

Lee Edelman, "Tearooms and Sympathy, or, The Epistemology of the Water Closet"

Marjorie Garber, "Spare Parts: The Surgical Construction of Gender"

Phillip Brian Harper, "Eloquence and Epitaph: Black Nationalism and the Homophobic Impulse in Responses to the Death of Max Robinson"

Kobena Mercer, "Looking for Trouble"

Richard Meyer, "Robert Mapplethorpe and the Discipline of Photography"

D.A. Miller, "Sontag's Urbanity"

Daniel L. Selden, " 'Just When You Thought It Was Safe to Go Back in the Water . . .' "

Sasha Torres, "Television/Feminism: *HeartBeat* and Prime Time Lesbianism"

Simon Watney, "The Spectacle of AIDS"

Literary Studies

Michèle Aina Barale, "When Jack Blinks: Si(gh)ting Gay Desire in Ann Bannon's *Beebo Brinker*"

Jonathan Dollimore, "Different Desires: Subjectivity and Transgression in Wilde and Gide"

Gloria T. Hull, " 'Lines She Did Not Dare': Angelina Weld Grimké, Harlem Renaissance Poet"

Biddy Martin, "Lesbian Identity and Autobiographical Difference[s]"

Deborah E. McDowell, " 'It's Not Safe. Not Safe At All': Sexuality in Nella Larsen's *Passing*"

Eve Kosofsky Sedgwick, "Epistemology of the Closet"

Catharine R. Stimpson, "The Somagrams of Gertrude Stein"

John J. Winkler, "Double Consciousness in Sappho's Lyrics"

Yvonne Yarbro-Bejarano, "De-constructing the Lesbian Body: Cherríe Moraga's *Loving in the War Years*"

NOTES

1. We have borrowed the idea for a "User's Guide" from *Cultural Studies*, ed. Lawrence Grossberg, Cary Nelson, and Paula A. Treichler (Routledge, 1992), pp. 17–22.

I

POLITICS AND REPRESENTATION

1

Thinking Sex:
Notes for a Radical Theory of the Politics of Sexuality*

GAYLE S. RUBIN

Gayle S. Rubin is a feminist anthropologist who has written on a wide range of subjects, including anthropological theory, s/m sex, and modern lesbian literature. In this essay, first published in 1984, Rubin argues that in the West, the 1880s, the 1950s, and the contemporary era have been periods of sex panic, periods in which the state, the institutions of medicine, and the popular media have mobilized to attack and oppress all whose sexual tastes differ from those allowed by the currently dominative model of sexual correctness. She also suggests that during the contemporary era the worst brunt of the oppression has been borne by those who practice s/m or cross-generational sex. Rubin maintains that if we are to devise a theory to account for the outbreak and direction of sexual panics, we shall need to base the theory on more than just feminist thinking. Although feminist thinking explains gender injustices, it does not and cannot provide by itself a full explanation for the oppression of sexual minorities. Gayle S. Rubin is presently at work on a collection of her essays—including her well-known work of theory, "The Traffic in Women"—and on a historical and ethnographic account of the gay male leather community of San Francisco.

I The Sex Wars

Asked his advice, Dr. J. Guerin affirmed that, after all other treatments had failed, he had succeeded in curing young girls affected by the vice of onanism by burning the clitoris with a hot iron. . . . I apply the hot point three times to each of the large labia and another on the clitoris. . . . After the first operation, from forty to fifty times a day, the number of voluptuous spasms was reduced to three or four. . . . We believe, then, that in cases similar to those submitted to your consideration, one should not hesitate to resort to the hot iron, and at an early hour, in order to combat clitoral and vaginal onanism in little girls. (Demetrius Zambaco[1])

The time has come to think about sex. To some, sexuality may seem to be an unimportant topic, a frivolous diversion from the more critical problems of poverty, war, disease, racism, famine, or nuclear annihilation. But it is precisely at times such as these, when we live with the possibility of unthinkable destruction, that people are likely to

*© Gayle S. Rubin, 1984, 1992. First published in Carole S. Vance, ed., *Pleasure and Danger: Exploring Female Sexuality* (1984).

become dangerously crazy about sexuality. Contemporary conflicts over sexual values and erotic conduct have much in common with the religious disputes of earlier centuries. They acquire immense symbolic weight. Disputes over sexual behavior often become the vehicles for displacing social anxieties, and discharging their attendant emotional intensity. Consequently, sexuality should be treated with special respect in times of great social stress.

The realm of sexuality also has its own internal politics, inequities, and modes of oppression. As with other aspects of human behavior, the concrete institutional forms of sexuality at any given time and place are products of human activity. They are imbued with conflicts of interest and political maneuvering, both deliberate and incidental. In that sense, sex is always political. But there are also historical periods in which sexuality is more sharply contested and more overtly politicized. In such periods, the domain of erotic life is, in effect, renegotiated.

In England and the United States, the late nineteenth century was one such era. During that time, powerful social movements focused on "vices" of all sorts. There were educational and political campaigns to encourage chastity, to eliminate prostitution, and to discourage masturbation, especially among the young. Morality crusaders attacked obscene literature, nude paintings, music halls, abortion, birth control information, and public dancing.[2] The consolidation of Victorian morality, and its apparatus of social, medical, and legal enforcement, was the outcome of a long period of struggle whose results have been bitterly contested ever since.

The consequences of these great nineteenth-century moral paroxysms are still with us. They have left a deep imprint on attitudes about sex, medical practice, child-rearing, parental anxieties, police conduct, and sex law.

The idea that masturbation is an unhealthy practice is part of that heritage. During the nineteenth century, it was commonly thought that "premature" interest in sex, sexual excitement, and, above all, sexual release, would impair the health and maturation of a child. Theorists differed on the actual consequences of sexual precocity. Some thought it led to insanity, while others merely predicted stunted growth. To protect the young from premature arousal, parents tied children down at night so they would not touch themselves; doctors excised the clitorises of onanistic little girls.[3] Although the more gruesome techniques have been abandoned, the attitudes that produced them persist. The notion that sex *per se* is harmful to the young has been chiseled into extensive social and legal structures designed to insulate minors from sexual knowledge and experience.

Much of the sex law currently on the books also dates from the nineteenth-century morality crusades. The first federal anti-obscenity law in the United States was passed in 1873. The Comstock Act—named for Anthony Comstock, an ancestral anti-porn activist and the founder of the New York Society for the Suppression of Vice—made it a federal crime to make, advertise, sell, possess, send through the mails, or import books or pictures deemed obscene. The law also banned contraceptive or abortifacient drugs and devices and information about them.[4] In the wake of the federal statute, most states passed their own anti-obscenity laws.

The Supreme Court began to whittle down both federal and state Comstock laws during the 1950s. By 1975, the prohibition of materials used for, and information about, contraception and abortion had been ruled unconstitutional. However, although the obscenity provisions have been modified, their fundamental constitutionality has been upheld. Thus it remains a crime to make, sell, mail, or import material which has no purpose other than sexual arousal.[5]

Although sodomy statutes date from older strata of the law, when elements of canon law were adopted into civil codes, most of the laws used to arrest homosexuals and prostitutes come out of the Victorian campaigns against "white slavery." These campaigns produced the myriad prohibitions against solicitation, lewd behavior, loitering for immoral purposes, age offenses, and brothels and bawdy houses.

In her discussion of the British "white slave" scare, historian Judith Walkowitz observes that: "Recent research delineates the vast discrepancy between lurid journalistic accounts and the reality of prostitution. Evidence of widespread entrapment of British girls in London and abroad is slim."[6] However, public furor over this ostensible problem

> forced the passage of the Criminal Law Amendment Act of 1885, a particularly nasty and pernicious piece of omnibus legislation. The 1885 Act raised the age of consent for girls from 13 to 16, but it also gave police far greater summary jurisdiction over poor working-class women and children ... it contained a clause making indecent acts between consenting male adults a crime, thus forming the basis of legal prosecution of male homosexuals in Britain until 1967 ... the clauses of the new bill were mainly enforced against working-class women, and regulated adult rather than youthful sexual behaviour.[7]

In the United States, the Mann Act, also known as the White Slave Traffic Act, was passed in 1910. Subsequently, every state in the union passed anti-prostitution legislation.[8]

In the 1950s, in the United States, major shifts in the organization of sexuality took place. Instead of focusing on prostitution or masturbation, the anxieties of the 1950s condensed most specifically around the image of the "homosexual menace" and the dubious specter of the "sex offender." Just before and after World War II, the "sex offender" became an object of public fear and scrutiny. Many states and cities, including Massachusetts, New Hampshire, New Jersey, New York State, New York City, and Michigan, launched investigations to gather information about this menace to public safety.[9] The term "sex offender" sometimes applied to rapists, sometimes to "child molesters," and eventually functioned as a code for homosexuals. In its bureaucratic, medical, and popular versions, the sex offender discourse tended to blur distinctions between violent sexual assault and illegal but consensual acts such as sodomy. The criminal justice system incorporated these concepts when an epidemic of sexual psychopath laws swept through state legislatures.[10] These laws gave the psychological professions increased police powers over homosexuals and other sexual "deviants."

From the late 1940s until the early 1960s, erotic communities whose activities did not fit the postwar American dream drew intense persecution. Homosexuals were, along with communists, the objects of federal witch hunts and purges. Congressional investigations, executive orders, and sensational exposés in the media aimed to root out homosexuals employed by the government. Thousands lost their jobs, and restrictions on federal employment of homosexuals persist to this day.[11] The FBI began systematic surveillance and harassment of homosexuals which lasted at least into the 1970s.[12]

Many states and large cities conducted their own investigations, and the federal witch hunts were reflected in a variety of local crackdowns. In Boise, Idaho, in 1955, a schoolteacher sat down to breakfast with his morning paper and read that the vice-president of the Idaho First National Bank had been arrested on felony sodomy charges; the local prosecutor said that he intended to eliminate all homosexuality from the community. The teacher never finished his breakfast. "He jumped up from his seat, pulled out his suitcases, packed as fast as he could, got into his car, and drove straight to San Francisco. ... The cold eggs, coffee, and toast remained on his table for two days before someone from his school came by to see what had happened."[13]

In San Francisco, police and media waged war on homosexuals throughout the 1950s. Police raided bars, patrolled cruising areas, conducted street sweeps, and trumpeted their intention of driving the queers out of San Francisco.[14] Crackdowns against gay individuals, bars, and social areas occurred throughout the country. Although anti-homosexual crusades are the best-documented examples of erotic repression in the 1950s, future research should reveal similar patterns of increased harassment against pornographic materials, prostitutes, and erotic deviants of all sorts. Research is needed to determine the full scope of both police persecution and regulatory reform.[15]

The current period bears some uncomfortable similarities to the 1880s and the 1950s. The 1977 campaign to repeal the Dade County, Florida, gay rights ordinance inaugurated a new wave of violence, state persecution, and legal initiatives directed against minority sexual populations and the commercial sex industry. For the last six years, the United States and Canada have undergone an extensive sexual repression in the political, not the psychological, sense. In the spring of 1977, a few weeks before the Dade County vote, the news media were suddenly full of reports of raids on gay cruising areas, arrests for prostitution, and investigations into the manufacture and distribution of pornographic materials. Since then, police activity against the gay community has increased exponentially. The gay press has documented hundreds of arrests, from the libraries of Boston to the streets of Houston and the beaches of San Francisco. Even the large, organized, and relatively powerful urban gay communities have been unable to stop these depredations. Gay bars and bath houses have been busted with alarming frequency, and police have gotten bolder. In one especially dramatic incident, police in Toronto raided all four of the city's gay baths. They broke into cubicles with crowbars and hauled almost 300 men out into the winter streets, clad in their bath towels. Even "liberated" San Francisco has not been immune. There have been proceedings against several bars, countless arrests in the parks, and, in the fall of 1981, police arrested over 400 people in a series of sweeps of Polk Street, one of the thoroughfares of local gay nightlife. Queerbashing has become a significant recreational activity for young urban males. They come into gay neighborhoods armed with baseball bats and looking for trouble, knowing that the adults in their lives either secretly approve or will look the other way.

The police crackdown has not been limited to homosexuals. Since 1977, enforcement of existing laws against prostitution and obscenity has been stepped up. Moreover, states and municipalities have been passing new and tighter regulations on commercial sex. Restrictive ordinances have been passed, zoning laws altered, licensing and safety codes amended, sentences increased, and evidentiary requirements relaxed. This subtle legal codification of more stringent controls over adult sexual behavior has gone largely unnoticed outside of the gay press.

For over a century, no tactic for stirring up erotic hysteria has been as reliable as the appeal to protect children. The current wave of erotic terror has reached deepest into those areas bordered in some way, if only symbolically, by the sexuality of the young. The motto of the Dade County repeal campaign was "Save Our Children" from alleged homosexual recruitment. In February 1977, shortly before the Dade County vote, a sudden concern with "child pornography" swept the national media. In May, the *Chicago Tribune* ran a lurid four-day series with three-inch headlines, which claimed to expose a national vice ring organized to lure young boys into prostitution and pornography.[16] Newspapers across the country ran similar stories, most of them worthy of the *National Enquirer*. By the end of May, a congressional investigation was underway. Within weeks, the federal government had enacted a sweeping bill against "child pornography" and many of the states followed with bills of their own. These laws have reestablished restrictions on sexual materials that had been relaxed by some of the important Supreme Court decisions. For instance, the Court ruled that neither nudity nor sexual activity *per se* were obscene. But the child pornography laws define as obscene any depiction of minors who are nude or engaged in sexual activity. This means that photographs of naked children in anthropology textbooks and many of the ethnographic movies shown in college classes are technically illegal in several states. In fact, the instructors are liable to an additional felony charge for showing such images to each student under the age of 18. Although the Supreme Court has also ruled that it is a constitutional right to possess obscene material for private use, some child pornography laws prohibit even the private possession of any sexual material involving minors.

The laws produced by the child porn panic are ill-conceived and misdirected. They represent far-reaching alterations in the regulation of sexual behavior and abrogate important sexual civil liberties. But hardly anyone noticed as they swept through Congress and state legislatures. With the exception of the North American Man/Boy Love Association and the American Civil Liberties Union, no one raised a peep of protest.[17]

A new and even tougher federal child pornography bill has just reached House-Senate conference. It removes any requirement that prosecutors must prove that alleged child pornography was distributed for commercial sale. Once this bill becomes law, a person merely possessing a nude snapshot of a 17-year-old lover or friend may go to jail for fifteen years, and be fined $100,000. This bill passed the House 400 to 1.[18]

The experiences of art photographer Jacqueline Livingston exemplify the climate created by the child porn panic. An assistant professor of photography at Cornell University, Livingston was fired in 1978 after exhibiting pictures of male nudes which included photographs of her seven-year-old son masturbating. *Ms. Magazine, Chrysalis,* and *Art News* all refused to run ads for Livingston's posters of male nudes. At one point, Kodak confiscated some of her film, and for several months, Livingston lived with the threat of prosecution under the child pornography laws. The Tompkins County Department of Social Services investigated her fitness as a parent. Livingston's posters have been collected by the Museum of Modern Art, the Metropolitan, and other major museums. But she has paid a high cost in harassment and anxiety for her efforts to capture on film the uncensored male body at different ages.[19]

It is easy to see someone like Livingston as a victim of the child porn wars. It is harder for most people to sympathize with actual boy-lovers. Like communists and homosexuals in the 1950s, boy-lovers are so stigmatized that it is difficult to find defenders for their civil liberties, let alone for their erotic orientation. Consequently, the police have feasted on them. Local police, the FBI, and watchdog postal inspectors have joined to build a huge apparatus whose sole aim is to wipe out the community of men who love underaged youth. In twenty years or so, when some of the smoke has cleared, it will be much easier to show that these men have been the victims of a savage and undeserved witch hunt. A lot of people will be embarrassed by their collaboration with this persecution, but it will be too late to do much good for those men who have spent their lives in prison.

While the misery of the boy-lovers affects very few, the other long-term legacy of the Dade County repeal affects almost everyone. The success of the anti-gay campaign ignited long-simmering passions of the American right, and sparked an extensive movement to compress the boundaries of acceptable sexual behavior.

Right-wing ideology linking non-familial sex with communism and political weakness is nothing new. During the McCarthy period, Alfred Kinsey and his Institute for Sex Research were attacked for weakening the moral fiber of Americans and rendering them more vulnerable to communist influence. After congressional investigations and bad publicity, Kinsey's Rockefeller grant was terminated in 1954.[20]

Around 1969, the extreme right discovered the Sex Information and Education Council of the United States (SIECUS). In books and pamphlets, such as *The Sex Education Racket: Pornography in the Schools* and *SIECUS: Corrupter of Youth,* the right attacked SIECUS and sex education as communist plots to destroy the family and sap the national will.[21] Another pamphlet, *Pavlov's Children (They May Be Yours),* claims that the United Nations Educational, Scientific and Cultural Organization (UNESCO) is in cahoots with SIECUS to undermine religious taboos, to promote the acceptance of abnormal sexual relations, to downgrade absolute moral standards, and to "destroy racial cohesion," by exposing white people (especially white women) to the alleged "lower" sexual standards of black people.[22]

New Right and neo-conservative ideology has updated these themes, and leans heavily on linking "immoral" sexual behavior to putative declines in American power. In 1977, Norman Podhoretz wrote an essay blaming homosexuals for the alleged inability of the United States to stand up to the Russians.[23] He thus neatly linked "the anti-gay fight in the domestic arena and the anti-communist battles in foreign policy."[24]

Right-wing opposition to sex education, homosexuality, pornography, abortion, and pre-marital sex moved from the extreme fringes to the political center stage after 1977, when right-wing strategists and fundamentalist religious crusaders discovered that these issues had mass appeal. Sexual reaction played a significant role in the right's electoral success in 1980.[25] Organizations like the Moral Majority and Citizens for Decency have acquired mass followings, immense financial resources, and unanticipated clout. The Equal Rights Amendment has been defeated, legislation has been passed that mandates new restrictions on abortion, and funding for programs like Planned Parenthood and sex education has been slashed. Laws and regulations making it more difficult for teenage girls to obtain contraceptives or abortions have been promulgated. Sexual backlash was exploited in successful attacks on the Women's Studies Program at California State University at Long Beach.

The most ambitious right-wing legislative initiative has been the Family Protection Act (FPA), introduced in Congress in 1979. The Family Protection Act is a broad assault on feminism, homosexuals, non-traditional families, and teenage sexual privacy.[26] The Family Protection Act has not and probably will not pass, but conservative members of Congress continue to pursue its agenda in a more piecemeal fashion. Perhaps the most glaring sign of the times is the Adolescent Family Life Program. Also known as the Teen Chastity Program, it gets some 15 million federal dollars to encourage teenagers to refrain from sexual intercourse, and to discourage them from using contraceptives if they do have sex, and from having abortions if they get pregnant. In the last few years, there have been countless local confrontations over gay rights, sex education, abortion rights, adult bookstores, and public school curricula. It is unlikely that the anti-sex backlash is over, or that it has even peaked. Unless something changes dramatically, it is likely that the next few years will bring more of the same.

Periods such as the 1880s in England, and the 1950s in the United States, recodify the relations of sexuality. The struggles that were fought leave a residue in the form of laws, social practices, and ideologies which then affect the way in which sexuality is experienced long after the immediate conflicts have faded. All the signs indicate that the present era is another of those watersheds in the politics of sex. The settlements that emerge from the 1980s will have an impact far into the future. It is therefore imperative to understand what is going on and what is at stake in order to make informed decisions about what policies to support and oppose.

It is difficult to make such decisions in the absence of a coherent and intelligent body of radical thought about sex. Unfortunately, progressive political analysis of sexuality is relatively underdeveloped. Much of what is available from the feminist movement has simply added to the mystification that shrouds the subject. There is an urgent need to develop radical perspectives on sexuality.

Paradoxically, an explosion of exciting scholarship and political writing about sex has been generated in these bleak years. In the 1950s, the early gay rights movement began and prospered while the bars were being raided and anti-gay laws were being passed. In the last six years, new erotic communities, political alliances, and analyses have been developed in the midst of the repression. In this essay, I will propose elements of a descriptive and conceptual framework for thinking about sex and its politics. I hope to contribute to the pressing task of creating an accurate, humane, and genuinely liberatory body of thought about sexuality.

II Sexual Thoughts

"You see, Tim," Phillip said suddenly, "your argument isn't reasonable. Suppose I granted your first point that homosexuality is justifiable in certain instances and under certain controls. Then there is the catch: where does justification end and degeneracy begin? Society must condemn to protect. Permit even the intellectual homosexual a place of respect and the first bar is down. Then comes the next and the next until the sadist, the flagellist, the criminally insane demand their places, and society ceases to exist. So I ask again: where is the line drawn? Where does degeneracy begin if not at the beginning of individual freedom in such matters?" (Fragment from a discussion between two gay men trying to decide if they may love each other, from a novel published in 1950.[27])

A radical theory of sex must identify, describe, explain, and denounce erotic injustice and sexual oppression. Such a theory needs refined conceptual tools which can grasp the subject and hold it in view. It must build rich descriptions of sexuality as it exists in society and history. It requires a convincing critical language that can convey the barbarity of sexual persecution.

Several persistent features of thought about sex inhibit the development of such a theory. These assumptions are so pervasive in Western culture that they are rarely questioned. Thus, they tend to reappear in different political contexts, acquiring new rhetorical expressions but reproducing fundamental axioms.

One such axiom is sexual essentialism—the idea that sex is a natural force that exists prior to social life and shapes institutions. Sexual essentialism is embedded in the folk wisdoms of Western societies, which consider sex to be eternally unchanging, asocial, and transhistorical. Dominated for over a century by medicine, psychiatry, and psychology, the academic study of sex has reproduced essentialism. These fields classify sex as a property of individuals. It may reside in their hormones or their psyches. It may be construed as physiological or psychological. But within these ethnoscientific categories, sexuality has no history and no significant social determinants.

During the last five years, a sophisticated historical and theoretical scholarship has challenged sexual essentialism both explicitly and implicitly. Gay history, particularly the work of Jeffrey Weeks, has led this assault by showing that homosexuality as we know it is a relatively modern institutional complex.[28] Many historians have come to see the contemporary institutional forms of heterosexuality as an even more recent development.[29] An important contributor to the new scholarship is Judith Walkowitz, whose research has demonstrated the extent to which prostitution was transformed around the turn of the century. She provides meticulous descriptions of how the interplay of social forces such as ideology, fear, political agitation, legal reform, and medical practice can change the structure of sexual behavior and alter its consequences.[30]

Michel Foucault's *The History of Sexuality* has been the most influential and emblematic text of the new scholarship on sex. Foucault criticizes the traditional understanding of sexuality as a natural libido yearning to break free of social constraint. He argues that desires are not preexisting biological entities, but rather, that they are constituted in the course of historically specific social practices. He emphasizes the generative aspects of the social organization of sex rather than its repressive elements by pointing out that new sexualities are constantly produced. And he points to a major discontinuity between kinship-based systems of sexuality and more modern forms.[31]

The new scholarship on sexual behavior has given sex a history and created a constructivist alternative to sexual essentialism. Underlying this body of work is an assumption that sexuality is constituted in society and history, not biologically ordained.[32] This does not mean the biological capacities are not prerequisites for human sexuality. It does mean that human sexuality is not comprehensible in purely biological terms. Human organisms with human brains are necessary for human cultures, but no examination of the body or its parts can explain the nature and variety of human social systems. The belly's hunger gives no clues as to the complexities of cuisine. The body, the brain, the genitalia, and the capacity for language are all necessary for human sexuality. But they do not determine its content, its experiences, or its institutional forms. Moreover, we never encounter the body unmediated by the meanings that cultures give to it. To paraphrase Lévi-Strauss, my position on the relationship between biology and sexuality is a "Kantianism without a transcendental libido."[33]

It is impossible to think with any clarity about the politics of race or gender as long as these are thought of as biological entities rather than as social constructs. Similarly, sexuality is impervious to political analysis as long as it is primarily conceived as a biological phenomenon or an aspect of individual psychology. Sexuality is as much a human product as are diets, methods of transportation, systems of etiquette, forms of labor, types of entertainment, processes of production, and modes of oppression. Once sex is understood in terms of social analysis and historical understanding, a more realistic politics of sex becomes possible. One may then think of sexual politics in terms of such phenomena as populations, neighborhoods, settlement patterns, migration, urban conflict, epidemiology, and police technology. These are more fruitful categories of thought than the more traditional ones of sin, disease, neurosis, pathology, decadence, pollution, or the decline and fall of empires.

By detailing the relationships between stigmatized erotic populations and the social forces which regulate them, work such as that of Allan Bérubé, John D'Emilio, Jeffrey Weeks, and Judith Walkowitz contains implicit categories of political analysis and criticism. Nevertheless, the constructivist perspective has displayed some political weaknesses. This has been most evident in misconstructions of Foucault's position.

Because of his emphasis on the ways that sexuality is produced, Foucault has been vulnerable to interpretations that deny or minimize the reality of sexual repression in the more political sense. Foucault makes it abundantly clear that he is not denying the existence of sexual repression so much as inscribing it within a large dynamic.[34] Sexuality in Western societies has been structured within an extremely punitive social framework, and has been subjected to very real formal and informal controls. It is necessary to recognize repressive phenomena without resorting to the essentialist assumptions of the language of libido. It is important to hold repressive sexual practices in focus, even while situating them within a different totality and a more refined terminology.[35]

Most radical thought about sex has been embedded within a model of the instincts and their restraints. Concepts of sexual oppression have been lodged within that more biological understanding of sexuality. It is often easier to fall back on the notion of a natural libido subjected to inhumane repression than to reformulate concepts of sexual injustice within a more constructivist framework. But it is essential that we do so. We need a radical critique of sexual arrangements that has the conceptual elegance of Foucault and the evocative passion of Reich.

The new scholarship on sex has brought a welcome insistence that sexual terms be restricted to their proper historical and social contexts, and a cautionary scepticism towards sweeping generalizations. But it is important to be able to indicate groupings of erotic behavior and general trends within erotic discourse. In addition to sexual essentialism, there are at least five other ideological formations whose grip on sexual thought is so strong that to fail to discuss them is to remain enmeshed within them. These are sex negativity, the fallacy of misplaced scale, the hierarchical valuation of sex acts, the domino theory of sexual peril, and the lack of a concept of benign sexual variation.

Of these five, the most important is sex negativity. Western cultures generally consider sex to be a dangerous, destructive, negative force.[36] Most Christian tradition, following Paul, holds that sex is inherently sinful. It may be redeemed if performed within marriage for procreative purposes and if the pleasurable aspects are not enjoyed too much. In turn, this idea rests on the assumption that the genitalia are an intrinsically inferior part of the body, much lower and less holy than the mind, the "soul," the "heart," or even the upper part of the digestive system (the status of the excretory organs is close to that of the genitalia).[37] Such notions have by now acquired a life of their own and no longer depend solely on religion for their perseverance.

This culture always treats sex with suspicion. It construes and judges almost any sexual practice in terms of its worst possible expression. Sex is presumed guilty until proven innocent. Virtually all erotic behavior is considered bad unless a specific reason to exempt it has been established. The most acceptable excuses are marriage, reproduction, and love. Sometimes scientific curiosity, aesthetic experience, or a long-term intimate relationship may serve. But the exercise of erotic capacity, intelligence, curiosity, or creativity all require pretexts that are unnecessary for other pleasures, such as the enjoyment of food, fiction, or astronomy.

What I call the fallacy of misplaced scale is a corollary of sex negativity. Susan Sontag once commented that since Christianity focused "on sexual behavior as the root of virtue, everything pertaining to sex has been a 'special case' in our culture."[38] Sex law has incorporated the religious attitude that heretical sex is an especially heinous sin that deserves the harshest punishments. Throughout much of European and American history, a single act of consensual anal penetration was grounds for execution. In some states, sodomy still carries twenty-year prison sentences. Outside the law, sex is also a marked category. Small differences in value or behavior are often experienced as cosmic threats. Although people can be intolerant, silly, or pushy about what constitutes proper diet, differences in menu rarely provoke the kinds of rage, anxiety, and sheer terror that routinely accompany differences in erotic taste. Sexual acts are burdened with an excess of significance.

Modern Western societies appraise sex acts according to a hierarchical system of sexual value. Marital, reproductive heterosexuals are alone at the top of the erotic pyramid. Clamoring below are unmarried monogamous heterosexuals in couples, followed by most other heterosexuals. Solitary sex floats ambiguously. The powerful nineteenth-century stigma on masturbation lingers in less potent, modified forms, such as the idea that masturbation is an inferior substitute for partnered encounters. Stable, long-term lesbian and gay male couples are verging on respectability, but bar dykes and promiscuous gay men are hovering just above the groups at the very bottom of the pyramid. The most despised sexual castes currently include transsexuals, transvestites, fetishists, sadomasochists, sex workers such as prostitutes and porn models, and the lowliest of all, those whose eroticism transgresses generational boundaries.

Individuals whose behavior stands high in this hierarchy are rewarded with certified mental health, respectability, legality, social and physical mobility, institutional support, and material benefits. As sexual behaviors or occupations fall lower on the scale, the individuals who practice them are subjected to a presumption of mental illness, disreputability, criminality, restricted social and physical mobility, loss of institutional support, and economic sanctions.

Extreme and punitive stigma maintains some sexual behaviors as low status and is an effective sanction against those who engage in them. The intensity of this stigma is rooted in Western religious traditions. But most of its contemporary content derives from medical and psychiatric opprobrium.

The old religious taboos were primarily based on kinship forms of social organization. They were meant to deter inappropriate unions and to provide proper kin. Sex laws derived from Biblical pronouncements were aimed at preventing the acquisition of the wrong kinds of affinal partners: consanguineous kin (incest), the same gender (homosexuality), or the wrong species (bestiality). When medicine and psychiatry acquired extensive powers over sexuality, they were less concerned with unsuitable mates than with unfit forms of desire. If taboos against incest best characterized kinship systems of sexual organization, then the shift to an emphasis on taboos against masturbation was more apposite to the newer systems organized around qualities of erotic experience.[39]

Medicine and psychiatry multiplied the categories of sexual misconduct. The section on psychosexual disorders in the *Diagnostic and Statistical Manual of Mental and Physical Disorders (DSM)* of the American Psychiatric Association (APA) is a fairly reliable map of the current moral hierarchy of sexual activities. The APA list is much more elaborate than the traditional condemnations of whoring, sodomy, and adultery. The most recent edition, *DSM–III,* removed homosexuality from the roster of mental disorders after a long political struggle. But fetishism, sadism, masochism, transsexuality, transvestism, exhibitionism, voyeurism, and pedophilia are quite firmly entrenched as psychological malfunctions.[40] Books are still being written about the genesis, etiology, treatment, and cure of these assorted "pathologies."

Psychiatric condemnation of sexual behaviors invokes concepts of mental and emotional inferiority rather than categories of sexual sin. Low-status sex practices are vilified as mental diseases or symptoms of defective personality integration. In addition, psychological terms conflate difficulties of psycho-dynamic functioning with modes of erotic conduct. They equate sexual masochism with self-destructive personality patterns, sexual sadism with emotional aggression, and homoeroticism with immaturity. These terminological muddles have become powerful stereotypes that are indiscriminately applied to individuals on the basis of their sexual orientations.

Popular culture is permeated with ideas that erotic variety is dangerous, unhealthy, depraved, and a menace to everything from small children to national security. Popular sexual ideology is a noxious stew made up of ideas of sexual sin, concepts of psychological inferiority, anti-communism, mob hysteria, accusations of witchcraft, and xenophobia. The mass media nourish these attitudes with relentless propaganda. I would call this system of erotic stigma the last socially respectable form of prejudice if the old forms did not show such obstinate vitality, and new ones did not continually become apparent.

All these hierarchies of sexual value—religious, psychiatric, and popular—function in much the same ways as do ideological systems of racism, ethnocentrism, and religious chauvinism. They rationalize the well-being of the sexually privileged and the adversity of the sexual rabble.

Figure 1 diagrams a general version of the sexual value system. According to this system, sexuality that is "good," "normal," and "natural" should ideally be heterosexual, marital, monogamous, reproductive, and non-commercial. It should be coupled, relational, within the same generation, and occur at home. It should not involve pornography,

The charmed circle:
Good, Normal, Natural, Blessed Sexuality

Heterosexual
Married
Monogamous
Procreative
Non-commercial
In pairs
In a relationship
Same generation
In private
No pornography
Bodies only
Vanilla

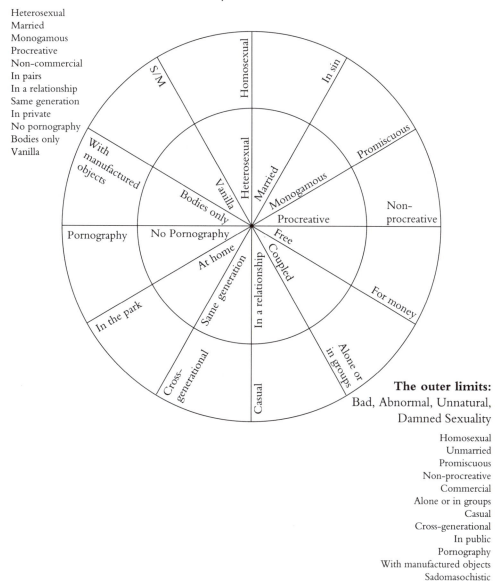

The outer limits:
Bad, Abnormal, Unnatural,
Damned Sexuality

Homosexual
Unmarried
Promiscuous
Non-procreative
Commercial
Alone or in groups
Casual
Cross-generational
In public
Pornography
With manufactured objects
Sadomasochistic

FIGURE 1. The sex hierarchy: the charmed circle vs. the outer limits

fetish objects, sex toys of any sort, or roles other than male and female. Any sex that violates these rules is "bad," "abnormal," or "unnatural." Bad sex may be homosexual, unmarried, promiscuous, non-procreative, or commercial. It may be masturbatory or take place at orgies, may be casual, may cross generational lines, and may take place in "public," or at least in the bushes or the baths. It may involve the use of pornography, fetish objects, sex toys, or unusual roles (see Figure 1).

Figure 2 diagrams another aspect of the sexual hierarchy: the need to draw and maintain an imaginary line between good and bad sex. Most of the discourses on sex, be they religious, psychiatric, popular, or political, delimit a very small portion of human sexual capacity as sanctifiable, safe, healthy, mature, legal, or politically correct. The "line" distinguishes these from all other erotic behaviors, which are understood to be the work of the devil, dangerous, psychopathological, infantile, or politically reprehensible. Arguments are then conducted over "where to draw the line," and to determine what other activities, if any, may be permitted to cross over into acceptability.*

All these models assume a domino theory of sexual peril. The line appears to stand between sexual order and chaos. It expresses the fear that if anything is permitted to cross this erotic DMZ, the barrier against scary sex will crumble and something unspeakable will skitter across.

Most systems of sexual judgment—religious, psychological, feminist, or socialist—attempt to determine on which side of the line a particular act falls. Only sex acts on the good side of the line are accorded moral complexity. For instance, heterosexual encounters may be sublime or disgusting, free or forced, healing or destructive, romantic or mercenary. As long as it does not violate other rules, heterosexuality is acknowledged to exhibit the full range of human experience. In contrast, all sex acts on the bad side

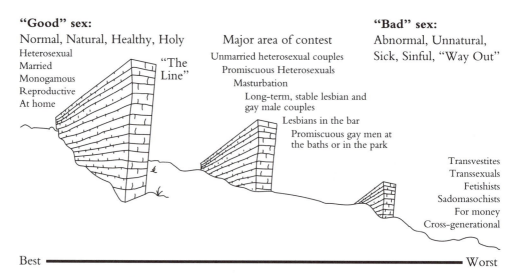

"Good" sex:
Normal, Natural, Healthy, Holy
Heterosexual
Married
Monogamous
Reproductive
At home

"The Line"

Major area of contest
Unmarried heterosexual couples
Promiscuous Heterosexuals
Masturbation
Long-term, stable lesbian and gay male couples
Lesbians in the bar
Promiscuous gay men at the baths or in the park

"Bad" sex:
Abnormal, Unnatural, Sick, Sinful, "Way Out"

Transvestites
Transsexuals
Fetishists
Sadomasochists
For money
Cross-generational

Best ——————————————————————————— Worst

FIGURE 2.   The sex hierarchy: the struggle over where to draw the line

*FN 1992. Throughout this essay I treated transgender behavior and individuals in terms of the sex system rather than the gender system, although transvestites and transsexuals are clearly transgressing gender boundaries. I did so because transgendered people are stigmatized, harassed, persecuted, and generally treated like sex "deviants" and perverts. But clearly this is an instance of the ways in which my classificatory system does not quite encompass the existing complexities. The schematic renderings of sexual hierarchies in Figures 1 and 2 were oversimplified to make a point. Although the point remains valid, the actual power relationships of sexual variation are considerably more complicated.

of the line are considered utterly repulsive and devoid of all emotional nuance. The further from the line a sex act is, the more it is depicted as a uniformly bad experience.

As a result of the sex conflicts of the last decade, some behavior near the border is inching across it. Unmarried couples living together, masturbation, and some forms of homosexuality are moving in the direction of respectability (see Figure 2). Most homosexuality is still on the bad side of the line. But if it is coupled and monogamous, the society is beginning to recognize that it includes the full range of human interaction. Promiscuous homosexuality, sadomasochism, fetishism, transsexuality, and cross-generational encounters are still viewed as unmodulated horrors incapable of involving affection, love, free choice, kindness, or transcendence.

This kind of sexual morality has more in common with ideologies of racism than with true ethics. It grants virtue to the dominant groups, and relegates vice to the underprivileged. A democratic morality should judge sexual acts by the way partners treat one another, the level of mutual consideration, the presence or absence of coercion, and the quantity and quality of the pleasures they provide. Whether sex acts are gay or straight, coupled or in groups, naked or in underwear, commercial or free, with or without video, should not be ethical concerns.

It is difficult to develop a pluralistic sexual ethics without a concept of benign sexual variation. Variation is a fundamental property of all life, from the simplest biological organisms to the most complex human social formations. Yet sexuality is supposed to conform to a single standard. One of the most tenacious ideas about sex is that there is one best way to do it, and that everyone should do it that way.

Most people find it difficult to grasp that whatever they like to do sexually will be thoroughly repulsive to someone else, and that whatever repels them sexually will be the most treasured delight of someone, somewhere. One need not like or perform a particular sex act in order to recognize that someone else will, and that this difference does not indicate a lack of good taste, mental health, or intelligence in either party. Most people mistake their sexual preferences for a universal system that will or should work for everyone.

This notion of a single ideal sexuality characterizes most systems of thought about sex. For religion, the ideal is procreative marriage. For psychology, it is mature heterosexuality. Although its content varies, the format of a single sexual standard is continually reconstituted within other rhetorical frameworks, including feminism and socialism. It is just as objectionable to insist that everyone should be lesbian, non-monogamous, or kinky, as to believe that everyone should be heterosexual, married, or vanilla—though the latter set of opinions are backed by considerably more coercive power than the former.

Progressives who would be ashamed to display cultural chauvinism in other areas routinely exhibit it towards sexual differences. We have learned to cherish different cultures as unique expressions of human inventiveness rather than as the inferior or disgusting habits of savages. We need a similarly anthropological understanding of different sexual cultures.

Empirical sex research is the one field that does incorporate a positive concept of sexual variation. Alfred Kinsey approached the study of sex with the same uninhibited curiosity he had previously applied to examining a species of wasp. His scientific detachment gave his work a refreshing neutrality that enraged moralists and caused immense controversy.[41] Among Kinsey's successors, John Gagnon and William Simon have pioneered the application of sociological understandings to erotic variety.[42] Even some of the older sexology is useful. Although his work is imbued with unappetizing eugenic beliefs, Havelock Ellis was an acute and sympathetic observer. His monumental *Studies in the Psychology of Sex* is resplendent with detail.[43]

Much political writing on sexuality reveals complete ignorance of both classical sexology and modern sex research. Perhaps this is because so few colleges and universities bother to teach human sexuality, and because so much stigma adheres even to scholarly investigation of sex. Neither sexology nor sex research has been immune to the prevailing sexual value system. Both contain assumptions and information which should not be accepted uncritically. But sexology and sex research provide abundant detail, a welcome posture of calm, and a well-developed ability to treat sexual variety as something that exists rather than as something to be exterminated. These fields can provide an empirical grounding for a radical theory of sexuality more useful than the combination of psychoanalysis and feminist first principles to which so many texts resort.*

III Sexual Transformation

As defined by the ancient civil or canonical codes, sodomy was a category of forbidden acts; their perpetrator was nothing more than the juridical subject of them. The nineteenth-century homosexual became a personage, a past, a case history, and a childhood, in addition to being a type of life, a life form, and a morphology, with an indiscreet anatomy and possibly a mysterious physiology. . . . The sodomite had been a temporary aberration; the homosexual was now a species. (Michel Foucault[44])

In spite of many continuities with ancestral forms, modern sexual arrangements have a distinctive character which sets them apart from preexisting systems. In Western Europe and the United States, industrialization and urbanization reshaped the traditional rural and peasant populations into a new urban industrial and service workforce. It generated new forms of state apparatus, reorganized family relations, altered gender roles, made possible new forms of identity, produced new varieties of social inequality, and created new formats for political and ideological conflict. It also gave rise to a new sexual system characterized by distinct types of sexual persons, populations, stratification, and political conflict.

The writings of nineteenth-century sexology suggest the appearance of a kind of erotic speciation. However outlandish their explanations, the early sexologists were witnessing the emergence of new kinds of erotic individuals and their aggregation into rudimentary communities. The modern sexual system contains sets of these sexual populations, stratified by the operation of an ideological and social hierarchy. Differences in social value create friction among these groups, who engage in political contests to alter or maintain their place in the ranking. Contemporary sexual politics should be

---

*FN 1992. The intention of this section was not to appeal to scientific authority, not to claim scientific objectivity for sexology, and certainly was not to privilege biological models as "tools [for] social inquiry" (Mariana Valverde, "Beyond Gender Dangers and Private Pleasures: Theory and Ethics in the Sex Debates," *Feminist Studies,* vol. 15, no. 2, Summer 1989, pp. 237–54). It was to suggest that sexology would be a rich vein to mine for analyses of sexuality, although it never occurred to me that those who did so would fail to subject sexological texts to analytic scrutiny. I did intend the claim that sexological studies have more direct relevance than the endless rehashings of Freud and Lacan on which so much feminist thought on sex has been based. I felt then, and still do now, that too much feminist sexual analysis is derived *a priori* from feminist first principles mixed with psychoanalysis. Such topographies are a bit like European maps of the world before 1492. They suffer from empirical deprivation. I am not a believer in "facts" unmediated by cultural structures of understanding. However, I do believe that social science theories which fail to recognize, assimilate, and account for the relevant information are useful primarily as calisthenics. Outside of mathematics most theory is anchored in some set of privileged data, and psychoanalytic feminism is hardly an exception. For an exemplary feminist history of twentieth-century American sexology see Janice Irvine, *Disorders of Desire,* Philadelphia, Temple University Press, 1990.

reconceptualized in terms of the emergence and on-going development of this system, its social relations, the ideologies which interpret it, and its characteristic modes of conflict.

Homosexuality is the best example of this process of erotic speciation. Homosexual behavior is always present among humans. But in different societies and epochs it may be rewarded or punished, required or forbidden, a temporary experience or a life-long vocation. In some New Guinea societies, for example, homosexual activities are obligatory for all males. Homosexual acts are considered utterly masculine, roles are based on age, and partners are determined by kinship status.[45] Although these men engage in extensive homosexual and pedophile behavior, they are neither homosexuals nor pederasts.

Nor was the sixteenth-century sodomite a homosexual. In 1631, Mervyn Touchet, Earl of Castlehaven, was tried and executed for sodomy. It is clear from the proceedings that the earl was not understood by himself or anyone else to be a particular kind of sexual individual. "While from the twentieth-century viewpoint Lord Castlehaven obviously suffered from psychosexual problems requiring the services of an analyst, from the seventeenth century viewpoint he had deliberately broken the Law of God and the Laws of England, and required the simpler services of an executioner."[46] The earl did not slip into his tightest doublet and waltz down to the nearest gay tavern to mingle with his fellow sodomists. He stayed in his manor house and buggered his servants. Gay self-awareness, gay pubs, the sense of group commonality, and even the term homosexual were not part of the earl's universe.

The New Guinea bachelor and the sodomite nobleman are only tangentially related to a modern gay man, who may migrate from rural Colorado to San Francisco in order to live in a gay neighborhood, work in a gay business, and participate in an elaborate experience that includes a self-conscious identity, group solidarity, a literature, a press, and a high level of political activity. In modern, Western, industrial societies, homosexuality has acquired much of the institutional structure of an ethnic group.[47]

The relocation of homoeroticism into these quasi-ethnic, nucleated, sexually constituted communities is to some extent a consequence of the transfers of population brought about by industrialization. As laborers migrated to work in cities, there were increased opportunities for voluntary communities to form. Homosexually inclined women and men, who would have been vulnerable and isolated in most pre-industrial villages, began to congregate in small corners of the big cities. Most large nineteenth-century cities in Western Europe and North America had areas where men could cruise for other men. Lesbian communities seem to have coalesced more slowly and on a smaller scale. Nevertheless, by the 1890s, there were several cafes in Paris near the Place Pigalle which catered to a lesbian clientele, and it is likely that there were similar places in the other major capitals of Western Europe.

Areas like these acquired bad reputations, which alerted other interested individuals of their existence and location. In the United States, lesbian and gay male territories were well established in New York, Chicago, San Francisco, and Los Angeles in the 1950s. Sexually motivated migration to places such as Greenwich Village had become a sizable sociological phenomenon. By the late 1970s, sexual migration was occurring on a scale so significant that it began to have a recognizable impact on urban politics in the United States, with San Francisco being the most notable and notorious example.[48]

Prostitution has undergone a similar metamorphosis. Prostitution began to change from a temporary job to a more permanent occupation as a result of nineteenth-century agitation, legal reform, and police persecution. Prostitutes, who had been part of the general working-class population, became increasingly isolated as members of an outcast group.[49] Prostitutes and other sex workers differ from homosexuals and other sexual minorities. Sex work is an occupation, while sexual deviation is an erotic preference. Nevertheless, they share some common features of social organization. Like homosexuals, prostitutes are a criminal sexual population stigmatized on the basis of sexual activity. Prostitutes and male homosexuals are the primary prey of vice police everywhere.[50] Like gay men, prostitutes occupy well-demarcated urban territories and battle with police to defend and maintain those territories. The legal persecution of both populations is justified by an elaborate ideology which classifies them as dangerous and inferior undesirables who are not entitled to be left in peace.

Besides organizing homosexuals and prostitutes into localized populations, the "modernization of sex" has generated a system of continual sexual ethnogenesis. Other populations of erotic dissidents—commonly known as the "perversions" or the "paraphilias"—also began to coalesce. Sexualities keep marching out of the *Diagnostic and Statistical Manual* and on to the pages of social history. At present, several other groups are trying to emulate the successes of homosexuals. Bisexuals, sadomasochists, individuals who prefer cross-generational encounters, transsexuals, and transvestites are all in various states of community formation and identity acquisition. The perversions are not proliferating as much as they are attempting to acquire social space, small businesses, political resources, and a measure of relief from the penalties for sexual heresy.

IV   Sexual Stratification

An entire sub-race was born, different—despite certain kinship ties—from the libertines of the past. From the end of the eighteenth century to our own, they circulated through the pores of society; they were always hounded, but not always by laws; were often locked up, but not always in prisons; were sick perhaps, but scandalous, dangerous victims, prey to a strange evil that also bore the name of vice and sometimes crime. They were children wise beyond their years, precocious little girls, ambiguous schoolboys, dubious servants and educators, cruel or maniacal husbands, solitary collectors, ramblers with bizarre impulses; they haunted the houses of correction, the penal colonies, the tribunals, and the asylums; they carried their infamy to the doctors and their sickness to the judges. This was the numberless family of perverts who were on friendly terms with delinquents and akin to madmen. (Michel Foucault[51])

The industrial transformation of Western Europe and North America brought about new forms of social stratification. The resultant inequalities of class are well known and have been explored in detail by a century of scholarship. The construction of modern systems of racism and ethnic injustice has been well documented and critically assessed. Feminist thought has analyzed the prevailing organization of gender oppression. But although specific erotic groups, such as militant homosexuals and sex workers, have agitated against their own mistreatment, there has been no equivalent attempt to locate particular varieties of sexual persecution within a more general system of sexual stratification. Nevertheless, such a system exists, and in its contemporary form it is a consequence of Western industrialization.

Sex law is the most adamantine instrument of sexual stratification and erotic persecution. The state routinely intervenes in sexual behavior at a level that would not be tolerated in other areas of social life. Most people are unaware of the extent of sex law, the quantity and qualities of illegal sexual behavior, and the punitive character of legal sanctions. Although federal agencies may be involved in obscenity and prostitution cases, most sex laws are enacted at the state and municipal level, and enforcement is largely in the hands of local police. Thus, there is a tremendous amount of variation in the laws applicable to any given locale. Moreover, enforcement of sex laws varies dramatically with the local political climate. In spite of this legal thicket, one can make some tentative and qualified generalizations. My discussion of sex law does not apply to laws against sexual coercion, sexual assault, or rape. It does pertain to the myriad prohibitions on consensual sex and the "status" offenses such as statutory rape.

Sex law is harsh. The penalties for violating sex statutes are universally out of proportion to any social or individual harm. A single act of consensual but illicit sex, such as placing one's lips upon the genitalia of an enthusiastic partner, is punished in many states with more severity than rape, battery, or murder. Each such genital kiss, each lewd caress, is a separate crime. It is therefore painfully easy to commit multiple felonies in the course of a single evening of illegal passion. Once someone is convicted of a sex violation, a second performance of the same act is grounds for prosecution as a repeat offender, in which case penalties will be even more severe. In some states, individuals have become repeat felons for having engaged in homosexual love-making on two separate occasions. Once an erotic activity has been proscribed by sex law, the full power of the state enforces conformity to the values embodied in those laws. Sex laws are notoriously easy to pass, as legislators are loath to be soft on vice. Once on the books, they are extremely difficult to dislodge.

Sex law is not a perfect reflection of the prevailing moral evaluations of sexual conduct. Sexual variation *per se* is more specifically policed by the mental-health professions, popular ideology, and extra-legal social practice. Some of the most detested erotic behaviors, such as fetishism and sadomasochism, are not as closely or completely regulated by the criminal justice system as somewhat less stigmatized practices, such as homosexuality. Areas of sexual behavior come under the purview of the law when they become objects of social concern and political uproar. Each sex scare or morality campaign deposits new regulations as a kind of fossil record of its passage. The legal sediment is thickest—and sex law has its greatest potency—in areas involving obscenity, money, minors, and homosexuality.

Obscenity laws enforce a powerful taboo against direct representation of erotic activities. Current emphasis on the ways in which sexuality has become a focus of social attention should not be misused to undermine a critique of this prohibition. It is one thing to create sexual discourse in the form of psychoanalysis, or in the course of a morality crusade. It is quite another to depict sex acts or genitalia graphically. The first is socially permissible in a way the second is not. Sexual speech is forced into reticence, euphemism, and indirection. Freedom of speech about sex is a glaring exception to the protections of the First Amendment, which is not even considered applicable to purely sexual statements.

The anti-obscenity laws also form part of a group of statutes that make almost all sexual commerce illegal. Sex law incorporates a very strong prohibition against mixing sex and money, except via marriage. In addition to the obscenity statutes, other laws impinging on sexual commerce include anti-prostitution laws, alcoholic beverage regulations, and ordinances governing the location and operation of "adult" businesses. The sex industry and the gay economy have both managed to circumvent some of this legislation, but that process has not been easy or simple. The underlying criminality of sex-oriented business keeps it marginal, underdeveloped, and distorted. Sex businesses can only operate in legal loopholes. This tends to keep investment down and to divert commercial activity towards the goal of staying out of jail rather than the delivery of goods and services. It also renders sex workers more vulnerable to exploitation and bad working conditions. If sex commerce were legal, sex workers would be more able to organize and agitate for higher pay, better conditions, greater control, and less stigma.

Whatever one thinks of the limitations of capitalist commerce, such an extreme exclusion from the market process would hardly be socially acceptable in other areas of activity. Imagine, for example, that the exchange of money for medical care, pharmacological advice, or psychological counseling were illegal. Medical practice would take place in a much less satisfactory fashion if doctors, nurses, druggists, and therapists could be hauled off to jail at the whim of the local "health squad." But that is essentially the situation of prostitutes, sex workers, and sex entrepreneurs.

Marx himself considered the capitalist market a revolutionary, if limited, force. He argued that capitalism was progressive in its dissolution of pre-capitalist superstition, prejudice, and the bonds of traditional modes of life. "Hence the great civilizing influence of capital, its production of a state of society compared with which all earlier stages appear to be merely local progress and idolatry of nature."[52] Keeping sex from realizing the positive effects of the market economy hardly makes it socialist.

The law is especially ferocious in maintaining the boundary between childhood "innocence" and "adult" sexuality. Rather than recognizing the sexuality of the young, and attempting to provide for it in a caring and responsible manner, our culture denies and punishes erotic interest and activity by anyone under the local age of consent. The amount of law devoted to protecting young people from premature exposure to sexuality is breath-taking.

The primary mechanism for insuring the separation of sexual generations is age of consent laws. These laws make no distinction between the most brutal rape and the most gentle romance. A 20-year-old convicted of sexual contact with a 17-year-old will face a severe sentence in virtually every state, regardless of the nature of the relationship.[53] Nor are minors permitted access to "adult" sexuality in other forms. They are forbidden to see books, movies, or television in which sexuality is "too" graphically portrayed. It is legal for young people to see hideous depictions of violence, but not to see explicit pictures of genitalia. Sexually active young people are frequently incarcerated in juvenile homes, or otherwise punished for their "precocity."

Adults who deviate too much from conventional standards of sexual conduct are often denied contact with the young, even their own. Custody laws permit the state to steal the children of anyone whose erotic activities appear questionable to a judge presiding over family court matters. Countless lesbians, gay men, prostitutes, swingers, sex workers, and "promiscuous" women have been declared unfit parents under such provisions. Members of the teaching professions are closely monitored for signs of sexual misconduct. In most states, certification laws require that teachers arrested for sex offenses lose their jobs and credentials. In some cases, a teacher may be fired merely because an unconventional lifestyle becomes known to school officials. Moral turpitude is one of the few legal grounds for revoking academic tenure.[54] The more influence one has over the next generation, the less latitude one is permitted in behavior and opinion. The coercive power of the law ensures the transmission of conservative sexual values with these kinds of controls over parenting and teaching.

The only adult sexual behavior that is legal in every state is the placement of the penis in the vagina in wedlock. Consenting adults statutes ameliorate this situation in fewer than half the states. Most states impose severe criminal penalties on consensual sodomy, homosexual contact short of sodomy, adultery, seduction, and adult incest. Sodomy laws vary a great deal. In some states, they apply equally to homosexual and heterosexual partners and regardless of marital status. Some state courts have ruled that married couples have the right to commit sodomy in private. Only homosexual sodomy is illegal in some states. Some sodomy statutes prohibit both anal sex and oral-genital contact. In other states, sodomy applies only to anal penetration, and oral sex is covered under separate statutes.[55]

Laws like these criminalize sexual behavior that is freely chosen and avidly sought. The ideology embodied in them reflects the value hierarchies discussed above. That is, some sex acts are considered to be so intrinsically vile that no one should be allowed under any circumstance to perform them. The fact that individuals consent to or even prefer them is taken to be additional evidence of depravity. This system of sex law is similar to legalized racism. State prohibition of same sex contact, anal penetration, and oral sex make homosexuals a criminal group denied the privileges of full citizenship. With such laws, prosecution is persecution. Even when they are not strictly enforced, as is usually the case, the members of criminalized sexual communities remain vulnerable to the possibility of arbitrary arrest, or to periods in which they become the objects of social panic. When those occur, the laws are in place and police action is swift. Even sporadic enforcement serves to remind individuals that they are members of a subject population. The occasional arrest for sodomy, lewd behavior, solicitation, or oral sex keeps everyone else afraid, nervous, and circumspect.

The state also upholds the sexual hierarchy through bureaucratic regulation. Immigration policy still prohibits the admission of homosexuals (and other sexual "deviates") into the United States. Military regulations bar homosexuals from serving in the armed forces.* The fact that gay people cannot legally marry means that they cannot enjoy the same legal rights as heterosexuals in many matters, including inheritance, taxation, protection from testimony in court, and the acquisition of citizenship for foreign partners. These are but a few of the ways that the state reflects and maintains the social relations of sexuality. The law buttresses structures of power, codes of behavior, and forms of prejudice. At their worst, sex law and sex regulation are simply sexual apartheid.

Although the legal apparatus of sex is staggering, most everyday social control is extra-legal. Less formal, but very effective social sanctions are imposed on members of "inferior" sexual populations.

In her marvelous ethnographic study of gay life in the 1960s, Esther Newton observed that the homosexual population was divided into what she called the "overts" and the "coverts." "The overts live their *entire* working lives within the context of the [gay] community; the coverts live their entire *nonworking* lives within it."[56] At the time of Newton's study, the gay community provided far fewer jobs than it does now, and the non-gay work world was almost completely intolerant of homosexuality. There were some fortunate individuals who could be openly gay and earn decent salaries. But the vast majority of homosexuals had to choose between honest poverty and the strain of maintaining a false identity.

Though this situation has changed a great deal, discrimination against gay people is still rampant. For the bulk of the gay population, being out on the job is still impossible. Generally, the more important and higher paid the job, the less the society will tolerate overt erotic deviance. If it is difficult for gay people to find employment where they do not have to pretend, it is doubly and triply so for more exotically sexed individuals. Sadomasochists leave their fetish clothes at home, and know that they must be especially careful to conceal their real identities. An exposed pedophile would probably be stoned out of the office. Having to maintain such absolute secrecy is a considerable burden. Even those who are content to be secretive may be exposed by some accidental event.

*FN 1992. For a wonderful history of the relationship between gays and the United States military, see Allan Bérubé, *Coming Out Under Fire: The History of Gay Men and Women in World War II*, New York, The Free Press, 1990.

Individuals who are erotically unconventional risk being unemployable or unable to pursue their chosen careers.

Public officials and anyone who occupies a position of social consequence are especially vulnerable. A sex scandal is the surest method for hounding someone out of office or destroying a political career. The fact that important people are expected to conform to the strictest standards of erotic conduct discourages sex perverts of all kinds from seeking such positions. Instead, erotic dissidents are channeled into positions that have less impact on the mainstream of social activity and opinion.

The expansion of the gay economy in the last decade has provided some employment alternatives and some relief from job discrimination against homosexuals. But most of the jobs provided by the gay economy are low-status and low-paying. Bartenders, bathhouse attendants, and disc jockeys are not bank officers or corporate executives. Many of the sexual migrants who flock to places like San Francisco are downwardly mobile. They face intense competition for choice positions. The influx of sexual migrants provides a pool of cheap and exploitable labor for many of the city's businesses, both gay and straight.

Families play a crucial role in enforcing sexual conformity. Much social pressure is brought to bear to deny erotic dissidents the comforts and resources that families provide. Popular ideology holds that families are not supposed to produce or harbor erotic non-conformity. Many families respond by trying to reform, punish, or exile sexually offending members. Many sexual migrants have been thrown out by their families, and many others are fleeing from the threat of institutionalization. Any random collection of homosexuals, sex workers, or miscellaneous perverts can provide heart-stopping stories of rejection and mistreatment by horrified families. Christmas is the great family holiday in the United States and consequently it is a time of considerable tension in the gay community. Half the inhabitants go off to their families of origin; many of those who remain in the gay ghettos cannot do so, and relive their anger and grief.

In addition to economic penalties and strain on family relations, the stigma of erotic dissidence creates friction at all other levels of everyday life. The general public helps to penalize erotic non-conformity when, according to the values they have been taught, landlords refuse housing, neighbors call in the police, and hoodlums commit sanctioned battery. The ideologies of erotic inferiority and sexual danger decrease the power of sex perverts and sex workers in social encounters of all kinds. They have less protection from unscrupulous or criminal behavior, less access to police protection, and less recourse to the courts. Dealings with institutions and bureaucracies—hospitals, police, coroners, banks, public officials—are more difficult.

Sex is a vector of oppression. The system of sexual oppression cuts across other modes of social inequality, sorting out individuals and groups according to its own intrinsic dynamics. It is not reducible to, or understandable in terms of, class, race, ethnicity, or gender. Wealth, white skin, male gender, and ethnic privileges can mitigate the effects of sexual stratification. A rich, white male pervert will generally be less affected than a poor, black, female pervert. But even the most privileged are not immune to sexual oppression. Some of the consequences of the system of sexual hierarchy are mere nuisances. Others are quite grave. In its most serious manifestations, the sexual system is a Kafkaesque nightmare in which unlucky victims become herds of human cattle whose identification, surveillance, apprehension, treatment, incarceration, and punishment produce jobs and self-satisfaction for thousands of vice police, prison officials, psychiatrists, and social workers.[57]

V Sexual Conflicts

The moral panic crystallizes widespread fears and anxieties, and often deals with them not by seeking the real causes of the problems and conditions which they demonstrate but by displacing them on to "Folk Devils" in an identified social group (often the "immoral" or "degenerate"). Sexuality has had a peculiar centrality in such panics, and sexual "deviants" have been omnipresent scapegoats. (Jeffrey Weeks[58])

The sexual system is not a monolithic, omnipotent structure. There are continuous battles over the definitions, evaluations, arrangements, privileges, and costs of sexual behavior. Political struggle over sex assumes characteristic forms.

Sexual ideology plays a crucial role in sexual experience. Consequently, definitions and evaluations of sexual conduct are objects of bitter contest. The confrontations between early gay liberation and the psychiatric establishment are the best example of this kind of fight, but there are constant skirmishes. Recurrent battles take place between the primary producers of sexual ideology—the churches, the family, the shrinks, and the media—and the groups whose experience they name, distort, and endanger.

The legal regulation of sexual conduct is another battleground. Lysander Spooner dissected the system of state-sanctioned moral coercion over a century ago in a text inspired primarily by the temperance campaigns. In *Vices Are Not Crimes: A Vindication of Moral Liberty,* Spooner argued that government should protect its citizens against crime, but that it is foolish, unjust, and tyrannical to legislate against vice. He discusses rationalizations still heard today in defense of legalized moralism—that "vices" (Spooner is referring to drink, but homosexuality, prostitution, or recreational drug use may be substituted) lead to crimes, and should therefore be prevented; that those who practice "vice" are *non compos mentis* and should therefore be protected from their self-destruction by state-accomplished ruin; and that children must be protected from supposedly harmful knowledge.[59] The discourse on victimless crimes has not changed much. Legal struggle over sex law will continue until basic freedoms of sexual action and expression are guaranteed. This requires the repeal of all sex laws except those few that deal with actual, not statutory, coercion; and it entails the abolition of vice squads, whose job it is to enforce legislated morality.

In addition to the definitional and legal wars, there are less obvious forms of sexual political conflict which I call the territorial and border wars. The processes by which erotic minorities form communities and the forces that seek to inhibit them lead to struggles over the nature and boundaries of sexual zones.

Dissident sexuality is rarer and more closely monitored in small towns and rural areas. Consequently, metropolitan life continually beckons to young perverts. Sexual migration creates concentrated pools of potential partners, friends, and associates. It enables individuals to create adult, kin-like networks in which to live. But there are many barriers which sexual migrants have to overcome.

According to the mainstream media and popular prejudice, the marginal sexual worlds are bleak and dangerous. They are portrayed as impoverished, ugly, and inhabited by psychopaths and criminals. New migrants must be sufficiently motivated to resist the impact of such discouraging images. Attempts to counter negative propaganda with more realistic information generally meet with censorship, and there are continuous ideological struggles over which representations of sexual communities make it into the popular media.

Information on how to find, occupy, and live in the marginal sexual worlds is also suppressed. Navigational guides are scarce and inaccurate. In the past, fragments of rumor, distorted gossip, and bad publicity were the most available clues to the location of underground erotic communities. During the late 1960s and early 1970s, better information became available. Now groups like the Moral Majority want to rebuild the ideological walls around the sexual undergrounds and make transit in and out of them as difficult as possible.

Migration is expensive. Transportation costs, moving expenses, and the necessity of finding new jobs and housing are economic difficulties that sexual migrants must overcome. These are especially imposing barriers to the young, who are often the most desperate to move. There are, however, routes into the erotic communities which mark trails through the propaganda thicket and provide some economic shelter along the way. Higher education can be a route for young people from affluent backgrounds. In spite of serious limitations, the information on sexual behavior at most colleges and universities is better than elsewhere, and most colleges and universities shelter small erotic networks of all sorts.

For poorer kids, the military is often the easiest way to get the hell out of wherever they are. Military prohibitions against homosexuality make this a perilous route. Although young queers continually attempt to use the armed forces to get out of intolerable hometown situations and closer to functional gay communities, they face the hazards of exposure, court martial, and dishonorable discharge.

Once in the cities, erotic populations tend to nucleate and to occupy some regular, visible territory. Churches and other anti-vice forces constantly put pressure on local authorities to contain such areas, reduce their visibility, or to drive their inhabitants out of town. There are periodic crackdowns in which local vice squads are unleashed on the populations they control. Gay men, prostitutes, and sometimes transvestites are sufficiently territorial and numerous to engage in intense battles with the cops over particular streets, parks, and alleys. Such border wars are usually inconclusive, but they result in many casualties.

For most of this century, the sexual underworlds have been marginal and impoverished, their residents subjected to stress and exploitation. The spectacular success of gay entrepreneurs in creating a variegated gay economy has altered the quality of life within the gay ghetto. The level of material comfort and social elaboration achieved by the gay community in the last fifteen years is unprecedented. But it is important to recall what happened to similar miracles. The growth of the black population in New York in the early part of the twentieth century led to the Harlem Renaissance, but that period of creativity was doused by the Depression. The relative prosperity and cultural florescence of the gay ghetto may be equally fragile. Like blacks who fled the South for the metropolitan North, homosexuals may have merely traded rural problems for urban ones.

Gay pioneers occupied neighborhoods that were centrally located but run down. Consequently, they border poor neighborhoods. Gays, especially low-income gays, end up competing with other low-income groups for the limited supply of cheap and moderate housing. In San Francisco, competition for low-cost housing has exacerbated both racism and homophobia, and is one source of the epidemic of street violence against homosexuals. Instead of being isolated and invisible in rural settings, city gays are now numerous and obvious targets for urban frustrations.

In San Francisco, unbridled construction of downtown skyscrapers and high-cost condominiums is causing affordable housing to evaporate. Megabuck construction is creating pressure on all city residents. Poor gay renters are visible in low-income neighborhoods; multimillionaire contracters are not. The specter of the "homosexual invasion" is a convenient scapegoat which deflects attention from the banks, the planning commission, the political establishment, and the big developers. In San Francisco, the well-being of the gay community has become embroiled in the high-stakes politics of urban real estate.

Downtown expansion affects all the territorial erotic underworlds. In both San Francisco and New York, high investment construction and urban renewal have intruded on the main areas of prostitution, pornography, and leather bars. Developers are salivating over Times Square, the Tenderloin, what is left of North Beach, and South of Market. Anti-sex ideology, obscenity law, prostitution regulations, and the alcoholic beverage codes are all being used to dislodge seedy adult businesses, sex workers, and leathermen. Within ten years, most of these areas will have been bulldozed and made safe for convention centers, international hotels, corporate headquarters, and housing for the rich.

The most important and consequential kind of sex conflict is what Jeffrey Weeks has termed the "moral panic." Moral panics are the "political moment" of sex, in which diffuse attitudes are channeled into political action and from there into social change.[60] The white slavery hysteria of the 1880s, the anti-homosexual campaigns of the 1950s, and the child pornography panic of the late 1970s were typical moral panics.

Because sexuality in Western societies is so mystified, the wars over it are often fought at oblique angles, aimed at phony targets, conducted with misplaced passions, and are highly, intensely symbolic. Sexual activities often function as signifiers for personal and social apprehensions to which they have no intrinsic connection. During a moral panic, such fears attach to some unfortunate sexual activity or population. The media become ablaze with indignation, the public behaves like a rabid mob, the police are activated, and the state enacts new laws and regulations. When the furor has passed, some innocent erotic group has been decimated, and the state has extended its power into new areas of erotic behavior.

The system of sexual stratification provides easy victims who lack the power to defend themselves, and a preexisting apparatus for controlling their movements and curtailing their freedoms. The stigma against sexual dissidents renders them morally defenseless. Every moral panic has consequences on two levels. The target population suffers most, but everyone is affected by the social and legal changes.

Moral panics rarely alleviate any real problem, because they are aimed at chimeras and signifiers. They draw on the pre-existing discursive structure which invents victims in order to justify treating "vices" as crimes. The criminalization of innocuous behaviors such as homosexuality, prostitution, obscenity, or recreational drug use, is rationalized by portraying them as menaces to health and safety, women and children, national security, the family, or civilization itself. Even when activity is acknowledged to be harmless, it may be banned because it is alleged to "lead" to something ostensibly worse (another manifestation of the domino theory).[61] Great and mighty edifices have been built on the basis of such phantasms. Generally, the outbreak of a moral panic is preceded by an intensification of such scapegoating.

It is always risky to prophesy. But it does not take much prescience to detect potential moral panics in two current developments: the attacks on sadomasochists by a segment of the feminist movement, and the right's increasing use of AIDS to incite virulent homophobia.

Feminist anti-pornography ideology has always contained an implied, and sometimes overt, indictment of sadomasochism. The pictures of sucking and fucking that comprise the bulk of pornography may be unnerving to those who are not familiar with them. But it is hard to make a convincing case that such images are violent. All of the early anti-porn slide shows used a highly selective sample of S/M imagery to sell a very flimsy analysis. Taken out of context, such images are often shocking. This shock value was mercilessly exploited to scare audiences into accepting the anti-porn perspective.

A great deal of anti-porn propaganda implies that sadomasochism is the underlying and essential "truth" towards which all pornography tends. Porn is thought to lead to S/M porn which in turn is alleged to lead to rape. This is a just-so story that revitalizes the notion that sex perverts commit sex crimes, not normal people. There is no evidence that the readers of S/M erotica or practicing sadomasochists commit a disproportionate number of sex crimes. Anti-porn literature scapegoats an unpopular sexual minority and its reading material for social problems they do not create.

The use of S/M imagery in anti-porn discourse is inflammatory. It implies that the way to make the world safe for women is to get rid of sadomasochism. The use of S/M images in the movie *Not a Love Story* was on a moral par with the use of depictions of black men raping white women, or of drooling old Jews pawing young Aryan girls, to incite racist or anti-Semitic frenzy.

Feminist rhetoric has a distressing tendency to reappear in reactionary contexts. For example, in 1980 and 1981, Pope John Paul II delivered a series of pronouncements reaffirming his commitment to the most conservative and Pauline understandings of human sexuality. In condemning divorce, abortion, trial marriage, pornography, prostitution, birth control, unbridled hedonism, and lust, the pope employed a great deal of feminist rhetoric about sexual objectification. Sounding like lesbian feminist polemicist Julia Penelope, His Holiness explained that "considering anyone in a lustful way makes that person a sexual object rather than a human being worthy of dignity."[62]

The right wing opposes pornography and has already adopted elements of feminist anti-porn rhetoric. The anti-S/M discourse developed in the women's movement could easily become a vehicle for a moral witch hunt. It provides a ready-made defenseless target population. It provides a rationale for the recriminalization of sexual materials which have escaped the reach of current obscenity laws. It would be especially easy to pass laws against S/M erotica resembling the child pornography laws. The ostensible purpose of such laws would be to reduce violence by banning so-called violent porn. A focused campaign against the leather menace might also result in the passage of laws to criminalize S/M behavior that is not currently illegal. The ultimate result of such a moral panic would be the legalized violation of a community of harmless perverts. It is dubious that such a sexual witch hunt would make any appreciable contribution towards reducing violence against women.

An AIDS panic is even more probable. When fears of incurable disease mingle with sexual terror, the resulting brew is extremely volatile. A century ago, attempts to control syphilis led to the passage of the Contagious Diseases Acts in England. The Acts were based on erroneous medical theories and did nothing to halt the spread of the disease. But they did make life miserable for the hundreds of women who were incarcerated, subjected to forcible vaginal examination, and stigmatized for life as prostitutes.[63]

Whatever happens, AIDS will have far-reaching consequences on sex in general, and on homosexuality in particular. The disease will have a significant impact on the choices gay people make. Fewer will migrate to the gay meccas out of fear of the disease. Those who already reside in the ghettos will avoid situations they fear will expose them. The gay economy, and the political apparatus it supports, may prove to be evanescent. Fear of AIDS has already affected sexual ideology. Just when homosexuals have had some success in throwing off the taint of mental disease, gay people find themselves metaphorically welded to an image of lethal physical deterioration. The syndrome, its peculiar qualities, and its transmissibility are being used to reinforce old fears that sexual activity, homosexuality, and promiscuity led to disease and death.

AIDS is both a personal tragedy for those who contract the syndrome and a calamity for the gay community. Homophobes have gleefully hastened to turn this tragedy against its victims. One columnist has suggested that AIDS has always existed, that the Biblical prohibitions on sodomy were designed to protect people from AIDS, and that AIDS is therefore an appropriate punishment for violating the Levitical codes. Using fear of infection as a rationale, local right-wingers attempted to ban the gay rodeo from Reno, Nevada. A recent issue of the *Moral Majority Report* featured a picture of a "typical" white family of four wearing surgical masks. The headline read: "AIDS: HOMOSEX-UAL DISEASES THREATEN AMERICAN FAMILIES."[64] Phyllis Schlafly has recently issued a pamphlet arguing that passage of the Equal Rights Amendment would make it impossible to "legally protect ourselves against AIDS and other diseases carried by homosexuals."[65] Current right-wing literature calls for shutting down the gay baths, for a legal ban on homosexual employment in food-handling occupations, and for state-mandated prohibitions on blood donations by gay people. Such policies would require the government to identify all homosexuals and impose easily recognizable legal and social markers on them.

It is bad enough that the gay community must deal with the medical misfortune of having been the population in which a deadly disease first became widespread and visible. It is worse to have to deal with the social consequences as well. Even before the AIDS scare, Greece passed a law that enabled police to arrest suspected homosexuals and force them to submit to an examination for venereal disease. It is likely that until AIDS and its methods of transmission are understood, there will be all sorts of proposals to control it by punishing the gay community and by attacking its institutions. When the cause of Legionnaires' Disease was unknown, there were no calls to quarantine members of the American Legion or to shut down their meeting halls. The Contagious Diseases Acts in England did little to control syphilis, but they caused a great deal of suffering for the women who came under their purview. The history of panic that has accompanied new epidemics, and of the casualties incurred by their scapegoats, should make everyone pause and consider with extreme scepticism any attempts to justify anti-gay policy initiatives on the basis of AIDS.*

VI The Limits of Feminism

We know that in an overwhelmingly large number of cases, sex crime is associated with pornography. We know that sex criminals read it, are clearly influenced by it. I believe that, if we can eliminate the distribution of such items among impressionable children, we shall greatly reduce our frightening sex-crime rate. (J. Edgar Hoover[66])

In the absence of a more articulated radical theory of sex, most progressives have turned to feminism for guidance. But the relationship between feminism and sex is

*FN 1992. The literature on AIDS and its social sequelae has mushroomed since this essay was published. A few of the important texts are Douglas Crimp, *AIDS: Cultural Analysis, Cultural Activism*, Cambridge, Mass., MIT Press, 1988; Douglas Crimp with Adam Rolston, *AIDS DEMOGRAPHICS*, Seattle, Bay Press, 1990; Elizabeth Fee and Daniel M. Fox, *AIDS: The Burdens of History*, Berkeley, University of California Press, 1988; Elizabeth Fee and Daniel M. Fox, *AIDS: The Making of a Chronic Disease*, Berkeley, University of California Press, 1992; Cindy Patton, *Sex and Germs: The Politics of AIDS*, Boston, South End Press, 1985; Cindy Patton, *Inventing AIDS*, New York, Routledge, 1990; Simon Watney, *Policing Desire: Pornography, AIDS, and the Media*, Minneapolis, University of Minnesota Press, 1987; Erica Carter and Simon Watney, *Taking Liberties: AIDS and Cultural Politics*, London, Serpent's Tail, 1989; Tessa Boffin and Sunil Gupta, *Ecstatic Antibodies*, London, Rivers Oram Press, 1990; and James Kinsella, *Covering the Plague: AIDS and the American Media*, New Brunswick, Rutgers University Press, 1989.

complex. Because sexuality is a nexus of the relationships between genders, much of the oppression of women *is* borne by, mediated through, and constituted within, sexuality. Feminism has always been vitally interested in sex. But there have been two strains of feminist thought on the subject. One tendency has criticized the restrictions on women's sexual behavior and denounced the high costs imposed on women for being sexually active. This tradition of feminist sexual thought has called for a sexual liberation that would work for women as well as for men. The second tendency has considered sexual liberalization to be inherently a mere extension of male privilege. This tradition resonates with conservative, anti-sexual discourse. With the advent of the anti-pornography movement, it achieved temporary hegemony over feminist analysis.

The anti-pornography movement and its texts have been the most extensive expression of this discourse.[67] In addition, proponents of this viewpoint have condemned virtually every variant of sexual expression as anti-feminist. Within this framework, monogamous lesbianism that occurs within long-term, intimate relationships and which does not involve playing with polarized roles, has replaced married, procreative heterosexuality at the top of the value hierarchy. Heterosexuality has been demoted to somewhere in the middle. Apart from this change, everything else looks more or less familiar. The lower depths are occupied by the usual groups and behaviors: prostitution, transsexuality, sadomasochism, and cross-generational activities.[68] Most gay male conduct, all casual sex, promiscuity, and lesbian behavior that does involve roles or kink or non-monogamy are also censured.[69] Even sexual fantasy during masturbation is denounced as a phallocentric holdover.[70]

This discourse on sexuality is less a sexology than a demonology. It presents most sexual behavior in the worst possible light. Its descriptions of erotic conduct always use the worst available example as if it were representative. It presents the most disgusting pornography, the most exploited forms of prostitution, and the least palatable or most shocking manifestations of sexual variation. This rhetorical tactic consistently misrepresents human sexuality in all its forms. The picture of human sexuality that emerges from this literature is unremittingly ugly.

In addition, this anti-porn rhetoric is a massive exercise in scapegoating. It criticizes non-routine acts of love rather than routine acts of oppression, exploitation, or violence. This demon sexology directs legitimate anger at women's lack of personal safety against innocent individuals, practices, and communities. Anti-porn propaganda often implies that sexism originates within the commercial sex industry and subsequently infects the rest of society. This is sociologically nonsensical. The sex industry is hardly a feminist utopia. It reflects the sexism that exists in the society as a whole. We need to analyze and oppose the manifestations of gender inequality specific to the sex industry. But this is not the same as attempting to wipe out commercial sex.

Similarly, erotic minorities such as sadomasochists and transsexuals are as likely to exhibit sexist attitudes or behavior as any other politically random social grouping. But to claim that they are inherently anti-feminist is sheer fantasy. A good deal of current feminist literature attributes the oppression of women to graphic representations of sex, prostitution, sex education, sadomasochism, male homosexuality, and transsexualism. Whatever happened to the family, religion, education, child-rearing practices, the media, the state, psychiatry, job discrimination, and unequal pay?

Finally, this so-called feminist discourse recreates a very conservative sexual morality. For over a century, battles have been waged over just how much shame, distress, and punishment should be incurred by sexual activity. The conservative tradition has promoted opposition to pornography, prostitution, homosexuality, all erotic variation, sex education, sex research, abortion, and contraception. The opposing, pro-sex tradition has included individuals like Havelock Ellis, Magnus Hirschfeld, Alfred Kinsey, and Victoria Woodhull, as well as the sex education movement, organizations of militant prostitutes and homosexuals, the reproductive rights movement, and organizations such as the Sexual Reform League of the 1960s. This motley collection of sex reformers, sex educators, and sexual militants has mixed records on both sexual and feminist issues. But surely they are closer to the spirit of modern feminism than are moral crusaders, the social purity movement, and anti-vice organizations. Nevertheless, the current feminist sexual demonology generally elevates the anti-vice crusaders to positions of ancestral honor, while condemning the more liberatory tradition as anti-feminist. In an essay that exemplifies some of these trends, Sheila Jeffreys blames Havelock Ellis, Edward Carpenter, Alexandra Kollantai, "believers in the joy of sex of every possible political persuasion," and the 1929 congress of the World League for Sex Reform for making "a great contribution to the defeat of militant feminism."[71]*

The anti-pornography movement and its avatars have claimed to speak for all feminism. Fortunately, they do not. Sexual liberation has been and continues to be a feminist goal. The women's movement may have produced some of the most retrogressive sexual thinking this side of the Vatican. But it has also produced an exciting, innovative, and articulate defense of sexual pleasure and erotic justice. This "pro-sex" feminism has been spearheaded by lesbians whose sexuality does not conform to movement standards of purity (primarily lesbian sadomasochists and butch/femme dykes), by unapologetic heterosexuals, and by women who adhere to classic radical feminism rather than to the revisionist celebrations of femininity which have become so common.[72] Although the anti-porn forces have attempted to weed anyone who disagrees with them out of the movement, the fact remains that feminist thought about sex is profoundly polarized.[73]

Whenever there is polarization, there is an unhappy tendency to think the truth lies somewhere in between. Ellen Willis has commented sarcastically that "the feminist bias is that women are equal to men and the male chauvinist bias is that women are inferior. The unbiased view is that the truth lies somewhere in between."[74] The most recent development in the feminist sex wars is the emergence of a "middle" that seeks to evade the dangers of anti-porn fascism, on the one hand, and a supposed "anything goes" libertarianism, on the other.[75] Although it is hard to criticize a position that is not yet fully formed, I want to draw attention to some incipient problems.**

*FN 1992. These trends have become much more fully articulated. Some of the key texts are Sheila Jeffreys, *The Spinster and Her Enemies: Feminism and Sexuality 1880–1930,* London, Pandora Press, 1985; Sheila Jeffreys, *Anti-Climax,* London, The Women's Press, 1990; Lal Coveney, Margaret Jackson, Sheila Jeffreys, Leslie Kay, and Pat Mahony, *The Sexuality Papers: Male Sexuality and the Social Control of Women,* London, Hutchinson, 1984; and Dorchen Leidholdt and Janice G. Raymond, *The Sexual Liberals and the Attack on Feminism,* New York, Pergamon, 1990.

**FN 1992. The label "libertarian feminist" or "sexual libertarian" continues to be used as a shorthand for feminist sex radicals. The label is erroneous and misleading. It is true that the Libertarian Party opposes state control of consensual sexual behavior. We agree on the pernicious quality of state activity in this area, and I consider the Libertarian program to repeal most sex legislation superior to that of any other organized political party. However, there the similarity ends. Feminist sex radicals rely on concepts of systemic, socially structured inequalities and differential powers. In this analysis, state regulation of sex is part of a more complex system of oppression which it reflects, enforces, and influences. The state also develops its own structures of interests, powers, and investments in sexual regulation.

As I have explained in this essay and elsewhere, the concept of consent plays a different role in sex law than it does in the social contract or the wage contract. The qualities, quantity, and significance of state intervention and regulation of sexual behavior need to be analyzed in context, and not crudely equated with analyses drawn from economic theory. Certain basic freedoms which are taken for granted in other areas of life do not exist in the area of sex. Those that do exist are not equally available to members of different sexual populations and are differentially applied to various sexual activities. People are not called "libertarian" for agitating for basic freedoms and legal equality for racial and ethnic groups; I see no reason why sexual populations should be denied even the limited benefits of liberal capitalist societies.

I doubt anyone would call Marx a liberal or libertarian, but he considered capitalism a revolutionary, if limited, social system. "Hence the great civilizing influence of capital, its production of a stage of society

The emergent middle is based on a false characterization of the poles of the debate, construing both sides as equally extremist. According to B. Ruby Rich, "the desire for a language of sexuality has led feminists into locations (pornography, sadomasochism) too narrow or overdetermined for a fruitful discussion. Debate has collapsed into a rumble."[76] True, the fights between Women Against Pornography (WAP) and lesbian sadomasochists have resembled gang warfare. But the responsibility for this lies primarily with the anti-porn movement, and its refusal to engage in principled discussion. S/M lesbians have been forced into a struggle to maintain their membership in the movement, and to defend themselves against slander. No major spokeswoman for lesbian S/M has argued for any kind of S/M supremacy, or advocated that everyone should be a sado-masochist. In addition to self-defense, S/M lesbians have called for appreciation for erotic diversity and more open discussion of sexuality.[77] Trying to find a middle course between WAP and Samois is a bit like saying that the truth about homosexuality lies somewhere between the positions of the Moral Majority and those of the gay movement.

In political life, it is all too easy to marginalize radicals, and to attempt to buy acceptance for a moderate position by portraying others as extremists. Liberals have done this for years to communists. Sexual radicals have opened up the sex debates. It is shameful to deny their contribution, misrepresent their positions, and further their stigmatization.

In contrast to cultural feminists, who simply want to purge sexual dissidents, the sexual moderates are willing to defend the rights of erotic non-conformists to political participation. Yet this defense of political rights is linked to an implicit system of ide-ological condescension.* The argument has two major parts. The first is an accusation that sexual dissidents have not paid close enough attention to the meaning, sources, or historical construction of their sexuality. This emphasis on meaning appears to function in much the same way that the question of etiology has functioned in discussions of homosexuality. That is, homosexuality, sadomasochism, prostitution, or boy-love are taken to be mysterious and problematic in some way that more respectable sexualities are not. The search for a cause is a search for something that could change so that these "problematic" eroticisms would simply not occur. Sexual militants have replied to such exercises that although the question of etiology or cause is of intellectual interest, it is not high on the political agenda and that, moreover, the privileging of such questions is itself a regressive political choice.

The second part of the "moderate" position focuses on questions of consent. Sexual radicals of all varieties have demanded the legal and social legitimation of consenting sexual behavior. Feminists have criticized them for ostensibly finessing questions about "the limits of consent" and "structural constraints" on consent.[78] Although there are deep problems with the political discourse of consent, and although there are certainly structural constraints on sexual choice, this criticism has been consistently misapplied in the sex debates. It does not take into account the very specific semantic content that consent has in sex law and sex practice.

As I mentioned earlier, a great deal of sex law does not distinguish between con-sensual and coercive behavior. Only rape law contains such a distinction. Rape law is based on the assumption, correct in my view, that heterosexual activity may be freely

---

compared with which all earlier stages appear to be merely *local progress* . . ." (Karl Marx, *The Grundrisse,* New York, Harper Torchbooks, 1971, pp. 94–95). The failure to support democratic sexual freedoms does not bring on socialism; it maintains something more akin to feudalism.

*FN 1992. A recent example of dismissive ideological condescension is this: "The Sadomasochists are not entirely 'valueless,' but they have resisted any values that might limit their freedom rather than someone else's judgement; and in this they show themselves as lacking in an understanding of the requirements of common life." It appears in Shane Phelan, *Identity Politics: Lesbian Feminism and the Limits of Community,* Philadelphia, Temple University Press, 1989, p. 133.

chosen or forcibly coerced. One has the legal right to engage in heterosexual behavior as long as it does not fall under the purview of other statutes and as long as it is agreeable to both parties.

This is not the case for most other sexual acts. Sodomy laws, as I mentioned above, are based on the assumption that the forbidden acts are an "abominable and detestable crime against nature." Criminality is intrinsic to the acts themselves, no matter what the desires of the participants. "Unlike rape, sodomy or an unnatural or perverted sexual act may be committed between two persons both of whom consent, and, regardless of which is the aggressor, both may be prosecuted."[79] Before the consenting adults statute was passed in California in 1976, lesbian lovers could have been prosecuted for committing oral copulation. If both participants were capable of consent, both were equally guilty.[80]

Adult incest statutes operate in a similar fashion. Contrary to popular mythology, the incest statutes have little to do with protecting children from rape by close relatives. The incest statutes themselves prohibit marriage or sexual intercourse between adults who are closely related. Prosecutions are rare, but two were reported recently. In 1979, a 19-year-old Marine met his 42-year-old mother, from whom he had been separated at birth. The two fell in love and got married. They were charged and found guilty of incest, which under Virginia law carries a maximum ten-year sentence. During their trial, the Marine testified, "I love her very much. I feel that two people who love each other should be able to live together."[81] In another case, a brother and sister who had been raised separately met and decided to get married. They were arrested and pleaded guilty to felony incest in return for probation. A condition of probation was that they not live together as husband and wife. Had they not accepted, they would have faced twenty years in prison.[82]

In a famous S/M case, a man was convicted of aggravated assault for a whipping administered in an S/M scene. There was no complaining victim. The session had been filmed and he was prosecuted on the basis of the film. The man appealed his conviction by arguing that he had been involved in a consensual sexual encounter and had assaulted no one. In rejecting his appeal, the court ruled that one may not consent to an assault or battery "except in a situation involving ordinary physical contact or blows incident to sports such as football, boxing, or wrestling."[83] The court went on to note that the "consent of a person without legal capacity to give consent, such as a child or insane person, is ineffective," and that "It is a matter of common knowledge that a normal person in full possession of his mental faculties does not freely consent to the use, upon himself, of force likely to produce great bodily injury."[84] Therefore, anyone who would consent to a whipping would be presumed *non compos mentis* and legally incapable of consenting. S/M sex generally involves a much lower level of force than the average football game, and results in far fewer injuries than most sports. But the court ruled that football players are sane, whereas masochists are not.

Sodomy laws, adult incest laws, and legal interpretations such as the one above clearly interfere with consensual behavior and impose criminal penalties on it. Within the law, consent is a privilege enjoyed only by those who engage in the highest-status sexual behavior. Those who enjoy low-status sexual behavior do not have the legal right to engage in it. In addition, economic sanctions, family pressures, erotic stigma, social discrimination, negative ideology, and the paucity of information about erotic behavior, all serve to make it difficult for people to make unconventional sexual choices. There certainly are structural constraints that impede free sexual choice, but they hardly operate to coerce anyone into being a pervert. On the contrary, they operate to coerce everyone toward normality.

The "brainwash theory" explains erotic diversity by assuming that some sexual acts are so disgusting that no one would willingly perform them. Therefore, the reasoning goes, anyone who does so must have been forced or fooled. Even constructivist sexual theory has been pressed into the service of explaining away why otherwise rational individuals might engage in variant sexual behavior. Another position that is not yet fully formed uses the ideas of Foucault and Weeks to imply that the "perversions" are an especially unsavory or problematic aspect of the construction of modern sexuality.[85] This is yet another version of the notion that sexual dissidents are victims of the subtle machinations of the social system. Weeks and Foucault would not accept such an interpretation, since they consider all sexuality to be constructed, the conventional no less than the deviant.

Psychology is the last resort of those who refuse to acknowledge that sexual dissidents are as conscious and free as any other group of sexual actors. If deviants are not responding to the manipulations of the social system, then perhaps the source of their incomprehensible choices can be found in a bad childhood, unsuccessful socialization, or inadequate identity formation. In her essay on erotic domination, Jessica Benjamin draws upon psychoanalysis and philosophy to explain why what she calls "sadomasochism" is alienated, distorted, unsatisfactory, numb, purposeless, and an attempt to "relieve an original effort at differentiation that failed."[86] This essay substitutes a psycho-philosophical inferiority for the more usual means of devaluing dissident eroticism. One reviewer has already construed Benjamin's argument as showing that sadomasochism is merely an "obsessive replay of the infant power struggle."[87]

The position which defends the political rights of perverts but which seeks to understand their "alienated" sexuality is certainly preferable to the WAP-style bloodbaths. But for the most part, the sexual moderates have not confronted their discomfort with erotic choices that differ from their own. Erotic chauvinism cannot be redeemed by tarting it up in Marxist drag, sophisticated constructivist theory, or retro-psychobabble.

Whichever feminist position on sexuality—right, left, or center—eventually attains dominance, the existence of such a rich discussion is evidence that the feminist movement will always be a source of interesting thought about sex. Nevertheless, I want to challenge the assumption that feminism is or should be the privileged site of a theory of sexuality. Feminism is the theory of gender oppression. To assume automatically that this makes it the theory of sexual oppression is to fail to distinguish between gender, on the one hand, and erotic desire, on the other.

In the English language, the word "sex" has two very different meanings. It means gender and gender identity, as in "the female sex" or "the male sex." But sex also refers to sexual activity, lust, intercourse, and arousal, as in "to have sex." This semantic merging reflects a cultural assumption that sexuality is reducible to sexual intercourse and that it is a function of the relations between women and men. The cultural fusion of gender with sexuality has given rise to the idea that a theory of sexuality may be derived directly out of a theory of gender.

In an earlier essay, "The Traffic in Women," I used the concept of a sex/gender system, defined as a "set of arrangements by which a society transforms biological sexuality into products of human activity."[88] I went on to argue that "Sex as we know it—gender identity, sexual desire and fantasy, concepts of childhood—is itself a social product."[89] In that essay, I did not distinguish between lust and gender, treating both as modalities of the same underlying social process.

"The Traffic in Women" was inspired by the literature on kin-based systems of social organization. It appeared to me at the time that gender and desire were systemically intertwined in such social formations. This may or may not be an accurate assessment of the relationship between sex and gender in tribal organizations. But it is surely not an adequate formulation for sexuality in Western industrial societies. As Foucault has pointed out, a system of sexuality has emerged out of earlier kinship forms and has acquired significant autonomy.

> Particularly from the eighteenth century onward, Western societies created and deployed a new apparatus which was superimposed on the previous one, and which, without completely supplanting the latter, helped to reduce its importance. I am speaking of the deployment of *sexuality*. . . . For the first [kinship], what is pertinent is the link between partners and definite statutes; the second [sexuality] is concerned with the sensations of the body, the quality of pleasures, and the nature of impressions.[90]

The development of this sexual system has taken place in the context of gender relations. Part of the modern ideology of sex is that lust is the province of men, purity that of women. It is no accident that pornography and the perversions have been considered part of the male domain. In the sex industry, women have been excluded from most production and consumption, and allowed to participate primarily as workers. In order to participate in the "perversions," women have had to overcome serious limitations on their social mobility, their economic resources, and their sexual freedoms. Gender affects the operation of the sexual system, and the sexual system has had gender-specific manifestations. But although sex and gender are related, they are not the same thing, and they form the basis of two distinct arenas of social practice.

In contrast to my perspective in "The Traffic in Women," I am now arguing that it is essential to separate gender and sexuality analytically to reflect more accurately their separate social existence. This goes against the grain of much contemporary feminist thought, which treats sexuality as a derivation of gender. For instance, lesbian feminist ideology has mostly analyzed the oppression of lesbians in terms of the oppression of women. However, lesbians are also oppressed as queers and perverts, by the operation of sexual, not gender, stratification. Although it pains many lesbians to think about it, the fact is that lesbians have shared many of the sociological features and suffered from many of the same social penalties as have gay men, sadomasochists, transvestites, and prostitutes.

Catherine MacKinnon has made the most explicit theoretical attempt to subsume sexuality under feminist thought. According to MacKinnon, "Sexuality is to feminism what work is to marxism . . . the molding, direction, and expression of sexuality organizes society into two sexes, women and men."[91] This analytic strategy in turn rests on a decision to "use sex and gender relatively interchangeably."[92] It is this definitional fusion that I want to challenge.*

There is an instructive analogy in the history of the differentiation of contemporary feminist thought from Marxism. Marxism is probably the most supple and powerful conceptual system extant for analyzing social inequality. But attempts to make Marxism the sole explanatory system for all social inequalities have been dismal exercises. Marxism is most successful in the areas of social life for which it was originally developed—class relations under capitalism.

In the early days of the contemporary women's movement, a theoretical conflict took place over the applicability of Marxism to gender stratification. Since Marxist theory

---

*FN 1992. MacKinnon's published oeuvre has also burgeoned: Catherine A. MacKinnon, *Toward a Feminist Theory of the State*, Cambridge, Mass., Harvard University Press, 1989; Catherine A. MacKinnon, *Feminism Unmodified: Discourses on Life and Law*, Cambridge, Mass., Harvard University Press, 1987.

is relatively powerful, it does in fact detect important and interesting aspects of gender oppression. It works best for those issues of gender most closely related to issues of class and the organization of labor. The issues more specific to the social structure of gender were not amenable to Marxist analysis.

The relationship between feminism and a radical theory of sexual oppression is similar. Feminist conceptual tools were developed to detect and analyze gender-based hierarchies. To the extent that these overlap with erotic stratifications, feminist theory has some explanatory power. But as issues become less those of gender and more those of sexuality, feminist analysis becomes misleading and often irrelevant. Feminist thought simply lacks angles of vision which can fully encompass the social organization of sexuality. The criteria of relevance in feminist thought do not allow it to see or assess critical power relations in the area of sexuality.

In the long run, feminism's critique of gender hierarchy must be incorporated into a radical theory of sex, and the critique of sexual oppression should enrich feminism. But an autonomous theory and politics specific to sexuality must be developed.

It is a mistake to substitute feminism for Marxism as the last word in social theory. Feminism is no more capable than Marxism of being the ultimate and complete account of all social inequality. Nor is feminism the residual theory which can take care of everything to which Marx did not attend. These critical tools were fashioned to handle very specific areas of social activity. Other areas of social life, their forms of power, and their characteristic modes of oppression, need their own conceptual implements. In this essay, I have argued for theoretical as well as sexual pluralism.

VII Conclusion

... these pleasures which we lightly call physical ... (Colette[93])

Like gender, sexuality is political. It is organized into systems of power, which reward and encourage some individuals and activities, while punishing and suppressing others. Like the capitalist organization of labor and its distribution of rewards and powers, the modern sexual system has been the object of political struggle since it emerged and as it has evolved. But if the disputes between labor and capital are mystified, sexual conflicts are completely camouflaged.

The legislative restructuring that took place at the end of the nineteenth century and in the early decades of the twentieth was a refracted response to the emergence of the modern erotic system. During that period, new erotic communities formed. It became possible to be a male homosexual or a lesbian in a way it had not been previously. Mass-produced erotica became available, and the possibilities for sexual commerce expanded. The first homosexual rights organizations were formed, and the first analyses of sexual oppression were articulated.[94]

The repression of the 1950s was in part a backlash to the expansion of sexual communities and possibilities which took place during World War II.[95] During the 1950s, gay rights organizations were established, the Kinsey reports were published, and lesbian literature flourished. The 1950s were a formative as well as a repressive era.

The current right-wing sexual counter-offensive is in part a reaction to the sexual liberalization of the 1960s and early 1970s. Moreover, it has brought about a unified and self-conscious coalition of sexual radicals. In one sense, what is now occurring is the emergence of a new sexual movement, aware of new issues and seeking a new theoretical basis. The sex wars out on the streets have been partly responsible for provoking a new intellectual focus on sexuality. The sexual system is shifting once again, and we are seeing many symptoms of its change.

In Western culture, sex is taken all too seriously. A person is not considered immoral, is not sent to prison, and is not expelled from her or his family, for enjoying spicy cuisine. But an individual may go through all this and more for enjoying shoe leather. Ultimately, of what possible social significance is it if a person likes to masturbate over a shoe? It may even be non-consensual, but since we do not ask permission of our shoes to wear them, it hardly seems necessary to obtain dispensation to come on them.

If sex is taken too seriously, sexual persecution is not taken seriously enough. There is systematic mistreatment of individuals and communities on the basis of erotic taste or behavior. There are serious penalties for belonging to the various sexual occupational castes. The sexuality of the young is denied, adult sexuality is often treated like a variety of nuclear waste, and the graphic representation of sex takes place in a mire of legal and social circumlocution. Specific populations bear the brunt of the current system of erotic power, but their persecution upholds a system that affects everyone.

The 1980s have already been a time of great sexual suffering. They have also been a time of ferment and new possibility. It is up to all of us to try to prevent more barbarism and to encourage erotic creativity. Those who consider themselves progressive need to examine their preconceptions, update their sexual educations, and acquaint themselves with the existence and operation of sexual hierarchy. It is time to recognize the political dimensions of erotic life.

Acknowledgments

It is always a treat to get to the point in a paper when I can thank those who contributed to its realization. Many of my ideas about the formation of sexual communities first occurred to me during a course given by Charles Tilly on "The Urbanization of Europe from 1500–1900." Few courses could ever provide as much excitement, stimulation, and conceptual richness as did that one. Daniel Tsang alerted me to the significance of the events of 1977 and taught me to pay attention to sex law. Pat Califia deepened my appreciation for human sexual variety and taught me to respect the much-maligned fields of sex research and sex education. Jeff Escoffier shared his powerful grasp of gay history and sociology, and I have especially benefited from his insights into the gay economy. Allan Bérubé's work in progress on gay history has enabled me to think with more clarity about the dynamics of sexual oppression. Conversations with Ellen Dubois, Amber Hollibaugh, Mary Ryan, Judy Stacey, Kay Trimberger, Rayna Rapp, and Martha Vicinus have influenced the direction of my thinking.

I am very grateful to Cynthia Astuto for advice and research on legal matters, and to David Sachs, book-dealer extraordinaire, for pointing out the right-wing pamphlet literature on sex. I am grateful to Allan Bérubé, Ralph Bruno, Estelle Freedman, Kent Gerard, Barbara Kerr, Michael Shively, Carole Vance, Bill Walker, and Judy Walkowitz for miscellaneous references and factual information. I cannot begin to express my gratitude to those who read and commented on versions of this paper: Jeanne Bergman, Sally Binford, Lynn Eden, Laura Engelstein, Jeff Escoffier, Carole Vance, and Ellen Willis. Mark Leger both edited and performed acts of secretarial heroism in preparing the manuscript. Marybeth Nelson provided emergency graphics assistance.

I owe special thanks to two friends whose care mitigated the strains of writing. E.S. kept my back operational and guided me firmly through some monumental bouts of writer's block. Cynthia Astuto's many kindnesses and unwavering support enabled me to keep working at an absurd pace for many weeks.

None of these individuals should be held responsible for my opinions, but I am grateful to them all for inspiration, information, and assistance.

A Note on Definitions

Throughout this essay, I use terms such as homosexual, sex worker, and pervert. I use "homosexual" to refer to both women and men. If I want to be more specific, I use terms such as "lesbian" or "gay male." "Sex worker" is intended to be more inclusive than "prostitute," in order to encompass the many jobs of the sex industry. Sex worker includes erotic dancers, strippers, porn models, nude women who will talk to a customer via telephone hook-up and can be seen but not touched, phone partners, and the various other employees of sex businesses such as receptionists, janitors, and barkers. Obviously, it also includes prostitutes, hustlers, and "male models." I use the term "pervert" as a shorthand for all the stigmatized sexual orientations. It used to cover male and female homosexuality as well but as these become less disreputable, the term has increasingly referred to the other "deviations." Terms such as "pervert" and "deviant" have, in general use, a connotation of disapproval, disgust, and dislike. I am using these terms in a denotative fashion, and do not intend them to convey any disapproval on my part.

NOTES

1. Demetrius Zambaco, "Onanism and Nervous Disorders in Two Little Girls," in François Peraldi (ed.), *Polysexuality, Semiotext(e)*, vol. IV, no. 1, 1981, pp. 31, 36.

2. Linda Gordon and Ellen Dubois, "Seeking Ecstasy on the Battlefield: Danger and Pleasure in Nineteenth Century Feminist Sexual Thought," *Feminist Studies*, vol. 9, no. 1, Spring 1983; Steven Marcus, *The Other Victorians*, New York, New American Library, 1974; Mary Ryan, "The Power of Women's Networks: A Case Study of Female Moral Reform in America," *Feminist Studies*, vol. 5, no. 1, 1979; Judith R. Walkowitz, *Prostitution and Victorian Society*, Cambridge, Cambridge University Press, 1980; Judith R. Walkowitz, "Male Vice and Feminist Virtue: Feminism and the Politics of Prostitution in Nineteenth-Century Britain," *History Workshop Journal*, no. 13, Spring 1982; Jeffrey Weeks, *Sex, Politics and Society: The Regulation of Sexuality Since 1800*, New York, Longman, 1981.

3. G.J. Barker-Benfield, *The Horrors of the Half-Known Life*, New York, Harper Colophon, 1976; Marcus, op. cit.; Weeks, op. cit., especially pages 48–52; Zambaco, op. cit.

4. Sarah Senefield Beserra, Sterling G. Franklin, and Norma Clevenger (eds.), *Sex Code of California*, Sacramento, Planned Parenthood Affiliates of California, 1977, p. 113.

5. Ibid., pp. 113–17.

6. Walkowitz, "Male Vice and Feminist Virtue," op. cit., p. 83. Walkowitz's entire discussion of the *Maiden Tribute of Modern Babylon* and its aftermath (pp. 83–5) is illuminating.

7. Walkowitz, "Male Vice and Feminist Virtue," op. cit., p. 85.

8. Beserra et al., op. cit., pp. 106–7.

9. Commonwealth of Massachusetts, *Preliminary Report of the Special Commission Investigating the Prevalence of Sex Crimes*, 1947; State of New Hampshire, *Report of the Interim Commission of the State of New Hampshire to Study the Cause and Prevention of Serious Sex Crimes*, 1949; City of New York, *Report of the Mayor's Committee for the Study of Sex Offences*, 1939; State of New York, *Report to the Governor on a Study of 102 Sex Offenders at Sing Sing Prison*, 1950; Samuel Hartwell, *A Citizen's Handbook of Sexual Abnormalities and the Mental Hygiene Approach to Their Prevention*, State of Michigan, 1950; State of Michigan, *Report of the Governor's Study Commission on the Deviated Criminal Sex Offender*, 1951. This is merely a sampler.

10. Estelle B. Freedman, " 'Uncontrolled Desire': The Threat of the Sexual Psychopath in America, 1935–1960," paper presented at the Annual Meeting of the American Historical Association, San Francisco, December 1983.

11. Allan Bérubé, "Behind the Spectre of San Francisco," *Body Politic*, April 1981; Allan Bérubé, "Marching to a Different Drummer," *Advocate*, October 15, 1981; John D'Emilio, *Sexual Politics, Sexual Communities: The Making of the Homosexual Minority in the United States, 1940–1970*, Chicago, University of Chicago Press, 1983; Jonathan Katz, *Gay American History*, New York, Thomas Y. Crowell, 1976.

12. D'Emilio, op. cit., pp. 46–7; Allan Bérubé, personal communication.

13. John Gerassi, *The Boys of Boise,* New York, Collier, 1968, p. 14. I am indebted to Allan Bérubé for calling my attention to this incident.

14. Allan Bérubé, personal communication; D'Emilio, op. cit.; John D'Emilio, "Gay Politics, Gay Community: San Francisco's Experience," *Socialist Review,* no. 55, January–February 1981.

15. The following examples suggest avenues for additional research. A local crackdown at the University of Michigan is documented in Daniel Tsang, "Gay Ann Arbor Purges," *Midwest Gay Academic Journal,* vol. 1, no. 1, 1977; and Daniel Tsang, "Ann Arbor Gay Purges," part 2, *Midwest Gay Academic Journal,* vol. 1, no. 2, 1977. At the University of Michigan, the number of faculty dismissed for alleged homosexuality appears to rival the number fired for alleged communist tendencies. It would be interesting to have figures comparing the number of professors who lost their positions during this period due to sexual and political offenses. On regulatory reform, many states passed laws during this period prohibiting the sale of alcoholic beverages to "known sex perverts" or providing that bars which catered to "sex perverts" be closed. Such a law was passed in California in 1955, and declared unconstitutional by the state Supreme Court in 1959 (Allan Bérubé, personal communication). It would be of great interest to know exactly which states passed such statutes, the dates of their enactment, the discussion that preceded them, and how many are still on the books. On the persecution of other erotic populations, evidence indicates that John Willie and Irving Klaw, the two premier producers and distributors of bondage erotica in the United States from the late 1940s through the early 1960s, encountered frequent police harassment and that Klaw, at least, was affected by a congressional investigation conducted by the Kefauver Committee. I am indebted to personal communication from J.B. Rund for information on the careers of Willie and Klaw. Published sources are scarce, but see John Willie, *The Adventures of Sweet Gwendoline,* New York, Belier Press, 1974; J.B. Rund, "Preface," *Bizarre Comix,* vol. 8, New York, Belier Press, 1977; J.B. Rund, "Preface," *Bizarre Fotos,* vol. 1, New York, Belier Press, 1978; and J.B. Rund, "Preface," *Bizarre Katalogs,* vol. 1, New York, Belier Press, 1979. It would be useful to have more systematic information on legal shifts and police activity affecting non-gay erotic dissidence.

16. "Chicago is Center of National Child Porno Ring: The Child Predators," "Child Sex: Square in New Town Tells it All," "U.S. Orders Hearings On Child Pornography: Rodino Calls Sex Racket an 'Outrage,' " "Hunt Six Men, Twenty Boys in Crackdown," *Chicago Tribune,* May 16, 1977; "Dentist Seized in Child Sex Raid: Carey to Open Probe," "How Ruses Lure Victims to Child Pornographers," *Chicago Tribune,* May 17, 1977; "Child Pornographers Thrive on Legal Confusion," "U.S. Raids Hit Porn Sellers," *Chicago Tribune,* May 18, 1977.

17. For more information on the "kiddie porn panic" see Pat Califia, "The Great Kiddy Porn Scare of '77 and Its Aftermath," *Advocate,* October 16, 1980; Pat Califia, "A Thorny Issue Splits a Movement," *Advocate,* October 30, 1980; Mitzel, *The Boston Sex Scandal,* Boston, Glad Day Books, 1980; Gayle Rubin, "Sexual Politics, the New Right, and the Sexual Fringe," in Daniel Tsang (ed.), *The Age Taboo,* Boston, Alyson Publications, 1981. On the issue of cross-generational relationships, see also Roger Moody, *Indecent Assault,* London, Word Is Out Press, 1980; Tom O'Carroll, *Paedophilia: The Radical Case,* London, Peter Owen, 1980; Tsang, *The Age Taboo,* op. cit.; and Paul Wilson, *The Man They Called A Monster,* New South Wales, Cassell Australia, 1981.

18. "House Passes Tough Bill on Child Porn," *San Francisco Chronicle,* November 15, 1983, p. 14.

19. George Stambolian, "Creating the New Man: A Conversation with Jacqueline Livingston," *Christopher Street,* May 1980; "Jacqueline Livingston," *Clothed With the Sun,* vol. 3, no. 1, May 1983.

20. Paul H. Gebhard, "The Institute," in Martin S. Weinberg (ed.), *Sex Research: Studies from the Kinsey Institute,* New York, Oxford University Press, 1976.

21. Phoebe Courtney, *The Sex Education Racket: Pornography in the Schools (An Exposé),* New Orleans, Free Men Speak, 1969; Dr. Gordon V. Drake, *SIECUS: Corrupter of Youth,* Tulsa, Oklahoma, Christian Crusade Publications, 1969.

22. *Pavlov's Children (They May Be Yours),* Impact Publishers, Los Angeles, California, 1969.

23. Norman Podhoretz, "The Culture of Appeasement," *Harper's,* October 1977.

24. Alan Wolfe and Jerry Sanders, "Resurgent Cold War Ideology: The Case of the Committee on the Present Danger," in Richard Fagen (ed.), *Capitalism and the State in U.S.-Latin American Relations*, Stanford, Stanford University Press, 1979.

25. Jimmy Breslin, "The Moral Majority in Your Motel Room," *San Francisco Chronicle*, January 22, 1981, p. 41; Linda Gordon and Allen Hunter, "Sex, Family, and the New Right," *Radical America*, Winter 1977–8; Sasha Gregory-Lewis, "The Neo-Right Political Apparatus," *Advocate*, February 8, 1977; Sasha Gregory-Lewis, "Right Wing Finds New Organizing Tactic," *Advocate*, June 23, 1977; Sasha Gregory-Lewis, "Unravelling the Anti-Gay Network," *Advocate*, September 7, 1977; Andrew Kopkind, "America's New Right," *New Times*, September 30, 1977; Rosalind Pollack Petchesky, "Anti-abortion, Anti-feminism, and the Rise of the New Right," *Feminist Studies*, vol. 7, no. 2, Summer 1981.

26. Rhonda Brown, "Blueprint for a Moral America," *Nation*, May 23, 1981.

27. James Barr, *Quatrefoil*, New York, Greenberg, 1950, p. 310.

28. This insight was first articulated by Mary McIntosh, "The Homosexual Role," *Social Problems*, vol. 16, no. 2, Fall 1968; the idea has been developed in Jeffrey Weeks, *Coming Out: Homosexual Politics in Britain from the Nineteenth Century to the Present*, New York, Quartet, 1977, and in Weeks, *Sex, Politics and Society*, op. cit.; see also D'Emilio, *Sexual Politics, Sexual Communities*, op. cit.; and Gayle Rubin, "Introduction" to Renée Vivien, *A Woman Appeared to Me*, Weatherby Lake, Mo., Naiad Press, 1979.

29. Bert Hansen, "The Historical Construction of Homosexuality," *Radical History Review*, no. 20, Spring/Summer 1979.

30. Walkowitz, *Prostitution and Victorian Society*, op. cit.; and Walkowitz, "Male Vice and Female Virtue," op. cit.

31. Michel Foucault, *The History of Sexuality*, New York, Pantheon, 1978.

32. A very useful discussion of these issues can be found in Robert Padgug, "Sexual Matters: On Conceptualizing Sexuality in History," *Radical History Review*, no. 20, Spring/Summer 1979.

33. Claude Lévi-Strauss, "A Confrontation," *New Left Review*, no. 62, July–August 1970. In this conversation, Lévi-Strauss calls his position "a Kantianism without a transcendental subject."

34. Foucault, op. cit., p. 11.

35. See the discussion in Weeks, *Sex, Politics and Society*, op. cit., p. 9.

36. See Weeks, *Sex, Politics and Society*, op. cit., p. 22.

37. See, for example, "Pope Praises Couples for Self-Control," *San Francisco Chronicle*, October 13, 1980, p. 5; "Pope Says Sexual Arousal Isn't a Sin If It's Ethical," *San Francisco Chronicle*, November 6, 1980, p. 33; "Pope Condemns 'Carnal Lust' As Abuse of Human Freedom," *San Francisco Chronicle*, January 15, 1981, p. 2; "Pope Again Hits Abortion, Birth Control," *San Francisco Chronicle*, January 16, 1981, p. 13; and "Sexuality, Not Sex in Heaven," *San Francisco Chronicle*, December 3, 1981, p. 50. See also footnote 62 below.

38. Susan Sontag, *Styles of Radical Will*, New York, Farrar, Straus, & Giroux, 1969, p. 46.

39. See Foucault, op. cit., pp. 106–7.

40. American Psychiatric Association, *Diagnostic and Statistical Manual of Mental and Physical Disorders*, 3rd edn, Washington, DC, American Psychiatric Association.

41. Alfred Kinsey, Wardell Pomeroy, and Clyde Martin, *Sexual Behavior in the Human Male*, Philadelphia, W.B. Saunders, 1948; Alfred Kinsey, Wardell Pomeroy, Clyde Martin, and Paul Gebhard, *Sexual Behavior in the Human Female*, Philadelphia, W.B. Saunders, 1953.

42. John Gagnon and William Simon, *Sexual Deviance*, New York, Harper & Row, 1967; John Gagnon and William Simon, *The Sexual Scene*, Chicago, Transaction Books, Aldine, 1970; John Gagnon, *Human Sexualities*, Glenview, Illinois, Scott, Foresman, 1977.

43. Havelock Ellis, *Studies in the Psychology of Sex* (two volumes), New York, Random House, 1936.

44. Foucault, op. cit., p. 43.

45. Gilbert Herdt, *Guardians of the Flutes*, New York, McGraw-Hill, 1981; Raymond Kelly, "Witchcraft and Sexual Relations," in Paula Brown and Georgeda Buchbinder (eds.), *Man and Woman in the New Guinea Highlands*, Washington, DC, American Anthropological Association, 1976; Gayle Rubin, "Coconuts: Aspects of Male/Female Relationships in New Guinea," unpublished ms., 1974; Gayle Rubin, review of *Guardians of the Flutes*, *Advocate*, December 23, 1982; J.

Van Baal, *Dema,* The Hague, Nijhoff, 1966; F.E. Williams, *Papuans of the Trans-Fly,* Oxford, Clarendon, 1936.

46. Caroline Bingham, "Seventeenth-Century Attitudes Toward Deviant Sex," *Journal of Interdisciplinary History,* Spring 1971, p. 465.

47. Stephen O. Murray, "The Institutional Elaboration of a Quasi-Ethnic Community," *International Review of Modern Sociology,* July–December 1979.

48. For further elaboration of these processes, see: Bérubé, "Behind the Spectre of San Francisco," op. cit.; Bérubé, "Marching to a Different Drummer," op. cit.; D'Emilio, "Gay Politics, Gay Community," op. cit.; D'Emilio, *Sexual Politics, Sexual Communities,* op. cit.; Foucault, op. cit.; Hansen, op. cit.; Katz, op. cit.; Weeks, *Coming Out,* op. cit.; and Weeks, *Sex, Politics and Society,* op. cit.

49. Walkowitz, *Prostitution and Victorian Society,* op. cit.

50. Vice cops also harass all sex businesses, be these gay bars, gay baths, adult book stores, the producers and distributors of commercial erotica, or swing clubs.

51. Foucault, op. cit., p. 40.

52. Karl Marx, in David McLellan (ed.), *The Grundrisse,* New York, Harper & Row, 1971, p. 94.

53. Clark Norton, "Sex in America," *Inquiry,* October 5, 1981. This article is a superb summary of much current sex law and should be required reading for anyone interested in sex.

54. Bessera et al., op. cit., pp. 165–7.

55. Sarah Senefeld Beserra, Nancy M. Jewel, Melody West Matthews, and Elizabeth R. Gatov (eds.), *Sex Code of California,* Public Education and Research Committee of California, 1973, pp. 163–8. This earlier edition of the *Sex Code of California* preceeded the 1976 consenting adults statute and consequently gives a better overview of sodomy laws.

56. Esther Newton, *Mother Camp: Female Impersonators in America,* Englewood Cliffs, New Jersey, Prentice-Hall, 1972, p. 21, emphasis in the original.

57. D'Emilio, *Sexual Politics, Sexual Communities,* op. cit., pp. 40–53, has an excellent discussion of gay oppression in the 1950s which covers many of the areas I have mentioned. The dynamics he describes, however, are operative in modified forms for other erotic populations, and in other periods. The specific model of gay oppression needs to be generalized to apply, with appropriate modifications, to other sexual groups.

58. Weeks, *Sex, Politics and Society,* op. cit., p. 14.

59. Lysander Spooner, *Vices Are Not Crimes: A Vindication of Moral Liberty,* Cupertino, Cal., Tanstaafl Press, 1977.

60. I have adopted this terminology from the very useful discussion in Weeks, *Sex, Politics and Society,* op. cit., pp. 14–15.

61. See Spooner, op cit., pp. 25–29. Feminist anti-porn discourse fits right into the tradition of justifying attempts at moral control by claiming that such action will protect women and children from violence.

62. "Pope's Talk on Sexual Spontaneity," *San Francisco Chronicle,* November 13, 1980, p. 8; see also footnote 37 above. Julia Penelope argues that "we do not need anything that labels itself purely sexual" and that "fantasy, as an aspect of sexuality, may be a phallocentric 'need' from which we are not yet free . . ." in "And Now For the Really Hard Questions," *Sinister Wisdom,* no. 15, Fall 1980, p. 103.

63. See especially Walkowitz, *Prostitution and Victorian Society,* op. cit., and Weeks, *Sex, Politics and Society,* op. cit.

64. *Moral Majority Report,* July 1983. I am indebted to Allan Bérubé for calling my attention to this image.

65. Cited in Larry Bush, "Capitol Report," *Advocate,* December 8, 1983, p. 60.

66. Cited in H. Montgomery Hyde, *A History of Pornography,* New York, Dell, 1965, p. 31.

67. See for example Laura Lederer (ed.), *Take Back the Night,* New York, William Morrow, 1980; Andrea Dworkin, *Pornography,* New York, Perigee, 1981. The *Newspage* of San Francisco's Women Against Violence in Pornography and Media and the *Newsreport* of New York Women Against Pornography are excellent sources.

68. Kathleen Barry, *Female Sexual Slavery,* Englewood Cliffs, New Jersey, Prentice-Hall, 1979; Janice Raymond, *The Transsexual Empire,* Boston, Beacon, 1979; Kathleen Barry, "Sadomasochism: The New Backlash to Feminism," *Trivia,* no. 1, Fall 1982; Robin Ruth Linden, Darlene R. Pagano, Diana E.H. Russell, and Susan Leigh Starr (eds.), *Against Sadomasochism,* East Palo Alto, Cal., Frog in the Well, 1982; and Florence Rush, *The Best Kept Secret,* New York, McGraw-Hill, 1980.

69. Sally Gearhart, "An Open Letter to the Voters in District 5 and San Francisco's Gay Community," 1979; Adrienne Rich, *On Lies, Secrets, and Silence,* New York, W.W. Norton, 1979, p. 225. ("On the other hand, there is homosexual patriarchal culture, a culture created by homosexual men, reflecting such male stereotypes as dominance and submission as modes of relationship, and the separation of sex from emotional involvement—a culture tainted by profound hatred for women. The male 'gay' culture has offered lesbians the imitation role-stereotypes of 'butch' and 'femme,' 'active' and 'passive,' cruising, sado-masochism, and the violent, self-destructive world of 'gay' bars."); Judith Pasternak, "The Strangest Bedfellows: Lesbian Feminism and the Sexual Revolution," *WomanNews,* October 1983; Adrienne Rich, "Compulsory Heterosexuality and Lesbian Existence," in Ann Snitow, Christine Stansell, and Sharon Thompson (eds.), *Powers of Desire: The Politics of Sexuality,* New York, Monthly Review Press, 1983.

70. Julia Penelope, op. cit.

71. Sheila Jeffreys, "The Spinster and Her Enemies: Sexuality and the Last Wave of Feminism," *Scarlet Woman,* no. 13, part 2, July 1981, p. 26; a further elaboration of this tendency can be found in Judith Pasternak, op. cit.

72. Pat Califia, "Feminism vs. Sex: A New Conservative Wave," *Advocate,* February 21, 1980; Pat Califia, "Among Us, Against Us—The New Puritans," *Advocate,* April 17, 1980; Califia, "The Great Kiddy Porn Scare of '77 and Its Aftermath," op. cit.; Califia, "A Thorny Issue Splits a Movement," op. cit.; Pat Califia, *Sapphistry,* Tallahassee, Florida, Naiad, 1980; Pat Califia, "What Is Gay Liberation," *Advocate,* June 25, 1981; Pat Califia, "Feminism and Sadomasochism," *Co-Evolution Quarterly,* no. 33, Spring 1981; Pat Califia, "Response to Dorchen Leidholdt," *New Women's Times,* October 1982; Pat Califia, "Public Sex," *Advocate,* September 30, 1982; Pat Califia, "Doing It Together: Gay Men, Lesbians, and Sex," *Advocate,* July 7, 1983; Pat Califia, "Gender-Bending," *Advocate,* September 15, 1983; Pat Califia, "The Sex Industry," *Advocate,* October 13, 1983; Deirdre English, Amber Hollibaugh, and Gayle Rubin, "Talking Sex," *Socialist Review,* July–August 1981; "Sex Issue," *Heresies,* no. 12, 1981; Amber Hollibaugh, "The Erotophobic Voice of Women: Building a Movement for the Nineteenth Century," *New York Native,* September 26–October 9, 1983; Maxine Holz, "Porn: Turn On or Put Down, Some Thoughts on Sexuality," *Processed World,* no. 7, Spring 1983; Barbara O'Dair, "Sex, Love, and Desire: Feminists Struggle Over the Portrayal of Sex," *Alternative Media,* Spring 1983; Lisa Orlando, "Bad Girls and 'Good' Politics," *Village Voice,* Literary Supplement, December 1982; Joanna Russ, "Being Against Pornography," *Thirteenth Moon,* vol. VI, nos. 1 and 2, 1982; Samois, *What Color Is Your Handkerchief,* Berkeley, Samois, 1979; Samois, *Coming to Power,* Boston, Alyson, 1982; Deborah Sundahl, "Stripping For a Living," *Advocate,* October 13, 1983; Nancy Wechsler, "Interview with Pat Califia and Gayle Rubin," part I, *Gay Community News,* Book Review, July 18, 1981, and part II, *Gay Community News,* August 15, 1981; Ellen Willis, *Beginning to See the Light,* New York, Knopf, ·1981. For an excellent overview of the history of the ideological shifts in feminism which have affected the sex debates, see Alice Echols, "Cultural Feminism: Feminist Capitalism and the Anti-Pornography Movement," *Social Text,* no. 7, Spring and Summer 1983.

73. Lisa Orlando, "Lust at Last! Spandex Invades the Academy," *Gay Community News,* May 15, 1982; Ellen Willis, "Who Is a Feminist? An Open Letter to Robin Morgan," *Village Voice,* Literary Supplement, December 1982.

74. Ellen Willis, *Beginning to See the Light,* op. cit., p. 146. I am indebted to Jeanne Bergman for calling my attention to this quote.

75. See, for example, Jessica Benjamin, "Master and Slave: The Fantasy of Erotic Domination," in Snitow et al., op. cit., p. 297; and B. Ruby Rich, review of *Powers of Desire, In These Times,* November 16–22, 1983.

76. B. Ruby Rich, op. cit., p. 76.

77. Samois, *What Color Is Your Handkerchief*, op. cit.; Samois, *Coming To Power*, op. cit.; Pat Califia, "Feminism and Sadomasochism," op. cit.; Pat Califia, *Sapphistry*, op. cit.

78. Lisa Orlando, "Power Plays: Coming To Terms With Lesbian S/M," *Village Voice*, July 26, 1983; Elizabeth Wilson, "The Context of 'Between *Pleasure* and *Danger*': The Barnard Conference on Sexuality," *Feminist Review*, no. 13, Spring 1983, especially pp. 35–41.

79. *Taylor* v. *State*, 214 Md. 156, 165, 133 A. 2d 414, 418. This quote is from a dissenting opinion, but it is a statement of prevailing law.

80. Bessera, Jewel, Matthews, and Gatov, op. cit., pp. 163–5. See note 55 above.

81. "Marine and Mom Guilty of Incest," *San Francisco Chronicle*, November 16, 1979, p. 16.

82. Norton, op. cit., p. 18.

83. *People* v. *Samuels*, 250 Cal. App. 2d 501, 513, 58 Cal. Rptr. 439, 447 (1967).

84. *People* v. *Samuels*, 250 Cal. App. 2d. at 513–514, 58 Cal. Rptr. at 447.

85. Mariana Valverde, "Feminism Meets Fist-Fucking: Getting Lost in Lesbian S & M," *Body Politic*, February 1980; Wilson, op. cit., p. 38.

86. Benjamin, op. cit., p. 292, but see also pp. 286, 291–7.

87. Barbara Ehrenreich, "What Is This Thing Called Sex," *Nation*, September 24, 1983, p. 247.

88. Gayle Rubin, "The Traffic in Women," in Rayna R. Reiter (ed.), *Toward an Anthropology of Women*, New York, Monthly Review Press, 1975, p. 159.

89. Rubin, "The Traffic in Women," op. cit., p. 166.

90. Foucault, op. cit., p. 106.

91. Catherine MacKinnon, "Feminism, Marxism, Method and the State: An Agenda for Theory," *Signs*, vol. 7, no. 3, Spring 1982, pp. 515–16.

92. Catherine MacKinnon, "Feminism, Marxism, Method, and the State: Toward Feminist Jurisprudence," *Signs*, vol. 8, no. 4, Summer 1983, p. 635.

93. Colette, *The Ripening Seed*, translated and cited in Hannah Alderfer, Beth Jaker, and Marybeth Nelson, *Diary of a Conference on Sexuality*, New York, Faculty Press, 1982, p. 72.

94. John Lauritsen and David Thorstad, *The Early Homosexual Rights Movement in Germany*, New York, Times Change Press, 1974.

95. D'Emilio, *Sexual Politics, Sexual Communities*, op. cit.; Bérubé, "Behind the Spectre of San Francisco," op. cit.; Bérubé, "Marching to a Different Drummer," op. cit.

Postscript

I finished writing "Thinking Sex" in the early Spring of 1984. For this reprint, I have corrected typographical errors, made some very minor editorial changes, and added several footnotes. While the essay remains largely the same, going over it again has sharpened my awareness of the extent to which the social, political, and intellectual contexts of sexuality have changed in the eight years since it was written. Moreover, the *rate* of such change seems to be accelerating madly and exponentially.

Only four months ago I prepared a lengthy afterword to accompany another reprint of "Thinking Sex" (Linda Kauffman, ed., *American Feminist Thought, 1982–1992*, Oxford, Basil Blackwell, forthcoming). In that afterword I detailed a few of the ways in which sex-politics and thought have shifted since the essay was published. I need not reiterate them here. Nevertheless, since I mailed off the afterword in mid-February there have been several developments that illustrate what is at stake in conflicts over sex and the increasingly giddy pace at which they occur. Three areas of critical activity are the codification of anti-pornography ideas into law, the growing criminalization of sadomasochistic representation and practice, and the alarming level of political gay-bashing taking place in the 1992 US elections.

Late in February, the Canadian Supreme Court upheld Canada's obscenity law in a decision (*Butler* v. *Her Majesty the Queen*) which redefined obscenity along the lines pursued by anti-pornography feminists since the late seventies.[1] The Canadian court adopted language similar to the definitions in the MacKinnon/Dworkin so-called "civil rights anti-pornography" ordinances. In Canada, the legal definition of obscenity is now based, in part, on depictions of sexual behavior considered to be "degrading and dehumanizing." This approach was rejected by the US Supreme Court as a violation of the First Amendment. Canada has nothing comparable to the Bill of Rights, and has fewer legal protections for speech and political expression.

Although the Canadian legal situation is different from that of the United States, the increasingly right-wing US Supreme Court may be influenced by the Canadian decision when it next considers similar legal wording. The logic of Senate Bill 1521 (the Pornography Victims Compensation Act) is based on the same flawed assumptions as the Butler decision. This bill was just passed out of the Senate Judiciary Committee late in June and now heads to the Senate floor.

In addition, it appears that the Butler decision was facilitated by the slow accumulation of legal precedent in lesser cases. In the US, anti-porn activists and attorneys are attempting to build a similar body of precedent in cases which might initially appear tangential to obscenity law. Anti-censorship feminist and civil rights lawyers should be alert to language that treats pornography as inherently "harmful" or "anti-woman" in, for example, sexual harassment cases (pornography, like Coca-Cola cans or any number of other objects, may in fact be used to harass; but it is far more tempting to think of pornography as harmful regardless of context than it is to make similar assumptions about less demonized items).

Many gay activists in Canada warned that the new obscenity definitions would be used differentially against gay and lesbian media. Glad Day Books, the gay and lesbian bookstore in Toronto, has already suffered through a decade of police harassment, and customs confiscations have already made many gay and lesbian publications unobtainable in Canada. Emboldened by the Butler definitions, police raided Glad Day on April 30 and charged the store manager with violating obscenity law for selling *Bad Attitude,* a US lesbian sex magazine which contained depictions of bondage and penetration. On May 4, the owner and corporation were also charged with obscenity.[2]

The new criteria for obscenity effectively make S/M erotica completely illegal in Canada, since such materials most closely resemble the category of "degrading and dehumanizing" pornography.[3] Moreover, gay male S/M materials appear to have played a key role in persuading the Court to adopt the new obscenity standards. One news article praising the Canadian decision contains a disturbing claim by one of the victorious attorneys. She is quoted as attributing the success of their litigation to showing the justices "violent and degrading *gay* movies. We made the point that the abused men in these films were being treated like women—*and the judges got it.* Otherwise, men can't put themselves in our shoes."[4] If this report is accurate, feminist lawyers sold their analysis by using gay male S/M movies to elicit the predictably defensive responses and homophobic repugnance such films were likely to produce among heterosexual men. For many years, feminist anti-porn activists have exploited ignorance and bigotry toward sadomasochism to substitute for their lack of evidence; in exploiting ignorance and bigotry toward male homosexuality they have sunk to new depths of political irresponsibility and opportunism.

This is particularly distressing in the wake of a recent court decision in England, and in the context of significant gay-baiting in the 1992 US elections. In England in 1990, fifteen men were convicted on various charges arising from consensual homosexual sadomasochistic activities. Many were given prison sentences, some up to four and a half years. None of the participants complained or brought charges; the men were arrested after police confiscated home-made sex videos which documented their activities.[5] The case was appealed. In late February, the Court of Appeal upheld the convictions, ruling that "the question of consent was immaterial," and effectively confirming that S/M sexual activity is illegal in England.[6] While the decision is based on earlier rulings, such prosecutions had been extremely rare. The fact that so many gay men were given lengthy prison sentences for private consensual adult sexual activities is ominous.

In the United States, homophobia has become a major political tactic in this year's elections. In February the presidential primary season was just heating up. As the elections have progressed, the National Endowment for the Arts (NEA), the Public Broadcasting System (PBS), representations of homosexuality, and homosexuality itself have all become hot buttons and hot targets. Funding for PBS has been attacked, and the former chair of the NEA has been sacked (for believing in the Constitution and the Bill of Rights). From Patrick Buchanan's neo-Nazi rantings to Dan Quayle's euphemistic emphasis on "family values," both overt and covert attacks on homosexuality have been prominent tactics in the 1992 election campaigns.[7]

In Oregon, the right-wing Oregon Citizens Alliance (OCA) is attempting to pass two initiatives which would amend the state constitution to define homosexuality, sadomasochism, pedophilia, bestiality, and necrophilia as "abnormal, wrong, unnatural, and perverse" *by law.* If passed, these initiatives would prevent such groups from using public facilities, would prohibit any civil rights legislation to protect sexual minorities, and would forbid teaching positive views of such behaviors in any state funded school, college, or university.

While the OCA claims its initiative would not change the criminal law or increase criminal penalties for these behaviors, the initiative is reminiscent of several aspects of National Socialist legislation. The OCA initiatives would, if passed, deprive sexual minorities of equal citizenship, make them "inferior" by law and public policy, mandate teaching such inferiority in all state-supported educational institutions, and suppress the promulgation of opinions or evidence that would contravene such legally dictated inferiority.[8]

I am now preparing to mail this postscript in early July. Four months remain until the 1992 elections. Who know what hysterias will be elicited, what fears drummed upon, what hostilities and antagonisms enticed, and to what base levels the political process will plunge in order to keep power, wealth, and privilege as concentrated as possible? Who knows how many more harmless people will be jailed, ostracized, harassed, financially destroyed, or physically assaulted? Who knows why ostensibly progressive and well-intentioned people continue to fail to oppose regressive policies with serious and devastating consequences? By now they should all know better.

Tune in next year for another exciting episode.

Gayle Rubin
San Francisco, July 4, 1992

Notes

1. Tamar Levin, "Canada Court Says Pornography Harms Women and Can Be Barred," *New York Times,* February 28, 1992, p. 1; Michele Landsberg, "Canada: Antipornography Breakthrough in the Law," *Ms.,* May/June 1992, pp. 14–15.

2. Shawn Syms and Carrie Wofford, "Obscenity Crackdown: Using obscenity laws, U.S. customs begins new tactic of seizing gay magazines; Toronto police raid a gay bookstore," *Gay Community News,* May 22–June 4, 1992, pp. 1, 7.

3. Kathryn E. Diaz, "The porn debates reignite," *Gay Community News,* June 6–19, 1992, pp. 3, 5.

4. Landsberg, op. cit., p. 15, my emphasis.

5. "Sado-masochists jailed for 'degrading' sex acts," *The Guardian,* December 1990; Rex Wockner, "SM Crackdown in London," *Bay Area Reporter,* January 24, 1991, p. 16; Rex Wockner, "London S/M Gays Fight Oppression," *Bay Area Reporter,* February 21, 1991, p. 20; "Taking Liberties," *Marxism Today,* March 1991, p. 16; T.A. Feldwebel, "Two Steps Backward," *DungeonMaster* 43, p. 3; "SM Gays—SM and the Law," *DungeonMaster* 43, p. 4.

6. Chris Woods, "SM sex was a crime, court rules," *Capital Gay,* February 21, 1992; Angus Hamilton, "Criminalizing gay sex," *The Pink Paper,* February 23, 1992, p. 9; "S&M is Illegal in England," *Growing Pains,* May 1992, pp. 1–2.

7. "Buchanan's New Anti-Bush Ad Shows Gay Scenes From PBS," *San Francisco Chronicle,* February 27, 1992, p. A-2; Susan Yoachum, "Buchanan Calls AIDS 'Retribution,' " *San Francisco Chronicle,* February 28, 1992, p. 1; Elizabeth Kolbert, "Bitter G.O.P. Air War Reflects Competitiveness of Georgia Race," *New York Times,* February 28, 1992, p. A-9; "Hitler's 'Courage' Etc.," *San Francisco Examiner,* March 8, 1992, p. A-12; Dawn Schmitz, "Riggs, Buchanan battle for public TV," *Gay Community News,* April 5-18, 1992, p. 5; Jerry Roberts, "Quayle Blames Riots on Decline of Family Values," *San Francisco Chronicle,* May 20, 1992, p. 1; Carl Irving, "Quayle: Marriage is key to ending poverty," *San Francisco Examiner,* May 20, 1992, p. A–14; Marsha Ginsburg and Larry D. Hatfield, " 'Murphy Brown' furor grows," *San Francisco Examiner,* May 20, 1992, p. 1; Jerry Roberts, "Uproar Over Comments By Quayle," *San Francisco Chronicle,* May 21, 1992, p. 1; George Raine, "Quayle planned attack on 'Murphy,' " *San Francisco Examiner,* May 21, 1992, p. A–1; "Bush Links Big-City Woes To Collapse of the Family," *San Francisco Chronicle,* March 10, 1992, p. A-4; Torie Osborn and David M. Smith, "Are Gays Being Made '92's Hate Symbol?," *San Francisco Chronicle,* March 9, 1992, p. A-21; Elaine Herscher, "Gays Under Fire in Presidential Race," *San Francisco Chronicle,* June 26, 1992, p. 1.

8. Information about these initiatives based on flyers prepared by the Right to Privacy PAC and the Campaign for a Hate-Free Oregon in Portland, Oregon.

2

Epistemology of the Closet

Eve Kosofsky Sedgwick

Eve Kosofsky Sedgwick is a poet and literary critic who has done pioneering and influential work in queer theory. In this essay, she begins to outline a theory of "the closet," arguing that the prevailing account of modern lesbian/gay history, as transformed by the liberationist movement following on the Stonewall rising of 1969, may be in some ways misleading. Sedgwick argues that "the closet," or what she also calls the regime of "the open secret," has been basic to lesbian/gay life for the last century, both before and after Stonewall. She further argues that this regime, with its contradictory and constraining rules about privacy and disclosure, public and private, knowledge and ignorance, has served to shape the way in which many questions of value and epistemology have been conceived and addressed in modern Western society as a whole. Eve Kosofsky Sedgwick is the author of Between Men: English Literature and Male Homosocial Desire *(1985), and of* Epistemology of the Closet *(1990), from which this essay is excerpted. She is Newman Ivy White Professor of English at Duke University.*

The lie, the perfect lie, about people we know, about the relations we have had with them, about our motive for some action, formulated in totally different terms, the lie as to what we are, whom we love, what we feel with regard to people who love us . . .—that lie is one of the few things in the world that can open windows for us on to what is new and unknown, that can awaken in us sleeping senses for the comtemplation of universes that otherwise we should never have known. (Proust, *The Captive***)**

The epistemology of the closet is not a dated subject or a superseded regime of knowing. While the events of June, 1969, and later vitally reinvigorated many people's sense of the potency, magnetism, and promise of gay self-disclosure, nevertheless the reign of the telling secret was scarcely overturned with Stonewall. Quite the opposite, in some ways. To the fine antennae of public attention the freshness of every drama of (especially involuntary) gay uncovering seems if anything heightened in surprise and delectability, rather than staled, by the increasingly intense atmosphere of public articulations of and about the love that is famous for daring not speak its name. So resilient and productive a structure of narrative will not readily surrender its hold on important forms of social meaning. As D.A. Miller points out in an aegis-creating essay, secrecy can function as

> the subjective practice in which the oppositions of private/public, inside/outside, subject/object are established, and the sanctity of their first term kept inviolate. And

the phenomenon of the "open secret" does not, as one might think, bring about the collapse of those binarisms and their ideological effects, but rather attests to their fantasmatic recovery.[1]

Even at an individual level, there are remarkably few of even the most openly gay people who are not deliberately in the closet with someone personally or economically or institutionally important to them. Furthermore, the deadly elasticity of heterosexist presumption means that, like Wendy in *Peter Pan,* people find new walls springing up around them even as they drowse: every encounter with a new classful of students, to say nothing of a new boss, social worker, loan officer, landlord, doctor, erects new closets whose fraught and characteristic laws of optics and physics exact from at least gay people new surveys, new calculations, new draughts and requisitions of secrecy or disclosure. Even an out gay person deals daily with interlocutors about whom she doesn't know whether they know or not; it is equally difficult to guess for any given interlocutor whether, if they did know, the knowledge would seem very important. Nor—at the most basic level—is it unaccountable that someone who wanted a job, custody or visiting rights, insurance, protection from violence, from "therapy," from distorting stereotype, from insulting scrutiny, from simple insult, from forcible interpretation of their bodily product, could deliberately choose to remain in or to reenter the closet in some or all segments of their life. The gay closet is not a feature only of the lives of gay people. But for many gay people it is still the fundamental feature of social life; and there can be few gay people, however courageous and forthright by habit, however fortunate in the support of their immediate communities, in whose lives the closet is not still a shaping presence.

To say, as I will be saying here, that the epistemology of the closet has given an overarching consistency to gay culture and identity throughout this century is not to deny that crucial possibilities around and outside the closet have been subject to most consequential change, for gay people. There are risks in making salient the continuity and centrality of the closet, in a historical narrative that does not have as a fulcrum a saving vision—whether located in past or future—of its apocalyptic rupture. A meditation that lacks that particular utopian organization will risk glamorizing the closet itself, if only by default; will risk presenting as inevitable or somehow valuable its exactions, its deformations, its disempowerment and sheer pain. If these risks are worth running, it is partly because the nonutopian traditions of gay writing, thought, and culture have remained so inexhaustibly and gorgeously productive for later gay thinkers, in the absence of a rationalizing or often even of a forgiving reading of their politics. The epistemology of the closet has also been, however, on a far vaster scale and with a less honorific inflection, inexhaustibly productive of modern Western culture and history at large. While that may be reason enough for taking it as a subject of interrogation, it should not be reason enough for focusing scrutiny on those who inhabit the closet (however equivocally) to the exclusion of those in the ambient heterosexist culture who enjoin it and whose intimate representational needs it serves in a way less extortionate to themselves.

I scarcely know at this stage a consistent alternative proceeding, however; and it may well be that, for reasons to be discussed, no such consistency is possible. At least to enlarge the circumference of scrutiny and to vary by some new assays of saltation the angle of its address will be among the methodological projects of this discussion.

In Montgomery County, Maryland, in 1973, an eighth-grade earth science teacher named Acanfora was transferred to a nonteaching position by the Board of Education when they learned he was gay. When Acanfora spoke to news media, such as "60 Minutes" and the Public Broadcasting System, about his situation, he was refused a new contract entirely. Acanfora sued. The federal district court that first heard his case supported the action and rationale of the Board of Education, holding that Acanfora's recourse to the media had brought undue attention to himself and his sexuality, to a degree that would be deleterious to the educational process. The Fourth Circuit Court of Appeals disagreed. They considered Acanfora's public disclosures to be protected speech under the First Amendment. Although they overruled the lower court's rationale, however, the appellate court affirmed its decision not to allow Acanfora to return to teaching. Indeed, they denied his standing to bring the suit in the first place, on the grounds that he had failed to note on his original employment application that he had been, in college, an officer of a student homophile organization—a notation that would, as school officials admitted in court, have prevented his ever being hired. The rationale for keeping Acanfora out of his classroom was thus no longer that he had disclosed too much about his homosexuality, but quite the opposite, that he had not disclosed enough.[2] The Supreme Court declined to entertain an appeal.

It is striking that each of the two rulings in *Acanfora* emphasized that the teacher's homosexuality "itself" would not have provided an acceptable ground for denying him employment. Each of the courts relied in its decision on an implicit distinction between the supposedly protected and bracketable fact of Acanfora's homosexuality proper, on the one hand, and on the other hand his highly vulnerable management of information about it. So very vulnerable does this latter exercise prove to be, however, and vulnerable to such a contradictory array of interdictions, that the space for simply existing as a gay person who is a teacher is in fact bayonetted through and through, from both sides, by the vectors of a disclosure at once compulsory and forbidden.

A related incoherence couched in the resonant terms of the distinction of *public* from *private* riddles the contemporary legal space of gay being. When it refused in 1985 to consider an appeal in *Rowland v. Mad River Local School District,* the U.S. Supreme Court let stand the firing of a bisexual guidance counselor for coming out to some of her colleagues; the act of coming out was judged not to be highly protected under the First Amendment because it does not constitute speech on a matter "of public concern." It was, of course, only eighteen months later that the same U.S. Supreme Court ruled, in response to Michael Hardwick's contention that it's nobody's business if he do, that it ain't: if homosexuality is not, however densely adjudicated, to be considered a matter of *public* concern, neither in the Supreme Court's binding opinion does it subsist under the mantle of the *private.*[3]

The most obvious fact about this history of judicial formulations is that it codifies an excruciating system of double binds, systematically oppressing gay people, identities, and acts by undermining through contradictory constraints on discourse the grounds of their very being. That immediately political recognition may be supplemented, however, by a historical hypothesis that goes in the other direction. I want to argue that a lot of the energy of attention and demarcation that has swirled around issues of homosexuality since the end of the nineteenth century, in Europe and the United States, has been impelled by the distinctively indicative relation of homosexuality to wider mappings of secrecy and disclosure, and of the private and the public, that were and are critically problematical for the gender, sexual, and economic structures of the heterosexist culture at large, mappings whose enabling but dangerous incoherence has become oppressively, durably condensed in certain figures of homosexuality. "The closet" and "coming out," now verging on all-purpose phrases for the potent crossing and recrossing of almost any politically charged lines of representation, have been the gravest and most magnetic of those figures.

The closet is the defining structure for gay oppression in this century. The legal couching, by civil liberties lawyers, of *Bowers v. Hardwick* as an issue in the first place of a Constitutional right to privacy, and the liberal focus in the aftermath of that decision on the image of the *bedroom invaded by policemen*—"Letting the Cops Back into Michael Hardwick's Bedroom," the *Native* headlined[4]—as though political empowerment were a matter of getting the cops back on the street where they belong and sexuality back into the impermeable space where *it* belongs, are among other things extensions of, and testimony to the power of, the image of the closet. The durability of the image is perpetuated even as its intelligibility is challenged in antihomophobic responses like the following, to *Hardwick,* addressed to gay readers:

> What can you do—alone? The answer is obvious. You're *not* alone, and you can't afford to try to be. That closet door—never very secure as protection—is even more dangerous now. You must come out, for your own sake and for the sake of all of us.[5]

The image of coming out regularly interfaces the image of the closet, and its seemingly unambivalent public siting can be counterposed as a salvational epistemologic certainty against the very equivocal privacy afforded by the closet: "If every gay person came out to his or her family," the same article goes on, "a hundred million Americans could be brought to our side. Employers and straight friends could mean a hundred million more." And yet the Mad River School District's refusal to hear a woman's coming out as an authentically public speech act is echoed in the frigid response given many acts of coming out: "That's fine, but why did you think I'd want to know about it?"

Gay thinkers of this century have, as we'll see, never been blind to the damaging contradictions of this compromised metaphor of *in* and *out* of the closet of privacy. But its origins in European culture are, as the writings of Foucault have shown, so ramified—and its relation to the "larger," i.e., ostensibly nongay-related, topologies of privacy in the culture is, as the figure of Foucault dramatized, so critical, so enfolding, so representational—that the simple vesting of some alternative metaphor has never, either, been a true possibility.

I recently heard someone on National Public Radio refer to the sixties as the decade when Black people came out of the closet. For that matter, I recently gave an MLA talk purporting to explain how it's possible to come out of the closet as a fat woman. The apparent floating-free from its gay origins of that phrase "coming out of the closet" in recent usage might suggest that the trope of the closet is so close to the heart of some modern preoccupations that it could be, or has been, evacuated of its historical gay specificity. But I hypothesize that exactly the opposite is true. I think that a whole cluster of the most crucial sites for the contestation of meaning in twentieth-century Western culture are consequentially and quite indelibly marked with the historical specificity of homosocial/homosexual definition, notably but not exclusively male, from around the turn of the century.[6] Among those sites are, as I have indicated, the pairings secrecy/disclosure and private/public. Along with and sometimes through these epistemologically charged pairings, condensed in the figures of "the closet" and "coming out," this very specific crisis of definition has then ineffaceably marked other pairings as basic to modern cultural organization as masculine/feminine, majority/minority, innocence/initiation, natural/artificial, new/old, growth/decadence, urbane/provincial, health/illness, same/different, cognition/paranoia, art/kitsch, sincerity/sentimentality, and voluntarity/addiction. So permeative has the suffusing stain of homo/heterosexual crisis been that to discuss any of these indices in any context, in the absence of an antihomophobic analysis, must perhaps be to perpetuate unknowingly compulsions implicit in each.

For any modern question of sexuality, knowledge/ignorance is more than merely one in a metonymic chain of such binarisms. The process, narrowly bordered at first in European culture but sharply broadened and accelerated after the late eighteenth century, by which "knowledge" and "sex" become conceptually inseparable from one another—so that knowledge means in the first place sexual knowledge; ignorance, sexual ignorance; and epistemological pressure of any sort seems a force increasingly saturated with sexual impulsion—was sketched in Volume I of Foucault's *History of Sexuality.* In a sense, this was a process, protracted almost to retardation, of exfoliating the biblical genesis by which what we now know as sexuality is fruit—apparently the only fruit—to be plucked from the tree of knowledge. Cognition itself, sexuality itself, and transgression itself have always been ready in Western culture to be magnetized into an unyielding though not an unfissured alignment with one another, and the period initiated by Romanticism accomplished this disposition through a remarkably broad confluence of different languages and institutions.

In some texts, such as Diderot's *La Religieuse,* that were influential early in this process, the desire that represents sexuality per se, and hence sexual knowledge and knowledge per se, is a same-sex desire.[7] This possibility, however, was repressed with increasing energy, and hence increasing visibility, as the nineteenth-century culture of the individual proceeded to elaborate a version of knowledge/sexuality increasingly structured by its pointed cognitive *refusal* of sexuality between women, between men. The gradually reifying effect of this refusal[8] meant that by the end of the nineteenth century, when it had become fully current—as obvious to Queen Victoria as to Freud—that knowledge meant sexual knowledge, and secrets sexual secrets, there had in fact developed one particular sexuality that was distinctively constituted *as* secrecy: the perfect object for the by now insatiably exacerbated epistemological/sexual anxiety of the turn-of-the-century subject. Again, it was a long chain of originally scriptural identifications of a sexuality with a particular cognitive positioning (in this case, St. Paul's routinely reproduced and reworked denomination of sodomy as the crime whose name is not to be uttered, hence whose accessibility to knowledge is uniquely preterited) that culminated in Lord Alfred Douglas's epochal public utterance, in 1894, "*I am* the Love that dare not speak its name."[9] In such texts as *Billy Budd* and *Dorian Gray* and through their influence, the subject—the thematics—of knowledge and ignorance themselves, of innocence and initiation, of secrecy and disclosure, became not contingently but integrally infused with one particular object of cognition: no longer sexuality as a whole but even more specifically, now, the homosexual topic. And the condensation of the world of possibilities surrounding same-sex sexuality—including, shall we say, both gay desires and the most rabid phobias against them—the condensation of this plurality to *the homosexual topic* that now formed the accusative case of modern processes of personal knowing, was not the least infliction of the turn-of-the-century crisis of sexual definition.

To explore the differences it makes when secrecy itself becomes manifest as *this* secret, let me begin by twining together in a short anachronistic braid a variety of exemplary narratives—literary, biographical, imaginary—that begin with the moment on July 1, 1986, when the decision in *Bowers v. Hardwick* was announced, a moment which, sandwiched between a weekend of Gay Pride parades nationwide, the announcement of a vengeful new AIDS policy by the Justice Department, and an upcoming media-riveting long weekend of hilarity or hysteria focused on the national fetishization in a huge hollow blind spike-headed female body of the abstraction Liberty, and occurring in an ambient medium for gay men and their families and friends of wave on wave of renewed loss, mourning, and refreshed personal fear, left many people feeling as if at any rate one's own particular car had finally let go forever of the tracks of the roller coaster.

In many discussions I heard or participated in immediately after the Supreme Court ruling in *Bowers v. Hardwick,* antihomophobic or gay women and men speculated—more or less empathetically or venomously—about the sexuality of the people most involved with the decision. The question kept coming up, in different tones, of what it could have felt like to be a closeted gay court assistant, or clerk, or justice, who might have had some degree, even a very high one, of instrumentality in conceiving or formulating or "refining" or logistically facilitating this ruling, these ignominious majority opinions, the assaultive sentences in which they were framed.

That train of painful imaginings was fraught with the epistemological distinctiveness of gay identity and gay situation in our culture. Vibrantly resonant as the image of the closet is for many modern oppressions, it is indicative for homophobia in a way it cannot be for other oppressions. Racism, for instance, is based on a stigma that is visible in all but exceptional cases (cases that are neither rare nor irrelevant, but that delineate the outlines rather than coloring the center of racial experience); so are the oppressions based on gender, age, size, physical handicap. Ethnic/cultural/religious oppressions such as anti-Semitism are more analogous in that the stigmatized individual has at least notionally some discretion—although, importantly, it is never to be taken for granted how much—over other people's knowledge of her or his membership in the group: one could "come out as" a Jew or Gypsy, in a heterogeneous urbanized society, much more intelligibly than one could typically "come out as," say, female, Black, old, a wheelchair user, or fat. A (for instance) Jewish or Gypsy identity, and hence a Jewish or Gypsy secrecy or closet, would nonetheless differ again from the distinctive gay versions of these things in its clear ancestral linearity and answerability, in the roots (however tortuous and ambivalent) of cultural identification through each individual's originary culture of (at a minimum) the family.

Proust, in fact, insistently suggests as a sort of limit-case of one kind of coming out precisely the drama of Jewish self-identification, embodied in the Book of Esther and in Racine's recasting of it that is quoted throughout the "Sodom and Gomorrah" books of *A la recherche.* The story of Esther seems a model for a certain simplified but highly potent imagining of coming out and its transformative potential. In concealing her Judaism from her husband, King Assuérus (Ahasuerus), Esther the Queen feels she is concealing, simply, her identity: "The King is to this day unaware who I am."[10] Esther's deception is made necessary by the powerful ideology that makes Assuérus categorize her people as unclean ("cette source impure" [1039]) and an abomination against nature ("Il nous croit en horreur à toute la nature" [174]). The sincere, relatively abstract Jew-hatred of this fuddled but omnipotent king undergoes constant stimulation from the grandiose cynicism of his advisor Aman (Haman), who dreams of an entire planet exemplarily cleansed of the perverse element.

> I want it said one day in awestruck centuries:
> "There once used to be Jews, there was an insolent race;
> widespread, they used to cover the whole face of the earth;
> a single one dared draw on himself the wrath of Aman,
> at once they disappeared, every one, from the earth."
>
> (476–80)

The king acquiesces in Aman's genocidal plot, and Esther is told by her cousin, guardian, and Jewish conscience Mardochée (Mordecai) that the time for her revelation has come;

at this moment the particular operation of suspense around her would be recognizable to any gay person who has inched toward coming out to homophobic parents. "And if I perish, I perish," she says in the Bible (Esther 4:16). That the avowal of her secret identity will have an immense potency is clear, is the premise of the story. All that remains to be seen is whether under its explosive pressure the king's "political" animus against her kind will demolish his "personal" love for her, or vice versa: will he declare her as good as, or better, dead? Or will he soon be found at a neighborhood bookstore, hoping not to be recognized by the salesperson who is ringing up his copy of *Loving Someone Jewish*?

The biblical story and Racinian play, bearable to read in their balance of the holocaustal with the intimate only because one knows how the story will end,[11] are enactments of a particular dream or fantasy of coming out. Esther's eloquence, in the event, is resisted by only five lines of her husband's demurral or shock: essentially at the instant she names herself, both her ruler and Aman see that the anti-Semites are lost ("*AMAN, tout bas:* Je tremble" [1033]). Revelation of identity in the space of intimate love effortlessly overturns an entire public systematics of the natural and the unnatural, the pure and the impure. The peculiar strike that the story makes to the heart is that Esther's small, individual ability to risk losing the love and countenance of her master has the power to save not only her own space in life but her people.

It would not be hard to imagine a version of *Esther* set in the Supreme Court in the days immediately before the decision in *Bowers v. Hardwick.* Cast as the ingenue in the title role a hypothetical closeted gay clerk, as Assuérus a hypothetical Justice of the same gender who is about to make a majority of five in support of the Georgia law. The Justice has grown fond of the clerk, oddly fonder than s/he is used to being of clerks, and . . . In our compulsive recursions to the question of the sexualities of court personnel, such a scenario was close to the minds of my friends and me in many forms. In the passionate dissenting opinions, were there not the traces of others' comings-out already performed; could even the dissents themselves represent such performances, Justice coming out to Justice? With the blood-let tatters of what risky comings-out achieved and then overridden—friends', clerks', employees', children's—was the imperious prose of the majority opinions lined? More painful and frequent were thoughts of all the coming out that had not happened, of the women and men who had not in some more modern idiom said, with Esther,

> I dare to beg you, both for my own life
> and the sad days of an ill-fated people
> that you have condemned to perish with me.
>   (1029–31)

What was lost in the absence of such scenes was not, either, the opportunity to evoke with eloquence a perhaps demeaning pathos like Esther's. It was something much more precious: evocation, articulation, of the dumb Assuérus in all his imperial ineloquent bathos of unknowing: "A périr? Vous? Quel peuple?" ("To perish? You? What people?" [1032]). "What people?" indeed—why, as it oddly happens, the very people whose eradication he personally is just on the point of effecting. But only with the utterance of these blank syllables, making the weight of Assuérus's powerful ignorance suddenly audible—not least to him—in the same register as the weight of Esther's and Mardochée's private knowledge, can any open flow of power become possible. It is here that Aman begins to tremble.

Just so with coming out: it can bring about the revelation of a powerful unknowing *as* unknowing, not as a vacuum or as the blank it can pretend to be but as a weighty and occupied and consequential epistemological space. Esther's avowal allows Assuérus to make visible two such spaces at once: "You?" "What people?" He has been blindly presuming about herself,[12] and simply blind to the race to whose extinction he has pledged himself. What? *you*'re one of *those*? Huh? *you*'re a *what*? This frightening thunder can also, however, be the sound of manna falling.

There is no question that to fixate, as I have done, on the scenario sketched here more than flirts with sentimentality. This is true for quite explicable reasons. First, we have too much cause to know how limited a leverage any individual revelation can exercise over collectively scaled and institutionally embodied oppressions. Acknowledgment of this disproportion does not mean that the consequences of such acts as coming out can be circumscribed within *predetermined* boundaries, as if between "personal" and "political" realms, nor does it require us to deny how disproportionately powerful and disruptive such acts can be. But the brute incommensurability has nonetheless to be acknowledged. In the theatrical display of an *already institutionalized* ignorance no transformative potential is to be looked for.

There is another whole family of reasons why too long a lingering on moments of *Esther*-style avowal must misrepresent the truths of homophobic oppression; these go back to the important differences between Jewish (here I mean Racinian-Jewish) and gay identity and oppression. Even in the "Sodom and Gomorrah" books of Proust, after all, and especially in *La Prisonnière,* where *Esther* is so insistently invoked, the play does not offer an efficacious model of transformative revelation. To the contrary: *La Prisonnière* is, notably, the book whose Racine-quoting hero has the most disastrous incapacity either to come out or *to be come out to.*

The suggested closeted Supreme Court clerk who struggled with the possibility of a self-revelation that *might* perceptibly strengthen gay sisters and brothers, but *would* radically endanger at least the foreseen course of her or his own life, would have an imagination filled with possibilities beyond those foreseen by Esther in her moment of risk. It is these possibilities that mark the distinctive structures of the epistemology of the closet. The clerk's authority to describe her or his own sexuality might well be impeached; the avowal might well only further perturb an already stirred-up current of the open secret; the avowal might well represent an aggression against someone with whom the clerk felt, after all, a real bond; the nongay-identified Justice might well feel too shaken in her or his own self-perception, or in the perception of the bond with the clerk, to respond with anything but an increased rigor; the clerk might well, through the avowal, be getting dangerously into the vicinity of the explosive-mined closet of a covertly gay Justice; the clerk might well fear being too isolated or self-doubting to be able to sustain the consequences of the avowal; the intersection of gay revelation with underlying gender expectations might well be too confusing or disorienting, for one or the other, to provide an intelligible basis for change.

To spell these risks and circumscriptions out more fully in the comparison with *Esther:*

1. Although neither the Bible nor Racine indicates in what, if any, religious behaviors or beliefs Esther's Jewish identity may be manifested, *there is no suggestion that that identity might be a debatable, a porous, a mutable fact about her.* "Esther, my lord, had a Jew for her father" (1033)—ergo, Esther is a Jew. Taken aback though he is by this announcement, Assuérus does not suggest that Esther is going through a phase, or is just angry at Gentiles, or could change if she only loved him enough to get counseling. Nor do such undermining possibilities occur to Esther. The Jewish identity in this play— whatever it may consist of in real life in a given historical context—has a solidity whose

very unequivocalness grounds the story of Esther's equivocation and her subsequent self-disclosure. In the processes of gay self-disclosure, by contrast, in a twentieth-century context, questions of authority and evidence can be the first to arise. "How do you know you're really gay? Why be in such a hurry to jump to conclusions? After all, what you're saying is only based on a few feelings, not real actions [or *alternatively:* on a few actions, not necessarily your real feelings]; hadn't you better talk to a therapist and find out?" Such responses—and their occurrence in the people come out to can seem a belated echo of their occurrence in the person coming out—reveal how problematical at present is the very concept of gay identity, as well as how intensely it is resisted and how far authority over its definition has been distanced from the gay subject her- or himself.

2. *Esther expects Assuérus to be altogether surprised by her self-disclosure; and he is.* Her confident sense of control over other people's knowledge about her is in contrast to the radical uncertainty closeted gay people are likely to feel about who is in control of information about their sexual identity. This has something to do with a realism about secrets that is greater in most people's lives than it is in Bible stories; but it has much more to do with complications in the notion of gay identity, so that no one person can take control over all the multiple, often contradictory codes by which information about sexual identity and activity can seem to be conveyed. In many, if not most, relationships, coming out is a matter of crystallizing intuitions or convictions that had been in the air for a while already and had already established their own power-circuits of silent contempt, silent blackmail, silent glamorization, silent complicity. After all, the position of those who think they *know something about one that one may not know oneself* is an excited and empowered one—whether what they think one doesn't know is that one somehow *is* homosexual, or merely that one's supposed secret is known to them. The glass closet can license insult ("I'd never have said those things if I'd *known* you were gay!"—yeah, sure); it can also license far warmer relations, but (and) relations whose potential for exploitiveness is built into the optics of the asymmetrical, the specularized, and the inexplicit.[13] There are sunny and apparently simplifying versions of coming out under these circumstances: a woman painfully decides to tell her mother that she's a lesbian, and her mother responds, "Yeah, I sort of thought you might be when you and Joan started sleeping together ten years ago." More often this fact makes the closet and its exits not more but less straightforward, however; not, often, more equable, but more volatile or even violent. Living in and hence coming out of the closet are never matters of the purely hermetic; the personal and political geographies to be surveyed here are instead the more imponderable and convulsive ones of the open secret.

3. *Esther worries that her revelation might destroy her or fail to help her people, but it does not seem to her likely to damage Assuérus, and it does not indeed damage him.* When gay people in a homophobic society come out, on the other hand, perhaps especially to parents or spouses, it is with the consciousness of a potential for serious injury that is likely to go in both directions. The pathogenic secret itself, even, can circulate contagiously *as* a secret: a mother says that her adult child's coming out of the closet with her has plunged her, in turn, into the closet in her conservative community. In fantasy, though not in fantasy only, against the fear of being killed or wished dead by (say) one's parents in such a revelation there is apt to recoil the often more intensely imagined possibility of its killing *them.* There is no guarantee that being under threat from a double-edged weapon is a more powerful position than getting the ordinary axe, but it is certain to be more destabilizing.

4. The inert substance of *Assuérus seems to have no definitional involvement with the religious/ethnic identity of Esther.* He sees neither himself nor their relationship differently when he sees that she is different from what he had thought her. The double-edged

potential for injury in the scene of gay coming out, by contrast, results partly from the fact that the erotic identity of the person who receives the disclosure is apt also to be implicated in, hence perturbed by it. This is true first and generally because erotic identity, of all things, is never to be circumscribed simply as itself, can never not be relational, is never to be perceived or known by anyone outside of a structure of transference and countertransference. Second and specifically it is true because the incoherences and contradictions of homosexual identity in twentieth-century culture are responsive to and hence evocative of the incoherences and contradictions of compulsory heterosexuality.

5. *There is no suggestion that Assuérus might himself be a Jew in disguise.* But it is entirely within the experience of gay people to find that a homophobic figure in power has, if anything, a disproportionate likelihood of being gay and closeted. Some examples and implications of this are discussed toward the end of Chapter 5 of *Epistemology;* there is more to this story. Let it stand here merely to demonstrate again that gay identity is a convoluted and off-centering possession if it is a possession at all; even to come out does not end anyone's relation to the closet, including turbulently the closet of the other.

6. *Esther knows who her people are and has an immediate answerability to them.* Unlike gay people, who seldom grow up in gay families; who are exposed to their culture's, if not their parents', high ambient homophobia long before either they or those who care for them know that they are among those who most urgently need to define themselves against it; who have with difficulty and always belatedly to patch together from fragments a community, a usable heritage, a politics of survival or resistance; unlike these, Esther has intact and to hand the identity and history and commitments she was brought up in, personified and legitimated in a visible figure of authority, her guardian Mardochée.

7. Correspondingly, *Esther's avowal occurs within and perpetuates a coherent system of gender subordination.* Nothing is more explicit, in the Bible, about Esther's marriage than its origin in a crisis of patriarchy and its value as a preservative of female discipline. When the Gentile Vashti, her predecessor as Ahasuerus's queen, had refused to be put on exhibition to his drunk men friends, "the wise men, which knew the times," saw that

> Vashti the queen hath not done wrong to the king only, but also to all the princes, and to all the people that are in all the provinces of the king Ahasuerus. For this deed of the queen shall come abroad unto all women, so that they shall despise their husbands in their eyes, when it shall be reported.
>
> (Esther 1:13–17)

Esther the Jew is introduced onto this scene as a salvific ideal of female submissiveness, her single moment of risk with the king given point by her customary pliancy. (Even today, Jewish little girls are educated in gender roles—fondness for being looked at, fearlessness in defense of "their people," nonsolidarity with their sex—through masquerading as Queen Esther at Purim; I have a snapshot of myself at about five, barefoot in the pretty "Queen Esther" dress my grandmother made [white satin, gold spangles], making a careful eyes-down toe-pointed curtsey at [presumably] my father, who is manifest in the picture only as the flashgun that hurls my shadow, pillaring up tall and black, over the dwarfed sofa onto the wall behind me.) Moreover, the literal patriarchism that makes coming out to *parents* the best emotional analogy to Esther's self-disclosure to her *husband* is shown with unusual clarity to function through the male traffic in women: Esther's real mission, as a wife, is to get her guardian Mardochée installed in place of Aman as the king's favorite and advisor. And the instability and danger that by contrast lurk in the Gentile Aman's relation to the king seem, Iago-like, to attach to the inadequate heterosexual buffering of the inexplicit intensities between them. If the story of Esther reflects a firm Jewish choice of a minority politics based on a conservative rein-scription of gender roles, however, such a choice has never been able to be made intel-ligibly by gay people in a modern culture (although there have been repeated attempts at making it, especially by men). Instead, both within and outside of homosexual-rights movements, the contradictory understandings of same-sex bonding and desire and of male and female gay identity have crossed and recrossed the definitional lines of gender identity with such disruptive frequency that the concepts "minority" and "gender" themselves have lost a good deal of their categorizing (though certainly not of their performative) force.

Each of these complicating possibilities stems at least partly from the plurality and the cumulative incoherence of modern ways of conceptualizing same-sex desire and, hence, gay identity; an incoherence that answers, too, to the incoherence with which *hetero*sexual desire and identity are conceptualized. A long, populous theoretical project of interrogating and historicizing the self-evidence of the pseudo-symmetrical opposition homosexual/heterosexual (or gay/straight) as categories of persons will be assumed rather than summarized here. Foucault among other historians locates in about the nineteenth century a shift in European thought from viewing same-sex sexuality as a matter of prohibited and isolated genital *acts* (acts to which, in that view, anyone might be liable who did not have their appetites in general under close control) to viewing it as a function of stable definitions of *identity* (so that one's personality structure might mark one as *a homosexual,* even, perhaps, in the absence of any genital activity at all). Thus, according to Alan Bray, "To talk of an individual [in the Renaissance] as being or not being 'a homosexual' is an anachronism and ruinously misleading,"[14] whereas the period stretch-ing roughly between Wilde and Proust was prodigally productive of attempts to name, explain, and define this new kind of creature, the homosexual person—a project so urgent that it spawned in its rage of distinction an even newer category, that of the heterosexual person.[15]

To question the natural self-evidence of this opposition between gay and straight as distinct kinds of persons is not, however, to dismantle it. Perhaps no one should wish it to do so; substantial groups of women and men under this representational regime have found that the nominative category "homosexual," or its more recent near-syn-onyms, does have a real power to organize and describe their experience of their own sexuality and identity, enough at any rate to make their self-application of it (even when only tacit) worth the enormous accompanying costs. If only for this reason, the cate-gorization commands respect. And even more at the level of groups than of individuals, the durability of any politics or ideology that would be so much as *permissive* of same-sex sexuality has seemed, in this century, to depend on a definition of homosexual persons as a distinct, minority population, however produced or labeled.[16] Far beyond any cog-nitively or politically enabling effects on the people whom it claims to describe, moreover, the nominative category of "the homosexual" has robustly failed to disintegrate under the pressure of decade after decade, battery after battery of deconstructive exposure—evidently not in the first place because of its meaningfulness to those whom it defines but because of its indispensableness to those who define themselves as against it.

For surely, if paradoxically, it is the paranoid insistence with which the definitional barriers between "the homosexual" (minority) and "the heterosexual" (majority) are fortified, in this century, by nonhomosexuals, and especially by men against men, that most saps one's ability to believe in "the homosexual" as an unproblematically discrete category of persons. Even the homophobic fifties folk wisdom of *Tea and Sympathy* detects that the man who most electrifies those barriers is the one whose own current is at most intermittently direct. It was in the period of the so-called "invention of the 'homosex-ual' " that Freud gave psychological texture and credibility to a countervalent, univer-salizing mapping of this territory, based on the supposed protean mobility of sexual desire and on the potential bisexuality of every human creature; a mapping that implies no presumption that one's sexual penchant will always incline toward persons of a single gender, and that offers, additionally, a richly denaturalizing description of the psycho-logical motives and mechanisms of male paranoid, projective homophobic definition and enforcement. Freud's antiminoritizing account only gained, moreover, in influence by being articulated through a developmental narrative in which heterosexist and mascu-linist ethical sanctions found ready camouflage. If the new common wisdom that hotly overt homophobes are men who are "insecure about their masculinity" supplements the implausible, necessary illusion that there could be a *secure* version of masculinity (known, presumably, by the coolness of its homophobic enforcement) and a stable, intelligible way for men to feel about other men in modern heterosexual capitalist patriarchy, what tighter turn could there be to the screw of an already off-center, always at fault, endlessly blackmailable male identity ready to be manipulated into any labor of channeled violence?[17]

It remained for work emerging from the later feminist and gay movements to begin to clarify why the male paranoid project had become so urgent in the maintenance of gender subordination; and it remained for a stunningly efficacious coup of feminist redefinition to transform lesbianism, in a predominant view, from a matter of female virilization to one of woman-identification.[18] Although the post-Stonewall, predomi-nantly male gay liberation movement has had a more distinct political presence than radical lesbianism and has presented potent new images of gay people and gay com-munities, along with a stirring new family of narrative structures attached to coming out, it has offered few new analytic facilities for the question of homo/heterosexual definition prior to the moment of individual coming out. That has not, indeed, been its project. In fact, except for a newly productive interest in historicizing gay definition itself, the array of analytic tools available today to anyone thinking about issues of homo/ heterosexual definition is remarkably little enriched from that available to, say, Proust. Of the strange plethora of "explanatory" schemas newly available to Proust and his contemporaries, especially in support of minoritizing views, some have been superseded, forgotten, or rendered by history too unpalatable to be appealed to explicitly. (Many of the supposedly lost ones do survive, if not in sexological terminology, then in folk wisdom and "commonsense." One is never surprised, either, when they reemerge under new names on the Science page of the *Times;* the men-women of Sodom matriculate as the "sissy boys" of Yale University Press.)[19] But there are few new entries. Most moderately to well-educated Western people in this century seem to share a similar understanding of homosexual definition, independent of whether they themselves are gay or straight, homophobic or antihomophobic. That understanding is close to what Proust's probably was, what for that matter mine is and probably yours. That is to say, it is organized around a radical and irreducible incoherence. It holds the minoritizing view that there is a distinct population of persons who "really are" gay; at the same time, it holds the universalizing views that sexual desire is an unpredictably powerful solvent of stable identities; that apparently heterosexual persons and object choices are strongly marked by same-sex influences and desires, and vice versa for apparently homo-sexual ones; and that at least male heterosexual identity and modern masculinist culture may require for their maintenance the scapegoating crystallization of a same-sex male desire that is widespread and in the first place internal.[20]

It has been the project of many, many writers and thinkers of many different kinds to adjudicate between the minoritizing and universalizing views of sexual definition and to resolve this conceptual incoherence. With whatever success, on their own terms, they have accomplished the project, none of them has budged in one direction or other the absolute hold of this yoking of contradictory views on modern discourse. A higher *valuation* on the transformative and labile play of desire, a higher *valuation* on gay identity and gay community: neither of these, nor their opposite, often far more potent depreciations, seems to get any purchase on the stranglehold of the available and ruling paradigm-clash. And this incoherence has prevailed for at least three-quarters of a century. Sometimes, but not always, it has taken the form of a confrontation or nonconfrontation between politics and theory. A perfect example of this potent incoherence was the anomalous legal situation of gay people and acts in this country after one recent legal ruling. The Supreme Court in *Bowers v. Hardwick* notoriously left the individual states free to prohibit any *acts* they wish to define as "sodomy," by whomsoever performed, with no fear at all of impinging on any rights, and particularly privacy rights, safeguarded by the Constitution; yet only shortly thereafter a panel of the Ninth Circuit Court of Appeals ruled (in *Sergeant Perry J. Watkins v. United States Army*) that homosexual *persons,* as a particular kind of person, *are* entitled to Constitutional protections under the Equal Protection clause.[21] To be gay in this system is to come under the radically overlapping aegises of a universalizing discourse of acts and a minoritizing discourse of persons. Just at the moment, at least within the discourse of law, the former of these prohibits what the latter of them protects; but in the concurrent public-health constructions related to AIDS, for instance, it is far from clear that a minoritizing discourse of persons ("risk groups") is not even more oppressive than the competing, universalizing discourse of acts ("safer sex"). In the double binds implicit in the space overlapped by the two, at any rate, every matter of definitional control is fraught with consequence.

The energy-expensive but apparently static clinch between minoritizing and universalizing views of *homo/heterosexual definition* is not, either, the only major conceptual siege under which modern homosexual and heterosexist fates are enacted. The second one, as important as the first and intimately entangled with it, has to do with defining the relation to gender of homosexual persons and same-sex desires. (It was in this conceptual register that the radical-feminist reframing of lesbianism as woman-identification was such a powerful move.) Enduringly since at least the turn of the century, there have presided two contradictory *tropes of gender* through which same-sex desire could be understood. On the one hand there was, and there persists, differently coded (in the homophobic folklore and science surrounding those "sissy boys" and their mannish sisters, but also in the heart and guts of much living gay and lesbian culture), the trope of inversion, *anima muliebris in corpore virili inclusa*—"a woman's soul trapped in a man's body"—and vice versa. As such writers as Christopher Craft have made clear, one vital impulse of this trope is the preservation of an essential *heterosexuality* within desire itself, through a particular reading of the homosexuality of persons: desire, in this view, by definition subsists in the current that runs between one male self and one female self, in whatever sex of bodies these selves may be manifested.[22] Proust was not the first to demonstrate—nor, for that matter, was the Shakespeare of the comedies—that while these attributions of "true" "inner" heterogender may be made to stick, in a haphazard way, so long as dyads of people are all that are in question, the broadening of view to include any larger circuit of desire must necessarily reduce the inversion or liminality trope to a choreography of breathless farce. Not a jot the less for that has the trope of inversion remained a fixture of modern discourse of same-sex desire; indeed, under the banners of androgyny or, more graphically, "genderfuck," the dizzying instability of this model has itself become a token of value.

Charged as it may be with value, the persistence of the inversion trope has been yoked, however, to that of its contradictory counterpart, the trope of gender separatism. Under this latter view, far from its being of the essence of desire to cross boundaries of gender, it is instead the most natural thing in the world that people of the same gender, people grouped together under the single most determinative diacritical mark of social organization, people whose economic, institutional, emotional, physical needs and knowledges may have so much in common, should bond together also on the axis of sexual desire. As the substitution of the phrase "woman-identified woman" for "lesbian" suggests, as indeed does the concept of the continuum of male or female homosocial desire, this trope tends to reassimilate to one another identification and desire, where inversion models, by contrast, depend on their distinctness. Gender-separatist models would thus place the woman-loving woman and the man-loving man each at the "natural" defining center of their own gender, again in contrast to inversion models that locate gay people—whether biologically or culturally—at the threshold between genders (see Figure 1).

The immanence of each of these models throughout the history of modern gay definition is clear from the early split in the German homosexual rights movement between Magnus Hirschfeld, founder (in 1897) of the Scientific-Humanitarian Committee, a believer in the "third sex" who posited, in Don Mager's paraphrase, "an exact equation . . . between cross-gender behaviors and homosexual desire"; and Benedict Friedländer, co-founder (in 1902) of the Community of the Special, who concluded to the contrary "that homosexuality was the highest, most perfect evolutionary stage of gender differentiation."[23] As James Steakley explains, "the true *typus inversus*," according to this latter argument, "as distinct from the effeminate homosexual, was seen as the founder of patriarchal society and ranked above the heterosexual in terms of his capacity for leadership and heroism."[24]

Like the dynamic impasse between minoritizing and universalizing views of homosexual definition, that between transitive and separatist tropes of homosexual gender has its own complicated history, an especially crucial one for any understanding of modern gender asymmetry, oppression, and resistance. One thing that does emerge with clarity from this complex and contradictory map of sexual and gender definition is that the possible grounds to be found there for alliance and cross-identification among various

	Separatist:	Integrative:
Homo/hetero *sexual* definition:	*Minoritizing*, e.g., gay identity, "essentialist," third-sex models, civil rights models	*Universalizing*, e.g., bisexual potential, "social constructionist," "sodomy" models, "lesbian continuum"
Gender definition:	*Gender separatist*, e.g., homosocial continuum, lesbian separatist, manhood-initiation models	*Inversion/liminality/transitivity*, e.g., cross-sex, androgyny, gay/lesbian solidarity models

FIGURE 1. Models of Gay/Straight Definition in Terms of Overlapping Sexuality and Gender

groups will also be plural. To take the issue of gender definition alone: under a gender-separatist topos, lesbians have looked for identifications and alliances among women in general, including straight women (as in Adrienne Rich's "lesbian continuum" model); and gay men, as in Friedländer's model—or more recent "male liberation" models—of masculinity, might look for them among men in general, including straight men. "The erotic and social presumption of women is our enemy," Friedländer wrote in his "Seven Theses on Homosexuality" (1908).[25] Under a topos of gender inversion or liminality, in contrast, gay men have looked to identify with straight women (on the grounds that they are also "feminine" or also desire men), or with lesbians (on the grounds that they occupy a similarly liminal position); while lesbians have analogously looked to identify with gay men or, though this latter identification has not been strong since second-wave feminism, with straight men. (Of course, the political outcomes of all these trajectories of potential identification have been radically, often violently, shaped by differential historical forces, notably homophobia and sexism.) Note, however, that this schematization over "the issue of gender definition alone" also does impinge on the issue of homo/heterosexual definition, as well, and in an unexpectedly chiasmic way. Gender-*separatist* models like Rich's or Friedländer's seem to tend toward *universalizing* understandings of homo/heterosexual potential. To the degree that gender-*integrative* inversion or liminality models, such as Hirschfeld's "third-sex" model, suggest an alliance or identity between lesbians and gay men, on the other hand, they tend toward gay-*separatist,* minoritizing models of specifically gay identity and politics. Steakley makes a useful series of comparisons between Hirschfeld's Scientific-Humanitarian Committee and Friedländer's Community of the Special: "Within the homosexual emancipation movement there was a deep factionalization between the Committee and the Community. . . . [T]he Committee was an organization of men and women, whereas the Community was exclusively male. . . . The Committee called homosexuals a third sex in an effort to win the basic rights accorded the other two; the Community scorned this as a beggarly plea for mercy and touted the notion of supervirile bisexuality."[26] These crossings are quite contingent, however; Freud's universalizing understanding of sexual definition seems to go with an integrative, inversion model of gender definition, for instance. And, more broadly, the routes to be taken across this misleadingly symmetrical map are fractured in a particular historical situation by the profound asymmetries of gender oppression and heterosexist oppression.

Like the effect of the minoritizing/universalizing impasse, in short, that of the impasse of gender definition must be seen first of all in the creation of a field of intractable, highly structured discursive incoherence at a crucial node of social organization, in this case the node at which *any* gender is discriminated. I have no optimism at all about the availability of a standpoint of thought from which either question could be intelligibly, never mind efficaciously, adjudicated, given that the same yoking of contradictions has presided over all the thought on the subject, and all its violent and pregnant modern history, that has gone to form our own thought. Instead, the more promising project would seem to be a study of the incoherent dispensation itself, the indisseverable girdle of incongruities under whose discomfiting span, for most of a century, have unfolded both the most generative and the most murderous plots of our culture.

NOTES

1. D.A. Miller, "Secret Subjects, Open Secrets," in his *The Novel and the Police* (Berkeley and Los Angeles: University of California Press, 1988), p. 207.

2. On this case see Michael W. La Morte, "Legal Rights and Responsibilities of Homosexuals in Public Education," *Journal of Law and Education* 4, no. 23 (July 1975): 449–67, esp. 450–53;

and Jeanne La Borde Scholz, "Comment: Out of the Closet, Out of a Job: Due Process in Teacher Disqualification," *Hastings Law Quarterly* 6 (Winter 1979): 663–717, esp. 682–84.

3. Nan Hunter, director of the ACLU's Lesbian and Gay Rights Project, analyzed *Rowland* in "Homophobia and Academic Freedom," a talk at the 1986 Modern Language Association National Convention. There is an interesting analysis of the limitations, for gay-rights purposes, of both the right of privacy and the First Amendment guarantee of free speech, whether considered separately or in tandem, in "Notes: The Constitutional Status of Sexual Orientation: Homosexuality as a Suspect Classification," *Harvard Law Review* 98 (April 1985): 1285–1307, esp. 1288–97. For a discussion of related legal issues that is strikingly apropos of, and useful for, the argument made in *Epistemology of the Closet* (Berkeley and Los Angeles: University of California Press, 1990), see Janet E. Halley, "The Politics of the Closet: Towards Equal Protection for Gay, Lesbian, and Bisexual Identity," *UCLA Law Review* 36 (1989): 915–76.

4. *New York Native,* no. 169 (July 14, 1986): 11.

5. Philip Bockman, "A Fine Day," *New York Native,* no. 175 (August 25, 1986): 13.

6. A reminder that "the closet" retains (at least the chronic potential of) its gay semantic specification: a media flap in June, 1989, when a Republican National Committee memo calling for House Majority Leader Thomas Foley to "come out of the liberal closet" and comparing his voting record with that of an openly gay Congressman, Barney Frank, was widely perceived (and condemned) as insinuating that Foley himself is gay. The committee's misjudgment about whether it could maintain deniability for the insinuation is an interesting index to how unpredictably full or empty of gay specificity this locution may be perceived to be.

7. On this, see my "Privilege of Unknowing," *Genders,* no. 1 (Spring 1988).

8. On this, see *Between Men: English Literature and Male Homosocial Desire* (New York: Columbia University Press, 1985).

9. Lord Alfred Douglas, "Two Loves," *The Chameleon* 1 (1894): 28 (emphasis added).

10. Jean Racine, *Esther,* ed. H.R. Roach (London: George G. Harrap, 1949), line 89; my translation. Further citations of this play will be noted by line number in the text.

11. It is worth remembering, of course, that the biblical story still ends with mass slaughter: while Racine's king *revokes* his orders (1197), the biblical king *reverses* his (Esther 8:5), licensing the Jews' killing of "seventy and five thousand" (9:16) of their enemies, including children and women (8:11).

12. In Voltaire's words, "un roi insensé qui a passé six mois avec sa femme sans savoir, sans s'informer même qui elle est" (in Racine, *Esther,* pp. 83–84).

13. On this, see "Privilege of Unknowing," esp. p. 120.

14. Alan Bray, *Homosexuality in Renaissance England* (London: Gay Men's Press, 1982), p. 16.

15. On this, see Jonathan Katz, *Gay/Lesbian Almanac: A New Documentary* (New York: Harper & Row, 1983), pp. 147–50. For more discussion, David M. Halperin, *One Hundred Years of Homosexuality* (New York: Routledge, 1989).

16. Conceivably, contemporary liberal/radical feminism, on the spectrum stretching from NOW to something short of radical separatism, could prove to be something of an exception to this rule—though, of course, already a much compromised one.

17. For a fuller discussion of this, see Chapter 4 of *Epistemology of the Closet.*

18. See, for example, Radicalesbians, "The Woman Identified Woman," reprinted in Anne Koedt, Ellen Levine, and Anita Rapone, eds., *Radical Feminism* (New York: Quadrangle, 1973), pp. 240–45; and Adrienne Rich, "Compulsory Heterosexuality and Lesbian Existence," in Catherine R. Stimpson and Ethel Spector Person, eds., *Women, Sex,* and *Sexuality* (Chicago: University of Chicago Press, 1980), pp. 62–91. Reprinted in this volume.

19. I'm referring here to the publicity given to Richard Green's *The "Sissy Boy Syndrome" and the Development of Homosexuality* on its 1987 publication. The intensely stereotypical, homophobic journalism that appeared on the occasion seemed to be legitimated by the book itself, which seemed, in turn, to be legitimated by the status of Yale University Press *itself.*

20. Anyone who imagines that this perception is confined to antihomophobes should listen, for instance, to the college football coach's ritualistic scapegoating and abjection of his team's "sissy" (or worse) personality traits. D.A. Miller's "*Cage aux folles:* Sensation and Gender in Wilkie

Collins's *The Woman in White*" (in his *The Novel and the Police,* pp. 146–91, esp. pp. 186–90) makes especially forcefully the point (oughtn't it always to have been obvious?) that this whole family of perceptions is if anything less distinctively the property of cultural criticism than of cultural enforcement.

21. When Watkins's reinstatement in the army was supported by the full Ninth Circuit Court of Appeals in a 1989 ruling, however, it was on narrower grounds.

22. Christopher Craft, " 'Kiss Me with Those Red Lips': Gender and Inversion in Bram Stoker's *Dracula,*" *Representations,* no. 8 (Fall 1984): 107–34, esp. 114.

23. Don Mager, "Gay Theories of Gender Role Deviance," *SubStance* 46 (1985): 32–48; quoted from 35–36. His sources here are John Lauritsen and David Thorstad, *The Early Homosexual Rights Movement* (New York: Times Change Press, 1974), and James D. Steakley, *The Homosexual Emancipation Movement in Germany* (New York: Arno Press, 1975).

24. Steakley, *The Homosexual Emancipation Movement in Germany,* p. 54.

25. Steakley, *The Homosexual Emancipation Movement in Germany,* p. 68.

26. Steakley, *The Homosexual Emancipation Movement in Germany,* pp. 60–61.

3

Deviance, Politics, and the Media

STUART HALL

Stuart Hall is a sociological theorist who has written extensively about race, class, and identity. He is widely regarded as one of the founders of the field now known as cultural studies, and he is also a prominent critic and opponent of the contemporary Tory regime in Great Britain. In this article, first published in 1974, he takes note of the emergence of new political movements in the late 1960s and early 1970s, movements for instance of black power advocates, welfare claimants, and lesbian and gay people; and he argues that the measure of the success of such new movements as these must depend crucially on whether they are publicly legitimated as political or are instead delegitimated because labeled as deviant. To devise, at least tentatively, a theory cogent and complex enough to explain why some movements are legitimated and others delegitimated is his objective; and in devising it he draws eclectically on several different sources, including both contemporary versions of Marxism and ethnography. Stuart Hall is the author of Policing the Crisis: Mugging, the State, and Law and Order *(1978), and of* New Times: The Changing Face of Politics in the 1990's *(1991); and he is Professor and Head of Sociology at the Open University.*

This paper is largely speculative.[1] It refers to a piece of work on the way certain forms of political deviance and political activism are handled by the mass media and labeled in the political domain. The research is still in its early stages. It is not, therefore, possible to present any substantive findings or a résumé of the empirical evidence. But we are now at the stage of sketching out our working hypotheses, and as these suggest certain links between the study of deviance, political behavior, and mass media research, it seems opportune to present, in a compressed and provisional form, the process of *ad hoc* theorizing for comment and discussion.

I

Political deviance does not figure prominently in the study of deviant behavior. Becker (1967) suggests that this is because, in many forms of social deviance, "The conflicting segments or ranks are not organized for conflict; no one attempts to alter the shape of the hierarchy." Yet it is clear that the process by which certain deviant acts come to be defined as "social problems," the labeling process itself, and the enforcement of social controls all contain an intrinsically political component. Horowitz and Liebowitz (1968) argue that "Deviance has been studied by employing a consensus welfare model rather than a conflict model." This model has tended to suppress the political element in deviant transactions with "straight" society. Lemert (1967) appears to be one of the earliest

deviancy theorists in the interactionist school to have openly acknowledged the close
interpenetration of labeling theory with power and ideology:

> Social action and control usually emanate from élite power groups who have their
> own systems of values, which differ from those of the general population, from those
> of other groups, and even from those of individual members of the élites. The or-
> ganizational values of such élites and their rules of procedure also have a strong bearing
> on controlling events. The position of groups and individuals at the point of their
> interaction in a social structure is of great significance in predicting the resultant
> action taken by a society to control or decontrol. . . .

Horowitz and Liebowitz (1968) argue that, conventionally, deviance theory has accepted
a "highly formalistic vision of politics" which confines politics "to the formal juridical
aspects of social life, such as the electoral process and to the maintenance of a party
apparatus through procedural norms. . . . In this view, only behavior within the electoral
process is defined as political in character."

From such a vantage point, certainly, the study of deviance and of politics have
little or nothing to say to one another. Yet events in the real world are increasingly
revealing the operational and ideological content of this formal proposition about politics.
From the normative point of view, all political action which is not expressed via the
electoral process, which does not contribute to the maintenance of party apparatuses,
and is not governed by procedural norms is, by definition, deviant with respect to politics.
But, as in all labeling theory, the question is, who defines which action belongs where?
Operationally, the maintenance of boundaries between "politics" and "non-politics" and
the casting of certain "political" acts into the "non-political" domain, are themselves
political acts, and reflect the structure of power and interest. These acts of labeling in
the political domain, far from being self-evident, or a law of the natural world, constitute
a form of continuing political "work" on the part of the élites of power: they are, indeed,
often the opening salvo in the whole process of political control.

The crisp distinction between socially and politically deviant behavior is increasingly difficult to sustain. There are at least five reasons for this. First, many socially
deviant groups are being politicized. Secondly, political activist groups are frequently
also "deviant" in life-style and values. Thirdly, the "politics" of deviant groups has, in
contrast with the more "objective" content of traditional class politics, a distinctive
cultural or existential content: their dissociation from the *status quo* is expressed as much
in cultural attitudes, ideology, and life-style, as in program or economic disadvantage.
Fourthly, the collective organization and activities of such political minorities have had
the effect of transferring some questions from the "social problem" to the "political
issue" category. In this way the hidden political element inside deviant behavior is
rendered transparent, and the map of social deviance is altered. Fifthly, under pressure
from events, the consensual nature of sociological theory—to which the earlier forms
of deviant theory of, say, the Mertonian variety, belonged—has been polarized and
fragmented.[2] Models of social action predicated on the assumption of an integrative and
self-regulative functional social order are progressively challenged by models in which,
precisely, the internal cohesiveness of the 'social system' and its ability to "tension-
manage" dissidents and deviants are rendered problematic. The elaboration of such
counter-theories clearly apply in equal measure to the analysis of socially deviant and
politically conflictful behavior. Thus, at different levels, both of action and theory, new,
more radical perspectives on the phenomenon of deviance have opened up, in which
hard-and-fast distinctions between deviance and politics are weakened. Horowitz and
Liebowitz (1968) therefore seem correct when they declare the distinction between

"political marginality" and "social deviance" to be, increasingly "an obsolete distinction." This presents us with new problems of definition which, in turn, open the lines of confluence once again between deviance and politics.

Lemert (1967) gives a classic formulation of the distinction between "deviant groups" and "political minorities."

> Groups of individuals whose values are being sacrificed by intoxication and drunkenness may have no structure to formulate their vaguely felt dissatisfactions. On the other hand, minorities, because their programmes are defined and their power is organized and well timed, more readily have their values cast into an emergent pattern of social action.

This distinction, too, is no longer so clear-cut. Certainly, we need some way of distinguishing between behavior labeled deviant, where the participants formulate no program of action, and require only to be left alone by the authorities of control, or more organized forms of political activism. Many so-called "crimes without victims" or "crimes" where the only victims are the participants themselves, fall within the first category. Such forms of action differ from the actions of political minorities whose "values" are more readily cast "into an emergent pattern of social action." Yet, deviant groups who regularly, because of their deviation, fall foul of the law, and are harassed by law-enforcing agencies and the courts, may, in response, develop programs, organizations, and actions directed at ending their stigmatization or redefining the legal injunctions against them. This represents, at the very least, the inception of a process of politicization of deviant subcultures along at least two dimensions: by opposing constituted authority in the form of the courts, political legislation, and social control agencies, such groups take up an organized existence against the locus of authority as such. They undertake projects "to alter the shape of the hierarchy." This, in turn, may lead to the forging of formal or informal coalitions with other groups who are also ranged against the hierarchy on other grounds. Secondly, in the course of organizing themselves, deviant groups come, retrospectively, to redefine the social stigmas against them in political terms. Hence, in recent years, many deviant groups—drug addicts, homosexuals, welfare claimants, etc.— have begun, on their own as well as in company with other, more overtly political groupings, to "pioneer the development of organization responses to harassment." In return (especially within the spectrum of "new left" politics) such deviant subcultures provide "a broad base for political organizing." The extent to which a "soft drug" culture is common both to deviant and political minority groupings in the United States is one indication of the coalescence of deviant and political elements within what might be broadly labeled a "generational underground" (Hall 1969). This process of mutual interpenetration has been facilitated by the fact that, in any case, the political groupings with which deviant subcultures are most likely to ally themselves rarely throw up clear and permanent organizational forms, and are only loosely, if at all, attached to a stated program of political reforms.[3] In many cases, the "members" of deviant groups and of politically activist minorities are one and the same. This process of coalescence is attested to in the widespread convergence of criminal and ideological labels applied, without much distinction, by labeling agencies to dissenting minorities of both a "deviant" and "political" type.

Horowitz and Liebowitz (1968) suggest that "the right to dissent" is traditionally accorded to many organized political minorities but traditionally denied to most deviant groups. But, as political minorities increasingly cross the line from legal demonstrations to illegal forms of protest, and as deviants cross the line from privatized deviancy to public protest, so the "traditional right to dissent," for both groups, becomes problematic and is contested.

Horowitz and Liebowitz (1968) also argue that the conventional wisdom about deviance in its liberal form is based on the "majoritarian formulation of politics."

> This is a framework limited to the political strategies available to majorities or to *powerful minorities* (my italics) having access to élite groups. The strategies available to disenfranchised minorities are largely ignored and thus the politics of deviance also go unexamined.

This suggests an important distinction which we cannot neglect. In classic democratic theory, of course, a very simple model was preserved in which political decisions were arrived at through the conflict and interaction of organized majorities representing the broad sections of the population, within the framework of a written or unwritten constitution, the electoral process, parliamentary representation, and the state. It is now clearly recognized, even by its defenders, that such a simple majoritarian model of democratic politics has little or no relevance as a portrait of the modern industrial state. "With the emergence of mass politics ... all hope of this immediacy and comprehensibility was irrevocably lost" (Wolff 1965). Between the organized majorities of an electorate and the process of political decision-taking there has grown up the great corporate industrial state-within-the-state, intermediary bureaucratic organizations associated with national and local administration and government, the web of voluntary organizations and the intricate network of private associations, pressure and interest groups, all of which, systematically, mediate and transform a simple, majoritarian model of the political process. While democratic theory in its simple sense is vestigially retained, as a sort of ideological and legitimating myth, political theory has itself had to come to terms with the much more complex and ramified nature of the modern state, and especially with the complex of intermediary associations which stand in between organized electoral majorities and the political process. As Partridge (1971) observes:

> Only the naive now entertain the model of a political system in which policy initiatives proceed from the body of the citizens and the function of government is to give effect to the popular will. For a great number of empirical reasons we recognize that the politics of complex societies cannot work like that; that political parties and other organizations, leaders and élites, bureaucracies and governments necessarily assume such functions as selecting and defining issues or problems, assembling and distributing information, proposing policies and advocating them, engaging in public persuasion, demonstrating the satisfactoriness of general lines of policy by initiating practical measures that are seen to work.... These are among the ways in which governments (and other influential political organizations and groups) may forge, consolidate, and expand the approval or support which enables them to continue to enjoy and deploy authority—or, as we commonly say, manufacture consent.

This modification in the simple variant of "majoritarian politics" is usually defined as a shift towards a theory of democratic élitism, or democratic pluralism. But, within the theory of democratic pluralism, there is all the distinction in the world between those large corporate institutions and the web of powerful minority interest or pressure groups which operate within and upon the organs of the state, on the one hand, and the small, emergent, marginal, disenfranchised minority groupings not institutionalized within the processes of political bargaining and compromise. While in theory democratic pluralism allows for the entry of new groups and associations into the political arena, concretely and in practice it operates in such a way as systematically to ignore and disenfranchise certain emergent groups and interests which are outside the consensus, while maintaining intact the existing structure of political interests. Writing about the application of democratic pluralism in the context of American political life, Wolff (1965) has observed:

> There is a very sharp distinction in the public domain between legitimate interests and those which are absolutely beyond the pale. If a group or interest is within the framework of acceptability, then it can be sure of winning some measure of what it seeks, for the process of national politics is distributive and compromising. On the other hand, if an interest falls outside the circle of the acceptable, it receives no attention whatsoever and its proponents are treated as crackpots, extremists, or foreign agents. With bewildering speed, an interest can move from "outside" to "inside" and its partisans, who have been scorned by the solid and established in the community, become presidential advisers and newspaper columnists. . . . Thus the "vector-sum" version of pluralist theory functions ideologically by tending to deny new groups or interests access to the political plateau. It does this by ignoring their existence in practice, not by denying their claim in theory.

For our purpose, then, the important distinction is not that between a "majoritarian" and a "minority" formulation of politics, but that between the powerful, legitimate minorities and the weak, emergent, marginal minorities. Powerful political minority groups, whether hereditary, voluntary, pressure-group, or interest based, share with élites and with organized majorities the right to exercise influence, to organize to further their views, and to dissent: they are understood to act in a "political" manner. Weak, marginal, non-institutionalized, and illegitimate political minorities share with social deviants the definition of their actions in terms of a "social problem" paradigm: they are "explained" within a welfare-state, therapeutic, or psychological framework: their actions are, by definition, "non-political."

If one looks at the political spectrum as a whole, within this perspective, it is clear that while some emergent minority interests gain ready access to the political process, are accorded a legitimate place within the process of bargaining about decisions or scarce resources, and flower as successfully formed interests, others—which share many social characteristics with deviant groups—are themselves defined as "deviant" with respect to the political process itself: different models of explanation are applied to the latter, and they are subject to quite different processes of social stigmatization and control.

We may now formulate one of the central problems of the emergence of deviant political minorities in the following way:

(1) When new political movements come into existence, it is a matter of critical importance whether they are legitimized publicly within the "political" category, or de-legitimized by being assigned to the "deviant" category. Deviant groups and individuals may be sick, disadvantaged, corrupted by others, led astray, or subject to social disorganization: but they are not exploited. Consequently, they can be made well again (therapeutic), isolated from contagion (segregated), or supported (welfare state)—but they cannot organize or dissent.

(2) Under certain circumstances, legitimate political minorities are subjected to severe "status degradation" ceremonies, and are lumped with the more marginal groups. They are then subject to quite different forms of public opprobrium, stigmatization, and exclusion. They have been symbolically de-legitimated.

In general terms, then, the line between social deviance and minority political militancy is disappearing. The alliance between some types of social deviance and political marginality has been strengthened: politics has become more "deviant" with respect to social norms, and deviancy is progressively politicized. The latent political content of the deviant process and the deviant element in radical politics now emerge together as a single phenomenon. "As this happens, political dissent by deviant means will become subject to the types of repression that have been a traditional response to social deviance" (Horowitz and Liebowitz 1968).

II

For the purpose of this paper, political deviance is very loosely defined.[4] The projects of such groups must contain some manifest political aim or goal, as well as perhaps a latent content of socially deviant attitudes and life-style. Their activities tend to fall outside the consensual norms which regulate political conflict, and they are willing to employ means commonly defined as "illegitimate" to further or secure their ends. In life-style, attitude, and relationships they are socially unorthodox, permissive, even subversive. They are marginal to the more powerful groups—organized majorities, legitimate minorities, interest-groups, élites—institutionalized in the political domain. They challenge the representative/electoral/parliamentary framework which stabilizes the British political structure, with its complicated mechanisms for negotiating conflict. They tend to by-pass the "reformism" of the organized mass parties of the "left" and the "economism" of the trade unions. The forms of political deviance I have in mind here all have a radical political perspective and are recent arrivals on the stage of political life in advanced industrial societies. Centrally, we are concerned here with movements involving students and young people, ethnic and religious minorities. These groupings and formations are complexly structured by class, but are not explicitly class-based. They are largely extra-parliamentary in form. The types of deviant political activities involved include student militancy and protest (confrontations with university authorities, sit-ins, occupations, etc.); militant extra-parliamentary demonstrations, which might involve conflict with the police; urban rioting and rebellion (e.g. Watts) and urban insurgency (e.g. Ulster); sporadic incidents of bombing incendiarism, attacks on property for political reasons (Weathermen or "Angry Brigade" activities); squatters' movements, rent strikes, militant tenants' action; ethnically oriented "Black Power" or Panther-style activities. It will at once be clear that all these groups' activities fall roughly within the category of the "new politics" or extra-parliamentary oppositional groups which have so decisively emerged on the political stage of the advanced capitalist societies in the West in the past decide. I want also to consider, as a special transitional category, the case of "unofficial strikes"—industrial strikes originating through shop floor organization rather than via the initiative of union bureaucracies, which, even when subsequently sanctioned by official sponsorship, are systematically defined as "deviant" to the political system as such, and contrary to "the national interest." One might also include the resistance—sometimes with official union sponsorship—to the recent attempts by both political parties to legislate for control over the unions by some form of Industrial Relations Bill.

Our concern is specifically with the way these emergent forms of political militancy are defined and labeled. But it is necessary, first, to understand their emergence and position in relation to the socio-political structure as a whole. This constitutes at least a paper on its own, and a full account cannot be attempted here. But, briefly, we may say that, in the years immediately following the Second World War, the armed rivalry between East and West served to stabilize the internal political systems of the West. The expansion of welfare capitalist structures, the dominance of mass parties of the center-left and center-right, and the evolution of social-democratic parties towards a general accommodation with capitalism were integral aspects of this process. This enforced stabilization of advanced capitalist societies has, in recent years, been broken: first, by the liberation movements and armed struggles of the "third world," second by the emergence of militant minority movements within the Western capitalist world itself. In the majority of cases, these latter emergent political groupings occupy positions marginal to the institutional power groups and the institutionalized forms of class conflict upon which the welfare-capitalist consensus was based. In many cases, these activist minorities also remain marginal to the traditional class agencies of change. Even where they openly and consciously espouse a revolutionary class perspective, they remain largely segregated from the organized industrial working class. Such groupings may work for, and temporarily succeed in forging, alliances and coalitions with class formations: events in France in May 1968 represent the clearest example of such a convergence. In other circumstances, such groupings are clearly in one sense or another "vanguard elements" in relation to class conflict, articulating and promoting protest from the outside amongst such wider sectors as well as on their behalf. Thus "black power" militants clearly speak and organize on behalf of the disenfranchised black majorities of the Deep South and the disadvantaged black poor of the urban ghettos; the early Civil Rights movement in Northern Ireland articulated the structural discontents of the poor, disenfranchised Catholic minorities of Ulster. There is, clearly, a spectrum here in terms of the relation between emergent political minorities of this new type and their real or potential "constituents." But, by and large, the pace, content, style, direction, and tempo of development among such minority activist groups move at a different rate from the growth of organized protest amongst the disadvantaged classes and majorities. The relation here between the extra-parliamentary opposition and the articulation of class conflict in the more traditional sense exhibits all the characteristics of a "combined and uneven development."[5] Their relative marginality, not only to the political heartland of their own societies, but also to the groups and classes on whose behalf they are active, remains one of their defining characteristics. As Raymond Williams (1971) has remarked,

> it seems to be true that in late capitalist societies some of the most powerful campaigns begin from specific unabsorbed (and therefore necessarily marginal) experiences and situations. Black Power in the United States, civil rights in Ulster, the language movement in Wales, are experiences comparable in this respect to the student movement and to women's liberation. In their early stages these campaigns tend to stress as absolutes those local experiences which are of course authentic and yet most important as indices of the crisis of the wider society.

Despite the many differences within and between such groups, they share, by and large, certain features in common. In social composition, they tend to recruit most successfully outside the sphere of productive relations proper: either—as in black movements, ghetto rebellions, tenants' and claimants' organizations, etc.—from the "*Lumpen*" under-classes, or from other groups—lower professionals, students, social deviants and drop-outs, intellectuals and bohemians—marginal to the structure of productive class relations. Typically, they define their alienation from the prevailing structure in social, cultural, and experiential, as well as economic, terms: as Juliet Mitchell (1971) remarks, their position enables them to embrace a "totalist" attack on capitalism—and thus to transcend the economism which has so effectively neutralized working-class organizations cast in the trade-union or social-democratic molds. In many cases, students have provided the core-recruits to such groupings—recruits precisely from the sphere of expanded higher and technical education, itself a consequence of the growing sophistication and differentiation of the modes of reproduction and the advanced division of labor in technically sophisticated, mature, capitalist societies. Typically, such groups do not seek to advance their cause via the traditional access to élite influence; they do not seek to enhance their position within the system of political bargaining. Instead, they embrace militant, activist, "extremist" political tactics, and explicitly challenge the system itself and its "rules of the game." Their techniques of protest and dissent contravene the norms of political legitimacy which institutionalize political conflict. They take up deviant issues, adopt deviant life-styles and attitudes, in part because of the elective affinity between their political aims and socially subversive values, in part as a way of dramatizing and symbolizing their alienation from the dominant orientations of the hegemonic system. Far from seeking to win their way by the traditional means of influence and negotiation, from the margins to the mainstream of power, they accent their disaffiliation from majority consensual values. They are especially sensitive to the hidden mechanisms by which the dominant system wins and manipulates consent to its own hegemony—socialization through the family and secondary institutions, the manipulative content and constraints of the education process, the creation of an environment of consensus in the mass media. That is, their position makes them acutely sensitive to the spheres of ideological domination and coercion.[6] This sensitivity occurs at precisely the stage, historically, when ideological domination plays a special role in the pacification of class conflict.

> In a consumer society the role of ideology is so important that it is within the sphere
> of ideology that the oppressions of the whole system sometimes manifest themselves
> most apparently. It is here that middle-class radicalism has its place. (Mitchell 1971)

It is essentially groupings, activities, strategies *of this type* which attract to themselves the stigma of political deviance.

Briefly, then, these emergent forms of political militancy appear at a highly contingent moment, historically, in the evolution of advanced, late-industrial capitalist societies. They are the product of, as well as the response to, the corporatist structure and consensual style of managed capitalist societies. (They are also the product of more specific, contingent structural features of such societies: their appearance in the same historical moment is, therefore, doubly determined, "over-determined.")

"Consensus politics" has become, in one variant or another, the stable form of institutional politics in managed capitalism.[7] In Britain in the postwar period, both major political parties have been in active pursuit of a basis of legitimacy rooted, not in class, or in group, or sectional interests, but in a loosely defined political consensus. Consensus politics does not represent a real decentralization of power and authority. Rather, it is the form in which élite class power manages the consent of "masses" in socially stratified, differentiated, so-called "pluralist" societies. In the ideology and rhetoric of "consensus politics," the "national interest" is represented as transcending all other collective social interests. We draw a distinction between the "welfare state" and "consensual" variants of capitalist politics: in the "welfare state" variant, conflicts of interest are recognized, but are mitigated by reforms and regulated; in the "consensual" model, "all good men and true," whatever their class and social position or outlook, are supposed to have an over-riding interest in maintaining and advancing the consensual goals. Conflict, especially of an open or radical kind, is symbolically displaced to the political margins. Those who engage in conflict-politics, or interpret society in conflict terms, are powerfully stigmatized. The essential task for consensus politics is:

> to construct around each issue by means of bargaining and compromise a coalition
> of interests; to associate with this legislative program the big battalions of power in
> the state; and from this base to manage public consent and isolate or exclude dissent.
> (Hall 1967)

In Britain, the move towards "consensus politics" has been underwritten by persistent economic stagnation and crisis. The rhetoric of "consensus politics" in Britain thus pivots on a basically economistic definition of "overriding national interest." The postwar effort, by Conservative and Labour administration alike, has been to win over the traditional agencies of working-class organization and defense to active integration within and collusion with the system of politico-economic management. Elsewhere (Williams 1968) we have argued that social democratic parties, like the Labour Party, have played a peculiarly adaptive role in pioneering the path of integration and incorporation, though nowhere has this process been successfully accomplished or completed.

The politics of the extra-parliamentary opposition is specifically the politics of this stage in the evolution of "integrated" capitalist societies. That is not to say it is the *only* form of politics—it exists as a new strand of political dissent alongside and in a complex relation to more traditional agencies of change: capitalism, in seeking stability at this higher level of integration, has not eliminated, but further compounded its untranscended contradictions. But the politics of deviance is a specific and contingent response to the specific stage of evolution of modern capitalism. This form of political protest emerges at just this stage (a) because the position of such groups is now more pivotal than at earlier stages of the system to the system's mode of reproduction; (b) because of the partial containment of the traditional agencies of change; and (c) because such groups are peculiarly responsive to modes of ideological domination which depend, in part upon the repressive and coercive functions of "the state," in part, upon the invisible lines of coordination and integration operating in the ideological and socializing spheres, or what have been called "ideological state apparatuses" (Althusser 1971). The protests from students—the privileged but alienated *cadres* of the new society—and from blacks—the permanently *Lumpen* strata of an "affluent" society—are the *loci* of political conflict in moments when the classic class agencies of change are temporarily contained inside the structures of the state, the mitigating institutions of welfare, laborism as a political practice and economism. Hegemonic demands arose, in their displayed, proto-political form, among supernumerary social strata which remain, nevertheless, neither developed nor evolved sufficiently to be, on their own account, pivotal to revolutionary political transformation.

Societies moving ambiguously towards "consensus politics" therefore provoke a specific counter-politics—the politics of deviance. Since the form and content of consensus is highly problematic, it has to be powerfully advanced in ideological terms. The drive to install consensual forms of domination at the heart of the political process itself is countered, specifically, in the ideological zone by the promulgation and articulation of counter-norms and values: that is, by counter-cultural or "deviant" forms of political action. Shared norms, values, and institutions—the "sacred" character of the consensus itself—are stressed: conflicts of outlook and interest are repressed. Alternative minority politics is therefore impelled, not simply to advance counter-interests within the pattern of regulated class conflict and "due process," but to exaggerate their degree of deviation from institutionalized processes *as such*. New systematic contradictions which arise are displaced, in the search for consensus, from the heart of political life. Groups which express these grievances and contradictions, having been given marginal political status, are labeled "marginal": they develop coalitions with groups and issues already so stigmatized, they crystallize their self-images in "deviant" terms: their deviance is then made the basis for public denunciation and symbolic status-degradation, which legitimates the enforcement of "consensual norms"—and repressive social control. A classic political version of a deviance amplification spiral is joined.[8] Thus the drift and drive to consensus politics not only engenders its own types of conflict, but tends to produce, as a response, a specific type of oppositional movement: political deviance. Political deviance is the form in which conflict reasserts itself at certain nodal points in a system drifting and driving towards "consensus" management of the state. The deviant character and form of minority politics is an unintended consequence—but also a determinate negation—of the movement towards consensualism in the institutionalized life and management of advanced capitalist societies.

III

We argue that militant political deviance is engendered—in its location incidence and form—as a counter-praxis to institutionalized consensual politics. But consensus, in either its political or its ideological form, does not spontaneously evolve: it must be actively constructed. That is the praxis to which deviant politics is a counter. The rise of conflict politics in its deviant form is, therefore, problematic for the society, and requires its own "interpretative work." Problematic situations are those in which the available public meanings and definitions fail to account for, and cannot easily be extended to cover, new developments.[9] New political developments, which are both dramatic and "meaningless" within the consensually validated norms, pose a challenge to the normative world. They render problematic not only how the political world is defined, but how it ought to be. They "breach our expectancies."[10] They interrupt the "seen but unnoticed, expected background features" of everyday political scenes which we use as schemes of interpretation for comprehending political life (Garfinkel 1967). When such practical reasons and accounts are breached, and we are "deprived" of consensual support for alternative definitions of social reality, the active work of constructing new meanings and "definitions of the situation" begins. This social construction of meanings is not to be confused with the elaboration of theories and explanatory models (though it often comprises the *ad hoc* element in them): the latter are systematic accounts, governed by a more formal logic of propositions, which attempt to be internally coherent and consistent. Political structures engender their own characteristic ideologies and theorizing or, better, political structures, ideological and theoretical forms are interpenetrating elements or "practices" in any specific social formation which is "structured in dominance" (Althusser 1971); but the work of public and pragmatic management of political reality cannot be accomplished at this level.[11] We are dealing, rather, with the construction of *ad hoc* "explanations," accounts "for all practical purposes," working definitions of political reality, with their own situational logic (or "logic-in-use") which serve to "make sense of" problematic situations, and which then become the "socially sanctioned grounds of inference and action that people use in their everyday affairs and which we assume others use in the same way" (Garfinkel 1967). As Berger and Luckmann (1967) have suggested:

> If the integration of an institutional order can be understood only in terms of the "knowledge" that its members have of it, it follows that the analysis of that "knowledge" will be essential for an analysis of the institutional order in question. It is important to stress that this does not exclusively or even primarily involve a preoccupation with complex theoretical systems serving as legitimations for the institutional order. Theories also have to be taken into account, of course. But theoretical knowledge is only a small part and by no means the most important part of what passes for knowledge in a society. . . . The primary knowledge about the institutional order is knowledge on the pre-theoretical level. . . . It is the sum total of "what everybody knows" about a social world, an assemblage of maxims, proverbial nuggets of wisdom, values and beliefs, myths and so forth, the theoretical integration of which requires considerable intellectual fortitude in itself. . . .

The social construction and the "interpretative work" involved in explanations at this level, which resolve problematic, troubling, or deviant events, is, nevertheless, a complex process. The work of establishing new kinds of "knowledge" about problematic features of social or political life is accomplished through the mediation of language: the trans-actions of public language are the specific *praxis*—the praxis of public signification—through which such new "knowledge" is objectivated.[12] The relationship between this "knowledge" and its social base "is a dialectical one":

> that is, knowledge is a social product *and* knowledge is a factor in social change. This principle of the dialectic between social production and the objectivated world that is its product has already been explicated. (Berger and Luckmann 1967)

The social production of new definitions in problematic areas produces both "expla-nations" and "justifications." "Legitimation" is this process of "explaining" and "justifying."

> Legitimation "explains" the institutional order by ascribing cognitive validity to its objectivated meanings. Legitimation justifies the institutional order by giving a nor-mative dignity to its practical imperatives. It is important to understand that legiti-mation has a cognitive as well as a normative element. . . . Legitimation not only tells the individual why he *should* perform one action and not another; it also tells him why things are what they are. (Berger and Luckmann 1967).

In complexly structured, socially differentiated societies like Britain or the United States, based on an advanced division of labor, groups lead highly segregated lives, and maintain apparently discrete, often contradictory, "maps of problematic social reality." In such societies, Durkheim observed, "*representations collectives* become increasingly in-determinate." This is especially true of the political domain, which progressively be-comes a segregated area, requiring a special expertise, familiarity, or commitment: a finite province of the social world.

> Modern mass societies, indeed, are made up of a bewildering variety of social worlds. Each is an organized outlook built up by people in their interaction with one another; hence each communication channel gives rise to a separate world. . . . Each of these worlds is a unity of order, a universe of regularized mutual response. Each is an area in which there is some structure which permits reasonable anticipation of the behavior of others, hence, an area in which one may act with a sense of security and confidence. Each social world, then, is a culture area, the boundaries of which are set neither by territory nor by formal group membership but by the limits of effective communi-cation. (Shibutani 1955)

This does not mean that there are no prevailing and dominant symbolic universes which "integrate different provinces of meaning and encompass the institutional order in a symbolic totality" (Berger and Luckmann 1967). But it does mean that such symbolic universes operate at a high degree of typification, and are experienced by the majority as, at best, sedimented and stereotypical constructs.[13] It also means that those who are not directly concerned with enforcing norms and definitions in a problematic or contested area of political life are heavily dependent for their "working definitions" on those agents, institutions, and channels which have access to power and have appropriated the means of signification. This accords with our knowledge about the situations in which typically the mass media exert innovatory power.

The mass media cannot imprint their meanings and messages on us as if we were mentally *tabula rasa*. But they do have an integrative, clarifying, and legitimating power to shape and define political reality, especially in those situations which are unfamiliar, problematic, or threatening: where no "traditional wisdom," no firm networks of per-sonal influence, no cohesive culture, no precedents for relevant action or response, and no first-hand way of testing or validating the propositions are at our disposal with which to confront or modify their innovatory power. The sort of "effectiveness" we have in mind here is not reflected at the primitive behavioral level normally pursued in traditional mass media studies. It is best expressed, as it has been by Halloran (1970), in the following terms:

> The sort of situation I have in mind is where television puts across an attitude or mode of behavior by presenting it as an essential component of required behavior in a valued group. It is stated or implied that certain forms of behavior, attitudes, possessions, etc. are necessary if the individual is to remain a member in a group.... Those who do not have what it takes or refuse to make the effort may be presented as deviants or non-conformists. The appropriate social sanctions for deviance and the modes of approval for acceptance are sometimes explained and illustrated. Adoption of the behavior or attitudes may also be presented as conducive to the integration and general welfare of the group.... What is involved in this type of influence is the provision of social realities where they did not exist before, or the giving of new directions to tendencies already present, in such a way that the adoption of the new attitude or form of behavior is made a socially acceptable mode of conduct, whilst failure to adopt is represented as socially disapproved deviance.

In the area of political deviance, the prevailing, emergent "commonsense" definitions have largely been the product of *three* main agencies: professional politicians (or trade union leaderships)—the legitimate "gate-keepers" of the political domain; agents or representatives of face-to-face control; and the mass media.[14] Each of these agencies for the definition of political reality has a different perspective on the phenomenon of political deviance: but, like all the elements in a social formation "structured in dominance," these perspectives show a strong disposition, in the fact of overt challenge, to "hang together." By political gate-keepers we mean, of course, both the organized mass parties, since each has a vested interest in the "sacred" nature of the consensus. By mass media we mean, essentially, television, the press (regional, national, and local), and radio. By "agencies of face-to-face control" we mean vice-chancellors and university administrators with respect to student militancy; public spokesmen and the army with respect to Ulster; official trade union functionaries with respect to "unofficial strikes"; the police and the social welfare agencies with respect to squatting, rent strikes, militant demonstrations, "Black Power" militants, etc.

IV

Geertz (1964) has argued that the study of ideology as a specific social *praxis* lacks "anything more than the most rudimentary conception of the processes of symbolic formulation."

> The links between the causes of ideology and its effects seem adventitious because the connecting element—the autonomous process of symbolic formulation—is passed over in virtual silence. Both interest theory and strain theory go directly from source analysis to consequence analysis without ever seriously examining ideologies as systems of interacting symbols, as patterns of interworking meanings. Themes are outlined, of course; among the content analysts, they are even counted. But they are referred for elucidation, not to other themes nor to any sort of semantic theory, but either backward to the affect they presumably mirror or forward to the society reality they presumably distort. The problem of how ideologies transform sentiment into significance and so make it socially available is short-circuited....

The new definitions of political deviance do not emerge once-and-for-all, as "full-bloom, inevitable totalities." The work of "classifying out" the political universe, of building up meaningful "semantic zones" to which deviant political acts can be assigned and within which they "make sense," the processes of telescoping, of ascription, of amplifying descriptions and the attribution of "secondary status traits," the use of charged associative metaphors which summon up old meanings in the service of explaining the unfamiliar, the way discrete events are selectively composed into composite "action-images" and "scenarios" of political action, the use of analogies and metaphors which "transform sentiment into significance," win plausibility and command the assent of uninformed and remote publics: these, and other processes, compose the specificity of the *praxis* of political signification as a discrete level within the "ensemble of social relations." Such interpretative work is, at one and the same moment, social and symbolic: its study constitutes a reflexive theoretical practice and its own—that study once described by Lévi-Strauss as "the study of the life of signs at the heart of social life."

> Not only is the semantic structure of an [ideological] figure a good deal more complex than it appears on the surface, but an analysis of that structure forces one into tracing a multiplicity of referential connexions between it and social reality, so that the final picture is one of a configuration of dissimilar meanings out of whose interworking both the expressive power and the rhetorical force of the final symbol derive. This interworking is itself a social process, an occurrence not "in the head" but in that public world where "people" talk together, name things, make assertions, and to a degree understand each other. (Geertz 1964)

Such theoretical work, as a necessary and integral part of the study of deviance (and of political deviance in particular), as well as of politics and the media, is only just beginning.[15] All too often we still employ the much cruder concepts of "intentional bias" and "deliberate distortion" (rather than, say, the more structural notions of "unwitting bias" and "systematically distorted communications").[16] These notions are based on either simple functionalist or simple reflexive models of the relation of consciousness to social being wholly inadequate to the situations they are called upon to explain. They repress the reciprocally structured interaction of social experience and the cultural forms in which experience is handled.

The process by which certain kinds of political deviance come to be signified in a distinctive way, and the relation of the agents of signification to this process are complex, and can only be enforced by detailed analysis. The events dealt with here, and the quotations, are intended for illustrative purposes only. Nor is there space to develop the argument about how this kind of analysis can be carried through. But we must insist that analysis of political signification through linguistic transaction in the public domain must give special weight to the linguistic mediation, and the process of symbolization itself, as Geertz (1964) has argued. In our analysis, we have adopted the method of "immanent structural analysis," in preference to quantitative analysis of the manifest content of political communications. This method is concerned both with the "interior relations" which linguistic forms establish within a "system" of discourse, and with the "codes" and the "logics-in-use" which integrate linguistic items within an inferential structure of argument. The logic is a "situated logic" proceeding (via the basic tropes of condensation and displacement) as much by inference as by direct statement. Special attention is paid to stylistic and rhetorical features of expression.

> Structural analysis proposes . . . such a framework in which the style is the level of integration of content in the code from which it arises. Thus, analysis of style, and particularly analysis of figures of rhetoric of content in the interior of the code is the

best way to reach the code. The figures of rhetoric are . . . the moment where the code (normally unconscious) betrays and confesses its presence. (Burgelin 1968)

Analysis of political communications concerning political deviance conducted by this method of semiological analysis reveals one dominant pervasive deep structure in the material.[17] This is the structure we call minorities/majorities. All the agents of signification when dealing with this type of political behavior employ the minority/ majority distinction. The world of political deviance is systematically "classified out" in terms of this basic opposition. Politicians of local and national status, in public speeches and reported statements, the media in all its forms, and the agents of face-to-face control all consistently employ the minority/majority explanatory model.

One brief comparison suggests how powerful this minority/majority structure is. The two cases concern the incidents around the destruction of the gates within the building at LSE in January/February 1969, and the occupation of the main administration block by students at Birmingham University in December 1968. The first was one incident in a series of militant confrontations between students and university authorities at LSE over a period of three years: the second was an isolated incident at a university noted for its conservative outlook and political quiescence. The first involved the destruction of property, several incidents of milling and scuffling: the second involved no destruction of property, and no incidents which could be labeled as "political violence." The first involved the closing of the School for several days: in the second, only the administration block was occupied, and normal teaching continued throughout. Yet a study of the way both incidents were signified reveals a convergent use of the minority/ majority paradigm. In both cases, the active political groups were defined as "small minorities" exploiting the majority of their compatriots, and holding their institutions and the public at large "up to ransom." This image of a conspiratorial group survives, in the LSE case, the virtually unanimous vote, on 3 February, in favor of two motions supporting militant action; and, in the Birmingham case, the fact that the occupation was supported by an overwhelming majority of those voting in the relevant extraordinary meeting of the Guild of Undergraduates.

The events at LSE were widely reported in the national press. The Birmingham occupation was sparsely reported, the main coverage being on the regional television and radio news, and in the local press. A clear example of the minority/majority paradigm as applied in the LSE situation is the following report in the *Daily Sketch* (27 January 1969):

> A cabal of about 300 students at the London School of Economics has, for patently selfish and confused reasons, caused 2,700 other students to be denied their studies.
>   They deliberately engineered a closure of the College. The majority suffer. The hooligan clique withdrew to repair their wounds and excite themselves in yet another storm of public outrage. . . . I believe that even the people who have been prepared to tolerate student idiosyncrasy have now had their fill of this calculated anarchy. The group of 300, including foreigners. . . .

Another example may be quoted from the *Evening News* (28 January 1969):

> It is an astonishing piece of anarchy . . . 3,000 students, the bulk of who want to work and appreciate their privileged position, are being deprived of their rights by a comparative handful of revolutionary socialists (probably not more than fifty) whose avowed aim is to create physical havoc to overthrow the LSE regime—and the nation's regime, too. . . . What these revolutionaries want is violence for its own sake.

This structure of argument was common to press reports of the LSE events as a whole, though there was the usual distinction, in terms of tone and sensationalism, between the popular and the "posh" papers. Thus the *Daily Telegraph* (3 February 1969) predicted, more sedately:

> Students from the LSE are likely to dissociate themselves from the militant minority at a Union meeting at Euston today.

The prediction was wrong. Reports in the press and television, as a whole, were full of the "wreckers of the School"; this was also the occasion of the now-famous remarks by the then Secretary for Education, Mr. Short, about "academic thugs" and "Brand X revolutionaries."

Exactly the same paradigm dominates the coverage of the Birmingham events in the local press (*Birmingham Post* and *Evening Mail*). The simplest way of characterizing this coverage is to quote from the lead editorial of the *Post* for Saturday, 30 November—the second of five editorials on the subject in the relevant eight days:

> The real affliction for Vice-Chancellors is that universities are also collecting grounds for small minorities who, under a multiplicity of labels, advocate revolution and are out to stir up trouble. Although their aims are principally political these can make effective use of genuine student discontents or aspirations. Vice-Chancellors have the duty to meet the just aspirations of the majority while at the same time giving no ground to deliberate trouble makers.

On the following Tuesday, the *Post* printed on the front page, running across the top of the page, and pre-empting the main news headlines of the day, a letter from 61 students, condemning "militant extremist minority." It introduced the letter to its readers thus:

> The *Post* believes that the activities at Birmingham university are stimulated by a minority group. Unhappily, there is growing evidence that the public is tending to associate all students with the extremists. This letter underlines what we feel is the attitude of the majority.

The same inferential structure of argument is to be found throughout the reports of comments made by local councillors and aldermen about the occupation, as well as by representatives of the university administration. One councillor spoke of "a small minority of agitating adolescents" holding up "the life of the whole university." Another said, "I believe that the majority of students are quite sound and want to get on with their studies. . . ."

In the vast majority of the press and television reports covering militant student protest in the period of high activity between 1967 and 1969, the majority/minority paradigm is employed. The same is true of public statements by representative politicians and by face-to-face agencies of control. It has become ubiquitous as a "common sense explanation" of the perplexing phenomenon of why student protest has made its appearance on the political stage, and of why it should assume such militant forms. It thus serves the latent function of resolving into intelligible terms a highly problematic phenomenon. It is a powerful labeling device. It has cognitive power, effectively classifying "students" into two groups. It has evaluative power, since it attaches to the favored group the preferred title of "majority," transferring to this category the sacred symbolism attaching to all "majorities" in a parliamentary democracy. It has crystallizing value, in that it separates out the complex groupings and proto-formations within student radicalism into simple, stereotypical units, resolving ambiguities. It has generative power. On the basis of this simple polarization, all sorts of "secondary status attributions" can be made. The classified groups can now be particularized and concretized by attributing to them status traits, drawn from other deviant areas, where the stereotypical classifications already exist. Thus "minorities" become "extremists," and, in the course of time, accrete a variety of other qualitative attributes: they are "hooligans" ... "a hooligan clique" ... "wreckers" ... "agitating adolescents" ... "a cabal" ... "thugs" ... "adolescent hooligans" ... "mentally disturbed" ... a "smash-now-and-think-later-caucus" ... "outside agitators" ... "rowdies" ... "plotters." It also has expressive power, providing a framework for the minting of new epithets which are powerfully picturesque: "Brand X revolutionaries" ... "a bunch of hairy coconuts." Above all, it has explanatory and predictive power. For it is only if the student world can be polarized into a minority-extremist-clique and a majority of dupes, "judgmental dopes," whose desire for legitimate reform and whose attention to their studies is being subverted and exploited by the minority "who have something else in mind," that the phenomenon of student militancy can be rendered accountable within the consensual norms of what politics should be. Finally, it has consolatory power: if only the small handful of agitators can be isolated—"probably not more than fifty" at LSE—normalcy can be restored, the *status quo* affirmed.

The minority/majority paradigm is also a persuasive definition. It is employed not simply to explain and account for the phenomenon of student militancy, but contains its own implicit strategies for containment and its own inferred call for retributive punishment. In almost all cases, the minority/majority paradigm attempts to build a *coalition* between the moderates and the agencies of control. It attempts to win over "majority dupes" to a position of active cooperation with the authorities. The clearest example of this is in the *Post* editorial already quoted:

> At the very least five-sixths of the 6,000 or so students at Birmingham University have held aloof from the movement that inaugurated the "direct action," and it is safe to assume that even more disapprove of the actual form this has now taken. The Vice-Chancellor is entitled to look for support not only to the public but to the general student body, because he is upholding their right not to have their studies and university life interfered with by a clamant and apparently intolerant minority group. Unfortunately, when in like circumstances, firm action has been contemplated elsewhere against an activist minority the majority has sometimes felt it should side with those being disciplined. The student majority should remember that if Birmingham University had to be closed because of student indiscipline, the general public would probably bear it with considerable fortitude. It is the student majority that would suffer.

The "explanation" thus frequently assumes a characteristic rhetorical form.[18] It *splits* the student body into two simple and opposed groups—the "pure" (but stupid) and the "polluted": it seeks to "win over" the majority to the side of the reasonable, the rational, the normal, the natural (all these normative elements are centrally built-in to the paradigm itself and are actively present in its actual use): but it also counterposes to students *as a whole*—as if audiences to a spectacle—the "general public," whose relation to what is going on, it is inferred, cannot be anything but distant, passive, disinterested, and remote. If the paradigm serves to stereotype the minority as military extremists, intent on violence for its own sake, and the majority as reasonable but simple men, whose good-will is being used and exploited, it also stereotypes the public, as a distant, heterogeneous, and uninvolved mass—spectators to a dangerous but diverting symbolic drama, linked only by their as yet unexpressed wish to see the reasonable, the normal— "due process"—resume its steady course once again: a silent majority. This process of splitting/isolation and projection is the precise *rhetorical* form assumed by élite power in the society of "masses." It is the new symbolic version of the ancient principle of "divide and rule."

The significant fact, for our purposes, is that this minority/majority paradigm in its amplified form has become one of the most persistent "inferential structures" in the signification of political deviance of all types in the political domain and in the media. It has long since become a standard "deep structure" in the definition and labeling of militant political demonstrations, such as the protests against the South African cricket and Springboks' tour, and the famous Hyde Park/Grosvenor Square demonstration against the Vietnam War of 27 October 1968. The *Times,* for example, reported Mr. Callaghan, then Home Secretary, as saying in the House of Commons on the Friday before the Vietnam demonstration:

> The organization of the demonstration, Mr. Callaghan said, carried a heavy respon-
> sibility when they called large numbers of people together. The overwhelming number
> of people in the march were likely to be concerned passionately with the issue of
> peace in Vietnam. They must be careful, he said, not to allow themselves to be
> exploited by a tiny minority who were basically not concerned with this issue but
> with undermining and destroying the institutions that enabled protests to be made.

Taking his cue from this paradigm, Mr. Marcus Lipton then undertook his own private piece of amplification, referring to the organizers as a "motley crew of crackpots. . . ."

It has for long also been the dominant definition applied to "unofficial strikes"—the notion of conspiratorial cliques, challenging the due authority of their own leaderships and holding the innocent public up to ransom. For a long period, the use of this paradigm in respect of "unofficial strikes" had a strong element of "coalition-building"—it was designed to "win over" union leaderships and the TUC to support for the Government in the effort to restrain certain types of trade union conflict, and to "distance" the mass of the public (the consumers/audience) from any commitment to the event.

Its use has certainly also been a common feature of the process of public signification associated with developments in Northern Ireland. With respect especially to events in Ulster since the later months of 1970, this paradigm has indeed attained the status of a "self-fulfilling prophecy," with the emergence of the IRA stigmatized, split off from, and counterposed to the vast majority of "good and reasonable folk" of both religious persuasions in Ulster, whose grievances are being exploited for the pursuance by a tiny minority of a "holy war" against Stormont, Whitehall, the army, and the forces of moderation and reform. Indeed, the emergence of the IRA—a known, labeled, stigmatized, extremist group, committed to the policies of armed insurrection and physical force—has powerfully crystallized and simplified the complex problems of signifying the Ulster crisis to the British public. It permitted the agencies of signification—the political manager both at Stormont and at Whitehall, the agents of face-to-face control in the shape of the army and its public relations machinery, and the media of press, radio, and television—to extract, isolate, and stereotype a small, organized, band of "foreign" insurgents, committed to violence against the state, from the complex structure of exploitation, disenfranchisement, and oppression of the Ulster minorities, and, behind that, from the interlocking complex of immediate class-rule at Stormont and distant colonial oppression in the continuing links between Britain and the Protestant ascendancy. Accounts of engagements between the para-military forces of the IRA and the army could now be depicted in simple form as a straight confrontation between a minority extremist element and a peace-keeping force. In the language of the weekly and nightly accounts of bombings, explosions, street encounters, etc., the IRA is consistently attributed an active, destructive role, the army a passive, neutral one. Thus the girl inadvertently shot by a sniper bullet is described in the press headline as "Girl shot by IRA sniper," but the girl inadvertently wounded by army fire is described as "Girl shot in IRA-Army crossfire."[19] The difficult task of extracting a political solution to the Ulster crisis has been, accordingly, suppressed, replaced by the call for military measures to "end the violence." On this basis, the public has been brought to collude with such developments as the imposition of internment without trial, and the use of repressive and coercive methods of interrogation on the basis of the inferred logic that "the gunmen and the bombers must be brought to heel." The power of the paradigm to crystallize a complex political situation in stereotypical and simplified terms may be evidenced in a BBC television news broadcaster of 27 February 1971. The Ulster correspondent observed that "the Northern Ireland situation is resolving itself into a straight battle between small groups of armed agitators and the British army." But this comment was accompanied by film clips from incidents in Belfast on that same day, showing a block of flats ("predominantly Catholic") where "youths" (but also, visibly, women and children) were involved in persistent stone-throwing and pan-rattling at soldiers and in which the army had to attack the flats in order to "root out the rioters." The form in which these events were signified simply left no room in which the most critical question could be posed: that which would have exposed the fact that the army were unlikely to isolate and destroy the IRA gunmen precisely because they were tacitly and actively sheltered, supported, forewarned, and assisted by the vast majority of the working-class Catholics in the predominantly Catholic areas. The power of signification to legitimate repressive control and methods of intimidation was nowhere so powerfully attested to as in the whole episode surrounding the revelation of the methods used to interrogate detainees. The plain fact is that the vast majority of the allegations of physical brutality investigated by the Compton Report, and widely reported on in the press and television, were confirmed: but the *meaning* of the physical forms of interrogation was symbolically legitimated by a purely semantic device: that of re-defining the methods not as "brutality" (unacceptable) but as "physical ill-treatment" (acceptable). As Compton (1971) asserts:

> Where we have concluded that physical ill-treatment took place, we are not making a finding of brutality on the part of those who handled these complainists. We consider that brutality is an inhuman or savage form of cruelty and that cruelty implies a disposition to inflict suffering, coupled with indifference to, or pleasure in, the victim's pain. We do not think this happened here.

It is a nice distinction. The generative and associative power of the paradigm is evidenced in an interview with a Stormont politician, transmitted in the 7.00 p.m. *Newsdesk* on BBC radio, in which, in reply to a question as to whether the "young hoodlums" on the street were organized, replied: "Yes, by men described as shadowy figures. . . . Just the sort of person of inelegant mentality such as lay behind the bombing incident with Mr. Carr . . . anarchists, proto-revolutionaries, call them what you will." These are only a few, brief examples taken at random from the coverage of the Ulster crisis. In any substantive analysis of the process of political signification, events in Ulster provides an almost paradigmatic instance.

The paradigm was also, significantly, employed with reference to the activities, not simply of the unofficial minorities in strike situations, but to the official trade union leaderships in so far as their wage demands threatened to attempt to control the level of wages by both Labour and Conservative governments: and more recently, as unions undertook strike action in defense of their claims, and one-day strikes in opposition to the proposed Industrial Relations Bill. The escalation of the use of the minority-extremists/majority moderates common sense explanation in response to the actions of groups which can in no sense be labeled "political deviants"—that is, the transfer of the more militant actions of powerful majorities and legitimate minorities to the "deviant" category—can be pin-pointed in the renowned speech by Mr. Wilson in June 1966 concerning the strike by the National Union of Seamen: "A natural democratic revolt is now giving way, in the name of militancy, to pressures which are anything but democratic . . . a few individuals have brought pressure to bear on a select few on the Executive Council of the NUS, who in turn have been able to dominate the majority of that otherwise sturdy union . . . this tightly knit group of politically motivated men. . . ." A more recent example was Mr. Carr's televised speech, on the eve of the second one-day strike against the IRB (17 March 1971), in which he described the action as one of "mindless militancy," a "denial of democratic leadership," the "acts of a small minority recognizing no responsibility to anyone or anything" and contrary to the wishes of the "vast majority, including those who oppose the Bill."

The minority/majority, extremist/moderate way of labeling acts of political deviance is now being applied to situations which are intrinsically quite different in manifest character. This process of "cross-attribution" and amplification is characteristic of persuasive inferential explanations which try to resolve ambiguities at the same time as they actively contain threatening and problematic political developments. A close analysis of the way this process of stigmatization and signification is carried through yields other deep paradigms which, in a similar way, tap sacred and symbolic values which are widely shared (e.g. the sanctity of majorities; the "due process" of negotiation as a way of resolving conflict; the taboo against violence and confrontation; the role of reasonableness, rationality, moderation, and compromise in the regulation of conflict—the sacred values of British institutional political life), and either 'map' them on to new, problematic situations, or "map" emergent political phenomena in terms of already known and legitimate values.[20]

V

Some problems of considerable complexity are posed by the model and account offered above. These can only be briefly resumed here. The first cluster of problems concerns the relationship, at both theoretical and empirical levels, between the dominant and subordinate forms of ideological consciousness present in a society at a specific historical moment on the one hand, and on the other the level of ideological "work" and praxis with which we have been primarily concerned. Such a discussion must take as its departure Gramsci's (1971) concept of hegemonic and corporate class formations and, linked with that, the essence of the Marxian notion of dominant and subordinate value systems—the classic formulation of which is *The German Ideology*. In a useful amplification of this model, Parkin (1971) suggests that we must concern ourselves with at least three levels of ideological consciousness: a *dominant* value-system—"those groups in society which occupy positions of the greatest power and privilege will also tend to have the greatest access to the means of legitimation"; a *subordinate* value system, the generating *milieu* of which is "the local working-class community," and whose content is both different from, but also subordinate to and accommodated within the dominant value-system—it is a "negotiated version of the dominant value system"—and what he calls a *radical* value-system, which is in effect a counter system of values to the hegemonic ideology. Though all ideological systems contain the interests of hegemonic class forces imprinted in them, dominant value-systems represent themselves as the natural mental environment and horizon of the whole society, and the explanations of or accounting for new problematic events tend to be accomplished within the mental universe, the symbolic forms and the embedded interests of such forms of consciousness. As Marx (1965) observed, "each new class ... is compelled ... to represent its interests as the common interest of all the members of a society ... expressed in ideal form: it has to give its ideas the form of universality and represent them as the only rational, universally valid ones." Installed ideological perspectives of this type are thus not only the symbolic bearers of the social interests of ruling groups, but tend to be amplified into what Lefebvre (1968) calls "a vision or conception of the world, a *Weltanschauung* based on extrapolations and interpretations." Their function is not simply to assert, in a naked, open, or direct manner, the establishment of class power, but to provide for society as a whole what Harris (1969) calls "a more or less coherent organization for our experience." Ideologies are one of the principal mechanisms which expand and amplify the dominance of certain class interests into a hegemonic formation. Their role, as Lefebvre remarks, "is to secure the assent of the oppressed and exploited. Ideologies represent the latter to themselves in such a way as to wrest from them, in addition to material wealth, their 'spiritual' acceptance of this situation, even their support." The crucial point, made by Poulantzas (1968) is that "the dominant ideology does not simply reflect the life conditions of the dominant class-subject 'pure and simple,' but the political relationship in a social formation between the dominant and dominated classes." In the gloss by Steadman-Jones (1972), "ideologies are not simply the subjective product of the 'will to power' of different classes: they are objective systems determined by the whole field of struggle between contending classes." Thus, though we can see, over time, the continuity in themes, interests, and content of a dominant ideological formation, we nevertheless have to deal with the process by which ideologies are reproduced, seek and win consent in a contending situation, the social praxis through which they renew themselves at the heart of social life, and gain legitimation as dominant perspectives. This process is compounded by at least two further factors. First, the social division of labor, the distribution of power, and the segmentation and differentiation of different classes and groups will work in such a way as "to stress different elements in the given orthodoxy." As Harris (1969) comments:

> Orthodoxies have an elastic quality to cover very different social groups, to unite them within a common terminology, but inevitably the version of the orthodoxy held by different social groups will be different, incorporating each group's specific perspective.

The second point is that ideologies survive only if they are able to change, transform, and amplify themselves so as to take account of, and integrate, within the existing mental environment, new events and developments in social conflict. As Geertz insists, ideologies are "maps of *problematic* social reality" (our italics). Ideologies which are thoroughly fixed in their forms and content are not flexible enough to sustain themselves in the face of problematic and threatening events. Thus, though ideologies may remain, at one level, stable and persistent over time, in terms of the class interests they represent and the constituent elements legitimate within them, at another level they require to be continually reproduced, amplified, and elaborated so as to "cover" the unexplained. As Lefebvre remarks: "No historical situation can ever be stabilized once and for all, though that is what ideologies aim at." The objectivation of social knowledge within the environment of a specific ideological formation is, therefore, an ongoing social process with its own specific contradictions (Althusser 1971). This process constitutes ideological work as a specific social praxis—and it is this aspect of elaboration which we have tried to "net" in our concept of "signification within the public discourse." It follows from this that ideological discourse is characterized by the rigidity of its structuring at the level of "deep" interests, and by the relative "openness"—the flexibility, the labile quality of its forms—at the "surface" level. The borrowing of a Chomskyian metaphor of "deep" and "surface" structures for the study of ideological discourse is not fortuitous, since the study of ideologies as a specific level of a social formation requires precisely such a model by which quite unrestricted elements give rise, via "rules" of transformation, and by way of specified forms of praxis (signification) and institutions (e.g. the mass media), to a heterodox variety of "surface" forms. Recent studies of the nature of ideological discourse stress its *polysemic* character. Althusser (1970) has observed that, though specific ideologies have a history, there can be no "history of ideology" as such:

> Unlike a science, an ideology is both theoretically closed and politically supple and adaptable. It bends to the interests of the times, but without apparent movement, being content to reflect the historical changes which is its mission to assimilate and master by some imperceptible modification of its peculiar internal relations. . . . Ideology changes therefore, but imperceptibly conserving its ideological form; it moves, but with an immobile motion which maintains it where it is, in its place and its ideological role.

The polysemic or polyvocal character of ideological discourse presents us with another set of problems whose range can only be sketchily touched upon here. The mediatory role played by rhetoric and symbolization in the elaboration of ideological formations has been emphasized by Geertz. Ideologies, like other cultural "systems," consist of symbolic items, rich and diverse in their connotational power, which have been ordered and disposed, through human use and through social structures into diverse and interpenetrating meaning-systems. Barthes (1971) and other semiologists have, correctly, drawn our attention to the fact that since individual items in such meaning-systems are "arbitrary," what matters is the relational system (correspondence and opposition) into which the elements are integrated. It is the relation between the elements in a constituted symbolic field—or, as Lévi-Strauss would put it, the relations of difference within a system of meanings—which specify and signify. Harris observes "The central role of culture . . . is to present us with a diversity of partial or coherent systems with which to organize our experience, so that by identifying objects and attributing systematic meaning to them, we shall be able to overcome the problems we face in seeking to survive. . . . Of course, the same object may be identified in a host of different ways within different systems." It is the structure of social relations which establish, maintain, and preserve certain meaning-systems in being, generating around them the quality of a stable, "taken-for-granted" world, which permits certain ideological clusters to retain their power to specify new and troubling events in old and legitimated terms, and which tend to "rule out of court" other, alternative meanings. In this way, through their continued production or objectivation within a special social formation, certain meanings come to represent what Berger and Luckmann call "the social stock of knowledge at hand" which supplies us with "typificatory schemes required for the major routines of social life, not only the typifications of others . . . but typifications of all sorts of events and experiences both social and natural."

> When government becomes as changeable as the men who constitute it, when the apparent objectivity of institutions dissolves into no more than the contradictory subjectivities of an uncoordinated mass of individual men, it is no wonder that some onlookers feel a "sense of meaninglessness." (Harris 1969)

Not only will ideological systems be polyvocal in their symbolic content: they will frequently be extended and amplified to deal with new situations by "putting together," often in an illogical or incoherent way, what were, previously, the fragments of more ordered or stable meaning-systems. As they evolve, ideologies employ what Gramsci has called *traces* embedded in previously accumulated cultural traditions. The process of ideological elaboration is thus closer, as Harris has noted, to Lévi-Strauss's process of *bricolage,* than it is to the consistent elaboration of theoretical or philosophical "world views." The usual mode of ideological analysis, common, say, in the work of Lukács or Goldmann, which analyses ideological formations at their most representative and coherent point, linking them with major philosophical totalizations, misses the critical *ad hoc* level at which ideologies are brought to bear on specific situations, and organize the experience of particular groups and classes of men. The distinction Harris suggests between "higher" and "lower order" meaning systems is an important one, because it distinguishes the great conceptual schemas and totalizations, historically embedded or sedimented over time, or articulated with a rare logical consistency, from "lower order" systems, which are more directly related to immediate experience, and which are concerned with "particular ways we use this logic, the association we make and unmake."

> It is the lower order systems about which men argue, which change, which vary between social groups, between studies of different kinds, between historical periods. Of higher order systems, philosophers examine perhaps the tip of the iceberg, giving an account of some of the rules presupposed by our ordinary use. . . .

In line with this, it seems to follow, as Berger and Luckmann argue, that the critical study of ideology must deal with the continued production of everyday knowledge itself, in so far as this knowledge provides us with the terms, categories, and the classifications within which social reality itself is apprehended and maintained. As they remark:

> Only a very limited group of people in any society engages in theorizing, in the business of "ideas" and the construction of *Weltanschauungen.* But everyone in society participates in its "knowledge" in one way or another.

Such a critical study must therefore take as its object of reflection the forms, content, and production of "everything that passes for 'knowledge' in society"—or, to put it another way, with the everyday forms of ideological consciousness, including the process by which new kinds of knowledge are legitimated and win assent for their plausibility in the real world.

This brings us to the third cluster of problems: the relationship between what we have called the different "agents of signification," or the role which the institutions charged with the production and amplification of "knowledge" play within a social formation which is complexly structured in dominance. The starting-point for such a discussion must be Gramsci's (1971) notion of the production and maintenance of social hegemony.

> What we can do . . . is to fix two major superstructural "levels": the one that can be called "civil society," that is the ensemble of organisms commonly called "private," and that of "political society" or the State. These two levels correspond on the one hand to the function of "hegemony" which the dominant group exercises throughout society and on the other hand to that of "direct domination" or command exercised through the State and "juridical" government. The functions in question are precisely organizational and connective. The intellectuals are the dominant group's "deputies" exercising the subaltern functions of social hegemony and political government.

The functions for this double structure which Gramsci anticipated included the organization of "spontaneous" consent, "given by the great masses of the population to the general direction imposed on social life by the dominant fundamental group," and the exercise of coercive power, which " 'legally' enforces discipline on those groups who do not 'consent' either actively or passively." Gramsci's (1971) formulations are based on the notion of the distinctive role and position within the State of "the coercive apparatus," which brings "the mass of the people into conformity with the specific type of production and the specific economy at a given moment," and the apparatus for the maintenance of social hegemony, "exercised through the so-called private organizations, like the Church, the trade unions, the schools, etc." He adds that "it is precisely in civil society that intellectuals operate especially." This distinction has recently been expanded by such theorists as Althusser and Poulantzas who, while differing precisely in the way they conceive the relations between what Althusser (1971) has called "the State Apparatus" and the "Ideological State Apparatuses," nevertheless share, with Gramsci, a fundamental determination to "think" the specificity of the ideological or superstructural level within a complex social formation. In essence, both insist that a dominant social class maintains its rule and legitimacy, not only through the coercive agencies of the state, but also via "the whole institutional superstructure of bourgeois class power: parties, reformist trade unions, newspapers, schools, churches, families . . ." (Steadman-Jones 1972): both insist, therefore, on the specificity, the "relative autonomy"—until the "last instance"—of the various levels of the superstructure. Poulantzas (1968) argues that though state power imposes limits on the ideological institutions, "power relations in the State ideological apparatuses do not depend directly on the class nature of the State power and are not exhaustively determined by it." Thus, "in a social formation several contradictory and antagonistic ideologies exist." Althusser (1971) argues that "ideologies are realized in institutions, their rituals and practices"—"it is by the installation of the Ideological State Apparatuses in which this ideology is realized itself that it becomes the ruling ideology."

> But this installation is not achieved all by itself; on the contrary, it is the stake in a bitter and continuous class struggle: first against the former ruling classes and their positions in the old and new ISAs, then against the exploited class. . . . In fact, the struggle in the ISAs is indeed an aspect of the class struggle, sometimes an important and symptomatic one. . . . But the class struggles in the ISAs is only one aspect of a class struggle which goes beyond the ISAs.

Despite the important differences of emphasis between these theorists, the important questions to which they are addressed concern the relations of unity and difference within the ideological or signifying agencies, between the ideological institutions of "indirect hegemony" and the State institutions of "direct domination." Only by concrete analysis can we determine the degree to which the signifying agencies may undertake their work of amplifying and elaborating a specific form of ideological consciousness within limits set by the prevailing structures of power and interest, *and yet* not be "exhaustively determined by it"—becoming, that is, the locus of contending and conflictful definitions of the situation, the focus of struggle at the level of authority and consent (as Althusser puts it), "the seat and the stake" of ideological class struggle.

> Ideologies are not "born" in the ISAs but from the social classes at grips in the class struggle: from their conditions of existence, their practices, their experiences of the struggle, etc. (Althusser 1971)

In any specific historical conjuncture, therefore, we are required to examine the specificity of the role and the work which such agencies of signification undertake; to acknowledge that contradictory definitions contend for hegemony within their orbit: at the same time recognizing that their form, content, and direction cannot be deduced from some abstract "dominant ideology" which is taken, in a process of conflict-free realization, to saturate all the complex levels of a social formation from one end to another in an unproblematic manner. As Gramsci observed:

> The dominant group is coordinated concretely with the general interests of the subordinate groups, and the life of the State is conceived of as a continuous process of formation and superseding of unstable equilibria ... between the interests of the fundamental group and those of the subordinate groups—equilibria in which the interests of the dominant group prevail, but only up to a certain point, i.e. stopping short of narrowly corporate economic interests.

In our case, we are required to offer an analysis which would clarify where the dominant paradigms of an ideological consensus originate: what the role of the media, the political apparatus, and the judicial and other agencies of face-to-face control play in elaborating those definitions: the existence of disjunctures between the different levels of civil and state institutions in the amplifying of such "maps of problematic social reality": the differences between the different institutions, and yet their complex unity-in-dominance: the locale of struggle and conflict in the elaboration of consensual perspectives: and the forms of class struggle expressed by these similarities and differences.

We cannot undertake such an analysis here. But this *résumé* of problems posed by our initial analysis allows us to formulate, more precisely, the nexus of issues which this paper explores. It is an attempt to explore the mediations between a rhetoric and ideological discourse, its social location and functions. The position adopted is that these levels must be studied, at once, with attention to their full specificity, and, simultaneously, in terms of their place in a complexly structured social formation. This attempt necessitates what might at first appear to be a theoretical *detour,* by way of certain key concepts and perspectives of phenomenology, symbolic interaction, and ethnomethodological ideas. In this detour, what in former paradigms which have given this problem a sustained attention is presented either as an unmediated determinism (vulgar Marxist) or a formal determinism (structuralism) is translated back into the concepts of praxis—signification maintaining and interpreting a social reality, definitional work, etc. Ideological discourse about problematic political events are not conceived as following, full blown, from the heads of practical bourgeois men and institutions, as unproblematic for them as they are for those who are enclosed with their horizons of thought. "Explanations" of political events are conceived as normative structures which have to be objectivated by their own specific social practices, evolved and realized by specific groups and institutions, maintained and sustained amidst contending definitions, in situations, and only with some difficulty winning assent among subordinate groups. Such "explanations" are related to more stable, more comprehensive historical ideological formations, in that, at a lower level of specificity, they rehearse, thematically, linguistically, rhetorically, the "vocabularies of motive," the historical interests and experience of dominant groups and classes which lie embedded within the environment of a public language, and which are drawn on—made active—in a persuasive sort of "labor," in specific settings of dominance. There are points at which such definitions are minted anew, when the work of ideological bricolage is accomplished for the first time: there are other times when these rhetorical elements, in their truncated form, lie sleeping in the public language, awaiting an appropriate sequence of events to awaken them. In crisis moments, when the *ad hoc* formulas which serve, "for all practical purposes," to classify the political world meaningfully and within the limits of legitimacy are rendered problematic, and new problems and new groupings emerge to threaten and challenge the ruling positions of power and their social hegemony, we are in a special position to observe the work of persuasive definition in the course of its formation. This is a privileged moment for the student of ideologies. In this process the mass media play an extremely important role: but they remain only *one* of the several institutions in which this process of signification is realized. The relation at any specific moment between the *ad hoc* definitions arrived at within their domain and the structure of a prevailing or dominant ideology: the relation between the work of managing the definition of social reality and reproducing the relations of production and power: the relation between the ideological and the coercive apparatuses of the state: the outcome of the groups which contend on its terrain over the means and modes of signification: the relation, above all, of the operative definitions of power and control which are employed by the state apparatus, to the structure of definitions "determined by the whole field of struggle between contending classes"—the area of consensus, to which the media seem too powerfully attached: these and other related issues can only be clarified by the study of a specific conjuncture between the different levels of practice and institution in a historical moment.

We said such a study was only possible on the basis of a theoretical detour. But the route by which such insight is gained into the specificity of ideological discourse cannot be the final resting place of theory. Phenomenology teaches us to attend, once again, to the level of *meaning:* symbolic interaction presses on us the decisive level of "definitions of the situation" as critical intervening variables: ethnomethodology refers us to the interactive work by which normative features of interpreted social situations are sustained, and the indexable character of expressions. Yet, in the end, these different aspects of the process by which abnormal political events are signified must be returned to the level of the social formation, via the critical concepts of power, ideology, and conflict.

"The question," Dreitzel (1970) has recently observed, "is to understand how the assignment of significance to social actions and events works. . . . We have to analyze the construction of such norms and typifications through the pattern of interpretive communication." But,

> in order to overcome the limitation imposed by phenomenological bracketing, studies of communicative behavior should be open to the fact that the rules of interpretation are not invariant essences of the social life-world, but are themselves subject to other social processes. . . . In fact, communicative behavior rests on work and power relations as well as on language; and if we comprehend the typification schemes of language as the most fundamental rules of everyday life, we also have to notice that even language is subject to distortions caused by the condition of our life-style. . . . The interpretive paradigm may well serve to bring a deeper understanding of the potentialities as well as the limitations of the patterns of communicative behavior that produce and reproduce the social reality. . . . However the social world is structured not only by language but also by the modes and forces of material production and by the systems of domination. . . .

VI

Militant political activity of the kind described in this paper is a real, new, emergent feature of political conflict in our society. Its significance as a form of "political deviance," while not wholly attributable to the cultural process by which such acts are labeled and defined as deviant, appears in large measure as an aspect best understood in terms of that process. Events are real enough, but they are appropriated in social consciousness only as they are culturally signified and defined. Our analysis must therefore attempt to discover the ideas, values, and attitudes which inform those definitions. It must also reveal the categories, conscious or unconscious, into which events are grouped and classified, ranked and ordered, so as to make them meaningful. These frameworks of value and meaning are "inferential normative structures" of social life. They are widely shared, though not by everyone, and are not understood in the same way by groups who have different life-situations and projects, and who may be the objects rather than the subjects or authors of such "accounts." These maps of meaning give plausibility, order, and coherence to discrete events, by placing them within a common world of meanings. Culture is knitted together by these overlapping, partially closed, incomplete mappings of problematic social reality. Such "structures" tend to define and limit the range of possible new meanings which can be constructed to explain new and unfamiliar events. In part, such normative structures are historical constructs, already objectivated and available as the informal social knowledge—"what everybody knows" about a social situation. They have been routinized and sedimented over time, and are available for the construction of new definitions and labels only in truncated form. They also exhibit varying degrees of "closure" and of "openness," of coherence or contradictoriness. They are "moving structures" in that they must be continuously revised and emended to "cover" new events. They are never stable. The process of emending and revising known definitions, or of constructing new ones, is a societal process, and like all processes in society, is "structured in dominance." Nor are they fixed. They contain or make use of their own "logic-in-use," which serves as a set of loose generative rules which governs the way the "explanation" can be used. Such normative definitions contain strong predispositions to "see" events in certain ways: they tend to "rule in" and "rule out" certain kinds of additional inferences.

In problematic situations, old normative structures are often "mapped" on to new situations, or new situations are "mapped" in terms of older meanings. While not limited to "social interest" in a narrow sense, such structures arise in and are maintained by the reciprocity of social life: they therefore have embedded in them the life-situations, outlooks, interests, and informal models of the social world of those who actively project them. They are structured by power and domination: inevitably, the normative *ad hoc* explanations of dominant groups tend to exert more power, to "cover" a wider range of topics, to provide more inclusive and comprehensive formulations, than those of subordinate groups. The conflicts between social groups are thus always and inevitably mediated by conflicts between contrasting normative definitions—indeed, the conflicts are understood only in so far as such outlooks exist. These structures thus "betray themselves" at different levels of social life, with respect to wider or narrower areas, with greater or lesser degrees of structuralism. At the level of everyday comprehension, the commonsense world is "classified out" in stereotypical ways which simplify and crystallize complex social processes in distinctive ways. At this level, then, they surface in the form of informal "models," *ad hoc* explanations, proverbs, maxims, routines, recipes, truncated social myths, images, and scenarios. At the level of social life as a whole they "surface" as full-blown ideologies, symbolic universes, secular versions of the sacred canopy.

NOTES

1. Empirical work relating to this project is currently being undertaken in the News/media project, Centre for Cultural Studies, University of Birmingham.

2. Deviance always represented a "deviant" area within the overall American structural-functionalist paradigm. Cf. Matza (1969) and Taylor, Walton, and Young (1973).

3. Elsewhere I tried to identify the alternating rhythm in American "new left" politics, between the "political" and "experiential" pole. Cf. "The Hippies: An American Moment" (Hall 1969).

4. Despite massive documentation, there is still no adequate typology of the tactics and forms of struggle of the oppositional movements of the 1960s. The American movement probably represents the widest range of tactics, though it omits some: see *inter alia* Teodori (1969). Part 2 of *Politics of the New Left* (Stolz 1971) contains extracts on "forms of action." Horowitz (1970) offers a list of anti-war activities arranged by tactics, in the Appendix to *The Struggle is the Message*. Oppenheimer (1970) deals exclusively with urban insurgency. See also Jacobs (1970).

5. No adequate theoretical account of these emergent movements is yet available. Habermas (1971), though abstract and moderate in perspective, is suggestive. Two modest but important attempts are Mitchell (1971) and Nairn (1968). Any adequate account would have to deal with what Gransci called "organic" and "conjunctual" features.

6. Though contemporary critiques retain both the notion of "dominant ideology" and of "consensus," there is little detailed work which analyses the mediations between them.

7. For a brief characterization of "consensus politics," see Williams (1968).

8. For the original notion of a "deviancy amplification spiral," see Wilkins (1967). For its application to the role of the media, see Young (1971).

9. On "problematic situations," cf. Douglas (1970a and 1970b).

10. The perspective employed here is, of course, "ethnomethodological." Cf. especially, Garfinkel (1967).

11. Althusser's formulations on the specificity of practices and contradictions within "the ever-pre-givenness of a structured complex unity" seem to us crucial and definitive. See, especially, "Contradiction and Over-Determination" and "On the Marxist Dialectic" in *For Marx* (Althusser 1969).

12. Work is only just beginning on the specificity of "signification" as a form of praxis. Apart from the work of Marxist structuralists, such as the *Tel Quel* group, see some suggestive remarks on *poiesis* as a praxis in Lefebvre (1968).

13. On degrees of "typification," see Berger and Luckmann (1967).

14. The media both serve as primary agents of signification, generating descriptions and explanations of their own account, and as secondary agents, relaying and amplifying accounts given by other agencies. Where its secondary function is concerned, the link must be made via the notion of the media's "accredited witnesses"—its sensitivity to other power-signifying agencies in society set against the problems of access by alternative minority groups. It is by way of some structure composed of accredited witnesses/limited access/notions of news values that the media reproduces the structure of dominance and subordination within the public discourse.

15. I am indebted here, especially, to Jock Young and Stan Cohen for the opportunity to discuss work in the area of the media and "deviance," much of it as yet unpublished, which considerably advanced this argument. See, *inter alia,* Jock Young (1974) and Stan Cohen (1972).

16. For the concepts of "unwitting bias" and "inferential structure," cf. Lang and Lang (1953 and 1965). For a recent application of these concepts, see Halloran, Elliot, and Murdock (1970). On the signification of protest, cf. *inter alia,* Lang and Lang (forthcoming), Edelman (1967), Turner (1969), and Grimshaw (1968).

17. The semiological analysis of ideological discourse now developing in France appears as yet to have made little or no impact on traditional content analysis or mass communications "effects" studies which use content analysis as a base.

18. For a very similar model, cf. Jock Young (1974).

19. See, for example, McCann (1971) and Foot (1972).

20. For the notion of "mapping," see Laing (1971).

References

Althusser, L. 1969. *For Marx.* London: Allen Lane.

——— 1970. *Reading Capital.* London: New Left Books.

——— 1971. Ideology in the State. In *Lenin and Philosophy, and Other Essays.* London: New Left Books.

Barthes, R. 1971. Rhetoric of the Image. *Working Papers in Cultural Studies* I (Spring): 37–50.

Becker, H.S. 1967. Whose Side Are We On? *Social Problems* **14** (Winter): 239–247.

Berger, P. and Luckmann, T. 1967. *The Social Construction of Reality.* New York: Anchor.

Burgelin, O. 1968. Structural Analysis and Mass Communication. *Studies of Broadcasting* **6**: 143–168.

Cohen, S. 1972. *Folk Devils and Moral Panics.* London: MacGibbon & Kee.

Compton, E. *Report of the Enquiry into Allegations against the Security Forces of Physical Brutality in Northern Ireland arising out of Events on 9 August 1971. Cmnd 4823.* London: HMSO.

Douglas, J. 1970a. Deviance and Respectability. In J. Douglas (ed.) *Deviance and Respectability.* New York: Basic Books.

—— 1970b. Deviance and Order in a Pluralistic Society. In J.C. McKinney and E.A. Tiryakian (eds.) *Theoretical Sociology.* New York: Appleton-Century-Crofts.

Dreitzel, H.P. 1970. Patterns of Communicative Behaviour. In H.P. Dreitzel (ed.) *Recent Sociology* Vol. 2. New York: Crowell Collier Macmillan.

Edelman, M. 1967. Myths, Metaphors, and Political Conformity. *Psychiatry* **30** (3): 217–228.

Foot, M. 1972. Ulster Coverage or Cover Up. *Ink* (7 January 1972).

Garfinkel, H. 1967. *Studies in Ethnomethodology.* Englewood Cliffs, N.J.: Prentice-Hall.

Geertz, C. 1964. Ideology as a Cultural System. In D. Apter (ed.) *Ideology and Discontent.* New York: Free Press.

Gramsci, A. 1971. The Intellectuals, Notes on Italian History, and The Modern Prince. In Q. Hoare and G. Nowell-Smith (eds.) *Selections from Prison Notebooks.* London: Lawrence & Wishart.

Grimshaw, A. 1968. Three Views of Urban Violence. *American Behavioral Scientist* (March/April).

Habermas, J. 1971. *Toward a Rational Society.* London: Heinemann.

Hall, S. 1967. The Condition of England Question. *People and Politics* (Easter).

—— 1969. The Hippies: an American Moment. In J. Nagel (ed.) *Student Power.* London: Merlin Press.

Halloran, J. 1970. The Social Effects of Television. In J. Halloran (ed.) *Effects of Television.* London: Panther.

Halloran, J., P. Elliott, and G. Murdoch. 1970. *Demonstrations and Communication.* Harmondsworth: Penguin.

Harris, N. 1969. *Beliefs in Society.* London: Watts.

Horowitz, I.L. and Liebowitz, M. 1968. Social Deviance and Political Marginality. *Social Problems* **15**: 280–296.

Horowitz, I.L. 1970. *The Struggle is the Message.* Berkeley: Glendessary Press.

Jacobs, H. (ed.) 1970. *Weatherman.* San Francisco: Ramparts Press.

Laing, R.D. 1971. *The Politics of the Family.* London: Tavistock Publications.

Lang, K. and Lang, L. 1953. The Unique Perspective of Television and Its Effect. *American Sociological Review* **18** (1).

Lang, K. and Lang, L. 1965. The Inferential Structure of Political Communications. *Public Opinion Quarterly* **19** (Summer).

Lefebvre, H. 1968. *The Sociology of Marx.* New York: Random House.

Lemert, E.T. 1967. Alcohol, Values and Social Control. In *Human Deviance, Social Problems and Social Control.* Englewood Cliffs, N.J.: Prentice Hall.

McCann, E. 1971. *The British Press and Northern Ireland.* The Northern Ireland Socialist Research Council.

Marx, K. and Engels, F. 1965. *The German Ideology* (trans. C. Dutt). London: Lawrence & Wishart.

Matza, D. 1969. *Becoming Deviant.* Englewood Cliffs, N.J.: Prentice-Hall.

Mitchell, J. 1971. *Woman's Estate.* Harmondsworth: Penguin.

Nairn, T. 1968. Why It Happened. In A. Quattrocchi and T. Nairn (eds.) *The Beginning of the End.* London: Panther.

Oppenheimer, M. 1970. *Urban Guerilla.* Harmondsworth: Penguin.

Parkin, F. 1971. *Class Inequality and Political Order.* London: MacGibbon & Kee.

Partridge, P. 1971. *Consent and Consensus.* London: Macmillan.

Poulantzas, N. 1966. *Vers une théorie marxiste.* Les temps modernes 240 (May).

—— 1968. *Pouvoir politique et classes sociales.* Paris: Maspero.

Shibutani, T. 1955. Reference Groups as Perspectives. *American Journal of Sociology* **60** (May).

Steadman-Jones, G. 1972. The Marxism of the Early Lukács. *New Left Review* **70.**

Stolz, M. 1971. *The Politics of the New Left.* New York: Free Press.

Taylor, I., Walton, P., and Young, J. 1973. *The New Criminology.* London: Routledge & Kegan Paul.

Teodori, M. 1969. *The New Left: a Documentary History.* New York: Bobbs Merrill.

Turner, R. 1969. The Public Perception of Protest. *American Sociological Review* **34** (6).

Williams, R. (ed.) 1968. *May Day Manifesto.* Harmondsworth: Penguin.

——— 1971. Who Speaks For Wales? *Guardian* (3 June).

Wilkins, L. 1967. *Social Policy, Action, and Research.* London: Tavistock Publications.

Wolff, R.P. 1965. Beyond Tolerance. In R.P. Wolfe, B. Moore, and H. Marcuse. *Critique of Pure Tolerance.* Boston: Beacon.

Young, J. 1971. The Role of the Police as Amplifiers of Deviancy. In S. Cohen (ed.) *Images of Deviance.* Harmondsworth: Penguin.

——— 1974. Mass Media, Drugs, and Deviance. In Paul Rock and Mary McIntosh, (eds.) *Deviance and Social Control* London: Tavistock.

4

Some Reflections on Separatism and Power

Marilyn Frye

Marilyn Frye is a lesbian writer, teacher, theorist, and philosopher who lives in Lansing, Michigan, and teaches at Michigan State University; she is the author of The Politics of Reality: Essays in Feminist Theory *(1983). In this 1977 essay, Frye takes up the issue of separatism, often regarded by both feminists and non-feminists as a fringe movement and solely lesbian practice, and redefines it in two fundamental ways. First, she argues that rather than a form of extremism, separatism is the basis of all feminism, present to a greater or lesser degree in all feminist practices. She then argues that separatism is not simply the withdrawal from men, but is a seizure of power that takes the form of denying to men the access to women that men take for granted as a natural right. By such redefinition, separatism becomes feminism's most characteristic expression, one practiced by feminists regardless of sexual preference.*

I have been trying to write something about separatism almost since my first dawning of feminist consciousness, but it has always been for me somehow a mercurial topic which, when I tried to grasp it, would softly shatter into many other topics like sexuality, man-hating, so-called reverse discrimination, apocalyptic utopianism, and so on. What I have to share with you today is my latest attempt to get to the heart of the matter.*

In my life, and within feminism as I understand it, separatism is not a theory or a doctrine, nor a demand for certain specific behaviors on the part of feminists, though it is undeniably connected with lesbianism. Feminism seems to me to be kaleidoscopic—something whose shapes, structures, and patterns alter with every turn of feminist creativity; and one element which is present through all the changes is an element of separation. This element has different roles and relations in different turns of the glass—it assumes different meanings, is variously conspicuous, variously determined or determining, depending on how the pieces fall and who is the beholder. The theme of separation, in its multitude variations, is there in everything from divorce to exclusive lesbian separatist communities, from shelters for battered women to witch covens, from women's studies programs to women's bars, from expansion of daycare to abortion on demand. The presence of this theme is vigorously obscured, trivialized, mystified, and

---

*This paper was first presented at a meeting of the Society for Women in Philosophy, Eastern Division, in December of 1977. It was first printed in *Sinister Wisdom 6,* Summer, 1978. Before it was published, I received many helpful comments from those who heard or read the paper. I have incorporated some, made notes of others. I got help from Carolyn Shafer in seeing the structure of it all, in particular, the connections among parasitism, access, and definition.

outright denied by many feminist apologists, who seem to find it embarrassing, while it is embraced, explored, expanded, and ramified by most of the more inspiring theorists and activists. The theme of separation is noticeably absent or heavily qualified in most of the things I take to be personal solutions and band-aid projects, like legalization of prostitution, liberal marriage contracts, improvement of the treatment of rape victims, and affirmative action. It is clear to me, in my own case at least, that the contrariety of assimilation and separation is one of the main things that guides or determines assessments of various theories, actions, and practices as reformist or radical, as going to the root of the thing or being relatively superficial. So my topical question comes to this: What is it about separation, in any or all of its many forms and degrees, that makes it so basic and so sinister, so exciting and so repellent?

Feminist separation is, of course, separation of various sorts or modes from men and from institutions, relationships, roles, and activities which are male-defined, male-dominated, and operating for the benefit of males and the maintenance of male privilege—this separation being initiated or maintained, at will, *by women*. (Masculist separatism is the partial segregation of women from men and male domains *at the will of men*. This difference is crucial.) The feminist separation can take many forms. Breaking up or avoiding close relationships or working relationships; forbidding someone to enter your house; excluding someone from your company, or from your meeting; withdrawal from participation in some activity or institution, or avoidance of participation; avoidance of communications and influence from certain quarters (not listening to music with sexist lyrics, not watching tv); withholding commitment or support; rejection of or rudeness toward obnoxious individuals.* Some separations are subtle realignments of identification, priorities, and commitments, or working with agendas which only incidently coincide with the agendas of the institution one works in.[1] Ceasing to be loyal to something or someone is a separation; and ceasing to love. The feminist's separations are rarely if ever sought or maintained directly as ultimate personal or political ends. The closest we come to that, I think, is the separation which is the instinctive and self-preserving recoil from the systematic misogyny that surrounds us.** Generally, the separations are brought about and maintained for the sake of something else like independence, liberty, growth, invention, sisterhood, safety, health, or the practice of novel or heretical customs.[2] Often the separations in question evolve, unpremeditated, as one goes one's way and finds various persons, institutions, or relationships useless, obstructive, or noisome and leaves them aside or behind. Sometimes the separations are consciously planned and cultivated as necessary prerequisites or conditions for getting on with one's business. Sometimes the separations are accomplished or maintained easily, or with a sense of relief, or even joy; sometimes they are accomplished or maintained with difficulty, by dint of constant vigilance, or with anxiety, pain, or grief.

Most feminists, probably all, practice some separation from males and male-dominated institutions. A separatist practices separation consciously, systematically, and probably more generally than the others, and advocates thorough and "broad-spectrum"

Adrienne Rich: ". . . makes me question the whole idea of 'courtesy' or 'rudeness'—surely their constructs, since women become 'rude' when we ignore or reject male obnoxiousness, while male 'rudeness' is usually punctuated with the 'Haven't you a sense of humor' tactic." Yes; me too. I embrace rudeness; our compulsive/compulsory politeness so often is what coerces us into their "fellowship."
**Ti-Grace Atkinson: *Should give more attention here to our vulnerability to assault and degradation, and to separation as protection.* Okay, but then we have to re-emphasize that it has to be separation at *our* behest—we've had enough of their imposed separation for our "protection." (There's no denying that in my real-life life, protection and maintenance of places for healing are major motives for separation.)

separation as part of the conscious strategy of liberation. And, contrary to the image of the separatist as a cowardly escapist,[3] hers is the life and program which inspires the greatest hostility, disparagement, insult, and confrontation and generally she is the one against whom economic sanctions operate most conclusively. The penalty for refusing to work with or for men is usually starvation (or, at the very least, doing without medical insurance[4]); and if one's policy of non-cooperation is more subtle, one's livelihood is still constantly on the line, since one is not a loyal partisan, a proper member of the team, or what have you. The penalties for being a lesbian are ostracism, harassment, and job insecurity or joblessness. The penalty for rejecting men's sexual advances is often rape and, perhaps even more often, forfeit of such things as professional or job opportunities. And the separatist lives with the added burden of being assumed by many to be a morally depraved man-hating bigot. But there is a clue here: if you are doing something that is so strictly forbidden by the patriarchs, you must be doing something right.

There is an idea floating around in both feminist and anti-feminist literature to the effect that females and males generally live in a relation of parasitism,[5] a parasitism of the male on the female ... that it is, generally speaking, the strength, energy, inspiration, and nurturance of women that keeps men going, and not the strength, aggression, spirituality, and hunting of men that keeps women going.

It is sometimes said that the parasitism goes the other way around, that the female is the parasite. But one can conjure the appearance of the female as parasite only if one takes a very narrow view of human living—historically parochial, narrow with respect to class and race, and limited in conception of what are the necessary goods. Generally, the female's contribution to her material support is and always has been substantial; in many times and places it has been independently sufficient. One can and should distinguish between a partial and contingent material dependence created by a certain sort of money economy and class structure, and the nearly ubiquitous spiritual, emotional, and material dependence of males on females. Males presently provide, off and on, a portion of the material support of women, within circumstances apparently designed to make it difficult for women to provide them for themselves. But females provide and generally have provided for males the energy and spirit for living; the males are nurtured by the females. And this the males apparently cannot do for themselves, even partially.

The parasitism of males on females is, as I see it, demonstrated by the panic, rage, and hysteria generated in so many of them by the thought of being abandoned by women. But it is demonstrated in a way that is perhaps more generally persuasive by both literary and sociological evidence. Evidence cited in Jesse Bernard's work in *The Future of Marriage* and in George Gilder's *Sexual Suicide* and *Men Alone* convincingly shows that males tend in shockingly significant numbers and in alarming degree to fall into mental illness, petty crime, alcoholism, physical infirmity, chronic unemployment, drug addiction, and neurosis when deprived of the care and companionship of a female mate, or keeper. (While on the other hand, women without male mates are significantly healthier and happier than women with male mates.) And masculist literature is abundant with indications of male cannibalism, of males deriving essential sustenance from females. Cannibalistic imagery, visual and verbal, is common in pornography: images likening women to food, and sex to eating. And, as documented in Millett's *Sexual Politics* and many other feminist analyses of masculist literature, the theme of men getting high off beating, raping, or killing women (or merely bullying them) is common. These interactions with women, or rather, these actions upon women, make men feel good, walk tall, feel refreshed, invigorated. Men are drained and depleted by their living by themselves and with and among other men, and are revived and refreshed, re-created, by going home and being served dinner, changing to clean clothes, having sex with the wife; or by dropping by the apartment of a woman friend to be served coffee or a drink and stroked in one way or another; or by picking up a prostitute for a quicky or for a dip in favorite sexual escape fantasies; or by raping refugees from their wars (foreign and domestic). The ministrations of women, be they willing or unwilling, free or paid for, are what restore in men the strength, will, and confidence to go on with what they call living.

If it is true that a fundamental aspect of the relations between the sexes is male parasitism, it might help to explain why certain issues are particularly exciting to patriarchal loyalists. For instance, in view of the obvious advantages of easy abortion to population control, to control of welfare rolls, and to ensuring sexual availability of women to men, it is a little surprising that the loyalists are so adamant and riled up in their objection to it. But look . . .

The fetus lives parasitically. It is a distinct animal surviving off the life (the blood) of another animal creature. It is incapable of surviving on its own resources, of independent nutrition; incapable even of symbiosis. If it is true that males live parasitically upon females, it seems reasonable to suppose that many of them and those loyal to them are in some way sensitive to the parallelism between their situation and that of the fetus. They could easily identify with the fetus. The woman who is free to see the fetus as a parasite* might be free to see the man as a parasite. The woman's willingness to cut off the life line to one parasite suggests a willingness to cut off the life line to another parasite. The woman who is capable (legally, psychologically, physically) of decisively, self-interestedly, independently rejecting the one parasite, is capable of rejecting, with the same decisiveness and independence, the like burden of the other parasite. In the eyes of the other parasite, the image of the wholly self-determined abortion, involving not even a ritual submission to male veto power, is the mirror image of death.

Another clue here is that one line of argument against free and easy abortion is the slippery slope argument that if fetuses are to be freely dispensed with, old people will be next. Old people? Why are old people next? And why the great concern for them? Most old people are women, indeed, and patriarchal loyalists are not generally so solicitous of the welfare of any women. Why old people? Because, I think, in the modern patriarchal divisions of labor, old people too are parasites on women. The anti-abortion folks seem not to worry about wife beating and wife murder—there is no broad or emotional popular support for stopping these violences. They do not worry about murder and involuntary sterilization in prisons, nor murder in war, nor murder by pollution and industrial accidents. Either these are not real to them or they cannot identify with the victims; but anyway, killing in general is not what they oppose. They worry about the rejection *by women, at women's discretion,* of something which lives parasitically on women. I suspect that they fret not because old people are next, but because men are next.

There are other reasons, of course, why patriarchal loyalists should be disturbed about abortion on demand; a major one being that it would be a significant form of female control of reproduction, and at least from certain angles it looks like the progress of patriarchy *is* the progress toward male control of reproduction, starting with possession of wives and continuing through the invention of obstetrics and the technology of extrauterine gestation. Giving up that control would be giving up patriarchy. But such

---

*Caroline Whitbeck: Cross-cultural evidence suggests it's not the fetus that gets rejected in cultures where abortion is common, it is the role of motherhood, the burden, in particular, of "illegitimacy"; where the institution of illegitimacy does not exist, abortion rates are pretty low. This suggests to me that the woman's rejection of the fetus is even more directly a rejection of the male and his world than I had thought.

an objection to abortion is too abstract, and requires too historical a vision, to generate the hysteria there is now in the reaction against abortion. The hysteria is, I think, to be accounted for more in terms of a much more immediate and personal presentiment of ejection by the woman-womb.[6]

I discuss abortion here because it seems to me to be the most publicly emotional and most physically dramatic ground on which the theme of separation and male parasitism is presently being played out. But there are other locales for this play. For instance,[7] women with newly raised consciousnesses tend to leave marriages and families, either completely through divorce, or partially, through unavailability of their cooking, housekeeping, and sexual services. And women academics tend to become alienated from their colleagues and male mentors and no longer serve as sounding board, ego booster, editor, mistress, or proofreader. Many awakening women become celibate or lesbian, and the others become a very great deal more choosy about when, where, and in what relationships they will have sex with men. And the men affected by these separations generally react with defensive hostility, anxiety, and guilt-tripping, not to mention descents into illogical argument which match and exceed their own most fanciful images of female irrationality. My claim is that they are very afraid because they depend very heavily upon the goods they receive from women, and these separations cut them off from those goods.

Male parasitism means that males *must have access* to women; it is the Patriarchal Imperative. But feminist no-saying is more than a substantial removal (redirection, reallocation) of goods and services because Access is one of the faces of Power. Female denial of male access to females substantially cuts off a flow of benefits, but it has also the form and full portent of assumption of power.

Differences of power are always manifested in asymmetrical access. The President of the United States has access to almost everybody for almost anything he might want of them, and almost nobody has access to him. The super-rich have access to almost everybody; almost nobody has access to them. The resources of the employee are available to the boss as the resources of the boss are not to the employee. The parent has unconditional access to the child's room; the child does not have similar access to the parent's room. Students adjust to professors' office hours; professors do not adjust to students' conference hours. The child is required not to lie; the parent is free to close out the child with lies at her discretion. The slave is unconditionally accessible to the master. Total power is unconditional access; total powerlessness is being unconditionally accessible. The creation and manipulation of power is constituted of the manipulation and control of access.

All-woman groups, meetings, projects seem to be great things for causing controversy and confrontation. Many women are offended by them; many are afraid to be the one to announce the exclusion of men; it is seen as a device whose use needs much elaborate justification. I think this is because conscious and deliberate exclusion of men by women, from anything, is blatant insubordination, and generates in women fear of punishment and reprisal (fear which is often well-justified). Our own timidity and desire to avoid confrontations generally keep us from doing very much in the way of all-woman groups and meetings. But when we do, we invariably run into the male champion who challenges our right to do it. Only a small minority of men go crazy when an event is advertised to be for women only—just one man tried to crash our women-only Rape Speak-Out, and only a few hid under the auditorium seats to try to spy on a women-only meeting at a NOW convention in Philadelphia. But these few are onto something their less rabid com-patriots are missing. The woman-only meeting is a fundamental challenge to the structure of power. It is always the privilege of the master to enter the slave's hut. The slave who decides to exclude the master from her hut is declaring herself not a slave. The exclusion of men from the meeting not only deprives them of certain benefits (which they might survive without); it is a controlling of access, hence an assumption of power. It is not only mean, it is arrogant.

It becomes clearer now why there is always an off-putting aura of negativity about separatism—one which offends the feminine pollyanna in us and smacks of the purely defensive to the political theorist in us. It is this: First: When those who control access have made you totally accessible, your first act of taking control must be denying access, or must have denial of access as one of its aspects. This is not because you are charged up with (unfeminine or politically incorrect) negativity; it is because of the logic of the situation. When we start from a position of total accessibility there *must* be an aspect of no-saying (which is the beginning of control) in *every effective* act and strategy, the effective ones being precisely those which *shift power,* i.e., ones which involve manipulation and control of access. Second: Whether or not one says "no," or withholds or closes out or rejects, on this occasion or that, the capacity and ability to say "no" (with effect) is logically necessary to control. When we are in control of access to ourselves there will be some no-saying, and when we are more accustomed to it, when it is more common, an ordinary part of living, it will not seem so prominent, obvious, or strained . . . we will not strike ourselves or others as being particularly negative. In this aspect of ourselves and our lives, we will strike ourselves pleasingly as active beings with momentum of our own, with sufficient shape and structure—with sufficient integrity— to generate friction. Our experience of our no-saying will be an aspect of our experience of our definition.

When our feminist acts or practices have an aspect of separation, we are assuming power by controlling access and simultaneously by undertaking definition. The slave who excludes the master from her hut thereby declares herself *not a slave.* And *definition* is another face of power.

The powerful normally determine what is said and sayable. When the powerful label something or dub it or baptize it, the thing becomes what they call it. When the Secretary of Defense calls something a peace negotiation, for instance, then whatever it is that he called a peace negotiation is an instance of negotiating peace. If the activity in question is the working out of terms of a trade-off of nuclear reactors and territorial redistributions, complete with arrangements for the resulting refugees, that is peace-making. People laud it, and the negotiators get Noble Piece Prizes for it. On the other hand, when I call a certain speech act a rape, my "calling" it does not make it so. At best, I have to explain and justify and make clear exactly what it is about this speech act which is assaultive in just what way, and then the others acquiesce in saying the act was *like* rape or could figuratively be called a rape. My counterassault will not be counted a simple case of self-defense. And what I called rejection of parasitism, they call the loss of the womanly virtues of compassion and "caring." And generally, when renegade women call something one thing and patriarchal loyalists call it another, the loyalists get their way.*

*This paragraph and the succeeding one are the passage which has provoked the most substantial questions from women who read the paper. One thing that causes trouble here is that I am talking from a stance or position that is ambiguous—it is located in two different and noncommunicating systems of thought-action. *Re* the patriarchy and the English language, there is general usage over which I/we do not have the control that elite males have (with the cooperation of all the ordinary patriarchal loyalists). *Re* the new being and meaning which are being created now by lesbian-feminists, we *do* have semantic authority, and, collectively, can and do define with effect. I think it is only by maintaining our boundaries through controlling concrete access to us that we can enforce on those who are not-us our definitions of ourselves, hence force on them *the fact of our existence* and thence open up the *possibility* of our having semantic authority with them. (I wrote

Women generally are not the people who do the defining, and we cannot from our isolation and powerlessness simply commence saying different things than others say and make it stick. There is a humpty-dumpty problem in that. But we are able to arrogate definition to ourselves when we repattern access. Assuming control of access, we draw new boundaries and create new roles and relationships. This, though it causes some strain, puzzlement, and hostility, is to a fair extent within the scope of individuals and small gangs, as outright verbal redefinition is not, at least in the first instance.

One may see access as coming in two sorts, "natural" and humanly arranged. A grizzly bear has what you might call natural access to the picnic basket of the unarmed human. The access of the boss to the personal services of the secretary is humanly arranged access; the boss exercises institutional power. It looks to me, looking from a certain angle, like institutions *are* humanly designed patterns of access—access to persons and their services. But institutions are artifacts of definition. In the case of intentionally and formally designed institutions, this is very clear, for the relevant definitions are explicitly set forth in by-laws and constitutions, regulations and rules. When one defines the term "president," one defines presidents in terms of what they can do and what is owed them by other offices, and "what they can do" is a matter of their access to the services of others. Similarly, definitions of *dean, student, judge,* and *cop* set forth patterns of access, and definitions of *writer, child, owner,* and of course, *husband, wife,* and *man* and *girl.* When one changes the pattern of access, one forces new uses of words on those affected. The term "man" has to shift in meaning when rape is no longer possible. When we take control of sexual access to us, of access to our nurturance and to our reproductive function, access to mothering and sistering, we redefine the word "woman." The shift of usage is pressed on others by a change in social reality; it does not await their recognition of our definitional authority.

~ When women separate (withdraw, break out, regroup, transcend, shove aside, step outside, migrate, say *no*), we are simultaneously controlling access and defining. We are doubly insubordinate, since neither of these is permitted. And access and definition are fundamental ingredients in the alchemy of power, so we are doubly, and radically, insubordinate.

If these, then, are some of the ways in which separation is at the heart of our struggle, it helps to explain why separation is such a hot topic. If there is one thing women are queasy about it is *actually taking power.* As long as one stops just short of that, the patriarchs will for the most part take an indulgent attitude. We are afraid of what will happen to us when we really frighten them. This is not an irrational fear. It is our experience in the movement generally that the defensiveness, nastiness, violence, hostility, and irrationality of the reaction to feminism tends to correlate with the blatancy of the element of separation in the strategy or project which triggers the reaction. The separations involved in women leaving homes, marriages, and boyfriends, separations from fetuses, and the separation of lesbianism are all pretty dramatic. That is, they are dramatic and blatant when perceived from within the framework provided by the pa-

some stuff that's relevant to this in the last section of my paper "Male Chauvinism—A Conceptual Analysis.")[8] Our unintelligibility to patriarchal loyalists is a source of pride and delight, in some contexts; but if we don't have an effect on their usage while we continue, willy nilly, to be subject to theirs, being totally unintelligible to them could be fatal. (A friend of mine had a dream where the women were meeting in a cabin at the edge of town, and they had a sort of inspiration through the vision of one of them that they should put a sign on the door which would connect with the patriarchs' meaning-system, for otherwise the men would be too curious/frightened about them and would break the door down to get in. They put a picture of a fish on the door.) Of course, you might say that *being* intelligible to them might be fatal. Well, perhaps it's best to be in a position to make tactical decisions about when and how to be intelligible and unintelligible.

triarchal world view and male parasitism. Matters pertaining to marriage and divorce, lesbianism and abortion touch individual men (and their sympathizers) because they can feel the relevance of these to themselves—they can feel the threat that they might be the next. Hence, heterosexuality, marriage, and motherhood, which are the institutions which most obviously and individually maintain female accessibility to males, form the core triad of antifeminist ideology; and all-woman spaces, all-woman organizations, all-woman meetings, all-woman classes, are outlawed, suppressed, harassed, ridiculed, and punished—in the name of that other fine and enduring patriarchal institution, Sex Equality.

To some of us these issues can seem almost foreign . . . strange ones to be occupying center stage. We are busily engaged in what seem to *us* our blatant insubordinations: living our own lives, taking care of ourselves and one another, doing our work, and in particular, telling it as we see it. Still, the original sin is the separation which these presuppose, and it is that, not our art or philosophy, not our speechmaking, nor our "sexual acts" (or abstinences), for which we will be persecuted, when worse comes to worst.

NOTES

1. Help from Claudia Card.

2. Help from Chris Pierce and Sara Ann Ketchum. See "Separatism and Sexual Relationships," in *A Philosophical Approach to Women's Liberation,* eds. S. Hill and M. Weinzweig (Wadsworth, Belmont, California, 1978).

3. Answering Claudia Card.

4. Levity due to Carolyn Shafer.

5. I first noticed this when reading *Beyond God the Father,* by Mary Daly (Beacon Press, Boston, 1973). See also *Women's Evolution,* by Evelyn Reed (Pathfinder Press, New York, 1975) for rich hints about male cannibalism and male dependence.

6. Claudia Card.

7. The instances mentioned are selected for their relevance to the lives of the particular women addressed in this talk. There are many other sorts of instances to be drawn from other sorts of women's lives.

8. In (improbably enough) *Philosophy and Sex,* edited by Robert Baker and Frederick Elliston (Prometheus Books, Buffalo, New York, 1976).

5

Homophobia: Why Bring It Up?

Barbara Smith

Barbara Smith is a Black feminist writer and activist. She is co-editor with Lorraine Bethel of Conditions: Five, The Black Women's Issue *(1979) and with Gloria T. Hull and Patricia Bell Scott of* All the Women Are White, All the Blacks Are Men, But Some of Us Are Brave: Black Women's Studies *(1982), editor of* Home Girls: A Black Feminist Anthology *(1983) and co-author, with Elly Bulkin and Minnie Bruce Pratt, of* Yours in Struggle: Three Feminist Perspectives on Anti-Semitism and Racism *(1984). She has written for* Sinister Wisdom; This Bridge Called My Back: Writings by Radical Women of Color *(1981); and* Lesbian Studies: Present and Future *(1982), among many other collections and journals. This essay was originally published in* The Interracial Books for Children Bulletin. *Beginning with an incident in 1982 when Blues, a gay, Black, working-class Times Square bar, was vandalized by the police, its patrons beaten and called racist and homophobic epithets, and neither the newspapers nor civil rights organizers responded, Smith argues that the refusal to recognize the intersection of oppressions sanctions homophobia as the one* ism *that otherwise progressive people tolerate. Gay and lesbian activism's impact on public awareness can only bring about real social progress, she argues, when the educational system itself adopts an anti-homophobic stance.*

In 1977 the Combahee River Collective, a Black feminist organization in Boston of which I was a member, wrote:

> The most general statement of our politics at the present time would be that we are actively committed to struggling against racial, sexual, heterosexual, and class oppression and see as our particular task the development of integrated analysis and practice based upon the fact that the major systems of oppression are interlocking.... We ... often find it difficult to separate race from class from sex oppression because in our lives they are most often experienced simultaneously.*

Despite the logic and clarity of Third World women's analysis of the simultaneity of oppression, people of all colors, progressive ones included, seem peculiarly reluctant to grasp these basic truths, especially when it comes to incorporating an active resistance to homophobia into their everyday lives. Homophobia is usually the last oppression to be mentioned, the last to be taken seriously, the last to go. But it is extremely serious, sometimes to the point of being fatal.

*The Combahee River Collective, "A Black Feminist Statement," in *All the Women Are White, All the Blacks Are Men, But Some of Us Are Brave: Black Women's Studies*, pp. 13, 16 (The Feminist Press), 1982.

Consider that on the night of September 29, 1982, 20–30 New York City policemen rushed without warning into Blues, a Times Square bar. They harassed and
severely beat the patrons, vandalized the premises, emptied the cash register, and left
without making a single arrest. What motivated such brutal behavior? The answer is
simple. The cops were inspired by three cherished tenets of our society: racism, classism,
and homophobia: the bar's clientele is Black, working class, and gay. As the police
cracked heads, they yelled racist and homophobic epithets familiar to every school child.
The attackers' hatred of both the queer and the colored, far from making them exceptional, put them squarely in the mainstream. If their actions were more extreme than
most, their attitudes certainly were not.

The Blues bar happens to be across the street from the offices of the *New York
Times*. The white, upper middle-class, presumably heterosexual staff of the nation's
premier newspaper regularly calls in complaints about the bar to the police. Not surprisingly, none of the New York daily papers, including the *Times*, bothered to report
the incident. A coalition of Third World and white lesbians and gay men organized a
large protest demonstration soon after the attack occurred. Both moderate and militant
civil rights and anti-racist organizations were notably absent, and they have yet to express
public outrage about a verifiable incident of police brutality, undoubtedly because the
Black people involved were not straight.

Intertwining "Isms"

What happened at Blues perfectly illustrates the ways in which the major "isms" *including* homophobia are intimately and violently intertwined. As a Black woman, a
lesbian, a feminist, and an activist, I have little difficulty seeing how the systems of
oppression interconnect, if for no other reason than that their meanings so frequently
affect my life. During the 1970s and 1980s political lesbians of color have often been
the most astute about the necessity for developing understandings of the connections
between oppressions. They have also opposed the building of hierarchies and challenged
the "easy way out" of choosing a "primary oppression" and downplaying those messy
inconsistencies that occur whenever race, sex, class, and sexual identity actually mix.
Ironically, for the forces on the right, hating lesbians and gay men, people of color,
Jews, and women go hand in hand. *They* make connections between oppressions in the
most negative ways with horrifying results. Supposedly progressive people, on the other
hand, who oppose oppression on every other level, balk at acknowledging the societally
sanctioned abuse of lesbians and gay men as a serious problem. Their tacit attitude is
"Homophobia, why bring it up?"

There are numerous reasons for otherwise sensitive people's reluctance to confront
homophobia in themselves and others. A major one is that people are generally threatened
about issues of sexuality, and for some the mere existence of homosexuals calls their
sexuality/heterosexuality into question. Unlike many other oppressed groups, homosexuals are not a group whose identity is clear from birth. Through the process of coming
out, a person might indeed acquire this identity at any point in life. One way to protect
one's heterosexual credentials and privilege is to put down lesbians and gay men at every
turn, to make as large a gulf as possible between "we" and "they."

There are several misconceptions and attitudes which I find particularly destructive
because of the way they work to isolate the concerns of lesbians and gay men:

    1. Lesbian and gay male oppression is not as serious as other oppressions. It is not a
       political matter, but a private concern. The life-destroying impact of lost jobs,
       children, friendships, and family; the demoralizing toll of living in constant fear

of being discovered by the wrong person which pervades all lesbians and gay men's lives whether closeted or out; and the actual physical violence and deaths that gay men and lesbians suffer at the hands of homophobes can be, if one subscribes to this myth, completely ignored.

2. "Gay" means gay white men with large discretionary incomes, period. Perceiving gay people in this way allows one to ignore that some of us are women *and* people of color *and* working class *and* poor *and* disabled *and* old. Thinking narrowly of gay people as white, middle class, and male, which is just what the establishment media want people to think, undermines consciousness of how identities and issues overlap. It is essential, however, in making connections between homophobia and other oppressions, not to fall prey to the distorted reasoning that the justification for taking homophobia seriously is that it affects some groups who are "verifiably" oppressed, for example, people of color, women, or disabled people. Homophobia is in and of itself a verifiable oppression and in a heterosexist system, all non-heterosexuals are viewed as "deviants" and are oppressed.

3. Homosexuality is a white problem or even a "white disease." This attitude is much too prevalent among people of color. Individuals who are militantly opposed to racism in all its forms still find lesbianism and male homosexuality something to snicker about or, worse, to despise. Homophobic people of color are oppressive not just to white people, but to members of their own groups—at least ten per cent of their own groups.

4. Expressions of homophobia are legitimate and acceptable in contexts where other kinds of verbalized bigotry would be prohibited. Put-downs and jokes about "dykes" and "faggots" can be made without the slightest criticism in circles where "nigger" and "chink" jokes, for instance, would bring instant censure or even ostracism. One night of television viewing indicates how very acceptable public expressions of homophobia are.

How can such deeply entrenched attitudes and behavior be confronted and changed? Certainly gay and lesbian/feminist activism has made significant inroads since the late 1960s, both in the public sphere and upon the awareness of individuals. These movements have served a highly educational function, but they have not had nearly enough impact upon the educational system itself. Curriculum that focuses in a positive way upon issues of sexual identity, sexuality, and sexism is still rare, particularly in primary and secondary grades. Yet schools are virtual cauldrons of homophobic sentiment, as witnessed by everything from the graffiti in the bathrooms and the put-downs yelled on the playground, to the heterosexist bias of most texts and the firing of teachers on no other basis than that they are not heterosexual.

In the current political climate schools are constantly under hostile scrutiny from well-organized conservative forces. More than a little courage is required to challenge students' negative attitudes about what it means to be homosexual, female, Third World, etc., but these attitudes *must* be challenged if pervasive taken-for-granted homophobia is ever to cease. I have found both in teaching and in speaking to a wide variety of audiences that making connections between oppressions is an excellent way to introduce the subjects of lesbian and gay male identity and homophobia, because it offers people a frame of reference to build upon. This is especially true if efforts have already been made in the classroom to teach about racism and sexism. It is factually inaccurate and strategically mistaken to present gay materials as if all gay people were white and male. Fortunately, there is an increasing body of work available, usually written by Third World feminists, that provides an integrated approach to the intersection of a multiplicity of identities and issues.

Perhaps some readers are still wondering, "Homophobia, why bring it up?" One reason to bring it up is that at least ten per cent of your students will be or already are lesbians and gay males. Ten per cent of your colleagues are as well. Homophobia may well be the last oppression to go, but it will go. It will go a lot faster if people who are opposed to *every* form of subjugation work in coalition to make it happen.

RECOMMENDED READING

Titles which contain useful information, particularly about lesbians of color, are:

All the Women Are White, All the Blacks Are Men, But Some of Us Are Brave: Black Women's Studies, Gloria T. Hull, Patricia Bell Scott and Barbara Smith, co-editors, The Feminist Press, Old Westbury, NY, 1982.

Black Lesbians: An Annotated Bibliography, J.R. Roberts, compiler, Naiad Press, Tallahassee, FL, 1981.

Conditions: Five, The Black Women's Issue, Lorraine Bethel and Barbara Smith, co-editors, Conditions, Brooklyn, NY, 1979.

Cuentos: Stories by Latinas, Alma Gomez, Cherríe Moraga, and Mariana Romo-Carmona, editors, Kitchen Table: Women of Color Press, Brooklyn, NY, 1983.

Home Girls: A Black Feminist Anthology, Barbara Smith, editor, Persephone Press, Watertown, MA, 1983.

This Bridge Called My Back: Writings by Radical Women of Color, Cherríe Moraga and Gloria Anzaldúa, editors, Persephone Press, Watertown, MA, 1981.

Zami: A New Spelling of My Name, Audre Lorde, Persephone Press, Watertown, MA, 1982.

Also recommended because they contain many works by women of color are:

Lesbian Fiction: An Anthology, Elly Bulkin, editor, Persephone Press, Watertown, MA, 1981.

Lesbian Poetry: An Anthology, Elly Bulkin and Joan Larkin, co-editors, Persephone Press, Watertown, MA, 1981.

6

One Is Not Born a Woman

MONIQUE WITTIG

*Monique Wittig is the author of novels—*Les guérillères *(1969; English trans. 1985) and* The Lesbian Body *(1975;* Le corps lesbian *1973) among others—and short stories as well as plays and essays, including the influential essay "The Straight Mind" (1981). She has been awarded the Prix Medicis and is Professor in the Department of French and Italian at the University of Arizona. First published in 1981, this essay offers a challenging alternative to previous explanations for the historical causes of gender oppression. Wittig disputes the naturalness of women as a social category and the biological origins of both gender difference and inequality, first arguing that women are culturally imagined and not born, and, in turn, that lesbians, because of heterosexuality's rigid two-gender system, are not women. Although lesbians, like women, are cultural artifacts, their meaning within Wittig's analysis is not defined in terms of the erotic but in terms that describe lesbianism's ability to evade heterosexuality's insistence on a firm connection between gender and sexuality.*

A materialist feminist[1] approach to women's oppression destroys the idea that women are a "natural group": "a racial group of a special kind, a group perceived *as natural,* a group of men considered as materially specific in their bodies."[2] What the analysis accomplishes on the level of ideas, practice makes actual at the level of facts: by its very existence, lesbian society destroys the artificial (social) fact constituting women as a "natural group." A lesbian society[3] pragmatically reveals that the division from men of which women have been the object is a political one and shows that we have been ideologically rebuilt into a "natural group." In the case of women, ideology goes far since our bodies as well as our minds are the product of this manipulation. We have been compelled in our bodies and in our minds to correspond, feature by feature, with the *idea* of nature that has been established for us. Distorted to such an extent that our deformed body is what they call "natural," what is supposed to exist as such before oppression. Distorted to such an extent that in the end oppression seems to be a consequence of this "nature" within ourselves (a nature which is only an *idea*). What a materialist analysis does by reasoning, a lesbian society accomplishes practically: not only is there no natural group "women" (we lesbians are living proof of it), but as individuals as well we question "woman," which for us, as for Simone de Beauvoir, is only a myth. She said: "One is not born, but becomes a woman. No biological, psychological, or economic fate determines the figure that the human female presents in society: it is civilization as a whole that produces this creature, intermediate between male and eunuch, which is described as feminine."[4]

However, most of the feminists and lesbian-feminists in America and elsewhere still believe that the basis of women's oppression *is biological as well as* historical. Some of them even claim to find their sources in Simone de Beauvoir.[5] The belief in mother right and in a "prehistory" when women created civilization (because of a biological predisposition) while the coarse and brutal men hunted (because of a biological predisposition) is symmetrical with the biologizing interpretation of history produced up to now by the class of men. It is still the same method of finding in women and men a biological explanation of their division, outside of social facts. For me this could never constitute a lesbian approach to women's oppression, since it assumes that the basis of society or the beginning of society lies in heterosexuality. Matriarchy is no less heterosexual than patriarchy: it is only the sex of the oppressor that changes. Furthermore, not only is this conception still imprisoned in the categories of sex (woman and man), but it holds onto the idea that the capacity to give birth (biology) is what defines a woman. Although practical facts and ways of living contradict this theory in lesbian society, there are lesbians who affirm that "women and men are different species or races (the words are used interchangeably): men are biologically inferior to women; male violence is a biological inevitability . . ."[6] By doing this, by admitting that there is a "natural" division between women and men, we naturalize history, we assume that "men" and "women" have always existed and will always exist. Not only do we naturalize history, but also consequently we naturalize the social phenomena which express our oppression, making change impossible. For example, instead of seeing giving birth as a forced production, we see it as a "natural," "biological" process, forgetting that in our societies births are planned (demography), forgetting that we ourselves are programmed to produce children, while this is the only social activity "short of war"[7] that presents such a great danger of death. Thus, as long as we will be "unable to abandon by will or impulse a lifelong and centuries-old commitment to childbearing as *the* female creative act,"[8] gaining control of the production of children will mean much more than the mere control of the material means of this production: women will have to abstract themselves from the definition "woman" which is imposed upon them.

A materialist feminist approach shows that what we take for the cause or origin of oppression is in fact only the *mark*[9] imposed by the oppressor: the "myth of woman,"[10] plus its material effects and manifestations in the appropriated consciousness and bodies of women. Thus, this mark does not predate oppression: Colette Guillaumin has shown that before the socioeconomic reality of black slavery, the concept of race did not exist, at least not in its modern meaning, since it was applied to the lineage of families. However, now, race, exactly like sex, is taken as an "immediate given," a "sensible given," "physical features," belonging to a natural order. But what we believe to be a physical and direct perception is only a sophisticated and mythic construction, an "imaginary formation,"[11] which reinterprets physical features (in themselves as neutral as any others but marked by the social system) through the network of relationships in which they are perceived. (They are seen as *black,* therefore they *are* black; they are seen as *women,* therefore, they *are* women. But before being *seen* that way, they first had to be *made* that way.) Lesbians should always remember and acknowledge how "unnatural," compelling, totally oppressive, and destructive being "woman" was for us in the old days before the women's liberation movement. It was a political constraint, and those who resisted it were accused of not being "real" women. But then we were proud of it, since in the accusation there was already something like a shadow of victory: the avowal by the oppressor that "woman" is not something that goes without saying, since to be one, one has to be a "real" one. We were at the same time accused of wanting to be men. Today this double accusation has been taken up again with enthusiasm in the context of the women's liberation movement by some feminists and also, alas, by some lesbians whose political goal seems somehow to be becoming more and more "feminine." To refuse to be a woman, however, does not mean that one has to become a man. Besides, if we take as an example the perfect "butch," the classic example which provokes the most horror, whom Proust would have called a woman/man, how is her alienation different from that of someone who wants to become a woman? Tweedledum and Tweedledee. At least for a woman, wanting to become a man proves that she has escaped her initial programming. But even if she would like to, with all her strength, she cannot become a man. For becoming a man would demand from a woman not only a man's external appearance but his consciousness as well, that is, the consciousness of one who disposes by right of at least two "natural" slaves during his life span. This is impossible, and one feature of lesbian oppression consists precisely of making women out of reach for us, since women belong to men. Thus a lesbian *has* to be something else, a not-woman, a not-man, a product of society, not a product of nature, for there is no nature in society.

The refusal to become (or to remain) heterosexual always meant to refuse to become a man or a woman, consciously or not. For a lesbian this goes further than the refusal of the *role* "woman." It is the refusal of the economic, ideological, and political power of a man. This, we lesbians, and nonlesbians as well, knew before the beginning of the lesbian and feminist movement. However, as Andrea Dworkin emphasizes, many lesbians recently "have increasingly tried to transform the very ideology that has enslaved us into a dynamic, religious, psychologically compelling celebration of female biological potential."[12] Thus, some avenues of the feminist and lesbian movement lead us back to the myth of woman which was created by men especially for us, and with it we sink back into a natural group. Having stood up to fight for a sexless society,[13] we now find ourselves entrapped in the familiar deadlock of "woman is wonderful." Simone de Beauvoir underlined particularly the false consciousness which consists of selecting among the features of the myth (that women are different from men) those which look good and using them as a definition for women. What the concept "woman is wonderful" accomplishes is that it retains for defining women the best features (best according to whom?) which oppression has granted us, and it does not radically question the categories "man" and "woman," which are political categories and not natural givens. It puts us in a position of fighting within the class "women" not as the other classes do, for the disappearance of our class, but for the defense of "woman" and its reenforcement. It leads us to develop with complacency "new" theories about our specificity: thus, we call our passivity "nonviolence," when the main and emergent point for us is to fight our passivity (our fear, rather, a justified one). The ambiguity of the term "feminist" sums up the whole situation. What does "feminist" mean? Feminist is formed with the word "femme," "woman," and means: someone who fights for women. For many of us it means someone who fights for women as a class and for the disappearance of this class. For many others it means someone who fights for woman and her defense— for the myth, then, and its reenforcement. But why was the word "feminist" chosen if it retains the least ambiguity? We chose to call ourselves "feminists" ten years ago, not in order to support or reenforce the myth of woman, nor to identify ourselves with the oppressor's definition of us, but rather to affirm that our movement had a history and to emphasize the political link with the old feminist movement.

It is, then, this movement that we can put in question for the meaning that it gave to feminism. It so happens that feminism in the last century could never resolve its contradictions on the subject of nature/culture, woman/society. Women started to fight for themselves as a group and rightly considered that they shared common features as a result of oppression. But for them these features were natural and biological rather than social. They went so far as to adopt the Darwinist theory of evolution. They did not believe like Darwin, however, "that women were less evolved than men, but they did believe that male and female natures had diverged in the course of evolutionary development and that society at large reflected this polarization."[14] "The failure of early feminism was that it only attacked the Darwinist charge of female inferiority, while accepting the foundations of this charge—namely, the view of woman as 'unique.' "[15] And finally it was women scholars—and not feminists—who scientifically destroyed this theory. But the early feminists had failed to regard history as a dynamic process which develops from conflicts of interests. Furthermore, they still believed as men do that the cause (origin) of their oppression lay within themselves. And therefore after some astonishing victories the feminists of this first front found themselves at an impasse out of a lack of reasons to fight. They upheld the illogical principle of "equality in difference," an idea now being born again. They fell back into the trap which threatens us once again: the myth of woman.

Thus it is our historical task, and only ours, to define what we call oppression in materialist terms, to make it evident that women are a class, which is to say that the category "woman" as well as the category "man" are political and economic categories not eternal ones. Our fight aims to suppress men as a class, not through a genocidal, but a political struggle. Once the class "men" disappears, "women" as a class will disappear as well, for there are no slaves without masters. Our first task, it seems, is to always thoroughly dissociate "women" (the class within which we fight) and "woman," the myth. For "woman" does not exist for us: it is only an imaginary formation, while "women" is the product of a social relationship. We felt this strongly when everywhere we refused to be called a *"woman's* liberation movement." Furthermore, we have to destroy the myth inside and outside ourselves. "Woman" is not each one of us, but the political and ideological formation which negates "women" (the product of a relation of exploitation). "Woman" is there to confuse us, to hide the reality "women." In order to be aware of being a class and to become a class we first have to kill the myth of "woman" including its most seductive aspects (I think about Virginia Woolf when she said the first task of a woman writer is to kill "the angel in the house"). But to become a class we do not have to suppress our individual selves, and since no individual can be reduced to her/his oppression we are also confronted with the historical necessity of constituting ourselves as the individual subjects of our history as well. I believe this is the reason why all these attempts at "new" definitions of woman are blossoming now. What is at stake (and of course not only for women) is an individual definition as well as a class definition. For once one has acknowledged oppression, one needs to know and experience the fact that one can constitute oneself as a subject (as opposed to an object of oppression), that one can become *someone* in spite of oppression, that one has one's own identity. There is no possible fight for someone deprived of an identity, no internal motivation for fighting, since, although I can fight only with others, first I fight for myself.

The question of the individual subject is historically a difficult one for everybody. Marxism, the last avatar of materialism, the science which has politically formed us, does not want to hear anything about a "subject." Marxism has rejected the transcendental subject, the subject as constitutive of knowledge, the "pure" consciousness. All that thinks per se, before all experience, has ended up in the garbage can of history, because it claimed to exist outside matter, prior to matter, and needed God, spirit, or soul to exist in such a way. This is what is called "idealism." As for individuals, they are only the product of social relations, therefore their consciousness can only be "alienated." (Marx, in *The German Ideology,* says precisely that individuals of the dominating class are also alienated, although they are the direct producers of the ideas that alienate the classes oppressed by them. But since they draw visible advantages from their own alienation they can bear it without too much suffering.) There exists such a thing as class consciousness, but a consciousness which does not refer to a particular subject, except as participating in general conditions of exploitation at the same time as the other subjects of their class, all sharing the same consciousness. As for the practical class problems—outside of the class problems as traditionally defined—that one could encounter (for example, sexual problems), they were considered "bourgeois" problems that would disappear with the final victory of the class struggle. "Individualistic," "subjectivist," "petit bourgeois," these were the labels given to any person who had shown problems which could not be reduced to the "class struggle" itself.

Thus Marxism has denied the members of oppressed classes the attribute of being a subject. In doing this, Marxism, because of the ideological and political power this "revolutionary science" immediately exercised upon the workers' movement and all other political groups, has prevented all categories of oppressed peoples from constituting themselves historically as subjects (subjects of their struggle, for example). This means that the "masses" did not fight for themselves but for *the* party or its organizations. And when an economic transformation took place (end of private property, constitution of the socialist state), no revolutionary change took place within the new society, because the people themselves did not change.

For women, Marxism had two results. It prevented them from being aware that they are a class and therefore from constituting themselves as a class for a very long time, by leaving the relation "women/men" outside of the social order, by turning it into a natural relation, doubtless for Marxists the only one, along with the relation of mothers to children, to be seen this way, and by hiding the class conflict between men and women behind a natural division of labor (*The German Ideology*). This concerns the theoretical (ideological) level. On the practical level, Lenin, *the* party, all the communist parties up to now, including all the most radical political groups, have always reacted to any attempt on the part of women to reflect and form groups based on their own class problem with an accusation of divisiveness. By uniting, we women are dividing the strength of the people. This means that for the Marxists women *belong* either to the bourgeois class or to the proletariat class, in other words, to the men of these classes. In addition, Marxist theory does not allow women any more than other classes of oppressed people to constitute themselves as historical subjects, because Marxism does not take into account the fact that a class also consists of individuals one by one. Class consciousness is not enough. We must try to understand philosophically (politically) these concepts of "subject" and "class consciousness" and how they work in relation to our history. When we discover that women are the objects of oppression and appropriation, at the very moment that we become able to perceive this, we become subjects in the sense of cognitive subjects, through an operation of abstraction. Consciousness of oppression is not only a reaction to (fight against) oppression. It is also the whole conceptual reevaluation of the social world, its whole reorganization with new concepts, from the point of view of oppression. It is what I would call the science of oppression created by the oppressed. This operation of understanding reality has to be undertaken by every one of us: call it a subjective, cognitive practice. The movement back and forth between the levels of reality (the conceptual reality and the material reality of oppression, which are both social realities) is accomplished through language.

It is we who historically must undertake the task of defining the individual subject in materialist terms. This certainly seems to be an impossibility since materialism and subjectivity have always been mutually exclusive. Nevertheless, and rather than despairing of ever understanding, we must recognize the *need* to reach subjectivity in the abandonment by many of us to the myth "woman" (the myth of woman being only a snare that holds us up). This real necessity for everyone to exist as an individual, as well as a member of a class, is perhaps the first condition for the accomplishment of a revolution, without which there can be no real fight or transformation. But the opposite is also true; without class and class consciousness there are no real subjects, only alienated individuals. For women to answer the question of the individual subject in materialist terms is first to show, as the lesbians and feminists did, that supposedly "subjective," "individual," "private" problems are in fact social problems, class problems; that sexuality is not for women an individual and subjective expression, but a social institution of violence. But once we have shown that all so-called personal problems are in fact class problems, we will still be left with the question of the subject of each singular woman—not the myth, but each one of us. At this point, let us say that a new personal and subjective definition for all humankind can only be found beyond the categories of sex (woman and man) and that the advent of individual subjects demands first destroying the categories of sex, ending the use of them, and rejecting all sciences which still use these categories as their fundamentals (practically all social sciences).

To destroy "woman" does not mean that we aim, short of physical destruction, to destroy lesbianism simultaneously with the categories of sex, because lesbianism provides for the moment the only social form in which we can live freely. Lesbian is the only concept I know of which is beyond the categories of sex (woman and man), because the designated subject (lesbian) is *not* a woman, either economically, or politically, or ideologically. For what makes a woman is a specific social relation to a man, a relation that we have previously called servitude,[16] a relation which implies personal and physical obligation as well as economic obligation ("forced residence,"[17] domestic corvée, conjugal duties, unlimited production of children, etc.), a relation which lesbians escape by refusing to become or to stay heterosexual. We are escapees from our class in the same way as the American runaway slaves were when escaping slavery and becoming free. For us this is an absolute necessity; our survival demands that we contribute all our strength to the destruction of the class of women within which men appropriate women. This can be accomplished only by the destruction of heterosexuality as a social system which is based on the oppression of women by men and which produces the doctrine of the difference between the sexes to justify this oppression.

NOTES

1. Christine Delphy, "Pour un féminisme matérialiste," *L'Arc* 61 (1975). Translated as "For a Materialist Feminism," *Feminist Issues* 1, no. 2 (Winter 1981).

2. Colette Guillaumin, "Race et Nature: Système des marques, idée de groupe naturel et rapports sociaux," *Pluriel,* no. 11 (1977). Translated as "Race and Nature: The System of Marks, the Idea of a Natural Group and Social Relationships," *Feminist Issues* 8, no. 2 (Fall 1988).

3. I use the word society with an extended anthropological meaning; strictly speaking, it does not refer to societies, in that lesbian societies do not exist completely autonomously from heterosexual social systems.

4. Simone de Beauvoir, *The Second Sex* (New York: Bantam, 1952), p. 249.

5. Redstockings, *Feminist Revolution* (New York: Random House, 1978), p. 18.

6. Andrea Dworkin, "Biological Superiority: The World's Most Dangerous and Deadly Idea," *Heresies* 6:46.

7. Ti-Grace Atkinson, *Amazon Odyssey* (New York: Links Books, 1974), p. 15.

8. Dworkin, op. cit.

9. Guillaumin, op. cit.

10. de Beauvoir, op. cit.

11. Guillaumin, op. cit.

12. Dworkin, op. cit.

13. Atkinson, p. 6: "If feminism has any logic at all, it must be working for a sexless society."

14. Rosalind Rosenberg, "In Search of Woman's Nature," *Feminist Studies* 3, no. 1/2 (1975): 144.

15. Ibid., p. 146.

16. In an article published in *L'Idiot International* (mai 1970), whose original title was "Pour un mouvement de libération des femmes" ("For a Women's Liberation Movement").

17. Christiane Rochefort, *Les stances à Sophie* (Paris: Grasset, 1963).

7

Silences:
"Hispanics," AIDS, and Sexual Practices

ANA MARIA ALONSO AND MARIA TERESA KORECK

Ana Maria Alonso and Maria Teresa Koreck are both anthropologists who study northern Mexico. Alonso is especially interested in gender, ethnicity, and class along the northern Mexican frontier from the eighteenth century to the present, and Koreck in state formation and popular resistance in the same region during the nineteenth and twentieth centuries. In this jointly written article Alonso and Koreck argue that the term "Hispanics," so commonly used by Anglo state officials and AIDS researchers, is a mystification that blurs important variations among Latino population groups. They also argue that the familiar Anglo categories of sexual orientation—homosexual, bisexual, heterosexual—are culturally specific rather than universal or natural, and cannot be applied to northern Mexican or Chicano populations without producing misrecognition. If work to prevent the sexual transmission of AIDS is to be undertaken and done well among these populations, then, Alonso and Koreck insist, it must be based on an informed understanding of their social and cultural differences. Ana Maria Alonso is assistant professor of Anthropology at the University of Arizona, and Maria Teresa Koreck is visiting assistant professor of Anthropology, Latino Studies, and Women's Studies at the University of Michigan.

Silence ... is less the absolute limit of discourse than an element that functions alongside the things said, with them and in relation to them. ... We must try to determine the different ways of saying ... how those who can and cannot speak ... are distributed, which type of discourse is authorized, or which form of discretion is required. ... There is not one but many silences, and they are an integral part of the strategies that underlie and permeate discourse. ((Foucault, *History* 27)[1]

In the "Belly of the Beast"[2]

Americans devour what they might otherwise fear to become. (Rodriguez 84)

Lately, Hollywood producers and multinational corporations have discovered a significant new segment of consumers: "Hispanics." Films such as *La Bamba* and *Stand and Deliver* are shown in commercial cinemas while "Hispanic" Barbie dolls are sold in toy shops. Consulting firms call up "Hispanic" housewives, promising to rationalize their home economics through a free evaluation of the products they use.

Simultaneously, public opinion is changing color as politicians court the "Hispanic vote." While Dukakis and Bentsen speak Spanish to "Hispanic" crowds in the hopes

110

of winning over "the nation's fastest-growing voter group," Bush lays claim to being *"simpatico,"* as reported in the *Austin American Statesman,* because his son married a Mexican-American and his grandchildren are "little brown ones" (Henry A7).

But "Hispanics" are not only being pursued as voters and consumers; their cultural productions are also being consumed by Anglos. "The Hispanic influence is exploding into the American cultural mainstream," media headliners proclaim in *Time.* "Shake your body. The 'Black Bean invasion' arrives: from Salsa to Hip-Hop, Latino sounds go Pop" (Rodriguez 84).

Clearly, the boundaries between "self" and "other" are being redrawn. As configurations of power and identity shift, the consumption of the "Hispanic" acquires new flavors and the culinary metaphors of nationality and ethnicity assume novel significances. No longer represented as just the Frito Banditos from south of the border or the tutti-frutti bombshells of banana republics, "Hispanics" are now being construed as the "cultural ingredients" of a purportedly pluralist melting-pot cuisine, the salsa that adds "color and spirit" to good ol' American home cooking (Rodriguez 84).

The media and transnational corporations are not alone in producing and circulating discourses which refashion subjects.[3] The federal government W–4 forms now carry official "RACE/ETHNIC CATEGORY DEFINITIONS" which fix the meaning of "Hispanic" (primarily in relation to that of "White" and "Black"):

1. White *(not of Hispanic origin): Persons having origins in any of the original peoples of Europe, North Africa, or the Middle East.*
2. Black *(not of Hispanic origin): Persons having origins in any of the black racial groups of Africa. . . .*
3. Hispanic: *Persons of Mexican, Puerto Rican, Cuban, Central or South American or other Spanish culture or origin, regardless of race.*

There is a slippage between those aspects of social identity represented as sources of primordial ontological substance, namely between "race" on the one hand and "ethnicity" (national origins/cultural practices) on the other, and this slippage produces a new category of being: "Hispanic." Regardless of race (class, national origin, culture), "Hispanics" are homogenized as members of the melting pot's race-which-is-not-a-race, while their differences from both "blacks" and "whites" are stressed and authorized.

"Hispanic" is a term that packages the Latino[4] as "a more attractive commodity"; it "whitens" by giving voice to a hypostasized Spanish essence while simultaneously erasing from the field of discourse the African and Indian heritage of peoples of Latin America (Acuña; Yankauer; Hayes-Bautista and Chapa). The redefinition and management of subjects effected by the deployment of this category is rooted in the politics of the early 1970s. As Rodolfo Acuña points out, the Nixon administration began using the term in the wake of the 1960s Chicano[5] movement in order to co-opt middle-class Mexican-Americans and to displace and preempt more radical forms of ethnic self-identification and political alliance (379–80).

The "whitening" and assimilationist connotations of "Hispanic," on the one hand, and the continuing construction of Spanish-speaking peoples as inferior (but useful) "brown" bodies, on the other, are among the contradictory practices which mark out the terrain of contemporary cultural and political struggle. Despite the new "attractive packaging," Latinos continue to be exploited, discriminated against, and politically under-represented. Discourses which applaud the latest addition to the melting pot coexist with "English Only" resolutions (such as the one passed in California in 1986) designed to excise all traces of otherness from national identity. The IRCA (a labor/immigration law which promises amnesty to people who have committed no crimes)[6] is deployed to regulate the influx of "brown" bodies—for while a supply of low-paid and poorly treated Mexican labor is seen to benefit the US economy, too many "aliens" are construed as a threat to the nation.

Yet current struggles are not only about living but also about dying. Cesar Chavez has fasted for more than a month to protest California growers' use of pesticides which harm the health of farm workers ("Chavez Ends Fast"). And media headlines which celebrated a domesticated "Hispanic" otherness coexist with yet other headlines representing ethnic differences as a deadly proposition.

US Minorities and AIDS[7]

Entire generation of minorities [i.e., blacks and "Hispanics"] at risk from AIDS virus. (Ryckman)

The reasons for this recurring *racial* disproportion of [AIDS] infection, whether behavioral or biologic, are not yet apparent. The higher rate of IV drug use among black and Hispanic groups, with consequent greater risk of HIV exposure, is clearly a contributing factor. ("Human Immunodeficiency Virus," henceforth "HIV," emphasis added)

Initially portrayed as primarily affecting gay white men, since 1986 AIDS has been increasingly recognized as having a disproportionate impact on US blacks and "Hispanics."[8] Indeed, as of October 5, 1987, blacks and "Hispanics" had accounted for almost 37 percent of the non-pediatric AIDS cases reported in the United States since 1981 (United States, *AIDS Public Information Data Set,* henceforth US *PIDS*).[9] Whereas blacks make up 12 percent of the total population of the United States, 25 percent of reported US AIDS cases have affected the black community; while "Hispanics" make up 6 percent of the population of the United States, 14 percent of reported US AIDS cases have occurred in this segment of the population ("Acquired Immunodeficiency Syndrome," henceforth "AIDS"). Furthermore, the overall cumulative incidence rates of AIDS cases per 1,000,000 population for blacks and "Hispanics" are disproportionately high compared with those for whites. Incidence data ("HIV") have shown the rate per million population to be 149 for whites, 422 for blacks, and 390 for "Hispanics"; this means that blacks were 3.0 times and "Hispanics" were 2.6 times more likely to contract AIDS than whites ("HIV").[10] In addition, blacks and "Hispanics" are over-represented not only among AIDS sufferers but also among persons infected with the HIV virus who are still asymptomatic.

Minority women and children have been at a higher risk than their white counterparts. Black and "Hispanic" women were 13.3 and 11.1 times, respectively, more likely to contract AIDS than white women ("AIDS"). The cumulative incidences for black and "Hispanic" children were 15.1 and 9.1 times, respectively, the incidence for white children ("AIDS"). As of October 5, 1987, black and "Hispanic" men accounted for 21 percent and 14 percent, respectively, of the cumulative 38,219 adult male AIDS cases. However, among the 2,747 women making up almost 7 percent of the non-pediatric AIDS cases, black and "Hispanic" women accounted for almost 49 percent and 20 percent, respectively. Thus, of women with AIDS, 70 percent were from ethnic minorities, compared to a figure of 35 percent for ethnic minority men (US *PIDS*).

Not only are blacks and "Hispanics" at a higher risk for contracting AIDS, but also, once they have developed the disease, poverty, malnutrition, and inadequate access to health resources make their fate a much harsher one than that of whites. The average life expectancy after diagnosis of US whites with AIDS is two years; of minorities, only nineteen weeks (Hammonds 31).

The disproportionate number of AIDS cases among US minority groups has been generally attributed to the higher incidence of intravenous (IV) drug use in the black and "Hispanic" communities.[11] Since black and "Hispanic" IV drug users are poorer than their white counterparts, they are also more likely to share needles and syringes and hence, to expose themselves to contaminated blood (Rogers and Williams 91). But as Hammonds points out, the statistics commonly used to "prove" that needle/syringe sharing is the preeminent mode of HIV transmission and the cause of the higher AIDS incidence rates in these groups are skewed: these frequently cited figures represent the percentage of drug-related cumulative AIDS cases that are black and "Hispanic," *not* the percentage of cumulative black and "Hispanic" AIDS cases that are drug related (35). Re-examining the data, we find that as of October 5, 1987, out of a cumulative total of 9,293 black non-pediatric AIDS cases, *only 45 percent of the cases were drug related,* while the remaining 55 percent were attributable to transmission categories that did not involve IV drug use; out of a cumulative total of 5,729 "Hispanic" non-pediatric AIDS cases, *only 42 percent were attributable to IV drug use* (US *PIDS*).

In contrast to the efforts made by the media, institutions, and researchers to establish and publicize the connection between AIDS and IV drug abuse, scant attention has been paid to possible links between sexual practices and the disproportionate number of AIDS cases affecting minorities. Hammonds argues that the conceptual association of ethnicity and IV drug abuse has been so pervasive that the fact that about 50% of black and "Hispanic" men who have contracted AIDS have been *non*-IV drug users, classified under the category "gay" or "bisexual," has remained buried (35). Hammonds's argument is validated by available AIDS case surveillance data. As of October 5, 1987, out of a cumulative total of 7,951 black male adult AIDS cases, *50.5 percent were attributable to "homosexual"/"bisexual" transmission with no IV exposure;* out of 5,182 AIDS cases affecting male adult "Hispanics," *53.8 percent occurred within the "homosexual"/"bisexual" transmission category* (US *PIDS*).

AIDS cases represent only a small proportion of the population infected with the HIV virus. One can assume, with some degree of assurance, that the pool of HIV-infected persons will possess characteristics similar to the group of diagnosed AIDS cases. Thus, the percentage of black and "Hispanic" male AIDS cases attributable to the "homosexual"/"bisexual" mode of transmission with no IV drug use may suggest that this is also an important mode of HIV transmission among persons so far asymptomatic. Significantly, Rogers and Williams have noted that once diagnosed with AIDS, a higher proportion of blacks and "Hispanics" report that they are "bisexual" as compared to "homosexual," than do whites:[12]

> Among whites transmitting AIDS through homosexual contact, 87 percent were exclusively homosexual and 13 percent bisexual. Among blacks, 70 percent were exclusively homosexual and 30 percent bisexual. Among Hispanics, 80 percent were exclusively homosexual and 20 percent bisexual. Bisexual men may be less likely to consider themselves gay, and thus at risk for HIV infection. (91)

Long overlooked by both the mainstream media and AIDS researchers, the link between sexuality and AIDS disease among minorities in the United States is now beginning to be addressed. For example, a 1988 published study by Castro and Manoff on the epidemiology of AIDS among "Hispanic" adolescents (age 15–19 years) and young adults (age 20–24 years) examines the geographic distribution of reported AIDS cases and the role of sexual practices versus IV drug use within these infected age groups. Castro and Manoff conclude that while AIDS cases among young "Hispanics" in Puerto Rico, New York, and New Jersey are mostly attributable to IV drug use and "heterosexual" contact, "homosexual" or "bisexual" contact accounts for a proportionately larger number of AIDS cases in California, Texas, and Florida.

Castro and Manoff have made a valuable contribution. However, their conclusions about the geographic distribution of AIDS cases and transmission categories need to be interpreted in relation to the diverse ethnic affiliations of their "Hispanic" subjects, rather than in terms of the random geographic distribution of their population sample. There is no doubt that the epidemiological patterns uncovered by their study are a function not of geography[13] but rather of socio-cultural differences among Latino groups, differences which are rendered invisible by the deployment of the category "Hispanic." What their study suggests is that whereas IV drug use is a more important factor in AIDS infection among persons who are probably mostly of Puerto Rican origins, living in New York, New Jersey, and their native Puerto Rico,[14] sexual practices play a more critical role in the epidemiology of AIDS among those of Mexican origins (the predominant "Hispanic" group in California and Texas), and among those of Cuban origins (the largest "Hispanic" group in Florida).

The pattern of HIV transmission among "Hispanics" which prevails in the literature has been generated through a synecdoche which generalizes the "high risk" IV drug use of Puerto Ricans (a "part" of the purported "whole") to other Latino groups. But as Castro and Manoff's results unwittingly imply, "Hispanic" is not a useful category for AIDS research since it obscures key differences in the epidemiology of the disease among diverse Latino groups. In order for AIDS research to advance, the category "Hispanic" needs to be dismantled.

A further problem with research categories is raised by differences between minority and Anglo-American constructions of sexuality. A number of researchers and even the media have pointed out that black and "Hispanic" men who would be construed as "homosexual" or "bisexual" by Anglos do not always identify themselves as such (Communication Technologies; Hammonds; Worth and Rodriguez; National Minority AIDS Council; Ryckman). This suggests that Anglo-American sexual distinctions—"heterosexual," "bisexual," and "homosexual"—which have been reified, grounded in a construction of a biologically sexed body, and given an alibi[15] in nature, are neither universal nor natural but instead socio-culturally and historically produced categories which cannot be presumed to be applicable to US minority groups or to other societies. Indeed, a lack of awareness among Anglo-American researchers of differences in the social and cultural construction of sexuality has helped to obscure the role of sexual practices in HIV transmission among minority groups. What is evident is that research on the epidemiology of AIDS among US minorities requires the deconstruction of Anglo-American categories of ethnic identity, such as "Hispanic," and of erotic practice, sexual being, and gender.

In order to further substantiate these points, we now turn to a discussion of the construction of sexual practices in northern Mexico. The socio-cultural constructs described for northern Mexicans cannot simply be generalized to persons of Mexican origins in the US. However, in the light of Castro and Manoff's epidemiological observations, and the statistical data presented here, we hope our discussion will highlight the need for research strategies and methodologies capable of uncovering socio-cultural constructions of sexuality.

AIDS and Sexual Practices in Mexico

It is generally agreed that AIDS is an "imported disease," brought into Mexico via North America through "homosexual" contacts between Mexicans and Anglos both in

Mexico and in the US. However, the Human Immunodeficiency Virus is already being transmitted in Mexico, and the disease is currently reaching epidemic proportions (Carrier, "Sexual Behavior" 1–3).

IV drug abuse does not appear to be prominent in Mexico and is not a significant source of HIV transmission. The "high risk" activities which have been identified as key to the epidemiology of AIDS are "homosexual" and "bisexual" practices, prostitution, transfusions of contaminated blood, and the injection of medications with contaminated needles or syringes (Carrier, "Sexual Behavior" 3).

The use of the terms "homosexuality," "bisexuality," and "heterosexuality" with reference to Mexico is rather misleading, however, for erotic practices and gender identities are differently construed by Mexicans and Anglos.[16] In order to distinguish Mexican from North American sexual practices, some consideration of what these categories mean in Anglo discourse is in order.

"Popular understanding of the concept of 'masculinity' among Anglo-Americans," Blumstein and Schwartz note, "implies that one must show erotic distaste (not merely neutrality) toward other males, and that one must demonstrate competent performance in the heterosexual arena" (quoted in Carrier, "Mexican Male" 83). In Anglo culture, any erotic act between persons who are considered to be "biologically male" demarcates not only a "deviant" category of practice but also a stigmatized category of being, radically opposed to normative forms of (hetero)sexual desire and identity: the "homosexual."

Rooted in a Western concept of the uses and mis-uses of biologically sexed bodies whose socially sanctioned and divinely ordained purpose is the reproduction of the species, the "perversity" ascribed to same-sex erotic practices excludes the "homosexual" from the category of "normal" heterosexual men (Lancaster 114). As Blumstein and Schwartz point out, for Anglo-Americans, "one drop of homosexuality makes a man 'totally homosexual'" (83). In the United States, those who "mis-use" their bodies are "ghettoized"—marginalized from the circuits of heterosexual male power and prestige, and bounded off as members of a distinct group possessing a particular "sub-culture" and identity.

Carrier's research with *mestizos* in urban zones, and our own preliminary work with non-Indian agriculturalists in rural areas, suggests that a radically different regime of pleasure and power characterizes northern Mexico. The distinctiveness of this regime has a particular set of implications for the nexus of sexuality and disease which cannot be assimilated by or understood in terms of Anglo-American models of gender identity, erotic practice, and HIV transmission.

Like Lancaster in Nicaragua, Carrier has found that "males who [only] play the active insertor role in homosexual encounters generally are not conceptualized as *homosexuals*," and neither is their masculinity diminished nor their identity stigmatized by such practices ("Mexican Male" 77). By contrast, "effeminate males" who *only* play "the passive insertee role in anal intercourse" are demarcated as a particular category of beings—*jotos* or *putos* ("Sexual Behavior" 78). Unlike their sexual partners, *jotos* are stigmatized for their "unmanly effeminate behavior" and are the butt of social ridicule expressed through jokes and verbal play ("Mexican Male" 78).

While *jotos* only have erotic relations with "masculine males" or *machos*,[17] the latter can engage in sexual activity with both *jotos* and women without being stigmatized:

> Some post-pubertal males utilize pre-pubertal boys as sexual outlets prior to marriage, and, after marriage, continue to utilize both heterosexual and homosexual outlets. Another pattern is that some males in their first year of sexual activity initiate sexual encounters both with post-pubertal girls and effeminate boys they find in their neigh-

borhoods, at school, at social outings. They continue to utilize both sexual outlets prior to marriage, but discontinue or only occasionally use, homosexual outlets following marriage. Still another pattern exists where some males utilize both genders as sexual outlets during the first couple of years of sexual activity. They have *novias* ["decent" women involved in male-female relationships which presumably lead to matrimony] and plan to marry, but they also become romantically involved with males prior to marriage. After they marry, they continue to have romantic and sexual relationships with males. ("Mexican Male" 78)

Sex between *machos* and women includes both vaginal and anal intercourse. According to Taylor, in Mexico, male-female anal intercourse is practiced in order to preserve the virginity of *novias,* and more generally, to prevent pregnancy (cited in "Mexican Male" 79). Though fellatio is often part of foreplay, in *macho-joto* sexual contact, anal intercourse is considered the culminating act ("Sexual Behavior" 15).

The privileging of anal intercourse in *macho-joto* sex is partly motivated by an analogy between this type of erotic contact and relationship, and that which occurs between *machos* and women. As Carrier notes, unlike *machos,* who are considered to be "active and impenetrable," *jotos* or "feminine males" are construed as "passive and penetrable, like females," and the anus is seen as a site of "sexual pleasure like the vagina" ("Sexual Behavior 8). This construction of erotic practice is consistent with Lancaster's remarks:

> Unlike oral intercourse, which may lend itself to reciprocal sexual practices, anal intercourse invariably produces an active partner and a passive partner. If oral intercourse suggests the possibility of an equal sign between partners, anal intercourse most likely produces an unequal relationship. (112–13)

Yet the inequality inscribed in *macho-joto* (and in *macho*-female) sexual practice is not "invariably" produced by the "nature" of these activities but instead, by a culture which finds its alibi in the very nature it invests with meaning.

In Mexico, sexual intercourse (whether vaginal or anal) is not a sign of equality but instead, a sign *of* and a source of tropes *for* domination and subordination. A verb which always connotes the sexual act, *chingar* is a polysemic term whose semantic range is close to that of the English "rape"—" 'the act of taking anything by force, violent seizure (of goods), robbery, and, after 1481, the violation of a woman' " (Vickers 214)—as well as to that of the English "fuck." As Octavio Paz glosses it, *chingar* "denotes violence, an emergence from oneself to penetrate another by force. It also means to injure, to lacerate, to violate—bodies, souls, objects—and to destroy" (76–77).

In the rural northern Mexican communities where we worked,[18] a *macho* is a *chingón,* that is, he who can *chingar* but who cannot be *chingado* by others, and hence, who demonstrates his possession of *huevos.*[19] The testicles (*huevos*) are viewed as the physical source of "natural" masculine attributes which include valor, autonomy, mastery, virility, and closure. The signifier (*huevos*) is apprehended as a *cause* of the signified ("natural" masculine qualities).[20] Endowed with physical closure, the potent male body is non-permeable as well as capable of opening, penetrating, and rupturing other selves, bodies, and domains.

In order to establish their masculine identities, males have to demonstrate qualities of autonomy, mastery, valor, and virility on a day-to-day basis; if they fail to do so, they stand in danger of being feminized. Since masculinity is a source of honor—of social value—for males, the embodiment of masculine qualities is an agonistic affair. In the competition for honor, some men succeed in claiming and defending a masculine identity whereas others become feminized.

In contrast to men, women are perceived as penetrable and as incapable of penetrating others. The "natural" qualities of femininity are contradictory. On the one hand, women are icons of the Virgin Mary and are "by nature" sexually pure, virtuous, and sacred. The signifier, the intact hymen, is subjectively apprehended as the cause of this signified purity of body and soul. On the other hand, women, by "nature," are capable of being opened by men: they are destined to have their bodily integrity shattered and their sexual purity sullied by intercourse. The signifier, the ruptured hymen, is interpreted as the cause of the signified, female pollution and profanation.

Like Mary, the ideal woman is the embodiment of a paradox: she is both virgin and mother. The sacralization of virginal maternity is seen to conflict with "the natural facts" of conception—the source of female shame. Indeed, in one community, the main reason women give for taking baths is to purify themselves from the pollution of sexual intercourse. Significantly, one informant commented that sex, even with one's wife, is always a "violation" (*violación*) of the woman by the man, a breaching of her bodily boundaries. If intercourse makes the man the *chingón*, it makes the woman the *chingada*[21]—the open, violated mother, steeped in corporality, whose name is invoked only in the most offensive and power-laden of Mexican insults.

Our research in rural northern Mexico has led us to conclude that the active, penetrating role in sexual intercourse is seen as a source of honor and power, an index of the attributes of masculinity, including virility. This is why the active role in *macho-joto* relations carries no stigma. Indeed, in the communities where we worked, men who have sex with both *jotos* and women are not distinguished from those who only have sex with females, for they are also *chingones*. There is no distinct linguistic term to designate *machos* who have sex with *jotos,* nor are they socially or culturally set off in any way. By contrast, the passive role in sexual intercourse (whether anal or vaginal) is seen as a source of pollution, reduced autonomy, shame, and powerlessness—whether for women or *jotos*. Indeed, the ambiguity of the *joto,* and the stigma he/she bears, is motivated precisely by the paradox presented by a being who is born with a closed male body but who subjects him/her-self to being opened and penetrated like a woman.

The simultaneous use of female and male pronouns in the preceding paragraph is meant to index the contradictory gender identity of the *joto*. In the rural areas where we conducted our research, *jotos* are perceived as having male bodies but they are symbolically construed as women in numerous contexts. For example, *jotos* dress as women on festive occasions, wear make-up, adopt female names, and use female pronouns to refer to each other. They often engage in feminized occupations such as work in restaurants. They never have sexual relations with each other but only with *machos*. Indeed, when one informant was asked whether *jotos* had sex with each other, she answered that this would be "impossible," since it would be like two women "going to bed" together (lesbianism is not a culturally acknowledged possibility).[22] She explained that *jotos* themselves said they were women born in men's bodies (and indeed, some of them take female hormones in order to make their bodies more feminine).

Neither wholly male nor wholly female, *jotos* are interstitial beings who transgress and confound the power-laden categories of gender. Part of the stigma borne by the *joto* is his/her very anomaly and, as Mary Douglas has argued, that which is ambiguous, anomalous, discordant, or interstitial vis-à-vis dominant categories of socio-cultural order is often stigmatized or made the object of humor, as indeed the *jotos* are.

Jotos are anomalous in numerous ways. On the one hand, they are beings with male bodies who are penetrated like women. On the other hand, they are symbolic women who behave with the sexual license of men and for whom sex is a source of pleasure and not a reproductive activity. Indeed, this is why *jotos* are also called *putos, putas* being women whose sexuality has escaped the bounds of the patriarchal family and is "mis-used" for pleasure and profit rather than for "legitimate" reproductive ends. Though *putas* are women, their deviation from the norms of "respectable" female sexuality paradoxically masculinizes them. Thus, the stigma borne by the *joto* (like his/her identity) is multiple and contradictory: he/she is stigmatized as a man for being feminine and as a woman for being masculine.

However, rural northern Mexicans' attitudes to *jotos* differ from Anglos' attitudes to homosexuals. Though the *joto* is stigmatized, he/she is not ostracized and marginalized in the same way as the North American homosexual. For example, in one community, *jotos* run a restaurant which is patronized by "respectable people" (*personas de respeto*). The owner, a *joto,* is a pillar of the community, who is respected for supporting his mother and siblings, and who is invited to important community functions. Another *joto,* (who is, however, closeted) is on the Church Committee (otherwise integrated by "decent" and respected women). Indeed, some of the women from this same Committee helped *jotos* to dress for the bathing suit competition which was one of the events of a non-public, regional *joto* beauty contest celebrated in the local restaurant. While it is not quite "respectable" for women to be too friendly with *jotos,* some mentioned lending *jotos* feminine apparel for wear on festive occasions, and others spoke highly of one *joto*'s domestic skills, commenting with approval on the cleanliness and orderliness of his/her home. On the whole, though *jotos* are stigmatized, they are more objects of pity and amusement than of horror and avoidance. And "decent" women's attitudes to *jotos* are more positive than their attitudes to "bad women" who have sex outside of the bonds of matrimony, to prostitutes (*putas, mujeres prostituidas*) who sell their bodies to men, or to concubines (*concubinas*) who are involved in more permanent extra-marital liaisons and who receive some economic support from men.[23]

Rural northern Mexicans' attitudes to male pre- and extra-marital sex are contradictory. On the one hand, pre-/extra-marital "conquests" are viewed as an expression of "masculine nature" and as a sign of masculine virility which can increase the symbolic capital of males. Men, unlike women, are perceived as having sex for pleasure and not just for reproduction, and are considered to have only a limited degree of control over their sexual "instincts." On the other hand, community sanctions militate against pre-/extra-marital sexual liaisons with "decent" women which sully the honor of these females and their families.

However, the pool of "prostituted women" who have no honor and thus are potential pre-/extra-marital sexual partners for men, has been decreased by the efforts and actions of "decent" women. In the communities we worked in, "good" women had succeeded in shutting down the houses of female prostitution which they saw as a threat to the family. These "decent" women tacitly demonstrated a greater tolerance for male sexual encounters with *jotos* than for those with female prostitutes or concubines. Whereas women did not fear that their husbands would abandon them for or divert household resources to supporting *jotos* who cannot have children, they perceived that there was always a risk of desertion or of diminished economic support if men's extra-marital partners were female prostitutes or concubines.

In short, community sanctions against extra-marital sex with "decent" women, as well as married women's opposition to their husbands' relations with female prostitutes or concubines, have contributed to making *jotos* more available as pre-/extra-marital sexual partners for men.[24] But *macho-joto* relations may not just be a function of limitations on the availability of female sexual partners. Carrier notes that there is a Mexican saying, " 'the woman for her beauty, the man for his narrowness,' the implication being that a man's tight anus is better than a woman's vagina" ("Sexual Behavior" 84). This suggests that *jotos* are themselves objects of masculine desire. Though more research is necessary on this issue, it is possible that for *machos,* anal penetration of *jotos* involves a particularly erotic intersection of power/pleasure–*chingar,* and hence, to emasculate, another man may represent the ultimate validation of masculinity.

In our examination of the regime of gender, power, and pleasure which characterizes northern Mexico, our preliminary investigation in rural areas has led us to concur with the results of Carrier's long-term research on sexuality in urban areas and with his identification of the "high risk" groups and activities which may be implicated in HIV transmission. Carrier and Mexican AIDS researchers have concluded that in Mexico, males engaging in "homosexual" and "bisexual" practices have the highest risk of becoming infected with HIV ("Sexual Behavior" 3). However, based on the results of a seroprevalence study conducted by Mexican researchers in Guadalajara, Carrier has observed that not all "homosexual"/"bisexual" males are at equal risk for seropositivity. Those who only engage in "receptive anal intercourse," are at much higher risk of contracting HIV than those only engaging in "insertive anal intercourse" ("Sexual Behavior" 14).

In addition, the Guadalajara study identified a group of "homosexual" males who differ from both *machos* and *jotos* in that they play both the active and the passive roles in anal intercourse. According to Carrier, those "males playing both ('ambos') sexual roles in anal intercourse appear to be at higher risk than the 'activos' but at lower risk than the 'pasivos' " ("Sexual Behavior" 5). Significantly, males playing both roles are called "internationals," a term which indexes the "foreignness" of practices which are much more like those of American gays than the ones discussed here. Carrier suggests that "internationals" tend to be middle class and that their divergence from the type of *macho-joto* relationship discussed here is a result of influences from the US and the impact of the gay liberation movement in Mexico ("Sexual Behavior" 9).[25] In the areas where we carried out our preliminary study, where the population is largely composed of agriculturalists and rural workers, there were no "internationals."

Though research on AIDS and sexuality in Mexico has focused more on men than on women, the female partners of "bisexual" males (whether *putas* or "decent" women) are also clearly at risk, especially if they practice anal intercourse to preserve their virginity or as a form of birth control ("Sexual Behavior" 16). In addition, since HIV can be transmitted *in utero,* fetuses can contract the virus from infected mothers.

Research on sexuality in Mexico is meager. However, information provided by other studies does suggest that the types of erotic practices and relationships discussed here are characteristic of both rural and urban areas outside of the northern region ("Sexual Behavior" 1, 17 note 1). In addition, Lancaster's work in Nicaragua demonstrates that these practices are not confined to Mexico.

Interviews conducted by J. Raul Magaña, Director of Community Research of the Orange County AIDS Community Education Project, with undocumented Mexican farmworkers in California, have uncovered patterns of male sexual behavior similar to those described in this paper ("Sexual Behavior" 17 note 1). These interviews provide additional support for the hypothesis advanced here, namely, that "homosexual" and "bisexual" practices may be key to HIV transmission among persons of Mexican origins in the United States, and possibly, among other Latino groups such as Cubans.[26] However, it is important to stress that there are key differences in class, ethnicity, etc., within as well as among Latino groups in the US. Neither the Cuban- nor the Mexican-origin population in the US is a homogeneous group. Variables such as class, ethnicity, locality, and the character of immigration (among others) must be taken into account when doing AIDS research. In addition, there may be significant differences in the epidemiology of

HIV between Mexican immigrants who have not been in the US for long and persons of Mexican origin born in the US. One goal for future research would be to determine the extent to which sexual practices among Mexican-Americans have been influenced by the Anglo model.

Our hypothesis is consonant with the available epidemiological AIDS data for US "Hispanics" presented in the preceding section. The evidence suggests that our hypothesis merits further investigation. This raises the issue of how such research should be conducted.

AIDS Research Among Latinos: Methodological Issues

A reliance on epistemological assumptions and research methodologies which ignore socio-cultural differences, as well as the use of Anglo categories of ethnicity and sexuality, has led researchers in the United States to overlook the role of sexual practices in the transmission of HIV among Latinos, particularly those of Mexican origins. In order to investigate patterns of HIV transmission and AIDS infection, the scientific community has delimited "risk behaviors" following a Western epidemiological pattern. The emerging profile of "at-risk populations" comprises male homosexuals, IV drug users, either male or female, and their sexual partners and children. But Western epidemiological profiles cannot automatically be generalized to minority groups in the US.

The stereotypical figure of the AIDS sufferer which still inhabits the popular imagination is that of the "homosexual white male." However, a scientific discourse which invests "risk" in individual behaviors and inscribes it in personal rather than social bodies, has displaced the earlier emphasis on "groups-at-risk" (i.e., the gay community), which characterized applied research and the warning messages delivered at the onset of the AIDS epidemic.[27] But this Western epistemological and methodological individualism ignores that patterns of disease transmission are socially and culturally produced. What is needed is a research methodology which is sensitive to the impact of cultural differences and social distinctions (class, ethnicity, etc.) on HIV transmission and AIDS infection. Though research on AIDS is best carried out by an inter-disciplinary team, the sensitivity to social and cultural differences which is the hallmark of anthropological methods of investigation and analysis, can make a key contribution to generating appropriate methodologies.

Research teams equipped with promptly designed survey questionnaires have been knocking at the doors of family dwellings in "Hispanic" barrios—whenever and wherever funding for such purposes is available—eliciting "confessions" and discerning "the truth," in other words, who is a self-confessed "homosexual" or IV drug user and how many are "out there." However, it is difficult to identify and investigate the role of sexual practices in HIV transmission through a methodology based on interviews and questionnaires which deploy an etic idiom, a "majority" discourse, and which are administered by researchers who do not establish relations of *confianza* (trust, openness) with their subjects. Among Latinos, a culturally motivated silence surrounds sexuality and makes the frank and open response to direct, explicit questions by a stranger to whom nothing is owed an unlikely outcome. Moreover, questions cast in etic terms are often culturally unintelligible. And precisely because the behaviors under scrutiny have been integral to the construction of a stigmatized "other," research on the prevalence of "risk-behaviors" in minority communities presents "poignant difficulties" (Communication Technologies 6). The issues raised by research on AIDS among Latinos are not just methodological but also political.

Conclusions: The Politics of Saying and Not-Saying

For years most Americans were content to imagine the Latin world as a tropical paradise or a giant border town, a torrid zone just across the line of sexual decorum, that most heavily policed boundary in the American psyche. (Rodriguez 84)

stigma ... 1 a *archaic*: a scar left by a hot iron: BRAND b: a mark of shame or discredit: STAIN c: an identifying mark or characteristic; *specif*: a specific diagnostic sign of a disease.... (*Webster's Seventh New Collegiate Dictionary*)

As Cerullo and Hammonds point out, the nexus of "exotic" sexual practices and disease has long characterized Western discourses of domination which have stigmatized "others" and legitimated their subordination. Not only blacks, but also Latinos have been the object of dominant discourses which promote constructions of an "other" sexuality beyond "the bounds of decency," of an out-of-control concupiscence as lush and as torrid as the tropical jungles which are our origin sites in the Anglo imagination.

Such Anglo stereotypes have blocked the investigation of the role of sexual practices in HIV transmission among minorities. For in the Anglo imagination, the sexuality of the ethnic "other" was torrid but always "heterosexual." Between the Anglo image of the "homosexual" on the one hand, and the "Latin macho" or "black superstud" on the other, there is a great gulf. But by dismantling these stereotypes and breaking the silences which have obscured issues of sexuality and AIDS in US minority communities, are we not providing dominant groups with a further pretext to stigmatize us? Engaging in a public discourse which articulates the connection between sexual practices and AIDS may expose minorities to the homophobia as well as the racism of Anglos.

In this era of the "attractive packaging" of the "Hispanic," fear of the stigma of "homosexuality" and "bisexuality" has contributed to the silence in the Latino community about AIDS in general and about the role of sexual practices in HIV transmission in particular. Indeed, Latino AIDS activists have criticized the leadership of the Latino community for their refusal to deal with the issue of AIDS in the face of the devastating impact of the disease on their constituencies (Johnson, Muñoz, and Pares). According to José Pares, a Puerto Rican working with the Multicultural Concerns Committee of the AIDS Action Committee of Boston:

> In the Latino community there is still resistance among the leadership.... AIDS is not a priority for their agencies. They have said that explicitly.... Some leaders are starting to get involved. I personally have problems with some of them because they want to address AIDS in the Latino community just as a health issue and keep the gay issue aside. Maybe they will address i.v. drug use, but nothing else. (Johnson, Muñoz, and Pares 31)

According to Hammonds, a parallel silence has characterized the black leadership's and media's response to AIDS; and when issues of sexuality and HIV transmission are raised, they are "dealt with in a very conservative and problematic fashion." But as she points out, this "sexual conservatism" falls into the trap of reproducing the dominant discourse's definition of the nexus of deviancy, sexuality, and disease (31–33).

Though the reasons for these silences are evident and understandable, the refusal to deal with AIDS and sexuality is deadly. Not only have these silences hindered research on the epidemiology of the disease, but what is worse, they have resulted in a lack of awareness about the forms of HIV transmission in minority communities, and that lack of awareness is killing people.

Clearly, the situation of minority "homosexuals" and "bisexuals" is very different from that of gay white men (Morales 3). As a result of these differences as well as of a lack of information about the links between their sexual practices and HIV transmission, many "homosexual" or "bisexual" Latinos still believe that AIDS is a "gay white disease." Since they do not think of themselves as either "gay" or "white," they do not realize that they are at risk. As concerned minority leaders have noted, "the principal identification may be with ethnicity, and not with sexual orientation. This is reflected in individuals who engage in homosexual activities, but who do not perceive themselves as gay" (National Minority AIDS Council 23). In this same vein, Peterson has commented that:

> Some minority gay men may erroneously perceive that anal intercourse is "safe" if they are the "active" rather than "receptive" partner [since the insertor role is not construed as "homosexual"] or that high-risk sexual activity is "safe" if they only engage in these activities with minority rather than white men. (5)

The implications of denial are particularly deadly for Latina women who have to contend with yet other silences. Because of the way in which gender and sexuality are constructed, Latino men are not accountable to their female partners for their sexual practices or histories. As Worth and Rodriguez note: "Many of the female sex partners of these men are unaware of their bisexuality, and, therefore, not aware that they are at risk of HIV infection" (64). For Latina women, to raise issues of sexuality is not only to challenge the male authority they are culturally enjoined to obey, but also to put their reputations as women on the line and to risk being perceived as "loose" or "immoral." Thus, Latina women may be reluctant to ask their men to engage in "safe sex practices" or to use condoms. For example, "Puerto Rican women . . . professed the wish to have their partners use condoms, but felt unable to ask them to do so for fear of being rejected or superseding their defined role" (65). For Latina women, breaking the silence involves particular risks and ultimately necessitates a politics which challenges the patriarchal constructions which have given men control over our bodies and sexuality.

We almost did not write this paper. But after much discussion, we decided that maintaining the silence is to cede terrain, is to let dominant discourses define the politics of ethnicity, disease, sexuality, and morality. As Hammonds writes:

> For progressives, feminists, and gay activists, the AIDS crisis represents a crucial time when the work we have done on sexuality and sexual politics will be most needed to frame the fight against AIDS in political terms that move the politics of sexuality out of the background and challenge the repressive policies that threaten not only the people with this disease but all of us. (36)

Challenging these policies will involve forming new coalitions based on a postmodernist consciousness of "affinity" rather than an essentialist construction of "identity,"[28] and establishing political alliances with those who are also "other" and "different." Such coalitions are already being formed: witness the Multicultural Concerns Committee of Boston (Johnson, Muñoz, and Pares). Through such alliances we can construct affinity out of otherness and forge an "oppositional consciousness" based on an "appropriation of negation" (Haraway) which revalues the signs of difference and contests the power of dominant discourses to define not only who we are and how we live, but also, how we die.

NOTES

1. We would like to express our gratitude to a number of persons who have helped us in writing this paper (though they are not responsible for its contents). Alberta Parker, MD, MPH, Clinical Professor of Community Health, Emeritus, School of Public Health, UC Berkeley, and

Warren Winkelstein, Jr., MD, MPH, Professor of Epidemiology, School of Public Health, UC Berkeley, spent a great deal of time discussing and reviewing, in the context of our argument, the statistical information and epidemiological patterns presented in this paper, and we are very grateful for their assistance. We are indebted to Mindy Fullilove, MD, Director, Multicultural Inquiry and Research on AIDS, Center for AIDS Prevention Studies, UC San Francisco, for providing us with copies of the Centers for Disease Control *PIDS* 1987 computer printouts. Thanks to Dr. Daniel Nugent, ILAS, University of Texas-Austin, for his criticisms, comments, and editorial assistance. Thanks to Silvia F. Villarreal, MD, Assistant Clinical Professor of Pediatrics, UC San Francisco, for providing unpublished papers and relevant information. We thank John Peterson, PhD, Research Associate, Multicultural Inquiry and Research on AIDS, Center for AIDS Prevention Studies, UC San Francisco, for bringing J.M. Carrier's work to our attention and providing copies of Carrier's papers. Thanks to DeAnn Pendry, PhD student in Anthropology, University of Texas-Austin, for providing information on the sexual practices of urban working-class Cuban immigrants in the early 1980s.

2. The trope is José Martí's.

3. We are using "subjects" in the Foucauldian sense: "There are two meanings of the word subject: subject to someone else by control and dependence, and tied to his own identity by a conscience or self-knowledge. Both meanings suggest a form of power which subjugates and makes subject to" ("The Subject" 212).

4. "Latino" has emerged as a politicized term which designates all Spanish-speaking peoples of Latin American origin in the US and is the counter-discourse alternative to "Hispanic." In this paper we use the third person plural pronoun when referring to "Hispanics" in order to signify the otherness of this category of dominant discourse, and the first person plural pronoun when referring to Latinos, to signify our inclusion in a category which despite its "artificiality" recognizes the links among peoples of Latin American origins without erasing their differences (cf. Acuña).

5. "Chicano," as Acuña states, "for many years was a pejorative term whose origin is unknown. Often, however, middle-class Mexicans used it disparagingly—meaning low-class Mexicans. In the late 1960s, youth movements and political activists gave 'Chicano' a political connotation (similar to the way 'Black' became a more political term for 'Negro')" (Acuña ix note).

6. This is a paraphrase of a comment by James Cockcroft.

7. AIDS (Acquired Immunodeficiency Syndrome) is an infectious disease caused by the Human Immunodeficiency Virus (HIV). The virus is transmitted in only three ways: 1) through sexual contact with infected persons; 2) through exposure to blood or blood products contaminated with HIV; and 3) perinatally, i.e., from infected mothers to their fetuses during pregnancy (*in utero*). The period between infection with HIV and development of AIDS (the ultimate stage of HIV infection) is variable, although estimated to be over seven years (Curran et al.).

8. E.g., see Bakeman et al.; Centers for Disease Control 1986; M. Fullilove; Hopkins; Morales 1987; Peterson; Rogers and Williams.

9. This information was obtained from the Centers for Disease Control, *AIDS Public Information Data Set* (*PIDS*). This data set includes information on sex, race/ethnic group, transmission category, etc. for AIDS cases reported to the Centers for Disease Control as of October 5, 1987; it excludes cases of non-whites born in Haiti and Central Africa.

10. The cumulative incidence rates represent the number of AIDS cases per million population occurring in each racial/ethnic group since 1981. The derived ratios suggest the relative chances of contracting AIDS in each racial/ethnic group.

11. See R. Fullilove; Johnson and Murray: 60.

12. However, as we go on to discuss at the end of this section, the use of "homosexual" and "bisexual" as categories in AIDS research among minorities is problematic since black and "Hispanic" men frequently do not use these categories to identify themselves (even though, from an Anglo point of view, they are "homosexual" and "bisexual"). Thus, though Rogers and Williams's observations are significant, the percentages of "homosexual" versus "bisexual" males that they provide must be seen as tentative.

13. This is not to say that location is never a significant variable; for example, urban areas in the United States and northern Europe with the largest concentrations of homosexual men—New York, San Francisco, Los Angeles, Paris, Geneva, Amsterdam, and Copenhagen—also have

the highest incidence rates of AIDS cases, and current research indicates that a high correlation exists between seropositivity and geographical closeness to these high-risk areas (Carrier, "Mexican Male" 6–7).

14. Dooley Worth and Ruth Rodriguez's study of HIV transmission among Puerto Rican women on Manhattan's Lower East Side is consonant with Castro and Manoff's results. Worth and Rodriguez conclude that the "AIDS deaths among Puerto Rican women in this neighborhood are predominantly intravenous drug abuse related," though they also raise the issue of HIV transmission through sex with "bisexual" male partners (63–64).

15. The "alibi" is a concept developed by Roland Barthes to characterize the cultural process whereby history is transformed into nature (127–31).

16. In what follows, we will try to avoid using these terms except 1) when writing about Anglos; 2) when citing other researchers; 3) when they are absolutely essential as shorthand English glosses for Mexican practices.

17. In Northern Mexico, *hombre* is the unmarked term, the equivalent of "man" in English. *Macho* is a marked term used to designate men who demonstrate their possession of the "natural" attributes of masculinity. In this paper, we have used *macho* instead of *hombre* in order to stress that those involved in relations with *jotos* are considered to be "normal," masculine men.

18. These rural communities are located in northern Mexico, in a geographic area different from that of the cities where Carrier worked. In order to protect the identities of our informants, we provide no information as to the location of their communities.

19. In Spanish, the primary meaning of *huevos* is eggs. However, in Mexico, *huevos* is also used to denote testicles and indeed, in practice, this has become the most common meaning of the term (eggs are called *blanquillos* instead). It seems that this extension of the semantic range of the term *huevos* has been effected through iconism based on a perceived resemblance between the respective shapes of testicles and eggs, and between the fragility of testicles and that of eggs.

20. The body, like myth, is not read as a "semiological system but as an inductive one. Where there is only an equivalence, he [the social actor] sees a kind of causal process: the signifier and the signified have, in his eyes, a natural relationship" (Barthes 131). The iconic and indexical character of many somatic signs facilitates their apprehension as facts of nature rather than culture, and gives these signs an alibi.

21. See Paz 84–86 on the *chingada;* however, in northern Mexico, the *chingada* is not identified with the *Malinche.* Due to the distinct character of the process of conquest and colonization in the north of Mexico, the *Malinche* is not a salient cultural sign.

22. Though women are objects of male desire, they are never subjects of their own desire. Sex is something they are polluted by, not something they enjoy. "Decent" women, it is thought, only engage in sex as a duty to their husbands and in order to have children. Thus, lesbianism is inconceivable.

23. Of course, these attitudes may be changing as information about the epidemiology of AIDS infection becomes more available.

24. The relationship between male "bisexuality" and the availability of pre-/extra-marital female sexual partners is also discussed by Carrier in terms similar to those advanced here ("Sexual Behavior" 77–79; "Mexican Male" 9–10).

25. See Lancaster for the impact of Western sexual models in Nicaragua. Lancaster argues that though the Western sexual lexicon is beginning to be used, "the logic of the sexual system remains traditional, native, and popular" (119), and the *machista-cochon* relationship (very similar to the *macho-joto* relationship discussed here) continues to predominate over Western-oriented "homosexuality."

26. DeAnn Pendry, PhD student, Department of Anthropology, University of Texas-Austin, worked during 1980–81 with Cubans in Fort Chaffee, Arkansas, who had immigrated to the US in 1980. She reports that the sexual practices of these Cubans, who were largely urban working class, were rather similar to those described for northern Mexicans in this paper and in Carrier's articles, and to those described for Nicaraguans by Lancaster (Pendry, personal communication). The socially and culturally "male" partner (probably the active partner in anal intercourse), sometimes called a *bugarón* by others, did not consider himself to be a "homosexual" but instead thought of himself as a "man." Indeed, one such man was offended when asked whether he were a

"homosexual." The feminized partner (probably the passive partner in anal intercourse), frequently called a *maricón,* a *pato* (duck), or a *ganso* (goose)—purportedly because of the way he/she walks—did answer positively when asked whether he/she were a "homosexual." *Maricones* used feminine pronouns and adjectives to refer to themselves and each other, dressed effeminately, wore make-up, used hair rollers, etc. In addition, some of them took hormones to feminize their bodies; those with breasts wore bras.

Though Pendry agrees that these erotic practices are socially and culturally constituted, she also raised the issue of the extent to which the sexuality of those 1980 Cuban immigrants who had been in jail had been conditioned by their prison experiences. As Lancaster points out, the *machista/cochon* relationship in Nicaragua (and the *macho/joto* in northern Mexico) is similar to the sorts of sexual relations characteristic in prison populations in the US. Clearly, prison experiences are an important factor to take into account in conducting AIDS research.

Pendry's information suggests that the hypothesis presented in this paper would be applicable to the group with which she worked. However, there may be differences in the construction of sexuality between middle-class Cubans who immigrated to the US after 1959 and who may have been influenced by the Anglo model, and these urban working-class Cubans who immigrated during 1980. Further research is needed on these issues.

27. This shift is clearly discernible in United States Dept. of Health and Human Services, *Understanding AIDS: A Message from the Surgeon General.* What is also evident in this report, written in order to "educate" the general public about AIDS, is the extent to which the disease is being used to argue against "deviancy" and as a pretext for inculcating "normal" behaviors, such as heterosexuality and monogamy ("safe" practices) as well as to discourage the use of all drugs, including alcohol.

28. See Haraway for a definition of these terms and for a discussion of a postmodernist politics of difference.

WORKS CITED

"Acquired Immunodeficiency Syndrome (AIDS) among Blacks and Hispanics—United States" *Morbidity and Mortality Weekly Reports* 35.42 (1986): 655–56.

Acuña, Rodolfo. *Occupied America: A History of Chicanos.* 3rd ed. New York: Harper, 1988.

Bakeman, R., J.R. Lumb, and D.W. Smith. "AIDS Statistics and the Risks for Minorities." *AIDS Research* 2 (1986): 249–52.

Bakeman, R., E. McCray, et al. "The Incidence of AIDS among Blacks and Hispanics." *Journal of the National Medical Association* 79.9 (1987): 921–28.

Barthes, Roland, *Mythologies.* New York: Hill and Wang, 1972.

Carrier, J.M. "Mexican Male Bisexuality." *Bisexualities: Theory and Research.* Ed. Fritz Klein, MD, and Thomas J. Wolf. New York: Haworth, 1985. 75–85.

———— "Sexual Behavior and the Spread of AIDS in Mexico." *Medical Anthropology,* 10: 1989. 129–142.

Castro, Kenneth G., MD, and Susan B. Manoff, MD. "The Epidemiology of AIDS in Hispanic Adolescents." *The AIDS Challenge Prevention: Education for Young People.* Ed. M. Quackenbush, M. Nelson, and K. Clark. Santa Cruz, CA: Network, 1988.

Cerullo, Margaret, and Evelynn Hammonds. "AIDS in Africa: The Western Imagination and the Dark Continent." *Radical America* 21.2–3 (1987–88): 17–23.

"Chavez Ends Fast over Pesticide Use." *New York Times* 22 Aug. 1988: A12.

Communication Technologies and Research and Decisions Corporation. *Reaching Ethnic Communities in the Fight against AIDS: Summary of Major Findings from Focus Groups with Leaders from Minority Communities.* Prepared for San Francisco AIDS Foundation: n.p., 1986.

Curran, J.W., et al. "Epidemiology of HIV Infection and AIDS in the United States." *Science* 239 (1988): 610–16.

Dvorchak, Robert, and Lisa Levitt Ryckman. "Cultural Practices, Poverty Working against Minorities." *San Francisco Examiner* 31 July 1988: A2.

Foucault, Michel. *The History of Sexuality.* Trans. Robert Hurley. Vol. 1. New York: Vintage, 1980.

———— "The Subject and Power." *Michel Foucault: Beyond Structuralism and Hermeneutics.* Ed. Hubert L. Dreyfus and Paul Rabinow. Chicago: Univ. of Chicago Press, 1982. 208–26.

Fullilove, Mindy, MD. "Ethnic Minority Women and AIDS." *Multicultural Inquiry and Research on AIDS Newsletter* 2.2 (1988): 4–5.

Fullilove, Robert. "Minorities and AIDS: A Review of Recent Publications." *Multicultural Inquiry and Research on AIDS Newsletter* 2.1 (1988): 3–5.

Hammonds, Evelynn. "Race, Sex, AIDS: The Construction of 'Other.' " *Radical America* 20.6 (1986–87): 28–36.

Haraway, Donna. "A Manifesto for Cyborgs: Science, Technology and Socialist Feminism in the 1980's." *Socialist Review* 80 (1985): 65–107.

Hayes-Bautista, David, and Jorge Chapa. "Latino Terminology: Conceptual Bases for Standardized Terminology." *American Journal of Public Health* 77.1 (1987): 61–68.

Henry, John C. "Texas Hispanics Starring in G.O.P. Campaign Script." *Austin American Statesman* 18 Aug. 1988: A7.

Hopkins, Donald. "AIDS in Minority Populations in the United States." *Public Health Reports* 102.6 (1987): 677–81.

"Human Immunodeficiency Virus Infection in the United States: A Review of Current Knowledge." *Morbidity and Mortality Weekly Report* 36.5–6 (1987): 1–48.

Johnson, Diane, and John F. Murray, MD. "AIDS without End." *New York Review of Books* 35.13 (1988): 57–63.

Johnson, Paula, Doralba Muñoz, and José Pares. "Multi-Cultural Concerns and AIDS Action: Creating an Alternative." *Radical America* 21.2–3 (1987): 24–34.

Lancaster, Roger N. "Subject Honor and Object Shame: The Construction of Male Homosexuality and Stigma in Nicaragua." *Ethnology* 28.2 (1988): 111–26.

Morales, Edward. "AIDS & Ethnic Minority Researches." *Multicultural Inquiry and Research on AIDS Newsletter* 1.3 (1987): 2.

———— "AIDS and HIV Infection among Latins and Other Ethnic and Racial Minorities in the United States." Unpublished essay, 1987.

National Minority AIDS Council. "Report on AIDS and Ethnic Minorities." Unpublished report, 1987.

Paz, Octavio. *The Labyrinth of Solitude; The Other Mexico; Return to the Labyrinth of Solitude; Mexico and the United States; The Philanthropic Ogre.* Trans. Lysander Kemp, Yara Milos, and Rachel Phillips Belash. New York: Grove, 1985.

Peterson, John L. "AIDS among Minority Men." *American Psychologist* 1988.

Rodriguez, Richard. "The Fear of Losing a Culture." *Time* 11 July 1988: 84.

Rogers, M., and W. Williams. "AIDS in Blacks and Hispanics: Implications for Prevention." *Issues in Science and Technology* 3.3 (1987): 89–94.

Ryckman, Lisa Levitt. "Entire Generation of Minorities at Risk from AIDS Virus." *San Francisco Examiner* 31 July 1988: A2.

United States. Dept. of Health and Human Services. *Understanding AIDS: A Message from the Surgeon General.* Washington: GPO, 1988.

United States. Dept. of Health and Human Services. Public Health Service. Centers for Disease Control. *AIDS Public Information Data Set (PIDS).* N.p.: n.p., 5 Oct. 1987.

Vickers, Nancy J. "This Heraldry in Lucrece's Face." *The Female Body in Western Culture.* Ed. Susan Rubin Suleiman. Cambridge, MA: Harvard Univ. Press, 1986. 209–22.

Webster's Seventh New Collegiate Dictionary. Springfield, MA: Merriam, 1972.

Worth, Dooley, and Ruth Rodriguez. "Latina Women and AIDS." *Radical America* 20.6 (1986–87): 63–67.

Yankauer, Alfred, MD. "Hispanic/Latino—What's in a Name?" *American Journal of Public Health* 77.1 (1987): 15–17.

8

From Nation to Family:
Containing African AIDS

Cindy Patton

Cindy Patton, a writer and a long-time activist in the lesbian/gay community, has in recent years focused her energies on the struggle against AIDS. In this essay, she argues that international health administrators have done all too little in Africa to promote the kinds of education, community organizing, and improved blood-banking which would truly aid in preventing the transmission of HIV. Instead they have mendaciously and disastrously urged on Africans the view that safety from AIDS can be found within the fold of the bourgeois family. Patton shows that just as formerly, under the colonialists, the nation was the chief unit of administration in Africa, so now the family is; that international health workers are in a sense the successors of the colonialists; and that administration now, as then, is murderous in its consequences. Cindy Patton is the author of Inventing AIDS *(1991), and she is assistant professor of Communications at Temple University.*

Current AIDS-control efforts have invented a heterosexual "African AIDS" that promotes a new kind of colonial domination by reconstructing Africa as an uncharted, supranational mass. Whatever the overt concerns of international health workers for containing AIDS in (within?) the continent, their construal of "Africa" as the margin of economic/cultural "development" and as the "heart" of the AIDS epidemic helps to stabilize a Euro-America adrift in a postmodern condition of lost metanarratives and occluded origins. As a totalizing grand history of nations has given way to a transcendent account of chance intersections of germs and bodies, the map of the postcolonial world has now been redrawn as a graph of epidemiologic strike rates. Because international AIDS policy has discouraged or overlooked serious attempts to prevent HIV transmission through health education, community organizing, and improved bloodbanking, this new Africa-with-no-borders functions as a giant agar plate, etched by the "natural history" of the AIDS epidemic.[1]

The very labeling of "African AIDS" as a heterosexual disease quiets the Western fear that heterosexual men will need to alter their own sexual practices and identity. If the proximate (homosexual) AIDS allows such men to ignore their local complicity in "dangerous" practices that lead to the infection of ("their") women, then a distant "African AIDS," by correlating heterosexual danger with Otherness/thereness, performs the final expiative act for a Western heterosexual masculinity that refuses all containment. Erased in this process are the colonially inscribed borders of sub-Saharan countries while new borders are drawn between the "African family" and a "modernizing society" populated by "single people" who have been dying at an appalling rate throughout the epidemic. The nation, once the colonial administrative unit *par excellence,* has been re-placed in the minds of healthworkers with (an image of) the bourgeois family, thereby constituting what had never truly existed before in Africa as the only defense against modernization and its "diseases." In what follows I explore some of the implications of this movement from nation to family as the preferred prophylaxis in the catastrophe of "African AIDS."

Mapping "African AIDS"

Accompanying a recent *New York Times* article "AIDS in Africa: A Killer Rages On" (whose headline continues "AIDS Is Spreading Rapidly and Ominously Throughout Africa") is a nearly full-page chart, "AIDS in Africa: An Atlas of Spreading Tragedy."[2] These headlines displace responsibility for the epidemic—who exactly is this killer? what is the tragedy?—and elide the disease's biological mechanics in exploiting its symbolic resonances. The article's spatialization of AIDS in its accompanying map of the continent simultaneously locates countries and underscores the irrelevance of their borders: in *this* Africa, disease transcends nation. Replacing what had been colonialism's heart of dark-ness is the calculated horror of a new interior density, represented on the map by dark-to-light shadings corresponding to HIV attack rates. The "AIDS belt" supposed to exist in central Africa is depicted here not only as the "heart" of the regional epidemic but as the imagined origin of the entire global pandemic. Yet the "evidence" employed by the map reveals the duplicities of Western discourse about AIDS in Africa: seroprevalence rates for the continent are concocted from sensationalist media accounts of specific locations and from the records of epidemiologists working from strictly limited samples (often as few as 100 people) of pregnant women, prostitutes, and clients with sexually transmitted diseases. When not enough AIDS is found, it needs to be imagined, as the key to the *Times'* map suggests:

> The shadings on this map indicate the percentage of sexually active adults believed to be infected with the AIDS virus in major urban areas. Rural rates tend to be much lower. The numbers are based on the latest available data, which may understate current rates. Blank spots do not necessarily mean an absence of AIDS.

Despite its disclaimers about "missing data," there are in fact no "blank spots" on the map; the *Times* fills in the *entire* surface, lumping together countries with "infection rates less than 5 percent" with those for which "data [is] not available." Although we are told that high attack rates (of HIV, which is consistently conflated here with AIDS) are characteristic only of urban areas, whole countries are shaded to indicate "At least 5 percent to 10 percent," "At least 10 percent to 20 percent," and "At least 20 percent." The curious use of the non-exclusive "at least" for the increasingly darker/denser shad-ings suggests that errors in data will always underestimate "AIDS" for a country. But the note on "sources" at the bottom of the map gives us a clearer indication of the accuracy of the epidemiologic data from which the map is derived:

> Surveys of subgroups are useful but must be interpreted with caution. Urban infection rates cannot be extrapolated to rural areas. Rates among prostitutes, soldiers, hospital patients, and patients at clinics for sexually transmitted diseases tend to be far higher than in the population at large. Blood donor figures may overstate prevalence if donors are recruited among high-risk groups or understate it if efforts are made to avoid high-risk donors. Often, surveys of pregnant women visiting prenatal clinics are considered the best indicator of infection among the adult population.

In this brief summary of data offered for the twenty-four countries which appear to have data (this leaves as "blank spots" another twenty-nine, which include some of the continent's largest[3]), the *Times* acknowledges that seroprevalence studies vary from nation to nation, but all of these studies have been used indiscriminately to present the worst case scenario within any given country.

While HIV is certainly an important African health concern, seroprevalence rates are rising *everywhere* and not just in African locales. The *Times,* however, suggests no reason for singling out Africa as exceptional and offers no comparative data on rates in Euro-American or other global regions (Asia, the Pacific Rim, Eastern Europe, Central and South America, and the Caribbean are the real "blank spots" on the *Times'* map). The article's one comparison to the U.S. serves to inscribe "their AIDS" as heterosexual in comparison with "our AIDS":

> In contrast with the pattern in the United States, AIDS in Africa is spreading mainly through heterosexual intercourse, propelled by long-neglected epidemics of venereal disease that facilitates viral transmission. . . . In the United States, gay men and residents of a few inner-city pockets face comparable devastation, but over all, fewer than 1 percent of adults are believed to be infected with the AIDS virus.

"Inner-city pockets" is of course a reference to poor people of color, the internal blank spot of the U.S. If the horror of the American crisis is the confrontation (of white heterosexuals) with both homosexuality and the feared black underclass, the tragedy in Africa seems rather more unthinkable: "Strange new issues are in the air. Where the disease spread earliest and large numbers have already died, as in Uganda, frightened young men and women are starting to realize that even marriage may be risky."

If AIDS has been thought to sail or jet[4] between the Euro-American countries, it is represented by the *Times* as traveling by truck throughout Africa. An insert showing trucks on a dusty road and entitled "Dangerous Traffic" tells us that:

> The highways of East and Central Africa, such as this one west of Kampala, Uganda, have been major conduits for AIDS. A study in Kenya of 317 truck drivers of varied nationalities found that three-fourths frequently visited prostitutes but that only 30% ever used condoms. One in four was infected with HIV. In 1986, 35% of drivers studied in Kampala were infected. Most prostitutes and barmaids along trucking routes are infected.

While the direction of infection is obscured here (truck drivers to prostitutes or prostitutes to truck drivers?), the conflation of truckers with their penises and of roads with vaginas is abundantly clear. If truck drivers "unloading" their "dangerous cargo" is a more compelling trope than the usual evocation of urban prostitutes spewing germs to hapless clients, this is because the spread of AIDS in Africa is itself hardly unrelated to the spread of "modernization."

Inventing African AIDS

By 1986, Western media and scientists worldwide had created the linguistic distinction between "AIDS" and "African AIDS" that makes the *Times'* map readable. These designations are informal names for the more technical World Health Organization terms, Pattern One and Pattern Two. Pattern One describes epidemiologic scenarios where "homosexual behavior" and "drug injection" are considered the primary means of HIV transmission. Because Pattern One (or, as the unmarked category, simply "AIDS") is coded racially as "white," African-American communities—where homosexuality is presumed to be absent—are now said to exhibit features of Pattern Two ("African AIDS").

Pattern Two indicates places where transmission is held to be "almost exclusively heterosexual."[5] Synonymous with "African AIDS," Pattern Two is a linguistic construction
confusing an epidemiologic description (however unuseful) with an emerging "history"
of the epidemic. The Caribbean has "African AIDS" but Latin America has "AIDS,"
an unprecedented if barely conscious recognition of indigenous homosexualities. A third
category, Pattern Three, recognizes the emergence of "heterosexual" AIDS outside
Euro-America and Africa in places where HIV arrived "late" and largely through postcolonial sex tourism and international bloodbanking.

The "history" of the epidemic reflected in these categories inverts the crucial
epidemiologic issues. Rather than asking how HIV moved from the Pattern One countries (where AIDS was diagnosed first by epidemiologists' accounts) to the Pattern Two
countries, the scientifically endorsed history of AIDS shows HIV originating in Africa
and then moving to North America.[6] The scientific distinction between AIDS/gay/
white/Euro-American and African AIDS/heterosexual/black/African/U.S.-inner-city
neatly fails to inquire how HIV traveled from the bodies of U.S. homosexual men into
the bodies of "Africans" a continent and ocean away, or how "African AIDS" then
returned to diasporal African communities in the U.S. The blank spot within the Euro-
American mind makes it far easier to imagine an alternative causal chain running from
monkeys to Africans to queers than to recall the simple fact that the West exports huge
quantities of unscreened blood to its Third World client states (much less acknowledge
that black and white Americans have sex—gay as well as straight—and share needles
with each other).

This difference between Patterns One and Two thus helps white, Euro-American
heterosexuals evade the idea that they might themselves be vulnerable since African (and
African-American) heterosexuality is so evidently different than Euro-American. Euro-
American heterosexuality is "not at risk" as long as local AIDS is identified as homosexual
and heterosexual AIDS remains distant. This projected difference of African heterosexuality and the asserted absence of African homosexuality[7] continue to drive not only the
forms of epidemiologic research (for example, researchers have been more interested in
finding bizarre and distinctive "African" sexual practices[8] than in documenting transfusion-related cases) but also the forms of educational intervention whose focus in Africa
is almost exclusively on promoting monogamy or, in more "sensitive" campaigns, "stable
polygamy."

My earlier work on "African AIDS" investigated how Western scientific representations of the national and sexual cultures of postcolonial Africa direct the international AIDS research agenda. Reading conference documents and media reports on
"AIDS in Africa," I marked the links between apparently innocuous or obviously fantastic assumptions made about Africa(ns) within Western discourse and the conduct and
direction of Western science. In particular, I showed how the persistent Western description of Africa as a "catastrophe" and as "heterosexual" justified as altruistic genocidal
Western practices and policies toward their client-state "Others."

Because "African AIDS" is simultaneously "different" and "similar," conflicts in
Western AIDS discourse, ethics, and medical research can be rationalized by drawing
upon research undertaken throughout the continent. For example, while data from
African clinics convinces Westerners that heterosexual transmission is possible (because
all intercourse is the same), this same data is also read as suggesting that widespread
transmission among heterosexuals is not likely enough to require the universal adoption
of the condom (because Africans engage in other exotic sexual practices and polygamy).[9]
Diagnosis of AIDS in Africa is said to be unreliable because medical facilities are alleged
to be poor; this licenses demographers to multiply known cases by exorbitant factors in

order to obtain a "true" (i.e., catastrophic) picture of AIDS in "Africa." But "African" diagnosis becomes a problem (and for epidemiologists rather than clinicians) only because the definition of AIDS is derived from the U.S. experience of largely well-cared-for middle-class men who become inexplicably weak and unable to fight common illness. The fall from "previous health" is not a feasible diagnostic distinction in countries (or among U.S. women or those living in the inner city, for that matter) where people have received little health care or where infectious diseases and nutritional deficiencies make it difficult to distinguish between clinical AIDS and malaria, anaemia, tuberculosis, etc.

An important note on the terms I've employed here: in Western discourse, Africa, a continent of roughly eleven and a half million square miles and fifty-three countries, is treated as a homogeneous sociopolitical block. Yet this supposedly "unknown" continent—unknown, that is, to its pale neighbors to the north—is in fact far more culturally, linguistically, religiously, and socially diverse than North America and Europe. Collapsing the many cultures residing on the continent into "Africa" is an act of political and cultural violence. In order to complicate "Africa" as a Western construction, I employ the equivalent constructions "North American" and "Euro-America" to indicate the collection of relatively homogeneous northern administrative states as we appear to our southern neighbors. The resultant vagueness Euro-Americans will experience in this strategy should be read back from the "Other" point of view: "North Americans" in particular should consider their own discomfort at having their cultural space discursively reduced in this way.

But this is not the only critical reduction occurring in Western discourse about Africa: as a term, "Africa" can mean both the land mass and its people precisely because the people of Africa have been considered to be coextensive with the continent, a conflation I evoke through the shorthand "Africa(ns)." This conflation has been eloquently described by Frantz Fanon: what is done to the "African body," especially woman's body, is a metaphor for what is to be done to the continent, and vice versa.[10]

Imploding Borders

The flattening out of the racial, ethnic, and cultural diversity of non-European-descended Africans into a singular autochthonous people performed an important function during the era of colonialism. Carving up the land was not sufficient; a narrative reconstruction of Africa's "uncivilized" prehistory was necessary to justify the colonial presence. The colonial taxonomist's "racial" distributions—"semites," "hamites," "negroes," "nilotes," "half-hamites," "bantus," "khoisans," not to mention "Italians" and peoples of the Asian subcontinent ("Indian," another site of colonialist reduction through arbitrary racial taxonomic schemes)—mapped an Africa prior to colonial border construction in order to deny the social orders and political/cultural groups of *people* ("Zulus," "Sabaeans," "Berbers," "Ibos," etc.) who lived, intermarried, fought battles, and traded culture and religion with one another before the incursion of Europeans. These are peoples whose racial and sexual histories seemed always to defy the new administrative borders, but the Europeans still insisted that "natives" must be placed somewhere—spatialized—and organized properly through sexual and genealogical successions—temporalized.

Such a displacement of the political and social onto the sexual and racial has returned today, with similarly self-justificatory motives, as the narrative logic underwriting Western accounts of AIDS among the peoples of Africa. Again, spatial demarcation and temporal sequence organize historical narrative. In obvious ways ("AIDS began in Africa"), insidious ways ("AIDS 'jumped species' from green monkeys to 'African' humans"), and subtle ways (persistent descriptions of truck drivers, miners, "prostitutes," and soldiers traversing the continent), the Euro-American story of "African AIDS" concerns not only racial difference but also territory transected and borders gone out of control. But rather than continuing to adduce African "backwardness" as an excuse for colonial plunder, AIDS epidemiology offers "African sexuality" as a rationale for unethical experimentation and unwillingness to pursue education and community organizing projects that could decrease transmission of HIV. No longer content to carve up a massified Africa into "proper" nations, AIDS media reportage offers a view of African sexuality—alternately described as traditional (polygamy) or condemned as modern (rural-urban social breakdown resulting in "prostitution")—which now requires rapid reorganization into bourgeois families.

This is the side of "African AIDS" I wish to take up here: "containment" through the promotion of racist and heterophobic conceptions of "safe sex." Reading the *Times'* map alongside the new pamphlet series "Strategies for Hope," collaboratively produced by British international relief organizations and two African national AIDS committees,[11] I want to show how "self-help" manuals for use in Anglophone communities in Africa recall previous border constructions in seeking to promote as "safe sex" a bourgeois "African family" that has never in fact existed.

Strategies For Hope

With an international recession underway, the only capital-intensive educational projects possible in poor countries are collaborative ones with (largely) European international relief organizations. The set of concepts underlying "African AIDS" have become so naturalized today that such projects must rewrite local experience to conform to the internationally adopted narrative. The Euro-American fascination with a "different" African sexuality can routinely be glimpsed in epidemiologic studies and newspaper accounts (witness this sidebar to the *Times* article discussed previously):

> Studies in the United States show that transmission of the AIDS virus during vaginal intercourse is usually quite difficult, especially from female to male. But research in Africa has revealed conditions that multiply the danger. . . . One is the rampant extent of sexually transmitted diseases . . . above all, chancroid, which causes festering ulcers. . . . A second major factor . . . is the lack of male circumcision in much of Africa. . . . Researchers are just now turning attention to little-known sexual practices that might also raise transmission odds. . . . In parts of Central Africa . . . women engage in a practice know as "dry sex." In variations of the practice, designed to increase friction during intercourse, women use herbs, chemical powders, stones, or cloth in the vagina to reduce lubrication and cause swelling. . . . Promiscuity helps drive the epidemic. While data do not exist for comparing sexual behavior on different continents, surveys do show that extramarital sex is commonplace in Africa.

The Western imaginary runs wild in these few lines: the easy slide between the gaping vagina and the gaping hole that, on the map, is the "heart" of African AIDS; the undisguised preoccupation with the shape and size of African penises; the assertion of a relative promiscuity which even the author admits has no data to support it; the conflation of "extramarital" and "promiscuous"—all of these together form a shorthand litany of the "difference" of African sexuality. Such accounts, however, are not limited to the Western media but can be discovered in educational materials designed specifically for "African" use. The following is taken from the "Strategies for Hope" pamphlet series:

> HIV infection in Africa is spread primarily by *heterosexual intercourse*. It affects sexually active men and women in equal numbers, rather than subgroups of the population

such as male homosexuals or intravenous drug users. (Homosexuality and intravenous drug use are rare in Africa.) High-risk sexual behavior therefore consists of sexual intercourse with more than one partner. (Pamphlet 1, 3)

The claim in the colonial voice-over to this ostensibly "local" pamphlet that "African" homosexuality is rare is extraordinarily duplicitous. Indeed, same-sex affective and domestic relations were not at all unusual in many precolonial cultures. When colonial and especially British administrators arrived, they were distressed by these relationships which often played key roles in the distribution of goods and the maintenance of lineages. Colonial law grouped these disparate practices together under one name, "homosexuality," which it pronounced uncivilized and banned by law. Thus contemporary denials by African leaders of the category "homosexuality" are as often a refusal of the European notion of static homosexual identity as they are a denial of same-sex affective and domestic relations. Neo-colonialists now can denigrate homosexuality as a Western import and thereby gain increased control over indigenous economic and social relations by tightening control over the remaining cross-sex relations.[12]

In the context of the reigning transnational distinctions between "AIDS" and "African AIDS," (bad) individuals are routinely figured against (good) families, a strategy that both denies the existence of Euro-American gay people's social networks and ex-communicates them from their blood relatives. The language employed in the pamphlets—"HIV infection in Africa is primarily a *family disease,* rather than a disease affecting mainly single people" (Pamphlet 1, 3; emphasis in original)—begins to reveal what is at stake. The homophobic Section 28 in Britain (similar to the Helms Amendments in the U.S.) was not content to refuse government funding to projects that "promote homosexuality" but also derided "pretend families." The unit to be sanctioned and protected is thus the statistical minority, the bourgeois family—white, heterosexual, mother and father, small number of children. The logo for the 1987 International AIDS Conference in Stockholm proposed a similarly compacted description of the AIDS epidemic: here was a stylized (and nude) mother and father, each holding a hand of the small child who stood between them. To the Western mind, AIDS is most importantly a threat to the family, and a double one—not simply the threat of an entire family being infected, but also the threat of growing numbers of single people challenging the supremacy of the family unit.

Besides "African AIDS," the only other media image of a "family with AIDS" that has received wide attention focuses on the hemophiliac, the less celebrated Other whose "feminine" bleeding shores up heterosexual masculinity. The October 1988 *Scientific American,* a special issue entitled "What Science Knows About AIDS," presents a full-page picture of a white, North American family (the Burkes, who were outspoken advocates for the rights of people with HIV). We are told that the father is a hemophiliac who "infected" his wife before he knew he was himself infected, and she in turn gave birth to an infected son. Even as the Burkes' membership in a community of blood-product users is completely elided in the magazine's account, this apparently isolated family encodes the story of the tragic innocence of those who lack knowledge, pitted against those who do or should have had it (gay men and drug users are said to infect "knowingly" or recklessly). Though the article's passive constructions describing how wife and son "became infected" minimize the heterosexual component of the "Burke's AIDS," the fact of the matter is that, throughout this account, Mr. Burke's hemophilia has itself been sufficient to undercut his masculine identity. We have a glimpse here of the power of heterosexual culture's own heterophobia: the horror of this North American "family with AIDS" is that the unit was actually engaging in the identity-bestowing activities of a small, well-disciplined family.

The African family's purported problem is its similar inability to construct itself properly as a small, well-disciplined unit. Oddly enough, the families (that is, everyone defined as "not an individual") in the "Strategies for Hope" pamphlets are comprised of multiple adults, not just "polygamous" units but "sisters" who "often visited the nearby rural bar, where they sold chicken . . . and sexual favors" (Pamphlet 1, 19). Like homosexuality, the Euro-American category of "the prostitute"—an individual with a professional identity as a sex worker—is seen as distinct from those who engage in the traditional practice of "selling favors." Located outside the confines of the family proper, "prostitutes" are singled out by the media to bolster support for "family values" and by epidemiologists to mark the historical progress of HIV through a country or city. Such "prostitutes" are said to have "Western" AIDS since they are constructed as "single people"; they are not as recuperable into families as are the women who seem to mimic traditional female roles by selling chicken and sexual favors. In the "Strategies for Hope" series, the various extramarital and nonmarital sexual relations that have resulted in "family AIDS" (as represented in the thirteen "true story" inserts in the pamphlets) are considered, in contrast, to form part of "family life." The issue, it becomes clear, is not sex per se but the failure to organize it within the disciplined borders of the bourgeois family.

The pamphlets invoke a nostalgia for a less urban Africa in which "traditional family values" once prevailed—and this despite the reality that polygamy and age-specific sexual experimentation were the dominant organizational strategies in the many different cultural strands of this "tradition." In a gesture remarkably like Thatcher's privatization and Reagan's New Altruism, the pamphlets posit the family as the idealized site for support, care, and education: "Even in urban communities the family retains much of its cohesive power, although weakened to some extent by the spread of 'modern' attitudes and values" (Pamphlet 3, 3). Instead of noticing how this conception of the family-as-primary-political-unit disempowers both women and the community, this odd *recto-verso* history of the rise of the bourgeois family in Africa secures as "traditional" the mother-father-child unit by conflating the image of the single urban person ("prostitute" and perhaps migrant workers and truck drivers) with the image of "the modern." But what, after all, could be more modern than the bourgeois family?

Legible throughout the pamphlets is the heterophobic dread of the condom. The litany that "Africans won't use condoms," which formed a crucial part of Western rationalizations for pursuing vaccine trials,[13] is repeated under the guise of "cultural sensitivity" in this Christian missionary/British neo-colonial collaboration:

> *Sexual attitudes and habits* are different from those of industrialized countries. Resistance to the idea of using condoms is widespread, especially among men. Many years of intensive health education and attitude-forming would be required to achieve sustained attitudinal and behavioral change in this area.
>
> Condoms do have a significant—but limited—role in AIDS control in Africa, but promoting the use of condoms is a diversion from the central issue of *sexual behavior.* The practice of having multiple sexual partners is the main causal factor in the transmission of HIV in Africa. Promoting the use of condoms does not address this issue. It advocates a technical solution to a problem which can be addressed only through fundamental changes in social attitudes, values, and behavior. (Pamphlet 3, 21)[14]

Such distinctions are of course completely ludicrous—Euro-American heterosexual men seem no less resistent to condom use than African men; condom use and sexual behavior are scarcely two separable matters; the spatial dispersions invoked in the image of HIV-infected truck drivers and wandering prostitutes are only slightly more imaginative than the idea of mobile yuppies with bicoastal lifestyles transporting HIV around the U.S. or, as Pattern Three implicitly suggests, around the world. The crucial point here is that bourgeois family units in Africa—understood, from the outset, to be free of infection—must not rely upon condom use to prevent infection, for how otherwise could they succeed in reproducing themselves? Conversely, since those outside the family must be prevented from reproducing, it is they alone who must be urged to use condoms. The already-infected persons, especially women, in their haphazard, defamilialized units are thus to be "eliminated" in a kind of final prophylactic solution. Advocated only for "people already infected with HIV or those who engage in recognizably high-risk sexual behavior" (such as sex with "prostitutes"), condoms "reduce but *do not eliminate the risk of transmission*" (Pamphlet 3, 21). "Elimination" of transmission slides easily into elimination of persons: what is implicit here is a brave new world of monogamous or faithful polygamous relationships[15] that will rise from the ashes of the "modernization" which, in its destruction of "traditional values," becomes the "cause" of AIDS.

If any doubts remain about the nature of the pamphlet series, its descriptions of AIDS counseling make it clear that the "cure" for AIDS in Africa lies in the proliferation of bourgeois families. "Communication" is repeatedly proscribed for counselors and families. Although noting that other social support networks continue to exist (though always fractured by "modernization"), the pamphlets urge one-on-one, paraprofessional counseling to replace functioning social relations involving grandmothers, cousins, or jokesters who teach about sexuality. In the abstract, such programs seem desirable in a crisis setting, but their longer-term effect is to destroy existing social relations while promoting disciplining interventions from the local clinic.

The TASO project of Uganda (Pamphlet 2) follows precisely from this model of the reconstructed bourgeois family and describes how the transition "back" to the family and the "elimination" of the already-infected will be managed. I do not want to undercut the important work of TASO, modeled on the grassroots "self-help" (though largely gay male) people-living-with-AIDS movement in the West.[16] Instead, I want to underline what is presented here as "appropriate" AIDS work. While this organization has been enormously helpful, it is crucial to realize that the conception of "self-help" as employed in its project is as culture-bound as the idea of the bourgeois family. *Self*-help arises only in the context of already existing (or already denied) *state*-mediated services, hence the emphasis on "self-" rather than on community mobilization. Not surprisingly, most of the TASO clients whose stories appear in this pamphlet are men who are themselves both counselors and clients of the five-year-old organization. These stories suggest in effect that the organization has become a kind of surrogate family; indeed, a client named Gilbert has moved to a house near the TASO office where he now works part time, so that he "can see a lot more of his children. . . . As a father I feel much closer to my children" (Pamphlet 2, 24). These transitional family units, "victims" of the modernization which permitted the disease of Western single people to invade the African family, are presented as evidence for the "safeness" of bourgeois families to come. Though never specifically addressed in the pamphlet, the paradigmatic act that defines the bourgeois family—regulated heterosexual intercourse—is itself to be protected from the condom. In one sweep, the pamphlet's refusal to promote universal condom use paves the way for the virtual genocide of anyone outside the chastity-before-marriage-monogamous-couple and enables Euro-American epidemiologists to name the "difference" constitutive of "African AIDS." *If only they'd had proper families.*[17]

African social patterns once were deemed unnatural or hypernatural (uncivilized) by the West, but African sex is still considered profoundly natural, too close to the body and its supposedly prediscursive desires to be able to accommodate the inhibiting condom. Having failed to demonstrate anatomical, behavioral, or even sociomedical differences between Euro-American and African sex acts, international AIDS workers now conclude that intercourse itself must ultimately be declared safe, and the "risk" situated in its practice outside the legitimate borders of the bourgeois family. Those who cannot be contained within this family will be simply left to die, but such an outcome will be rapid because "African AIDS" seems inexplicably to move faster than "AIDS" (largely because the Western drug companies cannot make any money there). "Africa" is thus once more experiencing border constructions that mask state-sponsored genocide as indigenous social and cultural formations are elided in the interests of a brave new world of disease-free—and controllable—bourgeois family units.

NOTES

This essay differs in its focus from the version given at the Nationalisms and Sexualities Conference, a version which has already appeared at several stages and in different forms: "Inventing African AIDS," *City Limits*.[London], 363 (September 1988); "Inventing African AIDS," *New Formations,* 10 (Spring 1990); and "Inventing African AIDS," in my *Inventing AIDS* (New York: Routledge, 1990). I am indebted to Erica Carter who spent a good deal of time preparing the latter two manuscripts, and to Andrew Parker who helped with this new version. I am grateful as well to Eve Kosofsky Sedgwick for hosting a symposium on this topic at Duke University in September 1989.

For related analyses see especially Paula A. Treichler, "AIDS and HIV Infection in the Third World: A First World Chronicle," in Barbara Kruger and Phil Mariani, eds., *Remaking History* (Seattle: Bay Press, 1989); Treichler, "AIDS, Africa, and Cultural Theory," *Transition,* 51 (1991); and Simon Watney, "Missionary Positions," *Critical Quarterly,* 30, 1 (Autumn 1989).

1. "Natural history" is the term employed within epidemiology to describe the development of a disease, epidemic, or pandemic if left to run its course. The desire to learn the natural history of HIV/AIDS has resulted in debates, for example, about whether the few remaining long-time infected but asymptomatic men in a San Francisco "natural history" cohort should now "be allowed" to take prophylactic AZT or pentamidine, two of the most widely accepted life-prolonging drugs. Researchers in Africa have expressed a similar wish to allow existing conditions to continue to "see what happens." In one study of the effectiveness of contraceptive sponges for interrupting HIV transmission, researchers gave half of the targeted women (who were sex workers) placebos—in essence a wad of cotton. Despite early data suggesting that both groups in the study were becoming infected at a rapid rate, the experiment continued for three years until "statistically sound samplings" were obtained. Tragically, the same research data showed that sex workers in an adjoining district had been able to get many of their male clients to use condoms, thereby decreasing not only HIV transmission in these women but other sexually transmitted diseases overall. For more on such experiments see my *Inventing AIDS*.

2. *New York Times,* September 16, 1990, pp. 1, 14. The map and accompanying article, "What Makes the 2 Sexes So Vulnerable To Epidemic," appear on p. 15.

3. Specific information is given for: "Most Severely Affected"—Malawi, Rwanda, Uganda, Zambia; "Urban Rate 10% to 20%"—Burundi, Ivory Coast, Tanzania, Zimbabwe, Central African Republic, Congo, Guinea Bissau, Kenya, and Zaire (Rwanda has the same percentages but is placed in the "Most Severely Affected" category apparently because of a single study showing a 30% rate of seroprevalence in a cohort of pregnant women in the capital city); and "Ominous Signs"—Angola, Burkina Faso, Mali, Ethiopia, Ghana, Namibia, Nigeria, Senegal, Sierra Leone, South Africa, and Sudan.

4. I am alluding here to the highly publicized accounts which suggest (based on fantasy) that either Tall Ships sailors who toured the world in 1976 or "Patient Zero," a steward on Air Canada in the early 1980s, brought AIDS to the U.S. See Randy Shilts, *And the Band Played On* (New York: St. Martin's Press, 1987).

5. This assumption of heterosexuality seems to be based only on the simple statistical fact that the male to female ratio in Africa as a whole is about 1:1. Scientists have been slow to recognize, however, that the number of women who receive transfusions (and thus the transfusion-related HIV infection) has been grossly underestimated. Since it is standard medical practice throughout much of Africa to give whole blood transfusion for malarial, nutritional, or maternal anaemia, scientists have consistently conflated pregnancy with transfusions as "risk" factors. See Alan Fleming, "Prevention of Transmission of HIV by Blood Transfusion in Developing Countries," Global Impact of AIDS Conference (London, March 8–10, 1988).

6. A scientist of the stature of Luc Montaigne has persistently maintained, despite contrary epidemiologic data, that "AIDS" started in "Africa." His claim is based on the genetic similarity of a simian immunodeficiency virus found in monkeys. This insistence is an updating of racist evolutionary theory, only in place of the old missing link between apes and homo sapiens, the new missing link connects monkeys with North Americans. By a clever sleight of hand, the AIDS-came-from-Africa theory first situates the virus as more or less dormant in Africa and then transports it to Europe and/or America, where it rapidly disseminates. At the same time, so this theory runs, a variant of the virus suddenly proliferates in Africa (urbanization is cited as an explanation—but this process was already well underway before the onset of the epidemic).

7. I remain perplexed by Westerners' insistence that there is no homosexuality in Africa—after all, it would have been much simpler to lay AIDS at the door of a single "perversion." Yet Western homosexual panic works overtime in AIDS discourse: homosexuality is more controllable if it can be retained as a category of Western bourgeois culture. To acknowledge other homosexualities would implicitly challenge Western notions that homosexuality is a symptom of cultural decadence, even if "primitive" homosexualities can be written off on that basis. But such panic also enables the denial of miscegenation through the denial of cross-race homosexual congress. This is nowhere clearer than in South African AIDS discourse, where both "white (homosexual)" AIDS and "black (heterosexual)" AIDS are said to exist. Well into the 1980s, South African commentators would wryly note that apartheid may have "saved" South African blacks from AIDS. Studies of male relations in the mines, conducted as gay history, were appropriated as "proof" of the effectiveness of sexual apartheid (perhaps the least violent but most fundamental aspect of racial separation): black miners, it was argued, did not acquire AIDS while in the male-only dormitories since they had "intercourse" only with their female partners.

8. The persistent effort to establish an African heterosexual "difference" began with allegations that Africans favored anal intercourse because it is, as many media reports called it, "a primitive form of birth control." This assumed that HIV transmission was paradigmatically sodomitic; the handful of Army cases in which men alleged that they had been infected by prostitutes also rested on this idea since, as one researcher told me, "their wives wouldn't do it (permit anal intercourse)." Sadly, for the Western sexual imagination, epidemiologists failed to find higher rates of anal intercourse, or any other exotic practice, to explain differences between "African" and "Euro-American" heterosexual practice. But researchers and journalists are still searching, as can be seen in a passage from the *Times* on "dry sex" that I discuss below. Who knows what lurks in the Euro-American male imaginary here—"African" penises smaller than fantasized? "African" vaginas even larger than feared?

9. See, for example, Robert E. Gould, "Reassuring News About AIDS: A Doctor Tells Why You May Not Be at Risk," *Cosmopolitan* (January 1988), p. 147: "The data I gathered concerning heterosexual intercourse in Africa show marked differences from the way it is usually practiced in the United States."

10. See especially Frantz Fanon, "Unveiling Algeria," in *A Dying Colonialism* (New York: Monthly Review Press, 1965). I am also indebted here to Kirstin McDougall, whose unpublished manuscript on maternal metaphors in AIDS discourse confirms that such slippage occurs not only in Western but also in Anglophone African media.

11. The three "Strategies for Hope" pamphlets, published jointly by ACTIONAID in London, the African Medical and Research Foundation in Nairobi, and World in Need in Colchester (U.K.), are now distributed widely by the World Health Organization Global Program on AIDS. The series includes two pamphlets about Zambia and one about Uganda; these have been reviewed, respectively, by the National AIDS Surveillance Committee of Zambia and the National

AIDS Control Programme of Uganda. Pamphlet One is entitled *From Fear to Hope: AIDS Care and Prevention at Chikankata Hospital, Zambia*, authored by U.K.-based Glen Williams, who is also the series editor. Pamphlet Two, by U.K.-based Janie Hampton, is called *Living Positively with AIDS: The AIDS Support Organisation (TASO), Uganda.* The third pamphlet is *AIDS Management: An Integrated Approach*, by Williams and Capt. (Dr.) Ian D. Campbell, Chief Medical Officer of the Salvation Army Hospital in Chikankata, Zambia.

12. For more general information on the inscription of sexual cultures as subaltern, see especially T. Dunbar Moody, "Migrancy and Male Sexuality in South African Gold Mines," *Journal of South African Studies,* 14, 2 (January 1988), pp. 228–56; Lourdes Arguelles and B. Ruby Rich, "Homosexuality, Homophobia, and Revolution: Notes Toward an Understanding of the Cuban Lesbian and Gay Male Experience," in Martin Duberman, Martha Vicinus, and George Chauncey, Jr., eds., *Hidden From History* (New York: New American Library, 1989); Pat Caplan, ed., *The Cultural Construction of Sexuality* (New York: Tavistock, 1987); "Homecoming," *Black/Out,* 2, 1 (Fall 1986); and Alfred Machela, "The Work of the Rand Gay Organization," Conference on Homosexual Identity Before, During, and After HIV (Stockholm, June 1988).

13. For the longer argument on Western medical ethics and proposed vaccine trials, see my *Inventing AIDS.*

14. To their credit, in Pamphlet 3, the authors emphasize that condoms are not currently being supplied to African countries in sufficient supply to meet potential demand (21). However, this can hardly be used as an excuse not to promote condom usage at all, since it is probably easier and quicker to increase condom supplies than it is to promote "monogamy." Indeed, the ease with which the lack-of-supply argument becomes an excuse for not promoting condoms is rooted in the widespread notion that "In Africa, AIDS is a disease of poverty."

15. See Pamphlet 1, which invokes "traditional values and norms of sexual behavior, which have been lost in the recent wave of 'modernization,' " and which defines "stable polygamy" as a form of "safe sex" (20).

16. It is critical to recognize how limiting are the terms of the international health regime; many local strategies remain "unreadable" because they defy the standardizations favored by the World Health Organization.

17. I am indebted here to the brief sections on the construction of the "Algerian" family in Malek Alloula, *The Colonial Harem*, trans. Myrna Godzich and Wlad Godzich (Minneapolis: University of Minnesota Press, 1986). A similar pattern occurs in the media reportage about AIDS in Africa, where the existing "African" family is often implicitly denigrated for having, besides a surfeit of children, either too many parents or too few (usually the father has died or has run off).

II

SPECTACULAR LOGIC

9

Sexual Indifference and Lesbian Representation

Teresa de Lauretis

Teresa de Lauretis is Professor of the History of Consciousness at the University of California, Santa Cruz, and author of Alice Doesn't: Feminism, Semiotics, Cinema *(1984) and* Technologies of Gender: Essays on Theory, Film, and Fiction *(1987), as well as articles on lesbian representation in literature, film, and feminist theory. She recently edited the "Queer Theory" issue of* differences *(3.2:1992) and is now working on "The Practice of Love," a book on lesbian subjectivity, sexual structuring, and fantasy. In the essay reprinted here, de Lauretis adopts the concept of* hom(m)osexuality *from the French Lacanian psychoanalyst and feminist theorist Luce Irigaray and applies it to the analysis of problems in lesbian visibility and lesbian representation. Rendering Irigaray's term in English by the phrase "sexual (in)difference," de Lauretis argues that feminist definitions of gender as "sexual difference" do not in fact escape the tyranny of male categories, because women's supposed difference remains implicitly a difference* from *men, and thereby preserves "men" as the standard against which "difference" is to be measured. Such a conceptual hierarchy, depending as it does on either the presence or the absence of male identity, cancels sexual difference in the very act of attempting to establish it by continually defining "woman" in terms of "man." "Sexual difference" is transformed in this way into "sexual (in)difference." Any notion of gender too closely tied to a notion of "sexual difference" will reproduce the discursive structures of male privilege and, in effect, be heterosexualized. Hence, de Lauretis argues, recent feminists have tried to tease apart the mutual implication, in gender, of sex and sexuality; in this they have followed the example of lesbian writers and artists who in their work have variously sought to escape from gender itself.*

If it were not lesbian, this text would make no sense. (Nicole Brossard, *L'Amèr*)

There is a sense in which lesbian identity could be assumed, spoken, and articulated conceptually as political through feminism—and, current debates to wit, *against* feminism; in particular through and against the feminist critique of the Western discourse on love and sexuality, and therefore, to begin with, the rereading of psychoanalysis as a theory of sexuality and sexual difference. If the first feminist emphasis on sexual difference as gender (woman's difference from man) has rightly come under attack for obscuring the effects of other differences in women's psychosocial oppression, nevertheless that emphasis on sexual difference did open up a critical space—a conceptual, representational, and erotic space—in which women could address themselves to women. And in the very act of assuming and speaking from the position of subject, a woman could concurrently recognize women as subjects *and* as objects of female desire.

It is in such a space, hard-won and daily threatened by social disapprobation, censure, and denial, a space of contradiction requiring constant reaffirmation and painful renegotiation, that the very notion of sexual difference could then be put into question, and its limitations be assessed, both *vis-à-vis* the claims of other, not strictly sexual, differences, and with regard to sexuality itself. It thus appears that "sexual difference" is the term of a conceptual paradox corresponding to what is in effect a real contradiction in women's lives: the term, at once, of a sexual *difference* (women are, or want, something different from men) and of a sexual *indifference* (women are, or want, the same as men). And it seems to me that the racist and class-biased practices legitimated in the notion of "separate but equal" reveal a very similar paradox in the liberal ideology of pluralism, where social difference is also, at the same time, social indifference.

The psychoanalytic discourse on female sexuality, wrote Luce Irigaray in 1975, outlining the terms of what here I will call sexual (in)difference, tells "that *the feminine occurs only within models and laws devised by male subjects.* Which implies that there are not really two sexes, but only one. A single practice and representation of the sexual."[1] Within the conceptual frame of that *sexual indifference,* female desire for the self-same, an other female self, cannot be recognized. "That a woman might desire a woman 'like' herself, someone of the 'same' sex, that she might also have auto- and homosexual appetites, is simply incomprehensible" in the phallic regime of an asserted sexual difference between man and woman which is predicated on the contrary, on a complete indifference for the "other" sex, woman's. Consequently, Irigaray continues, Freud was at a loss with his homosexual female patients, and his analyses of them were really about male homosexuality. "The object choice of the homosexual woman is [understood to be] determined by a *masculine* desire and tropism"—that is, precisely, the turn of so-called sexual difference into sexual indifference, a single practice and representation of the sexual.

> So there will be no female homosexuality, just a hommo-sexuality in which woman will be involved in the process of specularizing the phallus, begged to maintain the desire for the same that man has, and will ensure at the same time, elsewhere and in complementary and contradictory fashion, the perpetuation in the couple of the pole of "matter."[2]

With the term *hommo-sexuality* [*hommo-sexualité*]—at times also written *hom(m)osexuality* [*hom(m)osexualité*]—Irigaray puns on the French word for man, *homme,* from the Latin *homo* (meaning "man"), and the Greek *homo* (meaning "same"). In taking up her distinction between homosexuality (or homo-sexuality) and "hommo-sexuality" (or "hom(m)osexuality"), I want to remark the conceptual distance between the former term, homosexuality, by which I mean lesbian (or gay) sexuality, and the diacritically marked hommo-sexuality, which is the term of sexual indifference, the term (in fact) of heterosexuality; I want to re-mark both the incommensurable distance between them and the conceptual ambiguity that is conveyed by the two almost identical acoustic images. Another paradox—or is it perhaps the same?

There is no validation for sodomy found in the teaching of the ancient Greek philosophers Plato or Aristotle. (Michael Bowers, Petitioners Brief in *Bowers v. Hardwick.*)

To attempt to answer that question, I turn to a very interesting reading of Plato's *Symposium* by David Halperin which (1) richly resonates with Irigaray's notion of sexual indifference (see also her reading of "Plato's Hystera" in *Speculum*), (2) emphasizes the embarrassing ignorance of the present Attorney General of the State of Georgia in matters of classical scholarship, which he nevertheless invokes,[3] and (3) traces the roots of the paradoxes here in question to the very philosophical foundation of what is called Western civilization, Plato's dialogues. For in those master texts of hommo-sexuality, as Halperin proposes, it is the female, reproductive body that paradoxically guarantees true eròs between men, or as Plato calls it, "proper paederasty" (113).[4]

"Why Is Diotima a Woman?," Halperin argues, is a question that has been answered only tautologically: because she is not or cannot be a man. It would have been indecorous to imply that Socrates owed his knowledge of erotic desire to a former paederastic lover. But there is a reason more stringent than decorum why Socrates's teacher should have been a woman. Plato wanted to prescribe a new homoerotic ethos and a model of "proper paederasty" based on the reciprocity of erotic desire and a mutual access to pleasure for both partners, a reciprocity of eros whose philosophical import found ultimate expression in the dialogue form. His project, however, ran against the homoerotic sexual ethos and practices of the citizens of classical Athens, "locked as they were into an aggressive, phallic sexuality of domination—and, consequently, into a rigid hierarchy of sexual roles in their relations with males and females alike." For an adult male citizen of Athens could have legitimate sexual relations only with his social inferiors: boys, women, foreigners, and slaves. Plato repudiated such erotic asymmetry in relations between men and boys and, through the teaching of Socrates/Diotima, sought to erase "the distinction between the active and the passive partner—according to Socrates, both members of the relationship become active, desiring lovers; neither remains a merely passive object of desire" (130–37).

Hence the intellectual and mythopoetic function of Diotima: her discourse on erotic desire, unlike a man's, could appear directly grounded in the experiential knowledge of a non-hierarchical, mutualistic, and reproductive sexuality, i.e., female sexuality as the Greeks construed it. It is indeed so grounded in the text, both rhetorically (Diotima's language systematically conflates sexual pleasure with the reproductive or generative function) and narratively, in the presumed experience of a female character, since to the Greeks female sexuality differed from male sexuality precisely in that sexual pleasure for women was intimately bound up with procreation. Halperin cites many sources from Plato's *Timaeus* to various ritual practices which represented, for example, "the relation of man to wife as a domestic form of cultivation homologous to agriculture whereby women are tamed, mastered, and made fruitful. . . . [I]n the absence of men, women's sexual functioning is aimless and unproductive, merely a form of rottenness and decay, but by the application of male pharmacy it becomes at once orderly and fruitful" (137–42, esp. 141).

After remarking on the similarity between the Greek construction and the contemporary gynaecological discourses on female eroticism, Halperin raises the question of Plato's politics of gender, noting that "the interdependence of sexual and reproductive capacities is in fact a feature of male, not female, physiology," and that male sexuality is the one in which "sexual pleasure and reproductive function cannot be separated (to the chagrin of Augustine and others)." His hypothesis is worth quoting at length:

> Plato, then, would seem to be interpreting as feminine and allocating to men a form of sexuality which is masculine to begin with and which men had previously alienated from themselves by constructing it as feminine. In other words, it looks as if what lies behind Plato's doctrine is a double movement whereby men project their own sexuality onto women only to reabsorb it themselves in the guise of a feminine character. This is particularly intriguing because it suggests that in order to facilitate

their own appropriation of the feminine men have initially constructed femininity according to a male paradigm while creating a social and political ideal of masculinity defined by the ability to isolate what only women can *actually* isolate—namely, sexuality and reproduction, recreative and procreative sex (142–43).

Let me restate the significance of Halperin's analysis for my own argument here. Plato's repudiation of asymmetrical paederasty and of the subordinate position in which that placed *citizen* boys who, after all, were the future rulers of Athens, had the effect of elevating the status of all male *citizens* and thus of consolidating *male citizen* rule. It certainly was no favor done to women or to any "others" (male and female foreigners, male and female slaves). But his move was yet more masterful: the appropriation of the feminine for the erotic ethos of a male social and intellectual elite (an ethos that would endure well into the twentieth century, if in the guise of "heretical ethics" or in the femininity [*"dévenir-femme"*] claimed by his most deconstructive critics)[5] had the effect not only of securing the millenary exclusion of women from philosophical dialogue, and the absolute excision of non-reproductive sexuality from the Western discourse on love. The construction and appropriation of femininity in Western erotic ethos has also had the effect of securing the heterosexual social contract by which all sexualities, all bodies, and all "others" are bonded to an ideal/ideological hierarchy of males.[6]

The intimate relationship of sexual (in)difference with social (in)difference, whereby, for instance, the defense of the mother country and of (white) womanhood has served to bolster colonial conquest and racist violence throughout Western history, is nowhere more evident than in "the teaching of the ancient Greek philosophers," *pace* the Attorney General. Hence the ironic rewriting of history, in a female-only world of mothers and amazons, by Monique Wittig and Sande Zeig in *Lesbian Peoples: Material for a Dictionary*.[7] And hence, as well, the crucial emphasis in current feminist theory on articulating, specifying, and historicizing the position of the female social subject in the intricate experiential nexus of (often contradictory) heterogeneous differences, across discourses of race, gender, cultural, and sexual identity, and the political working through those differences toward a new, global, yet historically specific and even local, understanding of community.[8]

Pardon me, I must be going! (Djuna Barnes, *The Ladies Almanack*)

Lesbian representation, or rather, its condition of possibility, depends on separating out the two contrary undertows that constitute the paradox of sexual (in)difference, on isolating but maintaining the two senses of homosexuality and hommo-sexuality. Thus the critical effort to dislodge the erotic from the discourse of gender, with its indissoluble knot of sexuality and reproduction, is concurrent and interdependent with a rethinking of what, in most cultural discourses and sociosexual practices, is still, nevertheless, a gendered sexuality. In the pages that follow, I will attempt to work through these paradoxes by considering how lesbian writers and artists have sought variously to escape gender, to deny it, transcend it, or perform it in excess, and to inscribe the erotic in cryptic, allegorical, realistic, camp, or other modes of representation, pursuing diverse strategies of writing and of reading the intransitive and yet obdurate relation of reference to meaning, of flesh to language.

Gertrude Stein, for example, "encrypted" her experience of the body in obscure coding, her "somagrams" are neither sexually explicit or conventionally erotic, nor "radically visceral or visual," Catharine Stimpson argues.[9] Stein's effort was, rather, to develop a distinguished "anti-language" in which to describe sexual activity, her "delight in the female body" (38) or her ambivalence about it, as an abstract though intimate relationship where "the body fuses with writing itself" (36), an act "at once richly pleasurable and violent" (38). But if Stein does belong to the history of women writers, claims Stimpson, who also claims her for the history of lesbian writers, it is not because she wrote out of femaleness "as an elemental condition, inseparable from the body" (40), the way some radical feminist critics would like to think; nor because her writing sprung from a preoedipal, maternal body, as others would have it. Her language was not "female" but quite the contrary, "as genderless as an atom of platinum" (42), and strove to obliterate the boundaries of gender identity.

Djuna Barnes's *Nightwood,* which Stimpson calls a "parable of damnation,"[10] is read by others as an affirmation of inversion as homosexual difference. In her "Writing Toward *Nightwood*: Djuna Barnes's Seduction Stories," Carolyn Allen reads Barnes's "little girl" stories as sketches or earlier trials of the sustained meditation on inversion that was to yield in the novel the most suggestive portrait of the invert, the third sex.

> In that portrait we recognize the boy in the girl, the girl in the Prince, not a mixing of gendered behaviors, but the creation of a new gender, "neither one and half the other". . . . In their love of the same sex [Matthew, Nora, and Robin] admire their non-conformity, their sexual difference from the rest of the world.[11]

That difference, which for the lesbian includes a relation to the self-same ("a woman is yourself caught as you turn in panic; on her mouth you kiss your own," says Nora), also includes her relation to the child, the "ambivalence about mothering one's lover," the difficult and inescapable ties of female sexuality with nurture and with violence. In this light, Allen suggests, may we read Barnes's personal denial of lesbianism and her aloofness from female admirers as a refusal to accept and to live by the homophobic categories promoted by sexology: man and woman, with their respective deviant forms, the effeminate man and the mannish woman—a refusal that in the terms of my argument could be seen as a rejection of the hommo-sexual categories of gender, a refusal of sexual (in)difference.

Thus the highly metaphoric, oblique, allusive language of Barnes's fiction, her "heavily embedded and often appositional" syntax, her use of the passive voice, indirect style, and interior monologue techniques in narrative descriptions, which Allen admirably analyzes in another essay, are motivated less by the modernist's pleasure in formal experimentation than by her resistance to what *Nightwood* both thematizes and demonstrates, the failure of language to represent, grasp, and convey her subjects: "The violation [of reader's expectation] and the appositional structure permit Barnes to suggest that the naming power of language is insufficient to make Nora's love for Robin perceivable to the reader."[12]

"Dr. Knox," Edward began, "my problem this week is chiefly concerning rest-rooms." (Judy Grahn, "The Psychoanalysis of Edward the Dyke")

Ironically, since one way of escaping gender is to so disguise erotic and sexual experience as to suppress any representation of its specificity, another avenue of escape leads the lesbian writer fully to embrace gender, if by replacing femaleness with masculinity, as in the case of Stephen Gordon in *The Well of Loneliness,* and so risk to collapse lesbian homosexuality into hommo-sexuality. However, representation is related to experience by codes that change historically and, significantly, reach in both directions: the writer struggles to inscribe experience in historically available forms of representation, the reader accedes to representation through her own historical and experiential context; each reading is a rewriting of the text, each writing a rereading of (one's) experience. The contrasting readings of Radclyffe Hall's novel by lesbian feminist critics show that each critic reads from a particular position, experiential but also historically available to her, and, moreover, a position chosen, or even politically assumed, from the spectrum of contemporary discourses on the relationship of feminism to lesbianism. The contrast of interpretations also shows to what extent the paradox of sexual (in)difference operates as a semiotic mechanism to produce contradictory meaning effects.

The point of contention in the reception of a novel that by general agreement was the single most popular representation of lesbianism in fiction, from its obscenity trial in 1928 to the 1970s, is the figure of its protagonist Stephen Gordon, the "mythic mannish lesbian" of the title of Esther Newton's essay, and the prototype of her more recent incarnation, the working-class butch.[13] Newton's impassioned defense of the novel rests on the significance of that figure for lesbian self-definition, not only in the 1920s and 1930s, when the social gains in gender independence attained by the New Woman were being reappropriated via sexological discourses within the institutional practices of heterosexuality, but also in the 1970s and 1980s, when female sexuality has been redefined by a women's movement "that swears it is the enemy of traditional gender categories and yet validates lesbianism as the ultimate form of femaleness" (558).

Newton argues historically, taking into account the then available discourses on sexuality which asserted that "normal" women had at best a reactive heterosexual desire, while female sexual deviancy articulated itself in ascending categories of inversion marked by increasing masculinization, from deviant—but rectifiable—sexual orientation (or "homosexuality" proper, for Havelock Ellis) to congenital inversion. Gender crossing was at once a symptom and a sign of sexual degeneracy.[14] In the terms of the cultural representations available to the novelist, since there was no image of female sexual desire apart from the male, Newton asks, "Just how was Hall to make the woman-loving New Woman a sexual being?. . . . To become avowedly sexual, the New Woman had to enter the male world, either as a heterosexual on male terms (a flapper) or as—or with—a lesbian in male body drag (a butch)" (572–73). Gender reversal in the mannish lesbian, then, was not merely a claim to male social privilege or a sad pretense to male sexual behavior, but represented what may be called, in Foucault's phrase, a "reverse discourse": an assertion of sexual agency and feelings, but autonomous from men, a reclaiming of erotic drives directed toward women, of a desire for women that is not to be confused with woman identification.

While other lesbian critics of *The Well of Loneliness* read it as an espousal of Ellis's views, couched in religious romantic imagery and marred by a self-defeating pessimism, aristocratic self-pity, and inevitable damnation, what Newton reads in Stephen Gordon and in Radclyffe Hall's text is the unsuccessful attempt to represent a female desire not determined by "masculine tropism," in Irigaray's words, or, in my own, a female desire not hommo-sexual but homosexual. If Radclyffe Hall herself could not envision homosexuality as part of an autonomous female sexuality (a notion that has emerged much later, with the feminist critique of patriarchy as phallic symbolic order), and if she therefore did not succeed in escaping the hommo-sexual categories of gender ("Unlike Orlando, Stephen is trapped in history; she cannot declare gender an irrelevant game," as Newton remarks [570]), nevertheless the figure of the mannish female invert continues to stand as the representation of lesbian desire against both the discourse of hommo-sexuality and the feminist account of lesbianism as woman identification. The context of Newton's reading is the current debate on the relationship of lesbianism to feminism and the reassertion, on the one hand, of the historical and political importance of gender roles (e.g., butch-femme) in lesbian self-definition and representation, and on the other, of the demand for a separate understanding of sex and gender as distinct areas of social practice.

The latter issue has been pushed to the top of the theoretical agenda by the polarization of opinions around the two adverse and widely popularized positions on the issue of pornography taken by Women Against Pornography (WAP) and by S/M lesbians (Samois). In "Thinking Sex," a revision of her earlier and very influential "The Traffic in Women," Gayle Rubin wants to challenge the assumption that feminism can contribute very much to a theory of sexuality, for "feminist thought simply lacks angles of vision which can encompass the social organization of sexuality."[15] While acknowledging some (though hardly enough) diversity among feminists on the issue of sex, and praising "pro-sex" feminists such as "lesbian sadomasochists and butch-femme dykes," adherents of "classic radical feminism," and "unapologetic heterosexuals" for not conforming to "movement standards of purity" (303), Rubin nonetheless believes that a "theory and politics specific to sexuality" must be developed apart from the theory of gender oppression, that is feminism. Thus she goes back over her earlier feminist critique of Lacan and Lévi-Strauss and readjusts the angle of vision:

> "The Traffic in Women" was inspired by the literature on kin-based systems of social organization. It appeared to me at the time that gender and desire were systematically intertwined in such social formations. This may or may not be an accurate assessment of the relationship between sex and gender *in tribal organizations*. But it is surely not an adequate formulation for sexuality *in Western industrial societies*. (307, emphasis added)

In spite of Rubin's rhetorical emphasis (which I underscore graphically in the above passage), her earlier article also had to do with gender and sexuality in Western industrial societies, where indeed Rubin and several other feminists were articulating the critique of a theory of symbolic signification that elaborated the very notion of desire (from psychoanalysis) in relation to gender as symbolic construct (from anthropology)—a critique that has been crucial to the development of feminist theory. But whereas "The Traffic in Women" (a title directly borrowed from Emma Goldman) was focused on women, here her interest has shifted toward a non-gendered notion of sexuality concerned, in Foucault's terms "with the sensations of the body, the quality of pleasures, and the nature of impressions."[16]

Accordingly, the specificity of either female or lesbian eroticism is no longer a question to be asked in "Thinking Sex," where the term "homosexual" is used to refer to both women and men (thus sliding inexorably, it seems, into its uncanny hommosexual double), and which concludes by advocating a politics of "theoretical as well as sexual pluralism" (309). At the opposite pole of the debate, Catharine MacKinnon argues:

> If heterosexuality is the dominant gendered form of sexuality in a society where gender oppresses women through sex, sexuality and heterosexuality are essentially the same thing. This does not erase homosexuality, it merely means that sexuality in that form may be no less gendered.[17]

I suggest that, despite or possibly because of their stark mutual opposition and common reductivism, both Rubin and MacKinnon collapse the tension of ambiguity, the semantic duplicity, that I have tried to sort out in the two terms homosexual and hommo-sexual, and thus remain caught in the paradox of sexual (in)difference even as they both, undoubtedly, very much want to escape it, one by denying gender, the other by categorically asserting it. As it was, in another sense, with Radclyffe Hall, Newton's suggestive reading notwithstanding. I will return to her suggestions later on.

A theory in the flesh. (Cherríe Moraga, *This Bridge Called My Back*)

It is certain, however, as Rubin notes, that "lesbians are *also* oppressed as queers and perverts" (308, emphasis added), not only as women; and it is equally certain that some lesbians are also oppressed as queers and perverts, and *also* as women of color. What cannot be elided in a politically responsible theory of sexuality, of gender, or of culture is the critical value of that "also," which is neither simply additive nor exclusive but signals the nexus, the mode of operation of *interlocking* systems of gender, sexual, racial, class, and other, more local categories of social stratification.[18] Just a few lines from *Zami,* Audre Lorde's "biomythography," will make the point, better than I can.

> But the fact of our Blackness was an issue that Felicia and I talked about only between ourselves. Even Muriel seemed to believe that as lesbians, we were all outsiders and all equal in our outsiderhood. "We're all niggers," she used to say, and I hated to hear her say it. It was wishful thinking based on little fact; the ways in which it was true languished in the shadow of those many ways in which it would always be false.
> . . . .
> It was hard enough to be Black, to be Black and female, to be Black, female, and gay. To be Black, female, gay, and out of the closet in a white environment, even to the extent of dancing in the Bagatelle, was considered by many Black lesbians to be simply suicidal. And if you were fool enough to do it, you'd better come on so tough that nobody messed with you. I often felt put down by their sophistication, their clothes, their manners, their cars, and their femmes.[19]

If the black/white divide is even less permeable than the gay/straight one, it does not alone suffice to self-definition: "Being Black dykes together was not enough. We were different. . . . Self-preservation warned some of us that we could not afford to settle for one easy definition, one narrow individuation of self" (226). Neither race nor gender nor homosexual difference alone can constitute individual identity or the basis for a theory and a politics of social change. What Lorde suggests is a more complex image of the psycho-socio-sexual subject ("our place was the very house of difference rather [than] the security of any one particular difference") which does not deny gender or sex but transcends them. Read together with the writings of other lesbians of color or those committed to antiracism (see note 8 above), Lorde's image of the house of difference points to a conception of community not pluralistic but at once global and local—global in its inclusive and macro-political strategies, and local in its specific, micro-political practices.

I want to propose that, among the latter, not the least is the practice of writing, particularly in that form which the *québecoise* feminist writer Nicole Brossard has called *"une fiction théorique,"* fiction/theory: a formally experimental, critical and lyrical, autobiographical and theoretically conscious, practice of writing-in-the-feminine that crosses genre boundaries (poetry and prose, verbal and visual modes, narrative and cultural criticism), and instates new correlations between signs and meanings, inciting other discursive mediations between the symbolic and the real, language and flesh.[20] And for all its specific cultural, historical, and linguistic variation—say between francophone and anglophone contemporary Canadian writers, or between writers such as Gloria Anzaldúa, Michelle Cliff, Cherríe Moraga, Joanna Russ, Monique Wittig, or even the Virginia Woolf of *Three Guineas* and *A Room of One's Own*—the concept of fiction/theory does make the transfer across borderlines and covers a significant range of practices of lesbian (self-)representation.

Lesbians are not women. (Monique Wittig, "The Straight Mind")

In a superb essay tracing the intertextual weave of a lesbian imagination throughout French literature, the kind of essay that changes the landscape of both literature and reading irreversibly, Elaine Marks proposes that to undomesticate the female body one must dare reinscribe it in excess—as excess—in provocative counterimages sufficiently outrageous, passionate, verbally violent, and formally complex to both destroy the male discourse on love and redesign the universe.[21] The undomesticated female body that was first *concretely* imaged in Sappho's poetry ("she is suggesting equivalences between the physical symptoms of desire and the physical symptoms of death, not between Eros and Thanatos," Marks writes [372]) has been read and effectively recontained within the male poetic tradition—with the very move described by Halperin above—as phallic or maternal body. Thereafter, Marks states, no "sufficiently challenging counterimages" were produced in French literature until the advent of feminism and the writing of a lesbian feminist, Monique Wittig.

"Only the women's movement," concurred the writer in her preface to the 1975 English edition of *The Lesbian Body,* "has proved capable of producing lesbian texts in a context of total rupture with masculine culture, texts written by women exclusively for women, careless of male approval."[22] If there is reason to believe that Wittig would no longer accept the designation lesbian-feminist in the 1980s (her latest published novel in English, *Across the Acheron,* more than suggests as much), Marks's critical assessment of *The Lesbian Body* remains, to my way of seeing, correct:

> In *Le corps lesbien* Monique Wittig has created, through the incessant use of hyperbole and a refusal to employ traditional body codes, images sufficiently blatant to withstand reabsorption into male literary culture.... The J/e of *Le corps lesbien* is the most powerful lesbian in literature because as a lesbian-feminist she reexamines and redesigns the universe. (375–76)

Like Djuna Barnes's, Wittig's struggle is with language, to transcend gender. Barnes, as Wittig reads her, succeeds in "universalizing the feminine" because she "cancels out the genders by making them obsolete. I find it necessary to suppress them. That is the point of view of a lesbian."[23] And indeed, from the impersonal *on* [one] in *L'Opoponax,* to the feminine plural *elles* [they] replacing the generic masculine *ils* [they] in *Les guér-illères,* to the divided, linguistically impossible *j/e* [I], lover and writing subject of *The Lesbian Body,* Wittig's personal pronouns work to "lesbianize" language as impudently as her recastings of both classical and Christian myth and Western literary genres (the Homeric heroes and Christ, *The Divine Comedy* and *Don Quixote,* the epic, the lyric, the *Bildungsroman,* the encyclopaedic dictionary) do to literary history.[24] What will not do, for her purposes, is a "feminine writing" [*écriture féminine*] which, for Wittig, is no more than "the naturalizing metaphor of the brutal political fact of the domination of women" (63) and so complicit in the reproduction of femininity and of the female body as Nature.

Thus, as I read it, it is in the garbage dump of femininity, "In this dark adored adorned gehenna," that the odyssey of Wittig's *j/e-tu* in *The Lesbian Body* begins: "Fais tes adieux m/a très belle," "say your farewells m/y very beautiful . . . strong . . . indomitable . . . learned . . . ferocious . . . gentle . . . best beloved to what they call affection tenderness or gracious abandon. No one is unaware of what takes place here, it has no name as yet."[25] Here where?—in this book, this journey into the body of Western culture, this season in hell. And what takes place here?—the dismemberment and slow decomposition of the *female* body limb by limb, organ by organ, secretion by secretion. No one will be able to stand the sight of it, no one will come to aid in this awesome, excruciating, and exhilarating labor of love: dis-membering and re-membering, reconstituting the body in a new erotic economy, relearning to know it ("it has no name as yet") by another semiotics, reinscribing it with invert/inward desire, rewriting it other-wise, other-wise: a *lesbian* body.

The project, the conceptual originality and radical import of Wittig's lesbian as subject of a "cognitive practice" that enables the reconceptualization of the social and of knowledge itself from a position eccentric to the heterosexual institution, are all there in the first page of *Le corps lesbien*.[26] A "subjective cognitive practice" and a practice of writing as consciousness of contradiction ("the language you speak is made up of words that are killing you," she wrote in *Les guérillères*); a consciousness of writing, living, feeling, and desiring in the noncoincidence of experience and language, in the interstices of representation, "in the intervals that your masters have not been able to fill with their words of proprietors."[27] Thus, the struggle with language to rewrite the body beyond its precoded, conventional representations is not and cannot be a reappropriation of the female body as it is, domesticated, maternal, oedipally or preoedipally en-gendered, but is a struggle to transcend both gender and "sex" and recreate the body other-wise: to see it perhaps as monstrous, or grotesque, or mortal, or violent, and certainly also sexual, but with a material and sensual specificity that will resist phallic idealization and render it accessible to women in another sociosexual economy. In short, if it were not lesbian, this body would make no sense.

Replacing the Lacanian slash with a lesbian bar. (Sue-Ellen Case, "Toward a Butch-Femme Aesthetic")

At first sight, the reader of *The Lesbian Body* might find in its linguistically im-possible subject pronoun several theoretically possible valences that go from the more conservative (the slash in *j/e* represents the division of the Lacanian subject) to the less conservative (*j/e* can be expressed by writing but not by speech, representing Derridean *différance*), and to the radical feminist ("*j/e* is the symbol of the lived, rending experience which is *m/y* writing, of this cutting in two which throughout literature is the exercise of a language which does not constitute m/e as subject," as Wittig is reported to have said in Margaret Crosland's introduction to the Beacon paperback edition I own). Another reader, especially if a reader of science fiction, might think of Joanna Russ's brilliant lesbian-feminist novel, *The Female Man,* whose protagonist is a female genotype artic-ulated across four spacetime probabilities in four characters whose names all begin with J—Janet, Jeannine, Jael, Joanna—and whose sociosexual practices cover the spectrum from celibacy and "politically correct" monogamy to live toys and the 1970s equivalent of s/m.[28] What Wittig actually said in one of her essays in the 1980s is perhaps even more extreme:

> The bar in the *j/e* of *The Lesbian Body* is a sign of excess. A sign that helps to imagine an excess of "I," an "I" exalted. "I" has become so powerful in *The Lesbian Body* that it can attack the order of heterosexuality in texts and assault the so-called love, the heroes of love, and lesbianize them, lesbianize the symbols, lesbianize the gods and the goddesses, lesbianize the men and the women. This "I" can be destroyed in the attempt and resuscitated. Nothing resists this "I" (or this *tu* [you], which is its name, its love), which spreads itself in the whole world of the book, like a lava flow that nothing can stop.[29]

Excess, an exaltation of the "I" through costume, performance, *mise-en-scène,* irony, and utter manipulation of appearance, is what Sue-Ellen Case sees in the discourse of camp. If it is deplorable that the lesbian working-class bar culture of the 1950s "went into the feminist closet" during the 1970s, when organizations such as the Daughters of Bilitis encouraged lesbian identification with the more legitimate feminist dress codes and upwardly mobile lifestyles, writes Case, "yet the closet, or the bars, with their hothouse atmosphere [have] given us camp—the style, the discourse, the *mise-en-scène* of butch-femme roles." In these roles, "recuperating the space of seduction,"

> the butch-femme couple inhabit the subject position together. . . . These are not split subjects, suffering the torments of dominant ideology. They are coupled ones that do not impale themselves on the poles of sexual difference or metaphysical values, but constantly seduce the sign system, through flirtation and inconstancy into the light fondle of artifice, replacing the Lacanian slash with a lesbian bar.[30]

The question of address, of who produces cultural representations and for whom (in any medium, genre, or semiotic system, from writing to performance), and of who receives them and in what contexts, has been a major concern of feminism and other critical theories of cultural marginality. In the visual arts, that concern has focused on the notion of spectatorship, which has been central to the feminist critique of representation and the production of different images of difference, for example in women's cinema.[31] Recent work in both film and performance theory has been elaborating the film-theoretical notion of spectatorship with regard to what may be the specific relations of homosexual subjectivity, in several directions. Elizabeth Ellsworth, for one, surveying the reception of *Personal Best* (1982), a commercial man-made film about a lesbian relationship between athletes, found that lesbian feminist reviews of the film adopted interpretive strategies which rejected or altered the meaning carried by conventional (Hollywood) codes of narrative representation. For example, they redefined who was the film's protagonist or "object of desire," ignored the sections focused on heterosexual romance, disregarded the actual ending and speculated, instead, on a possible extratextual future for the characters beyond the ending. Moreover, "some reviewers named and illicitly eroticized moments of the film's 'inadvertent lesbian verisimilitude' [in Patrice Donnelly's performance] . . . codes of body language, facial expression, use of voice, structuring and expression of desire and assertion of strength in the face of male domination and prerogative."[32]

While recognizing limits to this "oppositional appropriation" of dominant representation, Ellsworth argues that the struggle over interpretation is a constitutive process for marginal subjectivities, as well as an important form of resistance. But when the marginal community is directly addressed, in the context of out-lesbian performance such as the WOW Cafe or the Split Britches productions, the appropriation seems to have no limits, to be directly "subversive," to yield not merely a site of interpretive work and resistance but a representation that requires no interpretive effort and is immediately, univocally legible, signaling "the creation of new imagery, new metaphors, and new conventions that can be read, or given new meaning, by a very specific spectator."[33]

The assumption behind this view, as stated by Kate Davy, is that such lesbian performance "undercut[s] the heterosexual model by implying a spectator that is not the generic, universal male, not the cultural construction 'woman,' but lesbian—a subject defined in terms of sexual similarity . . . whose desire lies outside the fundamental model or underpinnings of sexual difference" (47). Somehow, this seems too easy a solution to the problem of spectatorship, and even less convincing as a representation of "lesbian desire." For, if sexual similarity could so unproblematically replace sexual difference, why would the new lesbian theater need to insist on gender, if only as "the residue of sexual difference" that is, as Davy herself insists, worn in the "stance, gesture, movement, mannerisms, voice, and dress" (48) of the butch-femme play? Why would lesbian camp be taken up in theatrical performance, as Case suggests, to recuperate that space of seduction which historically has been the lesbian bar, and the Left Bank salon before it—spaces of daily-life performance, masquerade, cross-dressing, and practices constitutive of both community and subjectivity?

In an essay on "The Dynamics of Desire" in performance and pornography, Jill Dolan asserts that the reappropriation of pornography in lesbian magazines ("a visual space meant at least theoretically to be free of male subordination") offers "liberative fantasies" and "representations of one kind of sexuality based in lesbian desire," adding that the "male forms" of pornographic representation "acquire new meanings when they are used to communicate desire for readers of a different gender and sexual orientation."[34] Again, as in Davy, the question of lesbian desire is begged; and again the ways in which the new context would produce new meanings or "disrupt traditional meanings" (173) appear to be dependent on the presumption of a unified lesbian viewer/reader, gifted with undivided and non-contradictory subjectivity, and every bit as generalized and universal as the female spectator both Dolan and Davy impute (and rightly so) to the anti-pornography feminist performance art. For, if all lesbians had one and the same definition of "lesbian desire," there would hardly be any debate among us, or any struggle over interpretations of cultural images, especially the ones we produce.

What is meant by a term so crucial to the specificity and originality claimed for these performances and strategies of representation, is not an inappropriate question, then. When she addresses it at the end of her essay, Dolan writes: "Desire is not necessarily a fixed, male-owned commodity, but can be exchanged, with a much different meaning, between women" (173). Unless it can be taken as the ultimate camp representation, this notion of lesbian desire as commodity exchange is rather disturbing. For, unfortunately—or fortunately, as the case may be—commodity exchange does have the same meaning "between women" as between men, by definition—that is, by Marx's definition of the structure of capital. And so, if the "aesthetic differences between cultural feminist and lesbian performance art" are to be determined by the presence or absence of pornography, and to depend on a "new meaning" of commodity exchange, it is no wonder that we seem unable to get it off (our backs) even as we attempt to take it on.

The king does not count lesbians. (Marilyn Frye, *The Politics of Reality*)

The difficulty in defining an autonomous form of female sexuality and desire in the wake of a cultural tradition still Platonic, still grounded in sexual (in)difference, still caught in the tropism of hommo-sexuality, is not to be overlooked or willfully bypassed. It is perhaps even greater than the difficulty in devising strategies of representation which will, in turn, alter the standard of vision, the frame of reference of visibility, of *what can be seen*. For, undoubtedly, that is the project of lesbian performance, theater and film, a project that has already achieved a significant measure of success, not only at the WOW Cafe but also, to mention just a few examples, in Cherríe Moraga's *teatro, Giving Up the Ghost* (1986), Sally Potter's film *The Gold Diggers* (1983), or Sheila McLaughlin's *She Must Be Seeing Things* (1987). My point here is that redefining the conditions of vision, as well as the modes of representing, cannot be predicated on a single, undivided identity of performer and audience (whether as "lesbians" or "women" or "people of color" or any other single category constructed in opposition to its dominant other, "heterosexual women," "men," "whites," and so forth).

Consider Marilyn Frye's suggestive Brechtian parable about our culture's conceptual reality ("phallocratic reality") as a conventional stage play, where the actors—those committed to the performance/maintenance of the Play, "the phallocratic loyalists"—visibly occupy the foreground, while stagehands—who provide the necessary labor and framework for the material (re)production of the Play—remain invisible in the background. What happens, she speculates, when the stagehands (women, feminists) begin thinking of themselves as actors and try to participate visibly in the performance, attracting attention to their activities and their own role in the play? The loyalists cannot conceive that anyone in the audience may see or focus their attention on the stagehands' projects in the background, and thus become "disloyal" to the Play, or, as Adrienne Rich has put it, "disloyal to civilization."[35] Well, Frye suggests, there are some people in the audience who do see what the conceptual system of heterosexuality, the Play's performance, attempts to keep invisible. These are lesbian people, who can see it because their own reality is not represented or even surmised in the Play, and who therefore reorient their attention toward the background, the spaces, activities, and figures of women elided by the performance. But "attention is a kind of passion" that "fixes and directs the application of one's physical and emotional work":

> If the lesbian sees the women, the woman may see the lesbian seeing her. With this, there is a flowering of possibilities. The woman, feeling herself seen, may learn that she *can be* seen; she may also be able to know that a woman can see, that is, can author perception. . . . The lesbian's seeing undercuts the mechanism by which the production and constant reproduction of heterosexuality for woman was to be rendered *automatic.* (172)

And this is where we are now, as the critical reconsideration of lesbian history past and present is doing for feminist theory what Pirandello, Brecht, and others did for the bourgeois theater conventions, and avant-garde filmmakers have done for Hollywood cinema; the latter, however, have not just disappeared, much as one would wish they had. So, too, have the conventions of seeing, and the relations of desire and meaning in spectatorship, remained partially anchored or contained by a frame of visibility that is still heterosexual, or hommo-sexual, and just as persistently color blind.

For instance, what are the "things" the Black/Latina protagonist of McLaughlin's film imagines seeing, in her jealous fantasies about her white lover (although she does not "really" see them), if not those very images which our cultural imaginary and the whole history of cinema have constructed as the visible, what can *be seen,* and eroticized? The originality of *She Must Be Seeing Things* is in its representing *the question of* lesbian desire in these terms, as it engages the contradictions and complicities that have emerged subculturally, in both discourses and practices, through the feminist-lesbian debates on sex-radical imagery as a political issue of representation, as well as real life. It may be interestingly contrasted with a formally conventional film like Donna Deitch's *Desert Hearts* (1986), where heterosexuality remains off screen, in the diegetic background (in the character's past), but is actively present nonetheless in the spectatorial expectations set up by the genre (the love story) and the visual pleasure procured by conventional casting, cinematic narrative procedures, and commercial distribution. In sum, one film works *with and against* the institutions of heterosexuality and cinema, the other works *with* them. A similar point could be made about certain films with respect to the novels they derive from, such as *The Color Purple* or *Kiss of the Spider Woman,* where the critical and formal work of the novels against the social and sexual indifference built into the institution of heterosexuality is altogether suppressed and rendered invisible by the films' compliance with the apparatus of commercial cinema and its institutional drive to, precisely, commodity exchange.

So what *can* be seen? Even in feminist film theory, the current "impasse regarding female spectatorship is related to the blind spot of lesbianism," Patricia White suggests in her reading of Ulrike Ottinger's film *Madame X: An Absolute Ruler* (1977).[36] That film, she argues, on the contrary, displaces the assumption "that feminism finds its audience 'naturally' " (95); it does so by addressing the female spectator through specific scenarios and "figures of spectatorial desire" and "trans-sex identification," through figures of transvestism and masquerade. And the position the film thus constructs for its spectator is not one of essential femininity or impossible masculinization (as proposed by Mary Ann Doane and Laura Mulvey, respectively), but rather a position of marginality or "deviance" *vis-à-vis* the normative heterosexual frame of vision.[37]

Once again, what *can* be seen? "When I go into a store, people see a black person and only incidentally a woman," writes Jewelle Gomez, a writer of science fiction and author of at least one vampire story about a black lesbian blues singer named Gilda. "In an Upper West Side apartment building late at night when a white woman refuses to get on an elevator with me, it's because I am black. She sees a mugger as described on the late night news, not another woman as nervous to be out alone as she is."[38] If my suspicion that social and sexual indifference are never far behind one from the other is not just an effect of paranoia, it is quite possible that, in the second setting, the elevator at night, what a white woman sees superimposed on the black image of the mugger is the male image of the dyke, and both of these together are what prevents the white woman from seeing the other one like herself. Nevertheless, Gomez points out, "I can pass as straight, if by some bizarre turn of events I should want to . . . but I cannot pass as white in this society." Clearly, the very issue of passing, across any boundary of social division, is related quite closely to the frame of vision and the conditions of representation.

"Passing demands quiet. And from that quiet—silence," writes Michelle Cliff.[39] It is "a dual masquerade—passing straight/passing lesbian [that] enervates and contributes to speechlessness—to speak might be to reveal."[40] However, and paradoxically again, speechlessness can only be overcome, and her "journey into speech" begin, by "claiming an identity they taught me to despise"; that is, by passing black "against a history of forced fluency," a history of passing white.[41] The dual masquerade, her writing suggests, is at once the condition of speechlessness and of overcoming speechlessness, for the latter occurs by recognizing and representing the division in the self, the difference and the displacement from which any identity that needs to be claimed derives, and hence can be claimed only, in Lorde's words, as "the very house of difference."

Those divisions and displacements in history, memory, and desire are the "ghost" that Moraga's characters want to but cannot altogether give up. The division of the Chicana lesbian Marisa/Corky from the Mexican Amalia, whose desire cannot be re-defined outside the heterosexual imaginary of her culture, is also the division of Marisa/Corky from herself, the split produced in the girl Corky by sexual and social indifference, and by her internalization of a notion of hommo-sexuality which Marisa now lives as a wound, an infinite distance between her female body and her desire for women. If "the realization of shared oppression on the basis of being women and Chicanas holds the promise of a community of Chicanas, both lesbians and heterosexual," Yvonne Yarbro-Bejarano states, nevertheless "the structure of the play does not move neatly from pain to promise," and the divisions within them remain unresolved.[42] The character Marisa, however, I would add, has moved away from the hommo-sexuality of Corky (her younger self at age 11 and 17); and with the ambiguous character of Amalia, who loved a man almost as if he were a woman and who can love Marisa only when she (Amalia) is no longer one, the play itself has moved away from any simple opposition of "lesbian" to "heterosexual" and into the conceptual and experiential continuum of a female, Chicana subjectivity from where the question of lesbian desire must finally be posed. The play ends with that question—which is at once its outcome and its achieve-ment, its *éxito*.

What to do with the feminine invert? (Esther Newton, "The Mythic Mannish Lesbian")

Surveying the classic literature on inversion, Newton notes that Radclyffe Hall's "vision of lesbianism as sexual difference and as masculinity," and her "conviction that sexual desire must be male," both assented to and sought to counter the sociomedical discourses of the early twentieth century. "The notion of a feminine lesbian contradicted the congenital theory that many homosexuals in Hall's era espoused to counter the demands that they undergo punishing 'therapies' " (575). Perhaps that counter-demand led the novelist further to reduce the typology of female inversion (initially put forth by Krafft-Ebing as comprised of four types, then reduced to three by Havelock Ellis) to two: the invert and the "normal" woman who misguidedly falls in love with her. Hence the novel's emphasis on Stephen, while her lover Mary is a "forgettable and inconsistent" character who in the end gets turned over to a man. However, unlike Mary, Radclyffe Hall's real-life lover Una Troubridge "did not go back to heterosexuality even when Hall, late in her life, took a second lover," Newton points out. Una would then represent what *The Well of Loneliness* elided, the third type of female invert, and the most trou-blesome for Ellis: the "womanly" women "to whom the actively inverted woman is most attracted. These women differ in the first place from normal or average women in that . . . they seem to possess a genuine, though not precisely sexual, preference for women over men."[43] Therefore, Newton concludes, "Mary's real story has yet to be told" (575), and a footnote after this sentence refers us to "two impressive beginnings" of what could be Mary's real story, told from the perspective of a self-identified, con-temporary femme.[44]

The discourses, demands, and counter-demands that inform lesbian identity and representation in the 1980s are more diverse and socially heterogeneous than those of the first half of the century. They include, most notably, the political concepts of oppres-sion and agency developed in the struggles of social movements such as the women's movement, the gay liberation movement, and third world feminism, as well as an aware-ness of the importance of developing a theory of sexuality that takes into account the working of unconscious processes in the construction of female subjectivity. But, as I have tried to argue, the discourses, demands, and counter-demands that inform lesbian representation are still unwittingly caught in the paradox of socio-sexual (in)difference, often unable to think homosexuality and hommo-sexuality at once separately *and* to-gether. Even today, in most representational contexts, Mary would be either passing lesbian or passing straight, her (homo)sexuality being in the last instance what can not be seen. Unless, as Newton and others suggest, she enter the frame of vision *as or with* a lesbian in male body drag.[45]

NOTES

1. Luce Irigaray *"Cosí fan tutti,"* in *This Sex Which Is Not One,* trans. Catherine Porter (Ithaca: Cornell University Press, 1985), 86. The phrase "sexual indifference" actually appeared in Luce Irigaray, *Speculum of the Other Woman* [1974], trans. Gillian C. Gill (Ithaca: Cornell University Press, 1985), 28.

2. Irigaray, *Speculum,* 101–103.

3. See Petitioner's Brief in *Bowers v. Hardwick,* cited by Mary Dunlap, "Brief *Amicus Curiae* for the Lesbian Rights Project et al.," *Review of Law and Social Change* 14 (1986): 960.

4. David M. Halperin, "Why Is Diotima a Woman?," in Halperin, *One Hundred Years of Homosexuality and Other Essays on Greek Love* (New York: Routledge, 1990), 113–51. See also Halperin, "Plato and Erotic Reciprocity," *Classical Antiquity* 5:1 (1986): 60–80.

5. I am thinking in particular of Julia Kristeva, "Stabat Mater" (originally published as "Héréthique de l'amour") in *Tales of Love,* trans. Leon Roudiez (New York: Columbia University Press, 1987), and Jacques Derrida, *Spurs: Nietzsche's Styles,* trans. Barbara Harlow (Chicago: University of Chicago Press, 1979).

6. For a related reading of Aristotle and theater, see Sue-Ellen Case, "Classic Drag: The Greek Creation of Female Parts," *Theatre Journal* 37:3 (1985): 317–327. I have developed the notion of heterosexual contract (originally suggested in Monique Wittig, "The Straight Mind," *Feminist Issues* 1:1 [1980]: 103–111) in my "The Female Body and Heterosexual Presumption," *Semiotica* 67:3/4 (1987): 259–279.

7. Monique Wittig and Sande Zeig, *Lesbian Peoples: Material for a Dictionary* (New York: Avon Books, 1979).

8. See Biddy Martin and Chandra Mohanty, "Feminist Politics: What's Home Got to Do with It," in *Feminist Studies/Critical Studies,* ed. Teresa de Lauretis (Bloomington: Indiana University Press, 1986), 191–212, and Teresa de Lauretis, "Eccentric Subjects: Feminist Theory and Historical Consciousness," forthcoming in *Poetics Today.*

9. Catharine R. Stimpson, "The Somagrams of Gertrude Stein," reprinted in full in this volume.

10. Catharine R. Stimpson, "Zero Degree Deviancy: The Lesbian Novel in English," *Critical Inquiry* 8:2 (1981): 369.

11. Carolyn Allen, "Writing Toward *Nightwood:* Djuna Barnes' Seduction Stories," in *Silence and Power: A Reevaluation of Djuna Barnes,* ed. M.L. Broe (Carbondale: Southern Illinois University Press, 1987).

12. Carolyn Allen, " 'Dressing the Unknowable in the Garments of the Known': The Style of Djuna Barnes' *Nightwood,*" in *Women's Language and Style,* ed. Douglas Butturft and Edmund E. Epstein (Akron: L&S Books, 1978), 116.

13. Esther Newton, "The Mythic Mannish Lesbian: Radclyffe Hall and the New Woman," *Signs* 9:4 (1984): 557–575. See also Madeline Davis and Elizabeth Lapovsky Kennedy, "Oral History and the Study of Sexuality in the Lesbian Community: Buffalo, New York, 1940–1960," *Feminist Studies* 12:1 (1986): 7–26; and Joan Nestle, "Butch-Fem Relationships: Sexual Courage in the 1950s," *Heresies* 12 (1981): 21–24, now reprinted in Joan Nestle, *A Restricted Country* (Ithaca: Firebrand Books, 1987), 100–109.

14. See the discussion of Krafft-Ebing, Ellis, and others in George Chauncey, Jr., "From Sexual Inversion to Homosexuality: Medicine and the Changing Conceptualization of Female Deviance," *Salmagundi* 58–59 (1982–83): 114–146, and in Carroll Smith-Rosenberg, "The New Woman as Androgyne," in *Disorderly Conduct: Visions of Gender in Victorian America* (New York: Oxford University Press, 1985), 245–349.

15. Gayle Rubin, "Thinking Sex: Notes for a Radical Theory of the Politics of Sexuality," in *Pleasure and Danger: Exploring Female Sexuality,* ed. Carole S. Vance (Boston: Routledge & Kegan Paul, 1984), 309, reprinted with revisions, in this volume; "The Traffic in Women: Notes on the 'Political Economy' of Sex," in *Toward an Anthropology of Women,* ed. Rayna R. Reiter (New York: Monthly Review Press, 1975), 157–210. On the feminist "sex wars" of the 1970s and 1980s, see B. Ruby Rich, "Feminism and Sexuality in the 1980s," *Feminist Studies* 12:3 (1986): 525–561. On the relationship of feminism to lesbianism, see also Wendy Clark, "The Dyke, the Feminist and the Devil," in *Sexuality: A Reader,* ed. Feminist Review (London: Virago, 1987), 201–215.

16. Michel Foucault, *The History of Sexuality* (New York: Pantheon, 1978), 106, cited by Rubin, "Thinking Sex," 307. For a critical reading of the relevance and limitations of Foucault's views with regard to female sexuality, see Biddy Martin, "Feminism, Criticism, and Foucault," *New German Critique* 27 (1982): 3–30, and Teresa de Lauretis, *Technologies of Gender: Essays on Theory, Film, and Fiction* (Bloomington: Indiana University Press, 1987), chapters 1 and 2.

17. Catharine A. MacKinnon, *Feminism Unmodified: Discourses on Life and Law* (Cambridge: Harvard University Press, 1987), 60.

18. Combahee River Collective, "A Black Feminist Statement," in *This Bridge Called My Back: Writings by Radical Women of Color,* ed. Cherríe Moraga and Gloria Anzaldúa (New York: Kitchen Table: Women of Color Press, 1983), 210.

19. Audre Lorde, *Zami: A New Spelling of My Name* (Trumansburg, New York: The Crossing Press, 1982), 203 and 224.

20. "Writing. It's work. Changing the relationship with language. . . . Women's fictions raise theoretical issues: women's theorizing appears as/in fiction. Women's writing disturbs our usual understanding of the terms fiction and theory which assign value to discourses. . . . Fiction/theory has been the dominant mode of feminist writing in Québec for more than a decade," states Barbara Godard for the editorial collective of *Tessera* no. 3, a Canadian feminist, dual-language publication that has appeared annually as a special issue of an already established magazine ("Fiction/Theory: Editorial," *Canadian Fiction Magazine* 57 [1986]: 3–4). See Nicole Brossard, *L'Amèr ou Le Chapitre effrité* (Montréal: Quinze, 1977) and *These Our Mothers Or: The Disintegrating Chapter,* trans. Barbara Godard (Toronto: Coach House, 1983). On Brossard and other Canadian writers of fiction/theory, see Shirley Neuman, "Importing Difference," and other essays in *A Mazing Space: Writing Canadian Women Writing,* ed. Shirley Neuman and Smaro Kamboureli (Edmonton: Longspoon Press and NeWest Press, 1986).

21. Elaine Marks, "Lesbian Intertextuality," in *Homosexualities and French Literature,* ed. George Stambolian and Elaine Marks (Ithaca: Cornell University Press, 1979), 353–377.

22. Monique Wittig, *The Lesbian Body,* trans. David LeVay (New York: William Morrow, 1975), 9, cited by Marks, 373.

23. Monique Wittig, "The Point of View: Universal or Particular," *Feminist Issues* 3:2 (1983): 64.

24. See Hélène Vivienne Wenzel, "The Text as Body/Politics: An Appreciation of Monique Wittig's Writings in Context," *Feminist Studies* 7:2 (1981): 264–287, and Namascar Shaktini, "Displacing the Phallic Subject: Wittig's Lesbian Writing," *Signs* 8:1 (1982): 29–44, who writes: "Wittig's reorganization of metaphor around the lesbian body represents an epistemological shift from what seemed until recently the absolute, central metaphor—the phallus" (29).

25. Monique Wittig, *Le corps lesbien* (Paris: Minuit, 1973), 7. I have revised the English translation that appears in *The Lesbian Body,* 15.

26. The concept of "subjective, cognitive practice" is elaborated in Wittig, "One Is Not Born a Woman," *Feminist Issues* 1:2 (1981): 47–54. Reprinted in this volume. I discuss it at some length in my "Eccentric Subjects" (note 8 above).

27. Monique Wittig, *Les Guérillères,* trans. David LeVay (Boston: Beacon Press, 1985), 114.

28. Joanna Russ, *The Female Man* (New York: Bantam, 1975). See also Catherine L. McClenahan, "Textual Politics: The Uses of Imagination in Joanna Russ's *The Female Man,*" *Transactions of the Wisconsin Academy of Sciences, Arts and Letters* 70 (1982): 114–125.

29. Monique Wittig, "The Mark of Gender," *Feminist Issues* 5:2 (1985): 71.

30. Sue-Ellen Case, "Toward a Butch-Femme Aesthetic," in *Feminist Perspectives on Contemporary Women's Drama,* ed. Lynda Hart (Ann Arbor: University of Michigan Press, 1989). Reprinted in this volume. The butch-femme couple, like Wittig's *j/e-tu* and like the s/m lesbian couple—all of whom, in their respective self-definitions, are one the name and the love of the other—propose a dual subject that brings to mind again Irigaray's *This Sex Which Is Not One,* though they all would adamantly deny the latter's suggestion that a non-phallic eroticism may be traced to the preoedipal relation to the mother. One has to wonder, however, whether the denial has more to do with the committedly heterosexual bias of neo-Freudian psychoanalysis and object relations theory, with their inability to work through the paradox of sexual (in)difference on which they are founded but perhaps not destined to, or with our rejection of the maternal body which phallic representation has utterly alienated from women's love, from our desire for the self-same, by colonizing it as the "dark continent" and so rendering it at once powerless and inaccessible to us and to all "others."

31. See, for example, Judith Mayne, "The Woman at the Keyhole: Women's Cinema and Feminist Criticism," and B. Ruby Rich, "From Repressive Tolerance to Erotic Liberation: *Maedchen in Uniform,*" in *Re-vision: Essays in Feminist Film Criticism,* ed. Mary Ann Doane, Patricia Mellencamp, and Linda Williams (Frederick, Md.: University Publications of America and the American

Film Institute, 1984), 49–66 and 100–130; and Teresa de Lauretis, "Rethinking Women's Cinema: Aesthetics and Feminist Theory," in *Technologies of Gender,* 127–148.

32. Elizabeth Ellsworth, "Illicit Pleasures: Feminist Spectators and *Personal Best," Wide Angle* 8:2 (1986): 54.

33. Kate Davy, "Constructing the Spectator: Reception, Context, and Address in Lesbian Performance," *Performing Arts Journal* 10:2 (1986): 49.

34. Jill Dolan, "The Dynamics of Desire: Sexuality and Gender in Pornography and Performance," *Theatre Journal* 39:2 (1987): 171.

35. "To Be and Be Seen," in Marilyn Frye, *The Politics of Reality: Essays in Feminist Theory* (Trumansburg, New York: The Crossing Press, 1983), 166–173; Adrienne Rich, "Disloyal to Civilization: Feminism, Racism, Gynephobia," in *On Lies, Secrets, and Silence: Selected Prose 1966–1978* (New York: Norton, 1979), 275–310.

36. Patricia White, "Madame X of the China Seas," *Screen* 28:4 (1987): 82.

37. The two essays discussed are Mary Ann Doane, "Film and the Masquerade: Theorizing the Female Spectator," *Screen* 23:3–4 (1982): 74–87, and Laura Mulvey, "Afterthoughts on 'Visual Pleasure and Narrative Cinema' Inspired by *Duel in the Sun," Framework* 15/16/17 (1981): 12–15. Another interesting discussion of the notion of masquerade in lesbian representation may be found in Sue-Ellen Case, "Toward a Butch-Femme Aesthetic."

38. Jewelle Gomez, "Repeat After Me: We Are Different. We Are the Same," *Review of Law and Social Change* 14:4 (1986): 939. Her vampire story is "No Day Too Long," in *Worlds Apart: An Anthology of Lesbian and Gay Science Fiction and Fantasy,* ed. Camilla Decarnin, Eric Garber, and Lyn Paleo (Boston: Alyson Publications, 1986), 215–223.

39. "Passing," in Michelle Cliff, *The Land of Look Behind* (Ithaca: Firebrand Books, 1985), 22.

40. Michelle Cliff, "Notes on Speechlessness," *Sinister Wisdom* 5 (1978):7.

41. Michelle Cliff, "A Journey into Speech" and "Claiming an Identity They Taught Me to Despise," both in *The Land of Look Behind,* 11–17 and 40–47; see also her novel *No Telephone To Heaven* (New York: E.P. Dutton, 1987).

42. Yvonne Yarbro-Bejarano, "Cherríe Moraga's *Giving up the Ghost:* The Representation of Female Desire," *Third Woman* 3: 1–2 (1986): 118–119. See also Cherríe Moraga, *Giving Up the Ghost: Teatro in Two Acts* (Los Angeles: West End Press, 1986).

43. Havelock Ellis, "Sexual Inversion in Women," *Alienist and Neurologist* 16 (1895): 141–158, cited by Newton, "The Mythic Mannish Lesbian," 567.

44. Joan Nestle, "Butch-Fem Relationships" (see note 13 above) and Amber Hollibaugh and Cherríe Moraga, "What We're Rollin' Around in Bed With," both in *Heresies* 12 (1981): 21–24 and 58–62.

45. For many of the ideas developed in this essay, I am indebted to the other participants of the student-directed seminar on Lesbian History and Theory sponsored by the Board in Studies in History of Consciousness at the University of California, Santa Cruz in Fall 1987. For support of various kinds, personal and professional, I thank Kirstie McClure, Donna Haraway, and Michael Cowan, Dean of Humanities and Arts.

10

Eloquence and Epitaph:
Black Nationalism and the Homophobic Impulse in Responses to the Death of Max Robinson

PHILLIP BRIAN HARPER

Phillip Brian Harper, Assistant Professor of English and Afro-American Studies at Harvard University, is a literary and cultural critic. He is the author of Fiction and Fracture: The Social Text of Postmodernism *(1993) and of* The Same Difference: Social Division in African-American Culture *(forthcoming). In the essay reprinted here, Harper examines the vexed (and ultimately murderous) social and cultural contradictions that surrounded the figure of Max Robinson, a Black male television anchorman who died from AIDS in 1988. Caught between the simultaneous imperatives to project to Black people the image of a "positive role model" (but at the cost of appearing to achieve success and respectability in largely White terms) and to embody in his own person the entire range of African-American experience (but at the cost of remaining an alien presence in the predominantly White world of network news), Robinson occupied a position that both authorized him to speak and imposed on him the obligation to maintain several kinds of silence. Harper sees the contradictions that hemmed in Robinson's career reproduced in the public responses to his death; those contradictions powerfully dramatize some of the constraints on efforts to halt the spread of AIDS in U.S. communities of color.*

From June 1981 through February 1991, 167,803 people in the US were diagnosed as having Acquired Immune Deficiency Syndrome. Of that number of total reported cases, 38,361—or roughly 23%—occurred in males of African descent, although black males account for less than 6% of the total US population.[1] It is common enough knowledge that black men constitute a disproportionate number of people with AIDS in this country—common in the sense that, whenever the AIDS epidemic achieves a new statistical milestone (as it did in the Winter of 1991, when the number of AIDS-related deaths in the US reached 100,000), the major media generally provide a demographic breakdown of the figures. And yet, somehow the enormity of the morbidity and mortality rates for black men (like that for gay men of whatever racial identity) doesn't seem to register in the national consciousness as a cause for great concern. This is, no doubt, largely due to a general sense that the trajectory of the average African-American man's life must "naturally" be rather short, routinely subject to violent termination. And this sense, in turn, helps account for the fact that there has never been a case of AIDS that riveted public attention on the vulnerability of black men the way, for instance, the death of Rock Hudson shattered the myth of the invincible white male cultural hero.[2] This is not to say that no nationally known black male figure has died of AIDS-related causes, but rather that numerous and complex cultural factors conspire to prevent such deaths from effectively galvanizing AIDS activism in African-American communities. This essay represents an attempt to explicate several such factors that were operative in the case of one particular black man's bout with AIDS, and thus to indicate what further cultural intervention needs to take place if we hope to stem the ravages of AIDS amongst the African-American population.

The Sound of Silence

In December of 1988, National Public Radio broadcast a report on the death of Max Robinson, who had been the first black newsanchor on US network television, staffing the Chicago desk of ABC's *World News Tonight* from 1978 to 1983. Robinson was one of 4,123 African-American men to die in 1988 of AIDS-related causes (of a nationwide total of 17,119 AIDS-related deaths),[3] but rather than focus on the death itself at this point, I want to examine two passages from the broadcast that, taken together, describe an entire problematic that characterizes the existence of AIDS in many black communities in the United States. The first is a statement by a colleague of Robinson's both at ABC News and at WMAQ-TV in Chicago, where Robinson worked after leaving the network. Producer Bruce Rheins remembers being on assignment with Robinson on the streets of Chicago: "We would go out on the street a lot of times, doing a story . . . on the Southside or something . . . and I remember one time, this mother leaned down to her children, pointed, and said, 'That's Max Robinson. You learn how to speak like him.' " Immediately after this statement from Rheins, the NPR correspondent reporting the piece, Cheryl Duvall, informs us that "Robinson had denied the nature of his illness for months, but after he died . . . his friend Roger Wilkins said Robinson wanted his death to emphasize the need for AIDS awareness among black people."[4] These are the concluding words of the report, and as such they reproduce the epitaphic structure of Robinson's deathbed request, raising the question of just how well any of us is addressing the educational needs of black communities with respect to AIDS.

That these two passages should be juxtaposed in the radio report is striking because they testify to the power of two different phenomena that appear to be in direct contradiction. Bruce Rheins's statement underscores the importance of Robinson's speech as an affirmation of black identity for the benefit of the community from which he sprang. Cheryl Duvall's remarks, on the other hand, implicate Robinson's denial that he had AIDS in a general silence regarding the effects of the epidemic among the African-American population. I would like, in this essay, to examine how speech and silence actually interrelate to produce a discursive matrix that governs the cultural significance of AIDS in black communities. Indeed, Max Robinson, newsanchor, inhabited a space defined by the overlapping of at least two distinct types of discourse which, though often in conflict, intersect in a way that makes discussion of Robinson's AIDS diagnosis—and of AIDS among blacks generally—a particularly difficult activity.

As it happens, the apparent conflict between vocal affirmation and the peculiar silence effected through denial is already implicated in the nature of speech itself, in the case of Max Robinson. There is a potential doubleness in the significance of Robinson's "speaking" that the mother cited above urges upon her child as an example to be emulated. It is clear, first of all, that the reference is to Robinson's exemplification of the articulate, authoritative presence that is ideally represented in the television newsanchor—an exemplification noteworthy because of the fact that Robinson was black.

Bruce Rheins's comments illustrate this particularly well: "Max really was a symbol for a lot of people. . . . Here was a very good-looking, well-dressed, and very obviously intelligent black man giving the news in a straightforward fashion, and not on a black radio station or a black TV station or on the black segment of a news report—he was the anchorman" (*All Things Considered*). Rheins's statement indicates the power of Robinson's verbal performance before the camera, for it is through this performance that Robinson's "intelligence," which Rheins emphasizes, is made "obvious." Other accounts of Robinson's tenure as a television newsanchor recapitulate this reference. An article in the June 1989 issue of *Vanity Fair* remembers Robinson for "his steely, unadorned delivery, precise diction, and magical presence."[5] A *New York Times* obituary notes the "unforced, authoritative manner" that characterized Robinson's on-air persona, and backs its claim with testimony from current ABC newsanchor and Robinson's former colleague, Peter Jennings: "In terms of sheer performance, Max was a penetrating communicator. He had a natural gift to look in the camera and talk to people."[6] A 1980 *New York Times* reference asserts that Robinson was "blessed with a commanding voice and a handsome appearance."[7] A posthumous "appreciation" in the *Boston Globe* describes Robinson as "earnest and telegenic," noting that he "did some brilliant reporting . . . and was a consummate newscaster."[8] James Snyder, News director at WTOP–TV in Washington, D.C., where Robinson began his anchoring career, says that Robinson "had this terrific voice, great enunciation and phrasing. He was just a born speaker" (Boyer 72). Elsewhere, Snyder succinctly summarizes Robinson's appeal, noting his "great presence on the air."[9]

All of these encomia embody allusions to Robinson's verbal facility that must be understood as praise for his ability to speak articulate Received Standard English, which linguist Geneva Smitherman has identified as the dialect upon which "White America has insisted . . . as the price of admission into its economic and social mainstream."[10] The emphasis that commentators place on Robinson's "precise diction" or on his "great enunciation and phrasing" is an index of the general surprise evoked by his facility with the white bourgeois idiom considered standard in "mainstream" US life, and certainly in television news. The black mother cited above surely recognizes the opportunity for social advancement inherent in this facility with standard English, and this is no doubt the benefit she has in mind for her children when she urges them to "speak like" Max Robinson.

At the same time, however, that the mother's words can be interpreted as an injunction to speak "correctly," they might alternately be understood as a call for speech, *per se*—as encouragement to *speak out* like Max Robinson, to stand up for one's interests as a black person as Robinson did throughout his career. In this case, the import of her command is traceable to a black cultural nationalism that has waxed and waned in the US since the mid-nineteenth century, but which, in the context of the Black Power movement of the 1960s, underwent a revival that has continued to influence black cultural life in this country.[11] Geneva Smitherman notes the way in which this cultural nationalism has been manifested in black language and discourse, citing the movement "among writers, artists, and black intellectuals of the 1960s who deliberately wrote and rapped in the Black Idiom and sought to preserve its distinctiveness in the literature of the period" (11). Obviously, Max Robinson did not participate in this nationalistic strategy in the context of his work as a network newsanchor. Success in television newscasting, insofar as it depends upon one's conformity to models of behavior deemed acceptable by white bourgeois culture, largely precludes the possibility of one's exercising the "Black Idiom" and thereby manifesting a strong black consciousness in the broadcast context. We might say, then, that black people's successful participation in modes of discourse validated in mainstream culture—their facility with Received Standard English, for instance—actually implicates them in a profound *silence* regarding their African-American identity.

It is arguable, however, that Max Robinson, like all blacks who have achieved a degree of recognition in mainstream US culture, actually played both sides of the behavioral dichotomy that I have described—the dichotomy between articulate verbal performance in the accepted standard dialect of the English language and vocal affirmation of conscious black identity.[12] Though on the one hand, Robinson's performance before the cameras provided an impeccable image of bourgeois respectability that could easily be read as the erasure of consciousness of black identity, he was at the same time known for publicly affirming his interest in the various sociopolitical factors that affect blacks' existence in the United States, thus continually emphasizing his African-American identity. For example, in February 1981, Robinson became the center of controversy when he was reported as telling a college audience that the various network news agencies, including ABC, discriminated against their black journalists, and that the news media in general constitute "a crooked mirror" through which "white America views itself."[13] In this instance, not only does Robinson's statement manifest semantically his consciousness of his own black identity, but the very form of the entire incident can be said to embody an identifiably black cultural behavior. After being summoned to the offices of then-ABC News president Roone Arledge subsequent to making his allegations of network discrimination, Robinson said that "he had not meant to single out ABC for criticism" (Gerard), thus performing a type of rhetorical backstep by which his criticism, though retracted, was effectively lodged and registered both by the public and by the network. While this mode of protecting one's own interests is by no means unique to African-American culture, it does have a particular resonance within an African-American context. Specifically, Robinson's backstepping strategy can be understood as a form of what is called "loud-talking" or "louding"—a verbal device, common within many black-English-speaking communities, in which a person "says something of someone just loud enough for that person to hear, but indirectly, so he cannot properly respond," or so that, when the object of the remark *does* respond, "the speaker can reply to the effect, 'Oh, I wasn't talking to you.'"[14] Robinson's insistence that his remarks did not refer specifically to ABC News can be interpreted as a form of the disingenuous reply characteristic of loud-talking, thus locating his rhetorical strategy within the cultural context of black communicative patterns and underscoring his African-American identification.

Roone Arledge, in summoning Robinson to his offices after the incident, made unusually explicit the suppression of African-American identity generally effected by the networks in their news productions; such dramatic measures are not usually necessary because potential manifestations of strong black cultural identification are normally subdued by blacks' very participation in the discursive conventions of the network newscast.[15] Thus, the more audible and insistent Max Robinson's televised performance in Received Standard English and in the white bourgeois idiom of the network newscast, the more secure the silence imposed upon the vocal black consciousness that he always threatened to display. Robinson's articulate speech before the cameras always implied a silencing of the African-American idiom.

Concomitant with the silencing in the network-news context of black-affirmative discourse is the suppression of another aspect of black identity alluded to in the above-quoted references to Max Robinson's on-camera performance. The emphasis these commentaries place on Robinson's articulateness is coupled with their simultaneous insistence on his physical attractiveness: Bruce Rheins's remarks on Robinson's "obvious intelligence" are accompanied by a reference to his "good looks"; Tony Schwartz's inventory of Robinson's assets notes both his "commanding voice" and his "handsome appearance"; Joseph Kahn's "appreciation" of Robinson cites his "brilliant reporting" as well as his "telegenic" quality; it seems impossible to comment on Robinson's success as a newsanchor without noting simultaneously his verbal ability and his physical appeal.

Such commentary is not at all unusual in discussions of television newscasters, whose personal charms have taken on an increasing degree of importance since the early day of the medium. Indeed, Schwartz's 1980 *New York Times* article entitled "Are TV Anchormen Merely Performers?"—intended as a critique of the degree to which television news is conceived as entertainment—actually underscores the importance of a newscaster's physical attractiveness to a broadcast's success; and by the late 1980s that importance has become a truism of contemporary culture, assimilated into the popular consciousness, through the movie *Broadcast News,* for instance.[16] In the case of a black man, such as Max Robinson, however, discussions of a newsanchor's "star quality" become potentially problematic and, consequently, extremely complex, because such a quality is founded upon an implicitly acknowledged "sex appeal" the concept of which has always been highly charged with respect to black men in the US.

In the classic text on the subject, Calvin C. Hernton has argued that the black man has historically been perceived as the bearer of a bestial sexuality, as the savage "walking phallus" that poses a constant threat to an idealized white womanhood and thus to the whole US social order.[17] To the extent that this is true, then for white patriarchal institutions such as the mainstream media to note the physical attractiveness of any black man is for them potentially to unleash the very beast that threatens their power. Max Robinson's achievement of a professional, public position that mandates the deployment of a certain rhetoric—that of the newsanchor's attractive and telegenic persona—thus also raises the problem of taming the threatening black male sexuality that that rhetoric conjures up.

This taming, I think, is once again achieved through Robinson's articulate verbal performance, references to which routinely accompany acknowledgments of his physical attractiveness. In commentary on white newscasters, paired references to both their physical appeal and their rhetorical skill serve merely to defuse accusations that television journalism is superficial and "image-oriented." In Robinson's case, however, the acknowledgment of his articulateness also serves to absorb the threat of his sexuality that is raised in references to his physical attractiveness; in the same way that Robinson's conformity to the "rules" of standard English language performance suppresses the possibility of his articulating a radical identification with African-American culture, it also, in attesting to his refinement and civility, actually *domesticates* his threatening physicality that itself *must* be alluded to in conventional liberal accounts of his performance as a newsanchor. James Snyder's reference to Robinson's "great presence" is a most stunning example of such an account, for it neatly conflates and thus simultaneously acknowledges both Robinson's *physical* person (in the tradition of commentary on network news personalities) and his virtuosity in standard *verbal* performance in such a way that the latter mitigates the threat posed by the former. Max Robinson's standard English speech, then, serves not only to suppress black culturolinguistic forms that might disrupt the white bourgeois aspect of network news, but also to keep in check the black male sexuality that threatens the social order that the news media represent.[18] Ironically, in this latter function, white bourgeois discourse seems to share an objective with forms of black discourse, which themselves work to suppress certain threatening elements of black male sexuality, resulting in a strange reaction to Max Robinson's death in African-American communities.

Homophobia in African-American Discourse

Whether it is interpreted as a reference to his facility at Received Standard English, whereby he achieved a degree of success in the white-run world of broadcast media, or as a reference to his repeated attempts to vocalize, in the tradition of African-American discourse, the grievances of blacks with respect to their sociopolitical status in the US, to "speak like Max Robinson" is simultaneously to silence discussion of the various possibilities of black male sexuality. We have seen how an emphasis on Robinson's facility at "white-oriented" discourse serves to defuse the "threat" of rampant black male sexuality that constitutes so much of the sexuopolitical structure of US society. Indeed, some middle-class blacks have colluded in this defusing of black sexuality, attempting to explode whites' stereotypes of blacks as oversexed by stifling discussion of black sexuality generally.[19] At the same time, the other tradition from which Max Robinson's speech derives meaning also functions to suppress discussion about specific aspects of black male sexuality that are threatening to the black male image.

In her book on "the language of black America," Geneva Smitherman cites, rather non-self-consciously, examples of black discourse that illustrate this point. For instance, in a discussion of black musicians' adaptation of themes from the African-American oral tradition, Smitherman mentions the popular early-sixties recording of "Stagger Lee," based on a traditional narrative folk poem. The hero for whom the narrative is named is, as Smitherman puts it, "a fearless, mean dude," so that "it became widely fashionable [in black communities] to refer to oneself as 'Stag,' as in . . . 'Don't mess wif me, cause I ain't no fag, uhm Stag' " (52). What is notable here is not merely the homophobia manifested in the "rap" laid down by the black "brother" imagined to be speaking this line, but also that the rap itself, the very verbal performance, as Smitherman points out, serves as the evidence that the speaker is indeed *not* a "fag"; verbal facility becomes proof of one's conventional masculinity and thus silences discussion of one's possible homosexuality.[20] This point touches upon a truism in studies of black discourse. Smitherman herself implies the testament to masculine prowess embodied in the black "rap," explaining that, "While some raps convey social and cultural information, others are used for conquering foes and women" (82); and she further acknowledges the "power" with which the spoken word is imbued in the African-American tradition (as in others), especially insofar as it is employed in masculine "image-making," through braggadocio and other highly self-assertive strategies (83; 97).[21] Indeed, a whole array of these verbal strategies for establishing a strong masculine image can be identified in the contemporary phenomenon of "rap" music, a form indigenous to black-male culture, though increasingly appropriated and transformed by members of other social groups, notably black women.[22]

If verbal facility is considered as an identifying mark of masculinity in certain African-American contexts, however, this is only when it is demonstrated specifically through use of the vernacular. Indeed, a too evident facility in the standard white idiom can quickly identify one not as a strong black man, but rather as a white-identified Uncle Tom who must also, therefore, be weak, effeminate, and probably a "fag." To the extent that this process of homophobic identification reflects powerful cross-class hostilities, then it is certainly not unique to African-American culture. Its imbrication with questions of racial identity, however, compounds its potency in the African-American context. Simply put, within some African-American communities the "professional" or "intellectual" black male inevitably endangers his status both as black and as "male" whenever he evidences a facility with Received Standard English—a facility upon which his very identity as a professional or an intellectual in the larger society is founded in the first place. Max Robinson was not the first black man to face this dilemma;[23] a decade or so before he emerged on network television, a particularly influential group of black writers attempted to negotiate the problem by incorporating into their work the semantics of "street" discourse, thereby establishing an intellectual practice that was both "black" enough and virile enough to bear the weight of a stridently nationalist agenda. Thus, a strong "Stagger Lee"-type identification can be found in the poem "Don't Cry, Scream," by Haki Madhubuti (Don L. Lee):

> swung on a faggot who politely
> scratched his ass in my presence.
> he smiled broken teeth stained from
> his over-used tongue, fisted-face.
> teeth dropped in tune with ray
> charles singing 'yesterday.'[24]

Here the scornful language of the poem itself recapitulates the homophobic violence that it commemorates (or invites us to imagine as having occurred), the two together attesting to the speaker's aversion to homosexuality and, thus, to his own unquestionable masculinity. Though it is striking, the violent hostility evident in this piece is not at all unusual among the revolutionist poems of the Black Arts Movement. Much of the work by the Black Arts Poets is characterized by a violent language that seems wishfully conceived of as potent and performative—as capable, in itself, of wreaking destruction upon the white establishment to which the Black Power movement is opposed.[25] What is important to note, beyond the rhetoric of violence, is the way in which that rhetoric is conceived as part and parcel of a black nationalism to which all sufficiently proud African-Americans must subscribe. Nikki Giovanni, for instance, urges, "Learn to kill niggers/Learn to be Black men," indicating the necessity of cathartic violence to the transformation of blacks from victims into active subjects, and illustrating the degree to which black masculinity functions as the rhetorical stake in much of the Black Arts poetry by both men *and* women.[26] To the extent that such rhetoric is considered as an integral element in the cultural-nationalist strategy of Black Power politics, then a violent homophobia, too, is necessarily implicated in this particular nationalistic position, which since the late 1960s has filtered throughout black communities in the US as a major influence in African-American culture.

Consequently, Max Robinson was put in a very difficult position with respect to talking about his AIDS diagnosis. Robinson's reputation was based on his articulate outspokenness; however, as we have seen, that very well-spokenness derived its power within two different modes of discourse that, though they are sometimes at odds, both work to suppress issues of sexuality that are implied in any discussion of AIDS.[27] The white bourgeois cultural context in which Robinson derived his status as an authoritative figure in the mainstream news media must always keep a vigilant check on black male sexuality, which is perceived to be threatening generally (and it is assisted in this task by a moralistic black middle class that seeks to explode notions of black hypersexuality). At the same time, the African-American cultural context to which Robinson appealed for his status as a paragon of black pride and self-determination embodies an ethic which precludes sympathetic discussion of black male homosexuality. However rapidly the demography of AIDS in this country may be shifting as more and more people who are not gay men become infected with HIV, the historical and cultural conditions surrounding the development of the epidemic ensure its ongoing association with male homosexuality, so it is not surprising that the latter should emerge as a topic of discussion in any consideration of Max Robinson's death. The apparent *inevitability* of that emergence (and the degree to which the association between AIDS and male homosexuality would become threatening to Robinson's reputation and discursively problematic, given the contexts in which his public persona was created) is dramatically illustrated in the 9 January 1989 issue of *Jet* magazine, the black-oriented weekly. That number of *Jet* contains an obituary of Max Robinson that is very similar to those issued by the *New York Times* and other non-black media, noting Robinson's professional achievements and his controversial tenure at ABC News, alluding to the "tormented" nature of his life as a symbol of black success, and citing his secrecy surrounding his AIDS diagnosis and his wish that his death be used as the occasion to educate blacks about AIDS. The *Jet* obituary also notes that "the main victims [sic] of the disease [sic] have been intravenous drug users and homosexuals," leaving open the question of Robinson's relation to either of these categories.[28]

Printed right next to Robinson's obituary in the same issue of *Jet* is a notice of another AIDS-related death, that of the popular disco singer, Sylvester. Sylvester's obituary, however, offers an interesting contrast to that of Robinson, for it identifies Sylvester, in its very first sentence, as "the flamboyant homosexual singer whose high-pitched voice and dramatic on-stage costumes propelled him to the height of stardom on the disco music scene during the late 1970s." The piece goes on to indicate the openness with which Sylvester lived as a gay man, noting that he "first publicly acknowledged he had AIDS at the San Francisco Gay Pride March last June [1988], which he attended in a wheelchair with the People With AIDS group," and quoting his recollection of his first sexual experience, at age 7, with an adult male evangelist: "You see, I was a queen even back then, so it didn't bother me. I rather liked it."[29]

Obviously, a whole array of issues is raised by Sylvester's obituary and its juxtaposition with that of Max Robinson (not the least of which has to do with the complicated phenomenon of sex between adults and children). What is most pertinent for discussion here, however, is the difference between *Jet*'s treatments of Sylvester's and Max Robinson's sexualities, and the factors that account for that difference. It is clear, I think, that Sylvester's public persona emerges from contexts that are different from those that produced Max Robinson. If it is true that, as *Jet* puts it, "the church was . . . the setting for Sylvester's first homosexual experience" (18), it is also true that "Sylvester learned to sing in churches in South Los Angeles and went on to perform at gospel conventions around the state" (18). That is to say that the church-choir context in which Sylvester was groomed for a singing career has stereotypically served as a locus in which young black men both discover and sublimate their homosexuality, and also as a conduit to a world of professional entertainment generally conceived as "tolerant," if not downright encouraging, of diverse sexualities. In Sylvester's case, this was particularly true, since he was able to help create a disco culture characterized by a fusion of elements from black and gay communities and in which he and others could thrive as openly gay men. Thus, the black-church context, though ostensibly hostile to homosexuality and gay identity, nevertheless has traditionally provided a means by which black men can achieve a sense of themselves as homosexual and even, in cases such as Sylvester's, expand that sense into a gay-affirmative public persona.[30]

On the other hand, the public figure of Max Robinson, as we have seen, is cut from entirely different cloth, formed in the intersection of discursive contexts that do not allow for the expression of black male homosexuality in any recognizable form. The discursive bind constituted by Robinson's status both as a conventionally successful media personality and as exemplar of black male self-assertion and racial consciousness left him with no alternative to the manner in which he dealt with his diagnosis in the public forum—shrouding the nature of his illness in a secrecy that he was able to break only after his death, with the posthumous acknowledgment that he had AIDS. Consequently, obituarists and commentators on Robinson's death are faced with the "problem" of how to address issues relating to Robinson's sexuality—to his possible *homo*sexuality—the result being a large body of wrongminded commentary that actually hinders the educational efforts Max Robinson supposedly intended to endorse.

It is a mistake to think that, because most accounts of Robinson's death do not mention the possibility of his homosexuality, it is not conceived of as a problem to be reckoned with. On the contrary, since, as I have attempted to show, the discursive contexts in which Max Robinson derived his power as a public figure function to prevent discussion of black male homosexuality, the silence regarding the topic that characterizes most of the notices of Robinson's death actually marks the degree to which the possibility of black male homosexuality is worried over and considered problematic. The instances in which the possibility of Robinson's homosexuality *does* explicitly figure actually serve as proof of the anxiety that founds the more usual silence on the subject. A look at a few commentaries on Robinson's death will illustrate this well; examining these pieces in the chronological order of their appearance in the media will especially help us to see how, over time, the need to quell anxiety about the possibility of Robinson's homosexuality becomes increasingly desperate, thus increasingly undermining the educational efforts that his death was supposed to occasion.

In the two weeks after Robinson died, there appeared in *Newsweek* magazine an obituary that, once again, includes the obligatory references to Robinson's "commanding" on-air presence, to his attacks on racism in the media, and to the psychic "conflict" he suffered that led him to drink.[31] In addition to rehearsing this standard litany, however, the *Newsweek* obituary also emphasizes that "even [Robinson's] family . . . don't know how he contracted the disease." The reference to the general ignorance as to how Robinson became infected with HIV—the virus widely believed to cause the suppressed immunity that underlies AIDS—leaves open the possibility that Robinson engaged in "homosexual activity" that put him at risk for infection, just as the *Jet* notice leaves unresolved the possibility that he was a homosexual or an IV drug user. Yet, the invocation in the *Newsweek* piece of Robinson's "family," with all its conventional heterosexist associations, simultaneously indicates the anxiety that the possibility of Robinson's homosexuality generally produces, and constitutes an attempt to redeem Robinson from the unsavory implications of his AIDS diagnosis.

The subtlety of the *Newsweek* strategy for dealing with the possibility of Robinson's homosexuality gives way to a more direct approach by Jesse Jackson, in an interview broadcast on the NPR series on AIDS and blacks (*Morning Edition,* 5 April 1989). Responding to charges by black AIDS activists that he missed a golden opportunity to educate blacks about AIDS by neglecting to speak out about modes of HIV transmission soon after Robinson's death, Jackson provided this statement:

> Max shared with my family and me that he had the AIDS virus [sic], but that it did not come from homosexuality, it came from promiscuity. . . . And now we know that the number one transmission [factor] for AIDS is not sexual contact, it's drugs, and so the crises of drugs and needles and AIDS are connected, as well as AIDS and promiscuity are connected. And all we can do is keep urging people not to isolate this crisis by race, or by class, or by sexual preference, but in fact to observe the precautionary measures that have been advised, on the one hand, and keep urging more money for research immediately because it's an international health crisis and it's a killer disease.

A number of things are notable about this statement. First of all, Jackson, like the *Newsweek* writer, is careful to reincorporate the discussion of Robinson's AIDS diagnosis into the nuclear family context, emphasizing that Robinson shared his secret with Jackson *and his family,* and thereby attempting to mitigate the effects of the association of AIDS with male homosexuality. Second, Jackson invokes the problematic and completely unhelpful concept of "promiscuity," wrongly opposing it to homosexuality (and thus implicitly equating it with heterosexuality) in such a way that he actually appears to be endorsing it over that less legitimate option, contrary to what he must intend to convey about the dangers of unprotected sex with multiple partners; and, of course, since he does not actually mention safer sex practices, he implies that it is "promiscuity," *per se,* that puts people at risk of contracting HIV, when it is, rather, unprotected sex with however few partners that constitutes risky behavior. Third, by identifying IV drug use over risky sexual behavior as the primary means of HIV transmission, Jackson manifests a blindness to his own insight about the interrelatedness of various factors in the phenomenon of AIDS, for unprotected sexual activity is often part and parcel of the drug culture (especially that of crack) in which transmission of HIV thrives, as sex is commonly exchanged for access to drugs in that context.[32] Finally, Jackson's sense of "all we can do" to prevent AIDS is woefully inadequate: to "urge people to observe the precautionary measures that have been advised" obviously presupposes that everyone is already aware of what those precautionary measures are, for Jackson himself does not outline them in his statement; to demand more money for research is crucial, but it does not go the slightest distance toward enabling people to protect themselves from HIV in the present; and to resist conceptualizing AIDS as endemic to one race, class, or sexual orientation is of extreme importance (though it is equally important to recognize the relative degrees of interest that different constituencies have in the epidemic), but in the context of Jackson's statement this strategy for preventing various social groups from being stigmatized through their association with AIDS is utilized merely to protect Max Robinson in particular from speculation that his bout with AIDS was related to homosexual sex. Indeed, Jackson's entire statement centers on the effort to clear Max Robinson from potential charges of homosexuality, and his intense focus on this homophobic endeavor works to the detriment of his attempts to make factual statements about the nature of HIV transmission.[33]

Jackson is implicated, as well, in the third media response to Robinson's death that I want to examine, a response that, like those discussed above, represents an effort to silence discussion of the possibility of Max Robinson's homosexuality. In his June 1989 *Vanity Fair* article, Peter J. Boyer reports on the eulogy Jackson delivered at the Washington, D.C. memorial service for Max Robinson. Boyer cites Jackson's quotation of Robinson's deathbed request: "He said, 'I'm not sure and know not where [sic], but even on my dying bed . . . let my predicament be a source of education to our people.' " Boyer then asserts that "two thousand people heard Jesse Jackson keep the promise he'd made to Robinson . . . : 'It was not homosexuality,' [Jackson] told them, 'but promiscuity,' " implicitly letting people know that Robinson "got AIDS from a woman" (84). Apparently, then, the only deathbed promise that Jackson kept was the one he made to ensure that people would not think that Robinson was gay; no information about how HIV is transmitted or about how such transmission can be prevented has escaped his lips in connection with the death of Max Robinson, though Peter Boyer, evidently, has been fooled into believing that Jackson's speech constituted just such substantive information. This is not surprising, since Boyer's article itself is nothing more than an anxious effort to convince us of Max Robinson's heterosexuality, as if that were the crucial issue. Boyer's piece mentions Robinson's three marriages (74); it comments extensively on his "well-earned" reputation as an "inveterate womanizer," and emphasizes his attractiveness to women, quoting one male friend as saying, "He could walk into a room and you could just hear the panties drop," and a woman acquaintance as once telling a reporter, "Don't forget to mention he has fine thighs" (74); it notes that "none of Robinson's friends believe that he was a homosexual" (84); and it cites Robinson's own desperate attempt "to compose a list of women whom he suspected as possible sources of his disease" (84), as though to provide written corroboration of his insistence to a friend, "But I'm not gay" (82).

From early claims, then, that "even Robinson's family" had no idea how he contracted HIV, there developed an authoritative scenario in which Robinson's extensive heterosexual affairs were common knowledge and which posits his contraction of HIV from a female sex partner as a near-certainty. It seems that, subsequent to Robinson's death, a whole propaganda machine was put into operation to establish a suitable account of his contraction of HIV and of his bout with AIDS, the net result of which was to preclude the effective AIDS education that Robinson reputedly wanted his death to occasion, as the point he supposedly intended to make became lost in a homophobic shuffle to "fix" his sexual orientation and to construe his death in inoffensive terms.

In order to ensure that this essay not become absorbed in that project, then, which would deter us from the more crucial task of understanding how to combat the AIDS epidemic, it is important for me to state flat out that I have no idea whether Max Robinson's sex partners were male or female or both. I acknowledge explicitly my ignorance on this matter because to do so, I think, is to reopen sex in all its manifestations as a primary category for consideration as we review modes of HIV transmission in African-American communities. Such a move is crucial because the same homophobic impulse that informs efforts to establish Max Robinson's heterosexuality is also implicated in a general reluctance to provide detailed information about sexual transmission of HIV in black communities; indeed a deep silence regarding the details of such transmission has characterized almost all of what passes for government-sponsored AIDS education efforts throughout the US.

Sins of Omission: Inadequacy in AIDS-Education Programs

Even the slickest, most visible print and television ads promoting awareness about AIDS consistently thematize a silence that has been a major obstacle to effective AIDS education in communities of color. Notices distributed around the time of Max Robinson's death utilized an array of celebrities—from Rubén Blades to Patti Labelle—who encouraged people to "get the facts" regarding AIDS, but didn't offer any, merely referring readers elsewhere for substantive information on the syndrome.[34] A bitter testimony to the inefficacy of this ad campaign is offered by a 31-year-old black woman interviewed in the NPR series on AIDS and blacks. "Sandra" contracted HIV through unprotected heterosexual sex; the child conceived in that encounter died at ten months of age from an AIDS-related illness. In her interview, "Sandra" reflects on her lack of knowledge about AIDS at the time she became pregnant:

> I don't remember hearing anything about AIDS until either the year that I was pregnant, which would have been 1986, or the year after I had her; but I really believe it was when I was pregnant with her because I always remember saying, "I'm going to write and get that information," because the only thing that was on TV was to write or call the 1–800 number to get information, and I always wanted to call and get that pamphlet, not knowing that I was going to have first-hand information. I didn't know how it was transmitted. I didn't know that it was caused by a virus. I didn't know that [AIDS] stood for "Acquired Immune Deficiency Syndrome." I didn't know any of that. (*All Things Considered*, 4 April 1989)

By 1986, when Sandra believes she first began even to hear about AIDS, the epidemic was at least 5 years old.

If, even today, response to AIDS in black communities is characterized by a profound silence regarding actual sexual practices, either heterosexual or homosexual, this is largely because of the suppression of talk about sexuality generally and about male homosexuality in particular that is enacted in black communities through the discourses that constitute them. Additionally, however, this continued silence is *enabled* by the ease with which the significance of sexual transmission of HIV can be elided beneath the admittedly massive (but also, to many minds, more "acceptable") problem of IV drug-related HIV transmission that is endemic in some black communities. George Bellinger, Jr., a "minority outreach" worker at Gay Men's Health Crisis, the New York City AIDS service organization, recounted for the NPR series "the horrible joke that used to go around [in black communities] when AIDS first started: 'There's good news and bad news. The bad news is I have AIDS, the good news is I'm an IV drug user' " (*All Things Considered*, 3 April 1989); this joke indicates the degree to which IV drug use can serve as a shield against the implications of male homosexuality that are always associated with AIDS, and which hover as a threat over any discussion of sexual transmission of HIV. This phenomenon is at work even in the NPR series itself. For all its emphasis on the need for black communities to "recognize homosexuality and bisexuality" within them, and despite its inclusion of articulate black lesbians and gay men in its roster of interviewees, the radio series still elides sexual transmission of HIV beneath a focus on IV drug use. One segment in particular illustrates this point.

In an interview broadcast on *Morning Edition*, 4 April 1989, Harold Jaffe, from the federal Centers for Disease Control, makes a crucial point regarding gay male sexual behavior in the face of the AIDS epidemic: "The studies that have come out saying gay men have made substantial changes in their behavior are true, but they're true mainly for white, middle class, exclusively gay men." As correspondent Richard Harris reports, however, Jaffe "doesn't see that trend among black gays." Harris notes that "Jaffe has been studying syphilis rates, which are a good measure of safe sex practices." Jaffe himself proclaims his discoveries: "We find very major decreases [in the rate of syphilis] in white gay men, and either no change or even increases in Hispanic and black gay men, suggesting that they have not really gotten the same behavioral message." Harris continues: "White gay men have changed their behavior to such an extent that experts believe the disease has essentially peaked for them, so as those numbers gradually subside, minorities will make up a growing proportion of AIDS cases." Up to this point, Harris's report has focused on important differences between the rates of syphilis and HIV transmission among gay white men and among black and Latino gay men, suggesting the inadequacy of the educational resources made available to gay men of color. As his rhetoric shifts, however, to refer to the risk that *all* members of "minority" groups face, regardless of their sexual identification, the risky behaviors on which he focuses also change. After indicating the need for gay men of color to change their sexual behavior in the same way that white gay men have, and after a pause of a couple beats that would conventionally indicate the introduction of some narrative into the report to illustrate this point, Harris segues into a story about Rosina, a former IV drug user who has AIDS, and to a claim that "about the only way to stop AIDS from spreading in the inner city is to help addicts get off of drugs." Thus, Harris's early focus on AIDS among black and Latino gay men serves, in the end, merely as a bridge to discussion of IV drug use as the primary factor in the spread of AIDS in communities of color. Moreover, the diversity of those communities is effaced through the conventional euphemistic reference to the "inner city," which, because it disregards class differences among blacks and Latinos, falsely homogenizes the concerns of people of color, and glosses over the complex nature of HIV transmission among them, which, just as with whites, implicates drug use *and* unprotected sexual activity as high-risk behaviors. The ease with which middle-class blacks can construe IV drug use as a problem of communities that are completely removed from their everyday lives (and as unrelated to high-risk sexual activity in which they may engage) makes an exclusive emphasis on IV drug-related HIV transmission among blacks actually detrimental to efforts at effective AIDS education.

To the extent that Max Robinson hoped that his death would occasion efforts at *comprehensive* AIDS education in black communities, then we must consider programs that utilize the logic manifested in Richard Harris's NPR report as inadequate to meet the challenge that Robinson posed. The inadequacy of such efforts is rooted, as I have suggested, in a reluctance to discuss issues of black sexuality that is based simultaneously on whites' stereotyped notions (often defensively adopted by blacks themselves) about the need to suppress black [male] sexuality generally, and on the strictness with which traditional forms of black discourse preclude the possibility of the discussion of black male homosexuality specifically. Indeed, these very factors necessitated the peculiar response to his own AIDS diagnosis that Max Robinson manifested—initial denial and posthumous acknowledgment. I suggested at the beginning of this essay that Robinson's final acknowledgment of his AIDS diagnosis—in the form of his injunction that we use his death as the occasion to increase blacks' awareness about AIDS—performs a sort of epitaphic function. As the final words of the deceased that constitute an implicit warning to others not to repeat his mistakes, Robinson's request has been promulgated through the media with such a repetitive insistence that it might as well have been literally etched in stone. The repetitive nature of the request ought itself to serve as a warning to us, however, since repetition can recapitulate the very silence that it is meant to overcome. As Debra Fried has said, regarding the epitaph, it is both

> silent and . . . repetitive; [it] refuses to speak, and yet keeps on saying the same thing: refusal to say anything different is tantamount to a refusal to speak. Repetition thus becomes a form of silence. . . . According to the fiction of epitaphs, death imposes on its victims an endless verbal task: to repeat without deviation or difference the answer to a question that, no matter how many times it prompts the epitaph to the same silent utterance, is never satisfactorily answered.[35]

In the case of Max Robinson's death, the pertinent question is "how can transmission of HIV and thus AIDS-related death be prevented?" The burden of response at this point is not on the deceased, however, but on us. We must formulate educational programs that offer comprehensive information on the prevention of HIV transmission. In order to do so, we must break the rules of the various discourses through which black life in the US has traditionally been articulated. A less radical strategy cannot induce the widespread behavioral changes that are necessary in the face of AIDS, and our failure in this task would mean sacrificing black people to an epidemic that is enabled, paradoxically, by the very discourses that shape our lives.

NOTES

An earlier version of this paper was presented at the conference on "Nationalisms and Sexualities," held at the Center for Literary and Cultural Studies, Harvard University, June 1989.

The following people have assisted me in the preparation of this article by providing statistical information, directing me to source materials, or commenting on early drafts of the essay: Harold Dufour-Anderson, David Halperin, Paul Morrison, Timothy Murphy, Suzanne Poirier, Julie Rioux, and Thom Whitaker.

1. Centers for Disease Control, *HIV/AIDS Surveillance Report,* March 1991: Table 7, p. 2.

2. Or at least not until November 1991, after the body of this essay was written, when pro basketball player Earvin "Magic" Johnson announced his infection with the human immunodeficiency virus, believed to be the chief factor in the aetiology of AIDS. That announcement precipitated a public response unprecedented in the history of the epidemic. While I do not address directly the nature of that response in this essay, I do believe that it was shaped largely by the set of social phenomena that I have tried to describe here. Indeed, I would argue that the very status of the black basketball player as a sports superstar who thus warrants mass attention (in contrast, for example, to the relatively lower profile of black tennis champion Arthur Ashe, who in April 1992 announced that he himself had AIDS) derives in the main from the very intersection of racial, sexual, and class politics that comprise the primary subject matter of my essay. While the rapidly changing course of the epidemic will no doubt quickly render out-of-date the various topical observations that I make here, I fear that much time will pass before the validity of my analysis, and of the general claims based on it, expires.

3. National Center for Health Statistics, *Health, United States, 1989* (Hyattsville, MD: Public Health Service, 1990) Table 3, p. 151.

4. From a broadcast on *All Things Considered,* National Public Radio, 20 December 1988.

5. Peter J. Boyer, "The Light Goes Out," *Vanity Fair,* June 1989: 68–84; 70.

6. Jeremy Gerard, "Max Robinson, 49, First Black To Anchor Network News, Dies," *New York Times,* 21 December 1988: D19.

7. Tony Schwartz, "Are TV Anchormen Merely Performers?," *New York Times,* 27 July 1980: II, 1, 27.

8. Joseph P. Kahn, "Max Robinson: Tormented Pioneer," *Boston Globe,* 21 December 1988: 65, 67; 67.

9. "Max Robinson, 49, first black anchor for networks; of AIDS complications," obituary in the *Boston Globe,* 21 December 1988: 51.

10. Geneva Smitherman, *Talkin and Testifyin: The Language of Black America* (Boston: Houghton Mifflin, 1977) 12.

11. For an overview of the various black nationalist movements that have emerged in the US since the late 18th century, see John H. Bracey, Jr., August Meier, and Elliott Rudwick, eds., *Black Nationalism in America* (Indianapolis and New York: Bobbs-Merrill, 1970). It should be noted here that the different nationalisms (cultural, revolutionary, and economic, for instance) are not always considered as sharing a common objective. See, for example, Linda Harrison's commentary on the inadequacy of cultural nationalism with respect to a black revolutionary agenda ("On Cultural Nationalism," in Philip S. Foner, ed., *The Black Panthers Speak* [New York: Lippincott, 1970] 151–153). Nevertheless, it seems to me that a generalized cultural nationalism, more than any other form, has been a pervasive influence in Afro-American life since the 1960s, and it is to this brand of nationalism that I allude repeatedly in this essay.

12. This dichotomy corresponds, of course, to that described by W.E.B. DuBois in his classic discussion of blacks' "double-consciousness"—the effect of their inability to reconcile their blackness and their "American" identity. See *The Souls of Black Folk,* 1903, especially, Chapter 1, "Of Our Spiritual Strivings."

13. Tony Schwartz, "Robinson of ABC News Quoted as Saying Network Discriminates," *New York Times,* 11 February 1981: C21; also Gerard.

14. Roger D. Abrahams, *Talking Black* (Rowley, MA: Newbury House, 1976) 19, 54; see also, Claudia Mitchell-Kernan, "Signifying, loud-talking and marking," in Thomas Kochman, ed., *Rappin' and Stylin' Out: Communication in Urban Black America* (Urbana: Univ. of Illinois Press, 1972) 315–335.

15. An additional example of the networks' explicit suppression of Afro-American identity involves black newsman Ed Bradley, a correspondent on the CBS News program, *60 Minutes.* Bradley sent *60 Minutes* producer Don Hewitt into a panic when he decided to change his name to Shaheeb Sha Hab, thereby reflecting his allegiance with Islamic black nationalism. Hewitt was able to convince Bradley not to take this step, and thus to keep black nationalist politics out of the scope of the *60 Minutes* cameras. See Don Hewitt, *Minute by Minute* (New York: Random House, 1985) 170.

16. This development may indicate a perverse "feminization" of the television newsanchor insofar as an insistent emphasis on physical appearance to the neglect of professional accomplishment has historically characterized women's experience in the public sphere. An indication of the extent to which this tyranny of "beauty" can now shape mass cultural phenomena is provided in the field of contemporary pop music. Since the advent of music video in the 1980s, the importance of musical acts' eye appeal has increased to such a degree that models are sometimes hired to lip sync and otherwise "visualize" a song that is actually sung by someone else outside the audience's range of view. The most notorious such case involved the male duo, Milli Vanilli, but the mere fact that men are increasingly subject to the imperative of "sex appeal" by no means implies that they now suffer from a social oppression parallel or equal to that borne by women.

17. Calvin C. Hernton, *Sex and Racism in America* (New York: Doubleday, 1965). As support for his argument, Hernton cites numerous instances of white-perpetrated violence against black men perceived to embody a threat to white femininity. Though such instances may be much less frequent now than in 1965, a structure of sociosexual relations that confers an inordinately threatening status upon black men remains very firmly in place in the US. Consider, for instance, the intense response to the April 1989 attack by a group of black youths on a white woman jogger in Central Park. This response, like the incident itself, was highly overdetermined, and too complex to analyze here, but it culminated in a widely publicized call by real estate magnate Donald Trump for application of the death penalty. It was suggested by numerous people that the intensity of the response was a function of the racial and gender identities of the parties involved, and that a different configuration (white attackers or black or male victim) would not have produced the same degree of outrage or media coverage. See Craig Wolff, "Youths Rape Jogger on Central Park Road," *New York Times,* 21 April 1989: B1, B3; and the full-page display ad paid for by Donald Trump, *New York Times,* 1 May 1989: A13. See also the daily coverage provided by the *Times* during the period framed by these two editions of the paper.

18. I want to emphasize that I consider this management of sexuality to be an operation that the culture continually performs upon each individual black male. The very appearance of a black man on the network newscast may seem to indicate that *he,* at least, has been judged safe for exposure before the bourgeois white audience, and his use of articulate and "objective" journalistic language would then serve merely as a sort of seal of his innocuousness. This could only be true, though, if the recognizably "professional" black male were generally seen as distinct from the mass of black men whose presence on US streets is routinely considered a threat to the well-being of the larger community. As any of us who have been detained and questioned by white urban police for no reason can attest, however, this is not the case. Just as every black man might suddenly manifest an ideological challenge that would certainly have to be kept in check (by a Roone Arledge or a Don Hewitt, for instance, in the broadcast news context), so too does every black man represent an ongoing threat of untamed sexuality that must continually be defused. Thus Max Robinson's expert use of Received Standard English is not merely a mark of his already having been neutralized as a threat to white bourgeois interests; rather, it is itself the neutralization of the threat, continual proof against black male insurgency.

19. This phenomenon was noted in a report on the 5 April 1989 broadcast of National Public Radio's *Morning Edition.* The report was part of the NPR series, "AIDS & Blacks: Breaking the Silence," broadcast on *Morning Edition* and *All Things Considered* during the week of 3–9 April 1989.

20. Frequently in this essay I will use the term "homosexual" (and "homosexuality") rather than "gay" or the even more militant "queer" when talking about sexual identifications within an African-American context. I do this not because I prefer the clinical connotations of "homosexual" to what I, personally, experience as the infinitely more liberating resonances of "gay" or "queer"; but because I want to point out the limited degree to which many men of color feel identified with these latter terms. Indeed, "gay," especially, conjures up in the minds of many who hear it images of a population that is characteristically white, male, and financially well-off; thus it can actually efface, rather than affirm, the experiences of women and of men of color. (This is why some groups of black men who might have identified as gay have chosen instead to designate themselves by terms they feel reflect a specifically Afrocentric experience. Consider the case of "Adodi," which has been used by black men in both Philadelphia and Boston. [See Elizabeth

Pincus, "Black gay men in Boston organize," *Gay Community News* 15:46 (12–18 June 1988), pp. 3, 9.]) I use "homosexual," then, to signal the difficulty of fairly designating any "minority" group, due to the inevitably complex and multifaceted nature of minority identity.

21. Other researchers, too, have noted the peculiarly male-identified nature of the black "rap," among them Thomas Kochman (" 'Rapping' in the Black Ghetto," *Trans-action,* 6 [February 1969]: 26–34); Roger Abrahams ("Playing the Dozens," *Journal of American Folklore,* 75 [July–September 1962]: 209–220); and Claudia Mitchell-Kernan.

22. See Lauren Berlant, "The Female Complaint," *Social Text* 19/20 (Fall 1988): 237–259.

23. Nor was he the last. My own performance in this essay (let alone in the other sites of my intellectual practice) sets me up to be targeted as too white-identified or too effete (or both) to be a "real" black man in certain contexts. The fact that I already identify *myself* as gay may mitigate my vulnerability on that score somewhat. At the same time, the fact that my work takes the form of scholarly writing that does not generally circulate outside the academy largely insulates me from charges that I am not sufficiently engaged with the day-to-day concerns of the black populace, even as it substantiates the claim. This latter paradox constitutes a dilemma not for black intellectuals alone, certainly; but the embattled position that blacks still occupy in this country—socially, politically, economically—makes the problem especially pressing for us.

24. Don L. Lee (Haki R. Madhubuti), *Don't Cry, Scream* (Detroit: Broadside Press, 1969) 27–31.

25. An effective manifesto for such a poetic practice can be seen in Imamu Amiri Baraka's "Black Art," with its call for "poems that kill." See the *Selected Poetry of Amiri Baraka/Leroi Jones* (New York: William Morrow, 1979) 106–107.

26. Nikki Giovanni, "The True Import of Present Dialogue: Black vs. Negro," in Dudley Randall, ed., *The Black Poets* (New York: Bantam, 1971) 318–319.

27. There is an evident irony here, in that the intense masculinism of black nationalist discourse was developed as a reaction against the suppression of black manhood and black male sexuality (often taking the form of literal castration, and at any rate consistently rhetorically figured as such) enacted by the dominant white society. Of course, the emphasis on traditional masculinity is not unique to black nationalism, either in the US or elsewhere. For an extensive discussion of the relation between European nationalist ideologies and the promulgation of a masculine ideal, see George Mosse, *Nationalism and Sexuality: Respectability and Abnormal Sexuality in Modern Europe* (Madison: Univ. of Wisconsin Press, 1985).

28. The *Jet* obituary reflects a general journalistic ignorance of the appropriate terms to be used in reference to the AIDS epidemic. "AIDS victim," with its connotations of passivity, help-lessness, and immutable doom, and its reduction of the person under discussion to a medical condition, should be rejected in favor of "person with AIDS" (PWA) or "person living with AIDS" (PLWA). Additionally, AIDS is not a "disease," it is a "syndrome"—a constellation of symptoms (and in the instance of AIDS many of the characteristic symptoms are themselves diseases) that indicates an underlying condition—in the case of AIDS, suppressed immunity likely caused by infection with the human immunodeficiency virus (HIV).

29. "Max Robinson, First Black National TV News Anchor, Succumbs to AIDS in D.C."; "Singer Sylvester, 42, Dies of AIDS in Oakland, CA," *Jet,* 9 January 1989: 14–15, 18.

30. For some commentary on this phenomenon, see Joseph Beam, ed., *In The Life: A Black Gay Anthology* (Boston: Alyson, 1986), particularly essays by James S. Tinney ("Why a Black Gay Church?," 70–86), Bernard Branner (an interview with Blackberri, "Singing for Our Lives," 170–184), and Max C. Smith, ("By the Year 2000," 224–229).

31. "Max Robinson: Fighting the Demons," *Newsweek,* 2 January 1989: 65.

32. Noted in a report from the NPR series, "AIDS & Blacks," *All Things Considered,* 7 April 1989.

33. Among Jackson's misstatements is his reference to the "AIDS virus." There is no virus that "causes AIDS," only HIV, which produces the immunosuppression that allows the conditions that constitute AIDS to flourish. Moreover, neither HIV infection nor AIDS "comes from" either homosexuality or "promiscuity"; HIV is a virus extant in the biosphere that is merely *transmitted* through sexual contact. It is particularly ironic, by the way, that the homophobia-informed task

of legitimizing Robinson's AIDS diagnosis should be undertaken by Jackson, whose 1988 presidential campaign was characterized by support for a lesbian and gay political agenda.

34. For an extensive analysis of this characteristic of AIDS-education programs in the US, see Douglas Crimp, "How to Have Promiscuity in an Epidemic," *AIDS: Cultural Analysis/Cultural Activism,* (*October* 43, Winter 1987) 237–271.

35. Debra Fried, "Repetition, Refrain, and Epitaph," *ELH* 53:3 (Fall 1986): 615–632; 620.

11

Television/Feminism:
HeartBeat *and Prime Time Lesbianism*

SASHA TORRES

Sasha Torres, Assistant Professor of Film Studies at Dartmouth College, is the author of essays on thirtysomething *and on* Batman. *She is also completing a book on* National Television: U.S. Prime Time and the Public Sphere. *In the following essay on* HeartBeat, *a prime-time TV drama with a lesbian character, Torres examines the contradictions in the ways that mainstream television represents lesbianism. In particular, she discusses network television's alternating appeal to what she calls, following Eve Kosofsky Sedgwick, universalizing and minoritizing definitions of lesbian identity: on the one hand, the lesbian character helps to generate a vision of feminism as a kind of erotic bonding among all women, in which lesbians are simply part of what Adrienne Rich calls a "continuum"; on the other hand, the lesbian character serves to isolate in her own person and thus to contain the homosexual threat implied by the existence of female homosocial bonds unmediated by men, thereby clearing the other women-identified women in* HeartBeat *from the charge of being queer. One effect of this strategy, Torres shows, is to make lesbian sex unrepresentable except when it can be figuratively displaced onto other thematic material.*

Marilyn: When Jerry and I were breaking up—just before I came out of the closet—
I was doing fine, until one day I'm driving along the 405 freeway, and
suddenly all the lanes open up into a sea of on-ramps and off-ramps. All
those choices, possibilities! It was a long time before I could get back into
a car again.

Joanne: Do you think our mothers had it this hard?

Marilyn: They had a different kind of hard. We've come a long way, baby.

This remarkable exchange took place on television, between two central characters on
the short-lived ABC drama *HeartBeat:* Marilyn McGrath (played by Gail Strickland),
the first continuous lesbian character in the history of U.S. prime time, and her colleague
and friend, Dr. Joanne Halloran (Kate Mulgrew). With its dense metaphorization of
the stresses of coming out, Marilyn's statement transforms the geometric increase in
erotic possibility that has for her accompanied lesbian self-identification into the quintessential Southern California experience of freeway driving. In the process, this figure
renders Marilyn's journey toward a socially and culturally specific engagement with her
sexuality accessible to *HeartBeat*'s straight audience; it also makes it possible for the
script's writers to divert that journey toward a different, if related, destination, by turning
a particular set of sexual choices into the much more loosely defined set of feminist
choices suggested by the phrase "We've come a long way, baby."

The two problematics enacted by Marilyn and Joanne's conversation—the televisual tendency to use feminism and lesbianism as stand-ins for each other, and the difficulties, for network television, of articulating lesbian erotic possibility—will be my emphases in this essay. I will begin by considering *HeartBeat*'s appropriation and deployment of the political discourse of liberal feminism and by situating *HeartBeat* within a larger set of prime time programs aimed at women. I will then consider the persistent appearances of lesbian and gay characters within these fictions, and the contradictory ideological functions served by their presence. In the last section of the essay I return to *HeartBeat*, reading two episodes closely in order to map out Marilyn's ideological roles.

HeartBeat, an hour-long medical melodrama about a group of feminist health workers at a women's clinic in Southern California, was created by novelist Sara Davidson, who based the practice, called "Women's Medical Arts," on the Santa Monica medical group that delivered her own children.[1] Like their real-life counterparts, the staff at Women's Medical Arts espouse "mildly progressive and/or alternative medical philosophies,"[2] and practices which are clearly designed to respond to feminist critiques of the medical establishment. Indeed, the series' deployment of "feminist" signifiers is discernable from the first scene of the two-hour pilot that launched *HeartBeat*.[3] During the opening credits, we see a Black woman pulling up in a car and taking a young child into the clinic with her. We soon learn that this is Dr. Corey Banks (Lynn Whitfield) and that it is not unusual for staffers to bring their children to work with them: in the spirit of sisterhood, not one, but two nurses offer to watch the child until Corey's real sister comes to pick him up. A new nurse who calls Corey "Dr. Banks" is matter-of-factly instructed to use her first name instead, because using titles "creates too much of a barrier between doctor and patient." When a woman in labor comes into the clinic asking for Joanne, another of the doctors, Corey reassuringly calms her down, coordinates her difficult delivery ("it's a breach and the feet are out!"), and then compliments her on a job well done. In short, this scene tells us that Women's Medical Arts is a feminist utopia: a medical practice where doctors are not only expert, but respectful, nurturing, and forthcoming with information as well, largely because they are, as Dr. Eve Calvert (Laura Johnson) puts it, "women taking care of women."

HeartBeat, then, is TV medical melodrama with a twist: it not only recycles contemporary medical-ethical dilemmas and cashes in on the narrative potential of the "life-and-death" dramas that are the currency of the medical profession, but also investigates the ragged interface between gender and medical practice, for both women doctors and patients. Thus the narratives tend to focus on patients facing reproductive and gynecological health issues, and on doctors facing their feelings about how to do right by their patients, and their confusion about how to have professional and personal lives at the same time.

In the process of dramatizing all these quandaries, *HeartBeat*, of course, manages to mobilize a number of media clichés about feminism. All of *HeartBeat*'s female characters, for example, are constructed as "strong women" with the help of those two televisual signs of feminism, "power dressing and assertiveness training."[4] But with its inclusion of Marilyn, *HeartBeat* manages to mobilize one particular cliché about feminism in an unprecedented way. In accordance with *HeartBeat*'s liberal-feminist mission, Marilyn is an out-of-the-closet nurse practitioner who, as gay characters on television go, seems to be a made-to-order "positive image" of the "gay lifestyle": she is depicted as likable, attractive, fun, good at her job, as well as being a happy lesbian in a long-term, stable relationship. But of course there is more to the depiction of Marilyn's character than a "positive image"; *HeartBeat* was, after all, produced by Hollywood insiders for

a major network. There are thus limits on the kind of ideological work such a representation can do, given its context in this particular televisual space. And in order to
understand those limits, it seems crucial to consider what the producers and writers of
HeartBeat may have told themselves about what Marilyn was doing within them in the
first place. In order to do that, we need both to situate *HeartBeat* within the context of
other 1980s prime time programming for women, and to figure out what to make of
these televisual deployments of "feminism."

Theorists of televisual representations of "feminism" generally agree that such
representations treat feminism "ambivalently": even as these texts give space to "positive"
images of feminist discourse, politics, or persons, they also generally undercut such
images, either narratively or visually. There also seems to be consensus that depictions
of feminism are in this way little different than depictions of other oppositional or left
discourses. Robert Deming, for example, alludes to this consensus when he writes:

> As several critics have recently demonstrated, television works to integrate oppositional
> and resistant forces, including feminist discourses, by absorbing and naturalizing them,
> usually into dominant definitions of the family melodrama and heterosexual ro-
> mance.... Television packages oppositional values and repackages them within dom-
> inant terms.[5]

While Deming carefully allows for the possibility of "possibly contradictory interpretations," this passage clearly emphasizes TV's conservative work of "repackaging" oppositional discourses.[6] Judith Mayne helps explain the necessity of this work when she
insists that television relies upon the consumption and transformation of political discourses for the very production of its narratives:

> From sit-coms like *All in the Family* to prime-time soaps like *Dallas,* television narrative
> has relied centrally on principles of multiple identification and of narrative structure
> in which there is a fine line, if any line at all, between irony and rhetoric, between
> critique and celebration. Indeed, one of the most distinctive characteristics of con-
> temporary television narrative might well be the breaking-down of familiar bound-
> aries—between fiction and nonfiction, between transparency and self-reflexivity, be-
> tween progressive and reactionary vantage points.[7]

While I am substantially in agreement with this consensus about TV's relation to oppositional discourses of various kinds,[8] I want to emphasize here that feminism is for
televisual representation a special, particularly heightened case of this generalized ambivalence, for reasons having as much to do with the economic workings of the television
industry as with America's obsession with the meanings and functions of gender.

Chiefly because of the persistent identification of consumerism with women, "feminism"—meaning in this context bourgeois, liberal feminism, of the still-taking-adver-
tising *Ms.* magazine variety—has effectively been collated with consumption by those
with interests in the U.S. television industry.[9] In this way, feminism is unlike the vast
variety of political discourses articulated by other oppositional groups, and particularly
unlike those of people of color and Marxists. Because market research has shown that
images of "strong women"—the images at the heart of the programming strategies that
gave us *Cagney and Lacey, Kate and Allie, L.A. Law, China Beach, Designing Women, Murphy
Brown,* and *HeartBeat*—appeal to the young, middle- and upper middle-class urban women
whom advertisers particularly covet, the collation of feminism with consumerism means
that feminist audiences "count" for programmers in a way that few other minority
groups do.[10] The following passage from a 1989 *Newsweek* article describes network
motivation in developing programing aimed at women:

> The feminization of television has surprisingly little to do with feminism. At its roots
> lies an intriguing demographic shift: female viewers have seized control of the prime-
> time dial as the network's male audience increasingly drifts to the cable channels. . . .
> At the same time, market research reveals that women have become the principal
> purchasers of the products most advertised by prime-time sponsors (e.g. cosmetics
> and household goods). Such findings have spawned a theory: the network that most
> endears itself to the lady of the house has the best chance of survival. The theory
> also comes with a corollary: shows that capture the viewers sponsors prize most—
> women between the ages of 18 and 49—can charge "Cosby"-close ad rates even
> though they rest a tier below in the ratings.[11]

The assertion that "the feminization of television has . . . little to do with feminism,"
or, in other words, that programming about "strong women" is motivated by profit
rather than politics suggests that the networks' deployment of images of feminism may
be more cynical than ambivalent.

But within these cynical texts, one element marks the difficulty, for the male-
dominated television industry, of representing feminist politics in the interests of gar-
nering profits. These televisual versions of "strong women" persistently link feminism
with lesbianism, and these representations of lesbian characters certainly *could* be called
ambivalent, given that they serve two completely contradictory functions at once.[12] On
the one hand, shows seeking to deploy images of feminism to attract women viewers
are appropriating lesbianism as, in Katie King's term, "feminism's magical sign," as the
single privileged signifier of feminism to which whole systems of signifiers have been
reduced, both within feminist communities, and within (more or less homophobic) mass-
cultural representations of feminism.[13] On the other hand, even as Marilyn and the
lesbian characters who occasionally appear on *Kate and Allie, The Golden Girls,* and *L.A.
Law* signify "feminism," they also ease the ideological threat of such "feminist" programs by localizing the homosexuality which might otherwise pervade these homosocial
spaces. Both *Kate and Allie* and *The Golden Girls,* for example, have been visited by "real"
lesbians, whose difference from the regular characters has been sufficient to ease the
homophobic anxieties that might be generated by representations of unmarried women
living together.[14] For the latter of these two contradictory functions, gay men, too, have
occasionally been pressed into service: *Cagney and Lacey* reassures us about the homosocial
bounds of Chris and Mary Beth's relationship by offering us Chris's gay neighbor, Tony,
as a "real" gay person.[15] And somewhat more ambiguously, the homosocial space of
Designing Women's interior design firm is breached by the Black and thoroughly campy
Anthony, who serves not only to allay liberal Northern anxieties about the possibility
of racism among these Southern belles, but also as a "man around the house," and as
an at-least-potentially localizing site of homosexuality.

The two contradictory narrative roles played by lesbian characters—as privileged
signs of feminism and as homosexual guarantors of chaste homosociality—assume fundamentally different relations between lesbians and other women, but both participate
in TV's refusal to represent lesbian erotic life. On the one hand, for lesbian characters
like Marilyn to signify "feminism," they must be recognizable as *like* the other women
within the fictions they inhabit; they must plausibly be part of what prime time imagines
as a feminist collectivity. In explaining why "Marilyn was introduced . . . before her
homosexuality was disclosed," Sara Davidson told *People,* "We wanted people to see her
as a terrific person first, then find out she has a private life that at its core *is no different
from anyone else's.*"[16] In the process, such universalizing representations must de-empha-
size the specificity of lesbian eroticism or sexual practice. In this discourse, everyone
always already knows what lesbians do in bed. On the other hand, for lesbian figures

to function as localizing sites of homosexuality within a homosocial televisual space, they must be sufficiently *different from* the other female characters that every one—both within the diegesis and outside of it—can tell the difference. Such minoritizing representations tend to rely on the assumption that lesbian sexuality is so different from heterosexuality as to be unrepresentable; what lesbians do in bed is, in this discourse, truly unimaginable.[17] Thus these two ideological functions of prime time lesbianism both manage to blend remarkably well with TV liberalism and with American television's squeamishness about sex.[18] As *People* notes, "On-camera, physical intimacy between McGrath and her romantic partner, played by Gina Hecht, will be limited to eye contact [!] and the occasional hug."[19]

My task in the remainder of this essay will be to map out how *HeartBeat*'s depictions of Marilyn are constrained by the contradictory necessity that her lesbianism make her at once different and not-different from *HeartBeat*'s other female characters. Not surprisingly, this representational quandary is often marked by confusion about, or displacement of, lesbian sexuality. An episode from the second season, for example, in which Marilyn nurses a woman friend who is dying of cancer, provides a useful example of the series' universalizing tendencies by making clear *HeartBeat*'s desire to valorize female bonding (non-genital, but with a dash of sexual tension thrown in) over an explicitly sexual lesbian relationship.[20] Here's how this works: Marilyn's old friend Claire is dying of leukemia. Marilyn is aware that Claire has been in love with her for some time, but feels that she cannot reciprocate (in part, we understand, because of her relationship with her lover of three years, Patty). Much of the episode is taken up with Claire and Patty making manifest their jealousy of each other to Marilyn; friend and lover jockey for the coveted position of most important in Marilyn's life. In an extraordinary scene, Patty and Marilyn, out for dinner to celebrate their third anniversary, discuss this problem:

Marilyn:	I know what [Claire's] going through.
Patty:	You should. You're practically living in her room. . . . I mean, I'm not complaining. I know what Claire means to you.
Marilyn:	I wonder.
Patty:	How could I not know? I've heard the litany a thousand times—how she gave you a roof over your head, a sense of identity.
Marilyn:	Patty, she's my *friend*.
Patty:	. . . This has nothing to do with you sleeping with her or not.
Marilyn:	We didn't and you know it.
Patty:	It's more than that. . . . When Claire's around I feel like a fifth wheel . . . you guys have a history together—finish each other's sentences. I'm jealous of what you two have. I know I shouldn't be, but it eats me up. There's no way we could ever share the same things, ever get as close.
Marilyn:	It's true. For us to ever have the same kind of relationship—it's just not possible. And I wouldn't have it any other way. What we have together is our own. It's no less special, no less important. The difference is, we have a future.

This scene begins with a medium shot of Patty and Marilyn, then shifts to a consistent shot-reverse shot pattern with increasingly tight close-ups. Thus the editing of the scene, with its increasing intrusiveness, works hard first to construct Marilyn and Patty as a couple, then to persuade us that we are learning something important about them. And the final shot of Patty's relieved smile insists that this conflict has been resolved, an insistence reinforced by the fact that Patty does not reappear during the episode. But the dialogue belies this resolution: the palpable labor with which it struggles toward a conclusion which would reassert the primacy of the romantic couple—something that isn't usually very hard for television to manage—marks the show's difficulty in really distinguishing between Marilyn's relationship with Claire and her relationship with Patty. Marilyn's final remark, designed to tell the difference, for us and for Patty, doesn't help at all. "The difference is, we have a future" begs the question by deferring it; eventually, she seems to say, all this will be decided because Claire will die before Patty does. Crucially (if predictably), Marilyn doesn't make the obvious point, the point that has been perfectly set up by the preceding dialogue: she doesn't say "The difference is, we have sex."

The larger narrative in which the scene I've just described takes place is structured around Marilyn's similarity to her straight colleagues. In a related plot in this episode, Joanne discovers that she's pregnant and then has a miscarriage. The final scene, which takes place in the empty room of the now-deceased Claire, links their mourning when Marilyn is joined, not by Patty, but by Joanne. The price of this linkage is the refusal of any boundary between the homosocial and the homosexual, and the concomitant refusal to recognize lesbian relationships as sexual. Whatever its costs, though, this universalizing view of Marilyn is the one with which *HeartBeat* is most comfortable, since it meshes so well with the show's liberalism. *HeartBeat* offers viewers a sustained view of Marilyn's difference from her colleagues, and of its potentially catastrophic consequences, only once, in another episode from the second season. Significantly, this episode shrinks from articulating a minoritizing view of her sexuality, choosing instead to displace her difference from her sexual status as a lesbian to her professional status as a nurse practitioner.[21] Nevertheless, this narrative allows the series covertly to raise, manage, and resolve the destabilizing potential Marilyn's lesbianism has within the cozy homosocial world of Women's Medical Arts.

This episode stages the only full-scale confrontation we ever see between Marilyn and her co-workers. Explicitly at issue here is Marilyn's friend and mentor, Betty Cherney, a nurse-midwife who is renting space at the practice until her own offices are ready. In the process, she is also giving Marilyn, who is about to get her own midwifery certificate, a first-hand look at a midwifery practice. The doctors with whom Marilyn works feel crowded by Betty's patients (who are usually to be found in their bathrobes, and in labor, in the reception area), and by Betty's disdain for technologized modern medicine ("The birthing process isn't a life-threatening disease," she tells Marilyn); they also feel threatened by evidence that a nurse could have the kind of authoritative relationship with her patients that they have with their own. To make matters worse, the practice as a whole is facing pressure from the patriarchs at Bay General, the hospital with which they are affiliated, to sever their ties with Betty. One by one, Marilyn's colleagues withdraw their support for Betty's continued presence, underscoring the professional gulf between doctors and nurses, caving into the pressure from the male medical establishment, and making Marilyn feel that her future at the practice which she co-founded is uncertain. When Betty finally leaves of her own accord, Marilyn insists that *she* will not give up: "I'll have my midwife's certificate in six months," she says, "Nights, weekends, I'll be using it somewhere." Confronted with this challenge, Joanne and Eve face down the head patriarch at Bay General, threatening lawsuits and press conferences if the hospital doesn't stop conspiring against midwives and their practices.

There are two crucial markers that what is really at issue in this plot is Marilyn's sexuality, not her professional status. First, this is one of the few episodes in which Marilyn's sexuality is never alluded to directly; it becomes, in the context of this minoritizing discourse, unrepresentable. Of the twelve episodes aired during *HeartBeat*'s second season, four contain no mention of Marilyn's sexuality or her relationship with Patty. Of these four, the midwifery episode is the only one in which Marilyn is the subject of the episode's main plot; generally speaking, other episodes which focus on Marilyn are more clearly about her sexuality. In this sense, then, the midwifery episode is anomalous. It's unusual in another way as well: *HeartBeat's* narratives generally shift continually from the public sites of the practice and hospital to the private spaces of the characters' homes; discussions of problems at work are almost always continued in the domestic realm. It is thus particularly striking that we never see Marilyn discussing her struggles at work at home with Patty.

But if this episode succeeds in excising the domestic evidence of Marilyn's sexual preference, it is unable to dispense with the sexual altogether. For the problems posed by Betty—problems which are explicitly coded as a conflict between scientific/medical discourses and women's ways of knowing—are always discussed in sexual terms. This code crossing marks the limits of *HeartBeat's* appropriation of the lesbian continuum by insisting that the episode's repressed knowledge of Marilyn's lesbianism must continually return. Figures of lesbian sex, *HeartBeat's* haunting abject, erupt into virtually every conversation Marilyn and her co-workers have about Betty and about midwifery.

Betty's work is described as "pioneering," "progressive," "ground-breaking," and "revolutionary." As a woman-centered activity, midwifery is explicitly understood by the doctors as a threat to medical profit-making and medical professionalization, which *HeartBeat* generally codes as male. Marilyn understands it differently, though, linking midwifery throughout the episode to a discourse of "freedom of choice" which evokes the language not only of reproductive rights, but also of gay liberation. The centrality of this latter association becomes clear in the following scene, in which Marilyn and Corey face off about Betty:

Corey:	Betty around?
Marilyn:	Grabbing a few winks. Anything I can do?
Corey:	Oh, I just wanted to thank her. I mean, here I am, having such a busy day, patients coming and going, about to start juggling my appointments, and along comes Betty to unburden my life.
Marilyn:	Last night must have been a full moon.
Corey:	I'm talking about the Mannheims. . . . It seems they've been lured off to moan with Mother Nature.
Marilyn:	Corey . . . they didn't have a doctor. They were window shopping.
Corey:	No, this is pure Betty. We help her and she helps herself to my patients.
Marilyn:	Maybe they'd never considered midwifery.
Corey:	Maybe they got sold a bill of goods.
Marilyn:	Or they saw something they liked better.

Marilyn's suggestion that the Mannheims "saw something they liked better," is significant in relation to Corey's characterization of them as having "been lured off to moan with mother nature"—an allusion not only to Betty's tendency to pose midwifery as an alternative to the alienating operations of modern medicine, or to matriarchal religion, but also to lesbian sex, to "moaning" with a woman.

This slide from medical/scientific discourse to sexual discourse is repeated twice in the episode. When one of the doctors learns that the hospital's latest in a series of harassing moves is to cut off referrals to the practice, he is told, "it's this midwifery thing; you people got in bed with the wrong woman." And consider the following scene, in which Joanne and Eve discuss Betty and the problems with the hospital:

| Joanne: | One day, Evie, when we're in charge . . . the old boy's network will run screaming through the halls. |

Eve: Damn right.... Cutting my lab supplies, dressing me down—it's corporeal
          punishment.
Joanne: It's hard to miss the message.
Eve: Friedlander's scared of the competition; it's hitting him right in the pocket
          . . .
Joanne: I'll tell you what this is really all about: power. . . . Men don't want to turn
          over control of the woman's body to the woman.
Eve: So you'd let a midwife deliver your children?
Joanne: That's not fair.
Eve: I thought so.
Joanne: Well I believe in what we do.
Eve: So does Betty.
Joanne: Where does that leave Marilyn?
Eve: OK. I'll get naked if you will. I respect midwifery. I even respect Betty.
          But she scares the hell out of me.... We've got to throw Betty out.... I
          love Marilyn. Do I have to risk the practice to prove it?

Eve's challenge to Joanne, "I'll get naked if you will," marks the threat that the localizing presence of Marilyn's lesbianism is designed to contain: the possibility of the female members of the Women's Medical Arts staff getting naked together in various combinations. So reluctant is *HeartBeat* even to raise this possibility that this scene places it at a second remove; it is Betty, not Marilyn, who "scares the hell out of" Eve. The question Eve and Joanne debate in this scene—is their love for Marilyn generalizable to others like her?—allows the series to preserve Marilyn herself as non-threatening, because non-different, even as it implicitly works through the effects of her threatening difference.

These episodes of *HeartBeat,* with their self-conscious, gingerly dances around Marilyn's sexuality, certainly underscore the intractability, as well as the inextricability, of the conflicting dual roles she plays as signifier of close-knit feminist community and preserver of safe homosocial boundaries. But while I certainly mean this mapping-out of the ideological uses of television lesbianism as an indictment of the television industry's homophobic conservatism, I don't mean it to be only that. For I think that *HeartBeat*'s often-confused and always-implicit vacillations between universalizing and minoritizing depictions of Marilyn themselves demonstrate the productive possibility, as well as the evident limitations, of such liberal representations. Because of the constraints imposed by the television markets in which it is a commodity, *HeartBeat* is never able to settle on either depiction; in being forced to maintain, at once, Marilyn's difference from and similarity to the women around her, *HeartBeat* can neither keep her at arm's length nor assimilate her completely.

NOTES

This essay is for Judy Frank, who has known and contributed to it in all its forms. Sabrina Barton, Lila Hanft, Biddy Martin, Lisa Moore, and Sharon Willis read and commented on various drafts; I have benefited from their suggestions. I am also indebted to Michèle Barale for useful conversation on related topics and to Jennifer Koerber for research assistance.

1. *HeartBeat* first aired as a mid-season replacement on ABC in March 1988, and returned for a second season that fall. ABC canceled the series in April 1989; during parts of 1989 and 1990 it could be seen on the cable channel called Lifetime, which specializes in "women's programming" and medical information shows. *HeartBeat*'s Executive Producer was Aaron Spelling; it was produced by Frederick Rappaport and William A. Schwartz, and created by Sara Davidson.

2. Andy Meisler, "Opulence Yields to Stethoscopes," *New York Times,* 27 March 1988, sec. 2, p. H1.

3. The pilot aired 24 March 1988. Executive Producer: Esther Shapiro; written by Sara Davidson; directed by Harry Winer.

4. Judith Mayne, "*L.A. Law* and Prime-Time Feminism," *Discourse* X.2 (Spring–Summer 1988): 36. Cf. Constance Rosenblum, "Drop-Dead Clothes Make the Working Woman," *New York Times,* 26 February 1989, sec. 2, p. H1. Rosenblum notes that many media career women "have their high-powered careers in much the same way they have the high-powered wardrobes that go with them: [they're] impressive on the surface, but they only go so far."

5. Robert Deming, "*Kate and Allie:* 'New Women' and the Audience's Television Archive," *Camera Obscura* 16 (January 1988): 155.

6. Deming, "*Kate and Allie,*" 155.

7. Mayne, "*L.A. Law,*" 33.

8. I myself have participated in this consensus in characterizing *thirtysomething* as "giv[ing] voice to, and then recuperat[ing] ideological critique" of the nuclear family and the sexual division of labor. See my "Melodrama, Masculinity and the Family: *thirtysomething* as Therapy," *Camera Obscura* 19 (January 1989): 100.

9. On the television industry's collation of feminism and consumerism, see Lauren Rabinovitz, "Sitcoms and Single Moms: Representations of Feminism on American TV," *Cinema Journal* 29 (Fall 1989): 6–7; see also Deming, "*Kate and Allie,*" 156 ff. For a useful bibliography of material on women and consumerism, see Lynn Spigel and Denise Mann, "Women and Consumer Culture: A Selective Bibliography," *Quarterly Review of Film and Video* 11.1 (1989): 85–105.

10. I refer here to Eileen Meehan's excellent article on the construction of the "commodity audience" measured by television ratings, "Why We Don't Count," in *Logics of Television: Ess in Cultural Criticism,* ed. Patricia Mellencamp (Bloomington: Indiana University Press, 1990), 11 137. Meehan's conclusion that "unless you have a meter, you don't count. Unless you live i cable area and subscribe, you have almost no opportunity to count" (132), usefully debunks claims of "the networks, advertisers, and ratings monopolist that . . . programming is just a mi of public taste" (127).

11. Harry F. Waters and Janet Huck, "Networking Women," *Newsweek,* 13 March 19 p. 48. See also John J. O'Connor's "The New Woman Finds Her Place on the Small Scree *New York Times,* 4 November 1990, sec. 2, p. H33. It's worth noting that feminist media gro released studies condemning women's lack of representation on both sides of the camera dur the new fall seasons of 1989 and 1990; they were thus much less optimistic than the author the *Newsweek* piece. See "NCWW pans new TV season," *Broadcasting,* 13 November 1989 88; and Andrea Adelson, "Study Attacks Women's Roles in TV," *New York Times,* 19 November 1990.

12. My point here was enabled by Judith Mayne's assertion about *L.A. Law* that "allusions to gay sexuality are flirtations with sexual difference that assure, rather than challenge, heterosexuality as a norm. Yet such allusions also suggest a destabilization of that very norm" (35).

13. Katie King, "The situation of lesbianism as feminism's magical sign: Contests for meaning and the U.S. women's movement, 1968–1972," *Communications* 9 (1986): 66–67.

14. See Deming, 160ff., for a reading of the relevant episode of *Kate and Allie.*

15. For an account of how concerns about lesbianism figured in the early days of *Cagney and Lacey,* see Julie D'Acci, "The Case of *Cagney and Lacey,*" in *Boxed in: Women and Television,* ed. Helen Baehr and Gillian Dyer (London: Pandora, 1987), 213.

16. Susan Toepler, with David Hutchings, "Is Prime Time Ready for Its First Lesbian? Gail Strickland Hopes So—And She's About to Find Out," *People,* 25 April 1988; p. 96, my emphasis. In "Commodity Lesbianism in Advertising and Commercial Television," Danae Clark deftly sums up what is so offensive about this remark when she notes that "Davidson's statement confirms that the show's first obligation is to its straight audience (since few lesbians would find a contradiction between 'terrific person' and 'lesbian')." Paper presented at the 1990 Society for Cinema Studies Conference.

17. I borrow the terms "universalizing" and "minoritizing" from Eve Kosofsky Sedgwick, and deploy them not just as a useful shorthand, but also to import her insistence that "no epistemological grounding now exists" from which to "adjudicate" between these two views of homo/ heterosexual definition. See her *Epistemology of the Closet* (Berkeley: University of California Press,

1990), 1–2. For my purposes here, Sedgwick's insistence on the conceptual inextricability of universalizing and minoritizing discourses helps explain televisual ambivalence toward gay figures and gay issues, by grounding that ambivalence in larger cultural crises of meaning.

18. Of course, U.S. television's prudish sensibilities are enforced by those of its advertisers, who have in the past been reluctant to appear to "endorse" homosexuality by sponsoring shows with gay themes. ABC reportedly lost well over $1.5 million dollars in advertising revenues when advertisers pulled commercials from an episode of *thirtysomething* which depicted two gay men in bed. See Geraldine Fabrikant, "Ads Reportedly Lost Because of Gay Scene," *New York Times,* 14 November 1989, p. D21.

19. Toepfer, "Is Prime Time Ready?," 96.

20. The executive producer of this episode was Aaron Spelling; teleplay by Frederick Rappaport and Douglas Steinberg; story by William A. Schwartz; directed by Gregory Rose.

21. The executive producer of this episode was Aaron Spelling; teleplay by Frederick Rappaport, Douglas Steinberg, and William A. Schwartz; story by Joe Viola and Allison Hock; directed by Michael Fresco.

12

Commodity Lesbianism

DANAE CLARK

Danae Clark is Assistant Professor of Media Studies in the Department of Communication at the University of Pittsburgh and is the author of a book on actor's labor in Hollywood, forthcoming from the University of Texas Press. In this essay she focuses on recent media efforts to target the lesbian fashion consumer and discusses the convoluted relationship between capitalism and lesbian identity politics. While earlier feminism's anti-fashion stance has been largely replaced by a new sense of fashion as a site for female resistance and masquerade, capitalism's ability to re-style such transgressive self-representations into the trendy and the chic calls into question the possibilities of agency that resistance implies. At the same time, the ability of lesbian consumers to read dominant media images as lesbian-coded, or to find in purposefully ambiguous sexual and gender images aspects of lesbian culture that yet remain inaccessible and uncolonized, undercuts heterosexual feminist analyses of media which depict women as passive bodies for male spectatorship or as narcissistic self-observers.

A commodity appears, at first sight, a very trivial thing, and easily understood. Its analysis shows that it is, in reality, *a very queer thing* . . . (Karl Marx, *Capital*[1])

In an effort to articulate the historical and social formation of female subjectivity under capitalism, feminist investigations of consumer culture have addressed a variety of complex and interrelated issues, including the construction of femininity and desire, the role of consumption in media texts, and the paradox of the woman/commodity relationship. Implicit in these investigations, however, has been an underlying concern for the heterosexual woman as consuming subject.[2] Perhaps because, as Jane Gaines notes, "consumer culture thrives on heterosexuality and its institutions by taking its cues from heterosexual 'norms,' "[3] theories *about* consumerism fall prey to the same normalizing tendencies. In any event, analyses of female consumerism join a substantial body of other feminist work that "assumes, but leaves unwritten, a heterosexual context for the subject" and thus contributes to the continued invisibility of lesbians.[4]

But lesbians too are consumers. Like heterosexual women they are major purchasers of clothing, household goods, and media products. Lesbians have not, however, been targeted as a separate consumer group within the dominant configuration of capitalism, either directly through the mechanism of advertising or indirectly through fictional media representations; their relation to consumerism is thus necessarily different. This "difference" requires a careful look at the relation between lesbians and consumer culture, representations of lesbianism and consumption in media texts, and the role of the lesbian spectator as consuming subject. Such an investigation is especially timely since current trends in both advertising and commercial television show that lesbian viewers (or at least some segments of the lesbian population) are enjoying a certain pleasure as consumers that was not available to them in the past. An analysis of these pleasures should therefore shed light not only on the place that lesbians occupy within consumer culture, but on the identificatory processes involved in lesbian reading formations.

Dividing the Consumer Pie

Lesbians have not been targeted as consumers by the advertising industry for several historical reasons. First, lesbians as a social group have not been economically powerful; thus, like other social groups who lack substantial purchasing power (for example, the elderly), they have not been attractive to advertisers. Second, lesbians have not been easily identifiable as a social group anyway. According to the market strategies commonly used by advertisers to develop target consumer groups, four criteria must be met. A group must be: (1) identifiable, (2) accessible, (3) measurable, and (4) profitable.[5] In other words, a particular group must be "knowable" to advertisers in concrete ways. Lesbians present a problem here because they exist across race, income, and age (three determinants used by advertisers to segment and distinguish target groups within the female population). To the extent that lesbians are not identifiable or accessible, they are not measurable and, therefore, not profitable. The fact that many lesbians prefer not to be identified because they fear discrimination poses an additional obstacle to targeting them. Finally, most advertisers have had no desire to identify a viable lesbian consumer group. Advertisers fear that by openly appealing to a homosexual market their products will be negatively associated with homosexuality and will be avoided by heterosexual consumers.[6] Thus, although homosexuals (lesbians and gay men) reputedly comprise 10% of the overall U.S. market population—and up to 20–22% in major urban centers such as New York and San Francisco—advertisers have traditionally stayed in the closet when it comes to peddling their wares.[7]

Recently, however, this trend has undergone a visible shift—especially for gay men. According to a 1982 review in the *New York Times Magazine* called "Tapping the Homosexual Market," several of today's top advertisers are interested in "wooing ... the white, single, well-educated, well-paid man who happens to be homosexual."[8] This interest, prompted by surveys conducted by the *Advocate* between 1977 and 1980 that indicated that 70% of their readers aged 20–40 earned incomes well above the national median, has led companies such as Paramount, Seagram, Perrier, and Harper & Row to advertise in gay male publications like *Christopher Street* and the *Advocate*.[9] Their ads are tailored specifically for the gay male audience. Seagram, for example, ran a "famous men of history" campaign for Boodles Gin that pictured men "purported to be gay."[10]

A more common and more discreet means of reaching the gay male consumer, however, is achieved through the mainstream (predominately print) media. As one marketing director has pointed out, advertisers "really want to reach a bigger market than just gays, but [they] don't want to alienate them" either.[11] Thus, advertisers are increasingly striving to create a dual marketing approach that will "speak to the homosexual consumer in a way that the straight consumer will not notice."[12] As one observer explains:

> It used to be that gay people could communicate to one another, in a public place, if they didn't know one another, only by glances and a sort of *code behavior* ... to indicate to the other person, but not to anybody else, that you, too, were gay. Advertisers, if they're smart, can do that too (emphasis added).[13]

One early example of this approach was the Calvin Klein jeans series that featured "a young, shirtless blond man lying on his stomach" and, in another ad, "a young, shirtless blond man lying on his side, holding a blue-jeans jacket." According to Peter Frisch, a gay marketing consultant, one would "have to be comatose not to realize that it appeals to gay men" (I presume he is referring to the photographs' iconographic resemblance to gay pornography).[14] Calvin Klein marketing directors, however, denied any explicit gay element:

> We did not try *not* to appeal to gays. We try to appeal, period. With healthy, beautiful people. If there's an awareness in that community of health and grooming, they'll respond to the ads.[15]

This dual marketing strategy has been referred to as "gay window advertising."[16] Generally, gay window ads avoid explicit references to heterosexuality by depicting only one individual or same-sexed individuals within the representational frame. In addition, these models bear the signifiers of sexual ambiguity or androgynous style. But "gayness" remains in the eye of the beholder: gays and lesbians can read into an ad certain subtextual elements that correspond to experiences with or representations of gay/lesbian subculture. If heterosexual consumers do not notice these subtexts or subcultural codes, then advertisers are able to reach the homosexual market along with the heterosexual market without ever revealing their aim.

The metaphor of the window used by the advertising industry to describe gay marketing techniques is strikingly similar to feminist descriptions of women's relation to consumer culture and film representation. Mary Ann Doane, for example, remarks that "the film frame is a kind of display window and spectatorship consequently a form of window shopping."[17] Jane Gaines likewise suggests that cinema-going is "analogous to the browsing-without-obligation-to-buy pioneered by the turn-of-the-century department store, where one could, with no offense to the merchant, enter to peruse the goods, exercising a kind of *visual connoisseurship,* and leave without purchase" (emphasis added).[18] Gaines further argues that the show window itself is "a medium of circulation" and that "commodification seems to facilitate circulation by multiplying the number of possible contexts."[19] The metaphor of the window, in other words, posits an active reader as well as a multiple, shifting context of display.

The notion of duality that characterizes gay window advertising's marketing strategy is also embodied in various theoretical descriptions and approaches to consumer culture in general. Within the Frankfurt School, for example, Adorno speaks of the dual character or dialectic of luxury that "opens up consumer culture to be read as its opposite," and Benjamin suggests that consumer culture is a dual system of meaning whereby "the economic life of the commodity imping[es] upon its life as an object of cultural significance."[20] More recently, a duality has been located in feminist responses to consumer culture and fashion culture in particular. As Gaines notes, the beginning of the Second Wave of feminist politics and scholarship was marked by a hostility toward fashion, perceiving it as a patriarchal codification and commodification of femininity that enslaved women and placed their bodies on display. But this "anti-fashion" position is now joined by a feminist perspective that sees fashion culture as a site of female resistance, masquerade, and self-representation.[21] At the heart of this "fabrication," says Gaines, is a gender confusion and ambiguity that disrupts and confounds patriarchal culture.[22]

Lesbians have an uneasy relationship to this dual perspective on fashion. First of all, lesbians have a long tradition of resisting dominant cultural definitions of female beauty and fashion as a way of separating themselves from heterosexual culture politically and as a way of signaling their lesbianism to other women in their subcultural group. This resistance to or reformulation of fashion codes thus distinguished lesbians from straight women at the same time that it challenged patriarchal structures. As Arlene Stein explains in an article on style in the lesbian community:

> Lesbian-feminist anti-style was an emblem of refusal, an attempt to strike a blow against the twin evils of capitalism and patriarchy, the fashion industry and the female objectification that fueled it. The flannel-and-denim look was not so much a style as it was anti-style—an attempt to replace the artifice of fashion with a supposed naturalness, free of gender roles and commercialized pretense.[23]

Today, however, many lesbians, particularly younger, urban lesbians, are challenging this look, exposing the constructedness of "natural" fashion, and finding a great deal of pleasure in playing with the possibilities of fashion and beauty.

This shift, which is not total and certainly not without controversy, can be attributed to a number of factors. First of all, many lesbians are rebelling against a lesbian-feminist credo of political correctness that they perceive as stifling. As a *Village Voice* writer observes:

> A lesbian can wag her fingers as righteously as any patriarchal puritan, defining what's acceptable according to what must be ingested, worn, and especially desired. . . . In a climate where a senator who doesn't like a couple of photographs tries to do away with the National Endowment for the Arts, censorious attacks within the lesbian community begin to sound a lot like fundamentalism. . . . They amount to a policing of the lesbian libido.[24]

Stein thus notes that while the old-style, politically correct(ing) strain of lesbian feminism is on the wane, "life style" lesbianism is on the rise. Lifestyle lesbianism is a recognition of the "diverse subcultural pockets and cliques—corporate dykes, arty dykes, dykes of color, clean and sober dykes—of which political lesbians are but one among many."[25] But it may also be a response to the marketing strategies of consumer culture.

The predominate research trend in U.S. advertising for the past two decades has been VALS (values and life styles) research. By combining information on demographics (sex, income, educational level), buying habits, self-image, and aspirations, VALS research targets and, in the case of yuppies, effectively *creates* consumer lifestyles that are profitable to advertisers.[26] Given lesbian-feminism's countercultural, anti-capitalist roots, it is not surprising that lesbians who "wear" their lifestyles or flaunt themselves as "material girls" are often criticized for trading in their politics for a self-absorbed materialism. But there is more to "lipstick lesbians" or "style nomads" than a freewheeling attitude toward their status as consumers or a boredom with the relatively static nature of the "natural look" (fashion, after all, implies change). Fashion-conscious dykes are rebelling against the idea that there is a clear one-to-one correspondence between fashion and identity. As Stein explains:

> You can dress as a femme one day and a butch the next. You can wear a crew-cut along with a skirt. Wearing high heels during the day does not mean you're a femme at night, passive in bed, or closeted on the job.[27]

Seen in this light, fashion becomes an assertion of personal freedom as well as political choice.

The new attitudes of openness toward fashion, sexuality, and lifestyle would not have been possible, of course, without the lesbian-feminist movement of recent decades. Its emergence may also have an economic explanation. According to a recent survey in OUT/LOOK, a national gay and lesbian quarterly, the average annual income for individual lesbians (who read OUT/LOOK) is $30,181; the average lesbian household income is approximately $58,000.[28] Since lesbians as a group are beginning to raise their incomes and class standing, they are now in a position to afford more of the clothing and "body maintenance" that was once beyond their financial capabilities. Finally, some credit for the changing perspectives on fashion might also be given to the recent emphasis on masquerade and fabrication in feminist criticism and to the more prominent role of camp in lesbian criticism. At least within academic circles these factors seem to affect, or to be the effect of, lesbian theorists' fashion sensibilities.

But regardless of what has *caused* this shift, or where one stands on the issue of fashion, advertisers in the fashion industry have begun to capitalize upon it. Given the increasing affluence and visibility of one segment of the lesbian population—the predominantly white, predominantly childless, middle-class, educated lesbian with disposable income—it appears that advertisers are now interested in promoting "lesbian window advertising." (Even while recognizing the highly problematic political implications of such a choice, I will continue to use the term "gay" instead of "lesbian" when referring to this marketing strategy since "gay window advertising" is the discursive phrase currently employed by the advertising industry.) In fashion magazines such as *Elle* and *Mirabella,* and in mail-order catalogs such as *Tweeds, J. Crew,* and *Victoria's Secret,* advertisers (whether knowingly or not) are capitalizing upon a dual market strategy that packages gender ambiguity and speaks, at least indirectly, to the lesbian consumer market. The representational strategies of gay window advertising thus offer what John Fiske calls "points of purchase" or points of identification that allow readers to make sense of cultural forms in ways that are meaningful or pleasurable to them.[29] The important question here is how these consumer points of purchase become involved in lesbian notions of identity, community, politics, and fashion.

When Dykes Go Shopping . . .

In a recent issue of *Elle,* a fashion layout entitled "Male Order" shows us a model who, in the words of the accompanying ad copy, represents "the zenith of masculine allure." In one photograph (figure 1) the handsome, short-haired model leans against the handlebars of a motorcycle, an icon associated with bike dyke culture. Her man-styled jacket, tie, and jewelry suggest a butch lesbian style that offers additional points of purchase for the lesbian spectator. In another photograph from the series (figure 2), the model is placed in a more neutral setting, a cafe, that is devoid of lesbian iconography. But because she is still dressed in masculine attire and, more importantly, exhibits the "swaggering" style recommended by the advertisers, the model incorporates aspects of lesbian style. Here, the traditional "come on" look of advertising can be read as the look or pose of a cruising dyke. Thus, part of the pleasure that lesbians find in these ads might be what Elizabeth Ellsworth calls "lesbian verisimilitude," or the representation of body language, facial expression, and general appearance that can be claimed and coded as "lesbian" according to current standards of style within lesbian communities.[30]

A fashion layout from *Mirabella,* entitled "Spectator," offers additional possibilities for lesbian readings (figure 3). In this series of photographs by Deborah Turbeville, two women (not always the same two in each photograph) strike poses in a fashionable, sparsely decorated apartment. The woman who is most prominently featured has very short, slicked-back hair and, in three of the photographs, she is wearing a tank top (styled like a man's undershirt) and baggy trousers. With her confident poses, her broad shoulders and strong arms (she obviously pumps iron), this fashion model can easily be read as "high-style butch." The other women in the series are consistently more "femme" in appearance, though they occasionally wear masculine-style apparel as well. The lesbian subtext in this fashion layout, however, is not limited to the models' ap-

SUIT UP
FOR A SWAGGERING
SPRING

Far left: Jacket,
Margaret Howell.
T-shirt, trousers;
Angelo Tarlazzi.
Left: Jacket,
shirt, trousers, tie,
scarf; Jean-Paul
Gaultier. Motor-
cycle, courtesy
Harley Davidson.
For details, see
Retail Guide. Hair
(style and cut),
Michel Aleman for
Bruno Dessange;
makeup, Tomoko
for Marek &
Associates; stylist,
Patricia Boin.

FIGURE 1.   © Gilles Bensimon, 1990.

pearances. The adoption of butch and femme *roles* suggests the possibility of interaction or a "playing out" of a lesbian narrative. Thus, while the women are physically separated and do not interact in the photographs,[31] their stylistic role-playing invites the lesbian spectator to construct a variety of (butch-femme) scenarios in which the two women come together. The eroticism of these imaginary scenes is enhanced by compositional details such as soft lighting and a rumpled bedsheet draped over the apartment window to suggest a romantic encounter. The variation of poses and the different combination of models also invites endless possibilities for narrative construction. Have these two women just met? Are they already lovers? Is there a love triangle going on here?, and so on.

Masculine clothes paired with feminine intuition: the latest news in sex appeal. **Left:** Cardigan, Bill Ditfort for Manitalia. Suit, Moschino Couture Uomo. Satin vest, Helmut Lang, $398. At H. Lorenzo, Los Angeles. Silver box pendant necklaces, Tanah Kalb at Apropo, $120 each. At Simons & Green, South Miami. Watch, Omega at Aaron Faber, $825. At Aaron Faber, NYC. Sunglasses, Eyevan Craft by Oliver Peoples, $215. At Gruen Optica, NYC. **Right:** Cotton jacket, $550, cotton pants, $315, cotton shirt, $88; Zucca. At Serenella, Boston; Savannah, Santa Monica. Crystal pendant necklace, Querrelle, $28. Watch, Aaron Faber, $675. For more details, see Retail Guide.

FIGURE 2.   © Gilles Bensimon, 1990.

Much of what gets negotiated, then, is not so much the contradictions between so-called "dominant" and "oppositional" readings, but the details of the subcultural reading itself. Even so, because lesbians (as members of a heterosexist culture) have been taught to read the heterosexual possibilities of representations, the "straight" reading is never entirely erased or replaced. Lesbian readers, in other words, know that they are not the primary audience for mainstream advertising, that androgyny is a fashionable and profitable commodity, and that the fashion models in these ads are quite probably heterosexual. In this sense, the dual approach of gay window advertising can refer not

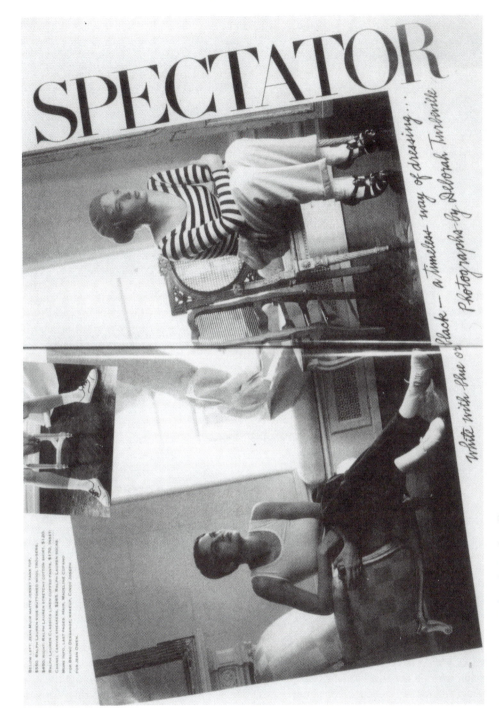

FIGURE 3. © Deborah Turbeville, 1990.

only to the two sets of readings formulated by homosexuals and heterosexuals, but to the dual or multiple interpretations that exist *within* lesbian reading formations. The straight readings, however, do not simply exist alongside alternative readings, nor do they necessarily diminish the pleasure found in the alternate readings. As "visual connoisseurs" lesbians privilege certain readings (styles) over others, or, in the case of camp readings, the straight reading itself forms the basis of (as it becomes twisted into) a pleasurable interpretation.

Here, as Sue-Ellen Case might argue, is the locus of a true masquerade of readership.[32] Lesbians are accustomed to playing out multiple styles and sexual roles as a tactic of survival and thus have learned the artifice of invention in defeating heterosexual codes of naturalism:

> The closet has given us the lie; and the lie has given us camp—the style, the discourse, the *mise-en-scène* of butch-femme roles. The survival tactic of hiding and lying [has] produced a camp discourse . . . in which gender referents are suppressed, or slip into one another, fictional lovers are constructed, [and] metaphors substitute for literal descriptions.[33]

I would not argue, as Case does, that "the butch-femme couple inhabit the [lesbian] subject position together"[34] since the butch-femme aesthetic is a historically specific (and even community and lifestyle specific) construct that ranges from the rigid butch-femme roles of the 1950s to the campy renaissance of today's butch-femme role-playing, and thus cannot represent a consistent subject position. But a lesbian subject's recognition of the butch-femme binarism, as it has been historically styled by lesbian communities, is an essential component of a reading practice that distances, subverts, and plays with both heterosexist representations and images of sexual indeterminacy. Another aspect of reading that must be considered is the pleasure derived from seeing the dominant media "attempt, but fail, to colonize 'real' lesbian space."[35] Even in representations that capitalize upon sexual ambiguity there are certain aspects of lesbian subculture that remain (as yet) inaccessible or unappropriated. By claiming this unarticulated space as something distinct and separable from heterosexual (or heterosexist) culture, lesbian readers are no longer outsiders, but insiders privy to the inside jokes that create an experience of pleasure and solidarity with other lesbians "in the know." Thus, as Ellsworth notes, lesbians "have responded to the marginalization, silencing, and debasement" found in dominant discourse "by moving the field of social pleasures . . . to the center of their interpretive activities" and reinforcing their sense of identity and community.[36]

This idea assumed concrete dimensions for me during the course of researching and presenting various versions of this paper. Lesbians across the country were eager to talk about or send copies of advertisements that had "dyke appeal" (and there was a good deal of consensus over how that term was interpreted). A number of lesbians admitted to having an interest in *J. Crew* catalogs because of a certain model they looked forward to seeing each month. Another woman told me of several lesbians who work for a major fashion publication as if to reassure me that gay window fashion photography is not an academic hallucination or a mere coincidence. Gossip, hearsay, and confessions are activities that reside at the center of lesbian interpretive communities and add an important discursive dimension to lesbians' pleasure in looking.

This conception of readership is a far cry from earlier (heterosexist) feminist analyses of advertising that argued that "advertisements help to endorse the powerful male attitude that women are passive bodies to be endlessly looked at, waiting to have their sexual attractiveness matched with *active* male sexual desire," or that women's relation to advertisements can only be explained in terms of anxiety or "narcissistic damage."[37]

These conclusions were based on a conspiracy theory that placed ultimate power in the hands of corporate patriarchy and relegated no power or sense of agency to the female spectator. Attempts to modify this position, however, have created yet another set of obstacles around which we must maneuver with caution. For in our desire and haste to attribute agency to the spectator and a means of empowerment to marginal or oppressed social groups, we risk losing sight of the interrelation between reading practices and the political economy of media institutions.

In the case of gay window advertising, for example, appropriation cuts both ways. While lesbians find pleasure (and even validation) in that which is both accessible and unarticulated, the advertising industry is playing upon a material and ideological tension that simultaneously appropriates aspects of lesbian subculture and positions lesbian reading practices in relation to consumerism. As John D'Emilio explains: "This dialectic—the constant interplay between exploitation and some measure of autonomy—informs all of the history of those who have lived under capitalism."[38] According to D'Emilio's argument that capitalism and the institution of wage labor have created the material conditions for homosexual desire and identity, gay window advertising is a logical outgrowth of capitalist development, one which presumably will lead to more direct forms of marketing in the future. But the reasons behind this development can hardly be attributed to a growing acceptance of homosexuality as a legitimate lifestyle. Capitalist enterprise creates a tension: materially it "weakens the bonds that once kept families together," but ideologically it "drives people into heterosexual families." Thus, "while capitalism has knocked the material foundations away from family life, lesbians, gay men, and heterosexual feminists have become the scapegoats for the social instability of the system."[39] The result of this tension is that capitalists welcome homosexuals as consuming subjects but not as social subjects. Or, as David Ehrenstein remarks, "the market is there for the picking, and questions of 'morality' yield ever so briefly to the quest for capital."[40]

The sexual indeterminacy of gay window advertising's dual market approach thus allows a space for lesbian identification, but must necessarily deny the representation of lesbian identity politics. This is a point that has so far been overlooked in the ongoing feminist and lesbian/gay debates over the issue of identity politics.[41] At the core of these debates is the poststructuralist challenge to essentialist definitions of identity. While theorists and activists alike agree that some shared sense of identity is necessary to build a cohesive and visible political community, some theorists argue that any unified conception of gay/lesbian identity is reductive and ahistorical. They thus opt for a historically constructed notion of *identities* that is contradictory, socially contingent, and rooted in progressive sexual politics. But while the controversies are raging over whether gay/lesbian identity is essential or constructed, media industries are producing texts that deny the very politics feminists and lesbians are busy theorizing.

Mainstream media texts employ representational strategies that generally refer to gays and lesbians in *anti-essentialist* terms. That is, homosexuals are not depicted as inherently different from heterosexuals; neither does there exist a unified or authentic "gay sensibility." As Mark Finch observes, "[t]he most recuperable part of the gay movement's message is that gay people are individuals."[42] The result is a liberal gay discourse that embraces humanism while rejecting any notion of a separate and authentic lesbian/gay subject. The homosexual, says John Leo, is thus "put together from disarticulating bits and pieces of the historical discourse on homosexual desire, which become a narrative pastiche for middle-class 'entertainment.' "[43] As a mode of representation that lacks any clear positioning toward what it shows, pastiche embodies "the popular" in the sense that people are free to make their own meanings out of the cultural bits and ideological pieces that are presented to them.

But this postmodern, anti-essentialist (indeed, democratic) discourse could also be interpreted as a homophobic response. As Jeffrey Weeks ironically points out, "The essentialist view lends itself most effectively to the defense of minority status."[44] (For example, if homosexuality were to be classified by the courts as biologically innate, discrimination would be more difficult to justify. By contrast, when a sense of lesbian or gay identity is lost, the straight world finds it easier to ignore social and political issues that directly affect gays and lesbians as a group.) The constructionist strategies of the media are thus not as progressive as anti-essentialist theorists (or media executives) might have us believe. The issue is not a matter of choosing between constructionism or essentialism, but a matter of examining the political motivations involved in each of these approaches—whether they appear in theory or media texts.

If we take politics as our starting point, then media and advertising texts can be analyzed in terms of their (un)willingness or (in)ability to represent the identity politics of current lesbian communities. Gay window advertising, as suggested earlier, consciously disavows any explicit connection to lesbianism for fear of offending or losing potential customers. At the same time, an appropriation of lesbian styles or appeal to lesbian desires can also assure a lesbian market. This dual approach is effective because it is based on two key ingredients of marketing success: style and choice. As Dick Hebdige has noted, "it is the subculture's stylistic innovations which first attract the media's attention."[45] Because style is a cultural construction, it is easily appropriated, reconstructed, and divested of its original political or subcultural signification. Style as resistance becomes commodifiable as chic when it leaves the political realm and enters the fashion world. This simultaneously diffuses the political edge of style. Resistant trends (such as wearing men's oversized jackets or oxford shoes—which, as a form of masquerade, is done in part for fun, but also in protest against the fashion world's insistence upon dressing women in tightly fitted garments and dangerously unstable footwear) become restyled as high-priced fashions.

In an era of "outing" (the practice of forcing gay and lesbian public figures to come out of the closet as a way to confront heterosexuals with our ubiquity as well as our competence, creativity, or civicmindedness), gay window advertising can be described as a practice of "ining." In other words, this type of advertising invites us to look *into* the ad to identify with elements of style, invites us *in* as consumers, invites us to be part of a fashionable "*in* crowd," but negates an identity politics based on the act of "coming out." Indeed, within the world of gay window advertising, there is no lesbian community to come out to, no lesbian community to identify with, no indication that lesbianism or "lesbian style" is a political issue. This stylization furthermore promotes a liberal discourse of choice that separates sexuality from politics and connects them both with consumerism. Historically, this advertising technique dates back to the 1920s, as Roland Marchand explains:

> The compulsion of advertising men to relegate women's modernity to the realm of consumption and dependence found expression not only in pictorial styles but also in tableaux that sought to link products with the social and political freedoms of the new woman. Expansive rhetoric that heralded women's march toward freedom and equality often concluded by proclaiming their victory only in the narrower realm of consumer products.[46]

Just as early twentieth-century advertisers were more concerned about women's votes in the marketplace than their decisions in the voting booth, contemporary advertisers are more interested in lesbian consumers than lesbian politics. Once stripped of its political underpinnings, lesbianism can be represented as a style of consumption linked to sexual preference. Lesbianism, in other words, is treated as merely a sexual style that can be chosen—or not chosen—just as one chooses a particular mode of fashion for self-expression.

But within the context of consumerism and the historical weight of heterosexist advertising techniques, "choice" is regulated in determinate ways. For example, gay window advertising appropriates lesbian subcultural style, incorporates its features into commodified representations, and offers it back to lesbian consumers in a packaged form cleansed of identity politics. In this way, it offers lesbians the opportunity to solve the "problem" of lesbianism: by choosing to clothe oneself in fashionable ambiguity, one can pass as "straight" (in certain milieux) while still choosing lesbianism as a sexual preference; by wearing the privilege of straight culture, one can avoid political oppression. Ironically, these ads also offer heterosexual women an alternative as well. As Judith Williamson notes, "[t]he bourgeois always wants to be in disguise, and the customs and habits of the oppressed seem so much more fascinating than his (sic) own."[47] Thus, according to Michael Bronski, "when gay sensibility is used as a sales pitch, the strategy is that gay images imply distinction and non-conformity, granting straight consumers a longed-for place outside the humdrum mainstream."[48] The seamless connections that have traditionally been made between heterosexuality and consumerism are broken apart to allow straight and lesbian women alternative choices. But these choices, which result in a rearticulated homogenized style, deny the differences among women as well as the potential antagonisms that exist between straight and lesbian women over issues of style, politics, and sexuality. As Williamson might explain, "femininity needs the 'other' in order to function . . . even as politically [it] seek[s] to eliminate it."[49]

Similar contradictions and attempts at containment occur within the discourses surrounding women's bodybuilding. As Laurie Schulze notes, "The deliberately muscular woman disturbs dominant notions of sex, gender, and sexuality, and any discursive field that includes her risks opening up a site of contest and conflict, anxiety and ambiguity."[50] Thus, within women's fashion magazines, bodybuilding has been recuperated as a normative ideal of female beauty that promotes self-improvement and ensures attractiveness to men. This discourse

> also assures women who are thinking about working out with weights that they need not fear a loss of privilege or social power; despite any differences that may result from lifting weights, they will still be able to "pass."[51]

The assurances in this case are directed toward heterosexual women who fear that bodybuilding will bring the taint of lesbianism. The connection between bodybuilding and lesbianism is not surprising, says Schulze, for "the ways in which female bodybuilders and lesbians disturb patriarchy and heterosexism . . . draw very similar responses from dominant culture."[52] Both the muscular female and the butch lesbian are accused of looking like men or wanting to be men. As Annette Kuhn puts it, "Muscles are rather like drag,"[53] Lesbian style, too, tends toward drag, masquerade, and the confusion of gender. Thus, both are subjected to various forms of control that either refuse to accept their physical or sexual "excesses" or otherwise attempt to domesticate their threat and fit them into the dominant constructions of feminine appearances and roles.

Both bodybuilders and lesbians, in other words, are given opportunities to "pass" in straight feminine culture. For bodybuilders, this means not flexing one's muscles while walking down the street or, in the case of competitive bodybuilders, exhibiting the signs of conventional feminine style (for example, makeup, coiffed hair, and string bikinis) while flexing on stage.[54] For lesbians, as discussed earlier, this means adopting more traditionally feminine apparel or the trendy accoutrements of gender ambiguity. But within these passing strategies are embodied the very seeds of resistance. As Schulze argues, muscle culture is a "terrain of resistance/refusal" as well as a "terrain of control."[55] It's simply a matter of how much muscle a woman chooses to flex. Within bodybuilding subculture, flexing is encouraged and admired; physical strength is valorized as a new form of femininity. Lesbians engage in their own form of "flexing" within lesbian subcultures (literally so for those lesbians who also pump iron) by refusing to pass as straight.

This physical and political flexing calls the contradictions of women's fashion culture into question and forces them out of the closet. It thus joins a long history of women's subversive and resistant responses to consumer culture in general. Although consumer culture has historically positioned women in ways that benefit heterosexist, capitalist patriarchy, women have always found ways to exert their agency and create their own pleasures and spaces. Fiske, for example, discusses the way that shopping has become a "terrain of guerrilla warfare" where women change price tags, shoplift, or try on expensive clothing without the intent of purchase.[56] The cultural phenomenon of shopping has also provided a homosocial space for women (for example, mothers and daughters, married and single adult women, teenage girls) to interact and bond. Lesbians have been able to extend this pleasure by shopping with their female lovers or partners, sharing the physical and erotic space of the dressing room, and, afterwards, wearing/ exchanging the fashion commodities they purchase. Within this realm, the static images of advertising have even less control over their potential consumers. Gay window advertising, for example, may commodify lesbian masquerade as legitimate high-style fashion, but lesbians are free to politicize these products or reappropriate them in combination with other products/fashions to act as new signifiers for lesbian identification or ironic commentaries on heterosexual culture.

This is not to suggest that there exists an authentic "lesbian sensibility" or that all lesbians construct the same, inherently progressive, meanings in the realm of consumption. One must be wary of the "affirmative character" of a cultural studies that leans toward essentialist notions of identity at the same time as it tends to overestimate the freedom of audience reception.[57] Since lesbians are never simply lesbians but also members of racial groups, classes, and so on, their consumption patterns and reading practices always overlap and intersect those of other groups. In addition, there is no agreement within lesbian communities on the "proper" response or relationship to consumer culture. This is precisely why the lesbian "style wars" have become a topic of such heated debate. Arlene Stein pinpoints the questions and fears that underlie this debate:

> Are today's lesbian style wars skin-deep, or do they reflect a changed conception of what it means to be a dyke? If a new lesbian has in fact emerged, is she all flash and no substance, or is she at work busily carving out new lesbian politics that strike at the heart of dominant notions of gender and sexuality?[58]

The answers are not simple, not a matter of binary logic. Some lesbians choose to mainstream. Others experience the discourse of fashion as an ambivalence—toward power, social investment, and representation itself.[59] Still others engage a camp discourse or masquerade that plays upon the lesbian's ambivalent position within straight culture. These responses, reading practices, interpretive activities—whatever one might call them—are as varied as the notions of lesbian identity and lesbian community.

Given the conflicts that lesbians frequently experience within their communities over issues of race, class, and lifestyle, lesbians are only too aware that a single, authentic identity does not exist. But, in the face of these contradictions, lesbians are attempting to forge what Stuart Hall calls an *articulation,* "a connection, a linkage that can establish a unity among different elements within a culture, under certain conditions."[60] For lesbians, the conditions are *political.* Lesbian identity politics must therefore be concerned with constructing political agendas and articulating collective identities that take into account our various needs and differences as well as our common experiences and oppressions *as a social group.* So too a theory of lesbian reading practices rooted in identity politics must stretch beyond analyses of textual contradictions to address the history of struggle, invisibility, and ambivalence that positions the lesbian subject in relation to cultural practices.

Ironically, now that our visibility is growing, lesbians have become the target of "capitalism's constant search for new areas to colonize."[61] This consideration must remain central to the style debates. For lesbians are not simply forming a new relationship with the fashion industry, *it* is attempting to forge a relationship with us. This imposition challenges us and is forcing us to renegotiate certain aspects of identity politics. (I can't help but think, for example, that the fashion controversy may not be about "fashion" at all but has more to do with the fact that it is the femmes who are finally asserting themselves.) In the midst of this challenge, the butch-femme aesthetic will undoubtedly undergo realignment. We may also be forced to reconsider the ways in which camp can function as a form of resistance. For once "camp" is commodified by the culture industry, how do we continue to camp it up?

The only assurance we have in the shadow of colonization is that lesbians *as lesbians* have developed strategies of selection, (re)appropriation, resistance, and subversion in order to realign consumer culture according to the desires and needs of lesbian sexuality, subcultural identification, and political action. Lesbian reading/social practices, in other words, are informed by an identity politics, however that politics may be formulated historically by individuals or by larger communities. This does not mean that the readings lesbians construct are always "political" in the strictest sense of the term (for example, one could argue that erotic identification is not political, and there is also the possibility that lesbians will identify with mainstreaming). Nonetheless, the discourses of identity politics—which arise out the lesbian's marginal and ambivalent social position—have *made it possible* for lesbians to consider certain contradictions in style, sexual object choice, and cultural representation that inform their reading practices, challenge the reading practices of straight culture, and potentially create more empowered, or at least pleasurable, subject positions as lesbians. Because identities are always provisional, lesbians must also constantly assert themselves. They must replace liberal discourse with camp discourse, make themselves visible, foreground their political agendas and their politicized subjectivities.

This may explain why feminists have avoided the issue of lesbian consumerism. Lesbians may present too great a challenge to the heterosexual economy in which they are invested, or lesbians may be colonizing the theoretical and social spaces they wish to inhabit. As long as straight women focus on the relation between consumer culture and women in general, lesbians remain invisible, or are forced to pass as straight, while heterosexual women can claim for themselves the oppression of patriarchal culture or the pleasure of masquerade that offers them "a longed for place outside the humdrum mainstream." On the other hand, straight feminists may simply fear that lesbians are better shoppers. When dykes go shopping in order to "go camping," they not only subvert the mix 'n' match aesthetic promoted by dominant fashion culture, they do it with very little credit.

NOTES

1. Karl Marx, *Capital,* Vol. I (London: Lawrence and Wishart, 1970) 71.

2. For a recent overview of the literature see Lynn Spigel and Denise Mann, "Women and Consumer Culture: A Selective Bibliography," *Quarterly Review of Film and Video* 11.1 (1989): 85–105. Spigel and Mann's compilation does not so much reproduce as *reflect* the heterosexual bias of scholarship in this field.

3. Jane Gaines, "The Queen Christina Tie-Ups: Convergence of Show Window and Screen," *Quarterly Review of Film and Video* 11.1 (1989): 50. Gaines is one of the few feminist critics who acknowledges gays and lesbians as consuming subjects.

4. Sue-Ellen Case, "Toward a Butch-Femme Aesthetic," *Discourse* 11.1 (1988–89): 56. Reprinted in this volume.

5. Roberta Astroff, "Commodifying Cultures: Latino Ad Specialists as Cultural Brokers," Paper presented at the 7th International Conference on Culture and Communication, Philadelphia, 1989.

6. Karen Stabiner, "Tapping the Homosexual Market," *New York Times Magazine,* May 2, 1982, p. 80.

7. Stabiner, 79.

8. Stabiner, 34.

9. Stabiner, 34.

10. Stabiner, 75.

11. Stabiner, 81.

12. Stabiner, 80.

13. Stabiner, 80.

14. Stabiner, 81.

15. Stabiner, 81.

16. Stabiner, 80.

17. Mary Ann Doane, "The Economy of Desire: The Commodity Form in/of the Cinema," *Quarterly Review of Film and Video* 11.1 (1989): 27.

18. Gaines, "The Queen Christina Tie-Ups," 35.

19. Gaines, "The Queen Christina Tie-Ups," 56.

20. Jane Gaines, "Introduction: Fabricating the Female Body," *Fabrications: Costume and the Female Body,* ed. Jane Gaines and Charlotte Herzog (New York: Routledge, 1990) 12–13.

21. Gaines, "Fabricating the Female Body," 3–9. Also see Kaja Silverman, "Fragments of a Fashionable Discourse," *Studies in Entertainment: Critical Approaches to Mass Culture,* ed. Tania Modleski (Bloomington: Indiana University Press, 1986) 139–152.

22. Gaines, "Fabricating the Female Body," 27.

23. Arlene Stein, "All Dressed Up, But No Place to Go? Style Wars and the New Lesbianism," *OUT/LOOK* 1.4 (1989): 37.

24. Alisa Solomon, "Dykotomies: Scents and Sensibility in the Lesbian Community," *Village Voice,* June 26, 1990, p. 40.

25. Stein, 39.

26. Stan LeRoy Wilson, *Mass Media/Mass Culture* (New York: Random House, 1989) 279.

27. Stein, 38.

28. "*OUT/LOOK* Survey Tabulations," Queery #10, Fall 1990.

29. John Fiske, "Critical Response: Meaningful Moments," *Critical Studies in Mass Communication* 5 (1988): 247.

30. Elizabeth Ellsworth, "Illicit Pleasures: Feminist Spectators and *Personal Best,*" Wide Angle 8.2 (1986): 54.

31. Cathy Griggers, "A Certain Tension in the Visual/Cultural Field: Helmut Newton, Deborah Turbeville and the VOGUE Fashion Layout," *differences* 2.2 (1990): 87–90. Griggers

notes that Turbeville's trademark is photographing women (often in pairs or groups) who "stand or sit like pieces of sculpture in interiors from the past in [a] grainy, nostalgic soft-focused finish."

32. Case, 64.

33. Case, 60.

34. Case, 58.

35. Ellsworth, 54.

36. Ellsworth, 54.

37. Jane Root, *Pictures of Women* (London: Pandora, 1984) 68; Rosalind Coward, *Female Desires* (New York: Grove Press, 1985) 80.

38. John D'Emilio, "Capitalism and Gay Identity," *Powers of Desire: The Politics of Sexuality,* ed. Ann Snitow, Christine Stansell, and Sharon Thompson (New York: Monthly Review Press, 1983) 102. Reprinted in this volume.

39. D'Emilio, 109.

40. David Ehrenstein, "Within the Pleasure Principle or Irresponsible Homosexual Propaganda," *Wide Angle* 4.1 (1980): 62.

41. See, for example, Teresa de Lauretis, "The Essence of the Triangle or, Taking the Risk of Essentialism Seriously: Feminist Theory in Italy, the U.S., and Britain," *differences* 1.2 (1989): 3–37; Diana Fuss, *Essentially Speaking* (New York: Routledge, 1989); Diana Fuss, "Reading Like a Feminist," *differences* 1.2 (1989): 72–92; Carol Vance, "Social Construction Theory: Problems in the History of Sexuality," *Which Homosexuality?* (London: GMP, 1989) 13–34; Jeffrey Weeks, "Against Nature," *Which Homosexuality?* 99–213; Jeffrey Weeks, *Sexuality and Its Discontents* (London: Routledge, 1985).

42. Mark Finch, "Sex and Address in 'Dynasty,' " *Screen* 27.6 (1986): 36.

43. John R. Leo, "The Familialism of 'Man' in American Television Melodrama," *South Atlantic Quarterly* 88.1 (1989): 42.

44. Weeks, *Sexuality,* 200.

45. Dick Hebdige, *Subculture: The Meaning of Style* (London: Methuen, 1979) 93.

46. Roland Marchand, *Advertising the American Dream* (Berkeley: University of California Press, 1985) 186.

47. Judith Williamson, "Woman Is an Island: Femininity and Colonization," *Studies in Entertainment: Critical Approaches to Mass Culture,* 116.

48. Michael Bronski, *Culture Clash: The Making of Gay Sensibility* (Boston: South End Press, 1984) 187.

49. Williamson, 109, 112.

50. Laurie Schulze, "On the Muscle," *Fabrications,* 59.

51. Schulze, 63.

52. Schulze, 73.

53. Annette Kuhn, "The Body and Cinema: Some Problems for Feminism," *Wide Angle* 11.4 (1989): 56.

54. Schulze, 68.

55. Schulze, 67.

56. John Fiske, *Reading the Popular* (Boston: Unwin Hyman, 1989): 14–17. Fiske cites the research of M. Pressdee, "Agony or Ecstasy: Broken Transitions and the New Social State of Working-Class Youth in Australia," Occasional Papers, S. Australian Centre for Youth Studies, S.A. College of A.E., Magill, S. Australia, 1986.

57. Mike Budd, Robert M. Entman, and Clay Steinman, "The Affirmative Character of U.S. Cultural Studies," *Critical Studies in Mass Communication* 7.2 (1990): 169–184.

58. Stein, 37.

59. Griggers, 101.

60. Jacqueline Bobo, "*The Color Purple:* Black Women as Cultural Readers," *Female Spectators,* ed. E. Deidre Pribram (London: Verso, 1988) 104–105. See also Stuart Hall, "Race, Articulation and Societies Structured in Dominance," *Sociological Theories: Race and Colonialism* (UNESCO, 1980) 305–345.

61. Williamson, 116.

13

The Spectacle of AIDS

Sᴍᴏɴ Wᴀᴛɴᴇʏ

Simon Watney is an art historian and AIDS activist. In this essay, first published in 1987, he focuses on the representation of AIDS in the United Kingdom. He argues that the extensive and costly public information campaign on AIDS run by the British government, along with the reporting on AIDS in the popular British media and the common discussions of it within the institutions of British medicine, are alike in conceiving of, and representing, gay men as the cause of AIDS, and as deserving punishment and marginalization, rather than support or health education. He also argues that this standard representation of gay men as source of plague and pollution serves to validate and reinforce the regime of what is now usually called "the family." Simon Watney is the author of Policing Desire: Pornography, AIDS, and the Media *(1987); he is the co-editor, with Erica Carter, of* Taking Liberties: AIDS and Cultural Politics *(1989); and he is the Director of the Red, Hot, and Blue Charitable Trust.*

And now what shall become of us without any barbarians? Those people were a kind of solution. (C.P. Cavafy, *Expecting the Barbarians*)

The question of identity—how it is constituted and maintained—is therefore the central issue through which psychoanalysis enters the political field. (Jacqueline Rose, "Feminism and the Psychic")

The "Truth" of AIDS

As I write, there have been "about" a thousand cases of AIDS in the United Kingdom. Writing on the subject of statistics, the great Polish poet Zbignev Herbert describes the fundamentally shameful nature of the word *about* when used in circumstances of disaster. For, in such matters,

accuracy is essential
we must not be wrong
even by a single one

we are despite everything
the guardians of our brothers

ignorance about those who have disappeared
undermines the reality of the world.[1]

Five years have passed since the isolation of the HIV retrovirus responsible for AIDS. Millions of pounds have been spent by the British government on public information campaigns. AIDS education workers have been appointed by local authorities throughout

Britain. Tens if not hundreds of thousands of lives have been directly affected by the consequences of HIV. Yet even the most fundamental medical facts concerning HIV and AIDS remain all but universally misunderstood. The entire subject continues to be framed by a cultural agenda that is as medically misinformed as it is socially misleading and politically motivated.[2] For those of us living and working in the various constituencies most devastated by HIV, it seems, as Richard Goldstein has pointed out, as if the rest of the population were tourists, casually wandering through the very height of a blitz of which they are totally unaware. This is hardly surprising at a time when the only sources of AIDS information are themselves so profoundly polluted and unreliable. Thus in England recently the *Guardian* noted that "by the end of August 1,013 cases had been reported, of whom 572 had died," while on the same day the *Star* informed *its* readers that "AIDS has now killed more than 1,000 people in Britain."[3]

Misreporting on such a scale has been regular and systematic since the earliest days of the epidemic, and is indicative of the values and priorities of an international information industry that continues to oscillate daily between meretricious gloating over the fate of those deemed responsible for their own misfortune, and the supposed "threat" of a "real" epidemic. Currently in the United States, someone dies of AIDS every half hour. An estimated six percent of all Africans have been infected by HIV, including nearly a quarter of the entire populations of Malawi and Uganda.[4] If statistics teach us anything, it is the sheer scale and efficiency of the cultural censorship within and between different countries and continents, which guarantees that the actual situation of the vast majority of people with HIV and/or AIDS is rarely if ever discussed. Moreover, this disappearance is strategic, and faithfully duplicates the positions the social groups most vulnerable to HIV found themselves in even before the epidemic began. Thus the Latino population of the two continents of America, IV drug users, workers in the sex industry, black Africans, and gay men are carefully confined in the penal category of the "high-risk group," from which position their experience and achievements may be safely ignored. In this manner a terrible ongoing human catastrophe has been ruthlessly denied the status of tragedy, or even natural disaster.

The British government's AIDS information campaign, which has been widely admired overseas, dutifully exhorted the "general public" not to die of ignorance.[5] Yet this campaign has still found itself unable to address one single word to British gay men, who constitute almost ninety percent of people with AIDS in Britain. At every level of "public" address and readership, ignorance is sustained on a massively institutionalized scale by British and American media commentary. The modes of address of such commentary reveal much about the ways in which the state and the media industry "think" the question of population. Indeed, the relentless monotony and sadism of AIDS commentary in the West only serve to manifest a sense of profound cultural uneasiness concerning the fragility of the nationalistic fantasy of an undifferentiated "general public," supposedly united above all divisions of class, region, and gender, yet totally excluding everyone who stands outside the institution of marriage. Popular perceptions of all aspects of AIDS thus remain all but exclusively informed by a cultural agenda that seriously and culpably impedes any attempt to understand the complex history of the epidemic, or to plan effectively against its future. In this context it is impossible to separate individual perceptions of risk, and endlessly amplified fears concerning the "threat" of "spread," from the drastically miniaturized "truth" of AIDS, which has remained impervious to challenge or correction since the syndrome was first identified in the ideologically constitutive and immensely significant name GRID (gay-related immunodeficiency) in 1981.[6]

In this manner a "knowledge" of AIDS has been uniformly constituted across the boundaries of formal and informal information, accurately duplicating the contours of other, previous "knowledges" that speak confidently on behalf of the "general public," viewed as a homogenous entity organized into discrete family units over and above all the fissures and conflicts of both the social and the psychic. This "truth" of AIDS also resolutely insists that the point of emergence of the virus should be identified as its *cause.* Epidemiology is thus replaced by a moral etiology of disease that can only conceive homosexual desire within a medicalized metaphor of contagion. Reading AIDS as the outward and visible sign of an imagined depravity of will, AIDS commentary deftly returns us to a premodern vision of the body, according to which heresy and sin are held to be scored in the features of their voluntary subjects by punitive and admonitory manifestations of disease. Moreover, this rhetoric of AIDS incites a violent siege mentality in the "morally well," a mentality that locks only too easily into other rhetorics of preemptive "defense."[7] Thus an essentially modern universalizing discourse of "family values," "standards of decency," and so on, recruits subjects to an ever more disciplinary "knowledge" of themselves and "their" world. This "knowledge" is effortlessly stitched in the likeness of an always-already-familiar *broderie Anglais* picture of seemingly timeless "national values" and the "national past."[8] At the same time, secular institutions appropriate and refashion an equally sober discourse of "promiscuity," which drifts out across the Mediterranean to incorporate the entire African subcontinent and beyond, recharging "the Orient" with a deadly cargo of exoticism that reminds "us" that negritude has always been, for whites, a sign of sexual excess and death.

The Government of the Home

All discussion of AIDS should proceed from the known facts concerning the modes of transmission of HIV in relation to lay perceptions of health and disease that mediate and "handle" this information. That this is far from the case in contemporary AIDS commentary remains in urgent need of explanation. To begin with, an overly rational model of health education continues to ignore all questions of cultural and psychic *resistance.* Similarly, the study of risk perception lacks a theory of the subject, even in its explicitly anti-economistic "culturalist" modes.[9] Both disciplines recognize that the localization of HIV infection in particular communities is no more intrinsically remarkable than the localization of any other infectious agent in any other specific constituencies. Yet the heavily concentrated and disseminated image of AIDS as a species of "gay plague" cannot be adequately explained by available sociological theories of scapegoating, boundary protection, or "moral panics." What is at stake here is the capacity of particular ideological configurations to activate deep psychic anxieties that run far beneath the tangible divisions of the social formation. In particular, we should consider the active legacy of eugenic theory, which is as much at work within the sociobiological dogmatics of contemporary familialism as it was in the biomedical politics of National Socialism. This is not to posit a crude parallel of objectives or identities between Thatcherite Britain and Nazi Germany, but merely to observe that whenever history is biologized with recourse to the authority of seemingly unquestionable and innate laws, "the perception of a natural order of social structure and stratification" is always "thought to be readily available in the evidence of the human body."[10] It is the sense of a *totalized* threat to a biologized identification of self with nation that characterizes both Nazi medical politics and modern familialism. Thus Jews, antifascists, gypsies, and "degenerates" (including, of course, large numbers of lesbians and gay men) were postulated as intrinsic and self-evident threats to the perceived unity and the very existence of the German *Volk*, and the policy of killing them all "as a therapeutic imperative" only emerged in relation to the deeply felt danger of *Volkstod*, or "death of the people" (or "nation," or "race").[11] It is in precisely this sense that people with HIV infection, usually misdescribed as "AIDS carriers," are widely understood to threaten the equally spurious unity of "the family," "the nation," and even "the species."[12] Hence the overriding need to return to the pressing question of the contemporary government of the home, especially in the light of Foucault's argument that in the modern period

> the family becomes an instrument rather than a model: the privileged instrument for the government of the population and not the chimerical model for good government: this shift from the level of the model to that of the instrument is, I believe, absolutely fundamental, and it is from the middle of the 18th century that the family appears in this dimension of instrumentality with respect to the population: hence the campaigns on morality, marriage, vaccinations, etc.[13]

This is why it is so important to avoid any temptation to think of the ongoing AIDS crisis as a form of "moral panic," which carries the implication that it is an entirely discrete phenomenon, distinct from other elements and dramas in the perpetual moral management of the home. On the contrary, homosexuality, understood by AIDS commentary as the "cause" of AIDS, is always available as a coercive and menacing category to entrench the institutions of family life and to prop up the profoundly unstable identities those institutions generate. The felt "problem" of sexual diversity is not established and imposed externally by the state, but rather internally, by the categorical imperatives of the modern organization of sexuality. The state, of course, responds to this situation, but it is not its originator. This, after all, is what sexuality *means*. Thus, consent to social policy is grafted from desire itself, as political prescriptions are understood to "protect" heterosexual identities, which are stabilized by an ever proliferating sense of permanent personal threat, with corresponding emotional responses ranging from "outrage" to actual violence against imaginary adversaries. Hence, as I have written elsewhere,

> We can begin to understand the seeming obsession with homosexuality in contemporary Britain, whether it is presented as a threat *within* the home, in the form of deviant members of the family who must be expelled, or as deviant images invading the "innocent" space of domesticity via TV or video; or as a supposedly *external* threat in the form of explicit sex education in schools, the (homo)sexuality of public figures, and above all, now, in the guise of AIDS.[14]

Homosexuality has lately come to occupy a most peculiar and centrally privileged position in the government of the home—homosexuality ideologically constructed as a regulative admonitory sign throughout the field of "popular" culture in the likeness of the ruthless pervert, justifying any amount of state intervention in the cause of "family values" and so on. Yet at the same time, the male homosexual becomes an impossible object, a monster that can only be engendered by a process of corruption through seduction, which is itself inexplicable, since familialism lacks any theory of desire beyond the supposed "needs" of reproduction. It is this rigorously anti-Freudian scenario that actively encourages the forward slippage from corruption theories of homosexuality to contagion theories of AIDS. In this manner the axiomatic identification of AIDS as a sign and symptom of homosexual behavior reconfirms the passionately held view of "the family" as a uniquely vulnerable institution. It also sanctions the strongest calls for "protectionist" measures, of an ever intensified censorship that will obliterate the evidently unbearable cultural evidence of that sexual diversity which stalks the terra incognita beyond the home.

Hence the incomparably strange reincarnation of the cultural figure of the male homosexual as a predatory, determined invert, wrapped in a Grand Guignol cloak of degeneracy theory, and casting his lascivious eyes—and hands—out from the pages of Victorian sexology manuals and onto "our" children, and above all onto "our" sons. Undoubtedly there is a real threat in the above scenario, which only serves to reveal the full extent to which the home is always a site of intense sexual fantasy. But the unspeakable that lurks in the very bosom of "the family" is not so much the real danger of child-molestation from *outside,* but the more radical possibility of acknowledging that the child's body is invariably an object of *parental* desire, and further, that the child itself is not only *desirable* but *desiring.* Calls for the quarantining of people infected with HIV, or the compulsory HIV testing of all gay men, immigrants, and other extra-familial categories, clearly derive from this prior, unconscious compulsion to censor and expel the signs of sexual diversity from the domestic field of vision, which is always equated with the child's point of view. Identifying with the child, the "good" parent is thus protected from troubling disturbances of adult identities, taking refuge in a projective fantasy of childhood "innocence" that significantly de-sexualizes all the actors involved. The utter violence of AIDS commentary suggests much about the force with which these repressed sexual materials return, and the forms of hysteria and hysterical identification that are responsible for successfully paralyzing the family ensemble into the rigidly stereotyped routines of "respectable" domesticity.

It is from this perspective that we may glimpse something of the political unconscious of the visual register of AIDS commentary, which assumes the form of a diptych. On one panel we are shown the HIV retrovirus (repeatedly misdescribed as the "AIDS virus") made to appear, by means of electron microscopy or reconstructive computer graphics, like a huge technicolor asteroid. On the other panel we witness the "AIDS victim," usually hospitalized and physically debilitated, "withered, wrinkled, and loathsome of visage"—the authentic cadaver of Dorian Gray.[15] This is the *spectacle of AIDS,* constituted in a regime of massively overdetermined images, which are sensitive only to the values of the dominant familial "truth" of AIDS and the projective "knowledge" of its ideally interpellated spectator, who already "knows all he needs to know" about homosexuality *and* AIDS. It is the principal and serious business of this spectacle to ensure that the subject of AIDS is "correctly" identified and that any possibility of positive sympathetic identification *with* actual people with AIDS is entirely expunged from the field of vision. AIDS is thus embodied as an exemplary and admonitory drama, relayed between the image of the miraculous authority of clinical medicine and the faces and bodies of individuals who clearly disclose the stigmata of their guilt. The principal target of this sadistically punitive gaze is the body of "the homosexual."

The Homosexual Body

Psychoanalysis understands identification as a psychological process whereby the subject "assimilates an aspect, property, or attribute of the other and is transformed, wholly or partially, after the model the other provides." Further, "it is by means of a series of identifications that the personality is constituted and specified."[16] But the substantive process of identifying operates in two modes: the transitive one of identifying the self in relation to the *difference* of the other, and the reflexive one of identifying the self in a relation of *resemblance* to the other. The homosexual body is an object that can only enter "public" visibility in the transitive mode, upon the strictly enforced condition that any possibility of identification *with* it is scrupulously refused. In the register of object-choice, the homosexual body inescapably evidences a sexual diversity that it is its ideological "function" to restrict. In the register of gender, it exposes the impossibility of the entire enterprise. Feminized in contempt, the homosexual body speaks too much of male "heterosexual" misogyny. Masculinized, it simply disappears. It is thus constituted as a *contradictio in objecto,* an objective contradiction. Psychoanalysis will pose this "problem" in a very different way, since the body with which it deals is "not some external realm but something that is internal to the psyche. . . . For psychoanalysis does not conceive of perceptions as unmediated registrations of the reality of a pregiven body. Rather, it has a libidinal theory of perception."[17]

The "problem," then, is the body itself, radically mute, yet rendered garrulous by projective, desiring fantasies all around it, which, as Leo Bersani reminds us, are "a frantic defense against the return of dangerous images and sensations to the surface of consciousness."[18] More precisely, these "desiring fantasies are by no means turned only towards the past; they are projective reminiscences."[19] Indeed, the very notion of a "homosexual body" only exposes the more or less desperate ambition to confine mobile desire in the semblance of a stable object, calibrated by its sexual aim, regarded as a "wrong choice." The "homosexual body" would thus evidence a fictive collectivity of perverse sexual performances, denied any psychic reality and pushed out beyond the furthest margins of the social. This, after all, is what the category of "the homosexual" (which we *cannot* continue to employ) was invented to do in the first place. The social sight lines of sexuality are thus permanently tensed against "mistakes" that might threaten to undermine the fragile stability of the heterosexual subject of vision. Hence the inestimable convenience of AIDS, reduced to a typology of signs that promises to identify the dreaded object of desire in the final moments of its own apparent self-destruction. AIDS is thus made to rationalize the impossibility of the "homosexual body," and reminds us only of the dire consequences of a failure to "forget". . . . Hence the social *necessity* of the "homosexual body," disclosed in the composite photography of nineteenth-century penal anthropology and sexology, and contemporary journalism. Hence also the voice of a contemporary English ex-police pathologist in a London teaching hospital, inviting his students, in the familiar pedagogic manner, to identify the physical symptoms of homosexuality, especially the "typical keratinized funnel-shaped rectum of the habitual homosexual."[20] Other constitutional symptoms of the "habitual homosexual" include softening of the brain. It is this order of "knowledge" of the "homosexual body" that precedes most clinical AIDS commentary and seeps out into the domestic register through the mediating services of medical correspondents, who report back from the clinical front lines on "our" behalf and ceaselessly refer us to the diagnostic AIDS diptych. In these densely coded *tableaux mourants* the body is subjected to extremes of casual cruelty and violent indifference, like the bodies of aliens, sliced open to the frightened yet fascinated gaze of uncomprehending social pathologists. Here, where the signs of homosexual "acts" have been entirely collapsed into the signs of death-as-the-deserts-of-depravity, there is still some chance that reflexive identification *with* the merely human fact of death might interrupt the last rites of psychic censorship, with the human body in extremis.

Thus, even and especially in the *clair-obscur* of death itself, the "homosexual body," which is also that of the "AIDS victim," must be publicly seen to be humiliated, thrown around in zip-up plastic bags, fumigated, denied burial, lest there be any acknowledgment of the slightest sense of *loss.* Thus the "homosexual body" continues to speak after death, not as a memento mori, but as its exact reverse, for a life that must at all costs be seen to have been devoid of value, unregretted, unlamented, and—final indignity—effaced into a mere anonymous statistic. The "homosexual body" is "disposed of," like so much rubbish, like the trash it was in life. Yet, as always, it is the very *excess* of the psychic operations informing this terminal "truth" of AIDS that signifies far beyond its own intentions. And, in these circumstances, ironically, the psychic consequences of the savage social organization of "sexuality" in the modern world can only serve ultimately to make instruments to plague us all. For it is precisely the displacement of epidemiology by a moralized etiology of disease, which regards AIDS as an intrinsic property of the fantasized "homosexual body," that is likely actively to encourage the real spread of HIV by distracting attention away from the well-proven means of blocking its transmission. Such attention would require listening to the voices of the "guilty" ones, would run the grave risk of acknowledging that HIV is no respector of persons or even bodies. But the spectacle of AIDS continues to protect us against any such ghastly eventuality, as we settle down before our TV screens to watch and to celebrate the long-prophesied and marvelous sight of the degenerates finally burning themselves out, comfortable and secure in our *gesundes Volksempfinden*—our healthy folk feelings.

The Spectacle of AIDS

In all its variant forms the spectacle of AIDS is carefully and elaborately stage-managed as a sensational didactic pageant, furnishing "us," the "general public," with further dramatic evidence of what "we" already "know" concerning the enormity of the dangers that surround us on all sides and at all times. It provides a purgative ritual in which we see the evildoers punished, while the national family unit—understood as the locus of "the social"—is cleansed and restored. Yet, as Jacques Donzelot has argued, "In showing the emergence of 'the social' as the concrete space of intelligibility of the family, it is the social that suddenly looms as a strange abstraction."[21]

Venerealizing AIDS, the spectacle reduces "the social" to the scale of "the family," from which miniaturized and impoverished perspective all aspects of consensual sexual diversity are systematically disavowed. We are thus returned to the question of "sexuality" in the modern world, but with a wholly different point of view from that which sustained earlier twentieth-century campaigns—conceived in terms of a right to privacy—on behalf of "sexual minorities." For it is precisely the concept of privacy that is the central term of familialism, now used to challenge the authority of the traditional liberal distinction between "public" and "private," which has defined the consensus view of how the space of "the social" has been thought for well over a century. That consensus is now up for grabs.[22]

The category of "homosexuality" has always in any case constituted a serious "problem" in relation to laws and social policies drawn up in the terms of a supposedly physical public/private distinction. Legitimated, to some extent, in the technical sphere of the private, it has been all the more problematized in the public domain. AIDS commentary demonstrates this very clearly, insofar as it is invariably addressed to a "family" that is also "the nation." Hence the extraordinary fact that even after 1,000 cases of AIDS, the British government has yet to direct a single item of information, advice, or support to the constituency most directly affected by the consequences of HIV since the early 1980s—gay men. This is evidently because we are not recognized as a part of "the social," from which we are paradoxically excluded by virtue of our partially legalized "private" status. And let us not forget that we are talking here about *at least* ten percent of the overall population of the United Kingdom. The spectacle of AIDS is thus always modified by the fear of being too "shocking" for its domestic audience, while at the same time it amplifies and magnifies the collective "wisdom" of familialism. AIDS commentary thus provides a unique perspective on the contemporary government of the home, which is experienced from within as a refuge of "privacy," and in the defense of which its members agree that it can hardly be sufficiently regulated. In this manner all aspects of "public" life are gradually annexed and subsumed by the precepts and "etiquette" of privacy at the very moment that its most eloquent advocates are drawing their curtains against what they perceive as a hostile and dangerous outside world.

Yet, as we have seen, the home itself is also recognized as a site of potential *inner* corruption, and the prosecution of the "public" by the "private" is ideally personified in the fantasy of the "homosexual body," whose sexual object-choice is displaced into the calibrated signs of AIDS. This body is as repulsive as the task of policing recalcitrant desire requires it to be. The spectacle of AIDS is thus placed in the service of the strongly felt need for constant domestic surveillance and the strict regulation of identity through the intimate mechanisms of sexual guilt, sibling rivalries, parental favoritism, embarrassment, hysterical modesty, house-pride, "keeping-up-with-the-Joneses," hobbies, diet, clothes, personal hygiene, and the general husbandry of the home. These are the concrete practices that authorize consent to "political" authority, and it is in relation to them that the entire spectacle of AIDS is unconsciously choreographed, with its studied emphasis on "dirt," "depravity," "license," and above all "promiscuity." Yet the proliferating agencies and voices that offer their "expertise" on behalf of "the family" are inevitably as uneven and inept as is the actual maintenance of power in the home itself. "The family" is thus frequently provided with mutually conflicting and contradictory messages from the very experts to which it has granted authority. Hence, for example, the glaring contemporary British conflict between popular consent for sex education in schools and an imperative against any form of education that is held to "advocate" homosexuality. "Public" sex education thus comes to duplicate the "knowledge" of "the family," which is duly inscribed in the national curriculum with the full force of law. In a very similar way, the strong lobby in favor of "AIDS education" in schools, and far beyond, is equally compelled to ignore the actual experience of most people with AIDS, or the communities most vulnerable to HIV infection, lest they also be accused of "advocating" homosexuality. Here, as in all similar instances, the concept of "advocacy" speaks from a discourse of sexual "acts" by which the "innocent" might become "corrupted" and turned into "habitual homosexuals." Such a concept functions within the powerful anti-Freudian project that aspires to erase all notions of desire from the epistemological field of "family," that is, "public," life.

In these circumstances, the spectacle of AIDS operates as a public masque in which we witness the corporal punishment of the "homosexual body," identified as the enigmatic and indecent source of an incomprehensible, voluntary resistance to the unquestionable governance of marriage, parenthood, and property. It is at precisely this point that opposition to the familial sovereignty of AIDS commentary can be posed most effectively. For, as I have argued, the overall spectacle of AIDS places its own audience at direct risk of HIV infection by distracting attention away from the demonstrably effective means of preventing its transmission. At the same time, the tremendous discursive responsibility that is placed upon the notion of "promiscuity" throughout AIDS commentary renders it especially vulnerable to challenge when it is isolated from the propping imagery of venerealized death. It can easily be demonstrated, for example, that HIV is not a venereal condition, since it is not necessarily or exclusively sexually transmitted. It is not difficult to grasp the fact that if every disease that can or may be sexually transmitted were classified as venereal, the list would include all the most common known medical ailments, as Kaye Wellings has pointed out in relation to the earlier venerealizing of herpes in the 1970s.[23] It must also be forcefully pointed out on every available occasion that those posing "monogamy" as a preferable alternative to prophylactic information are in turn responsible for increasing the spread of HIV by mischievously suggesting that monogamy affords some kind of intrinsic "moral" defense against a retrovirus. In such ways the entire authority of the spectacle of AIDS could be undermined by the protectionist rhetoric of the spectacle itself. This also permits the wider affirmation of sexual desire and diversity in the presentation of safer sex as an emancipatory and life-saving protectorate for the nation, posed in actively democratic terms that enlarge conceptions of the self beyond the narrowing confines of "citizenship." In these respects the challenge of AIDS reeducation exemplifies the insight of Ernesto Laclau and Chantal Mouffe that what is being exploded in the postmodern period

> is the idea and the reality itself of a unique space of constitution of the political. What we are witnessing is a politicization far more radical than any we have known in the past, because it tends to dissolve the distinction between the public and the private, not in terms of the encroachment on the private by a unified public space, but in terms of a proliferation of radically new and different political spaces. We are confronted with the emergence of a *plurality of subjects* whose forms of constitution and diversity it is only possible to think if we relinquish the category of "subject" as a unified and unifying essence.[24]

By insisting on the psychoanalytic perception of the *psychic reality* of desire, we may avoid the shortcomings of a sexual politics that continues to see "gay oppression" as a unitary and distinct phenomenon that might easily be rectified and remedied through direct political and legislative interventions, however intrinsically expedient these may be in relation to the only too concrete institutions that currently secure the meaning and practice of "justice." The spectacle of AIDS teaches us, however, that it is the structure, epistemology, and "decorum" of "sexuality" itself that have inexorably led us to the tragic impasse in which we find ourselves, where seemingly unified "sexual minorities" are widely and routinely regarded, in their entirety, as disposable constituencies. This point cannot be sufficiently emphasized. For let there be no mistake: the spectacle of AIDS calmly and constantly entertains the possible prospect of the death of all Western European and American gay men from AIDS—a total, let us say, of some twenty million lives—without the slightest flicker of concern, regret, or grief. Psychoanalysis may alert us to the psychological processes that can be activated in particular, complex historical circumstances in order to endorse an indifference that casually dehumanizes whole categories of persons. To turn back now to the prospect of a politics rooted in the subjectivity of public/private space can only serve to strengthen the powerful emergent forms of a secularized fundamentalism that will not cease to prosecute its own "projective reminiscences," picked out in the spotlights of its own displaced desires. In the meantime, all those who threaten to expose the brutal, hypocritical, and degrading implications of contemporary "family values" and "standards of decency" will undoubtedly continue to be stridently denounced—quite accurately—as "enemies of the family."

AIDS is increasingly being used to underwrite a widespread ambition to erase the distinction between "the public" and "the private," and to establish in their place a monolithic and legally binding category—"the family"—understood as the central term through which the world and the self are henceforth to be rendered intelligible. Consent to this strategy is sought by tapping into lay perceptions of health, sickness, and disease, unevenly accreted down the centuries, and sharing only the common human fear and disavowal of death. Health education thus emerges as the central site of hegemonic struggle in the coming decades—a struggle that refuses and eludes all known lines of previous party-political allegiance and observance. A new and essentially talismanic model of power is emerging, offering to protect subjectivities carefully nurtured in folklore and superstition, now rearticulated in a discourse of ostensibly medical authority. We are witnessing the precipitation of a moralized bio-politics of potentially awesome power—a cunning combination of leechcraft and radiotherapy, eugenics and a master narrative of "family health"—with social policies that aspire with sober fanaticism to the creation of a modernity in which *we* will no longer exist. The spectacle of AIDS thus promises a stainless world in which *we* will only be recalled, in textbooks and carefully edited documentary "evidence," as signs of plagues and contagions averted—intolerable interruptions of the familial, subjects "cured" and disinfected of desire, and "therapeutically" denied the right to life itself.

NOTES

1. Zbignev Herbert, "Mr. Cogito on the Need for Precision," in *Report from the Besieged City,* New York and Oxford, Oxford University Press, 1987, p. 67.

2. See Simon Watney, "The Subject of AIDS," *Copyright,* vol. 1, no. 1 (Fall 1987).

3. Andrew Veitch, "AIDS Cases Exceed 1,000," *Guardian,* September 8, 1987; Anthony Smith, "AIDS Death Toll Hits 1,000," *Star,* September 8, 1987.

4. Andrew Veitch, " 'Up to 10 Million' Have AIDS Virus," *Guardian,* June 24, 1986.

5. See Simon Watney, "AIDS: How Big Did It Have to Get?," *New Socialist,* March 1987.

6. See Dennis Altman, *AIDS in the Mind of America,* New York, Doubleday, 1986, p. 33.

7. See Simon Watney, "AIDS USA," *Square Peg,* no. 17 (Autumn 1987).

8. See Patrick Wright, *On Living in an Old Country,* London, Verso, 1985.

9. See, for example, Mary Douglas, *Risk Acceptability According to the Social Sciences,* London, Routledge & Kegan Paul, 1986.

10. David Green, "Veins of Resemblance: Photography and Eugenics," in Simon Watney et al. eds., *Photography/Politics: Two,* London, Commedia, 1987, p. 13.

11. See Robert Jay Lifton, *The Nazi Doctors: Medical Killing and the Psychology of Genocide,* New York, Basic Books, 1986, p. 25. This book should be read by anyone interested in the archeology of AIDS commentary.

12. For an example, see William E. Dannemeyer, "AIDS Infection Must Be Reportable," *Los Angeles Times,* June 12, 1987.

13. Michel Foucault, "On Governmentality," *Ideology & Consciousness,* no. 6 (Autumn 1979), p. 17.

14. Simon Watney, "AIDS: The Cultural Agenda," paper presented at the conference Homosexuality, Which Homosexuality? at the Free University, Amsterdam, December 1987. Forthcoming.

15. Oscar Wilde, *The Picture of Dorian Gray* (1891), New York and Oxford, Oxford University Press, 1974, p. 224.

16. J. Laplanche and J.-B. Pontalis, *The Language of Psycho-Analysis,* London, The Hogarth Press, 1983, p. 205.

17. Parveen Adams, "Versions of the Body," *m/f,* nos. 11–12 (1986), p. 29.

18. Leo Bersani, *Baudelaire and Freud,* Berkeley, University of California Press, 1977, p. 129.

19. *Ibid.,* pp. 41–42.

20. Meyrick Horton, "General Practices," paper presented at the second annual Social Meanings of AIDS conference, South Bank Polytechnic, London, November 1987.

21. Jacques Donzelot, *The Policing of Families: Welfare Versus the State,* London, Hutchinson & Co., 1979, p. xxvi.

22. See Simon Watney, *Policing Desire: Pornography, AIDS, and the Media,* Minneapolis, University of Minnesota Press, 1987, chapter 4.

23. Kaye Wellings, "Sickness and Sin: The Case of Genital Herpes," paper presented to the British Sociological Association, Medical Sociology Group, 1983, p. 10.

24. Ernesto Laclau and Chantal Mouffe, *Hegemony and Socialist Strategy: Towards a Radical Democratic Politics,* London, Verso, 1985, p. 181.

14

Sontag's Urbanity

D.A. Miller

D.A. Miller, Professor of English at Harvard University, is a literary and political critic of narrative representation in the novel and in film. Among his many publications are The Novel and the Police *(1988), "Anal* Rope" *(in* Inside/Out, *edited by Diana Fuss [1991]), and* Bringing Out Roland Barthes *(1992). In "Sontag's Urbanity," Miller reviews Susan Sontag's widely read book,* AIDS and its Metaphors *(New York: Farrar, Straus and Giroux, 1989), and he finds embedded in that seemingly humanistic meditation a deeply homophobic design. Specifically, Miller analyzes the discursive strategies by which ostensibly liberal commentary manages to shore up its own literary and cultural authority by casually and thus all the more effectively devaluing the lives of gay men. Miller's critique identifies "urbanity" as one of the most devastating and typical devices in the arsenal of homophobic discourse, devices that serve routinely and almost invisibly to support the political and ideological structures of heterosexual privilege.*

In the promotion of *AIDS and its Metaphors,* Susan Sontag has expressed irritation, disappointment, and even hurt that her book has been reviewed by experts on science and AIDS rather than as "writing." This is "a literary performance," she insists in one interview, that "has more to do with Emerson than Randy Shilts."[1] "Imagine," she invites us in another, "M.F.K. Fisher just reviewed for her recipes. First of all M.F.K. Fisher is a writer. Her subject just happens to be food."[2] The plausibility of such statements depends on assuming a difference, sharp enough to amount to an opposition, between one entity called writing and another called AIDS. It is not the derisory oyster that secretes the pearl of M.F.K. Fisher's prose, or that can help us estimate its luster. Likewise, the comparison implies, AIDS "just happens to be" the most recent incitement to what should more properly, or "first of all," engage our attention: Susan Sontag's ongoing writing project. The claim for the precession and superiority of form over a content whose main function is to justify the elaboration of artistic or literary devices is of course a familiar one, from Wilde, the Russian formalists, even Sontag's own early manifesto "Against Interpretation." As the case of Wilde best illustrates, however, the argument for the secondariness of content typically surfaces in contexts where the content in question, far from being trivial, enjoys a particular volatility whose ignition would catastrophically overwhelm both personal and public spheres together, obliterating whatever barriers had allowed, or required, them to be kept separate. The intellectually fatuous, politically repellent desire to scale AIDS down to the import of what one might cook for dinner ("one man's meat . . .") is only comprehensible, therefore, if we recognize how thoroughly it is determined by the dominant cultural reception of AIDS and grasp the continuity of this desire with what elsewhere Sontag herself is capable of recognizing as "practices of decontamination."[3] Accordingly, both Sontag's aggressive valorization of writing and her anxious defense of the distance writing must assume vis-à-vis its subject matter bespeak AIDS panic in its looniest form to date: a fear that the epidemic might breech—whether through the "one-dimensional reading"[4] of unlettered experts or perhaps even the unsedated importunity of persons with the disease—the all-but-ontological *cordon sanitaire* that protects literary essay writing, as a genre or form. Sontag's insistence on inhabiting and maintaining the boundaries of this category—as, explicitly, against the discourse on AIDS she is more Emerson than Shilts, and her book, she stresses, is "not another book on AIDS"[5]—thus inadvertently tends to situate her writing, from its general conception down to the grain of its prose, in the same irrationally phobic relation to AIDS that she alleges an interest in demystifying. In what follows, I will be suggesting that the most serious limitations of Sontag's consideration of AIDS and its metaphors inhere in what enters that consideration mainly tacitly, as the structuring frame of its rhetoric. The trouble—trouble, at any rate, for those engaged in what, against the express wish of Sontag's text, let me persist in calling the *fight* against AIDS—lies not in Sontag's "views" on AIDS (which are, to the admitted confusion of almost every reviewer, strangely hard to come by in any case), so much as in the *attitude of her writing*—by which I mean the unexamined and, I assume, largely unconscious complex of positionings, protocols, and poses that determine her deployment of language.

Near the end of her "Notes on 'Camp,'" the essay that did most to make her early reputation, Sontag addresses the "peculiar relation between Camp taste and homosexuality": "Homosexuals, by and large, constitute the vanguard—and the most articulate audience—of Camp," whose playfulness, Sontag contends, by dissolving the moral indignation that might otherwise oppress them, promotes their integration into society.[6] On this account, Camp is a primordially gay phenomenon, emerging within the formation of a specifically gay subculture, at the interface of that subculture with the homophobic culture at large. But when once Sontag has evoked the gay lineage of Camp, she proceeds to deny it any necessity: "Camp taste is much more than homosexual taste. Obviously, its metaphor of life as theater is peculiarly suited as a justification and projection of a certain aspect of the situation of homosexuals. (The Camp insistence on not being 'serious,' on playing, also connects with the homosexual's desire to remain youthful.) Yet one feels that if homosexuals hadn't more or less invented Camp, someone else would."[7] That unblinking embrace of counterfactuality can only be understood as not just expressing, but also fulfilling, a wish for a Camp theoretically detachable—and therefore already detached—from gay men (all of whom are parenthetically assumed to be clones of that familiar figure of psychopathology, "the" homosexual, with his self-evident desire to remain youthful, and the rest). The act of severance thus performed, the claim to Camp's origination goes up for grabs—someone else could invent Camp, and who better than the author of this manifestly inventive and authoritative essay? As early as her first page, this author has justified her phobic de-homosexualization of Camp as the necessary condition for any intelligent discourse on the subject. "I am strongly drawn to Camp, and almost as strongly offended by it. That is why I want to talk about it, and why I can. For no one who wholeheartedly shares in a given sensibility can analyze it; he can only, whatever his intentions, exhibit it. To name a sensibility, to draw its contours and recount its history, requires a deep sympathy modified by revulsion." In a memorably lapidary, lapidating conclusion, "To talk about Camp is therefore to betray it."[8]

Twenty-five years later, twenty years "after Stonewall," the same revulsion modifies—almost to the point of elision—Sontag's treatment of gay men in *AIDS and its Metaphors.*[9] On the mere handful of occasions when they are mentioned, gay men are still called "homosexual men" (25, 76), even "male homosexuals" (76), as though such a term, variously redolent of psychiatry, the police, and social science, and historically assisting in the attempt of such discourses to stigmatize those so named (as sick, criminal, or just "other"), could be—in this context, at this date—at all neutral. The sexual practices of gay men disappear into soft-focus names suitable for (continuing to mystify, refusing to educate) a "general population": such as the "deviance" of sociology (64), the "perversity" of psychoanalysis (26), or the "sodomy" of morality and law (65). (What Sontag calls "specifically the practice of sodomy" [65] is probably the least specific practice in the whole history of sexuality.) In Sontag's idiom, the sadly rich, even fundamental link between gay men and AIDS metaphors vanishes into wider categories ("groups at risk" [91], "despised and feared minorities" [54]) or broader questions. Thus, "denunciations of 'the gay plague' are part of a much larger complaint . . . about contemporary permissiveness" (63); "what moves [the neoconservatives' demagogic use of AIDS] is not just, or even principally, homophobia" (63); "risk-free sexuality" is "hardly an invention of the male homosexual subculture" (77); and "'the general population' may be as much a code phrase for whites as it is for heterosexuals" (82). One recalls all those advice columnists and student counselors who routinely offer the reassurance that just because something—a fantasy, a feeling, even an act—looks gay, this "does not necessarily mean" that it is. It is not that Sontag's statements, as such, are untrue; what is disingenuous is rather the pattern in which they are all made, a pattern that consists of denying, in the form of an invitation to move beyond, the specifically gay bearings of AIDS metaphors. A lexicon that not only prefers "homosexual" and "sodomy," say, to "gay" and "anal intercourse," but also, in the definitively heterosexist manner, lets its preference go without saying, puts writing in the service of the homophobic oppression that is exacerbated by AIDS and that underpins the stigmatization of those with AIDS, gay or not. Similarly, the compulsively repeated claim that homosexuality is not the only or even the main topic of AIDS metaphors, *when homosexuality hasn't been elaborated as a topic at all,* becomes a way of actively avoiding the question, of positively preventing its availability for discussion.

Inevitably, such homophobia "of omission" comes to betray its collusion with more active forms of abuse:

> An infectious disease whose principal means of transmission is sexual necessarily puts at greater risk those who are sexually more active—and *is easy to view as* a punishment for that activity. True of syphilis, this is even truer of AIDS, since not just promiscuity but a specific sexual "practice" *regarded as* unnatural *is named as* more endangering. Getting the disease through a sexual practice *is thought to be* more willful, therefore deserves more blame. Addicts who get the illness by sharing contaminated needles *are seen as* committing (or completing) a kind of inadvertent suicide. Promiscuous homosexual men practicing their vehement sexual customs under the illusory conviction, fostered by medical ideology with its cure-all antibiotics, of the relative innocuousness of all sexually transmitted diseases, *could be viewed as* dedicated hedonists—though it's now clear that their behavior was no less suicidal. (26, emphases added)

One needn't be an expert on AIDS to notice how, in this passage, the qualification of every view as *idée reçue,* contingent and hence modifiable cultural fantasy, abruptly ceases in the last sentence, where contestable doxa ("regarded, seen, viewed as") becomes immovable fact: "it's now clear" that the behavior of sexually active gay men "was no less suicidal." Yet insofar as a notion of suicide is inseparable from an intention to kill oneself, then one's infection by a life-threatening virus of whose existence and means of transmission one was entirely ignorant can hardly be considered suicidal outside the punitive fantasy about male homosexuality—in its blanched New Age form, that such men "chose" their disease—to which Sontag, meaning to demystify it, unwittingly surrenders.

The ethnological perspective, fixing those "promiscuous homosexual men" who practice "their vehement sexual customs" in an alterity without appeal, sparks a similarly uncontrolled backfire in the argument Sontag may believe she is making. If one form of the homophobia in Sontag's text takes the high ground of opposition to racism, by urging us to consider, instead of the gay men implied to be monopolizing all our unstintingly expended concern and resources, those who are sick or infected with AIDS in West Africa ("were AIDS only an African disease . . . few outside of Africa would be concerned with it" [83], "people are being told that heterosexual transmission is extremely rare, and unlikely—as if Africa did not exist" [26]), another form is by no means above relying on that very racism, however unintentionally, by inscribing gay men in the most abusive stereotypes of our popular anthropology of the African "tribe" (e.g., "in the 1970s . . . many male homosexuals reconstituted themselves as something like an ethnic group, one whose distinctive folkloric custom was sexual voracity" [76]). Equally, the moralism that insinuates notions of sexual "promiscuity," "vehemence," and "voracity" must also render Sontag's dismissal of Jerry Falwell, Pat Robertson, Norman Podhoretz, and their like as "specialists in ugly feelings" (63) merely gestural.

Neither the epidemic's changed demographics nor the changes in our awareness of them have much altered its poetics. As the vehicle of metaphor, the point of reference in what Paula Treichler has called "an epidemic of signification,"[10] AIDS remains centrally a gay disease, the disease of gayness itself. It is amazing that Sontag could imagine setting us free from the tyranny of AIDS metaphors without acknowledging the large and specific extent to which that tyranny, though exercised *over* every person or group sick, infected, at risk, or merely panicstricken, is exercised *through* activating and justifying homophobia against gay men; or without feeling therefore obliged to interrogate those metaphors as the precipitate of deep-seated and widespread cultural fantasies attaching to gay men, as intimately and forcibly as the tattoo that, in this sense, William F. Buckley, Jr.'s monstrous proposal allows us to recognize *has already been inscribed* on the "private" parts—say, for instance, on the fucking assholes—of their bodies.

It is, of course, the peculiar status of such fantasies that their relatively candid expression, as by Buckley, incurs a manifest risk. As anyone adept in the *bon usage* of homophobia knows, too much of it is as apt to be thought to betray homosexual desire as too little; becoming a fully entitled man in our society—not the usual fate of teenage gaybashers, who more likely grow up, for instance, pumping Buckley's gas—means not just learning homophobia, but also learning to acquire the calculation-become-intuition that would moderate it, or rather silence its expression just short of the point where it might start to show. It is homophobia, not homosexuality, that requires a closet, whence it characteristically makes its sorties only as a multiply coded allusion, or an unprovable, if not improbable, connotation. Such featherweight pressure, however, is all that is required to activate—via a chain of displacements to rival a Freudian dream—fantasy positions and defenses whose cumulative effect on gay men and on gay desire has been thus almost inarticulably harmful. (News still deemed fit to print: the *New York Times* speaks of the "limp blond hair" of Rock Hudson's lover, not to mention his wrist; and as it quotes John Tower apologetically saying, "I don't usually wear pink shirts," it notices "his powder-pink cuff" as a way of unpacking his own implicit evocation of the powderpuffs who usually affect this color.)

All this is why a sustained understanding of homophobia matters crucially to an attempt to intervene in the social construction of AIDS, and why the failure to offer such an understanding must compromise the integrity—I mean the coherence as well as the honesty—of any account of this construction. (Purporting to advance beyond mere homophobia, for instance, Sontag finds AIDS offering a reference to fantasies of apocalypse, as though such fantasies, starting from Sodom and Gomorrah, were at all extricable from the decor of a homosexualized decadence.) This is also why the operational effects of homophobia cannot be dismissed as self-evident, as Sontag's bored preteritions are apt (and anxious) to imply, for reading the homophobic social text in the sinuous process of its condensation-and-displacement into AIDS metaphors, as Simon Watney for example does in *Policing Desire,* requires no less deft or detailed attention than an analyst might give to a dream, a literary critic to a poem, or M.F.K. Fisher to her menus. (Sontag's valorization of writing would be more persuasive if it were accompanied by a valorization of the act of *reading* that any writing worthy of the name performs.) And this is why the call for an analysis along these lines will sound tendentious, shrill, "one-dimensional," while the various forms of denegation—it's not (just, mainly, at all) homophobia—retain the plausibility of urbanity itself.

Although Sontag perfectly sees through the notion of "the general population" in AIDS discourse, where it means (by seeming to not just mean) a white, heterosexual middle class, and where its use therefore reaffirms the agenda of this class at its most invisibly oppressive, her own writing on AIDS is nonetheless determined through and through by its imagined address to, and on behalf of, an analogously pseudo-universal and -unified entity she at one point calls, without apology or explanation, "general consciousness" (72). Such an address obliges the writing to simulate a disinterestedness that must be "proven" not just by the arrogant silence it keeps about whatever interests thereby retain all the power of presumption, but also by the anxious spectacle it always makes of itself—in those feats of keeping proper balance or distance, whose treachery is supposed to edify, or in that ever and evenly shifting attention, whose shortness of span can pass for an exhilarating breadth. The writer is—but must also be shown to be—unsituated in any noticeably peculiar and hence "partial" relation to her subject; her language is—but must also be shown to be—as impeccably detached as the thought whose motions it transcribes. In this sense Sontag's closing recommendation that military metaphors of illness be "retired" (94)—as though there were no violence in forced retirement—only reveals how high above the fray of competing interests and meanings she imagines situating what in fact can't help being her intervention, no less contentious than any other, in that struggle. (Even Sontag's one powerfully "personal" gesture—a resonant unsentimental account of the cancer that spurred her to write *Illness as Metaphor*—is doubly dislocated by the exactions of impersonality. In the first place, she is only able to confess her private interest in that "little book" [13] now that the interest, no longer current, has evolved into a story whose adventure is complete, and long after the book has consolidated a considerable reputation—as "a classic essay," the jacket reminds us—without benefit of such confession; and secondly, in the new little book where the story is interpolated, it necessarily acquires a new meaning—if Sontag wrote about cancer metaphors because she had cancer, then she writes about AIDS metaphors because . . . she had cancer = does not have AIDS—that reinforces her separateness from the epidemic, and makes the question of her relation to it all the more inscrutable, all the more urgent to pose.)

The pacification to which Sontag thinks to subject her writing finds its clearest articulation in the notion of metaphor that in various guises has long presided over her work. For Sontag, metaphor, or its earlier stand-in "interpretation," designates a dimension of discourse that is largely, if not entirely, dispensable—dispensable in principle, or cognitively, and dispensable as a matter of principle, or ethically, too. As she puts it in *Illness as Metaphor,* "The most truthful way of regarding illness—and the healthiest way of being ill—is the one most purified of, most resistant to, metaphoric thinking."[11] Her consequent aim, in *AIDS and its Metaphors* as well, is to liberate illness from the metaphors deforming it into the literality that is, she argues, the only state propitious for understanding and cure. As for the language employed on the rescue mission, it must imagine itself, as Peter Brooks has seen, inhabiting "a Platonic dream," where it "would give direct access to realities rather than the displaced symbols of realities."[12] It will do anything to remain in this dream, if necessary even feign to awaken from it. "Of course I know, say, with Emerson, that language is 'fossil poetry' and, with Nietzsche, that truth is 'a mobile army of metaphors' merely too worn out for us to recognize them as such. But because I know it, because I've said I know it, please let me be permitted to go on as though I *don't* know it." Thus, at the start of *AIDS and it Metaphors:* "Of course, one cannot think without metaphors. But that does not mean there aren't some metaphors we might well abstain from or try to retire. As, of course, all thinking is interpretation. But that does not mean it isn't sometimes correct to be 'against' interpretation" (5). The only interventions Sontag conceives making in the world of metaphor, even as she acknowledges that a speaking or writing subject can dwell in no other, involve retiring or abstaining from metaphor—and not, for instance, choosing, inventing, or modifying it. (Likewise, the purpose of the strategy she calls "against interpretation" is "not to confer meaning . . . but to deprive something of meaning" [14].) And the slide from abstaining from some metaphors to opposing interpretation *en bloc* is telling of the all-encompassing drift of her aversion. If *Illness as Metaphor* figures metaphor as illness—unhealthy, unhygienic, a kind of germ that thinking must resist and language needs to sterilize, *AIDS and its Metaphors* carries abhorrence still further and disgustedly construes metaphor as a kind of sexual transmission of disease. Sontag urges us to "abstain" from the "seductiveness" (5) of metaphor, as passionately as the legionnaires of the new decency counsel "abstinence as the best way of safeguarding against AIDS" (75). Just as for them truly safe sex means no sex at all, so for her the only secure practice of metaphor must avoid the practice—or rather, must assume it can. Through identifying writing with an ideal of its own neutrality, this untenable but tenacious attitude dispenses Sontag from ever having to consider the complicities of her language in any way that she can't meet with the perfunctoriness of disavowal. Such constant inattention accounts for why *AIDS and its Metaphors* is so often and variously to be found retracting its author's ostensible arguments, and why the book is positively haunted by metaphors and myths that, by no means having given up the ghost, contradict her values far more emphatically than she knows how to profess them. But it also explains why Sontag appears to enjoy an obliviously good conscience even as her language continues to ratify the prejudice, oppression, and violence that gay people and people with AIDS daily encounter. She is doubtless blissfully ignorant, for instance, about what packs the punch in so striking—I mean so assaultive—a phrase as "promiscuous homosexual men practicing their vehement sexual customs," where a kind of excess associated with gay male *sex* (promiscuity) and a kind of excess usually linked to *rhetoric* (vehemence) mutually provide the altogether phobic metaphors for describing one another and for inciting a desire to "retire" them both. The only good metaphor—whoever thought this belief would come so near to enacting the savagery of an AIDS joke?—is a dead one.

"General consciousness," moreover, has an unconscious whose cathexes belie (and hence necessitate keeping up) the appearances of neutrality: what this consciousness doesn't want to think, but determines nonetheless how it does think, is its smitten identification with the priorities of a transatlantic intelligentsia (white, heterosexual, and "generalist" in every other way as well), as these are manufactured and managed for the readership of the *New York Review of Books,* say, where a shortened version of *AIDS and its Metaphors* first appeared. It is the complaisant assumption of this readership, who may find reflected in Sontag's mandarin aloofness the fantasy of its own distance from the epidemic, that entails her unrelenting intellectualization of AIDS (via a rhetoric of cognitive advantage in which everything is "predictable" and nothing is "surprising"— except to readers who are therefore, as it used to be said of sailors, impressed) as well as her no less insistent colonization of AIDS for high culture (high on the order of whose business-as-usual is deciding where to situate the epidemic in relation to "modernity"). The particularity, not to speak of the urgency, of the epidemic is eclipsed in the need to show oneself "smart" about it—or just "smart," period. "Plague, from the Latin *plaga* (stroke, wound), has long been used metaphorically as the highest standard of collective calamity, evil, scourge. Procopius . . ." (44), and away we go, as in a certain kind of term paper that seems to have no point beyond its conspicuously consumable deftness in maneuvering among the monuments of culture. Yet though it is bad enough that AIDS is diminished to an occasion for a *son et lumières* of such monuments (Camus, Defoe, Donne, Manzoni, Poe, "but where is Boccaccio? and who is Čapek?"), it is perhaps worse when AIDS is taken to reaffirm the rightness of a whole mystified relation to them. With Debussy's *Pelléas et Mélisande,* Sontag suggests that "the theory [of miasma] inspired at least one great work of art" (42), and goes on to write a program note for the next major production. It is as though the erroneousness of the theory were to this extent redeemed, or, in general, as though the entelechy of everything were the great work of art that at once justifies and consoles us for the conditions of its making. In the treatment of AIDS that this piety must impose, whatever about the epidemic can't be banalized by being encoded in a network of cultural citations serves to legitimate the proliferation of such citations by vouching for their relevance. AIDS is thus transformed from a disease into a wonder drug—desperate times requiring desperate measures—applied to the agonies of a "traditional culture" imagined to be in critical condition, perhaps even in extremis. Sontag is right when she says that *AIDS and its Metaphors* is "not another book about AIDS"; rather it is another book (to be set next to Allan Bloom's or E.D. Hirsch's) that defends this culture, whose value ("these fragments I have shored against my ruins") the epidemic provides a usefully extreme opportunity for once again recommending.

It is then precisely its *refusal* to take itself as writing, with writing's constitutive metaphors and metaphors' constitutive social implication and reverberation, that allows this book to reinforce the very tendencies in the figuration of AIDS—the homophobia, racism, and cultural conservatism—that it otherwise might have more successfully challenged. AIDS anxiety, we learn, for a last instance, "inevitably" communicates a fear of polluting people (73); the end-of-the-world rhetoric that AIDS has evoked "inevitably" builds a case for repression (86); in the countdown to a millennium, a rise in apocalyptic thinking may be "inevitable" (87); and so on. What sort of "liberation" can be effected by an analysis whose terms make it thus consonant with "the standard plague story . . . of inexorability, inescapability" (53)? So thoroughly does that story come to take Sontag herself prisoner that by the end she gives up even pretending to be doing something besides retelling it: "AIDS"—not its metaphors—"may be extending the pro-

pensity for being inured to vistas of global annihilation which the stocking and bran-
dishing of nuclear arms has already promoted" (87). "Like the effects of industrial
pollution and the new system of global financial markets, the AIDS crisis is"—just is—
"evidence of a world in which nothing important is regional, local, limited; in which
everything that can circulate does, and every problem is, or is destined to become,
worldwide" (92). "AIDS is"—not, a myth of AIDS makes it—"one of the dystopian
harbingers of the global village, that future which is already here and always before us,
which no one knows how to refuse" (93). Just as what was identified as a variety of
views about sexually transmissible diseases suddenly yielded to the plain "truth" that
large numbers of gay men have lately taken to committing suicide, so, following a
similar warp, Sontag's overall project of critically examining AIDS myths ends by uncritically exemplifying what she has herself said is the most disabling of them. AIDS
makes its last fading appearance in her pages as just another figure of a world that
pollution, nuclear armament, mass communications, and international capitalism have
already brought to the verge of apocalypse, whose imminence, it is maintained, is now
permanent. Having only further generalized the *fin-de-siècle, fin du monde* spell of futility
she said she wanted to break, Sontag must give to her original project this holy-minded
twist, when she comes to sum it up: the effort to detach AIDS from its meanings and
metaphors is no longer just "liberating," but now also "even consoling" (94). Consolation
has to be "even" higher on Sontag's scale of values than liberation because it is meant
to make up for a liberation whose worse than inanity can no longer be hidden—except,
of course, as "consolation." Consolation for whom? for people with AIDS, many of
whom cannot even get treatment, whose disease has just been demeaned as one more
sign to the well and well off of their cultural competence? for those who, in exchange
for their dead, have just received a reading list of plague classics and some survey course
schemas to help them not have to get through it?

But consolation may in fact be all that is left to readers willing to follow Sontag's
modest proposal, in her next paragraph, that the military imagery around illness be
"retired" (94). Unwilling to specify which war metaphors are particularly demoralizing
to people with AIDS, Sontag characteristically rejects them all, as all contributing equally
powerfully to "the excommunication and stigmatizing of the ill" (94). In doing so, she
forgets how well one such military metaphor—the one conveyed in the word "polemic"
(15) (from the Greek *polemos* [war])—served her as a cancer patient, beset by debilitating
myths of "responsibility" and "predisposition." She also overlooks how vital another
such metaphor—the one conveyed in the word *militancy* (from the Latin *miles* [soldier])—
is proving to people with AIDS and to the AIDS activism of which they stand at the
center. "Fight back, fight AIDS," is a chant of this activism, one of whose many organizations calls itself Mobilization Against AIDS. It is almost unspeakably insulting to
suggest that "fighting AIDS" sooner or later means fighting people with AIDS in a
context where the notion has authorized the pursuit, *by* people with AIDS, first among
others, of such very different goals as increased research funding, expanded medical
resources, greater access to them, humane drug trials, safe sex education, and housing
and legal protection for the sick. Under these circumstances, Sontag's silence about people
with AIDS—with self-representations and agendas, too—amounts to a kind of silencing.
Acknowledging no duty to speak of them, her text makes a last recommendation that
would deny them the right to speak of themselves—polemically, militantly, in any voice
but that of victims who now have something else they need "consoling" for. No doubt
that recommendation, like much else in *AIDS and its Metaphors,* was drafted in ignorance;
but how can a writing so frequently allowing for no better defense achieve any relation
to AIDS that is not merely—to make use of an AIDS metaphor—opportunistic?

Notes

1. Kenny Fries, "*AIDS and Its Metaphors:* A Conversation with Susan Sontag," *Coming Up!,* March 1989, p. 49.

2. Leah Garchik, "Susan Sontag's Appetite for Life," *San Francisco Chronicle,* February 3, 1989, p. E1.

3. Susan Sontag, *Illness as Metaphor,* New York, Farrar, Straus and Giroux, 1978, p. 6.

4. Quoted in Garchik, p. E1.

5. Quoted in Fries, p. 49.

6. Susan Sontag, "Notes on 'Camp,'" in *Against Interpretation,* New York, Delta, 1979, p. 290.

7. *Ibid.,* pp. 290–291.

8. *Ibid.,* pp. 275–276.

9. Susan Sontag, *AIDS and its Metaphors,* New York, Farrar, Straus and Giroux, 1989. Page references to this book appear in parentheses in the text.

10. See Paula Treichler, "AIDS, Homophobia, and Biomedical Discourse: An Epidemic of Signification," *October,* no. 43 (Winter 1987), pp. 31–70.

11. Sontag, *Illness as Metaphor,* p. 3.

12. Peter Brooks, "Death of/As Metaphor," *Partisan Review,* vol. XLVI, no. 3 (1979), p. 443.

15

"Just When You Thought It Was Safe to Go Back in the Water..."

Daniel L. Selden

Daniel L. Selden, Associate Professor of Literature at the University of California, Santa Cruz, is a classicist, comparatist, and media critic. He is the co-editor of Innovations of Antiquity *(Routledge, 1992) and the author of a forthcoming book on poetics and politics in Graeco-Roman Egypt during the third century B.C. In the brief essay included here, Selden mounts a radical critique of AIDS discourse: he locates what is dangerous about media representations of the epidemic not in particular themes or images—not, that is, in the iconography of the disease—but in the underlying narrative formula of crisis and solution that structures almost all such representations and also informs popular responses to AIDS by everyone from activists to the police. He suggests that effective political resistance to AIDS discourse will ultimately consist not in efforts to eliminate bias and distortion, to produce more positive images of people with AIDS, or to achieve more enlightened journalistic standards, but rather in efforts to confront and to disrupt the process whereby patterns of institutional practice reflect, enact, and reproduce sequences of narrative plot.*

Hence the inestimable convenience of AIDS. (Simon Watney)

It makes a good deal of difference how we define the field of representation insofar as it relates to AIDS, and I would like to reflect for a moment on that problem by way of a specific text. In the present context, it is only possible to summarize its plot, and this runs more or less as follows:

Once upon a time in America, in the heyday of urban consumer culture, a primitive, but lethal organism begins to devastate unsuspecting individuals amid their assiduous pursuit of pleasure. Death comes swiftly, and it is particularly gruesome. The first victims are typed as sexually promiscuous and have a history of drug or alcohol abuse. Each is deviant or marginal to the mainstream in some way. The organism also attacks women and, most pathetically, young children, but only in the last instance white, middle-class, heterosexual males who remain monogamous or chaste.

Authorities are alerted to the danger early on. However, owing to a combination of political and economic factors, no effective action is taken, until the death rate escalates and the threat to society can no longer be ignored. There follow various campaigns of "disinformation," and the allegations of cover-up extend to medical practitioners themselves. Once the media catch on, however, there is a barrage of irresponsible and exploitative journalism. Anxieties run high, and produce hysterical fears that the peril may spread without limit, unless there are concerted efforts for precaution and general community surveillance.

221

> *In the end, three agencies rise up to meet the challenge: law and order, biomedical technology, and old-style ingenuity and self-reliance. Together these three forces join to do combat with the peril and, after much self-sacrifice and Herculean effort, the deadly organism is isolated, studied, and eventually wiped out. Many are dead, but American society can now return to normal.*

This is not the story of the eruption of HIV and its proposed eradication as we have witnessed it develop in the 1980s. It is the plot of Steven Spielberg's *Jaws,* a film that went into production nearly 10 years before anyone ever heard of AIDS. As all of us who are old enough will remember, the release of *Jaws* in 1975 galvanized the American imagination as few movies do. The film not only ranks as one of Hollywood's major achievements of the seventies. *Jaws* is a document that we now recognize to be central to contemporary mass culture, and it is in this capacity that its parallels with the events surrounding AIDS might give us pause for some reflection.

I do not mean to suggest that Spielberg's film is a prophetic allegory of AIDS or that AIDS is the only, or even the most obvious, thing the shark could symbolize. In fact, Fredric Jameson has argued that the very effectiveness of Spielberg's vehicle "lies less in any single message or meaning than in its [. . .] capacity to absorb and organize [. . .] quite distinct [historical] anxieties together."[1] I am actually less concerned here with the iconography of the shark *per se,* though it is depicted in terms that regularly resurface in more recent descriptions of the nature and impact of HIV. What interests me is how uncannily *Jaws* outlines the same sequence of reactions and set of solutions with which we are all familiar in the public backlash unleashed by AIDS. I am thinking here not only of the sociology of the so-called "victims," or the alleged complicity of government and science with self-serving political and economic ends. The triple partnership between surveillance, technology, and traditional moral fiber is precisely the nexus of forces that has banded together so conspicuously in America's attempt to combat the invisible, though evidently no less primitive and deadly, predator which threatens it today.

I draw two conclusions from this. First, public response to AIDS realizes in a complex, but entirely concrete way a scenario that is well attested in popular culture of the immediately preceding years. The forum, to be sure, is different, but the cast of characters and of institutions in the drama are all substantially the same, as are their roles and the general nature of the crisis that has engaged them. One way to explain this recurrence is to attribute it to the "cultivation" of the media, the industry's ability to "mainstream" public values, expectations, and beliefs,[2] and some effect of this nature should certainly not, I think, be ruled out. More problematically, however, it seems to me that *Jaws* and AIDS as cultural phenomena are both displaced spectacles that rehearse the same deeply entrenched psycho-social narrative and, as admonitory dramas, work to instill, though AIDS in an immeasurably more palpable and violent form, a similar ideological framing of knowledge and power, played out punitively across a lacerated body.

Secondly, this means that the question of AIDS and representation cannot be posed simply at the level of images, perceptions, and metaphors. Studies of the "iconography of AIDS" expose only one factor in a much more complex and insidious syntax of representational drives and forces. *Jaws* is a moving picture and, as such, is not simply a set of situational predicates or propositions, but an operator which establishes a series of transformational relationships between terms. "The minimal complete plot," Tzvetan Todorov reminds us, "consists in the *passage* from one equilibrium *to* another."[3] One of the things the script of *Jaws* suggests, then, is that the material *practices* of individuals in response to AIDS, the agitation of different interest groups, and even the agencies which we as a society look to, and invest in, for a solution, live out and thereby reconfirm a motivating narratival scheme. Consequently, a representational critique of AIDS can by no means simply be a matter of "improving" the ways in which the media depict the epidemic or of weeding out "corruptions" in the language of science.[4] However indispensable here an analysis of discourse or iconography may be, it is bound to remain tactically limited unless it goes on to address the larger social syntax which links and hence construes such images in relation to specific patterns of response.

Evidently, this is no less true of the enterprise that we are mutually engaged in here. If you look at Spielberg's film again, you will see that it contains a good deal of self-referential play with the ways in which shark attacks are represented, and there is a significant amount of attention devoted to how these images shape popular perception and affect the making of public policy. Whoever is committed to questioning the representational determinants of AIDS in full, will have to go on to ask, then, to what extent that demystificatory gesture itself, however progressively conceived, plays unwittingly into the same public spectacle that it set out to critique.

In the utopian ending of *Jaws,* the police chief and bio-whiz kid triumph over the violence of nature, though significantly the skipper who guides them, linked to an older ethic and an outmoded means of production, is sacrificed along the way. For those of us who reject surveillance as a viable solution to the problems posed by AIDS, science continues to hold out our best hope. If, however, what Simon Watney calls "the miraculous authority of clinical medicine"[5] does succeed in discovering a cure for the disease—as we can only have reason to believe it will—one begins to suspect that this remedy, among other things, will serve to ratify a cultural agenda which effectively organized the entire drama in the first place. If, in our relief, we accept this end uncritically and without resistance, do we not, I wonder, leave ourselves open potentially to the execution of a sequel, most likely in some other form, though equally as violent and where we least expect it—just (as the saying goes) when we thought it was safe to go back in the water?

NOTES

This essay originated as an intervention at the conference on "Sexuality and Disease: Metaphors, Perceptions, and Behavior in the AIDS Era" organized by June Machover Reinisch and held at The Kinsey Institute for Research in Sex, Gender, and Reproduction in December, 1988.

1. F. Jameson, "Reification and Utopia in Mass Culture," *Social Text* 1 (1979), 142.

2. G. Gerbner, L. Gross, M. Morgan, and N. Signorielli, "Living with Television: The Dynamics of the Cultivation Process," in *Perspectives on Media Effects,* ed. J. Bryant and D. Zillman (Hillsdale, NJ, 1986).

3. T. Todorov, *The Poetics of Prose,* trans. R. Howard (Ithaca, NY, 1977), 111; cf. 218–33.

4. S. Sontag, *Aids and its Metaphors* (New York, 1988), 94; S. Gilman, *Disease and Representation: Images of Illness from Madness to AIDS* (Ithaca, NY, 1988), 16.

5. S. Watney, "The Spectacle of AIDS," in *AIDS: Cultural Analysis/Cultural Activism,* ed. D. Crimp (Cambridge, MA, 1988), 78.

III

SUBJECTIVITY,
DISCIPLINE,
RESISTANCE

16

Compulsory Heterosexuality and Lesbian Existence

ADRIENNE RICH

Adrienne Rich, Professor in the Center for the Study of Women and Gender at Stanford, has been publishing poetry and essays for nearly forty years. Her most recent book of poetry is An Atlas of the Difficult World: Poems, 1988–1991 *(1991). With Michelle Cliff, Rich has been co-editor of the lesbian/feminist journal* Sinister Wisdom. *The essay reprinted here remains one of the foundational texts in lesbian studies. At the time of its first publication in 1980 it offered a new vision of personal and political bonding among women, one that could mend some of the rifts that had begun to divide the women's movement. At issue was a vocal and highly visible lesbian membership whose presence evoked homophobic fears within the movement and seemed to offer exactly the kinds of "evidence" that the wider culture sought in discrediting the claims of feminism. Rich here accounts for the origin and continuing dominance of heterosexuality as well as a corresponding neglect of the presence of lesbians. Postulating that the pre-historic bonds between mothers and daughters had been forcibly interrupted by sons, Rich offers her concept of a lesbian continuum as a political affiliation that can reestablish those lost same-sex loyalties by uniting women—heterosexual, bisexual, and lesbian—in a mutual, woman-focused vision. By naming all woman-identified women as lesbian, Rich unhinged lesbianism from a solely sexual definition, and gave impetus for the feminist political movement to reunite on the basis of shared gender. As the subsequently written Foreword and Afterword to the original text make clear, this essay is part of an ongoing discussion of sexual politics and is not her final word.*

Foreword [1982]

I want to say a little about the way "Compulsory Heterosexuality" was originally conceived and the context in which we are now living. It was written in part to challenge the erasure of lesbian existence from so much of scholarly feminist literature, an erasure which I felt (and feel) to be not just anti-lesbian, but anti-feminist in its consequences, and to distort the experience of heterosexual women as well. It was not written to widen divisions but to encourage heterosexual feminists to examine heterosexuality as a political institution which disempowers women—and to change it. I also hoped that other lesbians would feel the depth and breadth of woman identification and woman bonding that has run like a continuous though stifled theme through the heterosexual experience, and that this would become increasingly a politically activating impulse, not simply a validation of personal lives. I wanted the essay to suggest new kinds of criticism, to incite new questions in classrooms and academic journals, and to sketch, at least, some bridge over the gap between *lesbian* and *feminist*. I wanted, at the very least, for feminists to find it less possible to read, write, or teach from a perspective of unexamined heterocentricity.

Within the three years since I wrote "Compulsory Heterosexuality"—with this energy of hope and desire—the pressures to conform in a society increasingly conservative in mood have become more intense. The New Right's messages to women have been, precisely, that we are the emotional and sexual property of men, and that the autonomy and equality of women threaten family, religion, and state. The institutions by which women have traditionally been controlled—patriarchal motherhood, economic exploitation, the nuclear family, compulsory heterosexuality—are being strengthened by legislation, religious fiat, media imagery, and efforts at censorship. In a worsening economy, the single mother trying to support her children confronts the feminization of poverty which Joyce Miller of the National Coalition of Labor Union Women has named one of the major issues of the 1980s. The lesbian, unless in disguise, faces discrimination in hiring and harassment and violence in the street. Even within feminist-inspired institutions such as battered-women's shelters and Women's Studies programs, open lesbians are fired and others warned to stay in the closet. The retreat into sameness—assimilation for those who can manage it—is the most passive and debilitating of responses to political repression, economic insecurity, and a renewed open season on difference.

I want to note that documentation of male violence against women—within the home especially—has been accumulating rapidly in this period. At the same time, in the realm of literature which depicts woman bonding and woman identification as essential for female survival, a steady stream of writing and criticism has been coming from women of color in general and lesbians of color in particular—the latter group being even more profoundly erased in academic feminist scholarship by the double bias of racism and homophobia.[1]

There has recently been an intensified debate on female sexuality among feminists and lesbians, with lines often furiously and bitterly drawn, with *sadomasochism* and *pornography* as key words which are variously defined according to who is talking. The depth of women's rage and fear regarding sexuality and its relation to power and pain is real, even when the dialogue sounds simplistic, self-righteous, or like parallel monologues.

Because of all these developments, there are parts of this essay that I would word differently, qualify, or expand if I were writing it today. But I continue to think that heterosexual feminists will draw political strength for change from taking a critical stance toward the ideology which *demands* heterosexuality, and that lesbians cannot assume that we are untouched by that ideology and the institutions founded upon it. There is nothing about such a critique that requires us to think of ourselves as victims, as having been brainwashed or totally powerless. Coercion and compulsion are among the conditions in which women have learned to recognize our strength. Resistance is a major theme in this essay and in the study of women's lives, if we know what we are looking for.

I

Biologically men have only one innate orientation—a sexual one that draws them to women,—while women have two innate orientations, sexual toward men and reproductive toward their young.[2]

I was a woman terribly vulnerable, critical, using femaleness as a sort of standard or yardstick to measure and discard men. Yes—something like that. I was an Anna who invited defeat from men without ever being conscious of it. (But I am conscious of it. And being conscious of it means I shall leave it all behind me and become—but what?) I was stuck fast in an emotion common to women of our time, that can turn them bitter, or Lesbian, or solitary. Yes, that Anna during that time was . . .

[Another blank line across the page:][3]

The bias of compulsory heterosexuality, through which lesbian experience is perceived on a scale ranging from deviant to abhorrent or simply rendered invisible, could be illustrated from many texts other than the two just preceding. The assumption made by Rossi, that women are "innately" sexually oriented only toward men, and that made by Lessing, that the lesbian is simply acting out of her bitterness toward men, are by no means theirs alone; these assumptions are widely current in literature and in the social sciences.

I am concerned here with two other matters as well: first, how and why women's choice of women as passionate comrades, life partners, co-workers, lovers, community has been crushed, invalidated, forced into hiding and disguise; and second, the virtual or total neglect of lesbian existence in a wide range of writings, including feminist scholarship. Obviously there is a connection here. I believe that much feminist theory and criticism is stranded on this shoal.

My organizing impulse is the belief that it is not enough for feminist thought that specifically lesbian texts exist. Any theory or cultural/political creation that treats lesbian existence as a marginal or less "natural" phenomenon, as mere "sexual preference," or as the mirror image of either heterosexual or male homosexual relations is profoundly weakened thereby, whatever its other contributions. Feminist theory can no longer afford merely to voice a toleration of "lesbianism" as an "alternative life style" or make token allusion to lesbians. A feminist critique of compulsory heterosexual orientation for women is long overdue. In this exploratory paper, I shall try to show why.

I will begin by way of examples, briefly discussing four books that have appeared in the last few years, written from different viewpoints and political orientations, but all presenting themselves, and favorably reviewed, as feminist.[4] All take as a basic assumption that the social relations of the sexes are disordered and extremely problematic, if not disabling, for women; all seek paths toward change. I have learned more from some of these books than from others, but on this I am clear: each one might have been more accurate, more powerful, more truly a force for change had the author dealt with lesbian existence as a reality and as a source of knowledge and power available to women, or with the institution of heterosexuality itself as a beachhead of male dominance.[5] In none of them is the question ever raised as to whether, in a different context or other things being equal, women would *choose* heterosexual coupling and marriage; heterosexuality is presumed the "sexual preference" of "most women," either implicitly or explicitly. In none of these books, which concern themselves with mothering, sex roles, relationships, and societal prescriptions for women, is compulsory heterosexuality ever examined as an institution powerfully affecting all these, or the idea of "preference" or "innate orientation" even indirectly questioned.

In *For Her Own Good: 150 Years of the Experts' Advice to Women* by Barbara Ehrenreich and Deirdre English, the authors' superb pamphlets, *Witches, Midwives and Nurses: A History of Women Healers* and *Complaints and Disorders: The Sexual Politics of Sickness,* are developed into a provocative and complex study. Their thesis in this book is that the advice given to American women by male health professionals, particularly in the areas of marital sex, maternity, and child care, has echoed the dictates of the economic marketplace and the role capitalism has needed women to play in production and/or reproduction. Women have become the consumer victims of various cures, therapies, and normative judgments in different periods (including the prescription to middle-class women to embody and preserve the sacredness of the home—the "scientific" romanticization of the home itself). None of the "experts'" advice has been either particularly scientific or women-oriented; it has reflected male needs, male fantasies about women, and male interest in controlling women—particularly in the realms of sexuality and motherhood—fused with the requirements of industrial capitalism. So much of this book is so devastatingly informative and is written with such lucid feminist wit, that I kept waiting as I read for the basic proscription against lesbianism to be examined. It never was.

This can hardly be for lack of information. Jonathan Katz's *Gay American History*[6] tells us that as early as 1656 the New Haven Colony prescribed the death penalty for lesbians. Katz provides many suggestive and informative documents on the "treatment" (or torture) of lesbians by the medical profession in the nineteenth and twentieth centuries. Recent work by the historian Nancy Sahli documents the crackdown on intense female friendships among college women at the turn of the present century.[7] The ironic title *For Her Own Good* might have referred first and foremost to the economic imperative to heterosexuality and marriage and to the sanctions imposed against single women and widows—both of whom have been and still are viewed as deviant. Yet, in this often enlightening Marxist-feminist overview of male prescriptions for female sanity and health, the economics of prescriptive heterosexuality go unexamined.[8]

Of the three psychoanalytically based books, one, Jean Baker Miller's *Toward a New Psychology of Women,* is written as if lesbians simply do not exist, even as marginal beings. Given Miller's title, I find this astonishing. However, the favorable reviews the book has received in feminist journals, including *Signs* and *Spokeswoman,* suggest that Miller's heterocentric assumptions are widely shared. In *The Mermaid and the Minotaur: Sexual Arrangements and the Human Malaise,* Dorothy Dinnerstein makes an impassioned argument for the sharing of parenting between women and men and for an end to what she perceives as the male/female symbiosis of "gender arrangements," which she feels are leading the species further and further into violence and self-extinction. Apart from other problems that I have with this book (including her silence on the institutional and random terrorism men have practiced on women—and children—throughout history,[9] and her obsession with psychology to the neglect of economic and other material realities that help to create psychological reality), I find Dinnerstein's view of the relations between women and men as "a collaboration to keep history mad" utterly ahistorical. She means by this a collaboration to perpetuate social relations which are hostile, exploitative, and destructive to life itself. She sees women and men as equal partners in the making of "sexual arrangements," seemingly unaware of the repeated struggles of women to resist oppression (their own and that of others) and to change their condition. She ignores, specifically, the history of women who—as witches, *femmes seules,* marriage resisters, spinsters, autonomous widows, and/or lesbians—have managed on varying levels *not* to collaborate. It is this history, precisely, from which feminists have so much to learn and on which there is overall such blanketing silence. Dinnerstein acknowledges at the end of her book that "female separatism," though "on a large scale and in the long run wildly impractical," has something to teach us: "Separate, women could in principle set out to learn from scratch—undeflected by the opportunities to evade this task that men's presence has so far offered—what intact self-creative humanness is."[10] Phrases like "intact self-creative humanness" obscure the question of what the many forms of female separatism have actually been addressing. The fact is that women in every culture and throughout history *have* undertaken the task of independent, non-heterosexual, woman-connected existence, to the extent made possible by their context, often in the belief that they were the "only ones" ever to have done so. They have undertaken it even though few women have been in an economic position to resist marriage altogether, and even though attacks against unmarried women have ranged from aspersion and mockery to deliberate gynocide, including the burning and torturing of millions of widows and spinsters during the witch persecutions of the fifteenth, sixteenth, and seventeenth centuries in Europe.

Nancy Chodorow does come close to the edge of an acknowledgement of lesbian existence. Like Dinnerstein, Chodorow believes that the fact that women, and women only, are responsible for child care in the sexual division of labor has led to an entire social organization of gender inequality, and that men as well as women must become primary carers for children if that inequality is to change. In the process of examining, from a psychoanalytic perspective, how mothering by women affects the psychological development of girl and boy children, she offers documentation that men are "emotionally secondary" in women's lives, that "women have a richer, ongoing inner world to fall back on . . . men do not become as emotionally important to women as women do to men."[11] This would carry into the late twentieth century Smith-Rosenberg's findings about eighteenth- and nineteenth-century women's emotional focus on women. "Emotionally important" can, of course, refer to anger as well as to love, or to that intense mixture of the two often found in women's relationships with women—one aspect of what I have come to call the "double life of women" (see below). Chodorow concludes that because women have women as mothers, "the mother remains a primary internal object [*sic*] to the girl, so that heterosexual relationships are on the model of a nonexclusive, second relationship for her, whereas for the boy they re-create an exclusive, primary relationship." According to Chodorow, women "have learned to deny the limitations of masculine lovers for both psychological and practical reasons."[12]

But the practical reasons (like witch burnings, male control of law, theology, and science, or economic nonviability within the sexual division of labor) are glossed over. Chodorow's account barely glances at the constraints and sanctions which historically have enforced or ensured the coupling of women with men and obstructed or penalized women's coupling or allying in independent groups with other women. She dismisses lesbian existence with the comment that "lesbian relationships do tend to re-create mother-daughter emotions and connections, but most women are heterosexual" (implied: more mature, having developed beyond the mother-daughter connection?). She then adds: "This heterosexual preference and taboos on homosexuality, in addition to objective economic dependence on men, make the option of primary sexual bonds with other women unlikely—though more prevalent in recent years."[13] The significance of that qualification seems irresistible, but Chodorow does not explore it further. Is she saying that lesbian existence has become more *visible* in recent years (in certain groups), that economic and other pressures have changed (under capitalism, socialism, or both), and that consequently more women are rejecting the heterosexual "choice"? She argues that women want children because their heterosexual relationships lack richness and intensity, that in having a child a woman seeks to re-create her own intense relationship with her mother. It seems to me that on the basis of her own findings, Chodorow leads us implicitly to conclude that heterosexuality is *not* a "preference" for women, that, for one thing, it fragments the erotic from the emotional in a way that women find impoverishing and painful. Yet her book participates in mandating it. Neglecting the covert socializations and the overt forces which have channeled women into marriage and heterosexual romance, pressures ranging from the selling of daughters to the silences of literature to the images of the television screen, she, like Dinnerstein, is stuck with trying to reform a man-made institution—compulsory heterosexuality—as if, despite profound emotional impulses and complementarities drawing women toward women, there is a mystical/biological heterosexual inclination, a "preference" or "choice" which draws women toward men.

Moreover, it is understood that this "preference" does not need to be explained unless through the tortuous theory of the female Oedipus complex or the necessity for species reproduction. It is lesbian sexuality which (usually, and incorrectly, "included" under male homosexuality) is seen as requiring explanation. This assumption of female heterosexuality seems to me in itself remarkable: it is an enormous assumption to have glided so silently into the foundations of our thought.

The extension of this assumption is the frequently heard assertion that in a world of genuine equality, where men are nonoppressive and nurturing, everyone would be bisexual. Such a notion blurs and sentimentalizes the actualities within which women have experienced sexuality; it is a liberal leap across the tasks and struggles of here and now, the continuing process of sexual definition which will generate its own possibilities and choices. (It also assumes that women who have chosen women have done so simply because men are oppressive and emotionally unavailable, which still fails to account for women who continue to pursue relationships with oppressive and/or emotionally unsatisfying men.) I am suggesting that heterosexuality, like motherhood, needs to be recognized and studied as a *political institution*—even, or especially, by those individuals who feel they are, in their personal experience, the precursors of a new social relation between the sexes.

II

If women are the earliest sources of emotional caring and physical nurture for both female and male children, it would seem logical, from a feminist perspective at least, to pose the following questions: whether the search for love and tenderness in both sexes does not originally lead toward women; *why in fact women would ever redirect that search;* why species survival, the means of impregnation, and emotional/erotic relationships should ever have become so rigidly identified with each other; and why such violent strictures should be found necessary to enforce women's total emotional, erotic loyalty and subservience to men. I doubt that enough feminist scholars and theorists have taken the pains to acknowledge the societal forces which wrench women's emotional and erotic energies away from themselves and other women and from woman-identified values. These forces, as I shall try to show, range from literal physical enslavement to the disguising and distorting of possible options.

I do not assume that mothering by women is a "sufficient cause" of lesbian existence. But the issue of mothering by women has been much in the air of late, usually accompanied by the view that increased parenting by men would minimize antagonism between the sexes and equalize the sexual imbalance of power of males over females. These discussions are carried on without reference to compulsory heterosexuality as a phenomenon, let alone as an ideology. I do not wish to psychologize here, but rather to identify sources of male power. I believe large numbers of men could, in fact, undertake child care on a large scale without radically altering the balance of male power in a male-identified society.

In her essay "The Origin of the Family," Kathleen Gough lists eight characteristics of male power in archaic and contemporary societies which I would like to use as a framework: "men's ability to deny women sexuality or to force it upon them; to command or exploit their labor to control their produce; to control or rob them of their children; to confine them physically and prevent their movement; to use them as objects in male transactions; to cramp their creativeness; or to withhold from them large areas of the society's knowledge and cultural attainments."[14] (Gough does not perceive these power characteristics as specifically enforcing heterosexuality, only as producing sexual inequality.) Below, Gough's words appear in italics; the elaboration of each of her categories, in brackets, is my own.

Characteristics of male power include *the power of men*

1. *to deny women* [their own] *sexuality*—[by means of clitoridectomy and infibulation; chastity belts; punishment, including death, for female adultery; punishment, including death, for lesbian sexuality; psychoanalytic denial of the clitoris; strictures against masturbation; denial of maternal and postmenopausal sensuality; unnecessary hysterectomy; pseudolesbian images in the media and literature; closing of archives and destruction of documents relating to lesbian existence]

2. *or to force it* [male sexuality] *upon them*—[by means of rape (including marital rape) and wife beating; father-daughter, brother-sister incest; the socialization of women to feel that male sexual "drive" amounts to a right;[15] idealization of heterosexual romance in art, literature, the media, advertising, etc.; child marriage; arranged marriage; prostitution; the harem; psychoanalytic doctrines of frigidity and vaginal orgasm; pornographic depictions of women responding pleasurably to sexual violence and humiliation (a subliminal message being that sadistic heterosexuality is more "normal" than sensuality between women)]

3. *to command or exploit their labor to control their produce*—[by means of the institutions of marriage and motherhood as unpaid production; the horizontal segregation of women in paid employment; the decoy of the upwardly mobile token woman; male control of abortion, contraception, sterilization, and childbirth; pimping; female infanticide, which robs mothers of daughters and contributes to generalized devaluation of women]

4. *to control or rob them of their children*—[by means of father right and "legal kidnaping";[16] enforced sterilization; systematized infanticide; seizure of children from lesbian mothers by the courts; the malpractice of male obstetrics; use of the mother as "token torturer"[17] in genital mutilation or in binding the daughter's feet (or mind) to fit her for marriage]

5. *to confine them physically and prevent their movement*—[by means of rape as terrorism, keeping women off the streets; purdah; foot binding; atrophying of women's athletic capabilities; high heels and "feminine" dress codes in fashion; the veil; sexual harassment on the streets; horizontal segregation of women in employment; prescriptions for "full-time" mothering at home; enforced economic dependence of wives]

6. *to use them as objects in male transactions*—[use of women as "gifts"; bride price; pimping; arranged marriage; use of women as entertainers to facilitate male deals—e.g., wife-hostess, cocktail waitress required to dress for male sexual titillation, call girls, "bunnies," geisha, *kisaeng* prostitutes, secretaries]

7. *to cramp their creativeness*—[witch persecutions as campaigns against midwives and female healers, and as pogrom against independent, "unassimilated" women;[18] definition of male pursuits as more valuable than female within any culture, so that cultural values become the embodiment of male subjectivity; restriction of female self-fulfillment to marriage and motherhood; sexual exploitation of women by male artists and teachers; the social and economic disruption of women's creative aspirations;[19] erasure of female tradition][20]

8. *to withhold from them large areas of the society's knowledge and cultural attainments*—[by means of noneducation of females; the "Great Silence" regarding women and particularly lesbian existence in history and culture;[21] sex-role tracking which deflects women from science, technology, and other "masculine" pursuits; male

social/professional bonding which excludes women; discrimination against women in the professions]

These are some of the methods by which male power is manifested and maintained. Looking at the schema, what surely impresses itself is the fact that we are confronting not a simple maintenance of inequality and property possession, but a pervasive cluster of forces, ranging from physical brutality to control of consciousness, which suggests that an enormous potential counterforce is having to be restrained.

Some of the forms by which male power manifests itself are more easily recognizable as enforcing heterosexuality on women than are others. Yet each one I have listed adds to the cluster of forces within which women have been convinced that marriage and sexual orientation toward men are inevitable—even if unsatisfying or oppressive—components of their lives. The chastity belt; child marriage; erasure of lesbian existence (except as exotic and perverse) in art, literature, film; idealization of heterosexual romance and marriage—these are some fairly obvious forms of compulsion, the first two exemplifying physical force, the second two control of consciousness. While clitoridectomy has been assailed by feminists as a form of woman torture,[22] Kathleen Barry first pointed out that it is not simply a way of turning the young girl into a "marriageable" woman through brutal surgery. It intends that women in the intimate proximity of polygynous marriage will not form sexual relationships with each other, that—from a male, genital-fetishist perspective—female erotic connections, even in a sex-segregated situation, will be literally excised.[23]

The function of pornography as an influence on consciousness is a major public issue of our time, when a multibillion-dollar industry has the power to disseminate increasingly sadistic, women-degrading visual images. But even so-called soft-core pornography and advertising depict women as objects of sexual appetite devoid of emotional context, without individual meaning or personality—essentially as a sexual commodity to be consumed by males. (So-called lesbian pornography, created for the male voyeuristic eye, is equally devoid of emotional context or individual personality.) The most pernicious message relayed by pornography is that women are natural sexual prey to men and love it, that sexuality and violence are congruent, and that for women sex is essentially masochistic, humiliation pleasurable, physical abuse erotic. But along with this message comes another, not always recognized: that enforced submission and the use of cruelty, if played out in heterosexual pairing, is sexually "normal," while sensuality between women, including erotic mutuality and respect, is "queer," "sick," and either pornographic in itself or not very exciting compared with the sexuality of whips and bondage.[24] Pornography does not simply create a climate in which sex and violence are interchangeable; *it widens the range of behavior considered acceptable from men in heterosexual intercourse*—behavior which reiteratively strips women of their autonomy, dignity, and sexual potential, including the potential of loving and being loved by women in mutuality and integrity.

In her brilliant study *Sexual Harassment of Working Women: A Case of Sex Discrimination*, Catharine A. MacKinnon delineates the intersection of compulsory heterosexuality and economics. Under capitalism, women are horizontally segregated by gender and occupy a structurally inferior position in the workplace. This is hardly news, but MacKinnon raises the question why, even if capitalism "requires some collection of individuals to occupy low-status, low-paying positions . . . such persons must be biologically female," and goes on to point out that "the fact that male employers often do not hire qualified women, *even when they could pay them less than men* suggests that more than the profit motive is implicated" [emphasis added].[25] She cites a wealth of material documenting the fact that women are not only segregated in low-paying service jobs (as secretaries, domestics, nurses, typists, telephone operators, child-care workers, waitresses), but that "sexualization of the woman" is part of the job. Central and intrinsic to the economic realities of women's lives is the requirement that women will "market sexual attractiveness to men, who tend to hold the economic power and position to enforce their predilections." And MacKinnon documents that "sexual harassment perpetuates the interlocked structure by which women have been kept sexually in thrall to men at the bottom of the labor market. Two forces of American society converge: men's control over women's sexuality and capital's control over employees' work lives."[26] Thus, women in the workplace are at the mercy of sex as power in a vicious circle. Economically disadvantaged, women—whether waitresses or professors—endure sexual harassment to keep their jobs and learn to behave in a complaisantly and ingratiatingly heterosexual manner because they discover this is their true qualification for employment, whatever the job description. And, MacKinnon notes, the woman who too decisively resists sexual overtures in the workplace is accused of being "dried up" and sexless, or lesbian. This raises a specific difference between the experiences of lesbians and homosexual men. A lesbian, closeted on her job because of heterosexist prejudice, is not simply forced into denying the truth of her outside relationships or private life. Her job depends on her pretending to be not merely heterosexual, but a heterosexual *woman* in terms of dressing and playing the feminine, deferential role required of "real" women.

MacKinnon raises radical questions as to the qualitative differences between sexual harassment, rape, and ordinary heterosexual intercourse. ("As one accused rapist put it, he hadn't used 'any more force than is usual for males during the preliminaries.' ") She criticizes Susan Brownmiller[27] for separating rape from the mainstream of daily life and for her unexamined premise that "rape is violence, intercourse is sexuality," removing rape from the sexual sphere altogether. Most crucially she argues that "taking rape from the realm of 'the sexual,' placing it in the realm of 'the violent,' allows one to be against it without raising any questions about the extent to which the institution of heterosexuality has defined force as a normal part of 'the preliminaries.' "[28] "Never is it asked whether, under conditions of male supremacy, the notion of 'consent' has any meaning."[29]

The fact is that the workplace, among other social institutions, is a place where women have learned to accept male violation of their psychic and physical boundaries as the price of survival; where women have been educated—no less than by romantic literature or by pornography—to perceive themselves as sexual prey. A woman seeking to escape such casual violations along with economic disadvantage may well turn to marriage as a form of hoped-for protection, while bringing into marriage neither social nor economic power, thus entering that institution also from a disadvantaged position. MacKinnon finally asks:

> What if inequality is built into the social conceptions of male and female sexuality, of masculinity and femininity, of sexiness and heterosexual attractiveness? Incidents of sexual harassment suggest that male sexual desire itself may be aroused by female vulnerability.... Men feel they can take advantage, so they want to, so they do. Examination of sexual harassment, precisely because the episodes appear commonplace, forces one to confront the fact that sexual intercourse normally occurs between economic (as well as physical) unequals ... the apparent legal requirement that violations of women's sexuality appear out of the ordinary before they will be punished helps prevent women from defining the ordinary conditions of their own consent.[30]

Given the nature and extent of heterosexual pressures—the daily "eroticization of women's subordination," as MacKinnon phrases it[31]—I question the more or less psychoanalytic perspective (suggested by such writers as Karen Horney, H.R. Hayes, Wolfgang Lederer, and, most recently, Dorothy Dinnerstein) that the male need to control women sexually results from some primal male "fear of women" and of women's sexual insatiability. It seems more probable that men really fear not that they will have women's sexual appetites forced on them or that women want to smother and devour them, but that women could be indifferent to them altogether, that men could be allowed sexual and emotional—therefore economic—access to women *only* on women's terms, otherwise being left on the periphery of the matrix.

The means of assuring male sexual access to women have recently received searching investigation by Kathleen Barry.[32] She documents extensive and appalling evidence for the existence, on a very large scale, of international female slavery, the institution once known as "white slavery" but which in fact has involved, and at this very moment involves, women of every race and class. In the theoretical analysis derived from her research, Barry makes the connection between all enforced conditions under which women live subject to men: prostitution, marital rape, father-daughter and brother-sister incest, wife beating, pornography, bride price, the selling of daughters, purdah, and genital mutilation. She sees the rape paradigm—where the victim of sexual assault is held responsible for her own victimization—as leading to the rationalization and acceptance of other forms of enslavement where the woman is presumed to have "chosen" her fate, to embrace it passively, or to have courted it perversely through rash or unchaste behavior. On the contrary, Barry maintains, "female sexual slavery is present in ALL situations where women or girls cannot change the conditions of their existence; where regardless of how they got into those conditions, e.g., social pressure, economic hardship, misplaced trust, or the longing for affection, they cannot get out; and where they are subject to sexual violence and exploitation."[33] She provides a spectrum of concrete examples, not only as to the existence of a widespread international traffic in women, but also as to how this operates—whether in the form of a "Minnesota pipeline" funneling blonde, blue-eyed Midwestern runaways to Times Square, or the purchasing of young women out of rural poverty in Latin America or Southeast Asia, or the providing of *maisons d'abattage* for migrant workers in the eighteenth arrondissement of Paris. Instead of "blaming the victim" or trying to diagnose her presumed pathology, Barry turns her floodlight on the pathology of sex colonization itself, the ideology of "cultural sadism" represented by the pornography industry and by the overall identification of women primarily as "sexual beings whose responsibility is the sexual service of men."[34]

Barry delineates what she names a "sexual domination perspective" through whose lens sexual abuse and terrorism of women by men has been rendered almost invisible by treating it as natural and inevitable. From its point of view, women are expendable as long as the sexual and emotional needs of the male can be satisfied. To replace this perspective of domination with a universal standard of basic freedom for women from gender-specific violence, from constraints on movement, and from male right of sexual and emotional access is the political purpose of her book. Like Mary Daly in *Gyn/Ecology*, Barry rejects structuralist and other cultural-relativist rationalizations for sexual torture and anti-woman violence. In her opening chapter, she asks of her readers that they refuse all handy escapes into ignorance and denial. "The only way we can come out of hiding, break through our paralyzing defenses, is to know it all—the full extent of sexual violence and domination of women. . . . In *knowing*, in facing directly, we can learn to chart our course out of this oppression, by envisioning and creating a world which will preclude sexual slavery."[35]

"Until we name the practice, give conceptual definition and form to it, illustrate its life over time and in space, those who are its most obvious victims will also not be able to name it or define their experience."

But women are all, in different ways and to different degrees, its victims; and part of the problem with naming and conceptualizing female sexual slavery is, as Barry clearly sees, compulsory heterosexuality.[36] Compulsory heterosexuality simplifies the task of the procurer and pimp in worldwide prostitution rings and "eros centers," while, in the privacy of the home, it leads the daughter to "accept" incest/rape by her father, the mother to deny that it is happening, the battered wife to stay on with an abusive husband. "Befriending or love" is a major tactic of the procurer, whose job it is to turn the runaway or the confused young girl over to the pimp for seasoning. The ideology of heterosexual romance, beamed at her from childhood out of fairy tales, television, films, advertising, popular songs, wedding pageantry, is a tool ready to the procurer's hand and one which he does not hesitate to use, as Barry documents. Early female indoctrination in "love" as an emotion may be largely a Western concept; but a more universal ideology concerns the primacy and uncontrollability of the male sexual drive. This is one of many insights offered by Barry's work:

> As sexual power is learned by adolescent boys through the social experience of their sex drive, so do girls learn that the locus of sexual power is male. Given the importance placed on the male sex drive in the socialization of girls as well as boys, early adolescence is probably the first significant phase of male identification in a girl's life and development. . . . As a young girl becomes aware of her own increasing sexual feelings . . . she turns away from her heretofore primary relationships with girlfriends. As they become secondary to her, recede in importance in her life, her own identity also assumes a secondary role and she grows into male identification.[37]

We still need to ask why some women never, even temporarily, turn away from "heretofore primary relationships" with other females. And why does male identification—the casting of one's social, political, and intellectual allegiances with men—exist among lifelong sexual lesbians? Barry's hypothesis throws us among new questions, but it clarifies the diversity of forms in which compulsory heterosexuality presents itself. In the mystique of the overpowering, all-conquering male sex drive, the penis-with-a-life-of-its own, is rooted the law of male sex right to women, which justifies prostitution as a universal cultural assumption on the one hand, while defending sexual slavery within the family on the basis of "family privacy and cultural uniqueness" on the other.[38] The adolescent male sex drive, which, as both young women and men are taught, once triggered cannot take responsibility for itself or take no for an answer, becomes, according to Barry, the norm and rationale for adult male sexual behavior: a condition of *arrested sexual development.* Women learn to accept as natural the inevitability of this "drive" because they receive it as dogma. Hence, marital rape; hence, the Japanese wife resignedly packing her husband's suitcase for a weekend in the *kisaeng* brothels of Taiwan; hence, the psychological as well as economic imbalance of power between husband and wife, male employer and female worker, father and daughter, male professor and female student.

The effect of male identification means

> internalizing the values of the colonizer and actively participating in carrying out the colonization of one's self and one's sex. . . . Male identification is the act whereby women place men above women, including themselves, in credibility, status, and importance in most situations, regardless of the comparative quality the women may bring to the situation. . . . Interaction with women is seen as a lesser form of relating on every level.[39]

What deserves further exploration is the doublethink many women engage in and from which no woman is permanently and utterly free: However woman-to-woman relationships, female support networks, a female and feminist value system are relied on and cherished, indoctrination in male credibility and status can still create synapses in thought, denials of feeling, wishful thinking, a profound sexual and intellectual confusion.[40] I quote here from a letter I received the day I was writing this passage: "I have had very bad relationships with men—I am now in the midst of a very painful separation. I am trying to find my strength through women—without my friends, I could not survive." How many times a day do women speak words like these or think them or write them, and how often does the synapse reassert itself?

Barry summarizes her findings:

> Considering the arrested sexual development that is understood to be normal in the male population, and considering the numbers of men who are pimps, procurers, members of slavery gangs, corrupt officials participating in this traffic, owners, operators, employees of brothels and lodging and entertainment facilities, pornography purveyors, associated with prostitution, wife beaters, child molesters, incest perpetrators, johns (tricks) and rapists, one cannot but be momentarily stunned by the enormous male population engaging in female sexual slavery. The huge number of men engaged in these practices should be cause for declaration of an international emergency, a crisis in sexual violence. But what should be cause for alarm is instead accepted as normal sexual intercourse.[41]

Susan Cavin, in a rich and provocative, if highly speculative, dissertation, suggests that patriarchy becomes possible when the original female band, which includes children but ejects adolescent males, becomes invaded and outnumbered by males; that not patriarchal marriage, but the rape of the mother by the son, becomes the first act of male domination. The entering wedge, or leverage, which allows this to happen is not just a simple change in sex ratios; it is also the mother-child bond, manipulated by adolescent males in order to remain within the matrix past the age of exclusion. Maternal affection is used to establish male right of sexual access, which, however, must ever after be held by force (or through control of consciousness) since the original deep adult bonding is that of woman for woman.[42] I find this hypothesis extremely suggestive, since one form of false consciousness which serves compulsory heterosexuality is the maintenance of a mother-son relationship between women and men, including the demand that women provide maternal solace, nonjudgmental nurturing, and compassion for their harassers, rapists, and batterers (as well as for men who passively vampirize them).

But whatever its origins, when we look hard and clearly at the extent and elaboration of measures designed to keep women within a male sexual purlieu, it becomes an inescapable question whether the issue feminists have to address is not simple "gender inequality" nor the domination of culture by males nor mere "taboos against homosexuality," but the enforcement of heterosexuality for women as a means of assuring male right of physical, economic, and emotional access.[43] One of many means of enforcement is, of course, the rendering invisible of the lesbian possibility, an engulfed continent which rises fragmentedly into view from time to time only to become submerged again. Feminist research and theory that contribute to lesbian invisibility or marginality are actually working against the liberation and empowerment of women as a group.[44]

The assumption that "most women are innately heterosexual" stands as a theoretical and political stumbling block for feminism. It remains a tenable assumption partly because lesbian existence has been written out of history or catalogued under disease, partly because it has been treated as exceptional rather than intrinsic, partly because to acknowledge that for women heterosexuality may not be a "preference" at all but something that has had to be imposed, managed, organized, propagandized, and maintained by force is an immense step to take if you consider yourself freely and "innately" heterosexual. Yet the failure to examine heterosexuality as an institution is like failing to admit that the economic system called capitalism or the caste system of racism is maintained by a variety of forces, including both physical violence and false consciousness. To take the step of questioning heterosexuality as a "preference" or "choice" for women—and to do the intellectual and emotional work that follows—will call for a special quality of courage in heterosexually identified feminists, but I think the rewards will be great: a freeing-up of thinking, the exploring of new paths, the shattering of another great silence, new clarity in personal relationships.

III

I have chosen to use the terms *lesbian existence* and *lesbian continuum* because the word *lesbianism* has a clinical and limiting ring. *Lesbian existence* suggests both the fact of the historical presence of lesbians and our continuing creation of the meaning of that existence. I mean the term *lesbian continuum* to include a range—through each woman's life and throughout history—of woman-identified experience, not simply the fact that a woman has had or consciously desired genital sexual experience with another woman. If we expand it to embrace many more forms of primary intensity between and among women, including the sharing of a rich inner life, the bonding against male tyranny, the giving and receiving of practical and political support, if we can also hear it in such associations as *marriage resistance* and the "haggard" behavior identified by Mary Daly (obsolete meanings: "intractable," "willful," "wanton," and "unchaste," "a woman reluctant to yield to wooing"),[45] we begin to grasp breadths of female history and psychology which have lain out of reach as a consequence of limited, mostly clinical, definitions of *lesbianism*.

Lesbian existence comprises both the breaking of a taboo and the rejection of a compulsory way of life. It is also a direct or indirect attack on male right of access to women. But it is more than these, although we may first begin to perceive it as a form of naysaying to patriarchy, an act of resistance. It has, of course, included isolation, self-hatred, breakdown, alcoholism, suicide, and intrawoman violence; we romanticize at our peril what it means to love and act against the grain, and under heavy penalties; and lesbian existence has been lived (unlike, say, Jewish or Catholic existence) without access to any knowledge of a tradition, a continuity, a social underpinning. The destruction of records and memorabilia and letters documenting the realities of lesbian existence must be taken very seriously as a means of keeping heterosexuality compulsory for women, since what has been kept from our knowledge is joy, sensuality, courage, and community, as well as guilt, self-betrayal, and pain.[46]

Lesbians have historically been deprived of a political existence through "inclusion" as female versions of male homosexuality. To equate lesbian existence with male homosexuality because each is stigmatized is to erase female reality once again. Part of the history of lesbian existence is, obviously, to be found where lesbians, lacking a coherent female community, have shared a kind of social life and common cause with homosexual men. But there are differences: women's lack of economic and cultural privilege relative to men; qualitative differences in female and male relationships—for example, the patterns of anonymous sex among male homosexuals, and the pronounced ageism in male homosexual standards of sexual attractiveness. I perceive the lesbian experience as being, like motherhood, a profoundly *female* experience, with particular oppressions, meanings, and potentialities we cannot comprehend as long as we simply bracket it with other sexually stigmatized existences. Just as the term *parenting* serves to conceal the particular and significant reality of being a parent who is actually a mother, the term *gay* may serve the purpose of blurring the very outlines we need to discern, which are of crucial value for feminism and for the freedom of women as a group.[47]

As the term *lesbian* has been held to limiting, clinical associations in its patriarchal definition, female friendship and comradeship have been set apart from the erotic, thus limiting the erotic itself. But as we deepen and broaden the range of what we define as lesbian existence, as we delineate a lesbian continuum, we begin to discover the erotic in female terms: as that which is unconfined to any single part of the body or solely to the body itself; as an energy not only diffuse but, as Audre Lorde has described it, omnipresent in "the sharing of joy, whether physical, emotional, psychic," and in the sharing of work; as the empowering joy which "makes us less willing to accept powerlessness, or those other supplied states of being which are not native to me, such as resignation, despair, self-effacement, depression, self-denial."[48] In another context, writing of women and work, I quoted the autobiographical passage in which the poet H.D. described how her friend Bryher supported her in persisting with the visionary experience which was to shape her mature work:

> I knew that this experience, this writing-on-the-wall before me, could not be shared with anyone except the girl who stood so bravely there beside me. This girl said without hesitation, "Go on." It was she really who had the detachment and integrity of the Pythoness of Delphi. But it was I, battered and dissociated . . . who was seeing the pictures, and who was reading the writing or granted the inner vision. Or perhaps, in some sense, we were "seeing" it together, for without her, admittedly, I could not have gone on.[49]

If we consider the possibility that all women—from the infant suckling at her mother's breast, to the grown woman experiencing orgasmic sensations while suckling her own child, perhaps recalling her mother's milk smell in her own, to two women, like Virginia Woolf's Chloe and Olivia, who share a laboratory,[50] to the woman dying at ninety, touched and handled by women—exist on a lesbian continuum, we can see ourselves as moving in and out of this continuum, whether we identify ourselves as lesbian or not.

We can then connect aspects of woman identification as diverse as the impudent, intimate girl friendships of eight or nine year olds and the banding together of those women of the twelfth and fifteenth centuries known as Beguines who "shared houses, rented to one another, bequeathed houses to their room-mates . . . in cheap subdivided houses in the artisans' area of town," who "practiced Christian virtue on their own, dressing and living simply and not associating with men," who earned their livings as spinsters, bakers, nurses, or ran schools for young girls, and who managed—until the Church forced them to disperse—to live independent both of marriage and of conventual restrictions.[51] It allows us to connect these women with the more celebrated "Lesbians" of the women's school around Sappho of the seventh century B.C., with the secret sororities and economic networks reported among African women, and with the Chinese marriage-resistance sisterhoods—communities of women who refused marriage or who, if married, often refused to consummate their marriages and soon left their husbands, the only women in China who were not footbound and who, Agnes Smedley tells us, welcomed the births of daughters and organized successful women's strikes in the silk mills.[52] It allows us to connect and compare disparate individual instances of marriage resistance: for example, the strategies available to Emily Dickinson, a nineteenth-century white woman genius, with the strategies available to Zora Neale Hurston, a twentieth-century black woman genius. Dickinson never married, had tenuous intellectual friendships with men, lived self-convented in her genteel father's house in Amherst, and wrote a lifetime of passionate letters to her sister-in-law Sue Gilbert and a smaller group of such letters to her friend Kate Scott Anthon. Hurston married twice but soon left each husband, scrambled her way from Florida to Harlem to Columbia University to Haiti and finally back to Florida, moved in and out of white patronage and poverty, professional success, and failure; her survival relationships were all with women, beginning with her mother. Both of these women in their vastly different circumstances were marriage resisters, committed to their own work and selfhood, and were later characterized as "apolitical." Both were drawn to men of intellectual quality; for both of them women provided the ongoing fascination and sustenance of life.

If we think of heterosexuality as *the* natural emotional and sensual inclination for women, lives such as these are seen as deviant, as pathological, or as emotionally and sensually deprived. Or, in more recent and permissive jargon, they are banalized as "life styles." And the work of such women, whether merely the daily work of individual or collective survival and resistance or the work of the writer, the activist, the reformer, the anthropologist, or the artist—the work of self-creation—is undervalued, or seen as the bitter fruit of "penis envy" or the sublimation of repressed eroticism or the meaningless rant of a "man-hater." But when we turn the lens of vision and consider the degree to which and the methods whereby heterosexual "preference" has actually been imposed on women, not only can we understand differently the meaning of individual lives and work, but we can begin to recognize a central fact of women's history: that women have always resisted male tyranny. A feminism of action, often though not always without a theory, has constantly re-emerged in every culture and in every period. We can then begin to study women's struggle against powerlessness, women's radical rebellion, not just in male-defined "concrete revolutionary situations"[53] but in all the situations male ideologies have not perceived as revolutionary—for example, the refusal of some women to produce children, aided at great risk by other women;[54] the refusal to produce a higher standard of living and leisure for men (Leghorn and Parker show how both are part of women's unacknowledged, unpaid, and ununionized economic contribution). We can no longer have patience with Dinnerstein's view that women have simply collaborated with men in the "sexual arrangements" of history. We begin to observe behavior, both in history and in individual biography, that has hitherto been invisible or misnamed, behavior which often constitutes, given the limits of the counterforce exerted in a given time and place, radical rebellion. And we can connect these rebellions and the necessity for them with the physical passion of woman for woman which is central to lesbian existence: the erotic sensuality which has been, precisely, the most violently erased fact of female experience.

Heterosexuality has been both forcibly and subliminally imposed on women. Yet everywhere women have resisted it, often at the cost of physical torture, imprisonment, psychosurgery, social ostracism, and extreme poverty. "Compulsory heterosexuality" was named as one of the "crimes against women" by the Brussels International Tribunal on Crimes against Women in 1976. Two pieces of testimony from two very different cultures reflect the degree to which persecution of lesbians is a global practice here and now. A report from Norway relates:

> A lesbian in Oslo was in a heterosexual marriage that didn't work, so she started taking tranquillizers and ended up at the health sanatorium for treatment and rehabilitation. . . . The moment she said in family group therapy that she believed she was a lesbian, the doctor told her she was not. He knew from "looking into her eyes," he said. She had the eyes of a woman who wanted sexual intercourse with her husband. So she was subjected to so-called "couch therapy." She was put into a

comfortably heated room, naked, on a bed, and for an hour her husband was to . . . try to excite her sexually. . . . The idea was that the touching was always to end with sexual intercourse. She felt stronger and stronger aversion. She threw up and sometimes ran out of the room to avoid this "treatment." The more strongly she asserted that she was a lesbian, the more violent the forced heterosexual intercourse became. This treatment went on for about six months. She escaped from the hospital, but she was brought back. Again she escaped. She has not been there since. In the end she realized that she had been subjected to forcible rape for six months.

And from Mozambique:

> I am condemned to a life of exile because I will not deny that I am a lesbian, that my primary commitments are, and will always be to other women. In the new Mozambique, lesbianism is considered a left-over from colonialism and decadent West-ern civilization. Lesbians are sent to rehabilitation camps to learn through self-criticism the correct line about themselves. . . . If I am forced to denounce my own love for women, if I therefore denounce myself, I could go back to Mozambique and join forces in the exciting and hard struggle of rebuilding a nation, including the struggle for the emancipation of Mozambiquan women. As it is, I either risk the rehabilitation camps, or remain in exile.[55]

Nor can it be assumed that women like those in Carroll Smith-Rosenberg's study, who married, stayed married, yet dwelt in a profoundly female emotional and passional world, "preferred" or "chose" heterosexuality. Women have married because it was necessary, in order to survive economically, in order to have children who would not suffer economic deprivation or social ostracism, in order to remain respectable, in order to do what was expected of women, because coming out of "abnormal" childhoods they wanted to feel "normal" and because heterosexual romance has been represented as the great female adventure, duty, and fulfillment. We may faithfully or ambivalently have obeyed the institution, but our feelings—and our sensuality—have not been tamed or contained within it. There is no statistical documentation of the numbers of lesbians who have remained in heterosexual marriages for most of their lives. But in a letter to the early lesbian publication *The Ladder,* the playwright Lorraine Hansberry had this to say:

> I suspect that the problem of the married woman who would prefer emotional-physical relationships with other women is proportionally much higher than a similar statistic for men. (A statistic surely no one will ever really have.) This because the estate of woman being what it is, how could we ever begin to guess the numbers of women who are not prepared to risk a life alien to what they have been taught all their lives to believe was their "natural" destiny—AND—their only expectation for ECO-NOMIC security. It seems to be that this is why the question has an immensity that it does not have for male homosexuals. . . . A woman of strength and honesty may, if she chooses, sever her marriage and marry a new male mate and society will be upset that the divorce rate is rising so—but there are few places in the United States, in any event, where she will be anything remotely akin to an "outcast." Obviously this is not true for a woman who would end her marriage to take up life with another woman.[56]

This *double life*—this apparent acquiescence to an institution founded on male in-terest and prerogative—has been characteristic of female experience: in motherhood and in many kinds of heterosexual behavior, including the rituals of courtship; the pretense of asexuality by the nineteenth-century wife; the simulation of orgasm by the prostitute, the courtesan, the twentieth-century "sexually liberated" woman.

Meridel LeSueur's documentary novel of the Depression, *The Girl,* is arresting as a study of female double life. The protagonist, a waitress in a St. Paul working-class speakeasy, feels herself passionately attracted to the young man Butch, but her survival relationships are with Clara, an older waitress and prostitute, with Belle, whose husband owns the bar, and with Amelia, a union activist. For Clara and Belle and the unnamed protagonist, sex with men is in one sense an escape from the bedrock misery of daily life, a flare of intensity in the gray, relentless, often brutal web of day-to-day existence:

> It was like he was a magnet pulling me. It was exciting and powerful and frightening. He was after me too and when he found me I would run, or be petrified, just standing in front of him like a zany. And he told me not to be wandering with Clara to the Marigold where we danced with strangers. He said he would knock the shit out of me. Which made me shake and tremble, but it was better than being a husk full of suffering and not knowing why.[57]

Throughout the novel the theme of double life emerges; Belle reminisces about her marriage to the bootlegger Hoinck:

> You know, when I had that black eye and said I hit it on the cupboard, well he did it the bastard, and then he says don't tell anybody. . . . He's nuts, that's what he is, nuts, and I don't see why I live with him, why I put up with him a minute on this earth. But listen kid, she said, I'm telling you something. She looked at me and her face was wonderful. She said, Jesus Christ, Goddam him I love him that's why I'm hooked like this all my life, Goddam him I love him.[58]

After the protagonist has her first sex with Butch, her women friends care for her bleeding, give her whiskey, and compare notes.

> My luck, the first time and I got into trouble. He gave me a little money and I come to St. Paul where for ten bucks they'd stick a huge vet's needle into you and you start it and then you were on your own. . . . I never had no child. I've just had Hoinck to mother, and a hell of a child he is.[59]

> Later they made me go back to Clara's room to lie down. . . . Clara lay down beside me and put her arms around me and wanted me to tell her about it but she wanted to tell about herself. She said she started it when she was twelve with a bunch of boys in an old shed. She said nobody had paid any attention to her before and she became very popular. . . . They like it so much, she said, why shouldn't you give it to them and get presents and attention? I never cared anything for it and neither did my mama. But it's the only thing you got that's valuable.[60]

Sex is thus equated with attention from the male, who is charismatic though brutal, infantile, or unreliable. Yet it is the women who make life endurable for each other, give physical affection without causing pain, share, advise, and stick by each other. *(I am trying to find my strength through women—without my friends, I could not survive.)* LeSueur's *The Girl* parallels Toni Morrison's remarkable *Sula,* another revelation of female double life:

> Nel was the one person who had wanted nothing from her, who had accepted all aspects of her. . . . Nel was one of the reasons Sula had drifted back to Medallion. . . . The men . . . had merged into one large personality: the same language of love, the same entertainments of love, the same cooling of love. Whenever she introduced her private thoughts into their rubbings and goings, they hooded their eyes. They taught her nothing but love tricks, shared nothing but worry, gave nothing but money. She had been looking all along for a friend, and it took her a while to discover that a lover was not a comrade and could never be—for a woman.

But Sula's last thought at the second of her death is "Wait'll I tell Nel." And after Sula's death, Nel looks back on her own life:

> "All that time, all that time, I thought I was missing Jude." And the loss pressed down on her chest and came up into her throat. "We was girls together," she said as though explaining something. "O Lord, Sula," she cried, "Girl, girl, girlgirlgirl!" It was a fine cry—loud and long—but it had no bottom and it had no top, just circles and circles of sorrow.[61]

The Girl and *Sula* are both novels which examine what I am calling the lesbian continuum, in contrast to the shallow or sensational "lesbian scenes" in recent commercial fiction.[62] Each shows us woman identification untarnished (till the end of LeSueur's novel) by romanticism; each depicts the competition of heterosexual compulsion for women's attention, the diffusion and frustration of female bonding that might, in a more conscious form, reintegrate love and power.

IV

Woman identification is a source of energy, a potential springhead of female power, curtailed and contained under the institution of heterosexuality. The denial of reality and visibility to women's passion for women, women's choice of women as allies, life companions, and community, the forcing of such relationships into dissimulation and their disintegration under intense pressure have meant an incalculable loss to the power of all women *to change the social relations of the sexes, to liberate ourselves and each other*. The lie of compulsory female heterosexuality today afflicts not just feminist scholarship, but every profession, every reference work, every curriculum, every organizing attempt, every relationship or conversation over which it hovers. It creates, specifically, a profound falseness, hypocrisy, and hysteria in the heterosexual dialogue, for every heterosexual relationship is lived in the queasy strobe light of that lie. However we choose to identify ourselves, however we find ourselves labeled, it flickers across and distorts our lives.[63]

The lie keeps numberless women psychologically trapped, trying to fit mind, spirit, and sexuality into a prescribed script because they cannot look beyond the parameters of the acceptable. It pulls on the energy of such women even as it drains the energy of "closeted" lesbians—the energy exhausted in the double life. The lesbian trapped in the "closet," the woman imprisoned in prescriptive ideas of the "normal" share the pain of blocked options, broken connections, lost access to self-definition freely and powerfully assumed.

The lie is many-layered. In Western tradition, one layer—the romantic—asserts that women are inevitably, even if rashly and tragically, drawn to men; that even when that attraction is suicidal (e.g., *Tristan and Isolde,* Kate Chopin's *The Awakening*), it is still an organic imperative. In the tradition of the social sciences it asserts that primary love between the sexes is "normal"; that women *need* men as social and economic protectors, for adult sexuality, and for psychological completion; that the heterosexually constituted family is the basic social unit; that women who do not attach their primary intensity to men must be, in functional terms, condemned to an even more devastating outsiderhood than their outsiderhood as women. Small wonder that lesbians are reported to be a more hidden population than male homosexuals. The Black lesbian-feminist critic Lorraine Bethel, writing on Zora Neale Hurston, remarks that for a Black woman—already twice an outsider—to choose to assume still another "hated identity" is problematic indeed. Yet the lesbian continuum has been a life line for Black women both in Africa and the United States.

Black women have a long tradition of bonding together ... in a Black/women's community that has been a source of vital survival information, psychic and emotional support for us. We have a distinct Black woman-identified folk culture based on our experiences as Black women in this society; symbols, language and modes of expression that are specific to the realities of our lives. ... Because Black women were rarely among those Blacks and females who gained access to literary and other acknowledged forms of artistic expression, this Black female bonding and Black woman-identification has often been hidden and unrecorded except in the individual lives of Black women through our own memories of our particular Black female tradition.[64]

Another layer of the lie is the frequently encountered implication that women turn to women out of hatred for men. Profound skepticism, caution, and righteous paranoia about men may indeed be part of any healthy woman's response to the misogyny of male-dominated culture, to the forms assumed by "normal" male sexuality, and to *the failure even of "sensitive" or "political" men to perceive or find these troubling.* Lesbian existence is also represented as mere refuge from male abuses, rather than as an electric and empowering charge between women. One of the most frequently quoted literary passages on lesbian relationship is that in which Colette's Renée, in *The Vagabond,* describes "the melancholy and touching image of two weak creatures who have perhaps found shelter in each other's arms, there to sleep and weep, safe from man who is often cruel, and there to taste *better than any pleasure, the bitter happiness of feeling themselves akin, frail and forgotten* [emphasis added]."[65] Colette is often considered a lesbian writer. Her popular reputation has, I think, much to do with the fact that she writes about lesbian existence as if for a male audience; her earliest "lesbian" novels, the Claudine series, were written under compulsion for her husband and published under both their names. At all events, except for her writings on her mother, Colette is a less reliable source on the lesbian continuum than, I would think, Charlotte Brontë, who understood that while women may, indeed must, be one another's allies, mentors, and comforters in the female struggle for survival, there is quite extraneous delight in each other's company and attraction to each others' minds and character, which attend a recognition of each others' strengths.

By the same token, we can say that there is a *nascent* feminist political content in the act of choosing a woman lover or life partner in the face of institutionalized heterosexuality.[66] But for lesbian existence to realize this political content in an ultimately liberating form, the erotic choice must deepen and expand into conscious woman identification—into lesbian feminism.

The work that lies ahead, of unearthing and describing what I call here "lesbian existence," is potentially liberating for all women. It is work that must assuredly move beyond the limits of white and middle-class Western Women's Studies to examine women's lives, work, and groupings within every racial, ethnic, and political structure. There are differences, moreover, between "lesbian existence" and the "lesbian continuum," differences we can discern even in the movement of our own lives. The lesbian continuum, I suggest, needs delineation in light of the "double life" of women, not only women self-described as heterosexual but also of self-described lesbians. We need a far more exhaustive account of the forms the double life has assumed. Historians need to ask at every point how heterosexuality as institution has been organized and maintained through the female wage scale, the enforcement of middle-class women's "leisure," the glamorization of so-called sexual liberation, the withholding of education from women, the imagery of "high art" and popular culture, the mystification of the "personal" sphere, and much else. We need an economics which comprehends the institution of heterosexuality, with its doubled workload for women and its sexual divisions of labor, as the most idealized of economic relations.

The question inevitably will arise: Are we then to condemn all heterosexual relationships, including those which are least oppressive? I believe this question, though often heartfelt, is the wrong question here. We have been stalled in a maze of false dichotomies which prevents our apprehending the institution as a whole: "good" versus "bad" marriages; "marriage for love" versus arranged marriage; "liberated" sex versus prostitution; heterosexual intercourse versus rape; *Liebeschmerz* versus humiliation and dependency. Within the institution exist, of course, qualitative differences of experience; but the absence of choice remains the great unacknowledged reality, and in the absence of choice, women will remain dependent upon the chance or luck of particular relationships and will have no collective power to determine the meaning and place of sexuality in their lives. As we address the institution itself, moreover, we begin to perceive a history of female resistance which has never fully understood itself because it has been so fragmented, miscalled, erased. It will require a courageous grasp of the politics and economics, as well as the cultural propaganda, of heterosexuality to carry us beyond individual cases or diversified group situations into the complex kind of overview needed to undo the power men everywhere wield over women, power which has become a model for every other form of exploitation and illegitimate control.

Afterword [1986]

In 1980, Ann Snitow, Christine Stansell, and Sharon Thompson, three Marxist-feminist activists and scholars, sent out a call for papers for an anthology on the politics of sexuality. Having just finished writing "Compulsory Heterosexuality" for *Signs,* I sent them that manuscript and asked them to consider it. Their anthology, *Powers of Desire,* was published by the Monthly Review Press New Feminist Library in 1983 and included my paper. During the intervening period, the four of us were in correspondence, but I was able to take only limited advantage of this dialogue due to ill health and resulting surgery. With their permission, I reprint here excerpts from that correspondence as a way of indicating that my essay should be read as one contribution to a long exploration in progress, not as my own "last word" on sexual politics. I also refer interested readers to *Powers of Desire* itself.

Dear Adrienne,

. . . In one of our first letters, we told you that we were finding parameters of left-wing/feminist sexual discourse to be far broader than we imagined. Since then, we have perceived what we believe to be a crisis in the feminist movement about sex, an intensifying debate (although not always an explicit one), and a questioning of assumptions once taken for granted. While we fear the link between sex and violence, as do Women Against Pornography, we wish we better understood its sources in ourselves as well as in men. In the Reagan era, we can hardly afford to romanticize any old norm of a virtuous and moral sexuality.

In your piece, you are asking the question, what would women choose in a world where patriarchy and capitalism did *not* rule? We agree with you that heterosexuality is an institution created between these grind stones, but we don't conclude, therefore, that it is entirely a male creation. You only allow for female historical agency insofar as women exist on the lesbian continuum while we would argue that women's history, like men's history, is created out of a dialectic of necessity and choice.

All three of us (hence one lesbian, two heterosexual women) had questions about your use of the term "false consciousness" for women's heterosexuality. In general, we think the false-consciousness model can blind us to the necessities and desires that comprise the lives of the oppressed. It can also lead to the too easy denial of others' experience when that experience is different from our own. We posit, rather, a complex social model in which all erotic life is a continuum, one which therefore includes relations with men.

Which brings us to this metaphor of the continuum. We know you are a poet, not an historian, and we look forward to reading your metaphors all our lives—and standing straighter as feminists, as women, for having read them. But the metaphor of the lesbian continuum is open to all kinds of misunderstandings, and these sometimes have odd political effects. For example, Sharon reports that at a recent meeting around the abortion-rights struggle, the notions of continuum arose in the discussion several times and underwent divisive transformation. Overall, the notion that two ways of being existed on the same continuum was interpreted to mean that those two ways were the *same*. The sense of range and gradation that your description evokes disappeared. Lesbianism and female friendship became exactly the same thing. Similarly, heterosexuality and rape became the same. In one of several versions of the continuum that evolved, a slope was added, like so:

Lesbianism
  ↘ Sex with men, no penetration
       ↘ Sex with men, penetration
            ↘ Rape

This sloped continuum brought its proponents to the following conclusion: An appropriate, workable abortion-rights strategy is to inform all women that heterosexual penetration is rape, whatever their subjective experience to the contrary. All women will immediately recognize the truth of this and opt for the alternative of nonpenetration. The abortion-rights struggle will thus be simplified into a struggle against coercive sex and its consequences (since no enlightened woman would voluntarily undergo penetration unless her object was procreation—a peculiarly Catholic-sounding view).

The proponents of this strategy were young women who have worked hard in the abortion-rights movement for the past two or more years. They are inexperienced but they are dedicated. For this reason, we take their reading of your work seriously. We don't think, however, that it comes solely, or even at all, from the work itself. As likely a source is the tendency to dichotomize that has plagued the women's movement. The source of that tendency is harder to trace.

In that regard, the hints in "Compulsory" about the double life of women intrigue us. You define the double life as "the apparent acquiescence to an institution founded on male interest and prerogative." But that definition doesn't really explain your other references—to, for instance, the "intense mixture" of love and anger in lesbian relationships and to the peril of romanticizing what it means "to love and act against the grain." We think these comments raise extremely important issues for feminists right now; the problem of division and anger among us needs airing and analysis. Is this, by any chance, the theme of a piece you have in the works?

... We would still love it if we could have a meeting with you in the next few months. Any chance? ... Greetings and support from us—in all your undertakings.

We send love,
Sharon, Chris, and Ann

New York City
April 19, 1981

Dear Ann, Chris, and Sharon,

. . . It's good to be back in touch with you, you who have been so unfailingly patient, generous, and persistent. Above all, it's important to me that you know that ill health, not a withdrawal because of political differences, delayed my writing back to you. . . .

"False consciousness" can, I agree, be used as a term of dismissal for any thinking we don't like or adhere to. But, as I tried to illustrate in some detail, there is a real, identifiable system of heterosexual propaganda, of defining women as existing for the sexual use of men, which goes beyond "sex role" or "gender" stereotyping or "sexist imagery" to include a vast number of verbal and nonverbal messages. And this I call "control of consciousness." The possibility of a woman who does not exist sexually for men—the lesbian possibility—is buried, erased, occluded, distorted, misnamed, and driven underground. The feminist books—Chodorow, Dinnerstein, Ehrenreich and English, and others—which I discuss at the beginning of my essay contribute to this invalidation and erasure, and as such are part of the problem.

My essay is founded on the belief that we all think from within the limits of certain solipsisms—usually linked with privilege, racial, cultural, and economic as well as sexual—which present themselves as "the universal," "the way things are," "all women," etc., etc. I wrote it equally out of the belief that in becoming conscious of our solipsisms we have certain kinds of choices, that we can and must re-educate ourselves. I never have maintained that heterosexual feminists are walking about in a state of "brainwashed" false consciousness. Nor have such phrases as "sleeping with the enemy" seemed to me either profound or useful. *Homophobia* is too diffuse a term and does not go very far in helping us identify and talk about the sexual solipsism of heterosexual feminism. In this paper I was trying to ask heterosexual feminists to examine their experience of heterosexuality critically and antagonistically, to critique the institution of which they are a part, to struggle with the norm and its implications for women's freedom, to become more open to the considerable resources offered by the lesbian-feminist perspective, to refuse to settle for the personal privilege and solution of the individual "good relationship" within the institution of heterosexuality.

As regards "female historical agency," I wanted, precisely, to suggest that the victim model is insufficient; that there *is* a history of female agency and choice which has actually challenged aspects of male supremacy; that, like male supremacy, these can be found in many different cultures. . . . It's not that I think all female agency has been solely and avowedly lesbian. But by erasing lesbian existence from female history, from theory, from literary criticism . . . from feminist approaches to economic structure, ideas about "the family," etc., an enormous amount of female agency is kept unavailable, hence unusable. I wanted to demonstrate that that kind of obliteration continues to be acceptable in seriously regarded feminist texts. What surprised me in the responses to my essay, including your notes, is how almost every aspect of it has been considered, except this—to me—central one. I was taking a position which was neither lesbian/separatist in the sense of dismissing heterosexual women nor a "gay civil rights" plea for . . . openness to lesbianism as an "option" or an "alternate life style." I was urging that lesbian *existence* has been an unrecognized and unaffirmed claiming by women of their sexuality, thus a pattern of resistance, thus also a kind of borderline position from which to analyze and challenge the relationship of heterosexuality to male supremacy. And that lesbian existence, when recognized, demands a conscious restructuring of feminist analysis and criticism, not just a token reference or two.

I certainly agree with you that the term *lesbian continuum* can be misused. It was, in the example you report of the abortion-rights meeting, though I would think anyone who had read my work from *Of Woman Born* onward would know that my position on abortion and sterilization abuse is more complicated than that. My own problem with the phrase is that it can be, is, used by women who have not yet begun to examine the privileges and solipsisms of heterosexuality, as a safe way to describe their felt connections with women, without having to share in the risks and threats of lesbian existence. What I had thought to delineate rather complexly as a continuum has begun to sound more like "life-style shopping." *Lesbian continuum*—the phrase—came from a desire to allow for the greatest possible variation of female-identified experience, while paying a different kind of respect to *lesbian existence*—the traces and knowledge of women who have made their primary erotic and emotional choices for women. If I were writing the paper today, I would still want to make this distinction, but would put more caveats around *lesbian continuum*. I fully agree with you that Smith-Rosenberg's "female world" is not a social ideal, enclosed as it is within prescriptive middle-class heterosexuality and marriage.

My own essay could have been stronger had it drawn on more of the literature by Black women toward which Toni Morrison's *Sula* inevitably pointed me. In reading a great deal more of Black women's fiction I began to perceive a different set of valences from those found in white women's fiction for the most part: a different quest for the woman hero, a different relationship both to sexuality with men and to female loyalty and bonding. . . .

You comment briefly on your reactions to some of the radical-feminist works I cited [footnote no. 9]. I am myself critical of some of them even as I found them vitally useful. What most of them share is a taking seriously of misogyny—of organized, in-stitutionalized, normalized hostility and violence against women. I feel no "hierarchy of oppressions" is needed in order for us to take misogyny as seriously as we take racism, anti-Semitism, imperialism. To take misogyny seriously needn't mean that we perceive women merely as victims, without responsibilities or choices; it does mean recognizing the "necessity" in that "dialectic of necessity and choice"—identifying, describing, re-fusing to turn aside our eyes. I think that some of the apparent reductiveness, or even obsessiveness, of some white radical-feminist theory derives from racial and/or class solipsism, but also from the immense effort of trying to render woman hating visible amid so much denial. . . .

Finally, as to poetry and history: I want both in my life; I need to see through both. If metaphor can be misconstrued, history can also lead to misconstrual when it obliterates acts of resistance or rebellion, wipes out transformational models, or senti-mentalizes power relationships. I know you know this. I believe we are all trying to think and write out of our best consciences, our most open consciousness. I expect that quality in this book which you are editing, and look forward with anticipation to the thinking—and the actions—toward which it may take us.

In sisterhood,
Adrienne

Montague, Massachusetts
November 1981

NOTES

1. See, for example, Paula Gunn Allen, *The Sacred Hoop: Recovering the Feminine in American Indian Traditions* (Boston: Beacon, 1986); Beth Brant, ed., *A Gathering of Spirit: Writing and Art by North American Indian Women* (Montpelier, Vt.: Sinister Wisdom Books, 1984); Gloria Anzaldúa and Cherríe Moraga, eds., *This Bridge Called My Back: Writings by Radical Women of Color* (Water-town, Mass.: Persephone, 1981; distributed by Kitchen Table/Women of Color Press, Albany,

N.Y.); J.R. Roberts, *Black Lesbians: An Annotated Bibliography* (Tallahassee, Fla.: Naiad, 1981); Barbara Smith, ed., *Home Girls: A Black Feminist Anthology* (Albany, N.Y.: Kitchen Table/Women of Color Press, 1984). As Lorraine Bethel and Barbara Smith pointed out in *Conditions 5: The Black Women's Issue* (1980), a great deal of fiction by Black women depicts primary relationships between women. I would like to cite here the work of Ama Ata Aidoo, Toni Cade Bambara, Buchi Emecheta, Bessie Head, Zora Neale Hurston, Alice Walker. Donna Allegra, Red Jordan Arobateau, Audre Lorde, Ann Allen Shockley, among others, write directly as Black lesbians. For fiction by other lesbians of color, see Elly Bulkin, ed., *Lesbian Fiction: An Anthology* (Watertown, Mass.: Persephone, 1981).

See also, for accounts of contemporary Jewish-lesbian existence, Evelyn Torton Beck, ed., *Nice Jewish Girls: A Lesbian Anthology* (Watertown, Mass.: Persephone, 1982; distributed by Crossing Press, Trumansburg, N.Y.); Alice Bloch, *Lifetime Guarantee* (Watertown, Mass.: Persephone, 1982); and Melanie Kaye-Kantrowitz and Irena Klepfisz, eds., *The Tribe of Dina: A Jewish Women's Anthology* (Montpelier, Vt.: Sinister Wisdom Books, 1986).

The earliest formulation that I know of heterosexuality as an institution was in the lesbian-feminist paper *The Furies*, founded in 1971. For a collection of articles from that paper, see Nancy Myron and Charlotte Bunch, eds., *Lesbianism and the Women's Movement* (Oakland, Calif.: Diana Press, 1975; distributed by Crossing Press, Trumansburg, N.Y.).

2. Alice Rossi, "Children and Work in the Lives of Women," paper delivered at the University of Arizona, Tucson, February 1976.

3. Doris Lessing, *The Golden Notebook,* 1962 (New York: Bantam, 1977), p. 480.

4. Nancy Chodorow, *The Reproduction of Mothering* (Berkeley: University of California Press, 1978); Dorothy Dinnerstein, *The Mermaid and the Minotaur: Sexual Arrangements and the Human Malaise* (New York: Harper & Row, 1976); Barbara Ehrenreich and Deirdre English, *For Her Own Good: 150 Years of the Experts' Advice to Women* (Garden City, N.Y.: Doubleday, Anchor, 1978); Jean Baker Miller, *Toward a New Psychology of Women* (Boston: Beacon, 1976).

5. I could have chosen many other serious and influential books, including anthologies, which would illustrate the same point: e.g., *Our Bodies, Ourselves,* the Boston Women's Health Book Collective's best seller (New York: Simon and Schuster, 1976), which devotes a separate (and inadequate) chapter to lesbians, but whose message is that heterosexuality is most women's life preference; Berenice Carroll, ed., *Liberating Women's History: Theoretical and Critical Essays* (Urbana: University of Illinois Press, 1976), which does not include even a token essay on the lesbian presence in history, though an essay by Linda Gordon, Persis Hunt, *et al.* notes the use by male historians of "sexual deviance" as a category to discredit and dismiss Anna Howard Shaw, Jane Addams, and other feminists ("Historical Phallacies: Sexism in American Historical Writing"); and Renate Bridenthal and Claudia Koonz, eds., *Becoming Visible: Women in European History* (Boston: Houghton Mifflin, 1977), which contains three mentions of male homosexuality but no materials that I have been able to locate on lesbians. Gerda Lerner, ed., *The Female Experience: An American Documentary* (Indianapolis: Bobbs-Merrill, 1977), contains an abridgment of two lesbian-feminist-position papers from the contemporary movement but no other documentation of lesbian existence. Lerner does note in her preface, however, how the charge of deviance has been used to fragment women and discourage women's resistance. Linda Gordon, in *Woman's Body, Woman's Right: A Social History of Birth Control in America* (New York: Viking, Grossman, 1976), notes accurately that "it is not that feminism has produced more lesbians. There have always been many lesbians, despite the high levels of repression; and most lesbians experience their sexual preference as innate" (p. 410).

[A.R., 1986: I am glad to update the first annotation in this footnote. *"The New" Our Bodies, Ourselves* (New York: Simon and Schuster, 1984) contains an expanded chapter on "Loving Women: Lesbian Life and Relationships" and furthermore emphasizes *choices* for women throughout—in terms of sexuality, health care, family, politics, etc.]

6. Jonathan Katz, ed., *Gay American History: Lesbians and Gay Men in the U.S.A.* (New York: Thomas Y. Crowell, 1976).

7. Nancy Sahli, "Smashing Women's Relationships before the Fall," *Chrysalis: A Magazine of Women's Culture* 8 (1979): 17–27.

8. This is a book which I have publicly endorsed. I would still do so, though with the above caveat. It is only since beginning to write this article that I fully appreciated how enormous is the unasked question in Ehrenreich and English's book.

9. See, for example, Kathleen Barry, *Female Sexual Slavery* (Englewood Cliffs, N.J.: Prentice-Hall, 1979); Mary Daly, *Gyn/Ecology: The Metaethics of Radical Feminism* (Boston: Beacon, 1978); Susan Griffin, *Woman and Nature: The Roaring inside Her* (New York: Harper & Row, 1978); Diana Russell and Nicole van de Ven, eds., *Proceedings of the International Tribunal of Crimes against Women* (Millbrae, Calif.: Les Femmes, 1976); and Susan Brownmiller, *Against Our Will: Men, Women and Rape* (New York: Simon and Schuster, 1975); *Aegis: Magazine on Ending Violence against Women* (Feminist Alliance against Rape, Washington, D.C.).

[A.R., 1986: Work on both incest and on woman battering has appeared in the 1980s which I did not cite in the essay. See Florence Rush, *The Best-kept Secret* (New York: McGraw-Hill, 1980); Louise Armstrong, *Kiss Daddy Goodnight: A Speakout on Incest* (New York: Pocket Books, 1979); Sandra Butler, *Conspiracy of Silence: The Trauma of Incest* (San Francisco: New Glide, 1978); F. Delacoste and F. Newman, eds., *Fight Back!: Feminist Resistance to Male Violence* (Minneapolis: Cleis Press, 1981); Judy Freespirit, *Daddy's Girl: An Incest Survivor's Story* (Langlois, Ore.: Diaspora Distribution, 1982); Judith Herman, *Father-Daughter Incest* (Cambridge, Mass.: Harvard University Press, 1981); Toni McNaron and Yarrow Morgan, eds., *Voices in the Night: Women Speaking about Incest* (Minneapolis: Cleis Press, 1982); and Betsy Warrior's richly informative, multipurpose compilation of essays, statistics, listings, and facts, the *Battered Women's Directory* (formerly entitled *Working on Wife Abuse*), 8th ed. (Cambridge, Mass.: 1982).]

10. Dinnerstein, p. 272.

11. Chodorow, pp. 197–198.

12. *Ibid.,* pp. 198–199.

13. *Ibid.,* p. 200.

14. Kathleen Gough, "The Origin of the Family," in *Toward an Anthropology of Women,* ed. Rayna [Rapp] Reiter (New York: Monthly Review Press, 1975), pp. 69–70.

15. Barry, pp. 216–219.

16. Anna Demeter, *Legal Kidnapping* (Boston: Beacon, 1977), pp. xx, 126–128.

17. Daly, pp. 139–141, 163–165.

18. Barbara Ehrenreich and Deirdre English, *Witches, Midwives and Nurses: A History of Women Healers* (Old Westbury, N.Y.: Feminist Press, 1973); Andrea Dworkin, *Woman Hating* (New York: Dutton, 1974), pp. 118–154; Daly, pp. 178–222.

19. See Virginia Woolf, *A Room of One's Own* (London: Hogarth, 1929), and *id., Three Guineas* (New York: Harcourt Brace, [1938] 1966); Tillie Olsen, *Silences* (Boston: Delacorte, 1978); Michelle Cliff, "The Resonance of Interruption," *Chrysalis: A Magazine of Women's Culture* 8 (1979): 29–37.

20. Mary Daly, *Beyond God the Father* (Boston: Beacon, 1973), pp. 347–351; Olsen, pp. 22–46.

21. Daly, *Beyond God the Father,* p. 93.

22. Fran P. Hosken, "The Violence of Power: Genital Mutilation of Females," *Heresies: A Feminist Journal of Art and Politics* 6 (1979): 28–35; Russell and van de Ven, pp. 194–195.

[A.R., 1986: See especially "Circumcision of Girls," in Nawal El Saadawi, *The Hidden Face of Eve: Women in the Arab World* (Boston: Beacon, 1982), pp. 33–43.]

23. Barry, pp. 163–164.

24. The issue of "lesbian sadomasochism" needs to be examined in terms of dominant cultures' teachings about the relation of sex and violence. I believe this to be another example of the "double life" of women.

25. Catharine A. MacKinnon, *Sexual Harassment of Working Women: A Case of Sex Discrimination* (New Haven, Conn.: Yale University Press, 1979), pp. 15–16.

26. *Ibid.,* p. 174.

27. Brownmiller, *op. cit.*

28. MacKinnon, p. 219. Susan Schecter writes: "The push for heterosexual union at whatever cost is so intense that . . . it has become a cultural force of its own that creates battering. The ideology of romantic love and its jealous possession of the partner as property provide the mas-

querade for what can become severe abuse" (*Aegis: Magazine on Ending Violence against Women* [July–August 1979]: 50–51).

29. MacKinnon, p. 298.

30. *Ibid.,* p. 220.

31. *Ibid.,* p. 221.

32. Barry, *op. cit.*

[A.R., 1986: See also Kathleen Barry, Charlotte Bunch, and Shirley Castley, eds., *International Feminism: Networking against Female Sexual Slavery* (New York: International Women's Tribune Center, 1984).]

33. Barry, p. 33.

34. *Ibid.,* p. 103.

35. *Ibid.,* p. 5.

36. *Ibid.,* p. 100.

[A.R., 1986: This statement has been taken as claiming that "all women are victims" purely and simply, or that "all heterosexuality equals sexual slavery." I would say, rather, that all women are affected, though differently, by dehumanizing attitudes and practices directed at women as a group.]

37. *Ibid.,* p. 218.

38. *Ibid.,* p. 140.

39. *Ibid.,* p. 172.

40. Elsewhere I have suggested that male identification has been a powerful source of white women's racism and that it has often been women already seen as "disloyal" to male codes and systems who have actively battled against it (Adrienne Rich, "Disloyal to Civilization: Feminism, Racism, Gynephobia," in *On Lies, Secrets, and Silence: Selected Prose, 1966–1978* [New York: W.W. Norton, 1979]).

41. Barry, p. 220.

42. Susan Cavin, "Lesbian Origins" (Ph.D. diss., Rutgers University, 1978), unpublished, ch. 6.

[A.R., 1986: This dissertation was recently published as *Lesbian Origins* (San Francisco: Ism Press, 1986).]

43. For my perception of heterosexuality as an economic institution I am indebted to Lisa Leghorn and Katherine Parker, who allowed me to read the manuscript of their book *Woman's Worth: Sexual Economics and the World of Women* (London and Boston: Routledge & Kegan Paul, 1981).

44. I would suggest that lesbian existence has been most recognized and tolerated where it has resembled a "deviant" version of heterosexuality—e.g., where lesbians have, like Stein and Toklas, played heterosexual roles (or seemed to in public) and have been chiefly identified with male culture. See also Claude E. Schaeffer, "The Kuterai Female Berdache: Courier, Guide, Prophetess and Warrior," *Ethnohistory* 12, no. 3 (Summer 1965): 193–236. (Berdache: "an individual of a definite physiological sex [m. or f.] who assumes the role and status of the opposite sex and who is viewed by the community as being of one sex physiologically but as having assumed the role and status of the opposite sex" [Schaeffer, p. 231].) Lesbian existence has also been relegated to an upper-class phenomenon, an elite decadence (as in the fascination with Paris salon lesbians such as Renée Vivien and Natalie Clifford Barney), to the obscuring of such "common women" as Judy Grahn depicts in her *The Work of a Common Woman* (Oakland, Calif.: Diana Press, 1978) and *True to Life Adventure Stories* (Oakland, Calif.: Diana Press, 1978).

45. Daly, *Gyn/Ecology,* p. 15.

46. "In a hostile world in which women are not supposed to survive except in relation with and in service to men, entire communities of women were simply erased. History tends to bury what it seeks to reject" (Blanche W. Cook, " 'Women Alone Stir My Imagination': Lesbianism and the Cultural Tradition," *Signs: Journal of Women in Culture and Society* 4, no. 4 [Summer 1979]: 719–720). The Lesbian Herstory Archives in New York City is one attempt to preserve contemporary documents on lesbian existence—a project of enormous value and meaning, working against the continuing censorship and obliteration of relationships, networks, communities in other archives and elsewhere in the culture.

47. [A.R., 1986: The shared historical and spiritual "crossover" functions of lesbians and gay men in cultures past and present are traced by Judy Grahn in *Another Mother Tongue: Gay Words, Gay Worlds* (Boston: Beacon, 1984). I now think we have much to learn both from the uniquely female aspects of lesbian existence and from the complex "gay" identity we share with gay men.]

48. Audre Lorde, "Uses of the Erotic: The Erotic as Power," in *Sister Outsider* (Trumansburg, N.Y.: Crossing Press, 1984).

49. Adrienne Rich, "Conditions for Work: The Common World of Women," in *On Lies, Secrets, and Silence*, p. 209; H.D., *Tribute to Freud* (Oxford: Carcanet, 1971), pp. 50–54.

50. Woolf, *A Room of One's Own*, p. 126.

51. Gracia Clark. "The Beguines: A Mediaeval Women's Community," *Quest: A Feminist Quarterly* 1, no. 4 (1975): 73–80.

52. See Denise Paulmé, ed., *Women of Tropical Africa* (Berkeley: University of California Press, 1963), pp. 7, 266–267. Some of these sororities are described as "a kind of defensive syndicate against the male element," their aims being "to offer concerted resistance to an oppressive patriarchate," "independence in relation to one's husband and with regard to motherhood, mutual aid, satisfaction of personal revenge." See also Audre Lorde, "Scratching the Surface: Some Notes on Barriers to Women and Loving," in *Sister Outsider*, pp. 45–52; Marjorie Topley, "Marriage Resistance in Rural Kwangtung," in *Women in Chinese Society*, ed. M. Wolf and R. Witke (Stanford, Calif.: Stanford University Press, 1978), pp. 67–89; Agnes Smedley, *Portraits of Chinese Women in Revolution*, ed. J. MacKinnon and S. MacKinnon (Old Westbury, N.Y.: Feminist Press, 1976), pp. 103–110.

53. See Rosalind Petchesky, "Dissolving the Hyphen: A Report on Marxist-Feminist Groups 1–5," in *Capitalist Patriarchy and the Case for Socialist Feminism*, ed. Zillah Eisenstein (New York: Monthly Review Press, 1979), p. 387.

54. [A.R., 1986: See Angela Davis, *Women, Race and Class* (New York: Random House, 1981), p. 102; Orlando Patterson, *Slavery and Social Death: A Comparative Study* (Cambridge: Harvard University Press, 1982), p. 133.]

55. Russell and van de Ven, pp. 42–43, 56–57.

56. I am indebted to Jonathan Katz's *Gay American History* (*op. cit.*) for bringing to my attention Hansberry's letters to *The Ladder* and to Barbara Grier for supplying me with copies of relevant pages from *The Ladder*, quoted here by permission of Barbara Grier. See also the reprinted series of *The Ladder*, ed. Jonathan Katz *et al.* (New York: Arno, 1975), and Deirdre Carmody, "Letters by Eleanor Roosevelt Detail Friendship with Lorena Hickok," *New York Times* (October 21, 1979).

57. Meridel LeSueur, *The Girl* (Cambridge, Mass.: West End Press, 1978), pp. 10–11. LeSueur describes, in an afterword, how this book was drawn from the writings and oral narrations of women in the Workers Alliance who met as a writers' group during the Depression.

58. *Ibid.*, p. 20.

59. *Ibid.*, pp. 53–54.

60. *Ibid.*, p. 55.

61. Toni Morrison, *Sula* (New York: Bantam, 1973), pp. 103–104, 149. I am indebted to Lorraine Bethel's essay " 'This Infinity of Conscious Pain': Zora Neale Hurston and the Black Female Literary Tradition," in *All the Women Are White, All the Blacks Are Men, but Some of Us Are Brave: Black Women's Studies*, ed. Gloria T. Hull, Patricia Bell Scott, and Barbara Smith (Old Westbury, N.Y.: Feminist Press, 1982).

62. See Maureen Brady and Judith McDaniel, "Lesbians in the Mainstream: The Image of Lesbians in Recent Commercial Fiction," *Conditions* 6 (1979): 82–105.

63. See Russell and van de Ven, p. 40: "Few heterosexual women realize their lack of free choice about their sexuality, and few realize how and why compulsory heterosexuality is also a crime against them."

64. Bethel, " 'This Infinity of Conscious Pain,' " *op. cit.*

65. Dinnerstein, the most recent writer to quote this passage, adds ominously: "But what has to be added to her account is that these 'women enlaced' are sheltering each other not just

from what men want to do to them, but also from what they want to do to each other" (Dinnerstein, p. 103). The fact is, however, that woman-to-woman violence is a minute grain in the universe of male-against-female violence perpetuated and rationalized in every social institution.

66. Conversation with Blanche W. Cook, New York City, March 1979.

17

Chicano Men:
A Cartography of Homosexual Identity and Behavior

Tomás Almaguer

Tomás Almaguer is a sociologist who writes about racial difference in California history and culture. In this essay he undertakes to map the forms of homosexual desire, practice, and identity among contemporary Chicano men, and he argues that these forms are bound to be different from anything in Anglo gay life. He says that the Mexican/Latin-American sexual system, a crucial influence on many Chicanos, is inflected by a distinction not between straight and gay but rather between active and passive. In this system the passive, which is understood in a gender-coded way as feminine, is radically devalued. He also says that because Chicanos are subordinated in the United States, their family life, with the various kinds of support it provides them, is important to their survival; and therefore they are less free to violate family expectations than Anglos are. These and other such cultural factors mold the forms of Chicano male homosexuality. Tomás Almaguer is associate professor of American Studies at the University of California, Santa Cruz, and he has served as an editor of OUT/LOOK.

The sexual behavior and sexual identity of Chicano male homosexuals is principally shaped by two distinct sexual systems, each of which attaches different significance and meaning to homosexuality. Both the European-American and Mexican/Latin-American systems have their own unique ensemble of sexual meanings, categories for sexual actors, and scripts that circumscribe sexual behavior. Each system also maps the human body in different ways by placing different values on homosexual erotic zones. The primary socialization of Chicanos into Mexican/Latin-American cultural norms, combined with their simultaneous socialization into the dominant European-American culture, largely structures how they negotiate sexual identity questions and confer meaning to homosexual behavior during adolescence and adulthood. Chicano men who embrace a "gay" identity (based on the European-American sexual system) must reconcile this sexual identity with their primary socialization into a Latino culture that does not recognize such a construction: there is no cultural equivalent to the modern "gay man" in the Mexican/Latin-American sexual system.

How does socialization into these different sexual systems shape the crystallization of their sexual identities and the meaning they give to their homosexuality? Why does only a segment of homosexually active Chicano men identify as "gay"? Do these men primarily consider themselves *Chicano* gay men (who retain primary emphasis on their ethnicity) or *gay* Chicanos (who place primary emphasis on their sexual preference)?

How do Chicano homosexuals structure their sexual conduct, especially the sexual roles and relationships into which they enter? Are they structured along lines of power/dominance firmly rooted in a patriarchal Mexican culture that privileges men over women and the masculine over the feminine? Or do they reflect the ostensibly more egalitarian sexual norms and practices of the European-American sexual system? These are among the numerous questions that this paper problematizes and explores.

We know little about how Chicano men negotiate and contest a modern gay identity with aspects of Chicano culture drawing upon more Mexican/Latin-American configurations of sexual meaning. Unlike the rich literature on the Chicana/Latina lesbian experience, there is a paucity of writings on Chicano gay men.[1] There does not exist any scholarly literature on this topic other than one unpublished study addressing this issue as a secondary concern (Carrillo and Maiorana). The extant literature consists primarily of semi-autobiographical, literary texts by authors such as John Rechy, Arturo Islas, and Richard Rodriguez.[2] Unlike the writings on Chicana lesbianism, however, these works fail to discuss directly the cultural dissonance that Chicano homosexual men confront in reconciling their primary socialization into Chicano family life with the sexual norms of the dominant culture. They offer little to our understanding of how these men negotiate the different ways these cultural systems stigmatize homosexuality and how they incorporate these messages into their adult sexual practices.

In the absence of such discussion or more direct ethnographic research to draw upon, we must turn elsewhere for insights into the lives of Chicano male homosexuals. One source of such knowledge is the perceptive anthropological research on homosexuality in Mexico and Latin America, which has direct relevance for our understanding of how Chicano men structure and culturally interpret their homosexual experiences. The other, ironically, is the writings of Chicana lesbians who have openly discussed intimate aspects of their sexual behavior and reflected upon sexual identity issues. How they have framed these complex sexual issues has major import for our understanding of Chicano male homosexuality. Thus, the first section of this paper examines certain features of the Mexican/Latin-American sexual system which offer clues to the ensemble of cultural meanings that Chicano homosexuals give to their sexual practices. The second section examines the autobiographical writings of Chicana lesbian writer Cherríe Moraga. I rely upon her candid discussion of her sexual development as ethnographic evidence for further problematizing the Chicano homosexual experience in the United States.

The Cartography of Desire in the Mexican/Latin-American Sexual System

American anthropologists have recently turned their attention to the complex meaning of homosexuality in Mexico and elsewhere in Latin America. Ethnographic research by Joseph M. Carrier, Roger N. Lancaster, Richard Parker, Barry D. Adam, and Clark L. Taylor has documented the inapplicability of Western European and North American categories of sexual meaning in the Latin American context. Since the Mexican/Chicano population in the U.S. shares basic features of these Latin cultural patterns, it is instructive to examine this sexual system closely and to explore its impact on the sexuality of homosexual Chicano men and women.

The rules that define and stigmatize homosexuality in Mexican culture operate under a logic and a discursive practice different from those of the bourgeois sexual system that shaped the emergence of contemporary gay/lesbian identity in the U.S. Each sexual system confers meaning to homosexuality by giving different weight to the two fundamental features of human sexuality that Freud delineated in the *Three Essays on the*

Theory of Sexuality: sexual object choice and sexual aim. The structured meaning of homosexuality in the European-American context rests on the sexual object choice one makes—i.e., the biological sex of the person toward whom sexual activity is directed. The Mexican/Latin-American sexual system, on the other hand, confers meaning to homosexual practices according to sexual aim—i.e., the act one wants to perform with another person (of either biological sex).

The contemporary bourgeois sexual system in the U.S. divides the sexual landscape according to discrete sexual categories and personages defined in terms of sexual preference or object choice: same sex (homosexual), opposite sex (heterosexual), or both (bisexual). Historically, this formulation has carried with it a blanket condemnation of all same-sex behavior. Because it is non-procreative and at odds with a rigid, compulsory heterosexual norm, homosexuality traditionally has been seen as either 1) a sinful transgression against the word of God, 2) a congenital disorder wracking the body, or 3) a psychological pathology gripping the mind. In underscoring object choice as the crucial factor in defining sexuality in the U.S., anthropologist Roger Lancaster argues that "homosexual desire itself, without any qualifications, stigmatizes one as a homosexual" (116). This stigmatization places the modern gay man at the bottom of the dominant sexual hierarchy. According to Lancaster, "the object choice of the homosexual emarginates him from male power, except insofar as he can serve as a negative example and . . . is positioned outside the operational rules of normative (hetero)sexuality" (123–24).

Unlike the European-American system, the Mexican/Latin-American sexual system is based on a configuration of gender/sex/power that is articulated along the active/passive axis and organized through the scripted sexual role one plays.[3] It highlights sexual aim—the act one wants to perform with the person toward whom sexual activity is directed—and gives only secondary importance to the person's gender or biological sex. According to Lancaster, "it renders certain organs and roles 'active,' other body passages and roles 'passive,' and assigns honor/shame and status/stigma accordingly" (123). It is the mapping of the body into differentiated erotic zones and the unequal, gender-coded statuses accorded sexual actors that structure homosexual meaning in Latin culture. In the Mexican/Latin-American context there is no cultural equivalent to the modern gay man. Instead of discrete sexual personages differentiated according to sexual preference, we have categories of people defined in terms of the role they play in the homosexual act. The Latin homosexual world is divided into *activos* and *pasivos* (as in Mexico and Brazil) and *machistas* and *cochóns* (in Nicaragua).

Although stigma accompanies homosexual practices in Latin culture, it does not equally adhere to both partners. It is primarily the anal-passive individual (the *cochón* or *pasivo*) who is stigmatized for playing the subservient, feminine role. His partner (the *activo* or *machista*) typically "is not stigmatized at all and, moreover, no clear category exists in the popular language to classify him. For all intents and purposes, he is just a normal . . . male" (Lancaster, 113). In fact, Lancaster argues that the active party in a homosexual drama often gains status among his peers in precisely the same way that one derives status from seducing many women (113). This cultural construction confers an inordinate amount of meaning to the anal orifice and to anal penetration. This is in sharp contrast to the way homosexuality is viewed in the U.S., where the oral orifice structures the meaning of homosexuality in the popular imagination. In this regard, Lancaster suggests that the lexicon of male insult in each context clearly reflects this basic difference in cultural meaning associated with oral/anal sites (111). The most common derisive term used to refer to homosexuals in the U.S. is "cocksucker." Conversely, most Latin American epithets for homosexuals convey the stigma associated with their being anally penetrated.

Consider for a moment the meaning associated with the passive homosexual in Nicaragua, the *cochón*. The term is derived from the word *colchón* or mattress, implying that one man gets on top of another as one would a mattress, and thereby symbolically affirms the former's superior masculine power and male status over the other, who is feminized and indeed objectified (Lancaster, 112). *Cochón* carries with it a distinct configuration of power, delineated along gender lines that are symbolically affirmed through the sexual role one plays in the homosexual act. Consequently, the meaning of homosexuality in Latin culture is fraught with elements of power/dominance that are not intrinsically accorded homosexual practices in the U.S. As Lancaster notes,

> The resultant anal emphasis suggests a significant constraint on the nature of homo-erotic practices. Unlike oral intercourse, which may lend itself to reciprocal sexual practices, anal intercourse invariably produces an active partner and a passive partner. If oral intercourse suggests the possibility of an equal sign between partners, anal intercourse most likely produces an unequal relationship. (112–13)

Therefore, it is anal passivity alone that is stigmatized and that defines the subordinate status of homosexuals in Latin culture. The stigma conferred to the passive role is fundamentally inscribed in gender-coded terms.

> "To give" (*dar*) is to be masculine, "to receive" (*recibir, aceptar, tomar*) is to be feminine. This holds as the ideal in all spheres of transactions between and within genders. It is symbolized by the popular interpretation of the male sexual organ as active in intercourse and the female sexual organ (or male anus) as passive. (Lancaster, 114)

This equation makes homosexuals such as the *pasivo* and *cochón* into feminized men; biological males, but not truly men. In Nicaragua, for example, homosexual behavior renders "one man a machista and the other a cochón. The machista's honor and the cochón's shame are opposite sides of the same coin" (Lancaster, 114).

The Power of Myth and Male Cultural Fantasy: Mexican Female Betrayal and Male Masculinity

Psychoanalyst Marvin Goldwert argues that this patriarchal cultural equation has special resonance for Mexicans and remains deeply embedded in the Mexican psyche. He claims that it has symbolic roots in cultural myths surrounding the Spanish conquest of Mexico in the sixteenth century. This colonial drama unfolded with the Spanish conquistadores playing the role of active, masculine intruders who raped the passive, feminine Indian civilization. Goldwert suggests that

> ... there now exists in every Mexican male a culturally stereotyped polarity in which "masculinity" is synonymous with the active/dominant personality and "femininity" is passive/submissive. In mestizo society, the macho ... strove to overcome his sense of Indian femininity by asserting a true Spanish dominance over his women. (162)

In this formulation, Mexican men are disposed to affirm their otherwise insecure masculinity through the symbolic sexual conquest of women: "Male-female relations in Mexico thus were fit into a stereotypical mold of the dominant/aggressive male and the inferior *mujer abnegada,* the passive, self-sacrificing, dutiful woman" (162).

This gender-coded equation finds its clearest expression in the betrayal of Doña Marina (or *la Malinche*), the Indian woman who facilitated the Spanish conquest of Mexico. In *Labyrinth of Solitude,* Octavio Paz sums up the significance of her betrayal for the Mexican mestizo population in the phrase "los hijos de la chingada" ("the sons of the violated mother").[4] He perceptively notes that the distinction between el chingón and la chingada is not only a Spanish/Indian configuration, but is also fundamentally inscribed in male/female terms. According to Paz, the word chingar signifies "doing violence to another."

> The verb is masculine, active, cruel: it stings, wounds, gashes, stains. And it provokes a bitter, resentful satisfaction. The person who suffers this action is passive, inert and open, in contrast to the active, aggressive and closed person who inflicts it. The chingón is the macho, the male; he rips open the chingada, the female, who is pure passivity, defenseless against the exterior world. The relationship between them is violent and it is determined by the cynical power of the first and the impotence of the second. (77)

Mexican men often find a tenuous assurance of their masculinity and virility in aggressive manliness and through a rigid gender role socialization that ruthlessly represses their own femininity.[5] Psychoanalyst Santiago Ramirez identifies the Mexican family as the procrustean bedrock upon which this psychic structuring lies. From early childhood, the young Mexican male develops an ambivalence toward women, who are less valued than men in patriarchal Mexican society. This fundamental disdain for that which is feminine later gives way to an outpouring of resentment and humiliation onto one's wife or mistress and women in general (Goldwert, 165). The psychic consequences of this rejection of the feminine are profound. According to Goldwert,

> Identifying with an idealized paternal model and repressing the maternal model of tenderness, the young macho worships at the shrine of virility. During childhood the sign of virility for the Mexican male is courage to the point of recklessness, aggressiveness, and unwillingness to run away from a fight or break a deal (no rejarse). During adolescence the sign of virility is for the male to talk about or act in the sexual sphere.... From adolescence through his entire life, the Mexican male will measure virility by sexual potential, with physical strength, courage, and audacity as secondary factors. (166)

This cultural and psychic structure has particular significance for men who engage in homosexual behavior. Paz notes that the active/male and passive/female construction in Mexican culture has direct significance for the way Mexicans view male homosexuality. According to him, "masculine homosexuality is regarded with a certain indulgence insofar as the active agent is concerned. The passive agent is an abject, degraded being. Masculine homosexuality is tolerated, then, on condition that it consists in violating a passive agent" (40). Aggressive, active, and penetrating sexual activity, therefore, becomes the true marker of the Mexican man's tenuous masculinity. It is attained by the negation of all that is feminine within him and by the sexual subjugation of women. But this valorization of hyper-masculinity can also be derived by penetrating passive, anal-receptive men as well.

Male Homosexual Identity and Behavior in Mexico

Some of the most insightful ethnographic research on homosexuality in Mexico has been conducted by anthropologist J.M. Carrier. Like other Latin American specialists exploring this issue, Carrier argues that homosexuality is construed very differently in the U.S. and in Mexico. In the U.S., even one adult homosexual act or acknowledgment of homosexual desire may threaten a man's gender identity and throw open to question his sexual identity as well. In sharp contrast, a Mexican man's masculine gender and heterosexual identity are not threatened by a homosexual act as long as he plays the inserter's role. Only the male who plays the passive sexual role and exhibits feminine gender characteristics is considered to be truly homosexual and is, therefore, stigmatized. This "bisexual" option, an exemption from stigma for the "masculine" homosexual, can be seen as part of the ensemble of gender privileges and sexual prerogatives accorded Mexican men. Thus it is primarily the passive, effeminate homosexual man who becomes the object of derision and societal contempt in Mexico.

> Effeminate males provide easily identifiable sexual targets for interested males in Mexico. . . . The beliefs linking effeminate males with homosexuality are culturally transmitted by a vocabulary which provides the appropriate labels, by homosexually oriented jokes and word games and by the mass media. From early childhood on, Mexican males are made aware of the labels used to denote male homosexuals, and the connection is always clearly made that these homosexual males (usually called *putos* or *jotos*) are guilty of unmanly effeminate behavior. (Carrier, "Mexican Male," 78)

The terms used to refer to homosexual Mexican men are generally coded with gendered meaning drawn from the inferior position of women in patriarchal Mexican society. The most benign of these contemptuous terms is *maricón,* a label that highlights the non-conforming gender attributes of the (feminine) homosexual man. Its semantic equivalent in the U.S. is "sissy" or "fairy" (Carrier, "Cultural Factors," 123–24). Terms such as *joto* or *puto,* on the other hand, speak to the passive sexual role taken by these men rather than merely their gender attributes. They are infinitely more derogatory and vulgar in that they underscore the sexually non-conforming nature of their passive/receptive position in the homosexual act. The invective associated with all these appellations speaks to the way effeminate homosexual men are viewed as having betrayed the Mexican man's prescribed gender and sexual role. Moreover, it may be noted that the Spanish feminine word *puta* refers to a female prostitute while its male form *puto* refers to a passive homosexual, not a male prostitute. It is significant that the cultural equation made between the feminine, anal-receptive homosexual man and the most culturally stigmatized female in Mexican society (the whore) share a common semantic base.[6]

Carrier's research suggests that homosexuality in Mexico is rigidly circumscribed by the prominent role the family plays in structuring homosexual activity. Whereas in the U.S., at least among most European-Americans, the role of the family as a regulator of the lives of gay men and lesbians has progressively declined, in Mexico the family remains a crucial institution that defines both gender and sexual relations between men and women. The Mexican family remains a bastion of patriarchal privilege for men and a major impediment to women's autonomy outside the private world of the home.

The constraints of family life often prevent homosexual Mexican men from securing unrestricted freedom to stay out late at night, to move out of their family's home before marriage, or to take an apartment with a male lover. Thus their opportunities to make homosexual contacts in other than anonymous locations, such as the balconies of movie theaters or certain parks, are severely constrained (Carrier, "Family Attitudes," 368). This situation creates an atmosphere of social interdiction which may explain why homosexuality in Mexico is typically shrouded in silence. The concealment, suppression, or prevention of any open acknowledgment of homosexual activity underscores the stringency of cultural dictates surrounding gender and sexual norms within Mexican family life. Unlike the generally more egalitarian, permissive family life of white middle-class gay men and lesbians in the U.S., the Mexican family appears to play a far more important and restrictive role in structuring homosexual behavior among Mexican men ("Family Attitudes," 373).

Given these constraints and the particular meanings attached to homosexuality in Mexican culture, same-sex behavior in Mexico typically unfolds in the context of an age-stratified hierarchy that grants privileges to older, more masculine men. According to Carrier, these male homosexual transactions usually follow these basic patterns:

> Some post-pubertal males utilize boys as sexual outlets prior to marriage, and, after marriage, continue to utilize both heterosexual and homosexual outlets. Another pattern is that some males in their first year of sexual activity initiate sexual encounters both with post-pubertal girls, and effeminate boys, they find in their neighborhoods, at schools, at social outings. They continue to utilize both sexual outlets prior to marriage, but discontinue, or only occasionally use, homosexual outlets following marriage. Still another pattern exits where some males utilize both genders as sexual outlets during their first couple of years of sexual activity. They have *novias* and plan to marry, but they also become romantically involved with males prior to marriage. After they marry, they continue to have romantic and sexual relationships with males. ("Mexican Male," 81)

Carrier's research on mestizo homosexual men in Guadalajara found that the majority of the feminine, passive homosexual males become sexually active prior to puberty; many as young as from the ages of six to nine. Most of their homosexual contacts are with postpubescent cousins, uncles, or neighbors. They may occur quite frequently and extend over a long period or be infrequent and relatively short-lived in duration. These early experiences are generally followed by continued homosexual encounters into adolescence and adulthood. Only a segment of the homosexually active youth, however, develop a preference for the anal receptive, *pasivo* sexual role, and thus come to define their individual sense of gender in a decidedly feminine direction ("Gay Liberation," 228, 231).

It is very significant that in instances where two masculine, active men enter into a homosexual encounter, the rules that structure gender-coded homosexual relations continue to operate with full force. In these exchanges one of the men—typically he who is defined as being more masculine or powerful—assumes the active, inserter role while the other man is pressed into the passive, anal-receptive role. Moreover, men who may eventually adopt both active and passive features of homosexual behavior typically do not engage in such reciprocal relations with the same person. Instead, they generally only play the active role with one person (who is always viewed as being the more feminine) and are sexually passive with those they deem more masculine than themselves ("Cultural Factors," 120–21).

Although some cognitive dissonance is involved in Mexican male homosexual contacts, it appears to be primarily related to the extent of homosexual involvement and how one sets limits to the sexual exchange. Many of these men, who typically start out playing only the *activo* sexual role and begin meaningful homosexual relations while adolescents, experience some uneasiness over their homosexual activity if they stray from the exclusive inserter role. They often reduce this psychic conflict through increased heterosexual contacts (conquests) or by limiting their homosexuality to only the active sexual role ("Gay Liberation," 250).

In sum, it appears that the major difference between bisexually active men in Mexico and bisexual males in the U.S. is that the former are not stigmatized because they exclusively play the active, masculine, inserter role. Unlike in the North American context, "one drop of homosexuality" does not, ipso facto, make a Mexican male a *joto* or a *maricón*. As Carrier's research clearly documents, none of the active inserter participants in homosexual encounters ever considers himself a "homosexual" or to be "gay" ("Mexican Male," 83). What may be called the "bisexual escape hatch" functions to insure that the tenuous masculinity of Mexican men is not compromised through the homosexual act; they remain men, *hombres,* even though they participate in this sexual behavior. Moreover, the Mexican sexual system actually militates against the construction of discernable, discrete "bisexual" or "gay" sexual identities because these identities are shaped by and draw upon a different sexual system and foreign discursive practices. One does not, in other words, become "gay" or "lesbian" identified in Mexico because its sexual system precludes such an identity formation in the first place. These "bourgeois" sexual categories are simply not relevant or germane to the way gender and sexual meanings are conferred in Mexican society.

The Problematic Nature of a Gay Identity for Mexican Men

Given the contours of the Mexican sexual system, and the central role the Mexican family plays in structuring homosexual behavior, it is not surprising that North American sexual categories, identities, and identity-based social movements have only recently made their appearance in Mexico. Carrier has documented that the gay liberation movement is a very recent phenomenon in Mexico and one that has confronted formidable obstacles in taking root. For example, there existed as late as 1980 only a very small and submerged gay scene in large cities such as Mexico City, Guadalajara, and Acapulco. There are no distinct "gay neighborhoods" to speak of, and only a few gay bars and discos ("Gay Liberation," 225). Those Mexican men who define their sexual identity as "gay" have clearly adopted North American homosexual patterns, such as incorporating both passive and active sexual roles into their homosexual behavior. This more recent incarnation of the "modern Mexican homosexual" is widely considered to be based on North American sexual scripts, and the "foreign" nature of such sexual practices has caused the men who adopt them to be commonly referred to as *internacionales.*

> Gay Mexican males who fall into the *internacionales* category are difficult to assess as a group. . . . Most of them are masculine rather than feminine and during the early years of their sex lives play only the "activo" sexual role—the "pasivo" sexual role is incorporated later as they become more involved in homosexual encounters. Many "internacionales" state that although they may play both sex roles, they nevertheless retain a strong general preference for one over the other. ("Gay Liberation," 231)

It appears that gay liberation in Mexico is more readily advocated by the new, more masculine homosexual, who can utilize his gender conformity as a legitimating factor for embracing a gay lifestyle. These *macho maricas* (as they are referred to in Argentina [i.e., butch queens]) are most likely to develop a gay identity by "coming out of the closet" and becoming part of "los de Ambiente" (245). The masculine stance of the *internacionales* often places them at odds, however, with the more feminine *joto,* who also seeks self-affirmation and a less stigmatized status. Since these stigmatized, effeminate homosexuals have never thought of themselves as or claimed to be heterosexual, they reportedly experience less cognitive dissonance accepting a "gay" identity and fewer problems in coming out (250).

The recent emergence of this "gay" sexual identity in Mexico has brought with it a number of special problems for the homosexual Mexican man. Carrier argues that an ongoing source of tension within the emergent gay subculture typically crystallizes between

> . . . those homosexual males who are open and feminine and those who are not. Public demonstrations of feminine behavior by young gay males who consider it a basic part of their makeup is disturbing to those gay males who prefer to comport themselves

in more masculine ways and thus be less obvious in straight settings. . . . Although attempts have been made in the gay liberation movement to get its more masculine members to view feminine male behavior in a more positive way, they have had little success. ("Gay Liberation," 248)

Despite the incorporation of more bourgeois conceptions of sexuality, the privileging of masculinity among Mexican men—whether heterosexual or homosexual—remains a cornerstone of patriarchal Mexican society, which is very resistant to fundamental re-definition and cultural intrusion from the outside.

Implications for Chicano Gay Men in the U.S.

The emergence of the modern gay identity in the U.S. and its recent appearance in Mexico have implications for Chicano men that have not been fully explored. What is apparent, however, is that Chicanos, as well as other racial minorities, do not negotiate the acceptance of a gay identity in exactly the same way white American men do. The ambivalence of Chicanos vis-à-vis a gay sexual identity and their attendant uneasiness with white gay/lesbian culture do not necessarily reflect a denial of homosexuality. Rather, I would argue, the slow pace at which this identity formation has taken root among Chicanos is attributable to cultural and structural factors which differentiate the experiences of the white and non-white populations in the U.S.

Aside from the crucial differences discussed above in the way homosexuality is culturally constructed in the Mexican/Latin-American and European- or Anglo-American sexual systems, a number of other structural factors also militate against the emergence of a modern gay identity among Chicano men. In this regard, the progressive loosening of familial constraints among white, middle-class homosexual men and women at the end of the nineteenth century, and its acceleration in the post-World War II period, structurally positioned the white gay and lesbian population to redefine their primary self-identity in terms of their homosexuality. The shift from a family-based economy to a fully developed wage labor system at the end of the nineteenth century dramatically freed European-American men and women from the previously confining social and economic world of the family. It allowed both white men and the white "new woman" of the period to transgress the stifling gender roles that previously bound them to a compulsory heterosexual norm.[7] Extricating the nuclear family from its traditional role as a primary unit of production enabled homosexually inclined individuals to forge a new sexual identity and to develop a culture and community that were not previously possible. Moreover, the tremendous urban migration ignited (or precipitated) by World War II accelerated this process by drawing thousands of homosexuals into urban settings where the possibilities for same-sex intimacy were greater.

It is very apparent, however, that the gay identity and communities that emerged were overwhelmingly white, middle class, and male-centered. Leading figures of the first homophile organizations in the U.S., such as the Mattachine Society, and key individuals shaping the newly emergent gay culture were primarily drawn from this segment of the homosexual population. Moreover, the new communities founded in the postwar period were largely populated by white men who had the resources and talents needed to create "gilded" gay ghettos. This fact has given the contemporary gay community—despite its undeniable diversity—a largely white, middle-class, and male form. In other words, the unique class and racial advantages of white gay men provided the foundation upon which they could boldly carve out the new gay identity. Their collective position in the social structure empowered them with the skills and talents needed to create new gay institutions, communities, and a unique sexual subculture.

Despite the intense hostility that, as gay men, they faced during that period, nevertheless, as white gay men, they were in the best position to risk the social ostracism that this process engendered. They were *relatively* better situated than other homosexuals to endure the hazards unleashed by their transgression of gender conventions and traditional heterosexual norms. The diminished importance of ethnic identity among these individuals, due principally to the homogenizing and integrating impact of the dominant racial categories which defined them foremost as white, undoubtedly also facilitated the emergence of gay identity among them. As members of the privileged racial group—and thus no longer viewing themselves primarily as Irish, Italian, Jewish, Catholic, etc.—these middle-class men and women arguably no longer depended solely on their respective cultural groups and families as a line of defense against the dominant group. Although they may have continued to experience intense cultural dissonance leaving behind their ethnicity and their traditional family-based roles, they were now in a position to dare to make such a move.

Chicanos, on the other hand, have never occupied the social space where a gay or lesbian identity can readily become a primary basis of self-identity. This is due, in part, to their structural position at the subordinate ends of both the class and racial hierarchies, and in a context where ethnicity remains a primary basis of group identity and survival. Moreover, Chicano family life requires allegiance to patriarchal gender relations and to a system of sexual meanings that directly militate against the emergence of this alternative basis of self-identity. Furthermore, factors such as gender, geographical settlement, age, nativity, language usage, and degree of cultural assimilation further prevent, or at least complicate, the acceptance of a gay or lesbian identity by Chicanos or Chicanas respectively. They are not as free as individuals situated elsewhere in the social structure to redefine their sexual identity in ways that contravene the imperatives of minority family life and its traditional gender expectations. How they come to define their sexual identities as gay, straight, bisexual or, in Mexican/Latin-American terms, as an *activo, pasivo,* or *macho marica,* therefore, is not a straightforward or unmediated process. Unfortunately, there are no published studies to date exploring this identity formation process.

However, one study on homosexual Latino/Chicano men was conducted by Hector Carrillo and Horacio Maiorana in the spring of 1989. As part of their ongoing work on AIDS within the San Francisco Bay Area Latino community, these researchers developed a typology capturing the different points in a continuum differentiating the sexual identity of these men. Their preliminary typology is useful in that it delineates the way homosexual Chicanos/Latinos integrate elements of both the North American and Mexican sexual systems into their sexual behavior.

The first two categories of individuals, according to Carrillo and Maiorana, are: 1) Working-class Latino men who have adopted an effeminate gender persona and usually play the passive role in homosexual encounters (many of them are drag queens who frequent the Latino gay bars in the Mission District of San Francisco); and 2) Latino men who consider themselves heterosexual or bisexual, but who furtively have sex with other men. They are also primarily working class and often frequent Latino gay bars in search of discreet sexual encounters. They tend to retain a strong Latino or Chicano ethnic identity and structure their sexuality according to the Mexican sexual system. Although Carrillo and Maiorana do not discuss the issue, it seems likely that these men would primarily seek out other Latino men, rather than European-Americans, as potential partners in their culturally circumscribed homosexual behavior.

I would also suggest from personal observations that these two categories of individuals occasionally enter into sexual relationships with middle-class Latinos and European-American men. In so doing, these working-class Latino men often become the object of the middle-class Latino's or the white man's colonial desires. In one expression of this class-coded lust, the effeminate *pasivo* becomes the boyish, feminized object of the middle-class man's colonial desire. In another, the masculine Mexican/Chicano *activo* becomes the embodiment of a potent ethnic masculinity that titillates the middle-class man who thus enters into a passive sexual role.

Unlike the first two categories of homosexually active Latino men, the other three have integrated several features of the North American sexual system into their sexual behavior. They are more likely to be assimilated into the dominant European-American culture of the U.S. and to come from middle-class backgrounds. They include 3) Latino men who openly consider themselves gay and participate in the emergent gay Latino subculture in the Mission district; 4) Latino men who consider themselves gay but do not participate in the Latino gay subculture, preferring to maintain a primary identity as Latino and only secondarily a gay one; and, finally, 5) Latino men who are fully assimilated into the white San Francisco gay male community in the Castro District and retain only a marginal Latino identity.

In contrast to the former two categories, Latino men in the latter three categories are more likely to seek European-American sexual partners and exhibit greater difficulty in reconciling their Latino cultural backgrounds with their gay lifestyle. In my impressionistic observations, these men do not exclusively engage in homosexual behavior that is hierarchically differentiated along the gender-coded lines of the Mexican sexual system. They are more likely to integrate both active and passive sexual roles into their sexuality and to enter into relationships in which the more egalitarian norms of the North American sexual system prevail. We know very little, however, about the actual sexual conduct of these individuals. Research has not yet been conducted on how these men express their sexual desires, how they negotiate their masculinity in light of their homosexuality, and, more generally, how they integrate aspects of the two sexual system into their everyday sexual conduct.

In the absence of such knowledge, we may seek clues about the social world of Chicano gay men in the perceptive writings of Chicana lesbians. Being the first to shatter the silence on the homosexual experience of the Chicano population, they have candidly documented the perplexing issues Chicanos confront in negotiating the conflicting gender and sexual messages imparted by the coexisting Chicano and European-American cultures. The way in which Chicana lesbians have framed these problems, I believe, is bound to have major significance for the way Chicano men reconcile their homosexual behavior and gay sexual identity within a Chicano cultural context. More than any other lesbian writer's, the extraordinary work of Cherríe Moraga articulates a lucid and complex analysis of the predicament that the middle-class Chicana lesbian and Chicano gay man face in this society. A brief examination of her autobiographical writings offers important insights into the complexities and contradictions that may characterize the experience of homosexuality for all Chicanos and Chicanas in the U.S.

Cherríe Moraga and Chicana Lesbianism

An essential point of departure in assessing Cherríe Moraga's work is an appreciation of the way Chicano family life severely constrains the Chicana's ability to define her life outside of its stifling gender and sexual prescriptions. As a number of Chicana feminist scholars have clearly documented, Chicano family life remains rigidly structured along patriarchal lines that privilege men over women and children.[8] Any violation of these norms is undertaken at great personal risk because Chicanos draw upon the family to resist racism and the ravages of class inequality. Chicano men and women are drawn together in the face of these onslaughts and are closely bound into a family structure that exaggerates unequal gender roles and suppresses sexual non-conformity.[9] Therefore, any deviation from the sacred link binding husband, wife, and child not only threatens the very existence of *la familia* but also potentially undermines the mainstay of resistance to Anglo racism and class exploitation. "The family, then, becomes all the more ardently protected by oppressed people and the sanctity of this institution is infused like blood into the veins of the Chicano. At all costs, la familia must be preserved," writes Moraga. Thus, "we fight back . . . with our families—with our women pregnant, and our men as indispensable heads. We believe the more severely we protect the sex roles within the family, the stronger we will be as a unit in opposition to the anglo threat" (*Loving,* 110).

These cultural prescriptions do not, however, curb the sexually non-conforming behavior of certain Chicanos. As in the case of Mexican homosexual men in Mexico, there exists a modicum of freedom for the Chicano homosexual who retains a masculine gender identity while secretly engaging in the active homosexual role. Moraga has perceptively noted that the Latin cultural norm inflects the sexual behavior of homosexual Chicanos: "Male homosexuality has always been a 'tolerated' aspect of Mexican/Chicano society, as long as it remains 'fringe'. . . . But lesbianism, in any form, and male homosexuality which openly avows both the sexual and the emotional elements of the bond, challenge the very foundation of la familia" (111). The openly effeminate Chicano gay man's rejection of heterosexuality is typically seen as a fundamental betrayal of Chicano patriarchal cultural norms. He is viewed as having turned his back on the male role that privileges Chicano men and entitles them to sexual access to women, minors, and even other men. Those who reject these male prerogatives are viewed as non-men, as the cultural equivalents of women. Moraga astutely assesses the situation as one in which "the 'faggot' is the object of Chicano/Mexicano's contempt because he is consciously choosing a role his culture tells him to despise. That of a woman" (111).

The constraints that Chicano family life imposed on Moraga herself are candidly discussed in her provocative autobiographical essays "La Güera" and "A Long Line of Vendidas" in *Loving in the War Years.* In recounting her childhood in Southern California, Moraga describes how she was routinely required to make her brother's bed, iron his shirts, lend him money, and even serve him cold drinks when his friends came to visit their home. The privileged position of men in the Chicano family places women in a secondary, subordinate status. She resentfully acknowledges that "to this day in my mother's home, my brother and father are waited on, including by me" (90). Chicano men have always thought of themselves as superior to Chicanas, she asserts in unambiguous terms: "I have never met any kind of Latino who . . . did not subscribe to the basic belief that men are better" (101). The insidiousness of the patriarchal ideology permeating Chicano family life even shapes the way a mother defines her relationships with her children: "The daughter must constantly earn the mother's love, prove her fidelity to her. The son—he gets her love for free" (102).

Moraga realized early in life that she would find it virtually impossible to attain any meaningful autonomy in that cultural context. It was only in the Anglo world that freedom from oppressive gender and sexual strictures was remotely possible. In order to secure this latitude, she made a necessary choice: to embrace the white world and reject crucial aspects of her Chicana upbringing. In painfully honest terms, she states:

> I gradually became anglocized because I thought it was the only option available to
> me toward gaining autonomy as a person without being sexually stigmatized. . . . I

instinctively made choices which I thought would allow me greater freedom of movement in the future. This meant resisting sex roles as much as I could safely manage
and that was far easier in an anglo context than in a Chicano one. (99)

Born to a Chicana mother and an Anglo father, Moraga discovered that being fair-
complexioned facilitated her integration into the Anglo social world and contributed
immensely to her academic achievement. "My mother's desire to protect her children
from poverty and illiteracy" led to their being "anglocized," she writes; "the more
effectively we could pass in the white world, the better guaranteed our future" (51).
Consequently her life in Southern California during the 1950s and 1960s is described
as one in which she "identified with and aspired toward white values" (58). In the
process, she "rode the wave of that Southern California privilege as far as conscience
would let me" (58).

The price initially exacted by anglicization was estrangement from family and a
partial loss of the nurturing and love she found therein. In reflecting on this experience,
Moraga acknowledges that "I have had to confront that much of what I value about
being Chicana, about my family, has been subverted by anglo culture and my cooperation
with it. . . . I realized the major reason for my total alienation from and fear of my
classmates was rooted in class and culture" (54). She poignantly concedes that, in the
process, "I had disavowed the language I knew best—ignored the words and rhythms
that were closest to me. The sounds of my mother and aunts gossiping—half in English,
half in Spanish—while drinking cerveza in the kitchen" (55). What she gained, on the
other hand, was the greater autonomy that her middle-class white classmates had in
defining their emergent sexuality and in circumventing burdensome gender prescriptions. Her movement into the white world, however, was viewed by Chicanos as a great
betrayal. By gaining control of her life, Moraga became one of a "long line of vendidas,"
traitors or "sell-outs," as self-determined women are seen in the sexist cultural fantasy
of patriarchal Chicano society. This is the accusation that "hangs above the heads and
beats in the hearts of most Chicanas, seeking to develop our own autonomous sense of
ourselves, particularly our sexuality" (103).

Patriarchal Chicano culture, with its deep roots in "the institution of heterosexuality," requires Chicanas to commit themselves to Chicano men and subordinate to
them their own sexual desires. "[The Chicano] too, like any other man," Moraga writes,
"wants to be able to determine how, when, and with whom his women—mother, wife,
and daughter—are sexual" (110–11). But "the Chicana's sexual commitment to the
Chicano male [is taken as] proof of her fidelity to her people" (105). "It is no wonder,"
she adds, that most "Chicanas often divorce ourselves from conscious recognition of our
own sexuality" (119). In order to claim the identity of a Chicana lesbian, Moraga had
to take "a radical stand in direct contradiction to, and in violation of, the women [sic]
I was raised to be" (117); and yet she also drew upon themes and images of her Mexican
Catholic background. Of its impact on her sexuality Moraga writes:

> I always knew that I felt the greatest emotional ties with women, but suddenly I was
> beginning to consciously identify those feelings as sexual. The more potent my dreams
> and fantasies became and the more I sensed my own exploding sexual power, the
> more I *retreated* from my body's messages and into the region of religion. By giving
> definition and meaning to my desires, religion became the discipline to control my
> sexuality. Sexual fantasy and rebellion became "impure thoughts" and "sinful acts."
> (119)

These "contrary feelings," which initially surfaced around the age of twelve, unleashed
feelings of guilt and moral transgression. She found it impossible to leave behind the

Catholic Church's prohibitions regarding homosexuality, and religious themes found their way into how she initially came to define herself as a sexual subject—in a devil-like form. "I wrote poems describing myself as a centaur: half-animal/half-human, hairy-rumped and cloven-hoofed, como el diablo. The images emerged from a deeply Mexican and Catholic place" (124).

As her earliest sexual feelings were laden with religious images, so too were they shaped by images of herself in a male-like form. This is understandable in light of the fact that only men in Chicano culture are granted sexual subjectivity. Consequently, Moraga instinctively gravitated toward a butch persona and assumed a male-like stance toward other women.

> In the effort to avoid embodying la chingada, I became the chingón. In the effort not to feel fucked, I became the fucker, even with women. . . . The fact of the matter was that all those power struggles of "having" and "being had" were played out in my own bedroom. And in my psyche, they held a particular Mexican twist. (126)

In a candid and courageously outspoken conversation with lesbian activist Amber Hollibaugh, Moraga recounts that

> . . . what turned me on sexually, at a very early age, had to do with the fantasy of capture, taking a woman, and my identification was with the man. . . . The truth is, I do have some real gut-level misgivings about my sexual connection with capture. It might feel very sexy to imagine "taking" a woman, but it has sometimes occurred at the expense of my feeling, sexually, like I can surrender myself to a woman; that is, always needing to be the one in control, calling the shots. It's a very butch trip and I feel like this can keep me private and protected and can prevent me from fully being able to express myself. (Moraga and Hollibaugh, 396)

Moraga's adult lesbian sexuality defined itself along the traditional butch/femme lines characteristic of lesbian relationships in the postwar period.[10] It is likely that such an identity formation was also largely an expression of the highly gender-coded sexuality imparted through Chicano family life. In order to define herself as an autonomous sexual subject, she embraced a butch, or more masculine, gender persona, and crystallized a sexual desire for feminine, or femme, lovers. She discusses the significance of this aspect of her sexuality in these terms:

> I feel the way I want a woman can be a very profound experience. Remember I told you how when I looked up at my lover's face when I was making love to her (I was actually just kissing her breast at the moment) . . . I could feel and see how deeply every part of her was present? That every pore in her body was entrusting me to handle her, to take care of her sexual desire. This look on her face is like nothing else. It fills me up. She entrusts me to determine where she'll go sexually. And I honestly feel a power inside me strong enough to heal the deepest wound. (Moraga and Hollibaugh, 398)

In assuming the butch role, Moraga was not seeking simply to cast herself as a man or merely to mimic the male role in the sexual act. Becoming a butch Chicana lesbian was much more complex than that and carried with it a particular pain and uneasiness:

> I think that there is a particular pain attached if you identified yourself as a butch queer from an early age as I did. I didn't really think of myself as female, or male. I thought of myself as this hybrid or somethin. I just kinda thought of myself as this free agent until I got tits. Then I thought, oh no, some problem has occurred here. . . . For me, the way you conceive of yourself as a woman and the way I am attracted to women sexually reflects that butch/femme exchange—where a woman believes herself so woman that it really makes me want her.

But for me, I feel a lot of pain around the fact that it has been difficult for me to conceive of myself as thoroughly female in that sexual way. So retaining my "butchness" is not exactly my desired goal. . . . How I fantasize sex roles has been really different for me with different women. I do usually enter into an erotic encounter with a woman from the kind of butch place you described, but I have also felt very ripped off there, finding myself taking all the sexual responsibility. I am seriously attracted to butches sometimes. It's a very different dynamic, where the sexuality may not seem as fluid or comprehensible, but I know there's a huge part of me that wants to be handled in the way I described I can handle another woman. I am very compelled toward that "lover" posture. I have never totally reckoned with being the "beloved" and, frankly, I don't know if it takes a butch or a fem or what to get me there. I know that it's a struggle within me and it scares the shit out of me to look at it so directly. I've done this kind of searching emotionally, but to combine sex with it seems like very dangerous stuff. (Moraga and Hollibaugh, 400–01)

A crucial dimension of the dissonance Moraga experienced in accepting her lesbian sexuality and reconciling the Anglo and Chicano worlds was the conscious awareness that her sexual desires reflected a deeply felt love for her mother. "In contrast to the seeming lack of feelings I had for my father," she writes, "my longings for my mother and fear of her dying were the most passionate feelings that had ever lived inside of my young heart" (*Loving,* 93). These feelings led her to the realization that both the affective and sexual dimensions of her lesbianism were indelibly shaped by the love for her mother. "When I finally lifted the lid on my lesbianism, a profound connection with mother awakened in me" (52), she recalls. "Yes, this is why I love women. This woman is my mother. There is no love as strong as this, refusing my separation, never settling for a secret that would split us off, always at the last minute, like now, pushing me to [the] brink of revelation, speaking the truth" (102).

The Final Frontier: Unmasking the Chicano Gay Man

Moraga's experience is certainly only one expression of the diverse ways in which Chicana lesbians come to define their sense of gender and experience their homosexuality. But her odyssey reflects and articulates the tortuous and painful path traveled by working-class Chicanas (and Chicanos) who embrace the middle-class Anglo world and its sexual system in order to secure, ironically, the "right to passion expressed in our own cultural tongue and movements" (136). It is apparent from her powerful autobiographical writings, however, how much her adult sexuality was also inevitably shaped by the gender and sexual messages imparted through the Chicano family.

How this complex process of integrating, reconciling, and contesting various features of both Anglo and Chicano cultural life are experienced by Chicano gay men, has yet to be fully explored. Moraga's incisive and extraordinarily frank autobiographical account raises numerous questions about the parallels in the homosexual development of Chicana lesbians and Chicano gay men. How, for example, do Chicano male homosexuals internalize and reconcile the gender-specific prescriptions of Chicano culture? How does this primary socialization impact on the way they define their gender personas and sexual identities? How does socialization into a patriarchal gender system that privileges men over women and the masculine over the feminine structure intimate aspects of their sexual behavior? Do most Chicano gay men invariably organize aspects of their sexuality along the hierarchical lines of dominance/subordination that circumscribe gender roles and relationships in Chicano culture? My impression is that many Chicano gay men share the Chicano heterosexual man's underlying disdain for women and all that is feminine. Although it has not been documented empirically, it is likely that Chicano gay men incorporate and contest crucial features of the Mexican/Latin-American sexual system into their intimate sexual behavior. Despite having accepted a "modern" sexual identity, they are not immune to the hierarchical, gender-coded system of sexual meanings that is part and parcel of this discursive practice.

Until we can answer these questions through ethnographic research on the lives of Chicano gay men, we must continue to develop the type of feminist critique of Chicano male culture that is so powerfully articulated in the work of lesbian authors such as Cherríe Moraga. We are fortunate that courageous voices such as hers have irretrievably shattered the silence on the homosexual experience within the Mexican American community. Her work, and that of other Chicana lesbians, has laid a challenge before Chicano gay men to lift the lid on their homosexual experiences and to leave the closeted space they have been relegated to in Chicano culture. The task confronting us, therefore, is to begin interpreting and redefining what it means to be both Chicano and gay in a cultural setting that has traditionally viewed these categories as a contradiction in terms. This is an area of scholarly research that can no longer be left outside the purview of Chicano Studies, Gay and Lesbian Studies, or even more traditional lines of sociological inquiry.

NOTES

I gratefully acknowledge the valuable comments on an earlier version of this article by Jackie Goldsby, David Halperin, Teresa de Lauretis, Bob Blauner, Carla Trujillo, Patricia Zavella, Velia Garcia, and Ramón Gutiérrez.

1. See, for example, the writings by Chicana and Latina lesbians in Ramos; Alarcón, Castillo, and Moraga; Moraga and Anzaldúa; and Anzaldúa. See also the following studies on Latinas: Arguelles and Rich; Espin; and Hidalgo and Hidalgo-Christensen.

2. See Bruce-Novoa's interesting discussion of homosexuality as a theme in the Chicano novel.

3. There is a rich literature documenting the ways in which our sexuality is largely structured through sexual scripts that are culturally defined and individually internalized. See, for example, Gagnon and Simon; Simon and Gagnon; and Plummer. What is being referred to here as the Mexican/Latin-American sexual system is part of the circum-Mediterranean construction of gender and sexual meaning. In this regard, see the introduction and essays in Gilmore. For further discussion of this theme in the Mexican context, see Alonso and Koreck. Their essay, which uses many of the same sources as the present essay, explores male homosexual practices in Mexico in relation to AIDS.

4. For a Chicana feminist critique of Paz's discussion of *la Malinche,* see Alarcón.

5. Chicano machismo may also be seen as "a culturally defined hypermasculine ideal model of manliness through which a Mexican male may measure himself, his sons, and his male relatives and friends against such attributes as courage, dominance, power, aggressiveness, and invulnerability" (Carrier, "Gay Liberation," 228).

6. In "Birth of the Queen," Trumbach has perceptively documented that many of the contemporary terms used to refer to homosexual men in Western Europe and the United States (such as queen, punk, gay, faggot, and fairy) also were at one time the slang term for prostitutes (137). See also Alonso and Koreck, 111–13.

7. For a broad overview of the development of a gay and lesbian identity and community in the United States, see D'Emilio; D'Emilio and Freedman; and Katz. A number of articles in the important anthology edited by Duberman, Vicinus, and Chauncey document the white middle class-centered nature of gay/lesbian identity construction and community formation. In particular see Smith-Rosenberg; Newton; Rupp; and Martin.

8. Some of the very best research in Chicano Studies has been conducted by Chicana feminists who have explored the intersection of class, race, and gender in Chicanas' lives. Some recent examples of this impressive scholarship include Zavella; Segura; Pesquera; and Baca-Zinn.

9. This solidarity is captured in the early Chicano movement poster fittingly entitled "La Familia." It consists of three figures in a symbolic pose: a Mexican woman, with a child in her arms, is embraced by a Mexican man, who is centrally positioned in the portrait and a head taller. This poster symbolized the patriarchal, male-centered privileging of the heterosexual, nuclear family in Chicano resistance against white racism. For a provocative discussion of these themes in the Chicano movement see Gutiérrez.

10. For an interesting discussion of the butch/femme formulation among working class white women at the time, see Davis and Kennedy; and Nestle.

WORKS CITED

Adam, Barry D. "Homosexuality without a Gay World: Pasivos y Activos en Nicaragua." *Out/Look* 1.4 (1989): 74–82.

Alarcón, Norma. "Chicana's Feminist Literature: A Re-vision Through Malintzin/or Malintzin: Putting Flesh Back on the Object." Moraga and Anzaldúa, 182–90.

Alarcón, Norma, Ana Castillo, and Cherríe Moraga, eds. *Third Woman: The Sexuality of Latinas.* Berkeley: Third Woman, 1989.

Alonso, Ana Maria, and Maria Teresa Koreck. "Silences: 'Hispanics,' AIDS, and Sexual Practices." *differences: A Journal of Feminist Cultural Studies* 1.1 (1989): 101–24. Reprinted in this volume.

Anzaldúa, Gloria. *Borderlands/La Frontera: The New Mestiza.* San Francisco: Spinsters, 1987.

Arguelles, Lourdes, and B. Ruby Rich. "Homosexuality, Homophobia, and Revolution: Notes Toward an Understanding of the Cuban Lesbian and Gay Male Experience, Part 1." *Signs: Journal of Women in Culture and Society* 9 (1984): 683–99.

——— "Homosexuality, Homophobia, and Revolution: Notes Toward an Understanding of the Cuban Lesbian and Gay Male Experience, Part 2." *Signs: Journal of Women in Culture and Society* 11 (1985): 120–36.

Baca-Zinn, Maxine. "Chicano Men and Masculinity." *The Journal of Ethnic Studies* 10.2 (1982): 29–44.

——— "Familism Among Chicanos: A Theoretical Review." *Humboldt Journal of Social Relations* 10.1 (1982–83): 224–38.

Blackwood, Evelyn, ed. *The Many Faces of Homosexuality: Anthropological Approaches to Homosexual Behavior.* New York: Harrington Park, 1989.

Bruce-Novoa, Juan. "Homosexuality and the Chicano Novel." *Confluencia: Revista Hispanica de Cultura y Literatura* 2.1 (1986): 69–77.

Carrier, Joseph M. "Cultural Factors Affecting Urban Mexican Male Homosexual Behavior." *The Archives of Sexual Behavior: An Interdisciplinary Research Journal* 5.2 (1976): 103–24.

——— "Family Attitudes and Mexican Male Homosexuality." *Urban Life: A Journal of Ethnographic Research* 5.3 (1976): 359–76.

——— "Gay Liberation and Coming Out in Mexico." Herdt, 225–53.

——— "Mexican Male Bisexuality." *Bisexualities: Theory and Research.* Ed. F. Klein and T. Wolf. New York: Haworth, 1985. 75–85.

Carrillo, Hector, and Horacio Maiorana. "AIDS Prevention Among Gay Latinos in San Francisco: From Behavior Change to Social Change." Unpublished ms., 1989.

Davis, Madeline, and Elizabeth Lapovsky Kennedy. "Oral History and the Study of Sexuality in the Lesbian Community: Buffalo, New York, 1940–1960." Duberman et al., 426–40.

D'Emilio, John. "Capitalism and Gay Identity." Snitow, Stansell, and Thompson, 100–13.

——— *Sexual Politics, Sexual Communities: The Making of a Homosexual Minority in the United States, 1940–1970.* Chicago: Univ. of Chicago Press, 1983.

D'Emilio, John, and Estelle B. Freedman. *Intimate Matters: A History of Sexuality in America.* New York: Harper, 1988.

Duberman, Martin Bauml, Martha Vicinus, and George Chauncey Jr., eds. *Hidden from History: Reclaiming the Gay and Lesbian Past.* New York: NAL, 1989.

Espin, Oliva M. "Cultural and Historical Influences on Sexuality in Hispanic/Latin Women: Implications for Psychotherapy." *Pleasure and Danger: Exploring Female Sexuality*. Ed. Carol Vance. London: Routledge, 1984. 149–63.

———— "Issues of Identity in the Psychology of Latina Lesbians." *Lesbian Psychologies*. Ed. Boston Lesbian Psychologies Collective. Urbana: Univ. of Illinois Press, 1987. 35–55.

Freud, Sigmund. *Three Essays on the Theory of Sexuality*. 1905. *The Standard Edition of the Complete Psychological Works of Sigmund Freud*. Trans. and ed. James Strachey. Vol. 7. London: Hogarth, 1953. 123–243.

Gagnon, John H., and William Simon. *Sexual Conduct: The Social Sources of Human Sexuality*. Chicago: Aldine, 1973.

Gilmore, David D., ed. *Honor and Shame and the Unity of the Mediterranean*. No. 22. Washington: American Anthropological Association, 1987.

Goldwert, Marvin. "Mexican Machismo: The Flight from Femininity." *Psychoanalytic Review* 72.1 (1985): 161–69.

Gutiérrez, Ramón. "Community, Patriarchy, and Individualism: The Politics of Chicano History and the Dream of Equality." Forthcoming in *American Quarterly*.

Herdt, Gilbert, ed. *Gay and Lesbian Youth*. New York: Haworth, 1989.

Hidalgo, Hilda, and Elia Hidalgo-Christensen. "The Puerto Rican Lesbian and the Puerto Rican Community." *Journal of Homosexuality* 2 (1976–77): 109–21.

———— "The Puerto Rican Cultural Response to Female Homosexuality." *The Puerto Rican Woman*. Ed. Edna Acosta-Belen. New York: Praeger, 1979. 110–23.

Islas, Arturo. *Immigrant Souls*. New York: Morrow, 1990.

———— *The Rain God: A Desert Tale*. Palo Alto, CA: Alexandrian, 1984.

Katz, Jonathan Ned. *Gay/Lesbian Almanac: A New Documentary*. New York: Harper, 1983.

Lancaster, Roger N. "Subject Honor and Object Shame: The Construction of Male Homosexuality and Stigma in Nicaragua." *Ethnology* 27.2 (1987): 111–25.

Martin, Robert K. "Knights-Errant and Gothic Seducers: The Representation of Male Friendship in Mid-Nineteenth Century America." Duberman et al., 169–82.

Moraga, Cherríe. *Loving in the War Years: Lo que nunca pasó por sus labios*. Boston: South End, 1983.

Moraga, Cherríe, and Gloria Anzaldúa, eds. *This Bridge Called My Back: Writings by Radical Women of Color*. Watertown, MA: Persephone, 1981.

Moraga, Cherríe, and Amber Hollibaugh. "What We're Rollin Around in Bed With: Sexual Silences in Feminism." Snitow, Stansell, and Thompson, 394–405.

Nestle, Joan. "Butch-Fem Relationships: Sexual Courage in the 1950s." *Heresies* 12 (1981): 21–24.

Newton, Esther. "The Mythic Mannish Lesbian: Radclyffe Hall and the New Woman." Duberman et al., 281–93.

Parker, Richard. "Youth Identity, and Homosexuality: The Changing Shape of Sexual Life in Contemporary Brazil." Herdt, 269–89.

Paz, Octavio. *Labyrinth of Solitude: Life and Thought in Mexico*. New York: Grove, 1961.

Pesquera, Beatriz M. "Work and Family: A Comparative Analysis of Professional, Clerical and Blue-Collar Chicana Workers." PhD diss. Univ. of California, Berkeley, 1985.

Plummer, Kenneth. "Symbolic Interaction and Sexual Conduct: An Emergent Perspective." *Human Sexual Relations*. Ed. Mike Brake. New York: Pantheon, 1982. 223–44.

Ramos, Juanita, ed. *Compañeras: Latina Lesbians*. New York: Latina Lesbian History Project, 1987.

Rechy, John. *City of Night*. New York: Grove, 1963.

———— *Numbers*. New York: Grove, 1967.

———— *Rushes*. New York: Grove, 1979.

———— *The Sexual Outlaw*. New York: Grove, 1977.

Rodriguez, Richard. *Hunger of Memory: The Education of Richard Rodriguez, An Autobiography*. Boston: Godine, 1982.

———— "Late Victorians: San Francisco, AIDS, and the Homosexual Stereotype." *Harper's Magazine* (Oct. 1990): 57–66.

———— "Masculinity, Femininity, and Homosexuality: On the Anthropological Interpretation of Sexual Meanings in Brazil." Blackwood, 155–64.

Rupp, Leila J. "Imagine My Surprise: Woman's Relationships in Mid-Twentieth Century America." Duberman et al., 395–410.

Segura, Denise. "Chicanas and Mexican Immigrant Women in the Labor Market: A Study of Occupational Mobility and Stratification." PhD diss. Univ. of California, Berkeley, 1986.

——— "Chicana and Mexican Immigrant Women at Work: The Impact of Class, Race, and Gender on Occupational Mobility." *Gender and Society* 3.1 (1989): 37–52.

——— "The Interplay of Familism and Patriarchy on Employment Among Chicana and Mexican Women." *Renato Rosaldo Lecture Series* 5 (1989): 35–53.

Simon, William, and John H. Gagnon. "Sexual Scripts: Permanence and Change." *Archives of Sexual Behavior* 15.2 (1986): 97–120.

Smith-Rosenberg, Carroll. "Discourses of Sexuality and Subjectivity: The New Woman, 1870–1936." Duberman et al., 264–80.

Snitow, Ann, Christine Stansell, and Sharon Thompson, eds. *Powers of Desire: The Politics of Sexuality.* New York: Monthly Review, 1983.

Taylor, Clark L. "Mexican Male Homosexual Interaction in Public Contexts." Blackwood, 117–36.

Trumbach, Randolph. "The Birth of the Queen: Sodomy and the Emergence of Gender Equality in Modern Culture, 1660–1750." Duberman et al., 129–40.

Zavella, Patricia. *Women's Work and Chicano Families: Cannery Workers of the Santa Clara Valley.* Ithaca: Cornell Univ. Press, 1987.

18

Lesbian Identity and Autobiographical Difference[s]

Biddy Martin

Biddy Martin is a feminist theorist and a critic of German literature and culture. In this article she suggests that much of the lesbian autobiographical writing of the 1970s, however valuable, may be in some ways misleading. It may tend to promote a view of lesbian identity as uniform and monolithic, as based primarily on a shared psychological experience or perspective, and as devoid of any sort of sexuality except that stemming from the tradition of romantic friendship among women. But in autobiographical writings dating mostly from the 1980s and exemplified by This Bridge Called My Back, *Martin finds a cogent corrective to the earlier tendency. Here lesbian identity is neither monolithic nor reducible to psychology. Identity is instead a site of the complex interactions of many variables, including race, class, gender, and sexual practice. Biddy Martin is the author of* Woman and Modernity: The (Life)Styles of Lou Andreas-Salomé *(1991), and she is completing a book of essays on the construction of lesbian identities. She is associate professor of German Studies and Women's Studies at Cornell University.*

No theoretical reading of "lesbian autobiography" can fail to take up the question of the category itself. Under the circumstances, it seems almost obligatory to begin with a set of questions designed to introduce some margin of difference into that apparently airtight package. To write *about* lesbian autobiography or even lesbian autobiographies as if such a totalizable, intelligible object or its multiplication simply existed would be to beg a number of questions, for example, what a lesbian life is, what autobiography is, and what the relation between them could possibly be. There is no singular answer to such questions, however ingenious the attempt to mask partial, provisional, interested responses with claims to generality, universality, or authority. Any attempt to give a definitive or singular answer to these three questions must be rendered suspect.

Much recent lesbian writing is autobiographical, often taking the form of auto-biographical essay and coming-out stories, and I will return to that writing. There are full-blown, bound autobiographies by authors who define themselves quite explicitly as lesbians. If we lend credence to the lesbian reader's sensitivity to the ways in which lesbianism is encoded in only apparently "straight" autobiographical accounts, then there are many more lesbian autobiographies. And if we abandon the obsession with the author's identity, the text's mimetic function and the reader's necessary identification, if we then consider the reader's pleasure, the ways in which she feels addressed, her desire engaged, then the question of what is lesbian about a life or an account of a life shifts much more dramatically. In 1978 Bertha Harris suggested that lesbian writing engaged a desire and an excess that defied the fixity of identity, the boundaries drawn round individual subjects, around all forms of categorization and normalization. Her lobbying efforts for an avant-garde or modernist writing included the infamous and curious claim that *Jaws,* in its celebration of unassimilable monstrosity, was a far more lesbian novel than the far more "conventional" fiction written in the 1970s by self-declared lesbians.[1] In 1987 there are surely (lesbian) readers who would find, say, a Roland Barthes to be a far more "lesbian" autobiographer than some explicitly lesbian writers. I would not ordinarily go so far, but here, under the weight of that certain identification "lesbian autobiography," such extreme claims acquire a certain allure. They also constitute a certain danger, given the institutional privileges enjoyed by those who can afford to disavow "identity" and its "limits" over against those for whom such disavowals reproduce their invisibility.

Of course, "lesbian autobiography," in its bound singularity, could appear to be a match made in a rather conventional heaven, plagued as both terms are historically by "facile assumptions of referentiality."[2] Their combination brings out the most conventional interpretation in each, for the *lesbian* in front of *autobiography* reinforces conventional assumptions of the transparency of autobiographical writing. And the *autobiography* that follows *lesbian* suggests that sexual identity not only modifies but essentially defines a life, providing it with predictable content and an identity possessing continuity and universality. Set apart in a volume on women's life stories, "lesbian autobiography" suggests that there is something coherently different about lesbians' lives vis-à-vis other lives and that there is something coherently the same about all lesbians. We could attempt to introduce difference into the category by speaking of lesbians' autobiographies and emphasizing the differences between the experiences of various lesbians. Many of the collections of coming-out stories and autobiographical narratives are organized on this very principle. However, differences, for example, of race, class, or sexuality, are finally rendered noncontradictory by virtue of their (re)presentation as differences between individuals, reducible to questions of identity within the unifying context of feminism. What remains unexamined are the systemic institutional relationships between those differences, relationships that exceed the boundaries of the lesbian community, the women's movement, or particular individuals, and in which apparently bounded communities and individuals are deeply implicated.

The isolation of lesbian autobiography here may have strategic political value, given the continued, or perhaps renewed, invisibility of lesbians even in feminist work, but it also marks lesbianism in a way that gives "women's autobiography" a curiously unmarked and unifying quality, reproducing the marginality of lesbianism and its containment in particular types of people. Lesbianism loses its potential as a position from which to read against the grain of narratives of normal life course, and becomes simply the affirmation of something separated out and defined as "lesbian." Of course, the problem of essentialism inevitably plagues not only scholarly volumes committed to representing differences among women; it has plagued and continues to plague lesbian and gay politics and writing as well. In fact, it is the risk taken by any identity politics. Claims to difference conceived in terms of different identities have operated and continue to operate as interventions in facile assumptions of "sisterhood," assumptions that have tended to mask the operation of white, middle-class, heterosexual "womanhood" as the hidden but hegemonic referent. Challenges to the erasure of difference in the name of another identity, however, limit the potential for subversion and critique by recontaining the discursive/institutional operations of "differences" in discrete categories of individuals, thereby rendering difference a primarily psychological "problem." A number of marginalized communities now face important questions about the possibility of reconceptualizing identity without abandoning it and its strategic deployment altogether. I suggest that such reconceptualizations of identity and of community have emerged in recent autobiographical writing and on the very grounds of identity and community.

The work of Michel Foucault has been essential in gay studies to a critique of identity politics, of the ways in which sexuality comes to constitute the ground of identity, and autobiographical gestures the exclusive ground of politics.[3] Several claims have made their way into gay historiography and into discussions of the politics of "coming out": first, that homosexual identity, the "homosexual" as a particular type of personality, was an invention of the late nineteenth century, and further, that the creation of the homosexual as type was, in the words of Jeffrey Minson, part of "the efforts in the human sciences to regulate and control by way of the construction of definite categories of personality."[4] At the same time that "deviance" and "perversion" were located and confined in marginal types and communities, sexual pathologies of all kinds were discovered to be potentials in "the normal family," justifying the intervention of pedagogical, medical, psychiatric, and social welfare experts. At stake in late nineteenth-century Europe was the health of the "family" and its role in securing the health of the "race." Foucault locates the deployment of sexuality at the center of a racist eugenics.[5]

In contrast, then, to conventional assumptions that the Victorian age was characterized by the repression of sexuality, Foucault argues that sexualities and discourse on sexuality proliferated in the late nineteenth century; moreover, he asserts that the deployment of sexuality as an apparatus of normalization and control involved the inducement to speak the truth of one's sexuality, to locate the truth of one's self in a buried sexual essence, and to confuse autobiographical gestures with liberation. The "repressive hypothesis" itself served to mask the actual workings of power. Laying claim, then, to one's sexuality and the rights associated with it, insisting on the freedom to speak freely of one's sexuality, risks subjection to regulation and control. Foucault's critique of the association of sexuality and truth and their location in the depths of the only apparently autonomous individual externalizes questions presumed to be internal and psychological by throwing them onto social and discursive axes. Hayden White characterizes Foucault's challenge to the illusions of the bourgeois subject: "Foucault resists the impulse to seek an origin or transcendental subject which would confer any specific 'meaning' on human life. Foucault's discourse is willfully superficial. And this is consistent with the larger purpose of a thinker who wishes to dissolve the distinction between surfaces and depths, to show that wherever this distinction arises, it is evidence of the play of organized power."[6] Foucault challenges any belief in the autonomy of the psychological, thereby contesting what Arthur Brittan and Mary Maynard have called the derivation of both racism and sexism "from the operation of the irrational, from the hidden depths of the human psyche."[7] Foucault's critique pushes "identity politics" off the exclusive grounds of identity to questions of alternative social and communicative forms, away from claims to "rights" and "choice" to questions about "the social relationships in which choice becomes meaningful."[8] It may also, however, as a number of feminist critics have noted, work to suppress questions of subjective agency, indeed, to render self-determination unthinkable.

Teresa de Lauretis remains one of the most persistent critics of Foucault and discourse theory for neutralizing gender by conceiving it as pure discursive effect and for suppressing questions of subjective agency and self-representation. In her introduction to *Technologies of Gender,* de Lauretis also uses Foucault's work to criticize American cultural feminists for reproducing conceptions of gender as "sexual difference," i.e., woman's difference from man.[9] She identifies the heterosexual social contract and its constant assumption in feminist as well as nonfeminist writing as a primary site for the reproduction of "just two neatly divided genders." Such assumptions obscure the ways in which gender is constructed across a range of discursive and institutional lines, and always at the intersections of class, race, and ethnicity. Drawing on Foucault's technologies of sexuality, de Lauretis's conception of the "technologies of gender" serves not only to separate gender from any apparent continuity with biology but also to suggest that there is no one monolithic ideology of gender.

De Lauretis's double-edged critique of American feminist identity politics and of Foucault points to the importance of reconceptualizing "experience" and "identity" without abandoning attention to "the semiotic interaction of 'outer world' and 'inner world,' the continuous engagement of a self or subject in social reality."[10] To her earlier formulation of the tensions between that ideological distillate "Woman" and historical, empirical "women," de Lauretis adds a third term, "the subject of feminism," the space of an "elsewhere," in order to point to the irreducibility of "women" to any one ideology of gender:

> By the phrase "the subject of feminism" I mean a conception or an understanding of the (female) subject as not only distinct from Woman with the capital letter . . . but also distinct from women, the real historical beings and social subjects who are defined by the technology of gender and actually engendered in social relations. The subject of feminism I have in mind is one *not* so defined, one whose definition or conception is in progress.[11]

According to de Lauretis, this subject must be sought not in particular persons or groups— i.e., not in identities—but in "micropolitical practices," practices of self-representation which illuminate the contradictory, multiple construction of subjectivity at the intersections, but also in the interstices of ideologies of gender, race, and sexuality.

De Lauretis draws on the autobiographical writing of women of color to suggest that identity can be reconceptualized on its very grounds. She is one of several feminist critics who read recent autobiographical writing by women of color in the United States as "representational practices" that illuminate the "contradictory, multiple construction of subjectivity." This autobiographical writing actually complicates de Lauretis's own earlier formulation of the inevitable tensions between the negativity of theory and the positivity of politics by robbing theory of its exclusive claim to negativity and suggesting a new imbrication of theory and personal history.

I am interested here in recent autobiographical writings that work against self-evidently homogeneous conceptions of identity, writings in which lesbianism comes to figure as something other than a "totalizing self-identification" and to be located on other than exclusively psychological grounds.[12] These recent writings necessarily take up, even as they work against, already conventional lesbian-feminist narratives of lesbian experience. Encounters between and among feminists over racism and anti-Semitism have played a crucial role in pushing identity politics, generally, and lesbian identity, in particular, beyond the apparent impasses of the late 1970s and early 1980s. The autobiographical contributions to *This Bridge Called My Back,* edited by Cherríe Moraga and Gloria Anzaldúa (1981), serve as a concrete example of how the politics of identity has been challenged on its very grounds. For the writings of Moraga, Anzaldúa, and others participate in attempts to attend to the irreducibly complex intersections of race, gender, and sexuality, attempts that both directly and indirectly work against assumptions that there are no differences within the "lesbian self" and that lesbian authors, autobiographical subjects, readers, and critics can be conflated and marginalized as self-identical and separable from questions of race, class, sexuality, and ethnicity. I will conclude with a discussion of how the encounter with racism and its complexities has informed the autobiographical writing of two southern white lesbian writers, Minnie

Bruce Pratt and Mab Segrest. In the exchange between the work of women of color and that of white lesbian writers, only apparently discrete and unified identities are rendered complex by attention to the imbrications of different personal and community histories.

Before I take up these exchanges in more detail, let me recall the forms of lesbian identity against which recent autobiographical texts implicitly, when not explicitly, react and on which they necessarily rely. In her review of the most widely read collections of coming-out stories and autobiographical essays of the 1970s and early 1980s, Bonnie Zimmerman argues that the centrality of autobiography in lesbian writing is fundamentally connected with the emergence of a lesbian-feminist politics of experience and identity.[13] Self-worth, identity, and a sense of community have fundamentally depended on the production of a shared narrative or life history and on the assimilation of individuals' life histories into the history of the group. This autobiographical writing has specific purposes in the (not always synchronous) histories of the community and of the individuals who write or read them; it aims to give lesbian identity a coherence and legitimacy that can make both individual and social action possible. The coming-out stories and autobiographical essays collected in such volumes as *The Coming Out Stories, The Lesbian Path, The New Lesbians* are responses to the at least implicit question of what it means to be a lesbian, how lesbianism figures in a life, what it means to come out. In a stricter sense, they are accounts of the process of becoming conscious of oneself as a lesbian, about accepting and affirming that identity against enormous odds, including, of course, the authors' own resistance to the label. Hence, lesbianism becomes the central moment around which women's lives are reconstructed. These narratives appear in journals and anthologies committed quite explicitly to making the realities of lesbians' lives visible in accessible terms, committed, in short, to presence. They are addressed to a reading community assumed to be (or to have the potential to be) lesbian. They assume a mimetic relationship between experience and writing and a relationship of identification between the reader and the autobiographical subject. Moreover, they are explicitly committed to the political importance of just such reading strategies for the creation of identity, community, and political solidarity.

In an important sense, these written stories are imitations of oral narratives, the coming-out stories at the heart of community building, at the most everyday level. Indeed, many of the stories read as if they had been transcribed from taped accounts. But the oral exchange of stories is, of course, impossible to reproduce, despite the obviously dialogic quality of the individuals' written narratives, which identify the lesbian community as their origin and end. Like all spoken language, the language of many written coming-out stories is necessarily reductionist, all the more so in published accounts, for the pleasures and subtleties of oral exchange and storytelling traditions are eradicated. Here the communicative, performative, and provisional aspects of coming-out stories are subordinated to the claims of recorded speech; in print, the coming-out story appears to hold more claims on the "truth" of the life as a whole.

Telling, writing, and reading autobiographical stories are linked to the perceived importance of countering representations that have rendered homosexuality invisible, perverse, aberrant, or marginal. In her collection of autobiographical essays titled *My Mama's Dead Squirrel: Lesbian Essays on Southern Culture,* Mab Segrest attempts to link antiracist literary traditions with lesbian writing by suggesting that autobiography constitutes a critical "decolonization of self" in the lesbian community. Further, she defines lesbian storytelling as part of larger struggles for self-determination among oppressed and silenced groups.

> Now this literature I stumbled into was very different, you had better believe it, from what I had been reading while struggling to acquire a Ph.D. in English. . . . Most of the "great works" of this century traced the dissolution of Western white male culture, by male writers who could only identify with its demise. . . . With lesbian literature I remembered how it's supposed to be. No lesbian in the universe, I do believe, will tell you there's nothing left to say. We have our whole lives to say, lives that have been censored, repressed, suppressed, and depressed from millennia from official versions of literature, history, and culture. . . . The lesbian's knowledge that we all have stories to tell and that each of our cultures produces its own artists lessens the suicidal modern alienation between writer and audience. Lesbian literature, like all the best women's writing is fueled by the knowledge that what we have to say is essential to our own survival and to the survival of the larger culture which has tried so hard to destroy us. The lesbian's definition of herself is part of the larger movement by all oppressed people to define ourselves.[14]

Rendering lesbianism natural, self-evident, original, can have the effect of emptying traditional representations of their content, of contesting the only apparent self-evidence of "normal" (read heterosexual) life course. Lesbian autobiographical narratives are about remembering differently, outside the contours and narrative constraints of conventional models. Events or feelings that are rendered insignificant, mere "phases"—or permanent aberrations when a life is organized in terms of the trajectory toward adult heterosexuality, marriage, and motherhood—become differently meaningful in lesbian stories. They become signs that must be reread on the basis of different interpretive strategies. Whether the emphasis is on a tomboyish past, on childhood friendships, or on crushes on girl friends, teachers, or camp counselors—all now the stock-in-trade of lesbian humor—these narratives point to unsanctioned discontinuities between biological sex, gender identity, and sexuality.

But lesbian autobiographical writing has an affirmative as well as a critical relationship to questions of identity and self-definition. And lesbian identity comes to mean quite particular things in the seventies under the impact of feminist struggles for conceptual and political unity. It is now quite common to reconstruct the history of those struggles among American feminists as a shift from a "radical" to a "cultural" feminism concerned only with psychology and identity and guilty of reproducing the very gender divisions radical feminism set out to question.[15] A particular construction of lesbianism as a political stance for all women is seen to be at the heart of that shift, to have enabled and supported it. "Elevating" lesbianism to the status of a "sign" of political solidarity with women worked to challenge the homophobic reduction of lesbianism to sex. Alice Echols has argued that the "desexualization" of questions of lesbianism may have been the condition of possibility for any unity between lesbians and feminists at all, given the virulent homophobia in the women's movement and the use of homophobia to attack the movement from without.[16] It also had more positive effects, providing a name and a visibility for interpersonal and political solidarity among women and for the pleasures that women, whatever their sexuality, take in each other's company. As a political fantasy, it allowed for the convergence of legitimate (because not explicitly sexual) desire and political liberation. And it provoked and enabled analyses of the intersection of gender division and a heterosexist social contract. In the place of the "sexual minority," however, another figure emerged, one that could encompass both lesbians and heterosexual women, the "woman-identified woman" with a legacy in the history of (romantic) female friendship, a figure that proved disabling and reductionist in its own way. By the late 1970s, when pornography and sexual violence had become the focus of what are now called "cultural feminist analyses," heterosexuality itself, not just particular institutionalized forms and normalizations of heterosexuality, had been identified as the source of women's dependence and oppression. In the context of this emerging critique of heterosexuality, lesbianism came to figure more and more significantly as what Katie King has called "feminism's magical sign of liberation."[17] For the key to opposing male supremacy and the forms of false consciousness imposed on women through the myths of heterosexual desire and pleasure was withdrawal from men, now named lesbianism.

One of the effects of the monolithic and universal division between men and women suggested by this work was the disappearance of institutional analyses, a focus on psychology, and the suggestion that politics could be derived directly from experience or identity. In King's words, "Identifying with lesbianism falsely implies that one knows all about heterosexism and homophobia magically through identity or association. . . . The power of lesbianism as a privileged signifier makes analysis of heterosexism and homophobia difficult since it obscures the need for counter-intuitive challenges to ideology."[18] At the heart of the division is a conception not only of an inside and outside of oppression but of an inside and outside of ideology. Drawing on the work of the Furies Collective in the mid–1970s, Zimmerman suggests that the unity constructed between lesbianism and feminism and the links established between "the personal" and "the political" resulted in "a radically rationalistic rewriting of personal history" to conform to political stance[19]–hence, the often formulaic and noncontradictory quality of some autobiographical writing, hence, too, the forms of moralism and voluntarism that inhere in such demands for the identity of sexuality, subjectivity, and political stance.

As many critics have now argued, Adrienne Rich's "Compulsory Heterosexuality and Lesbian Existence" (1980) constitutes the ultimate formulation of a particular conception of the relationship between sexuality and politics, explicitly marking off lesbianism as an issue of gender identification and contrasting the interests of gay men and lesbians.[20] Indeed, Rich's essay can be read as the culmination of a textual and political tendency that begins with the Furies Tracts of the early 1970s, namely, the construction of lesbianism as "feminism's magical sign of liberation." Rich uses Freud himself to argue for the primacy and naturalness of women's erotic bond with another woman. The daughter is violently separated from the mother by the imperative of heterosexuality, a social imperative and a form of violence which serves to consolidate male power and to blind women to their own supposedly "essential" love or desire. The ultimate formulation of a politics of nostalgia, of a return to that state of innocence free of conflict conceived as women's primary emotional bonds with one another, enacts its own violence, as all dreams of perfect union do. A number of lesbian critics have remarked that Rich's lesbian continuum effectively erases sexuality and robs lesbianism of any specificity. As Hilary Allen argues, "In conventional terms, whatever is sexual about Political Lesbianism appears to be systematically attenuated: genitality will yield to an unspecified eroticism, eroticism to sensuality, sensuality to 'primary emotional intensity,' and emotional intensity to practical and political support."[21]

Many of the coming-out stories and autobiographical narratives collected in the 1970s quite clearly display the effects of feminist rhetoric on definitions of lesbianism. The narratives are written against the notion that lesbianism can be explained in terms of "penis envy" or the desire to be or imitate a man. And indeed, sexual desire is often attenuated and appears as "love" in these narratives. Lesbianism, understood to be first and foremost about love for other women and for oneself as a woman, becomes a profoundly life-saving, self-loving, political resistance to patriarchal definitions and limitations in these narratives. Virtually every contributor to *The Lesbian Path* and *The Coming Out Stories* acknowledges her debt to feminism for giving lesbianism the meaning it has come to have. A feminist analysis of the suppression of love and solidarity among women in a sexist society and the ensuing celebration of women's relationships with one another provide the lever with which many of the authors pry lesbianism loose from its homophobic reduction to sex, suggesting that the reduction of their desires and their relationships to sex stood in the way of their ability or willingness to accept a lesbian identity. Feminism and the collective rereadings and redefinitions it facilitated are credited with having created the possibility of taking on and redefining the label.

The debt is particularly clear in the editors' presentations of these collections. *The Coming Out Stories* are organized, according to the editors, on the basis of each author's access to a language for her feelings and desires.[22] The book begins with the stories of those contributors who came out when there were no words for the feelings they had, or only words that rendered them perverse, sick, or male; they end with the stories of those who could name their experience woman identification. The cover blurb of *The New Lesbians* makes the impact of feminist politics even more apparent; it suggests that "a majority of lesbians are woman-identified: they do not want to act like or look like men or to practice role-playing."[23] *The Lesbian Path* is introduced as "the book I never had: true stories of strong, women-identified women."[24] The opposition between negative stereotypes and new "truths" about the majority of lesbians masks the role of rhetoric in constructing this majority. The "old" lesbians, those who came out prior to feminism are rendered invisible, made anachronistic, or converted.

Clearly, access to lesbian and feminist communities, to the collective interpretive strategies and rhetoric developed there have made positive self-definition and political activism possible. As Joan Nestle suggests in her contribution to *The Lesbian Path,* self-definition shifts and changes as lesbian communities shift and grow. Nestle describes her own transformation under the impact of feminism from the bar butch/fem culture of the 1950s and 1960s to a lesbian-feminist culture of woman identification.[25] Joan Nestle has since become one of the most articulate critics of the constraints imposed on what it means to be a lesbian by the woman-identified woman, the rhetorical figure that effaced the subtleties of legacies other than romantic female friendship.[26] In the context of the "sexuality debates," renewed interest in butch/fem relationships, in role playing, and in sadomasochism has restored attention to the discontinuities of sex, gender, sexual desire, sexual object choice by introducing the elements of fantasy and play. This work not only has fractured the unity achieved in the woman-identified woman between lesbianism and feminism but has exposed the absence of any consensus about the definition of lesbian identity and its relation to politics.[27]

Many of the coming-out stories are tautological insofar as they describe a process of coming to know something that has always been true, a truth to which the author has returned. They also describe a linear progression from a past shrouded in confusion or lies to a present or future that represents a liberation from the past. Coming out is conceived, then, as both a return to one's true self and desire and a movement beyond distortion and constraint, grounding identity and political unity in moral right and truth. The titles alone, according to Zimmerman—*The Lesbian Path, Lesbian Crossroads, Coming Out Stories*—point to the conception of lesbianism and of life story as a journey, as a "metaethical" journey à la Mary Daly from patriarchal distortion to a woman-identified consciousness, a choice, finally, to be who one is in a new world of women.[28] The "happy end" to internal struggles, doubts, and contradictions in many coming-out stories depends, in part, on forgetting that "the community" and the feminist literature on which it relies construct rather than simply reflect the truth of experience and identity. It depends, moreover, on suppressing the fact that the past has been rendered not more diverse but homogeneous in a new way. Despite the dialogic exchange between individual and community, these narratives tend to erase the individual's and the group's active participation in their formation as social beings by relying on apparently transcendent "essences" lying in wait for discovery and language. The increasingly exclusive focus on shifts in consciousness and on identification with women leads Zimmerman to conclude that "although lesbian feminism evolved during the 1970s as a politics of transliteration, this power of the word has been used primarily to name, and thereby control, individual and group identity."[29]

In her review of lesbian autobiographical writing, Zimmerman points out that the critiques of lesbian-feminist unities by women of color, Jewish women, and sex radicals have themselves proceeded by way of autobiographical texts committed to the affirmation of multiple identities. In some sense, according to Zimmerman, anthologies like Evelyn Torton Beck's *Nice Jewish Girls* and Moraga's and Anzaldúa's *This Bridge Called My Back* reproduce a cultural politics that places its faith in identity and in writing.[30] Zimmerman warns against the fragmentation that results from the search for more authentic unities based on multiplication of identities. Like other critics of "cultural feminism" and identity politics, she concludes with an appeal for institutional analyses in place of the focus on identity. Challenges to increasingly identical constructions of the unity of "women" *have* at times simply expanded the conception of personal and group identities arithmetically without changing entrenched notions of identity and without furthering what Barbara Smith has called "our ability to analyze complicated intersections of privilege and oppression."[31] The autobiographical writings of women of color, however—indeed, the conception of that category itself—also have the potential to challenge conventional assumptions of identity and its relationship to politics and writing.[32]

I would like to look more closely at *This Bridge Called My Back: Writings by Radical Women of Color,* a collection of autobiographical essays, poems, and letters that move questions of identity off exclusively psychological ground. *This Bridge Called My Back* is a collection of writings by and for radical women of color which also addresses white feminists both directly and indirectly. *This Bridge* is a provocation to white feminists to educate themselves about racism, about the material lives and realities of communities other than their own, about the relationship between the histories of their communities or growing-up places and those of people of color in the United States and elsewhere. It also insists that we cease locating "race" in those individuals or groups in whom it is supposedly embodied, that we abandon the notion that to be "white" is to be unmarked by race. And further, it is a provocation to white feminists and lesbians to render their own histories, subjectivities, and writing complex by attending to their various implications in overlapping social/discursive divisions and their histories.

By demonstrating the complex discursive and institutional intersections of race, class, gender, and sexuality and their inscription on the bodies and psyches of women, these autobiographical essays, poems, and letters relate psychic and political struggles in ways that make "identity" irreducible to consciousness. Not all the contributors to *This Bridge* are lesbians; even for those who identify themselves as lesbians, sexual identity is not a singular focus. *This Bridge* is conceived as a discussion, between and among "women of color," of the contradictions, conflicts, and possibilities in that constructed but "potent fusion of outsider identities."[33] It is a text committed to exposing the complexities of "race" in the United States, complexities too often reduced to a black/ white divide. The contributions of women from a range of racial, ethnic, even national communities complicate "race" by focusing on the relationship between the histories and the current situations of different communities and individuals. The category "women of color," as it is elaborated in *This Bridge,* stands in a critical relation to assumptions of unity based on identity, assumptions of a "unity of the oppressed." For the forms of solidarity forged here are based on shared but not identical histories, shared but not identical structural positions, shared but not identical interests. Moreover, the forms of solidarity suggested here are grounded not in claims to victimization but, as Chela Sandoval has argued, in the convergence of shared perspectives, shared competences, and shared pleasures. For Sandoval, the very category "women of color" eschews reference to an essential, pregiven, natural, or self-evident "home" or whole; it is a category that operates as a form of "oppositional consciousness" as well as a source of new political unities, new pleasures and communities.[34] In her critique of Susan Krieger's work on lesbian communities, Sandoval formulates the challenge: "United States Third World feminists are pointing out the differences that exist among all women not in order to fracture any hope of unity among women but to propose a new order—one that provides a new possibility for unity without the erasure of differences. This new order would draw attention to the construction and ideological consequences of every order, of every community, of every identity."[35] The category "women of color" amounts to an acknowledgment of what Erica Carter, in her introduction to the work of a German feminist collective on ideology, has called "the disappearance of *any* one coherent subject whose history (individual or collective) might be mobilized as a force for political action," this without abandoning personal histories or politics altogether.[36]

The very title of *This Bridge* suggests its connections with a metaphorical tradition in lesbian-feminist writing of journeys, paths, and transformations.[37] Donna Rushin's "The Bridge Poem," however, and Moraga's preface suggest from the outset that *This Bridge* is critical of that tradition. Audre Lorde's "Open Letter to Mary Daly" makes it quite clear that too many lesbian-feminist "metaethical" journeys to an assumed new world of women have passed over the bodies, the differences, of women of color. And the text as a whole lodges a double-edged critique of feminist and antiracist politics, both of which can erase the interests, indeed, the very existence of women of color; again and again, the critiques echo the analysis embedded in the title of Barbara Smith and Gloria Hull's introduction to black women's studies, *All the Women Are White/All the Blacks Are Men/But Some of Us Are Brave.*[38]

Moraga asks in her preface, "How can we—this time—not use our bodies to be thrown over a river of tormented history to bridge the gap?" For the contributors to this volume, the journey, and hence the narrative, is neither coherently linear nor tautological. There is no linear progression toward some other world or new "home" with women and no restored origin in innocence and wholeness. In fact, for women of color, the very conception of a linear passage from the old to the new, the expectation that women shed a patriarchal past for a new home with women constitutes a form of cultural imperialism. For the feminist dream of a new world of women simply reproduces the demand that women of color (and women more generally) abandon their histories, the histories of their communities, their complex locations and selves, in the name of a unity that barely masks its white, middle-class cultural reference/referent. In the words of Judit Moschkovich,

> When Anglo-American women speak of developing a new feminist or women's culture, they are still working and thinking within an Anglo-American cultural framework. This new culture would still be just as racist and ethnocentric as patriarchal American culture. I have often confronted the attitude that anything different is male. Therefore if I hold on to my Latin culture I am holding on to hateful patriarchal constructs. Meanwhile, the Anglo woman who deals with the world in her Anglo way, with her Anglo culture, is being "perfectly feminist."[39]

Moraga complicates the question of lesbian journeys and paths by beginning her preface with a description of her trip from the white suburbs of Watertown, Massachusetts, to black Roxbury.

Take Boston alone, I think to myself, and the feminism my so-called sisters have constructed does nothing to help me make the trip from one end of town to another. Leaving Watertown, I board a bus and ride it quietly in my light flesh to Harvard Square, protected by the gold highlights my hair dares to take on, like an insult, in this miserable heat. **I transfer and go underground.** I am a lesbian. I want a movement that helps me make some sense of the trip from Watertown to Roxbury, from white to Black. I love women the entire way, beyond a doubt.

The passage, for Moraga, must be "*through,* not over, not by, not around, but through."[40]

For the contributors who identify themselves as lesbians, lesbianism clearly does not figure as the exclusive ground of either identity or politics; however, it is neither divisible from nor subordinate to other identities. Moraga, for example, rejects the concept of separate, even if multiple, identities by refusing to isolate the "self" and then divide it into neat and hierarchical categories. Even as attention to racism interrupts any conception of lesbianism as the exclusive ground of identity and politics, lesbianism interrupts other potentially totalizing self-identifications. For it often works to expose the exclusions required by the dreams of heterosexual complementarity and wholes which organize so many fantasies of "home" and unity. Lesbianism represents the threat of rejection "by one's own kind."[41] Conceived here too as women's love for other women and for ourselves as women, lesbianism is politicized less as an identity than as a desire that transgresses the boundaries imposed by structures of race, class, ethnicity, nationality; it figures not as a desire that can efface or ignore the effects of those boundaries but as a provocation to take responsibility for them out of the desire for different kinds of connections. Lesbianism, for Moraga, for example, is about connection but not about a total or automatic identification; it marks a desire for more complex realities, for relationships filled with struggle and risk as well as pleasure and comfort.

I would grow despairing if I believed . . . we were unilaterally defined by color and class. Lesbianism is then a hoax, a fraud. I have no business with it. Lesbianism is supposed to be about connection. What drew me to politics was my love of women, the agony I felt in observing the straight-jackets of poverty and repression I saw people in my own family in. But the deepest political tragedy I have experienced is how with such grace, such blind faith, this commitment to women in the feminist movement grew to be exclusive and reactionary. *I call my white sisters on this.*[42]

For a number of contributors, lesbian and not, the love of women, the pleasure in women's company, is said to sustain political analysis and struggle across divisions. This sense of a desire for connection, however partial and provisional, gives the pieces a particular force.

There is no attempt to specify the relationships among gender, sexuality, race, and ethnicity in the abstract; Moraga and other contributors instead address the question of relationships and priorities by examining how they intersect at specific historical sites. A significant number of poems and autobiographical narratives begin with the memories of the crowds, the noises, the smells, the languages of the streets, concrete sites that evoke memories of home even as they suggest a kind of homelessness. The invocation of the sights, smells, sounds, and meanings of "the street" works to locate the author concretely in geographic, demographic, architectural spaces, spaces with permeable boundaries and heterogeneous collectivities and communities. In "The Other Heritage," Rosario Morales uses the streets of Spanish Harlem to challenge the effects of racism and cultural imperialism on historical memory:

I forgot   I forgot the other heritage   the other strain refrain   the silver thread thru my sound   the ebony sheen to my life   to the look of things to the sound of how I grew up which was in Harlem right down in Spanish Harlem El Barrio and bounded I always say to foreigners from Minnesota   Ohio and Illinois bounded on the North by Italians and on the South by Black Harlem. . . . What I didn't forget was the look of Ithaca Rochester Minneapolis and Salt Lake. . . . so how come I come to feel   safe!   when I hit Harlem   when I hit a city with enough color   when a city gets moved in on   when Main Street Vermont looks mottled   agouti   black and brown and white. . . .[43]

Such attention to the ideological quality of memory itself interrupts conventional assumptions of a logical continuity between the past and present self, exposing the means by which such continuities are manufactured.

Virtually every contributor addresses the complex politics of language in postcolonial contexts, underlining the absence of "natural" linguistic unities. Donna Haraway has characterized Moraga's work in/on language: "Moraga's language is not 'whole': it is self-consciously spliced, a chimera of English and Spanish, both conqueror's languages. But it is this chimeric monster without claim to an original language before violation, that crafts the erotic, competent, potent identities of women of color."[44] Haraway's characterization of Moraga's work holds for many of the other contributors to *This Bridge* as well. The question of language is thrown onto historical axes that exceed and construct individual personal and community histories. The attention to "histories" carries an implicit, when not explicit, critique of the "dream of a common language," calling attention to the impossibility of neutral or unmediated speech.[45] These texts work concertedly against the ways in which "experience" has been coded within feminist texts so as to render the complex realities of everyday life invisible.

The critique of a reduction of politics to psychology is also manifest in the call for a "theory in the flesh," in the use of a language of the body's physical pains and pleasures and of the materiality of psychic and social life. Moraga suggests that "the materialism in this book lives in the flesh of these women's lives, the exhaustion we feel in our bones at the end of the day, the fire we feel in our hearts when we are insulted, the knife we feel in our backs when we are betrayed, the nausea we feel in our bellies when we are afraid, even the hunger we feel between our hips when we long to be touched."[46] The contributions to *This Bridge* concretely describe the inscription of social and institutional constraints but also the lived pleasures and sensations of community in/on their bodies, drawing attention to the imbrication of "inner and outer world" without reducing one to the other. "Here," writes Moraga,

we introduce you to the "color problem" as it was first introduced to us: "not white enuf, not dark enuf," always up against a color chart that first got erected far outside our families and our neighborhoods, but which invaded them both with systematic determination. . . . We were born into colored homes. We grew up with the inherent contradictions in the color spectrum right inside those homes: the lighter sister, the mixed-blood cousin, being the darkest one in the family. . . . We learned to live with those contradictions. This is the root of our radicalism.[47]

For Moraga, who describes herself as a light-skinned Chicana lesbian, the contradictions that she lives in and on her body provoke important questions about the workings of privilege and power, the difficulties of unities and of identities, the complexities, therefore, of her relations with other women of color. "Sisterhood" with other women of color, according to Moraga, is achieved, not assumed; it is based on affinities and shared but not identical histories. The attention to the difficulties of community are counterbalanced by the emphasis on its importance and its pleasures. These authors seek connections and forms of community that are chosen, negotiated, achieved, not simply given. But they do not deny the importance or the pleasure of shared memories, shared histories, of identifications, partial and provisional though they may be. They avoid an overly rationalistic critique of identity and unity as dangerous fictions, curable through rational thought and theoretical negativity.

Several of the lesbian contributors speak openly of the importance of making connections with lesbians who share their ethnic, linguistic, or racial backgrounds, connections that allow them to combine their politics with the pleasures and safety of "home." The sense of safety and security in being with one's own kind is not explained with recourse to essential identities or natural connections but described quite concretely in terms of histories that are erased by all forms of "unity through incorporation or appropriation."[48] In the company of lesbians with similar histories, it becomes possible to live rather than cut off the languages, the forms of social interaction and humor, the smells, the tastes, the sights of those growing up places in oneself. What becomes crucial is knowing how to distinguish between the indulgence of home and the forging of political coalition, knowing how to indulge the provisional, though no less essential, pleasures of "home" without retreating into what Bernice Johnson Reagon has called "little barred rooms" in which differences are held at bay.[49]

In these narratives, "family" figures in complex and critical ways. The authors refer to neighborhoods, kin networks, communities that include aunts, grandmothers, mothers, fathers, sisters, brothers, neighbors, and friends. Families still operate as constraints and obstacles to particular forms of self-expression and freedom but also provide support, warmth, security, solidarity, sensuality. Moreover, working through memories and relationships with kin constitutes a resistance to internalized negations or denigrations of the authors' pasts, of families and communities that "fail" to mirror a white, middle-class Christian ideal:

> I don't really understand first-hand what it feels like being shitted on for being brown. I understand much more about the joys of it—being Chicana and having family are synonymous for me. What I know about loving, singing, crying, telling stories, speaking with my heart and hands, even having a sense of my own soul comes from the love of my mother, aunts, cousins. . . . But at the age of twenty-seven, it is frightening to acknowledge that I have internalized a racism and classism, where the object of oppression is not only someone outside of my skin, but the someone inside my skin. In fact, to a large degree, the real battle with such oppression, for all of us, begins under the skin. I have had to confront the fact that much of what I value about being Chicana, about my family, has been subverted by anglo-culture and my own cooperation with it.[50]

However great the actual physical or emotional separation between mothers and daughters, a great many of the narratives, poems, and letters are addressed directly to the authors' mothers, or to that relationship. This particular "thinking back through the mothers" involves neither disavowal nor total identification. Merle Woo, Moraga, and Aurora Levins Morales point to the negative legacies in forms of denial and self-contempt, but they also draw on the skills, the strengths, the confidence that constitute the positive legacy, the legacy of survival. The struggles to "unravel the knot" demonstrate the complex imbrication of interpersonal, intrapsychic, and social relations in histories of colonialism, racism, and sexism. Aurora Levins Morales, daughter of Rosario Morales, another contributor to *This Bridge,* describes the work:

> I'm a latin woman in the United States, closely involved with Latin American movements in the rest of the continent. I *should* write about the connection. But when I tried, all I could think was: No, write about the separation. For me the point of

terror, the point of denial is the New York Puerto Rican. My mother was born in New York in 1930, raised in Spanish Harlem and the Bronx. I represent the generation of return. . . . For my mother, the Barrio is safety, warmth. For me, it's the fear of racist violence that clipped her tongue of all its open vowels, into crisp, imitation British.[51]

Finally, such attention to detail rather than to coherent life history succeeds in illuminating discontinuities between past and present and, as a consequence, opens up possibilities for a different future. In her account of the importance of personal historical memory to theoretical work on ideology, German feminist Frigga Haug characterizes the "object" of memory in terms that could describe the work in *This Bridge:* "Day-to-day struggles over the hearts and minds of human subjects are not located only within social structures or within the individual but in the *process* whereby they perceive and appropriate the outer world . . . in a field of conflict between dominant cultural values and oppositional attempts to wrest cultural meaning and pleasure from life."[52]

The work of Minnie Bruce Pratt and Mab Segrest, both of whom identify themselves as southern, white, lesbian writers, demonstrates the impact of feminist encounters over racism and identity. In an autobiographical essay, "Identity: Skin Blood Heart," Pratt sets out to locate her own personal history in concrete histories of racism and anti-Semitism.[53] Pratt begins by identifying herself as a white, southern, middle-class, Christian-raised lesbian and then proceeds to explore the exclusions and repressions that support the seeming homogeneity, stability, and self-evidence of those identities. As Chandra Mohanty and I have argued elsewhere, Pratt situates herself quite concretely in relation to geographical, demographic, and architectural sites, working to expose the illusory coherence and inclusiveness of the positions from which she is taught to see and to speak.[54] Like so many of the narratives in *This Bridge,* Pratt's begins on a street, on H Street, NW, in Washington, D.C., her current "home," a place that doesn't exist on most white folks' map of the city, except as " 'the H Street Corridor,' as in something to be passed through quickly, going from your place, on the way to elsewhere" (p. 11). Pratt chooses to live in and to write about a space that daily brings her face-to-face with the relationship between her own personal history and the very different but overlapping histories of the people and the communities among whom she now lives.

Lesbianism figures in Pratt's narrative as a basis for her political vision. It is also that which her "identity" and privilege as a white, middle-class, southern woman disallows; its denial is the price of her privilege and her acceptance, of her welcome in a number of "homes." Pratt succeeds in showing that the exclusions required of conventional "homes" include parts of her self as well as others. Lesbianism then figures as desire, pleasure, and possibility, as a desire that transgresses conventional boundaries, not only the boundaries between self and others but the boundaries around "identity" itself. That desire, however, is easily recontained when it simply reproduces a nostalgia for safe places, for sameness, for Reagon's little barred rooms. Far from guaranteeing political correctness, innocence, and truth, lesbianism, when it is conceived as automatic and essential commonality, can indeed stand in the way of analysis and of coalition. As for Moraga, lesbianism for Pratt is about connection but no longer about automatic connections or about substitute "homes." Pratt takes up the dangers of such substitutions: "Raised to believe that I could be where I wanted and have what I wanted, as a grown woman I thought I could simply claim what I wanted, even the making of a new place to live with other women. I had no understanding of the limits that I lived within, nor of how much my memory and my experience of a safe place was based on places secured by omission, exclusions or violence, and on my submitting to the limits of that place" (pp. 25–26). The connections Pratt struggles to make are conceived as expansions of a "constricted eye," a "living on the edge of the skin," on the borders, and are contrasted to the fearful isolation of homogenous "homes." Clearly, for Pratt a feminism that reproduces the constraints of the white, middle-class home constitutes a severe impoverishment of reality, a blindness to its complexities. Pratt's expansions proceed by way of her own efforts to educate herself about the histories of her family and of the peoples whose histories have been systemically obliterated, obscured by a systematic, an institutionalized and passionate forgetfulness, by racism and anti-Semitism.

Pratt attends quite concretely to her own family's implication in those histories and in their suppression. Pratt's return to her childhood home is rendered particularly complex and subtle by virtue of her attention to racism. Here, there is no attempt to efface either positive or negative connections with her past for the sake of coherence or political purity; rather, she attempts to work through her contradictory implication in structures of privilege and oppression, pain and pleasure by repeatedly relocating herself in relation to concrete structures and institutional forms. She, too, reconstructs and sorts through positive and negative legacies, the materiality, the very physicality of her connections with "home"; she opens the enclosed space of the family, the illusory promises of home to analysis and critique. Through specific demographic and architectural sites and figures, Pratt locates herself in a web of relationships of difference and similarity with her family, her father, their vision, and their deeds. For in Pratt's words, "I was shaped by my relation to those buildings and to the people in the buildings, by ideas of who should be in the Board of Education, of who should be in the bank handling money, of who should have the guns and the keys to the jail, of who should be *in* the jail; and I was shaped by what I didn't see, or didn't notice on those streets" (p. 17). The only apparent self-evidence and neutrality of her father's "white male" identity are exposed as bounded in terror and defense: "A month after I dreamed this he died; I honor the grief of his life by striving to change much of what he believed in: and my own grief by acknowledging that I saw him caught in the grip of racial, sexual, cultural fears that I still am trying to understand in myself" (p. 53). "Unraveling the knot" between herself and her father, working through the ways in which she is her father's daughter become central to Pratt's enterprise.

Antiracist politics inform Mab Segrest's autobiographical writing as well. Segrest also identifies herself as a white, southern, lesbian writer whose personal history is deeply implicated in the history of racism and bigotry in the South. In her attempt to draw connections between southern lesbian writing and antiracist writing, Segrest inevitably comes counter to a lesbian feminism that assumes the unity of women or of lesbians to be primary and essential, overriding other divisions and loyalties. In her critique of certain forms of lesbian autobiography, Segrest writes: "The assertion of the decolonized self . . . can trap the fugitive into a need to be too pure, too free—which leads back into a new repression, into another death-dealing denial of our complex selves. And if the decolonized self slips into the born-again self, we are really in trouble."[55] Racism, beginning with the forms it takes in her family and the community in which she grew up, becomes the lever by which she uncovers the stakes in particular forms of community and unity in the South and, indeed, in the women's movement. Like Pratt, Segrest recalls the pleasures of her family's brand of southern humor, social manners, styles of communication, and storytelling. Both succeed in working through the complex links between the pleasures of those social forms and the pain of the racism, misogyny, and homophobia inextricably embedded in them.

> Southerners raise their indirection to an art and call it *manners*. Manners are one thing that still, to this day, separate Southerners from Yankees. It is my experience that

Yankees have a hard time believing that Southerners can have so many manners, and Southerners cannot believe that Yankees do not.... Manners, lies, and truth were all intertwined in the world I grew up in. Manners were, in fact, elaborate rituals for getting at or avoiding the truth.... "Courtesy," my mother explained, "is the mortar of civilization." And anger, she implied, destroyed both. I think as a white Southern mother she knew her "civilization" needed a lot of mortar.[56]

Segrest's essays, ordered chronologically, move from the more exclusively auto-biographical to several final pieces that document her antiracist work in Klanwatch in North Carolina. In fact, Segrest reconstructs the history of lesbian writing in such a way as to emphasize the ongoing links between antiracist and southern lesbian writing. This attempt to establish a tradition of southern antiracist lesbian writing leads Segrest to the work of Angelina Weld Grimké, Carson McCullers, Lillian Smith, and more recently, Barbara Deming, Pat Parker, Judy Grahn, and Minnie Bruce Pratt. Segrest locates the roots of contemporary southern lesbian writing in the early antiracist work of the Combahee River Collective in Boston;[57] in so doing, she challenges reconstructions that make lesbianism the origin and end of a coherent tradition, reconstructions that too often represent a lesbian-feminist tradition (from the perspective of white lesbian feminists) in such a way as to suggest that the problem of racism was "discovered" at a particular point in a fairly linear history. For Segrest, an antiracist lesbian tradition stands in a critical relationship to "southern gentlemen" and the "disciplinary power" of the agrarians, or New Critics, Allen Tate, John Crowe Ransom, Donald Davidson, Robert Penn Warren, Stark Young, and John Peale Bishop, the guardians of traditions she studied as a graduate student in English literature. Segrest suggests that the "arrogance in this New Critical approach is the assumption that white, class-privileged, European men have produced a *complete* tradition; in Tate's words, 'the whole of experience ... the true knowledge which is poetry,' as opposed to society's 'unremitting imposition of partial formulas.' "[58] Though Segrest's polemical consolidation of antiracist and lesbian writing in opposition to white male culture tends to reproduce an overly simple division between oppressors and oppressed, it also represents the important effort to work back through the complex coimplication of histories in the South without completely reducing the relation between different histories to analogy.[59]

Segrest's work participates in attempts to remove questions of identity from the exclusive ground of the psychological or interpersonal and to open up questions about the relations between psychic and social life, between intrapsychic, interpersonal, and political struggles. Identity is thrown onto historically constructed discursive and social axes that crisscross only apparently homogeneous communities and bounded subjects. Experience itself, now exposed as deeply ideological, no longer guarantees knowledge and political correctness. In fact, experience and the identities on which it is presumed to rely stand in the way of analysis and solidarity. The circuits of exchange between the work of Moraga, Anzaldúa, Pratt, and Segrest, whether direct or indirect, have moved autobiographical writing in this context onto a different plane. In these exchanges there is no longer a simple side by side, but a provocation to examine the coimplication of "my" history in "yours," to analyze the relations between.

As a consequence of these developments, lesbianism ceases to be an identity with predictable contents, to constitute a total political and self-identification, and yet it figures no less centrally for that shift. It remains a position from which to speak, to organize, to act politically, but it ceases to be the exclusive and continuous ground of identity or politics. Indeed, it works to unsettle rather than to consolidate the boundaries around identity, not to dissolve them altogether but to open them to the fluidities and heterogeneities that make their renegotiation possible. At the same time that such autobiographical writing enacts a critique of both sexuality and race as "essential" and totalizing identifications, it also acknowledges the political and psychological importance, indeed, the pleasures, too, of at least partial or provisional identifications, homes, and communities. In so doing, it remains faithful to the irreducibly complex and paradoxical status of identity in feminist politics and autobiographical writing.

NOTES

1. Bertha Harris, "What We Mean to Say: Notes toward Defining the Nature of Lesbian Literature," *Heresies: A Feminist Publication on Art and Politics—Lesbian Art and Artists* (Fall 1977): 5–8. Harris's distinction between a literature of the grotesque and a literature of "winkieburgers" is certainly unsatisfying. For those, however, who felt somewhat isolated in 1977–78 in our critical response to increasingly homogeneous narratives of lesbian experience, Bertha Harris's pleas for monstrosity had particular polemical value.

2. Paul de Man, "Autobiography as Defacement," *MLN* 94 (Dec. 1979): 920.

3. I am interested here in the impact of Michel Foucault's *The History of Sexuality,* vol. 1 (New York: Pantheon Books, 1978).

4. Jeffrey Minson, "The Assertion of Homosexuality," *m/f* 5 (1981): 22. Also see Minson, *Genealogies of Morals: Nietzsche, Foucault, Donzelot and the Eccentricity of Ethics* (New York: St. Martin's Press, 1985).

5. I have argued this point in more detail in "Feminism, Criticism and Foucault," *New German Critique* 27 (Fall 1982): 3–30.

6. Hayden White, "Michel Foucault," in *Structuralism and Since,* ed. John Sturrock (Oxford: Oxford University Press, 1979), p. 82.

7. Arthur Brittan and Mary Maynard, *Sexism, Racism, and Oppression* (Oxford: Basil Blackwell, 1984), p. 29. Brittan and Maynard use the work of Foucault to critique orthodox Marxism, Frankfurt School Critical Theory, and radical feminisms for treating racism and sexism as derivative of more primary contradictions.

8. Jeffrey Weeks, *Sexuality and Its Discontents: Meanings, Myths and Modern Sexualities* (London: Routledge and Kegan Paul, 1985), p. 218. I agree with Weeks's reading of the strategic political implications for gay politics in Foucault's work, in particular his emphasis on reconceptualizing rights and choices in terms of the social conditions that make such notions meaningful.

9. Teresa de Lauretis, *Technologies of Gender: Feminism, Film and Fiction* (Bloomington: Indiana University Press, 1987), p. 1. De Lauretis works with and against Louis Althusser as well as Foucault. Her critique of Althusser draws on the interesting and important work of Wendy Hollway, "Gender Difference and the Production of Subjectivity," in Julian Henriques, Wendy Hollway, Cathy Urwin, Couze Venn, and Valerie Walkerdine, *Changing the Subject: Psychology, Social Regulation and Subjectivity* (London: Methuen, 1984), 225–63. For an excellent discussion by the German feminist Argument Collective of the uses of and problems with Foucault for feminists, see *Female Sexualization,* ed. Frigga Haug et al., trans. Erica Carter (London: Verso, 1987). Haug et al. make a critique of the suppression of subjective agency in Foucault's work which is very similar to that made by de Lauretis. The Argument Collective is interested in mobilizing historical memory in order to expose both processes of "individualization" and possibilities of resistance. See also *Feminism and Foucault,* ed. Irene Diamond and Lee Quinby (Boston: Northeastern University Press, 1988).

10. De Lauretis, *Alice Doesn't: Feminism, Semiotics, Cinema* (Bloomington: Indiana University Press, 1984), p. 182.

11. De Lauretis, *Technologies of Gender,* pp. 9–10.

12. I am indebted to Jeffrey Minson's "Assertions of Homosexuality" for this formulation and for his use of that formulation to criticize particular forms of the politics of coming out.

13. Bonnie Zimmerman, "The Politics of Transliteration: Lesbian Personal Narratives," in *The Lesbian Issue: Essays from Signs,* ed. Estelle B. Freedman, Barbara C. Gelpi, Susan L. Johnson, and Kathleen M. Weston (Chicago: University of Chicago Press, 1985), pp. 251–70.

14. Mab Segrest, *My Mama's Dead Squirrel: Lesbian Essays on Southern Culture* (Ithaca, N.Y.: Firebrand, 1985), pp. 101–2.

15. For two of the most influential reconstructions, see Alice Echols, "The Taming of the Id: Feminist Sexual Politics, 1968–83," in *Pleasure and Danger: Exploring Female Sexuality* (Boston: Routledge and Kegan Paul, 1984), pp. 50–72; and Echols, "The New Feminism of Yin and Yang," in *Powers of Desire: The Politics of Sexuality*, ed. Ann Snitow, Christine Stansell, and Sharon Thompson (New York: Monthly Review Press, 1983), pp. 439–59; see also Hester Eisenstein, *Contemporary Feminist Thought* (Boston: G.K. Hall, 1983). Ellen Willis, "Feminism, Moralism and Pornography," in *Powers of Desire*, pp. 460–67, has also popularized a narrative that moves from "radical" to "cultural" feminism. To the extent that these reconstructions rely on only apparently self-evident taxonomies, even as a position from which to assess the use of certain taxonomies, they tend to reproduce the problems they expose. Despite the importance of Echols's critique of what she calls "cultural feminism," the danger exists that all manner of cultural practices will be ossified as mere symptoms of a feminism gone wrong. It is also not clear what the status of "culture" is in many of these critical reconstructions. Since at least some such reconstructions have emerged in the context of a self-identified "socialist feminism," there is some danger that conventional distinctions between "real politics" and "cultural preoccupations" are reproduced in another guise.

16. Echols, "The Taming of the Id," pp. 55–56.

17. Katie King, "The Situation of Lesbianism as Feminism's Magical Sign: Contests for Meaning and the U.S. Women's Movement, 1968–1972," *Communication* 9 (1986): 65–91. King's work provides an explicit and implicit critique of historical reconstructions of feminism that rely on taxonomic identification and linear historical narratives.

18. King, "Situation of Lesbianism," p. 85.

19. Zimmerman, "Politics of Transliteration," p. 255.

20. Adrienne Rich, "Compulsory Heterosexuality and Lesbian Existence," *Signs* 5 (1980): 631–60. Reprinted in this volume.

21. Hilary Allen, "Political Lesbianism and Feminism—Space for a Sexual Politics?," *m/f* 7 (1982): 15–34. Allen's essay provides a particularly lucid exploration of the contradictions on which a political lesbian stance has relied, contradictions in the category "woman" and in conceptions of sexuality. For one of the most successful critiques of that once hegemonic figure, the "woman-identified-woman," and its effects on conceptions of lesbian sexuality, see Esther Newton's discussion of Radclyffe Hall, "The Mythic Mannish Lesbian: Radclyffe Hall and the New Woman," in *The Lesbian Issue*, pp. 7–25.

22. *The Coming Out Stories*, ed. Julia Penelope Stanley and Susan J. Wolfe (Watertown, Mass.: Persephone Press, 1980).

23. *The New Lesbians*, ed. Laurel Galana and Gina Cavina (Berkeley: Moon Books, 1977).

24. *The Lesbian Path*, ed. Margaret Cruikshank (San Francisco: Grey Fox Press, 1985).

25. Joan Nestle, "An Old Story," in *The Lesbian Path*, pp. 37–39.

26. For more detailed autobiographical accounts and analyses of the lesbian culture of the 1950s, see Nestle's collected essays, *A Restricted Country* (Ithaca, N.Y.: Firebrand Press, 1987).

27. Gayle Rubin has gone as far as to suggest that sexuality constitutes a separate axis, which intersects with but is irreducible to gender, so that feminism becomes inadequate to an analysis or politics of sexuality. Though Rubin's work on lesbian sadomasochism has been legitimately criticized for reproducing identity politics in the name of a different sexual community and for tending toward a sexual essentialism, it has served to contest the only apparent hegemony of particular constructions of lesbianism by introducing a complicating axis. See in particular Rubin's "Thinking Sex: Notes for a Radical Theory of the Politics of Sexuality," in *Pleasure and Danger*, pp. 267–319. Reprinted, with revisions, in this volume. For a critical assessment of the "prosex" and "antisex" divisions in the sexuality debates, see the review of the texts and major conferences of the so-called sexuality debates by B. Ruby Rich, "Feminism and Sexuality in the 1980s," *Feminist Studies* 12 (Fall 1986): 525–63.

28. Mary Daly, *Gyn/ecology: The Metaethics of Radical Feminism* (Boston: Beacon Press, 1978).

29. Zimmerman, "Politics of Transliteration," p. 270.

30. Zimmerman characterizes *Nice Jewish Girls: A Lesbian Anthology,* ed. Evelyn Torton Beck (Watertown, Mass.: Persephone Press, 1982) and *This Bridge Called My Back: Writings by Radical Women of Color,* ed. Cherríe Moraga and Gloria Anzaldúa (Watertown, Mass.: Persephone Press, 1981), both now published by Firebrand Books, as "more political" than *The Coming Out Stories* or *The Lesbian Path,* both of which include work primarily by white, middle-class women. According to Zimmerman, however, "it is the intensity and power of self-affirmation that dominates these volumes" (p. 265). I am less interested in contesting Zimmerman's assessment of the differences, an assessment with which I basically agree, than in specifying the differences between conceptions of identity in the two sets of texts in terms other than "political" versus "self-affirmative." Zimmerman also points to a number of what she calls imaginative personal narratives or autobiographical texts by women of color, which are producing "a new, more inclusive, and more accurate politics" (p. 264). She notes, in particular, Audre Lorde, *Zami: A New Spelling of My Name* (Trumansburg, N.Y.: Crossing Press, 1983); Michelle Cliff, *Claiming an Identity They Taught Me to Despise* (Watertown, Mass.: Persephone Press, 1980); Anita Cornwall, *Black Lesbian in White America* (Tallahassee, Fla.: Naiad Press, 1983); Cherríe Moraga, *Loving in the War Years* (Boston: South End Press, 1983); and Gloria Anzaldúa, *Borderlands/La Frontera: The New Mestiza* (San Francisco: Spinsters/aunt lute, 1987).

31. Barbara Smith, "Between a Rock and a Hard Place," in *Yours in Struggle: Three Feminist Perspectives on Anti-Semitism and Racism* (New York: Long Haul Press, 1984), p. 81.

32. For an excellent discussion of the possibilities of "postmodern autobiography," see Caren Kaplan, "The Poetics of Displacement in *Buenos Aires,*" *Discourse: Journal of Theoretical Studies in Media and Culture* 8 (Fall–Winter 1986–87): 84–102.

33. I am indebted for this formulation to Donna Haraway's discussion of "women of color" as a category and a form of coalition in "A Manifesto for Cyborgs: Science, Technology, and Socialist Feminism in the 1980s," *Socialist Review* 80 (April 1985): 93.

34. Chela Sandoval, "Dis-illusionment and the Poetry of the Future: The Making of Oppositional Consciousness" (Ph.D. qualifying essay, University of California–Santa Cruz, 1984), quoted in Haraway, "Manifesto," p. 73.

35. Sandoval, "Comment on Susan Krieger's 'Lesbian Identity and Community: Recent Social Science Literature,'" in *The Lesbian Issue,* p. 241–44.

36. Erica Carter, Introduction to *Female Sexualization,* p. 15.

37. Zimmerman calls attention to the prevalence of such metaphors and their implications in "Politics of Transliteration," p. 258.

38. *All the Women Are White/All the Blacks are Men/But Some of Us Are Brave: Black Women's Studies,* ed. Gloria T. Hull, Patricia Bell Scott, and Barbara Smith (Old Westbury, N.Y.: Feminist Press, 1982).

39. Judit Moschkovich, "—But I Know You, American Woman," in *This Bridge Called My Back,* p. 83.

40. Cherríe Moraga, Preface to *This Bridge Called My Back,* pp. xiii–xix.

41. See Barbara Smith's introduction to *Home Girls: A Black Feminist Anthology* (New York: Kitchen Table Press, 1984).

42. Moraga, Preface, p. xiv.

43. Rosario Morales, "The Other Heritage," in *This Bridge Called My Back,* p. 107.

44. Haraway, "Manifesto," p. 94.

45. In her call for a postmodern socialist feminism, Donna Haraway works quite explicitly against political myths like Adrienne Rich's *The Dream of a Common Language* (1978), the title of one of Rich's collections of poetry, and a section title in Haraway's "Manifesto."

46. Moraga, Preface, p. xviii.

47. Moraga, Introduction, to "Children Passing in the Street: The Roots of Our Radicalism," in *This Bridge Called My Back,* p. 5.

48. Haraway, "Manifesto," p. 67. She gives a critique of both radical and socialist feminism for reproducing conceptions of unity that amount to incorporation, appropriation, and erasure of differences.

49. Bernice Johnson Reagon, "Coalition Politics: Turning the Century," in *Home Girls,* pp. 356–68.

50. Moraga, "La Güera," in *This Bridge Called My Back,* p. 30.

51. Aurora Levins Morales, ". . . And Even Fidel Can't Change That!," in *This Bridge Called My Back,* pp. 53–56.

52. Haug, *Female Sexualization,* p. 41.

53. Minnie Bruce Pratt, "Identity: Skin Blood Heart," in Elly Bulkin, Minnie Bruce Pratt, and Barbara Smith, *Yours in Struggle: Three Feminist Perspectives on Anti-Semitism and Racism* (Brooklyn, N.Y.: Long Haul Press, 1984, now published by Firebrand Books), pp. 11–63, hereafter cited in the text.

54. See Biddy Martin and Chandra Talpade Mohanty, "Feminist Politics: What's Home Got to Do With It," in *Feminist Studies/Critical Studies,* ed. Teresa de Lauretis (Bloomington: Indiana University Press, 1986).

55. Segrest, *My Mama's Dead Squirrel,* p. 127.

56. Ibid., pp. 63–64.

57. "The Combahee River Collective Statement," in *Capitalist Patriarchy and the Case for a Socialist Feminism,* ed. Zillah Eisenstein (New York: Monthly Review Press, 1979), pp. 362–72.

58. Segrest, *My Mama's Dead Squirrel,* pp. 111–12.

59. The consolidation also constitutes the basis for Segrest's humor and is therefore more complex than I render it.

19

Toward a Butch-Femme Aesthetic

SUE-ELLEN CASE

Sue-Ellen Case is Professor of English at the University of California, Riverside. Her most recent article on queer theory, "Tracking the Vampire," appeared in differences (1992) and her forthcoming book from Indiana University Press will be on lesbians and the notion of the screen. She is editor of Performing Feminisms: Feminist Critical Theory and Theatre *(1990) and former editor of* Theatre Journal. *In this essay, she takes issue with feminist critics' adoption of the postmodernist theory of the subject: a conception of the individual as so completely a creation of ideology that agency—the power to change events, surroundings, and even ideology itself—is ultimately an impossibility. Too often, Case argues, feminist criticism has produced the female subject, one who remains trapped within the confines of heterosexual ideology, rather than the feminist subject, an individual who, conscious of herself as both inside and outside that ideology, is capable of change and of changing the conditions of her existence. Case suggests that the lesbian roles of butch and femme exemplify the kinds of self-determination that the feminist subject demands. First, however, feminist theory must recognize precisely those lesbians—working-class butches and femmes—it has excluded, since it is from bar life's rich campiness that the butch-femme couple emerged as self-conscious, feminist subjects. In the work of current performance artists, Case finds examples of butch-femme subjects who escape the kinds of theoretical assimilation that currently make queerness welcome even as it erases the individual presence of gays and, particularly, lesbians.*

In the 1980s, feminist criticism has focused increasingly on the subject position: both in the explorations for the creation of a female subject position and the deconstruction of the inherited subject position that is marked with masculinist functions and history. Within this focus, the problematics of women inhabiting the traditional subject position have been sketched out, the possibilities of a new heterogeneous, heteronomous position have been explored, and a desire for a collective subject has been articulated. While this project is primarily a critical one, concerned with language and symbolic structures, philosophic assumptions, and psychoanalytic narratives, it also implicates the social issues of class, race, and sexuality. Teresa de Lauretis's article "The Technology of Gender" (in *Technologies of Gender,* 1987) reviews the recent excavations of the subject position in terms of ideology, noting that much of the work on the subject, derived from Foucault and Althusser, denies both agency and gender to the subject. In fact, many critics leveled a similar criticism against Foucault in a recent conference on postmodernism, noting that while his studies seem to unravel the web of ideology, they suggest no subject position outside the ideology, nor do they construct a subject who has the agency to change ideology ("Postmodernism," 1987). In other words, note de Lauretis and others, most of the work on the subject position has only revealed the way in which the subject is trapped within ideology and thus provides no programs for change.

For feminists, changing this condition must be a priority. The common appellation of this bound subject has been the "female subject," signifying a biological, sexual difference, inscribed by dominant cultural practices. De Lauretis names her subject (one capable of change and of changing conditions) the feminist subject, one who is "at the same time inside and outside the ideology of gender, and conscious of being so, conscious of that pull, that division, that doubled vision" (1987, 10). De Lauretis ascribes a sense of self-determination at the micropolitical level to the feminist subject. This feminist subject, unlike the female one, can be outside of ideology, can find self-determination, can change. This is an urgent goal for the feminist activist/theorist. Near the conclusion of her article (true to the newer rules of composition), de Lauretis begins to develop her thesis: that the previous work on the female subject, assumes, but leaves unwritten, a heterosexual context for the subject and this is the cause for her continuing entrapment. Because she is still perceived in terms of men and not within the context of other women, the subject in heterosexuality cannot become capable of ideological change (1987, 17–18).

De Lauretis's conclusion is my starting place. Focusing on the feminist subject, endowed with the agency for political change, located among women, outside the ideology of sexual difference, and thus the social institution of heterosexuality, it would appear that the lesbian roles of butch and femme, as a dynamic duo, offer precisely the strong subject position the movement requires. Now, in order for the butch-femme roles to clearly emerge within this sociotheoretical project, several tasks must be accomplished: the lesbian subject of feminist theory would have to come out of the closet, the basic discourse or style of camp for the lesbian butch-femme positions would have to be clarified, and an understanding of the function of roles in the homosexual lifestyle would need to be developed, particularly in relation to the historical class and racial relations embedded in such a project. Finally, once these tasks have been completed, the performance practice, both on and off the stage, may be studied as that of a feminist subject, both inside and outside ideology, with the power to self-determine her role and her conditions on the micropolitical level. Within this schema, the butch-femme couple inhabit the subject position together—"you can't have one without the other," as the song says. The two roles never appear as . . . discrete. The combo butch-femme as subject is reminiscent of Monique Wittig's "j/e" or coupled self in her novel *The Lesbian Body*. These are not split subjects, suffering the torments of dominant ideology. They are coupled ones that do not impale themselves on the poles of sexual difference or metaphysical values, but constantly seduce the sign system, through flirtation and inconstancy into the light fondle of artifice, replacing the Lacanian slash with a lesbian bar.

However, before all of this *jouissance* can be enjoyed, it is first necessary to bring the lesbian subject out of the closet of feminist history. The initial step in that process is to trace historically how the lesbian has been assigned to the role of the skeleton in the closet of feminism; in this case, specifically the lesbian who relates to her cultural roots by identifying with traditional butch-femme role-playing. First, regard the feminist genuflection of the 1980s—the catechism of "working-class-women-of-color" feminist theorists feel impelled to invoke at the outset of their research. What's wrong with this picture? It does not include the lesbian position. In fact, the isolation of the social dynamics of race and class successfully relegates sexual preference to an attendant position, so that even if the lesbian were to appear, she would be as a bridesmaid and never the bride. Several factors are responsible for this ghosting of the lesbian subject: the first is the growth of moralistic projects restricting the production of sexual fiction or fantasy through the antipornography crusade. This crusade has produced an alliance between those working on social feminist issues and right-wing homophobic, born-again men and women who also support censorship. This alliance in the electorate, which aids in producing enough votes for an ordinance, requires the closeting of lesbians for the so-called greater cause. Both Jill Dolan and Alice Echols develop this position in their respective articles.

Although the antipornography issue is an earmark of the moralistic 1980s, the homophobia it signals is merely an outgrowth of the typical interaction between feminism and lesbianism since the rise of the feminist movement in the early 1970s. Del Martin and Phyllis Lyon describe the rise of the initial so-called lesbian liberatory organization, the Daughters of Bilitis (DOB), in their influential early book, *Lesbian/Woman* (1972). They record the way in which the aims of such organizations were intertwined with those of the early feminist, or more precisely, women's movement. They proudly exhibit the way in which the DOB moved away from the earlier bar culture and its symbolic systems to a more dominant identification and one that would appease the feminist movement. DOB's goal was to erase butch-femme behavior, its dress codes, and lifestyle from the lesbian community and to change lesbians into lesbian feminists.

Here is the story of one poor victim who came to the DOB for help. Note how similar this narrative style is to the redemptive, corrective language of missionary projects: "Toni joined Daughters of Bilitis . . . at our insistence, and as a result of the group's example, its unspoken pressure, she toned down her dress. She was still very butch, but she wore women's slacks and blouses . . . one of DOB's goals was to teach the lesbian a mode of behavior and dress acceptable to society. . . . We knew too many lesbians whose activities were restricted because they wouldn't wear skirts. But Toni did not agree. 'You'll never get me in a dress,' she growled, banging her fist on the table." The description of Toni's behavior, her animal growling noise, portrays her as uncivilized, recalling earlier, colonial missionary projects. Toni is portrayed as similar to the inappropriately dressed savage whom the missionary clothes and saves. The authors continue: "But she became fast friends with a gay man, and over the months he helped her to feel comfortable with herself as a woman" (*Lesbian/Woman* 1972, 77). Here, in a lesbian narrative, the missionary position is finally given over to a man (even if gay) who helps the butch to feel like a woman. The contemporary lesbian-identified reader can only marvel at the conflation of gender identification in the terms of dominant, heterosexual culture with the adopted gender role-playing within the lesbian subculture.

If the butches are savages in this book, the femmes are lost heterosexuals who damage birthright lesbians by forcing them to play the butch roles. The authors assert that most femmes are divorced heterosexual women who know how to relate only to men and thus force their butches to play the man's role, which is conflated with that of a butch (*Lesbian/Woman* 1972, 79). Finally, the authors unveil the salvationary role of feminism in this process and its power to sever the newly constructed identity of the lesbian feminist from its traditional lesbian roots: "The minority of lesbians who still cling to the traditional male-female or husband-wife pattern in their partnerships are more than likely old-timers, gay bar habituées or working-class women." This sentence successfully compounds ageism with a (homo)phobia of lesbian bar culture and a rejection of a working-class identification. The middle-class upward mobility of the lesbian feminist identification shifts the sense of community from one of working-class, often women-of-color lesbians in bars, to that of white upper-middle-class heterosexual women who predominated in the early women's movement. The book continues: "the old order changeth however" (here they even begin to adopt verb endings from the

King James Bible) "as the women's liberation movement gains strength against this pattern of heterosexual marriages, the number of lesbians involved in butch-femme roles diminishes" (*Lesbian/Woman* 1972, 80).

However, this compulsory adaptation of lesbian feminist identification must be understood as a defensive posture, created by the homophobia that operated in the internal dynamics of the early movement, particularly within the so-called consciousness-raising groups. In her article with Cherríe Moraga on butch-femme relations, Amber Hollibaugh, a femme, described the feminist reception of lesbians this way: "the first discussion I ever heard of lesbianism among feminists was: 'We've been sex objects to men and where did it get us? And here when we're just learning how to be friends with other women, you got to go and sexualize it' . . . they made men out of every sexual dyke" (1983, 402). These kinds of experiences led Hollibaugh and Moraga to conclude: "In our involvement in a movement largely controlled by white middle-class women, we feel that the values of their culture . . . have been pushed down our throats . . .," and even more specifically, in the 1980s, to pose these questions: "why is it that it is largely white middle-class women who form the visible leadership in the anti-porn movement? Why are women of color not particularly visible in this sex-related single issue movement?" (1983, 405).

When one surveys these beginnings of the alliance between the heterosexual feminist movement and lesbians, one is not surprised at the consequences for lesbians who adopted the missionary position under a movement that would lead to an antipornography crusade and its alliance with the Right. Perhaps too late, certain members of the lesbian community who survived the early years of feminism and continued to work in the grass-roots lesbian movement, such as Joan Nestle, began to perceive this problem. As Nestle, founder of the Lesbian Herstory Archives in New York, wrote: "We lesbians of the 1950s made a mistake in the 1970s: we allowed ourselves to be trivialized and reinterpreted by feminists who did not share our culture" (1981, 23). Nestle also notes the class prejudice in the rejection of butch-femme roles: "I wonder why there is such a consuming interest in the butch-fem lives of upper-class women, usually more literary figures, while real-life, working butch-fem women are seen as imitative and culturally backward . . . the reality of passing women, usually a working-class lesbian's method of survival, has provoked very little academic lesbian-feminist interest. Grassroots lesbian history research is changing this" (1981, 23).

So the lesbian butch-femme tradition went into the feminist closet. Yet the closet, or the bars, with their hothouse atmosphere have produced what, in combination with the butch-femme couple, may provide the liberation of the feminist subject—the discourse of camp. Proust described this accomplishment in his novel *The Captive:*

> The lie, the perfect lie, about people we know, about the relations we have had with them, about our motive for some action, formulated in totally different terms, the lie as to what we are, whom we love, what we feel in regard to those people who love us . . .—that lie is one of the few things in the world that can open windows for us on to what is new and unknown, that can awaken in us sleeping senses for the contemplation of universes that otherwise we should never have known. (Proust, 213; in Sedgwick 1987)

The closet has given us camp–the style, the discourse, the *mise en scène* of butch-femme roles. In his history of the development of gay camp, Michael Bronski describes the liberative work of late-nineteenth-century authors such as Oscar Wilde in creating the homosexual camp liberation from the rule of naturalism, or realism. Within his argument, Bronski describes naturalism and realism as strategies that tried to save fiction from the accusation of daydream, imagination, or masturbation and to affix a utilitarian goal to literary production—that of teaching morals. In contrast, Bronski quotes the newspaper *Fag Rag* on the functioning of camp: "We've broken down the rules that are used for validating the difference between real/true and unreal/false. The controlling agents of the status quo may know the power of lies; dissident subcultures, however, are closer to knowing their value" (1984, 41). Camp both articulates the lives of homosexuals through the obtuse tone of irony and inscribes their oppression with the same device. Likewise, it eradicates the ruling powers of heterosexist realist modes.

Susan Sontag, in an avant-garde assimilation of camp, described it as a "certain mode of aestheticism . . . one way of seeing the world as an aesthetic phenomenon . . . not in terms of beauty, but in terms of the degree of artifice" (1966, 275). This artifice, as artifice, works to defeat the reign of realism as well as to situate the camp discourse within the category of what can be said (or seen). However, the fixed quality of Sontag's characteristic use of camp within the straight context of aestheticization has produced a homosexual strategy for avoiding such assimilation: what Esther Newton has described as its constantly changing, mobile quality, designed to alter the gay camp sensibility before it becomes a fad (1972, 105). Moreover, camp also protects homosexuals through a "first-strike wit" as *Fag Rag* asserts: "Wit and irony provide the only reasonable modus operandi in the American Literalist Terror of Straight Reality" (1984, 46).

Oscar Wilde brought this artifice, wit, irony, and the distancing of straight reality and its conventions to the stage. Later, Genet staged the malleable, multiple artifice of camp in *The Screens,* which elevates such displacement to an ontology. In his play, *The Blacks,* he used such wit, irony, and artifice to deconstruct the notion of "black" and to stage the dynamics of racism. *The Blacks* displaced the camp critique from homophobia to racism, in which "black" stands in for "queer" and the campy queen of the bars is transformed into an "african queen." This displacement is part of the larger use of the closet and gay camp discourse to articulate other social realities. Eve Sedgwick attests to this displacement when she writes: "I want to argue that a lot of energy of attention and demarcation that has swirled around issues of homosexuality since the end of the nineteenth century . . . has been impelled by the distinctly indicative relation of homosexuality to wider mappings of secrecy and disclosure, and of the private and the public, that were and are critically problematical for the gender, sexual, and economic structures of the heterosexist culture at large. . . . 'the closet' and 'coming out' are now verging on all-purpose phrases for the potent crossing and recrossing of almost any politically charged lines of representation. . . . The apparent floating-free from its gay origins of that phrase 'coming out of the closet' in recent usage might suggest that the trope of the closet is so close to the heart of some modern preoccupations that it could be . . . evacuated of its historical gay specificity. But I hypothesize that exactly the opposite is true." Thus, the camp success in ironizing and distancing the regime of realist terror mounted by heterosexist forces has become useful as a discourse and style for other marginal factions.

Camp style, gay-identified dressing, and the articulation of the social realities of homosexuality have also become part of the straight, postmodern canon, as Herbert Blau articulated it in a special issue of *Salmagundi:* "becoming homosexual is part of the paraphilia of the postmodern, not only a new sexual politics but the reification of all politics, supersubtilized beyond the unnegotiable demands of the sixties, from which it is derived, into a more persuasive rhetoric of unsublimated desire" (1983, 233). Within this critical community, the perception of recognizable homosexuals can also inspire broader visions of the operation of social codes. Blau states: "there soon came pullulating toward me at high prancing amphetamined pitch something like the end of Empire or like the screaming remains of the return of the repressed—pearl-white, vinyl, in polo pants and scarf—an englistered and giggling outburst of resplendent queer . . . what was there to consent to and who could possibly legitimate that galloping specter I had seen, pure ideolect, whose plunging and lungless soundings were a full-throttled forecast of much weirder things to come?" (1983, 221–22). Initially, these borrowings seem benign and even inviting to the homosexual theorist. Contemporary theory seems to open the closet door to invite the queer to come out, transformed as a new, postmodern subject, or even to invite straights to come into the closet, out of the roar of dominant discourse. The danger incurred in moving gay politics into such heterosexual contexts is in only slowly discovering that the strategies and perspectives of homosexual realities and discourse may be locked inside a homophobic "concentration camp." Certain of these authors, such as Blau, even introduce homosexual characters and their subversions into arguments that conclude with explicit homophobia. Note Blau's remembrance of things past: "thinking I would enjoy it, I walked up Christopher Street last summer at the fag end of the depleted carnival of Gay Pride Day, with a disgust unexpected and almost uncontained by principle. . . . I'll usually fight for the right of each of us to have his own perversions, I may not, under the pressure of theory and despite the itchiness of my art, to try on yours and, what's worse, rather wish you wouldn't. Nor am I convinced that what you are doing isn't perverse in the most pejorative sense" (1983, 249). At least Blau, as in all of his writing, honestly and openly records his personal prejudice. The indirect or subtextual homophobia in this new assimilative discourse is more alluring and ultimately more powerful in erasing the social reality and the discursive inscriptions of gay, and more specifically, lesbian discourse.

Here, the sirens of sublation may be found in the critical maneuvers of heterosexual feminist critics who metaphorize butch-femme roles, transvestites and campy dressers into a "subject who masquerades," as they put it, or is "carnivalesque" or even, as some are so bold to say, who "cross-dresses." Even when these borrowings are nested in more benign contexts than Blau's, they evacuate the historical, butch-femme couples' sense of masquerade and cross-dressing the way a cigar-store Indian evacuates the historical dress and behavior of the Native American. As is often the case, illustrated by the cigar-store Indian, these symbols may only proliferate when the social reality has been successfully obliterated and the identity has become the private property of the dominant class. Such metaphors operate simply to display the breadth of the art collection, or style collection, of the straight author. Just as the French term *film noir* became the name for B-rate American films of the forties, these notions of masquerade and cross-dressing, standing in for the roles of working-class lesbians, have come back to us through French theory on the one hand and studies of the lives of upper-class lesbians who lived in Paris between the wars on the other. In this case, the referent of the term Left Bank is not a river, but a storehouse of critical capital.

Nevertheless, this confluence of an unresolved social, historical problem in the feminist movement and these recent theoretical strategies, re-assimilated by the lesbian critic, provide a ground that could resolve the project of constructing the feminist subject position. The butch-femme subject could inhabit that discursive position, empowering it for the production of future compositions. Having already grounded this argument within the historical situation of butch-femme couples, perhaps now it would be tolerable to describe the theoretical maneuver that could become the butch-femme subject position. Unfortunately, these strategies must emerge in the bodiless world of "spectatorial positions" or "subject positions," where transvestites wear no clothes and subjects tread only "itineraries of desire." In this terrain of discourse, or among theorized spectators in darkened movie houses with their gazes fixed on the dominant cinema screen, "the thrill is gone" as Nestle described it. In the Greenwich Village bars, she could "spot a butch 50 feet away and still feel the thrill of her power" as she saw "the erotic signal of her hair at the nape of her neck, touching the shirt collar; how she held a cigarette; the symbolic pinky ring flashing as she waved her hand" (1981, 21–22). Within this theory, the erotics are gone, but certain maneuvers maintain what is generally referred to as "presence."

The origins of this theory may be found in a Freudian therapist's office, where an intellectual heterosexual woman, who had become frigid, had given way to rages, and, puzzled by her own coquettish behavior, told her story to Joan Riviere sometime around 1929. This case caused Riviere to publish her thoughts in her ground-breaking article entitled "Womanliness as a Masquerade" that later influenced several feminist critics such as Mary Russo and Mary Ann Doane and the French philosopher Jean Baudrillard. Riviere began to "read" this woman's behavior as the "wish for masculinity" which causes the woman to don "the mask of womanliness to avert anxiety and the retribution feared from men" (1929, 303). As Riviere saw it, for a woman to read an academic paper before a professional association was to exhibit in public her "possession of her father's penis, having castrated him" (1929, 305–6). In order to do recompense for this castration, which resided in her intellectual proficiency, she donned the mask of womanliness. Riviere notes: "The reader may now ask how I define womanliness or where I draw the line between genuine womanliness and the 'masquerade' ... they are the same thing" (1929, 306). Thus began the theory that all womanliness is a masquerade worn by women to disguise the fact that they have taken their father's penis in their intellectual stride, so to speak. Rather than remaining the well-adjusted castrated woman, these intellectuals have taken the penis for their own and protect it with the mask of the castrated, or womanhood. However, Riviere notes a difference here between heterosexual women and lesbian ones—the heterosexual women don't claim possession openly, but through reaction-formations; whereas the homosexual women openly display their possession of the penis and count on the males' recognition of defeat (1929, 312). This is not to suggest that the lesbian's situation is not also fraught with anxiety and reaction-formations, but this difference in degree is an important one.

I suggest that this kind of masquerade is consciously played out in butch-femme roles, particularly as they were constituted in the 1940s and 1950s. If one reads them from within Riviere's theory, the butch is the lesbian woman who proudly displays the possession of the penis, while the femme takes on the compensatory masquerade of womanliness. The femme, however, foregrounds her masquerade by playing to a butch, another woman in a role; likewise, the butch exhibits her penis to a woman who is playing the role of compensatory castration. This raises the question of "penis, penis, who's got the penis," because there is no referent in sight; rather, the fictions of penis and castration become ironized and "camped up." Unlike Riviere's patient, these women play on the phallic economy rather than to it. Both women alter this masquerading subject's function by positioning it between women and thus foregrounding the myths of penis and castration in the Freudian economy. In the bar culture, these roles were always acknowledged as such. The bars were often abuzz with the discussion of who was or was not a butch or femme, and how good they were at the role (see Davis and Kennedy 1986). In other words, these penis-related posturings were always acknowledged as roles, not biological birthrights, nor any other essentialist poses. The lesbian roles are underscored as two optional functions for women in the phallocracy, while the heterosexual woman's role collapses them into one compensatory charade. From a theatrical point of view, the butch-femme roles take on the quality of something more like a character construction and have a more active quality than what Riviere calls a reaction-formation. Thus, these roles qua roles lend agency and self-determination to the historically passive subject, providing her with at least two options for gender identification and with the aid of camp, an irony that allows her perception to be constructed from outside ideology, with a gender role that makes her appear as if she is inside of it.

Meanwhile, other feminist critics have received this masquerade theory into a heterosexual context, retaining its passive imprint. In Mary Ann Doane's influential article entitled "Film and the Masquerade: Theorizing the Female Spectator," Doane, unfortunately, resorts to a rather biologistic position in constructing the female spectator and theorizing out from the female body. From the standpoint of something more active in terms of representation such as de Lauretis's feminist subject or the notion of butch-femme, this location of critical strategies in biological realities seems revisionist. That point aside, Doane does devise a way for women to "appropriate the gaze for their own pleasure" (1982, 77) through the notion of the transvestite and the masquerade. As the former, the female subject would position herself as if she were a male viewer, assimilating all of the power and payoffs that spectatorial position offers. As the latter, she would, as Riviere earlier suggested, masquerade as a woman. She would "flaunt her femininity, produce herself as an excess of femininity—foreground the masquerade," and reveal "femininity itself . . . as a mask" (1982, 81). Thus, the masquerade would hold femininity at a distance, manufacturing "a lack in the form of a certain distance between oneself and one's image" (1982, 82). This strategy offers the female viewer a way to be the spectator of female roles while not remaining close to them, nor identifying with them, attaining the distance from them required to enter the psychoanalytic viewing space. The masquerade that Doane describes is exactly that practiced by the femme—she foregrounds cultural femininity. The difference is that Doane places this role in the spectator position, probably as an outgrowth of the passive object position required of women in the heterosexist social structures. Doane's vision of the active woman is as the active spectator. Within the butch-femme economy, the femme actively performs her masquerade as the subject of representation. She delivers a performance of the feminine masquerade rather than, as Doane suggests, continue in Riviere's reactive formation of masquerading compensatorily before the male-gaze-inscribed-dominant-cinema-screen. *Flaunting* has long been a camp verb and here Doane borrows it, along with the notion of "excess of femininity," so familiar to classical femmes and drag queens. Yet, by reinscribing it within a passive, spectatorial role, she gags and binds the traditional homosexual role players, whose gender play has nothing essential beneath it, replacing them with the passive spectatorial position that is, essentially, female.

Another feminist theorist, Mary Russo, has worked out a kind of female masquerade through the sense of the carnivalesque body derived from the work of Mikhail Bakhtin. In contrast to Doane, Russo moves on to a more active role for the masquerader, one of "making a spectacle of oneself." Russo is aware of the dangers of the essentialist body in discourse, while still maintaining some relationship between theory and real women. This seems a more hopeful critical terrain to the lesbian critic. In fact, Russo even includes a reference to historical instances of political resistance by men in drag (1985, 3). Yet in spite of her cautions, like Doane, Russo's category is once again the female subject, along with its biologically determined social resonances. Perhaps it is her reliance on the male author Bakhtin and the socialist resonances in his text (never too revealing about gender) that cause Russo to omit lesbian or gay strategies or experiences with the grotesque body. Instead, she is drawn to depictions of the pregnant body and finally Kristeva's sense of the maternal, even though she does note its limitations and problematic status within feminist thought (1985, 6). Finally, this swollen monument to reproduction, with all of its heterosexual privilege, once more stands alone in this performance area of the grotesque and carnivalesque. Though she does note the exclusion, in this practice, of the "the already marginalized" (6), once again, they do not appear. Moreover, Russo even cites Showalter's notion that feminist theory itself is a kind of "critical cross-dressing," while still suppressing the lesbian presence in the feminist community that made such a concept available to the straight theorists (1985, 8). Still true to the male, heterosexual models from which her argument derives, she identifies the master of *mise en scène* as Derrida. Even when damning his characterization of the feminist as raging bull and asking "what kind of drag is this," her referent is the feminist and not the bull . . . dyke (1985, 9). This argument marks an ironic point in history: once the feminist movement had obscured the original cross-dressed butch through the interdiction of "politically incorrect," it donned for itself the strategies and characteristics of the role-playing, safely theorized out of material reality and used to suppress the referent that produced it.

In spite of their heterosexist shortcomings, what, in these theories, can be employed to understand the construction of the butch-femme subject on the stage? First, how might they be constructed as characters? Perhaps the best example of some workings of this potential is in Split Britches' production of *Beauty and the Beast*.[1] The title itself connotes the butch-femme couple: Peggy Shaw as the butch becomes the Beast who actively pursues the femme, while Lois Weaver as the excessive femme becomes Beauty. Within the dominant system of representation, Shaw, as butch Beast, portrays a bestial woman who actively loves other women. The portrayal is faithful to the historical situation of the butch role, as Nestle describes it: "None of the butch women I was with, and this included a passing woman, ever presented themselves to me as men; they did announce themselves as tabooed women who were willing to identify their passion for other women by wearing clothes that symbolized the taking of responsibility. Part of this responsibility was sexual expertise . . . this courage to feel comfortable with arousing another woman became a political act" (1981, 21). In other words, the butch, who represents by her clothing the desire for other women, becomes the beast—the marked taboo against lesbianism dressed up in the clothes of that desire. Beauty is the desired one and the one who aims her desirability at the butch.

This symbolism becomes explicit when Shaw and Weaver interrupt the Beauty/Beast narrative to deliver a duologue about the history of their own personal butch-femme roles. Weaver uses the trope of having wished she was Katharine Hepburn and casting another woman as Spencer Tracy, while Shaw relates that she thought she was James Dean. The identification with movie idols is part of the camp assimilation of dominant culture. It serves multiple purposes: (1) they do not identify these butch-femme roles with "real" people, or literal images of gender, but with fictionalized ones, thus underscoring the masquerade; (2) the history of their desire, or their search for a sexual partner becomes a series of masks, or identities that stand for sexual attraction in the culture, thus distancing them from the "play" of seduction as it is outlined by social mores; (3) the association with movies makes narrative fiction part of the strategy as well as characters. This final fiction as fiction allows Weaver and Shaw to slip easily from one narrative to another, to yet another, unbound by through-lines, plot structure, or a stable sense of character because they are fictional at their core in the camp style and through the butch-femme roles. The instability and alienation of character and plot is compounded with their own personal butch-femme play on the street, as a recognizable couple in the lower East Side scene, as well as within fugitive narratives onstage, erasing the difference between theater and real life, or actor and character, obliterating any kind of essentialist ontology behind the play. This allows them to create a play with scenes

FIGURE 1.   Peggy Shaw and Lois Weaver of Split Britches Company. Photo: Eva Weiss. Copyright Eva Weiss.

that move easily from the narrative of beauty and the beast, to the duologue on their butch-femme history, to a recitation from *Macbeth,* to a solo lip-synced to Perry Como. The butch-femme roles at the center of their ongoing personalities move masquerade to the base of performance and no narrative net can catch them or hold them, as they wriggle into a variety of characters and plots.

This exciting multiplicity of roles and narratives signals the potency of their agency. Somehow the actor overcomes any text, yet the actor herself is a fiction and her social self is one as well. Shaw makes a joke out of suturing to any particular role or narrative form when she dies, as the beast. Immediately after dying, she gets up to tell the audience not to believe in such cheap tricks. Dies. Tells the audience that Ronald Reagan pulled the same trick when he was shot—tells them that was not worth the suturing either. Dies. Asks for a Republican doctor. Dies. Then rises to seemingly close the production by kissing Weaver. Yet even this final butch-femme tableau is followed by a song to the audience that undercuts the performance itself.

Weaver's and Shaw's production of butch-femme role-playing in and out of a fairy tale positions the representation of the lesbian couple in a childhood narrative: the preadolescent proscription of perversity. Though they used *Beauty and the Beast* to stage butch-femme as outsiders, the quintessential childhood narrative that proscribes cross-dressing is *Little Red Riding Hood,* in which the real terror of the wolf is produced by his image in grandmother's clothing. The bed, the eating metaphor, and the cross-dressing by the wolf, provide a gridlock closure of any early thoughts of transgressing gender roles. Djuna Barnes wrote a version of this perspective in *Nightwood.* When Nora sees the transvestite doctor in his bed, wearing women's nightclothes, she remarks: "God, children know something they can't tell; they like Red Riding Hood and the wolf in bed!" Barnes goes on to explicate that sight of the cross-dressed one: "Is not the gown the natural raiment of extremity? . . . He dresses to lie beside himself, who is so constructed that love, for him, can only be something special. . . ." (1961, 78–80).[2] *Beauty and the Beast* also returns to a childhood tale of taboo and liberates the sexual preference and role-playing it is designed to repress, in this case, specifically the butch-femme promise. As some lesbians prescribed in the early movement: identify with the monsters!

What, then, is the action played between these two roles? It is what Jean Baudrillard terms *séduction* and it yields many of its social fruits. Baudrillard begins his argument in *De la séduction,* by asserting that seduction is never of the natural order, but always operates as a sign, or artifice (1979, 10). By extension, this suggests that butch-femme seduction is always located in semiosis. The kiss, as Shaw and Weaver demonstrate in their swooping image of it, positioned at its most clichéd niche at the end of the narrative, is always the high camp kiss. Again, Baudrillard: seduction doesn't "recuperate the autonomy of the body . . . truth . . . the sovereignty of this seduction is transsexual, not bisexual, destroying all sexual organization. . . ." (1979, 18). The point is not to conflict reality with another reality, but to abandon the notion of reality through roles and their seductive atmosphere and lightly manipulate appearances. Surely, this is the atmosphere of camp, permeating the *mise en scène* with "pure" artifice. In other words, a strategy of appearances replaces a claim to truth. Thus, butch-femme roles evade the notion of "the female body" as it predominates in feminist theory, dragging along its Freudian baggage and scopophilic transubstantiation. These roles are played in signs themselves and not in ontologies. Seduction, as a dramatic action, transforms all of these seeming realities into semiotic play. To use Baudrillard with Riviere, butch-femme roles offer a hypersimulation of woman as she is defined by the Freudian system and the phallocracy that institutes its social rule.[3]

Therefore, the female body, the male gaze, and the structures of realism are only sex toys for the butch-femme couple. From the perspective of camp, the claim these have to realism destroys seduction by repressing the resonances of vision and sound into its medium. This is an idea worked out by Baudrillard in his chapter on pornography, but I find it apt here. That is, that realism, with its visual organization of three dimensions, actually degrades the scene; it impoverishes the suggestiveness of the scene by its excess of means (1979, 49). This implies that as realism makes the spectator see things its way, it represses her own ability to free-associate within a situation and reduces the resonances of events to its own limited, technical dimensions. Thus, the seduction of the scene is repressed by the authoritarian claim to realistic representation. This difference is marked in the work of Weaver and Shaw in the ironized, imaginative theatrical space of their butch-femme role-playing. Contrast their freely moving, resonant narrative space to the realism of Marsha Norman, Beth Henley, Irene Fornes's *Mud,* or Sam Shepard's *A Lie of the Mind.* The violence released in the continual zooming-in on the family unit, and the heterosexist ideology linked with its stage partner, realism, is directed against women and their hint of seduction. In *A Lie of the Mind,* this becomes literally woman-battering. Beth's only associative space and access to transformative discourse is the result of nearly fatal blows to her head. One can see similar violent results in Norman's concerted moving of the heroine toward suicide in *'night, Mother* or Henley's obsession with suicide in *Crimes of the Heart* or the conclusive murder in Fornes's *Mud.* The closure of these realistic narratives chokes the women to death and strangles the play of symbols, or the possibility of seduction. In fact, for each of them, sexual play only assists their entrapment. One can see the butch Peggy Shaw rising to her feet after these realistic narrative deaths and telling us not to believe it. Cast the realism aside—its consequences for women are deadly.

In recuperating the space of seduction, the butch-femme couple can, through their own agency, move through a field of symbols, like tiptoeing through the two lips (as Irigaray would have us believe), playfully inhabiting the camp space of irony and wit, free from biological determinism, elitist essentialism, and the heterosexist cleavage of sexual difference. Surely, here is a couple the feminist subject might perceive as useful to join.

NOTES

A version of this article appears in the journal *Discourse* II, no. 1, from the Center for Twentieth Century Studies, University of Wisconsin-Milwaukee.

1. There is no published version of this play. In fact, there is no satisfactory way to separate the spoken text from the action. The play is composed by three actors, Deborah Margolin along with Shaw and Weaver. Margolin, however, does not play within the lesbian dynamics, but represents a Jewish perspective. For further discussions of this group's work see Kate Davy, "Constructing the Spectator: Reception, Context, and Address in Lesbian Performance," *Performing Arts Journal* 10, no. 2 (1986): 43–52; Jill Dolan, "The Dynamics of Desire: Sexuality and Gender in Pornography and Performance," *Theatre Journal* 39, no. 2 (1987): 156–74; and Sue-Ellen Case, "From Split Subject to Split Britches," *Contemporary Women Playwrights,* ed. Enoch Brater. Oxford, 1989.

2. My thanks to Carolyn Allen, who pointed out this passage in Barnes to me in discussing resonances of the fairy tale. In another context, it would be interesting to read the lesbian perspective on the male transvestite in these passages and the way he works in Barnes's narrative. "The Company of Wolves," a short story and later a screenplay by Angela Carter, begins to open out the sexual resonances, but retains the role of the monster within heterosexuality.

3. The term *hypersimulation* is borrowed from Baudrillard's notion of the simulacrum rather than his one of seduction. It is useful here to raise the ante on terms like artifice and to suggest, as Baudrillard does, its relation to the order of reproduction and late capitalism.

REFERENCES

Barnes, Djuna. 1961. *Nightwood.* New York: New Directions.

Baudrillard, Jean. 1979. *De la séduction.* Paris: Editions Galilee.

Blau, Herbert. 1983. "Disseminating Sodom." *Salmagundi* 58–59: 221–51.

Bronski, Michael. 1984. *Culture Clash: The Making of Gay Sensibility.* Boston: South End Press.

Davis, Madeline, and Kennedy, Elizabeth Lapovsky. 1986. "Oral History and the Study of Sexuality in the Lesbian Community: Buffalo, New York, 1940–1960." *Feminist Studies* 12, no. 1: 7–26.

de Lauretis, Teresa. 1987. *Technologies of Gender.* Bloomington: Indiana University Press.

Doane, Mary Ann. 1982. "Film and the Masquerade: Theorizing the Female Spectator." *Screen* 23: 74–87.

Dolan, Jill. 1987. "The Dynamics of Desire: Sexuality and Gender in Pornography and Performance." *Theatre Journal* 39, no. 2: 156–74.

Echols, Alice. 1983. "The New Feminism of Yin and Yang." In *Powers of Desire: The Politics of Sexuality,* ed. Ann Snitow, Christine Stansell, and Sharon Thompson, 440–59. New York: Monthly Review Press.

Hollibaugh, Amber, and Moraga, Cherríe. 1983. "What We're Rollin' Around in Bed With: Sexual Silences in Feminism." In *Powers of Desire: The Politics of Sexuality,* ed. Ann Snitow, Christine Stansell, and Sharon Thompson, 395–405. New York: Monthly Review Press.

Martin, Del, and Lyon, Phyllis. 1972. *Lesbian/Woman.* New York: Bantam.

Nestle, Joan. 1981. "Butch-Fem Relationships: Sexual Courage in the 1950s." *Heresies* 12: 21–24. All pagination here is from that publication. Reprinted in Joan Nestle. 1987. *A Restricted Country,* 100–109. Ithaca: Firebrand Books.

Newton, Esther. 1972. *Mother Camp: Female Impersonators in America.* Englewood Cliffs, N.J.: Prentice-Hall.

"Postmodernism: Text, Politics, Instruction." 1987. International Association for Philosophy and Literature. Lawrence, Kansas, April 30–May 2.

Riviere, Joan. 1929. "Womanliness as a Masquerade." *International Journal of Psycho-Analysis* 10: 303–13.

Russo, Mary. 1985. "Female Grotesques: Carnival and Theory." Working Paper no. 1. Center for Twentieth Century Studies, Milwaukee. Page citations for this text. Reprinted in *Feminist Studies/Critical Studies,* ed. Teresa de Lauretis. Bloomington: Indiana University Press, 1986.

Sedgwick, Eve. 1987. "The Epistemology of the Closet." Manuscript. Revised and published in Eve Kosofsky Sedgwick, 1990. *Epistemology of the Closet.* Berkeley and Los Angeles: University of California Press. "Epistemology of the Closet," from Sedgwick 1990, is reprinted in this volume.

Sontag, Susan. 1966. *Against Interpretation.* New York: Farrar, Straus & Giroux.

Wittig, Monique. 1975. *The Lesbian Body.* Trans. David LeVay. New York: William Morrow.

20

Imitation and Gender Insubordination[1]

Judith Butler

Judith Butler, Professor of Humanities at Johns Hopkins University, is a philosopher, critic, and theorist. She is the author of Gender Trouble: Feminism and the Subversion of Identity *(Routledge, 1990) and co-editor of* Feminists Theorize the Political *(Routledge, 1992). She has also written on a variety of topics in philosophy, pornography, film, feminist and psychoanalytic theory, and the politics of sexuality and race. In "Imitation and Gender Insubordination," reprinted here from* Inside/Out *(ed. Diana Fuss, 1991), Butler explores the ways in which the assumption of a lesbian identity can serve not only to affirm but also to constrain, legislate, determine, or specify one's identity in ways that support the categories of homophobic and heterosexist thought. Asserting that the only thing lesbians may have in common is their collective experiences of sexism and homophobia, Butler argues for subverting both gender and sexual identity by destabilizing the categories that make them up. Once you realize that gender is a kind of imitation for which there is no original, that heterosexuality constantly tries and fails to reproduce its own ideal image of itself, and that sex and gender achieve their supposed "naturalness" through social performance and psychic scripting alone, then (according to Butler) you can come out as lesbian or gay without trading one straitjacket for another—and the lesbian/gay community can practice a politics that not only emphasizes a shared sexual identity but embraces many kinds of sexual, social, racial, ethnic, economic, and gender difference.*

So what is this divided being introduced into language through gender? It is an impossible being, it is a being that does not exist, an ontological joke. (*Monique Wittig*[2])

Beyond physical repetition and the psychical or metaphysical repetition, is there an *ontological* repetition? . . . This ultimate repetition, this ultimate theater, gathers everything in a certain way; and in another way, it destroys everything; and in yet another way, it selects from everything. (*Gilles Deleuze*[3])

To Theorize as a Lesbian?

At first I considered writing a different sort of essay, one with a philosophical tone: the "being" of being homosexual. The prospect of *being* anything, even for pay, has always produced in me a certain anxiety, for "to be" gay, "to be" lesbian seems to be more than a simple injunction to become who or what I already am. And in no way does it settle the anxiety for me to say that this is "part" of what I am. To write or speak *as a lesbian* appears a paradoxical appearance of this "I," one which feels neither true nor false. For it is a production, usually in response to a request, to come out or write in

307

the name of an identity which, once produced, sometimes functions as a politically
efficacious phantasm. I'm not at ease with "lesbian theories, gay theories," for as I've
argued elsewhere,[4] identity categories tend to be instruments of regulatory regimes,
whether as the normalizing categories of oppressive structures or as the rallying points
for a liberatory contestation of that very oppression. This is not to say that I will not
appear at political occasions under the sign of lesbian, but that I would like to have it
permanently unclear what precisely that sign signifies. So it is unclear how it is that I
can contribute to this book and appear under its title, for it announces a set of terms
that I propose to contest. One risk I take is to be recolonized by the sign under which
I write, and so it is this risk that I seek to thematize. To propose that the invocation of
identity is always a risk does not imply that resistance to it is always or only symptomatic
of a self-inflicted homophobia. Indeed, a Foucauldian perspective might argue that the
affirmation of "homosexuality" is itself an extension of a homophobic discourse. And
yet "discourse," he writes on the same page, "can be both an instrument and an effect
of power, but also a hindrance, a stumbling-block, a point of resistance and a starting
point for an opposing strategy."[5]

So I am skeptical about how the "I" is determined as it operates under the title
of the lesbian sign, and I am no more comfortable with its homophobic determination
than with those normative definitions offered by other members of the "gay or lesbian
community." I'm permanently troubled by identity categories, consider them to be
invariable stumbling-blocks, and understand them, even promote them, as sites of necessary trouble. In fact, if the category were to offer no trouble, it would cease to be
interesting to me: it is precisely the *pleasure* produced by the instability of those categories
which sustains the various erotic practices that make me a candidate for the category
to begin with. To install myself within the terms of an identity category would be to
turn against the sexuality that the category purports to describe; and this might be true
for any identity category which seeks to control the very eroticism that it claims to
describe and authorize, much less "liberate."

And what's worse, I do not understand the notion of "theory," and am hardly
interested in being cast as its defender, much less in being signified as part of an elite
gay/lesbian theory crowd that seeks to establish the legitimacy and domestication of
gay/lesbian studies within the academy. Is there a pregiven distinction between theory,
politics, culture, media? How do those divisions operate to quell a certain intertextual
writing that might well generate wholly different epistemic maps? But I am writing
here now: is it too late? Can this writing, can any writing, refuse the terms by which
it is appropriated even as, to some extent, that very colonizing discourse enables or
produces this stumbling block, this resistance? How do I relate the paradoxical situation
of this dependency and refusal?

If the political task is to show that theory is never merely *theoria,* in the sense of
disengaged contemplation, and to insist that it is fully political (*phronesis* or even *praxis*),
then why not simply call this operation *politics,* or some necessary permutation of it?

I have begun with confessions of trepidation and a series of disclaimers, but perhaps
it will become clear that *disclaiming,* which is no simple activity, will be what I have to
offer as a form of affirmative resistance to a certain regulatory operation of homophobia.
The discourse of "coming out" has clearly served its purposes, but what are its risks?
And here I am not speaking of unemployment or public attack or violence, which are
quite clearly and widely on the increase against those who are perceived as "out" whether
or not of their own design. Is the "subject" who is "out" free of its subjection and
finally in the clear? Or could it be that the subjection that subjectivates the gay or lesbian
subject in some ways continues to oppress, or oppresses most insidiously, once "outness"

is claimed? What or who is it that is "out," made manifest and fully disclosed, when and if I reveal myself as lesbian? What is it that is now known, anything? What remains permanently concealed by the very linguistic act that offers up the promise of a transparent revelation of sexuality? Can sexuality even remain sexuality once it submits to a criterion of transparency and disclosure, or does it perhaps cease to be sexuality precisely when the semblance of full explicitness is achieved?[6] Is sexuality of any kind even possible without that opacity designated by the unconscious, which means simply that the conscious "I" who would reveal its sexuality is perhaps the last to know the meaning of what it says?

To claim that this is what I *am* is to suggest a provisional totalization of this "I." But if the I can so determine itself, then that which it excludes in order to make that determination remains constitutive of the determination itself. In other words, such a statement presupposes that the "I" exceeds its determination, and even produces that very excess in and by the act which seeks to exhaust the semantic field of that "I." In the act which would disclose the true and full content of that "I," a certain radical *concealment* is thereby produced. For it is always finally unclear what is meant by invoking the lesbian-signifier, since its signification is always to some degree out of one's control, but also because its *specificity* can only be demarcated by exclusions that return to disrupt its claim to coherence. What, if anything, can lesbians be said to share? And who will decide this question, and in the name of whom? If I claim to be a lesbian, I "come out" only to produce a new and different "closet." The "you" to whom I come out now has access to a different region of opacity. Indeed, the locus of opacity has simply shifted: before, you did not know whether I "am," but now you do not know what that means, which is to say that the copula is empty, that it cannot be substituted for with a set of descriptions.[7] And perhaps that is a situation to be valued. Conventionally, one comes out *of* the closet (and yet, how often is it the case that we are "outed" when we are young and without resources?); so we are out of the closet, but into what? what new unbounded spatiality? the room, the den, the attic, the basement, the house, the bar, the university, some new enclosure whose door, like Kafka's door, produces the expectation of a fresh air and a light of illumination that never arrives? Curiously, it is the figure of the closet that produces this expectation, and which guarantees its dissatisfaction. For being "out" always depends to some extent on being "in"; it gains its meaning only within that polarity. Hence, being "out" must produce the closet again and again in order to maintain itself as "out." In this sense, *outness* can only produce a new opacity; and *the closet* produces the promise of a disclosure that can, by definition, never come. Is this infinite postponement of the disclosure of "gayness," produced by the very act of "coming out," to be lamented? Or is this very deferral of the signified *to be valued,* a site for the production of values, precisely because the term now takes on a life that cannot be, can never be, permanently controlled?

It is possible to argue that whereas no transparent or full revelation is afforded by "lesbian" and "gay," there remains a political imperative to use these necessary errors or category mistakes, as it were (what Gayatri Spivak might call "catachrestic" operations: to use a proper name improperly[8]), to rally and represent an oppressed political constituency. Clearly, I am not legislating against the use of the term. My question is simply: which use will be legislated, and what play will there be between legislation and use such that the instrumental uses of "identity" do not become regulatory imperatives? If it is already true that "lesbians" and "gay men" have been traditionally designated as impossible identities, errors of classification, unnatural disasters within juridico-medical discourses, or, what perhaps amounts to the same, the very paradigm of what calls to be classified, regulated, and controlled, then perhaps these sites of disruption, error, confusion, and trouble can be the very rallying points for a certain resistance to classification and to identity as such.

The question is not one of *avowing* or *disavowing* the category of lesbian or gay, but, rather, why it is that the category becomes the site of this "ethical" choice? What does it mean to *avow* a category that can only maintain its specificity and coherence by performing a prior set of *disavowals?* Does this make "coming out" into the avoval of disavowal, that is, a return to the closet under the guise of an escape? And it is not something like heterosexuality or bisexuality that is disavowed by the category, but a set of identificatory and practical crossings between these categories that renders the discreteness of each equally suspect. Is it not possible to maintain and pursue heterosexual identifications and aims within homosexual practice, and homosexual identifications and aims within heterosexual practices? If a sexuality is to be disclosed, what will be taken as the true determinant of its meaning: the phantasy structure, the act, the orifice, the gender, the anatomy? And if the practice engages a complex interplay of all of those, which one of this erotic dimensions will come to stand for the sexuality that requires them all? Is it the *specificity* of a lesbian experience or lesbian desire or lesbian sexuality that lesbian theory needs to elucidate? Those efforts have only and always produced a set of contests and refusals which should by now make it clear that there is no necessarily common element among lesbians, except perhaps that we all know something about how homophobia works against women—although, even then, the language and the analysis we use will differ.

To argue that there might be a *specificity* to lesbian sexuality has seemed a necessary counterpoint to the claim that lesbian sexuality is just heterosexuality once removed, or that it is derived, or that it does not exist. But perhaps the claim of specificity, on the one hand, and the claim of derivativeness or non-existence, on the other, are not as contradictory as they seem. Is it not possible that lesbian sexuality is a process that reinscribes the power domains that it resists, that it is constituted in part from the very heterosexual matrix that it seeks to displace, and that its specificity is to be established, not *outside* or *beyond* that reinscription or reiteration, but in the very modality and effects of that reinscription? In other words, the negative constructions of lesbianism as a fake or a bad copy can be occupied and reworked to call into question the claims of hetero-sexual priority. In a sense I hope to make clear in what follows, lesbian sexuality can be understood to redeploy its "derivativeness" in the service of displacing hegemonic heterosexual norms. Understood in this way, the political problem is not to establish the specificity of lesbian sexuality over and against its derivativeness, but to turn the homophobic construction of the bad copy against the framework that privileges het-erosexuality as origin, and so "derive" the former from the latter. This description requires a reconsideration of imitation, drag, and other forms of sexual crossing that affirm the internal complexity of a lesbian sexuality constituted in part within the very matrix of power that it is compelled both to reiterate and to oppose.

On the Being of Gayness as Necessary Drag

The professionalization of gayness requires a certain performance and production of a "self" which is the *constituted effect* of a discourse that nevertheless claims to "represent" that self as a prior truth. When I spoke at the conference on homosexuality in 1989,[9] I found myself telling my friends beforehand that I was off to Yale to be a lesbian, which of course didn't mean that I wasn't one before, but that somehow then, as I spoke in that context, I *was* one in some more thorough and totalizing way, at least for the time being. So I *am* one, and my qualifications are even fairly unambiguous. Since I was sixteen, being a lesbian is what I've been. So what's the anxiety, the discomfort? Well, it has something to do with that redoubling, the way I can say, I'm going to Yale to be a lesbian; a lesbian is what I've been being for so long. How is it that I can both "be" one, and yet endeavor to be one at the same time? When and where does my being a lesbian come into play, when and where does this playing a lesbian constitute something like what I am? To say that I "play" at being one is not to say that I am not one "really"; rather, how and where I play at being one is the way in which that "being" gets established, instituted, circulated, and confirmed. This is not a performance from which I can take radical distance, for this is deep-seated play, psychically entrenched play, *and this "I" does not play its lesbianism as a role.* Rather, it is through the repeated play of this sexuality that the "I" is insistently reconstituted as a lesbian "I"; paradoxically, it is precisely the *repetition* of that play that establishes as well the *instability* of the very category that it constitutes. For if the "I" is a site of repetition, that is, if the "I" only achieves the semblance of identity through a certain repetition of itself, then the I is always displaced by the very repetition that sustains it. In other words, does or can the "I" ever repeat itself, cite itself, faithfully, or is there always a displacement from its former moment that establishes the permanently non-self-identical status of that "I" or its "being lesbian"? What "performs" does not exhaust the "I"; it does not lay out in visible terms the comprehensive content of that "I," for if the performance is "repeated," there is always the question of what differentiates from each other the moments of identity that are repeated. And if the "I" is the effect of a certain repetition, one which produces the semblance of a continuity or coherence, then there is no "I" that precedes the gender that it is said to perform; the repetition, and the failure to repeat, produce a string of performances that constitute and contest the coherence of that "I."

But *politically*, we might argue, isn't it quite crucial to insist on lesbian and gay identities precisely because they are being threatened with erasure and obliteration from homophobic quarters? Isn't the above theory *complicitous* with those political forces that would obliterate the possibility of gay and lesbian identity? Isn't it "no accident" that such theoretical contestations of identity emerge within a political climate that is performing a set of similar obliterations of homosexual identities through legal and political means?

The question I want to raise in return is this: ought such threats of obliteration dictate the terms of the political resistance to them, and if they do, do such homophobic efforts to that extent win the battle from the start? There is no question that gays and lesbians are threatened by the violence of public erasure, but the decision to counter that violence must be careful not to reinstall another in its place. Which version of lesbian or gay ought to be rendered visible, and which internal exclusions will that rendering visible institute? Can the visibility of identity *suffice* as a political strategy, or can it only be the starting point for a strategic intervention which calls for a transformation of policy? Is it not a sign of despair over public politics when identity becomes its own policy, bringing with it those who would "police" it from various sides? And this is not a call to return to silence or invisibility, but, rather, to make use of a category that can be called into question, made to account for what it excludes. That any consolidation of identity requires some set of differentiations and exclusions seems clear. But which ones ought to be valorized? That the identity-sign I use now has its purposes seems right, but there is no way to predict or control the political uses to which that sign will be put in the future. And perhaps this is a kind of openness, regardless of its risks, that ought to be safeguarded for political reasons. If the rendering visible of lesbian/gay identity now presupposes a set of exclusions, then perhaps part of what is necessarily excluded is *the future uses of the sign.* There is a political necessity to use some sign now, and we do, but how to use it in such a way that its futural significations are not *foreclosed?* How to use the sign and avow its temporal contingency at once?

In avowing the sign's strategic provisionality (rather than its strategic essentialism), that identity can become a site of contest and revision, indeed, take on a future set of significations that those of us who use it now may not be able to foresee. It is in the safeguarding of the future of the political signifiers—preserving the signifier as a site of rearticulation—that Laclau and Mouffe discern its democratic promise.

Within contemporary U.S. politics, there are a vast number of ways in which lesbianism in particular is understood as precisely that which cannot or dare not *be.* In a sense, Jesse Helms's attack on the NEA for sanctioning representations of "homo-eroticism" focuses various homophobic fantasies of what gay men are and do on the work of Robert Mapplethorpe.[10] In a sense, for Helms, gay men exist as objects of prohibition; they are, in his twisted fantasy, sadomasochistic exploiters of children, the paradigmatic exemplars of "obscenity"; in a sense, the lesbian is not even produced within this discourse as a prohibited object. Here it becomes important to recognize that oppression works not merely through acts of overt prohibition, but covertly, through the constitution of viable subjects and through the corollary constitution of a domain of unviable (un)subjects—*abjects,* we might call them—who are neither named nor pro-hibited within the economy of the law. Here oppression works through the production of a domain of unthinkability and unnameability. Lesbianism is not explicitly prohibited in part because it has not even made its way into the thinkable, the imaginable, that grid of cultural intelligibility that regulates the real and the nameable. How, then, to "be" a lesbian in a political context in which the lesbian does not exist? That is, in a political discourse that wages its violence against lesbianism in part by excluding les-bianism from discourse itself? To be prohibited explicitly is to occupy a discursive site from which something like a reverse-discourse can be articulated; to be implicitly pros-cribed is not even to qualify as an object of prohibition.[11] And though homosexualities of all kinds in this present climate are being erased, reduced, and (then) reconstituted as sites of radical homophobic fantasy, it is important to retrace the different routes by which the unthinkability of homosexuality is being constituted time and again.

It is one thing to be erased from discourse, and yet another to be present within discourse as an abiding falsehood. Hence, there is a political imperative to render les-bianism visible, but how is that to be done outside or through existing regulatory regimes? Can the exclusion from ontology itself become a rallying point for resistance?

Here is something like a confession which is meant merely to thematize the impossibility of confession: As a young person, I suffered for a long time, and I suspect many people have, from being told, explicitly or implicitly, that what I "am" is a copy, an imitation, a derivative example, a shadow of the real. Compulsory heterosexuality sets itself up as the original, the true, the authentic; the norm that determines the real implies that "being" lesbian is always a kind of miming, a vain effort to participate in the phantasmatic plenitude of naturalized heterosexuality which will always and only fail.[12] And yet, I remember quite distinctly when I first read in Esther Newton's *Mother Camp: Female Impersonators in America*[13] that drag is not an imitation or a copy of some prior and true gender; according to Newton, drag enacts the very structure of imper-sonation by which *any gender* is assumed. Drag is not the putting on of a gender that belongs properly to some other group, i.e. an act of *ex*propriation or *ap*propriation that assumes that gender is the rightful property of sex, that "masculine" belongs to "male" and "feminine" belongs to "female." There is no "proper" gender, a gender proper to one sex rather than another, which is in some sense that sex's cultural property. Where that notion of the "proper" operates, it is always and only *improperly* installed as the effect of a compulsory system. Drag constitutes the mundane way in which genders are appropriated, theatricalized, worn, and done; it implies that all gendering is a kind of impersonation and approximation. If this is true, it seems, there is no original or primary gender that drag imitates, but *gender is a kind of imitation for which there is no original;* in fact, it is a kind of imitation that produces the very notion of the original as an *effect* and consequence of the imitation itself. In other words, the naturalistic effects of heterosexualized genders are produced through imitative strategies; what they imitate is a phantasmatic ideal of heterosexual identity, one that is produced by the imitation as its effect. In this sense, the "reality" of heterosexual identities is performatively constituted through an imitation that sets itself up as the origin and the ground of all imitations. In other words, heterosexuality is always in the process of imitating and approximating its own phantasmatic idealization of itself—*and failing.* Precisely because it is bound to fail, and yet endeavors to succeed, the project of heterosexual identity is propelled into an endless repetition of itself. Indeed, in its efforts to naturalize itself as the original, heterosexuality must be understood as a compulsive and compulsory repetition that can only produce the *effect* of its own originality; in other words, compulsory heterosexual identities, those ontologically consolidated phantasms of "man" and "woman," are theatrically produced effects that posture as grounds, origins, the normative measure of the real.[14]

Reconsider then the homophobic charge that queens and butches and femmes are imitations of the heterosexual real. Here "imitation" carries the meaning of "derivative" or "secondary," a copy of an origin which is itself the ground of all copies, but which is itself a copy of nothing. Logically, this notion of an "origin" is suspect, for how can something operate as an origin if there are no secondary consequences which retrospectively confirm the originality of that origin? The origin requires its derivations in order to affirm itself as an origin, for origins only make sense to the extent that they are differentiated from that which they produce as derivatives. Hence, if it were not for the notion of the homosexual *as* copy, there would be no construct of heterosexuality *as* origin. Heterosexuality here presupposes homosexuality. And if the homosexual *as* copy *precedes* the heterosexual as *origin,* then it seems only fair to concede that the copy comes before the origin, and that homosexuality is thus the origin, and heterosexuality the copy.

But simple inversions are not really possible. For it is only *as* a copy that homosexuality can be argued to *precede* heterosexuality as the origin. In other words, the entire framework of copy and origin proves radically unstable as each position inverts into the other and confounds the possibility of any stable way to locate the temporal or logical priority of either term.

But let us then consider this problematic inversion from a psychic/political perspective. If the structure of gender imitation is such that the imitat*ed* is to some degree produced—or, rather, *re*produced—by imitation (see again Derrida's inversion and displacement of mimesis in "The Double Session"), then to claim that gay and lesbian identities are implicated in heterosexual norms or in hegemonic culture generally is not to *derive* gayness from straightness. On the contrary, *imitation* does not copy that which is prior, but produces and *inverts* the very terms of priority and derivativeness. Hence, if gay identities are implicated in heterosexuality, that is not the same as claiming that they are determined or derived from heterosexuality, and it is not the same as claiming that that heterosexuality is the only cultural network in which they are implicated. These are, quite literally, *inverted* imitations, ones which invert the order of imitated and imitation, and which, in the process, expose the fundamental dependency of "the origin" on that which it claims to produce as its secondary effect.

What follows if we concede from the start that gay identities as derivative inversions are in part defined in terms of the very heterosexual identities from which they are differentiated? If heterosexuality is an impossible imitation of itself, an imitation that performatively constitutes itself as the original, then the imitative parody of "heterosexuality"—when and where it exists in gay cultures—is always and only an imitation of an imitation, a copy of a copy, for which there is no original. Put in yet a different way, the parodic or imitative effect of gay identities works neither to copy nor to emulate heterosexuality, but rather, to expose heterosexuality as an incessant and *panicked* imitation of its own naturalized idealization. That heterosexuality is always in the act of elaborating itself is evidence that it is perpetually at risk, that is, that it "knows" its own possibility of becoming undone: hence, its compulsion to repeat which is at once a foreclosure of that which threatens its coherence. That it can never eradicate that risk attests to its profound dependency upon the homosexuality that it seeks fully to eradicate and never can or that it seeks to make second, but which is always already there as a prior possibility.[15] Although this failure of naturalized heterosexuality might constitute a source of pathos for heterosexuality itself—what its theorists often refer to as its constitutive malaise—it can become an occasion for a subversive and proliferating parody of gender norms in which the very claim to originality and to the real is shown to be the effect of a certain kind of naturalized gender mime.

It is important to recognize the ways in which heterosexual norms reappear within gay identities, to affirm that gay and lesbian identities are not only structured in part by dominant heterosexual frames, but that they are *not* for that reason *determined* by them. They are running commentaries on those naturalized positions as well, parodic replays and resignifications of precisely those heterosexual structures that would consign gay life to discursive domains of unreality and unthinkability. But to be constituted or structured in part by the very heterosexual norms by which gay people are oppressed is not, I repeat, to be claimed or determined by those structures. And it is not necessary to think of such heterosexual constructs as the pernicious intrusion of "the straight mind," one that must be rooted out in its entirety. In a way, the presence of heterosexual constructs and positionalities in whatever form in gay and lesbian identities presupposes that there is a gay and lesbian repetition of straightness, a recapitulation of straightness—which is itself a repetition and recapitulation of its own ideality—within its own terms, a site in which all sorts of resignifying and parodic repetitions become possible. The parodic replication and resignification of heterosexual constructs within non-heterosexual frames brings into relief the utterly constructed status of the so-called original, but it shows that heterosexuality only constitutes itself as the original through a convincing act of repetition. The more that "act" is expropriated, the more the heterosexual claim to originality is exposed as illusory.

Although I have concentrated in the above on the reality-effects of gender practices, performances, repetitions, and mimes, I do not mean to suggest that drag is a "role" that can be taken on or taken off at will. There is no volitional subject behind the mime who decides, as it were, which gender it will be today. On the contrary, the very possibility of becoming a viable subject requires that a certain gender mime be already underway. The "being" of the subject is no more self-identical than the "being" of any gender; in fact, coherent gender, achieved through an apparent repetition of the same, produces as its *effect* the illusion of a prior and volitional subject. In this sense, gender is not a performance that a prior subject elects to do, but gender is *performative* in the sense that it constitutes as an effect the very subject it appears to express. It is a *compulsory* performance in the sense that acting out of line with heterosexual norms brings with it ostracism, punishment, and violence, not to mention the transgressive pleasures produced by those very prohibitions.

To claim that there is no performer prior to the performed, that the performance is performative, that the performance constitutes the appearance of a "subject" as its effect is difficult to accept. This difficulty is the result of a predisposition to think of sexuality and gender as "expressing" in some indirect or direct way a psychic reality that precedes it. The denial of the *priority* of the subject, however, is not the denial of the subject; in fact, the refusal to conflate the subject with the psyche marks the psychic as that which exceeds the domain of the conscious subject. This psychic excess is precisely what is being systematically denied by the notion of a volitional "subject" who elects at will which gender and/or sexuality to be at any given time and place. It is this excess which erupts within the intervals of those repeated gestures and acts that construct the apparent uniformity of heterosexual positionalities, indeed which compels the repetition itself, and which guarantees its perpetual failure. In this sense, it is this excess which, within the heterosexual economy, implicitly includes homosexuality, that perpetual threat of a disruption which is quelled through a reenforced repetition of the same. And yet, if repetition is the way in which power works to construct the illusion of a seamless heterosexual identity, if heterosexuality is compelled to *repeat itself* in order to establish the illusion of its own uniformity and identity, then this is an identity permanently at risk, for what if it fails to repeat, or if the very exercise of repetition is redeployed for a very different performative purpose? If there is, as it were, always a compulsion to repeat, repetition never fully accomplishes identity. That there is a need for a repetition at all is a sign that identity is not self-identical. It requires to be instituted again and again, which is to say that it runs the risk of becoming *de*-instituted at every interval.

So what is this psychic excess, and what will constitute a subversive or *de*-instituting repetition? First, it is necessary to consider that sexuality always exceeds any given performance, presentation, or narrative which is why it is not possible to derive or read off a sexuality from any given gender presentation. And sexuality may be said to exceed any definitive narrativization. Sexuality is never fully "expressed" in a performance or practice; there will be passive and butchy femmes, femmy and aggressive butches, and both of those, and more, will turn out to describe more or less anatomically stable "males" and "females." There are no direct expressive or causal lines between sex, gender, gender presentation, sexual practice, fantasy and sexuality. None of those terms captures or determines the rest. Part of what constitutes sexuality is precisely that which does not appear and that which, to some degree, can never appear. This is perhaps the most fundamental reason why sexuality is to some degree always closeted, especially to the one who would express it through acts of self-disclosure. That which is excluded for a given gender presentation to "succeed" may be precisely what is played out sexually, that is, an "inverted" relation, as it were, between gender and gender presentation, and gender presentation and sexuality. On the other hand, both gender presentation and sexual practices may corollate such that it appears that the former "expresses" the latter, and yet both are jointly constituted by the very sexual possibilities that they exclude.

This logic of inversion gets played out interestingly in versions of lesbian butch and femme gender stylization. For a butch can present herself as capable, forceful, and all-providing, and a stone butch may well seek to constitute her lover as the exclusive site of erotic attention and pleasure. And yet, this "providing" butch who seems *at first* to replicate a certain husband-like role, can find herself caught in a logic of inversion whereby that "providingness" turns to a self-sacrifice, which implicates her in the most ancient trap of feminine self-abnegation. She may well find herself in a situation of radical need, which is precisely what she sought to locate, find, and fulfill in her femme lover. In effect, the butch inverts into the femme or remains caught up in the specter of that inversion, or takes pleasure in it. On the other hand, the femme who, as Amber Hollibaugh has argued, "orchestrates" sexual exchange,[16] may well eroticize a certain dependency only to learn that the very power to orchestrate that dependency exposes her own incontrovertible power, at which point she inverts into a butch or becomes caught up in the specter of that inversion, or perhaps delights in it.

Psychic Mimesis

What stylizes or forms an erotic style and/or a gender presentation—and that which makes such categories inherently unstable—is a set of *psychic identifications* that are not simple to describe. Some psychoanalytic theories tend to construe identification and desire as two mutually exclusive relations to love objects that have been lost through prohibition and/or separation. Any intense emotional attachment thus divides into either wanting to have someone or wanting to be that someone, but never both at once. It is important to consider that identification and desire can coexist, and that their formulation in terms of mutually exclusive oppositions serves a heterosexual matrix. But I would like to focus attention on yet a different construal of that scenario, namely, that "wanting to be" and "wanting to have" can operate to differentiate mutually exclusive position-alities internal to lesbian erotic exchange. Consider that identifications are always made in response to loss of some kind, and that they involve a certain *mimetic practice* that seeks to incorporate the lost love within the very "identity" of the one who remains. This was Freud's thesis in "Mourning and Melancholia" in 1917 and continues to inform contemporary psychoanalytic discussions of identification.[17]

For psychoanalytic theorists Mikkel Borch-Jacobsen and Ruth Leys, however, identification and, in particular, identificatory mimetism, *precedes* "identity" and constitutes identity as that which is fundamentally "other to itself." The notion of this Other *in* the self, as it were, implies that the self/Other distinction is *not* primarily external (a powerful critique of ego psychology follows from this); the self is from the start radically implicated in the "Other." This theory of primary mimetism differs from Freud's account of melancholic incorporation. In Freud's view, which I continue to find useful, incorporation—a kind of psychic miming—is a response to, and refusal of, *loss*. Gender as the site of such psychic mimes is thus constituted by the variously gendered Others who have been loved and lost, where the loss is suspended through a melancholic and imaginary incorporation (and preservation) of those Others into the psyche. Over and against this account of psychic mimesis by way of incorporation and melancholy, the theory of primary mimetism argues an even stronger position in favor of the non-self-identity of the psychic subject. Mimetism is not motivated by a drama of loss and wishful recovery, but appears to precede and constitute desire (and motivation) itself; in this sense, mimetism would be prior to the possibility of loss and the disappointments of love.

Whether loss or mimetism is primary (perhaps an undecidable problem), the psychic subject is nevertheless constituted internally by differentially gendered Others and is, therefore, never, as a gender, self-identical.

In my view, the self only becomes a self on the condition that it has suffered a separation (grammar fails us here, for the "it" only becomes differentiated through that separation), a loss which is suspended and provisionally resolved through a melancholic incorporation of some "Other." That "Other" installed in the self thus establishes the permanent incapacity of that "self" to achieve self-identity; it is as it were always already disrupted by that Other; the disruption of the Other at the heart of the self is the very condition of that self's possibility.[18]

Such a consideration of psychic identification would vitiate the possibility of any stable set of typologies that explain or describe something like gay or lesbian identities. And any efforts to supply one—as evidenced in Kaja Silverman's recent inquiries into male homosexuality—suffer from simplification, and conform, with alarming ease, to the regulatory requirements of diagnostic epistemic regimes. If incorporation in Freud's sense in 1914 is an effort to *preserve* a lost and loved object and to refuse or postpone the recognition of loss and, hence, of grief, then to become *like* one's mother or father or sibling or other early "lovers" may be an act of love and/or a hateful effort to replace or displace. How would we "typologize" the ambivalence at the heart of mimetic incorporations such as these?[19]

How does this consideration of psychic identification return us to the question, what constitutes a subversive repetition? How are troublesome identifications apparent in cultural practices? Well, consider the way in which heterosexuality naturalizes itself through setting up certain illusions of continuity between sex, gender, and desire. When Aretha Franklin sings, "you make me feel like a natural woman," she seems at first to suggest that some natural potential of her biological sex is actualized by her participation in the cultural position of "woman" as object of heterosexual recognition. Something in her "sex" is thus expressed by her "gender" which is then fully known and consecrated within the heterosexual scene. There is no breakage, no discontinuity between "sex" as biological facticity and essence, or between gender and sexuality. Although Aretha appears to be all too glad to have her naturalness confirmed, she also seems fully and paradoxically mindful that that confirmation is never guaranteed, that the effect of naturalness is only achieved as a consequence of that moment of heterosexual recognition. After all, Aretha sings, you make me feel *like* a natural woman, suggesting that this is a kind of metaphorical substitution, an act of imposture, a kind of sublime and momentary participation in an ontological illusion produced by the mundane operation of hetero-sexual drag.

But what if Aretha were singing to me? Or what if she were singing to a drag queen whose performance somehow confirmed her own?

How do we take account of these kinds of identifications? It's not that there is some kind of *sex* that exists in hazy biological form that is somehow *expressed* in the gait, the posture, the gesture; and that some sexuality then expresses both that apparent gender or that more or less magical sex. If gender is drag, and if it is an imitation that regularly produces the ideal it attempts to approximate, then gender is a performance that *produces* the illusion of an inner sex or essence or psychic gender core; it *produces* on the skin, through the gesture, the move, the gait (that array of corporeal theatrics understood as gender presentation), the illusion of an inner depth. In effect, one way that genders gets naturalized is through being constructed as an inner psychic or physical *necessity*. And yet, it is always a surface sign, a signification on and with the public body that produces this illusion of an inner depth, necessity, or essence that is somehow magically, causally expressed.

To dispute the psyche as *inner depth,* however, is not to refuse the psyche altogether. On the contrary, the psyche calls to be rethought precisely as a compulsive repetition, as that which conditions and disables the repetitive performance of identity. If every performance repeats itself to institute the effect of identity, then every repetition requires an interval between the acts, as it were, in which risk and excess threaten to disrupt the identity being constituted. The unconscious is this excess that enables and contests every performance, and which never fully appears within the performance itself. The psyche is not "in" the body, but in the very signifying process through which that body comes to appear; it is the lapse in repetition as well as its compulsion, precisely what the performance seeks to deny, and that which compels it from the start.

To locate the psyche within this signifying chain as the instability of all iterability is not the same as claiming that it is inner core that is awaiting its full and liberatory expression. On the contrary, the psyche is the permanent failure of expression, a failure that has its values, for it impels repetition and so reinstates the possibility of disruption. What then does it mean to pursue disruptive repetition within compulsory heterosexuality?

Although compulsory heterosexuality often presumes that there is first a sex that is expressed through a gender and then through a sexuality, it may now be necessary fully to invert and displace that operation of thought. If a regime of sexuality mandates a compulsory performance of sex, then it may be only through that performance that the binary system of gender and the binary system of sex come to have intelligibility at all. It may be that the very categories of sex, of sexual identity, of gender are produced or maintained in the *effects* of this compulsory performance, effects which are disingenuously renamed as causes, origins, disingenuously lined up within a causal or expressive sequence that the heterosexual norm produces to legitimate itself as the origin of all sex. How then to expose the causal lines as retrospectively and performatively produced fabrications, and to engage gender itself as an inevitable fabrication, to fabricate gender in terms which reveal every claim to the origin, the inner, the true, and the real as nothing other than the effects of *drag,* whose subversive possibilities ought to be played and replayed to make the "sex" of gender into a site of insistent political play? Perhaps this will be a matter of working sexuality *against* identity, even against gender, and of letting that which cannot fully appear in any performance persist in its disruptive promise.

Notes

1. Parts of this essay were given as a presentation at the Conference on Homosexuality at Yale University in October, 1989.

2. "The Mark of Gender," *Feminist Issues* 5, no. 2 (1985): 6.

3. *Différence et répétition* (Paris: PUF, 1968), 374; my translation.

4. *Gender Trouble: Feminism and the Subversion of Identity* (New York and London: Routledge, 1990).

5. Michel Foucault, *The History of Sexuality, Vol. I,* trans. John Hurley (New York: Random House, 1980), 101.

6. Here I would doubtless differ from the very fine analysis of Hitchcock's *Rope* offered by D.A. Miller. See "Anal *Rope,*" in *Inside/Out: Lesbian Theories, Gay Theories*, ed. Diana Fuss (New York: Routledge, 1991).

7. For an example of "coming out" that is strictly unconfessional and which, finally, offers no content for the category of lesbian, see Barbara Johnson's deftly constructed "Sula Passing: No Passing" presentation at UCLA, May 1990.

8. Gayatri Chakravorty Spivak, "Displacement and the Discourse of Woman." In *Displacement: Derrida and After,* ed. Mark Krupnick (Bloomington: Indiana University Press, 1983).

9. Let me take this occasion to apologize to the social worker at that conference who asked a question about how to deal with those clients with AIDS who turned to Bernie Segal and others for the purposes of psychic healing. At the time, I understood this questioner to be suggesting that such clients were full of self-hatred because they were trying to find the causes of AIDS in their own selves. The questioner and I appear to agree that any effort to locate the responsibility for AIDS in those who suffer from it is politically and ethically wrong. I thought the questioner, however, was prepared to tell his clients that they were self-hating, and I reacted strongly (too

strongly) to the paternalistic prospect that this person was going to pass judgment on someone who was clearly not only suffering, but already passing judgment on him or herself. To call another person self-hating is itself an act of power that calls for some kind of scrutiny, and I think in response to someone who is already dealing with AIDS, that is perhaps the last thing one needs to hear. I also happened to have a friend who sought out advice from Bernie Segal, not with the belief that there is an exclusive or even primary psychic cause or solution for AIDS, but that there might be a psychic contribution to be made to surviving with AIDS. Unfortunately, I reacted quickly to this questioner, and with some anger. And I regret now that I didn't have my wits about me to discuss the distinctions with him that I have just laid out.

Curiously, this incident was invoked at a CLAGS (Center for Lesbian and Gay Studies) meeting at CUNY sometime in December of 1989 and, according to those who told me about it, my angry denunciation of the social worker was taken to be symptomatic of the political insensitivity of a "theorist" in dealing with someone who is actively engaged in AIDS work. That attribution implies that I do not do AIDS work, that I am not politically engaged, and that the social worker in question does not read theory. Needless to say, I was reacting angrily on behalf of an absent friend with AIDS who sought out Bernie Segal and company. So as I offer this apology to the social worker, I wait expectantly that the CLAGS member who misunderstood me will offer me one in turn.

10. See my "The Force of Fantasy: Feminism, Mapplethorpe, and Discursive Excess," *differences* 2, no. 2 (Summer 1990). Since the writing of this essay, lesbian artists and representations have also come under attack.

11. It is this particular ruse of erasure which Foucault for the most part fails to take account of in his analysis of power. He almost always presumes that power takes place through discourse as its instrument, and that oppression is linked with subjection and subjectivation, that is, that it is installed as the formative principle of the identity of subjects.

12. Although miming suggests that there is a prior model which is being copied, it can have the effect of exposing that prior model as purely phantasmatic. In Jacques Derrida's "The Double Session" in *Dissemination,* trans. Barbara Johnson (Chicago: University of Chicago Press, 1981), he considers the textual effect of the mime in Mallarmé's "Mimique." There Derrida argues that the mime does not imitate or copy some prior phenomenon, idea, or figure, but constitutes—some might say *performatively*—the phantasm of the original in and through the mime:

> He represents nothing, imitates nothing, does not have to conform to any prior referent with the aim of achieving adequation or verisimilitude. One can here foresee an objection: since the mime imitates nothing, reproduces nothing, opens up in its origin the very thing he is tracing out, presenting, or producing, he must be the very movement of truth. Not, of course, truth in the form of adequation between the representation and the present of the thing itself, or between the imitator and the imitated, but truth as the present unveiling of the present. . . . But this is not the case. . . . We are faced then with mimicry imitating nothing: faced, so to speak, with a double that couples no simple, a double that nothing anticipates, nothing at least that is not itself already double. There is no simple reference. . . . This speculum reflects no reality: it produces mere "reality-effects". . . . In this speculum with no reality, in this mirror of a mirror, a difference or dyad does exist, since there are mimes and phantoms. But it is a difference without reference, or rather reference without a referent, without any first or last unit, a ghost that is the phantom of no flesh . . . (206)

13. Esther Newton, *Mother Camp: Female Impersonators in America* (Chicago: University of Chicago Press, 1972).

14. In a sense, one might offer a redescription of the above in Lacanian terms. The sexual "positions" of heterosexually differentiated "man" and "woman" are part of the *Symbolic,* that is, an ideal embodiment of the Law of sexual difference which constitutes the object of imaginary pursuits, but which is always thwarted by the "real." These symbolic positions for Lacan are by definition impossible to occupy even as they are impossible to resist as the structuring telos of desire. I accept the former point, and reject the latter one. The imputation of universal necessity to such positions simply encodes compulsory heterosexuality at the level of the Symbolic, and the "failure" to achieve it is implicitly lamented as a source of heterosexual pathos.

15. Of course, it is Eve Kosofsky Sedgwick's *Epistemology of the Closet* (Berkeley: University of California Press, 1990) which traces the subleties of this kind of panic in Western heterosexual epistemes.

16. Amber Hollibaugh and Cherríe Moraga, "What We're Rollin Around in Bed With: Sexual Silences in Feminism," in *Powers of Desire: The Politics of Sexuality,* ed. Ann Snitow, Christine Stansell, and Sharon Thompson (New York: Monthly Review Press, 1983), 394–405.

17. Mikkel Borch-Jacobsen, *The Freudian Subject* (Stanford: Stanford University Press, 1988); for citations of Ruth Leys's work, see the following two endnotes.

18. For a very fine analysis of primary mimetism with direct implications for gender formation, see Ruth Leys, "The Real Miss Beauchamp: The History and Sexual Politics of the Multiple Personality Concept," in *Feminists Theorize the Political,* eds. Judith Butler and Joan W. Scott (New York and London: Routledge, 1992). For Leys, a primary mimetism or suggestibility requires that the "self" from the start is constituted by its incorporations; the effort to differentiate oneself from that by which one is constituted is, of course, impossible, but it does entail a certain "incorporative violence," to use her term. The violence of identification is in this way in the service of an effort at differentiation, to take the place of the Other who is, as it were, installed at the foundation of the self. That this replacement, which seeks to be a displacement, fails, and must repeat itself endlessly, becomes the trajectory of one's psychic career.

19. Here again, I think it is the work of Ruth Leys which will clarify some of the complex questions of gender constitution that emerge from a close psychoanalytic consideration of imitation and identification. Her forthcoming book manuscript will doubtless galvanize this field: *The Subject of Imitation.*

21

Spare Parts:
The Surgical Construction of Gender

Marjorie Garber

Marjorie Garber, Professor of English and Director of the Center for Literary and Cultural Studies at Harvard University, is a Shakespearean scholar as well as a literary and cultural critic. In addition to a number of books on Elizabethan culture and its modern reception, she has recently published a major survey of the varieties of transvestism and their cultural significance, Vested Interests: Cross-Dressing and Cultural Anxiety *(Routledge, 1992). In the essay reprinted here, Garber examines the figure of the transsexual—of the person who acquires by means of surgery the anatomy and morphology of a different sex—in order to bring out the fundamental asymmetries that govern the social identities and definitions of "male" and "female." She notes that the blurring of sexual boundaries caused by the transsexual motivates a series of efforts to fix more precisely the meanings of both sex and gender—efforts which ultimately serve only to reveal, however, the instability and insubstantiality of each of those categories. Garber's approach to sex adds an unexpectedly literal dimension to the meaning and practice of what critical theorists call "deconstruction."*

The Maserati I picked up in Modena was a reconditioned model. Previously owned, the car had been lovingly rebuilt by the craftsman who had originally made it. The guarantee was the same as if it had been new. My automobile seemed a perfect reflection of my personal state. I too was reconditioned or at least on the way to being so. (Renée Richards, *Second Serve*)

Although I originally wrote this essay for a special issue of *differences* concerned with male subjectivity, what I aim to do in it, at least initially, is to put the viability of such a concept in question. I suspect that "male subjectivity" is a recuperative cultural fantasy, a theoretical back formation from "female subjectivity," where the latter evolved as a politically necessary critique of the universal subject, "man." Does "male subjectivity," conceptualized, represent anything more than a wishful logic of equality, which springs from a feminist desire to make "man" part rather than whole? Is "male subjectivity" not, in fact, like "female fetishism," a theoretical tit-for-tat which finally demonstrates the limits of theorization when it comes to matters of gender construction?

Consider, for instance, the dissymmetry in the following rhetorical matter. Long before critics wrote so eloquently about the constructedness (rather than the innateness) of gender, writers and ordinary citizens spoke readily about experiences that would "make a man" of some (male) candidate: war, perhaps, or sexual initiation, or some

Hemingwayesque test of hunting or shooting or a battle one-on-one with nature. These things would, it used to be said, "make a man" of the hapless boy, test his mettle; hence a whole literature of male sexual and martial initiation, from—say—Coriolanus to Norman Mailer. Businessmen boasted of being "self-made men," and (in a slightly different spirit) Stephen Greenblatt writes of "Renaissance self-fashioning" in a book that, without regarding the fact as odd, treats only men. Mafiosi, we are told by popular fiction and film, speak of "making one's bones"—of the first murder that makes a boy a man. Teenage boys in my adolescence spoke, and presumably still speak, of "making it" with a girl, of "making out," of "making" her; my dictionary gives as definition 26 under "make": "*Slang.* To persuade to have sexual intercourse." The dictionary does not give a gender to the implied speaker, but I have never heard a woman speak of "making" a man in this way. To "make" a man is to test him; to "make" a woman is to have intercourse with her. Like the dissymmetry of reference in Spanish between a "public man" (a statesman) and a "public woman" (a whore), "making a man" and "making a woman" mean two very different things, culturally speaking.

When we refer to maturation for a girl, we speak, usually, of a passive process: "becoming a woman," a process at the mercy of biology and custom. To "become a woman" is to get one's period, to develop rounded hips, full breasts—and, concurrently, to put away childish things. In my adolescence this meant, generally, male sports and games, which gave way to eye makeup and the junior prom. Happily, we now live in a more enlightened age, an age that can produce a Florence Griffith Joyner (as well as a Martina Navratilova and, indeed, a Renée Richards). But the sociology of gender construction—as distinguished from its theorization—still encodes a dissymmetry. If sexual initiation can mean "becoming a woman"—and it can—this is still not the same as, not entirely the equivalent of, "making a woman" of oneself, or of being taken to a place of initiation, like a brothel, by some kindly older relative or more experienced friend, to be "made a woman." "Male subjectivity" to many custodians of Western culture—whether literary critics, psychoanalysts, or rock musicians, should they ever have recourse to the term—is still a phallic redundancy. To be a subject is to have a phallus, to be male literally or empowered "as" male in culture and society.

In what follows, I will propose the cultural discourses of transvestism and transsexualism as limit cases for "male subjectivity"—places where the very concept of "male subjectivity" is stretched to the vanishing point—perhaps. My intent is to test the "differences" between theory and praxis on the question of gender construction, by noting a number of curious and compelling dissymmetries between "male" and "female" subjectivity as they are read backward from the borderlines of gender. What does a male transvestite theorize about his subjectivity? How is it inscribed in his dress, behavior, sexual object choice, core gender identity? What about a male-to-female transsexual? Is she culturally, politically, sexually the mirror image of her counterpart, the former woman who has undergone hormone treatment and phalloplasty (the surgical construction of a penis) to become a man? What does, or might, the concept of "male subjectivity" mean to a transsexual, whether male-to-female or female-to-male?

The Absolute Insignia of Maleness

Can you imagine the effect you will have on your partner as you enter a room dressed in the most elegant of feminine attire right down to these European stretch pantless pantyhose! These "surprise pantyhose" will complete your web of intrigue as you slowly raise your skirt to that delectable area where "lo & behold" your male member will be anxiously awaiting introduction. (ad for Surprise Pantyhose, *Crossdressers Forum*)

Let me begin this inquiry by citing the views of an expert, one of the most widely respected interpreters of gender identity today. Dr. Robert Stoller, a psychoanalyst and professor of psychiatry at UCLA, is the author of numerous books and articles on gender dysphoria, including *Sex and Gender* Volumes I and II, *Splitting, Perversion, Sexual Excitement,* and *Observing the Erotic Imagination.* Here, from the influential first volume of *Sex and Gender,* is a passage widely quoted in both medical articles and TV–TS (transvestite-transsexual) journals, describing the mechanism of transvestite behavior:

> The whole complex psychological system that we call transvestism is a rather efficient method of handling very strong feminine identifications without the patient having to succumb to the feeling that his sense of masculinity is being submerged by feminine wishes. The transvestite fights this battle against being destroyed by his feminine desires, first by alternating his masculinity with the feminine behavior, and thus reassuring himself that it isn't permanent; and second, by being always aware even at the height of the feminine behavior—when he is fully dressed in women's clothes—that he has the absolute insignia of maleness, a penis. And there is no more acute awareness of its presence than when he is reassuringly experiencing it with an erection. (Stoller, *Sex* 1:186)

Almost twenty years later, Stoller repeated this assertion—in much the same language:

> [T]he transvestite states the question, "When I am like a female, dressed in her clothes and appearing to be like her, have I nonetheless escaped the danger? Am I still male, or did the women succeed in ruining me?" And the perversion—with its exposed thighs, ladies' underwear, and coyly covered crotch—answers, "No. You are still intact. You are a male. No matter how many feminine clothes you put on, you did not lose that ultimate insignia of your maleness, your penis." And the transvestite gets excited. What can be more reassuringly penile than a full and hearty erection? (Stoller, *Observing* 30)

Stoller's narrative style is both sympathetic and empathetic, adopting the affective subject position of the transvestite ("*reassuringly* experiencing it with an erection"; "*reassuringly* penile"; "a *full and hearty* erection"). In the earlier passage, the phrase "absolute insignia of maleness" is implicitly ventriloquized, the transvestite's eye-view given in indirect discourse; the later passage puts the equivalent phrase, "that ultimate insignia of your maleness," firmly in quotes, as "the perversion," an allegorized voice of Transvestism, is permitted to speak for itself. In both, however, and thus over a span of two decades, Stoller points to the primacy of the penis as the fetishized self-object of transvestite subjectivity. "The transvestite needs his penis as an insignia of maleness," he writes elsewhere in *Sex and Gender.* "One cannot be a male transvestite without *knowing, loving, and magnificently expanding* the importance of one's own phallus" (1: 188; emphasis added).

I have used Stoller as my chief evidence here because he is the most frequently cited of gender identity specialists. But he is far from alone. A vast medical literature exists on this question, overwhelmingly confirming the phallessentialist description of male transvestism and transsexualism.[1] Nor do we have to have recourse to doctors to test this hypothesis. Any pornographic bookstore or magazine stand will attest to the same facts: on page after page of magazines for male transvestites like *Great Pretenders, Transvestite Key Club, Petticoat Power* ("Like Father, Like Son"), *Meet-a-Mimic* ("Gorgeous Fun Loving Guys") and *Crossdressers' Forum,* photographs, both illustrations and "personals ads," depict transvestites in panties, garter belts, maids' uniforms, boots and chains, each with naked, erect, and prominently displayed cock and balls. The Stoller scenario of reassurance as potency—which is clearly indebted to the Freudian scenario of fetishistic display ("Fetishism" 149–59)—is visible or readable in every chapter of *Mario in Makeup* and *Bobby's New Panties*. What is the gendered subjectivity of these representations?

It is not clear to me who reads these novels and magazines, but statistically, we know, male transvestites are largely middle class, heterosexual, and married. Their wives frequently belong to TV support groups, and join them on cross-dressed weekends in Provincetown and other, less obvious locales. Transvestites, cross-dressed, choose women's names, which they use in their personals ads, and also in their daily or episodic cross-dressing activities. Their wives will address them as "Donna" or "Jeanne" or whatever, when they are wearing women's clothes. Yet this is clearly not "female subjectivity," even though it goes by women's names. It is a man's idea of what "a woman" is; it is male subjectivity in drag. The discourse of reassurance is the manifestation of what Adler called "male protest": *despite* the female clothing and nomenclature, the male transvestite asserts his masculinity. As Stoller puts it in the passage quoted above: "The transvestite fights this battle against being destroyed by his feminine desires, first by alternating his masculinity with the feminine behavior, and thus reassuring himself that it isn't permanent; and second, by being always aware even at the height of the feminine behavior—when he is fully dressed in women's clothes—that he has the absolute insignia of maleness, a penis" (Stoller, *Sex* 1: 186). Paradoxically, then, the male transvestite represents the extreme limit case of "male subjectivity," "proving" that he is male against the most extraordinary odds. Dressed in fishnet stockings, garter belt, and high heels, or in a housedress, the male transvestite is the paradoxical embodiment of male subjectivity. For it is his anxiety *about* his gendered subjectivity that engenders the masquerade.

And what of the transsexual male? By the same reasoning, the male transsexual—the person who believes that he is a "woman trapped in a man's body"—marks the other pole of male subjectivity. For him "[t]he insignia of maleness is what causes his despair. He does not wish to be a phallic 'woman'; he wishes to be a biologically normal woman" (Stoller, *Sex* 1: 188). But in this case too the "insignia of maleness," present or absent, desired or despised, is the outward sign of gendered subjectivity. Erections, says Stoller, "force a sense of maleness" upon the transsexual; "the more intensely excited the organ is the more his need to be rid of it" (188).

The desire "to be rid of" the penis, by surgical or less permanent and costly means, has led to some ingenious arrangements. Thus in his youthful cross-dressing forays, the transsexual Richard Raskind, later to become Renée Richards, regularly stretched his penis backward between his legs to hide it, binding it with heavy adhesive tape, and used the same tape to tuck his testicles up into his abdomen. Over the years, Richards writes,

> I became more and more strict in this regard, increasing the strains and inventing new ways to eliminate the hated body parts. Sometimes I would knot a piece of fishing line or strong twine around the head of my penis and use that to pull it backward between my legs. The other end would be secured to a piece of rope cinched tightly around my waist . . . I could pass the string between the cheeks of my ass and up under the rope. Then I would pull the string taut causing my penis to be stretched brutally around the curve of my torso. Believe me, I have great respect for the resiliency of the human penis. (56–57)

The male-to-female transsexual's obsessive concern with "the absolute insignia of maleness" as a mistaken sign or a false signal of gender identity is based on the same conviction instrumental to the male transvestite: the conviction that masculine identity, male subjectivity, is determined and signified by the penis. Interestingly, this is the case even after sex change surgery has removed the unwanted organ. Thus Jan (formerly James) Morris, the travel writer whose autobiography, *Conundrum,* is subtitled *An Extraordinary Narrative of Transsexualism,* offers her account of her own transformation from the penile point of view:

> A neurotic condition common among women is called penis envy, its victims supposing that there is inherent to the very fact of the male organs some potent energy of spirit. There is something to this fancy. It is not merely the loss of androgens that has made me more retiring, more ready to be led, more passive: the removal of the organs themselves has contributed, for there was to the presence of the penis something positive, thrusting, and muscular. My body then was made to push and initiate, and it is made now to yield and accept, and the outside change has had its inner consequences. (152–53)

Seldom has "function follows form" been more ardently argued in gender terms. Whatever we may think of the politics (or psychology) of this statement, it unmistakably gives rise to the same overdetermination of the penis that has characterized both the male transvestite and the male-to-female transsexual in the examples I have considered. In fact, the transsexual male represents the *other* extreme limit case of "male subjectivity" as it is constructed in Western culture. For the phallus is the insignia not only of maleness but of sexuality as such. Rather than regarding the penis (or the phallus) as incidental equipment contributory towards a general sense of "male subjectivity" that transcends the merely anatomical, both male transvestites and transsexuals radically and dramatically *essentialize* their genitalia. "The absolute insignia of maleness" *is* for them the index of male identity. Male subjectivity in this case is objectivity. And what I am suggesting is these apparently marginal or aberrant cases, that of the transvestite and the transsexual, both define and problematize the entire concept of "male subjectivity." It is by looking at them, and at the cultural gaze that both constructs and regards them, that we can best test out the viability of the term.

"A Real One"

They call it easing the Spring; it is perfectly easy
If you have any strength in your thumb: like the bolt,
And the breech, and the cocking-piece, and the point of balance,
Which in our case we have not got . . .
(Henry Reed, "Lessons of the War: Naming of Parts")

What then of the wish—perfectly "natural," in cultural if not political terms—that is to say, in a phallocentric culture, dominated by male discourses in medicine, law, psychology, however traversed by feminism—to "be" a man? What do *female* transvestites and *female-to-male* transsexuals have to do with "male subjectivity"?

In his 1968 book, *Sex and Gender,* Robert Stoller maintained that there was no such thing as a transvestite *woman,* a woman who would become erotically excited by the wearing of male clothing. Such women, he suggested, were really transsexuals, who really wanted to be men—which meant, to have a penis. In the cultural milieu of the mid-to-late sixties, with a new wave of feminism only beginning to manifest itself as a vital political movement, the mainstream expectation that the desire to be a man was "natural" seems to underlie Stoller's (and other clinicians') theories. The "perversion gap," the implication that women have neuroses (like hysteria) and only men have psychoses, perversions, and "paraphilias" (like fetishism and transvestism) grows out of this same dissymmetrical expectation. Psychiatrists and psychoanalysts might not subscribe to the Orthodox Jewish man's creed, thanking God daily for not making him a woman, but the assumptions on which they posited their canons of "normality" reflected a temporal cultural bias. Women who habitually cross-dressed were not psychotic (Stoller, *Sex* 1: 196); they merely wanted to be men, which in their society was a highly reasonable, indeed healthy, desire. "I have never seen or heard of a woman who is a biologically normal female and does not question that she was properly assigned as a female, who is an intermittent, fetishistic cross-dresser," Stoller wrote in 1968 (195). Such women were really *transsexuals,* who thought of themselves as men trapped in the bodies of women.

> If—imagine for a moment—in dead seriousness we should ever offer a penis to any of our women patients who are not transsexual, we would see that she would be horrified. But not the transsexual female. She would be most grateful indeed. (197)

The "absolute insignia of maleness" becomes the *sine qua non* of the "male subjectivity" of the transsexual woman. To "offer [her] a penis," "in dead seriousness," became the ambivalent task of the specialist in gender dysphoria, the "sex change doctor."

Some years later, returning to the question of "Female Transvestism," Stoller was willing to revise his absolute pronouncement against it. Clinical data, he explained, remains at a minimum—he discusses only three cases, and still maintains that fetishistic cross-dressing in women is "so rare it is almost nonexistent" (*Observing* 135), but he was now ready to acknowledge that specific items of clothing, like "blue denim Levi's" (142), "engineer boots" (147), or a false moustache (140), can produce erotic and orgasmic sensations in women. This problem—that of female fetishism in general and fetishistic cross-dressing by women in particular—is a fascinating one, which deserves and has received interesting treatment recently by a number of feminist theorists, and I will not address it directly here.[2] But I do want to point out that Stoller, in comparing and contrasting transvestite women to women with other "disorders," distinguishes them from transsexuals, butch homosexuals, and "women with 'penises,'" whom he characterizes as "biologically intact women [who] feel and openly state that they are anatomically equipped with an intraabdominal or intravaginal penis, truly physically present." One of his transvestite cases was a "woman with a 'penis,'" two were not, and the other two "women with 'penises'" he has treated were not erotically stimulated by wearing male clothing (*Splitting*). The transvestite "woman with a 'penis'" testifies that she wore pants to school at a time when it was not customary for girls to do so: "I was thin and I protruded in the front as though I had a penis. . . . Even when I wore a straight skirt (rather than a gathered full skirt) there would be a swelling, or my pubic area protruded" (*Observing* 148–50).

In another case history, this one describing a female transsexual, Stoller describes a young woman who had always thought of herself as a boy. All her childhood pictures showed her in boys' clothes, especially cowboy suits. She and her mother engage in a lively conversation about the guns she used to play with that fairly bristles with double entendre.

> Patient: I have always wanted—in fact, I still do—a good holster, because I like to shoot. I can't shoot a pistol very well, but I can shoot a rifle.
> Mother: When you were small you always had guns strapped around you. . . . On summer vacation, she had a gun—some kind of pistol. What kind was it?
> Patient: Was that a real one?
> Mother: Sure it was real.
> Patient: A thirty-eight.

Mother: She slept with it under her pillow.
Patient: I slept with it because I felt it was real good. I didn't need it, but I liked
           it a lot; it was real; it was a real gun and lots of kids didn't have them.
           (*Sex* 1: 198–99)

No gloss is offered, or needed, for this testimony to the importance of having a "real one." This patient managed to attend an all-girl's school in the daytime and, cross-dressed as a boy, dated some of her unsuspecting classmates at night. Stoller, who calls this impersonation "brilliant," comments that "he [the female-to-male transsexual] was able to disguise his physical sexual characteristics by inventing and manufacturing for himself a camisole for his chest and an artificial penis which would give the right bulge to his pants. At one point, he was so successful (and had constructed such an excellent 'penis') that he had 'intercourse' with a girl. For several months she failed to have a period and was fearful that he had gotten her pregnant" (203–04).

The word "constructed" in Stoller's account is of interest, for here, indeed, is a self-made man. Although both the word "penis" and the word "intercourse" are in quotation marks, indicating that from Stoller's point of view they are not the real thing, the patient's girlfriend plainly disagreed. Is it possible to think of "penis" and "intercourse" here as concepts under erasure, "barred" words? Does "male subjectivity" in fact require the putting of the "absolute insignia" in question in this way? This quest for the "real one" led ultimately to surgical intervention. Was *this* patient's subjectivity "male"? What would "male subjectivity" mean in such a case?

Notice that in this case the actual gender identification precedes the surgical make-over by many years; one of the interviewing doctors even told the patient's mother that in talking about her child as "she" she was "making a mistake," and the case history regularly refers to the patient as "he." Pronominal confusion (pronominal dysphoria) is a constant pitfall in discussions of the transsexual phenomenon, and is, again, an indicator of the boundary crossing that makes gendered subjectivity so problematic in such cases.[3]

Many "pre-op" transsexuals have chosen to halt their progress toward surgery, retaining both male and female attributes induced by hormone treatment, and "passing" for the chosen sex in dress and manner (a stage still mandated by doctors who treat transsexual patients) but declining (for reasons variously economic, philosophical, prag-matic, and social) to undergo the final surgical translation into the "other" gender. What this means is that male-to-female transsexuals may, and increasingly do, retain "the absolute insignia of maleness" together with their hormone-enhanced breasts, their women's clothes, and their new female names. Their "core gender identity," according to doctors, is that of the gender toward which they are crossing. But is their gendered subjectivity mimicry, or a "real one"? What would "real" and "mimic" mean in the cultural milieu in which all gender roles are constructed?

And what happens when technology catches up with cultural fantasy? When it becomes possible, in the context of a culture in which maleness is normative, to "make" a man?

"A Possible Artifact": Eve's Rib, Adam's Apple

Snips and snails and puppy dogs' tails. ("What Are Little Boys Made Of?")

After years in which transsexualism was viewed as a largely male phenomenon, the situation of female transsexuals has lately come in for more direct scrutiny. The reasons for the emphasis on males (that is to say, persons who feel that they are women trapped in a man's body) are concisely outlined by Dr. Leslie Martin Lothstein, the co-director of the Case Western Reserve Gender Identity Clinic: 1) most gender clinics were set up to provide services for only the male transsexual; 2) the majority of transsexuals applying for sex reassignment surgery (SRS) were male (as Dr. Lothstein—a man—points out, this is "a possible artifact," since female transsexual surgery was not possible until fairly recently); 3) most transsexual researchers were males, and may have exhibited a bias toward male patients, together with a "homocentric" or "patricentric" discouragement of women who inquire about clinical treatment; 4) social pressures made it easier for female transsexuals to acclimate themselves to society in their unchanged status (a characteristic double bind for women: they often are not considered psychotic enough or distressed enough for treatment, since wishing to be or act like a man is considered "normal" or "natural" in this culture); and, finally, 5) men have traditionally had more latitude to express concern about sexual dysfunction than have women—or, put slightly differently, men have been allowed to have sex lives and to place importance upon sexual performance and response, while women have—until recently—been acculturated to deny, repress, or veil sexual feeling (6–7; 14).

Each of these "reasons" for the clinical neglect of female-to-male transsexuals, then, is based at least in part on the dissymmetry between the cultural status of males and of females. While much has been said about the "construction of women" in Western culture, women considered as an artifact of patriarchy, Petrarchism, primogeniture, and the necessities of domestic economy,[4] we hear much less about the "construction of men." That process is more usually, and more optimistically, called "self-fashioning," and, while queried as a realizable goal by even its strongest advocates, it persists as a male ideal of intentionality and control. There remains some desire to see men as not constructed but "natural," or essential—hence, again, the "naturalness" of women's desire to be more like men.

Transsexualism, manifestly, puts in question this very essentialism of gender identity, offering both surgical and hormonal—as well as psychological—"solutions" to gender undecidability. If a "man trapped in a woman's body" or a "woman trapped in a man's body" is claiming what doctors call a "core gender identity," and what literary and psychoanalytic theorists describe as female or male subjectivity, then the task (or art) of the surgeon is to refashion the body to suit the subjectivity. Again, it is instructive to note that this refashioning, or reconstruction, is far more readily and easily done with male-to-female than with female-to-male transsexuals. Indeed, the terms of reference here are themselves highly revealing; men who wish to become biological women are generally referred to, in medical terminology, as "*male* transsexuals." Although their "core gender identity" is female, the culture still designates them male. In fact, the terms "transsexual" and "transvestite" are themselves normatively male in general usage; recent work on the early modern period, for example, has begun to speak of the visibility of "female transvestites" in London, while "transvestite" without a gender qualification is usually taken to refer to men in women's clothing.

What lies behind some of the resistance to or neglect of the female-to-male transsexual is, I think, a sneaking feeling that it should not be so easy to "construct" a "man"—which is to say, a male body. Psychoanalysts since Freud have paid lip service, at least, to the maxim that "what constitutes masculinity or femininity is an unknown characteristic which anatomy cannot lay hold of" ("Femininity" 114), but it seems clear, as we have already seen, that there is one aspect of gender identity that can be laid hold of: the penis. Yet the surgical construction of the penis, what is technically known as *phalloplasty,* is consistently referred to in the medical literature as "not accomplished easily," "fraught with rather serious hazards," "still quite primitive and experimental," and likely to produce "poor cosmetic results" (which, as Lothstein notes, is "surgical jargon for a rather grotesque appearance" [293]).

The first "total reconstruction" of the penis (on a biological male) was performed in 1936 (Gelb, Malament, and LoVerme 62–73), but fifty years later "few, if any, surgeons, can construct a phallus that is aesthetically and surgically acceptable" (Lothstein 299). Among the complaints of female-to-male post-operative patients have been: scarring of the abdominal area; a penis that was too small (not a complaint only of transsexuals); an inability to urinate; a dysfunctional penis that could not become erect except with the insertion of a rod. One doctor reported having seen a female transsexual's newly constructed penis fall off, which, he said "caus[ed] the patient to become extremely anxious" (Lothstein 300). The penis had to be totally reconstructed. Another patient had to have reconstructive surgery after a tissue graft failed to take. "Both patients," their psychiatrist records, "developed massive castration anxiety" (Lothstein 300).

Here is a new aspect of penis envy. The female-to-male transsexual (note that the doctors call him/her a "female transsexual," although the patient, having endured all this reconstructive surgery, would doubtless prefer to be described as a "man") gets more than he (or she) bargained for: together with the penis, he/she (how meaningful that slash mark becomes) gets not only castration *anxiety,* but something that sounds very much like *castration:* his (or her) penis falls off, and has to be replaced (again). To become an anatomical male in this case is to become a caricature of the psychological male, essentialized, literalized, made into a grotesque cartoon: the penis *does* fall off, as had always been threatened. And it *doesn't* become hard, as had always been feared. So the transsexual gets the name, but not the game. In early procedures for phalloplasty the surgeon sometimes used a piece of the patient's rib to permanently stiffen the new penis; this New Eve is reconstructed as Adam, the first-made "man," begotten from her *own* rib. (The role for which the surgeon is cast in this transformation needs no comment.)

Female-to-male breast surgery, the flattening of the chest by mastectomy, has likewise been described as often yielding "poor cosmetic results." In fact, patients are warned against surgeons who are hostile to the idea of transsexualism. Some surgeons have strong reactions to transsexual patients and often, if the surgery is done in a teaching hospital, the surgeon turns out to be a resident or staff member who is offended by the procedure. "In one case, with which I am familiar," writes a doctor, "the patient's massive scars were probably the result of the surgeon's unconscious sadism and wish to scar the patient for "going against nature" (Lothstein 293). In spite of such unaesthetic results, transsexual patients often go barechested, displaying what doctors call a "poor reality" sense along with their flattened chests. Another way of describing this, and a less condemnatory one, might be to say that the patient is regarding his new body *theoretically;* it is, he is, *male,* however attractive or unattractive the appearance.

Nonetheless, fears about gross physical scarring, an "unaesthetic neo-phallus" (Lothstein 301), and an incapacity for erection and ejaculation makes sexual reassignment surgery for females-to-males less common, and less clinically "satisfactory," than the converse procedure for males-to-females. I regard this as a political as much as a medical fact. Research money and scientific discovery have historically been tied to a strong desire within the culture for medical progress, whether in the development of vaccines to combat infectious disease or in the great advances in, say, plastic surgery as a result of disfiguring and disabling injuries suffered in wartime. The example of AIDS and its (mis)treatment by the Reagan and Bush administrations points out the opposite dynamic; a refusal to acknowledge, and therefore to make effective progress against, a major disease whose victims, and etiology, the dominant culture wants to wish (or throw) away. In sex reassignment surgery there remains an implicit privileging of the phallus, a sense that a "real one" can't be made, but only born. The (predominantly male) surgeons who do such reconstructive surgery have made individual advances in technique, but the culture does not yet strongly support the construction of "real men" by this route, preferring cold baths, rugged physical labor, and male-bonding rituals from fraternity beer bashes to the Skull and Bones society and the Fly Club, depending on the economic and cultural context.

In rounding out this discussion it may be of interest merely to chronicle the number and nature of surgical operations undergone by one transsexual subject, Renée Richards. Richards comments in her autobiography that the name she chose as her fantasy cross-dressed other quite early in her childhood suddenly occurred to her, on the operating table, to carry a special meaning: "Renée. Reborn." She does not mention the emblematic meaning of the name by which she was known to family and friends throughout her early life when *not* cross-dressed as Renée: that name, of course, was *Dick*. It is the cutting off, by surgery, of the name and identity of "Dick"—in effect the quintessential penectomy, the amputation of male subjectivity—that enables the rebirth of Renée.

Dick Raskind took female hormones (in both injection and suppository form) to round his hips, thighs, and breasts, and, after a brief period when he grew a beard at a psychiatrist's suggestion ("if the thought of Renée came to mind, I needed only to stroke my chin and her specter was banished" [140]), he underwent electrolysis to remove his beard growth forever. These procedures, like the penectomy and the construction of a vagina, are standard for most male-to-female transsexuals. While hardly trivial, they fall within a new surgical "norm." But Richards also had what I like to think of as a "pomectomy"—that is, an operation to remove his Adam's apple, the "one aspect of his outward appearance that displeased" him (211). The surgeon, using a device like a dentist's drill, let his hand slip, and broke through the delicate larynx, leaving Richards with a permanently gravelly voice. (Disguised as an exotic dancer, rather than "out" in the doctor's office as a fellow physician, Richards felt doubly disempowered, unable to claim his subjectivity as a mainstream professional. Thinking him a gay female impersonator, the doctors and nurses treated him, in the hospital, without the deference he had come to expect as "professional courtesy"; here, hardly for the first time, presumptions about gender and class conspire to make the patient an object rather than a subject.)

After the Adam's apple operation Richards went to Casablanca, but had doubts about the ultimate surgical step, and returned to New York ("Dick's back!") and married a woman. His feminized breasts became a "continuing source of embarrassment" (263) and so he underwent breast reduction surgery ("This time I could go in as a doctor and be given due respect" [264]), not without some sense of irony: "I was probably the only person in the world who had ever had breast reduction under such bizarre circumstances" (266). In his "newly created silhouette" he was soon back on the tennis court, and, barechested, on the beach. But three years later his marriage ended, and he began the whole cycle all over again. In 1975, six years after first inquiring into the possibility of transsexual surgery, and 72 hours after locating a sex change doctor in New York who would accord him professional courtesy, Dick Raskind was surgically transformed into Renée Richards. Dick was gone. Or was he? Is the subjectivity exhibited in Richards's autobiography "female" or "male"?

As a college student Dick Raskind had attended Yale, where he apparently received a suitable education in canonical English literature, for his autobiography is filled with references to Milton. As many recent studies have pointed out, Milton had some interesting ideas about subjectivity, gender identity, and the construction of womanhood, and those ideas come into fascinating play in *Second Serve*. Before undergoing surgery, but after her body had been modified by female hormones and electrolysis, Renée reflects en route to Casablanca, "I was like one of Milton's spirits in *Paradise Lost*: 'for spirits when they like can either sex assume or both' " (228). After the sex change operation, when she is briefly permitted to play tennis on the women's circuit, she remembers, "I was like Eve in the Garden of Eden but with a tennis ball instead of an apple" (313). The Adam's apple surgery itself does not seem to have reminded her of Milton, however, and it is difficult to tell whether the book's most Miltonic moment is at all ironized for her—the moment when, like Eve, she gazes into a mirror and falls in love with what she sees. It is, for Renée Richards, the post-operative moment, when the surgeon holds up a mirror that reflects her newly constructed vagina. And even—or especially—here, the question of male vs. female subjectivity is far from simple: "What I saw was essentially what I had seen so many times between the legs of the women with whom I'd been intimate—a normal looking introitus but incredibly distinctive because it was mine" (284). The "I" of this statement is, at least in part, Dick, however much the "mine" belongs to Renée.

Changing the Subject

Dr. Paul Walker: *I think it's important not to call it sex change because these people felt this way from day one. It's not that they felt like little girls and one day decided, "gee, maybe I'm a boy."*
Phil Donahue: *It's not what, doctor?*
Dr. Paul Walker: *It's not a sex change. They've always felt this way.*

(Donahue, 1982)

But what *is* a transsexual? Is he or she a member of one sex "trapped" in the other's body? Or someone who has taken hormones and undergone other somatic changes to more closely resemble the gender into which he (or she) was not born? Most pertinent to this inquiry, does a transsexual *change subjects?* Or just bodies—or body parts?

"Transsexuals," writes Dr. John Money of the Johns Hopkins University Gender Identity Clinic, a respected expert in the field,

> undergo hormonal reassignment so that their body-sex will be more congruous with their self-perceived mental sex. Mentally, masculine has already metamorphosed into feminine (or vice versa) before the taking of hormones. Thus the transsexual condition does not provide information on the effect of sex hormones, if any, on bringing about the metamorphosis. . . . [T]he time for such a hormonal metamorphosis, if ever, is during prenatal life, with a possible short extension into neonatal life. (58)

Money is sure, then, medically speaking, that "transexuals" (his preferred spelling)[5] are "natural," that is, produced by a gendered subjectivity which precedes acculturation, and most probably precedes birth. Yet, interestingly, Money also describes transsexuals in terms of semiology—and while some of his "insignia" are biological or anatomical, others are the products of custom or culture:

> Forfeiture of the insignia of the sex of birth is the defining characteristic of transexualism as compared with other manifestations of gender crosscoding. For female-to-male transexuals, it means having a man's haircut, flattening or amputation of the breasts, having no menstrual periods, having nothing insertable into the vagina, and modulating the pitch and intonation of the voice to be more baritone and mannish. For male-to-female transexuals, forfeiture means becoming a eunuch with no testicles, penis, or scrotum, losing facial or body hair, not cutting the head hair, and modulating the pitch and intonation of the voice to a feminine-sounding husky falsetto. (89)

Having no menstrual periods and losing body hair are medically produced effects; castration and "having nothing insertable into the vagina" are surgical alterations; and short (or long) haircuts are clearly social choices or erotic styles without medical consequence or pertinence. The lowering or raising of the voice in pitch and intonation falls somewhere in between, since its effect is that of style but its achievement is dependent upon hormones. Yet all of these attributes are linked together as "insignia" of gendered subjectivity. Precisely where we might wish to turn to medical discourses for specificity and distinction, we find, instead, a blurring of categories and boundaries.

The term "transsexual" is used to describe persons who are either "pre-op" or "post-op"—that is, whether or not they have undergone penectomy, hysterectomy, phallo- or vaginoplasty. Transsexualism is not a surgical product but social, cultural, and psychological zone. Gender identity clinics administer a battery of tests to candidates for sexual reassignment, including Wechsler Adult Intelligence Scale, House-Tree-Person, Rorschach, Drawing of Self-Concept, Thematic Apperception, MMPI, and the Jenkins test. It is possible to "fail" these tests for transsexualism, as well as to "pass" them.

Here is how Jan (formerly James) Morris describes another such "test"—a moment in which her subjectivity (and her body) deconstructs the binary. Prior to surgery, her body transformed by hormones, and equipped thus with both female breasts and a penis, Morris approached the security check at Kennedy airport after an international flight:

> Dressed as I am in jeans and a sweater, I have no idea to which sex the policeman will suppose me to belong, and must prepare my responses for either decision. I feel their silent appraisal down the corridor as I approach them, and as they search my sling bag I listen hard for a "Sir" or a "Ma'am" to decide my course of conduct. Beyond the corridor, I know, the line divides, men to the male frisker, women to the female, and so far I have no notion of which to take. . . . An awful moment passes. Everyone seems to be looking at me. Then "Move along there lady, please, don't hold up the traffic"—and instantly I join the female queue, am gently and (as it proves) not all that skillfully frisked by a girl who thanks me for my co-operation, and emerge from another small crisis pleased (for of course I have hoped for this conclusion all along) but shaken too. (110)

But the transsexual surgery itself brought to a close Morris's halcyon if confusing days of biological multivalence. In a characteristically self-dramatizing moment on the eve of his sex change surgery, Morris writes, "I went to say good-bye to myself in the mirror. We would never meet again, and I wanted to give that other self a long last look in the eye and a wink of luck" (140). Nora Ephron, reviewing the book for *Esquire* in 1974 when it was first published, adds her tart gloss: "The wink of luck did that other self no good at all; the next morning it was lopped off, and James Morris woke up to find himself as much a woman as hormones and surgery could make him" (203). Ephron's response exhibits both a feminist consternation about this medical construction of "woman" and a residual sense that gender identity inevitably involves loss or partialness. For Ephron this is still "James Morris," however bizarrely altered by surgery. She objects to Morris's girlishness, her pleasure in "feminine" helplessness when there are willing males about to put cars in reverse and open bottles, her eagerness to spend her day in gossip sessions with village ladies. To Ephron this self-image made Morris not a "woman" but "a forty-seven-old *Cosmopolitan* girl" (204), whose consciousness needs raising whatever the gender of her subjectivity (or her sexual organs).

But in point of fact, even for a feminist like Ephron the "absolute insignia of maleness" remains the prime indicator of gender, whether or not it happens to remain attached to the subject's body. She reads Morris's subjectivity, his/her "self," as precisely a reference to male anatomy. "The wink of luck did that other self no good at all; next morning it was lopped off." Metonymically, the penis becomes the "subject" both of the sentence and of *Conundrum*. Despite the fact that Morris considers her subjectivity to be conditioned by nurture as well as surgery—"the more I was treated as a woman, the more woman I became. If I was assumed to be incompetent . . . oddly, incompetent I found myself becoming"—for Ephron "it"—the "it" that was unceremoniously "lopped off"—is still the determinative sign of gender.

In reviewing Morris's book at all Ephron underscores a central cultural fact about the surgical discourse of gender: transsexualism as depicted in films, novels, and memoirs, paradoxically, amounted in effect to a *new essentialism,* while it focused attention on the twin anxieties of technology and gender. The body was again the focus of gender determination.

The boundary lines of gender and of subjectivity, never clear or precise, their very uncertainty the motivation behind the anxious desire to define, to delimit, to *know,* are not only being constantly redrawn, but also are receding inward, *toward* the mysterious locale of "subjectivity," away from the visible body and its artifacts. To see how this has happened, it may be useful to return briefly, one last time, to the tribulations of Renée Richards, the transsexual opthalmologist and tennis player, to see how "trans-sexualism" is itself undergoing a kind of reconstructive surgery.

When Dick became Renée through surgery, some tournament players protested that because of her superior muscle development and larger frame Renée was really a man playing women's tennis. The proof of gender, they claimed, was not in sex organs at all, but rather in chromosomes. X—or Y—still marked the spot. It was not the phallus or the penis ("lopped off" by surgery) nor the reconstructed vagina lined with penile skin that identified Renée Richards's true gender, but rather the apparently unalterable pattern of genes and chromosomes with which Richards had been born. The U.S. Open Committee declared that Renée could play if she could pass the so-called Barrbody test, in which some cells are scraped from the mucous membranes lining the cheek and placed under a microscope; certain bodies that indicate femaleness, called Barrbodies, are counted, and their presence in appropriate numbers indicates that the subject is female. The ground of the medical argument, in other words, had shifted from surgery to genetics. A new essentialism stood ready to take the place of the old. Although, as Richards herself explains, "even normal women occasionally fail it because the number of Barrbodies is not consistent from one day to the next," and despite the fact that she had done the test on herself previously and had "achieved borderline results" (355) the United States Tennis Association insisted that this test was the necessary, and determinant, indicator of gender.

In the case of Renée Richards, this argument failed. Barred from the Open for a deficiency in Barrbodies, Richards was later invited to compete professionally by a promoter who had been the main force in the development of the Virginia Slims Circuit—a sponsor whose cigarette slogan, appropriately enough, was "You've come a long way, baby." After playing exhibition matches with Billy Jean King (who was later pilloried in the press for an extramarital lesbian relationship) and Bobby Riggs (who had been known to play tennis in a dress) Richards filed suit with the help of lawyer Roy Cohn and won. She was permitted to play tournament tennis on the women's circuit.

But the replacement of the surgical by the medical, of the seen by the unseen borderline, is omnipresent in competitive sports today, in the controversy about the use of steroids. A recent political cartoon by *Atlanta Constitution* artist Doug Marlette showed a huge, hairy, lantern-jawed athlete in a singlet, being told in the first frame by a tiny coach, "You're disqualified. You failed the test for steroids." In the second frame the coach comments, as a tear rolls down the athlete's cheek, "I hate to see a woman cry." In the last several Olympics, U.S. media commentators have pointed out the solidity of body mass on Eastern European female athletes, with the clear implication that their training is augmented by steroid use. Dan Duchaine, a former body builder and self-styled "steroid consultant," contends in his 1980 pamphlet "The Underground Steroid Handbook" that steroids should be regarded as a technological advancement "like the creation of better running shoes." Commenting on the steroid drug Maxibolan, he writes, "Maxibolan is used by a lot of women body builders as it is not very androgenic [that is, it doesn't produce major male characteristics, unlike some other steroids], and of course, doesn't leave needle marks that the girls in the lockerroom can gossip about" (Alfano 49).

This shift in the grounds of medical definition raises further, and important questions, which I will not have room to explore in depth here. After the boom in transsexual surgery in the seventies, there is some evidence that those who once looked toward surgery for the solution to the conundrum of sexual identity are considering other options. As Renée Richards points out wryly at the end of her autobiography, "the flood of transsexuals" predicted by the U.S.T.A. (males who would presumably undergo sex change operations in order to make a fortune on the women's tennis circuit) failed to materialize (344; 365). And, in the meantime, the medical proving grounds of gender identity have moved inward away from anatomy and toward boundary lines invisible to the naked eye (chromosomes, Barrbodies, body chemistries, as well as body shapes altered by steroids). This further invalidation of the test of anatomical gender identity, whether "natural" or surgically wrought, has translated the anxieties of gender to a new register, a new kind of uncertainty and artifactuality.

Jan Morris writes in a 1986 postscript to *Conundrum,*

> I have a feeling . . . that the specifically transsexual urge is less common now than it was in 1974; perhaps the slow overlapping of the genders has weakened it, certainly homosexuals have been spared their agonized and misguided search for physical escape. In recent years I have had few requests for Dr. B's address in Casablanca; more and more my correspondents recognize that this book is not really about sex at all. (176)

But if the story of transsexualism is not about sex at all, is it about subjectivity, specifically, "male subjectivity"? Does subjectivity follow the knife, or guide it? If a "woman trapped in a man's body" is "really" a woman, and a "man trapped in a woman's body" is "really" a man, what is the force of that "really"?

The phenomenon of transsexualism is both a confirmation of the constructedness of gender and a secondary recourse to essentialism—or, to put it a slightly different way, transsexualism demonstrates that essentialism *is* cultural construction. Nora Ephron accuses Jan Morris of essentializing stereotypes (believing in an essentializing stereotype as what a woman is). But according to what principle does she argue? That anatomy is destiny? That subjectivity follows the sign of the genitals? Or rather is she arguing that there is a difference between social construction and surgical construction, that to be a woman one needs to have been socialized as one? But if that is the case, is social construction "natural," and surgical construction "artificial"?

The transsexual body is not an absolute insignia of anything. Yet it makes the referent ("man" or "woman") seem knowable. Paradoxically, it is to transsexuals and transvestites that we need to look if we want to understand what gender categories mean. For transsexuals and transvestites are *more* concerned with maleness and femaleness than persons who are neither transvestite nor transsexual. They are emphatically not interested in "unisex" or "androgyny" as erotic styles, but rather in gender-marked and gender-coded identity structures.

So those who problematize the binary are those who have a great deal invested in it. In putting in question the age-old boundary between "male" and "female," they also put in question a newer binarism which has become something of a theoretical commonplace, and which now begs to be deconstructed, if we are to come to terms with "subjectivity" as a category to be linked with gender-identification in the nineties: that between "constructed" and "essential."

NOTES

1. Here are some selections from a vast (and growing) medical literature: Benjamin, Ellis, Fenichel, Gutheil, Money, Prince and Bentler, and Rubenstein.

2. See, for example, Schor, who cites medical as well as literary arguments in her bibliography.

3. One such "pre-op" transsexual, in this case a male-to-female transsexual, Merissa Sherrill Lynn (born Wade Southwick), is the founder of the International Foundation for Gender Education, an organization for transvestites and transsexuals based in Waltham, Massachusetts. Lynn was recently interviewed by the *Boston Globe,* and the interview transcript as printed in the newspaper manifested pronomial anxiety in an extreme degree:

> "The bottom line is that it is a turn-on," said a smiling Lynn, smoothing *her* blue and white floral print dress with well-manicured nails.

> "This is all me," Lynn said, squeezing *his* breast through *his* dress. "I don't have a double D-cup, but this keeps me stable and happy. It gives me peace." (Jacobs; emphasis added)

4. The case is well argued by Catherine Belsey, in a deliberately polemical articulation of "the construction of the subject":

> Man, the center and hero of liberal humanism, was produced in contradistinction to the objects of his knowledge and in terms of the relations of power in the economy and the state. Woman was procured in contradistinction to man, and in terms of the relations of power in the family. (9)

5. According to Money, the term "transexual" was coined by D.O. Cauldwell in an article, published in 1949, "Psychopathia Transexualis." Dr. Harry Benjamin popularized the term in his 1966 textbook (the first on the topic), *The Transsexual Phenomenon.* Benjamin's spelling, with two *s*'s, is thus the one most generally in use (Money, 88). I have spelled "transsexual" in the conventional way except when quoting Money directly.

WORKS CITED

Alfano, Peter, with Michael Janofsky. "A Guru Who Spreads the Gospel of Steroids." *New York Times,* 19 November 1988: 49.

Belsey, Catherine. *The Subject of Tragedy: Identity & Difference in Renaissance Drama.* London: Methuen, 1985.

Benjamin, H. *The Transsexual Phenomenon.* New York: Julian, 1966.

Cauldwell, D.O. "Psychopathia Transexualis." *Sexology* 16 (1949): 274–80.

Crossdressers Forum. 1.1 (1987): 35.

Ellis, Havelock. *Studies in the Psychology of Sex.* New York: Modern Library, 1942.

Ephron, Nora. "Conundrum." *Crazy Salad: Some Things about Women.* New York: Bantam, 1976. 203–08.

Fenichel, Otto. "The Psychology of Transvestitism." *International Journal of Psycho-Analysis* 11 (1930): 211–27.

Freud, Sigmund. "Femininity." 1933. *The Standard Edition of the Complete Psychological Works of Sigmund Freud.* Trans. and ed. James Strachey. Vol. 22. London: Hogarth, 1966; rpt. 1986. 112–35. 24 vols. 1953–74.

———— "Fetishism." 1927. Trans. Joan Riviere. *The Standard Edition.* Vol. 21. 149–57.

Gelb, J., M. Malament, and S. LoVerme, "Total Reconstruction of the Penis." *Plastic and Reconstructive Surgery* 24 (1959): 62–73.

Gutheil, Emil. "Analysis of a Case of Transvestism." *Sexual Aberrations.* Ed. W. Stekel. Vol. 2. New York: Liveright, 1930. 281–318. 2 vols.

Hoopes, J. "Operative Treatment of the Female Transsexual." *Transsexualism and Sex Reassignment.* Ed. R. Green and J. Money. Baltimore: The Johns Hopkins Univ. Press, 1969.

Jacobs, Sally. "You Do What You Need to Do." *Boston Globe,* 2 Aug. 1988: 2.

Lothstein, Leslie Martin. *Female-to-Male Transsexualism: Historical, Clinical, and Theoretical Issues.* Boston: Routledge, 1983.

Money, J. *Gay, Straight, and In-Between: The Sexology of Erotic Orientation.* New York: Oxford Univ. Press, 1988.

Morris, Jan. *Conundrum: An Extraordinary Narrative of Transsexualism.* 1974. New York: Holt, 1986.

Prince, V. and P.M. Bentler. "Survey of 504 Cases of Transvestism." *Psychological Reports* 31 (1972): 903–17.

Reed, Henry. "Lessons of the War: Naming of Parts." *Introduction to Literature: Poems.* New York: Macmillan, 1963. 486.

Richards, Renée, with Jack Ames. *Second Serve.* New York: Stein, 1983.

Rubenstein, L.H. "The Role of Identification in Homosexuality and Transvestism in Men and Women." *The Pathology and Treatment of Sexual Deviation.* Ed. I. Rosen. London: Oxford Univ. Press, 1964.

Schor, Naomi. "Female Fetishism: The Case of George Sand." *The Female Body in Western Culture.* Ed. Susan Rubin Suleiman. Cambridge: Harvard Univ. Press, 1986. 363–73.

Stoller, Robert J. *Observing the Erotic Imagination.* New York: Oxford Univ. Press, 1985.

———— *Perversion.* New York: Pantheon, 1975.

———— *Sex and Gender.* 2 vols. London: Hogarth. 1968–75.

———— *Sexual Excitement.* New York: Pantheon, 1979.

———— *Splitting.* New York: Quadrangle, 1973.

"Transsexual Twins." *Donahue.* Metromedia. Transcript 062382. 1982.

IV

"THE USES OF THE EROTIC"

22

The Uses of the Erotic:
The Erotic as Power

AUDRE LORDE

Audre Lorde died in November, 1992. Audre Lorde was author of more than a dozen books of poetry and prose, recipient of national and international awards, and a founding member of Kitchen Table: Women of Color Press. Her most recent poetry includes Undersongs: Chosen Poems Old and New Revised *(1992) and* Our Dead Behind Us *(1986); in* Zami: A New Spelling of My Name *(1982) she writes her own bio-mythography, and her recent essays and speeches can be found in* A Burst of Light *(1988) and* Sister Outsider *(1984), which includes the essay reprinted here. Anti-ascetic in her demands that desire be made conscious and sensuality affirmed, Lorde responds in this 1978 essay to Second Wave Feminists' debates over whether or not pornography creates and maintains sexual oppression. By disentangling women's eroticism from its cultural misuse and calling for a realization of the erotic as the most self-responsible source of women's power, Lorde, locating that power in women's acknowledgment of desire, blurs the boundaries between the erotic, on the one hand, and political, creative, and everyday activities, on the other. And in issuing her call to all women, regardless of their sexual identity, Lorde erases erotic differences between straight, bisexual, and lesbian desire in order to promote such desire as a creative force for revolutionary change.*

There are many kinds of power, used and unused, acknowledged or otherwise.* The erotic is a resource within each of us that lies in a deeply female and spiritual plane, firmly rooted in the power of our unexpressed or unrecognized feeling. In order to perpetuate itself, every oppression must corrupt or distort those various sources of power within the culture of the oppressed that can provide energy for change. For women, this has meant a suppression of the erotic as a considered source of power and information within our lives.

We have been taught to suspect this resource, vilified, abused, and devalued within Western society. On the one hand, the superficially erotic has been encouraged as a sign of female inferiority; on the other hand, women have been made to suffer and to feel both contemptible and suspect by virtue of its existence.

It is a short step from there to the false belief that only by the suppression of the erotic within our lives and consciousness can women be truly strong. But that strength is illusory, for it is fashioned within the context of male models of power.

As women, we have come to distrust that power which rises from our deepest and nonrational knowledge. We have been warned against it all our lives by the male world,

*Paper delivered at the Fourth Berkshire Conference on the History of Women, Mount Holyoke College, August 25, 1978.

which values this depth of feeling enough to keep women around in order to exercise it in the service of men, but which fears this same depth too much to examine the possibilities of it within themselves. So women are maintained at a distant/inferior position to be psychically milked, much the same way ants maintain colonies of aphids to provide a life-giving substance for their masters.

But the erotic offers a well of replenishing and provocative force to the woman who does not fear its revelation, nor succumb to the belief that sensation is enough.

The erotic has often been misnamed by men and used against women. It has been made into the confused, the trivial, the psychotic, the plasticized sensation. For this reason, we have often turned away from the exploration and consideration of the erotic as a source of power and information, confusing it with its opposite, the pornographic. But pornography is a direct denial of the power of the erotic, for it represents the suppression of true feeling. Pornography emphasizes sensation without feeling.

The erotic is a measure between the beginnings of our sense of self and the chaos of our strongest feelings. It is an internal sense of satisfaction to which, once we have experienced it, we know we can aspire. For having experienced the fullness of this depth of feeling and recognizing its power, in honor and self-respect we can require no less of ourselves.

It is never easy to demand the most from ourselves, from our lives, from our work. To encourage excellence is to go beyond the encouraged mediocrity of our society is to encourage excellence. But giving in to the fear of feeling and working to capacity is a luxury only the unintentional can afford, and the unintentional are those who do not wish to guide their own destinies.

This internal requirement toward excellence which we learn from the erotic must not be misconstrued as demanding the impossible from ourselves nor from others. Such a demand incapacitates everyone in the process. For the erotic is not a question only of what we do; it is a question of how acutely and fully we can feel in the doing. Once we know the extent to which we are capable of feeling that sense of satisfaction and completion, we can then observe which of our various life endeavors bring us closest to that fullness.

The aim of each thing which we do is to make our lives and the lives of our children richer and more possible. Within the celebration of the erotic in all our endeavors, my work becomes a conscious decision—a longed-for bed which I enter gratefully and from which I rise up empowered.

Of course, women so empowered are dangerous. So we are taught to separate the erotic demand from most vital areas of our lives other than sex. And the lack of concern for the erotic root and satisfactions of our work is felt in our disaffection from so much of what we do. For instance, how often do we truly love our work even at its most difficult?

The principal horror of any system which defines the good in terms of profit rather than in terms of human need, or which defines human need to the exclusion of the psychic and emotional components of that need—the principal horror of such a system is that it robs our work of its erotic value, its erotic power and life appeal and fulfillment. Such a system reduces work to a travesty of necessities, a duty by which we earn bread or oblivion for ourselves and those we love. But this is tantamount to blinding a painter and then telling her to improve her work, and to enjoy the act of painting. It is not only next to impossible, it is also profoundly cruel.

As women, we need to examine the ways in which our world can be truly different. I am speaking here of the necessity for reassessing the quality of all the aspects of our lives and of our work, and of how we move toward and through them.

The very word *erotic* comes from the Greek word *eros,* the personification of love in all its aspects—born of Chaos, and personifying creative power and harmony. When I speak of the erotic, then, I speak of it as an assertion of the lifeforce of women; of that creative energy empowered, the knowledge and use of which we are now reclaiming in our language, our history, our dancing, our loving, our work, our lives.

There are frequent attempts to equate pornography and eroticism, two diametrically opposed uses of the sexual. Because of these attempts, it has become fashionable to separate the spiritual (psychic and emotional) from the political, to see them as contradictory or antithetical. "What do you mean, a poetic revolutionary, a meditating gunrunner?" In the same way, we have attempted to separate the spiritual and the erotic, thereby reducing the spiritual to a world of flattened affect, a world of the ascetic who aspires to feel nothing. But nothing is farther from the truth. For the ascetic position is one of the highest fear, the gravest immobility. The severe abstinence of the ascetic becomes the ruling obsession. And it is one not of self-discipline but of self-abnegation.

The dichotomy between the spiritual and the political is also false, resulting from an incomplete attention to our erotic knowledge. For the bridge which connects them is formed by the erotic—the sensual—those physical, emotional, and psychic expressions of what is deepest and strongest and richest within each of us, being shared: the passions of love, in its deepest meanings.

Beyond the superficial, the considered phrase, "It feels right to me," acknowledges the strength of the erotic into a true knowledge, for what that means is the first and most powerful guiding light toward any understanding. And understanding is a hand-maiden which can only wait upon, or clarify, that knowledge, deeply born. The erotic is the nurturer or nursemaid of all our deepest knowledge.

The erotic functions for me in several ways, and the first is in providing the power which comes from sharing deeply any pursuit with another person. The sharing of joy, whether physical, emotional, psychic, or intellectual, forms a bridge between the sharers which can be the basis for understanding much of what is not shared between them, and lessens the threat of their difference.

Another important way in which the erotic connection functions is the open and fearless underlining of my capacity for joy. In the way my body stretches to music and opens into response, hearkening to its deepest rhythms, so every level upon which I sense also opens to the erotically satisfying experience, whether it is dancing, building a bookcase, writing a poem, examining an idea.

That self-connection shared is a measure of the joy which I know myself to be capable of feeling, a reminder of my capacity for feeling. And that deep and irreplaceable knowledge of my capacity for joy comes to demand from all of my life that it be lived within the knowledge that such satisfaction is possible, and does not have to be called *marriage,* nor *god,* nor *an afterlife.*

This is one reason why the erotic is so feared, and so often relegated to the bedroom alone, when it is recognized at all. For once we begin to feel deeply all the aspects of our lives, we begin to demand from ourselves and from our life-pursuits that they feel in accordance with that joy which we know ourselves to be capable of. Our erotic knowledge empowers us, becomes a lens through which we scrutinize all aspects of our existence, forcing us to evaluate those aspects honestly in terms of their relative meaning within our lives. And this is a grave responsibility, projected from within each of us, not to settle for the convenient, the shoddy, the conventionally expected, nor the merely safe.

During World War II, we bought sealed plastic packets of white, uncolored margarine, with a tiny, intense pellet of yellow coloring perched like a topaz just inside the clear skin of the bag. We would leave the margarine out for a while to soften, and then we would pinch the little pellet to break it inside the bag, releasing the rich yellowness into the soft pale mass of margarine. Then taking it carefully between our fingers, we would knead it gently back and forth, over and over, until the color had spread throughout the whole pound bag of margarine, thoroughly coloring it.

I find the erotic such a kernel within myself. When released from its intense and constrained pellet, it flows through and colors my life with a kind of energy that heightens and sensitizes and strengthens all my experience.

We have been raised to fear the *yes* within ourselves, our deepest cravings. But, once recognized, those which do not enhance our future lose their power and can be altered. The fear of our desires keeps them suspect and indiscriminately powerful, for to suppress any truth is to give it strength beyond endurance. The fear that we cannot grow beyond whatever distortions we may find within ourselves keeps us docile and loyal and obedient, externally defined, and leads us to accept many facets of our oppression as women.

When we live outside ourselves, and by that I mean on external directives only rather than from our internal knowledge and needs, when we live away from those erotic guides from within ourselves, then our lives are limited by external and alien forms, and we conform to the needs of a structure that is not based on human need, let alone an individual's. But when we begin to live from within outward, in touch with the power of the erotic within ourselves, and allowing that power to inform and illuminate our actions upon the world around us, then we begin to be responsible to ourselves in the deepest sense. For as we begin to recognize our deepest feelings, we begin to give up, of necessity, being satisfied with suffering and self-negation, and with the numbness which so often seems like their only alternative in our society. Our acts against oppression become integral with self, motivated and empowered from within.

In touch with the erotic, I become less willing to accept powerlessness, or those other supplied states of being which are not native to me, such as resignation, despair, self-effacement, depression, self-denial.

And yes, there is a hierarchy. There is a difference between painting a back fence and writing a poem, but only one of quantity. And there is, for me, no difference between writing a good poem and moving into sunlight against the body of a woman I love.

This brings me to the last consideration of the erotic. To share the power of each other's feelings is different from using another's feelings as we would use a kleenex. When we look the other way from our experience, erotic or otherwise, we use rather than share the feelings of those others who participate in the experience with us. And use without consent of the used is abuse.

In order to be utilized, our erotic feelings must be recognized. The need for sharing deep feeling is a human need. But within the European-American tradition, this need is satisfied by certain proscribed erotic comings-together. These occasions are almost always characterized by a simultaneous looking away, a pretense of calling them something else, whether a religion, a fit, mob violence, or even playing doctor. And this misnaming of the need and the deed give rise to that distortion which results in pornography and obscenity—the abuse of feeling.

When we look away from the importance of the erotic in the development and sustenance of our power, or when we look away from ourselves as we satisfy our erotic needs in concert with others, we use each other as objects of satisfaction rather than share our joy in the satisfying, rather than make connection with our similarities and our differences. To refuse to be conscious of what we are feeling at any time, however comfortable that might seem, is to deny a large part of the experience, and to allow ourselves to be reduced to the pornographic, the abused, and the absurd.

The erotic cannot be felt secondhand. As a Black lesbian feminist, I have a particular feeling, knowledge, and understanding for those sisters with whom I have danced hard, played, or even fought. This deep participation has often been the forerunner for joint concerted actions not possible before.

But this erotic charge is not easily shared by women who continue to operate under an exclusively European-American male tradition. I know it was not available to me when I was trying to adapt my consciousness to this mode of living and sensation.

Only now, I find more and more women-identified women brave enough to risk sharing the erotic's electrical charge without having to look away, and without distorting the enormously powerful and creative nature of that exchange. Recognizing the power of the erotic within our lives can give us the energy to pursue genuine change within our world, rather than merely settling for a shift of characters in the same weary drama.

For not only do we touch our most profoundly creative source, but we do that which is female and self-affirming in the face of a racist, patriarchal, and anti-erotic society.

23

The Boys in My Bedroom

Douglas Crimp

Douglas Crimp, Visiting Professor at Sarah Lawrence College, is a cultural critic and an AIDS activist. His essays on contemporary art and postmodernism are collected in On the Museum's Ruins *(1993); he is also the editor of the anthology,* AIDS: Cultural Analysis/ Cultural Activism *(1988) and the author, with Adam Rolston, of* AIDS Demo Graphics *(1990). In "The Boys in My Bedroom" Crimp reflects on the defects in his earlier theory of postmodernism. Specifically, he notes that one effect of his own previous shift in emphasis from a concern with the formal features of an artwork to a concern with the artwork's function in the institutional context of the art world was an inability to recognize the many different ways that images get appropriated, particularly by viewers outside the art world who may respond directly to the content of homoerotic images—with sexual interest or with homophobic rage, as the case may be. Crimp finds in the graphics of ACT UP and of other radical activist groups an indication that the opportunities for reaching various marginalized communities by means of appropriated images are greater than postmodern artists might initially have supposed; the opportunities for homophobic attack, however, are not necessarily diminished by the supposedly distancing strategy of appropriation.*

In 1983, I was asked to contribute to the catalogue of an exhibition about the postmodernist strategy of appropriation, organized by the Institute for Contemporary Art in Philadelphia—a museum now placed on probation by the National Endowment for the Arts.[1] I chose as a negative example—an example, that is, of old-fashioned *modernist* appropriation—the photography of Robert Mapplethorpe. Here is part of what I wrote:

> Mapplethorpe's photographs, whether portraits, nudes, or still lifes (and it is not coincidental that they fall so neatly into these traditional artistic genres), appropriate the stylistics of prewar studio photography. Their compositions, poses, lighting, and even their subjects (*mondain* personalities, glacial nudes, tulips) recall *Vanity Fair* and *Vogue* at that historical juncture when such artists as Edward Steichen and Man Ray contributed to those publications their intimate knowledge of international art photography. Mapplethorpe's abstraction and fetishization of objects thus refer, through the mediation of the fashion industry, to Edward Weston, while his abstraction of the *subject* refers to the neoclassical pretenses of George Platt Lynes.[2]

In contrast to Mapplethorpe's conventional borrowings, I posed the work of Sherrie Levine:

> When Levine wished to make reference to Edward Weston and to the photographic variant of the neoclassical nude, she did so by simply rephotographing Weston's

pictures of his young son Neil—no combinations, no transformations, no additions, no synthesis. . . . In such an undisguised theft of already existing images, Levine lays no claim to conventional notions of artistic creativity. She makes use of the images, but not to constitute a style of her own. Her appropriations have only functional value for the particular historical discourses into which they are inserted. In the case of the Weston nudes, that discourse is the very one in which Mapplethorpe's photographs naively participate. In this respect, Levine's appropriation reflects on the strategy of appropriation itself—the appropriation by Weston of classical sculptural style; the appropriation by Mapplethorpe of Weston's style; the appropriation by the institutions of high art of both Weston and Mapplethorpe, indeed of photography in general; and finally, photography as a tool of appropriation.[3]

For several years I had hanging in my bedroom Levine's series of Weston's young male nudes. On a number of occasions, a certain kind of visitor to my bedroom would ask me, "Who's the kid in the photographs?" generally with the implication that I was into child pornography. Wanting to counter that implication, but unable easily to explain what those photographs meant to *me,* or at least what I *thought* they meant to me, I usually told a little white lie, saying only that they were photographs by a famous photographer of his son. I was thereby able to establish a credible reason for having the pictures without having to explain postmodernism to someone I figured—given the nature of these encounters—wouldn't be particularly interested anyway.

But some time later I was forced to recognize that these questions were not so naive as I'd assumed. The men in my bedroom were perfectly able to read—in Weston's

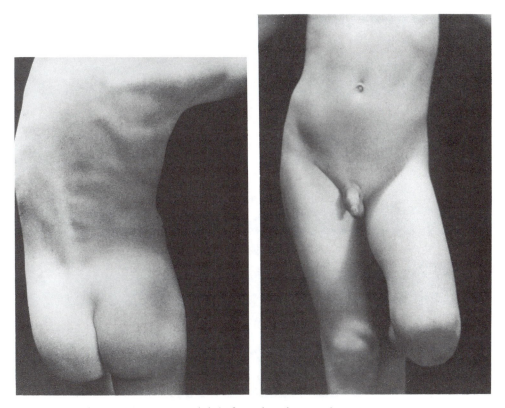

FIGURE 1.   Sherrie Levine, *Untitled (After Edward Weston)*, 1981.

posing, framing, and lighting the young Neil so as to render his body a classical sculpture—the long-established codes of homoeroticism. And in making the leap from those codes to the codes of kiddie porn, they were stating no more than what was enacted, in the Fall of 1989, as the law governing federal funding of art in the United States. That law—proposed by right-wing senator Jesse Helms in response to certain of Mapplethorpe's photographs—directly equated homoeroticism with obscenity and with the sexual exploitation of children.[4] Of course, all of us know that neither Weston's nor Mapplethorpe's photographs would be declared obscene under the Supreme Court's *Miller v. California* ruling, to which the appropriations bill pretended to defer; but we also know that NEA grant applications do not come before a court of law.[5] For those considering whether to fund arts projects, it is the equation itself that would matter. As Jesse Helms himself so aptly said of his victory: " 'Old Helms will win every time' on cutting Federal Money for art projects with homosexual themes."[6] And indeed he will. As I hope everyone remembers, in 1987, when gay men still constituted over 70% of all reported cases of AIDS in the United States, 94 senators voted for the Helms amendment to prevent safe sex information directed at us from being funded by Congress.[7]

Given these assaults on our sexuality and indeed on our lives, what are we to say now of the ways we first theorized postmodernism? To stay with the parochial debate with which I began, what does the strategy of appropriation matter now? My answer is that we only now know how it might really matter.

In October of 1989, the third annual conference of the Lesbian and Gay Studies Center at Yale began with violence unleashed on the participants by the Yale and New Haven police forces.[8] The trouble started with the arrest of Bill Dobbs, a lawyer and member of Art Positive, a group within New York's AIDS Coalition to Unleash Power (ACT UP) that was formed in response to the Helms amendment. Dobbs was presumed to be responsible for putting up a series of what the police claimed were obscene posters

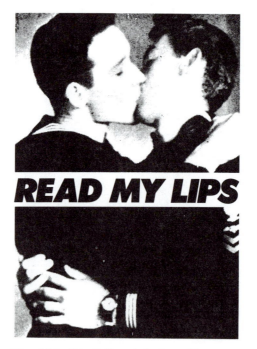

FIGURE 2.   "Read My Lips" (boys) designed by Gran Fury 1988.

around the sites of the conference. The 11 × 17 xerox posters—showing various images of and texts about sex appropriated from such sources as old sex education manuals, sexology texts, and pulp novels, and accompanied by the words "Sex Is" or "Just Sex"— were produced by the anonymous San Francisco collective Boy with Arms Akimbo, also formed to fight the Helms amendment. The collective's goal was to get as many people as possible involved in placing in public places imagery showing various cultural constructions of sexuality. Four thousand of the "Sex Is" posters were wheatpasted around San Francisco, and they also appeared in Sacramento, on various Bay Area college campuses, in Boston, New York, Tel Aviv, and Paris, as well as, of course, New Haven. For the month prior to the Yale lesbian and gay conference, the "Sex Is" xeroxes were shown in the city-sponsored San Francisco Arts Commission Gallery, situated across from San Francisco City Hall, in an exhibition titled "What's Wrong with this Picture? Artists Respond to Censorship."

But it is precisely the censorial intent of the Helms amendment, to which Boy with Arms Akimbo's pictures were intended to call attention at the Yale conference, that was effaced in the reporting of the events of that weekend. While charges against

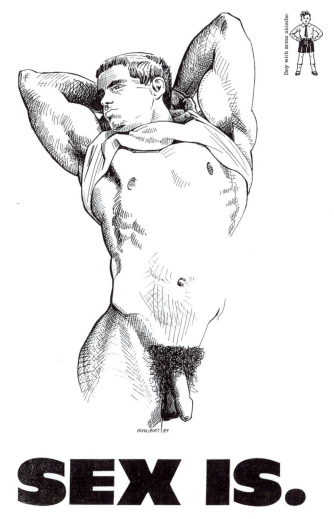

FIGURE 3.   *Sex Is*. Boy With Arms Akimbo 1989.

others arrested in the fracas were quickly dropped, those against Dobbs were not. And Yale president Benno Schmidt adopted an uncompromising stance.[9] Rather than apologize for the homophobic actions of his police, he sought to exonerate them through an "impartial" investigation, conducted as usual by the police themselves, to adjudicate the obscenity call and to consider possible police misconduct.[10] Moreover, Schmidt was quoted in the *New Haven Register* as saying that he thought at least one of the posters would be considered obscene using the Supreme Court's definition. The Court's caveat regarding "serious literary, artistic, political, or scientific value" was simply disregarded by this so-called expert in First Amendment law, since the serious *political* value of Boy with Arms Akimbo's posters—that they constitute a form of political speech about Helms's equation of homoeroticism with obscenity—was never even admitted as an issue.

Boy with Arms Akimbo is only one example of how the postmodernist strategy of appropriation has been transformed through its shift from a grounding in art world discourse to a grounding in movement politics. Within the AIDS activist movement, and especially within ACT UP New York, a certain savvy about this narrow aspect of postmodernist theory has been especially enabling. The graphic work of the Silence= Death Project, Gran Fury, and many others, the video activism of DIVA TV (for Damned Interfering Video Activist Television) grows very directly out of propositions of postmodernist theory. Assaults on authorship have led to anonymous and collective production. Assaults on originality have given rise to dictums like "if it works, use it"; "if it's not yours, steal it." Assaults on the institutional confinement of art have resulted in seeking means of reaching affected and marginalized communities more directly.[11]

But finally, I want to say something about what was excluded from postmodernist theory, which made it considerably less enabling—excluded not only from the aesthetic theory I've been addressing, but also from more global theories. My own blindness in the Mapplethorpe/Levine comparison is symptomatic of a far greater blindness. My failure to take account of what those men in my bedroom insisted on seeing was a failure of theory generally to consider what we are now only beginning to be able to consider—what, in fact, was being variously considered at the Yale lesbian and gay studies conference: the dangerous, even murderous, ways in which homophobia structures every aspect of our culture. Sadly, it has taken the horror of AIDS and the virulent backlash against gays and lesbians that AIDS has unleashed to teach us the gravity of this theoretical omission. What must be done now—if only as a way to begin rectifying our oversight—is to *name* homophobia, the very thing that Yale's President Schmidt so adamantly refused to do, the very thing that the entire membership of Congress refuses to do.

Returning once again to the comparison with which I began, but this time taking into consideration what the boys in my bedroom saw, the photographs by Mapplethorpe and Levine no longer seem definitional of postmodernism through their opposition. Appropriating Weston's photographs of Neil, Levine claimed them as her own. Seen thus in the possession of a woman, the nude pictures of the young boy no longer appear, though their deployment of a classical vocabulary, as universal aesthetic expression. Because Levine has "taken" the photographs, we recognize the contingency of gender in looking at them. Another consequence of that contingency is made explicit by Mapplethorpe. Appropriating Weston's style, Mapplethorpe puts in the place of Weston's child the fully sexualized adult male body. Gazing at that body, we can no longer overlook its eroticism. That is to say, we must abandon the formalism that attended *only* to the artwork style. In both cases, then, we learn to experience Weston's modernist photographs not as universal images, but as images of the universal constituted by disavowing gender and sexuality; and it is such deconstructions of modernism's claims to universality—as well as its formalism—that qualify as postmodernist practices.

What made Boy with Arms Akimbo's posters a provocation to the Yale police and its president was perhaps after all not their imputed obscenity, but rather their *variety*, their proliferation of different ways of showing *Sex Is . . . Just Sex*. Or rather, as Jesse Helms has made clear, difference, in our culture, *is* obscenity. And it is this with which postmodern theory must contend.

NOTES

1. As punishment for having organized *Robert Mapplethorpe: The Perfect Moment* with funding approved by the National Endowment for the Arts, the ICA was subjected, through an amendment to a 1989 congressional appropriations measure, to a five-year probationary period during which its activities would be specially scrutinized by the NEA.

2. Douglas Crimp, "Appropriating Appropriation," in *Image Scavengers: Photographer,* Philadelphia, Institute of Contemporary Art, 1982, p. 30.

3. *Ibid.*

4. The compromise language of the notorious Helms amendment to the NEA/NEH appropriations bill read: "None of the funds authorized to be appropriated for the National Endowment for the Arts or the National Endowment for the Humanities may be used to promote, disseminate, or produce materials which in the judgment of the National Endowment for the Arts or National Endowment for the Humanities may be considered obscene, including but not limited to, depictions of sadomasochism, homo-eroticism, the sexual exploitation of children, or individuals engaged in sex acts and which, when taken as a whole, do not have serious literary, artistic, political, or scientific value" (*Congressional Record—House,* October 2, 1989, p. H6407).

5. Moreover, in flagrant disregard of their own inclusion of the *Miller* language, the new law declared a sense of the Congress, clearly referring to photographs by Mapplethorpe and Andres Serrano, "that recently works have been funded which are without artistic value but which are criticized as pornographic and shocking by any standards" (*Congressional Record—House,* October 2, 1989, p. H6407). For an illuminating discussion of *Miller* in relation to the Right's attack on the NEA, see Carole S. Vance, "Misunderstanding Obscenity," *Art in America* 78, no. 5 (May 1990), pp. 39–45.

6. Maureen Dowd, "Jesse Helms Takes No-Lose Position on Art," *New York Times,* 28 July 1989, p. A1.

7. See my discussion of this other notorious Helms amendment in "How to Have Promiscuity in an Epidemic," in *AIDS: Cultural Analysis/Cultural Activism,* ed. Douglas Crimp, Cambridge, Massachusetts, MIT Press, 1988, esp. pp. 256–265.

8. The conference, titled "Outside/Inside," was held on the weekend of October 27–29, 1989. The police-instigated violence occurred on Friday evening, October 27.

9. As keynote speaker for the "Inside/Outside" conference, I wrote an open letter of protest to President Schmidt, reiterating the demands of the conferees that he forcefully condemn the violence perpetrated against us and publicly declare his support for our fight against homophobia. Perhaps needless to say, Schmidt saw fit to respond neither to my letter nor to the conferees' demands.

10. On November 30, the *New York Times* reported that "charges against Mr. Dobbs were eventually dropped," and that "two Yale police officers will be disciplined for using 'poor judgment.' " Thus, for what many of us experienced as extreme violence by both Yale and New Haven police against those of us protesting the initial arrests, the officers' disciplining will consist of a reprimand for one and three days without pay for the other. This accords perfectly with a number of recent cases in which the police have investigated their own abuses, as well as with a general failure to take attacks against gay men and lesbians seriously.

11. See Douglas Crimp and Adam Rolston, *AIDS Demo Graphics,* Seattle, Bay Press, 1990.

24

Looking for Trouble

KOBENA MERCER

Kobena Mercer, Assistant Professor of Art History at the University of California, Santa Cruz, is a critic of the visual arts, politics, and culture. A number of his writings are edited and assembled in "Race, Sexual Politics and Black Masculinity: A Dossier" (with Isaac Julien) in Male Order: Unwrapping Masculinity, *ed. Rowena Chapman and Jonathan Rutherford (1988). Among his other essays are "Skin Head Sex Thing: Racial Difference and the Homoerotic Imaginary" (in* How Do I Look?, *ed. Bad Object Choices, 1991), and " '1968': Periodizing Politics and Identity" (in* Cultural Studies, *ed. Lawrence Grossberg, Cary Nelson, and Paula Treichler, 1991). In "Looking for Trouble," Mercer reconsiders Robert Mapplethorpe's photographs of Black males and his own earlier responses to them. The publication of a retrospective catalogue of Mapplethorpe's work (Richard Marshall, ed.,* Robert Mapplethorpe, *with essays by Richard Howard and Ingrid Sischy [Boston and New York: Bullfinch Press, 1988]) provides Mercer with the occasion to assess the ambivalent qualities of the "shock effect" produced by those photographs: although Mapplethorpe's objectification and fetishizing of his Black models encourages the viewer (of whatever race) to assume a posture of racial and sexual mastery over them, Mercer suggests that Mapplethorpe's visual strategy also has the effect of motivating the viewer to confront her or his own implication in the racial and sexual fantasies that the images arouse. By "contaminating" the genre of the fine art nude with the "polluted" mass culture stereotype of the Black male body, Mapplethorpe dramatizes the interdependency of whiteness on Otherness, thereby revealing "whiteness" to be a specific, culturally constituted racial identity.*

Lawd, Jesse, I can't believe what I'm seeing. (Mrs. Helms)

Look, a Negro! Mama, see the Negro! I'm frightened! (Frantz Fanon)

To shock was always the key verb in the avant-garde vocabulary. Over the past year, the shocking eroticism of Robert Mapplethorpe's exquisite and perverse photography has been at the center of a major controversy in the United States concerning public funding of contemporary art. Led by Senator Jesse Helms, the campaign to prevent the National Endowment for the Arts from funding exhibitions of so-called "obscene and indecent materials" has helped bring Mapplethorpe's work to the attention of a wider public audience. Paradoxically, Mapplethorpe, who died of AIDS in March 1989, now enjoys enhanced notoriety and a far wider audience than he ever did during his twenty years of art practice on the margins of the New York avant-garde. Based on the retrospective show held at the Whitney Museum of American Art in 1988, this paperback edition of the catalogue is therefore particularly timely as it makes it possible to stand back and reassess the aesthetic and political issues at stake in the recent exhibition history of Mapplethorpe's sublime "immoral trash."

Undoubtedly, it is the question of sexual representation that intersects across the conflicting political readings which have been produced in response to Mapplethorpe's homoerotic work. More than the still lifes of dead flowers or the portraits of art-world celebrities, it is the photographs depicting gay sadomasochism and the nude studies of black men that have caused all the trouble. To enter into the "dark" world of pleasure and danger mapped out in Mapplethorpe's erotica, we cannot assume that black audiences are somehow exempt from its modernist "shock effect," although it seems black voices have been curiously silent and muted in the recent furor. In my own case, however, I can still quite vividly recall my first encounter with Mapplethorpe's black male nudes precisely because I was so shocked by what I saw! The profile of a black man, whose head was cropped or "decapitated," so to speak, holding his semitumescent penis through the y-fronts of his underpants: which is the first image that confronts you in *Black Males* (1982).

When a friend lent me his copy of the book it circulated between us as an illicit and highly problematic object of desire. We were fascinated by the beautiful bodies and drawn in by the pleasure of looking as we went over the repertoire of images again and again. We wanted to look, but we didn't always find what we wanted to see. We were, of course, disturbed by the racial dimension of the imagery and, above all, angered by the aesthetic objectification that reduced these black male bodies to abstract visual "things," silenced in their own right as subjects and serving only to enhance the name of the white gay male artist in the privileged world of art photography. In other words, we were stuck in an intransitive "structure of feeling"; caught out in a liminal experience of textual ambivalence.

In an attempt to make sense of this experience I drew on elements of feminist cultural theory to loosen the grip of this uncomfortable, and ambivalent, fascination. The first thing to notice about Mapplethorpe's black males—so obvious, it goes without saying—is that all the men are *nude*. Framed within such generic conventions of the fine art nude, their bodies are aestheticized and eroticized as "objects" of the gaze and thus offer an erotic source of pleasure in the act of looking. But whose pleasure is being served? Regarding the position of women in dominant regimes of visual representation, feminist theory has shown that the female image functions predominantly as a mirror image of what men want to see. In the mise-en-scène of heterosexual wish fulfillment, the visual depiction of the female nude serves primarily to stabilize the phallocentric fantasy in which the omnipotent male gaze sees but is never itself seen. The binary relations of seeing/being seen that structure dominant regimes of representation in Western traditions are organized by the subject/object dichotomy in which, to put it crudely, men look and women are there to be looked at. However, in Mapplethorpe's case, the fact that both artist and model are male sets up a tension of sameness which thereby transfers the frisson of "difference" from gendered to racialized polarity. The black/white duality overdetermines the subject/object dichotomy of seeing/being seen.

In this sense, what is represented in the pictorial space of Mapplethorpe's photographs is a "look," or a certain "way of looking," in which the pictures reveal more about the absent and invisible white male subject who is the agent of representation than they do about the black men whose beautiful bodies we see depicted. Insofar as the nude studies facilitate the projection of certain sexual and racial fantasies about the "difference" that black masculinity is assumed to embody, they reveal the tracing of desire on the part of the I/eye placed at the center of the camera's monocular perspective. On this view, the position to which the spectator is invited to identify can be described as a white male subject-position, not so much because Robert Mapplethorpe is himself white and male, but because of the fantasy of mastery inscribed in the "look" which implies a hierarchical ordering of racial identity historically congruent with the power and privilege of hegemonic white masculinity. Through a combination of formal conventions—the posing and posture of the body in the studio; strong chiaroscuro lighting; the cropping, framing, and fragmentation of body parts—the fantasy of mastery in Mapplethorpe's "look" structures the viewer's affective disposition towards the image. Moreover, as any social or historical contextualization is effaced and withheld from the pictorial frame, the cool distance of the detached gaze enables the circulation of fantasies that saturate the black man's body in sexual predicates. Whereas the gay sadomasochism photographs portray a subcultural sexuality that consists of "doing" something, the black men are defined and confined to "being" purely sexual and nothing but sexual, hence hypersexual, endowed with an excess of sexuality. In pictures like *Man in a Polyester Suit* (1980), apart from his hands, it is the penis and the penis alone that identifies the model as a black man (figure 1).

Considering the way in which the glossy allure of the high-quality monochrome print becomes consubstantial with the shiny texture of black skin, I argued that fetishism is an important element in the pleasures (and displeasures) that Mapplethorpe brings into play. Such fetishism not only eroticizes the most visible aspect of racial difference—skin color—but also lubricates the ideological reproduction of "colonial fantasy" based on the desire for mastery and power over the racialized Other. Hence, alongside the codes of the fine art nude, Mapplethorpe seems to appropriate the regulative function of the commonplace stereotype—the black man as athlete, savage, or mugger—in order

FIGURE 1. *Man in a Polyester Suit*, 1980.
Copyright 1983 The Estate of Robert Mapplethorpe.

to stabilize the masculine economy of the "look" and to thereby "fix" the black subject in its place as the object that holds a mirror to white male fears and fantasies. According to the literary critic Homi Bhabha, "an important feature of colonial discourse is its dependence on the concept of 'fixity' in the ideological construction of otherness." As in the serialized shots of body-builder Lady Lisa Lyon, in which Mapplethorpe's "look" processes her body through a thousand cultural stereotypes of femininity, the obsessive undercurrent in his black nudes would appear to confirm this emphasis on fixity. The scopic fixation on the signifying difference of black skin thus implies a kind of "negrophilia," an aesthetic idealization of racial Otherness that merely inverts and reverses the binary axis of the repressed fears and anxieties that are projected onto the Other in the psychic representations of "negrophobia." Both positions, whether they overvalue or devalue the visible signs of blackness, inhabit the shared space of colonial fantasy. These elements for a psychoanalytic reading of racial fetishization in visual representation are forcefully brought together in a photograph such as *Man in a Polyester Suit*.

The use of framing and scale emphasizes the sheer size of the big black penis. As Fanon said, diagnosing the terrifying figure of "the Negro" in the fantasies of his white psychiatric patients, "One is no longer aware of the Negro, but only of a penis: the Negro is eclipsed. He is turned into a penis. He *is* a penis." By virtue of the purely formal device of scale, Mapplethorpe summons up from the political unconscious one of the deepest mythological fears in the supremacist imagination: namely, the belief that all black men have monstrously huge willies. In the fantasmatic space of the supremacist imaginary, the big black phallus is perceived as a threat not only to the white master (who shrinks in impotence from the thought that the subordinate black male is more sexually powerful than he), but to civilization itself, since the "bad object" represents a danger to white womanhood and therefore the threat of miscegenation, eugenic pollution, and racial degeneration. Historically, white males eliminated the overwhelming anxiety which black male sexuality is constantly constructed to incite through rituals of aggression and negation in which the lynching of black American men routinely involved the literal castration of the Other's strange fruit. The historical myth of penis size amounts to a "primal fantasy" in that it is shared and collective in nature and, moreover, so pervasive that the modern science of sexology repeatedly embarked upon the task of measuring empirical pricks to demonstrate its ideological untruth. Now that liberal orthodoxy provides no available legitimation for the phantasm of such racial folk myths, it is as if Mapplethorpe's picture enacts a disavowal of the wish fulfillment inscribed in the myth: *I know* (it's not true that all black guys have big willies), *but* (nevertheless, in my photographs they do).

In the picture, the binarisms of everyday racial discourse are reproduced by the jokey irony of the contrast between the black man's private parts and the public respectability signified by the three-piece business suit. The oppositions hidden/exposed and denuded/clothed play upon the Manichean oppositions of nature/culture and savage/civilized to bring about a condensation of libidinal looking. The binarisms repeat the assumption that hypersexuality is the essential "nature" of the black man, while the cheap and tacky polyester suit confirms his failure to gain access to "culture." The camouflage of respectability fails to conceal the fact that the Other originates, like his dick, from somewhere anterior to civilization. However, while the Freudian concept of fetishism allows us to investigate the fears and fantasies that make this picture so shocking to behold, because it is grounded in the Oedipal scenario that privileges the normative developmental path of heterosexual gender identity, it is not so useful as an analytic tool for opening the perverse economy of the homoerotic imaginary. The analogy drawn from feminism enables recognition of similar patterns in the objectification and "othering" of race and gender in dominant regimes of representation: but as a gay artist, Mapplethorpe is hardly representative of the hegemonic model of heterosexual white male identity which has historically been the privileged subject and agent in control of the apparatus of visual representation. Despite its value in cultural criticism, the residual moralistic connotation of the term *fetishism* tends to flatten out the affective ambivalence that viewers of Mapplethorpe's work experience as its characteristic "shock effect."

Indeed, in recognition of this intractable ambivalence that Mapplethorpe arouses with such perverse precision, I have come to change my mind about my earlier reading of his racial fetishism. To put it another way: the textual ambivalence of the black nude photographs is strictly undecidable because Mapplethorpe's photographs do not provide an unequivocal yes/no answer to the question of whether they reinforce or undermine commonplace racist stereotypes—rather, he throws the binary structure of the question back to the spectator, where it is torn apart in the disruptive "shock effect." The shock of recognition of the unconscious sex-race fantasies is experienced precisely as an emotional disturbance which troubles the spectator's secure sense of identity. As reader-response theory shows, we habitually attempt to resolve such textual ambivalence by appealing to authorial intentions; yet, as the "death of the author" argument put forward by poststructuralism has also shown, authorial intentions can never finally determine the meaning or value of a text because readers play an interactive role in determining the range of meanings that can be derived from a polyvocal, modernist, text.

In our case, the recent actual death of the author entails a reconsideration of the subject-positions in Mapplethorpe's theater of racial/sexual fantasy, and requires that we move towards a more relational and dialogic view of the violent kind of ambivalence which arises at the interface between the social and the emotional.

Once we accept the role of the reader, I should come out with regard to the specificity of my own subject-position as a black gay reader in Mapplethorpe's text. Looking back at the angry tone of my earlier analysis of objectification and fetishization, it expressed only one aspect of the ambivalent structure of feeling I experienced in that initial "shock." On the one hand, I was angry and emphasized the implicitly exploitative process of racial othering because I felt identified with the black men depicted in the field of vision; an emotional tie or identification that might best be described, again in Fanon's words, as the feeling that "I am laid bare. I am overdetermined from without. I am the slave not of the 'idea' that others have of me but of my own appearance. I am being dissected under white eyes. I am *fixed* . . . Look, it's a Negro." Subject to the isolation effect, whereby it is only ever one black man who occupies the field of vision at any one time (thus enabling the fantasy of mastery by denying the representation of a collective and contextualized black male identity), the black models seemed to become mere raw material, to be sculpted and molded by the agency of the white artist into an abstract and idealized aesthetic form—as in the picture of Derrick Cross: with the tilt of the pelvis, the black man's bum becomes a Brancusi (figure 2). It was my anger at the process of "ironic" appropriation that informed the description of Mapplethorpe's fetishism as resulting in the reduction of beautiful black male bodies to abject, alienated "things," each enslaved like a juju doll in the white male imaginary to arouse its unspeakable fantasies of racial Otherness.

But now I am not so sure whether the perverse strategy of visual fetishism is necessarily a bad thing, in the sense that as the locus of the destabilizing "shock effect" it encourages the viewer to examine his or her own implication in the fantasies that the images arouse. Once I acknowledge my own implication in the image reservoir as a gay subject, as a desiring subject for whom the aestheticized object of the look represents an object choice already there in my own fantasies, then I am forced to confront the

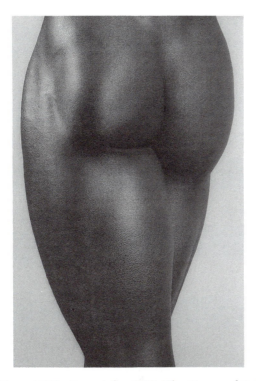

FIGURE 2. *Derrick Cross*, 1983. Copyright 1983 The Estate of Robert Mapplethorpe.

unwelcome fact that as a spectator I actually inhabit the same position in the fantasy of mastery which I said earlier was that of the hegemonic white male subject! There must be some way out of here, said the joker to the thief. I now wonder, as I wander back through the text, whether the anger was not also intermixed, on the other hand, with the expression of envy and jealousy?

If I shared the same desire to look, which would position me in the same place as that attributed to the white (gay) male author, the anger becomes intelligible as the expression of a certain aggressive rivalry over the same unobtainable object of desire, predicated on a shared homosexual identification. If this was the case, the implication is not simply that black subjects are equally "interpellated" into the psychic structures of social fantasy, but that by projecting my frustration onto the author I was myself involved in a denial or disavowal of the emotional disturbance that Mapplethorpe's pictures provoked. I refuse to believe that black gay male readers somehow have privileged access to this uncomfortable structure of feeling—the point, rather, is to recognize that Mapplethorpe's work is powerful and disturbing precisely because it forces such acknowledgment of the ambivalence of identity and identification we actually inhabit in living with difference. In rereading the nude studies and changing my mind, I would say that my ambivalent positioning as a black gay reader entailed two contradictory identifications "lived" at one and the same time. Insofar as the anger and envy were an effect of my identifications with both object and subject of the look, I inhabited a "stereophonic" space (in Barthes's phrase) that was subject to closure in the earlier reading by simply projecting the ambivalence onto the author.

It was the death of the author, and the sense of loss by which the AIDS crisis has affected all our lives, that made me reread the subversive and deconstructive dimension of Mapplethorpe's modernist erotica. Previously, I argued that the fixative function of the stereotype played the decisive role in reproducing colonial fantasy: now, however, in relation to Mapplethorpe's authorial identity as an explicitly gay artist (located, like other gay artists, on the margins of mainstream art-world institutions), it becomes possible, and necessary, to reverse that view and recognize the way in which his aesthetic strategy begins to subvert the hierarchy of the cultural codes that separate the pure and noble values of the fine art nude from the filthy and degraded form of the commonplace racist stereotype.

The nude is one of the most valued genres in Western art history because the human figure embodies the central values of liberal humanism. In this sense, the model of physical perfection embodied in classical Greek sculpture serves as the mythological origin of the ethnocentric fantasy that there was only one "race" of human beings who represented what was good and true and beautiful. In Enlightenment aesthetics, the Negro was none of these: ugly, animalistic, and ultimately inhuman, the black subject, whether male or female, was necessarily excluded from access to aesthetic idealization on account of its Otherness. The reason why that forgotten slogan of the sixties—"Black Is Beautiful"—had so much political and existential force was precisely because as a statement of ontology it subverted the naturalized hegemony of supremacist ideology which made the linguistic conjunction of the two terms logically "unthinkable." In the discourse of Western aesthetics, as Kant and Hegel both emphasized, it was unthinkable that Africans could embody the aesthetic ideal by which the narcissistic self-image of the West saw itself at the transcendental center of world civilization. The a priori exclusion of the racial Other was not unrelated to the hierarchical separation of "art" from "everyday life," as the value invested in high culture necessarily depends on the denial of value in what is regarded as low culture.

In his own perverse way, Mapplethorpe invites us to see hidden intertextual connections in the dominant regimes of the representation of racial and sexual difference. By virtue of a strategy of promiscuous intertextuality, whereby the over-valued genre of the fine art nude is "contaminated" by the connotative yield of racist fears and fantasies secreted into mass media stereotypes, he shows the interdependency between systems of representation at opposite ends of the hierarchy of aesthetic and cultural value. The pure and the polluted fold together in the same pictorial space, which is to suggest that what is experienced in the viewer's salient "shock effect" is the disruption of our normative expectations and the radical unfixing of the spectator's ideological positioning. The responses of Senator and Mrs. Helms would seem to confirm this view. What is so troubling about the black male nudes is that Mapplethorpe stages the return of the repressed in the ethnocentric unconscious. The psychic/social boundary that separates "high" and "low" culture is transgressed and decentered precisely by the superimposition of two ways of looking, which thus throws the spectator into the flux of uncertainty and undecidability, experienced as the feeling of ambivalence and disturbance in which one's subject-position has been called into question.

In social, economic, and political terms, black males constitute one of the "lowest" social classes in the United States: disenfranchised, disadvantaged, and disempowered as a distinct group identity in the late capitalist underclass. Yet in Mapplethorpe's studio, some of the men who in all probability came from this underclass are elevated onto the pedestal of the transcendental Western aesthetic ideal. Paradoxically, the humanist model of physical beauty said to originate with the Greeks is brought to life by the grace of men who were probably too busy hustling a means of daily survival to be bothered with an appreciation of ancient sculptures in their local art museum. Mapplethorpe's supremely ironic achievement as a postmodern "society photographer" is to render visible such "invisible men" (in Ralph Ellison's phrase) within a cultural system of representation—art photography—that always historically denied their existence. As he put it in an interview before his death,

> At some point I started photographing black men. It was an area that hadn't been explored intensively. If you went through the history of nude male photography, there were very few black subjects. I found that I could take pictures of black men that were so subtle, and the form was so photographical.

As Ingrid Sischy notes, Mapplethorpe's passion as a photographer came "from subjects that have been forced by our culture to be hidden like secrets." Homosexuality is often forced into hiding as a dirty little secret (and not just in Western societies, either), and I would therefore add that what Mapplethorpe achieved in his art was not simply the making visible of the psychic and social splitting that is normally repressed into invisibility, but that he used his homosexuality as a creative resource with which to explore and open up a politics of marginality across the multiform relations of class, race, gender, and sexuality in which it is actually lived.

In this review I have focused on the black nudes, to the exclusion of other aspects of his oeuvre, for two reasons. First, because it seems to me they represent a culmination of an aesthetic strategy. During the 1970s, Mapplethorpe's homoerotica paralleled the development of an urban gay male subculture: what makes the "difficult" sadomasochism pictures from the late seventies so disturbing, after all, is the nonchalant matter-of-factness of the author's nonjudgmental stance, which throws the question of aesthetic or moral judgment back into the field of the spectator. During this period, Mapplethorpe kept the erotica separate from the formalist concerns seen in his sculptural approach to the pictorial frame and in the figuration of lighting in the floral still lifes. The black nude studies are shaped by a synthesis between these two tendencies: the sense of ambivalence is exacerbated by the way the "cool" technology of neoclassical lines and minimalist space is brought to bear on the "hot" eroticism of the sex-race phantasm that haunts the representational space of the scene.

In this respect, we should acknowledge the collaborative relationship between the privileged white male artist on the margins of the avant-garde and the anonymous black male models on the margins of the late modern underclass. It may not have been entirely equal, but in the specific historical context of the "imagined community" created by the new social movements over the past twenty years, the photographs can be read as a document of relations of mutuality under shared conditions of marginality, which is something Mapplethorpe alluded to when he remarked, "Most of the blacks don't have health insurance and therefore can't afford AZT. They all died quickly, the blacks. If I go through my *Black Book,* half of them are dead." The AIDS crisis has changed all our lives, in the black communities of Europe and America as much as in Africa and the Caribbean. In this context, when mourning and melancholia become routine, what does it mean to acknowledge the loss of this strange, marginal, white gay male photographer?

By posing the question like this, I want to suggest that Mapplethorpe confronts black spectators and critics with a unique and difficult intellectual challenge. Can we afford to assume that black artists have privileged access to insights into the politics of race and racism simply by virtue of being black? Stuart Hall's often-quoted remarks on "the end of the innocent notion of the essential black subject" point to the legacy of essentialism in black cultural politics. His argument, that the aesthetic or political value of a text cannot be guaranteed by the racial or ethnic identity of the author who creates it, has disturbing consequences for the commonsense "theory" we habitually practice as black spectators, audiences, and critics: it means we can no longer have recourse to empirical evidence about the author's quotient of melanin to decide the aesthetic or political value of a text.

Recent works by black gay artists engage with these questions directly. Black British filmmaker Isaac Julien, whose *Looking for Langston* (1989) initiates an archeological inquiry into the enigmatic sexuality of Langston Hughes in the era of the Harlem Renaissance, and Nigerian-British photographer Rotimi Fani-Fayode, whose first published collection, *Black Male/White Male* (1988), opens an aperture onto an Afrocentric homoerotic image world, are directly engaged in a critically dialogic relationship with Mapplethorpe's work. It is through this critical dialogue that they have negotiated a mode of enunciation for black gay male subjectivity in the visual arts, which, against the quirky assumption that all black men are supposedly heterosexual, is something to celebrate indeed. But more than mere "celebration," this new wave of cultural work, which has developed in black lesbian and gay communities alongside the impact of black women's voices over the last decade, enables us to theorize a more pluralistic conception of identity in the cultural politics of race and ethnicity.

Robert Mapplethorpe was not a black artist: but on the rereading I have put forward, his subversive use of visual fetishism can be seen as a strategic move that reveals what is "unconscious" in the cultural construction of whiteness as a "racial" identity. By laying bare the supplementary relationship between the purified fine art nude and the polluted mass culture stereotype, he confronts white identity with its interdependency on the Otherness that allows it to be constituted as such. In other words, the trope of visual fetishism paradoxically decenters and denaturalizes whiteness by showing its dependence on what is denied as Other to it. Writing in the 1940s, an eccentric organic intellectual from the British West Indies, J.A. Rogers, assembled a heterogenous collection of "facts" and narratives in evidence of the black presence in Western history, ordinarily effaced in school textbooks. In *Your History* (1940), one of these hidden stories concerns the origins of classical Greek sculpture—"Several sculptors and scientists have said that the finest physiques in the world are to be found among the Negro peoples. Dr. Sargeant, Director of Physical Culture at Harvard University, said in 1903 that he thought the Greeks modeled the bodies of some of their finest statues from Negroes and that the Apollo Belvedere, the most superb of all, was modeled from a Negro." In the light of recent research such as Martin Bernal's *Black Athena,* there is probably no reason to be shocked or surprised at what Rogers uncovered: that Western ethnocentrism, predicated on the desire for mastery, entails the denial and disavowal of that upon which it depends for its existence and identity. Maybe Mapplethorpe has done something similar each time his images have shocked and frightened and disturbed us: by showing, and giving to be seen, that which is repressed and denied as Other as a condition of existence of an identity based on the desire for mastery.

I have another reason for concentrating on the nude studies, especially in the current context where the voices and visions of black lesbian and gay artists, among others, have widened and pluralized theoretical debates about sexuality, desire, and representation. A symptomatic reading of the relative silence of black voices in the Mapplethorpe/NEA controversy suggests that questions of repression, denial, and disavowal bear directly on the social relations of black culture itself. During the mid-eighties moral panic on AIDS, when media scapegoating switched from urban gays and turned in the direction of Haiti and Africa, one prevalent response within diaspora societies was a rhetoric of denial. All too often, the repudiation of racial stigmatization was based on the homophobic premise that homosexuality, and therefore AIDS, is a "white man's disease"—even though we could all see that black people were dying. This cruel rhetoric of denial, like the psychic mechanism of disavowal (the refusal to believe) on which it is based, can only imply a negation of diversity and difference in black society.

It was after Mapplethorpe's death that the New Right initiative began, first in protest against a second exhibition of "The Perfect Moment" in Philadelphia, and then given further momentum by the decision of the Corcoran Gallery in Washington to cancel its exhibition of the show, which was supported by NEA grants. Like the Salman Rushdie affair in Britain, the public debates about the politics of representation have tended to polarize into the stark dichotomy of censorship versus freedom of expression, yet this crude binary frontier serves only to obscure the complex field of antagonism, brought to light in Cincinnati earlier this year when antipornography feminists joined forces with the city police department in an attempt to foreclose the show. The politics at stake cannot be reduced to the stereotype of bigoted philistines on the one side versus cultured liberals on the other, because what is at stake in the everyday postmodern politics of difference is the fact that the new social actors of race, gender, ethnicity, and sexuality are just as capable of antidemocratic politics as the old social actors of class, party, and nation-state.

I should emphasize that I've changed my mind about Mapplethorpe's shocking eroticism not for the fun of it, but because I have no particular desire to form an alliance with the New Right. We have seen how the initial emancipatory aims of feminist antipornography arguments have been appropriated, translated, and rearticulated into the coercive cultural agenda of the New Right. Paradoxically, the success of late-seventies radical feminism lies in the way that reductive arguments about representation have been literally translated into the official discourse of the state, such as the Report of the Meese Commission in 1986. Such alliances are rarely controlled by authorial intentions, yet feminist discourses have helped to strengthen and extend neoconservative definitions of "offensive" material into more and more areas of popular culture. In contemporary rap music, for instance, "explicit lyrics" warning labels indicate the extension of what should be censored by consent. The worrying thing about the original 1989 Helms amendment was that it sought a broader remit for cultural censorship not only on the traditional moral grounds of "obscenity and indecency," but on the new cultural grounds of "offensiveness" to minorities. Helms said he objected to publicly funded art that "denigrates, debases, or reviles a person, group, or class of citizens on the basis of race, creed, sex, handicap, or national origin." By means of such a rhetorical move the discourse of liberal antidiscrimination is reversed and reappropriated to promote a politics of coercion based on the denial of difference. With ambivalent adversaries like that, it becomes possible for a reductive "antiracist" reading of Mapplethorpe's racial fetishism, however progressively intended, to serve the antidemocratic aims of the Right.

The fact that Mapplethorpe's photographs are open to a range of antagonistic political readings means that different actors are in a struggle to hegemonize one preferred version over another. The risky business of ambivalence by which his images can elicit a homophobic reading as easily as a homoerotic one, can confirm a racist reading as much as produce an antiracist one, suggests that indeterminacy doesn't happen "inside" the text, but in the social relations of difference that different readers bring to bear on the text, in the worldly relations "between."

25

Robert Mapplethorpe and the Discipline of Photography

RICHARD MEYER

Richard Meyer, a graduate student in Art History at the University of California, Berkeley, is the author of essays on "Rock Hudson's Body" (in Inside/Out, *ed. Diana Fuss, 1991) and on "Warhol's Clones" (forthcoming). In this essay, on Robert Mapplethorpe's photographs of sadomasochistic scenes, Meyer discusses the ways in which Mapplethorpe both continues and deviates from the traditions of documentary photography. He concludes that Mapplethorpe stages S/M scenes in such a way as to enable his subjects to defy the objectifying, voyeuristic gaze of the camera and, instead, to perform in a theatrically explicit fashion the power games that are conventionally, though usually more discreetly, played between photographer and subject.*

Censored

In the Spring of 1978, 80 Langton Street, an alternative art space in San Francisco, mounted an exhibition of Robert Mapplethorpe's photography. The show consisted of 19 black and white photographs cataloguing a range of sadomasochistic practices including penis piercing, latex bondage, single and double fist-fucking, and anal-penetration with a bull-whip. An image of this last practice was the only self-portrait in the exhibit and was, not incidentally, selected as the gallery announcement for the show (figure 1).

The exhibit's title, *Censored,* referred to the curatorial circumstances surrounding and suppressing Mapplethorpe's work at the time. After attempting without success to show his s/m photographs in New York, Mapplethorpe secured an agreement from the Simon Lowinsky gallery in downtown San Francisco to exhibit that work alongside some of his other portraits and still-lifes. Shortly before the opening of the show, however, the Lowinsky gallery "edited" out the most overt of the s/m images, belatedly declaring them unfit for commercial exhibition. 80 Langton Street then stepped in, agreeing to exhibit the censored photographs on the proviso that they would not be sold via the exhibition.[1]

In this case, the censorship of Mapplethorpe's photography resulted in the return of the work to the space of its subculture: the 80 Langton Street gallery was located just off Folsom Street, the center (then as now) of San Francisco's gay leather scene.[2] This fringe venue, just around the corner from the Ramrod, the Rivet, and the Brig, imbued the *Censored* exhibit with a certain glamor of the margin. Listen, for example, to the description of the show's opening night reception which appeared in the *San Francisco Art Dealer's Associated Newsletter:*

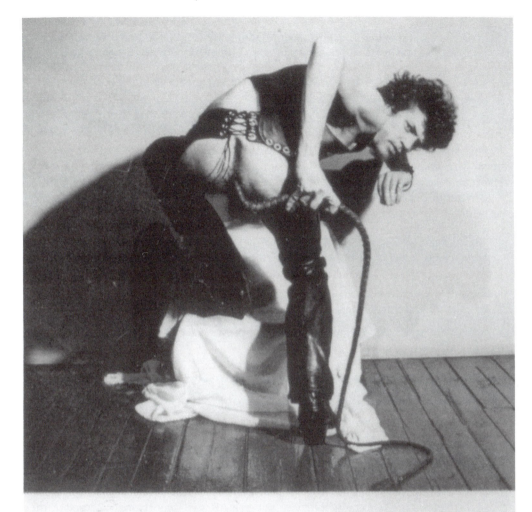

CENSORED

Robert Mapplethorpe

March 21
through April 1, 1978
Reception:
Monday, March 20,
6–8 p.m.

80 Langton Street
San Francisco
(415) 626-5416
Gallery Hours: 1–5 p.m.
Tuesday–Saturday

FIGURE 1.   Robert Mapplethorpe, *Self-Portrait*, 1978 (Gallery announcement, "Censored" exhibit at 80 Langton Street). Photograph copyright 1978 The Estate of Robert Mapplethorpe.

> A fascinating cross-section of San Francisco society, and visitors from elsewhere, drank wine and bottled beer as they congratulated the New York photographer on his exhibition of photographs which explore the world of sadomasochism and its ritualistic trappings. Among those in the crowd, rubbing shoulders with the men in black leather, were popular ceramic artist Anita Mardikian, art collector Byron Meyer, University Art Museum Director James Elliot, male model Peter Berlin . . . San Francisco art dealers Simon Lowinsky, Ursula Gropper . . .[3]

The smug clubbiness of this account might give us some pause in celebrating Mapplethorpe's resistance to the commercial censorship of his work in 1978. It is the photographer, after all, who straddles the "world of sado-masochism" and that of the art market, forming the singular join in that "fascinating cross-section." Mapplethorpe is celebrated as an avatar of the erotic transgressions he photographs, the gay male artist engaging in the wild side of subculture in order to frame (and tame) its image for the gallery crowd. Patrons of the San Francisco art circuit may now "rub shoulders" with the "men in black leather" while safely installed within the chic propriety of the art opening.[4]

The *Censored* exhibit would seem to fulfill the conventional function of documentary photography, namely, the framing of the subject as victim, freak, or specimen in relation to an enfranchised, implicitly normative viewing audience. Martha Rosler describes the signifying procedures of such "concerned" photography as follows:

> Documentary testifies . . . to the bravery or (dare we name it?) the manipulativeness and savvy of the photographer who entered a situation of physical danger, social restrictedness, human decay, or combinations of these and saved us the trouble. Or who, like the astronauts, entertained us by showing us places we never hope to go: War photography, slum photography, "subculture" or cult photography, photography of the foreign poor, photography of deviance . . .[5]

This passage describes the *Censored* exhibit in significant ways: Mapplethorpe did recover gay sadomasochism from the sites of its subcultural practice and bring it back to the avant-garde "safe space" of the alternative art gallery. The artist's commodification of gay subculture and his complicity with the procedures of the commercial art market should be admitted, even and perhaps especially at our present moment.[6] As I will argue below, however, such an admission does not exhaust the importance or describe the achievement of Mapplethorpe's work on gay sadomasochism. There were other pressures applied by these photographs, ways in which they could not be, and still cannot be, dismissed as just so much subcultural profiteering or avant-garde exploitation.

Far from "saving us the trouble" of going there ourselves, Mapplethorpe announces the impossibility of "visiting" gay sadomasochism through its photographic representation. Rather than framing s/m as the curious object of concerned photography, he emphasizes the insufficiency of the camera to document leather sex and subculture. In stressing the premeditations of the studio session (pose, props, lighting, cropping), Mapplethorpe marks his photographs as highly mediated and willfully incomplete representations of gay s/m. At its best, Mapplethorpe's work calls upon the intrinsic theatricality of sadomasochism not to stage some truth of leather subculture but to reveal the very artifice and fetishisms of photography.[7]

"Sex Without the Camera is Sexier"

The 1978 *Self-Portrait* offers Mapplethorpe, outfitted in a black leather vest, chaps and boots, penetrating his asshole with a bullwhip. The portrait announces the artist's stake in the subculture he photographs, making its selection as gallery announcement for the *Censored* show declarative of considerably more than the opening night reception and gallery hours. Specifically, the *Self-Portrait* asserts that when Mapplethorpe photographs other practitioners of gay s/m the lens of his camera is not pointed, metaphorically, downward. In rendering his sadomasochistically engaged body visible to the camera, Mapplethorpe repudiates what Susan Sontag has called the "supertourist" stance of documentary photography.[8] The 1978 *Self-Portrait* graphically insists on Mapplethorpe's double investment in gay s/m, as both photographer and erotic participant:

> I was a part of it, yeah, that's where most of the time people—photographers—who move in that direction have a disadvantage, I think a disadvantage, in that they're not part of it. They're just voyeurs moving in on a scene, and with me it was quite different. Some of those experiences that I later recorded I had experienced first-hand, without a camera.[9]

This claim for the insider status of Mapplethorpe's photography is substantiated by the 1978 *Son of Drummer* magazine, a leather and s/m porn publication which showcased the *Censored* exhibit with a "Mapplethorpe gallery" of nine photographs.[10] A commentary accompanying the pictures affirmed that "Mapplethorpe is no 'concerned' photographer smug with social significance. He chronicles SM fetishism from the inside out. He's a man who knows night territory."[11] Mapplethorpe's first-hand experience of s/m is here invoked as evidence of the authenticity of his images. Not surprisingly, the 1978 *Self-Portrait,* Mapplethorpe's most explicit credential of s/m experience, is featured prominently in the *Son of Drummer* gallery.

The *Self-Portrait* does far more, however, than confirm Mapplethorpe's knowledge of night territory; it rewrites the conventions of artistic self-representation along manifestly homo- and anal-erotic lines. The bravado of the photograph derives largely from the spectacle of its anality and from the fact that the asshole on offer is the photographer's own. By offering, indeed flaunting, his anus to the camera while also self-penetrating it, Mapplethorpe presents his body as a sadomasochistic receptacle of both the bull-whip and the viewer's gaze. Within the history of art, one is hard-pressed to recall another self-portrait, whether painterly or photographic, which depicts its artist as anally penetrable. As against the conventional self-portrait's claim to phallic mastery and professional self-regard, Mapplethorpe insists on the productive potential of his opened asshole. "Gay men," writes Richard Fung in another context, are "disruptive of masculine norms because we assert the pleasure of being fucked and the eroticism of the anus."[12] The visibility of Mapplethorpe's asshole (alongside that of his leather chaps, vest, boots, and bull-whip) in the 1978 *Self-Portrait* activates a specifically and spectacularly gay form of self-representation.

Even as the *Self-Portrait* articulates Mapplethorpe's audacious anality, it reminds us that such an articulation is occurring within the space of the studio, the space of white walls, varnished floorboards, draped chairs. In this context, the fact that Mapplethorpe is both the agent and object of anal penetration (both top and bottom) refers as well to the procedure of creating a self-portrait, to the simultaneity of serving as both productive agent and receptive object of photography. In short, the reflexivity of Mapplethorpe's auto-penetration mirrors the reflexivity of his auto-portraiture.

To extend this reading of the image, consider the way Mapplethorpe's bull-whip snakes not only out of his body but out of the visual field, leading from his opened asshole to our position of gazing. The bull-whip resembles nothing so much as an extension cord or cable tying Mapplethorpe's body to the clicking camera off-frame. Notice the photographer's careful fingering of the whip and the way his cupped left hand mimics the action of triggering a shutter-release. The bull-whip, a fetish object of gay s/m, here stands in for the mechanisms of photography, mechanisms implied by the metaphor to be themselves fetishistic.

But if the bull-whip (and by metaphoric extension, the camera) is a fetish object of pleasure-in-pain, the very composure of Mapplethorpe's expression seems at odds with it. It is as though he is performing anal penetration without seeming to experience it, or at least, without offering the traces of that experience to the viewer's gaze: there is no erotic release, no register of sexualized pain, no expressive evidence of the fact of being fucked. Instead, Mapplethorpe seems consummately in control of his appearance before the camera. While the surliness of the artist's gaze acknowledges that he is being caught in an act of auto-penetration, it also signifies an extreme mastery over the photographic image and the self depicted in it.[13]

I suggested above that Mapplethorpe's work on gay s/m refutes the conventional distance between the empowered viewer and the curious object of documentary photography. There is, however, a quite different distance on which the 1978 *Self-Portrait* insists, namely, the distance between Mapplethorpe's practice of sadomasochism (say, at the Mineshaft or the Catacombs) and his masquerade of it in the studio, for the camera. What we are offered in the *Self-Portrait* is not a documentary image of gay sadomasochism but an acknowledged simulation of it, a self-styled performance of penetration which visually glosses Mapplethorpe's own statement that "sex without the camera is sexier."[14]

Where the 1978 *Self-Portrait* signifies a confidence in being looked at rather than a pleasure in being penetrated (thereby stressing the photographic circumstance over the sexual one), Mapplethorpe's *Self-Portrait* from five years earlier (figure 2) employs a quite different visual strategy to make a similar point. The rapid movement of the artist's face together with his tit-clamp and tensed musculature suggests a spontaneous and kinesthetic response to sexual pain. The visual illegibility of that response, however, marks it as one too fugitive to be caught by the camera, too intense to be photographically captured as a "perfect moment."[15] Although the 1973 *Self-Portrait* offers Mapplethorpe in the midst of a sexual episode, the specific content of that episode (is he jerking off or receiving a blow-job? is he coming?) cannot be recovered by the viewer of the photograph.

In addition to its somewhat illegible image, the 1973 *Self-Portrait* also features a red and black leather frame of Mapplethorpe's own design. By refashioning the frame, that most conventional of pictorial devices, in leather, Mapplethorpe overlays the visual codes of sadomasochism and art-photography. The fetishized texture of s/m frames an image of Mapplethorpe's own body which is similarly encased, if only incompletely, by a leather vest. While both image and frame of the 1973 *Self-Portrait* metonymically refer to leather sex, neither attempts to embody or document it fully.

Mapplethorpe's cross-coding of sadomasochism and photography extends well beyond the occasions of his self-portraiture. The 1979 photograph of *Helmut* (figure 3), for example, emphasizes its spare art-studio backdrop (that framing swath of fabric) and the elegant if unlikely pose of the leatherman atop a pedestal. Mapplethorpe's formal play with light and shade is insistent and unapologetic, the leather jacket becoming blackest, for instance, when it overlaps the white muslin fabric behind it. The preparations and beautifications of *Helmut* conform to the traditions of the studio still-life far more than to those of documentary or "subculture" photography.

The still-life was, of course, one of Mapplethorpe's specialties and comparisons are frequently drawn between his photographs of flowers and his portraits of leathermen. Consider, for example, the parallel structure of a 1979 *Artforum* advertisement (figure 4) in which the portrait of *Helmut* is opposed to an equally stylized composition of white blossoms in a black bowl. The letter "x" centered beneath *Helmut* refers to Map-

FIGURE 2.   Robert Mapplethorpe, *Self-Portrait*, 1973. Copyright The Estate of Robert Mapplethorpe.

plethorpe's "x" portfolio, an edition of thirteen s/m photographs which were viewed (and marketed) against a contrasting "y" portfolio of floral studies (a "z" series of black male nudes was later added). Once cock-ring and carnation inhabit the same photographic lexicon, then even the hottest of leathermen may be "tamed" into elegant abstraction and the gentlest of floral arrangements freighted with a sexual charge.[16] Such, in any event, would seem to be the logic proposed by the coordination of Mapplethorpe's alternate photographic practices ("faces, flowers, and fetishes") into parallel portfolios.[17]

For all its affinity to a still-life, however, Mapplethorpe's *Helmut* can never be divorced outright from the specificity of leather sex and subculture. Certain visual details (the spreading of Helmut's legs, the outlining of his ass by the leather tie-strings, the suggestion of jerking-off made by the placement of his right arm) will assert themselves should the viewer become too interested in photographic *chiaroscuro* or abstraction for abstraction's sake. The rear perspective of the portrait blocks access to Helmut's face, cock, and hands, and thus to any explicit scene of sexual activity. As beholders, we are thus left to imagine the frontal view which the portrait denies. My own such view sees Helmut, now in the midst of jerking off, taking a hit of amyl nitrate, hence the crook of his left elbow as that arm reaches upward and the droop of his head as it receives the poppers. *Helmut,* as Roland Barthes writes in the context of another Mapplethorpe

FIGURE 3.   Robert Mapplethorpe, *Helmut*, 1979. Copyright The Estate of Robert
Mapplethorpe.

photograph, has "launched desire beyond what it permits us to see,"[18] directing the
viewer to the space, just past the camera's grasp, of leather sex and self-pleasure.

As with *Helmut*, Mapplethorpe's 1978 portrait of *Joe* (figure 5) is not concerned
with catching its subject in the midst of spontaneous sexual activity but with describing
his erotic costume: the strap-on tube extending from the mouth, the ridges of the rubber
hood, the studded collar, the industrial rubber gloves, the sheen and torsion of the latex
uniform. The premeditation of Joe's pose, the fact that he has donned his latex and is
stilling his body for Mapplethorpe's camera, is emphasized by the visual evidence of
the image. This is no *verité* realm of the street or sex club but an acknowledged artistic
set-up, the studio space of bare floorboards and benches, of backdrops and strobe lights.

Even less than *Helmut* or *Joe* does Mapplethorpe's *Untitled* photograph of 1978
(figure 6) abstract its model out of the specificity of his subculture. Indeed, it appears
that the sitter has here become subordinated to his s/m fetish-object, as though through
the very posturing of his body, he is attempting to conform to the demands of his
cowboy boot. Note the rounding over of the shoulders, the loss of the lower part of
the face, the way in which the body, however we trace its contours, continually returns
our gaze to the boot. Once again, Mapplethorpe takes the fetishistic capabilities of
photography—the way it can deploy light, texture, and cropping to isolate and eroticize
an object—and crosses them with the fetishisms of gay s/m.[19]

It is on this point that I would distinguish Mapplethorpe's s/m project from his
subsequent series of black male nudes. In the s/m work, fetish objects and sexual par-

X   Y

FIGURE 4. Advertisement for exhibit of Robert Mapplethorpe's X and Y portfolios, Robert Miller Gallery, New York, from *Artforum*, March 1979, pp. 10–11. Used with permission.

aphernalia mark the body of the (white) male subject and signify his preferred erotic practice. We may not have very much information about Helmut but we do know that the biker jacket, boots, and harness are his favored sexual costume just as we know that Joe's latex-wear is his, and so on. The sheer quantity of the erotic paraphernalia on offer in the s/m photographs (leather and latex, boots and chaps, hoods and harnesses, whips and chains, clamps and restraints . . .) confirms that Mapplethorpe is cataloguing a *community* of sexual practitioners and not merely his own desires or favorite practices as one member of that community. But in Mapplethorpe's photographs of black male nudes, in the 1981 portrait of *Ajitto,* for example (figure 7), the model's body is stripped of any marker of subjectivity or preferred sexual practice; no traces here of the black man's own erotic investments and fetish objects. Writing on these portraits, Kobena Mercer and Isaac Julien rightly suggest that

> [a]s all references to a social, political, or cultural context are ruled out of the frame . . . the images reveal more about what the eye/I behind the lens wants to see than they do about the relatively anonymous black male models whose beautiful bodies we see.[20]

Where the s/m project displays the sexual costumes and fetish objects of white gay men (including but not limited to those of Mapplethorpe himself), the series of black male nudes frames the model's body as the very fetish of Mapplethorpe's camera.

In turning back to the s/m project, I want to suggest that Mapplethorpe's insistence on the premeditations of photography applies not only to his portraits of individual practitioners but to those of s/m couples as well. Although it is in photographs of the couple that we might reasonably expect to witness active sexual exchange, it is here that Mapplethorpe most pointedly refuses that representation.[21] In the double-portrait *Elliot and Dominick* (figure 8), for instance, both sitters present their erotic roles and s/m equipment to the viewer. But while Dominick is strung up and enchained by the bondage apparatus and while Elliot grabs both his own crotch and that of his submissive partner,

FIGURE 5.   Robert Mapplethorpe, *Joe*, 1978. Copyright The Estate of Robert Mapplethorpe.

neither man seems enthralled by the sexual act. It is as though they are waiting, perhaps resentfully, for the camera to absent itself so that the pleasure-session might begin or resume. Rather than enact a pretense of photographic transparency, these men insist upon the artifice of their pose; they challenge our spectatorial power to see and freeze them by allowing us only a *limited* view of their sadomasochistic practice. As a significant part of their refusal to be seen as subcultural freaks, Elliot and Dominick project a resolute awareness of their roles, not only as sexual master and slave, but as subjects before the camera's stilling gaze.[22]

To support the claim that Mapplethorpe distances his work from the conventions of "subculture" photography, we might compare *Elliot and Dominick* to a 1982 photograph by Mark I. Chester (figure 9) which accompanied an *Advocate* expose on gay sadomasochism entitled "To the Limits and Beyond." Note that the two men pictured by Chester are seemingly oblivious to the presence of the camera, that their spectacular fucking has been caught *in medias res* though also from some distance, and that the subordinate details of the image (long shadows, crushed mattress, tangle of chains) seem randomly composed and spontaneously registered. Such are the visual codes which testify to an authentic documentary adventure, to the photographic capture of gay sex "beyond the limits." Such are the codes which Mapplethorpe's *Elliot and Dominick* avoids at all costs.

If Mapplethorpe's work defies the codes of subculture photography, so too does it avoid the typical strategies of s/m pornography, strategies which will here be exemplified by a photograph from *Son of Drummer* (figure 10).[23] As viewers of this image, we are invited to disregard its material production (the presence of the photographer, the lighting of the scene, the hire and costuming of the models) so as to take more consummate pleasure in its erotic content. Apart from assigning the roles of sexual dominance and submission, the photograph extends little sense of subjectivity to the beautiful male bodies it displays. Indeed, even the men's s/m roles appear reversible since both models are similarly outfitted for sex (tit-clamps, leather harnesses and hoods) and are, so far as one can make out, physically identical. In contrast to this image of muscular sadomasochism, Mapplethorpe's *Elliot and Dominick* emphasizes both the specific identity of its sitters and the premeditated terms of their representation. Elliot and Dominick appear before us as self-possessed, self-aware subjects of their own (largely off-stage) sadomasochistic practice, not as ciphers of the beholder's fantasy.

FIGURE 6.   Robert Mapplethorpe, *Untitled*, 1978. Copyright The Estate of Robert Mapplethorpe.

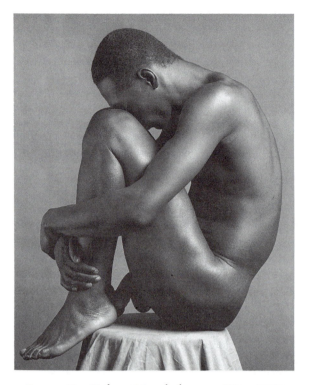

FIGURE 7.   Robert Mapplethorpe, *Ajitto*, 1981.
Copyright The Estate of Robert Mapplethorpe.

Ironically, it is Mapplethorpe's very acknowledgment of the premeditations of photography for which his work has been criticized. In an *Artnews* review from February 1984, Mapplethorpe's photographs of s/m are dismissed on the grounds that they are "stagey, the shots just don't ring true."[24] Yet Mapplethorpe's project is not to register the truth of sadomasochistic subculture but the fact of it, a fact which resides beyond the photographic frame and has been signified as such by the very "staginess" of Mapplethorpe's idiom.

The self-conscious theatricality of the s/m project is perhaps best characterized by the 1979 portrait of *Bryan Ridley and Lyle Heeter* (figure 11). In this image, Mapplethorpe exploits a mismatch between the couple's sadomasochistic outfitting and their domestic interior; between their leather, chains, and master/slave hierarchy on the one hand and their wingback chair, oriental rug, grasscloth wall covering, and white antlers endtable on the other. This spectacular disjunction not only defuses the leather machismo of Ridley and Heeter, it also asserts that neither their erotic costume nor their domestic context, neither their chains nor their faux rococo table clock, are sufficient metaphors for their identity. The contradictions of this portrait defeat any essentialist interpretation of Ridley and Heeter in (or as) their sadomasochistic roles.

In terms of the photograph's surprising overlay of sadomasochism and domesticity, consider the way in which the couple's stance mimics a conventional marriage-portrait pose, with the dominant partner standing behind his seated and submissive mate. For an example of this pose in its more conventional format, we may look to Cecil Beaton's photograph of Queen Elizabeth and the Prince Consort taken on the occasion of the Queen's coronation in 1953 (figure 12). Even here, however, the standard positions of (male) dominance and (female) subservience are revised insofar as the Queen's superior authority is marked by the elaborate regalia which unfurl from her seated position and by the marginalized position of the Prince within the visual field. Needless to say, Mapplethorpe's portrait of Ridley and Heeter provides a more radical revision of this pose than Beaton's since the "husband" is now a leather-daddy who restrains his strapping male mate with chains in one hand and a riding crop in the other.

Although Ridley and Heeter signify their respective roles of erotic dominance and submission, each man is equally dominant or better, defiant, in the face of the camera. While a sexual economy of "top" and "bottom" exists between Ridley and Heeter, neither man will readily submit to the gaze of the camera. The intensity of the couple's look out at the camera (at Mapplethorpe, at us) was necessary if the portrait was to avoid condescending to its sitters. We can imagine how easily the contradictions of the scene might otherwise have framed Ridley and Heeter as deluded or pathetic.

We can imagine, for example, how a photographer like Diane Arbus would have handled the portrait. Arbus's 1963 photograph, *A Widow in Her Bedroom,* like Mapplethorpe's *Brian Ridley and Lyle Heeter,* pivots around the relation of sitter to domestic space.[25] In Arbus's scene, however, the widow's bedroom frames the subject within her own freakishness. The uneven lighting and eclectic furnishings of the room (Buddhist curios, baroque étagère, chrome trash-basket, damask drapes) overpower the widow and seem to crowd her out of the space. Ridley and Heeter, on the other hand, preside over their space and dictate its scale, with Ridley securely inhabiting his large wingback chair and Heeter perfectly filling the gap formed by the parted curtains. While the widow appears awkward and indecisive in her own bedroom (an awkwardness no doubt provoked by the presence of the camera), Ridley and Heeter project a certain stance and self-confident look. Mapplethorpe's portrait admits no disdain for its sitters, none of that Arbus certainty that the photographed subject will always "bottom" for both the photographer and the viewer.

In *Brian Ridley and Lyle Heeter,* as in most of the photographs in the s/m series, Mapplethorpe is after something rather more ambitious than subcultural verisimilitude. In allowing his subjects to display their sexual paraphernalia while turning away from, or better, looking resolutely at the camera, Mapplethorpe stages gay sadomasochism as an erotic theater whose *players* determine their own props and costumes, their own pleasures and script; a theater whose performances occur beyond the frame of art photography and are therefore not accessible to the avant-garde viewer in search of otherness. In *Subculture, the Meaning of Style,* Dick Hebdige writes that

> What distinguishes the visual ensembles of spectacular subcultures from those favored in the surrounding culture [is that] they are *obviously* fabricated [and] they *display* their own codes or at least demonstrate that codes are there to be used and abused. In this they go against the grain of a mainstream culture whose principal defining characteristic ... is a tendency to masquerade as nature.[26]

The achievement of Robert Mapplethorpe's work on s/m is that it displays the codes and erotic fabrications of gay sadomasochism all the while acknowledging, and indeed actively calling into signifying use, the masquerades of photography.

Shockers

When these [s/m] pictures first appeared there were shivers and most often people turned away, myself included. Eventually they became the portion of his work which stayed in drawers, only appearing on the rarest of occasions and many of them never

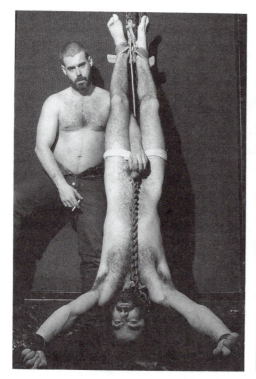

FIGURE 8.　Robert Mapplethorpe, *Elliot and Dominick*, 1979. Copyright The Estate of Robert Mapplethorpe.

FIGURE 9.　Copyright 1992 Mark I. Chester, *Slot Rm. 328*, in *The Advocate*, July 8, 1982.

again seen. But no one who knew about them forgot those scenes, even if the knowledge was only by rumor. They stayed in the back of the mind, tugging a little every time another Mapplethorpe work went by.[27]

Robert Mapplethorpe's photographs of gay s/m represent a relatively small portion of his overall artistic output: still-lifes, nudes (most often of black men), and commissioned portraits are all more heavily represented than sadomasochism. But, to hear a number of critics and one senator tell it, it is the work on s/m which has inflected, informed, even "deformed" the rest of Mapplethorpe's oeuvre. For these viewers, real or imagined scenes of sadomasochism attach to even the most anodyne of Mapplethorpe photographs as a kind of signifying afterimage or residue.[28] It is doubtful, for example, that Mapplethorpe's portraits of children would have stirred such paranoia about pedophilia had not Senator Helms (et al.) seen or heard about the photographs of leather sex. Indeed, as Carole Vance suggests, Helms's "laundry list" of indecencies (sadomasochism, homoeroticism, child pornography) is probably best interpreted as a chain of hysterical association.[29]

Another association now affixed, and often hysterically, to Mapplethorpe's work is that of the artist's AIDS-related death. In writing about Mapplethorpe's 1988 retrospective at the Whitney Museum, Dominick Dunne warned the readers of *Vanity Fair* that

However much you may have heard that this exhibition was not a shocker, believe me, it was a shocker. Robert Mapplethorpe was described by everyone I interviewed

FIGURE 10. Untitled image from *Son of Drummer* magazine, 1978.

as the man who had taken the sexual experience to the limits in his work, a docu-
mentarian of the homoerotic life in the 1970s at its most excessive, resulting, possibly,
in the very plague that was killing its recorder.[30]

Dunne rewrites the express homosexuality of Mapplethorpe's work as an etiology of
disease. The plague metaphor is used to "contaminate" both the general practice of gay
sex in the 1970s and Mapplethorpe's particular documentation of it. In a similar if yet
more ferocious move, *Artnews* critic Susan Weiley suggested that, in light of AIDS, the
most explicit of Mapplethorpe's s/m images ". . . provoke a shudder similar to the one
we feel looking at smiling faces in photographs of the Warsaw ghetto."[31]

Such an escalation of rhetoric (from AIDS to plague to the Holocaust) characterizes
both the recent reception of Mapplethorpe's work and the justifications given for the
censorship of it. Throughout the N.E.A. episode, the continued invocation of Mapplethorpe's death as a result of AIDS and the frequent representation of his body as conspicuously ailing served as the frame through which his s/m photographs, and sometimes
his entire photographic output, were to be re-viewed. Mapplethorpe, once the most
explicitly gay of gay male artists, now became the most explicitly diseased of artists with
AIDS. During the Congressional hearings on the funding of the National Endowment

FIGURE 11.   Robert Mapplethorpe, *Bryan Ridley and Lyle Heeter*, 1979. Copyright
The Estate of Robert Mapplethorpe.

for the Arts, Senator Helms, after mentioning Mapplethorpe's "recent death from
AIDS," declared of his photography:

> There are unspeakable portrayals which I cannot describe on the floor of the Sen-
> ate. . . . this pornography is sick. But Mapplethorpe's sick art does not seem to be an
> isolated incident. Yet another artist exhibited some of this sickening obscenity in my
> own state . . . I could go on and on, Mr. President, about the sick art that has been
> displayed around the country.[32]

Helms denounces Mapplethorpe's art as epidemic, suggesting that it is not an "isolated
incident" but a spreading "obscenity" which must be contained and eradicated. HIV
infection is thus displaced from Mapplethorpe's body to the body of his work as his
photographs are said to pollute (the neo-conservative fantasy of) a "clean" American
culture.[33] As Ingrid Sischy observes,

> The press coverage of the Corcoran's cancellation made it clear just how glued together
> Mapplethorpe and AIDS have become. Practically every time his name was mentioned,
> AIDS was mentioned too, as his I.D . . . Now the physical sickness that the man
> endured is being used to confirm ideas that the work itself is sick.[34]

FIGURE 12.   Cecil Beaton, *Queen Elizabeth II's Coronation*, 1953. Copyright Cecil Beaton/Camera Press/Globe Photos, Inc.

In this context, Sischy discusses the fact that Mapplethorpe's late self-portraits were often published in the popular press to signify the "illness" of both the artist and his imagery, the 1988 *Self-Portrait* (figure 13) being the photograph most often reprinted to this end.

But what is most striking about the 1988 *Self-Portrait* is that, like Mapplethorpe's work on gay sadomasochism, it explicitly refutes the economy of concerned or "victim" photography.[35] Mapplethorpe's *Self-Portrait* signifies anger as well as illness, confidence in the face of cultural fear. Through its very theatricality (white fist grasping death's-head cane in near space, white face floating in deeper space, all set within a monochrome of black), the *Self-Portrait* asserts Mapplethorpe's authority over his self-representation. While the visual repercussions of AIDS are there to be seen in the face of Robert Mapplethorpe, the very force of his photographic abstraction contests the patheticizing operations of victim photography.

Douglas Crimp has observed that "photography is a very impoverished medium for representing anything so complex as AIDS, as *living* with AIDS."[36] Unlike most

FIGURE 13.   Robert Mapplethorpe, *Self-Portrait*, 1988. Copyright The Estate of Robert Mapplethorpe.

other art photographs of a person with AIDS, Mapplethorpe's 1988 *Self-Portrait* admits that impoverishment, even insists upon it. In this image, as in the self-portrait with bull-whip from a decade earlier, Mapplethorpe meets and then defies the gaze of his own camera. In so doing, he signals the radical insufficiency of photography to describe the experiences, and here the vulnerabilities, of his sentient body.

NOTES

I am grateful to Whitney Davis, Douglas Melton, Paul Morrison, David Halperin, Abigail Solomon-Godeau, and Susan Scott Parish for their assistance with this essay.

1. The *Censored* episode in San Francisco should be seen as a prelude to the recent and more repressive censorship of Mapplethorpe's work: the July 1989 cancellation of a full-scale retrospective of Mapplethorpe's career, by the Corcoran Gallery of Art in Washington D.C. (the show was subsequently revived by the Washington Project for the Arts, an alternative arts space, and then traveled to Berkeley, Cincinnati, and Boston); a punitive reduction in the federal funding of the National Endowment for the Arts in the amount of $45,000, the sum of the grants awarded by the N.E.A. to the Mapplethorpe retrospective and to Andres Serrano, another photographer whose work was deemed "obscene" by members of Congress; new restrictions on the N.E.A.'s funding procedure based on the perceived content and "decency" of the work under consideration (the restrictions have since been repealed); and, in April 1990, the temporary closing of the *The Perfect Moment* by Cincinnati police and the indictment of its local exhibitor on obscenity charges—charges on which the defendant was tried and acquitted.

Curatorial information concerning the *Censored* show was provided by Renny Pritikin, director of the New Langton Art gallery, in a phone interview on November 11, 1989 and confirmed by Robert McDonald, former board member of the 80 Langton Street gallery, in a phone interview on November 14, 1989.

2. The emergence, beginning in the mid-1960s, of an extensive gay leather subculture in San Francisco's South of Market district is documented by Gayle Rubin in "Valley of the Kings," *Sentinel* (September 13, 1984): 10–11 and "The Catacombs: A Temple of the Butthole," in *Leatherfolk: Radical Sex, People, Politics, and Practice,* Mark Thompson, ed. (Boston: Alyson Publications, 1991): 119–141.

3. Rita Brooks, "Censored," *San Francisco Art Dealer's Associated Newsletter* (unpaginated), May/June 1978.

4. We might note that Lowinsky, the very dealer who suppressed Mapplethorpe's work, is named on the list of prominent guests at the *Censored* opening. In one of the photographs accompanying the notice, Lowinsky and Mapplethorpe are seen posing together for the opening night camera, the former in jacket and tie, the latter in full leather. Although Lowinsky could not sell any work through 80 Langton Street, it stands to reason that the *Censored* exhibit would have drawn attention to Lowinsky's concurrent show of Mapplethorpe portraits and still-lifes across town, lending it a *frisson* of the transgressive. For a review of the Lowinsky exhibit, see Thomas Albright, "Realism, Romanticism, and Leather," in *San Francisco Chronicle,* February 24, 1978: 64.

5. Martha Rosler, *3 Works* (Halifax: Nova Scotia: Press of the Nova Scotia College of Art and Design, 1981): 73.

6. The status of Mapplethorpe's photography is no less paradoxical today than it was in 1978: even as it is now censored and censured, Mapplethorpe's work, at up to $35,000 per print, defines the very apex of the contemporary photographic market. The recent battle over the putative "indecency" of Mapplethorpe's work served, among other purposes, to inflate the market value of that work. See Grace Glueck, "Publicity is Enriching Mapplethorpe Estate," *New York Times,* April 16, 1990: B1.

7. On the theatrics of gay male sadomasochism, see Don Miesen, "SM: A View of Sadomasochism," *Drummer* 10, No. 87: 15–17, 100–103 and Jeffrey Weeks, *Sexuality and Its Discontents: Meanings, Myths, & Modern Sexualities* (London: Routledge & Kegan Paul, 1986): 236–41. For an

account of the theatricality of lesbian s/m, see Pat Califia's "Unraveling the Sexual Fringe: A Secret Side of Lesbian Sexuality," *Advocate,* December 27, 1979: 19ff.

It should be noted that there are several Mapplethorpe pictures that exploit the spectacle of sadomasochism without referencing the artifice of photography. Foremost among these is *Richard* (1978) an image of a bound, ostensibly bloodied penis seen in close-up. (For a reproduction, see *Robert Mapplethorpe,* New York: Whitney Museum, 1988: 69.) There are also the fist-fucking photographs from the *Censored* show which have not to my knowledge been reproduced in any American publication of Mapplethorpe's work. The problems raised by these images (i.e. the denial of agency to the male body photographed, the fact that Mapplethorpe seems voyeuristically to "invade" s/m subculture rather than provide a partial and patently mediated view of it) distinguishes them from the photographs under consideration in this essay.

8. Sontag uses the term to criticize the work of Diane Arbus:

> "Photography was a license to go wherever I wanted and to do what I wanted to do," Arbus wrote. The camera is a kind of passport that annihilates moral boundaries and social inhibitions, freeing the photographer from any responsibility toward the people photographed. The whole point of photographing people is that you are not intervening in their lives, only visiting them. The photographer is supertourist, an extension of the anthropologist, visiting natives and bringing back news of their exotic doings and strange gear.

See Susan Sontag, *On Photography* (New York: Dell Publishing, 1977): 41–42.

9. Mapplethorpe interviewed in "Robert Mapplethorpe," a broadcast documentary produced by Arena films, 1988, Great Britain.

10. *Son of Drummer* (San Francisco: 1978) was a special, one-time-only issue of *Drummer,* the premier American porn magazine devoted to leather sex and gay sadomasochism.

11. "The Robert Mapplethorpe Gallery," *Son of Drummer* (San Francisco: 1978): 15.

12. Richard Fung, "Looking for My Penis: The Eroticized Asian in Gay Video Porn," *How Do I Look? Queen Film and Video,* ed. Bad Object Choices (Seattle: Bay Press, 1991): 153.

Eve Kosofsky Sedgwick writes that the anus is "the place that is signally not under one's own ocular control." In the 1978 *Self-Portrait,* Mapplethorpe calls upon his camera to overcome this blind-spot and thereby to enunciate anality as central to both his professional and sexual identities.

See Eve Kosofsky Sedgwick, "A Poem is Being Written," *Representations* 17 (Winter 1987): 126.

13. According to Susan Sontag, "I once asked Mapplethorpe what he does with himself when he poses for the camera, and he replied that he tries to find that part of himself that is self-confident." "Certain Mapplethorpes," preface to *Certain People* (Pasadena: Twelvetrees Press, 1985): unpaginated. While the registration of self-confidence is central to all of Mapplethorpe's self-portraits, it is particularly significant when the self, as in the 1978 *Self-Portrait,* would seem to be in a position of submission.

14. This was Mapplethorpe's response when asked whether he derived sexual pleasure from photographing gay s/m. Quoted in an unpublished transcript of a public discussion of the *Censored* exhibition held at 80 Langton Street, April 1978, and subsequently cited by Robert McDonald in "Censored," *Advocate,* June 28, 1978, Issue 244: 21 (Second Section).

15. *The Perfect Moment* was the title of the 1988 Mapplethorpe retrospective organized by the Institute of Contemporary Art at the University of Pennsylvania and later canceled by the Corcoran Gallery in Washington D.C. The modernist implications of that title and the ways in which Mapplethorpe alternately invites and cuts against them are discussed by Paul Morrison in his extraordinary essay "Coffee Table Sex: Robert Mapplethorpe and the Sadomasochism of Everyday Life," *Genders* 11 (Fall 1991): 17–36.

16. It has become nearly a cliché of the art-critical writing on Mapplethorpe to note that his still-lifes emphasize the fact and metaphor of flowers as sexual organs. See, for example, Alan Hollinghurst's 1983 catalogue essay for the London retrospective of Mapplethorpe's work:

> Mapplethorpe's flowers are subjected to a scrutiny which discovers their tense sensuality. Their staring eyes, their extended fingers, their dropping or thrusting penile leaves com-

plement the concentrated postures of Mapplethorpe's men. Flowers, which are the sexual organs of plants, are brilliantly deployed as a subject both abstract and heavily metaphorical at the same time.

Robert Mapplethorpe 1970–1983, ICA, London: 1983: 17.

Similarly, Gary Indiana in the *Village Voice* claims that within the vocabulary of Mapplethorpe's oeuvre,

> . . . a white man's fist clutching his enormous, stiff, bent dick has the same harsh elegance as the numerous, voluptuous studies of flowers (which are, lest we forget, sexual organs).

Gary Indiana, "Mapplethorpe," *Village Voice,* May 14, 1985: 97.

17. The reference to "faces, flowers, and fetishes" is taken from a commentary on Mapplethorpe in the 1978 *Son of Drummer*:

> He lunches afternoons at One Fifth Avenue. He maneuvers after midnight at the Mineshaft. He photographs princesses like Margaret, bodybuilders like Arnold, rockstars like his best friend Patti Smith, and night trippers nameless in leather, rubber, and ropes. He's famous for his photographs of faces, flowers, and fetishes.

"The Robert Mapplethorpe Gallery," *Son of Drummer* (San Francisco, 1978): 15.

18. Roland Barthes, *Camera Lucida: Reflections on Photography,* trans. by Richard Howard (New York: Farrar, Straus & Giroux, 1981): 59.

19. On the photograph's capacity to serve as fetish see Christian Metz, "Photography and Fetish," in Carol Squiers, ed., *The Critical Image: Essays on Contemporary Photography* (Seattle: Bay Press, 1990): 155–164.

20. Kobena Mercer and Isaac Julien, "Imaging the Black Man's Sex," *Photography/Politics: Two,* 1987, reprinted in *Male Order: Unwrapping Masculinity,* ed. Rowena Chapman and Jonathan Rutherford (London: Lawrence and Wishart, 1988): 143–144. See also Mercer's revision of his earlier work on Mapplethorpe, "Skin Head Sex Thing: Racial Difference and the Homoerotic Imaginary" in *How Do I Look?* (note 12 above): 169–222, and "Looking for Trouble," reprinted in this volume.

21. Mapplethorpe's now notorious *Jim and Tom,* 1977–78, a portrait of two men engaging in "water sports" in a Sausalito bunker, is the clearest exception to this rule. See *Robert Mapplethorpe* (New York: Whitney Museum of American Art, 1988): 63.

22. On the ways in which the subject may use posing to contest the power of the (camera's) gaze, Craig Owens writes,

> To strike a pose is to present oneself to the gaze of the other as if one were already frozen, immobilized, suspended, that is, already a picture . . . pose has a strategic value: doubling, mimicking the immobilizing power of the gaze, reflecting it back on itself, pose forces the gaze to surrender. Confronted with a pose, the gaze itself is immobilized, brought to a standstill . . . to strike a pose is to pose a threat.

Craig Owens, *Beyond Recognition: Representation, Power, and Culture,* ed. Scott Bryson et al. (Berkeley: University of California Press, 1992): p. 198.

23. Figure ten is part of a larger layout in *Son of Drummer* entitled "Color Shots from 'The Room': David Warner's Hot New Leather Film." My selection of this image as a comparison piece to Mapplethorpe's work was in part prompted by the fact that it was published in the same *Son of Drummer* which ran the "Mapplethorpe Gallery."

24. C.S. Manegold, "Robert Mapplethorpe, 1970–1983: On the 1983–84 Retrospective," *Artnews* 58 (February 1984): 98.

25. Unfortunately, rights to reproduce *A Widow in Her Bedroom* could not be secured from the Arbus estate. The photograph is reproduced in *Diane Arbus: An Aperture Monograph* (New York: Aperture, 1972): unpaginated.

26. Dick Hebdige, *Subculture, the Meaning of Style* (London: Methuen, 1979): 191–192.

27. Ingrid Sischy, "A Society Artist," *Robert Mapplethorpe* (New York: Whitney Museum, 1988): 84.

28. As discussed above, this effect was at least partially choreographed by Mapplethorpe and his dealers.

29. See Vance's excellent "Misunderstanding Obscenity," *Art in America* (May 1990): 49–55.

30. Dominick Dunne, "Robert Mapplethorpe's Proud Finale," *Vanity Fair* (February 1989): 126.

31. Susan Weiley, "Prince of Darkness, Angel of Light," *Artnews* 87 (December 1988): 109.

32. *Proceedings and Debates of the 101st Congress*, First Session, July 26, 1989: S8807.

33. As Carole Vance has pointed out, the descriptive language employed by neo-conservative censors of Mapplethorpe's work closely resembles the National-Socialist (Nazi) rhetoric of degenerate art. Vance cites the following passage from *Washington Times* columnist Patrick Buchanan as one such example:

> As with our rivers and lakes, we need to clean up our culture: for it is a well from which we must all drink. Just as poisoned land will yield poisonous fruits, so a polluted culture, left to fester and stink, can destroy a nation's soul . . . we can not subsidize decadence.

See Carole S. Vance "The New Censorship," *Art in America* (September 1989): 40.

34. Ingrid Sischy, "White and Black," *New Yorker* (November 13, 1989): 139–140.

35. An excellent critique of "victim" photography is offered by Douglas Crimp in "Portraits of People With AIDS," *Cultural Studies,* ed. Lawrence Grossberg, Cary Nelson, and Paula Treichler (New York: Routledge, 1991): 117–133.

36. Ibid., 132.

26

Freud, Male Homosexuality, and the Americans

Henry Abelove

Henry Abelove is a cultural historian who works especially on the history of sex. In this essay, first published in 1985, Abelove shows that Freud's view of male homosexuality was much less pathologizing and much more complex than has usually been supposed. He also shows that Freud actively despised the more pathologizing and less complex view of the moralistic United States psychoanalysts who were his contemporaries and followers. Abelove then goes on to argue that in recent years, long after Freud's death, many United States psychoanalysts have come closer to his less pathologizing view, without, however, achieving any of its complexity or relinquishing much of their traditional moralism. Henry Abelove is the author of The Evangelist of Desire: John Wesley and the Methodists *(1990), and he is one of the editors of this volume. He is completing a book titled* The Making of the Modern Heterosexual, *and he is professor of English at Wesleyan University.*

Anybody inquiring about Freud's attitude to male homosexuality is likely to come across a letter he wrote in April of 1935. The letter is now almost famous. It was first printed in 1951; it has been reprinted since many times; and it is conveniently available in Ernest Jones's standard biography. Freud wrote it in English as a courtesy to his correspondent, who was an American, a mother, distressed and embarrassed because her young son was homosexual. What the letter tells her is that she has less cause for distress than she may think and none for embarrassment. "I gather," Freud says, ". . . that your son is a homosexual. I am most impressed by the fact that you do not mention this term yourself in your information about him. May I question you, why you avoid it? Homosexuality is assuredly no advantage, but it is nothing to be ashamed of, no vice, no degradation, it cannot be classified as an illness, we consider it to be a variation of the sexual function produced by a certain arrest of sexual development." He goes on to say more:

> Many highly respectable individuals of ancient and modern times have been homosexuals, several of the greatest among them (Plato, Michelangelo, Leonardo da Vinci, etc.) It is a great injustice to persecute homosexuality as a crime and cruelty too. If you do not believe me, read the books of Havelock Ellis.
>
> By asking me if I can help, you mean, I suppose, if I can abolish homosexuality and make normal heterosexuality take its place. The answer is, in a general way, we cannot promise to achieve it. In a certain number of cases we succeed in developing the blighted germs of heterosexual tendencies which are present in every homosexual,

in the majority of cases it is no more possible. It is a question of the quality and the age of the individual. The result of treatment cannot be predicted.

What analysis can do for your son runs in a different line. If he is unhappy, neurotic, torn by conflicts, inhibited in his social life, analysis may bring him harmony, peace of mind, full efficiency, whether he remains a homosexual or gets changed. If you make up your mind he should have analysis with me. I don't expect you will. He has to come over to Vienna. I have no intention of leaving here. However, don't neglect to give me your answer.

> Sincerely yours with kind wishes,
> Freud[1]

The American mother said that she was grateful for the letter, sent a copy eventually to the sex-researcher Alfred Kinsey, and told him that Freud was a "great and good" man. Presumably she found the letter helpful, maybe also comforting, even though it had probed her fearfulness and prejudice. Jones is probably right to describe the letter, in his biography, as a remarkable "kindness."[2] After all Freud had no previous acquaintance with the woman. Yet he took the time to write to her when he was himself deathly ill.

But the letter was more than just a "kindness." It was also the considered expression of a viewpoint which Freud had long deeply felt and tenaciously held. Everything about homosexuality that he says in the letter had been an article of conviction with him for more than thirty years. Summarized: That homosexuality is no advantage. That it is also no illness. That it should neither be prosecuted as a crime nor regarded as a disgrace. That no homosexual need be treated psychoanalytically unless he also, and quite incidentally, happened to be neurotic. Freud had expressed himself on the subject before, often, and on occasion very publicly.

As early as 1903 he had given an interview to the Vienna newspaper *Die Zeit,* which was doing a feature story on a local scandal: a prominent Vienna professional man was on trial, charged with homosexual practices. A reporter had come to get Freud's reaction, and Freud had said:

> . . . I advocate the standpoint that the homosexual does not belong before the tribunal of a court of law. I am even of the firm conviction that homosexuals must not be treated as sick people, for a perverse orientation is far from being a sickness. Wouldn't that oblige us to characterize as *sick* many great thinkers and scholars whom we admire precisely because of their mental health?

He had then repeated himself, apparently for the sake of emphasis: "*Homosexual persons are not sick,* but they also *do not belong in a court of law!*" He had added finally, and by way of qualification, that if however a homosexual molested a child below "the age of consent," then he should be charged in the courts, just as a heterosexual should be charged under analogous circumstances.[3]

In 1930 Freud again spoke in the Vienna public press on the subject of homosexuality. This time he appeared as a co-signatory to a statement addressed to a joint Austro-German legal commission, which was considering the revision of the penal code. Among the other signatories were Artur Schnitzler, Franz Werfel, and Moritz Schlick. The statement noted that the commission was reported as deadlocked over a proposal to repeal the laws penalizing homosexual relations between "consenting adult males." But the deadlock should be broken. "Humanity, justice, and reason" all required the repeal, and it should be agreed to immediately. "Homosexuality," the statement continued, had "been present throughout history and among all peoples." The laws which penalized it represented an "extreme violation of human rights." For they denied homosexuals "their very sexuality." They also gave a wide opening to "blackmail" and indirectly drove some homosexuals to "suicide." There was yet another bad consequence of these laws. By stigmatizing homosexuality as "criminal," they often forced homosexuals into "anti-social" postures and attitudes. The statement concluded with the "demand" that homosexuals be allowed the same "rights" as everyone else.[4]

These were Freud's public interventions; privately he took a similar line. For instance he held that there was no good reason why homosexuals should necessarily be refused permission to become psychoanalysts. This position of his turned out to be objectionable to most of his associates. The issue surfaced in 1920. The Dutch Psychoanalytic Association had an application for membership from a doctor known to be "manifestly homosexual." Uncertain how to respond, they turned for advice to a member of Freud's inner circle, Ernest Jones, the same who later wrote the standard biography. Jones kept Freud informed by letter. "I advised against it," he said, "and now I hear . . . that the man has been detected and committed to prison." He then asked whether or not Freud thought that to always refuse homosexual applicants would be "a safe general maxim to act on." Freud consulted with another member of the inner circle, Otto Rank, who was also a close friend; and then Rank and Freud jointly wrote back to Jones and censured his propriety:

> Your query dear Ernest concerning prospective membership of homosexuals has been considered by us and we disagree with you. In effect we cannot exclude such persons without other sufficient reasons, as we cannot agree with their legal prosecution. We feel that a decision in such cases should depend upon a thorough examination of the other qualities of the candidate.

Rank and Freud wrote of course from Vienna. Jones, who got their letter, was in London. Within about a month news of the exchange had reached the analysts of Berlin, whereupon three of them, Hanns Sachs, Karl Abraham, and Max Eitingon, all alarmed, wrote to Rank and Freud in criticism of their position. The criticism was put tactfully but firmly: "We have not yet decided," they began, "about the question of admitting homosexual analysts to our Society. . . ." This was no doubt meant to remind Freud that the decision at least in Berlin was constitutionally theirs rather than his. "But," they went on, "we have had some thoughts on this matter." Their "thoughts" were that "homosexuality appears in many forms as part of a neurosis," that in such instances the homosexuality "should be analyzed," that neurotic homosexuals might and often did refuse to let their analysis go deep, and that when they so refused they could hardly turn out to be good analysts themselves. Sachs, Abraham, and Eitingon then concluded: "We agree that we only should accept homosexuals into our membership when they have other qualities in their favor." This conclusion both restated the Rank-Freud position and modified it subtly. Their letter had stipulated that homosexuality ought to be a neutral factor or a non-factor in the evaluation of applicants; the Berlin letter on the other hand suggested that homosexuality might well make for a presumption against an applicant but that he should nevertheless be admitted if he were judged good enough. The wording of both letters is, however, close; and Freud chose to be, or had to be, content with the Berlin response.[5]

As a clinician, Freud refused to treat homosexuals, unless he thought them markedly neurotic, too.[6] Otherwise there was nothing to treat. Homosexuality was not in his view an illness, and whenever associates who assumed that it was in fact an illness tried to refer homosexuals to him for treatment, he turned them away, if he knew in advance that they were just homosexuals. He could not always know in advance, and he must on occasion have had to see if only for a single session a patient who was homosexual and relatively unneurotic but forced to consult him by a psychiatrist, a family doctor, a friend, or a relative, like the American mother with whom Freud corresponded in 1935. It would be interesting to know how he handled such patients; but he has left us no account of his dealings with any of them. For him, they were not cases, and so there was never any reason to write up a case-history. But there is one account of a single session with Freud written by a patient who may fit into this category. It is hard to be entirely sure; the account is moving as a portrait of the psychoanalyst but disappointingly sparse about the patient himself, whose name was Bruno Goetz. At the time Goetz consulted Freud, he was a student at the University of Vienna, an aspiring poet, poor, afflicted with eye-trouble and bad headaches, and apparently sexually unconventional, too. One of his professors, who was worried about Goetz, had arranged for the consultation and sent Freud some of the man's poems as well. Goetz did not want to go, but the professor's authority was sufficient to make him do so, and he went. Once he got to Freud's office, he began to feel better immediately. The headaches disappeared, and he talked eagerly about his life and loves. He talked about masturbating, about once loving a woman older than himself, about his fascination with the sea, about his attraction to sailors, whom he wanted "to kiss," and about his not marrying. Freud said, "And the matter with the sailors has never upset you"? Goetz answered, "Never . . . I was very much in love. And when you're in love, everything is fine. Right?" Freud replied, "For you certainly . . ." and laughed. Toward the end of the consultation, Freud asked him when he had last eaten a steak. Goetz said four weeks before. Freud then handed him a sealed envelope, told him it was a "prescription," and then turned "shy" as he concluded the session by saying:

> Please accept this envelope and allow me to play your father this time. A small fee
> for the joy you have brought me with your poems and the story of your youth.

When Goetz left and opened the envelope, he found that it contained money, 200 kronen, more than enough to buy a big steak dinner.[7]

Freud was perfectly consistent on the subject of homosexuality. What he told the American mother in his letter of 1935, that it was neither advantage, crime, illness, nor disgrace, he had long believed and long acted on. His viewpoint wasn't wholeheartedly shared by most of his fellow-analysts, though no analyst so far as I know directly and avowedly rejected it during Freud's lifetime. But his colleagues did show some hesitation about it, some edginess. The Dutch wondered whether or not a homosexual should be admitted to practice analysis; Jones, in England, thought not; the Berliners said maybe yes, maybe no, but were probably inclined to say no; and some analysts referred relatively unneurotic homosexuals to Freud for treatment, though he of course thought there was no need. Jung too may have felt rather differently from Freud on the subject of homosexuality. His viewpoint, during the years when he was still associated with psychoanalysis, is hard to reconstruct fully; but there is a suggestive comment in one of his letters. He and Freud were corresponding about where a certain essay of Freud's was to be published. The *Zeitschrift für Sexualwissenschaft,* a journal edited by a homosexual, had been mentioned, and Jung advised against using it. "If the '175'ers' are in charge, that will hardly be a guarantee of its scientific attitude," Jung wrote. One Hundred Seventy-five was the number of the clause in the German law code in which the penalties for homosexual practice were specified.[8] The term '175'ers' meant homosexuals and was derogatory. Jung's comment, in substance, was also of course prejudicious. Freud replied by saying that he had not intended the essay for the *Zeitschrift,* which might become the voice of the homosexual emancipation movement in Germany, and therefore was too political. He said that he had intended the essay for the *Jahrbuch für Sexuelle Zwis-*

chenstufen—another journal edited by the same homosexual who edited the *Zeitschrift.* Jung made no further comment.[9] So far as I can tell, only three analysts can be tentatively identified as sharing perhaps without reservation in Freud's viewpoint on homosexuality. They are Rank, first of all, who co-signed the letter to Jones calling for the admission of qualified homosexuals to the practice of psychoanalysis; Isidor Sadger, whose position can be deduced from some essays that he published;[10] and Victor Tausk. One of Tausk's colleagues reported him as saying this in about 1914 on the treatment of a particular neurotic homosexual: ". . . his therapeutic goal for the patient was to rid him of feelings of guilt about his homosexuality so that he could be free to satisfy his homosexual needs."[11] But if Rank, Sadger, and Tausk stood in this matter firmly with Freud, they were the exceptions. Most analysts had room for other thoughts.

It was in America, however, that Freud's viewpoint on homosexuality was least accepted or maybe most resisted. Jung may in a careless moment have let slip a prejudicious slur; Jones may have wanted to draw the line at having homosexual colleagues; the Dutch and Germans may also have felt some of his reserve; but from the very beginnings of the transplanting of psychoanalysis onto these shores, American analysts have tended to view homosexuality with disapproval and have actually wanted to get rid of it altogether. As early as 1916, when Freud was still very active, Smith Ely Jeliffe, a prominent New York analyst and a founder of the *Psychoanalytic Review,* declared that "individual training" and "education" should control the "homogenic" tendency and "direct it" to a "normal, well-adjusted sexual life" so that there need be no homosexuality.[12]

Jeliffe's declaration is perhaps distinctively American; it reflects the outlook which historians usually call moralistic and that has always dominated psychoanalytic thinking in this country. It is an outlook which Freud knew, despised, and opposed, but never succeeded in overcoming or even mitigating. Why he never succeeded may require an explanation. He was after all a domineering leader, with little patience for any deviationism; and presumably he could have cut off the offending American analysts, just as he eventually cut off such Europeans as Adler and Jung. Perhaps he was afraid that too much severity on the American front would put the whole future of psychoanalysis at risk. It was clear, certainly by the 1930s, that the movement's greatest growth area was going to be America. Then too he may have held back partly out of a kind of indifference. What Americans said and thought was less important to him than what his fellow-Europeans said and thought. Finally, he believed that the American analysts' outlook was not accidental but necessary, derived directly from what he took to be the root conditions of American life. If that were true, what good could come of cutting off particular analysts?

Still he argued with them, teased, parried. His most frequent butt was James Jackson Putnam of Harvard, the American analyst whom he liked most or maybe disliked least. Their correspondence, stretching over a period of about seven years, was on Freud's part one long effort to get Putnam to relinquish his moralism (specific allusions to homosexuality, or indeed any sexuality, hardly came up, so elevated were Putnam's ideas, so obliging was Freud as a correspondent); on Putnam's part, one long refusal. Putnam met Freud in 1909, and had on that occasion apparently been firmly told that he should not try to hold up before his analytic patients some ethical goal of his own. "It still appears to me," he wrote later that year, "that . . . the psychoanalytic method needs to be supplemented by methods which seek to hold up before the patient some goal toward which he may strive." Putnam went on to note that he was currently treating a "lady" who was "a great sufferer from morbid self-consciousness and blushing," that he was making "good headway" in tracing out the origins of her "symptoms," but that he found himself confronted by the "difficulty" that she had "lost all interest in life and living." Should he not try, in a hortatory way, to provide her with such an interest? Freud replied that no analyst could "compensate" a patient for giving up an "illness." But that was not the analyst's fault.

> What would you have us do when a woman complains about her thwarted life, when, with youth gone, she notices that she has been deprived of the joy of loving for merely conventional reasons? She is quite right, and we stand helpless before her, for we cannot make her young again. But the recognition of our therapeutic limitations reinforces our determination to change other social factors so that men and women shall no longer be forced into hopeless situations.

This was Freud at his most militantly political; American moralism always brought it out in him. But the militancy made no apparent impact on Putnam, who soon wrote back that patients need "more than to simply learn to know themselves," they need also to know the "reasons why they should adopt higher views of their obligations". He then wrote back yet again, "As I study patients and try to relieve them of their symptoms, I find that I must also try to improve their moral characters and temperaments." Soon after, he told Freud one of his childhood fantasies—it was of a happy family life—and asked for an interpretation. This request gave Freud an opening which he gleefully took:

> On the whole I see that you are suffering from a too early and too strongly repressed sadism expressed in over-goodness and self-torture. Behind the fantasy of a happy family life, you would discover the normal repressed fantasies of rich sexual fulfillment.

Later Freud responded again on a note less personal but still very naughty, gibing at the Christian rhetoric that lay just below the surface of Putnam's letters:

> You make psychoanalysis seem so much nobler and more beautiful: in her Sunday clothes I scarcely recognize the servant who performs my household tasks.

Next, undaunted, Putnam wrote to say that he wanted to compose something rather big on the subject of "sublimation," with special reference "to the work of Dante and Emerson." Freud replied that he looked forward to it "with great interest." Putnam then wrote more about his personal commitment to sublimation and to the task of helping his patients achieve it satisfactorily. Freud replied this time with bitterness rather than irony: "As soon," he wrote, as analysts take on "the task of leading the patient toward sublimation, they hasten away from the arduous tasks of psychoanalysis so that they can take up the much more comfortable . . . duties of the teacher and paragon of virtue." Finally Freud turned very direct. He dropped all obliquity, all his tones except candor, and in one of the last few letters he wrote to Putnam, shortly before Putnam's death separated them forever, attacked his moralism straight on:

> Sexual morality as society—and at its most extreme, American society—defines it, seems very despicable to me. I stand for a much freer sexual life.

That too made no apparent impact on Putnam, and in his next letter he ignored altogether Freud's remark about America.[13]

If Freud thought that American sexual morality was despicable, he also thought he knew how it had come to be that way. He visited America only once, in the fall of 1909, when he came here to deliver five introductory lectures on psychoanalysis at Clark University to an audience that, incidentally, included both William James and Emma Goldman. During his stay, he got to see New York, New Haven, Boston, Worcester, and Niagara Falls, and he also spent some time in the Adirondacks. Still the trip was brief, the itinerary limited, and his conclusions exceptionally positive and firm. No doubt he had made up his mind at least tentatively before the trip had begun, largely on the basis of his reading and his personal contacts with individual Americans, partly probably on the basis of the prejudice against America which is perennially common in European intellectual circles.

When asked once he returned to Vienna what exactly he thought was wrong here, he would usually treat the question as unserious and respond lightly. He hated the food. It gave him indigestion. Or he might say he hated the accent. Only the British knew how to speak English right. But sometimes he treated the question as serious and responded accordingly; and there is no difficulty now in making out his actual view. First of all he thought that Americans were extraordinarily overrepressed. He found them sexually vapid, flavorless. As his Viennese colleague Paul Federn tactlessly reported years later when in 1947 he spoke in New York at the dedication of a Freud bust in the headquarters of the New York Psychoanalytic Society, Freud had always held that in America there was not "enough libido actually to be found and felt by him."[14] Why were the Americans such nonentities sexually? Because they sublimated their sexual energy so completely. As for their despicable moralism, that was the rationale for the sublimation. And was the goal of American sublimation the production of art, science, law, architecture, music, literature? No: the goal was cash, acquisition, accumulation. All the energy that was not loosed sexually was going toward making money and toward very little else. Jones, in his autobiography *Free Associations,* put the point delicately: Freud had an "unfavorable impression" of America. "I imagine," Jones added, "that the aversion had something to do with a feeling that commercial success dominated the scale of values in the United States . . ."[15]

Freud himself put the point still more delicately, but nonetheless very definitely, while actually speaking to his one American audience at Clark. To be sure, his primary rhetorical strategy in those five lectures was to flatter his hearers in the hopes of securing their favorable interest in what he had to say concerning psychoanalysis. He told them that theirs was a "New World"; he added that in the old, benighted European world there was unreasoning prejudice against psychoanalysis; and he intimated that in the New World no such prejudice was likely. He told them that he had originally planned to speak chiefly about "dream interpretation" but upon consideration had rejected the plan. It seemed to him, he said, somehow wrong to focus on dreams in a country so admirably "devoted to practical aims." He told them that "hysteria" might perhaps be best understood as analogous to a kind of overinvolvement in history. Imagine, he said, a "Londoner" unable to live joyfully in the present because he could not escape from the clutch of the past and so spent all his time mourning at spots like "Charing Cross" or "the Monument," consecrated to ancient losses. In developing this analogy, Freud was hinting broadly and quite mendaciously that since Americans had much less history than, say, Londoners, they were much better off. All this was flattery, and thickly applied, too. But in the midst of the flattery, Freud also managed to say what he thought. His moment came when he explained how jokes are to be interpreted psychoanalytically. First he gave an example of a joke:

> Two not particularly scrupulous businessmen had succeeded, by dint of a series of highly risky enterprises, in amassing a large fortune, and they were now making efforts to push their way into good society. One method, which struck them as a likely one, was to have their portraits painted by the most celebrated and highly paid artist in the city . . . The precious canvasses were shown for the first time at a large evening party, and the two hosts led the most influential connoisseur . . . up to the wall on which the portraits were hanging side by side. He studied the works for a

long time, and then, shaking his head, as though there was something he had missed, pointed to the gap between the pictures and asked quietly: "But where's the Savior?"

The audience laughed. Freud went on:

> Clearly what the connoisseur meant to say was: "You are a couple of rogues, like the two thieves between whom the Savior was crucified." But he did not say this. Instead he made a remark which seems at first sight strangely inappropriate . . . but which we recognize later as an *allusion* to the insult that he had in mind . . .

Having explained how to interpret the joke, Freud proceeded to ask: "Why" did the connoisseur "not tell the rogues straight out what he wanted to say?" Why did he tell them only indirectly via the joke? He then answered his own question. The connoisseur had

> excellent counter-motives working against his desire to say it to their faces. There are risks attendant upon insulting people who are one's hosts.[16]

It takes but a moment's reflection to realize that at Clark, Freud himself was the honored guest, the Americans his hosts, and that he was insulting them, though indirectly, with the joke he told. They were the unscrupulous businessmen; they were the thieves. From this opinion of them or rather of us as thieves—and as consequently also sexless and despicably moralistic—Freud never budged.

What happened to homosexuals who found themselves in treatment with American psychoanalysts of the era of Putnam and Jeliffe? Putnam, who thought he should inspire his patients with his own ethical vision? Jeliffe, who thought that training and education should control homosexual feeling and reshape it into "normal, well-adjusted" sexuality? First of all, such patients could feel physically safe; they ran no risk, so long as they were in the hands of the analysts, of getting castrated. This disaster sometimes overtook homosexuals in non-analytic treatment. Analysts only talked. Just what the talk was we of course cannot now know exactly and fully. But we can know partially, fragmentarily, a small sample of it, a sample that concerns an American homosexual named C.M. Otis, who in 1911 found himself in successive consultations with two different Boston analysts, Isador Coriat and Louville Emerson. Of these analysts the second, Emerson, took notes which are still extant. From them we learn that Otis described himself as having never had intercourse with a woman, as having more than occasionally had sexual contact with boys, as having long felt both persecuted and sure that he could never become heterosexual. Emerson saw Otis for six therapy sessions. During the sixth Emerson ended their connection. In his notes he recorded the reason for his making so decisive and abrupt an ending: The patient "shows no adequate emotional reaction to my suggestions." He did not specify what the suggestions were.[17] Some eight years later Emerson published in the *Psychoanalytic Review* a brief and courteous critique of Freud. The point of the critique was that Freud was wrong to try to exclude "ethics" from psychoanalysis. All analysts must try to tell which social relations were, and which were not, "righteous."[18] Whatever were the suggestions that Emerson made and Otis rejected, we can surely conclude that Otis's experience with his analyst was significantly different from Goetz's with his.

To return to Freud's letter to the American mother. His motive in writing it was by no means just "kindness," nor was it just a determination to restate a position he had long held. He wanted also to hit back at us Americans, at our moralism and our misuse of psychoanalysis. He knew perfectly well that the letter would be noticed. He intended it to be noticed. It was a deliberate provocation, and perhaps the heart of it was the passage where he ended:

If you make up your mind he should have analysis with me. I don't expect you will. He has to come over to Vienna.[19]

Freud had no need of more patients, and the woman was a stranger. His object was to tell her, and everybody else too, that her son could not be properly treated in America.

It may be surprising, in the light of what this paper has said so far, to find that Freud was very much at odds with the homosexual emancipation movement of his own day. But in fact he was. On one important matter he disagreed adamantly with the line taken by the movement, and he expressed the disagreement in his psychological writings on three separate occasions.

The movement was then based mostly in Germany, where it had originated during the latter part of the nineteenth century. Its progenitor had been Karl Heinrich Ulrichs (1825–1895), a Hanoverian lawyer, who in a series of books had propounded the view that homosexuals constituted a "third sex," possessed of a "female soul" in a "male body." Ulrichs's spiritual successor and the movement's first great leader had been Magnus Hirschfeld (1868–1935), a Berlin Jewish doctor, who as a publicist, organizer, lobbyist, and clinical investigator, had worked long and tirelessly for the repeal of the laws penalizing homosexuality and for public recognition of its widespread incidence. Like Ulrichs, Hirschfeld had also thought of homosexuals as a biologically and psychically distinct group. He had called them "sexual intermediates."[20]

As we have already seen, Freud willingly endorsed the movement's law reform objectives. What he rejected was the theory which lay behind them, the theory of the "third sex," of "sexual intermediates." In *Three Essays on the Theory of Sexuality* (1905), he criticized Ulrichs directly, referring to him by name as "a spokesman of the male inverts," and mentioning his notion of "a feminine brain in a masculine body" in order to brush it aside.[21] In *Leonardo da Vinci* (1910), he again took note of the movement's line:

> Homosexual men, who have in our times taken vigorous action against the restrictions imposed by law on their sexual activity, are fond of representing themselves, through their theoretical spokesmen, as being from the outset a distinct sexual species, as an intermediate sexual stage, as a "third sex."

He added that this representation should be viewed with "some reserve." For it took no account of the findings of psychoanalysis. Later, in the 1919 edition, he inserted in a footnote a firmer critical comment: ". . . those who speak for the homosexuals in the field of science have been incapable of learning anything from the established findings of psychoanalysis."[22] Yet again in *Introductory Lectures* (1917), he made much the same point. He said that homosexuals "through the mouth of their scientific spokesmen" were endeavoring to "represent themselves as a special variety of the human species—a 'third sex' . . ." This representation was, however, mistaken; psychoanalysis proved it wrong.[23]

But how did psychoanalysis prove it wrong? Freud thought that analysis showed that all people were "capable of making a homosexual object choice" and that all had "in fact made one in their unconscious." He thought that analysis also showed that

> . . . libidinal attachments to persons of the same sex play no less a part in normal mental life, and a greater part as a motive force for illness, than do similar attachments to the opposite sex.[24]

With these findings in mind, he could hardly accept that homosexuals were "a distinct sexual species" or "a special variety of the human species." On the contrary he held that all people were psychologically like the ones called homosexuals. No doubt homosexual men would on the whole tend to have sex with men, while non-homosexual men would on the whole tend to have sex with women. This difference, though of "practical significance," was of small "theoretical" significance. What *was* theoretically significant, what must never be forgotten or denied or elided, was that everybody's sexuality was homosexual in large part.

Homosexuals, Freud insisted, were not "exceptions," and psychoanalysis was "decidedly opposed to any attempt" to separate them off "from the rest of mankind as a group of a special character."[26] To do so would be to reject, in fact to repress, the psychoanalytic theory of sex.

So Freud argued, but the movement was not much interested by his argument. Notions like the "third sex" or, to glance ahead for a moment to modern-day America, "gay people," can play an important role in enabling homosexual assertiveness. It's bracing to think of oneself as part of a group. One feels less odd, maybe less vulnerable, maybe even prouder. Besides, groups can organize to advance their members' common interests. In a parliamentary culture, as the Germany of Freud's day in some measure was, or as modern-day America is, group organizational strength can often translate directly into political influence. Freud understood all this, and he cannot have been surprised when the homosexual emancipation movement ignored him. But he took his stand against their line anyway, just as he had also taken his stand against American moralism, and for the same reason: Both line and moralism were, as he saw the matter, in effect repressions.

Freud died in 1939, four years after he had written his letter to the American mother. Almost as soon as he was safely cremated, a host of revisionist essays started rolling off the psychoanalytic presses, especially in America. One of the subjects most eagerly canvassed was homosexuality. We may here review briefly and in a very foreshortened way what the American analysts said about it once they could be sure that Freud was gone. Sandor Rado (1890–1972) of the Columbia Psychoanalytic Clinic in New York was the first to declare himself. In a series of pieces published in the 1940s, he argued that male-female pairing was healthy, that it was moreover the "standard pattern," that homosexuality was an illness based on a fear of women, and that it could often be cured in psychoanalysis.[27]

Following Rado's lead, Irving Bieber (b. 1908) conducted a big study in the 1950s and published his results in 1962. His purpose was not, he said, to establish that homosexuality was an illness. All "psychoanalytic theories," he went on, effectually ignoring Freud, "*assume* that homosexuality is psychopathologic." His purpose was rather to come to understand the etiology of the illness; and he argued that it derived primarily from a certain sort of bad family situation: a domineering mother, a cold father. He too was relatively optimistic about achieving cures. Charles Socarides (b. 1922) went farthest perhaps of any of the American analysts. He argued, in a series of pieces published mostly in the 1960s, that homosexuality wasn't just an illness but a severe illness, accompanied often by psychotic manifestations like schizophrenia or manic-depressive mood swings. While heterosexual pairings could make for "cooperation, solace, stimulation, enrichment, healthy challenge and fulfillment," homosexual pairings could bring only "destruction, mutual defeat, exploitation of the partner and the self, oral-sadistic incorporation, aggressive onslaughts, attempts to alleviate anxiety, and a pseudo-solution to the aggressive and libidinal urges which dominate and torment the individual." Socarides also said that cures were possible.[28]

Influenced perhaps especially by Rado, the American Psychiatric Association in 1952 formally classified homosexuality as an illness. When the gay liberation movement grew strong in America in the 1960s, this classification, still very much on the books,[29] became a major issue for its adherents, and they devoted much effort to getting it rescinded. Through a mix of agitation and argument, they eventually succeeded. In 1973 the Association removed homosexuality from their official list of illnesses.[30] In announcing the declassification, the president of the Association said that he hoped the result would be a "more accommodative climate of opinion for the homosexual minority in our country. . . ."[31] Here the word to note is minority. What the president assumed was that homosexuals were indeed a minority, a group of a special character. He assumed as much both because the gay liberation movement was predictably saying so and because their psychoanalytic allies were loudly agreeing.

Psychoanalytic allies? Yes: the movement had such allies, of whom the two most influential were Judd Marmor (b. 1910) and Robert Stoller (b. 1924). During the sixties and seventies, both these analysts clashed repeatedly with the Bieber-Socarides set. Both, denying that homosexuality was an illness, described it instead as the sexual orientation of a minority. In so describing it they of course rejected the view which Freud had thought theoretically crucial—the view that *everybody's* sexuality was in large part homosexual. Marmor put his rejection tactfully: Freud had held that homosexuality was a "universal trend." That view was not "illogical," but it was "non-operational" and should be discarded.[32] Stoller said much the same: By sticking to Freud's view we could never have clear grounds for saying of anybody that he was not homosexual. That would be "troublesome." We would probably be well advised to revert to a "less complicated definition of homosexuality" and think of it as just the preserve of homosexuals, as "that state in which sexual practices are performed by preference, in conscious fantasy or in reality, with a person of the same sex."[33] So, Marmor and Stoller both saw homosexuality as belonging to homosexuals alone, who were therefore different from everybody else, and thus a minority. But homosexuals were not necessarily ill any more than was any other minority—Blacks, Latinos, Jews—and they were entitled to be free of the stigma which official psychiatry had placed on them so unfairly. Of course the corollary of the humane ascription of minority status was this: that people outside the minority need no longer think of themselves as in some important way homosexual, too.

At the Association meetings which had led up to the eventual decision to rescind the classification of homosexuality as an illness, all of the major protagonists had been psychoanalysts. On one side, Bieber and Socarides. On the other side, Marmor and Stoller. A strange spectacle: Two sets of moralistic psychoanalysts, each opposing the other, each claiming to stand in the tradition of Freud, and each espousing a position which Freud had himself rejected as wrong and repressive. In America Freudianism continues as it began.

NOTES

1. "A Letter from Freud," *American Journal of Psychiatry,* April 1951, p. 786. A photostat of the holograph letter is reproduced here.

2. Ernest Jones, *The Life and Work of Sigmund Freud,* 3 vols. (New York: Basic Books, 1953–57), 3:195.

3. Quoted by Herb Spiers and Michael Lynch, "The Gay Rights Freud," *Body Politic,* May 1977, p. 9.

4. Quoted by Spiers and Lynch, p. 9.

5. Quoted by Spiers and Lynch, p. 9. This set of letters is part of a group known as the "Rundbriefe," preserved in the Otto Rank Collection and deposited at the Columbia University

Library. I am grateful for the Library's permission to quote. I use translations prepared, and kindly made available to me, by Professor James Steakley (Rank Collection IIa/238, IIa/243, and IIa/248). Probably the most crucial unpublished source for the history of psychoanalytic thought, the "Rundbriefe" are still very little known. But see Patrick Mahony, *Freud as a Writer* (New York: International Universities Press, 1982), pp. 97–98; M. Grotjahn, "Notes on Reading the 'Rundbriefe,'" *Journal of the Otto Rank Association* 8 (1973–74), pp. 35–38; and E. Salomon, "Reactions to Reading the 'Rundbriefe,'" *Journal of th Otto Rank Association* 8 (1973–74), pp. 89–91.

6. See, for instance, Freud's letter of April 13, 1919 to Oscar Pfister, in *The Letters of Sigmund Freud and Oscar Pfister,* H. Meng and E. Freud, eds. (New York: Basic Books, 1963), p. 68.

7. An excerpt from Goetz's memoir in English translation is printed in *Freud as We Knew Him,* H. Ruitenbeek, ed. (Detroit: Wayne State University Press, 1973), pp. 264ff. For the full text in the original German, see Bruno Goetz, "Erinnerungen an Sigmund Freud," *Neue Schweizer Rundschau,* May 1952, pp. 3ff. This translation, slightly modified by me, is Dr. Ruitenbeek's.

8. See Jürgen Baumann, *Paragraph 175: Über die Möglichkeit, die einfache, nicht jugendgefährdende und nicht öffentliche Homosexualität unter Erwachsenen straffrei zu lassen* (Berlin/Neuwied: Luchterhand, 1968).

9. *The Freud-Jung Letters: The Correspondence of Sigmund Freud and C.G. Jung,* W. McGuire, ed. (Princeton: Princeton University Press, 1974), pp. 97, 125, 126. But about three years later in their correspondence, Jung let slip another slur. He was writing about a man named Römer, who was homosexual, and said: "He is, like all homosexuals, no delicacy." See *Freud-Jung,* p. 423.

10. See, for instance, Isidor Sadger, "Ist die Konträre Sexualempfindung heilbar?," *Zeitschrift für Sexualwissenschaft* 1 (1908), pp. 712ff. I am grateful to Professor Steakley for bringing this essay to my attention.

11. The colleague was the Italian analyst Edoardo Weiss. See Edoardo Weiss, *Sigmund Freud as Consultant* (New York: Intercontinental Medical Book Corp., 1970), p. 9. On Tausk and his relation to Freud, see Paul Roazen, *Brother Animal* (New York: Knopf, 1969); K.R. Eissler, *Talent and Genius* (New York: Grove, 1971); and Neil Hertz, "Freud and the Sandman," *Textual Strategies,* J. Harari, ed. (Ithaca: Cornell University Press, 1979), pp. 296–321.

12. Quoted by Nathan Hale, *Freud and the Americans: The Beginning of Psychoanalysis in the United States, 1876–1971* (New York: Oxford University Press, 1971), p. 339.

13. *James Jackson Putnam and Psychoanalysis,* N. Hale, ed. (Cambridge, Mass.: Harvard University Press, 1971), pp. 87, 90, 91, 95, 117, 130, 137, 152, 153, 161, 168, 171, 189.

14. Ruitenbeek, p. 220.

15. Ernest Jones, *Free Associations: Memoirs of a Psychoanalyst* (London: Hogarth, 1959), p. 190.

16. *The Standard Edition of the Complete Psychological Works of Sigmund Freud,* J. Strachey et al., trs. and eds., 24 vols. (London: Hogarth, 1966–74), vol. 11, pp. 9, 39, 33, 16, 17, 30, 31. I am grateful to my student Andrew Tully, who made a comment in classroom discussion that helped me to focus my ideas about the *Five Lectures.*

17. Martin Duberman, "The Therapy of C.M. Otis: 1911," *Christopher Street,* November, 1977, p. 33ff.

18. Hale, *Freud and the Americans,* p. 346.

19. See above, Note 1.

20. I follow John Lauritsen and David Thorstad, *The Early Homosexual Rights Movement, 1864–1935* (New York: Times Change, 1974); James Steakley, *The Homosexual Emancipation Movement in Germany* (New York: Arno, 1975); and Timothy Roe Lyman, "Homosexual Movements in Perspective: The Emergence of Homosexual Identity in Germany, 1900–1933" (A.B. Honors Thesis, Harvard College, 1980). I am grateful to Timothy Lyman for his kindness in permitting me to read his excellent thesis.

21. *Standard Edition,* 7:142.

22. *Standard Edition,* 11:98, 99.

23. *Standard Edition,* 16:304, 307, 308.

24. *Standard Edition,* 12:145.

25. *Standard Edition,* 16:308.

26. *Standard Edition,* 16:307; 7:145.

27. Quoted by Ronald Bayer, *Homosexuality and American Psychiatry: The Politics of Diagnosis* (New York: Basic Books, 1981), pp. 28, 29. In my account of Rado, Bieber, and Socarides, I generally and gratefully follow Bayer. So perhaps I should note that I cannot follow his treatment of Freud. There Bayer goes wrong. He tends to accept that Freud believed what American analysts have said he believed.

28. Bayer, pp. 30, 31, 34, 35, 36, 37.

29. This classification was also reflected in the attitudes of a substantial number of American health-care professionals. As late as 1971, just two years before the classification was rescinded, a study of a random sample of 163 such professionals in the San Francisco area (63 social workers, 50 psychiatrists, and 50 clinical psychologists) showed that only 64% overall were prepared to say that homosexuality wasn't an illness. See Joel Fort, Claude M. Steiner, and Florence Conrad, "Attitudes of Mental Health Professionals toward Homosexuality and Its Treatment," *Psychological Reports* 29 (1971), p. 349. One way of gauging the enduring force of American moralism may be to compare these results with those of a rather similar study done the same year in England. A random sample of 300 health-care professionals (150 general practitioners, 150 psychiatrists) showed that 94.3% overall were prepared to say that homosexuality wasn't an illness. See Philip A. Morris, "Doctors' Attitudes to Homosexuality," *British Journal of Psychiatry* 72 (1973), p. 436.

30. Bayer, p. 136.

31. Quoted by Bayer, p. 138.

32. *Sexual Inversion,* ed. J. Marmor (New York: Basic Books, 1965), pp. 2, 3, 4.

33. Robert Stoller, *Sex and Gender* (New York: Science House, 1968), pp. 142, 143, 144.

V

"THE EVIDENCE
OF EXPERIENCE"

27

The Evidence of Experience

JOAN W. SCOTT

Joan W. Scott is an historian who is especially concerned with what is sometimes called "difference," the marking off of some groups of people like women and gay men as "other," as distinguishable from a taken-for-granted norm. But in writing about these groups she has not been content just to make them visible, to rescue them from the oblivion to which they had been consigned by old-fashioned historians. In fact she has been critical of the new social historians who have made such rescue operations their business. Scott says that the rescue operations are often based on the assumption that we know what women or gay men are, that their character or identity is obvious if undervalued. In this essay she argues that by so assuming we wrongly reaffirm the naturalness of "difference," instead of trying as we should to analyze how it is historically produced. Joan W. Scott is the author of Gender and the Politics of History *(1988), and she is professor of Social Science at the Institute of Advanced Study, Princeton.*

Becoming Visible

There is a section in Samuel Delany's magnificent autobiographical meditation, *The Motion of Light in Water,* that dramatically raises the problem of writing the history of difference, the history, that is, of the designation of "other," of the attribution of characteristics that distinguish categories of people from some presumed (and usually unstated) norm.[1]

Delany (a gay man, a black man, a writer of science fiction) recounts his reaction to his first visit to the St. Marks bathhouse in 1963. He remembers standing on the threshold of a "gym-sized room" dimly lit by blue bulbs. The room was full of people, some standing, the rest

> an undulating mass of naked, male bodies, spread wall to wall.
>
> My first response was a kind of heart-thudding astonishment, very close to fear.
>
> I have written of a space at certain libidinal saturation before. That was not what frightened me. It was rather that the saturation was not only kinesthetic but visible.[2]

Watching the scene establishes for Delany a "fact that flew in the face" of the prevailing representation of homosexuals in the 1950s as "isolated perverts," as subjects "gone awry." The "apprehension of massed bodies" gave him (as it does, he argues, anyone, "male, female, working or middle class") a "sense of political power":

> what *this* experience said was that there was a population—not of individual homosexuals ... not of hundreds, not of thousands, but rather of millions of gay men, and

that history had, actively and already, created for us whole galleries of institutions, good and bad, to accommodate our sex. [*M*, p. 174]

The sense of political possibility is frightening and exhilarating for Delany. He emphasizes not the discovery of an identity, but a sense of participation in a movement; indeed, it is the extent (as well as the existence) of these sexual practices that matters most in his account. Numbers—massed bodies—constitute a movement and this, even if subterranean, belies enforced silences about the range and diversity of human sexual practices. Making the movement visible breaks the silence about it, challenges prevailing notions, and opens new possibilities for everyone. Delany imagines, even from the vantage of 1988, a future utopian moment of genuine sexual revolution, "once the AIDS crisis is brought under control":

> That revolution will come precisely because of the infiltration of clear and articulate language into the marginal areas of human sexual exploration, such as this book from time to time describes, and of which it is only the most modest example. Now that a significant range of people have begun to get a clearer idea of what has been possible among the varieties of human pleasure in the recent past, heterosexuals and homosexuals, females and males will insist on exploring them even further. [*M*, p. 175]

By writing about the bathhouse Delany seeks not, he says, "to romanticize that time into some cornucopia of sexual plenty," but rather to break an "absolutely sanctioned public silence" on questions of sexual practice, to reveal something that existed but that had been suppressed.

> Only the coyest and the most indirect articulations could occasionally indicate the boundaries of a phenomenon whose centers could not be spoken or written of, even figuratively: and that coyness was medical and legal as well as literary; and, as Foucault has told us, it was, in its coyness, a huge and pervasive discourse. But what that coyness means is that there is no way to gain from it a clear, accurate, and extensive picture of extant public sexual institutions. That discourse only touched on highly select margins when they transgressed the legal and/or medical standards of a populace that firmly wished to maintain that no such institutions existed. [*M*, pp. 175–76]

The point of Delany's description, indeed of his entire book, is to document the existence of those institutions in all their variety and multiplicity, to write about and thus to render historical what has hitherto been hidden from history.

As I read it, a metaphor of visibility as literal transparency is crucial to his project. The blue lights illuminate a scene he has participated in before (in darkened trucks parked along the docks under the West Side Highway, in men's rooms in subway stations), but understood only in a fragmented way. "No one ever got *to see* its whole" (*M*, p. 174; emphasis added). He attributes the impact of the bathhouse scene to its visibility: "You could *see* what was going on throughout the dorm" (*M*, p. 173; emphasis added). Seeing enables him to comprehend the relationship between his personal activities and politics: "the first direct sense of political power comes from the apprehension of massed bodies." Recounting that moment also allows him to explain the aim of his book: to provide a "clear, accurate, and extensive *picture* of extant public sexual institutions" so that others may learn about and explore them (*M*, pp. 174, 176; emphasis added). Knowledge is gained through vision; vision is a direct apprehension of a world of transparent objects. In this conceptualization, the visible is privileged; writing is then put at its service.[3] Seeing is the origin of knowing. Writing is reproduction, transmission—the communication of knowledge gained through (visual, visceral) experience.

This kind of communication has long been the mission of historians documenting the lives of those omitted or overlooked in accounts of the past. It has produced a wealth of new evidence previously ignored about these others and has drawn attention to dimensions of human life and activity usually deemed unworthy of mention in conventional histories. It has also occasioned a crisis for orthodox history by multiplying not only stories but subjects, and by insisting that histories are written from fundamentally different—indeed irreconcilable—perspectives or standpoints, none of which is complete or completely "true." Like Delany's memoir, these histories have provided evidence for a world of alternative values and practices whose existence gives the lie to hegemonic constructions of social worlds, whether these constructions vaunt the political superiority of white men, the coherence and unity of selves, the naturalness of heterosexual monogamy, or the inevitability of scientific progress and economic development. The challenge to normative history has been described, in terms of conventional historical understandings of evidence, as an enlargement of the picture, a correction to oversights resulting from inaccurate or incomplete vision, and it has rested its claim to legitimacy on the authority of experience, the direct experience of others, as well as of the historian who learns to see and illuminate the lives of those others in his or her texts.

Documenting the experience of others in this way has been at once a highly successful and limiting strategy for historians of difference. It has been successful because it remains so comfortably within the disciplinary framework of history, working according to rules that permit calling old narratives into question when new evidence is discovered. The status of evidence is, of course, ambiguous for historians. On the one hand, they acknowledge that "evidence only counts as evidence and is only recognized as such in relation to a potential narrative, so that the narrative can be said to determine the evidence as much as the evidence determines the narrative."[4] On the other hand, historians' rhetorical treatment of evidence and their use of it to falsify prevailing interpretations, depends on a referential notion of evidence which denies that it is anything but a reflection of the real.[5] Michel de Certeau's description is apt. Historical discourse, he writes,

> gives itself credibility in the name of the reality which it is supposed to represent, but this authorized appearance of the "real" serves precisely to camouflage the practice which in fact determines it. Representation thus disguises the praxis that organizes it.[6]

When the evidence offered is the evidence of "experience," the claim for referentiality is further buttressed—what could be truer, after all, than a subject's own account of what he or she has lived through? It is precisely this kind of appeal to experience as uncontestable evidence and as an originary point of explanation—as a foundation on which analysis is based—that weakens the critical thrust of histories of difference. By remaining within the epistemological frame of orthodox history, these studies lose the possibility of examining those assumptions and practices that excluded considerations of difference in the first place. They take as self-evident the identities of those whose experience is being documented and thus naturalize their difference. They locate resistance outside its discursive construction and reify agency as an inherent attribute of individuals, thus decontextualizing it. When experience is taken as the origin of knowledge, the vision of the individual subject (the person who had the experience or the historian who recounts it) becomes the bedrock of evidence on which explanation is built. Questions about the constructed nature of experience, about how subjects are constituted as different in the first place, about how one's vision is structured—about language (or discourse) and history—are left aside. The evidence of experience then becomes evidence for the fact of difference, rather than a way of exploring how difference is established, how it operates, how and in what ways it constitutes subjects who see and act in the world.[7]

To put it another way, the evidence of experience, whether conceived through a metaphor of visibility or in any other way that takes meaning as transparent, reproduces rather than contests given ideological systems—those that assume that the facts of history speak for themselves and those that rest on notions of a natural or established opposition between, say, sexual practices and social conventions, or between homosexuality and heterosexuality. Histories that document the "hidden" world of homosexuality, for example, show the impact of silence and repression on the lives of those affected by it and bring to light the history of their suppression and exploitation. But the project of making experience visible precludes critical examination of the workings of the ideological system itself, its categories of representation (homosexual/heterosexual, man/ woman, black/white as fixed immutable identities), its premises about what these categories mean and how they operate, and of its notions of subjects, origin, and cause. Homosexual practices are seen as the result of desire, conceived as a natural force operating outside or in opposition to social regulation. In these stories homosexuality is presented as a repressed desire (experience denied), made to seem invisible, abnormal, and silenced by a "society" that legislates heterosexuality as the only normal practice.[8] Because this kind of (homosexual) desire cannot ultimately be repressed—because experience is there—it invents institutions to accommodate itself. These institutions are unacknowledged but not invisible; indeed, it is the possibility that they can be seen that threatens order and ultimately overcomes repression. Resistance and agency are presented as driven by uncontainable desire; emancipation is a teleological story in which desire ultimately overcomes social control and becomes visible. History is a chronology that makes experience visible, but in which categories appear as nonetheless ahistorical: desire, homosexuality, heterosexuality, femininity, masculinity, sex, and even sexual practices become so many fixed entities being played out over time, but not themselves historicized. Presenting the story in this way excludes, or at least understates, the historically variable interrelationship between the meanings "homosexual" and "heterosexual," the constitutive force each has for the other, and the contested and changing nature of the terrain that they simultaneously occupy. "The importance—an importance—of the category 'homosexual,'" writes Eve Kosofsky Sedgwick,

> comes not necessarily from its regulatory relation to a nascent or already-constituted minority of homosexual people or desires, but from its potential for giving whoever wields it a structuring definitional leverage over the whole range of male bonds that shape the social constitution.[9]

Not only does homosexuality define heterosexuality by specifying its negative limits, and not only is the boundary between the two a shifting one, but both operate within the structures of the same "phallic economy"—an economy whose workings are not taken into account by studies that seek simply to make homosexual experience visible. One way to describe this economy is to say that desire is defined through the pursuit of the phallus—that veiled and evasive signifier which is at once fully present but unattainable, and which gains its power through the promise it holds out but never entirely fulfills.[10] Theorized this way, homosexuality and heterosexuality work according to the same economy, their social institutions mirroring one another. The social institutions through which gay sex is practiced may invert those associated with dominant heterosexual behavior (promiscuous versus restrained, public versus private, anonymous versus known, and so on), but they both operate within a system structured according to presence and lack.[11] To the extent that this system constructs desiring subjects (those who are legitimate as well as those who are not), it simultaneously establishes them and itself as given and outside of time, as the way things work, the way they inevitably are.

The project of making experience visible precludes analysis of the workings of this system and of its historicity; instead, it reproduces its terms. We come to appreciate the consequences of the closeting of homosexuals and we understand repression as an interested act of power or domination; alternative behaviors and institutions also become available to us. What we don't have is a way of placing those alternatives within the framework of (historically contingent) dominant patterns of sexuality and the ideology that supports them. We know they exist, but not how they have been constructed; we know their existence offers a critique of normative practices, but not the extent of the critique. Making visible the experience of a different group exposes the existence of repressive mechanisms, but not their inner workings or logics; we know that difference exists, but we don't understand it as relationally constituted. For that we need to attend to the historical processes that, through discourse, position subjects and produce their experiences. It is not individuals who have experience, but subjects who are constituted through experience. Experience in this definition then becomes not the origin of our explanation, not the authoritative (because seen or felt) evidence that grounds what is known, but rather that which we seek to explain, that about which knowledge is produced. To think about experience in this way is to historicize it as well as to historicize the identities it produces. This kind of historicizing represents a reply to the many contemporary historians who have argued that an unproblematized "experience" is the foundation of their practice; it is a historicizing that implies critical scrutiny of all explanatory categories usually taken for granted, including the category of "experience."

The Authority of Experience

History has been largely a foundationalist discourse. By this I mean that its explanations seem to be unthinkable if they do not take for granted some primary premises, categories, or presumptions. These foundations (however varied, whatever they are at a particular moment) are unquestioned and unquestionable; they are considered permanent and transcendent. As such they create a common ground for historians and their objects of study in the past and so authorize and legitimize analysis; indeed, analysis seems not to be able to proceed without them.[12] In the minds of some foundationalists, in fact, nihilism, anarchy, and moral confusion are the sure alternatives to these givens, which have the status (if not the philosophical definition) of eternal truths.

Historians have had recourse to many kinds of foundations, some more obviously empiricist than others. What is most striking these days is the determined embrace, the strident defense, of some reified, transcendent category of explanation by historians who have used insights drawn from the sociology of knowledge, structural linguistics, feminist theory, or cultural anthropology to develop sharp critiques of empiricism. This turn to foundations even by antifoundationalists appears, in Fredric Jameson's characterization, as "some extreme form of the return of the repressed."[13]

"Experience" is one of the foundations that has been reintroduced into historical writing in the wake of the critique of empiricism; unlike "brute fact" or "simple reality," its connotations are more varied and elusive. It has recently emerged as a critical term in debates among historians about the limits of interpretation and especially about the uses and limits of poststructuralist theory for history. In these debates those most open to interpretive innovation—those who have insisted on the study of collective mentalities, of economic, social, or cultural determinations of individual behavior, and even of the influences of unconscious motives on thought and action—are among the most ardent defenders of the need to attend to "experience." Feminist historians critical of biases in "malestream" histories and seeking to install women as viable subjects, social historians insisting on the materialist basis of the discipline on the one hand and on the "agency" of individuals or groups on the other, and cultural historians who have brought symbolic analysis to the study of behavior, have joined political historians whose stories privilege the purposive actions of rational actors and intellectual historians who maintain that thought originates in the minds of individuals. All seem to have converged on the argument that experience is an "irreducible" ground for history.

The evolution of "experience" appears to solve a problem of explanation for professed anti-empiricists even as it reinstates a foundational ground. For this reason it is interesting to examine the uses of "experience" by historians. Such an examination allows us to ask whether history can exist without foundations and what it might look like if it did.

In *Keywords* Raymond Williams sketches the alternative senses in which the term *experience* has been employed in the Anglo-American tradition. These he summarizes as "(i) knowledge gathered from past events, whether by conscious observation or by consideration and reflection; and (ii) a particular kind of consciousness, which can in some contexts be distinguished from 'reason' or 'knowledge.' "[14] Until the early eighteenth century, he says, experience and experiment were closely connected terms, designating how knowledge was arrived at through testing and observation (here the visual metaphor is important). In the eighteenth century, experience still contained this notion of consideration or reflection on observed events, of lessons gained from the past, but it also referred to a particular kind of consciousness. This consciousness, in the twentieth century, has come to mean a "full and active 'awareness,' " including feeling as well as thought (*K,* p. 127). The notion of experience as subjective witness, writes Williams, is "offered not only as truth, but as the most authentic kind of truth," as "the ground for all (subsequent) reasoning and analysis" (*K,* p. 128). According to Williams, experience has acquired another connotation in the twentieth century different from these notions of subjective testimony as immediate, true, and authentic. In this usage it refers to influences external to individuals—social conditions, institutions, forms of belief or perception—"real" things outside them that they react to, and does not include their thought or consideration.[15]

In the various usages described by Williams, "experience," whether conceived as internal or external, subjective or objective, establishes the prior existence of individuals. When it is defined as internal, it is an expression of an individual's being or consciousness; when external, it is the material on which consciousness then acts. Talking about experience in these ways leads us to take the existence of individuals for granted (experience is something people have) rather than to ask how conceptions of selves (of subjects and their identities) are produced.[16] It operates within an ideological construction that not only makes individuals the starting point of knowledge, but that also naturalizes categories such as man, woman, black, white, heterosexual, and homosexual by treating them as given characteristics of individuals.

Teresa de Lauretis's redefinition of experience exposes the workings of this ideology. "Experience," she writes, is the

> process by which, for all social beings, subjectivity is constructed. Through that process one places oneself or is placed in social reality, and so perceives and comprehends as subjective (referring to, originating in, oneself) those relations—material, economic, and interpersonal—which are in fact social and, in a larger perspective, historical.[17]

The process that de Lauretis describes operates crucially through differentiation; its effect is to constitute subjects as fixed and autonomous, and who are considered reliable sources of a knowledge that comes from access to the real by means of their experience.[18] When talking about historians and other students of the human sciences it is important to note that this subject is both the object of inquiry—the person one studies in the present or the past—and the investigator him- or herself—the historian who produces knowledge of the past based on "experience" in the archives or the anthropologist who produces knowledge of other cultures based on "experience" as a participant observer.

The concepts of experience described by Williams preclude inquiry into processes of subject-construction; and they avoid examining the relationships between discourse, cognition, and reality, the relevance of the position or situatedness of subjects to the knowledge they produce, and the effects of difference on knowledge. Questions are not raised about, for example, whether it matters for the history they write that historians are men, women, white, black, straight, or gay; instead, as de Certeau writes, "the authority of the 'subject of knowledge' [is measured] by the elimination of everything concerning the speaker" ("H," p. 218). His knowledge, reflecting as it does something apart from him, is legitimated and presented as universal, accessible to all. There is no power or politics in these notions of knowledge and experience.

An example of the way "experience" establishes the authority of an historian can be found in R.G. Collingwood's *Idea of History,* the 1946 classic that has been required reading in historiography courses for several generations. For Collingwood, the ability of the historian to reenact past experience is tied to his autonomy, "where by autonomy I mean the condition of being one's own authority, making statements or taking action on one's own initiative and not because those statements or actions are authorized or prescribed by anyone else."[19] The question of where the historian is situated—who he is, how he is defined in relation to others, what the political effects of his history may be—never enters the discussion. Indeed, being free of these matters seems to be tied to Collingwood's definition of autonomy, an issue so critical for him that he launches into an uncharacteristic tirade about it. In his quest for certainty, the historian must not let others make up his mind for him, Collingwood insists, because to do that means

> giving up his autonomy as an historian and allowing someone else to do for him what, if he is a scientific thinker, he can only do for himself. There is no need for me to offer the reader any proof of this statement. If he knows anything of historical work, he already knows of his own experience that it is true. If he does not already know that it is true, he does not know enough about history to read this essay with any profit, and the best thing he can do is to stop here and now.[20]

For Collingwood it is axiomatic that experience is a reliable source of knowledge because it rests on direct contact between the historian's perception and reality (even if the passage of time makes it necessary for the historian to imaginatively reenact events of the past). Thinking on his own means owning his own thoughts, and this proprietary relationship guarantees an individual's independence, his ability to read the past correctly, and the authority of the knowledge he produces. The claim is not only for the historian's autonomy, but also for his originality. Here "experience" grounds the identity of the researcher as an historian.

Another, very different use of "experience" can be found in E.P. Thompson's *Making of the English Working Class,* the book that revolutionized social and labor history. Thompson specifically set out to free the concept of "class" from the ossified categories of Marxist structuralism. For this project "experience" was a key concept. "We explored," Thompson writes of himself and his fellow New Left historians, "both in theory and in practice, those junction-concepts (such as 'need,' 'class,' and 'determine') by which, through the missing term, 'experience,' structure is transmuted into process, and the subject re-enters into history."[21]

Thompson's notion of experience joined ideas of external influence and subjective feeling, the structural and the psychological. This gave him a mediating influence between social structure and social consciousness. For him experience meant "social being"—the lived realities of social life, especially the affective domains of family and religion and the symbolic dimensions of expression. This definition separated the affective and the symbolic from the economic and the rational. "People do not only experience their own experience as ideas, within thought and its procedures," he maintained, "they also experience their own experience as *feeling*" ("PT," p. 171). This statement grants importance to the psychological dimension of experience, and it allows Thompson to account for agency. Feeling, Thompson insists, is "handled" culturally as "norms, familial and kinship obligations and reciprocities, as values or (through more elaborated forms) within art and religious beliefs" ("PT," p. 171). At the same time it somehow precedes these forms of expression and so provides an escape from a strong structural determination: "For any living generation, in any 'now,' " Thompson asserts, "the ways in which they 'handle' experience defies prediction and escapes from any narrow definition of determination" ("PT," p. 171).[22]

And yet in his use of it, experience, because it is ultimately shaped by relations of production, is a unifying phenomenon, overriding other kinds of diversity. Since these relations of production are common to workers of different ethnicities, religions, regions, and trades they necessarily provide a common denominator and emerge as a more salient determinant of "experience" than anything else. In Thompson's use of the term, experience is the start of a process that culminates in the realization and articulation of social consciousness, in this case a common identity of class. It serves an integrating function, joining the individual and the structural, and bringing together diverse people into that coherent (totalizing) whole which is a distinctive sense of class.[23] " 'Experience' (we have found) has, in the last instance, been generated in 'material life,' has been structured in class ways, and hence 'social being' has determined 'social consciousness' " ("PT," p. 171). In this way unequivocal and uniform identity is produced through objective circumstances and there is no reason to ask how this identity achieved predominance—it had to.

The unifying aspect of experience excludes whole realms of human activity by simply not counting them as experience, at least not with any consequences for social organization or politics. When class becomes an overriding identity, other subject-positions are subsumed by it, those of gender, for example (or, in other instances of this kind, of history, race, ethnicity, and sexuality). The positions of men and women and their different relationships to politics are taken as reflections of material and social arrangements rather than as products of class politics itself; they are part of the "experience" of capitalism. Instead of asking how some experiences become more salient than others, how what matters to Thompson is defined as experience, and how differences are dissolved, experience becomes itself cumulative and homogenizing, providing the common denominator on which class consciousness is built.

Thompson's own role in determining the salience of certain things and not others is never addressed. Although his author's voice intervenes powerfully with moral and ethical judgments about the situations he is recounting, the presentation of the experiences themselves is meant to secure their objective status. We forget that Thompson's history, like the accounts offered by political organizers in the nineteenth century of what mattered in workers' lives, is an interpretation, a selective ordering of information that through its use of originary categories and teleological accounts legitimizes a particular kind of politics (it becomes the only possible politics) and a particular way of doing history (as a reflection of what happened, the description of which is little influenced by the historian if, in this case, he only has the requisite moral vision that permits identification with the experiences of workers in the past).

In Thompson's account class is finally an identity rooted in structural relations that preexist politics. What this obscures is the contradictory and contested process by which class itself was conceptualized and by which diverse kinds of subject-positions were assigned, felt, contested, or embraced. As a result, Thompson's brilliant history of the English working class, which set out to historicize the category of class, ends up essentializing it. The ground may seem to be displaced from structure to agency by insisting on the subjectively felt nature of experience, but the problem Thompson sought to address isn't really solved. Working-class "experience" is now the ontological foundation of working-class identity, politics, and history.[24]

This kind of use of experience has the same foundational status if we substitute "women's" or "black" or "lesbian" or "homosexual" for "working class" in the previous sentence. Among feminist historians, for example, "experience" has helped to legitimize a critique of the false claims to objectivity of traditional historical accounts. Part of the project of some feminist history has been to unmask all claims to objectivity as an ideological cover for masculine bias by pointing out the shortcomings, incompleteness, and exclusiveness of mainstream history. This has been achieved by providing documentation about women in the past that calls into question existing interpretations made without consideration of gender. But how do we authorize the new knowledge if the possibility of all historical objectivity has been questioned? By appealing to experience, which in this usage connotes both reality and its subjective apprehension—the experience of women in the past and of women historians who can recognize something of themselves in their foremothers.

Judith Newton, a literary historian writing about the neglect of feminism by contemporary critical theorists, argues that women, too, arrived at the critique of objectivity usually associated with deconstruction or the new historicism. This feminist critique came "straight out of reflection on our own, that is, women's experience, out of the contradictions we felt between the different ways we were represented even to ourselves, out of the inequities we had long experienced in our situations."[25] Newton's appeal to experience seems to bypass the issue of objectivity (by not raising the question of whether feminist work can be objective) but it rests firmly on a foundational ground (experience). In her work the relationship between thought and experience is represented as transparent (the visual metaphor combines with the visceral) and so is directly accessible, as it is in historian Christine Stansell's insistence that "social practices," in all their "immediacy and entirety," constitute a domain of "sensuous experience" (a prediscursive reality directly felt, seen, and known) that cannot be subsumed by "language."[26] The effect of these kinds of statements, which attribute an indisputable authenticity to women's experience, is to establish incontrovertibly women's identity as people with agency. It is also to universalize the identity of women and thus to ground claims for the legitimacy of women's history in the shared experience of historians of women and those women whose stories they tell. In addition, it literally equates the personal with the political, for the lived experience of women is seen as leading directly to resistance to oppression, that is, to feminism.[27] Indeed, the possibility of politics is said to rest on, to follow from, a preexisting women's experience.

"Because of its drive towards a political massing together of women," writes Denise Riley, "feminism can never wholeheartedly dismantle 'women's experience,' however much this category conflates the attributed, the imposed, and the lived, and then sanctifies the resulting mélange." The kind of argument for a women's history (and for a feminist politics) that Riley criticizes closes down inquiry into the ways in which female subjectivity is produced, the ways in which agency is made possible, the ways in which race and sexuality intersect with gender, the ways in which politics organize and interpret experience—in sum, the ways in which identity is a contested terrain, the site of multiple and conflicting claims. In Riley's words, "it masks the likelihood that . . . [experiences] have accrued to women not by virtue of their womanhood alone, but as traces of domination, whether natural or political."[28] I would add that it masks the necessarily discursive character of these experiences as well.

But it is precisely the discursive character of experience that is at issue for some historians because attributing experience to discourse seems somehow to deny its status as an unquestionable ground of explanation. This seems to be the case for John Toews, who wrote a long article in the *American Historical Review* in 1987 called "Intellectual History after the Linguistic Turn: The Autonomy of Meaning and the Irreducibility of Experience." The term *linguistic turn* is a comprehensive one used by Toews to refer to approaches to the study of meaning that draw on a number of disciplines, but especially on theories of language "since the primary medium of meaning was obviously language."[29] The question for Toews is how far linguistic analysis has gone and should go, especially in view of the poststructuralist challenge to foundationalism. Reviewing a number of books that take on questions of meaning and its analysis, Toews concludes that

> the predominant tendency [among intellectual historians] is to adapt traditional historical concerns for extralinguistic origins and reference to the semiological challenge, to reaffirm in new ways that, in spite of the relative autonomy of cultural meanings, human subjects still make and remake the worlds of meaning in which they are suspended, and to insist that these worlds are not creations *ex nihilo* but responses to, and shapings of, changing worlds of experience ultimately irreducible to the linguistic forms in which they appear. ["IH," p. 882]

By definition, he argues, history is concerned with explanation; it is not a radical hermeneutics, but an attempt to account for the origin, persistence, and disappearance of certain meanings "at particular times and in specific sociocultural situations" ("IH," p. 882). For him explanation requires a separation of experience and meaning: experience is that reality which demands meaningful response. "Experience," in Toews's usage, is taken to be so self-evident that he never defines the term. This is telling in an article that insists on establishing the importance and independence, the irreducibility of "experience." The absence of definition allows experience to resonate in many ways, but it also allows it to function as a universally understood category—the undefined word creates a sense of consensus by attributing to it an assumed, stable, and shared meaning.

Experience, for Toews, is a foundational concept. While recognizing that meanings differ and that the historian's task is to analyze the different meanings produced in societies and over time, Toews protects "experience" from this kind of relativism. In doing so he establishes the possibility for objective knowledge and for communication among historians, however diverse their positions and views. This has the effect (among others) of removing historians from critical scrutiny as active producers of knowledge.

The insistence on the separation of meaning and experience is crucial for Toews, not only because it seems the only way to account for change, but also because it protects the world from "the hubris of wordmakers who claim to be makers of reality" ("IH," p. 906). Even if Toews here uses "wordmakers" metaphorically to refer to those who produce texts, those who engage in signification, his opposition between "words" and "reality" echoes the distinction he makes earlier in the article between language (or meaning) and experience. This opposition guarantees both an independent status for human agents and the common ground on which they can communicate and act. It produces a possibility for "intersubjective communication" among individuals despite differences between them, and also reaffirms their existence as thinking beings outside the discursive practices they devise and employ.

Toews is critical of J.G.A. Pocock's vision of "intersubjective communication" based on rational consensus in a community of free individuals, all of whom are equally masters of their own wills. "Pocock's theories," he writes, "often seem like theoretical reflections of familiar practices because the world they assume is also the world in which many contemporary Anglo-American historians live or think they live" ("IH," p. 893). Yet the separation of meaning and experience that Toews offers does not really provide an alternative. A more diverse community can be posited, of course, with different meanings given to experience. Since the phenomenon of experience itself can be analyzed outside the meanings given to it, the subjective position of historians then can seem to have nothing to do with the knowledge they produce.[30] In this way experience authorizes historians and it enables them to counter the radical historicist stance that, Toews says, "undermines the traditional historians' quest for unity, continuity, and purpose by robbing them of any standpoint from which a relationship between past, present, and future could be objectively reconstructed" ("IH," p. 902). Here he establishes as self-evident (and unproblematic) the reflective nature of historical representation, and he assumes that it will override whatever diversity there is in the background, culture, and outlook of historians. Attention to experience, he concludes, "is essential for our self-understanding, and thus also for fulfilling the historian's task of connecting memory with hope" ("IH," p. 907).[31]

Toews's "experience" thus provides an object for historians that can be known apart from their own role as meaning makers and it then guarantees not only the objectivity of their knowledge, but their ability to persuade others of its importance. Whatever diversity and conflict may exist among them, Toews's community of historians is rendered homogeneous by its shared object (experience). But as Ellen Rooney has so effectively pointed out, using the field of literary theory as her example, this kind of homogeneity can exist only because of the exclusion of the possibility that "historically irreducible interests divide and define reading communities."[32] Inclusiveness is achieved by denying that exclusion is inevitable, that difference is established through exclusion, and that the fundamental differences that accompany inequalities of power and position cannot be overcome by persuasion. In Toews's article no disagreement about the meaning of the term *experience* can be entertained, since experience itself lies somehow outside its signification. For that reason, perhaps, Toews never defines it.

Even among those historians who do not share all of Toews's ideas about the objectivity or continuous quality of history writing, the defense of "experience" works in much the same way: it establishes a realm of reality outside of discourse and it authorizes the historian who has access to it. The evidence of experience works as a foundation providing both a starting point and a conclusive kind of explanation, beyond which few questions can or need to be asked. And yet it is precisely the questions precluded—questions about discourse, difference, and subjectivity, as well as about what counts as experience and who gets to make that determination—that would enable us to historicize experience, and to reflect critically on the history we write about it, rather than to premise our history on it.

Historicizing "Experience"

Gayatri Chakravorty Spivak begins an essay addressed to the Subaltern Studies collective with a contrast between the work of historians and literary scholars:

> A historian confronts a text of counterinsurgency or gendering where the subaltern has been represented. He unravels the text to assign a new subject-position to the subaltern, gendered or otherwise.
>
> A teacher of literature confronts a sympathetic text where the gendered subaltern has been represented. She unravels the text to make visible the assignment of subject-positions. . . .
>
> The performance of these tasks, of the historian and the teacher of literature, must critically "interrupt" each other, bring each other to crisis, in order to serve their constituencies; especially when each seems to claim all for its own.[33]

Spivak's argument here seems to be that there is a difference between history and literature that is both methodological and political. History provides categories that enable us to understand the social and structural positions of people (as workers, subalterns, and so on) in new terms, and these terms define a collective identity with potential political (maybe even revolutionary, but certainly subversive) effects. Literature relativizes the categories history assigns, and exposes the processes that construct and position subjects. In Spivak's discussion, both are critical operations, although she clearly favors the deconstructive task of literature.[34] Although her essay has to be read in the context of a specific debate within Indian historiography, its general points must also be considered. In effect, her statements raise the question of whether historians can do other than construct subjects by describing their experience in terms of an essentialized identity.

Spivak's characterization of the Subaltern Studies historians' reliance on a notion of consciousness as a "*strategic* use of positivist essentialism" doesn't really solve the problem of writing history either, since whether it's strategic or not, essentialism appeals to the idea that there are fixed identities, visible to us as social or natural facts.[35] A refusal of essentialism seems particularly important once again these days within the field of history, as disciplinary pressure builds to defend the unitary subject in the name of his or her "experience." Neither does Spivak's invocation of the special political status of the subaltern justify a history aimed at producing subjects without interrogating and relativizing the means of their production. In the case of colonial and postcolonial peoples, but also of various others in the West, it has been precisely the imposition of a categorical (and universal) subject-status (*the* worker, *the* peasant, *the* woman, *the* black) that has masked the operations of difference in the organization of social life. Each category taken as fixed works to solidify the ideological process of subject-construction, making the process less rather than more apparent, naturalizing rather than analyzing it.

It ought to be possible for historians (as for the teachers of literature Spivak so dazzlingly exemplifies) to "make visible the assignment of subject-positions," not in the sense of capturing the reality of the objects seen, but of trying to understand the operations of the complex and changing discursive processes by which identities are ascribed, resisted, or embraced, and which processes themselves are unremarked and indeed achieve their effect because they are not noticed. To do this a change of object seems to be required, one that takes the emergence of concepts and identities as historical events in need of explanation. This does not mean that one dismisses the *effects* of such concepts and identities, nor that one does not explain behavior in terms of their operations. It does mean assuming that the appearance of a new identity is not inevitable or determined, not something that was always there simply waiting to be expressed, not something that will always exist in the form it was given in a particular political movement or at a particular historical moment. Stuart Hall writes:

> The fact is "black" has never been just there either. It has always been an unstable identity, psychically, culturally, and politically. It, too, is a narrative, a story, a history. Something constructed, told, spoken, not simply found. People now speak of the society I come from in totally unrecognizable ways. Of course Jamaica is a black society, they say. In reality it is a society of black and brown people who lived for three or four hundred years without ever being able to speak of themselves as "black." Black is an identity which had to be learned and could only be learned in a certain moment. In Jamaica that moment is the 1970s.[36]

To take the history of Jamaican black identity as an object of inquiry in these terms is necessarily to analyze subject-positioning, at least in part, as the effect of discourses that placed Jamaica in a late twentieth-century international racist political economy; it is to historicize the "experience" of blackness.[37]

Treating the emergence of a new identity as a discursive event is not to introduce a new form of linguistic determinism, nor to deprive subjects of agency. It is to refuse a separation between "experience" and language and to insist instead on the productive quality of discourse. Subjects are constituted discursively, but there are conflicts among discursive systems, contradictions within any one of them, multiple meanings possible for the concepts they deploy.[38] And subjects do have agency. They are not unified, autonomous individuals exercising free will, but rather subjects whose agency is created through situations and statuses conferred on them. Being a subject means being "subject to definite conditions of existence, conditions of endowment of agents and conditions of exercise."[39] These conditions enable choices, although they are not unlimited. Subjects are constituted discursively and experience is a linguistic event (it doesn't happen outside established meanings), but neither is it confined to a fixed order of meaning. Since discourse is by definition shared, experience is collective as well as individual. Experience can both confirm what is already known (we see what we have learned to see) and upset what has been taken for granted (when different meanings are in conflict we readjust our vision to take account of the conflict or to resolve it—that is what is meant by "learning from experience," though not everyone learns the same lesson or learns it at the same time or in the same way). Experience is a subject's history. Language is the site of history's enactment. Historical explanation cannot, therefore, separate the two.

The question then becomes how to analyze language, and here historians often (though not always and not necessarily) confront the limits of a discipline that has typically constructed itself in opposition to literature. (These are not the same limits Spivak points to; her contrast is about the different kinds of knowledge produced by history and literature, mine is about different ways of reading and the different understandings of the relationship between words and things implicit in those readings. In neither case are the limits obligatory for historians; indeed, recognition of them makes it possible for us to get beyond them.) The kind of reading I have in mind would not assume a direct correspondence between words and things, nor confine itself to single meanings, nor aim for the resolution of contradiction. It would not render process as linear, nor rest explanation on simple correlations or single variables. Rather it would grant to "the literary" an integral, even irreducible, status of its own. To grant such status is not to make "the literary" foundational, but to open new possibilities for analyzing discursive productions of social and political reality as complex, contradictory processes.

The reading I offered of Delany at the beginning of this essay is an example of the kind of reading I want to avoid. I would like now to present another reading—one suggested to me by literary critic Karen Swann—as a way of indicating what might be involved in historicizing the notion of experience. It is also a way of agreeing with and appreciating Swann's argument about "the importance of 'the literary' to the historical project."[40]

For Delany, witnessing the scene at the bathhouse (an "undulating mass of naked male bodies" seen under a dim blue light) was an event. It marked what in one kind of reading we would call a coming to consciousness of himself, a recognition of his authentic identity, one he had always shared, would always share with others like himself. Another kind of reading, closer to Delany's preoccupation with memory and the self in this autobiography, sees this event not as the discovery of truth (conceived as the reflection of a prediscursive reality), but as the substitution of one interpretation for another. Delany presents this substitution as a conversion experience, a clarifying moment, after which he sees (that is, understands) differently. But there is all the difference between subjective perceptual clarity and transparent vision; one does not necessarily follow from the other even if the subjective state is metaphorically presented as a visual experience. Moreover, as Swann has pointed out, "the properties of the medium through which the visible appears—here, the dim blue light, whose distorting, refracting qualities produce a wavering of the visible"—make any claim to unmediated transparency impossible. Instead, the wavering light permits a vision beyond the visible, a vision that contains the fantastic projections ("millions of gay men" for whom "history had, actively and already, created . . . whole galleries of institutions") that are the basis for political identification. "In this version of the story," Swann notes, "political consciousness and power originate, not in a presumedly unmediated experience of presumedly real gay identities, but out of an apprehension of the moving, differencing properties of the representational medium—the motion of light in water."

The question of representation is central to Delany's memoir. It is a question of social categories, personal understanding, and language, all of which are connected, none of which are or can be a direct reflection of the others. What does it mean to be black, gay, a writer, he asks, and is there a realm of personal identity possible apart from social constraint? The answer is that the social and the personal are imbricated in one another and that both are historically variable. The meanings of the categories of identity change and with them the possibilities for thinking the self:

> At that time, the words "black" and "gay"—for openers—didn't exist with their current meanings, usage, history. 1961 had still been, really, part of the fifties. The political consciousness that was to form by the end of the sixties had not been part of my world. There were only Negroes and homosexuals, both of whom—along with artists—were hugely devalued in the social hierarchy. It's even hard to speak of that world. [*M*, p. 242]

But the available social categories aren't sufficient for Delany's story. It is difficult, if not impossible to use a single narrative to account for his experience. Instead he makes entries in a notebook, at the front about material things, at the back about sexual desire. These are "parallel narratives, in parallel columns" (*M*, p. 29). Although one seems to be about society, the public, and the political, and the other about the individual, the private, and the psychological, in fact both narratives are inescapably historical; they are discursive productions of knowledge of the self, not reflections either of external or internal truth. "That the two columns must be the Marxist and the Freudian—the material column and the column of desire—is only a modernist prejudice. The autonomy of each is subverted by the same excesses, just as severely" (*M*, p. 212). The two columns are constitutive of one another, yet the relationship between them is difficult to specify. Does the social and economic determine the subjective? Is the private entirely separate from or completely integral to the public? Delany voices the desire to resolve the problem: "Certainly one must be the lie that is illuminated by the other's truth" (*M*, p. 212). And then he denies that resolution is possible since answers to these questions do not exist apart from the discourses that produce them:

> If it *is* the split—the space between the two columns (one resplendent and lucid with the writings of legitimacy, the other dark and hollow with the voices of the illegitimate)—that constitutes the subject, it is only after the Romantic inflation of the private into the subjective that such a split can even be located. That locus, that margin, that split itself first allows, then demands the appropriation of language—now spoken, now written—in both directions, over the gap. [*M*, pp. 29–30]

It is finally by tracking "the appropriation of language . . . in both directions, over the gap," and by situating and contextualizing that language that one historicizes the terms by which experience is represented, and so historicizes "experience" itself.

Conclusion

Reading for "the literary" does not seem at all inappropriate for those whose discipline is devoted to the study of change. It is not the only kind of reading I am advocating, although more documents than those written by literary figures are susceptible to such readings. Rather it is a way of changing the focus and the philosophy of our history, from one bent on naturalizing "experience" through a belief in the unmediated relationship between words and things, to one that takes all categories of analysis as contextual, contested, and contingent. How have categories of representation and analysis—such as class, race, gender, relations of production, biology, identity, subjectivity, agency, experience, even culture—achieved their foundational status? What have been the effects of their articulations? What does it mean for historians to study the past in terms of these categories and for individuals to think of themselves in these terms? What is the relationship between the salience of such categories in our own time and their existence in the past? Questions such as these open consideration of what Dominick LaCapra has referred to as the "transferential" relationship between the historian and the past, that is, of the relationship between the power of the historian's analytic frame and the events that are the object of his or her study.[41] And they historicize both sides of that relationship by denying the fixity and transcendence of anything that appears to operate as a foundation, turning attention instead to the history of foundationalist concepts themselves. The history of these concepts (understood to be contested and contradictory) then becomes the evidence by which "experience" can be grasped and by which the historian's relationship to the past he or she writes about can be articulated. This is what Foucault meant by genealogy:

> If interpretation were the slow exposure of the meaning hidden in an origin, then only metaphysics could interpret the development of humanity. But if interpretation is the violent or surreptitious appropriation of a system of rules, which in itself has no essential meaning, in order to impose a direction, to bend it to a new will, to force its participation in a different game, and to subject it to secondary rules, then the development of humanity is a series of interpretations. The role of genealogy is to record its history: the history of morals, ideals, and metaphysical concepts, the history of the concept of liberty or of the ascetic life; as they stand for the emergence

of different interpretations, they must be made to appear as events on the stage of historical process.[42]

Experience is not a word we can do without, although, given its usage to essentialize identity and reify the subject, it is tempting to abandon it altogether. But *experience* is so much a part of everyday language, so imbricated in our narratives that it seems futile to argue for its expulsion. It serves as a way of talking about what happened, of establishing difference and similarity, of claiming knowledge that is "unassailable."[43] Given the ubiquity of the term, it seems to me more useful to work with it, to analyze its operations and to redefine its meaning. This entails focusing on processes of identity production, insisting on the discursive nature of "experience" and on the politics of its construction. Experience is at once always already an interpretation *and* something that needs to be interpreted. What counts as experience is neither self-evident nor straightforward; it is always contested, and always therefore political. The study of experience, therefore, must call into question its originary status in historical explanation. This will happen when historians take as their project *not* the reproduction and transmission of knowledge said to be arrived at through experience, but the analysis of the production of that knowledge itself. Such an analysis would constitute a genuinely nonfoundational history, one which retains its explanatory power and its interest in change but does not stand on or reproduce naturalized categories.[44] It also cannot guarantee the historian's neutrality, for deciding which categories to historicize is inevitably political, necessarily tied to the historian's recognition of his or her stake in the production of knowledge. Experience is, in this approach, not the origin of our explanation, but that which we want to explain. This kind of approach does not undercut politics by denying the existence of subjects; it instead interrogates the processes of their creation and, in so doing, refigures history and the role of the historian and opens new ways for thinking about change.[45]

NOTES

I am grateful to Tom Keenan for inviting me to the conference ("History Today—and Tonight," Rutgers and Princeton Universities, March 1990) where I tried out some of these ideas, and to the many people there whose questions and comments led to a first round of revisions and reformulations. The students in my graduate seminar at Rutgers in the Spring of 1990 helped immeasurably in the clarification of my ideas about "experience" and about what it means to historicize. Criticism from members of the "History" seminar during 1990–91 in the School of Social Science at the Institute for Advanced Study helped give this paper its final—and, I think, much improved—form. As usual, Elizabeth Weed provided the crucial suggestions for the conceptualization of this paper. I also appreciate the important contributions of Judith Butler, Christina Crosby, Nicholas Dirks, Christopher Fynsk, Clifford Geertz, Donna Haraway, Susan Harding, Gyan Prakash, Donald Scott, and William Sewell, Jr. Karen Swann's astute comments led me to rethink and rewrite the final section of this paper. I learned a great deal from her and from that exercise. In a letter he wrote in July 1987, Reginald Zelnick challenged me to articulate a definition of "experience" that might work for historians. Although I'm not sure he will find this essay the answer he was looking for, I'm indebted to him for that early provocation.

1. For an important discussion of the "dilemma of difference," see Martha Minow. "Justice Engendered," foreword to "The Supreme Court, 1986 Term," *Harvard Law Review* 101 (Nov. 1987): 10–95.

2. Samuel R. Delany, *The Motion of Light in Water: Sex and Science Fiction Writing in the East Village, 1957–1965* (New York, 1988), p. 173; hereafter abbreviated *M*.

3. On the distinction between seeing and writing in formulations of identity, see Homi K. Bhabha, "Interrogating Identity," in *Identity: The Real Me*, ed. Lisa Appignanesi (London, 1987), pp. 5–11.

4. Lionel Gossman, *Towards a Rational Historiography,* Transactions of the American Philosophical Society, n.s. 79, pt. 3 (Philadelphia, 1989), p. 26.

5. On the "documentary" or "objectivist" model used by historians, see Dominick LaCapra, "Rhetoric and History," *History and Criticism* (Ithaca, N.Y., 1985), pp. 15–44.

6. Michel de Certeau, "History: Science and Fiction," in *Heterologies: Discourse on the Other,* trans. Brian Massumi (Minneapolis, 1986), p. 203; hereafter abbreviated "H."

7. Vision, as Donna Haraway points out, is not passive reflection. "All eyes, including our own organic ones, are active perceptual systems, building in translations and specific *ways* of seeing—that is, ways of life" (Donna Haraway, "Situated Knowledges: The Science Question in Feminism and the Privilege of Partial Perspective," *Feminist Studies* 14 [Fall 1988]: 583). In another essay she pushes the optical metaphor further: "The rays from my optical device diffract rather than reflect. These diffracting rays compose *interference* patterns, not reflecting images. . . . A diffraction pattern does not map where differences appear, but rather where the *effects* of differences appear" (Haraway, "The Promises of Monsters: Reproductive Politics for Inappropriate/d Others," typescript). In this connection, see also Minnie Bruce Pratt's discussion of her eye that "has only let in what I have been taught to see," in her "Identity: Skin Blood Heart," in Elly Bulkin, Pratt, and Barbara Smith, *Yours in Struggle: Three Feminist Perspectives on Anti-Semitism and Racism* (Brooklyn, N.Y., 1984), and the analysis of Pratt's autobiographical essay by Biddy Martin and Chandra Talpade Mohanty, "Feminist Politics: What's Home Got to Do with It?," in *Feminist Studies/ Critical Studies,* ed. Teresa de Lauretis (Bloomington, Ind., 1986), pp. 191–212.

8. On the disruptive, antisocial nature of desire, see Leo Bersani, *A Future for Astyanax: Character and Desire in Literature* (Boston, 1976).

9. Eve Kosofsky Sedgwick, *Between Men: English Literature and Male Homosocial Desire* (New York, 1985), p. 86.

10. See Jane Gallop, *The Daughter's Seduction: Feminism and Psychoanalysis* (Ithaca, N.Y., 1982); de Lauretis, *Alice Doesn't: Feminism, Semiotics, Cinema* (Bloomington, Ind., 1984), esp. chap. 5, "Desire in Narrative," pp. 103–57; Sedgwick, *Between Men;* and Jacques Lacan, "The Signification of the Phallus," *Écrits: A Selection,* trans. Alan Sheridan (New York, 1977), pp. 281–91.

11. Discussions with Elizabeth Weed on this point were helpful.

12. I am grateful to Judith Butler for discussions on this point.

13. Fredric Jameson, "Immanence and Nominalism in Postmodern Theory," *Postmodernism, or, the Cultural Logic of Late Capitalism* (Durham, N.C., 1991), p. 199.

14. Raymond Williams, *Keywords: A Vocabulary of Culture and Society,* rev. ed. (New York, 1985), p. 126; hereafter abbreviated *K.*

15. On the ways knowledge is conceived "as an assemblage of accurate representations," see Richard Rorty, *Philosophy and the Mirror of Nature* (Princeton, N.J., 1979), esp. p. 163.

16. Bhabha puts it this way: "*To see* a missing person, or *to look* at Invisibleness, is to emphasize the subject's *transitive* demand for a *direct* object of self-reflection; a point of presence which would maintain its privileged enunciatory position *qua subject*" (Bhabha, "Interrogating Identity," p. 5).

17. De Lauretis, *Alice Doesn't,* p. 159.

18. Gayatri Chakravorty Spivak describes this as "positing a metalepsis":

> A subject-effect can be briefly plotted as follows: that which seems to operate as a subject may be part of an immense discontinuous network . . . of strands that may be termed politics, ideology, economics, history, sexuality, language, and so on. . . . Different knottings and configurations of these strands, determined by heterogeneous determinations which are themselves dependent upon myriad circumstances, produce the effect of an operating subject. Yet the continuist and homogenist deliberative consciousness symptomatically requires a continuous and homogeneous cause for this effect and thus posits a sovereign and determining subject. This latter is, then, the effect of an effect, and its positing a metalepsis, or the substitution of an effect for a cause. [Gayatri Chakravorty Spivak, *In Other Worlds: Essays in Cultural Politics* (New York, 1987), p. 204]

19. R.G. Collingwood, *The Idea of History* (Oxford, 1946), pp. 274–75.

20. Ibid., p. 256.

21. E.P. Thompson, "The Poverty of Theory or an Orrery of Errors," *The Poverty of Theory and Other Essays* (New York, 1978), p. 170; hereafter abbreviated "PT."

22. Williams's discussion of "structures of feeling" takes on some of these same issues in a more extended way. See Williams, *The Long Revolution* (New York, 1961), and the interview about it in his *Politics and Letters: Interviews with New Left Review* (1979; London, 1981), pp. 133–74. I am grateful to Chun Lin for directing me to these texts.

23. On the integrative functions of "experience," see Judith Butler, *Gender Trouble: Feminism and the Subversion of Identity* (New York, 1990), pp. 22–25.

24. For a different reading of Thompson on experience, see William H. Sewell, Jr., "How Classes Are Made: Critical Reflections on E.P. Thompson's Theory of Working-class Formation," in *E.P. Thompson: Critical Debates,* ed. Harvey J. Kay and Keith McClelland (Philadelphia, 1990), pp. 50–77. I also have benefitted from Sylvia Schafer's "Writing about 'Experience': Workers and Historians Tormented by Industrialization," typescript.

25. Judith Newton, "History as Usual? Feminism and the 'New Historicism,' " *Cultural Critique* 9 (Spring 1988): 93.

26. Christine Stansell, "A Response to Joan Scott," *International Labor and Working-Class History,* no. 31 (Spring 1987): 28. Often this kind of invocation of experience leads back to the biological or physical "experience" of the body. See, for example, the arguments about rape and violence offered by Mary E. Hawkesworth, "Knowers, Knowing, Known: Feminist Theory and Claims of Truth," *Signs* 14 (Spring 1989): 533–57.

27. This is one of the meanings of the slogan "the personal is the political." Personal knowledge, that is, the experience of oppression is the source of resistance to it. This is what Mohanty calls "the feminist osmosis thesis: females are feminists by association and identification with the experiences which constitute us as female" (Mohanty, "Feminist Encounters: Locating the Politics of Experience," *Copyright* 1 [Fall 1987]: 32). See also an important article by Katie King, "The Situation of Lesbianism as Feminism's Magical Sign: Contests for Meaning and the U.S. Women's Movement, 1968–1972," *Communication* 9 (1986): 65–91.

28. Denise Riley, *"Am I That Name?" Feminism and the Category of Women in History* (Minneapolis, 1988), pp. 100, 99.

29. John E. Toews, "Intellectual History after the Linguistic Turn: The Autonomy of Meaning and the Irreducibility of Experience," *American Historical Review* 92 (Oct. 1987): 881; hereafter abbreviated "IH."

30. De Certeau puts in this way:

> That the particularity of the place where discourse is produced is relevant will be naturally more apparent where historiographical discourse treats matters that put the subject-producer of knowledge into question: the history of women, of blacks, of Jews, of cultural minorities, etc. In these fields one can, of course, either maintain that the personal status of the author is a matter of indifference (in relation to the objectivity of his or her work) or that he or she alone authorizes or invalidates the discourse (according to whether he or she is "of it" or not). But this debate requires what has been concealed by an epistemology, namely, the impact of subject-to-subject relationships (men and women, blacks and whites, etc.) on the use of apparently "neutral" techniques and in the organization of discourses that are, perhaps, equally scientific. For example, from the fact of the differentiation of the sexes, must one conclude that a woman produces a different historiography from that of a man? Of course, I do not answer this question, but I do assert that this interrogation puts the place of the subject in question and requires a treatment of it unlike the epistemology that constructed the "truth" of the work on the foundation of the speaker's irrelevance. ["H," pp. 217–18]

31. Here we have an example of what Foucault characterized as "continuous history": "the indispensable correlative of the founding function of the subject: the guarantee that everything that has eluded him may be restored to him; the certainty that time will disperse nothing without restoring it in reconstituted unity" (Michel Foucault, *The Archaeology of Knowledge,* trans. A.M. Sheridan Smith [New York, 1972], p. 12).

32. Ellen Rooney, *Seductive Reasoning: Pluralism as the Problematic of Contemporary Theory* (Ithaca, N.Y., 1989), p. 6.

33. Spivak, "A Literary Representation of the Subaltern: A Woman's Text from the Third World," *In Other Worlds,* p. 241.

34. Her argument is based on a set of oppositions between history and literature, male and female, identity and difference, practical politics and theory, and she repeatedly privileges the second set of terms. These polarities speak to the specifics of the debate she is engaged in with the (largely male) Subaltern Studies collective, historians working within a Marxist, especially Gramscian, frame.

35. Spivak, "Subaltern Studies: Deconstructing Historiography," *In Other Worlds,* p. 205. See also Spivak (with Rooney), "In a Word. *Interview,"* *differences* 1 (Summer 1989): 124–54, esp. p. 128. On essentialism, see Diana Fuss, *Essentially Speaking: Feminism, Nature and Difference* (New York, 1989).

36. Stuart Hall, "Minimal Selves," in *Identity: The Real Me,* p. 45. See also Barbara J. Fields, "Ideology and Race in American History," in *Region, Race, and Reconstruction: Essays in Honor of C. Vann Woodward,* ed. J. Morgan Kousser and James M. McPherson (New York, 1982), pp. 143–77. Fields's article is notable for its contradictions: the way, for example, that it historicizes race, naturalizes class, and refuses to talk at all about gender.

37. An excellent example of the historicizing of black women's "experience" is Hazel Carby's *Reconstructing Womanhood: The Emergence of the Afro-American Woman Novelist* (New York, 1987).

38. For discussions of how change operates within and across discourses, see James J. Bono, "Science, Discourse, and Literature: The Role/Rule of Metaphor in Science," in *Literature and Science: Theory and Practice,* ed. Stuart Peterfreund (Boston, 1990), pp. 59–89. See also, Mary Poovey, *Uneven Developments: The Ideological Work of Gender in Mid-Victorian England* (Chicago, 1988), pp. 1–23.

39. Parveen Adams and Jeff Minson, "The 'Subject' of Feminism," *m/f,* no. 2 (1978), p. 52. On the constitution of the subject, see Foucault, *The Archaeology of Knowledge,* pp. 95–96; Felicity A. Nussbaum, *The Autobiographical Subject: Gender and Ideology in Eighteenth-Century England* (Baltimore, 1989); and Peter de Bolla, *The Discourse of the Sublime: Readings in History, Aesthetics, and the Subject* (New York, 1989).

40. Karen Swann's comments on this paper were presented at the Little Three Faculty Colloquium on "The Social and Political Construction of Reality" at Wesleyan University in January 1991. The comments exist only in typescript.

41. See LaCapra, "Is Everyone a *Mentalité* Case? Transference and the 'Culture' Concept," *History and Criticism,* pp. 71–94.

42. Foucault, "Nietzsche, Genealogy, History," *Language, Counter-Memory, Practice: Selected Essays and Interviews,* trans. Donald F. Bouchard and Sherry Simon, ed. Bouchard (Ithaca, N.Y., 1977), pp. 151–52.

43. Ruth Roach Pierson, "Experience, Difference, and Dominance in the Writings of Women's History," typescript.

44. Conversations with Christopher Fynsk helped clarify these points for me.

45. For an important attempt to describe a poststructuralist history, see Peter de Bolla, "Disfiguring History," *Diacritics* 16 (Winter 1986): 49–58.

28

Is There a History of Sexuality?

David M. Halperin

David M. Halperin, Professor of Literature at the Massachusetts Institute of Technology and a co-editor of this volume, is a classicist, comparatist, and activist. He is the founder of the Lesbian/Gay Caucus of the American Philological Association, a founding editor of GLQ: A Journal of Lesbian and Gay Studies, and the series editor of "Ideologies of Desire" at Oxford University Press. In addition to his writings on Greek and Roman poetry, on Plato's erotic theory, and on various topics in modern literature and film, he is also the co-editor of Before Sexuality: The Construction of Erotic Experience in the Ancient Greek World *(1990) and the author of* One Hundred Years of Homosexuality *and other essays on* Greek Love *(Routledge, 1990). In the essay reprinted here, Halperin contends that the history of sexuality, in order to qualify as a genuinely historical enterprise, must treat sexuality not as a purely conceptual, and therefore timeless, category of historical analysis but as an object of historical scrutiny in its own right. The case of sexual relations between free males in the ancient Greek world provides a telling illustration of the need to historicize not only sexual attitudes and conventions but sexual orientation itself.*

Sex has no history.[1] It is a natural fact, grounded in the functioning of the body, and, as such, it lies outside of history and culture. Sexuality, by contrast, does not properly refer to some aspect or attribute of bodies. Unlike sex, sexuality is a cultural production: it represents the *appropriation* of the human body and of its physiological capacities by an ideological discourse.[2] Sexuality is not a somatic fact; it is a cultural effect. Sexuality, then, does have a history—though (as I shall argue) not a very long one.

To say that, of course, is not to state the obvious—despite the tone of assurance with which I just said it—but to advance a controversial, suspiciously fashionable, and, perhaps, a strongly counter-intuitive claim. The plausibility of such a claim might seem to rest on nothing more substantial than the prestige of the brilliant, pioneering, but largely theoretical work of the late French philosopher Michel Foucault.[3] According to Foucault, sexuality is not a thing, a natural fact, a fixed and immovable element in the eternal grammar of human subjectivity, but that "set of effects produced in bodies, behaviors, and social relations by a certain deployment" of "a complex political technology."[4] "Sexuality," Foucault insists in another passage,

> must not be thought of as a kind of natural given which power tries to hold in check, or as an obscure domain which knowledge tries gradually to uncover. It is the name that can be given to a historical construct [*dispositif*]: not a furtive reality that is difficult to grasp, but a great surface network in which the stimulation of bodies, the intensification of pleasures, the incitement to discourse, the formation of special knowl-

edges, the strengthening of controls and resistances, are linked to one another, in accordance with a few major strategies of knowledge and power.[5]

Is Foucault right? I believe he is, but I also believe that more is required to establish the historicity of sexuality than the mere weight of Foucault's authority. To be sure, a great deal of work, both conceptual and empirical, has already been done to sustain Foucault's central insights and to carry forward the historicist project that he did so much to advance.[6] But much more needs to be accomplished if we are to fill in the outlines of the picture that Foucault had time only to sketch—hastily and inadequately, as he was the first to admit[7]—and if we are to demonstrate that sexuality is indeed, as he claimed, a uniquely modern production.

The study of classical antiquity has a special role to play in this historical enterprise. The sheer interval of time separating the ancient from the modern world spans cultural changes of such magnitude that the contrasts to which they give rise cannot fail to strike anyone who is on the lookout for them. The student of classical antiquity is inevitably confronted in the ancient record by a radically unfamiliar set of values, behaviors, and social practices, by ways of organizing and articulating experience that challenge modern notions about what life is like, and that call into question the supposed universality of "human nature" as we currently understand it. Not only does this historical distance permit us to view ancient social and sexual conventions with particular sharpness; it also enables us to bring more clearly into focus the ideological dimension—the purely conventional and arbitrary character—of our own social and sexual experiences.[8] One of the currently unquestioned assumptions about sexual experience which the study of antiquity calls into question is the assumption that sexual behavior reflects or expresses an individual's "sexuality."

Now that would seem to be a relatively harmless and unproblematic assumption to make, empty of all ideological content, but what exactly do we have in mind when we make it? What, in particular, do we understand by our concept of "sexuality"? I think we understand "sexuality" to refer to a positive, distinct, and constitutive feature of the human personality, to the characterological seat within the individual of sexual acts, desires, and pleasures—the determinate source from which all sexual expression proceeds. "Sexuality" in this sense is not a purely descriptive term, a neutral representation of some objective state of affairs or a simple recognition of some familiar facts about us; rather, it is a distinctive way of constructing, organizing, and interpreting those "facts," and it performs quite a lot of conceptual work.

First of all, sexuality defines itself as a separate, sexual domain within the larger field of human psychophysical nature. Second, sexuality effects the conceptual demarcation and isolation of that domain from other areas of personal and social life that have traditionally cut across it, such as carnality, venery, libertinism, virility, passion, amorousness, eroticism, intimacy, love, affection, appetite, and desire—to name but a few of the older claimants to territories more recently staked out by sexuality. Finally, sexuality generates sexual identity: it endows each of us with an individual sexual nature, with a personal essence defined (at least in part) in specifically sexual terms; it implies that human beings are individuated at the level of their sexuality, that they differ from one another in their sexuality and, indeed, belong to different types or kinds of being by virtue of their sexuality.

These, at least, appear to me to be some of the significant ramifications of "sexuality," as it is currently conceptualized. I shall argue that the outlook it represents is alien to the recorded experience of the ancients. Two themes, in particular, that seem intrinsic to the modern conceptualization of sexuality but that hardly find an echo in ancient sources will provide the focus of my investigation: the autonomy of sexuality as a separate sphere of existence (deeply implicated in other areas of life, to be sure, but distinct from them and capable of acting on them at least as much as it is acted on by them), and the function of sexuality as a principle of individuation in human natures. In what follows, I shall take up each theme in turn, attempting to document in this fashion the extent of the divergence between ancient and modern varieties of sexual experience.

First, the autonomy of sexuality as a separate sphere of existence. The basic point I should like to make has already been made for me by Robert Padgug in a now-classic essay on conceptualizing sexuality in history. Padgug argues that

> what we consider "sexuality" was, in the pre-bourgeois world, a group of acts and institutions not necessarily linked to one another, or, if they were linked, combined in ways very different from our own. Intercourse, kinship, and the family, and gender, did not form anything like a "field" of sexuality. Rather, each group of sexual acts was connected directly or indirectly—that is, formed part of—institutions and thought patterns which we tend to view as political, economic, or social in nature, and the connections cut across our idea of sexuality as a thing, detachable from other things, and as a separate sphere of private existence.[9]

The ancient evidence amply supports Padgug's claim. In classical Athens, for example, sex did not express inward dispositions or inclinations so much as it served to position social actors in the places assigned to them, by virtue of their political standing, in the hierarchical structure of the Athenian polity. Let me expand this formulation.

In classical Athens a relatively small group made up of the adult male citizens held a virtual monopoly of social power and constituted a clearly defined élite within the political and social life of the city-state. The predominant feature of the social landscape of classical Athens was the great divide in status between this superordinate group, composed of citizens, and a subordinate group, composed of women, children, foreigners, and slaves—all of whom lacked full civil rights (though they were not all equally subordinate). Sexual relations not only respected that divide but were strictly polarized in conformity with it.

Sex is portrayed in Athenian documents not as a mutual enterprise in which two or more persons jointly engage but as an action performed by a social superior upon a social inferior. Consisting as it was held to do in an asymmetrical gesture—the penetration of the body of one person by the body (and, specifically, by the phallus)[10] of another—sex effectively divided and distributed its participants into radically distinct and incommensurable categories ("penetrator" versus "penetrated"), categories which in turn were wholly congruent with superordinate and subordinate social categories. For sexual penetration was thematized as domination: the relation between the insertive and the receptive sexual partner was taken to be the same kind of relation as that obtaining between social superior and social inferior.[11] Insertive and receptive sexual roles were therefore necessarily isomorphic with superordinate and subordinate social status; an adult, male citizen of Athens could have legitimate sexual relations *only* with statutory minors (his inferiors not in age but in social and political status): the proper targets of his sexual desire included, specifically, women of any age, free males past the age of puberty who were not yet old enough to be citizens (I'll call them "boys," for short), as well as foreigners and slaves of either sex.[12]

Moreover, the physical act of sex between a citizen and a statutory minor was stylized in such a way as to mirror in the minute details of its hierarchical arrangement the relation of structured inequality that governed the wider social interaction of the two lovers. What an Athenian did in bed was determined by the differential in status that distinguished him or her from his or her sexual partner; the (male) citizen's superior prestige and authority expressed themselves in his sexual precedence—in his power to initiate a sexual act, his right to obtain pleasure from it, and his assumption of an insertive rather than a receptive sexual role. Different social actors had different sexual roles: to assimilate both the superordinate and the subordinate member of a sexual relationship to the same "sexuality" would have been as bizarre, in Athenian eyes, as classifying a burglar as an "active criminal," his victim as a "passive criminal," and the two of them alike as partners in crime—it would have been to confuse what, in reality, were supposedly separate and distinct identities.[13] Each act of sex was no doubt an expression of real, personal desire on the part of the sexual actors involved, but their very desires had already been shaped by the shared cultural definition of sex as an activity that generally occurred only between a citizen and a non-citizen, between a person invested with full civil status and a statutory minor.

The "sexuality" of the classical Athenians, then, far from being independent of "politics" (each construed as an autonomous sphere) *was constituted by the very principles* on which Athenian public life was organized. In fact, the correspondences in classical Athens between sexual norms and social practices were so strict that an inquiry into Athenian "sexuality" *per se* would be nonsensical: such an inquiry could only obscure the phenomenon it was intended to elucidate, for it would conceal the sole context in which the sexual protocols of the classical Athenians make any sense—namely, the structure of the Athenian polity. The social articulation of sexual desire in classical Athens thus furnishes a telling illustration of the interdependence in culture of social practices and subjective experiences. Indeed, the classical Greek record strongly supports the conclusion drawn (from a quite different body of evidence) by the French anthropologist Maurice Godelier: "it is not sexuality which haunts society, but society which haunts the body's sexuality."[14]

For those inhabitants of the ancient world about whom it is possible to generalize, sexuality did not hold the key to the secrets of the human personality. (In fact, the very concept of and set of practices centering on "the human personality"—the physical and social sciences of the blank individual—belong to a much later era and bespeak the modern social and economic conditions that accompanied their rise.) In the Hellenic world, by contrast, the measure of a free male was most often taken by observing how he fared when tested in public competition against other free males, not by scrutinizing his sexual constitution. War (and other agonistic contests), not love, served to reveal the inner man, the stuff a free Greek male was made of.[15] A striking instance of this emphasis on public life as the primary locus of signification can be found in the work of Artemidorus, a master dream-interpreter who lived and wrote in the second century of our era and whose testimony, there is good reason to believe, accurately represents the sexual norms of ancient Mediterranean culture.[16] Artemidorus saw public life, not erotic life, as the principal tenor of dreams. Even sexual dreams, in Artemidorus's system, are seldom *really* about sex: rather, they are about the rise and fall of the dreamer's public fortunes, the vicissitudes of his domestic economy.[17] If a man dreams of having sex with his mother, for example, his dream signifies to Artemidorus nothing in particular about the dreamer's own sexual psychology, his fantasy life, or the history of his relations with his parents; it's a very common dream, and so it's a bit tricky to interpret precisely, but basically it's a lucky dream: it may signify—depending on the family's circumstances at the time, the postures of the partners in the dream, and the mode of penetration—that the dreamer will be successful in politics ("success" meaning, evidently, the power to screw one's country), that he will go into exile or return from exile, that he will win his lawsuit, obtain a rich harvest from his lands, or change professions, among many other things (1.79). Artemidorus's system of dream interpretation resembles the indigenous dream-lore of certain Amazonian tribes who, despite their quite different sociosexual systems, share with the ancient Greeks a belief in the predictive value of dreams. Like Artemidorus, these Amazonian peoples reverse what modern bourgeois Westerners take to be the natural flow of signification in dreams (from images of public and social events to private and sexual meanings): in both Kagwahiv and Mehinaku culture, for example, dreaming about the female genitalia portends a wound (and so a man who has such a dream is especially careful when he handles axes or other sharp instruments the next day); dreamt wounds do not symbolize the female genitalia.[18] Both these ancient and modern dream-interpreters, then, are innocent of "sexuality": what is fundamental to their experience of sex is not anything *we* would regard as essentially sexual;[19] it is instead something essentially outward, public, and social. "Sexuality," for cultures not shaped by some very recent European and American bourgeois developments, is not a cause but an effect. The social body precedes the sexual body.

I now come to the second of my two themes—namely, the individuating function of sexuality, its role in generating individual sexual identities. The connection between the modern interpretation of sexuality as an autonomous domain and the modern construction of individual sexual identities has been well analyzed, once again, by Robert Padgug:

> the most commonly held twentieth-century assumptions about sexuality imply that it is a separate category of existence (like "the economy," or "the state," other supposedly independent spheres of reality), almost identical with the sphere of private life. Such a view necessitates the location of sexuality within the individual as a fixed essence, leading to a classic division of individual and society and to a variety of psychological determinisms, and, often enough, to a full-blown biological determinism as well. These in turn involve the enshrinement of contemporary sexual categories as universal, static, and permanent, suitable for the analysis of all human beings and all societies.[20]

The study of ancient Mediterranean societies clearly exposes the defects in any such essentialist conceptualization of sexuality. Because, as we have seen in the case of classical Athens, erotic desires and sexual object-choices in antiquity were generally not determined by a typology of anatomical sexes (male versus female), but rather by the social articulation of power (superordinate versus subordinate), the currently fashionable distinction between homosexuality and heterosexuality (and, similarly, between "homosexuals" and "heterosexuals" as individual types) had no meaning for the classical Athenians: there were not, so far as they knew, two different kinds of "sexuality," two differently structured psychosexual states or modes of affective orientation, but a single form of sexual experience which all free adult males shared—making due allowance for variations in individual tastes, as one might make for individual palates.[21]

Thus, in the Third Dithyramb by the classical poet Bacchylides, the Athenian hero Theseus, voyaging to Crete among the seven youths and seven maidens destined for the Minotaur and defending one of the maidens from the advances of the libidinous Cretan commander, warns him vehemently against molesting *any one* of the Athenian youths (*tin' ēïtheôn:* 43)—that is, any girl *or* boy. Conversely, the antiquarian *littérateur* Athenaeus, writing six or seven hundred years later, is amazed that Polycrates, the tyrant of Samos in the sixth century B.C., did not send for any boys *or women* along with the other luxury articles he imported to Samos for his personal use during his reign, "despite his passion for relations with males" (12.540c–e).[22] Now *both* the notion that an act of heterosexual aggression in itself makes the aggressor suspect of homosexual tendencies *and* the mirror-opposite notion that a person with marked homosexual tendencies is bound to hanker after heterosexual contacts are nonsensical to us, associating as we do sexual object-choice with a determinate kind of "sexuality," a fixed sexual nature, but it would be a monumental task indeed to enumerate all the ancient documents in which the alternative "boy or woman" occurs with perfect nonchalance in an erotic context, as if the two were functionally interchangeable.[23]

A particularly striking testimony to the imaginable extent of male indifference to the sex of sexual objects can be found in a marriage-contract from Hellenistic Egypt dating to 92 B.C.[24] This not untypical document stipulates that "it shall not be lawful for Philiscus [the prospective husband] to bring home another wife in addition to Apollonia or to have a concubine *or boy-lover.* . . ."[25] The possibility that one's husband might take it into his head at some point during one's marriage to set up another household with his boyfriend evidently figured among the various potential domestic disasters that a prudent fiancée would be sure to anticipate and to indemnify herself against. A somewhat similar expectation is articulated in an entirely different context by Dio Chrysostom, a moralizing Greek orator from the late first century A.D. In a speech denouncing the corrupt morals of city life, Dio asserts that even respectable women are so easy to seduce nowadays that men will soon tire of them and will turn their attention to boys instead—just as addicts progress inexorably from wine to hard drugs (7.150–152). According to Dio, then, paederasty is not simply a second best; it is not "caused," as many modern historians of the ancient Mediterranean appear to believe, by the supposed seclusion of women, by the practice (it was more likely an ideal) of locking them away in the inner rooms of their fathers' or husbands' houses and thereby preventing them from serving as sexual targets for adult men. In Dio's fantasy, at least, paederasty springs not from the insufficient but from the superabundant supply of sexually available women; the easier it is to have sex with women, on his view, the less desirable sex with women becomes, and the more likely men are to seek sexual pleasure with boys. Scholars sometimes describe the cultural formation underlying this apparent refusal by Greek males to discriminate categorically among sexual objects on the basis of anatomical sex as a bisexuality of penetration[26] or—even more intriguingly—as a heterosexuality indifferent to its object,[27] but I think it would be advisable not to speak of it as a sexuality at all but to describe it, rather, as a more generalized ethos of penetration and domination,[28] a sociosexual discourse structured by the presence or absence of its central term: the phallus.[29] It may be worth pausing now to examine one text in particular which clearly indicates how thoroughly ancient cultures were able to dispense with the notion of sexual identity.

The document in question is the ninth chapter in the Fourth Book of the *De morbis chronicis,* a mid-fifth-century A.D. Latin translation and adaptation by the African writer Caelius Aurelianus of a now largely lost work on chronic diseases by the Greek physician Soranus, who practiced and taught in Rome during the early part of the second century A.D. Caelius's work is not much read nowadays, and it is almost entirely neglected by modern historians of "sexuality";[30] its date is late, its text is corrupt, and, far from being a self-conscious literary artifact, it belongs to the despised genre of Roman technical writing. But, despite all these drawbacks, it repays close attention, and I have chosen to discuss it here partly in order to show what can be learned about the ancient world from works that lie outside the received canon of classical authors.

The topic of this passage is *molles* (*malthakoi* in Greek)—that is, "soft" or unmasculine men, men who depart from the cultural norm of manliness insofar as they actively desire to be subjected by other men to a "feminine" (that is, receptive) role in sexual intercourse.[31] Caelius begins with an implicit defense of his own unimpeachable masculinity by noting how difficult it is to believe that such people actually exist;[32] he then goes on to observe that the cause of their affliction is not natural (that is, organic) but is rather their own excessive desire, which—in a desperate and foredoomed attempt to satisfy itself—drives out their sense of shame and forcibly converts parts of their bodies to sexual uses not intended by nature. These men willingly adopt the dress, gait, and other characteristics of women, thereby confirming that they suffer not from a bodily disease but from a mental (or moral) defect. After some further arguments in support of that point, Caelius draws an interesting comparison: "For just as the women called *tribades* [in Greek], because they practice both kinds of sex, are more eager to have sexual intercourse with women than with men and pursue women with an almost masculine jealousy . . . so they too [i.e., the *molles*] are afflicted by a mental disease" (132–133). The mental disease in question, which strikes both men and women alike and seems to be defined as a perversion of sexual desire, would certainly appear to be nothing other than homosexuality as it is often understood today.

Several considerations combine to prohibit that interpretation, however. First of all, what Caelius treats as a pathological phenomenon is not the desire on the part of either men or women for sexual contact with a person of the same sex; quite the contrary: elsewhere, in discussing the treatment of satyriasis (a state of abnormally elevated sexual desire accompanied by itching or tension in the genitals), he issues the following advice to those who suffer from it (*De morbis acutis*, 3.18.180–181).[33]

> Do not admit visitors and particularly young women and boys. For the attractiveness of such visitors would again kindle the feeling of desire in the patient. Indeed, *even healthy persons,* seeing them, would in many cases seek sexual gratification, stimulated by the tension produced in the parts [i.e., in their own genitals].[34]

There is nothing medically problematical, then, about a desire on the part of males to obtain sexual pleasure from contact with males—so long as the proper phallocentric protocols are observed; what is of concern to Caelius,[35] as well as to other ancient moralists,[36] is the male desire to be sexually penetrated by males, for such a desire represents a voluntary abandonment of the culturally constructed masculine identity in favor of the culturally constructed feminine one. It is sex-role reversal, or gender-deviance, that is problematized here and that also furnishes part of the basis for Caelius's comparison of unmasculine men to masculine women, who assume a supposedly masculine role in their relations with other women and actively "pursue women with an almost *masculine* jealousy."

Moreover, the ground of the similitude between these male and female gender-deviants is not that they are both homosexual but rather that they are both *bisexual* (in our terms), although in that respect at least they do not depart from the ancient sexual norm. The tribads "are [*relatively*] more eager to have sexual intercourse with women *than with men*" and "practice both kinds of sex"—that is, they have sex with both men and women.[37] As for the *molles,* Caelius's earlier remarks about their extraordinarily intense sexual desire implies that they turn to receptive sex because, although they try, they are not able to satisfy themselves by means of more conventionally masculine sorts of sexual activity, including insertive sex with women.[38] Far from having desires that are structured differently from those of normal folk, these gender-deviants desire sexual pleasure just as most people do, but they have such strong and intense desires that they are driven to devise some unusual and disreputable (though ultimately futile) ways of gratifying them. This diagnosis becomes explicit at the conclusion of the chapter when

Caelius explains why the disease responsible for turning men into *molles* is the only chronic disease that becomes stronger as the body grows older.

> For in other years when the body is still strong and can perform the normal functions of love, the sexual desire [of these persons] assumes a dual aspect, in which the soul is excited sometimes while playing a passive and sometimes while playing an active role. But in the case of old men who have lost their virile powers, all their sexual desire is turned in the opposite direction and consequently exerts a stronger demand for the feminine role in love. In fact, many infer that this is the reason why boys too are victims of this affliction. For, like old men, they do not possess virile powers; that is, they have not yet attained those powers which have already deserted the aged. [137][39]

"Soft" or unmasculine men, far from being a fixed and determinate sexual species with a specifically sexual identity, are evidently either men who once experienced an orthodoxly masculine sexual desire in the past or who will eventually experience such a desire in the future. They may well be men with a constitutional tendency to gender-deviance, according to Caelius, but they are not homosexuals: being a womanish man, or a mannish woman, after all, is not the same thing as being a homosexual. Furthermore, all the other ancient texts known to me, which assimilate both males who enjoy sexual contact with males and females who enjoy sexual contact with females to the same category, do so—in conformity with the two taxonomic strategies employed by Caelius Aurelianus—either because such males and females both *reverse* their proper sex-roles and adopt the sexual styles, postures, and modes of copulation conventionally associated with the opposite gender, or because they both *alternate* between the personal characteristics and sexual practices proper, respectively, to men and to women.[40]

Caelius's testimony makes an important historical point. Before the scientific construction of "sexuality" as a positive, distinct, and constitutive feature of individual human beings—an autonomous system within the physiological and psychological economy of the human organism—certain kinds of sexual *acts* could be individually evaluated and categorized, and so could certain sexual tastes or inclinations, but there was no conceptual apparatus available for identifying a person's fixed and determinate sexual *orientation,* much less for assessing and classifying it.[41] That human beings differ, often markedly, from one another in their sexual tastes in a great variety of ways (including sexual object-choice), is an unexceptionable and, indeed, an ancient observation[42]: Plato's Aristophanes invents a myth to explain why some men like women, why some men like boys, why some women like men, and why some women like women (*Symposium* 189c–193d). But it is not immediately evident that patterns of sexual object-choice are by their very nature more revealing about the temperament of individual human beings, more significant determinants of personal *identity,* than, for example, patterns of dietary object-choice.[43] And yet, it would never occur to us to refer a person's dietary preference to some innate, characterological disposition,[44] to see in his or her strongly expressed and even unvarying preference for the white meat of chicken the symptom of a profound psychophysical orientation, leading us to identify him or her in contexts quite removed from that of the eating of food as, say, a "pectoriphage" or a "stethovore"; nor would we be likely to inquire further, making nicer discriminations according to whether an individual's predilection for chicken breasts expressed itself in a tendency to eat them quickly or slowly, seldom or often, alone or in company, under normal circumstances or only in periods of great stress, with a clear or a guilty conscience ("ego-dystonic pectoriphagia"), beginning in earliest childhood or originating with a gastronomic trauma suffered in adolescence. If such questions did occur to us, moreover, I very much doubt whether we would turn to the academic disciplines of anatomy, neurology, clinical psychology, genetics, or sociobiology in the hope of obtaining a clear causal solution to them. That is because (1) we regard the liking for certain foods as a matter of taste; (2) we currently lack a theory of taste; and (3) in the absence of a theory we do not normally subject our behavior to intense, scientific or aetiological, scrutiny.

In the same way, it never occurred to the ancients to ascribe a person's sexual tastes to some positive, structural, or constitutive sexual feature of his or her personality. Just as we tend to assume that human beings are not individuated at the level of dietary preference and that we all, despite many pronounced and frankly acknowledged differences from one another in dietary habits, share the same fundamental set of alimentary appetites, and hence the same "dieticity" or "edility," so most premodern and non-Western cultures, despite an awareness of the range of possible variations in human sexual behavior, refuse to individuate human beings at the level of sexual preference and assume, instead, that we all share the same fundamental set of sexual appetites, the same "sexuality." For most of the world's inhabitants, in other words, "sexuality" is no more a "fact of life" than "dieticity." Far from being a necessary or intrinsic constituent of human life, "sexuality" seems indeed to be a uniquely modern, Western, even bourgeois production—one of those cultural fictions which in every society give human beings access to themselves as meaningful actors in their world, and which are thereby objectivated.

If there is a lesson that we should draw from this picture of ancient sexual attitudes and behaviors, it is that we need to de-center *sexuality* from the focus of the cultural interpretation of sexual experience—and not only ancient varieties of sexual experience. Just because modern bourgeois Westerners are so obsessed with sexuality, so convinced that it holds the key to the hermeneutics of the self (and hence to social psychology as an object of historical study), we ought not therefore to conclude that everyone has always considered sexuality a basic and irreducible element in, or a central feature of, human life. Indeed, there are even sectors of our own societies to which the ideology of "sexuality" has failed to penetrate. A sociosexual system that coincides with the Greek system, insofar as it features a rigid hierarchy of sexual roles based on a set of socially articulated power-relations, has been documented in contemporary America by Jack Abbott, in one of his infamous letters written to Norman Mailer from a federal penitentiary; because the text is now quite inaccessible (it was not reprinted in Abbott's book), and stunningly apropos, I have decided to quote it here at length.

> It really was years, many years, before I began to actually realize that the women in my life—the prostitutes as well as the soft, pretty girls who giggled and teased me so much, my several wives and those of my friends—it was years before I realized that they were not women, but men; years before I assimilated the notion that this was unnatural. I still only know this intellectually, for the most part—but for the small part that remains to my ken, I know it is like a hammer blow to my temple and the shame I feel is profound. Not because of the thing itself, the sexual love I have enjoyed with these women (some so devoted it aches to recall it), but because of shame—and anger—that the world could so intimately betray me; so profoundly touch and move me—and then laugh at me and accuse my soul of a sickness, when that sickness has rescued me from mental derangement and despairs so black as to cast this night that surrounds us in prison into day. I do not mean to say I never knew the physical difference—no one but an imbecile could make such a claim. I took it, without reflection or the slightest doubt, that this was a natural sex that emerged within the society of men, with attributes that naturally complemented masculine attributes. I thought it was a natural phenomenon in the society of women as well. The attributes were feminine and so there seemed no gross misrepresentation of facts

to call them (among us men) "women." . . . Many of my "women" had merely the appearance of handsome, extremely neat, and polite young men. I have learned, analyzing my feelings today, that those attributes I called feminine a moment ago were not feminine in any way as it appears in the real female sex. These attributes seem now merely a tendency to need, to depend on another man; to need never to become a rival or to compete with other men in the pursuits men, among themselves, engage in. It was, it occurs to me now, almost boyish—not really feminine at all.

This is the way it always was, even in the State Industrial School for Boys—a penal institution for juvenile delinquents—where I served five years, from age twelve to age seventeen. They were the possession and sign of manhood and it never occurred to any of us that this was strange and unnatural. It is how I grew up—a natural part of my life in prison.

It was difficult for me to grasp the definition of the clinical term "homosexual"—and when I finally did it devastated me, as I said.[45]

Abbott's society surpasses classical Athenian society in the extent to which power relations are gendered. Instead of the Greek system which preserves the distinction between males and females but overrides it when articulating categories of the desirable and undesirable in favor of a distinction between dominant and submissive persons, the system described by Abbott wholly assimilates categories of sociosexual identity to categories of gender identity—in order, no doubt, to preserve the association in Abbott's world between "masculinity" and the love of "women." What determines gender, for Abbott, is not anatomical sex but social status and personal style. "Men" are defined as those who "compete with other men in the pursuits men, among themselves, engage in," whereas "women" are characterized by the possession of "attributes that naturally complement masculine attributes"—namely, a "tendency to need, to depend on another man" for the various benefits won by the victors in "male" competition. In this way "a natural sex emerges within the society of men" and qualifies, by virtue of its exclusion from the domain of "male" precedence and autonomy, as a legitimate target of "male" desire.

The salient features of Abbott's society are uncannily reminiscent of those features of classical Athenian society with which we are already familiar. Most notable is the division of the society into superordinate and subordinate groups and *the production of desire* for members of the subordinate group in members of the superordinate one. Desire is sparked in this system, as in classical Athens, only when it arcs across the political divide, only when it traverses the boundary that marks out the limits of intramural competition among the élite and that thereby distinguishes subjects from objects of sexual desire. Sex between "men"—and, therefore, "homosexuality"—remains unthinkable in Abbott's society (even though sex between anatomical males is an accepted and intrinsic part of the system), just as sex between citizens, between members of the empowered social caste, is practically inconceivable in classical Athenian society. Similarly, sex between "men" and "women" in Abbott's world is not a private experience in which social identities are lost or submerged; rather, in Abbott's society as in classical Athens, the act of sex—instead of implicating both sexual partners in a common "sexuality"—helps to articulate, to define, and to actualize the differences in status between them.

To discover and to write the history of sexuality has long seemed to many a sufficiently radical undertaking in itself, inasmuch as its effect (if not always the intention behind it) is to call into question the very naturalness of what we currently take to be essential to our individual natures. But in the course of implementing that ostensibly radical project many historians of sexuality seem to have reversed—perhaps unwittingly—its radical design: by preserving "sexuality" as a stable category of historical analysis not only have they not denaturalized it but, on the contrary, they have newly idealized it.[46] To the extent, in fact, that histories of "sexuality" succeed in concerning themselves with *sexuality*, to just that extent are they doomed to fail as *histories* (Foucault himself taught us that much), unless they also include as an essential part of their proper enterprise the task of demonstrating the historicity, conditions of emergence, modes of construction, and ideological contingencies of the very categories of analysis that undergird their own practice.[47] Instead of concentrating our attention specifically on the history of sexuality, then, we need to define and refine a new, and radical, historical sociology of psychology, an intellectual discipline designed to analyze the cultural poetics of desire, by which I mean the processes whereby sexual desires are constructed, mass-produced, and distributed among the various members of human living-groups.[48] We must train ourselves to recognize conventions of feeling as well as conventions of behavior and to interpret the intricate texture of personal life as an artifact, as the determinate outcome, of a complex and arbitrary constellation of cultural processes. We must, in short, be willing to admit that what seem to be our most inward, authentic, and private experiences are actually, in Adrienne Rich's admirable phrase, "shared, unnecessary/and political."[49]

A little less than fifty years ago W.H. Auden asked, in the opening lines of a canzone, "When shall we learn, what should be clear as day, We cannot choose what we are free to love?"[50] It is a characteristically judicious formulation: love, if it is to be love, must be a free act, but it is also inscribed within a larger circle of constraint, within conditions that make possible the exercise of that "freedom." The task of distinguishing freedom from constraint in love, of learning to trace the shifting and uncertain boundaries between the self and the world, is a dizzying and, indeed, an endless undertaking. If I have not significantly advanced this project here, I hope at least to have encouraged others not to abandon it.

NOTES

Most of the material contained in this article appears, in slightly different form, in the title essay of my collection, *One Hundred Years of Homosexuality and Other Essays on Greek Love* (New York: Routledge, 1989), or in the Editors' Introduction to *Before Sexuality: The Construction of Erotic Experience in the Ancient Greek World,* ed. David M. Halperin, John J. Winkler, and Froma I. Zeitlin (Princeton, 1990).

1. Or, if it does, that history is a matter for the evolutionary biologist, not for the historian; see Lynn Margulis and Dorion Sagan, *The Origins of Sex* (New Haven, 1985).

2. I adapt this formulation from a passage in Louis Adrian Montrose, " 'Shaping Fantasies': Figurations of Gender and Power in Elizabethan Culture," *Representations* 2 (1983), 61–94 (passage on p. 62), which describes in turn the concept of the "sex/gender system" introduced by Gayle Rubin, "The Traffic in Women: Notes on the 'Political Economy' of Sex," in *Toward an Anthropology of Women,* ed. Rayna R. Reiter (New York, 1975), 157–210.

3. Volumes Two and Three of Foucault's *History of Sexuality,* published shortly before his death, depart significantly from the theoretical orientation of his earlier work in favor of a more concrete interpretative practice; see my remarks in "Two Views of Greek Love: Harald Patzer and Michel Foucault," *One Hundred Years of Homosexuality,* 62–71, esp. 64.

4. Michel Foucault, *The History of Sexuality, Volume I: An Introduction,* transl. Robert Hurley (New York, 1978), 127. See Teresa de Lauretis, *Technologies of Gender: Essays on Theory, Film, and Fiction* (Bloomington, 1987), 1–30, esp. 3, who extends Foucault's critique of sexuality to gender.

5. Foucault, *The History of Sexuality,* 105–106.

6. Of special relevance are: Robert A. Padgug, "Sexual Matters: On Conceptualizing Sexuality in History," *Radical History Review* 20 (1979), 3–23; George Chauncey, Jr., "From Sexual Inversion to Homosexuality: Medicine and the Changing Conceptualization of Female Deviance," in *Homosexuality: Sacrilege, Vision, Politics,* ed. Robert Boyers and George Steiner = *Salmagundi* 58–59 (1982–1983), 114–146; Arnold I. Davidson, "Sex and the Emergence of Sexuality," *Critical*

Inquiry 14 (1987–1988), 16–48. See also *The Cultural Construction of Sexuality,* ed. Pat Caplan (London, 1987); T. Dunbar Moodie, "Migrancy and Male Sexuality on the Southern African Gold Mines," *Journal of Southern African Studies* 14 (1987–1988), 228–256; George Chauncey, Jr., "Christian Brotherhood or Sexual Perversion? Homosexual Identities and the Construction of Sexual Boundaries in the World War One Era," *Journal of Social History* 19 (1985–1986), 189–211.

7. E.g., Michel Foucault, *The Use of Pleasure: The History of Sexuality, Volume Two,* transl. Robert Hurley (New York, 1985), 92, 253.

8. In applying the term "ideological" to sexual experience, I have been influenced by the formulation of Stuart Hall, "Culture, the Media, and the 'Ideological Effect,' " in *Mass Communication and Society,* ed. James Curran, Michael Gurevitch, Janet Woolacott, *et al.* (London, 1977), 315–348, esp. 330: "ideology as a *social practice* consists of the 'subject' positioning himself in the specific complex, the objectivated field of discourses and codes which are available to him in language and culture at a particular historical conjuncture" (quoted by Ken Tucker and Andrew Treno, "The Culture of Narcissism and the Critical Tradition: An Interpretative Essay," *Berkeley Journal of Sociology* 25 [1980], 341–355 [quotation on p. 351]); see also Hall's trenchant discussion of the constitutive role of ideology in "Deviance, Politics, and the Media," in *Deviance and Social Control,* ed. Paul Rock and Mary McIntosh, Explorations in Sociology 3 (London, 1974), 261–305, and reprinted in this volume.

9. Padgug, 16.

10. I say "phallus" rather than "penis" because (1) what qualifies as a phallus in this discursive system does not always turn out to be a penis (see note 29, below) and (2) even when phallus and penis have the same extension, or reference, they still do not have the same intension, or meaning: "phallus" betokens not a specific item of the male anatomy *simpliciter* but that same item *taken under the description* of a cultural signifier; (3) hence, the meaning of "phallus" is ultimately determined by its function in the larger sociosexual discourse; i.e., it is that which penetrates, that which enables its possessor to play an "active" sexual role, and so forth: see Rubin, 190–192.

11. Foucault, *The Use of Pleasure,* 215, puts it very well: "sexual relations—always conceived in terms of the model act of penetration, assuming a polarity that opposed activity and passivity—were seen as being of the same type as the relationship between a superior and a subordinate, an individual who dominates and one who is dominated, one who commands and one who complies, one who vanquishes and one who is vanquished."

12. In order to avoid misunderstanding, I should emphasize that by calling all persons belonging to these four groups "statutory minors," I do not wish either to suggest that they enjoyed the *same* status as one another or to obscure the many differences in status that could obtain between members of a single group—e.g., between a wife and a courtesan—differences that may not have been perfectly isomorphic with the legitimate modes of their sexual use. Nonetheless, what is striking about Athenian social usage is the tendency to collapse such distinctions as did indeed obtain between different categories of social subordinates and to create a single opposition between them all, *en masse,* and the class of adult male citizens: on this point, see Mark Golden, "*Pais,* 'Child' and 'Slave,' " *L'Antiquité classique* 54 (1985), 91–104, esp. 101 and 102, n. 38.

13. I have borrowed this analogy from Arno Schmitt, who uses it to convey what the modern sexual categories would look like from a traditional Islamic perspective: see Gianni De Martino and Arno Schmitt, *Kleine Schriften zu zwischenmännlicher Sexualität und Erotik in der muslimischen Gesellschaft* (Berlin, 1985), 19. Note that even the category of anatomical sex, defined in such a way as to include both men and women, seems to be absent from Greek thought for similar reasons: the complementarity of men and women as sexual partners implies to the Greeks a polarity, a difference in species, too extreme to be bridged by a single sexual concept equally applicable to each. In Greek medical writings, therefore, "the notion of sex never gets formalized as a functional identity of male and female, but is expressed solely through the representation of asymmetry and of complementarity between male and female, indicated constantly by abstract adjectives (*to thêly* ['the feminine'], *to arren* ['the masculine'])," according to Paola Manuli, "Donne mascoline, femmine sterili, vergini perpetue: La ginecologia greca tra Ippocrate e Sorano," in Silvia Campese, Paola Manuli, and Giulia Sissa, *Madre materia: Sociologia e biologia della donna greca* (Turin, 1983), 147–192, esp. 151 and 201n.

14. Maurice Godelier, "The Origins of Male Domination," *New Left Review* 127 (May–June, 1981), 3–17 (quotation on p. 17); cf. Maurice Godelier, "Le sexe comme fondement ultime de l'ordre social et cosmique chez les Baruya de Nouvelle-Guinée. Mythe et réalité," in *Sexualité et pouvoir,* ed. Armando Verdiglione (Paris, 1976), 268–306, esp. 295–296.

15. I am indebted for this observation to Professor Peter M. Smith of the University of North Carolina at Chapel Hill, who notes that Sappho and Plato are the chief exceptions to this general rule.

16. See John J. Winkler, "Unnatural Acts: Erotic Protocols in Artemidoros' *Dream Analysis,*" *Constraints of Desire: The Anthropology of Sex and Gender in Ancient Greece* (New York, 1989), 17–44, 221–224.

17. S.R.F. Price, "The Future of Dreams: From Freud to Artemidorus," *Past and Present* 113 (November, 1986), 3–37, abridged in *Before Sexuality: The Construction of Erotic Experience in the Ancient Greek World,* ed. David M. Halperin, John J. Winkler, and Froma I. Zeitlin (Princeton, 1990), 365–387; see also Michel Foucault, *The Care of the Self,* The History of Sexuality, Volume Three, transl. Robert Hurley (New York, 1986), 3–36, esp. 26–34.

18. See Waud H. Kracke, "Dreaming in Kagwahiv: Dream Beliefs and Their Psychic Uses in an Amazonian Indian Culture," *The Psychoanalytic Study of Society* 8 (1979), 119–171, esp. 130–132, 163 (on the predictive value of dreams) and 130–131, 142–145, 163–164, 168 (on the reversal of the Freudian direction of signification—which Kracke takes to be a culturally constituted defense mechanism and which he accordingly undervalues); Thomas Gregor, " 'Far, Far Away My Shadow Wandered . . .': The Dream Symbolism and Dream Theories of the Mehinaku Indians of Brazil," *American Ethnologist* 8 (1981), 709–720, esp. 712–713 (on predictive value) and 714 (on the reversal of signification), largely recapitulated in Thomas Gregor, *Anxious Pleasures: The Sexual Lives of an Amazonian People* (Chicago, 1985), 152–161, esp. 153. Foucault's comments on Artemidorus, in *The Care of the Self,* 35–36, are relevant here: "The movement of analysis and the procedures of valuation do not go from the act to a domain such as sexuality or the flesh, a domain whose divine, civil, or natural laws would delineate the permitted forms; they go from the subject as a sexual actor to the other areas of life in which he pursues his [familial, social, and economic] activity. And it is in the relationship between these different forms of activity that the principles of evaluation of a sexual behavior are essentially, but not exclusively, situated."

19. Note that even the human genitals themselves do not necessarily figure as sexual signifiers in all cultural or representational contexts: for example, Caroline Walker Bynum, "The Body of Christ in the Later Middle Ages: A Reply to Leo Steinberg," *Renaissance Quarterly* 39 (1986), 399–439, argues in considerable detail that there is "reason to think that medieval people saw Christ's penis not primarily as a sexual organ but as the object of circumcision and therefore as the wounded, bleeding flesh with which it was associated in painting and in text" (p. 407).

20. Padgug, 8.

21. Paul Veyne, in "La famille et l'amour sous le Haut-Empire romain," *Annales (E.S.C.)* 33 (1978), 35–63, remarks (p. 50) that Seneca's *Phaedra* is the earliest text to associate homosexual inclinations with a distinct type of subjectivity. The question is more complex than that, however, and a thorough exploration of it would require scrutinizing more closely the ancient figure of the *kinaidos,* a now-defunct sexual life-form: for details, see Maud W. Gleason, "The Semiotics of Gender: Physiognomy and Self-Fashioning in the Second Century C.E.," in *Before Sexuality,* 389–415; John J. Winkler, "Laying Down the Law: The Oversight of Men's Sexual Behavior in Classical Athens," *Constraints of Desire,* 45–70, 224–226.

22. See Padgug, 3, who mistakenly ascribes Athenaeus's comment to Alexis of Samos (Jacoby, *Fragmente der griechischen Historiker* 539, fr. 2).

23. See K.J. Dover, *Greek Homosexuality* (London, 1978), 63–67, for an extensive, but admittedly partial, list; also, Robert Parker, *Miasma: Pollution and Purification in Early Greek Religion* (Oxford, 1983), 94. For some Roman examples, see T. Wade Richardson, "Homosexuality in the *Satyricon,*" *Classica et Mediaevalia* 35 (1984), 105–127, esp. 111.

24. I wish to emphasize that I am *not* claiming that all Greek men must have felt such indifference: on the contrary, plenty of ancient evidence testifies to the strength of individual preferences for a sexual object of one sex rather than another (see note 42, below). But many ancient documents bear witness to a certain constitutional reluctance on the part of the Greeks

to predict, in any given instance, the sex of another man's beloved merely on the basis of that man's past sexual behavior or previous pattern of sexual object-choice.

25. *P. Tebtunis* I 104, translated by A.S. Hunt and C.C. Edgar, in *Women's Life in Greece and Rome*, ed. Mary Lefkowitz and Maureen B. Fant (Baltimore, 1982), 59–60; another translation is provided, along with a helpful discussion of the document and its typicality, by Sarah B. Pomeroy, *Women in Hellenistic Egypt from Alexander to Cleopatra* (New York, 1984), 87–89.

26. "Une bisexualité de sabrage": Veyne, 50–55; see the critique by Ramsay MacMullen, "Roman Attitudes to Greek Love," *Historia* 32 (1983), 484–502, esp. 491–497. Other scholars who describe the ancient behavioral phenomenon as "bisexuality" include Luc Brisson, "Bisexualité et médiation en Grèce ancienne," *Nouvelle revue de psychanalyse* 7 (1973), 27–48; Alain Schnapp, "Une autre image de l'homosexualité en Grèce ancienne," *Le Débat* 10 (1981), 107–117, esp. 116–117; Lawrence Stone, "Sex in the West," *The New Republic* (July 8, 1985), 25–37, esp. 30–32 (with doubts). *Contra*, Padgug, 13: "to speak, as is common, of the Greeks as 'bisexual' is illegitimate as well, since that merely adds a new, intermediate category, whereas it was precisely the categories themselves which had no meaning in antiquity."

27. T.M. Robinson, [Review of Dover's *Greek Homosexuality*], *Phoenix* 35 (1981), 160–163, esp. 162: "the reason why a heterosexual majority might have looked with a tolerant eye on 'active' homosexual practice among the minority, and even in some measure within their own group [!], . . . is predictably a sexist one: to the heterosexual majority, to whom (in a man's universe) the 'good' woman is *kata physin* [i.e., naturally] passive, obedient, and submissive, the 'role' of the 'active' homosexual will be tolerable precisely because his goings-on can, without too much difficulty, be equated with the 'role' of the male *heterosexual*, i.e., to dominate and subdue; what the two have in common is greater than what divides them." But this seems to me to beg the very question that the distinction between heterosexuality and homosexuality is supposedly designed to solve.

28. An excellent analysis of the contemporary Mediterranean version of this ethos has been provided by David Gilmore, "Introduction: The Shame of Dishonor," in *Honor and Shame and the Unity of the Mediterranean*, ed. Gilmore, Special Publication of the American Anthropological Association, 22 (Washington, D.C., 1987), 2–21, esp. 8–16.

29. By "phallus" I mean a culturally constructed signifier of social power: for the terminology, see note 10, above. I call Greek sexual discourse phallic because (1) sexual contacts are polarized around phallic action—i.e., they are defined by who has the phallus and by what is done with it; (2) sexual pleasures other than phallic pleasures do not count in categorizing sexual contacts; (3) in order for a contact to qualify as sexual, one—and no more than one—of the two partners is required to have a phallus (boys are treated in paederastic contexts as essentially un-phallused [see Martial, 11.22; but cf. *Palatine Anthology* 12.3, 7, 197, 207, 216, 222, 242] and tend to be assimilated to women; in the case of sex between women, one partner—the "tribad"—is assumed to possess a phallus-equivalent [an over-developed clitoris] and to penetrate the other: sources for the ancient conceptualization of the tribad—no complete modern study of this fascinating and long-lived fictional type, which survived into the early decades of the twentieth century, is known to me—have been assembled by Friedrich Karl Forberg, *Manual of Classical Erotology*, transl. Julian Smithson [Manchester, 1884; repr. New York, 1966], II, 108–167; Paul Brandt [pseud. "Hans Licht"], *Sexual Life in Ancient Greece*, transl. J.H. Freese, ed. Lawrence H. Dawson [London, 1932], 316–328; Gaston Vorberg, *Glossarium eroticum* [Hanau, 1965], 654–655; and Werner A. Krenkel, "Masturbation in der Antike," *Wissenschaftliche Zeitschrift der Wilhelm-Pieck-Universität Rostock* 28 [1979], 159–178, esp. 171. For a recent discussion, see Judith P. Hallett, "Female Homoeroticism and the Denial of Roman Reality in Latin Literature," *Yale Journal of Criticism* 3.1 [1989], 209–238.

30. Exceptions include Vern L. Bullough, *Homosexuality: A History* (New York, 1979), 3–5, and John Boswell, *Christianity, Social Tolerance, and Homosexuality: Gay People in Western Europe from the Beginning of the Christian Era to the Fourteenth Century* (Chicago, 1980), 53n., 75n.

31. For an earlier use of *mollis* in this almost technical sense, see Juvenal, 9.38.

32. See P.H. Schrijvers, *Eine medizinische Erklärung der männlichen Homosexualität aus der Antike (Caelius Aurelianus DE MORBIS CHRONICIS IV 9)* (Amsterdam, 1985), 11.

33. I have borrowed this entire argument from Schrijvers, 7–8; the same point about the passage from *De morbis acutis* had been made earlier—unbeknownst to Schrijvers, apparently—by Boswell, *Christianity, Social Tolerance, and Homosexuality*, 53, n. 33; 75, n. 67.

34. Translation (with my emphasis and amplification) by I.E. Drabkin, ed. and transl., *Caelius Aurelianus: ON ACUTE DISEASES and ON CHRONIC DISEASES* (Chicago, 1950), 413.

35. As his chapter title, "De mollibus *sive subactis*," implies.

36. See especially the pseudo-Aristotelian *Problemata* 4.26, well discussed by Dover, 168–170, and by Winkler, "Laying Down the Law," 67–69; generally, Boswell, *Christianity, Social Tolerance, and Homosexuality*, 53; Foucault, *The Use of Pleasure*, 204–214.

37. The Latin phrase *quod utranque Venerem exerceant* is so interpreted by both Drabkin, 901n., and Schrijvers, 32–33, who secures this reading by citing Ovid, *Metamorphoses* 3.323, where Teiresias, who had been both a man and a woman, is described as being learned in the field of *Venus utraque*. Compare Petronius, *Satyricon* 43.8: *omnis minervae homo*.

38. I follow, once again, the insightful commentary by Schrijvers, 15.

39. I quote from the translation by Drabkin, 905, which is based on his plausible, but nonetheless speculative, reconstruction (accepted by Schrijvers, 50) of a desperately corrupt text. For the notion expressed in it, compare Marcel Proust, *A la recherche du temps perdu*, ed. Pierre Clarac and André Ferré (Paris, 1954), III, 204, 212; *Remembrance of Things Past*, transl. C.K. Scott Moncrieff and Terence Kilmartin (New York, 1981), III, 203, 209; discussion by Eve Kosofsky Sedgwick, "Epistemology of the Closet (II)," *Raritan* 8 (Summer, 1988), 102–130, and reprinted, with revisions, in this volume.

40. Anon., *De physiognomonia* 85 (vol. ii, p. 114.5–14 Förster); Vettius Valens, 2.16 (p. 76.3–8 Kroll); Clement of Alexandria, *Paedagogus* 3.21.3; Firmicus Maternus, *Mathesis* 6.30.15–16 and 7.25.3–23 (esp. 7.25.5).

41. See Foucault, *The History of Sexuality*, 43: "As defined by the ancient civil or canonical codes, sodomy was a category of forbidden acts; their perpetrator was nothing more than the juridical subject of them. The nineteenth-century homosexual became a personage, a past, a case history, and a childhood, in addition to being a type of life, a life form, and a morphology, with an indiscreet anatomy and possibly a mysterious physiology. Nothing that went into his total composition was unaffected by his sexuality. It was everywhere present in him: at the root of all his actions because it was their insidious and indefinitely active principle; written immodestly on his face and body because it was a secret that always gave itself away. It was consubstantial with him, less as a habitual sin than as a singular nature." See also Randolph Trumbach, "London's Sodomites: Homosexual Behavior and Western Culture in the 18th Century," *Journal of Social History* 11 (1977), 1–33, esp. 9; Richard Sennett, *The Fall of Public Man* (New York, 1977), 6–8; Padgug, 13–14; Jean-Claude Féray, "Une histoire critique du mot homosexualité, [IV]," *Arcadie* 28, no. 328 (1981), 246–258, esp. 246–247; Schnapp (note 26, above), 116 (speaking of Attic vase-paintings): "One does not paint acts that characterize persons so much as behaviors that distinguish groups"; Pierre J. Payer, *Sex and the Penitentials: The Development of a Sexual Code 550–1150* (Toronto, 1984), 40–44, esp. 40–41: "there is no word in general usage in the penitentials for homosexuality as a category. . . . Furthermore, the distinction between homosexual acts and people who might be called homosexuals does not seem to be operative in these manuals" (also, pp. 14–15, 140–153); Bynum, "The Body of Christ," 406.

42. For attestations to the strength of individual preferences (even to the point of exclusivity) on the part of Greek males for a sexual partner of one sex rather than another, see Theognis, 1367–1368; Euripides, *Cyclops* 583–584; Xenophon, *Anabasis* 7.4.7–8; Aeschines, 1.41, 195; the *Life of Zeno* by Antigonus of Carystus, cited by Athenaeus, 13.563e; the fragment of Seleucus quoted by Athenaeus, 15.697de (= *Collectanea Alexandrina*, ed. J.U. Powell [Oxford, 1925], 176); an anonymous dramatic fragment cited by Plutarch, *Moralia* 766f–767a (= *Tragicorum Graecorum Fragmenta*, ed. August Nauck, 2d ed. [Leipzig, 1926], 906, #355; also in Theodor Kock, *Comicorum Atticorum Fragmenta* [Leipzig, 1880–1888], III, 467, #360); Athenaeus, 12.540e, 13.601e and ff.; Achilles Tatius, 2.35.2–3; pseudo-Lucian, *Erôtes* 9–10; Firmicus Maternus, *Mathesis* 7.15.1–2; and a number of epigrams by various hands contained in the *Palatine Anthology*: 5.19, 65, 116, 208, 277, 278; 11.216; 12.7, 17, 41, 87, 145, 192, 198, and *passim* (cf. P.G. Maxwell-Stuart, "Strato and the Musa Puerilis," *Hermes* 100 [1972], 215–240). See, generally, Dover, 62–63; John Boswell,

"Revolutions, Universals and Sexual Categories," in *Homosexuality: Sacrilege, Vision, Politics* (note 6, above), 89–113, esp. 98–101; Winkler, "Laying Down the Law"; and, for a list of passages, Claude Courouve, *Tableau synoptique de références à l'amour masculin: Auteurs grecs et latins* (Paris, 1986).

43. Hilary Putnam, in *Reason, Truth and History* (Cambridge, Eng., 1981), 150–155, in the course of analyzing the various criteria by which we judge matters of taste to be "subjective," implies that we are right to consider sexual preferences more thoroughly constitutive of the human personality than dietary preferences, but his argument remains circumscribed, as Putnam himself points out, by highly culture-specific assumptions about sex, food, and personhood.

44. Foucault, *The Use of Pleasure*, 51–52, remarks that it would be interesting to determine exactly when in the evolving course of Western cultural history sex became more morally problematic than eating; he seems to think that sex won out only at the turn of the eighteenth century, after a long period of relative equilibrium during the middle ages: see also *The Use of Pleasure*, 10; *The Care of the Self*, 143; "On the Genealogy of Ethics: An Overview of Work in Progress," in Hubert L. Dreyfus and Paul Rabinow, *Michel Foucault: Beyond Structuralism and Hermeneutics*, 2d ed. (Chicago, 1983), 229–252, esp. 229. The evidence lately assembled by Stephen Nissenbaum, *Sex, Diet, and Debility in Jacksonian America: Sylvester Graham and Health Reform*, Contributions in Medical History, 4 (Westport, Conn., 1980), and by Caroline Walker Bynum, *Holy Feast and Holy Fast: The Religious Significance of Food to Medieval Women* (Berkeley, 1987), suggests that moral evolution may not have been quite such a continuously linear affair as Foucault appears to imagine.

45. Jack H. Abbott, "On 'Women,' " *New York Review of Books* 28:10 (June 11, 1981), 17. It should perhaps be pointed out that this lyrical confession is somewhat at odds with the more gritty account contained in the edited excerpts from Abbott's letters that were published a year earlier in the *New York Review of Books* 27:11 (June 26, 1980), 34–37. (One might compare Abbott's statement with some remarks uttered by Bernard Boursicot in a similarly apologetic context and quoted by Richard Bernstein, "France Jails Two in a Bizarre Case of Espionage," *New York Times* [May 11, 1986]: "I was shattered to learn that he [Boursicot's lover of twenty years] is a man, but my conviction remains unshakable that for me at that time he was really a woman and was the first love of my life.")

46. See Davidson (note 6, above), 16.

47. I wish to thank Kostas Demelis for helping me with this formulation. Compare Padgug, 5: "In any approach that takes as predetermined and universal the categories of sexuality, real history disappears."

48. Stephen Greenblatt, "Fiction and Friction," in *Reconstructing Individualism: Autonomy, Individuality, and the Self in Western Thought*, ed. Thomas C. Heller, Morton Sosna, and David E. Wellbery, with Arnold I. Davidson, Ann Swidler, and Ian Watt (Stanford, 1986), 30–52, 329–332, esp. 34, makes a similar point; arguing that "a culture's sexual discourse plays a critical role in shaping individuality," he goes on to say, "It does so by helping to implant in each person an internalized set of dispositions and orientations that governs individual improvisations." See also Padgug; generally, Julian Henriques, Wendy Holloway, Cathy Urwin, Venn Couze, and Valerie Walkerdine, *Changing the Subject: Psychology, Social Regulation and Subjectivity* (London, 1984).

49. "Translations" (1972), lines 32–33, in Adrienne Rich, *Diving into the Wreck: Poems 1971–1972* (New York, 1973), 40–41 (quotation on p. 41).

50. "Canzone" (1942), lines 1–2, in W.H. Auden, *Collected Poems*, ed. Edward Mendelson (New York, 1976), 256–257 (quotation on p. 256).

29

"They Wonder to Which Sex I Belong": The Historical Roots of the Modern Lesbian Identity

Martha Vicinus

Martha Vicinus, Professor of English, of History, and of Women's Studies at the University of Michigan, Ann Arbor, is the author of Independent Women *(1985) as well as number of essays, and is co-editor of* Hidden from History *(1989). She is currently writing on women who dressed as men, in the period 1660 to 1950. In this survey of current work in lesbian history, Vicinus describes the pitfalls accompanying some historians' concern with the origins of individual and group identity—a concern that can limit its possibilities for inquiry by focusing solely on Euro-American instances where identity and sexuality are intertwined and where identity itself is a cultural value; she also indicates the ways in which lesbian history can begin more fully to reflect intersecting and conflicting identities. Locating lesbian history's focus in the cultural margins, and denying that any specific sexual expression can provide a key to understanding the lesbian past, Vicinus argues that lesbian history must be written so as to include not only the dyke, butch, witch, and amazon, but the invert, femme, androgyne, and even the merely occasional lover of women.*

In 1884 the aging French painter, Rosa Bonheur, wrote her sister, from Nice, where she had gone in her usual smock and trousers to sketch:

> It amuses me to see how puzzled the people are. They wonder to which sex I belong. The ladies especially lose themselves in conjectures about "the little old man who looks so lively." The men seem to conclude: "Oh, he's some aged singer from St. Peter's at Rome, who has turned to painting in his declining years to console himself for some misfortune." And they shake their beards triumphantly.[1]

Bonheur's bemused description of the impact her androgynous appearance had upon the general public pinpoints many of the major difficulties historians face in reconstructing the history of the lesbian. Bonheur spent her adult life living with a woman and wearing male attire, but she used a specifically Victorian vocabulary, reveling in her gender freedom, rather than her specific sexual identity. In describing her life-long friendship with Nathalie Micas, Bonheur spoke appreciatively of those who understood that "two women may delight in an intense and passionate friendship, in which nothing can debase its purity."[2] Did she have an active sexual life with Micas? Was she a lesbian? Did she identify as a lesbian? Whom should we include and why in the history of the modern lesbian?

Lesbian history is in its initial stages, inhibited both by the suspect nature of the subject and the small number of individuals willing and able to pursue half-forgotten, half-destroyed, or half-neglected sources. Nevertheless, the past fifteen years have seen an encouraging efflorescence of work, breaking from the old psychological paradigms and insisting upon the necessity of a historical understanding of women's same-sex sexual behavior. These studies have concentrated on issues of concern to lesbians, especially the origins of an individual and a group identity.

This attention to identity politics, past and present, has had two obvious pitfalls. As the editors of *Signs* pointed out in the introduction to their 1984 special issue on lesbians, "Such focus on identity may in fact limit inquiry to those cultures in which lesbian identity and survival *as lesbians* are crucial matters of concern; it may hinder cross-cultural analysis, for example, because it provides inadequate vocabulary for discussion of relationships among Third World women. . . . Discussion of lesbianism in these terms has relevance only where identity and sexuality are intertwined and where personal identity is itself a cultural value."[3] Such pioneering collections as *This Bridge Called My Back: Writings by Radical Women of Color* (1981), edited by Cherríe Moraga and Gloria Anzaldúa; *Nice Jewish Girls: A Lesbian Anthology* (1982), edited by Evelyn Torton Beck; and *Home Girls; A Black Feminist Anthology* (1984), edited by Barbara Smith have problematized the contemporary relationship between a lesbian identity and a racial identity in the United States. But possible role conflicts, personal opportunities, or individual self-definition in the past remain largely unknown. Moreover, the homosexual possibilities for women in the Third World, past or present, are still little understood by Western writers.

Lesbian desire is everywhere, even as it may be nowhere. Put bluntly, we lack any general agreement about what constitutes a lesbian. Jackie Stacey has suggested one alternative to any rigid definition of the lesbian identity. In an essay questioning feminist psychoanalysis, she recommends instead that "it might be possible to consider questions of lesbian identity and desire within the models of fragmented subjectivity":

> [T]he diversity of our experience of lesbianism is enormous . . . We cannot assume any coherent or unified collective identity when we recognize the diversity of definitions and experiences of lesbians . . . Lesbian experiences are not only fragmented within "lesbian cultures," but also within culture dominated by heterosexuality, in which lesbians are ascribed the contradictory positions of the invisible presence.[4]

"Diversity" is a salutary reminder that not all questions can be answered, but it hardly resolves the problems facing a historian. If we are to make sense of our history, we must look for connections embedded in differences and contradictions.

Virtually every historian of sexuality has argued that the present-day sexual identity of both homosexuals and heterosexuals is socially constructed and historically specific. Yet same-sex erotic attraction appears to be transhistorical and transcultural and to appear repeatedly in a limited range of behaviors. As Eve Kosofsky Sedgwick has pointed out, most of us hold contradictory notions in regard to sexual preference without attempting to resolve them: we recognize a distinct group of homosexual peoples or individuals, and also understand that sexual behavior is unpredictable, various, and strongly influenced by both same-sex and opposite-sex desires and influences.[5]

The history of lesbianism also demonstrates a continual jostling of two competing perspectives on the origins of homosexual feeling: is it a product of social conditions or of one's innate propensity? Onlookers have usually chosen the former, but medical experts have chosen the latter, although by the twentieth century the two models are often postulated simultaneously. Lesbians themselves seem to use both explanations, although those privileging butch-femme relations lean toward a model of innate predisposition, and those preferring romantic friendships favor a conditioned, sexual continuum. Moreover, in spite of the many different forms of actual behavior, lesbians, past and present, are assigned to a few readily recognizable types. As Steven Epstein has pointed out, "Each society seems to have a limited range of potential storylines for its sexual scripts. . . . It may be that we're all acting out scripts—but most of us seem to be typecast. . . . To paraphrase Marx, people make their own identities, but they do not make them just as they please."[6] The remaining sections of this essay document the "scripts" of the modern Western lesbian.

I. The Parameters of Lesbian Historiography

Conceptual confusion is perhaps inevitable in regard to lesbians, given the historical suppression of female sexuality in general. All societies that I know of have denied, controlled, or muted the public expression of active female sexuality. We must first decode female sexual desire, and then within it, find same-sex desire. By necessity we need to be sensitive to nuance, masks, secrecy, and the unspoken. If we look to the margins, to the ruptures and breaks, we will be able to piece together a history of women speaking to each other. Nevertheless, lesbian history will remain a history of discontinuities: we rarely know precisely what women in the past did with each other in bed or out, and we are not able to reconstruct fully how and under what circumstances lesbian communities evolved. Our history includes teen-age crushes, romantic friendships, Boston marriages, theatrical cross-dressing, passing women, bulldykes and prostitutes, butches and femmes, and numerous other identifications which may—and may not—include genital sex. When we can't even claim a specific sexual expression as a key to our past, we must accept a fragmentary and confusing history.

To date, lesbian historiography has concentrated on three areas of research: (1) the retrieval and reconstruction of both individual lesbians and lesbian communities; (2) the exploration of the two major paradigmatic forms of lesbian behavior, namely, romantic friendships and butch-femme roles; and (3) the question of when the modern lesbian identity arose and under what circumstances. Although all three of these have generated valuable preliminary work, all have weaknesses. Because scholars have spent so much time excavating a lost past, few cross-cultural or cross-national comparisons have yet been made. We also know all too little about the legal position of lesbians, in comparison with the far richer documentation of the oppression of gay men.[7] In spite of the extensive debates about the influence of the late nineteenth-century sexologists, we do not yet have detailed studies of how their theories were popularized within and outside the medical profession.[8] And we are still woefully ignorant about women's sexual behavior before the early modern period.[9]

The rediscovery of past lesbians has focused either upon the lives of well-known writers, artists, and activists who have left extensive documentation; upon an unproblematic celebration of the most famous lesbian communities;[10] or more recently, on oral histories of self-identified lesbians.[11] We look to the personal life to define a woman, whether by her sexual acts or her sexual identity. Biddy Martin, in her literary deconstruction of contemporary lesbian coming-out stories, has shown the ways in which

> they assume a mimetic relationship between experience and writing and a relationship
> of identification between the reader and the autobiographical subject. Moreover, they

are explicitly committed to the political importance of just such reading strategies
for the creation of identity, community, and political solidarity.[12]

She recommends considering multiple roles, rather than a single overriding identity,
and points to recent autobiographies by American women of color who have both used
and problematized issues of identity and identity politics.[13] Coming-out stories, with
their affirmation of a personal self, seldom critique the lesbian community which made
this fulfillment possible. A shift in focus so that both an individual's multiple roles and
the communities that have sustained (or rejected) her are examined may yield richer
biographies and autobiographies.

Far too much energy has probably been consumed discussing a very American
concern—whether romantic friendships or butch-femme relationships are most characteristic of lesbianism. Following Lillian Faderman's pioneering work, *Surpassing the
Love of Men: Romantic Friendships and Love Between Women from the Renaissance to the
Present* (1981), some scholars have privileged romantic friendships. Blanche Wiesen
Cook and Adrienne Rich have pointed to the historical suppression of homosexuality
and argued for the essential unity of all women-identified-women. Cook's definition,
for example, has been influential in encouraging women to rethink the broader social
and political context of their own lives and of women in the past: "Women who love
women, who choose women to nurture and support and to create a living environment
in which to work creatively and independently, are lesbians."[14] This definition usefully
reminds us that women's sexuality is not a matter of either/or choices, but can be many
things in different contexts. But for many lesbians, it neglects both the element of sexual
object-choice and of marginal status that was (and continues to be) so important in
lesbian relationships. Moreover, the different patterns of sexual behavior in the working
class and aristocracy are neglected in favor of a middle class that closely resembles the
present feminist movement.

These broad definitions have been largely rejected after several lesbians pointed
out that scholars were in danger of draining sexuality from lesbians' lives. In an important
special issue of *Heresies* (1981), several lesbians challenged the feminist vision of an
egalitarian, "mutually orgasmic, struggle-free, trouble-free sex." Amber Hollibaugh insisted that "by focusing on roles in lesbian relationships, we can begin to unravel who
we really are in bed. When you hide how profoundly roles can shape your sexuality,
you can use that as an example of other things that get hidden."[15] Depending as it does
upon self-definition and active sexuality, this definition can become insensitive to the
very different lives of women in the past. How are we ever to know, definitively, what
someone born a hundred or two hundred years ago did in bed? And as Cook has pointed
out, does it really matter so much?[16]

The question of when and under what circumstances the modern lesbian identity
arose is, perhaps, impossible to answer. If we turn to the larger historical context within
which such an identity might have grown, all the usual criteria used by historians to
explain social change do not seem sufficient. A lesbian identity did not result from
economic independence or from an ideology of individualism or from the formation of
women's communities, although all these elements were important for enhancing wom-
en's personal choices. In 1981 Ann Ferguson argued that financial independence was a
necessary precondition for the formation of a lesbian identity, but this does not seem
to be the case.[17] We have examples from the eighteenth and nineteenth centuries of
women who were economically dependent upon their families, and yet were successfully
involved with women. The sexually active upper-class Anne Lister (1791–1840) was
often frustrated that she had to live with her wealthy uncle and aunt in provincial

Yorkshire, but she arranged her social life to take advantage of every sexual opportunity. Over the course of eight years she managed numerous meetings with her married lover and had several affairs.[18]

The onset of the industrial revolution appears to have had little impact upon the formation of a lesbian culture, although it led to more occupational opportunities for women of all social classes. The development of a mercantile economy in seventeenth- and eighteenth-century Northern Europe may have encouraged some women to think of themselves as individuals apart from their families. Both religion and politics united to emphasize the importance of the individual's soul; those women who found strength through their religious beliefs to seek non-traditional roles may also have felt—and acted upon—nonconforming sexual desires.

The formation of self-conscious women's communities can be seen as a necessary precondition for a lesbian identity. But here again we find a tradition going back into the Middle Ages that yielded feminine and proto-feminist independence and bonding but hardly anything one could recognize as a lesbian identity. During the eighteenth and nineteenth centuries women organized salons, artistic coteries, religious organizations, and educational institutions. Although these were rarely self-consciously lesbian, such groups clearly provided opportunities for the development of intense friendships.[19]

Despite the weaknesses of all current explanatory models, fragmentary evidence and ghostly immanences tease scholars. The polymorphous, even amorphous sexuality of women is an invitation to multiple interpretative strategies. Discontinuity and reticence do not mean silence or absence. Many lesbian histories, contradictory, complicated and perhaps uncomfortable, can be told.

II. The Seventeenth and Eighteenth Centuries: Theatrics or Nature?

By the late seventeenth and eighteenth centuries, when the traditional hierarchies of social order, private and public, were giving way, among Europeans and Europeans in the Americas, to ideas of individualism and egalitarianism, lesbian desire appears to have been defined in four dominant ways, closely linked to the social class of the women concerned. This correlation between class, public appearance, and sexual behavior suggests an effort to categorize women's deviancy in a satisfactory manner that did not threaten the dominant heterosexual and social paradigms of the age. Biological explanations seem to have been confined to educated, often medical, men, but the general public preferred a "social constructionist" approach that emphasized the individual's circumstances.

The most common figure of female deviance was the transvestite. Early modern Europeans took cross-dressed women in their stride, even as they excoriated the effeminate man.[20] Virtually all the examples of "passing women" that have survived (and many women must have died with their true identity unknown) are of working-class and peasant women who sought more job opportunities, better pay, and greater freedom.[21] Contemporaries accepted such economic necessity, but often reinterpreted it in more romantic, heterosexual terms. Eighteenth-century broadside ballads praised the "female warrior" who went into battle in order to find her beloved. Most versions raised the possibility of sexual transgression but resolved matters in the final verse with a happy marriage or other appropriate female destiny.

The precursor to the modern "butch" cannot be traced back to those women who passed as "female soldiers." As Dianne Dugaw points out, such women retained their biological identity as women and simply donned the outward clothing of men. They managed to be courageous fighters, gentle helpers, and loyal wives simultaneously—and to be universally admired.[22] In her examination of the records of modern "military maids," Julie Wheelwright documents how many women depended upon the collusion of fellow soldiers to safeguard their secret.[23] When faced with a heterosexual proposition, the "soldier" either deserted or capitulated to a common-law marriage.

The female soldier's closest relative was the immensely popular cross-dressed actress of the eighteenth-century stage. Wandering actresses, or even less reputable vagrants, made up most of this group. Most of these women were notoriously heterosexual; only the infamous Londoner Charlotte Charke wore breeches in public. She delighted in playing with the possibilities of sexual transgression; her 1755 memoir robustly declared on the title page, "Her Adventures in Mens Cloaths, going by the Name of Mr. *Brown*, and being belov'd by a Lady of great Fortune, who intended to marry her."[24] However, she cast her autobiography in terms of a theatrical comedy, so as to mitigate the dangerous implications of her actions. Neither theatrical nor military dress implied a permanent identity, but rather a temporary, if bold, seizing of opportunity.

More troubling, because more difficult to place, were those women who either appeared "mannish" or continued to cross-dress after the wars were over. Rudolph Dekker and Lottie van de Pol have argued that in Holland women who dressed as men did so because they could conceive of love for another woman only in terms of the existing heterosexual paradigm. If this was so, the highly risky marriages that so many cross-dressed women undertook make sense, for they were "the logical consequence of, on the one hand, the absence of a social role for lesbians and the existence of, on the other hand, a tradition of women in men's clothing."[25] Although this suggestion is attractive, we lack sufficient personal information to generalize with confidence about the many and complicated psycho-social reasons why a woman might have cross-dressed in the past.

Elaine Hobby has usefully reminded us that the modern lesbian identity may go further back than early theorists admitted. Hobby argues that the types are familiar to us but that the explanatory models are different. Mannish women came from distant or past peoples, or possessed an elongated clitoris, said to resemble a penis, or were cursed by the stars or witchcraft; or, if all other explanations failed, they might just be born that way. Hobby quotes a 1671 account of a German woman trader which illustrates these diverse explanations, in order to show the early existence of someone whose sexual identity appears to have been both self-determined and innate:

> [Gretta] loved the young daughters, went after them and bought them pedlars' goods; and she also used all bearing and manners, as if she had a masculine *affect*. She was often considered to be a hermaphrodite or androgyne, but this did not prove to be the case, for she was investigated by cunning, and was seen to be a true, proper woman. To note: She was said to be born under an inverted, unnatural constellation. But amongst the learned and well-read one finds that this sort of thing is often encountered amongst the Greeks and Romans, although this is to be ascribed rather to the evil customs of those corrupted nations, plagued by sins, than to the course of the heavens or stars.[26]

Rather than looking for a societal or economic explanation for Gretta's behavior, suitable for cross-dressers, commentators sought an "essentialist" argument rooted either in biology or birth. In effect, she was a precursor to the "mannish lesbian."

Far more common, however, was the "free woman" who seemed to choose a flagrantly varied sexuality. Her appearance and behavior could signal an erotic interest in women, but at other times—as prostitute, courtesan, or mistress—she chose men. The subject of gossip or pornography, she was invariably portrayed as consuming both women and men. I would label this third category of publicly identified lesbian desire as the occasional lover of women. This woman was frequently attacked as a danger to the normal political hierarchies because of her undue influence upon male leaders. The evidence for her activities can be best described as "porn and politics," pamphlets, gossip, and similarly suspect sources describing flagrant sexual freedom. The connection between sexual deviance and political deviance is hardly unique to women; indeed, the libertine libertarian John Wilkes (1727–97) was the subject of an intense pamphlet war linking him with excessive freedoms of all sorts.[27]

The most famous example of this kind of political linkage is Marie Antoinette, who was repeatedly accused of political intrigue and bisexual debauchery.[28] Although her female lovers were of her own social class, she was accused of taking on male lovers from the lower classes. Much of the evidence against her was generated by those determined to destroy an effeminate aristocracy and to replace it with a purified masculine democracy. In several cases Marie Antoinette was woven into pre-existing pornographic plots with little consideration for historical facts.[29] But we should not dismiss this material, for such culturally influential male fantasies, derived from both pornography and high art, had a lasting impact upon the public (and occasionally, the private) image of the lesbian.

The fourth and increasingly common form that lesbian desire took is the romantic friendship. Nancy Cott has documented the ways in which the definition of "friend" changed in the eighteenth century to refer specifically to an elective, non-familial relationship of particular importance.[30] Maaike Meijer in her description of the friendship of two famous late eighteenth-century Dutch bluestockings, Betje Wolff and Aagje Deken, points to the importance of a shared interest in learning, often in the face of family and public opposition, as a crucial element in romantic friendships.[31] A sense of being different, of wanting more than other young women, symbolized by a love of learning, characterizes many of the romantic friendships described by Faderman in *Surpassing the Love of Men*. Yet even here, women's friendships were tightly controlled by external definitions of respectability. All bourgeois families feared any emotions that would overturn the conventional hierarchies in the private and public spheres. The discipline of study was supposed to teach women friends to be rational, to control their love for each other. In actuality, it probably led to a desire for greater independence—and consequently, an increased labeling of such friendships as deviant.[32]

Elaine Marks has wittily labeled "the Sapphic fairy tale," the common variation on romantic friendship in which an older woman teaches a younger woman about sexual desire and life; in most cases the relationship is brief, as the younger woman outgrows her initial attraction.[33] The degree of sexual involvement in this relation has been a subject of some controversy among scholars. But descriptions by participants invariably include a combination of emotional and physical feelings, creating, in the words of Constance Maynard (1849–1935), founder of Westfield College, London, that delicious "long, long clasp of living love that needs no explanation."[34] Participants emphasized the totality of the relationship, rather than one's outward appearance or a sexual act.

These four forms of lesbian sexual desire were united less by the behavior or attitudes of the women than by the ways in which men interpreted women's same-sex desire. On the one hand, we have amusement, curiosity, and romanticization; on the other, we have horror, punishment, and expulsion. In either response, however, women's same-sex behavior remained marginal to male sexual and societal discourses.[35] The vocabulary used to define these visibly aberrant women, drawn from the classical world, emphasized either an unnatural act or a congenital defect. The Greek word "tribade" appears only in the sixteenth and early seventeenth centuries in France and England, as a description of a woman who rubbed her genitals against another woman's. Well before the pioneering sexologists of the late nineteenth century, medical theorists assigned an essentialist identity to same-sex behavior, arguing that it must be rooted in the individual's physiology. The most common medical term was "hermaphrodite." "Sapphic," the word used most frequently in memoirs, does not even merit a sexual definition in the *Oxford English Dictionary*.[36]

Only when a woman seemed to contravene directly masculine priorities and privileges was she punished. But even in these cases, sexual deviancy had to be compounded by a trespassing upon the male preserves of religion or politics in order to draw the full wrath of masculine authority. Lesbian sexuality remained a muted discourse. The usual punishment for a woman who married another woman was a public whipping and banishment. One notable exception, however, was the early eighteenth-century case of the respectable inn-keeper, "James How." Mary East and her friend had opened a public house in the 1730s in a village north of London and by dint of hard work and honesty, they prospered. But East, known everywhere as "James How," had been forced to pay a blackmailer for years. Finally, after the death of her partner, she took her case to the magistrates; they did not arrest her for fraud but imprisoned the blackmailer. All surviving accounts of How treat her sympathetically.[37] The most acceptable model for understanding her thirty-five-year "marriage" was the female-warrior ballad, and reports were circulated that she and her "wife" must have decided to join together after they had been jilted by men. Marjorie Garber has labeled this "normalization" of the transvestite as a "progress narrative," which recuperates an individual into a bourgeois tale of economic struggle and social success.[38] Ironically, it also bears close resemblance to the lesbian autobiography which Biddy Martin critiqued for its seamless movement toward self-actualization.

This casual and seeming indifference to women's relationships needs to be contrasted with those occasions when women clearly threatened the dominance of men or of the traditional family. The actress Charlotte Charke, in spite of her notoriety, was never a public threat because she remained a liminal figure of farce, but the multifarious sins of the German Catharina Margaretha Linck led to her trial for sodomy and her execution in 1721. She had joined an egalitarian, woman-led religion, and later had converted to Roman Catholicism and then Lutheranism. Dressed as a man, she served in a Prussian volunteer corps, worked as a weaver, and married a woman, with whom she had sex, using a homemade dildo. After hearing complaints from her daughter, Linck's mother-in-law and a neighbor "attacked her, took her sword, ripped open her pants, examined her, and discovered that she was indeed not a man but a woman."[39] In her defense, Linck insisted she had been deluded by Satan, and that it was no sin for a maiden to wear men's clothes. Both reasons depend upon circumstances; Linck did not argue that she was biologically different or that she had been born "that way."

Women who avoided a direct confrontation with male prerogatives, whether sexual or political, fared best. The most famous example of romantic friendship in the eighteenth century was the upper-class "Ladies of Llangollen," who ran away from threats of marriage and the convent to live with each other in remote north Wales. Eleanor Butler (1739–1829) and Sarah Ponsonby (1755–1831) succeeded because they each had a small income, and made a determined effort to reproduce a happy marriage in rural retirement. (James How and his "wife" had followed the working-class equivalent of this pattern in their moral probity, modesty, and hard work.) In their riding habits and short, powdered hair they looked like a pair of old men when seated (they still wore skirts), and their eccentricities were brushed aside by a wide circle of admirers. Yet even they were subject to gossip. In 1790 a journalist described Lady Eleanor as "tall and masculine" and appearing "in all respects a young man, if we except the petticoats she retains."[40] She was actually short, dumpy, and fifty-one at the time. During their long lives they faced down snide comments by appearing intellectual, desexualized, and otherworldly.

Samuel Johnson's friend, the well-known gossip Mrs. Piozzi, made a distinction that was typical of the age, in respecting the intellectual Ladies of Llangollen and loathing the sexual antics of the aristocracy. In 1789 she noted, "The Queen of France is at the Head of a Set of Monsters call'd by each other *Sapphists,* who boast her example and deserve to be thrown with the *He* Demons that haunt each other likewise, into Mount Vesuvius. *That* Vice increases hourly in Extent—while expected *Parricides* frighten us no longer . . ."[41] The dislike of such behavior seems to have stemmed from the growing political hatred of the dissolute aristocracy as much as a distaste for their frolics. Nevertheless, the fear of active female sexuality in places of power was a potent threat, as Marie-Jo Bonnet reminds us. She argues that the Revolutionary crowd's decapitation and mutilation of Mme. Lamballe's genitals was an effort to destroy lesbian friendships, and not just the friend of the imprisoned queen.[42]

III. The Nineteenth Century and Twentieth Centuries: Natural Affection or *Femme Damnée*?

By the early years of the nineteenth century we can see two changes in same-sex relations. First, male commentary on occasional lesbian love-making, whether hearsay, journalism, or literature, became much more common. Public gossip shifted from Marie Antoinette's bedroom politics to the overtly sexual, unconventional women in artistic circles. Now women who were not necessarily prostitutes or well-connected could—at the price of respectability—choose to live a sexually free life. In addition, a few middle-class working women began to wear masculine (or simply practical) clothing. The active, mannish woman from the middle classes can be found throughout Europe and America by the 1820s. Most insisted upon their sexual respectability, but also asserted their right to enter such predominantly male arenas as medicine, literature, art, and travel. While professional single women emphasized their emotional ties, the bohemians flaunted their sexuality. George Sand (1804–76) is the most important representative of the former type, and Rosa Bonheur (1822–99) of the latter; not coincidentally both were economically independent artists.

Sometime in the early nineteenth century the cross-dressed masculine woman— the mannish lesbian—appeared whose primary emotional, and probably also her sexual commitment, was to women—the Rosa Bonheurs about whom society wondered to which sex they belonged. In effect, these women combined the outward appearance of the cross-dressed woman and the inner, emotional life of a romantic friendship. The mannish lesbian, a forerunner of the twentieth-century "butch," is the result of this double inheritance. It is one which denies the theatricality of gender, and instead inscribes it upon the body as a permanent identity. As I will discuss below, this figure became the identified deviant "invert" in the late nineteenth- and early twentieth-century work of such sexologists as Richard von Krafft-Ebing, Havelock Ellis, and Sigmund Freud. At the same time, both romantic friendships and passing women continued well into the twentieth century. In 1929, for example, in the midst of Radclyffe Hall's *The Well of Loneliness* obscenity trial, a Colonel Barker was arrested after passing as a World War I hero for over a decade; she had been "married" for three years before deserting her wife.[43] Romantic friendships flourished among women activists in the National Woman's Party in the 1940s and 1950s, according to Leila Rupp.[44]

None of these familiar types includes what we would now call the "femme" of the butch-femme couple.[45] Like the younger woman in a Sapphic romance, she was presumed to be only an occasional lover of women—someone who could, like Mary in *The Well of Loneliness* (1928), be lured away from her aberration by a handsome man. Teresa de Lauretis concludes: "Even today, in most representational contexts Mary would be either passing lesbian or passing straight, her (homo)sexuality being in the last instance what can not be seen. Unless . . . she enter the frame of vision *as* or *with* a lesbian in male body drag."[46] The impossibility of defining her by appearance or behavior baffled the sexologists. Havelock Ellis, by defining the sexual invert as someone who possessed the characteristics of the opposite sex, was unable to categorize the feminine invert. As Esther Newton has pointed out, he argued tentatively, "they are always womanly. One may perhaps say that they are the pick of the women whom the average man would pass by. . . . So far as they may be said to constitute a class they seem to possess a genuine, though not precisely sexual, preference for women over men."[47] Perhaps Ellis sensed that the "femme" was not a passive victim, but an active agent in defining her own sexual preference. Certainly by the late 1950s, scandal sheets had identified her as the consummate actress who deceived unsuspecting husbands—in effect, she had overtaken the butch as the threatening female who undermined masculinity.[48] An instability of gender identity adheres to the feminine invert in spite of every effort to categorize her.

The recent publication of excerpts of Anne Lister's diaries for the years 1817–24 has given us new insight into the life of a self-consciously mannish lesbian.[49] Her entries reveal that many educated women had covert sexual relations with other women, often as a pleasurable interlude before or during marriage, sometimes as part of a long-term commitment. Lister, twenty-five when her published diary begins, spends little time analyzing why she preferred a masculine demeanor, even at the expense of public effrontery. But she was deeply distressed when her more conventional (and married) lover was uneasy about being seen with her at a small seaside resort because she looked "unnatural." Lister defended her carefully contrived appearance, recording in her diary that "her conduct & feelings [were] surely natural to me in as much as they are not taught, not fictious, but instinctive."[50] Lister was a forerunner of those women who sought to change their appearance to accord with their souls; she assumed that her behavior was innate and instinctual, even though she had gradually and self-consciously adopted more masculine accoutrements. Her lover, on the other hand, denied that she might be pursuing an adulterous affair with "Freddy" Lister; economic circumstances had driven her into marriage and emotional circumstances had led her into Lister's arms. Both were choices made under social constraints, but in no way were they part of her intrinsic identity.[51] Within a self-consciously sexual couple two conflicting justifications for their behavior coexisted uneasily.

George Sand dressed as a male student in order to sit in the cheap seats at the theater, and into her forties she wore informal male dress at home. She was also for a brief period madly in love with the actress Marie Dorval; each of the men in Sand's life was convinced that the two women were having an affair specifically to torment him.[52] Given her reputation as a sexually free woman, rumors swirled around Sand, inviting different interpretations of her identity then and now. Sand, as Isabelle de Courtivon has pointed out, fit male fantasies of the devouring lesbian, of the woman who is all body. When this remarkable woman cross-dressed, it represented not her soul but her all-too-dominating body.[53] The bisexual Sand symbolized the strong woman who devoured weak men and found her pleasure in the arms of other women. The 1830s in

France spawned novels about monsters, of whom lesbians were among the most titillating. This male-generated image of sexual deviance proved to be especially powerful and one that would return repeatedly in twentieth-century portrayals of the lesbian *femme damnée*.[54]

We are now familiar with the public lives of numerous respectable professional women during the Victorian period. One of the most famous was the American sculptor Harriet Hosmer (1830–1908), who led a group of expatriate women artists in Rome. Charlotte Cushman (1816–76), an American actress of the period, frequently acted in male roles and wore men's clothes off stage. She and Hosmer, keen advocates of physical activity for women, took midnight horse rides, sat astride, and followed the hounds with the men.[55] The highly esteemed Rosa Bonheur was granted special permission to dress in trousers when she visited abattoirs and livestock auctions in order to study the anatomy of animals. She wore her trousers and smock, however, on all but formal occasions.

Lillian Faderman has defined the nineteenth century as the heyday of romantic friendships, when women could love each other without fear of social stigma.[56] In New England the longevity and the erotic undertones of relations between women appear to have been publicly accepted, for so-called "Boston marriages" were commonplace in literary circles; we have numerous other well-documented examples in every Northern European country where women were making inroads into the professions. Most of these highly respectable couples had one partner who was more active and public, while the other was more retiring. The nineteenth-century English educational reformers, Constance Maynard and Louisa Lumsden, for example, spoke of each other as wife and husband respectively; as headmistress of a girls' school, Lumsden expected her "wife" to support her decisions and to comfort her when difficulties arose.[57] Lumsden was repeatedly described by her friends as assertive, even "leonine," although photographs reveal her to our eyes as an upper-class lady much like her peers in physical appearance.

The mannish Bonheur worked hard to keep the image of respectable independence which characterized romantic friendships. Nevertheless, her square, craggy features and men's clothes placed her in a suspect category. When French taste turned against her realistic paintings, she hinted to friends that the criticism was as much a personal attack on her life with Nathalie Micas as it was her artistry.[58] However proud she may have been of her androgynous appearance, Bonheur was also self-conscious enough to insist that her lifelong relations with Micas and Anna Klumpke were pure. Both Lister and George Sand, one moneyed, the other aristocratic, were willing to risk public slander, but Bonheur needed public acceptance to succeed as a painter.

I think that we may have exaggerated the acceptability of romantic friendships. A fear of excess—whether of learning or of emotion—may well have been a cover for opposition to the erotic preference implied by a close friendship. The vituperation launched against Marie Antoinette and her best-known lovers had political roots, but it is only an extreme form of similar warnings found in etiquette books, medical tracts, and fiction, describing the dangers of overheated friendships. The Queen could endanger the state; less lofty women could endanger the state of marriage. The notorious example of the feminist Emily Faithfull (1835–95) provided ample opportunity to editorialize against romantic friendships. In 1864 Admiral Henry Codrington petitioned for divorce on the grounds of his wife's adultery; in addition, Faithfull was accused of alienating the Admiral's wife's affections. Helen Codrington, in turn, accused him of attempted rape upon Faithfull one night when the two women were sleeping together.[59] Faithfull herself first signed an affidavit claiming that this incident had taken place, but in court she refused to confirm it. The scandal permanently damaged her standing with other feminists, and she never regained the position of leadership she had held as the founder of the Victoria Press and *The Victoria Magazine.*

During the first half of the nineteenth century we can see the accelerating efforts of the medical and legal professions to define, codify, and control all forms of sexuality, and thereby to replace the church as the arbiters of sin and morality. Women's deviant sexual behaviors, whether heterosexual prostitution or homosexuality, continued to be male-defined transgressions dominated by male language, theories, and traditions. Such narrow terms as "hermaphrodite" were replaced with a plethora of competing words, such as "urning," "lesbian," "third sex," and "invert." Writing in the 1830s, Alexandre Jean-Baptiste Parent-Duchâtelet, the pioneering French medical hygienist, linked the lives of prostitutes with those of cross-dressed lesbians. Both represented possibilities and fears for men, for each embodied an active, independent, uncontrollable sexuality.[60] Underneath their veneer of scientific language, the medical and legal tracts betray many of the same interests and biases as pornography and literature.

It has become a truism that the sexologists, such as Richard von Krafft-Ebing and Havelock Ellis, did not so much define a lesbian identity as describe and categorize what they saw about them. Ellis drew his small sample of six lesbians from his bisexual wife and her friends. All his other examples are either historical or literary; many are drawn from the French writers who had been so shocked by Sand's flamboyance. Like Krafft-Ebing, he identified lesbians by their "masculine" behavior, such as smoking, speaking loudly, and wearing comfortable clothes. Carroll Smith-Rosenberg has pointed out that "Krafft-Ebing's lesbians seemed to desire male privileges and power as ardently as, perhaps more ardently than, they sexually desired women."[61] However revolutionary these men may have thought their descriptions to be, both were simply confirming the long-standing representation of women's social transgression as both the symptom and the cause of their sexual transgression. The incipient biologism of an earlier generation of medical men now moved to the forefront. These theorists all insisted upon the primacy of the body as the definer of public, social behavior. The long-familiar descriptions of deviant sexual activity were now labeled innate characteristics, rather than immoral choices.

Several feminist historians in Britain, following the lead of Lillian Faderman, have argued that the sexologists created a climate of opinion that stigmatized single women and their relationships and favored heterosexuality.[62] Others have argued that the sexologists stimulated the formation of a lesbian identity[63] or that their influence has been greatly exaggerated.[64] All these scholars have, to date, looked almost exclusively at the medical debates, rather than placing these debates in a wider historical context. A host of competing socio-biological ideologies and disciplines grew at the end of the nineteenth century, including social Darwinism, eugenics, criminology, and anthropology; women's sexual relations could hardly remain unaffected by them.

Have we too readily categorized these early sexologists and their embarrassingly crude classifications of sexual behavior? Rather than labeling the sexologists' descriptions benighted misogyny, we might learn more from them about both contemporary lesbian mores and masculine attitudes. Esther Newton has suggested that Havelock Ellis's biological determinism at the very least made available a sexual discourse to middle-class women, who "had no developed female sexual discourse; there were only male discourses—pornographic, literary, and medical—*about* female sexuality."[65] I would add that these three male discourses had long affected the traditional categories of transvestite, romantic friend, occasional lover, and androgynous woman; all four types had already been defined as suspect before they were taken up by Krafft-Ebing and Ellis. In effect, women's sexual behavior has never been isolated from or independent of the dominant male discourses of the age.

This dependence upon male theory can be seen in Germany, where lesbians—in spite of their very visible and active culture—remained quite marginal to the leading male theoreticians, Magnus Hirschfeld (1868–1935) and Benedict Friedlander (1866–1908). The former, a physician, worked all his life for the social acceptance of the congenital invert, which he defined as a female soul trapped in a male body or vice-versa, and for the repeal of the German law criminalizing homosexuality. Women connected with his Scientific Humanitarian Committee played a minor role in their Association for the Legal Protection of Mothers and for Sexual Reform, which combined an emphasis upon better maternity and sexual choice. Friedlander's "Gemeinschaft der Eigenen" promoted male friendship, with a special focus on "pedagogical eros," modeled on Greek boy-man relations. Friedlander and his followers championed bisexuality in all people, arguing that women were meant to bear children, while men should bond together to create culture and lead the nation. The women connected with this movement saw themselves as closer to Nature than men, and therefore as carriers of the spirit of Mother Nature.[66] They too promoted eroticized cross-age friendships, best exemplified by the film *Mädchen in Uniform* (1931), in which Manuela in the climactic scene is dressed as the hero in the school play and confesses her love for a favorite teacher before all the girls.[67]

By the end of the nineteenth century, wealthy and/or intrepid women had consciously migrated not only to Paris, but also to Berlin, Amsterdam, New York, San Francisco, Chicago, and other cities, where they hoped to find other homosexuals.[68] They were specifically attracted to cities with bohemian subcultures, which promised to give women space to explore their sexuality, their bodies. An extraordinary number of homosexual clubs and bars—surviving photographs indicate a passion for elegant butch-femme attire—flourished in Berlin, Munich, Hamburg, and other German cities, attesting to the cultural richness of Weimar Germany; none survived the Nazi takeover of 1933.

Some of the excitement and fragility of Germany's lively gay night life was also characteristic of Harlem of the 1920s. As Lillian Faderman has argued, it was a decade when bisexuality was fashionable, and the sexually freer world of Harlem attracted both white and Black women.[69] The wealthy A'Lelia Walker threw large and popular cross-race, cross-gender, and cross-class parties; lesbian "marriages" were celebrated with exuberant panache. Ma Rainey, Bessie Smith, Alberta Hunter, Jackie "Moms" Mabley, Josephine Baker, Ethel Waters, and above all, Gladys Bentley, celebrated lesbian sex. Bentley, a star at the famous Clam House, performed in a white tuxedo and married a woman in a civil ceremony in New Jersey. Many of the blues songs she and others sang mocked male sexual anxieties and reveled in female sexual subjectivity:

> Went out last night with a crowd of my friends,
> They must've been women, 'cause I don't like no men . . .
> . . . .
> They say I do it, ain't nobody caught me,
> They sure got to prove it on me . . . . [70]

But for literary English and American lesbians Paris symbolized sexual freedom.[71] It was already known for its lesbian subculture, thanks not only to Sand's reputation, but also to the poetry and fiction of such notable male writers as Balzac, Gautier, Baudelaire, Louÿs, Zola, Maupassant, and Daudet. In Paris the passing woman was embodied in the cross-dressed Marquise de Belbeuf, Colette's lover, or in Radclyffe Hall.

The enthusiasm for learning languages and the arts, so characteristic of earlier generations of romantic friends, continued. Renée Vivien and Natalie Barney took Greek lessons in order to read Sappho in the original; both made trips to Greece and participated in Greek theatricals. The Sapphic parties of Marie Antoinette were revived in Barney's famous entertainments. The militant respectability of Rosa Bonheur was transformed into the militant demand for recognition, best embodied in Hall's decision to write a book defending the "true invert." The bohemian world of George Sand did not need to be recreated because these women were living their own version of it.[72]

The most striking aspect of the lesbian coteries of the 1910s and 1920s was their self-conscious effort to create a new sexual language for themselves that included not only words but also gestures, costume, and behavior.[73] These women combined the essentialist biological explanation of lesbianism with a carefully constructed self-presentation. The parties, plays, and masquerades of the wealthy American Natalie Barney (1876–1970) are the best known "creations." They are commemorated in Djuna Barnes's privately published mock-heroic epic, *The Ladies' Almanack* (1928), in which Barney appears as Evangeline Musset. Although a "witty and learned Fifty," she was "so much in Demand, and so wide famed for her Genius at bringing up by Hand, and so noted and esteemed for her Slips of the Tongue that it finally brought her in the Hall of Fame . . ."[74] Barney herself said, "Men have skins, but women have flesh—flesh that takes and gives light."[75]

An insistence upon the flesh, the very body of the lesbian, distinguishes this generation. But if Barney celebrated the tactile delights of a woman's body, for Radclyffe Hall the lesbian body could be a curse because society refused to acknowledge its inherent validity. Without public, and especially family, acceptance, self-hatred was inevitable for her heroine Stephen in *The Well of Loneliness:* "She hated her body with its muscular shoulders, its small compact breasts, and its slender flanks of an athlete. All her life she must drag this body of hers like a monstrous fetter imposed on her spirit. This strangely ardent yet sterile body."[76] Moreover, contemporaries had the example of Renée Vivien (1877–1909) to remind them of the psychic dangers of lesbian love. Vivien embodied the doomed lesbian by changing her name, her religion, and her body, finally drinking and starving herself to death by the age of 31.

The privileged Barney declared that a woman's body was her greatest pleasure, but Hall contended that a woman's body was her unavoidable destiny, sterile or fertile. Both positions have an altogether too familiar ring, for both had long been encoded in male discourse. This generation of extraordinary women could not escape a familiar paradox that feminists still confront: by privileging the body, positively or negatively, women necessarily became participants in an already defined language and debate. Woman as body had been a male trope for too long to be overcome by a spirited or tragic rejection.[77]

Esther Newton has argued that Radclyffe Hall chose to portray Stephen as a congenital invert, based upon Havelock Ellis's theories, because it was her only alternative to the asexuality of romantic friendships. Actually, by the late 1920s Hall had numerous other alternatives, including Barney's hedonistic lesbianism, Vivien's self-created tragedy, Colette's theatrical affair with the marquise, and the many less colorful monogamous couples in Paris's literary world. For Hall, these women were either too secretive or too ostentatious and therefore too close to heterosexual fantasies about the life of the deviant.[78] Hall's militant demand for recognition made Ellis's congenital invert the most natural choice. This model, with its emphasis upon an innate, and therefore unchangeable, defect, also carried the status of scientific veracity. Ironically, as soon as a woman's body—specifically Stephen's "monstrous" body—became the focus of discussion, the book was legally banned in England. Only in 1968 was *The Well of Loneliness* available in England in a popular edition. A book that proclaimed a woman's free sexual choice as overtly as *The Well* was a dangerous as Catharina Margaretha Linck's dildo.

The demand for respect, for acceptance of one's innate difference, assumed a kind of sexual parity with men which has never been widely accepted. Hall's radical message was lost, but her portrait of Stephen remained. The complex heritage of the first generation of self-identified lesbians, experimental and flamboyant, collapsed into the public figure of the deprived and depraved *femme damnée*. The open-ended confidence and playfulness of the 1910s and 1920s did not survive the court case against *The Well of Loneliness*. The politically and economically turbulent 1930s narrowed women's sexual options. The lesbian community in Paris continued but shorn of its former glamor. Those who could find work often had to support relatives. The women's movement itself seemed increasingly irrelevant in the face of such competing ideologies as communism and fascism. Unfortunately generalizations are difficult to make, for we know little about the isolated lesbian of the 1930s. Characteristic of the decade, class divisions appear to have increased, so that the middle-class lesbian disappeared into discreet house parties, the aristocratic lesbian popped up at favorite expatriate spas, and the working-class lesbian could be found among the unemployed hitchhikers described by Box-Car Bertha.[79] Our only evidence of her public role is fleeting references in popular psychology books—like Krafft-Ebing—labeling her as dangerously independent.

The doomed lesbian was a remarkably durable image. By the 1950s everyone knew what a lesbian was; she had been assigned a clearly defined role. Defiance and loneliness marked her life, according to the pulp romances. The *femme damnée* was not simply a product of a fevered literary imagination; if her sexual preference became public knowledge during the witch-hunts of the McCarthy period she became literally outlawed. After acceptance during the labor-hungry years of World War II, lesbians and gays faced expulsion from military and government jobs.[80] Nevertheless, Elizabeth Wilson in England found the *femme damnée* an attractive alternative to bourgeois marriage in the 1950s; she was disappointed when progressive friends told her she was sick, not damned.[81]

In the 1950s both the general public and lesbians themselves privileged the predictable figure of the mannish lesbian. Romantic excess, forbidden desires, and social marginality were all represented by her cross-dressing. But, as I have demonstrated, she was also the product of a tangled history which embodied the outlawry of passing, the idealism of romantic friendship, and the theatricality of aristocratic play. What adhered to her identity most powerfully during these years, however, was a sense of being born different, of having a body that reflects a specific sexual identity. The femme who could pass had disappeared. Although the American Joan Nestle has argued forcefully for her importance, Wilson experienced being a woman's woman as "the lowest of the low" in the liberal heterosexual world she inhabited.[82]

But the old playfulness of an earlier generation never completely died. Now it has returned not to recreate the past, but rather to celebrate the identification of homosexuality with defined, and inescapable, roles or to imagine a utopian world of transformed women. Like the women of the early twentieth century, many lesbians of our time have set themselves the task of creating a lesbian language, of defining lesbian desire, and of imagining a lesbian society. Monique Wittig, in *Les guérillères* (1969), *Le corps lesbien* (1973), and *Brouillon pour un dictionnaire des amantes* (1975), has presented the most sustained alternative world. Her wholesale rewriting of history, in which all mention of man is eliminated, makes it possible to imagine a woman's body outside male discourse. Even here, however, our history is incomplete. In their heroic comedy, *Brouillon pour un dictionnaire des amantes,* Wittig and her co-author Sande Zeig leave a blank page for the reader to fill in under Sappho. Dyke, butch, amazon, witch, and such "obsolete" words as woman and wife are included. But androgyne, femme, invert, and friendship are missing.[83] Rosa Bonheur, who so disliked rigid sex roles, is strangely absent from this world. And what about the occasional lover of women? Historians are more confined to their evidence than writers of fiction, and cannot create utopias, but they can and do create myths. When we rewrite, indeed, recreate, our lost past, do we too readily drop those parts of our past that seem unattractive or confusing to us? Can (and should) utopian language and ideas help us recuperate a history full of contradictions?

NOTES

This is a revised and updated version of a paper originally presented at the "Homosexuality, Which Homosexuality? conference (Amsterdam, December 1987). The paper appears in Dennis Altman, et al., *Homosexuality, Which Homosexuality?* (Amsterdam: An Dekker, 1989). I am indebted to Anja van Kooten Niekerk, Theo van der Meer, and the other organizers of the conference for providing such a supportive environment for the testing of new ideas. My thanks to Anna Davin, Karin Lützen and Marlon Ross for their help; their probing questions and detailed suggestions have improved this essay immensely. Special thanks go to Alice Echols and Anne Herrmann, who read and critiqued each version with such encouragement and good will.

1. Theodore Stanton, ed., *Reminiscences of Rosa Bonheur* (1910, New York: Hacker Books, 1976), p. 199.

2. Anna Klumpke, *Rosa Bonheur, sa vie, son oeuvre* (Paris: Flammarion, 1908), p. 356: "Deux femmes peuvent sentir l'une pour l'autre le charme d'une amitié vive et passionée, sans que rien n'en altére la pureté." I am indebted to Karin Lützen for this reference.

3. Estelle B. Freedman, et al., Editorial, The Lesbian Issue, *Signs*, 9/4 (Summer 1984), 554.

4. Jackie Stacey, "The Invisible Difference: Lesbianism and Sexual Difference Theory," unpub. conference paper, "Homosexuality, Which Homosexuality?"

5. Eve Kosofsky Sedgwick, *Epistemology of the Closet* (Berkeley: University of California Press, 1990), p. 85. Chapter 1, "Epistemology of the Closet," is reprinted in this volume. See also Carole S. Vance, "Social Construction Theory: Problems in the History of Sexuality," in *Homosexuality, Which Homosexuality?, pp. 13–34.

6. Steven Epstein, "Gay Politics, Ethnic Identity: The Limits of Social Constructionism," *Socialist Review*, no. 93/94 (May–August 1987), 24, 30.

7. There are, however, at least two case studies: See Brigitte Ericksson, trans., "A Lesbian Execution in Germany, 1721: The Trial Records," *Historical Perspectives on Homosexuality*, ed. Salvatore J. Licata and Robert P. Petersen (New York: Haworth Press, 1981), p. 33; for the notorious Miss Pirie and Miss Woods vs. Lady Cumming Gordon, see Lillian Faderman, *Scotch Verdict* (New York: Quill Press, 1983). See also Louis Crompton, "The Myth of Lesbian Impunity: Capital Laws from 1270 to 1791," in *Historical Perspectives on Homosexuality*, pp. 11–26.

8. But see George Chauncey, Jr., "From Sexual Inversion to Homosexuality: Medicine and the Changing Conceptualization of Female Desire," *Salmagundi*, no. 58/59 (Fall/Winter 1982–83), 114–46; and Myriam Everard, "Lesbianism and Medical Practice in the Netherlands, 1897–1930," unpub. conference paper, "Homosexuality, Which Homosexuality?"

9. See Judith C. Brown's *Immodest Acts: The Life of A Lesbian Nun* (New York: Oxford University Press, 1986) for a case study of a seventeenth-century Italian nun. See also the preliminary study of Elaine Hobby, "Seventeenth-Century English Lesbianism: First Steps," unpub. conference paper, "Homosexuality, Which Homosexuality?"

10. See the early Bertha Harris, "The More Profound Nationality of their Lesbianism: Lesbian Society in Paris in the 1920's," *Amazon Expedition: A Lesbian Feminist Anthology* (New York: Times Change Press, 1973), pp. 77–88; and Lillian Faderman and Brigitte Eriksson, eds., *Lesbian-Feminism in Turn-of-the-Century Germany* (Tallahassee: Naiad Press, 1980). But see also the pioneering literary history of Shari Benstock, *Women of the Left Bank, Paris, 1900–1940* (Austin:

University of Texas Press, 1986). Blanche Wiesen Cook and Jane Marcus have always insisted upon the importance of a women's community during the 1920s. See Cook, "Female Support Networks and Political Activism: Lillian Wald, Crystal Eastman, Emma Goldman," in *A Heritage of Her Own: Toward a New Social History of American Women,* ed. Nancy Cott and Elizabeth Pleck (New York: Simon and Schuster, 1979), pp. 412–44, and for Marcus on Virginia Woolf, see especially her "The Niece of a Nun" and "Sapphistry: Narration as Lesbian Seduction" in Jane Marcus, *Virginia Woolf and the Languages of Patriarchy* (Bloomington: Indiana University Press, 1987).

11. See, for example, Hall=Carpenter Archives, Lesbian Oral History Group, *Inventing Ourselves: Lesbian Life Stories* (London: Routledge, 1989).

12. Biddy Martin, "Lesbian Identity and Autobiographical Difference[s]," reprinted in this volume, p. 278.

13. Biddy Martin specifically compares the life-stories in *This Bridge Called My Back: Writings by Radical Women of Color,* ed. Cherríe Moraga and Gloria Anzaldúa (Watertown, Mass: Persephone Press, 1981) with those in the predominantly white and middle-class collections, *The Coming Out Stories,* eds. Julia Penelope Stanley and Susan J. Wolfe (Watertown, Mass: Persephone Press, 1980) and *The Lesbian Path,* ed. Margaret Cruikshank (San Francisco: Grey Fox Press, 1985).

14. See my discussion of this debate in "Sexuality and Power: A Review of Current Work in the History of Sexuality," *Feminist Studies,* 8 (Spring 1982), 133–56.

15. Amber Hollibaugh and Cherríe Moraga, "What We're Rollin Around in Bed With: Sexual Silences in Feminism: A Conversation toward Ending them," *Heresies,* no. 12 (1981), 58.

16. Blanche Wiesen Cook, "The Historical Denial of Lesbianism," *Radical History Review,* no. 20 (Spring/Summer 1979), 64.

17. See Ann Ferguson, "Patriarchy, Sexual Identity, and the Sexual Revolution, *Signs,* 7 (Autumn 1981), 158–72.

18. Anne Lister, *I Know My Own Heart: The Diaries of Anne Lister,* ed. Helena Whitbread (London: Virago, 1988), passim. Lillian Faderman's *Surpassing the Love of Men: Romantic Friendship between Women from the Renaissance to the Present* (New York: William Morrow, 1981) contains the best account of the pleasures and limitations of romantic friendship without financial means.

19. I am indebted to Laurence Senelick for drawing my attention to Pidansat de Mairobert's pre-revolutionary quasi-pornographic romance, *Histoire d'une jeune fille* (Paris: Biblothèque des Curieux, n.d. [1789]), in which a fictional "Secte des Anandrynes" meet for lesbian frolics under the leadership of a statuesque woman described as possessing "something of the masculine in her appearance" ("quelque chose d'hommasse dans toute sa personne," p. 23).

20. Randolph Trumbach has documented the shift from the rake's bisexual freedom to the effeminate sodomite in "Gender and the Homosexual Role in modern Western Culture: The Eighteenth and Nineteenth Centuries Compared," in *Homosexuality, Which Homosexuality?,* pp. 149–70.

21. The one obvious exception to this generalization is Dr. James Barry (1795?–1865), a well-known British army surgeon, whom contemporaries assumed was a hermaphrodite on account of her small stature, lack of beard, and high voice. See Isobel Rae, *The Strange Story of Dr. James Barry* (London: Longmans, 1958).

22. Dianne Dugaw, *Warrior Women and Popular Balladry, 1650–1850* (Cambridge: Cambridge University Press, 1989), pp. 148–58.

23. See especially the case of the Civil War volunteer Frank Thompson (Emma Edmonds) in Julie Wheelwright, *Amazons and Military Maids* (London: Pandora, 1989), pp. 62–66.

24. See the facsimile reprint of the second edition (1755), *A Narrative of the Life of Charlotte Charke,* ed. Leonard R.N. Ashley (Gainesville, Fla: Scholars' Facsimiles and Reprints, 1969).

25. Rudolph Dekker and Lottie van de Pol, *The Tradition of Female Transvestism in Early Modern Europe* (London: Macmillan, 1988), pp. 54–55, 71.

26. See Hobby, "Seventeenth-Century English Lesbianism." Hobby is currently writing a book on lesbianism in the early modern period.

27. See Richard Sennett's discussion of the ways in which John Wilkes's body—and sexual freedom—came to represent political freedom in, *The Fall of the Public Man: On the Social Psychology of Capitalism* (New York: Vintage, 1978), pp. 99–106.

28. Marie-Jo Bonnet, *Un choix sans équivoque* (Paris: Denoel, 1981), pp. 137–65. See also Faderman, *Surpassing the Love of Men,* pp. 42–43.

29. See Lynn Hunt, "The Many Bodies of Marie Antoinette: Political Pornography and the Problem of the Feminine in the French Revolution," in *Eroticism and the Body Politic,* ed. Lynn Hunt (Baltimore: The Johns Hopkins University Press, 1991), pp. 108–30.

30. Nancy Cott, *The Bonds of Womanhood: "Woman's Sphere" in New England, 1780–1835* (New Haven: Yale University Press, 1977), p. 186.

31. Maaike Meijer, "Pious and Learned Female Bosomfriends in Holland in the Eighteenth Century," unpub. conference paper, "Among Men, Among Women" (Amsterdam, June 1983). These ideals also characterized the friendship of Ruth and Eva in *Dear Girls: The Diaries and Letters of Two Working Women, 1897–1917,* ed. Tierl Thompson (London: Women's Press, 1987), a century later.

32. These issues are touched on, but not completely developed, in Martha Vicinus, "Distance and Desire: English Boarding-School Friendships," in Martin Bauml Duberman, Martha Vicinus, and George Chauncey, Jr., eds., *Hidden from History: Reclaiming the Gay and Lesbian Past* (New York: New American Library, 1989), pp. 212–29.

33. Elaine Marks, "Lesbian Intertexuality," *Homosexualities and French Literature,* ed. George Stambolian and Elaine Marks (Ithaca: Cornell University Press, 1979), pp. 356–58.

34. Constance Maynard describing her relationship with Louisa Lumsden, quoted in Martha Vicinus, *Independent Women: Work and Community for Single Women, 1850–1920* (Chicago: University of Chicago Press, 1985), p. 201.

35. Joanne Glasgow argues that "misogyny, thus, accounts in significant ways for the official neglect of lesbianism" in the Roman Catholic church. See her "What's a Nice Lesbian Like You Doing in the Church of Torquemada? Radclyffe Hall and Other Catholic Converts," *Lesbian Texts and Contexts: Radical Revisions,* ed. Karla Jay and Joanne Glasgow (New York: New York University Press, 1990), p. 249.

36. The *Oxford English Dictionary,* not always the most reliable source on sexual matters, records the first use of tribade in 1601; tribady in 1811–19, in reference to the famous Miss Woods and Miss Pirie vs. Lady Cumming Gordon trial of 1811. Hermaphrodite receives the most complete coverage, with the first reference to its use as 1398. Sapphic is defined simply as "of or pertaining to Sappho, the famous poetess of Lesbos," or "a meter used by Sappho or named after her." Sapphism is not mentioned. Bonnet traces a similar linguistic development in French, beginning with the sixteenth-century use of tribade, *Un choix,* pp. 25–67. She gives three examples from the *Dictionnaire érotique latin-français,* a seventeenth-century erotic dictionary (published only in the nineteenth century) which mentions tribade, lesbian, and *fricatrix* (someone who rubs/caresses another person "for pleasure or for health"). See p. 43.

37. Faderman, *Surpassing the Love of Men,* p. 56 and Bram Stoker, *Famous Imposters* (New York: Sturgis & Walton, 1910), pp. 241–46. Similar revelations were always fair game for the prurient and pornographic. See, for example, Henry Fielding's titillating (and inaccurate) account of Mary Hamilton, *The Female Husband* (1746). The actual events are described by Sheridan Baker, "Henry Fielding's *The Female Husband:* Fact and Fiction," *PMLA* 74 (1959), 213–24.

38. Marjorie Garber, *Vested Interests: Cross-Dressing and Cultural Anxiety* (New York: Routledge, 1991), pp. 69–70. Garber's discussion is in regard to the jazz musician Billy Tipton, whose sexual identity was revealed at "his" death in 1989.

39. Ericksson, "A Lesbian Execution," p. 33. See also Theo van der Meer, "Tribades on Trial: Female Same-Sex Offenders in Late Eighteenth-Century Amsterdam," *Journal of the History of Sexuality,* 1 (January 1991), 424–45. These women, drawn from a similar class as Linck's, were seen as public nuisances and prostitutes, as well as tribades.

40. Butler's and Ponsonby's lives are recounted in Elizabeth Mavor, *The Ladies of Llangollen* (London: Michael Joseph, 1971), p. 74.

41. See *Thraliana: The Diary of Hester Lynch Thrale (Later Mrs. Piozzi),* ed. Katharine Balderston, 2d ed. (Oxford: Clarendon Press, 1951), vol. 1, p. 740. Randolph Trumbach, in "London's Sapphists: From Three Sexes to Four Genders in the Making of Modern Culture," *Body Guards: The Cultural Politics of Gender Ambiguity,* ed. Julia Epstein and Kristina Straub (New York: Rout-

ledge, 1991), pp. 112–41, documents Mrs. Piozzi's growing awareness of English "sapphists," and the reference to them in slang as early as 1782 as "tommies."

42. Bonnet, *Un choix,* p. 165. See also Terry Castle's recent examination of the continued interest in Marie Antoinette among lesbians, "Marie Antoinette Obsession," *Representations* 38 (Spring 1992), 1–38.

43. The fullest account of "Colonel" Barker can be found in Wheelwright, pp. 1–11, 159. Wheelwright points out that Barker married only after her father-in-law caught the two women living together. In court "his" wife, Elfrida Haward, denied all knowledge of her husband's true sex. Characteristically, the judge was most concerned with Barker's deception of the Church of England. See also Michael Baker, *Our Three Selves: The Life of Radclyffe Hall* (London: Hamish Hamilton, 1985), 254.

44. See Leila Rupp's essay, " 'Imagine My Surprise': Women's Relationships in Mid-Twentieth Century America," in *Hidden from History,* pp. 395–410.

45. But see Colette's attempt to define her in an evocative recreation of Sarah Ponsonby in *The Pure and the Impure,* trans. Herma Briffault (New York: Farrar, Straus & Giroux, 1966), pp. 114–29.

46. Teresa de Lauretis, "Sexual Indifference and Lesbian Representation," *Theatre Journal,* 40 (May 1988), 177. Reprinted in this volume.

47. Quoted by Esther Newton, "The Mythic Mannish Lesbian: Radclyffe Hall and the New Woman," in *Hidden from History,* p. 288.

48. See, for example, "The Shocking Facts about Those Lesbians," *Hush-Hush,* 5 (September 1959), unpaginated; "Do Lesbian Wives Swap Husbands?," *On the Q.T.,* 5 (July 1961), 28–29, 56–57, 60; Sharon Tague, "How Many U.S. Wives are Secret Lesbians?," *Uncensored,* 14 (February 1965), 20–21, 58. I am indebted to Laurence Senelick and the Lesbian Herstory Archives for these references.

49. See also the more elusive life described in Betty T. Bennett's biography, *Mary Diana Dods: A Gentleman and A Scholar* (New York: William Morrow, 1991). One of two illegitimate daughters of the fifteenth earl of Morton, Dods earned a precarious living as a writer using several different male pseudonyms. In 1827 Mary Shelley helped Dods escape from England to the continent as Walter Sholto Douglas, "husband" of the pregnant Isabel Robinson. Although they gained entry to the highest literary circles in Paris, the Douglases were totally dependent upon funds from their families. Dods appears to have died in penury in 1829, freeing her "wife" to make a highly respectable marriage to an Anglican minister resident in Florence, Italy.

50. Lister, *I Know My Own Heart,* 28. For examples of attacks on her by men, see pp. 48–49, 106, 110, 113–15.

51. We have, of course, only Lister's interpretation of her behavior, but see Lister, p. 104: "I felt she was another man's wife. I shuddered at the thought & at the conviction that no soffistry [sic] could gloss over the criminality of our connection. It seemed not that the like had occurred to her." The use of a masculine (or androgynous) nickname for the more mannish partner can be found repeatedly in these relations.

52. As Ruth Jordan describes it, "George was credited with at least three simultaneous affairs [with men]: one with Sandeau, unwanted but still officiating, another with Latouche, who had retired to the country, and yet another with Gustave Planche, the unkempt, uncombed, unwashed brilliant critic of the *Revue des Deux Mondes.* Marie Dorval was the latest, most sensational addition to a cohort of unproven lovers." See her *George Sand: A Biography* (London: Constable, 1976), p. 68. Biographers of Sand fall into two camps, those who sensationalize her life and those who normalize it; the latter, of course, are most reluctant to identify her relationship with Dorval as sexual.

53. Isabelle de Courtivon, "Weak Men and Fatal Women: The Sand Image," in *Homosexualities and French Literature,* pp. 214–16.

54. In addition to de Courtivon, see also Faderman, *Surpassing the Love of Men,* pp. 274–99, and Dorelies Kraakman, "Sexual Ambivalence of Women Artists in Early Nineteenth-Century France," unpub. conference Paper, "Homosexuality, Which Homosexuality?" I am indebted to Dorelies Kraakman for discussing with me the importance of the 1830s and 1840s in France for understanding the formation of a new public discourse about women's sexuality.

55. See Emmanuel Cooper, *The Sexual Perspective: Homosexuality and Art in the Last 100 Years in the West* (London: Routledge and Kegan Paul, 1986), pp. 55–58. See also the biography, Emma Stebbins, ed., *Charlotte Cushman: Her Life and Memories of Her Life* (Boston: Houghton Mifflin, 1991).

56. Faderman, *Surpassing the Love of Men,* pp. 190–230. See also Lillian Faderman, "The Morbidification of Love between Women by Nineteenth-Century Sexologists," *Journal of Homosexuality,* 4 (Fall 1978), 73–90.

57. Martha Vicinus, " 'One Life to Stand Beside Me': Emotional Conflicts in First-Generation College Women in England," *Feminist Studies* 8 (Fall 1982), 610–11.

58. Dore Ashton and Denise Browne Hare, *Rosa Bonheur: A Life and a Legend* (New York: Viking Press, 1981), p. 162.

59. The known facts are briefly outlined in Olive Banks, *The Biographical Dictionary of British Feminists, 1800–1930* (New York: New York University Press, 1985), p. 74. I am indebted to Gail Malmgreen for reminding me of this example.

60. A.J.B. Parent-Duchâtelet claimed that "lesbians have fallen to the last degree of vice to which a human creature can attain, and, for that very reason, they require a most particular surveillance on the part of those charged with the surveillance of prostitutes . . ." (*La prostitution dans la ville de Paris* [1836], vol. 1, p. 170), quoted in *Homosexualities and French Literature,* p. 148. I am indebted to Marjan Sax for pointing out the connection between prostitutes and lesbians in medical and legal texts.

61. Carroll Smith-Rosenberg, "The New Woman as Androgyne: Social Disorder and Gender Crisis, 1870–1936," *Disorderly Conduct: Visions of Gender in Victorian America* (New York: Alfred Knopf, 1985), pp. 271–72.

62. See Lal Coveney, et al., *The Sexuality Papers: Male Sexuality and the Sexual Control of Women* (London: Hutchinson, 1984) and Sheila Jeffreys, *The Spinster and Her Enemies: Feminism and Sexuality, 1880–1930* (London: Pandora, 1985). I am grateful for the opportunity to discuss these issues and their current popularity in England with Alison Oram.

63. Sonia Ruehl, "Inverts and Experts: Radclyffe Hall and the Lesbian Identity," *Feminism, Culture, and Politics,* ed. Rosalind Brunt and Caroline Rowan (London: Lawrence and Wishart, 1982), pp. 15–36.

64. See Chauncey, "From Sexual Inversion," and Vicinus, "Distance and Desire."

65. Newton, "Mythic Mannish Lesbian," p. 291.

66. See Heidi Schupmann, " 'Homosexuality' in the Journal *Die Neue Generation,*" unpub. conference paper, "Homosexuality, Which Homosexuality?" and Marian de Ras, "The 'Tribadic Revolt': Hans Blüher and the Girls' Unions," unpub. conference paper, "Homosexuality, Which Homosexuality?" See also Lillian Faderman and Brigitte Erickson, *Lesbians in Germany: 1890s–1920s* (Tallahassee: Naiad Press, 1990) and John Steakley, *The Homosexual Emancipation Movement in Germany* (New York: Arno Press, 1975).

67. For a discussion of the political implications of this lesbianism, see B. Ruby Rich, "*Maedchen in Uniform:* From Repressive Tolerance to Erotic Liberation," *Radical America,* 15 (1981), 18–36.

68. Gayle Rubin has coined the phrase "sexual migrations" to describe "the movement of people to cities undertaken to explore specialized sexualities not available in the traditional family arrangements, and often smaller towns, where they grew up." Quoted by Rayna Rapp, "An Introduction to Elsa Gidlow: Memoirs," *Feminist Studies* 6 (Spring 1980), 106, n. 4. In her autobiography, *Elsa: I Come with My Songs* (San Francisco: Booklegger Press, 1986), Gidlow (1898–1986) makes clear that until the 1970s her homosexual community was comprised primarily of men and a few close women friends.

69. Lillian Faderman, *Odd Girls and Twilight Lovers: A History of Lesbian Life in Twentieth-Century America* (New York: Columbia University Press, 1991), pp. 62–92. See also Eric Garber, "A Spectacle in Color: The Lesbian and Gay Subculture of Jazz Age Harlem," in *Hidden from History,* pp. 318–31, and "Gladys Bentley: The Bulldagger Who Sang the Blues," *Out/Look* (Spring 1988), 52–61.

70. "Prove It On Me Blues," sung by Ma Rainey, cited in Faderman, *Odd Girls and Twilight Lovers,* p. 77. See also Hazel V. Carby, "It Jus Be's Dat Way Sometimes: The Sexual Politics of Women's Blues," *Radical America,* 20 (1986), 9–22.

71. The literary relations in this subculture have been explored by Benstock, *Women of the Left Bank;* see also the numerous biographies of the most famous figures. Benstock quotes Elyse Blankley (p. 49) in characterizing Paris as "a double-edged sword, offering both free sexual expression and oppressive sexual stereotyping. It might cultivate lesbianism like an exotic vine, but it would never nourish it. In front of [Renée] Vivien—and indeed, every lesbian—yawned the immense, unbridgeable chasm separating men's perceptions of lesbian women and lesbian women's perceptions of themselves." See Elyse Blankley, "Return to Mytilène: Renée Vivien and the City of Women," in *Women Writers and the City,* ed. Susan Merrill Squier (Knoxville: University of Tennessee Press, 1984), pp. 45–67.

72. We have very little evidence of a working-class lesbian subculture at this time. Elsa Gidlow's memoirs (pp. 68–71) seem to indicate a similar pattern of seeking out a bohemian artistic culture. During World War I she started a literary group in Montreal which attracted a young gay man who introduced her to the Decadent writers of the late nineteenth century, avant-garde music, and modern art.

73. In her essay "The New Woman as Androgyne" Smith-Rosenberg discusses the revolutionary nature of this project—and its failure, which she attributes to the writers' unsuccessful effort to transform the male discourse on female sexuality (pp. 265–66, 285–96).

74. Quoted in Meryle Secrest, *Between Me and Life: A Biography of Romaine Brooks* (London: Macdonald & Jones, 1976), p. 335. See also George Wickes, *The Amazon of Letters: The Life and Loves of Natalie Barney* (London: W.H. Allen, 1977).

75. Secrest, *Between Me and Life,* p. 336.

76. Radclyffe Hall, *The Well of Loneliness* (London: Corgi Books, 1968), p. 217.

77. The feminist literature on this equation is vast, but see, most recently, Susan R. Suleiman, ed., *The Female Body in Western Culture: Contemporary Perspectives* (Cambridge: Harvard University Press, 1986).

78. This point is also made by Gillian Whitlock, " 'Everything is Out of Place': Radclyffe Hall and the Lesbian Literary Tradition," *Feminist Studies,* 13 (Fall 1987), 576. See also Benstock's comment (*Women of the Left Bank,* p. 59) about this generation of lesbian writers as a whole: "Without historical models, [their] writing was forced to take upon itself the double burden of creating a model of lesbian behavior while recording the personal experience of that behavior."

79. See Vern Bullough and Bonnie Bullough, "Lesbianism in the 1920s and 1930s: A Newfound Study," *Signs* 2 (1977), 895–904; Marion K. Sanders, *Dorothy Thompson, A Legend in Her Time* (Boston: Houghton Mifflin, 1973) [Thompson was the lover of Christa Winsloe, playwright and author of the play and novel upon which *Mädchen in Uniform* was based]; Box-Car Bertha, *Sister of the Road: An Autobiography,* as told to Ben L. Reitman (1937; New York: Harper and Row, 1975). See also Faderman, *Odd Girls,* pp. 93–117 and Gidlow, *Elsa,* pp. 250–81.

80. See Allan Bérubé, *Coming Out Under Fire: The History of Gay Men and Women in World War II* (New York: Free Press, 1990).

81. Elizabeth Wilson, "Forbidden Love," in *Hidden Agendas: Theory, Politics and Experience in the Women's Movement* (London: Tavistock, 1986), p. 175.

82. Joan Nestle, "Butch-Femme Relationships: Sexual Courage in the 1950s," in *A Restricted Country* (Ithaca: Firebrand Books, 1987), pp. 100–09; and Elizabeth Wilson, "Gayness and Liberalism," in *Hidden Agendas,* p. 141.

83. I am using the English translation, *Lesbian Peoples: Materials for a Dictionary* (London: Virago, 1980).

30

"Lines She Did Not Dare":
Angelina Weld Grimké,
Harlem Renaissance Poet

GLORIA T. HULL

Gloria T. Hull is Professor of Women's Studies and Literature, University of California, Santa Cruz. Her essay, "Tracing Her Evolution as Radical Scholar," appears in Changing Subjects: The Making of Feminist Criticism, *edited by Gayle Greene and Coppélia Kahn (Routledge); she is also the author of* Color, Sex, and Poetry: Three Women Writers of the Harlem Renaissance *(1987), from which this essay has been excerpted. Here Hull asks how we can account for the self-isolation and meager creative output of Angelina Weld Grimké (1880–1958), given the prominent presence and immense productivity of such Harlem Renaissance women writers as Alice Dunbar-Nelson and Georgia Douglas Johnson. A well-educated, racially mixed Black woman of comfortable means and prominent family, Grimké's refusal to take advantage of opportunities to speak and write, her surprisingly scant oeuvre, and her poetry's thematic insistence on loss are explained, Hull argues, at least in significant part, when we permit the covert lesbianism of her published love poetry to emerge as it so clearly does in her unpublished love lyrics. It is important in understanding Grimké's position at the beginning of the twentieth century to read her not only as a Black poet and a woman poet but also as a lesbian poet.*

... The third period of Angelina Weld Grimké's life finds her in her middle forties, sharing in the glory and good fortune of the Harlem Renaissance. It also brings her into focus as a poet. Though she had already been writing poems, they did not receive really widespread attention until this time. The effort that she poured into her drama and fiction notwithstanding, poetry was truly Grimké's major genre. However much she was applauded for *Rachel*, it was as a poet that she retains a valid place in literary history.

During the mid–1920s, her work was frequently published in *Opportunity* magazine. Perhaps because of her allegiance to *Opportunity* or some seeming antipathy that existed between her family and W.E.B. Du Bois, only two or three of her poems appear in *The Crisis*, the N.A.A.C.P. magazine edited by Du Bois.[1] Every anthology or special magazine issue of black poetry during the period includes her work—Alain Locke's *The New Negro* (1925), Countee Cullen's *Caroling Dusk* (1927), where she is represented by more poems than any other female poet, Charles S. Johnson's *Ebony and Topaz* (1927), *The Carolina Magazine* (May 1928), and so on. The one unexplainable exception is James Weldon Johnson's *Book of American Negro Poetry*, which, in neither its 1922 nor 1931 edition, reprints any poems by her. Grimké even received a request in 1928 from one Dr. Anna Nussbaum for permission to translate some of her poems into German for an anthology of black poetry.[2]

Grimké also tried to widen the journals in which she published and to enhance further her poetic reputation. Earlier, before she had produced her best poems, she had pieces rejected by magazines like *Harper's* and *The Smart Set*.[3] Now, with the aid of Charles Johnson, she looked again for other publishing outlets. On February 6, 1924, he writes her: "I sent some of the poems which you gave me . . . to Clement Wood and he has expressed considerable interest in them. . . . Meanwhile, I am trying out some other of the poetry magazines."[4] He also submitted some of her poems to *Century Magazine* in 1925; they were returned on June 16. Not readily placing her work caused her anxiety, for on June 25, 1925, Johnson is counseling her to "cease fretting for a spell."

Sometime either before or during this period, Grimké was planning a collection of her poetry. She tentatively called it *Dusk Dreams* and set down a list of twenty-three titles that would constitute the book. Oddly enough, only five of these are published poems and the bulk of them do not represent her at her best—suggesting perhaps that the collection was projected earlier in her career. Whatever the case, it never materialized, although if Grimké had taken the poems that she had published in magazines and anthologies by 1928 (which constitute her most mature work) and added some others to them, she could have assembled a very respectable volume. As it turned out, her name as a poet was kept alive after the 1920s by her inclusion in various textbooks and, of course, by editors of black poetry volumes who kept recycling the same poems.[5] Seemingly, she stopped writing altogether. On May 1, 1932, a friend of hers in Philadelphia, the artist Henry B. Jones, playfully—but earnestly—chided her for not using her gift and writing poetry.[6] Furthermore, none of her extant poems appears to have been produced after this date.

For the sake of convenience, Grimké's poetry can be roughly grouped into five general categories: (1) elegies, (2) love lyrics, (3) nature lyrics, (4) racial poems, and (5) philosophical poems about the human condition.

Throughout her career, Grimké eulogized family and close friends, beginning with Joseph Lee, described as "the Boston Negro caterer and hotel-keeper who was long Mr. W.D. Howells's admired host at Auburndale,"[7] and ending with Clarissa Scott Delany, another black female poet, who died in 1927 when she was only twenty-six years old. Recalling her poem to Clarissa, one of Grimké's correspondents, Julia Parks, made a relevant remark: "You surely do appreciate your friends—and can give your thought such exquisitely enduring form."[8] However, she wrote her finest elegy for her famous aunt, Charlotte Forten (the only other black woman besides Alice Dunbar-Nelson whose booklength diary has been published). Forten married Grimké's uncle Francis late in her life and died in 1914. Grimké loved and respected her "Aunt Lottie" (although they had some slight difficulty as two women living in the same house),[9] and the poem that she wrote for her, "To Keep the Memory of Charlotte Forten Grimké," reflects her intimate knowledge and appreciation of this gentle woman. The poem begins:

> Still are there wonders of the dark and day;
> The muted shrilling of shy things at night,
> So small beneath the stars and moon;
> The peace, dream-frail, but perfect while the light
> Lies softly on the leaves at noon.
> These are, and these will be

Until Eternity;
But she who loved them well has gone away[10]

Three more stanzas with the same form and pattern ensue, each one repeating as refrain the last two lines. The entire poem—as do all of Grimké's elegies—allays grief by accepting death as a beautiful phenomenon, placing the departed one in the natural schema, and evoking a sense of her/his continuing presence.

The second category of Grimké's poems, love lyrics, constitute one of the largest groups. These poems are, as a rule, very delicate, musical, romantic, and pensive. "A Mona Lisa" and "When the Green Lies Over the Earth," two of her best-known works, probably belong in this category. Practically all of these lyrics are addressed to women. One that she never published is called either "Rosabel" or "Rosalie":

I
Leaves that whisper whisper ever
    Listen, listen, pray!
Birds that twitter twitter softly
    Do not say me nay.
Winds that breathe about, upon her
    (Lines I do not dare)
Whisper, turtle, breathe upon her
    That I find her fair.
II
Rose whose soul unfolds white petaled
    Touch her soul, use white
Rose whose thoughts unfold gold petaled
    Blossom in her sight
Rose whose heart unfolds, red petaled
    Prick her slow heart's stir
Tell her white, gold, red my love is—
    And for her,—for her.

In these poems, Grimké was probably not simply assuming the mask of a traditional male persona, but writing from her own true feelings and experiences. In February 1896 one of her school friends, Mamie (Mary) Burrill, sent her a youthful letter, where, mixed in with apologies, school gossip, and church news, she recalled their secret good times together and reaffirmed her love: "Could I just come to meet thee once more, in the old sweet way, just coming at your calling, and like an angel bending o'er you breathe into your ear, 'I love you.' "[11] For her part, Angelina was even more ardent. In a letter written later that year while she was in Northfield, Minnesota, at the Carleton Academy, she overflows: "Oh Mamie if you only knew how my heart beats when I think of you and it yearns and pants to gaze, if only for one second upon your lovely face." With naïve sweetness, she asks Mamie to be her "wife" and ends the letter: "Now may the Almighty father bless thee little one and keep thee safe from all harm, Your passionate lover."[12]

Mamie went on to become a teacher in the Washington, D.C., public school system, an actress, and a playwright. Her 1919 one-act drama *They That Sit In Darkness* concerns a poor black woman with too many children who is mired in childbearing and poverty because the system denies women access to birth-control information.[13] It appeared in the same special issue of the *Birth Control Review* as Grimké's story "The Closing Door." Exactly what happened between Grimké and Burrill is not clear. She may or may not have been the partner in the disastrous love affair mentioned earlier that Grimké set down in her diary, July 18–September 10, 1903 (although it is a bit hard to imagine Grimké speaking forthrightly about a female lover to her father). Later in their lives, Mamie alluded to their girlhood relationship in a brief note that she wrote to Grimké in July 1911 after Grimké had been injured in a train wreck: "If I can serve you at all, for the sake of the days that are a long way behind us both, I trust you will let me do so."

The manuscript poems that Grimké wrote during the early 1900s parallel the diary's story of heartbreak and unhappiness and indicate, further, that the lover was female—either Mamie or some other woman. "If"—one copy of which is dated July 31, 1903—is divided into halves. The first speculates that if every thought, hope, and dream the speaker has of her love became a pansy, rose, or maidenhair, then the world would be overrun with "rosy blooms, and pansy glooms and curling leaves of green." The second part, though, posits that if every look, word, and deed of the lover became ice, sleet, and snow, then "this old world would fast be curled beneath a wintry moon/ With wastes of snow that livid glow—as it is now in June." Another poem, entitled "To Her of the Cruel Lips" and ending "I laugh, yet—my brain is sad," was written November 5, 1903. And, on January 16, 1904, Grimké is asking "Where is the Dream?" and "Why do I Love you so?"

Nothing else exists to tell if and whom and how she loved after this. She followed the external resolutions that she made in her diary to forego marriage and children and occupy her life with writing and her father—and probably continued to desire women, in silence and frustration. Unlike Dunbar-Nelson, Grimké does not appear to have acted on her lesbian feelings with continuous and mature assurance. But—perhaps because she did not—they provided greater impetus for her verse.

Her first developed piece, "El Beso," reveals one way that Grimké handled in her public art what seem to be woman-to-woman romantic situations. Here, she writes of "your provocative laughter,/The gloom of your hair;/Lure of you, eye and lip"; and then "Pain, regret—your sobbing." Because of the "feel" of the poem and its diction ("sobbing," for example), the "you" visualizes as a woman—despite the absence of the third-person pronouns and the usual tendency most readers have (knowledge of persona, notwithstanding) to image the other in a love poem as being opposite in sex from the poem's known author. "A Mona Lisa" is similar in tone and approach. It begins:

> I should like to creep
> Through the long brown grasses
>   That are your lashes.[14]

As one might predict, Grimké's unpublished poetry contains an even heavier concentration of love lyrics. In these can be found the raw feeling, feminine pronouns, and womanly imagery that have been excised or muted in the published poems:

> Thou are to me a lone white star,
> That I may gaze on from afar;
> But I may never never press
> My lips on thine in mute caress,
> E'en touch the hem of thy pure dress,
>   Thou art so far, so far. . . .

Or:

My sweetheart walks down laughing ways
Mid dancing glancing sunkissed ways
 And she is all in white . . .

Most of these lyrics either chronicle a romance that is now dead or record a cruel and unrequited love. The longest poem in this first group is "Autumn." Its initial stanza describes a bleak autumn with spring love gone; stanza two recalls that bygone spring, with its "slim slips of maiden moons, the shimmering stars;/And our love, our first love, glorious, yielding"; the final stanza paints the present contrasting scene where "Your hand does not seek mine . . . the smile is not for me . . . [but] for the new life and dreams wherein I have no part." The anguish of the second type is captured in poems like "Give Me Your Eyes" and "Caprichosa," and distilled in lines such as:

If I might taste but once, just once
 The dew
Upon her lips

Another work in this group, "My Shrine," is interesting for its underlying psychological and artistic revelations. The speaker builds a shrine to/for her "maiden small, . . . divinely pure" inside her heart—away from those who might widen their eyes and guffaw. There she kneels, only then daring to speak her soulful words. This poem was carried to the typescript stage and, having reached this point, Grimké substituted "he" for "she" where it was unavoidable. In many of these lyrics, the loved one is wreathed in whiteness (even to the mentioning of "her sweet white hands").

Needless to say, most of this poetry is fragmentary and unpolished. One reads it sensing the poet's tremendous need to voice, to vent, to share—if only on paper—what was pulsing within her, since it seems that sometimes she could not even talk to the woman she wanted, let alone anyone else. "Close your eyes," she says in one poem, "I hear nothing but the beating of my heart."

These romantic poems, as well as all the other types of Grimké's poetry, draw heavily on the natural world for allusions, figures of speech, and imagery. However, some of her work can be strictly classified as pure nature lyrics. Perhaps the best of these are "A Winter Twilight" and "Dusk." The latter reads:

Twin stars through my purpling pane,
 The shriveling husk
Of a yellowing moon on the wane—
 And the dusk.[15]

She also writes about the dawn ("Dawn," "At the Spring Dawn"), "Grass Fingers," and the "green of little leaves" ("Greenness").

Grimké produced relatively few racial poems. Of her works with racial overtones, the one most often reprinted is "Tenebris," which is about a shadow hand "huge and black" that plucks at the bricks of "the white man's house": "The bricks are the color of blood and very small./Is it a black hand,/Or is it a shadow?"[16] These poems are indirect and merely suggest the sensitivity to injustice and the political zeal that characterize her prose.

Finally, there are her philosophical poems about life. A varied lot, these treat regret, religious themes, the need for peace, "The Ways O' Men," a "puppet player" who "sits just beyond the border of our seeing,/Twitching the strings with slow sardonic grin,"[17] the "Paradox" of two people who are spiritually closer when physically apart than when "face to face,"[18] and many other subjects of universal human experience.

Generally, her first-person observations resonate more broadly, as in these lines from "The Eyes of My Regret":

> Always at dusk, the same tearless experience,
> . . . .
> Over it, the same slow unlidding of twin stars,
> Two eyes unfathomable, soul-searing,
> . . . .
> The same two eyes that keep me sitting late into the
>   night, chin on knees,
> Keep me there lonely, rigid, tearless, numbly miserable,
> —The eyes of my Regret.[19]

Grimké was not a literary theoretician, but on one occasion, she impressively explained her own creative process. A young man named Adolph Hult, Jr., a senior at Augustana College, Rock Island, Illinois, was studying her poetry as part of a class project in black literature. He wrote her on November 28, 1925, requesting information about her work. Almost immediately, she responded; what she wrote is one of the few self-critical statements that exists from a black writer of the period. It is introspective, sophisticated, even philosophical:

> I think most [poems] that I do are the reflections of moods. These appear to me in clearly defined forms and colors—remembered from what I have seen, felt. The mood is the spiritual atmosphere. Symbolic also. I love colors and contrasts. Suggestion.
>
> Whatever I have done it seems to me is a reflection of some mood which gives the spiritual atmosphere and significance. The mood has a physical counterpart in Nature in colors concrete images brought out by contrasts. Often to me the whole thing is not only a mood but symbolic as well. The more vivid the physical picture the more vivid the vibrations in the mind of the reader or listener. Each word has its different wavelength, vibration. Colors, trees flowers skies meadows. The more concrete, definite vivid the picture the more vivid the vibration of word in the reader or listener.
>
> And what is word? May it not be a sort of singing in the harp strings of the mind? Then on the principle of sympathetic vibration is there not in nature a harp singing also to be found. . . .[20]

Her theory of composition here is essentially romantic (even more theoretically so than Dunbar-Nelson's). First of all, the poetry arises from within herself; it is, as she puts it, the reflection of a mood. Her "appear to me" suggests the kind of spontaneous coming of a poem that Coleridge, for "Kubla Khan," called a "rising up." As for the romantic poets, nature is also a primary force that, in her case, furnishes the physical analogues for her moods. And nature, as well as the experience of it and the images in which it is clothed, is symbolic. Finally, she states, in the favorite romantic harp image, the sympathetic correspondence that was supposed to exist between the poet's mind and external nature.

Grimké's poetry accords very closely with her theoretical description of how she writes. Being expressions of the moment, her poems are usually brief. They present the scene or thought as swiftly as possible in sharp, concrete images, and then abandon it. This trait causes critics (like Robert Kerlin, for example) to compare her with the imagists. However, Grimké cannot usually refrain from comment, and thus violates the suggestive objectivity that is a part of their creed. Her poem "The Black Finger" is an excellent case in point. Here is its middle section:

Slim and still,
Against a gold, gold sky,
  A straight cypress,
  Sensitive,
    Exquisite,
A black finger
Pointing upwards.[21]

Those seven lines have the haiku-like, symbolic compression that the imagists prized. However, the poem consists of three additional lines—a beginning statement, "I have just seen a beautiful thing," and two closing questions, "Why, beautiful, still finger are you black?/And why are you pointing upwards?"—which alter considerably its tone and effect by making attitude and meaning too explicit.

Ironically, this predilection for brevity is also the source of one of Grimké's weaknesses as a poet—her occasional over-reliance on fragmentation and understatement. Sometimes, more often in early poems, her lines are too cropped and ejaculatory, resulting in a series of disjunct, giddy phrases. Something of this can be seen in the second half of "El Beso."

Without a doubt, Grimké's greatest strength is her affinity for nature, her ability to really see it and then describe what she has seen with precision and subtlety. Take, for example, this stanza from her elegy "To Clarissa Scott Delany":

Does the beryl in tarns, the soft orchid in haze,
The primrose through treetops, the unclouded jade
Of the north sky, all earth's flamings and russets and grays
  Simply smudge out and fade?[22]

Describing nature gives Grimké her freshest, most original and graphic expressions and helps her avoid the trite or threadbare diction that now and then entraps her. As she says in her poetic statement, she loves color and contrast. She handles them well and builds many of her finest effects upon them.

The mood of Grimké's poetry is predominantly sad and hushed (one of her favorite words). Colors—even when vivid—are not the primary ones, but saffron, green-gold, lilac. Sounds are muted; effects are delicate. Emotion—even when intense—is quiet and refined.

A hint of gold where the moon will be:
Through the flocking clouds just a star or two:
Leaf sounds, soft and wet and hushed,
And oh! the crying want of you.[23]

Grimké's poems are written in both rhyme and meter, and in what Sterling Brown calls "a carefully worded and cadenced free verse."[24] In some poems, she wavers between the two. Related to this metrical uncertainty is her major fault of repeating words, phrases, and lines in a manner that suggests padding. It seems that when inspiration waned, she sometimes resorted to the stock poetic technique of repetition to try to achieve some easy lyricism. Very few of her poems are written in the jazzy, syncopated style that was in vogue with black writers of the 1920s like Langston Hughes and Helene Johnson. One of them which is, "At April," has this rhythmic beginning:

Toss your gay heads,
  Brown girl trees;
Toss your gay lovely heads; . . .[25]

Generally speaking, Grimké's excellencies as a poet outweigh her weaknesses—
especially in the handful of well-wrought lyrics that secure her literary fame. However,
assessing her accurately requires thoughtful consideration of the personal and social
conditions under which she wrote. Clearly, her poetic themes of sadness and void,
longing and frustration (which commentators have been at a loss to explain) relate
directly to Grimké's convoluted life and thwarted sexuality. One also notes the self-
abnegation and diminution that mark her work. It comes out in her persistent vision of
herself as small and hidden, for instance, and in the death-wishing verses of "A Mona
Lisa" and other poems.

Equally obvious is the connection between her lesbianism and the slimness of her
creative output. Because of psychic and artistic constraints, the "lines she did not dare"
went almost as unwritten as they were unspoken. Being a black lesbian poet in America
at the beginning of the twentieth century meant that one wrote (or half wrote)—in
isolation—a lot that she did not show and could not publish. It meant that when one
did write to be printed, she did so in shackles—chained between the real experience and
the conventions that would not give her voice. It meant that one fashioned a few race
and nature poems, transliterated lyrics, and double-tongued verses that sometimes got
published. It meant, finally, that one stopped writing altogether, dying "with her real
gifts stifled within,"[26] and leaving behind the little that managed to survive of one's
true self in fugitive pieces. Ironically, the fact that Grimké did not write and publish
enough is given as a major reason for the scanty recognition accorded her (and also
other women poets of the Harlem Renaissance).

Especially during the culturally active 1920s, Grimké was called upon to write
articles and deliver speeches. It does not appear that she did many of these—which is
not surprising given her retiring personality. Dunbar-Nelson could rise almost spontaneously and, as a posthumous column put it, "deliver the most brilliant speeches . . .
new, vitalizing talks that made you think."[27] Grimké considered carefully—almost to
the point of inhibition—everything she did and said that was not prompted by pique or
anger. However, a few of her miscellaneous writings are important enough to mention.
(These do not include her brief diaries, which do not even begin to approach the literary
significance of Dunbar-Nelson's.) There is a sketch of her father's life for the February
1925 *Opportunity* magazine, and included in Brown, Davis, and Lee's 1941 collection,
Negro Caravan; the editors refer to it as "one of the few intimate biographical sketches
in the literature of the Negro."[28] In her characteristically readable prose, she reveals the
Grimké boys street-fighting in Charleston and showing up with canes and high silk hats
at the Welds' simple Quaker household; she also imparts necessary biographical and
personal data about her father. One of her correspondents singled out her "pen picture"
of her grandmother, Mrs. Nancy Weston, for special praise.

Grimké also reviewed Lillie B.C. Wyman's historical novel *Gertrude of Denmark,*
combining with it information about Wyman and Wyman's family's antislavery activities.[29] On September 27, 1925, she was invited by the Dubois Circle, "a club of women
interested in literature and art," to speak about "The Contribution of Negro Women
to Poetry." In addition to her remarks about the short story mentioned above, Grimké
wrote two other extant speeches, one entitled "Woman in the Home" and the other,
"The Social Emancipation of Woman" (holograph manuscripts). The first is unliberated
and Victorian. It views home as woman's proper sphere and praises her for her good,
calming influence. The other, a longer and more polished essay, jibes more closely with
what Grimké's life indicates that she believed. It espouses the opposite position, seeing
woman as man's equal and pressing for societal reforms that would allow women to
vote, participate actively in worldly affairs, escape the drudgery and subservience of

traditional marriages, and not be penalized any more severely than men for "social sins" such as gambling, drinking, and personal indiscretions.

She begins this second essay with a parable about a garden, gardener, and two plants:

> Now it happened one morning in the early spring, he [the gardener] came forth with two seeds in his hand, and not seeing that they were of the same kind (for he was a narrow, short-sighted, old, man) he planted one in the middle of the garden in the fertile soil, where the sun shone, and the rains and the dews fell; but the other, supposing it to need a different treatment and too delicate to stand the rough rains and winds, he planted in a far corner in the gloom and shelter of the walls.

The middle plant flourishes while the sheltered, weed-choked one is stunted—until a storm comes and exposes it to sun and rain, whereupon it blossoms out, to the astonishment of the gardener, who must now decide how he should henceforth tend the plants. The meaning is obvious (with the storm being reform and the gardener public opinion). Grimké concludes her explanation of the parable by asserting that "the one great overmastering power of growth is freedom," and ends the speech with this impassioned peroration:

> I hope that the time may come when the garden of the world may lie wallless, treeless, weedless, that the man plant and the woman plant may grow drinking alike of the same sun, the same rain, and the same dew, that their blossoms of thought may bloom in transcending beauty, and that their seed may spring in the coming years into plants so wonderful and flowers so glorious that all our grander dreams together are not able to match the reality.

One would have liked to know why Grimké wrote this essay and what, if anything, she did with it.

These few miscellaneous pieces and her significant body of published (and unpublished) poetry represent Grimké during this, the second high point, of her life. Her final years present, by contrast, a disappointingly blank picture.

Both Dunbar-Nelson and Georgia Douglas Johnson come into sharp focus as strong, colorful individuals. It is much harder to see who Grimké really was. Besides writing and teaching, she occupied herself largely with family activities and reading. One chapter of Anna Cooper's *Life and Writings of the Grimké Family* provides an intimate treatment of the Grimké family's Saturday and Sunday evening activities and amusements, which included art study and musical entertainment. In an autobiographical statement (which exists in an undated draft), Angelina wrote: "I am a voracious reader and possess something of a private library." She perused the classics, current books, and periodical magazines such as the *Nation* and the *New Republic*.

Grimké also sewed, danced, played tennis, and took almost yearly vacations in Massachusetts and Connecticut. Her circle of friends and acquaintances included members of Old Line Massachusetts families such as Ellen B. Stebbins,[30] as well as many of the prominent black leaders, educators, writers, and artists of the day. She received friendly notes from Langston Hughes (who wrote nice letters to everybody) on May 8, 1927, and June 4, 1937. She also corresponded and visited with Hallie Q. Brown, the noted elocutionist and author, Jessie Fauset, and Georgia Douglas Johnson. She was particularly close to her sister poet Georgia Johnson, writing her a charming poem about the things she liked about her and receiving from her an invitation to visit her in Washington as late as 1955.[31] On a more official level, she acted as an authority on and representative of the Grimké family (both Archibald and Francis) throughout her life—

for instance, helping to dedicate the Archibald H. Grimké School in Washington on November 9, 1938.

As Grimké mentioned, she was very "light." She was also very small, weighing only ninety-two pounds in 1899 and one hundred pounds in 1912, after she had matured.[32] She was a pretty little girl and an attractive woman, and she dressed well, judging from her schoolday letters asking her father for clothes and her later department-store bills. As a child, her demeanor was solemn, and in succeeding years, her face attained a "haughty sadness."[33] Interestingly enough, she generally made the girls in her plays and stories petite, cute, and dark-haired, like herself.

Her health, though, was not robust. Correspondence between her and her father and close friends frequently refers to her various ailments. She suffered from enlarged glands, nerves, headaches, bone and bilious conditions. In July 1911 her back was seriously injured in a railway accident. The July 3, 1926, document that granted her retirement as of June 30, 1926, states the grounds as her being "incapable of satisfactorily performing her duties as a teacher." And it appears that two years later, she was extremely unwell.[34]

As everything that has been said about her would indicate, Grimké was not an easygoing extrovert. Describing her as a child, Anna Cooper uses the words "sweet" and "sadfaced" and calls her an "undemonstrative intelligent child."[35] Another lady, Lillian Lewis, wrote her a letter on September 5, 1900, congratulating her on her "Black Is, As Black Does" and marveling: "You quiet, demure, little girl—who would think you dreamed such dreams!" Angelina also disliked crowds, saying once "the fewer [people] the better as far as I am concerned."[36] However, by her own admission, she possessed a number of personality traits that made her difficult. A diary entry that she wrote on New Year's Eve 1911 is most revealing. It reads in part:

> . . . My faith in myself is not profound. On this the last day of the year 1911 I am brought face to face with myself. I cannot say I am proud. My hands are not clean. . . . There are so many, many things I could have left undone, unkind thoughts . . . so many times when I have depressed others unnecessarily because I selfishly was blue; and the shadows black of many other disagreeable and disgusting things. Remorse and regret two unpleasant visitors on the last day yet here they are beside me hugging me close and I can do nought but entertain them civilly for they are rightful guests. . . . I am too critical, too impatient about trifles in my friends. Help me to . . . not be a cad. . . .

Perhaps some of what Grimké writes here can be dismissed as New Year's Eve depression. However, a friend of hers named Joseph B. Robinson, with whom she had a personal relationship, says much the same thing in a January 5, 1934, letter to her:

> I don't know of any friend of yours whom you have known intimately over any length of time, that you don't accuse of trying to rob you or that you don't quarrel with on some pretext or other sooner or later. . . . I do wish you would take hold of yourself quit suspecting everybody. You would certainly find life much more pleasant.

It seems that the final illness and death of her father from 1928 to 1930 marked a turning point in her life, with Grimké becoming more irritable, litigious, and possibly neurotic. Certainly, the strain of nursing her father—even with professional help—was severe. This was complicated, too, by their extremely close relationship, which was, it seems, almost incestuous. Lacking a mother for balance, she was doubly (and probably ambivalently) bound to him with the iron of affection and chastisement—even writing literature to prove her worth and win his approbation. Lacking lovers, husband, her own family, these ties grew into an unhealthy, lifetime dependency. Clearly, his loss would have been traumatic.

During this period, she quarreled with her Uncle Francis and threatened to disinter her father from the "demeaning" plot where he had him buried, wrote haranguing letters to their medical doctor about a nurse who had supposedly bilked them, charged that her uncle had called her "crazy," and procured a May 7, 1930, notarized statement from Dr. William C. McNeill that she was "competent of conducting her business affairs."[37] Her friends, among them Dr. Solomon Fuller (Meta Warrick's husband) and Anna Cooper, all counseled her to "keep the upper hand," "get a fresh grip on yourself," and so forth.[38]

After her father died, Grimké moved to New York, ostensibly for her work, but produced little or nothing thereafter.[39] Unlike practically every other black writer of that period, she had not even applied for the prestigious awards in black literature offered by the Harmon Foundation from 1926 to 1930.[40] Anna Cooper wrote in her 1955 book: "It is regrettable that in later years Miss Grimké has not kept up the line of creative work which her earlier successes foreshadowed."[41] Arna Bontemps states that she "spent the last years of her life in quiet retirement in a New York City apartment."[42]

Other factors also help to explain why Grimké stopped writing. The drying up of interest and literary markets after 1930 has already been mentioned. The New York that Grimké moved to was far less encouraging to black writers than the glorious city of the 1920s. Grimké herself reveals an additional factor in the autobiographical statement that she wrote while she was teaching at Dunbar. The document appears to be a response to questions on an application for a short-story course. Grimké wrote:

> I am not in school at the present and shall have more time than otherwise to devote to this course. I wish to take "short story writing" for I am inherently lazy and I believe that if I set myself the task of working under a competent and exacting teacher I shall get back into the routine of writing. I have not written anything besides a few verses for five or six years.

Clearly, for reasons personal to her, Grimké lost the requisite motivation, mentality, and industry for writing and did so at a time that roughly coincided with and was to some extent influenced by the external conditions that ended the Harlem Renaissance.

A few key statements can serve to summarize Grimké and her achievement. From a progressive and cultivated biracial background, she developed into a versatile, socially conscious writer who was particularly concerned with the plight of black people in a racist society and the special problems that faced black women. Her three-act drama, *Rachel* (1920), attacks the evil of lynching with feeling and a fair amount of dramaturgical skill—as does her later unpublished play, "Mara." Her short stories, the least significant of her writings, also confront prejudice. In the poetry that she wrote throughout her entire career but never collected, Grimké is most successful, treating predominantly love and nature themes in compact, sensitive lyrics. Her miscellaneous pieces reveal her interest in topical issues as well as her adeptness at handling occasional prose. In all of her works, she seems to write autobiographically and utilizes material and experiences relevant to herself.

Considered from a personal standpoint, Grimké's position as a comfortable, educated, racially mixed black woman during the first part of the twentieth century was both advantageous and problematical. It buffered her from the harsher indignities of being black in America at that time and allowed her to develop her literary talent. Yet, at the same time, her extraordinary circumstances probably made it more difficult for her to achieve psychic peace and emotional happiness. She had an unusually intimate relationship with her father, and women were of paramount importance in her real life as in her literary imagination. It seems, however, that personal factors contributed in a major way to the loss of inspiration that terminated her writing career more than twenty-five years before her death in 1958.

What Grimké did accomplish is valuable and worthwhile. It earned her participation in the renaissance of the 1920s and insures her lasting fame as a noteworthy figure in black American literary history, particularly as a woman writer and lesbian poet.

On October 22, 1936, Grimké wrote Harold Jackman a letter that provides the last concrete glimpse of her.[43] Vacationing in Massachusetts, she apologizes for not answering him sooner, but confesses, "I am afraid I am still trifling." She informs him of her plans to return to New York and then comments: "I hate coming back also but not because of the dirt [?] as you know [?], but because it probably means a return to loneliness and uselessness." Apparently, there had been talk among her, Jackman, and Georgia Douglas Johnson of her assuaging this "loneliness and uselessness" by marrying someone, for she tells Jackman: "What Drago [a mutual friend] said is interesting. You could have made it even stronger about my desire to marry." Jackman is one of Johnson's homosexual "sons" and Drago one of the neurotic "mixed breeds" whom she nurtured. Grimké is ambivalent about the efforts to match her with Drago and says in her brusque fashion: "I sent him [Drago] a second card and told him I didn't know whether I had anything to say to him or not that, Georgia to the contrary, one could not write to order. I have heard nothing since. Ahem!!!" The conclusion of her letter reads:

> I do hope I see you soon and that I shall see you often this coming year. You are good for me. I am not certain but I feel, now, that I may write again.
>
> Hoping to see you very soon
> Nana

Of course, she did not "write again," and from all available evidence, she retreated even further into the almost unimaginable solitariness of her inner-city apartment. How did she spend so many idle hours and empty months? In a December 26, 1944, letter to Jackman, Johnson asks: "Why is it Nina does not write to me. Please tell her to. I hope she is not sick."[44] The earnestness of her statements reflects Johnson's effort to connect with Grimké and to "dig her out," as it were, from her self-imposed isolation. Johnson was no more successful than modern readers who attempt to find this buried woman. One researches and resurrects—but must struggle to reach her, for she had no spirit left to send. Unlike Dunbar-Nelson and Johnson herself, who saw through adversity to triumph and bring courage in the midst of tears, Grimké was torn and flattened. Her obituary in the *New York Times* on June 11, 1958, begins: "Miss Angelina Weld Grimké, poet and retired school teacher, died yesterday at her home, 208 West 151st Street, after a long illness. She was 78 years old."[45] Long before this, she had inadvertently written her own problematic epitaph in an unpublished poem entitled "Under the Days":

> The days fall upon me;
> One by one, they fall,
> Like Leaves . . . .
> They are black,
> They are gray.
> They are white;
> They are shot through with gold and fire.
> They fall,

They fall
Ceaselessly.
They cover me,
They crush,
They smother.
Who will ever find me
Under the days?

Notes*

1. In 1905, Du Bois asked if his wife and daughter Yolande could stop with them, the Grimkés, in Washington. Archibald questioned his motives, wondering if the request should be interpreted as an olive branch or a move toward the Howard presidency (Letter to Angelina Weld Grimké, June 24, 1905). It seems also that the Grimkés were loyal to Roscoe Bruce, whom Du Bois did not particularly like. As Grimké phrased it in a November 13, 1910, letter to her father: ". . . there is so little good blood between the two men" (Archibald H. Grimké Collection).

2. Letter of Dr. Anna Nussbaum from Vienna to Angelina Weld Grimké, January 25, 1928.

3. Harper & Bros. returned her "Grief and Despair" (Letter of Archibald H. Grimké to Angelina Weld Grimké, June 24, 1905, in which he mentions this). *The Smart Set* rejected one of her manuscripts in a note postmarked February 28, 1913.

4. Letter of Charles S. Johnson to Angelina Weld Grimké, February 6, 1924.

5. For example, poems by her appear in the following: Cromwell, Turner, and Dykes, *Readings from Negro Authors for Schools and Colleges* (ca. 1931—letter of thanks to her March 5, 1931); Woolbert and Smith, *Fundamentals of Speech* (letter from Harper & Bros. asking her permission April 12, 1934); Walter Loban, *Adventures in Appreciation* (ca. 1947—she received a letter prior to her complimentary copy March 14, 1947); and, of course, standard anthologies such as Langston Hughes and Arna Bontemps, *The Poetry of the Negro* (1949, 1970).

6. Letter of Henry B. Jones to Angelina Weld Grimké, May 1, 1932.

7. *Boston Evening Transcript,* November 11, 1908, in prefacing her poem "Joseph Lee."

8. Letter of Julia Parks to Angelina Weld Grimké, postmarked May 4, 1928.

9. In an October 24, 1909, diary entry, Grimké grumbles about the trouble she is having with Lottie while Frank (Francis Grimké) is away, mentioning such things as their spatting over who will fix the fires: "Things she never dreams of doing while he is here she does when he is not. She gets real sprightly." (At this point in her life, Lottie is semi-invalid.) And on November 11, 1910, Grimké's father writes: "I am particularly pleased that your Aunt Lottie no longer disputes your position in the home. That I know makes your management much easier."

10. Robert Kerlin, ed., *Negro Poets and Their Poems,* Washington, D.C., Associated Publishers, 1935, p. 155.

11. Letter of Mamie Burrill to Angelina Weld Grimké, February 25, 1896.

12. This letter exists in a draft written on the back of some physics notes dated October 27, 1896.

13. This play is included in *Black Theater, U.S.A.: Forty-five Plays by Black Americans, 1847–1974,* ed. James V. Hatch with Ted Shine (New York: The Free Press, 1974).

14. Quoted from *Caroling Dusk: An Anthology of Verse by Negro Poets,* ed. Countee Cullen (New York: Harper and Row, 1927), p. 42.

15. Quoted from *Caroling Dusk,* p. 46.

16. Ibid., p. 41.

17. "The Puppet Player," *Caroling Dusk,* p. 46.

18. "Paradox," *Caroling Dusk,* pp. 43–44.

19. Quoted from *Caroling Dusk,* p. 37.

*Unless otherwise noted, all quotations from unpublished sources are from the Angelina Weld Grimké Collection deposited in the Manuscript Division of the Moorland-Spingarn Research Center, Howard University Library, Washington, D.C. The Archibald H. Grimké Collection is on deposit at the same library.

20. These remarks exist in an incomplete holograph draft.

21. Quoted from *American Negro Poetry,* ed. Arna Bontemps (New York: Hill and Wang, 1963), p. 17. This version of the poem has been slightly revised from its form in Alain Locke's *The New Negro* (New York, 1925).

22. Quoted from *American Negro Poetry,* p. 16.

23. "The Want of You," *Negro Poets and Their Poems,* p. 154.

24. Sterling Brown, *Negro Poetry and Drama* (1937; New York: Atheneum, 1969), p. 62.

25. This poem is reprinted in Louise Bernikow, ed., *The World Split Open: Four Centuries of Women's Poetry in England and America, 1552–1990* N.Y., Vintage Books, 1974, p. 262.

26. Alice Walker, "In Search of Our Mothers' Gardens," *MS* Magazine (May 1974), p. 67.

27. Julia Bumry Jones, "Talk O' Town," the Pittsburgh *Courier,* September 28, 1935.

28. *The Negro Caravan,* ed. Sterling Brown, Arthur P. Davis, and Ulysses Lee (1941; New York: Arno Press and the *New York Times,* 1969), p. 804.

29. In *Opportunity* magazine, December 1924.

30. Ellen B. (Nelly) Stebbins wrote Grimké a long, very interesting letter dated January 21, 1936, in which she recalls her relationship with her and her father. In it, she gives accounts of such events as the Grimké-Stanley wedding and of seeing Angelina as a baby "in short clothes." She also confesses to once kissing Mr. Grimké, a fact "*Not* for incorporation in your biography." This last statement suggests that Grimké was thinking about writing the life of her father at the time.

31. Letter of Georgia Douglas Johnson to Angelina Weld Grimké, December 2, 1955.

32. Letter of Angelina Weld Grimké to her father, December 6–11, 1899 (Archibald H. Grimké Collection); letter of Archibald H. Grimké to Angelina Weld Grimké, August 28, 1912.

33. Charles S. Johnson in a letter to her on June 1, 1927, after receiving her photograph: "I should not alter the haughty sadness of your face even if it were possible to do it."

34. Letter of Archibald Grimké to Angelina Weld Grimké, September 7, 1897. Angelina Weld Grimké to her father, November 13, 1910 (Archibald H. Grimké Collection); letter of Angelina Weld Grimké to her father, April 3, 1921 (AHG Collection); letters of Nelly Stebbins to Angelina Weld Grimké, January 17, 1928, and May 6, 1931.

35. Anna Cooper, *Life and Writings of the Grimké Family* (Copyright Anna J. Cooper, 1951), p. 27.

36. Letter to her father, August 22, 1913. Also see Angelina Weld Grimké to Archibald H. Grimké, August 26, 1913, August 9 and August 11, 1914. All in the Archibald H. Grimké Collection.

37. Her arguments with her uncle and the doctor exist in rough drafts of letters and a long list of charges.

38. Letter of Solomon C. Fuller to Angelina Weld Grimké, March 24, 1929; letter of Anna J. Cooper to Angelina Weld Grimké, "Easter Day 1930."

39. In a January 30, 1934, letter to her, Joseph Robinson states: "I hope you will now be able to find interest in your work, for which you originally came to New York."

40. This conclusion results from perusal of the Harmon Foundation Records, Manuscript Division, The Library of Congress, Washington, D.C.

41. Cooper, p. 27.

42. "Biographical Notes," *American Negro Poetry,* p. 190.

43. This letter is the sole item in the Angelina Grimké–Harold Jackman correspondence file, Small Collections, James Weldon Johnson Memorial Collection, Yale University Library, New Haven, Connecticut.

44. Letter from Georgia Douglas Johnson to Harold Jackman, December 26, 1944. The Cullen-Jackman Collection, Trevor Arnett Library, Atlanta University, Atlanta, Georgia.

45. "Angelina W. Grimké, Poet, Ex-Teacher, 78," the *New York Times,* June 11, 1958. Vertical File, the Schomburg Center, New York Public Library.

31

Capitalism and Gay Identity

John D'Emilio

John D'Emilio is a historian of the United States, and lesbian/gay United States history is one of his chief research interests. In this essay he explains that lesbian and gay people have not been present throughout history, that in the United States for instance there was no lesbian or gay identity and subculture until sometime in the nineteenth century, when the development of capitalism made our emergence possible. Capitalism required a system of labor based on wages, rather than on either a largely self-sufficient household or slavery; and wages gave individuals a relative autonomy, which was the necessary material condition for the making of lesbianism and gayness. A sound lesbian/gay politics in our own times, D'Emilio concludes, must be grounded in just such a demystified view of our past as he hopes his work in this essay and elsewhere may help to provide. John D'Emilio is the author of Sexual Politics, Sexual Communities: The Making of a Homosexual Minority *(1983), and of* Making Trouble: Essays on Gay History, Politics, and the University *(1992); and he is professor of History at the University of North Carolina, Greensboro.*

For gay men and lesbians, the 1970s were years of significant achievement. Gay liberation and women's liberation changed the sexual landscape of the nation. Hundreds of thousands of gay women and men came out and openly affirmed same-sex eroticism. We won repeal of sodomy laws in half the states, a partial lifting of the exclusion of lesbians and gay men from federal employment, civil rights protection in a few dozen cities, the inclusion of gay rights in the platform of the Democratic Party, and the elimination of homosexuality from the psychiatric profession's list of mental illnesses. The gay male subculture expanded and became increasingly visible in large cities, and lesbian feminists pioneered in building alternative institutions and an alternative culture that attempted to embody a liberatory vision of the future.

In the 1980s, however, with the resurgence of an active right wing, gay men and lesbians face the future warily. Our victories appear tenuous and fragile; the relative freedom of the past few years seems too recent to be permanent. In some parts of the lesbian and gay male community, a feeling of doom is growing: analogies with McCarthy's America, when "sexual perverts" were a special target of the Right, and with Nazi Germany, where gays were shipped to concentration camps, surface with increasing frequency. Everywhere there is the sense that new strategies are in order if we want to preserve our gains and move ahead.

I believe that a new, more accurate theory of gay history must be part of this political enterprise. When the gay liberation movement began at the end of the 1960s, gay men and lesbians had no history that we could use to fashion our goals and strategy. In the ensuing years, in building a movement without a knowledge of our history, we instead invented a mythology. This mythical history drew on personal experience, which we read backward in time. For instance, most lesbians and gay men in the 1960s first discovered their homosexual desires in isolation, unaware of others, and without resources for naming and understanding what they felt. From this experience, we constructed a myth of silence, invisibility, and isolation as the essential characteristics of gay life in the past as well as the present. Moreover, because we faced so many oppressive laws, public policies, and cultural beliefs, we projected this into an image of the abysmal past: until gay liberation, lesbians and gay men were always the victims of systematic, undifferentiated, terrible oppression.

These myths have limited our political perspective. They have contributed, for instance, to an overreliance on a strategy of coming out—if every gay man and lesbian in America came out, gay oppression would end—and have allowed us to ignore the institutionalized ways in which homophobia and heterosexism are reproduced. They have encouraged, at times, an incapacitating despair, especially at moments like the present: How can we unravel a gay oppression so pervasive and unchanging?

There is another historical myth that enjoys nearly universal acceptance in the gay movement, the myth of the "eternal homosexual." The argument runs something like this: gay men and lesbians always were and always will be. We are everywhere; not just now, but throughout history, in all societies and all periods. This myth served a positive political function in the first years of gay liberation. In the early 1970s, when we battled an ideology that either denied our existence or defined us as psychopathic individuals or freaks of nature, it was empowering to assert that "we are everywhere." But in recent years it has confined us as surely as the most homophobic medical theories, and locked our movement in place.

Here I wish to challenge this myth. I want to argue that gay men and lesbians have *not* always existed. Instead, they are a product of history, and have come into existence in a specific historical era. Their emergence is associated with the relations of capitalism; it has been the historical development of capitalism—more specifically, its free labor system—that has allowed large numbers of men and women in the late twentieth century to call themselves gay, to see themselves as part of a community of similar men and women, and to organize politically on the basis of that identity.[1] Finally, I want to suggest some political lessons we can draw from this view of history.

What, then, are the relationships between the free labor system of capitalism and homosexuality? First, let me review some features of capitalism. Under capitalism, workers are "free" laborers in two ways. We have the freedom to look for a job. We own our ability to work and have the freedom to sell our labor power for wages to anyone willing to buy it. We are also freed from the ownership of anything except our labor power. Most of us do not own the land or the tools that produce what we need, but rather have to work for a living in order to survive. So, if we are free to sell our labor power in the positive sense, we are also freed, in the negative sense, from any other alternative. This dialectic—the constant interplay between exploitation and some measure of autonomy—informs all of the history of those who have lived under capitalism.

As capital—money used to make more money—expands, so does this system of free labor. Capital expands in several ways. Usually it expands in the same place, transforming small firms into larger ones, but it also expands by taking over new areas of production: the weaving of cloth, for instance, or the baking of bread. Finally, capital expands geographically. In the United States, capitalism initially took root in the Northeast, at a time when slavery was the dominant system in the South and when noncapitalist Native American societies occupied the western half of the continent. During the nineteenth century, capital spread from the Atlantic to the Pacific, and in the twentieth, U.S. capital has penetrated almost every part of the world.

The expansion of capital and the spread of wage labor have effected a profound transformation in the structure and functions of the nuclear family, the ideology of family life, and the meaning of heterosexual relations. It is these changes in the family that are most directly linked to the appearance of a collective gay life.

The white colonists in seventeenth-century New England established villages structured around a household economy, composed of family units that were basically self-sufficient, independent, and patriarchal. Men, women, and children farmed land owned by the male head of household. Although there was a division of labor between men and women, the family was truly an interdependent unit of production: the survival of each member depended on the cooperation of all. The home was a workplace where women processed raw farm products into food for daily consumption, where they made clothing, soap, and candles, and where husbands, wives, and children worked together to produce the goods they consumed.

By the nineteenth century, this system of household production was in decline. In the Northeast, as merchant capitalists invested the money accumulated through trade in the production of goods, wage labor became more common. Men and women were drawn out of the largely self-sufficient household economy of the colonial era into a capitalist system of free labor. For women in the nineteenth century, working for wages rarely lasted beyond marriage; for men, it became a permanent condition.

The family was thus no longer an independent unit of production. But although no longer independent, the family was still interdependent. Because capitalism had not expanded very far, because it had not yet taken over—or socialized—the production of consumer goods, women still performed necessary productive labor in the home. Many families no longer produced grain, but wives still baked into bread the flour they bought with their husbands' wages; or, when they purchased yarn or cloth, they still made clothing for their families. By the mid-1800s, capitalism had destroyed the economic self-sufficiency of many families, but not the mutual dependence of the members.

This transition away from the household family-based economy to a fully developed capitalist free labor economy occurred very slowly, over almost two centuries. As late as 1920, 50 percent of the U.S. population lived in communities of fewer than 2,500 people. The vast majority of blacks in the early twentieth century lived outside the free labor economy, in a system of sharecropping and tenancy that rested on the family. Not only did independent farming as a way of life still exist for millions of Americans, but even in towns and small cities women continued to grow and process food, make clothing, and engage in other kinds of domestic production.

But for those people who felt the brunt of these changes, the family took on new significance as an affective unit, an institution that produced not goods but emotional satisfaction and happiness. By the 1920s among the white middle class, the ideology surrounding the family described it as the means through which men and women formed satisfying, mutually enhancing relationships and created an environment that nurtured children. The family became the setting for a "personal life," sharply distinguished and disconnected from the public world of work and production.[2]

The meaning of heterosexual relations also changed. In colonial New England, the birthrate averaged over seven children per woman of childbearing age. Men and women needed the labor of children. Producing offspring was as necessary for survival as producing grain. Sex was harnessed to procreation. The Puritans did not celebrate *hetero*sexuality but rather marriage; they condemned *all* sexual expression outside the marriage bond and did not differentiate sharply between sodomy and heterosexual fornication.

By the 1970s, however, the birthrate had dropped to under two. With the exception of the post-World War II baby boom, the decline has been continuous for two centuries, paralleling the spread of capitalist relations of production. It occurred even when access to contraceptive devices and abortion was systematically curtailed. The decline has included every segment of the population—urban and rural families, blacks and whites, ethnics and WASPs, the middle class and the working class.

As wage labor spread and production became socialized, then, it became possible to release sexuality from the "imperative" to procreate. Ideologically, heterosexual expression came to be a means of establishing intimacy, promoting happiness, and experiencing pleasure. In divesting the household of its economic independence and fostering the separation of sexuality from procreation, capitalism has created conditions that allow some men and women to organize a personal life around their erotic/emotional attraction to their own sex. It has made possible the formation of urban communities of lesbians and gay men and, more recently, of a politics based on a sexual identity.

Evidence from colonial New England court records and church sermons indicates that male and female homosexual behavior existed in the seventeenth century. Homosexual *behavior,* however, is different from homosexual *identity.* There was, quite simply, no "social space" in the colonial system of production that allowed men and women to be gay. Survival was structured around participation in a nuclear family. There were certain homosexual acts—sodomy among men, "lewdness" among women—in which individuals engaged, but family was so pervasive that colonial society lacked even the category of homosexual or lesbian to describe a person. It is quite possible that some men and women experienced a stronger attraction to their own sex than to the opposite sex—in fact, some colonial court cases refer to men who persisted in their "unnatural" attractions—but one could not fashion out of that preference a way of life. Colonial Massachusetts even had laws prohibiting unmarried adults from living outside family units.[3]

By the second half of the nineteenth century, this situation was noticeably changing as the capitalist system of free labor took hold. Only when *individuals* began to make their living through wage labor, instead of as parts of an interdependent family unit, was it possible for homosexual desire to coalesce into a personal identity—an identity based on the ability to remain outside the heterosexual family and to construct a personal life based on attraction to one's own sex. By the end of the century, a class of men and women existed who recognized their erotic interest in their own sex, saw it as a trait that set them apart from the majority, and sought others like themselves. These early gay lives came from a wide social spectrum: civil servants and business executives, department store clerks and college professors, factory operatives, ministers, lawyers, cooks, domestics, hoboes, and the idle rich: men and women, black and white, immigrant and native born.

In this period, gay men and lesbians began to invent ways of meeting each other and sustaining a group life. Already, in the early twentieth century, large cities contained male homosexual bars. Gay men staked out cruising areas, such as Riverside Drive in New York City and Lafayette Park in Washington. In St. Louis and the nation's capital, annual drag balls brought together large numbers of black gay men. Public bathhouses and YMCAs became gathering spots for male homosexuals. Lesbians formed literary societies and private social clubs. Some working-class women "passed" as men to obtain better paying jobs and lived with other women—lesbian couples who appeared to the world as husband and wife. Among the faculties of women's colleges, in the settlement houses, and in the professional associations and clubs that women formed one could find lifelong intimate relationships supported by a web of lesbian friends. By the 1920s and 1930s, large cities such as New York and Chicago contained lesbian bars. These patterns of living could evolve because capitalism allowed individuals to survive beyond the confines of the family.[4]

Simultaneously, ideological definitions of homosexual behavior changed. Doctors developed theories about homosexual*ity,* describing it as a condition, something that was inherent in a person, a part of his or her "nature." These theories did not represent scientific breakthroughs, elucidations of previously undiscovered areas of knowledge; rather, they were an ideological response to a new way of organizing one's personal life. The popularization of the medical model, in turn, affected the consciousness of the women and men who experienced homosexual desire, so that they came to define themselves through their erotic life.[5]

These new forms of gay identity and patterns of group life also reflected the differentiation of people according to gender, race, and class that is so pervasive in capitalist societies. Among whites, for instance, gay men have traditionally been more visible than lesbians. This partly stems from the division between the public male sphere and the private female sphere. Streets, parks, and bars, especially at night, were "male space." Yet the greater visibility of white gay men also reflected their larger numbers. The Kinsey studies of the 1940s and 1950s found significantly more men than women with predominantly homosexual histories, a situation caused, I would argue, by the fact that capitalism had drawn far more men than women into the labor force, and at higher wages. Men could more easily construct a personal life independent of attachments to the opposite sex, whereas women were more likely to remain economically dependent on men. Kinsey also found a strong positive correlation between years of schooling and lesbian activity. College-educated white women, far more able than their working-class sisters to support themselves, could survive more easily without intimate relationships with men.[6]

Among working-class immigrants in the early twentieth century, closely knit kin networks and an ethic of family solidarity placed constraints on individual autonomy that made gayness a difficult option to pursue. In contrast, for reasons not altogether clear, urban black communities appeared relatively tolerant of homosexuality. The popularity in the 1920s and 1930s of songs with lesbian and gay male themes—"B.D. Woman," "Prove It on Me," "Sissy Man," "Fairey Blues"—suggests an openness about homosexual expression at odds with the mores of whites. Among men in the rural West in the 1940s, Kinsey found extensive incidence of homosexual behavior, but, in contrast with the men in large cities, little consciousness of gay identity. Thus even as capitalism exerted a homogenizing influence by gradually transforming more individuals into wage laborers and separating them from traditional communities, different groups of people were also affected in different ways.[7]

The decisions of particular men and women to act on their erotic/emotional preference for the same sex, along with the new consciousness that this preference made them different, led to the formation of an urban subculture of gay men and lesbians. Yet at least through the 1930s this subculture remained rudimentary, unstable, and difficult to find. How, then, did the complex, well-developed gay community emerge that existed by the time the gay liberation movement exploded? The answer is to be found during World War II, a time when the cumulative changes of several decades coalesced into a qualitatively new shape.

The war severely disrupted traditional patterns of gender relations and sexuality, and temporarily created a new erotic situation conducive to homosexual expression. It plucked millions of young men and women, whose sexual identities were just forming, out of their homes, out of towns and small cities, out of the heterosexual environment of the family, and dropped them into sex-segregated situations—as GIs, as WACs and WAVEs, in same-sex rooming houses for women workers who relocated to seek employment. The war freed millions of men and women from the settings where heterosexuality was normally imposed. For men and women already gay, it provided an opportunity to meet people like themselves. Others could become gay because of the temporary freedom to explore sexuality that the war provided.[8]

Lisa Ben, for instance, came out during the war. She left the small California town where she was raised, came to Los Angeles to find work, and lived in a women's boarding house. There she met for the first time lesbians who took her to gay bars and introduced her to other gay women. Donald Vining was a young man with lots of homosexual desire and few gay experiences. He moved to New York City during the war and worked at a large YMCA. His diary reveals numerous erotic adventures with soldiers, sailors, marines, and civilians at the Y where he worked, as well as at the men's residence club where he lived, and in parks, bars, and movie theaters. Many GIs stayed in port cities like New York, at YMCAs like the one where Vining worked. In his oral histories of gay men in San Francisco, focusing on the 1940s, Allan Bérubé has found that the war years were critical in the formation of a gay male *community* in the city. Places as different as San Jose, Denver, and Kansas City had their first gay bars in the 1940s. Even severe repression could have positive side effects. Pat Bond, a lesbian from Davenport, Iowa, joined the WACs during the 1940s. Caught in a purge of hundreds of lesbians from the WACs in the Pacific, she did not return to Iowa. She stayed in San Francisco and became part of a community of lesbians. How many other women and men had comparable experiences? How many other cities saw a rapid growth of lesbian and gay male communities?[9]

The gay men and women of the 1940s were pioneers. Their decisions to act on their desires formed the underpinnings of an urban subculture of gay men and lesbians. Throughout the 1950s and 1960s, the gay subculture grew and stabilized so that people coming out then could more easily find other gay women and men than in the past. Newspapers and magazines published articles describing gay male life. Literally hundreds of novels with lesbian themes were published.[10] Psychoanalysts complained about the new ease with which their gay male patients found sexual partners. And the gay subculture was not just to be found in the largest cities. Lesbian and gay male bars existed in places like Worcester, Massachusetts, and Buffalo, New York; in Columbia, South Carolina, and Des Moines, Iowa. Gay life in the 1950s and 1960s became a nationwide phenomenon. By the time of the Stonewall Riots in New York City in 1969—the event that ignited the gay liberation movement—our situation was hardly one of silence, invisibility, and isolation. A massive, grass-roots liberation movement could form almost overnight precisely because communities of lesbians and gay men existed.

Although gay community was a precondition for a mass movement, the oppression of lesbians and gay men was the force that propelled the movement into existence. As the subculture expanded and grew more visible in the post-World War II era, oppression by the state intensified, becoming more systematic and inclusive. The Right scapegoated "sexual perverts" during the McCarthy era. Eisenhower imposed a total ban on the employment of gay women and men by the federal government and government contractors. Purges of lesbians and homosexuals from the military rose sharply. The FBI instituted widespread surveillance of gay meeting places and of lesbian and gay organizations, such as the Daughters of Bilitis and the Mattachine Society. The Post Office placed tracers on the correspondence of gay men and passed evidence of homosexual activity on to employers. Urban vice squads invaded private homes, made sweeps of lesbian and gay male bars, entrapped gay men in public places, and fomented local witch hunts. The danger involved in being gay rose even as the possibilities of being gay were enhanced. Gay liberation was a response to this contradiction.

Although lesbians and gay men won significant victories in the 1970s and opened up some safe social space in which to exist, we can hardly claim to have dealt a fatal blow to heterosexism and homophobia. One could even argue that the enforcement of gay oppression has merely changed locales, shifting somewhat from the state to the arena of extralegal violence in the form of increasingly open physical attacks on lesbians and gay men. And, as our movements have grown, they have generated a backlash that threatens to wipe out our gains. Significantly, this New Right opposition has taken shape as a "pro-family" movement. How is it that capitalism, whose structure made possible the emergence of a gay identity and the creation of urban gay communities, appears unable to accept gay men and lesbians in its midst? Why do heterosexism and homophobia appear so resistant to assault?

The answers, I think, can be found in the contradictory relationship of capitalism to the family. On the one hand, as I argued earlier, capitalism has gradually undermined the material basis of the nuclear family by taking away the economic functions that cemented the ties between family members. As more adults have been drawn into the free labor system, and as capital has expanded its sphere until it produces as commodities most goods and services we need for our survival, the forces that propelled men and women into families and kept them there have weakened. On the other hand, the ideology of capitalist society has enshrined the family as the source of love, affection, and emotional security, the place where our need for stable, intimate human relationships is satisfied.

This elevation of the nuclear family to preeminence in the sphere of personal life is not accidental. Every society needs structures for reproduction and childbearing, but the possibilities are not limited to the nuclear family. Yet the privatized family fits well with capitalist relations of production. Capitalism has socialized production while maintaining that the products of socialized labor belong to the owners of private property. In many ways, childrearing has also been progressively socialized over the last two centuries, with schools, the media, peer groups, and employers taking over functions that once belonged to parents. Nevertheless, capitalist society maintains that reproduction and childrearing are private tasks, that children "belong" to parents, who exercise the rights of ownership. Ideologically, capitalism drives people into heterosexual families: each generation comes of age having internalized a heterosexist model of intimacy and personal relationships. Materially, capitalism weakens the bonds that once kept families together so that their members experience a growing instability in the place they have come to expect happiness and emotional security. Thus, while capitalism has knocked the material foundation away from family life, lesbians, gay men, and heterosexual feminists have become the scapegoats for the social instability of the system.

This analysis, if persuasive, has implications for us today. It can affect our perception of our identity, our formulation of political goals, and our decisions about strategy.

I have argued that lesbian and gay identity and communities are historically created, the result of a process of capitalist development that has spanned many generations. A corollary of this argument is that we are *not* a fixed social minority composed for all time of a certain percentage of the population. *There are more of us* than one hundred years ago, more of us than forty years ago. And there may very well be more gay men and lesbians in the future. Claims made by gays and nongays that sexual orientation is fixed at an early age, that large numbers of visible gay men and lesbians in society, the media, and the schools will have no influence on the sexual identities of the young, are wrong. Capitalism has created the material conditions for homosexual desire to express itself as a central component of some individuals' lives; now, our political movements are changing consciousness, creating the ideological conditions that make it easier for people to make that choice.

To be sure, this argument confirms the worst fears and most rabid rhetoric of our political opponents. But our response must be to challenge the underlying belief that homosexual relations are bad, a poor second choice. We must not slip into the opportunistic defense that society need not worry about tolerating us, since only homosexuals become homosexuals. At best, a minority group analysis and a civil rights strategy pertain to those of us who already are gay. It leaves today's youth—tomorrow's lesbians and gay men—to internalize heterosexist models that it can take a lifetime to expunge.

I have also argued that capitalism has led to the separation of sexuality from procreation. Human sexual desire need no longer be harnessed to reproductive imperatives, to procreation; its expression has increasingly entered the realm of choice. Lesbians and homosexuals most clearly embody the potential of this split, since our gay relationships stand entirely outside a procreative framework. The acceptance of our erotic choices ultimately depends on the degree to which society is willing to affirm sexual expression as a form of play, positive and life-enhancing. Our movement may have begun as the struggle of a "minority," but what we should now be trying to "liberate" is an aspect of the personal lives of all people—sexual expression.[11]

Finally, I have suggested that the relationship between capitalism and the family is fundamentally contradictory. On the one hand, capitalism continually weakens the material foundation of family life, making it possible for individuals to live outside the family, and for a lesbian and gay male identity to develop. On the other, it needs to push men and women into families, at least long enough to reproduce the next generation of workers. The elevation of the family to ideological preeminence guarantees that capitalist society will reproduce not just children, but heterosexism and homophobia. In the most profound sense, capitalism is the problem.[12]

How do we avoid remaining the scapegoats, the political victims of the social instability that capitalism generates? How can we take this contradictory relationship and use it to move toward liberation?

Gay men and lesbians exist on social terrain beyond the boundaries of the heterosexual nuclear family. Our communities have formed in that social space. Our survival and liberation depend on our ability to defend and expand that terrain, not just for ourselves but for everyone. That means, in part, support for issues that broaden the opportunities for living outside traditional heterosexual family units: issues like the availability of abortion and the ratification of the Equal Rights Amendment, affirmative action for people of color and for women, publicly funded daycare and other essential social services, decent welfare payments, full employment, the rights of young people—in other words, programs and issues that provide a material basis for personal autonomy.

The rights of young people are especially critical. The acceptance of children as dependents, as belonging to parents, is so deeply ingrained that we can scarcely imagine what it would mean to treat them as autonomous human beings, particularly in the realm of sexual expression and choice. Yet until that happens, gay liberation will remain out of our reach.

But personal autonomy is only half the story. The instability of families and the sense of impermanence and insecurity that people are now experiencing in their personal relationships are real social problems that need to be addressed. We need political solutions for these difficulties of personal life. These solutions should not come in the form of a radical version of the pro-family position, of some left-wing proposals to strengthen the family. Socialists do not generally respond to the exploitation and economic inequality of industrial capitalism by calling for a return to the family farm and handicraft production. We recognize that the vastly increased productivity that capitalism has made possible by socializing production is one of its progressive features. Similarly, we should not be trying to turn back the clock to some mythic age of the happy family.

We do need, however, structures and programs that will help to dissolve the boundaries that isolate the family, particularly those that privatize childrearing. We need community- or worker-controlled daycare, housing where privacy and community coexist, neighborhood institutions—from medical clinics to performance centers—that enlarge the social unit where each of us has a secure place. As we create structures beyond the nuclear family that provide a sense of belonging, the family will wane in significance. Less and less will it seem to make or break our emotional security.

In this respect gay men and lesbians are well situated to play a special role. Already excluded from families as most of us are, we have had to create, for our survival, networks of support that do not depend on the bonds of blood or the license of the state, but that are freely chosen and nurtured. The building of an "affectional community" must be as much a part of our political movement as are campaigns for civil rights. In this way we may prefigure the shape of personal relationships in a society grounded in equality and justice rather than exploitation and oppression, a society where autonomy and security do not preclude each other but coexist.

NOTES

This essay is a revised version of a lecture given before several audiences in 1979 and 1980. I am grateful to the following groups for giving me a forum in which to talk and get feedback: the Baltimore Gay Alliance, the San Francisco Lesbian and Gay History Project, the organizers of Gay Awareness Week 1980 at San Jose State University and the University of California at Irvine, and the coordinators of the Student Affairs Lectures at the University of California at Irvine.

Lisa Duggan, Estelle Freedman, Jonathan Katz, Carole Vance, Paula Webster, Bert Hansen, Ann Snitow, Christine Stansell, and Sharon Thompson provided helpful criticisms of an earlier draft. I especially want to thank Allan Bérubé and Jonathan Katz for generously sharing with me their own research, and Amber Hollibaugh for many exciting hours of nonstop conversation about Marxism and sexuality.

1. I do not mean to suggest that no one has ever proposed that gay identity is a product of historical change. See, for instance, Mary McIntosh, "The Homosexual Role," *Social Problems* 16 (1968): 182–92; Jeffrey Weeks, *Coming Out: Homosexual Politics in Britain* (New York: Quartet Books, 1977). It is also implied in Michel Foucault, *The History of Sexuality,* vol. 1: *An Introduction,* tr. Robert Hurley (New York: Pantheon, 1978). However, this does represent a minority viewpoint and the works cited above have not specified how it is that capitalism as a system of production has allowed for the emergence of a gay male and lesbian identity. As an example of the "eternal homosexual" thesis, see John Boswell, *Christianity, Social Tolerance, and Homosexuality* (Chicago: University of Chicago Press, 1980), where "gay people" remains an unchanging social category through fifteen centuries of Mediterranean and Western European history.

2. See Eli Zaretsky, *Capitalism, the Family, and Personal Life* (New York: Harper and Row, 1976); and Paula Fass, *The Damned and the Beautiful: American Youth in the 1920s* (New York: Oxford University Press, 1977).

3. Robert F. Oaks, " 'Things Fearful to Name': Sodomy and Buggery in Seventeenth-Century New England," *Journal of Social History* 12 (1978): 268–81; J.R. Roberts, "The Case of Sarah Norman and Mary Hammond," *Sinister Wisdom* 24 (1980): 57–62; and Jonathan Katz, *Gay American History* (New York: Crowell, 1976), pp. 16–24, 568–71.

4. For the period from 1870 to 1940 see the documents in Katz, *Gay American History,* and idem, *Gay/Lesbian Almanac* (New York: Crowell, 1983). Other sources include Allan Bérubé, "Lesbians and Gay Men in Early San Francisco: Notes Toward a Social History of Lesbians and Gay Men in America," unpublished paper, 1979; Vern Bullough and Bonnie Bullough, "Lesbianism in the 1920s and 1930s: A Newfound Study," *Signs* 2 (Summer 1977): 895–904.

5. On the medical model see Weeks, *Coming Out,* pp. 23–32. The impact of the medical model on the consciousness of men and women can be seen in Louis Hyde, ed., *Rat and the Devil: The Journal Letters of F.O. Matthiessen and Russell Cheney* (Hamden, Conn.: Archon, 1978), p. 47, and in the story of Lucille Hart in Katz, *Gay American History,* pp. 258–79. Radclyffe Hall's classic novel about lesbianism, *The Well of Loneliness,* published in 1928, was perhaps one of the most important vehicles for the popularization of the medical model.

6. See Alfred Kinsey et al., *Sexual Behavior in the Human Male* (Philadelphia: W.B. Saunders, 1948) and *Sexual Behavior in the Human Female* (Philadelphia: W.B. Saunders, 1953).

7. On black music, see "AC/DC Blues: Gay Jazz Reissues," Stash Records, ST–106 (1977) and Chris Albertson, *Bessie* (New York: Stein and Day, 1974); on the persistence of kin networks in white ethnic communities see Judith Smith, "Our Own Kind: Family and Community Networks in Providence," in *A Heritage of Her Own,* ed. Nancy F. Cott and Elizabeth H. Pleck (New York: Simon and Schuster, 1979), pp. 393–411; on differences between rural and urban male homoeroticism see Kinsey et al., *Sexual Behavior in the Human Male,* pp. 455–57, 630–31.

8. The argument and the information in this and the following paragraphs come from my book *Sexual Politics, Sexual Communities: The Making of a Homosexual Minority in the United States, 1940–1970* (Chicago: University of Chicago Press, 1983). I have also developed it with reference to San Francisco in "Gay Politics, Gay Community: San Francisco's Experience," *Socialist Review* 55 (January–February 1981): 77–104.

9. Donald Vining, *A Gay Diary, 1933–1946* (New York: Pepys Press, 1979); "Pat Bond," in Nancy Adair and Casey Adair, *Word Is Out* (New York: New Glide Publications, 1978), pp. 55–65; and Allan Bérubé, "Marching to a Different Drummer: Coming Out During World War II," a slide/talk presented at the annual meeting of the American Historical Association, December 1981, Los Angeles. A shorter version of Bérubé's presentation can be found in *The Advocate,* October 15, 1981, pp. 20–24.

10. On lesbian novels see *The Ladder,* March 1958, p. 18; February 1960, pp. 14–15; April 1961, pp. 12–13; February 1962, pp. 6–11; January 1963, pp. 6–13; February 1964, pp. 12–19; February 1965, pp. 19–23; March 1966, pp. 22–26; and April 1967, pp. 8–13. *The Ladder* was the magazine published by the Daughters of Bilitis.

11. This especially needs to be emphasized today. The 1980 annual conference of the National Organization for Women, for instance, passed a lesbian rights resolution that defined the issue as one of "discrimination based on affectional/sexual preference/orientation," and explicitly disassociated the issue from other questions of sexuality such as pornography, sadomasochism, public sex, and pederasty.

12. I do not mean to suggest that homophobia is "caused" by capitalism, or is to be found only in capitalist societies. Severe sanctions against homoeroticism can be found in European feudal society and in contemporary socialist countries. But my focus in this essay has been the emergence of a gay identity under capitalism, and the mechanisms specific to capitalism that made this possible and that reproduce homophobia as well.

VI

COLLECTIVE IDENTITIES/ DISSIDENT IDENTITIES

32

Androgynous Males and Deficient Females:
Biology and Gender Boundaries in Sixteenth- and Seventeenth-Century China

CHARLOTTE FURTH

Charlotte Furth is Professor of History at the University of Southern California, and is presently writing a book on medicine and gender in China in the 17th and 18th centuries. The Glossary of ideographs pertinent to this essay can be found in the journal Late Imperial China *(1988) from which this essay is reprinted. Examining late Ming accounts of sexual transformation— men suddenly becoming women and women changing into men—Furth demonstrates how the sexual can construct the social. Arising at a time when the visibility of powerful eunuchs and gender-deviant men was unusually high, the narratives suggest a risky expansion of the boundaries of the permissible for males. In response, succeeding Manchu rulers mandated a variety of sexual prohibitions, including declaring illegal, for the first time in imperial history, male homosexual fornication. Accounts of female transformation, on the other hand, inspired welcome rather than scandal and were regarded as auspicious. Definitions of the anomalous and attempts to explain it thereby become clues to the meaning of female and male as social and biological categories, Furth argues, and it is the "strange" that comes to establish the "normal."*

Introduction[1]

Anomaly by contrast establishes the normal. What is "normal" easily becomes normative, in nature and for human beings as well. My topic here is the medical, political, and literary discourse surrounding some famous reported cases of sexual and reproductive anomaly in late Ming China. Such definitions of the "strange" [*i, ch'i*] and attempts to explain it become clues to the meaning of female and male as biological and social categories. It is well known that Chinese cosmology based on the interaction of the forces of yin and yang made sexual difference, a relative and flexible bipolarity in natural philosophy. On the other hand, Confucianism constructed gender around strict hierarchical kinship roles. When late Ming Chinese observers considered ambiguous bodies they had to confront the contradictory nature of these gender paradigms; they also had to talk about the ordinarily submerged category of the sexual itself.

An analysis of the kind offered here depends upon interpretative strategies first pioneered by Michel Foucault, Ivan Illich, and others who have shown that the human body has a history.[2] Gendered bodies are understood through culturally specific repertories of gestures and emotions which assign significance to acts and define objects of

479

desire at the level of the erotic; as well as by codes of the masculine and feminine at the level of psychic experience and personal identity. This way of thinking has intersected with feminist analysis of gender as socially constructed through kinship, religion, and other roles, and feminist rejection of "biology" as a natural basis of gender distinctions. Accordingly, sex, referring to physical characteristics and biological capabilities, is distinguished from gender, which represents the cultural and social meaning attached to sexed bodies. The "sexual" becomes that aspect of gender which deals with culturally constructed biological and erotic meanings.

The issue of biological variation in physical sex characteristics was addressed most systematically in Ming-Ch'ing China by medical writers. As experts on reproductive success or failure, they were the source of biological understanding of fertility. They attempted to classify and explain reproductive anomalies: sterility and impotence, abnormal births, from twins to monsters; hermaphroditism and sex change. Mapping a code of the sexually normal, they also sought to define patterns of nature shaping reproductive processes and so bounding human beings as a species. Among medical authorities of this period (largely the sixteenth and seventeenth centuries), Li Shih-chen, author of the *Pen ts'ao kang mu,* the classic study of the traditional *materia medica,* posed these questions in the most thoughtful and far-reaching way.[3]

But physicians were not the only ones to pay attention to such matters. Sexual anomaly attracted official notice, in keeping with old traditions concerning omens that assigned political significance to weird natural phenomena. Further, narratives claiming to be reports of extraordinary sexual and reproductive phenomena showed up in the informal writings (*pi chi*) of unofficial literati historians like Shen Te-fu (1578–1642) and Hsieh Chao-che (1567–1624).[4] Then in turn short stories by such authors as Li Yü and P'u Sung-ling embroidered on accounts of anomalous individuals which had attracted public attention in these other settings, giving further clues as to how sexuality and reproduction were socially interpreted.

One is led into a bizarre world of seemingly outlandish phenomena—of eunuchs and stone maidens, of males who give birth, of men who turn into women and women who turn into men; and even of individuals who are said to be capable of manipulating their genital organs so as to appear now male, now female. Whether today's biomedicine recognizes any modern pathologies here is less important than the position such stories occupied on the horizons of the possible in the late Ming imagination. As medical anomalies, they were part of a discourse on reproductive health. As examples of the "strange" they were part of a philosophical inquiry into order and disorder in the cosmos. Finally, as sexual phenomena they must be understood in the context of the gender system of the day. Through analyzing them we are able to see complexities in the relationship between the social and the sexual in establishing gender identity, and to understand how this relationship differed for women and men.

Biological Sex and its Boundaries in Medicine: The False Male and the False Female

Biological anomaly—the appearance in one individual of physical characteristics which are sexually disfunctional or thought appropriate to the opposite sex—seems to challenge accepted norms in a particularly disturbing way. However, in Chinese biological thinking, based as it was on yin-yang cosmological views, there was nothing fixed and immutable about male and female as aspects of yin and yang. These two aspects of primary ch'i are complementary and interacting, so that each at all times dynamically influences the other and each enjoys times of ascendancy in the periodic rhythms of things. In medicine yin and yang permeate the body and pattern its functions, and here as elsewhere they are interdependent, mutually reinforcing, and capable of turning into their opposites. This natural philosophy would seem to lend itself to a broad and tolerant view of variation in sexual behavior and gender roles.

In Chinese accounts of human biology we can see these classic cosmological notions at work in the standard interpretations of conception and sexual differentiation. "What is it that congeals at the time of sexual union to make the fetus? Though it is none other than the [male] essence (*ching*) and [female] blood (*hsueh*), made up of material dregs that exist in the world below, a tiny bit of pre-existent (*hsien t'ien*) true ch'i, moved to germinate by the feelings of desire, subtly mediates between them." This is the account in *Systematic Aid for the Disorders of Yin,* an authoritative seventeenth-century gynecological text.[5] Here female blood is not on a grosser material level than male semen; both are body fluids in one aspect and partake of heavenly ch'i in another. The sex of the child is determined simply by the relative ascendancy of yin or yang ch'i present at the moment of conception. In medical literature these forces are at times envisaged as internal to the bodies of the partners, as reproductive vitality. At times they are imagined as environmental influences, since yin and yang qualities inhering in such things as time of day, date or month or season of year, direction, moment in menstrual cycle of a woman, wind, weather—all are part of the total environmental forcefield bearing on the event.

Thus we can see that human males are not "pure yang" or females "pure yin," and sexual differentiation depends upon the momentary balance of fluid forces in dynamically interacting relationship with one another. This fluidity further suggested to medical authorities ways to explain certain kinds of biological anomalies in human beings. Disorderly configurations of yin-yang influences at the time of conception were held responsible for multiple births and for physical and functional defects. "Scattered" or "dispersed" ch'i produces twins; "deficient" yang or yin ch'i produces sterile individuals; "contrary," "variegated," or "disordered" ch'i (*po ch'i, luan ch'i*) produces "*fei nan fei nü*" (those who are neither male nor female; or false males and false females).[6]

"Old mothers and young fathers produce overripe daughters; vigorous mothers and feeble (*shuai*) fathers produce weakling sons."[7] This is how medical authorities categorized the milder, borderline cases of biological insufficiency in men and women. Believing that individuals with subnormal reproductive capacities still had the potential for fruitfulness, doctors recommended that such girls be married early, while weddings be delayed for these boys. Only time would tell whether in fact such individuals were among those whose yin and yang ch'i was so fatally aberrant as to make them barren.

Serious anomaly began with barrenness in the functionally normal, and extended to those with reproductively "useless bodies." Li Shih-chen's *Systematic Materia Medica* provides the best synthesis of the traditions concerning this in medicine and natural philosophy:

> Normally ch'ien and k'un [active and latent aspects of the cosmos] make [human beings into] fathers and mothers; but there are five kinds of false males [*fei nan*] who cannot become fathers and five kinds of false females [*fei nü*] who cannot become mothers. Can it indeed be the case that defective males are deficient in yang ch'i while defective females have blocked yin ch'i? The false females are the corkscrew, the striped, the drum, the horned, and the pulse. . . . The false males are the natural eunuch, the bullock [castrated], the leaky, the coward, and the changeling.[8]

As explained by Li and other medical writers who repeated these classifications, four of the five terms applied to women refer to genital abnormalities of the sort that would make sexual penetration impossible. The fifth or "pulse" is a woman with highly erratic menses. One of five physical abnormalities, the "drum" (or in other versions "small door"), was well known in popular lore as a "stone maiden"—one whose hymen is impenetrable.[9]

By contrast with false females, false males are largely the functionally impotent, not the physically marred. The "coward" for example is "he who sees the enemy and refuses to engage."[10] The "leaky" is a male subject to uncontrolled or excessive seminal losses,—a serious disorder in light of the medical view of reproductive fluids as measurable "vital essences" (*ching*) whose conservation is essential to both potency and longevity. Even the "natural eunuch" (*t'ien yen*)—a category defined in the ancient *Nei ching* medical classic as a male whose beard does not grow—in Li Shih-chen's later formulation is simply one "whose yang is impotent and of no use." Among males clear-cut physical anomaly is reserved for the "changeling."

"The changeling (*pien*) body is both male and female, what the common people call 'those with two forms' (*erh hsing*). The dynastic history of the Chin [Western Chin AD 265–419] considered them the product of disordered ch'i and called them 'human anomalies' (*jen k'o*). There are three types: those who can [both] serve men as women and serve women as men; those who are yin half the month and yang the other half; and those who can act as wife but not as husband. All of these have useless bodies."[11]

Although superficially parallel, false males and false females in fact were gendered classifications, the product of social assumptions about men and women. In accounts of borderline deficiency, an oversexed ("overripe") girl is produced by an excess of her youthful father's "yang ch'i." Vigorous mothers, if unchecked, weaken the sexual vitality of their sons. Yin energy doesn't lead to fecundity in girls but to weakness in men, and medical authorities don't identify any pathology of undersexed females or oversexed males. Similarly females fail biologically because of physical deformity; men are those whose sexual adequacy is defined in terms of performance. Moreover, the changelings with "two forms" are classed with males and described as capable of bisexual roles, in a manner that echos old Chinese legends of hermaphrodites as fantastic beings with superabundant erotic capabilities.[12] All of these asymmetries reflect the assumption that sexual action or initiative is a male attribute. Finally, false females merely fail to attain the proper role of women; only false males, in particular the eunuch and the changeling, are not merely deficient, but appear to move toward the opposite, feminine, sexual pole.

Medical authority, then, defined the sexually normal in terms of reproductive capabilities alone. From one end of this spectrum the sterile person, even though she or he looks ordinary and is capable of intercourse, is classed among those with a basic biological defect. From the other end, the physically anomalous person is fully human but simply useless. Beyond this no kind of sex act or object of desire was singled out in medical literature as pathological. Commonplace medical recommendations for moderation and restraint in sexual activity had the sole aim of conserving reproductive vitality. They included no catalogue of "perversions," and procreative efficacy alone defined the sexually healthy.[13]

In keeping with this there was no category of homosexual as a kind of false male. Medical literature appeared in harmony with Ming social images of homosexual behavior as a kind of male dissipation. As such potentially it could distract from family responsibilities and was perhaps imprudent in its wasteful expenditure of vital essence, but it was not in principle incompatible with proper male sexuality.[14] There is only the "coward" who rejects the family duty of paternity, and the castrati who are incapable of it. One finds here neither the Christian notion of "unnatural" sexual acts nor its modern medicalized outgrowth, the concept of perversion as the manifestation of a psychologically deviant personality.

In the foregoing medical analysis, reproductive incapacity occurs at a deep biological level. It is part of "native endowment" bestowed by Heaven and suggests that the physical boundaries between the sexes, including phenomena which blur those boundaries, are fixed inalterably before birth. But yin and yang constantly change and interact both in the human body and in the environment at large, and throughout life human beings are never free from their influences.

Li Shih-chen's essay on "human anomaly" (*jen k'uei*) which stands as the last chapter of his *Systematic Materia Medica,* was in fact a wide-ranging inquiry into biological processes as they govern human reproduction and produce our species norms. If false males and false females were shaped by events at work at conception, other sexual anomalies appeared spontaneously in adults. Can it be, he asked, that women sometimes grow beards, and men's breasts secrete milk; or that males have given birth, and adults have changed from one sex to the other? As a natural philosopher, Li was working within a long-standing Chinese view of cosmological pattern that sought to incorporate anomaly rather than reject the irregular as inconsistent with the harmony of natural pattern. Where patterns are seen as temporal processes, regularities are probabilities, not absolutes, and the "strange" as a unique event, like snow in summer, will—as the philosopher Chu Hsi put it in the Sung dynasty—occasionally intrude on the scene without undermining the intelligibility of the whole.

At the same time, anomaly posed problems for Li Shih-chen which had not troubled Chu Hsi five centuries earlier. As John Henderson has argued, late Ming thinkers were beginning to question the tradition of "correlative thinking" which assumed that natural, moral, and cosmological phenomena were rendered intelligible by an underlying pattern of affinities (*kan ying*).[15] Where the older view accommodated omens and magic as well as the rich lore of numerical and qualitative correspondences to make the anomalous a sign of unseen order, Li Shih-chen struck a newer note with these questions about "strange" reproductive events: he was dissatisfied with available explanations of the mechanisms involved. Nonetheless, this was a skepticism about the limits of human understanding more than a query about the believability of events. As food for seventeenth-century natural philosophy, the "strange" was a challenge to conventional canons of intelligibility, not superstition to be dismissed. Li Shih-chen concluded that changes of sex were among the possible "transformations of yin and yang."[16]

Males Who Become Female

From time to time in late Ming China stories circulated of men who were transformed into women and women who were transformed into men. They gained visibility when they surfaced in the form of reports to government authorities of omens, where they played a ritual role in court politics. Like epidemics, natural disasters, astronomical events, and multiple births of males, these had traditionally been understood in light of the theory of cosmological correlations as signs, for good or ill, of the health of the Heavenly Mandate. A zealous quarrier of historical curiosities could find a number of instances of such omens in the dynastic histories of the medieval period, especially the Wei and Chin dynasties (AD 220–419). Literati writings over the centuries also occasionally noted such things. But the "Omen" (*Wu hsing*) sections of the Sung and Yuan dynastic histories contained no such accounts.[17]

Then, beginning in the fifteenth century, such stories began to crop up in the informal literature, and two reached the Ming dynastic history: it was reported in the

"Omen" section that a female changed into a male in Kansu in 1548, while in Shansi in 1568, a male changed into a female.[18] Li Shih-chen took particular note of this second case, noting that its reliability was attested by the recent nature of the event and the rank of the circuit intendant who reported it to the throne. His account reads as follows:

> In the second year of the Lung-ching emperor, the Shansi governor, Shih Sung-hsu reported that in Ching-lo county a man named Li Liang-yü was married for four years to a woman named Chang. Later due to poverty he divorced his wife and went to work as a laborer. In the first month of the first year of the Lung-ching reign he suffered a stomach ache that came and went. On the ninth day of the second month of the second year he suffered sharp protracted pain. By sometime in the fourth month he could no longer feel his testicles [*shen nang*], which shrank, withdrew within his body and became a vagina. The following month he began to menstruate and to dress like a woman. At the time he was 28 years old.[19]

A more circumstantial narrative of the incident comes from the informal essays of Li Hsu (1505–93), a late Ming literatus who was writing from Kiangsu, far from the actual scene, and about 25 years after the event. Its style suggests that Li Hsu or his source derived their facts from an official report at either local or higher level. The presence of a detailed discussion from the pen of such a distant observer shows the case was well known:

> In the second year of the reign of the Lung-ching emperor [1568], in Dragon Spring township [*tu*] of Ching-lo county, T'ai-yuan prefecture in the province of Shansi, one Li Liang-yü, younger brother of a commoner named Li Liang-yun, suddenly changed into female form. Subsequently she became the wife of Pai Shang-hsiang of Ts'en-ch'eng township.
>   Formerly [Li Liang] Yun's father Li Huai gave birth to younger brother [Li Liang] Yü. Li Huai fell ill and died in Chia-ching 31 [1552] when Yü was twenty-eight sui. In 1558 Yü married the eldest daughter of one Chang Hao of Ma-chi township. In 1562 the couple had a falling out and Yü cast off his wife, giving her to Kao Ming-chin of the same place. Yü had no means of livelihood, so he went to work as a laborer in Yeh-p'a village, in the home of his elder sister's husband, Chia Chung-ao.
>   In the first month of the first year of the Lung-ching emperor's reign [1567], Yü suddenly developed a stomach ache, which came and went. On the ninth day of the second month of the second year [1568] he was unable to get out of bed. A fellow villager, Pai Shang-hsiang, was also a bachelor and while Yü was sick Pai shared his chamber day and night. In the fourth month, imperceptibly Yü's testicles [*nang*] shrank within his belly and changed into a yin [organ], and so she/he began to cohabit indecently with Pai. In the fifth month she/he began to have a menstrual pulse. At first the menses stopped on the third day; afterwards they came every month without fail. Then Yü began to arrange her/his hair in the style of a servant girl, to wear women's dress, to bind her/his feet and wear different shoes. But, afraid of shame, she/he kept out of view so that no one should know.
>   In the ninth month [elder brother] Yun made inquiries concerning this, and ordered his own wife, Mistress Nan, to look into it. In the second day of the eleventh month, the affair was reported to the district magistrate, who apprehended Yü. Pai went along to the hearings. A midwife, Mistress Fang, was led to the stable to make an inspection, and [verified] that Yü indeed had undergone a change of form and was no different physically from a woman. His ex-wife, Mistress Chang, also was called and officially made known that for three years after marriage sexual relations between them were normal, though without issue; later due to poverty they quarreled and she was sold to a neighboring hamlet.

The reports of Yao Han-chou and others [concerning these events] are the same as above. On the twenty-fifth day of the twelfth month of that same year the circuit inspector Sung Hsun sent a memorial to the throne with the news. Announcing that for a male to turn into a female was an omen of yin ascendency and yang eclipse, he recommended the promotion of the worthy and the retirement of the unworthy in order to correct the functioning of the natural order. Assenting to this, the emperor called for prayers and self-criticism [on the part of officialdom].[20]

It is clear from this account first of all that whatever the theoretically possible "transformations of yin and yang," it was not easy for this account of gender change to be accepted as credible. Family, community, and the state all suspected a hoax. On the other hand, efforts to substantiate omens resulted in just the sort of circumstantial detail that lent verisimilitude, growing out of official inquiry.

Thus the problem of credibility, while serious, was not insurmountable. The narrative, an official recounting of what actors said, reveals the authorities' effort to verify facts: the parade of witnesses, physical examiners, and so on. It also suggests what the principals, Li, his/her lover, and perhaps family members, thought was a plausible scenario. The day named as marking the beginning of the change, the first month of the first year of the reign of a new emperor, is rich in the symbolism of cosmic renewal that would support such a transformation. The feminization of the male body through the self-cultivation techniques of "internal alchemy" was an established ideal of Taoist longevity cults, and said to be marked by just such a shrinking of external genitals, though the Taoists' goal in this was not the attainment of female sexuality.[21] Finally, as a woman Li embraced the social and physical markers of this new role, including not only dress but bound feet and conventions of modesty as well.

The narrative also establishes that the community and the state had slightly different concerns in the affair. For the state, the presence of the circuit intendant on a tour of inspection may have been significant. Sung Hsun, who prepared the report to the throne, was at the time a young official just embarking on his career. He had received imperial commendation the year before for his investigation of some military trials associated with the pacification of the nearby Mongol-Chinese frontier. For whatever reason, Sung's report, with its supporting documentation and solemn ritual warning of an inversion of cosmic and social hierarchy, prompted a formal imperial statement of concern for the moral health of officialdom. The case is mentioned in Sung Hsun's biography as something which helped launch a successful career.[22]

Within the local community, however, what was important was the satisfactory disposal of a family scandal. The issue is Liang-yü's social place, in what family, under whose charge. When Li Liang-yü was acknowledged as a woman, family problems were solved. It effectively ended Liang-yun's headship over his younger brother and Liang-yü's claims to any of the obviously miniscule family property. Instead, Liang-yü was established as the dependent of the lover, Pai. As another impoverished bachelor, Pai was just the sort who could expect no prize in a "wife." So there were social as well as cosmological and political grounds for accepting the claims of a "transformation of yin and yang."

The case of Li Liang-yü was commented upon by the emperor, one of the greatest natural philosophers of the day (Li Shih-chen) and by at least three authors of pi chi (Li Hsu, Shen Te-fu, Wang Shih-chen). In addition, several seventeenth-century short stories depict a male who assumes a feminized physical and social identity, and may be taken as commentaries on the inversion of sexual roles, even if it cannot be proved that they were directly inspired by the scandal itself. The stories include a particularly brilliant one by Li Yü, "A Male 'Mother Mencius.' "[23] Li Yü gives a quasi-naturalistic interpretation of the phenomenon. The hero castrates himself, and thereby is transformed from an ordinary youth involved in a homosexual love affair to a feminized inhabitant of the inner quarters.

By treating his castratus protagonist sympathetically as lover, wife, foster-mother, and chaste widow on the model of the mother of Mencius, Li Yü shocks his readers with an account of gender inversion which is psychologically as well as socially radical. The narrative clearly establishes the line separating such an individual from the ordinary "dragon yang" (*lung yang*) homosexual male who in the story is made to joke about "the seven disagreeable things about a woman."[24] At the same time, conventional heterosexual attitudes are parodied at the end in a deadpan satire of a moralist's homily: "Cast your vital essence (*ching shen*) in a useful place. Isn't it beneficial to increase the Empire's household registers and produce progeny for your ancestors? Why would you take your 'golden fluid' and throw it away in some filthy receptacle?"[25]

The Li Yü story is framed by a narrator's social analysis of a "southern wind" (*nan feng*, punning on *nan feng**, "male fashion") of gender transgression currently sweeping China. It suggests that in the permissive atmosphere of the late Ming, homosexual activity threatened to break out of its accustomed pattern as a sporadic masculine dissipation to entangle men in what most would see as degrading, eunuch-like female roles.

The issue of the new "southern wind" was also raised by both Shen Te-fu and Hsieh Chao-che in their essays. Shen contrasted what he saw as the normal pattern of homosexual activity, "laughable but also pitiful," with a new "southern wind" of homosexual profligacy. For men to take males as lovers was to be expected among unmarried and impoverished bachelors, or in the all-male environment of shipboard, barracks, prison, or monastery. But the new fashionable sodomy [*nan seh*] was practiced by upper-class "gentlemen of ambition," spreading from its original home in the far south (Fukien) to the Yangtze delta regions, penetrating the entertainment quarters of Nanking and only half-resisted even in the north.[26] Hsieh Chao-che saw it as a revival of practices which had died out since the Sung under the influence of Neo-Confucianism. In his words, "The whole country has gone crazy." (*chü kuo ju k'uang*).[27]

Li Liang-yü was extraordinary, even for the sixteenth and seventeenth centuries. No other case like his appeared in either formal or informal literature of the Ming that I have seen. Later the Ch'ing dynastic history included two reports of male-to-female sex change, but details are lost. However, I have found three late Ming accounts of males who were said to have given birth, in contexts which suggest that many associated this phenomenon also with current fashions in sodomy. A traditional explanation for male pregnancy as for other kinds of anomalous birth was spirit possession, which is the interpretation offered in the case reported by Li Hsu.[28] However, another man claimed that someone had spied upon him while he was bathing,[29] while a third was said to have borne twin sons by his homosexual lover, a military officer from Fukien.[30] Hsieh Chao-che reported an incident in which male pregnancy was portrayed as a lesson to sodomites: "In our own dynasty when Chao Wen-hsiang was at Soochow a report came in that a male had given birth. He did not reply [to this announcement] but looked straight at his disciples and said, 'Be warned! Recently buggery [*nan se*] has become more commonplace than fornication with females. It will certainly lead to this sort of thing.' "[31] Nonetheless, however they understood the mechanisms involved, those who reported such anomalies did not question that this strange thing happened to certain people as men.[32]

In sum, late Ming male gender identity was not easily compromised by the sexually "strange." Social role normally overshadowed the sexual in gender construction, and the result for males was that mutability of bodies and diversity of objects of desire need not render male gender problematic. Relations between older and younger partners or between genteel and servile ones did not upset established notions of social hierarchy. Even male pregnancy was capable of being interpreted not as the result of possession by demonic influences but as an enlargement, however risky, of male powers. Broad and flexible notions of what was sexually compatible with maleness stopped only at the extreme: only the eunuch could be seen as a concubine. It took a case like that of Li Liang-yü for the sexual to construct the social. Accordingly, at the biological frontier of "strange" sexual transformations there was ample room for the philosophical detachment of a naturalist like Li Shih-chen or the emotional sympathy for a castrated feminized male depicted in the Li Yü story. These men were able to use the anomalous phenomena around them as means to a dispassionate, iconoclastic, and at the same time humane exploration of the boundaries of male gender.

Nonetheless, Li Liang-yü aroused passions because the figure of the eunuch concubine was associated with socially novel patterns of homosexual behavior in late Ming society. As we have seen, literati warnings about homosexual fashion in the late Ming revealed a new sense of unease. Such warnings also translated into a politics of class. When, as Frederick Wakeman has observed, the scholar Li Tung decried the effeminate behavior of late Ming Chiangnan dandies, he chided them *as scholars:* "All of those people in feminine finery/actually turned out to be literati."[33] Such criticism of homosexual fashion expressed anxieties about the inversion of Confucian moral order and the authority of officialdom which depended upon that order for legitimacy.

Beyond this, Li Liang-yü was identified with the sexually and politically charged figure of the eunuch. Here gender boundaries would seem to be clear cut, given the reproductive death castration implies, and given the affront to Confucian values represented in the unprecedented political power of the eunuch establishment at the Ming court. Yet even here ambiguities abounded. If eunuchs were servile, feminized inhabitants of the inner quarters, they were also part of a powerful political institution. Scholars routinely accused them of deliberate "self-castration" in search of the advancement that a successful palace post offered. Bodily deficiencies did not prevent some eunuchs from serving as ministers, generals, envoys, or admirals. Accordingly, in the folklore surrounding them, these powers were even occasionally genderized as sexual potency. Shen Te-fu, who chronicled their world in clinical detail, repeated stories of eunuchs said to have violated virgins, frequented brothels, married, or had heterosexual love affairs; and he chronicled famous men of antiquity said to have been born with "hidden palaces."[34] These were by no means always interpreted as sexual shams. Such rumors particularly clustered around Wei Chung-hsien, the most notorious of late Ming palace eunuchs, who virtually wielded the powers of a prime minister between 1620 and 1627. Others were subject to gossip that by bribery, drugs, or more mysterious means, they were eunuchs in name only.[35]

Li Liang-yü was humble and powerless: this made it easier for those who commented upon this scandal to privilege the sexual over the social in their discourse about him. As a symbol of the sexual itself as a source of threat to social order, Li's case pointed to the subversive potential of late Ming sexual politics: the homosexual fashion that threatened elite moral legitimacy and the eunuch power that eroded bureaucratic authority. The literati sense of outrage is captured in the following poem on the scandal composed by the famous man of letters, Wang Shih-chen (1526–90), which has been preserved in the Taiyuan prefectural gazette:

Nature's Changes ring their tune
But none like Shansi's sun turned moon

Unknown his birth; none saw him die.
Cock or hen—which now flies by? . . . .
Today such trash infests the land
One is ashamed to be a man.[36]

Beneath their worldly facades, literati commentators like Shen and Hsieh shared these sentiments.

Females Who Become Male

By contrast with Li Liang-yü, the case reported in the Ming history of a female who turned into a male attracted little literati notice as a scandal. We learn from the omen section of the dynastic history only that in 1549 this happened to a "young woman, seventeen [sui]," daughter of a member of a guard unit (Wei) near Ta-t'ung in Kansu.[37] However, three other cases were discussed in seventeenth century pi chi, all involving adolescent girls, all also in the north-west in Kansu. The most circumstantial, by Wang Shih-chen (1634–1711), reads as follows:

> The case of Li Liang-yü of Shansi who turned into a woman in the Chia-ching era, has already been recorded in earlier histories. But recently I saw in the "Miscellany of the Hall of Benevolence and Reciprocity" an account of two most strange events concerning Chuang-liang [a county in Kansu]. A woman named Chuang, widow of a soldier in the Red Deer Regiment, had a daughter. She was already promised in marriage when at age twelve, she suddenly turned into a male. Ashamed, she [sic] told no one, until her marriage took place and her husband appealed to the local magistrate to dissolve the union and return her to her father's household, permitting him to marry again. However, the girl's [sic] mother-in-law, finding her compliant and agreeable, pitied her and took her back. Today his name is "Chuang Ch'i-sheng" ["prosperity begins"], and he works in the district library.[38]

Wang reported a second similar case in Chuang-liang ten years later; while T'an Ch'ien (1594–1658) picked up a report of a case in P'ing-liang, Kansu, dating from 1514, in which it was claimed that a young woman changed sex, grew a beard, married, and fathered children. As a male, this individual's personal name was Kao-lei ("distant thunder").[39]

If these Ming accounts are supplemented by the ten reports of female-to-male sex change that appeared in the Ch'ing dynastic history,[40] and by seventeenth- and eighteenth-century narratives by P'u Sung-ling, Yuan Mei, and others, there is ample evidence for a pattern in the reported events and in their social interpretation. Although the official Ch'ing cases do not come from Kansu, but from scattered locations all over China, five of them (i.e. one-half) give the individual's age. She was young—typically an adolescent, though one of the five involved a child of seven who underwent the change, it was said, after recovering from smallpox.

The narratives constructed around these events show a common set of themes. The youngster's marriage provokes a crisis; the approaching wedding day may even lead to illness, and one narrative of such a case presents it as a "miracle cure" of the well-known mid-Ch'ing doctor, Yeh Kuei.[41] There are rejected brides; but families gain a son. There is a new, auspicious name, and a happy ending, especially if the stock theme of heirless parents figures in. The event is not explained or described, but presented as a rebirth mediated by some extraordinary power. P'u Sung-ling encapsulated all the idealized elements of this topos in his narrative, "Transformed into a Boy" ("Hua nan") in Liao chai:

In Soochow ... a girl one night was sitting in the family courtyard. Suddenly she was struck on the forehead by a meteorite from the sky. She fell down as if dead. Her parents were old and had no son; they wept bitterly. But she revived, and on being restored to life announced, laughing, "now I am a male." They investigated and indeed it was so. The parents did not consider him a monster (*yao jen*) but welcomed this violent and sudden gift of a son.[42]

Accounts of females who turn into males differ markedly, then, from those which describe such a transformation in the opposite direction. We do not know whether as an omen, female-to-male change was considered auspicious, along the lines of male multiple births. But socially it could be welcomed by the individuals and families that experienced it. Instead of being given elaborate rationalizations from the cosmological repertory as in the case of Li Liang-yü, female-to-male changes were explained simply. They were also subject to less questioning, scrutiny, and skepticism. However, there is no reason for thinking that this was because of any biologically based intuition that one kind of claim was likely to be less valid than another. In both directions the phenomenon was presented and interpreted as a change, not as a case of mistaken identity.[43]

Significantly, narratives of female-to-male changes were marked by a total suppression of the sexual in favor of the social. In spite of the fact that the actual feelings hinted of in these tales were more often the "feminine" ones of modesty and shame, the transition to male gender was presented as a psychologically unproblematic shift of role. Thus the discourse about transformations of sex subtly genderized the different protagonists' relationship to their bodily changes. Girls become male passively and modestly, like good girls; their new gender was accomplished through social placement untouched by sexual feelings. The male has taken an active role in his transformation, and narrators imply erotic motivation and moral complicity in subverting orthodox relationships.

Hermaphrodites and Female Deficiency

By the standards of today's biomedicine, it is probable that some if not all of these cases could be classified as recognized anomalies—the sort labeled by the old-fashioned name of "hermaphroditism." To modern science this is not a single condition. Authorities don't agree whether the complex chromosomal and hormononal interactions that cause people to be born with ambiguous external genitalia even always mask a "true sex." However, it is still the case that there is no way simply by observation to tell the gonadal or chromosomal sex of an anomalous newborn. Nor are such conditions extremely rare. Moreover, there are several kinds of conditions which lead such a child to masculinize as it grows, especially at puberty. Finally, children born with ambiguous genitalia who have come under modern medical observation in the West are found more likely to have been reared as girls than as boys. For example, sex of rearing has proved female by a ratio of about 3 to 1 among the 226 recorded cases of "hermaphroditism" treated at Johns Hopkins medical center between 1951 and 1972.[44] All of this is enough to explain the phenomenon of girls who transformed into boys in late traditional China. Cosmological and biological beliefs allowed such phenomena to be seen dynamically as "changing" body functions, rather than as static structural irregularities, and to be accepted as within the bounds of genuine if imperfectly understood natural phenomena.

However, the complementary bipolarity of yin-yang biological theory was overshadowed by socially hierarchical interpretations of sex change in practice. On the one hand the social valuation of sons and the repression of the sexual eased the transition from one gender to another of a certain group of children raised as girls. On the other hand, male change of social gender was seen as problematic while those recognized as social males enjoyed greater latitude in the sexually permissible. For both, there was no social room for an intermediate status between the sexes. These same patterns reappear in other Ming-Ch'ing narratives of unfortunates with ambiguous bodies who risked rejection as reproductively unfit. There are some hints in the same sixteenth- and seventeenth-century informal literature of how their bodies were likely to be genderized and what may have been their social fates.

The most precise and accurate description of a hermaphrodite infant that I have found is not in any medical book, but in another short story by Li Yü, which also demonstrates the social impossibility of intermediate status. "The Clever Bodhisattva Who Turns Girls into Boys" is a mocking yet at times tragi-comic narrative of an elderly man who prays for an heir. To punish him for his sins the Buddha answers his prayer— with a hermaphrodite baby. The reader is made to share graphically in the appalled father's first look at his child:

> Between its legs a clove kernel [penis] lacks the shape but preserves its
>   traces;
> A cardemon bud [vulva] is open without but closed within.
> What should be indented isn't; what should project doesn't—like a
>   flattened won-ton;
> Round here, truncated there—like a meat dumpling
> Beyond yin or yang, inbetween male and female.[45]

This otherwise healthy and handsome infant serves none of the purposes of the Confucian family. The accumulation of property, sons to inherit it, and the transmission of a patrilineal line—this is the "family selfishness" the old man is guilty of. "Even a girl would save my name," the anguished father is made to cry, forced to give up the possibility of a "second best" uxorilocal son-in-law. The anomalous child is rejected and put in the care of nurses; it cannot be named. As omnipotent author, Li Yü ends this story happily with the tongue-in-cheek divine intervention of the title, thus playing on the topos of the sex change as a gift of a son.

However, the title and narrative indicate that on some level Li Yü expects his readers to see this baby as female. This, he says, is "not male not female" (*pu nan pu nü*) but "one of those stone maidens, half hen but no cock" (*pan tz'u pu hsiung ti shih nü*).[46] The hermaphrodite child fits squarely within the Chinese medical classification of deficient females. Another contemporary, Hsieh Chao-che, made the same association. A "stone maiden" he said, is one whose "body is neither male nor female."[47] As an example he mentioned a court official's wife [sic] in Wu-chin county whose husband had cast her out, and who afterwards served several men in turn as concubine. "One who shared her pillow reported afterward that the body was not very different from a male's but the organ was small and weak."[48] Yet another kind of description of a "stone maiden" comes from the famous late Ming play, *Peony Pavillion,* in which Sister Stone of Purple Light Convent is a bawdy nun, failed in marriage, fit only for the "shaman's robe."

> My bumhole produces garden vines of turds;
> My tinkle hole trickles amid flowering buds
> But that hole in the middle, that good grotto there, is blocked up, a stony
>   well.
> Though stone highways are good to walk on there's no planting in a
>   stone field.[49]

It would seem that in everyday language the name "stone maiden" applied to the victims of a wide range of genital anomalies, identified in the passive bodies of infants as defective females rather than incomplete males. Moreover, as the burlesque character of Sister Stone suggests, in popular idiom the "stone maiden" could be a figure of fun, an old crone, perhaps, or a termagant wife.

There is no way of proving that these "stone maidens" outnumbered hermaphrodites identified at birth as boys—those who would grow up as "natural eunuchs."[50] However, it is a conclusion consistent with the prevailing Chinese medical classifications of abnormality, and with what is known of cross-cultural patterns. If the "stone maiden" reflected a cultural construction of the female as deficient, it should not be thought, however, that the assignment of sexual identity was literally made by male authority. The standard medical classifications used by Li Shih-chen and his contemporaries were ancient ones,[51] and there is little reason to think they were reinforced by personal observation. On the contrary, the most vivid late Ming recorded observations I have seen come from adventurous literary men, not doctors. Instead, narratives about sexual transformation show that the determination of sex, which normally took place at childbirth, was women's work. When magistrates had to judge in a case like that of Li Liang-yü, midwives or "old women" were called in.[52] Li Yü's story shows the midwife's judgment in a difficult case as unquestioned. Gender shaped medical decision-making through the perceptions of women themselves, who were organized to manage reproduction as part of an inferior female sphere.

However much they were socially marginalized, "stone maidens" were seen as harmless unfortunates. But there was a more sinister alternative—the *yao jen* or "monster." Such a case was reported by Hsieh Chao-che, Huang Wei, and Lu Ts'an, among other authors of *pi chi*.[53] All of these literati understood it to be an instance of a female impersonator, and remarked upon the strangeness of a male choosing to play a female role.

Sang Ch'ung of T'ai yuan prefecture in Shansi, an orphan, was reared during the Ch'eng-hua reign [1465–88] as a girl with bound feet. She/he did not marry but made a living as a teacher of needlework to daughters of good family. Traveling from district to district, she/he lived in intimate companionship with dozens of girl students until one day, after about ten years of this itinerant life, a male relative of an employer attempted rape. Exposed, physically inspected, and hauled before the magistrate's court, Sang Ch'ung was pronounced a male "monster" (*yao jen*)—one who treacherously manipulated his genitals to appear female to the world, but male to the girls he lived to debauch. Sang Ch'ung and a number of named confederates were executed. The earliest known account of the case, that of Lu Ts'an, who claimed to have taken it from an old copy of a court record, portrayed Sang Ch'ung as the leader of a whole gang of similar tricksters, who included his brother and several others from the same home district.

This story, which became famous, possessed in all of its versions lurid trappings of eroticism, sorcery, and deception. Hsieh and others assumed that female dress had to be a stratagem, that the victims were drugged, and that the criminal possessed weird sexual powers. These assumptions were in keeping with legal views of transvestism, which was normally prosecuted as a form of criminal fraud.[54] In *pi chi* and fictional accounts of the Sang Ch'ung case, the protagonist's ambiguous sexuality above all offered opportunities for romantic fantasy. Old Chinese traditions about hermaphroditism were built not so much on empirical observation as on the concept of an erotically protean individual with "two forms." They survived here in a quasi-rationalized form as a drama of deceit.[55]

However, P'u Sung-ling's story based on the case, "The Prodigy" (*Jen yao*), illustrates that not everyone accepted the demonic view of this scandal. In P'u's narrative the "female impersonator," one of Sang Ch'ung's gang, acquires a male lover in the house of his employer. However, "pitying his beauty," the lover castrates his exotic paramour, who is thus saved from the wrath of the law, and transformed into a harmless eunuch concubine.[56] In the eighteenth century Yuan Mei commented upon the case in even stronger terms, stating that Sang Ch'ung's sexual transgressions were not deserving of death and that his ghost remained unappeased.[57] However, detractors and defenders agreed on two things: Sang Ch'ung had lived a life of undreamed-of amorous exploits—and was in fact a male. Possessing freedom of movement and active sexuality, Sang Ch'ung achieved male status—in legend and in death.

Here we see intimations of the social fates which may have awaited real "false males and false females." Bodily ambiguity was translated into social gender according to patterns that identified the female with sexual deficiency and the male with androgynous erotic capabilities. These patterns show that although social gender overshadowed sexuality, this dominance was not total. Gender also involved sexual criteria ordering male and female around the oppositions of active/passive, presence/absence. Moreover, gender accommodated the sexual in asymmetrical ways. Where individuals were socially powerful and/or had capacity to act upon the world, their sexual organs and sexual acts could be genderized as male. Female gender, on the other hand, was identified with those powerless persons whose bodies were read as defective and whose sexuality was passive or absent.

Through their consideration of anomaly, medical opinion, literati narrative, and the social practice hinted of here all offered a common construction of female deficiency. They render more problematic those interpretations of Chinese females as sexually inexhaustible which scholars like Van Gulik have based upon medical bedchamber manuals of the earlier medieval period and on Ming pornography.[58]

Gender Transgression in the Ming-Ch'ing Historical Transition

Was the late Ming fascination with gender transgression a historically specific phenomenon? From the point of view of natural philosophy, of course, it fit in with a wide-ranging contemporary interest in all kinds of natural irregularities, evidence of glacial shifts in cosmological paradigms and canons of intelligibility. However, given the power of gender and politics to construct one another, anomalies in the form of reversals of gender hierarchy always carry social meaning. Gender transgression often merely serves to reinforce accepted social hierarchies by a controlled display of their inversion. Chinese culture, unlike many others, had no formal ritual festivals marked for such display. Still, political rituals involving omens had a perennial life in China, and hardly a year passed without the appearance of some local gazette record of cock-crowing hen or bearded woman. But there is reason to think that the discourse on anomaly outlined here points to the emergence of a sexual politics peculiar to the Ming-Ch'ing transition.

It was a time when eunuchs and homosexuals were unusually visible at the pinnacles of society, suggesting a socially risky expansion of the boundaries of the permissible for males. In this situation, the sexual constructed the social as an aspect of late Ming "decadence" associated later with the fall of the dynasty and its attendant disasters. In keeping with this interpretation, we find that the succeeding Manchu rulers used their power to mandate curbs on pornography and eunuch influence at court. Explicitly erotic fiction, and medical texts which discussed sexual technique, even in the context of advice on procreation, dropped out of sight. "Natural eunuchs" were strictly forbidden to enter royal service, and regular bureaucrats of the Imperial Household Department supervised the inner court. For the first time in imperial history homosexual fornication was declared illegal, and laws against rape became more stringent for both heterosexual and homosexual situations.[59] It is still hard to say whether such state actions simply drove the old permissive mores underground, or whether, as McMahon has suggested, male centrality in Ch'ing China consolidated around a stricter Confucian sexual orthodoxy.

What is clear is that the late Ming expansion of the possible and the social dangers it represented appear here as largely male affairs. The narrow range of the sexually permissible for females and the unproblematic character of female-to-male change all suggest that late Ming sexual politics was not connected to perceptions of new social assertiveness among women. Rather, as far as women were concerned, the Ming-to-Ch'ing transition in gender norms encouraged the intensification of the chaste widow cult.[60] If in these years the androgynous male body was the object of politically charged discourse suggesting its unfitness to represent the Confucian moral order, the asexual female body escaped from the ascription of deficiency when offered up as an icon of Confucian virtue uncompromised.

NOTES

1. I would like to thank the American Council of Learned Societies and the National Institute of Health History of Science Program for grant support which assisted me in my research. I am also grateful to the faculty and staff of the East Asian Studies Department and the Gest Library at Princeton University for their expertise and guidance in the sources for Ming history. Tani Barlow, Paul Gatz, Keith McMahon, Nathan Sivin, Marilyn Young, Judith Zeitlin, and the anonymous reviewer for *Late Imperial China* all offered criticisms and suggestions which improved and broadened the final draft.

2. Foucault 1978; Illich 1982. See also Laqueur 1986 and Duden 1987.

3. Li Shih-chen, *Pen ts'ao kang mu* [Systematic Materia Medica], pub 1596. See chüan 52, "Jen k'uei" ["human anomaly"].

4. Shen Te-fu, *Wan-li yeh huo pien*, pref 1606. Reprinted Peking 1959, 1980; Hsieh Chao-che, *Wu tsa tsu*. Reprinted in the *Pi-chi hsiao-shuo ta-kuan pa pien*, vols 6 and 7.

5. Wu Chih-wang, *Chi yin kang mu* [Systematic Aid for the Disorders of Yin], pref 1620. Shanghai 1958 ed.: 179. This text, heavily derivative of the Ming medical master Wang K'en-t'ang, was reprinted dozens of times in the Ch'ing dynasty.

6. *Chi yin kang mu*, 183–85. See also the standard eighteenth-century medical encyclopedia, Wu Ch'ien, et al., *I tsung chin chien* [Golden Mirror of Medicine], published 1742. Peking 1981 ed. 3:47. A frequently cited classical authority on reproductive anomaly was Ch'u Ch'eng (fl. Southern Ch'i dynasty AD 479–501). See *Ch'u shih i shu* [Posthumous Essay of Master Ch'u], reprinted in T'ao Tsung-i, *Shuo fu*, Taipei: Hsin hsing shu chü, 1963.

7. Ch'i Chung-fu, *Nü k'o pai wen* [One Hundred Questions on Medicine for Women]. Pref 1220. This work was widely reprinted in the late Ming. See *hsia* chüan: 1a. See also *Chi yin kang mu*: 183; and Shen Chin-ao (1717–1767), *Fu k'o yü ch'ih* [Jade Rule of Medicine for Women], published 1774.

8. *Pen ts'ao kang mu*, chüan 52.

9. A variant of "stone maiden" (*shih nü*) is "solid maiden" (*shih nü*). Shen Yao-feng, [fl late eighteenth century?] author of *Shen shih nü k'o chi yao* [Master Shen's Essentials of Medicine for Women], 1850 preface by Wang Shih-hsiung, has a slightly different list of "false males and false females." Interestingly, he suggests that "drums" can be cured in infancy by surgery. Hongkong 1956 reprint: 19.

10. *Pen ts'ao kang mu*, chüan 52.

11. *Pen ts'ao kang mu*, chüan 52. Another classification of "false males," derived from Buddhism, may be found in Shen Te-fu: 922. It was presented as a typology of "natural eunuchs" and not used by medical men.

12. The annals of the Chin dynasty, alluded to by Li Shih-chen, presents one common Chinese version of the hermaphrodite as erotic wizard. It was said of a palace favorite of the emperor Hui-ti [AD 290–307] that he assumed the form of a woman for one half the month and of a man for the other half. Judith Zeitlin quotes a Southern Sung miscellany, *Lu chun hsin hua*, which uses the same topos. A dissolute "maidservant" seduces her mistress. "Though I am a woman, both forms are present in me. When I encounter a woman I assume a male form: when I encounter a male, then I become a woman again," Zeitlin 1987:10.

13. Typical late Ming medical advice on sexuality and health may be found in Wan Ch'üan, *Wan Mi-chai shu* [Works of Wan Mi-chai], Wan-li edition, "Yang sheng" ["Long Life"] section; and in Kung T'ing-hsien, *Wan ping hui chun* [Rejuvenation from All Ills], publ 1587.

14. See Shen Te-fu:622; Hsieh Chao-che, chüan 5:3533; chüan 8:3743–45; 3780–81. Useful information may be found in two secondary works: "Wei hsing shih kuan chai" [pseud], *Chung-kuo t'ung-hsing-lien mi shih* [Secret History of Homosexual Love in China], 2 vols, Hongkong, n.d.; and "Xiaomingxiong" [pseud], *Zhongguo tongxing'ai shilu* [Veritable Record of Chinese Homosexuality], Hongkong 1984. Michel Foucault (1978) has shaped our understanding of the social construction of sexuality in Europe by his analysis of the nineteenth-century emergence of the "homosexual" and "lesbian" as personality types. As the power to define sexual norms shifted from the church to the emerging sciences and professions, sexual transgressions ceased to be defined as discrete carnal acts, and came to be associated with deep-rooted personal dispositions constituting a social identity.

15. Henderson 1984. See also the review by Willard Peterson in the *Harvard Journal of Asiatic Studies* 46.2 (December 1986). In a related discussion of late imperial astronomy, Nathan Sivin (1986) has argued that considerations of "cosmic indeterminancy" led astronomers to doubt the possibility of perfectly accurate prediction.

16. *Pen ts'ao kang mu,* chüan 52.

17. The *Chin shih,* 3:907–8, with three cases, represented a high point of official reporting of sex change as omens. The annalist assumed these occurred under the influence of the homosexual fashion at the court of the emperor Hui-ti [AD 290–307]. Later official histories largely dropped the issue, though there is one report of a male birth in the *Sung shih,* 5:1369. Reports of sex change in the "Omen" sections of the Ming and Ch'ing dynastic histories are summarized in Ch'en 1982:349, 388.

18. *Ming shih,* 2:441–2.

19. *Pen ts'ao kang mu,* chüan 52.

20. Li Hsu, *Chieh-an lao jen man-pi,* published 1597. Reprint in *Yuan-Ming shih-liao pi-chi ts'ung-k'an* series. Peking 1982:181–82.

21. Taoists commonly used symbols of gender inversion to signify rejection of outer worldly power in favor of inner spiritual mastery. See Schipper 1982:161. Somewhat similar is the tradition that the Buddha's male organ is sheathed within his body, an indication of his victory over carnality. See "Wei hsing shih kuan chai," 2:154.

22. *Ming Shih-lu,* 93:0730–31. See also Sung's biography in *Ku chin t'u shu chi-ch'eng,* vol. 280, chüan 303.

23. Li Yü, "Nan Meng mu chiao ho san ch'ien" [A Male 'Mother Mencius' Teaches the 'Three Removals'], *Li Yü ch'üan chi,* 13:5381–5454. See also P'u Sung-ling, "Jen yao" in *Liao chai chih i,* 3:1711–13. Late Ming pornographic short stories with similar homosexual themes are analyzed in McMahon 1984, 1987.

24. "They wear makeup, substituting the false for the true; they bind feet and pierce ears to make themselves beautiful; their breasts stick out and hang down like tumorous swellings; they can't go out, but are tied to home like a melon to its vine; they are bound to their children and have no freedom; their monthly blood flow soaks the matting and stains their lower garments; babies come one after another with no end in sight." "Nan Meng mu," 5389.

25. "Nan Meng mu," 5453.

26. Shen Te-fu:622.

27. Hsieh Chao-che, 8:3744–45, 3780–81.

28. *Chieh-an lao-jen man pi:22.*

29. *Ch'ing pai lei ch'ao,* "i pin" section, 25:2, reporting a case of 1644.

30. Wang Shih-chen (1634–1711), *Ch'ih pei ou t'an* 2:182. P'u Sung-ling has a version of this story in *Liao chai chih i* 2:1037.

31. Hsieh Chao-che 5:3533.

32. Religion supported folklore concerning male pregnancy, since *"nei tan"* internal alchemy taught seekers of immortality to cultivate an "immortal embryo" within. In the late Ming or even today, any visitor to temples dedicated to the "five hundred lohan" would find images of pregnant monks, skin peeled back to reveal the child. See Needham 1983. A comic burlesque is found in the magical pregnancies of Tripitaka and Chu Pa-chieh in chapter 53 of *Journey to the West*. My thanks to Ann Waltner for calling my attention to this reference.

33. Wakeman 1985, 1:95–96. Fu I-ling (1963), who is the source of the quotation from this rare *pi chi*. believes that such untraditional fashions reflected the influence of new commercial wealth. See p. 106–7.

34. Shen Te-fu, 157–179, 922. I interpret *"yin kung"* to allude to the biological belief that sexual function—identified with the "kidney system"—had two loci, in external genitals and internally at the "vital gate" (*ming men*) below the navel.

35. "Wei hsing shih kuan chai," 123–48. In the context of Confucian orthodoxy, to become a eunuch was to be guilty of sacrilege against the ancestor cult, and the late Ming court eunuch vogue for marriages—which emperors could not prevent—constituted an illegitimate manipulation of it. For Wei Chung-hsien and his cronies see Mammitzsch 1968:108–110.

36. *Tai-yuan fu-chih*, Wan li 40 (1610), chüan 25:8b.

37. *Ming shih*, 2:442.

38. Wang Shih-chen, *Ch'ih pei ou t'an*, chüan *hsia*: 185.

39. T'an Chi'en, *Tsao lin tsa tsu*, "I chi" section:6.

40. *Ch'ing shih kao* 14.41:19b24b.

41. Yang Chih-i and Chu Chen-sheng 1961:185–86.

42. P'u Sung-ling, 2:1060. Yuan Mei. *Tzu pu yü*, chüan 17:8b/9a has a similar anecdote.

43. This contrasts with the commentaries on reports of female-to-male sex change found in European sources from Pliny to Montaigne. These were taken as credible evidence of the mutability of bodies based on the Galenic belief that female reproductive organs are homologous with male, only turned outside in. However, these European authorities believed that such transformations worked only in one direction, "up the great chain of being." See Laqueur 1986:13–14.

44. For the Johns Hopkins study, see Money and Ehrhardt 1972:x–xi. A standard text is *Hermaphroditism, Genital Anomalies and Related Endocrine Disorders* by H. Jones and N. Scott (1958), who also note this pattern in childrearing. See p. 53. They say that in the United States the commonest form of hermaphroditism, occurring once in about every 5,000 births, is due to "congenital adrenal hyperplasia." It produces progressive genital virilization in girls. Imperato-McGinley et al. (1979) have isolated a type of genetic defect which delays masculinization in boys until puberty.

45. *"Pien nü wei erh p'u-sa ch'iao," Li Yü chüan chi*, 13:5577–5625.

46. *"Pien nü wei erh p'u-sa ch'iao,"* 5611.

47. Hsieh Chao-che, chüan 5:3530. The same observation is found in the eighteenth-century *pi chi* by Yuan Mei, *Tzu pu yü*, chüan 20:10a. Yuan contrasted the antiquity of the term "stone woman" (*shih fu*) with the novelty of a recently discovered "stone man" (*shih nan*) in Yangchow. From his description it is clear this individual suffered from serious bowel as well as genital abnormalities.

48. Hsieh Chao-che, 5:3530.

49. T'ang Hsien-tsu (1550–1616), *Mu tan t'ing* [Peony Pavillion], scene 17. I have slightly modified Cyril Birch's translation. My thanks to Andrew Plaks for calling my attention to this reference.

50. In the nineteenth century "stone maidens" more of the Sister Stone type turned up occasionally in the clinics of missionary doctors, brought by mothers hoping to make them fit as brides. See *Report of the Medical Missionary Society of China: 1866*, Hongkong, 1867, p. 15; *Chinese Medical Missionary Journal* 3.4:146, 155 (1889), 5.4:118, 208–09 (1891).

51. See footnote 6.

52. The same is true in the case of Sang Ch'ung discussed below.

53. Lu Ts'an (1494–1551), *Keng ssu pien, Tsung shu chi-ch'eng* ed., vol. 2910:204–8 (chüan 9): Huang Wei (b. 1438, *chin shih* 1490). *Peng hsuan wu chi, pieh chi*, preface 1526, 1a/b; Hsieh Chao-che, 8:3739. In Huang Wei's account Sang Ch'ung was known as a "widow" and operated around the capital. Huang did not mention any confederates. See also "Wei hsing shih kuan chai," 1:167–68.

54. Meijer 1985:115.

55. Judith T. Zeitlin (1987) has sensitively analyzed the most famous literary treatments of the Sang Ch'ung case. She stresses the "superhuman virility" attributed to Sang Ch'ung as a seducer, and the "superabundance of erotic possibilities" developed in short stories by Feng Meng-leng and Ling Meng-ch'u as well as P'u Sung-ling. I wish to thank her for calling my attention to several of the most important *pi chi* sources on the case. Readers will have to decide whether Sang Ch'ung, on the basis of present knowledge, is best understood as a transvestite, a trickster, or—as I have suggested here—as possibly a biological hermaphrodite. The Chinese terms used to describe Sang Ch'ung were rich in ambiguity: *yao jen,* meaning freak/monster but also sorcerer; and *jen yao,* suggesting freak/prodigy, but also someone who practices sexual travesty.

56. P'u Sung-ling, 3.1711–13.

57. Yuan Mei, *Tzu pu yü,* chüan 23:3a/b.

58. Van Gulik 1951 and 1974.

59. For Ch'ing law see Meijer 1985 and Ng 1987; for censorship and erotic fiction see McMahon 1984 and 1987; for curbs on eunuchs see "Wei hsing shih kuan chai" 1:145–54.

60. See Elvin 1984, and Mann 1987. Elvin notes that the cult first grew in popularity in the late Ming among elite families, who repeatedly defied imperial edicts designed to limit it to the common people. My argument here implies that to understand it we should look to sexual politics, and not just to the political discourse concerning "loyalty."

REFERENCES

Ch'en, Pan-kuan. 1982. *Erh-shih-liu shih i-hsueh shih-liao hui-pien* [Documentary Collection of Materials on Medicine in the Twenty-six Dynastic Histories]. Peking: Chung-i yen-chiu yuan.

Duden, Barbara. 1987. *Repertory on Body History: An Annotated Bibliography.* Pasadena, California: Humanities Working Paper 125, California Institute of Technology.

Elvin, Mark. 1984. "Female Virtue and the State in China," *Past and Present* 104.

Foucault, Michel. 1978. *The History of Sexuality. Vol. 1: An Introduction.* Trans. Robert Hurley. New York: Pantheon Books.

Fu I-ling. 1963. *Ming tai chiang-nan shih min ching chi shih t'an* [Investigation of the Urban Economic Life of Ming Dynasty Chiang-nan]. Shanghai: Jen-min ch'u-pan she.

Henderson, John B. 1984. *The Development and Decline of Chinese Cosmology.* New York: Columbia University Press.

Illich, Ivan. 1982. *Gender.* New York: Pantheon Books.

Imperato-McGinley, J., et al. 1979. "Androgens and the Evolution of Male Gender Identity Among Male Pseudohermaphrodites with Five-alpha Reductose Deficiency." *New England Journal of Medicine* 300 (22): 1233–37.

H. Jones and N. Scott. 1958. *Hermaphroditism, Genital Anomalies, and Related Endocrine Disorders.* Baltimore: Williams and Wilkins.

Laqueur, Thomas. 1986. "Orgasm, Generation, and the Politics of Reproductive Biology." *Representations* 14 (Spring).

Li Yü. 1970. *Li Yü chüan chi* [Collected Works of Li Yü]. Helmut Martin, compiler. 15 vols., Taipei.

Mammitzsch, Hans-Richard. 1968. *Wei Chung-hsien: A Reappraisal of the Eunuch and the Factional Strife at the Late Ming Court.* University of Hawaii Ph.D.

Mann, Susan. 1987. "Widows in the Kinship, Class and Community Structures of Qing Dynasty China." *Journal of Asian Studies* 46.1 (February).

McMahon, Keith. 1987. "Eroticism in Late Ming, Early Qing Fiction." *T'oung Pao* LXXIII.

McMahon, Keith. 1984. *The Gap in the Wall: Containment and Abandon in Seventeenth-century Chinese Fiction.* Princeton University Ph.D.

Meijer, M.J. 1985. "Homosexual Offences in Ch'ing Law." *T'oung Pao* LXXI.

Ming shih. 28 vols., 332 chüan. 1974 reprint. Taipei: Chung-hua shu-chü ch'u-pan she.

Money, John and Ehrhardt, Anke. 1972. *Man and Woman, Boy and Girl: The Differentiation and Dimorphism of Gender Identity from Conception to Maturity.* Baltimore and London: The Johns Hopkins University Press.

Needham, Joseph. 1983. *Science and Civilization in China. Vol. 5, Pt. 5: Spagyrical Discovery and Invention: Physiological Alchemy.* Cambridge: Cambridge University Press.

Ng, Vivien W. 1987. "Ideology and Sexuality: Rape Laws in Qing China." *Journal of Asian Studies* 46.1 (February).

P'u Sung-ling. 1962. *Liao chai chih i* [Strange Stories from a Chinese Studio]. 3 vols., Shanghai.

Schipper, Kristofer. 1982. *Le corps Taoiste: corps physique—corps social.* Paris: Fayard.

Sivin, Nathan. 1986. "On the Limits of Empirical Knowledge in the Traditional Chinese Sciences." In J.T. Fraser, N. Lawrence, and F.C. Haber, eds., *Time, Science, and Society in China and the West,* Amherst: University of Massachusetts Press.

Van Gulik, R.H. 1951. *Erotic Colour Prints of the Ming Period.* 3 vols. Tokyo: privately printed.

Van Gulik, R.H. 1974. *Sexual Life in Ancient China.* Leiden: E.J. Brill.

Wakeman, Frederick. 1985. *The Great Enterprise.* 2 vols. Berkeley: University of California Press.

"Wei hsing shih kuan chai" [pseud]. n.d. *Chung-kuo t'ung-hsing-lien mi shih* [Secret History of Homosexual Love in China]. 2 vols. Hongkong: Yu-chou ch'u-pan she.

"Xiaomingxiong" ("Samshasha") [pseud]. 1984. *Zhongguo tongxing'ai shihlu* [Veritable Record of Homosexual Love in China]. Hongkong.

Yang Chih-i and Chu Chen-sheng. 1961. *Ku-chin ming i kuai ping ch'i chih mi-chi shih-lu* [Veritable Record of the Precious Raft of Marvelous Cures of Strange Illnesses by Famous Doctors Ancient and Modern]. Taipei.

Zeitlin, Judith T. 1987. "Over the Borderline: Transvestites and Transsexuals in Seventeenth-century Chinese Literature." Unpublished manuscript.

33

The Bow and the Burden Strap:
A New Look at Institutionalized
Homosexuality in Native North America

Harriet Whitehead

Harriet Whitehead, a Research Associate in Anthropology at Duke University, is the author of Renunciation and Reformulation: A Study of Conversion in an American Sect *(1987) and co-editor, with Sherry B. Ortner, of* Sexual Meanings: The Cultural Construction of Gender and Sexuality *(1981) from which this essay was taken. She is currently completing an analysis of Papua New Guinea culture. Here Whitehead argues that cross-cultural investigations of homosexuality have too often been used to support various interpretations of the Western homosexual; thus, studies which posit an underlying identity between the Native American berdache—gender-crosser—and the modern "homosexual" only serve to obscure the berdache's meaning within Native American culture, since it is precisely in the area of sexuality that differences begin to emerge. Western society foregrounds erotic orientation as the basis for dividing people into socially significant categories, but for Native Americans, occupational pursuits and dress/demeanor were the important determinants of an individual's social classification, and sexual object choice was its trailing rather than its leading edge.*

Sexual exoticisms in exotic lands, when they are highlighted in the social science literature, typically appear not exotic at all but seem instead to be familiar items from our own sexual behavioral repertoire dressed up in foreign garb. The moral of the social scientist's discussion is often that a particular element of our sexual behavior appears in other cultures, but in other places meets a different cultural fate. Sexuality itself, that infinitely variable human capacity, paradoxically presents us with few surprises, but cultural responses to it are wildly unpredictable.

Nowhere does this construction of the data appear more commonly than in the case of what is called in the literature "institutionalized homosexuality." The homosexuality that other societies prescribe or condone is immediately taken to be something very much like one of the forms of homosexuality familiar to the modern West, and the explanation of the foreign culture's institutionalizing response, when offered, proceeds in accordance with the chosen meaning of the behavior in our own culture. Is homosexual behavior the result of an enduring erotic disposition to which a certain percentage of the population will inevitably fall prey? If so, it is noted that certain other cultures meet this universal problem by providing a specialized niche for such individuals (Kroeber 1940). Is homosexuality the result of irregularities in the early socialization process? In that case, those cultures in which it is widespread or institutionalized must have a correspondingly widespread or institutionalized kink in their early socialization processes (Slater 1968). Is homosexuality a practice to which people resort when heterosexual outlets are unavailable? Then look to the barriers that exist in some cultures against heterosexual expression (Bullough 1976). And so on. It is evident from the approaches cited that there is not much agreement as to what this phenomenon is that is supposedly the same wherever we find it. In fact, a good many of the cross-cultural investigations have been, explicitly or implicitly, aimed at mustering support for one or another interpretation of "our" homosexuality rather than at laying bare the meaning of "theirs."

A corollary of this ethnocentrism of interest is an anthropological solecism that often appears in studies of this sort, that of interpreting the styles of homosexuality that are fully institutionalized in the light of those that are not (again, "theirs" in the light of "ours"). Intriguing though the similarity of types often is, brief reflection should counsel us that cultural processes (and psychological ones as well) operate in a quite different fashion in behaviors that are formally instituted as opposed to those that are spontaneously expressed. Sexual behaviors that occur within the context of normative expectations tell us something about normative expectations but very little about human desire; and conversely, spontaneous (noninstituted) sexual expressions indicate the presence of characteristic desires without giving us any clear message about the operations of the formal cultural system. The cross-cultural data on spontaneous homosexuality around the world is too deficient to permit much clarification of its nature, but the rate of it in any particular area appears to vary independently of the official cultural "attitude" toward it. The rate may be high where it is condemned (twentieth-century America) or low (Trobriands); low where it is permitted (Nambikwara) or high (Desana). And it is not universal. Some groups genuinely have never heard of homosexuality in any form.[1] In other words, spontaneous expression is neither an automatic outcome of human psychological and social processes, nor is it an artifact of culture in any straightforward sense. (Heterosexual expression might appear equally elusive were it not, in some form, universally "institutionalized.") Whatever the forces are that generate homosexual desires in the population at large and bring these desires to expression, there is no evidence that these same forces, even when intensified, necessarily cause the expression to become formally instituted. Consider the relatively simple case of lack of heterosexual outlet as a motive for homosexual behavior. Among the Azande of Central Africa, young bachelors, deprived of women during their military service to the king, substituted "boy wives" in their place; the practice was explained in terms of substitution, and it was embedded in its own set of rules and standards of decorum (Evans-Pritchard 1970). Here we seem to have an "institution" of sorts flowing straightforwardly from a structurally engendered need. But we cannot predict when such a principle will operate. Neither the heterosexual deprivation nor the emotional intensity of the sex-segregated upper-class boarding school environment in European societies has been, in the entire history of these establishments, sufficient to produce any comparable acceptance of the resulting homosexual relationships. In native America, as we shall see, spontaneous homosexual expressions appear in societies where a fully institutionalized form is available, but the former, rather than being channeled into the latter is dismissed as some type of possibly dangerous foolishness. If in such cases the natives see no meaningful connection between an instituted form and a spontaneous one, should the anthropologist?

In all fairness to the discipline of cultural anthropology, the theoretical weaknesses in the cross-cultural study of sexuality (not just homosexuality) of which I complain, are largely confined to the "Culture and Personality" school and to assorted theorists from other fields similarly dominated by biological or psychiatric models. More strictly cultural studies have much better fulfilled the anthropological mandate that one put a practice into its cultural context before attempting to generalize about its meaning. These studies have often helped considerably to illuminate the meaning of certain sexual exoticisms, even when not always directly addressing them. The recent studies of New Guinea belief systems and social organization are notable examples. These studies include Kelly (1976), Meigs (1976), Schieffelin (1976), Buchbinder and Rappaport (1976), and Poole (1981). Because of the nature of New Guinea culture, these studies focus upon sex-roles and sex-related practices and ideas.

One of the customs clarified in this recent literature is that of prescribed man-boy homosexual relationships common throughout the south-central lowlands of New Guinea. These relationships, of limited duration, are similar in intention to ancient Greek pederasty. In both instances it is thought that the younger male generation is raised to full manhood through erotic connection to the older male generation, but the New Guineans, unlike the more abstract Greeks, consider this beneficial result to be a function of the fact that "manhood," in both its physical and cultural aspect, is embodied in semen, hence some regular mode of transmitting the stuff is in order (Kelly 1976: 450; Schieffelin 1976: 124; Van Baal 1966: 493–4). Comparably, full "womanhood," throughout New Guinea, is held to be embodied in menstrual and parturitional blood, and the males of pederastic tribes speculate that women too have some means of transmitting their substance to the next generation (Kelly 1976: 47).

What findings like this make clear is that a particular instituted sexual custom—in this case pederasty—is but one manifestation among many of a way of classifying and thinking about the sexes that, if traced in all its detail (a task I will not undertake here) is found to be rooted both in a wider set of cosmological premises and a characteristic pattern of social privilege and obligation that divides the sex and age categories. Furthermore, it is often the "offbeat" (to our eyes) sexual and sex-related practices such as pederasty (or ritual semen eating, or menstrual pollution taboos, or the use in head-hunting of weapons that symbolize copulation, to mention only a few items from the Southern Lowland New Guinea repertoire) that help to bring the native theory most clearly to the fore, probably because being unclouded by obvious utilitarian aims their "symbolic" nature stands out more boldly.

The "peculiarity" reveals the underlying thought system and the underlying thought system explains the peculiarity. This is, of course, one of cultural anthropology's classic findings, now used as a starting premise in most cultural studies. This starting premise is gradually coming into more frequent and more rigorous use in studies of gender and sex-related beliefs and practices everywhere, including the West (see Barker-Benfield 1976; Smith-Rosenberg 1978). This trend has been greatly inspired by recent feminist rejection of the conservative natural-destiny idiom that prevailed in so much previous theory. As the cultural and ideological dimension of sex and gender is made clearer, it is to be hoped that this dimension will be more revealing of the social—as opposed to natural—processes at work in the shaping of sex roles, sexual identity, and even eroticism itself.

In the interests of furthering this enterprise and simultaneously introducing more clarity into the subject of institutionalized homosexuality, it is my intention here to examine the cultural and social underpinnings of another ethnographically well-known style of homosexuality, the transvestitic version that abounded among tribal peoples of northern Asia and North America.[2] In contrast to New Guinea pederasty wherein a boy was considered to become fully a man through homosexual intercourse, in native North America, it was permissible for a man to become, in important social respects, a woman. Homosexual practice was one of the common accompaniments to this alteration in gender status. In some areas too, a female-to-male transition was possible. These two styles of institutionalized homosexuality, the New Guinea and the North American (which are the two styles most often encountered in tribal societies), could not be further apart in their primary meaning, and indeed as far as I can determine, they never coexist. The meaning of each is also significantly different from the culturally "recognized" but not instituted homosexuality of the modern West. Yet there is a dimension of similarity (aside from the common element of homoerotic contact) that continues to prompt "theirs"-to-"ours" comparisons, especially in the North American case. The differences and similarities can be sorted out and understood, I will argue, if it is realized that each of the "homosexualities" rests upon a different cultural construction of gender—a different gender system, so to speak—while, at the same time, cultural constructions of gender, however dissimilar in content, all have certain points of structural similarity.

When I speak of cultural constructions of gender, I mean simply the ideas that give social meaning to physical differences between the sexes, rendering two biological classes, male and female, into two social classes, men and women, and making the social relationships in which men and women stand toward each other appear reasonable and appropriate. A social gender dichotomy is present in all known societies in the sense that everywhere anatomic sexual differences observable at birth are used to start tracking the newborn into one or the other of two social role complexes. This minimal pegging of social roles and relationships to observable anatomic sex differences is what creates what we call a "gender" dichtomy in the first place, but in no culture does it exhaust the ideas surrounding the two classes thus minimally constituted. Additional defining features of gender status, some related to further real or further supposed physiological differences between the sexes, and some related to a host of other dimensions, such as fate, temperament, spiritual power, ability, and mythical history, are brought into play as well, and it is these additional hypothesized attributes of the sexes that vary significantly from culture to culture. As we shall see in the case of native North America these additional defining features often form clusters, with one or another feature being, in a sense, the "core" of the cluster. Cultural variation in "gender systems" may then appear both in regard to the content of clusters and in regard to their core features. In addition, as long as gender is not fully defined by any one feature alone, there is always the possibility that for various reasons—and the reasons will vary depending on the gender system—a mixed gender or deficient gender status may arise for certain persons or categories of persons. In New Guinea, boys are "deficient" in manhood, for instance. Although homosexuality does not inevitably accompany such situations, they may provide occasions where it is deemed appropriate: In both New Guinea and native North America the institutionalization of homosexual relations is occasioned by peculiar gender statuses constituted on other grounds. In our own society, by contrast, it is spontaneous homosexual activity as such that occasions the cultural recognition—if not condonement—of a peculiar gender status, that of the "homosexual." All of these points will be considered in further detail as I proceed with the analysis of the native North American gender system and the "gender-crossers" who proliferated in the context of it.

A word of caution is needed about the concept "gender system." My ambitions for this term are modest. I am positing here only that there will be some degree of structure in any culture's notions of manhood and womanhood, sexual relations and reproduction. I am not implying that the content of this "system" is in any way self-contained. Rather, starting off in the selected area of sex and gender, the investigator will soon find him/herself handling meanings that seemingly take their shape from the "kinship," "religious," "economic," and other systems of the culture in question, just as starting off in any of the latter areas one is apt to receive meanings from the "gender system." Culture is like this: a hall of mirrors. My viewpoint on the culture of gender is close to David Schneider's views on the culture of kinship (Schneider 1968, 1972, 1973). I also take a page from Schneider's book by easing into the analysis of gender systems through a "defining-features" approach. I do not wish to imply, however, that such an approach exhausts the analysis.

North American Indian Gender Concepts and the Berdache Status

Gender-crossers of some variety have been reported in almost every culture area of native North America. A word is necessary about the objectivity of some of these reports. Very early accounts are typically of this sort:

> It must be confessed that effeminacy and lewdness were carried to the greatest excess in those parts; men were seen to wear the dress of women without a blush, and to debase themselves so as to perform those occupations which are peculiar to the sex, from whence followed a corruption of morals past all expression; it was pretended that this custom came from I know not what principle of religion. [Charlevoix, in Katz 1976: 290 in reference to the Iroquois and Illinois]

> Among the women I saw some men dressed like women, with whom they go about regularly, never joining the men . . . From this I inferred they must be hermaphrodites, but from what I learned later I understood that they were sodomites, dedicated to nefarious practices. From all the foregoing I conclude that in this matter of incontinence there will be much to do when the Holy Faith and the Christian religion are established among them. [Font, in Katz 1976: 291 in reference to the Yuman]

Despite the obvious indifference of these early travelers to the niceties of native form and concept, later accounts lead us to believe that their judgments did not so seriously distort the facts as one might at first think. American Indian gender-crossing, which largely takes the form of anatomic males dressing as women and assuming the tasks of women, appears to have been a relatively visible phenomenon. Early travelers and missionaries remark upon the incongruity of these transvestite figures among the natives and we may assume that no extensive knowledge of the indigenous language or close rapport with members of the culture was required to uncover the practice. Even the frequent horrified assertions about sodomy did not necessarily represent a hasty conclusion on the part of these reporters (whose first impulse was to consider them hermaphrodites rather than homosexuals), and such assertions have not proved inconsistent with later, and better, documentation. It is, however, difficult to establish from such accounts the native attitude toward the gender-crosser. One wonders whether in those cases where the ordinary natives were said to share the visitor's disgust with the berdache, he was in fact despised, whereas in those cases where the "nation" as a whole was dismissed as depraved he was respected; but this is undoubtedly too crude a rule of thumb. What is not to be doubted is that some practice similar to the gender-crossing that later and more sophisticated ethnographers have detailed for us existed at one time over an extensive area of the continent. Kroeber was inclined to consider the trait present unless proven absent. Some geographical constriction of it, however, seems to have been afoot from the beginning of the historical period. The berdache role appears to have dwindled drastically or vanished altogether from much of the subarctic and northwest coastal areas by the late nineteenth century, and there is some question of how strong its foothold in these parts ever was (Bancroft 1875, v. 1: 58, 81–2, 92, 415, 515, 773–4; Hallowell 1955: 291–305; Landes 1938: 177, 180; Delaguna 1954: 178). There is no report of it among the Eskimo. Even moving southward, where one begins to encounter the custom extensively, there are occasional tribal groups that seem to have been abstainers: the Comanche of the Plains for instance, and the Maidu of California (Munroe et al. 1969; Dixon 1905: 241). One Plateau group, the Kaska, manifests the anomaly (perhaps an artifact of poor reporting) of having had only female-to-male crossers, not the more usual male-to-female (Honigmann, in Katz 1976: 237). These occasional gaps and anomalies aside, however, the presence of the berdache and his less frequent female counterpart is traceable throughout the Plateau, Plains, Southwest, Prairie, and Southeastern regions of the continental United States and deep into Mesoamerica. (Data are missing for the Atlantic and Northeastern states regions. In the case of the Mesoamerican civilizations, early Spanish accounts provide little more than allusions to effeminate male prostitutes and to sanctions against homosexuality.)

Rather than search for a focal or "classic" version of the custom, an approach that tends to beg more questions than it resolves, I will begin with a few simple common denominators and statistical generalities. Minimally, gender-crossing in North America consisted of the permissibility of a person of one anatomic sex assuming part or most of the attire, occupation, and social—including marital—status, of the opposite sex for an indeterminate period. The most common route to the status was to manifest, in childhood or early adolescence, behavior characteristic of the opposite sex. These manifestations were greeted by family and community with a range of responses from mild discouragement to active encouragement according to prevailing tribal sentiment, but there was seldom any question as to the meaning of certain opposite-sex-tending behaviors: They were signals that the youth might be destined for the special career of the gender-crossed. Supplementing and sometimes substituting for youthful behavioral cues were messages that came to the future gender-crosser in dreams and visions. Less commonly, men acquired the gender-crossed status by being taken captive in war and integrated into the household of a captor in the status of "wife." Although it was not inconsistent with North American notions of gender to assimilate anatomically intersexed (hermaphroditic) persons, or animals, to the gender-crossed category, there is little reason to believe that physical hermaphroditism occurred any more frequently among native Americans than among other populations or that the occasional appearance of such figures in any way inspired the gender-crossing custom. Despite the probings of Western observers predisposed toward physiological explanations, the number of cases of genuine hermaphrodites reported is negligible.

All evidence suggests that the gender-crossed status was more fully instituted for males than for females. The vast majority of reported cases are ones of anatomic males assuming aspects of the status of women. For these the term "berdache" (from the French word for male prostitute) has come down to us in the ethnographic literature. Female deviations into aspects of the male role were far from infrequent, but in most areas—with exceptions to be discussed—these excursions were not culturally organized into a named, stable status category comparable to that of "berdache." The asymmetry in the ease with which passage was made into the status of the opposite sex is consistent with the status asymmetry of the sexes in North America. The man was everywhere considered superior in worth to the woman. As in most hierarchical systems, downward mobility was more easily achieved than upward mobility. In more particular terms, however, the asymmetry of gender-crossing must be seen as a function of the relative weight given the principal defining features of gender, which differed inversely for the two sexes.

The institution of gender-crossing can be used analytically as a means of discerning the principal defining dimensions of gender and the proportions in which these dimensions were weighted for each sex. My focus will be first upon the man, then the woman.

The defining features of gender in North America can be seen as falling into two broad clusters, the one having to do with anatomy and physiology, the other with behavior and social role. In regard to the first, the sexual anatomy visible at birth was, in North America (as in every other part of the world), the baseline for the social differentiation of the sexes. The kind of genitalia established a prima facie case for the individual's social destiny. According to this criterion, normally the child was routed to one or the other side of the division of productive labor, to one or the other set of marital, parental, and kinship responsibilities, and to either a partially restricted (for women) role or an unrestricted (for men) role in political affairs and communal ceremonies. Even in the case of the berdache, as we shall see, the sheer fact of anatomic masculinity was never culturally "forgotten," however much it may have been counterbalanced by other principles. Yet beyond this basic anatomical marker, little attention devolved upon the details of male reproductive physiology. Unlike the New Guinea peoples mentioned earlier, American Indians were not given to using semen as a reification of manhood, vitality, and so forth, nor did they try, magically, to rid themselves of, or conversely acquire, the reproductive attributes of women. In a word, the physiological obsessions so common in Oceanic cultures do not appear in North America, at least not in regard to the male.[3]

The Male Berdache

Turning now to those aspects of social behavior most definitive of gender status in North America, the evidence from the material on male gender-crossing indicates overwhelmingly that pride of place was given to participation in productive labor. In instance after instance, he became "woman" who did woman's work, preferred the tools of the female trades, or had this work or those tools, through perverse fate, thrust upon him.

From the Yurok of northern California:

> The *wergen* usually manifested the first symptoms of his proclivities by beginning to weave baskets. Soon he donned women's clothing and pounded acorns. [Kroeber 1925: 46]

The Crow of the Plains:

> I was told that when very young, those persons manifested a decided preference for things pertaining to female duties ... as soon as they passed out of the jurisdiction of their parents ... they donned women's clothing. [Simms 1903: 581]

The prairie-dwelling Miami:

> There were men who are bred for this purpose from their childhood. When they are seen frequently picking up the spade, the spindle, the axe, but making no use of the bow and arrows, as all the other small boys are wont to do, they are girt with a piece of leather or cloth which envelops them from the belt to the knees, a thing all women wear ... They omit nothing that can make them like the women. [Liette, in Katz 1976: 288]

Similar accounts of the importance of cross-sex occupational preferences in childhood or adolescence can be found for the Southwest (Hill 1935: 274–5; Underhill 1939: 186; Devereux 1937: 501–3). When tests were used to confirm the nature of the opposite-sex-tending child, these took the form of a forced choice between characteristic male and female implements (Underhill 1939), and when it was a vision that commanded the change, the stereotypic elements of the vision again involved the posing of occupational alternatives:

> It is said that the moon would appear to a man having in one hand a burden strap, in the other a bow and arrows, and the man would be bidden to make a choice. When he reached for the bow, the moon would cross its hands and try to force the strap on the man. [Fletcher and LaFlesche 1972: 132]

That this strong association of manhood and womanhood with specific areas of productive activity was not confined to a narrow complex surrounding the berdache is shown by the fact that tests and visions to establish the sex of an unborn child follow the same pattern. Among the Omaha, a pregnant woman seeking to learn the sex of her future child presented the young child of a neighbor with a choice between bow and burden strap, in this case taking the child's choice to be conditioned by the influence of the fetus, not the inclinations of the chooser (Fletcher and LaFlesche 1972: 329). The Mohave expectant mother paid attention to whether her dreams were primarily of male or female implements and clothing (Devereux 1937: 501). Given the gender-defining character of labor activities, there is no particular contradiction between the usual reports that the berdache was a self-recruited position and the reports that in certain Woodlands and Prairie tribes male war captives were incorporated into the capturing group as berdaches (Angelino and Shedd 1955: 122). Lurie points out that both routes to berdachehood existed among the Winnebago, the self-initiated route being the honorable one, the enforced route dishonorable (Lurie 1953: 712). (The Plains and Western tribes did not as a rule take adult male captives.)

Clothing and mannerisms were also strongly defining of gender in North America. Spontaneous use of female speech patterns, a piping voice, or feminine ways of laughing and walking are sometimes mentioned as identifying the budding berdache (Fletcher and LaFlesche 1972: 132; Devereux 1937: 502; Lowie, in Katz 1976: 319), and cross-dressing (or attempted cross-dressing) was an almost invariable concomitant of gender transformation. Typically this dimension of gender was in harmony with occupational choice, but it was possible in the twentieth century for persons to maintain the gender-crossed status by occupation alone while dressing, in response to white pressure, as befitted anatomic sex (Landes 1970: 201–2; Stevenson, in Katz 1976: 314). It is not known whether a gender-crossed status could be maintained by cross-dressing alone, because examples of this are not reported. Probably the two "social" criteria, work and external appearance, were mutually reinforcing. Each in itself was suggestive of a gender-crossed destiny and conducive to reclassification, but it was expected that with the appearance of one cross-over trait, the other would and should follow. Of the two attributes, occupational preference and dress, it is the first that is most often mentioned and commented upon, inclining us to believe that it was the most central of the social attributes definitive of gender.

By anatomy the berdache was a man, by occupational pursuit and garb, a woman. In the eyes of the American Indians, he was therefore a mixed creature. The most frequent thumbnail description of the berdache given investigators is "man-woman," "part-man, part-woman," or, phrased in the negative, "not-man, not-woman" (Mc-Kenny, in Katz 1976: 299–300; Holder, in Katz 1976: 312; Simms, in Katz 1976: 318, Munroe et al. 1969: 90; Kroeber 1925: 180). Hermaphroditism was the analog to berdachehood in the animal kingdom when such an analogy was drawn (Lurie 1953: 709; Hill 1935: 273–4). Navajo, Cheyenne, and Mohave lore about the berdache's exceptional abilities as a matchmaker, love magician, or curer of venereal disease again expresses the logic that the berdache unites in himself both sexes, therefore he is in a position to facilitate the union of the sexes (Hill 1935: 275; Hoebel 1960: 77; Devereux 1937: 506). Although he was not infrequently dubbed "coward," that is, less than a full man, the male gender-crosser was at the same time viewed as more than a mere woman—for reasons I will discuss later (see Landes 1938: 136). It was not unheard of for the berdache, while taking on female tasks, to retain certain of the male ones as well, excluding those strongly stamped with the seal of masculinity such as warfare. The Navajo, for instance, prized the berdache precisely because he was thought capable of doing the productive work of both sexes. The Navajo *nadle* was often promoted to the head of his natal household, the family holding to the idea that his presence guaranteed them wealth (Hill 1935: 275). Because there is only the finest line between doing what both sexes do and doing what neither sex does (neither sex ordinarily does what both sexes do), we find in several instances specialized duties reserved only for the berdache. Among the Yokuts, the berdaches were corpse handlers (Kroeber 1940: 314), and this seems to have been the case as well in parts of Florida where, in addition, berdaches tended the ill and carried provisions for war parties (LeMoyne, in Katz 1976: 286). Specialized ritual functions, such as the cutting of a particular ritual lodge pole (Crow), or officiating at scalp dances (Papago and Cheyenne) are also reported (Lowie 1956: 48; Hoebel 1960: 77; Underhill 1939: 186). Judging from the usual American Indian division of labor and ritual activity, these special berdache functions were probably appropriated from the women's sphere; but not all instances can be so neatly diagnosed. Among the Illinois for example, the berdache could go to war but bearing only a club, not, as in the case of ordinary men, the bow and arrow (Marquette, in Katz 1976: 287).

In order for this peculiar mixed status to come into being, the two defining dimensions of gender—anatomical and social—had to be given equivalent weight, for then, when a nonconcordance arose, when occupational interest was one way and anatomy another, neither criterion was used as a final determinant of gender status. Instead, the individual became half the one thing, half the other. Attempts can be made to circumvent this logical outcome only by mystifying anatomy, as Westerners do when they say of an effeminate man or a masculine woman, "his/her genes are mixed up." But this reasoning has the ultimate effect of making anatomy the final determinant. In most areas of North America, Indian informants seem to have quickly disabused investigators of the idea, which the investigators favored, that the berdache was anatomically intersexed. But mystifications of anatomy were not entirely absent from North America. They crop up primarily in the Southwest and there for two superficially contrary reasons—either to shore up the gender-crossed status by appeal to the inevitability of the anatomical, or conversely, to undermine the status on the same grounds! In either case a certain insecurity concerning the gender-crossing practice is suggested. The Navajo, who respected the gender-crosser, furnish an example of the "shoring-up" strategy. Their term for gender-crosser, *nadle,* which is derived etymologically from the expression "changing" or "being transformed," has come to mean "hermaphrodite," and the Navajo will claim that the "real" *nadle* is physically intersexed. Gender-crossers not actually hermaphroditic are called "pretend" *nadle.* However, no distinction is made between "real" and "pretend" in degree of social worth; rather, the implicit idea seems to be that a status that is mixed because social appearance contradicts anatomy should really be thought of in terms of a mixed or "changing" anatomy. The ideal validates the imitation. (Hill 1935: 273. One of the Navajo *nadle* known to Hill may have been a genuine hermaphrodite.)

The Mohave present a contrasting situation. Here the gender-crossing custom was "humoristically viewed" according to Devereux, and ordinary Mohave seized upon every opportunity to bait the gender-crosser with the charge of anatomic fraudulence.[4] The gender-crossers in turn responded with apparently serious attempts at fakery to support their position. Several known *alyha* (berdaches) were said to have shammed a menstrual flow and even pregnancy (Devereux 1937: 511–12). In other words, baited with the "real" facts of anatomy, called in effect an imposter, the Mohave gender-crosser was thrown back upon the only defense he thought would be acceptable, namely, that in his case the "real" facts were otherwise.

With one or two possible exceptions (see note 5), this anatomical flummery seems to be confined to the Southwest. Throughout most of the continent, the "part-man, part-woman," was not thought to be, nor forced into the pretense of being, woman in the physiological "parts." It was sufficient that he do as women did in regard to occupation, dress, and demeanor. This established the female component of his identity as anatomy did the male and the mixture of the two dimensions gave rise to his special cross-sex status.

The Female Berdache

For someone whose anatomic starting point was female, the infusion of an official opposite-sex component into her identity was by no means so easily effected. Throughout most of North America, there was no recognized female counterpart to the male berdache. Yet women willing and able to traverse the sex boundary do not seem to have been in short supply. Wherever ethnographic attention has been turned to this subject, the impression is given that for every boy who dreamed of the burden strap, there was a woman who actually picked up the bow. Not uncommonly the examples are of married women, sometimes with children, whose excursions into the male domain were episodic. On occasion, economic necessity drove them to the hunt or other male tasks (Landes 1938: 163–6, 169); at other times, they, like men, took to the warpath in response to a sudden vision or the requirement to avenge a slain kinsman (Landes 1938: 152; 1968: 152–3, 166, 212; De Smet, in Katz 1976: 303). Whereas in some cases it was the absence of a husband, or his ineptitude, that provided the occasion for a woman's masculine debut (Landes 1970: 36; 1938: 126–77), just as often we hear of a husband or father encouraging the women to learn male skills or to act in his place in male curing, ceremonial, or even warlike duties (Landes 1970: 37; 1938: 124–77; Denig, in Katz 1976: 309). With appropriate circumstances or encouragement, some women consistently cultivated male skills from an early age (Landes 1968: 49; Denig, in Katz 1976: 308–11). All such transgressors, if successful in their actions, were honored by the community as a man would be.

> Women of the preceding tales, receive the title and symbolic eagle feather of "brave," *ogitcida,* which is a male title ideally, and grammatically is not conjugated for female sex gender ... The people are untroubled by the contradiction between a woman's carrying this title and the conventional belief that war is a male occupation. [Landes 1938: 144. The Ojibwa]

> A few individual women in each village did drive buffalo on horseback, and did stalk, scalp, and mutilate the enemy; often they were young women, of childbearing age. Their deeds were accepted simply by the men, who not only failed to criticize them but even accorded them the honors of men. [Landes 1968: 49. The Sioux]

One captured Gros Ventre girl ultimately rose to the position of a chief among the Crow, having from girlhood practiced masculine arts and, as an adult, repeatedly distinguished herself in battle and in horse raiding. This woman, after apparently trying and failing to find a husband, converted her horse wealth into marriage payments and founded a household by taking wives (Denig, in Katz 1976: 310). But was she reclassified as a man, or as "part-man, part-woman"? It seems not, for the Crow had no such slot for the anatomic female, nor did most of the other Plains, Prairie, and Woodland groups, many of which sported splendid examples of the male berdache.

What was the problem here? It might be thought significant that none of these women reportedly cross-dressed (not even the Crow chief), but the importance of this feature is equivocal given that berdaches were not always consistently transvestites; and the absence of full-scale imitations of the opposite sex can be explained as proceeding from the absence of a cross-sex category as easily as the other way round. Landes has speculated that a crystallized masculine status for women was rendered unlikely by the casual and sporadic approach of most women to manly activities. This in contrast to the single-minded dedication of the male berdache to his feminine tasks, or, for that matter, of ordinary men to their careers. Men were, in her view, "careerist" in whatever they did; women, inconstant and undisciplined (Landes 1938: 136, 156). But again, the lack of a masculine "career" for women might be the explanation for casualness and inconstancy in male pursuits rather than the other way round. Besides, some women were reported to have been disciplined and steady in their orientation to male activities. The young male berdache's career was commonly launched on the basis of less evidence of cross-sex talent than that shown by a number of the reported female cases. In short, when women did the equivalent of what men did to become berdaches, nothing happened.

The reason for this, I would suggest, is that throughout the continent, the anatomic-physiological component of gender was more significant in the case of the female than in the case of the male, and was thus less easily counter-balanced by the occupational component. The greater significance of the anatomical for the female had to do with the reproductive capacities of the mature women. As in so many other parts of the world, in North America, menstrual and birth blood was the symbolic door at which women's social disadvantage in relation to the men was laid (Lowie 1924: 205–17; Landes 1938: 124; Underhill 1939: 163). This area-wide belief in the inimical effect of female blood upon male activities, upon sacred power, or simply upon men, was ostensibly used to justify the exclusion of women from the occupational and ceremonial domain of men. In fact, this belief served more as simply a rationalization of women's less frequent participation in the male world for everywhere it seems, people shrugged at female intrusions as long as the woman nominally observed the monthly restrictions. Nevertheless, female blood and its attendant associations seems to have anchored women more firmly in their womanly identity than male anatomy anchored the man in his masculinity.

Support for this interpretation can be derived from those North American groups in which there was a cross-sex identity for women. Significantly, almost all reported cases are found in the Southwest. A female-to-male type, sometimes called by the same term as the berdache, is reported for the Mohave, the Cocopa, the Zuni, the Apache, and the Navajo. In these tribes women, either through dream inspiration or cross-sex occupational preferences, or both, established themselves as destined for the cross-sex identity early in life and thereafter cross-worked, cross-dressed, and even cross-married (Hill 1935: 273; Devereux 1937: 501–2; Forde, in Katz 1976: 324; Gifford, in Katz 1976: 325). Although there do not seem to have been many takers for the position because parents and community more actively discouraged the female-to-male crosser than the male-to-female, nevertheless the position was available. Southwestern tribes placed symbolic emphasis upon women's menstrual and parturitional blood just as did the other North American groups, but it was in the Southwest that a mystique of anatomical change had crept into the gender-crossing custom. As male crossers were found claiming that they menstruated, so, conversely it was bruited that female crossers did not. Gifford noted female transvestites in the Cocopa:

> Female transvestites (war'hameh). Male proclivities indicated by desire to play with boys, make bows and arrows, hunt birds and rabbits. Young men might love such a girl, but she cared nothing for them; wished only to become a man. Hair dressed like a man's, nose pierced. Such females not menstruate or develop large breasts. Like men in muscular build, but external sexual organs of women. (Gifford, in Katz 1976: 325)

Forde wrote on "female inverts" among the Yuman:

> Female inverts (kwe'rhame) are rare, but they too realize their character through a dream at puberty. The characteristic dream is of men's weapons. As a small child the kwe'rhame plays with boy's toys. Such women never menstruate; their secondary sexual characteristics are undeveloped or in some instances are male. [Forde, in Katz 1976: 324]

Obviously it could not be clear during the supposedly tomboyish childhood of such a woman whether or not she would grow up to menstruate or develop her secondary sexual characteristics; therefore all that one can conclude from this sketchily recorded lore is that the postpubertal indicators of cross-sex identity were made to jibe with the prepubertal ones, or vice versa, in the minds of informants, and that the absence of the mature woman's reproductive process was one of the critical attributes of the gender-crossed. Only one case of a known Southwestern female "berdache" has ever been detailed—that of the nineteenth-century Mohave, Sahaykwisa, remembered by Devereux's informants. She claimed and others believed that she did not menstruate, but she was otherwise of fully developed female form (Devereux 1937: 523).

   Whether or not the claim of nonmenstruation in any particular case was true, the point remains: Inasmuch as the gender-crossing custom had become mixed up with redefinitions of physiology, females could, by accident or design, find themselves relieved of that physiological factor that made them so resolutely women. The occupational component of their identity could then hold effective sway. The vast majority of other North American groups lacked the physiological elaborations on gender-crossing known to the Southwest, and lacked as well the female berdache.[5]

   A type of masculine status for women, that of the "manly heart" as it was called, existed in one Plains-culture group, the Piegan (Canadian Blackfoot). It has been well documented for us by Oscar Lewis (Lewis 1941). Although the "manly heart" was not the equivalent of the berdache, the category is significant for our understanding of gender-crossing and I will consider it again when I turn to the larger cultural and social context of the custom. For the moment let me note that this status, for various social reasons, grew upon a woman with advancing age, so that even though menopause was not mentioned as a prerequisite to the title, the overwhelming majority of known "manly hearts" were postmenopausal.

   To recapitulate: Two dimensions of personal identity stood out as central to North American Indian notions of gender. On the one hand, there was one's sexual anatomy and physiology, on the other, one's participation in the sexual division of labor and—somewhat less salient—one's public appearance (dress, demeanor). For those starting off as anatomically male, no further bodily processes came into play to reinforce the image of their masculinity—at least not in the official cultural mind of the American Indian. The masculine identity had thus to be reinforced, or conversely contradicted by a feminine identity, through the social medium of work and dress. When not reinforced by the quintessentially manly activities of hunting and warfare, and at the same time contradicted by stereotypically feminine tasks, the male identity that emerged was that of the "part-man, part-woman," the berdache. For the female, by contrast, the phenomena of adult reproductive processes added to and underscored an image of femininity that could weaken and be counter-balanced by masculine occupations only if the physiological processes themselves were held to be eliminable. Throughout most of North America, they were not so held, at least not for that period of a woman's life when she was realistically capable of taking up the hunter-warrior way of life. Becoming a member of the opposite sex was, therefore, predominantly a male game.

Gay Americans?

The sexual life of the berdache has been the subject of endless curiosity on the part of Westerners, for reasons that are not hard to discern. American Indian berdaches, male and female, conformed for the most part to a social, rather than anatomic, heterosexuality. In our terms, then, their sexual activity was heavily "homosexual." Apparently under no necessity to marry, the male berdache rather resembled in status the woman who, after several marriages and sundry affairs, had attained a certain looseness of reputation (Catlin, in Katz 1976: 301–2; Devereux 1937: 513). In the Plains and Prairie area, he might be treated as the village bawd or as everyman's "sister-in-law" or "cross-cousin," the kin categories with whom a man enjoyed, in Landes's words, "extensive and boorish flirting privileges" (Landes 1968: 98). Men might boast publicly of their exploits with the berdache (Catlin, in Katz 1976: 301–2), or he of his exploits with them (Hill 1935: 278). Fragmentary evidence suggests that the same "secondary marriage market" of divorced and widowed women to which the male berdache was assimilated, provided the female gender-crosser with a source of (real female) lovers and mates (Devereux 1937: 515).

When marriages between gender-crossed and ordinary individuals took place, they seem to have been in the form of secondary marriages—the taking of an additional wife by a polygynist in the Plains area (Boscana, in Katz 1976: 614; Tanner, in Katz 1976: 301), the rematch of divorcees in the Southwest (Devereux 1937: 515). The data on these marriages are insufficient to permit much generalization. Economic motives were cited as the reason for an ordinary person marrying a gender-crosser, but this did not imply an asexual relationship (Devereux 1937: 513–14, 515, 521–6; Parsons 1916: 526).

Given these practices, berdaches appeared in the eyes of Western observers as dominated by a homoerotic drive. Because spontaneous erotic orientation in our culture is the basis for dividing people into socially significant categories and is strongly linked in our view with gender identity as a whole (the more so in the late nineteenth century when homosexuality was considered a sign of gender "inversion"), it is not surprising that attention has been riveted upon this feature in the literature and that it has been the starting point for some of the more influential theories of institutionalized gender-crossing. But the need to gratify a conviction of underlying identity between the American Indian berdache and the homosexual of Western society has threatened to obscure the meaning of the former in American Indian culture, as well as to obscure the nature of cultural processes. I will take up these difficulties *seriatim*.

Foremost among the explanations of the North American berdache is that given by Kroeber, who saw institutionalized gender-crossing as part of a larger pattern whereby American Indian society made accommodation for instances of individual abnormality. He explicitly assumes that a certain number of sex variants appear in any population and they must be dealt with somehow; a regularized status was the American Indian way of dealing with them. Implicitly Kroeber also assumes that cultural institutions may arise out of the need to accommodate individual deviance (Kroeber 1940).

Let me start with the first assumption. Although Kroeber himself was hesitant on this point, not a few writers have interpreted the recurrent "sex variant" in question to be the person of homosexual erotic orientation. In their *Patterns of Sexual Behavior,* Ford and Beach classified the native American custom as one of the forms of "institutionalized homosexuality" (Ford and Beach 1951). Jonathan Katz, on whose careful scholarship I have relied heavily in putting this essay together, felt no hesitation in subsuming native American gender-crossers under the rubric "gay Americans" for his *Gay American History.* The most insistent anthropological exponent of the homosexuality interpretation is George Devereux, whose essay, "Institutionalized Homosexuality of the Mohave Indians," is something of a classic in the literature on the subject. Devereux sums up his understanding as follows:

> Socially speaking Mohave civilization acted wisely in acknowledging the inevitable. The airing of the abnormal tendencies of certain individuals achieved several aims ... In creating metaphorically speaking, "reserved quarters" for permanent homosexuals and for the passing whim of bisexually inclined active male homosexuals and passive female ones, they [the Mohave] gave the latter an opportunity to satisfy their passing longings, and left the door wide open for a return to normalcy. [Devereux 1937: 320]

In support of this paralleling of berdachehood with Western-style homosexuality (though not of Devereux's evaluative slant), there is not only the documented homosexual activity of gender-crossers, but also the strong element of self-selection to the role. The Mohave explain it—and their statements are echoed in other tribes:

> When there is a desire in a child's heart to become a transvestite, that child will act different. It will let people become aware of that desire. They may insist on giving the child the toys and garments of its true sex, but the child will throw them away and do this every time there is a big [social] gathering. [Mohave informant quoted by Devereux 1937: 503]

However, assessed against the data more closely and its logic scrutinized, the "niche-for-homosexuals" argument begins to unravel at the edges. First, there is no evidence that homosexual behavior as such was used as a reason for promoting reclassification of an individual to the gender-crossed status. In contradistinction to occupational and clothing choice, cross-sex erotic choice is never mentioned as one of the indicators of the budding berdache.[6] It was not as if homosexual behavior was unrecognized in North America. Homosexual acts between persons of ordinary gender status were known to occur or were recognized as a possibility among a number of tribes on which data are available. In some cases such behavior seems to have met with no objection (Forde, in Katz 1976: 324; Honigmann, in Katz 1976: 327; Holder, in Katz 1976: 313); more often, it was negatively sanctioned as some sort of evil, inadequacy, or foolishness (Hill 1935: 276; Jones, in Katz 1976: 317–18; Lowie, in Katz 1976: 321–2; Landes 1938: 103). But homosexual acts were not in any way immediately suggestive of an enduring disposition such as that which characterized the gender-crosser (or the "homosexual" in our culture), and such acts were not confused with gender-crossing in the native mind. Forde's ethnography of the Yuman tribes (closely related to the Mohave) brings this point out clearly:

> Male and female inverts are recognized; the females are known as kwe'rhame, the males as elxa' ... Casual secret homosexuality among both women and men is well

known. The latter is probably more common. This is not considered objectionable
but such persons would resent being called elxa' or kwe'rhame. [Forde, in Katz 1976:
324]

As to the practice of (anatomic) homosexuality by recognized gender-crossers, the social
expectation of it as well as its permissibility seems to have been the consequence of the
crosser's social redefinition. The process did not work the other way round. Hill reports
of the Navajo:

> The usual tabu placed on abnormal sex relations by normal individuals are lifted in
> the case of the nadle ... Sodomy with a nadle is countenanced by the culture and
> the insanity believed to follow such an act with a normal person does not occur if
> the relation is with a nadle. [Hill 1935: 276]

One wonders of course why the process did not work the other way around, as
one way seems to logically imply the other. If sexual object choice should conform to
public gender, then why should not public gender conform to sexual object choice? The
American Indians seem to have followed only one step of this logic, and even that not
consistently. That is, berdaches seem to have lapsed into anatomic heterosexuality and
on occasion even marriage without any loss of their cross-sex status (Liette, in Katz
1976: 288; Devereux, in Katz 1976: 305, 307; DuLac, in Katz 1976: 612; Fletcher and
LaFlesche 1972: 133; Stevenson, in Katz 1976: 314). Hill records of the Navajo, "Transvestites are known to marry both people of the same and opposite sexes," and "Transvestites have sex relations both normally and unnaturally with both sexes" (Hill 1935:
276). One of Hill's *nadle* was known to have a *nadle* grandfather and a Zuni *la'mana*
(male berdache) of Stevenson's acquaintance was credited with having fathered several
children (Stevenson, in Katz 1976: 314).

One way of construing this rather contradictory state of affairs is to say that sexual
object choice was indeed gender-linked, along heterosexual lines (man to woman, woman
to man), but that because the berdache had a foot in both camps, being by anatomy one
thing, by occupation the other, he had a claim on the favors of either sex. His (or her)
partners meanwhile retained their ordinary gender status because, whatever their gender,
they could be interpreted as conforming to the heterosexual norm. (There is never a
report of a berdache getting together with another berdache.) But this begs the question
of why homosexual acts between ordinary individuals had no gender-transformative
consequences. The only solution to this paradox is to conclude that sexuality, heterosexually typed though it may have been in the native mind, fell outside the realm of
what was publicly and officially important about the roles of the two sexes. Sexual object
choice was very much the trailing rather than the leading edge of gender definition. In
itself, it did not set in motion the process of gender reclassification. And the inconsistency
of some berdaches in regard to object choice was a function of the lesser relevance of
this feature to the maintenance of their gender-crossed status.

Some may wish to carry Kroeber's "sex variant" argument onto deeper ground
and rather than view the berdache as a homosexual, place him in the recently conceived
Western category of "transsexual." As defined by Benjamin, transsexualism, the drive
to assume the behavior and public identity of the opposite sex, is a psychological orientation in its own right, distinct from homosexuality. Anatomically homosexual behavior within the context of the transsexual orientation is merely the expression of a
psychological heterosexuality; it follows from rather than leads to the transsexual orientation (Benjamin 1966: 27 ff.). Just so, in the American Indian mind, the salient fact
about the gender-crosser was his/her preference for the external social identity of the
opposite sex. If all a person really wanted to do was engage in homosexual activity,

there were opportunities for doing so without all the ballyhoo of a special identity. But proponents of the homosexuality view, moving onto deeper ground themselves, can counterargue, as Jonathan Katz is inclined to do, that "transsexualism," as a psychological stance, whether appearing in our own culture or any other, arises by default from the absence of cultural categories sophisticated enough to permit homosexuals to conceptualize their nature. Having inadequate cultural tools for self-understanding, they tend to cast their desires into the socially dominant heterosexual framework (Katz 1976: 278).

Obviously, one can go round and round with this. Without attempting to resolve the debate as to the actual psychodynamics of the berdache, and leaving aside the strong political and social motivations that enter into this discussion, let me try to clarify what it is in the cultural logic of the West that strains theory toward positing an identity between berdache and Western homosexual. In the last couple of centuries, the homosexual has come to be the nearest thing to a cross-sex, or dual-gender, category in Western society. Although there have been and still are competing understandings of homosexuality, a recurrent one stresses the "intermediate" sexuality or androgynous character of the homosexual practitioner. Medical investigators keep returning to the possibility that opposite sex genetic or hormonal material lurks in the body of the homosexual (Ellis 1963), whereas social reformers have frequently adopted the "body of a man, mind of a woman" (conversely in the case of a lesbian) formula (De Becker 1969: 153–88). The homosexual thus emerges as part the one thing, part the other. At this level of abstraction (and ignoring that the condition was anathematized in the West), the Western homosexual *is* the logical counterpart of the native American berdache. But when we move down to the level of which features are conceived to be the crux of this gender dualism, the two types, "homosexual" and "berdache," part company. I say the "crux," because in both American Indian and Western gender systems, the same three social attributes of gender appear: occupation, dress/demeanor, and sexual object choice. What differs is the center of gravity in the two gender systems. For the American Indians, occupational pursuits clearly occupy the spotlight, with dress/demeanor coming in a close second. Sexual object choice is part of the gender configuration, but its salience is low; so low that by itself it does not provoke the reclassification of the individual to a special status. In the Western system, the order of salience is virtually the reverse. A marked cross-sex occupation may engender "suspicions," to be sure (decreasingly so in modern times), but by itself it has never defined a unique sex-gender status. Homosexual activity, on the other hand, has been so strongly definitive of an enduring, gender-anomalous condition that it has long been impossible to engage in it casually. In both Western and native American gender systems, dress and demeanor function as strong but not essential supports for the dualistic status established through the core variable. Esther Newton's comments on the relationship in our culture between dress/demeanor ("sex-role presentation of self" in her words) and homosexuality deserve to be repeated here:

> Homosexuality consists of sex-role deviation made up of two related but distinct parts: "wrong" sexual objects and "wrong" sex-role presentation of self. The first deviation is shared by all homosexuals ... The second deviation logically (in this culture) corresponds with the first, *which it symbolizes.* [my emphasis] It becomes clear that the core of the stigma is in "wrong" sexual object when it is considered that there is little stigma in simply being effeminate, or even in wearing feminine apparel in some contexts, as long as the male is known to be heterosexual, that is, known to sleep with women or, rather, not to sleep with men.

Newton makes note of the fact that there is class variation in this system: lower-class men consider a man "gay" only when he assumes the feminine role in the sex act with another man (Newton 1977: 341).

The new Western mixed type, the transsexual, who emerged with the dawn of the sex-change operation, is still persistently seen in terms of the dominant mixed type, the homosexual. That is, he/she, like the berdache, is thought to be a homosexual who misunderstands him/herself, or is misinterpreted by society. Yet, as one recent treatise argues, the rise of Western "transsexualism," with its formidable array of psychiatric, medical, and legal mediators, may in fact represent a movement within Western culture for the reestablishment of a strong connection between gender and dichotomized occupational spheres (see Raymond 1979). This reestablishment will not be easy for the trend of history is in the opposite direction, one probable reason why erotic object choice, not occupation, has been drawn into the foreground of Western gender identity.

To return to the North American berdache, and to give the arguments of Kroeber and others their due, the indifferent role of homosexuality in the establishment of berdache status does not in any way prove that homoerotic desires were absent from the psyche of the budding gender-crosser, or that such desires might not develop as a psychological offshoot of the young crosser's resocialization into the public status of the opposite sex. But it does make it hard to argue that the institution of gender-crossing was the way in which American Indian culture "dealt with" homosexuality.

There is another reason for demurring from this interpretation, one that applies with equal force to the now tempting proposal that institutionalized gender-crossing was the way in which American Indian culture "dealt with" sex-role deviance in the occupational realm. Hoebel has proposed this second explanation (Hoebel 1949: 459). The male berdache, according to his reasoning, is a fellow too timid to face the daunting warrior role of the adult Indian male, whereas the female-crosser is a girl too aggressive for feminine pursuits. Although accurate in terms of native American gender criteria, these suggestions, like those of Kroeber and Devereux, posit cultural forms as simple reactions to personality patterns, and minority patterns at that. If culture were by its nature so accommodating, one would expect deviants and role failures the world over to be provided with institutionalized "niches," "reserved quarters," and the like; this is far from being the case. Thus even if we were to clear up the mystery of the American Indian gender-crosser's inner psychic orientation, the cultural mystery would remain unsolved. We would still have to ask, if native American culture was permissive in regard to this particular "variation," why was it permissive?

The Larger Cultural and Social Context of Gender-crossing

Any really thorough answer to the question just posed takes us so deeply into the warp and woof of native American society and culture as to exceed the scope of this essay. I will content myself here with merely making some headway on this issue. Two lines of speculation present themselves. One is that American Indian culture was, in some sense, very permissive, and that therefore all sorts of—to our mind—surprising things received a routine stamp of approval. The other is that there was something special about the sex-role organization of Indian society, something we have not fully uncovered yet, that made it permissible, or at the very least understandable, for an occasional individual to stray over the sexual line, the institutionalization of this straying constituting a statement that the culture was, for these as yet obscure reasons, not unhappy to make. Both lines of speculation carry us a certain distance. The first thought takes its inspiration again from Kroeber, who had a way of being close to if not always on the point. As explained earlier, he was of the opinion that the gender-crossing custom was part of a larger pattern whereby American Indian culture made accommodation for instances of individual abnormality. There is virtue to the idea of a larger pattern, but it is not well understood as one of providing niches for individual abnormality. Rather, it consisted of a principle of letting all individual careers, sex-related or otherwise, be shaped by an extrasocietal destiny.

It does not require social identities as dramatic as that of the berdache to illustrate the pattern in question. All over North America, as persons matured they were expected to show special luck or ability in certain areas more than in others, and the consequent social differentiation of individuals was rationalized in terms of a fate over which neither the individual nor the community had much control. In wide areas of the continent—the Plains, Plateau, Prairie, Woodland, and Subarctic areas in particular—men and occasionally women received their particular destiny through visions of supernatural helpers who bestowed upon them special powers and protections. Usually supernatural visions were deliberately solicited through fasting, solitude, and self-mortification. Landes's characterization of the Ojibwa philosophy surrounding visions is widely applicable:

> All those talents and traits of character which we think of as functions of a total personality are regarded by the Ojibwa as isolated, objective items which may be acquired in the course of life by individuals who are fortunate enough to coerce them from the supernaturals. In Ojibwa thought, there is no original and absolute "self"—a person freshly born is "empty" of characteristics and identity. Consequently tremendous pressure is exerted upon a young person to pursue the supernaturals and move them to fill up his "emptiness." [Landes 1938: 124]

Appearing in the vision was the spiritual manifestation (often in human form) of some natural species or phenomenon—bear, crow, rabbit, morning star, thunder, and so forth—who taught the visionary songs and instructions that, if used properly, would insure success in some designated area. Treating the vision casually or ignoring the instructions (which often included taboos of one sort or another), occasioned not just the loss of the special powers bestowed by the guardian but often additional misfortune as well. Typically, men hoped for visions that would bring them success in the conventional male pursuits of warfare and hunting, although receiving a special curing or craft ability through vision was by no means despised. But fate could be cantankerous. A vision could deceive and the expected success fail to materialize. Some were blessed with abundant visions, whereas some received none at all; and not everyone received the powers he (or she) purported to want. Visions that instructed berdachehood, and those that involved the individual in the more rigorous forms of shamanism are often mentioned as unwanted destinies; but the individual ignored such a calling at his risk. Among many of the vision-questing tribes, it was possible to pass on vision-inspired luck to someone else by selling the collection of symbolic items—the "medicine bundle"—that the original visionary had constructed to embody and preserve his/her special fortune. Like the vision itself, bundle ownership inspired the possessor toward feats he or she might ordinarily fear to undertake and rallied community confidence behind the possessor's leadership of collective enterprises (or his/her curing activities). However, a bundle was not guaranteed to retain its powers any more than was a vision, and the new possessor might find himself out of luck.

In those areas where the vision ideology was highly developed, a complex casuistry of supernatural assistance, trickery, or neglect underlay the gradual differentiation of social identities that took place as each generation reached its social prime, and gender-crossing, along with many another distinctive idiosyncrasy, was readily encompassed by this ideology.

One might speak of the vision complex as simply a full articulation of attitudes that were generally present in American Indian society. Even in areas where vision was of minor significance, personal proclivity, talent, or peculiarity was handled with a vocabulary of preconceived stereotypes that excused both individual and community from worrying very deeply over why someone was the way he or she was or whether this should be changed. Among the Pima and the Papago for instance, some women eschewed the burdens of marriage, engaged in casual liaisons with men of their choice, and spent their time embellishing their appearance and going to dances. They were called "light women" or "playful women" and, as it was considered in their nature to be this way, their parents offered little protest against the behavior (Underhill 1939: 183–4). In parts of California, "bear men"—men born with the nature of the bear— were a culturally recognized category. A case is reported by Kroeber:

> When [the] child was born, he had tufts of hair on each shoulder. He grew up apparently stupid and sluggish, not participating much in ordinary activities. Once, when he was being teased, he grew angry, growled, turned into a bear, scattered the coals of the fire, and began to cuff people around. After this incident, he was carefully let alone, except when his anger could be directed against the enemy Yuki. [Kroeber 1940: 315]

A young man behaved and appeared rather like a bear: Very well then, he was a "bear-man." The same principle could be, and was, applied if he behaved rather like a woman; he became a "woman-man."

Although recognizing that the berdache fell under a broader rubric of culturally stereotyped individual careers, Kroeber interpreted this as "culture" putting the best face on a psychopathological condition of some sort. The "bear man" is an overgrown dullard, the shaman a stabilized psychotic, the berdache a sexual deviant. But the phenomenon of American Indian individualism extended well beyond the area of what, to our minds, is the "problematic" or the "abnormal." The able hunter had his stereotypic destiny too, as did the woman with a knack for curing low back pains. Rather than being a special dispensation, the institutionalization of gender deviation was only one of the many examples of the use, in North America, of various forms of distinctiveness as a guideline for future conduct on the part of the individual, and as a signal to the community of how destiny had decided to carve up the human landscape.

Undoubtedly the notion of a whimsical personal destiny to some degree fostered a generalized acceptance of all varieties of nonnormative personal outcomes; but this may be of less relevance to the understanding of gender-crossing than the fact that the ethic of individual destiny was invoked primarily in regard to activity patterns that established a person's productiveness and prestige within the community. What the ethic "said" about these activity patterns, and thus about wealth and prestige as well, was that their social distribution was unpredictable and that they could not be anchored to any sure determinants. In this respect, religious individualism (or just plain individualism among groups such as the Southwestern Pueblo where the vision quest was undeveloped) accorded well with the status organization of the majority of American Indian societies. Prosperity, or at the very least a brief moment of glory, was available through a diversity of avenues, for American Indian society was profuse with semispecialized trades and part-time communal positions: the war leader, the hunt leader, the various prophets and diviners, the unscatheable warrior, the craft adepts, the many curers of such delimited ailments as snowblindness, bear-bite, or urinary disorder in horses. The relative absence of heritable forms of wealth and status made it possible for personal determination and talent, in combination with a number of unobvious processes such as the careful man- agement of kin obligations and marriages, to result, each generation, in an unforeseen distribution of these leadership, ritual, curing, and craft functions that underlay social prominence (see Collier 1977). True, the odds were tipped in favor of the vigorous and well-connected for these were the persons best in a position to cultivate and capitalize upon semispecialized activities; but even within their ranks, a strong element of chance entered into social fortune. Doctrines of a capricious supernatural underlined this element of chance and pacified the unfortunate with the belief that their misery, if sufficiently extreme, might move the supernaturals to pity. Plains Indian legend, for example, abounds with "Horatio Alger" tales of downcast orphans who, having inspired the pity of the supernaturals, turn the tables on their persecutors, capture many horses, or win over the supercilious maiden (Lowie 1956: 237).

In such a context, in which prestige- and wealth-garnering skills and activities settled upon individuals in what seemed, and what many could only hope was, a rather haphazard manner, and in which, as we have seen, many of these activities and skills were gender-linked, it was not so unusual that there should be a certain haphazardness to gender as well, especially in the case of the male who was less firmly rooted in the physiological component of sex status. It was as if the various occupational complexes dragged with them, connotatively, the gender category with which they were most commonly associated, while being at the same time cut loose, on the ideal plane, from such automatic determinants. The potential "wandering" of sex-associated activity patterns and social attributes was all of a piece with the potential wandering of activity patterns and social attributes generally. If the attributes of a wealthy man could alight upon a poor orphan, why not those of a woman upon a man?[7] Another way of explaining this is that, as in all cultures, so in American Indian culture, gender was a "status," in the sense of a rank or standing. As such it was drawn into, in this case placed on a par with, all other available status positions and participated (to a degree) in their mode of allocation. In a vast number of American Indian societies, social distinction was linked to luck and ability in some established pursuit or set of pursuits, and so too was masculinity and femininity. Accordingly, just as a knack for these other pursuits was allocated by unobvious and officially unpredictable processes, so likewise—in its social as opposed to anatomic aspect—was gender.

Thus, it is apparent that the idea that North American Indian society was simply "permissive" in regard to individual variation must be significantly modified. Whether one calls the value complex of which the vision-quest ideology was the fullest expression, "permissiveness" in the sense of a passive acceptance of individual behavior, or "individualism" in the sense of an active encouragement of individual expression, the pattern in question was of a more specialized emphasis than noted by previous theorists. Rather than being simply supportive of individuality in all its personal ramifications, including the erotic, the American Indian ethic was really centered largely upon individual variation in prestige-relevant occupations. The reason this ideology bore upon gender-anomalous behavior at all is that gender itself was heavily defined in terms of prestige-relevant occupations.

It is this matter of the prestige potential of occupational specializations that leads us from the question of "permissiveness" to the other question raised earlier, that is, whether gender-crossing cannot be seen as tied in some more specific way to the sex-role organization of American Indian society. Obviously, it can, and the strong association of gender with occupational specialization leads us to look for the social sources of gender-crossing in the sexual division of labor.

It would be inadequate to argue that the way for gender-crossing was paved by the mere existence of a sexual division of labor. All known societies have some degree of division of labor by sex; thus, all known societies lay the groundwork for an association of manhood and womanhood with certain predetermined areas of work. I would venture that all known societies give some cultural expression to this association as well. Yet one need run only a quick survey of ethnographic cases to realize that not every cultural system brings occupation to the forefront of gender definition in the way that American Indian culture has done, nor does every system treat transgressions of the occupational boundary in the same accommodating manner as the American Indians. I am not arguing that American Indian society was unique in this respect; certainly there are other societies with similar types of organization (Shore, 1981). But a sexual division of labor alone is insufficient to account for either a strong cultural association of gender with work specialty or for the toleration of gender "individualism." In short, it is insufficient to account for the meaning complex we are examining here.

New Guinean systems, for instance, offer a striking contrast to native North America. In New Guinea, there is men's work and there is women's work, but New Guineans seldom seem to elaborate upon this particular dimension of masculinity and femininity: Rather, their focus is upon the reproductive substances associated with the sexually mature male and female. (American Indians, as we have seen, are not immune from this concern, but for the moment I am putting their relatively abbreviated use of this concept to one side.) And in paradoxical contrast to the gender-defining occupations that in North America are assigned by "fate," the gender-defining substances of New Guinea are believed to be controlled by the collectivity (the male collectivity to be precise) so that any gender redefinition to be done must be engineered by collective ritual action (Poole, 1981; Kelly 1976; Schieffelin 1976; Van Baal 1966). Finally, in New Guinea, the occupational boundary between the sexes, although culturally unstressed, is strongly defended in an indirect way through sanctions that warn the errant individual that his or her intrusions into the gardens, ritual lodges, or seating areas of the opposite sex (any of which might happen if cross-sex occupations were attempted) will result in mystical harm to self or opposite-sex kinfolk.

What is it then that the North American Indians (and others with similar cultural conventions) are doing differently? To begin with, it is important to reassert what numerous investigators into the status of women have already been at pains to make clear: The "sexual division of labor" is a term that tells us very little about the political and social significance of an organization of production. There is the "work" of simple production for instance, and there is the "work" of surplus appropriation, to name only the most crucial distinction that gets glossed over by bland "division of labor" concepts. Furthermore, even within the sphere of production, different labors are of different consequence for the eminence and social power of the "laboring" group. With these perspectives in mind, some observations can be made about the sex-divided organization of production in native North America that bear upon the cultural salience of occupation in the conceptualization of gender and upon the acceptability of gender-crossing. These observations illuminate as well the differences between the North American system and such culturally antithetical examples as the New Guinea one. Let me caution that my interpretation here will be sketchy and unrefined; I wish only to propose a line of thinking rather than to hone one to perfection.

First, almost everywhere in native North America, the woman's domain of economic activity included within it the production of significant durable goods: basketry in California; textiles, basketry, and pottery in the Southwest; in the buffalo-rich Plains and Prairie areas, a huge inventory of leather-goods including tipis, parfleches, garments, and the multipurpose robe, any of which might be decorated by painting, quillwork, or (in later periods) beadwork; in the Eastern Woodland areas, basketry, pottery, leather, and fur goods. These female products entered into intratribal gift exchange and intertribal trade, their circulation in both spheres accelerating with the arrival of the European trader. Many of the more difficult and time-consuming crafts—pottery in the Southwest, quilling, beadwork, tipi and earth-lodge construction in the Plains and Prairie areas— became the preserve of part-time female specialists who were remunerated both for supplying the craftwork and for passing on the skill. Various curing specializations tended to fall to women (different ones in different areas), and these were similarly a source of remuneration. Men of course had their own craftwork and curing specialties as well and were more apt than women to command and transmit expensive supernatural lore; but the point is that a woman's productive labor was not necessarily exhausted, any more than a man's, in the service of immediate consumption needs, and a woman's products circulated beyond the bounds of the domestic unit.

Second and more importantly, a good deal of a woman's wealth and talent re-dounded to her own credit officially, and not simply informally. Women's labor was not subject to total or even very extensive appropriation by men. Men, because of their position in warfare, intertribal contact, and the organization of often wide-scale coop-erative hunting, held sway in communal decision-making and were, as a class, accorded greater social esteem than women. But they were not privileged to appropriate the products of female labor into some higher distributive game from which women qua women were excluded. They were not organized in relation to women as "transactors" to "producers," to borrow the terms M. Strathern has applied to the New Guinea sex-role organization (Strathern 1972).

This is not to say that North American society lacked distributional structures whereby some parties could lay claim to the labor of others while simultaneously gaining rank through the economic generosity that these labor claims made possible. Such sys-tems were present, but they did not sharply divide the sexes. To generalize from the better-analyzed Plains culture examples, it seems that insofar as the labor of some was appropriated to the prestige machinations of others, it was the well-positioned elder or household head of either sex who benefited from claims on the labor of his/her juniors. The mature householder with the right assortment of married or marriage-age children, junior in-laws, wives—or in the case of women, junior co-wives—and a credible record of personal achievement, was the individual in a position to begin sponsoring ceremonials, purchasing ritual memberships and renowned "bundles," obligating others through timely acts of generosity, and devoting him/herself more fully to lucrative craft spe-cializations (Collier 1977; Lewis 1941). Wives and husbands often worked in concert to put together the admission feasts and gifts for, and were admitted jointly to, select religious societies; there were single-sex societies for women as well as for men in those areas where such "sodalities" were present (Fletcher and LaFlesche 1972: 440–540; Lowie 1924: 206, 211; Driver 1969: 351–4). Wealth objects produced (or stolen in raids) by one sex could circulate to and through either sex, because it was generally the case that women had the right to dispose of property independently of their husbands (Fletcher and LaFlesche 1972: 363; Driver 1969: 284; Lowie 1956: 61; Lewis 1941: 177–80). The ability to be an independent economic actor would, of course, buttress the position of the industrious female craft or curing specialist. It should be pointed out that this pattern of production and allocation did not favor *all* women, but it routinely favored a certain percentage of women in every generation. This female elite consisted heavily of first or favorite wives in polygynous households (because divorce was not difficult an ambitious woman could sometimes engineer a better marital "location" for herself) and only or favorite children of a prosperous parent (Lewis 1941: 178–9; Fletcher and LaFlesche 1972: 507–9).

The situation just outlined bore upon gender-crossing in a number of ways. Because prestigious goods and services (such as curing) were located within the realm of female, and not just male, production, and because women, and not just men, had the right to dispose of property and command the labor of others, the "meaning" of the gender distinction in native American society rested more heavily upon differences in productive specialization than upon position within a system of sexual-political interaction. Sexual identities were not overwhelmed by hierarchical relational attributes such as "overlord/ward" or "exchanger/exchanged," but were pinned primarily to the traditionally de-marcated spheres of activity. This laid the groundwork for a cross-sex category based upon cross-sex occupation, and it suggests, in part, how "crossing" came to be acceptable. An occasional gender maverick did not threaten to prick the bubble of an elaborate domination mystique, because sexual domination in North America was not elaborate, therefore neither were its mystiques. Thus the boundary between the sexual spheres was not strongly defended. (Only in one respect was male hegemony encoded in "ab-solutist" terms: This was in the notion that women's menstrual and parturitional blood was antipathetic to male enterprise, hence to true preeminence. The woman's child-tending responsibility, to which the symbolism of blood metonymically alluded, was not seen as an occupation of the sort that any human—including a man—could take up; and not having the status of a fully social activity, which translated into American Indian terms meant a supernaturally bestowed activity [!], it was not subject to variable allo-cation. As a consequence an asymmetry in access to the cross-sex status did appear throughout most of North America.)

However, the relatively nonthreatening character of occupational boundary transgressions only accounts in a negative way for the permissibility of gender-crossing. There may have been more positive influences at work as well. The prestige available to women operating simply as women in many ways narrowed the social gap that the gender-crosser of either sex had to jump in taking up cross-sex status, and may indeed have increased the incentive for "jumping," at least in the case of the male. Limited but striking evidence suggests that a woman's work and capacity to command resources (including kin obligations) could, when carried to its full potential, "masculinize" her status in and of itself. Witness the status of "manly hearted women" among the North Piegan, a Canadian Plains-culture group. "Manly heart" was not a title bestowed upon a girl who manifested cross-sex inclinations in occupation and dress; indeed there is no evidence that a manly heart ever had to participate in the strongly male-connotive hunting-and-warfare activity patterns. Rather, manly heartedness was a position toward which all successful Piegan matrons gravitated with age, economic achievement, spon-sorship of ceremonials, and the ability to dominate husbands and co-wives (Lewis 1941: 175–7). Wealth, if not sufficient, seems to have been the most "necessary" prerequisite for the status. ("Informants laughed at our question, Are manly hearted women poor? The answer invariably was that a poor woman would not have the nerve to do the things that are considered manly hearted." [Lewis 1941: 177]). Wealth could be accumulated through established female routes—the gifts of husbands and parents, the woman's own excellence in her crafts.

> It takes most women six days to tan a hide which a manly hearted woman can do in four or five days. A manly hearted woman can bead a dress or a man's suit in a week of hard work, while it takes most women a month. An average worker makes a pair of moccasins in a week, while a manly hearted woman can make it in little over a day. These excellent workers were able to produce over and above the personal needs of the household. A manly hearted woman was therefore an economic asset, which is the only justification the Piegan give for a woman dominating her husband. [Lewis 1941: 178]

Although we do not have any indication of the existence of this masculine label in other parts of the Plains, there is no reason to believe that the Piegan manly heart was anything more than the Plains matron at her epitome.[8] The fact that she was then called manly hearted reveals that, at the height of her powers, she came close to matching the successful male in prestige. She must certainly have surpassed the unsuccessful male.

If success in the female sphere could hold a reasonable candle to success in the male, if, at the very least, femininity represented a positive sort of power rather than being, as it is in many cultures, overwhelmingly connotive of powerlessness, then it is conceivable that the female sphere held an attraction for men over and above anything to do with the erotic. If manliness did not, for whatever reason, seem available to a boy, why not manly heartedness? The berdache, while quitting the battlefront (quite literally) of male prestige rivalry, found it possible to take up a respectable sort of lateral position—that of ultra-successful female. To be sure, such a status was not as high as the higher masculine statuses. The berdache had to renounce a higher status potential when turning into the female channel, and, in doing so, he took on, to a degree that varied by tribal area, the stigma of masculine failure. But, in compensation, he took on as well—again, to a degree that varied by tribal area—the charisma that tends to attach itself to those who voluntarily renounce social position. And he made available to himself the forms of material prosperity and cultural respect that accrued to the assiduous practitioner of female crafts.[9]

In the latter regard, we are reminded of the frequent assertions made to (or by) investigators about the berdache's excellence and prosperity in his chosen career. The two Zuni berdaches of Stevenson's acquaintance were "the finest potters and weavers in the tribe," and one of them among the richest men in the village (Stevenson, in Katz 1976: 314). Simms was told of Crow berdaches that they often had "the largest and best appointed tipis" (Simms 1903: 580). The Navajo berdaches who were mystically associated with wealth already seem typically to have laid an empirical foundation under their mystical reputations:

> They knit, tan hides, make moccasins, are said to be excellent sheep raisers, and excel as weavers, potters, and basket makers. The last three pursuits contribute substantially to their wealth, as especially are basketry and pottery making restricted technics and they are able to trade these products extensively with their own and other people. [Hill 1935: 275]

Among the Yurok of California, women apparently had cornered the market on a particularly lucrative form of shamanism, and it was precisely this specialty into which the Yurok berdaches (*wergen*) moved. The Yurok themselves interpreted the berdaches' motives in this light:

> The Yurok explanation of the phenomenon is that such males are impelled by the desire to become shamans. This is certainly not true, since male shamans are not unknown. It is a fact, however, that all the *wergen* seem to have been shamans and esteemed as such. [Kroeber 1925: 46]

The merit of psychosexual explanations of gender-crossing notwithstanding, the Yurok explanation embodies an important point: In Yurok society (as I would argue in many American Indian societies), the ways of woman could lead to material prosperity and social distinction *and were so perceived*. In the long run, it does not matter whether such perceptions entered into the consciousness of gender-deviating pubescent boys, as long as the prevailing culture was content to view the matter in this light and in doing so extend its toleration. At the same time, it is simplistic to discount such motivations in the young berdache, or arbitrarily oppose them to psychosexual ones. Certainly at the level of individual consciousness, prestige and psychosexual concerns are often bound up in indissoluble combinations.

It must be added that the cultural perception of women's potential was a complicated one. Common explanations of the successful berdache, as of the successful woman, testify to this. In actuality, it does not appear that berdaches were inevitably successful in their feminine careers. Besides the esteemed berdaches, some rather buffoonlike characters are reported in the literature (Katz 1976: 292, 300–1). Nor is it clear that, when successful, their achievements were of a higher order than those of women who, through age and household dominance, also enjoyed freedom from child-rearing responsibilities.[10] Nonetheless, investigators were frequently told that the berdache performed the tasks of women better than actual women. After all, he was a man! (Landes 1938: 136; Underhill 1939: 186; Simms 1903: 580; Stevenson, in Katz 1976: 314). Comparably, the Piegan case illustrates the (less pronounced) tendency of the culture to view successful women as "manly." Both reactions reveal an unwillingness or inability to distinguish the sources of prestige—wealth, skill, personal efficacy (among other things)—from masculinity. Rather there is the innuendo that if a person performing female tasks can attain excellence, prosperity, or social power, it must be because that person is, at some level, a man.

At the same time, the entire male berdache institution, the predominant form of gender-crossing in native North America, demonstrates a reverse lack of distinction between the sources of prestige in the female sphere and femininity in a larger sense. Thus if men were to aspire to the socially and economically significant achievements available to a person in the feminine role, they had to infiltrate the realm of woman in the guise of women. Again, sources of prestige were conflated with gender, only the other gender.

The point here is not to fault a cultural system for conflations and contradictions that show up only within an analytic framework that the culture has no particular access to nor reason to adopt. As the reflex of persons inhabiting a certain social order, and as their way of understanding it, the various gender-crossovers, recategorizations, and double-entendres of American Indian culture were an ingenious comprehension of a situation in which social and economic powers tended to assume more complex distributions than those that could be readily encompassed by a simple gender hierarchy and in which, at the same time, class or caste structures were not sufficiently consolidated so as to delineate a transgender system of rank. Stated broadly, the culturally dominant American Indian male was confronted with a substantial female elite not perceivable as simply dependents of powerful men. Within such a context, the response to feminine transgressions into the traditional male sphere (hunting, warfare) was amazingly dispassionate: A woman who could succeed at doing the things men did was honored as a man would be. Few, if any, tortured rationalizations were brought to bear upon her achievement. What seems to have been more disturbing to the culture—which means, for all intents and purposes, to the men—was the possibility that women, within their own department, might be onto a good thing. It was into this unsettling breach that the berdache institution was hurled. In their social aspect, women were complimented by the berdache's imitation. In their anatomic aspect, they were subtly insulted by his vaunted superiority. Through him, ordinary men might reckon that they still held the advantage that was anatomically given and inalterable.

Conclusion

The primary purpose of this essay has been to show what sorts of meanings emerge from the ethnographic data regarding sex and sexual practices when proper respect is accorded the native cultural system. In many respects, I have simply tried to perform upon an ethnographic example of "institutionalized homosexuality" the sorts of contextualizing operations anthropologists typically perform upon cultural items that they feel require explanation. As it happens, in the area of gender, sex, and sex-related matters, neither anthropologists nor anyone else have, until recently, cared to take these well-established analytic steps, a situation that can be attributed in part to neglect of the subject matter in general, and in part to the theoretical hegemony of biological-psychiatric models in this field over the past three decades.

It would be disingenuous to assert, however, that respect for the native categories is all that is involved in cultural interpretation. Anthropologists are certainly familiar with the more intuitive and solipsistic forms of culture-specific interpretation. These typically consist of endless circles of metaphors aimed at conjuring up in our minds what is presumed to be going on in the native's, but in terms of social and cultural theory they are often, in the end, quite sterile. If this style of interpretation is to be avoided, some deeper sociological theoretical grounding, and theoretical persuasion, must inform the analysis from the start.

In terms of the analytic method used here, I have absorbed, partly from Max Weber, partly from the Durkheim-inspired British social anthropology tradition, the conviction that sociocultural orders, however special each may be, are never so unique as to be incomparable. Indeed, it is only by relentless comparison that useful understanding of specific cases is achieved and the theoretical framework of social science expanded. The very switching of our perspective back and forth from one system to another helps to bring out the essential features of each, while simultaneously causing more abstract social or cultural principles to precipitate out in our thinking (or, alternately, confirming or disconfirming abstractions already present).

In the foregoing pages I have been always implicitly, and at points explicitly, comparing the gender meanings of native North America with both those of my own culture (an inevitable implicit comparison) and those of tribal New Guinea. Within this cross-cultural framework, I have performed a great many "internal" comparisons of details from one culture area, native North America, to try to bring into relief the defining features of North American Indian gender, and the relative weights of these features.

What emerges from this comparative analysis is first what one might call the basic "Margaret Mead" points. One is that the principal attributes of manhood and womanhood, outside of birth anatomy, are culturally variable. Closely linked to this point is a second: that particular sexual practices and beliefs must be understood within the context of the specific gender-meaning system of the culture in question. Although these ideas have been accepted in anthropology for years, there has been little systematic application and illustration of them. I hope this essay stirs interest in further attempts of this sort.

But my ambition has been to proceed beyond these basic and accepted ideas, especially beyond the position of unanchored cultural relativism in which they, by themselves, leave us. To say that gender definitions and concepts pertaining to sex and gender are culturally variable is not necessarily to say that they can vary infinitely or along any old axis. Look again, for instance, at the three "homosexualities" touched upon in this essay. In New Guinea, homosexual practice is part of a set of theoretically dictated ritual practices designed to grow boys into men. In native North America, homosexual practice was anomalous, faintly suspect, but largely meaningless behavior except when practiced by someone whose gender had been redefined to a mixed-gender type in accordance with this person's preference for opposite-sex occupation and clothing. It was acceptable in such cases for this person's sexual orientation, like his or her clothing, to imitate that of the opposite sex. Finally, in our own culture, homosexual behavior itself tends to redefine a person to the status of an intermediate (and, except in liberal circles, strongly disapproved) sex type.

Although it is true that the three homosexualities could hardly be more different from the point of view of actors living within any one of these systems, there is, at a higher level of abstraction, a limit to their difference. In the New Guinea case, homosexual practice is deemed appropriate because one of the two parties is held to be deficient in the traits normally associated with his anatomic sex; in native North America, homosexual practice was deemed appropriate because one of the two parties was held to be possessed of traits normally associated with the opposite anatomic sex; and in modern Western culture, homosexual practice, although not deemed appropriate, gives rise, when it occurs, to the idea that one or both of the parties involved is mixed and/or deficient in their expected gender attributes. In a word, in all three cases, we see some manifestation of the dominance of heterosexuality as the model for sexual exchange. Those familiar with Gayle Rubin's provocative essay, "The Traffic in Women," will recall that in surveying the varieties of culturally recognized homosexuality, she noted, "the rules of gender division and obligatory heterosexuality are present even in their transformations" (Rubin 1975: 182). The findings here reaffirm this observation.

But should we consider the dominance of the heterosexual paradigm a case of "nature" exercising a constraint upon cultural variation? Certainly nature constrains at some level; but the question is, which level? Rubin points out that the omnipresence of gender division and obligatory heterosexuality is in line with the presence everywhere of socially organized kinship systems and the marital alliances that reproduce these systems while reproducing human beings (Rubin 1975: 178–83). Thus one might just as well argue that what we are seeing in the common denominator of the styles of homosexuality discussed here is *society* exercising a constraint upon cultural variation, and upon the nature of the individual organism as well.

Outside of looking for biological irreducibles, which go only so far and then ambiguously, if we are to get to the bottom of both the "Meadian" cultural variation in sexual and gender conceptions and the limits of that variation, we must begin to work through the range of variation of social and cultural systems, placing gender relations within this context. This brings us to the next aspect of my theoretical emphasis.

One line of sociological inquiry that I have tried to suggest here is investigation of the relationship between gender constructs and the organization of prestige in a given society. The reasons and methods for such an investigation are discussed in the Introduction to this collection. Let me here summarize the nature of the interlock in the North American case.

In the sorts of North American societies in which the institution of gender-crossing was to be found, there was little development of general social stratification. Instead, as in many tribal societies, age and sex were the principal lines along which prestige hierarchy manifested itself. It is not uncommon in such societies to find further development of individual prestige-differentiating mechanisms operating among men as well, and this was so in native North America. The very military, hunting, ritual, and material craft skills that served ascriptively to establish men's higher standing vis-à-vis women continued on, so to speak, to create achieved status differences between men. However, at the same time, for reasons having to do with the sorts of productive activities charged to women and for reasons that I would speculate lay in the organization of kinship and marriage (a subject inadequately treated here), a distinctive arena of female prestige differentiation existed as well. Moreover, it was an arena of prestige that could not have remained trivial in men's eyes, for some women seemed regularly capable, through their own doings, of rivaling men in wealth and social influence.

Gender stratification, which was strongly linked to the occupational specializations of the two sexes, had, shall we say, begun to leak around the edges. The leak, or more precisely contradiction, did not exist because it was unclear which sex should be doing what, but because the doing of these clear things did not generate the consistent inequalities in power and influence associated with full prestige differentiation. Accordingly, gender differentiation, which is a prestige differentiation, manifested its contradiction as well—the mixed-gender figure. Inasmuch as women's activities generated wealth and influence comparable to that of men, men appeared who were willing to take up these activities. Inasmuch, however, as these activities were still marked as monopolies of the female sex, the men who took them up had to be those who were willing to assume the general guise—dress, demeanor, even sexual object—of women. In this analysis then, North American gender-crossing was a cultural compromise formation founded on an incipient, though never fully realized, collapse of the gender-stratification system.

NOTES

1. Wyatt MacGaffey, personal communication in reference to the BaKongo (Africa); Michelle Rosaldo, personal communication in reference to the Ilongot (Philippines); Sherry Ortner, personal communication in reference to the Sherpa (Nepal).

2. I am indebted to Jane Collier, Lynn Eden, Sherry Ortner, Michelle Rosaldo, and Judith Shapiro for invaluable critical and editorial assistance in the preparation of this essay.

3. Jane Collier has pointed out to me that some ambiguity in regard to these generalizations exists in the case of the Cheyenne. Cheyenne had notions that a man's supernatural vitality was depleted by sexual intercourse—also by childrearing and by hunting. They did not, however manipulate sexual substances in rituals of manhood as New Guinea people do (personal communication).

4. From Devereux's account, the Mohave closely resemble unsophisticated Anglo-Americans in their attitude toward gender ambiguity. Because Devereux's study is one of the more recent ones, the influence of acculturation cannot be ruled out. On the other hand, another anthropologist has commented that attitudes toward the berdache are more ambivalent among the Southwestern tribes (Hill 1938: 339n).

5. The Kaska, a Plateau group, considered it acceptable for a girl to be raised as a boy if the family had no sons. In this case, she had to wear from early childhood a magical talisman, the dried ovaries of a bear, to prevent conception. No mention is made of her menstruation (Honigmann, in Katz 1976: 327). Another Plateau group, the Kutenai, was the home tribe of a female "berdache" figure widely known among European traders in the early nineteenth century. This transvestite woman was definitely an idiosyncracy among the Kutenai who seem to have lacked even male berdaches, and it is likely that she adopted the idea of switching her sex from the example of male berdaches in neighboring groups (she was known among the Flathead). At any rate, returning home after a long sojourn with a Canadian husband, she perpetrated the hoax that her former husband had "operated" upon her and changed her into a man. Her brother, discovering that there was no anatomical foundation to the claim, exposed her to the community. She returned to wandering among tribal groups (Schaeffer, in Katz 1976: 293–8).

6. Even Devereux's data let him down on this point. The homosexual play of Mohave adolescents was not considered "homosexuality," he writes, meaning by this that it was not associated with their gender-crossing custom. Also, "A subsidiary informant . . . claimed that if a man was found to have submitted to rectal intercourse he was compelled to undergo the initiation [to berdache status], but this statement has been unanimously discredited" (Devereux 1937: 507–8).

7. Age status as well could be disassociated from chronological age because of the association of age with experience and knowledge. Thus among the Santee Sioux, persons experienced in an

activity were always spoken of as "old" in comparison to novices, and shamans of whatever chronological age were referred to as "old ones" (Landes 1968: 46, 209).

8. The "manly heart's" public display of domination over her husband may, however, have been atypical of the Plains matron pattern. It should be added as well that not every Plains group had this "wealthy matron" syndrome. Jane Collier, from whose excellent study of Plains marriage and labor organization I have abstracted this dimension of the female role, points out that among the Comanche, senior wives chose to maximize leisure rather than generate wealth, and used their free time to accompany their husbands on raiding expeditions (Collier 1977: 10). The Comanche, however, are said to have no berdaches.

9. Examining geographically just the connection between surplus-based female craft specializations and the institution of male gender-crossing, we find that in the wealthy and socially stratified Northwest Coast societies, the greater number of prestigious crafts were in the hand of male specialists and there were few, if any, berdaches. In the stratified Mesoamerican area, the same situation obtained in regard to craft specialization, but there is mention of male prostitutes; one might speculate that some wholly eroticized version of the berdache existed there but evidence is too skimpy to permit conclusions (see Guerra 1971). In much of the subarctic area, there were no berdaches, but there was also little surplus and craft specialization. Among the Eskimo, curing and artistic craftwork was entirely the domain of men as was much of the crucial foraging; high rates of female infanticide give one an idea of the position of women. There were no berdaches (see Driver 1969).

10. In some areas, the berdache was subject to a disadvantage not suffered by the dominant female householder—no household to dominate. The Potawatomi actually exiled the berdache from his natal village (Landes 1968: 31–2). Among Plains groups, a berdache, when married, seems to have been taken as a subsidiary wife, never the first, and this in all likelihood cut him off from household leadership (at least in his marital household). Only in the Southwest, among Zuni and Navajo, do we find definite reports of his being permitted a position of domestic headship, and here in his natal, not marital, household (Stevenson, in Katz 1976: 314; Hill 1935: 275). Obviously, in other areas, some arrangements must have existed whereby the berdache was supplied with the raw materials needed to practice female crafts, but the ethnography on this point is silent.

REFERENCES

Angelino, Henry, and Shedd, C.L. 1955. "A Note on Berdache." *American Anthropologist* 57: 121–6.

Barker-Benfield, G.J. 1976. *The Horrors of the Half-Known Life: Male Attitudes toward Women and Sexuality in Nineteenth-Century America.* New York: Harper and Row.

Benjamin, Harry, *The Transsexual Phenomenon.* New York: Warner Books, 1966.

Buchbinder, G. and Rappaport, R. 1976. "Fertility and Death among the Maring." In *Man and Woman in the New Guinea Highlands,* ed. P. Brown and G. Buchbinder. Special publication of the American Anthropological Association, no. 8, pp. 13–35.

Bullough, Vern. 1976. *Sexual Variance in Society and History.* New York: Wiley.

Collier, Jane F. 1977. "Women's Work, Marriage, and Stratification in Three Nineteenth–Century Plains Tribes." Unpublished manuscript.

De Becker, R. 1969. *The Other Face of Love.* New York: Bell Publishing.

Devereux, G. 1937. "Institutionalized Homosexuality of the Mohave Indians." *Human Biology* 9: 498–527.

Driver, H.E. 1969. *Indians of North America.* 2d ed. Chicago: University of Chicago Press.

Ellis, Albert. 1963. "Constitutional Factors in Homosexuality: A Reexamination of the Evidence." In *Advances in Sex Research,* ed. Hugo G. Beigel, pp. 161–86. New York: Harper & Row.

Evans-Pritchard, E.E. 1970. "Sexual Inversion among the Azande." *American Anthropologist* 72: 1428–34.

Fletcher, Alice, and LaFlesche, Frances. 1972. *The Omaha Tribe.* Lincoln: University of Nebraska Press.

Ford, C.S. and Beach, F.A. 1951. *Patterns of Sexual Behavior.* New York: Harper & Bros.

Guerra, Francisco. 1971. *The Pre-Columbian Mind: A Study into the Aberrant Nature of Sexual Drives, Drugs affecting Behavior and the Attitude towards Life and Death, With a Survey of Psychotherapy, in Pre-Columbian America.* London: Seminar.

Hallowell, A.I. 1955. *Culture and Experience.* Philadelphia: University of Pennsylvania Press.

Hill, W.W. 1935. "The Status of the Hermaphrodite and Transvestite in Navaho Culture." *American Anthropologist* 37: 273–9.

—— 1938. "Note on the Pima Berdache." *American Anthropologist* 40: 338–40.

Hoebel, A.E. 1949. *Man in the Primitive World: An Introduction to Anthropology.* New York: McGraw-Hill.

—— 1960. *The Cheyennes: Indians of the Great Plains.* New York: Holt, Rinehart & Winston.

Katz, Jonathan. 1976. *Gay American History: Lesbians and Gay Men in the U.S.A.* New York: Crowell.

Kelly, Raymond, 1976. "Witchcraft and Sexual Relations: An Exploration of the Social and Semantic Implications of the Structure of Belief." In *Man and Woman in the New Guinea Highlands,* ed. P. Brown and G. Buchbinder. Special publication of the American Anthropological Association, no. 8, pp. 36–53.

Kroeber, A.L. 1925. *Handbook of the Indians of California.* U.S. BAE Bulletin No. 78. Washington, D.C.: U.S. GPO.

—— 1940. "Psychosis or Social Sanction." In A.L. Kroeber, *The Nature of Culture.* Chicago: University of Chicago Press, 1952, pp. 310–19.

Landes, Ruth. 1938. *The Ojibwa Woman.* New York: Norton.

—— 1968. *The Mystic Lake Sioux: Sociology of the Mdewakantonwan Santee.* Madison: University of Wisconsin Press.

—— 1970. *The Prairie Potawatomi.* Madison: University of Wisconsin Press.

Lewis, Oscar. 1941. "The manly-hearted woman among the North Piegan." *American Anthropologist* 43: 173–87.

Lowie, Robert. 1924. *Primitive Religion.* New York: Liveright.

—— 1956. *The Crow Indians.* New York: Rinehart.

Lurie, Nancy O. 1953. "Winnebago Berdache." *American Anthropologist* 55: 708–12.

Meigs, Anna S. 1976. "Male Pregnancy and the Reduction of Sexual Opposition in a New Guinea Highlands Society." *Ethnology* 14: 393–407.

Munroe, Robert; Whiting, John W.M.; and Hally, David J. 1969. "Institutionalized Male Transvestism and Sex Distinctions." *American Anthropologist* 71: 87–91.

Newton, Esther. 1977. "Role Models," in *Symbolic Anthropology: A Reader in the Study of Symbols and Meaning,* ed. J. Dolgin et al. New York: Columbia University Press.

Parsons, E.C. 1916. "The Zuni La'Mana." *American Anthropologist* 18: 521–8.

Raymond, J.G. 1979. *The Transsexual Empire: The Making of the She-Male.* Boston: Beacon Press.

Rubin, Gayle. 1975. "The Traffic in Women: Notes on the 'Political Economy' of Sex." In *Toward an Anthropology of Women,* ed. R. Reiter, pp. 157–210. New York: Monthly Review Press.

Schieffelin, Edward. 1976. *The Sorrow of the Lonely and the Burning of the Dancers.* New York: St. Martin's Press.

Schneider, David. 1968. *American Kinship: A Cultural Account.* Englewood Cliffs: Prentice-Hall.

—— 1972. "What is Kinship All About?" In *Kinship Studies in the Morgan Centennial Year,* ed. P. Reining, pp. 32–63. Washington D.C.: Washington Anthropological Society.

—— and Smith, R.T. 1973. *Class Differences in American Kinship.* Ann Arbor: University of Michigan Press.

Simms, S.C. 1903. "Crow Indian Hermaphrodites." *American Anthropologist* 5: 580–1.

Slater, Philip. 1968. *The Glory of Hera: Greek Mythology and the Greek Family.* Boston: Beacon Press.

Smith-Rosenberg, Carroll. 1978. "Sex as Symbol of Victorian Purity." In *Turning Points: Historical and Sociological Essays on the Family,* ed. John Demos and Sarane Spence Boocock. Chicago: University of Chicago Press.

Strathern, M. 1972. *Women In Between.* London: Seminar (Academic) Press.

Underhill, Ruth M. 1939. *The Social Organization of the Papago Indians.* New York: Columbia University Press.

Van Baal, J. 1966. *Dema: Description and Analysis of Marind-Anim Culture.* The Hague: Martinus Nijhoff.

34

Just One of the Boys:
Lesbians in Cherry Grove, 1960–1988

Esther Newton

Esther Newton is Associate Professor of Anthropology and teaches Gay and Lesbian Studies and Women's Studies at the State University of New York at Purchase. She is the author of Mother Camp: Female Impersonators in America *(1972), and "The Mythic, Mannish Lesbian: Radclyffe Hall and the New Woman" (in* Hidden From History, *ed. Martin Bauml Duberman, Martha Vicinus, and George Chauncey, Jr., 1989). This essay is part of her newest work,* Pleasure Island, *forthcoming from Beacon Press. Highly conscious of the need for gay histories, Newton studies here the lesbians of Cherry Grove, a summer community of predominantly gay men, and demonstrates the inadequacy of a concept of lesbian communities that understands them as unified in their self-conceptions or as separate from the history of gay men. Newton describes three separate lesbian populations who joined Cherry Grove between 1930 and 1988: the "ladies," the "dykes," and the "postfeminists." She shows how attention to class, ethnic, racial, and political differences among the groups—rather than assumptions of similarity based on shared sexuality—provides a more specific and hence a more complex picture of succeeding generations of lesbians whose various responses to sexism, male sexuality, and lesbian "families" have little in common.*

I joined the fire department in '76. But this was more accepted because things were loosening up. So women could more or less invade as long as we did it very quietly. It was none of this, go down and demonstrate because there were no women on the fire department. You got to know the guys very subtly. You didn't push them . . . I was accepted . . . not necessarily that I was a woman, but for the work I could do.[1]

The "Ladies"

Cherry Grove is a summer community in the New York Metropolitan area which is different from every other resort in the world in that gay men and lesbians are the majority. Located on an Atlantic barrier beach called Fire Island, the "Grove" consists of about 275 houses, a small commercial center, and a ruggedly beautiful ocean beach. You can walk all around the community—there are no roads or cars—in a few minutes. It is accessible from the mainland only by boat or jeep, and separated from other Fire Island communities by sand dunes and brush.

First arriving in the 1930s, by the 1950s gay summer renters from New York City were becoming home owners and creating an underground gay Mecca. "Camp culture," a pre-Stonewall gay sensibility of gender-bending, hard drinking, theatricality, and cruising was the norm. Although the community tone was quickly dominated by gay men, an intrepid group of lesbians were among the founders. Throughout the Grove's fifty-year gay history, lesbians as home owners, renters, and "daytrippers" maintained a fragile presence.

Gay women came to the Grove in cohorts, the first from about 1936 to the end of World War II. Most of the first generation were WASPs and almost all of them were financially comfortable. Some had inherited wealth, while many were businesswomen or professionals in such fields as publicity, media, and theater, including some famous names like Cheryl Crawford, founder of the Group Theatre and Actor's Studio, and writers Carson McCullers, Patricia Highsmith, and Janet Flanner and her companion, Natalia Murray. The second cohort, currently in their fifties and sixties, arrived during the years 1945–1955. Very much of the same class as their elders, they were quickly accepted. These women referred to themselves as "gay girls," or "ladies." Although there had always been many more "gay boys" than "girls"—about eight to one—these affluent and sophisticated women participated as equals with their male peers in costume parties, the little theater, and community governance, every domain in fact except the important one of specifically sexual activities. But in the late fifties and early sixties, as men flooded into the exclusive "gay country club" and as the Grove became more developed and commercial, most "ladies" left for Connecticut or for the Hamptons further out on Long Island. A contributing factor to their departure was the arrival of some younger lesbians with whom the "ladies" had no intention of socializing.[2]

The "Dykes"

They weren't Broadway celebrities and they weren't wealthy, but the mostly Jewish and Italian women, most from blue collar backgrounds, who started coming into the Grove during the 1960s were just as determined and personally resourceful as the "ladies" who had come before them.[3] The remaining "ladies" intended an ethnic and class slur by calling the new women "dykes."[4] The working-class women identified with the word, which was "an affectionate term to us like 'fag' and 'queen' " when used among themselves.[5] Then in their twenties and thirties, the "dykes" heard about the Grove not from "ladies" who had been there, but in fifties and sixties mafia-controlled bars, which, whether they were patrons or bar workers, played a central role in their lesbianism.[6]

Butch/femme identities had been critical in fifties and sixties bars and the "dykes" often came in butch/femme couples, another point which set them off from the "ladies," most of whom had downplayed role distinctions. The term "dyke" was associated primarily with butches; Lyn explained that her ex-lover Amelia

> Is a dyke but she's not a dyke [because] I think when I crossdress I look rather masculine
> . . . I've been to parties in the city and been to leather bars where they did not know
> I was a woman. Amelia can't pull that off.[7]

Although Amelia and other femme women played important roles in Grove history, the butches—because they fought for public space, because they were the erotic focus of bar life and because they were "obvious" homosexuals—tended to personify this generation.[8]

Different as they may have been from the "ladies," the newcomers like Amelia and her friends reacted to the Grove in 1960 very much as Natalia Murray had back in 1936:

> It was the whole romantic feeling of taking a boat and going to an island and then
> coming here and it was a beautiful day and the water was marvelous. And the whole

romance of being, you know, in a gay community, being totally free, being O.K. . . .
and we all fell in love with it.[9]

During the early sixties the number of resident women was small. Unless they
worked for gay bar impresario Jimmy Merry, who tended to find housing for his own
help, it was not easy for them to become part of the community. Amelia and her friends
had a hard time translating their love for the Grove into a summer rental contract. One
of the realtors made his opposition very plain:

> I remember his face got very close to mine, and he said, "There is nothing available
> for you. There is nothing available for you." And I said, "Everything is rented?" He
> says, "No, but we don't rent to women, they put things down the toilet."[10]

But toward the middle of the decade the new generation of "gay girls" began to
take shape. For Amelia, "going to the gay clubs was home," and that's where she heard
about the Grove:

> . . . I had never heard of Cherry Grove. I never even envisioned a community that
> was gay . . . And a friend of mine came up with this idea: "Let's go to the beach,
> you know there's this place Cherry Grove. . . ."[11]

Not all the blue collar "girls" worked in Grove bars, but few of them could afford
the rents without working; many saw in the Grove economic opportunity. They worked
as waitresses, haircutters, housepainters, whatever they could find. Eventually some of
them did what virtually none of the "ladies" had done, they started Grove businesses.[12]

Because of the social gap between the "ladies" and the "dykes," there was little
connection between them. The younger "girls" hardly realized there had been an older
generation and tended to see themselves as "firsts." To this day, few of them realize
how many lesbians were among the Grove's gay pioneers. "Jeri," a sixties arrival, explained, erroneously, that before her time,

> There weren't that many women because they couldn't afford houses and they couldn't
> get mortgages. And also in the early days, there wasn't electricity, there wasn't running
> water. No woman, whether dyke or femme, wanted to put up with that.[13]

The "ladies" had socialized and identified with their gay male peers. In contrast,
many of the "dykes" had come out in lesbian-only bars in New York City and had little
experience of gay men before coming to the Grove, which they saw simply as a safe
space for women where one could be openly gay. Most came to the Grove with a lover
and a few other female friends. Amelia recalled that when she first started daytripping
in the sixties,

> . . . I was only interested in women and in my friends. It was only after, when I met
> Lyn, that I got involved in the community, you know, including men. Of course now
> I realize how much I *do* like them, but at that time I was very frightened of men
> and it didn't matter whether they were straight or gay, I just wanted to keep my
> distance . . .[14]

The dramatic population growth during the 1960s worked against the chumminess
of the previous "country club" era. The new lesbian arrivals spent their summer weekends in closed "cliques" made up of a few women who would share a summer rental
and socialize with other lesbian households. One clique was made up of bartenders and
waitresses who spent every off hour playing poker together. Another was mainly physical
education teachers. The cliques remained isolated from community men and from each
other. Jan Felshin remembered that

... we had a very communal ... life. On rainy days we'd all gather and play Bingo, we had potluck suppers on Sunday night, everybody would bring the last of their week-end food ... we had a very active group of about twelve or so people ... We sort of hung together, I think, as women.[15]

Gradually during the 1970s more women came. The situation they faced in the Grove was very different from the 1930s and forties when women, although vastly outnumbered, had participated in Grove life as near equals. Grove men, who had consolidated their hegemony during the 1960s, mostly saw the "dykes" as intruders and treated them as such. In the early seventies women, Ricki recalled, had to leave big tips for the bartenders just in order to be waited on.

As the "girls" got to know some men better and to appreciate the "camp" sensibility, they began to take part in male-controlled community institutions and organizations—the theater, the art show, the volunteer fire department, the annual costume ball—at first in very secondary roles. When "Jeri" went to the theater and said she wanted to participate the men said, "Can't you see we don't want women here?" But she hung around, and they "let" her "sweep the floor." Little by little she moved up.

Through their friendships with men and participation in local institutions the "dykes" began to break out of their cliques and get to know each other. "Dykes' corner," they called a couple of tables in a woman-owned restaurant claimed by one crowd on Friday nights during the seventies. In the 1960s there had been no lesbian group large enough to claim even a corner of public space.

While some of the "ladies" had owned imposing bay houses when most "boys" were still renting, the "dykes" "started in the low rent district." But as they prospered during the second half of the seventies, some of the "girls" bought homes in the Grove. Whereas the "ladies" had bought homes with cash, most "dykes" had to stretch financially. Lyn recalled that in 1975 she and Amelia had saved $11,000, had another $2000 from Amelia's father and calculated they could just make mortgage payments, but the seller, a straight man,

Didn't want to sell it to us ... It was "Well these fellows are supposed to come out" and "This other group I'm supposed to hear from" and Amelia said "I'm here and here's my check." It was made out for $1200 ... "Here's money ..." [We were] almost on our knees. Even with a check. 'Cause women were not buying. It was bad enough to have them renting here, let alone buying.[16]

Although the couple, through persistence, finally bought the first house, the owner refused to sell them two adjoining houses as an investment. When another lesbian couple wanted to buy a large house on the bay some "pretentious [male] property" owners intervened and manipulated the sale to a straight couple instead because they "didn't want girls as neighbors," an event about which these women were understandably bitter.[17] Men grumbled that "girls" were driving up house prices because they were willing to pay more, without acknowledging that their own discrimination *forced* women to pay more.

Once women owned houses, they were in a position to throw the kind of large parties that men had traditionally given to establish themselves socially. But mostly they didn't. Aside from the expense of giving large parties, many "dykes" disliked the traditional Grove party where:

Jan: There wasn't a salted peanut in the house. They were just belting hard liquor ...

Edrie: You could hardly call them parties. They were occasions for posturing and gesturing [laughs].[18]

By the late seventies even men had abandoned the large theme parties, a trend which suited most lesbians, who preferred dinner parties for groups of closer friends. One exception were the "Ziti" parties of 1975–1979, given by Lyn and Amelia to establish themselves in the neighborhood, which were the first of the larger parties since the 1950s to really mix genders. In contrast to the traditional hard-drinking Grove parties the Ziti party, as its name implies, centered on Italian food.

Lyn and Amelia invited about 120 people and "We were panicked," Lyn remembered, "because 60 of them were women and 60 were men and this was not done!" A lot of thought went into the "Ziti party":

> We decided we'd have the women on the lower deck and the men on the upper deck . . . But surprisingly it worked. We introduced everybody as best we could. The guys that knew me had accepted me and were starting to accept women and Amelia was starting to accept the men so our friends saw that these were . . . property owners out here . . . They weren't just the day tripper one-summer-rental type people . . .[19]

Whether homeowners or renters, by the late seventies, most "girls" had become active or at least participated in one or more phases of community life. Surmounting considerable male opposition, Lyn became chief of the fire department; she and Amelia bought a house, then a restaurant. A legitimate actress starred in *Little Mary Sunshine,* one of the most successful theater productions of the decade. Four "girls" became active in a mixed gender "band of rebels" who sought to mobilize the entire community against an influx of straight tourists in the late seventies.

One group of "girls" "paid their dues" by participating in the costume competition in the Arts Project of Cherry Grove's 30th anniversary ball in 1978.[20] The theme of the ball that year was "Arabian Nights." "Sisters of the Sand," their all-woman entry— only the second since the mid-1950s[21]—included two women inside a large camel suit ridden by a camel driver, guards with wooden swords, skimpily clad dancing girls, and Grove homeowner Jan Felshin as the "sultan"—the women referred to her affectionately (she is strongly Jewish-identified) as the "sheiksa"—who was carried in by litter-bearers.

Their entry played according to unspoken Grove rules. The women formed group households to compete, they rehearsed endlessly as secretly as they could, and the theme of the "queen" being carried by her bearers goes back to the first Grove parties in the 1930s. While in men's entries female parts were played by men in drag, here the dancing girls were played by "r.g.'s" or "real girls." Instead of the usual muscular "pretty boys" carrying in a drag "queen," solemn butch lesbians were the litter bearers for Jan dressed in men's Arab robes.

Ten years later the participants remembered doing the "Sisters of the Sand" with great pleasure, but emphasized that they could never spend the hours and hours of time and effort to enter a ball again. Yet the community response, Edrie Ferdun, one of the dancing girls, recalled, was a great reward:

> The whole community was absolutely thrilled. And loved our whole number and so forth. It was just totally supportive.[22]

As home owners, neighbors, community activists, stage hands and actors, the women of the sixties and seventies eventually came to see their destiny entwined with community men. As their sense of belonging grew so did their investment in the well-being of Cherry Grove. When they contemplated the Grove's future, these women all said they loved the community as it was, or cited the same problems of garbage disposal, overcrowding, and beach erosion that the men did. The goal of most "dykes" was to be accepted as equals by gay men on male terms, and "boys" and "girls" of this generation, like the founders before them, have mostly made peace with each other, agreeing to live and let live, or even help live:

> "Louise" said she was down in the sand by her house cutting a tree. Willy [a neighbor] walked by saying, "that's no work for a woman." "Damn it," "Louise" said, "so let him get down here and do it." Then Peaches [another neighbor] walked by saying, "That's no work for a woman." But then he came back with a "humungous" saw and helped her finish the job.[23]

"Postfeminists"

Since about 1985 a third and by far the largest influx of women has dramatically changed the Grove's gender balance. Opinions vary as to the cause of this change, but most point to the larger number of women who could afford to rent and buy. Certainly when I first rented in 1985, rental prices were depressed; although the Grove has always experienced cycles of price inflation and deflation, fear generated by the AIDS epidemic in the early eighties probably hit Grove property values especially hard. The temptations of easy cruising put men at more risk, Amelia reasoned:

> AIDS for the most part is a male disease. So if the men are not coming, it makes room for the women to come. And the women don't have to be frightened to come here, because they're not having the same kind of anonymous sex.[24]

Word of the Grove's charms spread fast because during 1987 and 1988 the women poured in. Still only perhaps fifteen percent of home owners, they now make up almost half of all renters, and many renters want to buy. Such sudden and massive change poses a real challenge to the community.

In calling the newest wave "postfeminists" I am not concurring with some conservatives that feminism is over but just the opposite, that whether these women are explicitly feminist or not, they have been irrevocably influenced by feminist gains and attitudes.[25] They vary in age and class background. Professional women in their thirties and forties tend to own or rent seasonally, with the youngest, least affluent renting weekly or sharing, and minority and working-class lesbians daytripping.

The "postfeminists" come from a larger, more complex, and varied lesbian world than any of their predecessors and the younger women especially look quite different from members of the preceding generations, I noted:

> No hard defensive look like Lyn Hutton and I have. No beefy body that says fuck you to men and I can take anything you can dish out. No dyke slump. These gals stand up straight. They have expensive stylish short haircuts and pressed, all cotton sportswear. They look a lot like smaller, softer versions of men in GQ; in other words like young gay men in the Pines.[26]

Many male Grovers are anxious and unhappy about the sudden influx of women, especially since the young men whom they consider desirable overwhelmingly prefer the neighboring and more "modern" community, Fire Island Pines. Young ambitious white men may actually shun the Grove, seeing it as old fashioned, un-trendy, and full of old unattractive, effeminate "queens."

I assume that because I am a woman, Grove men downplayed their fears and their sexism in my presence. Some men volunteered very positive statements about lesbians, especially about our work in the AIDS crisis. Nevertheless, many—even very polite men—told me that they had nothing against women but—they hog the boardwalks, or are too pushy, or rude in the bars, or . . . etc. etc. Others would compare the "dykes" and "postfeminists" unfavorably to the "real ladies" of the pioneer generation.

Sometimes women were directly insulted. Lucy was furious when in the course of her job picking up bags of garbage along the beach she stopped for a moment to empty the sand from her sandals. A man yelled out, "Don't empty your sand in front of my house!" Lucy made some mild reply to which he shouted, "Damn lesbian!"

Sexist hostility was directed not only at the newer women but down the well-trodden path leading to Cherry Grove's much admired Volunteer Fire Department, led since the mid-seventies by Chief Lyn Hutton, and about a fourth of whose members are women. Some of the stories about the department were sexist to the point of absurdity, yet men repeated them, even to me, almost unself-consciously. Dick admitted that the fire department was "a joke" before Lyn took it over, but

> Sometimes they take credit for things that maybe they shouldn't get the credit for. When Pete and Win had a small fire, a couple of guys noticed it and they went by and pissed on it . . . that actually happened . . . they pulled the alarm and Lyn got there and said "All right, out of the way" and they said "We saved it already" . . . that's the story you hear—(laughs uneasily) I don't know how true it is.[27]

Even men like long-time Grover Teri Warren who expressed very positive attitudes toward women had their reservations:

> TW: The community this year [1986] has gone very gay woman-oriented for some reason—a lot of the renters are girls, and they're just wonderful as far as I'm concerned.
>
> EN: Do you think there's hostility on the part of some of the men, that they don't like it?
>
> TW: I don't think so. I think there may be hostility on the part of the women toward the men, but that works two ways.[28]

With almost all of the "ladies" having died, left the Grove or having had to abdicate active participation in the community, the pioneers of the "dyke" generation are caught between male ambivalence or outright angst over the new arrivals and the sometimes alien attitudes of the "postfeminists."

Building on their 1970s accomplishments and riding the crest of the "postfeminist" population bulge, the "dykes" have become important community—not just lesbian—figures. Lyn and Amelia have bought and manage one of the two biggest local restaurants. Lois "Mac," who started as a waitress in 1960, is owner/manager of Cherry's, the most successful community-oriented bar. "Carol" established an independent hair-cutting business and is an acknowledged leader in AIDS work. Betty Ward was elected the president of the largest community organization, the Arts Project.[29] Jan and Edrie's household organized a women's volleyball team called the Cherry Tarts that has competed in recent summers with lesbians in neighboring Fire Island Pines. The Broadway actress and her lover bought a large and imposing house on the dunes and rent primarily to women.

Grove "dykes" in general are pleased that more women are coming in. Lyn admitted,

> I do like to see a lot more women around. I feel more comfortable in The Monster or some place if there's another couple of women . . . gay women in there . . .[30]

Even though it is axiomatic that women don't spend as much money as men, a welcoming attitude toward the newcomers prevails among women business owners Lois "Mac" and Lyn and Amelia, all of whom have also hired more women workers:

> I feel protective of women. Women probably don't spend as much, but that's because in the past women haven't had as much to spend. Of course sometimes the waiters

will say to me, "Oh all you did tonight was give me dykes, how could I make any money?" Then they joke around about "dyke dollars." Like eight dyke dollars are equivalent to twelve male dollars . . . it's a good tip.[31]

But there are important differences in outlook between the "dykes" and the "postfeminists." The "dykes," who came as a timid minority at a time of male power and control, have a keen sense that

It's just traditionally been [men's] island and we have definitely invaded their space.[32]

Arriving in the mid-eighties when many male home owners were either sick or elderly, the postfeminists saw themselves filling a vacuum. They have few personal ties to men and the gap between the aging male home owners and renters and the younger postfeminists doesn't help foster understanding. Bitching and complaints about men and male attitudes are more freely expressed:

"Minna" said she can't stand tea dance in the Pines; all those large muscular sweaty male bodies. She can't hear, can't see, can't breathe.[33]

Very few "dykes" were as outspoken and as bitter as "Leslie," who had been coming to the Grove since the seventies:

There's a lot of old queens here who hate so many women coming out, but we love it here too. We own property. We plant flowers, make it beautiful. So fuck 'em.[34]

Most "dykes" like the Grove the way it is, and want the new women to fit into the existing male framework. Tension hovers over the "postfeminist" use of the word "lesbian" which has taken hold in the titles of almost all gay organizations. Male Grovers often asked me why women wanted to be separate, even while treating them as if they were. Teri Warren corrected my use of the word "lesbian" with the words "gay people." I tried to explain to him why women would want to identify with a different word:

EN: I came out in the fifties and to me everyone was "gay."
TW: Right.
EN: But . . . a lot of times when you just use the term "gay," the women get lost—a lot of gay men unfortunately and certainly straight people assume that if you say "gay" it just means men, so lesbians get dropped by the wayside.
TW: Yeah, but it makes it to straight people like we don't get along.[35]

"Dykes" largely shared these attitudes. Lyn was especially clear that part of her antipathy to the word "lesbian" emerged from her loyalty to the Grove:

Lesbians come from the Isle of Lesbos, it's a very separated group and I don't think the guys out here although they aren't really in love with the women and the volume of women here . . . don't want one type of gay separated from another type of gay. . . . In other words, we don't have a drag queen bar, a leather bar, a women's bar, a this bar a that bar. We've got three major meeting places and we all fit into those three bars.[36]

"Jeri" told me she hated the word "lesbian," and criticized other women who gave all-woman parties "because it took us so long to be accepted out here." Amelia said flatly that feminism had nothing to do with the Grove. "Anyway," she added, "I don't believe in it" because

I don't believe in abortion, and I can't condone any organization that does. And that's just as basic as it is.[37]

Jan Felshin and her companion Edrie Ferdun, two college professors of physical education, *do* consider themselves lesbian-feminists. As far back as the 1976 bicentennial their household baked a cake with a flag reading "stars and dykes forever," and invited "all the women in the Grove"—"You could still get them all in one house"—to celebrate. And yet, in explaining why she had come back to the Grove since the sixties and become a homeowner Jan said:

> I really believe that my primary identification is as a homosexual. . . . And I have organized my social life around it, and everything else, . . . I can remember the olden days when every homosexual was your friend. I mean I have put my life on the line for terrible people because they were gay.[38]

These women were atypical of the "dyke" cohort in several ways, certainly in being strongly feminist politically. Yet they feared that some younger lesbians—"functionettes," they called them—didn't understand "the poetry and romance," and the value on "the symbolic life," which they loved about Cherry Grove. Jan and Edrie didn't identify as a butch/femme couple, but were terribly offended by an incident in the 1970s when some "functionettes":

> [Accused] me of not being a real feminist because the woman I was with was too attractive. . . . They saw Edrie and they started to hoot at me. And I didn't get it. And the idea was, oh, you're passing yourself off as a feminist, but look. (laughter).[39]

One of the most difficult issues between the postfeminists and Grove old-timers of both genders may be that of children. The Grove is not prepared for the lesbian baby boom. While older Grovers are very proud of the children who were raised at the beach by straight families, they also boast that none of these children are reputed to have turned out homosexual. The idea of lesbian "families" makes many Grovers uncomfortable.

In the Spring of 1988, a homeowning, well-established, "postfeminist" couple adopted an infant daughter. One of the "ladies" flatly refused her invitation to the baby shower, telling me that Cherry Grove and families don't mix. She said in effect that the two worlds—"normal" and "gay" as she put it—are separate and they should be, for the mutual comfort of both sides. A woman of the "dyke" generation told me at the shower itself that "Children don't belong here."

A second area of potential friction between "postfeminists" and old-timers may occur over the men's sexual practices and prerogatives. Grove gay "girls" of all generations expressed incomprehension of gay "boys'" promiscuity. It was just taken as a given that

> . . . men had more of a sexual drive and a desire, and they didn't care who they had it with . . . When we came out here, it never shocked us, because we understood, men's and women's sexuality were just completely different.[40]

Grove "ladies" and "dykes," who were in no position to object, were amused or indifferent, as long as sexual activity was confined to the so-called "meat rack," an open strip of brush and dunes which separates Cherry Grove from the Pines. The "girls'" shadowy and ambiguous relationship to the "boys" and their sexual practices was symbolized in the widely told stories about a "doughnut rack," a gay version of American gender iconography which contrasts the substantial "meaty" male genitals with the negative (though possibly sweet) space of the vagina.

The legendary origins of the doughnut rack were said by some to lie back in the 1950s or sixties.[41] For some men, it was only a male projection:

> I don't believe there was [a doughnut rack]. If it was it was the best kept secret. I think it was just a boys' joke to be honest.[42]

Some of the women liked the joke too, while denying that women could ever want or need such an institution. In Betty Ward's version the notion of separate spheres was preserved:

Betty: We used to tell women about a doughnut rack, and they'd go crazy, we'd never tell them where it was. Of course it never existed.

Randi: You know we never really had one [but] ... You know where we used to pretend it was? On the ocean side of the dunes. But then so many people started walking through that way, we couldn't use that as our spot any more, so we had to just play it cool like we're not telling you where it is ...[43]

The "absurdity" of the idea was employed to reinforce the supposedly immutable differences between men's and women's sexuality. Amelia laughed about the doughnut rack and added,

Of course there is no such place ... because women's sexuality is totally different from men's and women, generally speaking of course, do not have anonymous sex, and women have to be wined and dined and (laughs) be brought flowers. No, no. Of course, I say, *of course* there is no such place.[44]

For the "dyke" generation, the doughnut rack story symbolized their assertion of Grove citizenship as separate but equal partners to men. Once I was asking some Grovers about the Bridge of Sighs, a part of the Grove which had once been a male cruising spot, when "Jeri" quipped, "You mean the doughnut rack?" Relatively new to the Grove, I had never heard of this so "Jeri" explained, "*They* have the meat rack, *we* have the doughnut rack." Everyone was laughing heartily when one of the men said slyly, "I always thought it was the 'Bridge of Size.' " Subtly, the doughnut rack had disappeared.

The territorial, symbolic, and institutional compromises the "ladies" and "dykes" have made in order to be accepted will be sorely tested if the "postfeminist" generation stays and grows even larger. Although many women, even some of the "ladies," resented the beautiful meat rack area being off-limits to them, they accepted the trade-off: no women in the meat rack in exchange for no men having sex on the boardwalks, decks, beach, etc.

But the "postfeminists" have fewer scruples about male-only space. In recent years Lyn Hutton, acting on complaints from male Grovers, has "spoken to" particular women who were walking through the area. In 1986 someone painted "Gay Only" and a male sign on the boardwalk leading into the wooded part of the 'rack. Even assuming that no lesbians prove Amelia wrong by trying to set up their own sexual networks in the meat rack, it is perfect for such established lesbian activities as picnics, dog exercise, bird-watching, and tête-à-têtes on days when the beach is too windy. It is also by far the shortest walk to the Pines, where women are also renting and buying:

"Leona" and "Ellen" were pissed because walking along the path in the rack from the Pines they came across a Pakistani man who was totally naked with an erection. He didn't even turn his back as they passed, and "Leona" had to control her panic. She said "A naked man with an erection means one thing to me, rape." "Ellen" said the guys should go back into the bushes. Okay, that was their space. But don't do it on the public path. "I guess they think *all* of it is theirs, there *is* no public path," she added angrily.[45]

The Grove has no formal mechanisms for conflict resolution. It will just have to muddle toward solution of these and other potential problems on a case-by-case basis, calling on strong traditions of community loyalty, tolerance, neighborliness, and social decorum, along with slowly forming bonds of personal friendship between women and men. Meanwhile, the "dykes" and most "postfeminists" who are settling in the Grove share a common desire, despite the tensions, that the community stay mixed. It was no surprise when Lyn said:

> The guys . . . are projecting in the next ten years this is gonna be a women's island [and] . . . I don't think I'd like it.[46]

But some women who had just bought a house and were strong feminists expressed similar sentiments:

> In the course of airing complaints about men, "Linda" speculated "What would the Grove be like if it were all women?" "Kim" said, "Not as much fun" and "Miriam" added, "We wouldn't like it as much."[47]

The Three "Be's"

Until now not one scholarly book or article on the rich and fascinating history of gay men and women in Cherry Grove has been available to interested readers. The most important conclusion to be drawn from this essay is how much—almost everything—remains to be done to construct the history of gays in many parts of the world. Specifically in working on lesbian identity and culture, three principles have guided my thinking. First of all, *Be Descriptive.* Those of us doing primary source work are inscribing names on a big blank map with reference points as disparate as late 18th century England; the turn-of-the-century American South; 1920s Paris, Harlem, and Salt Lake City; World War Two; and mid-twentieth-century Buffalo, New York.[48] We should be asking Who, What, Where, When, Why?

For example, although both "ladies" and "dykes" acknowledged having the same sexual orientation, they lived in antagonistic class-bound spheres, even in as small a place as Cherry Grove. It really makes no sense to talk about "*the* lesbian community" or "lesbian history" in abstract generalities. Ideas that "lesbian" equals "lesbian-feminist" or that lesbian history begins in 1969 are just wrong. We need to document the variety of lesbian lives, past and present.

Deconstructionist, anti-positivist historical approaches offer a more subtle challenge. Intellectually seductive, they might collapse gay history into "broader" (and more abstract) discourses on gender, sexual behaviors, or power in general. However, deconstructionist history implies a prior hegemonic (mainstream, official, canonical) account which—in the gay instance—does not exist. Lesbians are null, and gay men are reduced to stiff sex organs and limp wrists. Yet the "native" accounts are mostly unwritten and informal. As scholars we can and should "tell truth to power" and to our community by making gay experience into texts. No deconstructionist theory yet has persuaded me that what I see as an anthropologist and live as a human being—gay communities—don't, or shouldn't, exist.

If lesbian history is not reducible to debates about discourse, neither is it just an aspect of women's or feminist history, as is posited in some female bonding/friendship approaches.[49] *Don't Be Gobbled Up.* Since at least the turn of the century and perhaps earlier, women in Western cultures have formed named groups based on self-conscious, nominally exclusive sexual orientation, and we who study lesbian cultures should focus primarily on "inverts," "gay girls," "bulldaggers," "dykes," "lesbian-feminists," not generic women's networks or groupings.[50] Nor is lesbian history as a whole, despite the subordination of women in Cherry Grove, just a footnote to gay male history.

But Don't Be Separatist. Understanding lesbians means seeing them *in relation to* nations and regions, and to the histories of women as a gender class, of gay men, of socio-economic classes and of American race categories. Although lesbians (and some straight women) played critical roles in founding the gay Grove, the common framework for Grove lesbians has been provided by gay men. Without their determination to preserve gay space, after most "ladies" left the Grove in the late fifties there would have been no turf in the next decade for a new generation of lesbians to claim.

The Grove as a gay and lesbian seaside resort beginning in the mid-1930s should be compared to what was simultaneously going on in the Catskill Mountains—the commercial development of Russian-Jewish resort hotels.[51] The summer enclaves expressed both the growing power of these New York City minority groups and their continuing ghettoization. After World War II ethnic whites began to leave New York City for the suburbs, an exodus supported by the federal government in the form of G.I. home mortgage loans. On the national level this phenomenon has been called "ethnic succession"—e.g. the way class in America has been expressed as an outward migration (city slum to exurb) by an ethnic hierarchy (with blacks on the bottom, "ethnic" Europeans in the middle, and WASPS on top) over time.

How many upwardly mobile ethnic gays tried to participate in the suburban migration we don't know, but it's a fair guess that just as many or more may have moved the opposite way, toward the protective cloak of city centers. Being Italian or Jewish was very important to most lesbians and gay men who came to the WASP "gay country club" in the 1960s in their own ethnic succession—at least ten years behind their straight peers' move to the suburbs. Gay ethnics may have moved into WASP space more slowly because secrecy—which represents both gay resistance and assent to oppression—kept such a desirable resort hidden. Not until mafia-controlled bars drew large numbers of working-class lesbians together did they learn of the Grove's existence.

Or consider the effects of money and race in the Grove. However important gender differences were, in the long run Grovers also identified as property owners, renters, and daytrippers. Many of the "ladies" were early property owners, while "dykes" "started in the low rent district," as Lyn Hutton told me. Class background and resources determined how, when, and if lesbians entered Grove life. And as important as economic factors are, they don't fully explain the virtual absence of black and latino lesbians in the Grove until recently (even now they are mostly daytrippers, not renters or owners). Racism has been no less effective in denying access to the Grove as elsewhere in American life.

The complex counterpoint between homophobia, camp culture, and capitalism has orchestrated the history of Cherry Grove. Desperate refugees from homophobia and mainstream sexism, "ladies", "dykes," and "postfeminists" accepted the secondary roles to which they were relegated in male camp culture in exchange for a leisure space where they could be free as gay people. Now, if "dykes" and "postfeminists" can learn to work together they could make lesbians—for the first time—equal partners with gay men in Grove life.

NOTES

1. Lyn Hutton, Interview by author, 5 August 1988. Only the first date of multiple interview sessions is cited. Second references in the text to the same interview subject are abbreviated "IBA." Most Grovers whom I interviewed gave me permission to use their real names, mainly as a sign of their immense pride in the community and desire to be associated with its history. Pseudonyms are in quotation marks. This material is part of a larger ethnohistory of Cherry Grove's men and

women, *Pleasure Island: Fifty Years of Gay Cherry Grove in the American Dream* to be published by Beacon Press.

2. The "ladies" are the subject of my earlier paper, "The Fun Gay Ladies: Lesbians in Cherry Grove, 1938–1960" to be published in a special issue of the *Journal of Homosexuality,* Randolph Trumbach and Theo van der Meer, eds.

3. My primary source of information about the "dykes" is interviews with eleven women who first came to Cherry Grove during the years 1960–1975.

4. Most Grovers are not aware that since the 1969 Stonewall Rebellion the word "dyke" has been appropriated by lesbian-feminists as a positive term.

5. Lyn Hutton, IBA.

6. The only published scholarly account of fifties lesbian bar culture is by Madeleine Davis and Elizabeth Lapovsky Kennedy, "Oral History and the Study of Sexuality in the Lesbian Community: Buffalo, New York, 1940–1960," in Martin Bauml Duberman, Martha Vicinus, and George Chauncey, Jr., eds., *Hidden From History: Reclaiming the Gay and Lesbian Past* (New York: New American Library, 1989) 426–440. When Davis and Kennedy's work is published in its entirety lesbian studies will have its first detailed community history. My own research indicates parallel developments in New York City. The social history of these bars will necessarily be a central task of lesbian history.

7. Lyn Hutton, IBA.

8. On this point see my paper, "The Mythic Mannish Lesbian," in *Hidden From History,* 281–293.

9. Amelia Migliaccio, Interview by author, 5 August 1988.

10. Amelia Migliaccio, IBA.

11. Amelia Migliaccio, IBA.

12. The exception was "lady" Peggy Fears, who started Peggy's Place which became the Botel, not in the Grove but in Fire Island Pines.

13. "Jeri," author's fieldnotes, 15 August 1986.

14. Amelia Migliaccio, IBA.

15. Jan Felshin, Interview by author, 18 July 1988.

16. Amelia Migliaccio, IBA.

17. One of the male property owners whom these women named confirmed his dislike of women and his intervention in this case: "Ed Bridges," Interview by author, 15 July 1986.

18. Jan Felshin and Edrie Ferdun, IBA.

19. Lyn Hutton, IBA.

20. A woman named Marge was cited by several narrators as a real go-getter who participated in everything and encouraged women to do the same.

21. In 1975 or 1976 Amelia Migliaccio and her household participated in a rerun of an "all girl orchestra" which had been performed by "ladies," without realizing that this had been done in the early 1950s.

22. Edrie Ferdun, IBA.

23. Author's fieldnotes, 30 June 1986.

24. Amelia Migliaccio, IBA.

25. Jocelyn Taylor, one of the young developers of New York's Clit Club, a "floating" lesbian nightclub, justified the demise of the traditional lesbian bar saying "The postfeminist lesbian is maybe a little bit different than her predecessor . . . The whole community is shifting, and if you're not shifting and changing with that community, you're going to wake up and say 'Whoa, what's happening here?,' " quoted in "Women Behind Bars: Lesbians Lock Horns Over the Changing Generational Face of the Lesbian Bar Business," by Kelly Harmon and Cindy Kirshman in the *Advocate,* December 31, 1991, p. 48. The authors argue that it is expanded access and opportunities for lesbians that threatens the old ghettoized bar.

26. Author's fieldnotes, 8 August 1988.

27. Richard, Interview by author, 30 July 1987.

28. Teri Warren, Interview by author, 8 July 1986.

29. The Arts Project of Cherry Grove. She is only the third woman and second lesbian to hold that position in the forty-year history of the organization.

30. Lyn Hutton, IBA.

31. Amelia Migliaccio, IBA.

32. Lyn Hutton, IBA.

33. Author's fieldnotes, 27 July 1989.

34. Author's fieldnotes, 14 June 1989.

35. Teri Warren, IBA.

36. Lyn Hutton, IBA.

37. Amelia Migliaccio, IBA.

38. Jan Felshin, IBA.

39. Jan Felshin, IBA.

40. Betty L. Ward, Interview by author, 2 July 1988.

41. None of the "ladies" ever mentioned this and I assume that no female cruising spot actually existed.

42. Thom "Panzi" Hansen, Interview by author, 4 September 1988.

43. Betty L. Ward and Randi-Gail Robinson, IBA.

44. Amelia Migliaccio, IBA.

45. Author's fieldnotes, 27 July 1989.

46. Lyn Hutton, IBA.

47. Author's fieldnotes, 25 July 1989.

48. For England, see Randolph Trumbach, "London's Sapphists: From Three Sexes to Four Genders in the Making of Modern Culture," in Julia Epstein and Kristina Straub, eds., *Body Guards: The Cultural Politics of Gender Ambiguity* (New York and London: Routledge, 1991) 112–141; for the South the as-yet-unpublished work of Lisa Duggan on the Alice Mitchell murder trial in "The Trials of Alice Mitchell: Love, Murder and the Emergence of Lesbian Subjectivity in Turn-of-the-Century America," paper read at the 4th Annual Lesbian Bisexual & Gay Studies Conference, Harvard University, October 26–28, 1990; for Paris numerous works documenting the Natalie Barney circle of which the most detailed is Shari Benstock, *Women of the Left Bank: Paris, 1900–1940* (Austin: University of Texas Press, 1986); for Harlem, Eric Garber, "A Spectacle in Color: The Lesbian and Gay Subculture of Jazz Age Harlem," in *Hidden From History,* 318–331; for Salt Lake City, Vern and Bonnie Bullough, "Lesbianism in the 1920s and 1930s: A Newfound Study," *Signs* 2, no. 4 (Summer 1977): 895–904; for the Armed Forces, Allan Bérubé, *Coming Out Under Fire: The History of Gay Men and Women in World War Two* (New York: The Free Press, 1990); and for Buffalo, Davis and Kennedy, "Oral History and the Study of Sexuality in the Lesbian Community: Buffalo, New York, 1940–1960."

49. The most influential and interesting of these is Adrienne Rich's "Compulsory Heterosexuality and Lesbian Existence," in Ann Snitow, Christine Stansell, and Sharon Thompson, eds., *Powers of Desire: The Politics of Sexuality* (New York: Monthly Review Press, 1983) 177–205. Reprinted, with revisions, in this volume.

50. The most sophisticated discussion of how to think about "woman-committed women" in relation to lesbian groups in this century is in Leila J. Rupp, " 'Imagine My Surprise' ": Women's Relationships in Mid-Twentieth Century America," in *Hidden From History,* 395–410.

51. See Stefan Kanfer, *A Summer World: The Attempt to Build a Jewish Eden in the Catskills From the Days of the Ghetto to the Rise and Decline of the Borscht Belt* (New York: Farrar, Straus, and Giroux, 1989).

35

Hijras as Neither Man Nor Woman

SERENA NANDA

Serena Nanda is a cultural anthropologist. In this piece, a chapter drawn from her book,
Neither Man Nor Woman: The Hijras of India *(1988), Nanda explains that the hijras
are Indians with a particular gender and social role. They may be born as men or as hermaphrodites. If men, they may as they mature come to feel themselves impotent with women.
If hermaphrodites, they may be raised as women; and their identity as hijras may be discovered
only when they prove to be incapable of menstruating. However they may be born or raised,
they typically undergo a surgical "emasculation," as she terms it, after joining the hijra community, and they dress as women. Nanda says that the hijras, though often objects of abuse
and ridicule, are also granted special powers in Indian society; and she argues that Indians
more than Westerners find meaningfulness in what she calls "in-between" categories such as
transvestism and transgenderism. Serena Nanda is professor of Anthropology at John Jay College
of Criminal Justice, City University of New York.*

In the time of the Ramayana, Ram fought with the demon Ravenna and went to Sri
Lanka to bring his wife, Sita, back to India. Before this, his father commanded Ram
to leave Ayodhya [his native city] and go into the forest for 14 years. As he went,
the whole city followed him because they loved him so. As Ram came to the banks
of the river at the edge of the forest, he turned to the people and said, "Ladies and
gents, please wipe your tears and go away." But those people who were not men and
not women did not know what to do. So they stayed there because Ram did not ask
them to go. They remained there 14 years and when Ram returned from Lanka he
found those people there, all meditating. And so they were blessed by Ram.

"And that is why we hijras are so respected in that part of India," added Gopi,
the hijra who told me this story. Gopi was about 40 years old, a Hindu from South
India who had just returned to the hijra household I was visiting in Bastipore. She had
recently spent several years telling fortunes outside a Hindu temple in another city and
was well versed in Hindu religious lore. The story she told me, in response to my
question, "What is a hijra?," expresses the most common view, held by both hijras and
people in the larger society, that the hijras are an alternative gender, neither men or
women. This story, and others like it, makes explicit both the cultural definition of this
role in India, and for many (though not all) hijras, it defines a personally experienced
gender identity as well.

The story is thus an origin myth, similar to those told by many Indian castes. Such
myths "explain" the caste's origin by linking the caste to Hindu deities, providing
religious sanction for its claimed place in Indian society. The many myths, such as the

one that opens this chapter, validate a positive identity for hijras by identifying their alternative gender role with deities and mythic figures of the Great Tradition of Hinduism.

The view of hijras as an alternative gender category is supported by linguistic evidence. The most widely used English translations of the word *hijra,* which is of Urdu origin, is either "eunuch" or "hermaphrodite" (intersexed). Both terms, as used in India, connote impotence—an inability to function in the male sexual role—and the word *hijra* primarily implies a physical defect impairing the male sexual function (Opler, 1960:507). In both cases the irregularity of the male genitalia is central to the definition: *Eunuch* refers to an emasculated male and *intersexed* to a person whose genitals are ambiguously male-like at birth. When this is discovered, the child, previously assigned to the male sex, would be recategorized as intersexed—as a hijra. Although historically in North India a linguistic distinction was made between "born hijras" (hermaphrodites) and "made hijras" (eunuchs) (Ibbetson et al., 1911:331), the term *hijra* as it is currently used collapses both of these categories.

Impotence is the force behind both the words *eunuch* and *hermaphrodite* as they are used in India, and impotence is central to the definition of the hijra as not man. Some 19th-century accounts report that impotence was an essential qualification for admission into the hijra community and that a newcomer initiated into the community was on probation for as long as a year. During this time his impotence was carefully tested, sometimes by making the person sleep four nights with a prostitute.[1] Only after impotence was established would the newcomer be permitted to undergo the emasculation operation and become a full member of the community (Bhimbhai, 1901:506). Another 19th-century account of the hijras also reports that "all state that they were incapable of copulation and that becoming [hijras] was on that account only" (Preston, 1987:375).

While in South India, where hijras do not have the cultural role that they do in North India, the terms used for hijra, such as *kojja* in Telegu (Anderson, 1977) or *pottai* in Tamil, are epithets that connote a derogatory meaning of a cowardly or feminine male, the term *hijra* itself is rarely used this way. Nor does hijra mean homosexual; I have never heard it given that English translation. Because it is widely believed in India that a man may become impotent through engaging in homosexual relations in the receiver role in anal intercourse, passive homosexuals who become impotent may identify themselves as hijras, not because they have sexual relations with men, but because they are impotent.

In parts of North India, effeminate males who are assumed to play the passive role in homosexual relationships are referred to as zenana (Ibbetson et al., 1911:332), literally meaning woman: By becoming a hijra, one removes oneself from this category (see Lynton and Rajan, 1974). Zenana are said to think of themselves in the male gender, generally wear male clothing, and sometimes may be married and have children. Some zenana may live with hijras (Ranade, 1983) and perform with them, but they are not "real" hijras (Sinha, 1967). Although hijras assert that such men are "fake" hijras, merely "men who impersonate hijras," some zenana do go through the formal initiation into the hijra community. Whereas hijras are sometimes cited in the literature as transvestites (Kakar, 1981:35) or transvestite prostitutes (Freeman, 1979), it is clear, as we will see, that the role refers to much more than a man who dresses in women's clothing.

Hijras as "Not Men"

We go into the house of all, and never has a eunuch looked upon a woman with a bad eye; we are like bullocks [castrated male cattle].

As indicated by this quote (Ibbetson et al., 1911:331), the view of hijras as an "in-between" gender begins with their being men who are impotent, therefore not men, or as Wendy O'Flaherty aptly puts it, "As eunuchs, hijras are man minus man" (1980:297). But being impotent is only a necessary and not sufficient condition for being a hijra. Hijras are men who are impotent for one reason or another and only become hijras by having their genitals cut off. Emasculation is the *dharm* (religious obligation) of the hijras, and it is this renunciation of male sexuality through the surgical removal of the organ of male sexuality that is at the heart of the definition of the hijra social identity. This understanding is true for both hijras and their audiences.

That the core meaning of the hijra role centers on the aberrant male genitals was brought home to me many times by hijras, who in response to my question, "What is a hijra?," would offer to show me their ambiguous or mutilated genitals. In some cases, a hijra I was talking with would jump to her feet, lift up her skirt, and, displaying her altered genitals, would say, "See, we are neither men nor women!"

Hijras' expressions of what they are often take the form of stating that they are in-between, neither men nor women, but the term *hijra* itself is a masculine noun suggesting, as does the word *eunuch,* a man that is less than a perfect man. In fact, however, several hijras I met were raised from birth as females; only as they failed to develop secondary female sexual characteristics (breast development and menarche) at puberty, did they change their gender role to hijra (see also Anderson, 1977; Mehta, 1947).[2] Indeed, hijras claim that one of their founders was "a woman, but not a normal woman, she did not menstruate," a point about which I shall have more to say later.

The primary cultural definition of hijras, however, is that they begin life as men, albeit incomplete men; this is consistent with my observations that those hijras who exclaim that they are neither man nor woman always begin with an explanation of how they are *not men.*

The hijra view of themselves as "not men" as it occurred in my conversations with them focused primarily on their anatomy—the imperfection or absence of a penis—but also implicated their physiology and their sexual capacities, feelings, and preferences. These definitions incorporated both the ascribed status of "being born this way" and the achieved status of renouncing sexual desire and sexual activity.

Lakshmi, a beautiful young hijra dancer, who had undergone the emasculation operation a year before I met her, said, "I was born a man, but not a perfect man." Neelam, a transvestite homosexual who had not yet had the emasculation operation, told me, "I was born a man, but my male organ did not work properly so I became a hijra." Shabnam, a hijra elder who now only wears women's clothing, showed me some photographs of her youth. Pointing to one in which she appears dressed as a man, with a mustache, she said, most casually, "See, that is when I was a boy. In those days I lived and worked for a Christian family." Sonya, a middle-aged hijra who had not had the emasculation operation and who looked very masculine, but who otherwise had adopted all of the clothing and gestures of a woman, explained, "We are not like men, we do not have the sexual desires men have." Krishna, a slim young man who mainly dressed in men's clothes, except for important hijra social occasions, when he put on female attire, said, "We are not men with the ordinary desires of men to get married and have families. Otherwise, why would we choose to live this life?" Bellama, a hijra elder, told me, "We hijra are like sannyasis (ascetics), we have renounced all sexual desire and family life."

But Kamladevi, a hijra prostitute, is skeptical: "Of course we have the sexual desires," she said. "Older hijras like Bellama and Gopi, now they say they don't have the sexual desires and all, they have become very religious minded and don't do all that.

But when they were young, I can tell you, they were just like me. We hijras are born as boys, but then we 'get spoiled' and have sexual desires only for men."

Lalitha, a hijra whose sexual relationships with her "man" dominated her life, told me:

> See, we are all men, born as men, but when we look at women, we don't have any desire for them. When we see men, we like them, we feel shy, we feel some excitement. We want to live and die as women. We have the same feelings you have, Serena, just as you women fall in love and are ready to sacrifice your life for a man, so we are also like that. Just like you, whenever a man touches us, we get an excitement out of it.

Shakuntala is a hijra who had once been a dancer and a prostitute, but who now has a husband and only does domestic chores for a hijra household. She had the emasculation operation in 1978, 3 years prior to my meeting her. One day, as we were talking about what a hijra is, she burst out in anger:

> In many places men who are perfect men have joined this community only for the sake of earning a living. This is not good. Only men who have not spoiled any lady or got any children should come into the hijra company. You should not have had any affairs with ladies, not have loved ladies, or done any sexual thing with them or have married a lady. We true hijras are like this from childhood. From a small age we like to dance and dress as women. Even when we go away from this world, in our death, we must wear the sari. That is our desire.

If hijras, as eunuchs, are man minus maleness, they are also, in their outward appearance and behavior, man plus woman.[3] The most obvious expression of hijras as women is in their dress. Although some hijras do wear male clothing—sometimes because they work outside their traditional occupations or for other reasons—wearing female attire is an essential and defining characteristic of the hijra. It is absolutely required for their performances, when asking for alms, and when they visit the temple of their goddess Bahuchara. Hijra prostitutes also invariably wear women's clothes. This clothing may follow the custom of the region: In South India, hijras wear saris, whereas in North India they may wear *salwar-kameez* (the loose shirt and pants worn by women in North India) or even Western fashions. All hijras who dress in women's clothes wear a bra, which may be padded or, more likely, stuffed, as padded bras are expensive; sometimes it just is there, empty, on the flat male chest.

Hijras enjoy dressing in women's clothing, and their female dress is typically accompanied by traditionally feminine jewelry, such as wrist bangles, nose rings, and toe rings, as well as *bindi*—the colored dot applied to the forehead of all Hindu women who are not widows. Long hair is a must for a hijra. One of the punishments meted out by the elders to a hijra who has misbehaved is to cut her hair. This is considered a disgrace and an insult; even hijras who normally dress in men's clothing keep their hair long. Some wear it merely pulled back in a ponytail or tied up and covered with a male head covering; others wear it openly in a woman's hairstyle. Arjun, the hero of one of the two great Hindu epics, the Mahabharata, is required to live for 1 year as a eunuch, and he specifically refers to how he shall wear his hair like a woman and adorn himself with bangles. Hijras are forbidden to shave but rather must pluck out their facial hair so that their skin remains smooth like a woman's.[4]

Hijras also adopt female behavior: They imitate, even exaggerate, a woman's "swaying walk," sit and stand like women, and carry pots on their hips, which men do not. But hijras may engage in male occupations: One hijra I knew delivered milk on a bicycle and another was an electrician; some work on construction, which in India is a woman's as well as a man's job. Nevertheless, most hijras who work outside traditional hijra occupations take jobs that are generally held by both men and women, for example, as household servants and cooks.

Hijras also take female names when they join the community, and they use female kinship terms for each other, such as "sister," "aunty," and "grandmother" (mother's mother).[5] In some parts of India they also have a special, feminized language, which consists of the use of feminine expressions and intonations (Freeman, 1979:295). In public transport or other public accommodations, hijras request "ladies only" seating, and they periodically demand to be counted as females in the census.

Hijras As "Not Women"

If hijras are clearly not men by virtue of anatomy, appearance, and psychology, they are also not women, though they are "like" women. Their female dress and mannerisms are often exaggerations, almost to the point of caricature, and they act in sexually suggestive ways that would be considered inappropriate, and even outrageous, for ordinary women in their significant and traditional female roles as daughters, wives, and mothers. Hijra performances are most often burlesques of female behavior, and much of the fun of the performance derives from the incongruities between their behavior and that of women of the larger society whom they pretend to imitate. Their very act of dancing in public is contrary to what ordinary women would do. They also use coarse and abusive speech and gestures, again in opposition to the Hindu ideal of demure and restrained femininity. The act of a hijra who lifts up her skirt and exposes her mutilated genitals is considered shameless and thoroughly unfeminine. In Gujarat, an important center of hijra culture, hijras smoke the *hookah* (water pipe), which is normally done only by men; and in Panjab, hijras are noted for smoking cigarettes, which is ordinarily done only by men. Although some emasculated hijras do experience bodily feminization, for example, in the rounding of the hips, hijras who have not been emasculated may retain a heavy male facial structure and body muscularity and facial hair (Rao, 1955).

The "not woman" aspect of the hijra role is attested to by 18th-century reports which note that hijras were required by native governments to distinguish themselves by wearing a man's turban with their female clothing. A century later hijras were also noted to wear "a medley of male and female clothing," in this case wearing the female sari under the male coatlike outer garment (Preston, 1987:373). However, today, this mixture of clothing is not required, and hijras who wear any female clothing at all wear completely female attire.

As I suggested, it is the absence of menstruation that is the most important signal that a person who has been assigned to the female sex at birth and raised as a female, is a hijra. This sign—the absence of the onset of a female's reproductive ability—points to the essential criterion of the feminine gender that hijras themselves make explicit: They do not have female reproductive organs, and because they cannot have children they cannot be considered real women.

To help me understand this, a hijra told me this story:

> See, two people got into a fight, a man and a hijra. The hijra said, "I am a lady," and the man said, "No, you are not." The fight went so long that they went to the magistrate. The magistrate said, "I agree, you look like a woman, you act like a woman, but I'll ask you a simple question—can you give birth to a baby? If that is not possible, then you don't win." The hijra answered, no, she could not give birth to a baby, so the magistrate said, "You are only a hijra, you are not a woman."

The hijras I was sitting with nodded vigorously in assent to the tale's conclusion. This story was immediately followed by another, which is further testimony to the hijra view of themselves as "not women," at least not real women:

> In Ajmer, in North India, there is a holy place that belongs to the hijras. It is called Baba Darga, and it is on top of a hill. One time, during Urs [a Muslim festival], many people were going up the hill to pay respects to Baba. One hijra was also there. She saw a lady with four children and offered to carry one or two of them. The lady became very angry and told the hijra, "You are a hijra, so don't touch my children."
>
> This made the hijra feel very sad, so she asked Baba for his blessings for a child of her own. But she only asked for a child and didn't ask Baba to bring the child out. The pregnancy went on for ten months, and her stomach became very bloated. She went to the doctors but they didn't want to perform an operation [Caesarean section] on her. Eventually she couldn't stand the weight any longer so she prayed to the Baba to redeem her from this situation. But Baba could only grant her the boon, he could not reverse it.
>
> When the hijra felt she could stand it no more, she found a sword at the *darga* [Muslim shrine] and slit herself open. She removed the child and placed in on the ground. The child died and the hijra also died. Now at this darga prayers are performed to this hijra and the child and then to the Baba.

This story reveals an ambivalence: On the one hand, it expresses the wish of some hijras to have a child, yet on the other hand acknowledges its impossibility. The death of the hijra and the child suggests that hijras cannot become women—in the most fundamental sense of being able to bear a child—and that they are courting disaster to attempt something so contrary to their nature. Meera, the hijra who told me this story, was convinced it was true. She had many times expressed to me her wish for a child and said that she had read in a magazine that in America doctors would help people like her have babies. The other hijras sitting with us laughed at this suggestion.[6]

Alternative Genders in Indian Culture and Society

The hijra role is a magnet that attracts people with many different kinds of cross-gender identities, attributes, and behaviors—people whom we in the West would differentiate as eunuchs, homosexuals, transsexuals, hermaphrodites, and transvestites. Such individuals, of course, exist in our own and perhaps all societies. What is noteworthy about the hijras is that the role is so deeply rooted in Indian culture that it can accommodate a wide variety of temperaments, personalities, sexual needs, gender identities, cross-gender behaviors, and levels of commitment without losing its cultural meaning. The ability of the hijra role to succeed as a symbolic reference point giving significant meaning to the lives of the many different kinds of people who make up the hijra community, is undoubtedly related to the variety and significance of alternative gender roles and gender transformations in Indian mythology and traditional culture.

Whereas Westerners feel uncomfortable with the ambiguities and contradictions inherent in such in-between categories as transvestism, homosexuality, hermaphroditism, and transgenderism, and make strenuous attempts to resolve them, Hinduism not only accommodates such ambiguities, but also views them as meaningful and even powerful.

In Hindu mythology, ritual, and art—important vehicles for transmitting the Hindu world view—the power of the combined man/woman is a frequent and significant theme. Indian mythology contains numerous examples of androgynes, impersonators of the opposite sex, and individuals who undergo sex changes, both among deities and humans. These mythical figures are well known as part of Indian popular culture, which helps explain the ability of the hijras to maintain a meaningful place for themselves within Indian society in an institutionalized third gender role.

One of the most important sexually ambivalent figures in Hinduism with whom hijras identify is Shiva, a deity who incorporates both male and female characteristics.[7] Shiva is an ascetic—one who renounces sex—and yet he appears in many erotic and procreative roles. His most powerful symbol and object of worship is the phallus—but the phallus is almost always set in the *yoni,* the symbol of the female genitals. One of the most popular forms of Shiva is that of *Ardhanarisvara,* or half-man/half-woman, which represents Shiva united with his shakti (female creative power). Hijras say that worshipers of Shiva give them special respect because of this close identification, and hijras often worship at Shiva temples.

Other deities also take on sexually ambiguous or dual gender manifestations. Vishnu and Krishna (an *avatar,* or incarnation, of Vishnu) are sometimes pictured in androgynous ways. In one myth, Vishnu transforms himself into Mohini, the most beautiful woman in the world, in order to take back the sacred nectar from the demons who have stolen it. In another well-known myth, Krishna takes on the form of a female to destroy a demon called Araka. Araka's strength came from his chasteness. He had never set eyes on a woman, so Krishna took on the form of a beautiful woman and married him. After 3 days of the marriage, there was a battle and Krishna killed the demon. He then revealed himself to the other gods in his true form. Hijras, when they tell this story, say that when Krishna revealed himself he told the other gods that "there will be more like me, neither man nor woman, and whatever words come from the mouths of these people, whether good [blessings] or bad [curses], will come true."

In Tamil Nadu, in South India, an important festival takes place in which hijras, identifying with Krishna, become wives, and then widows, of the male deity Koothandavar. The story behind this festival is that there were once two warring kingdoms. To avert defeat, one of the kings agreed to sacrifice his eldest son to the gods, asking only that he first be allowed to arrange his son's marriage. Because no woman could be found who would marry a man about to be sacrificed, Krishna came to earth as a woman to marry the king's son, and the king won the battle as the gods promised.

For this festival, men who have made vows to Koothandavar dress as women and go through a marriage ceremony with him. The priest performs the marriage, tying on the traditional wedding necklace. After 1 day, the deity is carried to a burial ground. There, all of those who have "married" him remove their wedding necklaces, cry and beat their breasts, and remove the flowers from their hair, as a widow does in mourning for her husband. Hijras participate by the thousands in this festival, coming from all over India. They dress in their best clothes and jewelry and ritually reaffirm their identification with Krishna, who changes his form from male to female.

Several esoteric Hindu ritual practices involve male transvestism as a form of devotion. Among the Sakhibhava (a sect that worships Vishnu) Krishna may not be worshiped directly. The devotees in this sect worship Radha, Krishna's beloved, with the aim of becoming her attendant: It is through her, as Krishna's consort, that Krishna is indirectly worshiped. The male devotees imitate feminine behavior, including simulated menstruation; they also may engage in sexual acts with men as acts of devotion, and some devotees even castrate themselves in order to more nearly approximate a female identification with Radha (Bullough, 1976:267–268; Kakar, 1981; Spratt, 1966:315).

Hinduism in general holds that all persons contain within themselves both male and female principles. In the Tantric school of Hinduism, the Supreme Being is conceptualized as one complete sex containing male and female sexual organs. Hermaphroditism is the ideal. In some of these sects, male (never female) transvestism is used as a way of transcending one's own sex, a prerequisite to achieving salvation. In other Tantric sects, religious exercises involve the male devotee imitating a woman in order to realize the woman in himself: Only in this way do they believe that true love can be realized (Bullough, 1976:260).

Traditional Hinduism makes many specific references to alternative sexes and sexual ambiguity among humans as well as among gods. Ancient Hinduism, for example, taught that there was a third sex, which itself was divided into four categories: the male eunuch, called the "waterless" because he had desiccated testes; the "testicle voided," so called because he had been castrated; the hermaphrodite; and the "not woman," or female eunuch (which usually refers to a woman who does not menstruate). Those who were more feminine (whether males or females) wore false breasts and imitated the voice, gestures, dress, delicacy, and timidity of women (Bullough, 1976:268). All of these categories of persons had the function of providing alternative techniques of sexual gratification, some of which are mentioned in the classical Hindu sex manual, the *Kamasutra.*

Another ancient reference to a third sex, one that sounds similar to the hijras, is a prostitute named Sukumarika ("good little girl"), who appears in a Sanskrit play. Sukumarika is accused of being sexually insatiable. As a third sex, she has some characteristics advantageous in her profession: "She has no breasts to get in the way of a tight embrace, no monthly period to interrupt the enjoyment of passion, and no pregnancy to mar her beauty" (O'Flaherty, 1980:299).

As just suggested, ancient Hindus, like contemporary ones, appeared to be ambivalent about such third gender roles and the associated alternative sexual practices. The figure of Sukumarika, for example, was considered inauspicious to look upon and, not coincidentally, similar to the hijras today, inspired both fear and mockery. Historically, both eunuchism and castration were looked down on in ancient India, and armed women and old men were preferred to eunuchs for guarding court ladies (Basham, 1954:172). Whereas homosexuality was generally not highly regarded in ancient India, such classic texts as the *Kamasutra,* however, did describe, even prescribe, sexual practices for eunuchs, for example, "mouth congress."[8]

Homosexuality was condemned in the ancient lawbooks. *The Laws of Manu,* the first formulation of the Hindu moral code, held that men who engaged in anal sex lost their caste. Other medieval writers held that men who engaged in oral sex with other men were reborn impotent. But homosexuals were apparently tolerated in reality. Consistent with the generally "sex positive" attitude of Hinduism, Vatsyayana, author of the *Kamasutra,* responded to critics of oral and anal sex by saying that "in all things connected with love, everybody should act according to the custom of his country, and his own inclination," asking a man to consider only whether the act "is agreeable to his nature and himself" (Burton, 1964:127).

Even the gods were implicated in such activities: Krishna's son Samba was notorious for his homosexuality and dressed as female, often a pregnant woman. As Sambali, Samba's name became a synonym for eunuch (Bullough, 1976:267). An important ritual at the Jagannatha temple in Orissa involves a sequence in which Balabhadra, the ascetic elder brother of the deity Jagannatha, who is identified with Shiva, is homosexually seduced by a transvestite (a young man dressed as a female temple dancer) (Marglin, 1985:53). In some Hindu myths a male deity takes on a female form specifically to experience sexual relations with another male deity.

Islam also provides a model of an in-between gender—not a mythological one, but a true historical figure—in the traditional role of the eunuch who guarded the ladies of the harem, under Moghul rule. Hijras often mention this role as the source of their prestige in Indian society. In spite of the clear connection of hijras with Hinduism, Islam not only provides a powerful positive model of an alternative gender, but also contributes many elements to the social organization of the hijra community. Hijras today make many references to the glorious, pre-independence Indian past when the Muslim rulers of princely states were exceedingly generous and renowned for their patronage of the hijras (see Lynton and Rajan, 1974).

Today the religious role of the hijras, derived from Hinduism, and the historical role of the eunuchs in the Muslim courts have become inextricably entwined in spite of the differences between them. Hijras are distinguished from the eunuchs in Muslim courts by their transvestism and their association with men. Muslim eunuchs dressed as males and associated with women and, unlike the hijras, were sexually inactive. More importantly, the role of hijras as ritual performers is linked to their sexual ambiguity as this incorporates the elements of the erotic and the ascetic; Muslim eunuchs had no such powers or roles. Today, the collapsing of the role of the hijra and that of the Muslim eunuchs leads to certain contradictions, but these seem easily incorporated into the hijra culture by hijras themselves; only the Western observer seems to feel the need to separate them conceptually.

The hijras, as human beings who are neither man nor woman, call into question the basic social categories of gender on which Indian society is built. This makes the hijras objects of fear, abuse, ridicule, and sometimes pity. But hijras are not merely ordinary human beings: they are also conceptualized as special, sacred beings, through a ritual transformation. The many examples that I have cited above indicate that both Indian society and Hindu mythology provide some positive, or at least accommodating, roles for such sexually ambiguous figures. Within the context of Indian social roles, sexually ambiguous figures are associated with sexual specializations; in myth and through ritual, such figures become powerful symbols of the divine and of generativity.

Thus, where Western culture strenuously attempts to resolve sexual contradictions and ambiguities, by denial or segregation, Hinduism appears content to allow opposites to confront each other without resolution, "celebrating the idea that the universe is boundlessly various, and . . . that all possibilities may exist without excluding each other" (O'Flaherty, 1973:318). It is this characteristically Indian ability to tolerate, even embrace, contradictions and variation at the social, cultural, and personality levels that provides the context in which the hijras cannot only be accommodated, but even granted a measure of power.

NOTES

1. The theme of attempted seduction of ascetics by prostitutes, in order to test (and strengthen) their commitment to chastity, occurs frequently in Hindu mythology (see O'Flaherty, 1973:43).

2. Anderson (1977) had several interviews with a hijra who was brought up as a girl. She did menstruate, but at puberty a gynecological examination indicated that she had a rudimentary penis. As a result of this discovery, she joined the hijras. In a study of 18 hijras in North India, Pimpley and Sharma (1985:44) found 7 who claimed to have been brought up as females from birth.

3. In South India there is a role similar to the hijra, which is called *jogappa*. The jogappas are male temple servants of the goddess Yellamma. Hijras in South India, who are familiar with Yellamma, say that she is the sister of their own goddess, Bahucharaji. Nicholas Bradford does not describe the jogappas as "neither men nor women," but rather as "men who become women; or . . . more precisely, ordinary men who have become sacred female men" (1983:311). Jogappas are similar in some ways to hijras: They wear female dress, take female names, wear their hair

long in a woman's style, engage in bawdy bantering and flirting with men in public "on pretext of demanding alms," and perform at auspicious life-cycle ceremonies such as marriage and after the birth of a male child. While impotence is one of the symptoms by which a man knows he has been "caught" by Yellamma, sexual identity problems are not normally mentioned by jogappas as part of their recruitment to the cult. Unlike hijras, jogappas do not get emasculated and are never called eunuchs or referred to as such. Though Bradford says that jogappas are "invariably homosexuals," he believes that they do not become involved with ordinary men as male prostitutes. Like hijras, jogappas are viewed as vehicles of the power of their goddess, and attitudes toward them include both fear and respect.

4. According to Bradford, jogappas never shave, but rather use a special instrument for plucking out their facial hair. Jogappas say that if they were to shave, they would break out in skin diseases with which the goddess Yellamma afflicts people who displease her (1983:311).

5. There is some inconsistency in historical sources on this point. Ibbetson, MacLagen, and Rose (1911:331) say that hijras "affect the names of men," but most sources—for example, Faridi (1899), Bhimbhai (1901), and Preston (1987)—say that hijras take women's names. Most hijras I met had female names, but some did keep male names, for example, Raj Dev, an important hijra elder in Bastipore.

6. But Wendy O'Flaherty cites the following from an unidentified newspaper headline: "In California, recently, a man who underwent a sex-change operation was able to become pregnant and then took hormone injections so that he could breast-feed the baby" (1980:298). I'm not sure if Meera was referring to this incident or not.

7. The Hindu Triad, or Trinity, is made up of Brahma, the creator; Vishnu, the preserver (protector and sustainer of the world); and Shiva, the destroyer. Brahma is the Supreme Being and the creator of all creatures. Vishnu is believed to descend into the world in many different forms (avataras, or incarnations) and is worshiped throughout India. One of Vishnu's incarnations is Ram. Krishna is sometimes considered an aspect or incarnation of Vishnu, but more commonly is worshiped as a god in his own right. Shiva is the god of destruction or absorption, but he also creates and sustains life. In addition to the Triad, Hinduism includes a large number of deities, both male and female, all of whom are aspects of the Absolute. This concept of the Absolute Reality also includes matter and finite spirits as its integral parts; the divine spirit is embodied in the self and the world, as well as in more specifically religious figures. The religious concepts of Hinduism are expressed in the two great Hindu epics, the Mahabharata and the Ramayana, both of which are familiar to every Hindu and many nonHindus as well. These epics, along with other chronicles of the gods and goddesses, are frequently enacted in all forms of popular and elite culture. Thus, for the hijras, particularly the Hindu hijras, the incorporation of these divine models of behavior into their own world view and community image is in no way unusual.

8. In an editor's note, Burton (1962:124) suggests that this practice is no longer common in India and has been replaced by sodomy, which was introduced after the Muslim period began in the 10th century. Meera, a hijra elder, specifically says that oral sex is "not a good thing and goes against the wishes of the hijra goddess" and that it brings all kinds of problems for those who practice it.

REFERENCES

Anderson, Christopher. 1977. *Gay Men in India*. Unpublished manuscript. University of Wisconsin, Madison.

Bhimbhai, K. 1901. *Pavayas* in Gujarat Population, Hindus. In J.M. Campbell (Compiler), *Gazetteer of the Bombay Presidency* (vol. 9, pt. 1, pp. 586–588). Bombay: Government Central Press.

Bradford, Nicholas J. 1983. Transgenderism and the Cult of Yellamma: Heat, Sex, and Sickness in South Indian Ritual. *Journal of Anthropological Research, 39*(3), 307–322.

Burton, R.F. (Trans.). 1964. *The Kama Sutra of Vatsyayana*. New York: E.P. Dutton.

Ibbetson, D.C.J., MacLagen, M.E., and Rose, H.A. 1911. *A Glossary of the Tribes and Castes of the Panjab and North-West Frontier Province* (vol. II, pp. 331–333). Lahore, Pakistan: Civil and Military Gazette Press.

O'Flaherty, Wendy Doniger. 1973. *Siva: The Erotic Ascetic.* New York: Oxford University Press.

Pimpley, P.N., and Sharma, S.K. 1985. Hijaras: A Study of an Atypical Role. *Avadh Journal of Social Sciences (India), 2,* 42–50.

Preston, Laurence W. 1987. A Right to Exist: Eunuchs and the State in Nineteenth-Century India. *Modern Asian Studies, 21*(2), 371–387.

36

Tearooms and Sympathy, or, The Epistemology of the Water Closet

LEE EDELMAN

Lee Edelman, Associate Professor of English at Tufts University, is a literary and cultural critic whose work distinctively combines gay theory with the critical approach known as deconstruction and with Jacques Lacan's brand of psychoanalysis. He has written gay-inflected essays on American poetry, critical theory, and film, as well as two books, Transmemberment of Song: Hart Crane's Anatomies of Rhetoric and Desire *(1987) and* Homographesis: Essays in Gay Literary and Cultural Theory *(1993). In "Tearooms and Sympathy," Edelman examines a 1964 Washington D.C. sex scandal for the way it illuminates the intersection of sexual, national, political, and bodily anxieties in the male culture of Cold War America. Specifically, Edelman analyzes the crisis of homosexual representation provoked by the scandal and by the simultaneous but contradictory impulses to which it gave rise—namely, an impulse to insist on the legibility of the gay male body, on the ease with which gay men can be recognized by straight society, and an impulse to resist representing gay sexuality as anything but an invisible, ubiquitous, and threatening possibility in all men. The paranoid tendency to construct the gay man on the analogy of the Communist, as a kind of internal émigré, springs at least in part, according to Edelman's analysis, from heterosexual men's repressed awareness of their own anatomical vulnerability to penetration—a repression that produces the strategies of denial and displacement embodied not only in media portrayals of homosexuality but in the physical articulation of public space in the men's room itself and, ultimately, in the psychic and social structures of male heterosexism and homophobia.*

On October 16, 1964, a correspondent for the *Times* of London made the following observation about the intertwining of sexuality and nationalistic ideology in the United States: "In the post war political primer for beginners perversion is synonymous with treason. A surviving McCarthyism is that homosexuality and other sexual aberrations are both dangerous to the national security and rife in Washington."[1] These remarks were prompted by the disclosure, less than three weeks before America's Presidential election, that Walter Jenkins, Lyndon Johnson's chief of staff, had been arrested with another man (identified, significantly, as "Hungarian-born") and charged with performing "indecent gestures" in a basement restroom of the Y.M.C.A. two blocks from Jenkins's office in the White House. This arrest, which Laud Humphreys would later characterize as "perhaps the most famous tearoom arrest in America,"[2] precipitated the furor of a political scandal, one that some thought capable of swaying the election, when it was learned that Jenkins had not only been arrested in the very same men's room five years earlier—leaving him with a police record on which had been marked: "disorderly conduct (pervert)"—but that this prior arrest had escaped detection by both the White House and the F.B.I. Jenkins, therefore, had had access to a variety of classified materials, including documents that were submitted to the National Security Council, and he had been granted the top-secret "Q" clearance from the Atomic Energy Commission.

The paranoid logic that echoed throughout the clamor provoked by these revelations found canonical expression in a column written by Arthur Krock for the *New York Times*. After sympathizing with Jenkins and his family, and asserting with self-congratulatory satisfaction that "sympathy in such circumstances is a foremost trait of the American people," Krock went on to admonish his readers: "But it would be irresponsible if the American people felt no anxiety over the fact . . . that a Government official to whom the most secret operations of national security were accessible . . . is among those unfortunates who are most readily subject to the blackmail by which security secrets are often obtained by enemy agents."[3] For this reason—and because, as the editor of the *New York Times* observed, "sexual perversion," like alcoholism and drug addiction, "is increasingly understood as an emotional illness"—America's paper of record, the public voice of "liberal" sentiment, editorialized in support of the anti-gay policies that had informed the federal government's hiring practices for over a decade: "there can be no place on the White House staff or in the upper echelons of government," the *Times* declared, "for a person of markedly deviant behavior."[4]

For several days the Jenkins affair earned front-page attention in newspapers throughout the country before being dislodged by events that seemed more immediately to threaten the nation's well-being: events such as the overthrow of Khrushchev in Russia and China's first explosion of a nuclear device. Aspects of the Jenkins case resurfaced in news reports during the weeks leading up to the election, but the political ramifications of the scandal were largely contained within ten days of the initial revelations. As soon as the story broke (and it did so despite efforts by Clark Clifford and Abe Fortas to persuade Washington editors to suppress it) Jenkins resigned as special assistant to the President; said to be suffering from "high blood pressure and nervous exhaustion,"[5] he was admitted to George Washington University Hospital where his room was kept under twenty-four-hour surveillance. On October 14, the day Jenkins resigned, President Johnson ordered the F.B.I. to "make an immediate and comprehensive inquiry"[6] into the affair. The document generated by that investigation, released on October 22 and consisting of some 100 pages of text under the chillingly broad and encompassing title "Report on Walter Wilson Jenkins,"[7] reassuringly offered its official conclusion that Jenkins at no time had "compromised the security or interests of the United States."[8]

In the process, however, the report inadvertently offered tantalizing insights into the discursive contexts within which it was possible in 1964 to conceptualize both homosexual activity and the susceptibility to participation in such activity of men not overtly homosexually identified: Jenkins himself, after all, had been married for some nineteen years at the time of the scandal and was the father of six children. According to Victor Lasky, President Johnson personally insisted that the final report "state that Jenkins was overly tired, that he was a good family man and a hard worker, and that he was not 'biologically' a homosexual."[9] Consequently, even though the incident in 1964 involved Jenkins's arrest for a second time in a men's room that *Time* magazine would describe as "a notorious hangout for deviates,"[10] and even though Jenkins acknowledged to the F.B.I. that he had had "limited association with some individuals who are alleged to be, or who admittedly are, sex deviates,"[11] and even though he admitted his participation in "the indecent acts for which he was arrested in 1959 and 1964," and even though he severely qualified his denial of participation in other homosexual encounters by saying that "he did not recall any further indecent acts" and that "if he had been involved in any such acts he would have been under the influence of alcohol and in a state of fatigue and would not remember them,"[12] despite all of this it was possible for the F.B.I. to reinforce the rationale for Jenkins's sexual behavior as publicly set forth by the White House: Jenkins had been suffering from high blood pressure, nervous tension, and physical exhaustion as a result of being severely overworked.[13] As Lady Bird Johnson expressed this notion in one of the earliest official responses to the scandal: "My heart is aching for someone who has reached the endpoint of exhaustion in dedicated service to his country."[14]

Though I will return to this framing, in every way *political,* of the interpretive context within which, according to the White House and the F.B.I., Walter Jenkins's homosexual encounters were properly to be construed, my interest here extends beyond the specific events that followed from the public disclosure of his arrests. I want in this essay to consider three apparently heterogenous pieces of information, each related in some way to the Jenkins affair, and then see what sort of analysis they permit of the interpenetration of nationalism and sexuality, or rather, of nationalism and the figurations of sexuality—and, in particular, the figurations of homosexuality—in dominant cultural expression at that historical moment in America. For insofar as it marked a turning point in the formulation of nationalistic ideology in the United States—insofar, that is, as it signaled the end of what Michael Rogin has called the "cold war consensus"[15] and initiated the period of national redefinition provoked by the emergence of a sizeable middle-class culture of opposition that would crystallize around the incipient anti-war movement—1964 constitutes a signal moment in which to examine the shifting ideological frameworks within which homosexuality could be read in relation to American national identity.

I would begin, then, by calling attention to the fact that Jenkins was apprehended in 1964 by two members of the District of Columbia vice squad who had placed the restroom of Washington's G-Street "Y" under surveillance on the evening of October 7 by concealing themselves behind the padlocked door of a shower room no longer in use. *Time* magazine explained the mechanics of the policemen's stake-out in the following terms: "They ... stationed themselves at two peepholes in the door that gave them a view of the washroom and enabled them to peep over the toilet partitions. (There are two peepholes in this and several other washrooms in the area because two corroborating officers are required in such cases)."[16] Let me place a second item beside this description of the State's operations in the public men's rooms of our nation's capitol: this one a statement made six months earlier, in May of 1964, by Senator Barry Goldwater as he set his sights on the White House. Responding to national anxiety about America's technological prowess—an anxiety that had dominated our forays into space since the Soviet triumph with the Sputnik satellite in 1957—Goldwater, implicitly acknowledging the connection between space exploration and the military development of missile and weapons technology, declared with characteristic immoderation: "I don't want to hit the moon. I want to lob one into the men's room of the Kremlin and make sure I hit it."[17] Finally, I would adduce one further item for consideration as a cultural text: the words with which Lyndon Johnson, in a televised comment, expressed his reaction to the discovery that his oldest and closest advisor and friend had been arrested for engaging in homosexual activities in the restroom of the Y.M.C.A.: "I was shocked," he said, "as if someone had told me my wife had murdered her daughter."[18]

In order to sketch some relationship among these fragments of the historical record, I want to consider another event that took place in 1964; for *Life* magazine, in June of that year, entered thousands of middle-class homes across the country with a photo-essay offering a spectacular view of what it called the "secret world" of "Homosexuality in America."[19] In thus breaking new ground for a family-oriented, mass circulation American periodical—and in the process establishing the journalistic conditions that would enable *Time* magazine to present so explicit and sensational an account of the Jenkins affair—the editors of *Life* felt compelled to provide some contextualizing remarks that would justify their devotion of so much attention to what that they identified as a "sad and often sordid world" (66). The terms in which they framed that justification, presenting it in a sort of exculpatory preface to the two essays on homosexuality that followed, are worth considering here:

> . . . today, especially in big cities, homosexuals are discarding their furtive ways and openly admitting, even flaunting, their deviation. Homosexuals have their own drinking places, their special assignation streets, even their own organizations. And for every obvious homosexual, there are probably nine nearly impossible to detect. This social disorder, which society tries to suppress, has forced itself into the public eye because it does present a problem—and parents especially are concerned. The myth and misconception with which homosexuality has so long been clothed must be cleared away, not to condone it but to cope with it. (66)

The prurience with which the accompanying photographs produce the spectacle of the gay male body for consumption by an audience presumed to be heterosexual finds its warrant here in the editors' claim that nine out of ten homosexuals are "nearly impossible to detect." *Life,* therefore, undertakes to expose the gay male body as social "problem" by exposing the problem of seeing or recognizing the gay male body itself: a purpose tellingly figured in the editors' insistence upon "clear[ing] away" the obfuscating garb with which homosexuality has, in their words, "so long been clothed."[20] Whatever else this fantasy of an unclothed homosexuality may bespeak, it establishes a sociological rationale for the journalistic depiction of gay men, and in the process it draws attention to the physicality of their bodies, in terms of which the notion of a "homosexual difference" continues to be construed; for even that ninety percent of homosexuals whose sexuality is not immediately "obvious" are only, the preface informs us, "nearly" impossible to detect.[21] As the magazine later tells its readers, with the goal of making them *better* readers of homosexuality and homosexual signs: "Often the only signs are a very subtle tendency to over-meticulous grooming, plus the failure to cast the ordinary man's admiring glance at every pretty girl who walks by" (77). Thus a falseness in relation to the body, a disparity between the "truth" of gender as articulated by anatomy and the ways in which that gender is represented by the individual, can serve both to assist the heterosexual in the recognition of the gay body and to effect the cultural reification of "the homosexual" itself. That is, as a "secret" or unarticulated condition that demands journalistic scrutiny and exposure, homosexuality falls from the outset of the article under the aegis of inauthenticity and of a difference all the more subversive because simultaneously threatening ("parents especially are concerned") and potentially unidentifiable.

That this ability of most homosexuals to "pass" produces an extraordinary degree of interpretive anxiety for heterosexuals—and especially for heterosexual men—becomes clear in the first of the two essays in *Life* when its author, Paul Welch, recounts the way in which one gay executive enacts his deep-rooted "bitterness . . . toward the 'straight' public." Tellingly, the article contextualizes these remarks only by announcing in advance that the executive "has been under a psychiatrist's care":

> I have to make believe all day long. If we're out for lunch, I go through the same complimenting and flirting routine with girls that you "straight" fellows do. I have

to be constantly on my guard not to say or do something that will make them suspect I'm "gay."

At night I have to get out and forget it. I don't like to go to "gay" bars night after night; but I'll tell you what I do like to do. I like to go to "straight" bars, find some guy with a good-looking girl and take her away from him. I couldn't be less interested in the girl, but it's a way of getting even. (74)

Here, condensed into the narrative space of a single anecdote attributed only to an anonymous gay man, the article unfolds its reading of homosexuality as a threat not merely to the moral and spiritual well-being of those who happen to be gay, but more importantly, to the happiness of "innocent" heterosexual men and women as well. Trailing his familiar cloak of psychological maladaption and misogyny, the male homosexual, according to the cultural stereotype that this story puts into play, vengefully makes use of his ability to "pass" in order to frustrate the happy ending of a heterosexual romance. A dangerous spy in the house of love, his "perversity" consists not merely in the orientation of his sexuality, but in the fact that he takes less pleasure in the pursuit of his own desires ("I don't like to go to 'gay' bars night after night") than he does in sabotaging heterosexual couples in the act of pursuing theirs.

The anecdote thus reinforces the more common cultural interpretation of the way in which homosexuality threatens the security of heterosexual unions—an interpretation in which a married man, a man like Walter Jenkins, for example, betrays his spouse through a series of anonymous homosexual encounters. Such a scenario appears at the outset of Welch's article when he evokes the following as a representative vignette of homosexual life: "By Chicago's Bughouse Square, a small park near the city's fashionable Gold Coast on the North Side, a suburban husband drives his car slowly down the street, searching for a 'contact' with one of the homosexuals who drift around the square. A sergeant on Chicago's vice squad explains: 'These guys tell their wives they're just going to the corner for the evening paper. Why, they even come down here in their slippers!' " (68). The coziness of suburban domestic ritual, figurally evoked through the culturally freighted images of newspaper and slippers, loses its anticipated coherence as an index of intimacy and familiarity through the revelation of the husband's attraction to the homosexual "drift[ers]" who frequent the park. The very stability of family life, the solidity rooted in such material acquisitions as the house in the suburbs—the historical signifier of the actualization of the "American dream"—is called into question in the context of this anecdote by the disruptive and aimless circulation of men who "drift around the square" while they wait for what is presumed to be an impersonal and transient "contact." As in the subsequent account of the gay executive, moreover, this male-authored narrative protectively displaces its own masculinist concern that gay sexuality threatens metonymically to effeminize even heterosexual males, as it effeminizes the man who had the woman he was pursuing lured away from him by, of all things, a homosexual. Instead, it solicits the reader to sympathize with the plight of the (presumptively heterosexual) woman victimized by a gay man not recognized as such—a gay man who is liable not only to misrepresent himself as "straight" but even to violate the sanctity of the marital relation.[22]

If the article in this way displays an anxiety about the dangers that can result from the cultural invisibility enjoyed by homosexuals, it also reproduces the culture's inconsistent assumptions about the identification and recognition of gay men. The preface to the article insists, after all, that the vast majority of homosexuals are "nearly impossible to detect," and the article itself seeks to drive that point home by remarking of a group of "tough-looking" men gathered on a block just west of Times Square that "few of the passers-by recognize them as male hustlers." But the captions to the photographs that illustrate the essay—and that necessarily attempt to capture the elusive "homosexual difference" in visual terms—indicate a textual imperative to reassert the knowability of homosexual men by focusing on the markers or "signs" by which homosexuality can be discerned. The pictures, therefore, present images such as that of a tailor's mannequin wearing a flamboyant scarf and capped by an enormous—and enormously extravagant—hat while the caption explains to the uninitiate that "this New York Greenwich Village store which caters to homosexuals is filled with the colorful, off-beat, attention-calling clothes that the 'gay' world favors" (68). Just opposite this, the magazine offers a full-page photograph of two couples—one gay, one straight—passing each other on the street; this picture emblematizes, as the caption makes clear, the essay's insistence on the presentation of the gay male body as public spectacle: "Two fluffy-sweatered young men stroll in New York City, ignoring the stare of a 'straight' couple. Flagrant homosexuals are unabashed by reactions of shock, perplexity, disgust" (68).

Such representations of gay men as identifiably different thus coexist in the essay with avowals of the disturbing invisibility that homosexuals generally rely upon, and the tension of contradiction between these competing assertions produces a space for the discursive enterprise that I have designated as *homographesis*.[23] For the article seeks to posit homosexuality as a readable phenomenon while simultaneously accounting for the frequency with which it manages to escape detection; it undertakes to construct male homosexuality in terms of what the "public eye" can recognize even as it situates it in a perpetual ontological shuttle between sameness and difference. One contemporary strategy for representing this double aspect of "homosexual difference" appears in *The Sixth Man* (1961), Jess Stearn's best-selling account of homosexual life in America. In a passage that recapitulates some of the astonishment with which Proust's narrator of *Cities of the Plain* witnessed what he described as the "transformation of M. de Charlus," Stearn identifies the metamorphic duplicity not only of gay men but of the gay body as well:

> They have a different face for different occasions. In conversation with each other, they often undergo a subtle change. I have seen men who appeared to be normal suddenly smile roguishly, soften their voices, and simper as they greeted homosexual friends. . . . Many times I saw these changes occur after I had gained a homosexual's confidence and he could safely risk my disapproval. Once as I watched a luncheon companion become an effeminate caricature of himself, he apologized. "It is hard to always remember that one is a man."

As was the case with M. de Charlus, the visibility of homosexuality in this account registers the emergence of an "effeminate caricature" or distortion of male identity, and yet, as Stearn goes on to note, "effeminate features or mannerisms . . . do not necessarily signify homosexuality."[24]

This rhetorical gesture whereby homosexuality becomes discernible in cognitive relation to effeminacy even as the necessity of that association is itself put into question, finds its anticipated place in the discussion of homosexuality in *Life*, which simultaneously published a companion piece to its exposé of America's "gay world" in which it explored "scientific" perspectives on the etiology of homosexual orientation. Ernest Havemann (can this *not* be a pseudonym?), the author of the article (titled plaintively, "Why?"), may evoke the "loneliness" of homosexual life by comparing the lot of a middle-aged gay man to that of an "aging party girl in the other kind of society" (76), but he sets out nonetheless to correct "the mistaken notion, still held by many people, that all homosexuals have effeminate, 'swishy' manners and would like nothing better, if only they could get away with it, than to dress like women, pluck their eyebrows, and use lipstick." Virtually echoing Jess Stearn, he follows this full-bodied description of a widely held but "mistaken notion" with the rather flat assertion, "in actual fact, there are many effeminate men who are not homosexual at all" (77).

The recurrence of this topos, the necessary return to this moment of "scientific" disavowal in which male homosexuality and effeminacy are denied the essential connection that the author has already laboriously, even tendentiously, delineated, pinpoints the homographic imperative to resolve the vertiginous confusion of sameness and difference by reading the gay male body in relation to the (ostensibly) determinate, (ostensibly) visible difference between the sexes. Male homosexuality, in other words, must be conceptualized in terms of femaleness not only because the governing heterosexual mythology interprets gay men as implicitly wanting to be or to be like women, but because the heterosexual himself wants to believe that the gay man *is*, in fact, like a woman to the extent that his difference can somehow be discerned through or inscribed upon his body, thereby making him subject to discrimination in more ways than one. In consequence, where the ideological contours within which homosexuality can be recognized remain those of inauthenticity, dissimulation, and disguise, even the most emphatically "masculine" aspects of male homosexuality are susceptible to interpretation in terms of a displaced or occluded effeminacy.

In his piece in *Life*, for instance, Paul Welch quotes the owner of a leather bar in San Francisco, cannily putting into this gay man's mouth the article's first explicitly misogynistic and effeminophobic pronouncements: "We throw out anybody who is too swishy. If one is going to be homosexual, why have anything to do with women of either sex?" As the article goes on, however, to describe the customers who frequent these "so called S & M bars" (68), it implicitly extends the phobic repudiation of "women of either sex" to include the brawny specimens who dress up in leather and chains. "The effort of these homosexuals to appear manly is obsessive," the author writes, reinforcing the suggestion of misrepresentation implicit in the word "appear" by recourse to the language of clinical diagnosis in "obsessive." Such an exposure of the "masculinity" of gay men as merely parodic or self-deceiving—as a gesture whose logic implicitly substantiates the "truth" or self-identity of heterosexual maleness—finds an echo, conveniently enough, in the words of the man who owns the bar. "Those screaming faggots," he says, referring to effeminate homosexual men, are "afraid to come here because everything looks tough. But we're probably the most genteel bar in town" (70). Underscoring the notion that "looks" can be deceptive, the acknowledged gentility of this seamy-seeming establishment situates even the most assertively "masculine" version of gay male life reassuringly, for the dominant culture, in the register of effeminacy. Seen properly, through the dominant cultural optic, the self-representations of gay men thus reveal an essential internal element of effeminacy-as-difference whereby it is possible for the educated eye to see them as gay in the first place.

Through all of this *Life* engages in the ideological labor of constructing homosexuality as a problem or social concern for its readers that cannot be disentangled from the processes by which "homosexuals become more visible to the public" (74). Insofar as the magazine itself participates in this project by making the "secret world" of homosexuality visible to its (presumptively heterosexual) readership, it does so in order to encourage their internalization of the repressive supervisory mechanisms of the State—an internalization that it seeks to effect by reproducing in its readers the magazine's interest in becoming aware of and learning to recognize those denizens of the gay world who are "nearly impossible to detect." And in the process of conjuring homosexuality as an often invisible yet omnipresent concern, the magazine evokes the Cold War equation of homosexuality with Communist infiltration and subversion—an equation that becomes explicit when Ernest Havemann begins his article by inquiring: "Do the homo-sexuals, like the Communists, intend to bury us?"

Now it is significant that when Guy George Gabrielson, the Republican National Chair, helped to popularize this equation in 1950 by warning that homosexuals in the government's employ were "perhaps as dangerous as actual Communists"—and the word "actual" in this phrase is worth noting—he also explained the public's relative ignorance about the extent of this "problem" by pointing to the moral constraints that prevented the mass media from exploring the issue: "The country would be more aroused over this tragic angle of the situation," he wrote, "if it were not for the difficulties of the newspapers and radio commentators in adequately presenting the facts, while respecting the decency of their American audiences."[25] With this the question of textual repre-sentation, especially in the media that shape popular opinion, finds itself enmeshed in the cold war rhetoric that conflated homosexuality with Communism. The very pos-sibility of a public, non-medical discourse of homosexuality comes to depend upon the political interests that such a discourse can be made to serve. Far from disallowing, therefore, the discussion of homosexuality, remarks such as Gabrielson's *encouraged* a certain public consideration of the issue to the extent that such consideration furthered the promotion of a homophobic—and therefore, if only metonymically, anti-Commu-nist—agenda sufficient to "arouse," to use his own word, the unwary American public. The result, of course, was that Senator McCarthy's campaign against subversives in the American government had the effect of focusing public attention on the unrecognized pervasiveness of homosexuality.[26]

Less constrained in 1964 by the representational "difficulties" to which Gabrielson alluded, the media were able to flesh out or give body to the abstract Cold War rhetoric of homosexuality as public and political threat by resituating it within the framework of concern about the definitional barriers between the social and the privately domestic—a concern that had served implicitly to support the ideological construction of American nationalism at the end of the forties and throughout the fifties. For the backward looking ideology of domesticity that governed the American national consciousness in the wake of World War II sought not only to achieve such regressive social policies as the return of white middle-class women to the unpaid labor of heterosexual home-making, it also attempted to establish for America the fictive cohesiveness of a suburban national-cultural identity. Even as American cities expanded, the white middle-class imaginary was en-thralled by the consumerist fantasy of the "American Dream": the bourgeois family safely ensconced in a home that was detached and privately owned. This national self-image can be viewed as a reaction against the political realities of a postwar world in which American power could no longer detach itself from military involvement in international affairs, a world in which atomic bombs and the pirated missile technologies of the Nazis, technologies simultaneously undergoing development by East and West alike, made American isolationism strategically impossible and therefore all the more powerful as a spur to ideological formation.

As the development of weapons technology—a phrase that is already perhaps a redundancy—deprived America of the geopolitical privilege of its historical distance from powerful enemies, the idealization of domestic security, for both the nuclear family and the nuclear state, became an overriding national concern. Yet that ideal of a private domestic preserve could only be articulated through an insistence upon the need for new technologies of social control. Refinements in techniques of interrogation, sur-veillance, and security examination marked the dependence of the white bourgeois family's expectation of a privileged domestic space upon the state's girding up of that notion even—or especially—by ceaselessly violating the domain of domestic privacy itself.

Such violations, however, gained considerable acceptance as necessary weapons in the effort to expose the activities of subversives who were widely depicted as misdirecting or abusing their constitutional liberties in order to bring the United States under foreign domination. Thus the postwar machinery of American nationalism operated by enshrining and mass-producing the archaic bourgeois fantasy of a self-regulating familial sanctuary at a time when the idea of the domestic was embroiled in an anxious and unstable relation to the manifold social imperatives of the State.

If the reactionary aftermath of World War II, then, saw a massive intensification of the State's efforts to control homosexual behavior, those efforts responded to the widespread perception of gay sexuality as an alien infestation, an unnatural because un-American practice, resulting from the entanglement with foreign countries—and foreign nationals—during the war.[27] And as the importance of international and domestic surveillance became a central preoccupation of postwar America, so the campaigns against gays by local police departments, spurred by the national political identification of homosexuality with domestic subversion, made use of new modes of subterfuge and dissimulation, including the techniques of surveillance in public restrooms that would lead to the arrest of Walter Jenkins in 1964.

Now in the twentieth-century American social landscape, the institutional men's room constitutes a site at which the zones of the public and the private overlap with a distinctive current of psychic charge. That charge, of course, carries, at a much stronger voltage, the tension of ambivalence that the bathroom as such is sufficient to evoke. In May of 1964, for example—the same month that Senator Goldwater declared his interest in making a preemptive strike against the men's room of the Kremlin—*Life* published an article in which it noted with satisfaction that "Americans already have nearly 50 million bathrooms, more than the rest of the world put together. Now they are demanding even more—and are demanding that they be bigger and fancier."[28] Yet if this metonymic index of American cleanliness—itself, proverbially, a metonym of Godliness—suggests an element of national pride that centers on the ongoing proliferation of its bathrooms, the opening sentence of the article sounds a note potentially more ominous: "Bedecked, bejeweled, and splashed with color, the bathroom is blossoming with a flair unapproached since the fall of the Roman Empire." Caught between its honorific associations with industrial progress and hygienic purity, and its more pejorative associations with weakness, luxury, and aesthetic indulgence of the perverse, the American bathroom in 1964 constituted an unacknowledged ideological battleground in the endless—because endlessly anxious—campaign to shore up "masculinity" by policing the borders at which sexual difference is definitionally produced.

Nowhere are the psychic stakes in that conflict more intense than when the bathroom in question is a public or institutional facility. Already set aside as a liminal zone in which internal poisons are cast out and disavowed, the institutional men's room typically emblematizes the intrinsic uncertainty of its positioning between the public and the private through its spatial juxtaposition of public urinals and private stalls. Indeed, the effort to provide a space of privacy interior to the men's room itself, a space that would still be subject to some degree of regulation and control, had encouraged by 1964 the increasing popularity of that monument to capitalist ingenuity, the pay toilet stall in the public washroom. And it was in the anticipated privacy of just such a stall that Walter Jenkins found himself spied upon by representatives of the D.C. police department as he engaged in illegal sexual behavior with a Hungarian-born veteran of the U.S. army.

The transformation of Walter Jenkins from retiring and camera-shy chief of staff to a man whose sexual behavior was subject to sensationalized depiction, however, was accomplished not so much by the police as by the social policing carried out by the press. For when Jenkins chose, on the night of his arrest, to forfeit his $50 bond, he waived his right to trial (without confessing guilt) and, as far as the law was concerned, that brought the matter to a close. Only when the news of his arrest was leaked to the Republican National Committee, and then leaked again by the RNC to members of the press, did Jenkins become the central figure in what many called Johnson's Profumo scandal[29]—and only then because the media coverage of the case re-enacted on an enormously magnified scale the regulatory surveillance that the vice squad detectives carried out from behind the shower room door.

Yet the scandal that led editors to pontificate about its ominous implications for American security produced a radically different response among members of the public at large. *Time* magazine acknowledged "a nationwide wave of ribald jokes" while *Newsweek* referred to the widespread outpouring of "sick jokes and leering sloganeering." Johnson's re-election motto—"All the way with LBJ"—was parodistically rewritten as "Either way with LBJ";[30] and wags insisted that Johnson was determined to stand "behind" Jenkins to the bitter end. Like the media's sensationalistic fascination with the case—*Time,* for instance, even gave its readers the measurements of the "notorious" restroom, describing it as a "9-ft. by 11-ft. spot reeking of disinfectant and stale cigars"— these jokes symptomatize a cultural fascination that can help to illuminate Senator Goldwater's remark ("I want to lob one into the men's room of the Kremlin") wherein he implied a symbolic connection that defined the "men's room" no less than "the Kremlin" as the source of his anxiety.

The public staging of the men's room in the Senator's martial rhetoric, as in the surveillance operations of the vice squad and the journalistic narratives of the Jenkins affair, takes much of its significance from the concern about the indeterminacy of "homosexual difference" in postwar America. Consider, for example, the language with which *Time* contextualized, in 1959, the social invisibility enjoyed by the majority of gay men examined in a contemporary book by Dr. Edmund Bergler: "Despite all the washroom jokes, most of Dr. Bergler's homosexuals look and act perfectly masculine." The washroom here serves as the locus of a universally recognizable heterosexual mythologizing (no specification of these "jokes" is necessary since the audience can be assumed already to know them) that defensively seeks to establish a sign by which homosexual difference can be determined—a sign that would establish such a difference as explicitly as the sign on the washroom door would insist on the certainty of distinctions between the sexes.

But that latter sign, of course, figures crucially in a celebrated diagram employed by Lacan: a diagram in which what he designates as "the laws of urinary segregation" produce the signifiers "Ladies" and "Gentlemen" in order to differentiate between identical doors. It is not insignificant that Lacan should elaborate a fable from this diagram in which "Ladies" and "Gentlemen" become, through the misrecognitions of a young boy and girl sitting across from each other on a train, "two countries" that are subject to "the unbridled power of ideological warfare," even though, as Lacan assures us, "they are actually one country."[31] Nor is it insignificant that in this fable "anatomical difference," as Jacqueline Rose observes, "comes to *figure* sexual difference," so that, as she goes on to note, "the phallus thus indicates the reduction of difference to an instance of visible perception."[32] For I want to suggest that the men's room, whose very signifier in this fable enshrines the phallus as the token not only of difference, but of difference as determinate, difference as knowable, is the site of a particular heterosexual anxiety about the inscriptions of homosexual desire and about the possibility of knowing or recognizing whatever would constitute the "homosexual difference."

This can be intuited more readily when the restroom is considered, not, as by Lacan, in terms of "urinary segregation"—a context that establishes the phallus from the outset as the token of anatomical difference—but instead as the site of a loosening or relaxation of sphincter control, with the subsequent evocation of an eroticism undifferentiated by gender, in Freudian etiology, because anterior to the genital tyranny that raises the phallus to its privileged position. Precisely because the phallus marks the putative stability of the divide between "Ladies" and "Gentlemen," because it articulates the concept of sexual difference in terms of "visible perception," the "urinary" function in the institutional men's room customarily takes place within view of others—as if to indicate its status as an act of definitional display; but the private enclosure of the toilet stall signals the potential anxiety at issue in the West when the men's room becomes the locus not of urinary but of intestinal relief. For the satisfaction that such relief affords abuts dangerously on homophobically abjectified desires, and because that satisfaction suggests an opening onto difference within the signifier on the men's room door, it must both be isolated and kept in view lest its erotic potential come out, as it were.[33] The Freudian pleasure or comfort stationed in that movement of the bowel overlaps too extensively with the Kristevan abjection that recoils from such evidence of the body's inescapable implication in its death; and the disquieting conjunction of these contexts informs, with predictably volatile and destructive results, the ways in which dominant American culture could interpret the notion of homosexual activity in 1964.

As a result, in the representations of the Jenkins case and in Senator Goldwater's remark, the historical framing of the men's room as theater for heterosexual anxiety condenses a variety of phobic responses to the inter-implication of sphinctral relaxation and the popular notion of gay male sexuality as a yielding to weakness or a loss of control—a notion invoked in the Jenkins scandal when James Reston, in the pages of the *New York Times,* defined Jenkins's behavior as an instance of nothing more serious than "personal weakness."[34] In fact, in a novel that made its first appearance on the *New York Times'* best-seller list the week Walter Jenkins was arrested, the title character of Saul Bellow's *Herzog* watches as a young man is brought before a magistrate to answer charges stemming from his pursuit of erotic gratification in the underground men's room of Grand Central Station. Herzog, whose analyses of American history led him earlier to complain of the *"invasion of the private sphere (including the sexual) by techniques of exploitation and domination"*[35] (emphasis in original), decries the young man's prosecution in terms that reassert the heterosexual identification of the men's room with epistemological crisis and the anxiety of lost control: "You don't destroy a man's career because he yielded to an impulse in that ponderous stinking cavern below Grand Central, in the cloaca of the city, where no mind can be sure of stability" (227).[36] The threat to stability—that is, to the fixity of (heterosexual) identity and to (heterosexual) mastery of the signifiers of difference—portended here by the men's room itself, gains figural reinforcement from its contiguity to the image of the "cloaca," a term that designates not only a sewer or a water closet, but also, as the *Random House Dictionary* phrases it, "the common cavity into which the intestinal, urinary, and generative canals open in birds, reptiles, amphibians, many fishes, and certain mammals." The "stinking cavern" of Grand Central Station recapitulates the anatomical "cavity" to which the "cloaca" refers, and together these displaced but insistent spatial tropes suggest the anxiety of an internal space of difference, an overdetermined opening or invagination within the male, of which the activity of defecation may constitute an unnerving reminder. Indeed, it is worth recalling, in this context, the words of Kristeva: "It is . . . not lack of cleanliness or health that cause abjection but what disturbs identity, system, order. What does not respect borders, positions, rules."[37]

It should come as no surprise, therefore, that in the sex-segregated environment of the institutional men's room the act of defecation remains, in most circumstances, discreetly closeted. For a host of reasons—including childhood fantasies of phallic detachability that are linked with the release of the faeces; the substitutability in the unconscious, according to Freud, of "the concepts *faeces*, . . . *baby*, and *penis*";[38] and a psychic ambivalence "memorialize[d]" in the anus, as Eve Sedgwick puts it, as the site of a struggle "over private excitations, adopted controls, the uses of shame, and the rhythms of productivity"[39]—the heightened awareness in the men's room of the presence and the possibilities of this internal space of difference threatens to vitiate the assurance of those identities that the signifiers "Ladies" and "Gentlemen" undertake to affirm. And by threatening the stable relations between those two heavily defended "countries," the disturbing psychic configurations for which the public men's room serves as arena make possible the figurative interchangeability of a (perceived) threat to the integrity of the nation's (male) bodies and a (perceived) threat to the integrity of the body of the nation, especially when that nation, like postwar America, finds its defenses subject to penetration for the first time by the superior missile technology of its foes.

In a sense, then, the arrest of Walter Jenkins can be viewed as one spectacular instance of the "false arrest" of what Herman Rapaport describes, in another context, as "the sliding that occurs between signified and signified, door one and two" in the Lacanian representation of the restrooms.[40] For Jenkins, like thousands of other men— not all of them gay or gay-identified—booked on such charges before and after, could be understood by his contemporaries in one of three ways: a) as a homosexual whose identity *as* a homosexual reinforced the binarism of "Ladies" and "Gentlemen" precisely by standing outside that binarism as the recognizable "mistake" within the system itself; or b) as the victim of some illness, physical or emotional, whose transgressive behavior therefore did not symptomatize his (homosexual) identity but rather bespoke an exceptional *falling away* from his (true, i.e. heterosexual) identity;[41] or c) as a threat to the interpretive certainty invested in the phallus as the privileged signifier of that "identity" upon which patriarchal epistemology definitionally depends. That is to say, insofar as male homosexuality continued to signify as a condition indissociable from the normative constructions of gender in the popular imagination, the only alternative to defining Jenkins as, essentially, "a homosexual" or to explaining his behavior in terms of some sort of illness or mental breakdown, was to posit a category-subverting alterity within the conceptual framework of "the masculine" itself. But it was, after all, to secure the integrity of that always embattled framework that the surveillance of public restrooms was undertaken in the first place, and that same defensive imperative determined the strategic response to the Jenkins affair as orchestrated by President Johnson and the members of his staff.

In seeking, however, to circumscribe the scandal by defining it outside the context of homosexuality as such—by insisting, for instance, as Victor Lasky reports the President to have done, that Jenkins was not "biologically" a homosexual—the White House entered into the unavoidable contradictions that permeate the discourse on homosexuality in America. Thus the image of Jenkins that it disseminated portrayed a family man finally victimized by the extraordinary professional demands that were placed on his energy, time, and attention. As one former insider, adhering to this line, subsequently wrote: "Whatever the nature of Jenkins's difficulty, he was obviously no simple or habitual homosexual. He was a man who for years had been destroying himself in the service of Lyndon Johnson, ten to sixteen hours a day, six or seven days a week, and finally something had snapped."[42] *Newsweek*, in its presentation of this interpretation of the affair, quoted from the F.B.I. report in which a colleague asserted that Jenkins "would walk 'on his hands and knees on broken glass to avoid giving President Johnson any problem,' "[43] while *Time* cited a "friend of Jenkins' " who declared, "There were two great devotions in his life: L.B.J. and his own family."[44] These testimonials, of course, endeavor rhetorically to "protect" Jenkins from any assumption that his acknowledged participation in male-male sexual acts should be read as an index of "homosexuality." By presenting him as man whose difficulties sprang from an excess of those celebrated American attributes of industriousness and loyalty, they dissociate him from a homosexuality conceived in terms of indolence, luxury, and the lack—or worse, the repudiation—of generative productivity. Those same testimonials, however, produce retroactively an inescapable question about the "meaning" of such excess and such "devotion." They produce, that is, the homographic imperative to reconstruct experience after the fact in order to discern the inscriptions (understood to have been present, necessarily, all along) that convey a "meaning"—homosexuality—that might earlier have been perceived.

Such retroactive productions of "homosexual difference" as an unrecognized but belatedly *recognizable* "meaning" leave their trace even on those accounts of Jenkins's breakdown that are offered in order to "defend" him against charges of homosexual orientation. Max Frankel, for instance, in the front-page story with which the *New York Times* first reported on the Jenkins affair, produced a slightly out-of-focus portrait of the President's advisor by combining an interest in the representation of the (potentially) homosexual body with a nod toward the official explanation that over-exertion was the cause of Jenkins's behavior: "A man of compact build, a slightly florid face, with heavy, graying hair, Mr. Jenkins has been described as a 'nervous type.' But he was also known for extremely hard work on behalf of the President."[45] The syntax of the first sentence establishes the logic of some unarticulated relationship between the reporter's attention to the details of Jenkins's appearance and the subsequent, unattributed description of Jenkins as a "nervous type." Whether the morphology at issue confirms or confounds the conventional stereotypes of the homosexual physique, the very fact that that morphology is subject to analysis, that it is understood as somehow telling with regard to the content of the report, indicates the effort to read into it retroactively the sexual connotations already implicit in that ambiguous characterological epithet that the *Times* surrounds with meaningful quotation marks, a "nervous type." The particulars of his bodily representation, therefore, matter less than does the fact that such representation has now become appropriate, for that representation itself effeminizes by subjecting the male body to interrogation. And it is axiomatic in the social context within which this representation occurs that a masculinity subject to questioning is no masculinity at all.

Against this "homosexualizing" reading, however, the second sentence offers the "heterosexualizing" assertion of Jenkins's reputation for "extremely hard work." The contradiction between these two ideologically determined contexts for the interpretation of Jenkins's behavior accounts for the unexpected conjunction, "but," by which the sentences are joined. The distinction that this conjunction would insist upon, however, very quickly comes undone. For the logic that seeks to exempt Jenkins from the "taint" of homosexuality by ascribing his actions to nervous exhaustion precipitated by too much work, gets tangled in the nexus of cultural associations whereby "nervous" conditions are themselves perceived as inherently effeminizing, and such effeminacy, as the rhetoric of protestation adopted by Havemann and Stearn makes clear, remains the dominant cultural signifier of male homosexuality. "Hard work" can only account for an emotional breakdown, after all, insofar as the worker in question is already a "nervous type" to begin with—insofar, that is, as he can be categorized in terms of an effeminizing typology that defines an essential condition always subject, within its historical context, to a reading that would fix its "meaning" as homosexuality. So powerful is the force-field of that signification that even Lyndon Johnson, who aggressively denied that his closest advisor might "be" homosexual, engaged in a loaded act of cross-gender figuration when he remarked, we may recall, that the discovery of Jenkins's arrest was as shocking to him "as if someone had told me my wife had murdered her daughter."

Not despite, but because of the grandiosity with which this statement showcases the anxiety underlying the heterosexual responses to the Jenkins affair, I have chosen to conclude my discussion by considering a few of the densely layered ideological assumptions that striate this extravagant metaphor. For the President's remark, like the popular joke that rewrote his campaign slogan as "Either way with LBJ," metonymically displaces the cognitive instability or epistemological uncertainty associated with homosexuality in order to produce a miniature model of the "conspiracy theory" of homophobic paranoia. The joke, of course, implicates the President in the sexual activities of his advisor by construing as suspect the bond of "devotion" that was so frequently insisted upon after Jenkins's resignation. Coming less than a month after the Warren Commission released, to a largely skeptical audience, its controversial report, and coming, as well, amid a campaign in which Senator Goldwater repeatedly attacked Johnson's integrity by associating him with financial impropriety and moral failure, the Jenkins scandal, perhaps inevitably, was read as a metonym for corruption at the very highest levels of power. The questions and uncertainty that had surrounded Johnson since his ascent to the Presidency the year before—questions that occasionally centered, as in the off-Broadway play, *MacBird,* on paranoid speculation about his involvement in Kennedy's death—could find expression in the charge of essential ambiguity or insidious duplicity that the popular jokes implicitly leveled through their suggestions that Johnson might go "either way," or that he would stand resolutely "behind" his advisor because they were linked, conspiratorially, in the commission of illicit deeds.

But if the metonymic "contagion" of epistemological doubt evoked by the subject of homosexuality led some members of the public to question their ability to know or trust the President, the President's more lurid figure of speech articulates a response to homosexual activity in terms that question his own ability to know or trust his wife. The news, that is, of an unrecognized "crime" committed by one of his intimates finds displaced expression through his conjuring of a very different crime imagined as having been committed by a very different intimate. The scene of desire between two men gets transformed into a scenario of violence between two women, and the "shock" that responds to the "foreignness" of the homosexual encounter in the men's room is translated into a betrayal interior to the structure of heterosexual marital domesticity. Johnson thus images his advisor's arrest as a violation of trust and cognitive security by dwelling upon its exposure of an unrecognized quality that calls into question the intimate knowledge and familiarity on which their relationship was based. By emphasizing the defamiliarization effected by such a sudden revelation, the comment implicitly diverges from the official explanation that Jenkins had strayed from the straight, if not the narrow, as a result of too much work; instead, it positions the shock of the affair in the disclosure of what should have been known in advance. The shock, therefore, derives as much from the President's having to receive from someone else ("as if someone had told me") such information about his friend (a friend close enough to be represented in the figure by Johnson's wife), as it does from the specific nature of the information he receives. In his framing of the shock, then, as in the cross-gender elaboration through which he situates Jenkins's behavior in relation to effeminacy, the President implicitly endorses the "homosexualizing" interpretation of his advisor's actions. Significantly, moreover, the logic at work in the mobilization of this figure places homosexuality in a conceptual space contiguous with, and impinged upon by, an anxiety-producing image of the power inherent in the woman's position as mother.

This bespeaks not merely the popular assumption of the interchangeability of same-sex desire and the disturbance of gender distinctions and roles, but also the psychological truism of the period that male homosexuality both resulted from, and constituted an inappropriate identification between, the mother and her son. The President's comment invokes the contradictory reasoning whereby male homosexuals were assumed, derisively, to be overly fond of and close to their mothers, even as they were assumed, projectively, to hate women—"especially," as the editors of the Catholic journal, *America,* wrote in 1962, "the woman who is a mother."[46] Tellingly, those who charged gay men with denigrating women and "especially" motherhood, did not scruple to read homosexuality as a "problem" for which the mother should herself be blamed. It was, after all, the too loving mother that heterosexual culture loved to hate, the smothering mother who destroyed her son through over-protection or over-indulgence. Just four months before the Jenkins affair, Ernest Havemann, borrowing heavily from the work of Irving Bieber, summarized these notions in his article for *Life:* "On the one hand, the homosexual's mother kept him utterly dependent on her, unable to make his own decisions. On the other, she pampered him, catered to his every whim and smothered him with affection" (78). As the language of this passage makes clear, the mother stands accused here of effeminizing her son, of preventing his "natural" development into manhood and thus, effectively, of consigning him to a life of non-generative sexuality. The abjection of male homosexuality, therefore, carries the burden of an archaic patriarchal anxiety about the mother's relation to power; as Kristeva puts it: "The abject confronts us . . . with our earliest attempts to release the hold of *maternal* entity even before existing outside of her, thanks to the autonomy of language. It is a violent, clumsy breaking away, with the constant risk of falling back under the sway of a power as securing as it is stiffling."[47] If the security of that power allows homosexual relations to be figured in terms of indulgence and weakness—in stark contrast to the masculinizing rigor and renunciation involved in the break from maternal control—the "stiffling" that the mother allegedly effects provokes a "violent" disavowal that gets displaced and reenacted in the phobic response to male homosexuality. Hence the logic by which Johnson can substitutively represent homosexual eros and desire in terms of a projective violence; hence too his anxious evocation of the slippage from "wife," a position of subordination within the dynamics of heterosexual marriage, to mother, a position of power within the mother-child dyad.[48]

It should come as no surprise that the same social pressures that conspired to "blame" the mother for male homosexuality produced the Cold War discourse of "mom-ism" that implicated mothers in narratives of subversion through the weakening of masculine resolve against Communism. In his compelling and well-documented analysis of Cold War cinema in America, Michael Rogin demonstrates how films of the fifties and early sixties "identif[y] Communism with secret, maternal influence. . . . The films suggest that the menace of alien invasion lay not so much in the power of a foreign state as in the obliteration of paternal inheritance."[49] Brilliantly exposing the contra-dictory implications of domestic ideology, Rogin shows how the security state of Cold War America adopted the very mechanisms of illicit power that it anxiously identified with its enemies: "Men comprise the state, to be sure; but they use the techniques of motherhood and Communism—intrusion, surveillance, and secret domination" (21). These techniques, as Rogin makes clear, were then turned against motherhood and Communism both so as to prevent the disappropriation of American masculinity. It is within this context that I want to suggest that by representing male homosexuality through the figure of a mother who murders her child, and who therefore participates in the destruction of (patriarchal) familial continuity, Johnson's comment not only restages the abjection of the mother, it also recapitulates the anxiety invoked when *Life* magazine inquired if "the homosexuals, like the Communists, intend to bury us." It figurally positions homosexual behavior in the context of "the obliteration of paternal inheritance" and signals an interpretation of male-male desire not only through the filter of sentimental self-pity writ large in the melodrama of (domestic) betrayal that President Johnson so vividly imagines, but also in a specific relation to history that equally informs Senator Goldwater's remark and the staging of the men's room in the Jenkins affair.

For when homosexuality enters the field of vision in each of these fragments of the social text it occasions a powerful disruption of that field by virtue of its uncontrollably figuralizing effects; and that disruption of the field of vision is precisely what homosexuality comes to represent: so radical a fracturing of the linguistic and epistemic order that it figures futurity imperiled, it figures history as apocalypse, by gesturing toward the precariousness of familial and national survival. If momism is the theory, then homosexuality is the practice, for it is seen as enacting the destabilization of borders, the subversion of masculine identity from within, that momism promotes. Such a reading of male homosexuality, of course, is not unique to America in the early sixties; indeed, it reactivates an anxiety about male-male sexual interaction that is older than Voltaire's expression of concern in his discussion of "Socratic Love." My point, however, is that the historical pressures upon the nationalistic self-image of postwar America found articulation through the portrayal of homosexual activity as the proximate cause of perceived danger to the nation at a time of unprecedented concern about the real possibility of national—and global—destruction. Employing late nineteenth-century arguments about racial degeneration in the context of contemporary socio-political conflicts, historically deployed readings that envisioned male homosexuality in terms of the abjection emblematized by the men's room could bemoan the threat that homosexuality posed to the continuity of civilization itself. Norman Mailer, in an essay from 1961, offers one blatant formulation of this idea: "As a civilization dies, it loses its biology. The homosexual, alienated from the biological chain, becomes its center."[50] Mailer clarifies the phobic logic that underlies this statement in an essay titled "Truth and Being: Nothing and Time," published in 1962 and reprinted (ironically?) in *The Presidential Papers* as part of a section labeled "On Waste": ". . . if excrement is the enforced marriage of Tragic Beauty and Filth, why then did God desert it, and leave our hole to the Devil, unless it is because God has hegemony over us only as we create each other. God owns the creation, but the Devil has power over all we waste—how natural for him to lay seige where the body ends and weak tragic air begins."[51] Heterosexuality alone possesses the divine attribute of creativity here; homosexual activity, by contrast, leads only to waste, as Mailer insisted in an interview in 1962: "I think one of the reasons that homosexuals go through such agony when they're around 40 or 50 is that their lives have nothing to do with procreation. . . . They've used up their being."[52]

The erotic behavior proscriptively associated with the men's room as the scene of the voiding of waste thus becomes entangled in the national imaginary with a fantasy of cultural and historical vastation. But the surveillance by which the law expresses the state's "need" to see homosexuality, like the sensationalism involved as that "need" is reenacted by the popular media, reveals a scarcely suppressed *desire* to see, to recognize, and to expose the alterity of homosexuality and homosexual tendencies. That desire bespeaks a narcissistic anxiety about the definition of (sexual) identity that can only be stabilized and protected by a process of elimination or casting out. It betokens, that is, a cultural imperative to anal sadistic behavior that generates the homophobic definition

21. One might note that in the *NYT* article first announcing Jenkins's arrest, the mere fact of his having been charged with homosexual behavior seems to authorize an invocation of his body as spectacle, as if his body might testify as to the truth of the allegations against him: "A man of compact build, a slightly florid face, with heavy, graying hair, Mr. Jenkins has been described as a 'nervous type.' " See n. 45 for a further citation of this quotation.

22. In "Superman in the Supermarket," written in 1960, Norman Mailer evokes this "treachery" in terms that bear significantly on the argument of this essay; describing Los Angeles' Pershing Square, he views it as "the town plaza for all those lonely, repectable, small-town homosexuals who lead a family life, make children, and have the Philbrick psychology (How I Joined the Communist Party and Led Three Lives)" (*The Presidential Papers* [New York: G.P. Putnam's Sons, 1963], p. 34).

23. "Homographesis," as I employ the term, refers to the disciplinary and projective fantasy that homosexuality is visibly, morphologically, or semiotically, written upon the flesh, so that homosexuality comes to occupy the stigmatized position of writing itself within the Western metaphysics of presence.

In order to assist the reader in understanding the concept of "homographesis," the editors requested that I include the following footnote that presents, in slightly different form, material from the essay in which I introduced that term ("Homographesis," *Yale Journal of Criticism* 3:1 [Fall 1989], 189–207): "I want in particular to call attention, by the use of the term 'homographesis,' to the historical formation of a category of homosexual person whose very condition of possibility—both cognitively and anatomically—is a determining relationship to writing or textuality. This inscription of the homosexual within a tropology that produces him in constitutive relation to inscription is the first of the things that I intend 'homographesis' to denote. This neologism literally incorporates within its structure—and figuratively incorporates by referring back to the body—the notion of 'graphesis,' which I appropriate from the title of an issue of *Yale French Studies*. In her introduction to that issue, Marie-Rose Logan defined graphesis as 'the nodal point of the articulation of a text' since it 'delimits the locus where the question of writing is raised' and 'de-scribes the action of writing as it actualizes itself in the text independently of the notion of intentionality' (Marie-Rose Logan, "Graphesis . . . ," *Graphesis: Perspectives in Literature and Philosophy, Yale French Studies* 52 [1975], 12). Homographesis, then, would refer to the process by which homosexuality is put into writing through a rhetorical or tropological articulation that raises the question of writing as difference by constituting the homosexual as text. This process whereby homosexuality becomes a subject of discourse, and therefore a subject on which one may write, coincides with the process whereby the homosexual as subject is conceived of as being, even more than as inhabiting, a body on which his sexuality is written.

Just as the superimposition of metaphoric significance upon the metonymic category of desire makes possible conventional figurations of the legibility of homosexuality in the literal figure—the (morphology)—of the homosexual, so it produces the *need* to construe an emblem of homosexual difference that will securely situate that difference within the register of visibility. This reference to a visible analogue of difference draws, of course, upon cultural associations that joined sodomy with effeminacy in the European mind long before the so-called 'invention' of the homosexual.

In the discursive transformation toward which Foucault's work gestures, these contingent connections between sodomy and effeminacy undergo translation into essential or metaphorical equivalences as soon as sexuality itself is metaphorized as essential and largely exclusive. Once sexuality becomes so intimately bound up with a strict ideology of gender binarism, and once male sexuality in particular becomes susceptible to (mis)reading in relation to absolutely discontinuous heterosexual and homosexual identities, it becomes both possible and necessary to posit the homosexual difference in terms of visual representation—the very terms that psychoanalysis posits as central to the process whereby gender distinctions become meaningful in the symbolic order of sexuality. Unlike gender difference, however, which many feminist and psychoanalytic critics see as grounding the notion of difference itself, homosexual difference produces the imperative to recognize and expose it precisely to the extent that it threatens to remain unmarked and undetected, and thereby to disturb the stability of the paradigms through which sexual difference can be interpreted and gender difference can be enforced.

Thus while homographesis signifies the act of putting homosexuality into writing under the aegis of writing itself, it also suggests the putting into writing—and therefore the putting into the realm of difference—of the sameness, the similitude, or the metaphors of identity that the graphesis of homosexuality historically deconstructs. For the insistent tropology of the inscribed gay body testifies to a deep-seated heterosexual concern that a widely available conceptualization of homosexual personhood might subvert the cognitive security that the categories of sameness and difference serve to anchor; it indicates, by its defensive assertion of a visible marker of sexual otherness, a fear that the categorical institutionalization of homosexual difference may challenge the integrity and reliability of sameness as the guarantor of identity, that this hypostatized difference between socially constructed and biologically determined understandings of maleness can vitiate the certainty by which one's own self-identity can be known.

To frame this in another way, homographesis can be unpacked not only as the graphesis of the homosexual, the putting of homosexuality into discourse as form of differential articulation, but also as the inscription of the homosexual within the purview of the homograph. As an explicitly graphemic structure, the homograph provides a useful point of reference for the consideration of a gay graphesis. A homograph, after all, refers to a 'word of the same written form as another but of different origin and meaning'; it posits, therefore, the necessity of reading difference within graphemes that appear to be the same. The *OED,* for instance, cites a definition from 1873 that describes homographs as 'identical to the eye,' and another that refers to 'groups of words identical in spelling, but perhaps really consisting of several distinct parts of speech, or even of words having no connexion.' The homographic nature of homographesis would thus point to the potential for misreading inherent in the graphesis of homosexuality to the extent that such a graphesis exposes the non-coincidence of what appears to be identical or what passes for identity. Recalling in this context metaphor's appeal to the idea of essence or totalizable identity, we can say that the homographic element in the notion of homographesis reinterprets what seems to be a mirroring or a (re)production of identity—which is to say, a structure of metaphoric correspondence—as a relation of contiguity, of items so close in the graphic register that they share a single signifier though they may be radically different in meaning and derivation both."

24. Jess Stearn, *The Sixth Man* (New York: McFadden Publications, Inc., 1963), p. 29.

25. *New York Times,* April 19, 1950, p. 25.

26. The publication of the Kinsey Report in 1948, of course, provided a context in which the concern about widespread and unrecognized homosexual behavior could be mobilized.

27. This sort of argument about the "sources" of homosexual behavior in a given society is, of course, quite common historically. Louis Crompton, in his study of Byron, cites a passage from the British anti-war newspaper, the *Morning Chronicle,* from 1810, which offers a strikingly similar analysis by ascribing the "prevalence" of homosexuality in England to "the unnecessary war in which we have been so long involved. It is not merely the favour which has been shewn to foreigners, to foreign servants, to foreign troops, but the sending of our own troops to associate with foreigners, that may truly be regarded as the source of evil" (*Byron and Greek Love,* p. 167).

American fiction of the fifties suggests in a number of different ways the connection between war-time experiences and homosexual behavior. In Dennis Murphy's novel, *The Sergeant,* for instance, published in 1958, the title character's coercive expressions of his erotic interest in the private, Tom Swanson, signify in terms of the text's initial recollection of the sergeant's decoration-earning bravery during an ambush in World War II; the narrative, evoking that primal moment, lingers provocatively over his violent and intimate struggle with a German soldier and thus underscores the element of desire that first finds expression in this lethal encounter. Allen Drury's *Advise and Consent,* published the following year, similarly implies a link between homosexuality and the war by situating Senator Brigham Anderson's fateful exploration of his homosexual tendencies during a rest period in Honolulu in the midst of World War II. When this episode, which Anderson has concealed throughout his subsequent marriage, finally surfaces as his political opponents attempt to control the Senator's vote, Anderson must finally try to explain his homosexual encounter to his wife: "People go off the track sometimes, under pressures like the war" (*Advise and Consent* [Garden City, New York: Doubleday & Company, 1959], p. 432). More interestingly, the novel establishes a structural analogy between homosexuality and Communism by pairing them as the guilty secrets that "come out" in the course of the political maneuvers prompted by the effort to confirm Robert Leffingwell as Secretary of State.

28. "Elegant Decor in Bathrooms," *Life*, May 15, 1964, p. 68.

29. In a front-page article for the *Wall Street Journal* on October 16, 1964, for instance, Henry Gemmill quotes "one prominent Republican Senator," as follows: "It seems to me there's now a direct parallel to Britain's Profumo case—except here it's boys instead of girls." The coverage of the scandal in *Newsweek*'s article on October 26, 1964 also features a photograph in which demonstrators protest at a Johnson rally in Pittsburgh by raising an enormous banner that queries, "Jenkins, LBJ's Profumo?" (p. 32).

30. Shelley Ross, *Fall from Grace: Sex, Scandal, and Corruption in American Politics from 1702 to the Present* (New York: Ballantine Books, 1988), p. 213.

31. Jacques Lacan, "The Agency of the Letter in the Unconscious," *Ecrits: A Selection*, trans. Alan Sheridan (New York: Norton, 1977), p. 152.

32. Jacqueline Rose, "Introduction-II," *Feminine Sexuality*, ed. Juliet Mitchell and Jacqueline Rose, trans. Jacqueline Rose (London: MacMillan Press, 1983), p. 42.

33. Significantly, one common response, especially in the fifties and early sixties, to the fear of homosexual activity in men's rooms, particularly in those on college campuses, was the removal of the doors from toilet stalls so as to produce a space enclosed on three sides which thereby continued to gesture toward privacy, while simultaneously functioning, as the absent fourth wall hints, as a stage upon which the actor could always be subject to surveillance.

34. *New York Times*, October 15, 1964, p. 31.

35. Saul Bellow, *Herzog* (Harmondsworth, Middlesex: Penguin Books, 1988), p. 166.

36. Note how close this comes to the words with which Lyndon Johnson's brother described the arguments made by Abe Fortas and Clark Clifford as they tried to persuade the Washington press not to publish the reports of Jenkins's arrest: "You can't condemn a man for one single moment of weakness" (Sam Houston Johnson, *My Brother Lyndon*, ed. Enrique Lopez [New York: Cowles Books, 1969], p. 175).

37. Julia Kristeva, *Powers of Horror: An Essay on Abjection*, trans. Leon Roudiez (New York: Columbia University Press, 1982), p. 4.

38. Sigmund Freud, "On Transformations of Instinct as Exemplified in Anal Erotism," *On Sexuality*, trans. James Strachey, The Pelican Freud Library, Volume 7 (Harmondsworth, Middlesex: Penguin, 1983), p. 296.

39. Eve Kosofsky Sedgwick, "A Poem is Being Written," *Representations* 17 (1987), 126.

40. Herman Rapaport, "Lacan Disbarred: Translation as Ellipsis," *Diacritics* (Winter 1976), 58.

41. Three days after Walter Jenkins resigned, the *New York Times* carried a story under the headline: "Ex-Homosexual Got U.S. Job Back." The article reports that the administrator of the Federal Aviation Agency, Najeeb H. Halaby, had ordered reinstatement of a 32-year-old employee who had been fired in 1960 when he admitted having engaged in four homosexual acts when he was 18. Mr. Halaby explained that the employee was "fully rehabilitated and competent" and "should not be scarred for life for a youthful mistake." The article substantiated this notion by then observing: "The employe [sic], now 32 years old, is married and the father of three children. The Government, in effect, conceded that he now had a normal sex life and that the homosexual incidents had been youthful indiscretions." In addition, however, the article offers two other interesting pieces of information: first, although the employee was ordered to be reinstated, the report concludes by assuring the public, "He will not actually control air traffic"; second, the article notes that despite the reinstatement, a memorandum from the White House had recently been circulated calling for more stringent security screening before hiring employees in order to avoid other cases in which such questions could arise. The memorandum, in an ironic twist that the author of the article clearly relished, turns out to have been, of course, none other than Walter Jenkins.

42. Eric Goldman, *The Tragedy of Lyndon Johnson*, (New York: Knopf, 1969) pp. 250–251.

43. "The Jenkins Report," *Newsweek*, November 2, 1964, p. 26.

44. "The Senior Staff Man," *Time*, October 23, 1964, p. 21.

45. *New York Times*, October 15, 1964, p. 1.

46. Editorial: "The 'Mother' Image," *America,* May 12, 1962, p. 227. In this virulently homophobic article the editors endorse an assertion by Eric Sevareid that homosexuals exercise pernicious international control over the worlds of fashion, theater, film, and design. The implications of a conspiracy are reinforced by Sevareid's description of homosexual power imposed through "loose but effective combines." Sevareid's vehement denunciation of gay men, as quoted in the editorial, touches so many of the familiar bases in this sort of rhetorical outburst that it seems worthwhile to quote from it here: "The homosexual is usually capable of neither loving nor understanding a woman; so, in his fashions, the woman's body is merely a skeletal frame for his artistic experiments in design; in his films the woman is generally a prostitute or an overbearing clod. In the theater, they [homosexuals] portray neither high triumph nor high tragedy, for these involve acts of will and decision. In their world there is no decision and no will; there is only a degraded helplessness against 'forces,' because being sick themselves, they must see society as the sickness" (p. 227). The occasion for this outburst in the pages of *America* was the celebration of a "antidote," one described as "providential," to the "malevolent . . . influence of the homosexual" in "defiling the image of mother." That "antidote" was the decision of Pope John XXIII to allow the 1964 World's Fair in New York to exhibit the "Pietà" of Michelangelo. The irony of *such* an "antidote," as the language of the article would have it, can hardly fail to recall Derrida's reading of the *pharmakon* in "Plato's Pharmacy" (*Disseminations*).

47. Kristeva, *Powers of Horror,* p. 13.

48. It may be worth noting that the name by which Johnson's wife was known, "Lady Bird," foregrounds the distinction of sex that bears so decisively on questions of power. The fact that the mother's destructive power is unleashed upon the female child responds, of course, to the historical circumstance that Johnson had two daughters and no sons. His naming of those daughters, however, suggests his eagerness to perpetuate the paternal inheritance insofar as both daughters were given names that made their initials identical to his (and to his wife's after her marriage to him): LBJ. The murderousness of the mother in this figure might position "Lady Bird" in the role of another lady, "Lady MacBeth," in which case she, as a tropological substitution for Walter Jenkins, would articulate male homosexuality in relation to the notion of being "unsex[ed]."

49. Rogin, "Kiss Me Deadly: Communism, Motherhood, and Cold War Movies," p. 9.

50. Norman Mailer, "Theatre: *The Blacks,*" *The Presidential Papers,* p. 210.

51. Mailer, *The Presidential Papers,* p. 275.

52. Mailer, *The Presidential Papers,* p. 144.

53. *Time,* October 23, 1964, p. 21.

54. *Wall Street Journal,* October 16, 1964, p. 14.

VII

BETWEEN THE PAGES

37

Double Consciousness in Sappho's Lyrics

John J. Winkler

John J. Winkler, who at the time of his death, from AIDS, in 1990, held the rank of Professor in the Department of Classics at Stanford University, was an activist, a scholar, and a leading interpreter of Greek and Roman culture; he pioneered a variety of feminist, narratological, and anthropological approaches to the study of ancient texts and authored a number of influential works, including Auctor & Actor: A Narratological Reading of Apuleius' "Golden Ass" *(1985),* The Constraints of Desire: The Anthropology of Sex and Gender in Ancient Greece *(Routledge, 1990), and* Rehearsals of Manhood: Athenian Drama as Social Practice *(forthcoming). In this essay on Sappho, the 7th-century B.C. Greek lyric poet, Winkler combines a lesbian-feminist approach, emphasizing the significance of erotic bonds among women, with an anthropological and postcolonial approach, emphasizing the phenomenon of dual literacy—a necessary survival skill by means of which members of marginalized groups learn to read the language of the dominant culture while continuing to communicate among themselves in a language of their own. By using this combination of critical methods, Winkler is able to render the complexity and delicacy of Sappho's poetry—its sensual richness, its literary politics, its negotiation of public and private meanings—and to situate it in a modern tradition of lesbian writing.*

Monique Wittig and Sande Zeig in their *Lesbian Peoples: Material for a Dictionary*[1] devote a full page to Sappho. The page is blank. Their silence is one quite appropriate response to Sappho's lyrics, particularly refreshing in comparison to the relentless trivialization, the homophobic anxieties, and the sheer misogyny that have infected so many ancient and modern responses to her work.[2] As Mary Barnard (1980: 34) puts it:

> I wanted to hear
> Sappho's laughter
> and the speech of
> her stringed shell.
>
> What I heard was
> whiskered mumble-
> ment of grammarians:
>
> Greek pterodactyls
> and Victorian dodos.

The very eminent classical scholars from F.G. Welcker to Denys Page who have assembled and sifted through so much of what can or might be known of Sappho, and whose work is indispensable to us, had their own matrices of understanding, their own concerns and commitments, which were, I should think, no more and no less time-bound and culture-specific than are ours.[3] But I doubt that those scholars would have understood our matrices (feminist, anthropological, pro-lesbian), given that their expertise was in such things as ancient metrics ("pterodactyls") rather than in ancient mores, whereas we are able in some good measure to understand theirs. This is an example of what I will refer to below as double consciousness, a kind of cultural bilingualism on our part, for we must be aware of and fluent in using two systems of understanding. Because Lobel and Page assumed the validity of Victorian no-no's, they were (it now seems to us) deaf to much of what Sappho was saying, tone-deaf to her deeper melodies. The forms of both worship and anxiety that have surrounded Sappho in the ancient and modern records require some analysis.[4] Part of the explanation is the fact that her poetry is continuously focused on women and sexuality, subjects which provoke many readers to excess.[5]

But the centering on women and sexuality is not quite enough to explain the mutilated and violent discourse which keeps cropping up around her. After all Anakreon speaks of the same subjects. A deeper explanation refers to the *subject* more than the object of her lyrics—the fact that it is a *woman* speaking about women and sexuality. To some audiences this would have been a double violation of the ancient rules which dictated that a proper woman was to be silent in the public world (defined as men's sphere) and that a proper woman accepted the administration and definition of her sexuality by her father and her husband.

I will set aside for the present the question of how women at various times and places actually conducted their lives in terms of private and public activity, appearance, and authority. If we were in a position to know more of the actual texture of ancient women's lives and not merely the maxims and rules uttered by men, we could fairly expect to find that many women abided by these social rules or were forced to, and that they sometimes enforced obedience on other women; but, since all social codes can be manipulated and subverted as well as obeyed, we would also expect to find that many women had effective strategies of resistance and false compliance by which they attained a working degree of freedom for their lives.* Leaving aside all these questions, however, I simply begin my analysis with the fact that there was available a common understanding that proper women ought to be publicly submissive to male definitions, and that a very great pressure of propriety could at any time be invoked to shame a woman who acted on her own sexuality.

This is at least the public ethic and the male norm. It cannot have been entirely absent from the society of Lesbos in Sappho's time. Unfortunately, our knowledge of that period and place is limited to a few general facts and rumors—a culture of some luxury, at least for the wealthy; aristocratic families fighting each other for power; the typical sixth-century emergence of tyrannies (Myrsilos) and mediating law-givers (Pittakos). Sappho's kin were clearly active in this elite feuding since she was banished with them from Lesbos to Sicily around the turn of the century. Lacking a reasonably dense texture of social information, and given the fragmentary state of her literary remains, anthropological investigation becomes much more difficult.

---

*There was also the category of heroic, exceptional woman, e.g. Herodotos' version of Artemisia, who is used to "prove the rule" every time he mentions her (7.99, 8.68, 8.87f., 8.101), and the stories collected by Plutarch in *de virtutibus mulierum*. The stated purpose of this collection is to show that *aretê,* "virtue" or "excellence," is the same in men and women, but the stories actually show only that some women in times of crisis have stepped out of their regular anonymity and performed male roles when men were not available (Schaps 1982).

What I want to recover are the traces of Sappho's consciousness in the face of these masculine norms of behavior, her attitude to the public ethic, and her allusions to private reality. This is becoming a familiar topic and problem in feminist anthropology: Do women see things in the same way as men? How can gender-specific differences of cultural attitude be discerned when one group is muted? Does their silence give consent? Or have we merely not found the right questions to ask and ways of asking them? My way of "reading what is there"* focuses on the politics of space—the role of women as excluded from public male domains and enclosed in private female areas—and on Sappho's consciousness[†] of this ideology. My analysis avowedly begins with an interest in sexual politics—the relations of power between women and men as two groups in the same society. In some sense the choice of a method will predetermine the kind and range of results which may emerge: a photo-camera will not record sounds, a non-political observer will not notice facts of political significance. Thus my readings of Sappho are in principle not meant to displace other readings but to add to the store of perceptions of "what is there."

There are various "publics and privates" which might be contrasted. What I have in mind here by "public" is quite specifically the recitation of Homer at civic festivals considered as an expression of common cultural traditions. Samuel Butler notwithstanding, Homer and the singers of his tradition were certainly men and the homeric epics as we have them cannot readily be conceived as women's songs. Women are integral to the social and poetic structure of both *Iliad* and *Odyssey,* and the *notion* of a woman's consciousness is particularly vital to the *Odyssey.* But Nausikaa and Penelope live in a male-prominent world, coping with problems of honor and enclosure which were differentially assigned to women, and their "subjectivity" in the epic must ultimately be analyzed as an expression of a male consciousness. Insofar as Homer presents a set of conventional social and literary formulas, he inescapably embodies and represents the definition of public culture as male territory.[‡]

Archaic lyric, such as that composed by Sappho, was also not composed for private reading but for performance to an audience (Merkelbach 1957; Russo 1973–4). Sappho often seems to be searching her soul in a very intimate way but this intimacy is in some measure formulaic (Lanata 1966) and is certainly shared with some group of listeners. And yet, maintaining this thesis of the public character of lyric, we can still propose three senses in which such song may be "private": first, composed in the person of a woman (whose consciousness was socially defined as outside the public world of men); second, shared only with women (that is, other "private" persons: "and now I shall sing this beautiful song to delight the women who are my companions," frag. 160 L–P[6]); and third, sung on informal occasions, what we would simply call poetry readings,

---

*"A feminist theory of poetry would begin to take into account the context in history of these poems and their political connections and implications. It would deal with the fact that women's poetry conveys . . . a special kind of consciousness. . . . Concentrating on consciousness and the politics of women's poetry, such a theory would evolve new ways of reading what is there" (Bernikow 1974: 10–1).

†Consciousness of course is not a solid object which can be discovered intact like an Easter egg lying somewhere in the garden (as in the Sapphic fragment 166 Leda is said to have found an egg hidden under the hyacinths). Sappho's lyrics are many-layered constructions of melodic words, images, ideas, and arguments in a formulaic system of sharable points of view (personas). I take it for granted that the usual distinctions between "the real Sappho" as author and speaker(s) of the poems will apply when I speak here of Sappho's consciousness.

‡In this territory and at these recitations women are present—Homer is not a forbidden text to women, not an arcane *arrhêton* of the male mysteries. In the *Odyssey* (1.325–9) Penelope hears and reacts to the epic poetry of a bard singing in her home, but her objections to his theme, the homecoming from Troy, are silenced by Telemakhos. Arete's decision to give more gifts to Odysseus (*Od.* 11.335–41) after he has sung of the women he saw in the Underworld may be an implicit sign of her approval of his poetry. Helen in *Iliad* 6 delights in the fact that she is a theme of epic poetry (357–8) and weaves the stories of the battles fought for her into her web (125–8).

rather than on specific ceremonial occasions such as sacrifice, festival, leave-taking, or initiation.* The lyric tradition, as Nagy argues, may be older than the epic, and if older perhaps equally honored as an achievement of beauty in its own right.

The view of lyric as a subordinate element in celebrations and formal occasions is no more compelling than the view, which I prefer, of song as honored and celebrated at least sometimes in itself. Therefore I doubt that Sappho always needed a sacrifice or dance or wedding *for which* to compose a song; the institution of lyric composition was strong enough to occasion her songs *as songs*. Certainly Sappho speaks of goddesses and religious festivities, but it is by no means certain that her own poems are either for a cult-performance or that her circle of women friends (*hetairai*) is identical in extension with the celebrants in a festival she mentions.† It is possible that neither of these latter two senses of "private" were historically valid for Sappho's performances. Yet her lyrics, as compositions which had some publicity, bear some quality of being in principle from another world than Homer's, not just from a different tradition, and they embody a consciousness both of her "private," woman-centered world and the other, "public" world. This chapter is an experiment in using these categories to unfold some aspects of Sappho's many-sided meaning.

Poem 1:   Many-Mindedness and Magic

One of the passages in Sappho which has been best illuminated in recent criticism is her first (and now only) complete poem, *poikilophron athanat' Aphrodita*. The reason for thinking that it stood first in a collection of her works is that Hephaistion, writing a treatise on meters in the second century C.E., took it as his paradigm of what was by then called the Sapphic stanza. The very notion, however, of a first poem in a first book hardly makes sense in Sappho's world, where the text seems to have circulated at first as a script and score for professional and amateur performers. Then we have to allow for some three to four hundred years in which single songs, groups of songs, various collections which interested performers made for their own use were in circulation before the scholar-librarians at Alexandria assembled, sorted, and compared the many variant versions to produce a canonical corpus of Sappho's lyrics in eight or nine books.

There were in fact at least two editions produced at the Alexandrian library, one by Aristophanes (who seems to have invented the convention that there were exactly nine great lyric poets of early Greece; Pfeiffer 1968: 205) and one by his pupil and successor Aristarchos.[7] Two of her fragments survive in written copies which may actually pre-date those standard editions: one scrawled on a shard and one on papyrus, both of the third century B.C.E. (fragments 2 and 98). The survival of poem 1 is due to the fact that Dionysios of Halikarnassos, writing a treatise on style, chose it for quotation as an example of perfect smoothness. This is sheer good luck for us; he might have quoted Simonides.

In the handing on of the text from one scribe or performer to another until it reaches our modern editors, who fiddle with it some more before handing it over to us, further uncertainties are introduced. The works of Dionysios and Hephaistion were

---

*Homer seems to include this possibility in the range of performing *klea andrôn* ["deeds of men"] when he presents Achilles singing to his own *thumos* ["spirit"], while Patroklos sits in silence, not listening as an audience but waiting for Achilles to stop (*Il.* 9.186–91).

†Sappho is only one individual, and may have been untypical in her power to achieve a literary life and renown. Claims that society in her time and place allowed greater scope for women in general to attain a measure of public esteem are based almost entirely on Sappho's poems (including probably Plutarch *Lykourgos* 18.4, *Theseus* 19.3, Philostratos *Life of Apollonios* 1.30). The invention of early women poets is taken to extremes by Tatian in his *adversus Graecos* and by Ptolemy Chennos (Winkler 1990: 143–44).

themselves copied many times over before they reached us. The sort of problem which infects even canonical book texts is illustrated by the first word in Sappho's poem 1. Some manuscripts of Dionysios and some of Hephaistion write *poikilothron'*, which all modern editors prefer, and other manuscripts have *poikilophron* (Neuberger-Donath 1969), for which a strong and interesting argument may be made. *Poikilophron* means "having a mind (*-phron*) which is *poikilos*," a notion usually translated by words like "dappled," "variegated," "changeful," "complex." It designates the quality of having many internal contrasts, whether perceived by the eye or by the mind. An embroidered robe is *poikilos*, Odysseus' crafty mind is *poikilos*.

I call attention to this not only as a lesson in the almost immeasurable distance, with all its stages of loss and distortion, which separates Sappho and her whole world from us but also because poem 1 is an astonishing example of *many-mindedness* (for want of a more elegant term). Other Greek lyric poets sing marvelous poems of hate and sorrow and personal ecstasy which is somehow never very far from regret and chagrin, but they do so from a single perspective, elaborating the mind and feelings of a single persona in a fixed situation. Sappho's poem 1, however, contains several personal perspectives, whose multiple relations to each other set up a field of voices and evaluations. This field-effect makes the rest of Greek lyric appear, by contrast, relatively single-minded, or as we can now say, not-*poikilos*. The field in poem 1 includes at least three Sappho's, two Aphrodite's, an unnamed girlfriend (representative of many), and (in virtue of echoing and parody effects) several homeric characters as well.

Let us consider the last first. Several analyses have developed the idea that Sappho is speaking in an imagined scene which represents that of Diomedes on the battlefield in *Iliad* 5 (Cameron 1949; Page 1955: 7; Svenbro, 1975; Stanley, 1976; Rissman, 1983). Sappho uses a traditional prayer formula, of which Diomedes' appeal to Athena at *Iliad* 5.115–7 is an example ("Hear me, Atrytone, child of aegis-bearing Zeus; if ever you stood beside my father supporting his cause in bitter battle, now again support me, Athena"), and she models Aphrodite's descent to earth in a chariot on the descent of Athena and Hera (5.719–72), who are coming to help the wounded Diomedes (5.781). Sappho asks Aphrodite to be her ally, literally her companion in battle, *summachos*.

> Intricate, undying Aphrodite, snare-weaver, child of Zeus, I pray thee,
> do not tame my spirit, great lady, with pain and sorrow. But come to me
> now if ever before you heard my voice from afar and leaving your father's
> house, yoked golden chariot and came. Beautiful sparrows swiftly brought
>   you
> to the murky ground with a quick flutter of wings from the sky's height
> through clean air. They were quick in coming. You, blessed goddess,
> a smile on your divine face, asked what did I suffer, this time again,
> and why did I call, this time again, and what did I in my frenzied heart
> most want to happen. Whom am I to persuade, this time again . . .
> to lead to your affection? Who, O Sappho, does you wrong? For one who
>   flees will
> soon pursue, one who rejects gifts will soon be making offers, and one
>   who
> does not love will soon be loving, even against her will. Come to me even
>   now
> release me from these mean anxieties, and do what my heart wants done,
> you yourself be my ally.*

*Translations of Sappho are my own; ellipses indicate that the Greek is incomplete.

One way of interpreting the correspondences which have been noticed is to say that Sappho presents herself as a kind of Diomedes on the field of love, that she is articulating her own experience in traditional (male) terms and showing that women too have manly excellence (*aretê;* Bolling 1959, Marry 1979). But this view that the poem is mainly about *erôs* and *aretê* and uses Diomedes merely as a background model, falls short.[8] Sappho's use of homeric passages is a way of allowing us, even encouraging us, to approach her consciousness as a woman and poet reading Homer. The homeric hero is not just a starting point for Sappho's discourse about her own love, rather Diomedes as he exists in the *Iliad* is central to what Sappho is saying about the *distance* between Homer's world and her own. A woman listening to the *Iliad* must cross over a gap which separates her experience from the subject of the poem, a gap which does not exist in quite the same way for male listeners. How can Sappho murmur along with the rhapsode the speeches of Diomedes, uttering and impersonating his appeal for help? Sappho's answer to this aesthetic problem is that she can only do so by substituting her concerns for those of the hero while maintaining the same structure of plight / prayer / intervention. Poem 1 says, among other things, "This is how I, a woman and poet, become able to appreciate a typical scene from the *Iliad.*"

Though the Diomedeia is a typical passage, Sappho's choice of it is not random, for it is a kind of test case for the issue of women's consciousness of themselves as participants without a poetic voice of their own at the public recitations of traditional Greek heroism. In *Iliad* 5, between Diomedes' appeal to the goddess and the descent of Athena and Hera, Aphrodite herself is driven from the battlefield after Diomedes stabs her in the hand. Homer identifies Aphrodite as a "feminine" goddess, weak, *analkis,* unsuited to take part in male warfare (331, 428). Her appropriate sphere, says Diomedes exulting in his victory over her, is to seduce weak women (*analkides,* 348–9). By implication, if "feminine" women (and all mortal women are "feminine" by definition and prescription) try to participate in men's affairs—warfare or war poetry—they will, like Aphrodite, be driven out at spear point.

Poem 1 employs not only a metaphorical use of the *Iliad* (transferring the language for the experience of soldiers to the experience of women in love) and a familiarization of the alien poem (so that it now makes better sense to women readers), but a *multiple identification* with its characters. Sappho is acting out the parts both of Diomedes and of Aphrodite as they are characterized in *Iliad* 5. Aphrodite, like Sappho, suffers pain (*odunêisi,* 354), and is consoled by a powerful goddess who asks "Who has done this to you?" (373). Aphrodite borrows Ares' chariot to escape from the battle and ride to heaven (358–67), the reverse of her action in Sappho's poem (Benedetto 1973, who refers to the poem as "Aphrodite's revenge"). Sappho therefore is in a sense presenting herself both as a desperate Diomedes needing the help of a goddess (Athena/Aphrodite) and as a wounded and expelled female (Aphrodite/Sappho) seeking a goddess' consolation (Dione/Aphrodite).

This multiple identification with several actors in an Iliadic scene represents on another level an admired feature of Sappho's poetics—her adoption of multiple points of view in a single poem. This is especially noteworthy in poem 1 where she sketches a scene of encounter between a victim and a controlling deity. The intensification of both pathos and mastery in the encounter is due largely to the ironic *double consciousness* of the poet-Sappho speaking in turn the parts of suffering "Sappho" and impassive goddess. Consider the cast of characters in poem 1, each different and each regarding the others with a look of mingled admiration and distrust. There is first the speaker in need, whose name we learn in line 15 is Psappo.* She is praying for help to Aphrodite,

---

*We may take it as another measure of our distance from her that the pep and bite of the consonants in "Psappo," with all the p's sounded, have evaporated into the tired fizz of "Saffo."

who is therefore the implied fictional audience of the entire poem and is to be imagined listening to all its words. Part of what Aphrodite hears is a narrative account of how she herself on a previous occasion mounted her sparrow-drawn chariot and drove down the sky and answered Sappho's prayers with a series of questions. This past-Aphrodite is not at all the same as the present-Aphrodite: the past-Aphrodite is an active character in the praying-Sappho's narrative, while the present-Aphrodite says nothing, does nothing, only listens—and presumably smiles.

One might wonder at the lengthy elaboration of the chariot-narrative, full of circumstantial detail, but I think the point is to create a slow build-up from distance to nearness, the goddess coming gradually closer to the speaker, taking her time (poetically, in the movement of the verse, even though she twice says it was a quick journey). As Aphrodite comes physically closer, she also becomes more vivid. First, her words are reported in indirect speech, and then she breaks into direct speech, so that Sappho the singer, impersonating Sappho in needful prayer, now suddenly is speaking in the voice of Aphrodite herself, so that the word "you," which from the beginning has been directed to Aphrodite, in line 15 now refers to Sappho. Fictional speaker and fictional audience change places, or rather the present-Aphrodite now hears from the mouth of praying Sappho the words which the past-Aphrodite spoke to the past-Sappho. The slow approach to this direct speech, starting far away (*pêloi*) in heaven, makes Aphrodite's words a kind of epiphany, a reported epiphany in a prayer asking for a repetition of the same.

For Sappho is once again tied up in a state of anxious desire. The three times repeated word for this is *dêute*, which is a contraction of *aute*, "again," and *dê*, an intensifying particle, something like "indeed," which gives a flavor to "again" which we might read as quizzical or ironic or pretended disappointment. Since the past-Aphrodite says "once again" to the past-Sappho, we are led to think of yet another Sappho, the one who got into the same fix before. The doubling of Aphrodite (present and past) and the tripling of Sappho (present, past, and . . . pluperfect) leads like the mirrors in a fun house to receding vistas of endlessly repeated intercessions, promises, and love affairs.

The appearance of an infinite regress, however, is framed and bounded by another Sappho. The person who we must think of as designing the whole is functionally and indeed practically quite different from any of the Sappho's in the poem. The author-performer who impersonates a character-in-need is not at the moment, at least *qua* performer, in need. In fact my primary impression of poem 1 is one of exquisite control, which puts Sappho-the-poet in a role analogous to Aphrodite's as the smiling, tolerant, ever helpful ally of her own *thumos*, "spirit." The guileful weaver, the many-minded one who performs intricate shifts of perspective, is fictionally Aphrodite but poetically Sappho herself.

But if such weaving and complexity give *poikilophron* a good claim to being the first word of Sappho's poem 1, there are also attractive reasons on the side of *poikilothron'*, which is most often taken to mean "sitting on an elaborately wrought throne." Although there certainly were, as Page (1955: 5) catalogues, elaborately wrought thrones, the interesting side of this compound word is not *thronos* meaning "throne" but a much rarer root, *throna*, found once in Homer, once in Theokritos, and several times in the Alexandrian poets Nikandros and Lykophron (Lawler 1948; Bolling 1958; Putnam 1960–1; see also Bonner 1949). In the later poets it refers to some kind of magic drugs. Theokritos' young woman in Idyll 2 is trying to perform a ceremony which will enchant her lover and bring him back to her. She tells her servant to smear the drugs, *throna*, on the threshold of Delphis' house and say "I am sprinkling the bones of Delphis."

"Sprinkle" is the standard translation of the verb *passô*, but homeric physicians also "sprinkle" drugs (*pharmaka*) onto wounds, so possibly the verb can include the more general action of applying or putting on.[9]

The homeric occurrence of the word is highly suggestive. Andromache is sitting at her loom, soon to hear the news of her husband Hektor's death. "She was weaving loom-cloth in a corner of the high house, a red double cloak, and she was sprinkling variegated *throna* on it" (*Iliad* 22.440–1): *en de throna poikil' epasse.* The conjunction of *throna* and *poikila* here might well tempt us to wonder whether Sappho actually did sing *poikilothron'*, and if so what would it mean. The usual interpretation of *throna* in *Iliad* 22 is "embroidered flowers." "Embroidered flowers" is surely too diminished a translation of the *throna* which Andromache is "sprinkling" onto her cloth. Instead I would sketch the semantic field of *throna* as somehow including both drugs and weaving.

I have already noted that "sprinkle" (*passô*) is what one does with *throna*, whether they are put on wounds or on loom-cloth. For further connections between drugs and weaving, I would cite the figure of Helen the weaver, who not only weaves (literally, "sprinkles") the story of the *Iliad* into her loom-cloth (3.125–8) but when she is home with Menelaos sits near him with a basket of wool and a spindle and when the war-tales they tell make everyone melancholy she puts drugs (*pharmaka*) into the wine-bowl and has it served around (*Odyssey* 4.120–35, 219–33).

Another locus for the conjunction of weaving and drugs is the *kestos*, the girdle, of Aphrodite, which too is described as *poikilos* and contains worked into it the powers to charm and enchant (*Iliad* 14.214–21). Helen's drugs and Aphrodite's charmed girdle are powerful magic, using the word loosely to designate many forms of alternate, un-official therapy. Since women did sing while spending long hours at the loom (so Kirke at *Odyssey* 10.221–2), I can readily imagine that some of those chants would wish good things onto the cloth and even that filaments of lucky plants and patterns of luck-bringing design would be woven into the best fabric.

In 1979 a new papyrus fragment of a Greek magical handbook was published which is very important for the fragmentary and suppressed history of that subject (Brashear 1979; Maltomini 1988; Obbink; and Janko 1988). Since most of the surviving collections of spells exist in copies made in the second to fourth centuries C.E., it is easy enough for traditional historians to dismiss all that as a late and alien intrusion into the sanctuary of rational Greek culture. But the new papyrus belongs to the late first century B.C.E. and confirms what is likely enough on other grounds—that the writing down of magic has a history comparable to other kinds of writing. Magical spells to produce love or cure a headache (both contained in the new papyrus) are like collections of natural marvels and folktales, the sort of cultural product which has a long and detailed oral history but which no one thought to write down until the changed social conditions of the Alexandrian and Roman empires. Certainly in the one area of magic which does have a continuous textual history from the sixth century B.C.E. to the sixth century C.E.—viz., curses written on lead and buried, sometimes with tortured dolls, in graves of the untimely dead—we can assert with confidence that the practice itself is ancient and uninterrupted.

For students of Sappho the fascinating feature of the new magical papyrus is that its language has some resemblance to that of poem 1. It involves an enchanted apple which is to be thrown in the direction of the intended love-object. The throwing of apples as a token of erotic interest is a quite widespread custom in Greek communities.[10] The incantation is a hexameter prayer to Aphrodite, asking her to "perfect this perfect song," or "fulfill a song of fulfillment," using the same word which Sappho repeats in her last stanza, "accomplish what my heart desires to accomplish." This is fairly standard in the language of prayer and request (*Iliad* 14.195–6). Standard too is the address to a great goddess as *potnia thea,* "lady goddess," found both in poem 1 and in the magical papyrus, but in the fragmentary magical text it is found next to the word *apothanô,* "I may die," which is found several times in Sappho (fragment 94: "I wish without guile to die;" fragment 31: "I seem to be little short of dying"). Closer still are the words *katatrechô, autos de me pheugei,* "I am running after, but he is fleeing from me" (column 2, line 12). Other magical papyri contain calls for assistance in terms as immediate and direct as Sappho's to Aphrodite to come and stand beside her in battle as a fellow-fighter: e.g., "Come and stand beside me for this project and work with me" (PGM XII.95). All of this may mean no more than that the magical papyrus shows the influence of Sappho, but the magical associations of *throna* (if that is the right reading) might explain why the later enchanter would naturally be drawn to echoing Sappho poem 1.

Poised between two possibilities—the many-mindedness of *poikilophron,* the magic of *poikilothron'*—I can see no way to decide that one must be right and the other wrong. Better to allow both to be heard and to appreciate how Sappho in poem 1 may be alluding to a goddess' magic and certainly is demonstrating her many-mindedness. Such multiple self-mirroring in the face of another, along with the alternation of viewpoints so that we in turn sympathize with and stand apart from each of the poem's five characters, is an achievement which reaches out into a different dimension, compared with the other Greek poets of the seventh and sixth centuries B.C.E. This complexity of understanding, which generates a field of personal perspectives, each regarding the other as alike but different, shows how comparable lyrics by poets of her time are quite truly and profoundly solo performances.

Such many-mindedness is intrinsic to the situation of Greek women understanding men's culture, as it is to any silenced group within a culture which acknowledges its presence but not its authentic voice. This leads to an interesting reversal of the standard (and oppressive) stricture on women's literature that it represents only a small and limited area of the larger world.[11] Such a view portrays women's consciousness according to the *social* contrast of public/private, as if women's literature occupied but a small circle somewhere inside the larger circle of men's literature, just as women are restricted to a domestic enclosure. But insofar as men's public culture is truly public, displayed as the governing norm of social interaction "in the streets," it is accessible to women as well as to men. Because men define and exhibit their language and manners as *the* culture and segregate women's language and manners as a subculture, inaccessible to and pro-tected from extra-familial men, women are in the position of knowing two cultures where men know only one.

From the point of view of *consciousness* (rather than physical space) we must diagram the circle of women's literature as a larger one which includes men's literature as one phase or compartment of women's cultural knowledge. Women in a male-prominent society are thus like a linguistic minority in a culture whose public actions are all conducted in the majority language. To participate even passively in the public arena the minority must be bilingual; the majority feels no such need to learn the minority's language. Sappho's consciousness therefore is necessarily a double consciousness, her participation in the public literary tradition always contains an inevitable alienation.

Poem 1 contains a statement of how important it is to have a double consciousness. Aphrodite reminds "Sappho" of the ebb and flow of conflicting emotions, of sorrow succeeded by joy, of apprehensiveness followed by relief, of loss turning into victory. The goddess' reminder not to be single-mindedly absorbed in one moment of experience can be related to the pattern of the *Iliad* in general, where the tides of battle flow back and forth, flight alternating with pursuit. This is well illustrated in *Iliad* 5, which is also the homeric locus for the specific form of alternation in fortunes which consists of wounding and miraculous healing. Two gods (Aphrodite and Ares) and one hero (Aineias) are injured and saved.

Recuperative alternation is the theme of poem 1, as it is of *Iliad* 5. But because of Sappho's "private" point of view and double consciousness it becomes not only the theme but the *process* of the poem, in the following sense: Sappho appropriates an alien text, the very one which states the exclusion of "weak" women from men's territory; she implicitly reveals the inadequacy of that denigration; and she restores the fullness of Homer's text by isolating and alienating its deliberate exclusion of the feminine and the erotic.

For when we have absorbed Sappho's complex re-impersonation of the homeric roles (male and female) and learned to see what was marginal as encompassing, we notice that there is a strain of anxious self-alienation in Diomedes' expulsion of Aphrodite. The overriding need of a battling warrior is to be strong and unyielding; hence the ever-present temptation (which is also a desire) is to be weak. This is most fully expressed at *Iliad* 22.111–30, where Hektor views laying down his weapons to parley with Achilles as effeminate and erotic. Diomedes' hostility to Aphrodite (= the effeminate and erotic) is a kind of scapegoating, his affirmation of an ideal of masculine strength against his *own* possible "weakness." For, in other contexts outside the press of battle, the homeric heroes have intense emotional lives and their vulnerability there is much like Sappho's: they are as deeply committed to friendship networks as Sappho ("He gave the horses to Deipylos, his dear comrade, whom he valued more than all his other age-mates," 325–6); they give and receive gifts as Sappho does; they wrong each other and re-establish friendships with as much feeling as Sappho and her beloved. In a "Sapphic" reading, the emotional isolation of the Iliadic heroes from their domestic happiness stands out more strongly ("no longer will his children run up to his lap and say 'Papa,'" 408). We can reverse the thesis that Sappho uses Homer to heroize her world and say that insofar as her poems are a reading of Homer (and so lead us back to read Homer again) they set up a feminine perspective on male activity which shows more clearly the inner structure and motivation of the exclusion of the feminine from male arenas.

I return to the image of the double circle—Sappho's consciousness is a larger circle enclosing the smaller one of Homer. Reading the *Iliad* is for her an experience of double consciousness. The movement thus created is threefold: by temporarily restricting herself to that smaller circle she can understand full well what Homer is saying; when she brings *her* total experience to bear she sees the limitation of his world; by offering her version of this experience in a poem she shows the strengths of her world, the apparent incompleteness of Homer's, and casts new illumination on some of the marginal and easily overlooked aspects of Homer. This threefold movement of appropriation from the "enemy," exposure of his weakness, and recognition of his worth is like the actions of homeric heroes who vanquish, despoil, and sometimes forgive. Underlying the relations of Sappho's persona to the characters of Diomedes and Aphrodite are the relations of Sappho the author to Homer, a struggle of reader and text (audience and tradition), of woman listening and man reciting.

Poem 16: What Men Desire

A sense of what we now call the sexual politics of literature seems nearly explicit in poem 16:

Some assert that a troup of horsemen, some of foot-soldiers, some that a
fleet of ships is the most beautiful thing on the dark earth; but I
assert that it is whatever anyone desires. It is quite simple to make
this intelligible to all, for she who was far and away preeminent in beauty
of all humanity—Helen—abandoning her husband, the . . . ,
went sailing to Troy and took no thought for child or dear parents, but
beguiled . . . herself . . . , for . . . lightly . . . reminds me now of Anaktoria
absent: whose lovely step and shining glance of face I would prefer
to see than Lydians' chariots and fighting men in arms . . . cannot be . . .
human . . . to wish to share . . . unexpectedly.

[This is a poem of eight stanzas, of which the first, second, third and fifth are almost
intact, the rest lost or very fragmentary.]

It is easy to read this as a comment on the system of values in heroic poetry. Against
the panoply of men's opinions on beauty (all of which focus on military organizations,
regimented masses of anonymous fighters), Sappho sets herself—"but I"—and a very
abstract proposition about desire. The stanza first opposes one woman to a mass of men
and then transcends that opposition when Sappho announces that "the most beautiful"
is "whatever you or I or anyone may long for." This amounts to a re-interpretation of
the kind of meaning the previous claims had, rather than a mere contest of claimants
for supremacy in a category whose meaning is agreed upon (Wills 1967; duBois 1978).
According to Sappho, what men mean when they claim that a troup of cavalrymen is
very beautiful is that they intensely desire such a troup. Sappho speaks as a woman
opponent entering the lists with men, but her proposition is not that men value military
forces whereas she values desire, but rather that all valuation is an act of desire. Men
are perhaps unwilling to see their values as erotic in nature, their ambitions for victory
and strength as a kind of choice. But it is clear enough to Sappho that men are in love
with masculinity and that epic poets are in love with military prowess.

Continuing the experiment of reading this poem as about poetry, we might next
try to identify Helen as the Iliadic character. But Holmer's Helen cursed herself for
abandoning her husband and coming to Troy; Sappho's Helen, on the contrary, is held
up as proof that it is right to desire one thing above all others, and to follow the beauty
perceived no matter where it leads. There is a charming parody of logical argumentation
in these stanzas; the underlying, real argument I would re-construct as follows, speaking
for the moment in Sappho's voice. "Male poets have talked of military beauty in positive
terms, but of women's beauty (especially Helen's) as baneful and destructive. They will
probably never see the lineaments of their own desires as I do, but let me try to use
some of their testimony against them, at least to expose the paradoxes of their own
system. I shall select the woman whom men both desire and despise in the highest
degree. What they have damned her for was, in one light, an act of the highest courage
and commitment, and *their own poetry* at one point makes grudging admission that she
surpasses all the moral censures leveled against her—the Teichoskopia [Survey from the
Wall, *Iliad* 3.121–244]. Helen's abandonment of her husband and child and parents is
mentioned there (139, 174), and by a divine manipulation she feels a change of heart,
now desiring her former husband and city and parents (139) and calling herself a bitch
(180). But these are the poet's sentiments, not hers; he makes her a puppet of his feeling,
not a woman with a mind of her own. The real Helen was powerful enough to leave
a husband, parents, and child whom she valued less than the one she fell in love with.
(I needn't and won't mention her lover's name: the person—male or female—is not
relevant to my argument.) Indeed she was so powerful that she *beguiled Troy itself* at that

moment when, in the midst of its worst suffering, the senior counselors watched her walk along the city wall and said, in their chirpy old men's voices, 'There is no blame for Trojans or armored Achaians to suffer pains so long a time for such a woman' (156–7)."

So far I have been speaking Sappho's mind as I see it behind this poem. There is an interesting problem in lines 12ff., where most modern editors of Sappho's text have filled the gaps with anti-Helen sentiments, on the order of "but (Aphrodite) beguiled her . . . , for (women are easily manipulated,) light(-minded . . .)." We do not know what is missing, but it is more consistent with Sappho's perspective, as I read it, to keep the subject of *paragag'*, "beguiled," the same as in the preceding clause—Helen. "Helen beguiled . . . itself (or, herself)," some feminine noun, such as "city" (*polis*), "blame" (*nemesis*), or the like. What is easily manipulated and light-minded (*kouphôs*) are the senior staff of Troy, who astonishingly dismiss years of suffering as they breathe a romantic sigh when Helen passes.

Poem 31: Sappho Reading the Odyssey

Perhaps Sappho's most impressive fragment is poem 31:

> That one seems to me to be like the gods, the man whosoever sits facing you and listens nearby to your sweet speech and desirable laughter—which surely terrifies the heart in my chest; for as I look briefly at you, so can I no longer speak at all, my tongue is silent, broken, a silken fire suddenly has spread beneath my skin, with my eyes I see nothing, my hearing hums, a cold sweat grips me, a trembling seizes me entire, more pale than grass am I, I seem to myself to be little short of dead. But everything is to be endured, since even a pauper. . . .

The first stanza is a *makarismos,* a traditional formula of praise and well-wishing, "happy the man who . . . ," and is often used to celebrate the prospect of a happy marriage (Snell 1931; Koniaris 1968; Saake 1971; 17–38). For instance, "That man is far and away blessed beyond all others who plies you with dowry and leads you to his house; for I have never seen with my eyes a mortal person like you, neither man nor woman. A holy dread grips me as I gaze at you" (*Odyssey* 6.158–61). In fact this passage from Odysseus' speech to Nausikaa is so close in structure (*makarismos* followed by a statement of deep personal dread) to poem 31 that I should like to try the experiment of reading the beginning of Sappho's poem as a re-creation of that scene from the *Odyssey.*

If Sappho is speaking to a young woman ("you") as Nausikaa, with herself in the role of an Odysseus, then there are only two persons present in the imagined scene (Del Grande 1959). This is certainly true to the emotional charge of the poem, in which the power and tension flow between Sappho and the woman she sees and speaks to, between "you" and "I." The essential statement of the poem is, like the speech of Odysseus to Nausikaa, a lauding of the addressee and an abasement of the speaker which together have the effect of establishing a working relationship between two people of real power. The rhetoric of praise and of submission are necessary because the poet and the shipwrecked man are in fact very threatening. Most readers feel the paradox of poem 31's eloquent statement of speechlessness, its powerful declaration of helplessness; as in poem 1, the poet is masterfully in control of herself as victim. The underlying relation of power then is the opposite of its superficial form: the addressee is of a delicacy and fragility which would be shattered by the powerful presence of the poet unless she makes elaborate obeisance, designed to disarm and, by a careful planting of hints, to seduce.

The anonymous "that man whosoever" (*kênos ônêr ottis* in Sappho, *keinos hos ke* in Homer) is a rhetorical cliché, not an actor in the imagined scene. Interpretations which *focus* on "that someone (male)" as a bridegroom (or suitor or friend) who is actually present and occupying the attention of the addressee miss the strategy of persuasion which informs the poem and in doing so reveal their own androcentric premises. In depicting "the man" as a concrete person central to the scene and god-like in power, such interpretations misread a figure of speech as a literal statement and thus add the weight of their own pro-male values to Sappho's woman-centered consciousness. "That man" in poem 31 is like the military armament in poem 16, an introductory set-up to be dismissed. We do not imagine that the speaker of poem 16 is actually watching a fleet or infantry; no more need we think that Sappho is watching a man sitting next to her beloved. To whom, in that case, would Sappho be addressing herself? Such a reading makes poem 31 a modern lyric of totally internal speech, rather than a rhetorically structured public utterance which imitates other well known occasions for public speaking (prayer, supplication, exhortation, congratulation).

My reading of poem 31 explains why "that man" has assumed a grotesque prominence in discussions of it. Androcentric habits of thought are part of the reason, but even more important is Sappho's intention to hint obliquely at the notion of a bridegroom just as Odysseus does to Nausikaa. Odysseus the stranger designs his speech to the princess around the roles which she and her family will find acceptable--helpless suppliant, valorous adventurer, and potential husband (Austin 1975: 191–200). The ordinary protocols of marital brokerage in ancient society are a system of discreet offers and counter-offers which must maintain at all times the possibility for saving face, for declining with honor and respect to all parties. Odysseus' speech to Nausikaa contains these delicate approaches to the offer of marriage which every reader would appreciate, just as Alkinoos understands Nausikaa's thoughts of marriage in her request to go wash her brothers' dancing clothes: "So she spoke, for she modestly avoided mentioning the word 'marriage' in the presence of her father; but he understood her perfectly" (*Odyssey* 6.66f.). Such skill at innuendo and respectful obliquity is one of the ordinary-language bases for the refined art of lyric speech. Sappho's hint that "someone" enjoys a certain happiness is, like Odysseus' identical statement, a polite self-reference and an invitation to take the next step. Sappho plays with the role of Odysseus as suitor extraordinary, an unheard of stranger who might fulfill Nausikaa's dreams of marriage contrary to all the ordinary expectations of her society. She plays too with the humble formalities of self-denigration and obeisance, all an expansion of *sebas m' echei eisoroôsa*, "holy dread grips me as I gaze on you" (*Odyssey* 161).

"That man is equal to the gods": this phrase has another meaning too. Sappho as reader of the *Odyssey* participates by turn in all the characters; this alternation of attention is the ordinary experience of every reader of the epic and is the basis for Sappho's multiple identification with both Aphrodite and Diomedes in *Iliad* 5. In reading *Odyssey* 6 Sappho takes on the roles of both Odysseus and Nausikaa, as well as standing outside them both. I suggest that "that man is equal to the gods," among its many meanings, is a reformulation of Homer's description of the sea-beaten Odysseus whom Athena transforms into a god-like man: *nun de theoisin eoike toi ouranon eurun echousin*, "but now he is like the gods who control the expanse of heaven" (6.243). This is Nausikaa's comment to her maids as she watches Odysseus sit on the shore after emerging from his bath, and she goes on to wish that her husband might be such.[12] The point of view from which Sappho speaks as one struck to the heart is that of a mortal visited by divine power and beauty, and this is located in the *Odyssey* in the personae of Odysseus (struck by Nausikaa, or so he says), of Nausikaa (impressed by Odysseus), and of the homeric audience, for Sappho speaks not only as the strange suitor and the beautiful princess but as the *Odyssey* reader who watches "that man" (Odysseus) face to face with the gently laughing girl.[13]

In performing this experiment of reading Sappho's poems as expressing, in part, her thoughts while reading Homer, her consciousness of men's public world, I think of her being naturally drawn to the character of Nausikaa, whose romantic anticipation (6.27) and delicate sensitivity to the unattainability of the powerful stranger (244f., 276–84) are among the most successful presentations of a woman's mind in male Greek literature.[14] Sappho sees herself both as Odysseus admiring the nymph-like maiden and as Nausikaa cherishing her own complex emotions. The moment of their separation has what is in hindsight, by the normal process of re-reading literature in the light of its own reformulations, a "Sapphic" touch: *mnêsêi emei'*, "Farewell, guest, and when you are in your homeland remember me who saved you—you owe me this" (*Odyssey* 8.461–2). These are at home as Sappho's words in poem 94.6–8: "And I made this reply to her, 'Farewell on your journey, and remember me, for you know how I stood by you' " (Schadewaldt 1936: 367).

Gardens of Nymphs

The idyllic beauty of Phaiakia is luxuriously expressed in the rich garden of Alkinoos, whose continuously fertile fruits and blossoms are like the gardens which Sappho describes (esp. poems 2, 81b, 94, 96), and it reminds us of Demetrios' words, "Virtually the whole of Sappho's poetry deals with nymphs' gardens, wedding songs, eroticism." The other side of the public/private contrast in Sappho is a design hidden in the lush foliage and flower cups of these gardens. There are two sides to double consciousness: Sappho both re-enacts scenes from public culture infused with her private perspective as the enclosed woman and she speaks publicly of the most private, woman-centered experiences from which men are strictly excluded. They are not equal projects, the latter is much more delicate and risky. The very formulation of women-only secrets, female *arrhêta*, runs the risk not only of impropriety (unveiling the bride) but of betrayal by misstatement. Hence the hesitation in Sappho's most explicit delineation of double consciousness: *ouk oid' otti theô, dicha moi ta noêmmata*, "I am not sure what to set down, my thoughts are double," could mean "I am not sure which things to set down and which to keep among ourselves, my mind is divided" (51).

Among the thoughts which Sappho has woven into her poetry, in a way which both conceals and reveals without betraying, are sexual images. These are in part private to women, whose awareness of their own bodies is not shared with men, and in part publicly shared, especially in wedding songs and rites, which are a rich store of symbolic images bespeaking sexuality (Bourdieu 1979: 105; Abbott 1903: chap. 11). The ordinary ancient concern with fertility, health, and bodily function generated a large family of natural metaphors for human sexuality and, conversely, sexual metaphors for plants and body parts. A high degree of personal modesty and decorum is in no way compromised by a daily language which names the world according to genital analogies or by marriage customs whose function is to encourage fertility and harmony in a cooperative sexual relationship.

I have been able to find no *simple* sexual imagery in Sappho's poems. For her the sexual is always something else as well. Her sacred landscape of the body is at the same time a statement about a more complete consciousness, whether of myth, poetry, ritual, or personal relationships. In the following fragment, 94, which contains a fairly explicit sexual statement in line 23 (West 1970: 322), we find Sappho correcting her friend's view of their relation.

... Without guile I wish to die. She left me weeping copiously and said, "Alas, what fearful things we have undergone, Sappho; truly I leave you against my will." But I replied to her, "Farewell, be happy as you go and remember me, for you know how we have stood by you. Perhaps you don't—so I will remind you ... and we have undergone beautiful things. With many garlands of violets and roses ... together, and ... you put around yourself, at my side, and flowers wreathed around your soft neck with rising fragrance, and ... you stroked the oil distilled from royal cherry blossoms and on tender bedding you reached the end of longing ... of soft ... and there was no ... nor sacred ... from which we held back, nor grove ... sound. ...

As usual the full situation is unclear, but we can make out a contrast of Sappho's view with her friend's. The departing woman says *deina peponthamen,* "fearful things we have suffered," and Sappho corrects her, *kal' epaschomen,* "beautiful things we continuously experienced." Her reminder of these beautiful experiences (which Page 1955: 83 calls a "list of girlish pleasures") is a loving progression of intimacy, moving in space—down along the body—and in time—to increasing sexual closeness: from flowers wreathed on the head to flowers wound around the neck to stroking the body with oil to soft bed-clothes and the full satisfaction of desire. I would like to read the meager fragments of the succeeding stanza as a further physical landscape: we explored every sacred place of the body. To paraphrase the argument, "When she said we had endured an awful experience, the ending of our love together, I corrected her and said it was a beautiful experience, an undying memory of sensual happiness that knew no limit, luxurious and fully sexual. Her focus on the termination was misplaced; I told her to think instead of our mutual pleasure which itself had no term, no stopping-point, no unexplored grove."

Poem 2 uses sacral language to describe a paradisal place (Turyn) which Aphrodite visits:

Hither to me from Krete, unto this holy temple, a place where there is a lovely grove of apples and an altar where the incense burns, and here is water which ripples cold through apple branches, and all the place is shadowed with roses, and as the leaves quiver a profound quiet ensues. And here is a meadow where horses graze, spring flowers bloom, the honeyed whisper of winds. ... This is the very place where you, Kypris ..., drawing into golden cups the nectar gorgeously blended for our celebration, then pour it forth.

The grove, Page comments, is "lovely," a word used "elsewhere in the Lesbians only of *personal* charm" (1955: 36). But this place is, among other things, a personal place, an extended and multi-perspectival metaphor for women's sexuality. Virtually every word suggests a sensuous ecstasy in the service of Kyprian Aphrodite (apples, roses, quivering followed by repose, meadow for grazing, spring flowers, honey, nectar flowing). Inasmuch as the language is both religious and erotic, I would say that Sappho is not describing a public ceremony for its own sake but is providing a way to experience such ceremonies, to infuse the celebrants' participation with memories of lesbian sexuality. The twin beauties of burning incense on an altar and of burning sexual passion can be held together in the mind, so that the experience of either is the richer. The accumulation of topographic and sensuous detail leads us to think of the interconnection of all the parts of the body in a long and diffuse act of love, rather than the genital-centered and more relentlessly goal-oriented pattern of love-making which men have been known to employ.

I have tried to sketch two areas of Sappho's consciousness as she has registered it in her poetry: her reaction to Homer, emblematic of the male-centered world of public

Greek culture, and her complex sexual relations with women in a world apart from men. Sappho seems always to speak in many voices—her friends', Homer's, Aphrodite's—conscious of more than a single perspective and ready to detect the fuller truth of many-sided desire. But she speaks as a woman to women: her eroticism is both subjectively and objectively woman-centered. Too often modern critics have tried to restrict Sappho's *erôs* to the strait-jacket of spiritual friendship.

A good deal of the sexual richness which I detect in Sappho's lyrics is compatible with interpretations such as those of Lasserre 1974 and Hallett 1979,[15] but what requires explanation is their insistent denial that the emotional lesbianism of Sappho's work has any physical component. We must distinguish between the physical component as a putative fact about Sappho in her own life and as a meaning central to her poems. Obviously Sappho as poet is not an historian documenting her own life but rather a creative participant in the erotic-lyric tradition.* My argument has been that this tradition includes pervasive allusions to physical *erôs* and that in Sappho's poems both subject and object of shared physical love are women. We now call this lesbian.† To admit that Sappho's discourse is lesbian but insist that she herself was not seems quixotic. Would anyone take such pains to insist that Anakreon in real life might not have felt any physical attraction to either youths or women?

It seems clear to me that Sappho's consciousness included a personal and subjective commitment to the holy, physical contemplation of the body of Woman, as metaphor and reality, in all parts of life. Reading her poems in this way is a challenge to think both in and out of our time, both in and out of a phallocentric framework, a reading which can enhance our own sense of this womanly beauty *as subject and as object* by helping us to un-learn our denials of it.

NOTES

1. English translation of *Brouillon pour un dictionnaire des amantes* (New York, 1976). There are some uncritical myths in Wittig's own account of Sappho in her essay "Paradigm," in Stambolian and Marks 1979.

2. Lefkowitz 1973 and Hallett 1979 analyze the bias and distortions found in critical comments, ancient and modern, on Sappho.

3. Calder 1988 analyzes Welcker's treatise "Sappho Liberated from a Prevalent Prejudice" (1816), suggesting that Welcker's determination to prove that Sappho was not a lesbian can be traced to his idealization of the mother figures in his life (155–6).

4. This has now been done for the French tradition by DeJean 1989.

5. My statement that this is Sappho's central topic throughout her nine books is based not merely on the few fragments (obviously), but on ancient testimonies, especially those of Demetrios (". . . nymphs' gardens, wedding songs, eroticism—in short the whole of Sappho's poetry") and Himerios ("Sappho dedicated all of her poetry to Aphrodite and the Erotes, making the beauty and charms of a maiden the occasion for her melodies"). These and the other testimonia are collected in Gallavotti 1947 and in Campbell 1982.

6. The text of Sappho used here is that of Edgar Lobel and D. Page (abbreviated L–P), *Poetarum Lesbiorum Fragmenta* (Oxford, 1955).

7. The evidence is found in Hephaistion, *peri sêmêiôn* 138, quoted by Hooker 1977: 11.

8. As Boedeker 1979 shows for fragment 95: "a consciously 'anti-heroic' persona, specifically perhaps an anti-Odysseus. . . . The poem becomes a new personal statement of values, a denial and reshaping of epic-heroic ideals" (52).

*Late Greek rhetoric maintains the tradition of praising a public official at a ceremonial event by a declaration of love. Himerios (48) and Themistios (13) tell their audiences that the honored official is their *erômenos*, boyfriend.

†"Women who love women, who choose women to nurture and support and create a living environment in which to work creatively and independently, are lesbians" (Cook 1979: 738).

9. That would solve the problem felt at Theokritos 2.61, where editors emend *passô* to *massô*.

10. "The classic custom of wooing a damsel by throwing an apple into her lap still exists, though it is condemned by public opinion as improper, and is strongly resented by the maid's kinsfolk as an impertinence" (Abbott 1903: 147–8).

11. E.g., J.B. Bury, ". . . while Sappho confined her muse within a narrower circle of feminine interests" (*Cambridge Ancient History* IV, 1953, 494f.) and similarly Werner Jaeger, *Paideia* (English translation, B. Blackwell: Oxford, 1965), vol. 1, p. 132.

12. The comparison to gods runs throughout the Phaiakian scenes: Nausikaa (16, 105–9), her maids (18), the Phaiakians (241), Nausikaa's brothers, *anthanatois enalinkioi* (7.5).

13. One could also experiment with reading the speaker's symptoms (fever, chill, dizziness) as the result of an erotic spell. The deadening of the speaker's tongue (so beautifully contradicted, of course, by the eloquence and precision of the poet herself) is a typical affliction brought on by a *katadesmos*.

14. Apollonios of Rhodes' Medeia is conscious of love in terms drawn from Sappho (Privitera 1969), and note especially the characteristic presentation of Medeia's mental after-images and imaginings (3.453–8, 811–6, 948–55), which is the technique of Sappho 1, 16, and 96.

15. "It would be most welcome if the adjective 'filthy,' as it is applied [by commentators] to the loves of Sappho, in a gesture that is as anachronistic as it is moralistic, were to fall entirely out of use": Gentili 1966: 48 n. 55. Stehle 1979 is excellent.

REFERENCES

Abbott, G.F. 1903. *Macedonian Folklore* (Cambridge).

Austin, Norman. 1975. *Archery at the Dark of the Moon* (Berkeley).

Barnard, Mary. 1980. "Static," in *Woman Poet, I: The West* (Reno).

Benedetto, V. di. 1973. "Il volo di Afrodite in Omero e in Saffo." *Quaderni urbinati di cultura classica* 16: 121–3.

Bernikow, Louise. 1974. *The World Split Open* (New York).

Boedeker, D.D. 1979. "Sappho and Acheron": 40–52 in G.W. Bowersock, W. Burkert, and M. Putnam, eds., *Arktouros: Hellenic Studies Presented to Bernard W.M. Knox on the occasion of his 65th birthday* (New York).

Bolling, G. 1958. "POIKILOS and THRONA." *American Journal of Philology* 79: 275–82.

Bolling, G. 1959. "Restoration of Sappho, 98a 1–7." *American Journal of Philology* 80: 276–87.

Bonner, C. 1949. "KESTOS IMAS and the Saltire of Aphrodite." *American Journal of Philology* 70: 1–6.

Bourdieu, Pierre. 1979. *Algeria 1960* (Cambridge).

Brashear, W. 1979. "Ein Berliner Zauberpapyrus." *Zeitschrift für Papyrologie und Epigraphik* 33: 261–78.

Butler, Samuel. 1922. *The Authoress of the Odyssey: Where and when she wrote, who she was, the use she made of the Iliad, & how the poem grew under her hands.* 2nd ed., corrected and reset (London).

Calder, W.M. 1988. "F.G. Welcker's *Sapphobild* and its Reception in Wilamowitz": 131–56 in Calder, et al., eds., *Friedrich Gottlieb Welcker, Werk und Wirkung.* Hermes Einzelschrift 49 (Stuttgart).

Cameron, A. 1949. "Sappho's Prayer to Aphrodite." *Harvard Theological Review* 32: 1–17.

Campbell, David A. 1982. *Greek Lyric, I: Sappho, Alcaeus* (Cambridge, MA).

Cook, B.W. 1979. " 'Women Alone Stir My Imagination': Lesbianism and the Cultural Tradition." *Signs* 4: 718–39.

DeJean, Joan. 1989. *Fictions of Sappho, 1546–1937* (Chicago).

Del Grande, C. 1959. "Saffo, Ode *phainetai moi kênos isos.*" *Euphrosyne* 2: 181–8.

duBois, Page. 1978. "Sappho and Helen." *Arethusa* 11: 88–99.

Gallavotti, C. 1947. *Saffo e Alceo: Testimonianze e frammenti* (Naples).

Gentili, B. 1966. "La veneranda Saffo." *Quaderni urbinati di cultura classica* 2: 37–62.

Hallett, J.P. 1979. "Sappho and her Social Context." *Signs* 4: 447–64.

Hooker, J.T. 1977. *The Language and Text of the Lesbian Poets.* Innsbrucker Beiträge zur Sprachwissenschaft 26 (Innsbruck).

Janko, R. 1988. "Berlin Magical Papyrus 21243: A Conjecture." *Zeitschrift für Papyrologie und Epigraphik* 72: 293.

Koniaris, G. 1968. "On Sappho fr. 31 (L–P)." *Philologus* 112: 173–86.

Lanata, C. 1966. "Sul linguaggio amoroso di Saffo." *Quaderni urbinati di cultura classica* 2: 63–79.

Lasserre, F. 1974. "Ornements érotiques dans la poésie lyrique archaïque": 5–33 in John L. Heller, ed., *Serta Turyniana* (Urbana, IL).

Lawler, L.B. 1948. "On Certain Homeric Epithets." *Philological Quarterly* 27: 80–4.

Lefkowitz, Mary R. 1973. "Critical Stereotypes and the Poetry of Sappho." *Greek Roman and Byzantine Studies* 14: 113–23.

Maltomini, F. 1988. "P. Berol. 21243 (Formulario Magico): Due Nuove Letture." *Zeitschrift für Papyrologie und Epigraphik* 74: 247–8.

Marry, J.D. 1979. "Sappho and the Heroic Ideal." *Arethusa* 12: 271–92.

Merkelbach, Reinhold. 1957. "Sappho und ihr Kreis." *Philologus* 101: 1–29.

Nagy, Gregory. 1974. *Comparative Studies in Greek and Indic Meter* (Cambridge, MA).

Neuberger-Donath, R. 1969. "Sappho Fr. 1.1: POIKILOTHRON' oder POIKILOPHRON." *Wiener Studien* 82: 15–7.

Obbink, Dirk. Forthcoming. "Apples and Eros: Hesiod frag. 72–75 M.-W." *Zeitschrift für Papyrologie und Epigraphik.*

Page, Denys. 1955. *Sappho and Alcaeus* (Oxford).

Pfeiffer, Rudolf. 1968. *A History of Classical Scholarship, I: From the Beginnings to the End of the Hellenistic Age* (Oxford).

Privitera, G.A. 1969. "Ambiguità antitesi analogia nel fr. 31 L–P di Saffo." *Quaderni urbinati di cultura classica* 8: 37–80.

Putnam, M. 1960/1. "*Throna* and Sappho 1.1." *Classical Journal* 56: 79–83.

Rissman, Leah. 1983. *Love as War: Homeric Allusion in the Poetry of Sappho.* Beiträge zur klassischen Wissenschaft 157 (Königstein).

Russo, J. 1973(/4). "Reading the Greek Lyric Poets (Monodists)." *Arion* n.s. 1: 707–30.

Saake, H. 1971. *Zur Kunst Sapphos* (Munich).

Schadewaldt, W. 1936. "Zu Sappho." *Hermes* 71: 363–73.

Schaps, David. 1982. "The Women of Greece in Wartime." *Classical Philology* 77: 193–213.

Snell, B. 1931. "Sapphos Gedicht *phainetai moi kênos.*" *Hermes* 66: 71–90.

Stambolian, G. and E. Marks, eds. 1979. *Homosexualities and French Literature* (Ithaca, NY).

Stanley, K. 1976. "The Role of Aphrodite in Sappho Fr. 1." *Greek Roman and Byzantine Studies* 17: 305–21.

Stehle [Stigers], E. 1979. "Romantic Sensuality, Poetic Sense: A Response to Hallett on Sappho." *Signs* 4: 464–71.

Svenbro, J. 1975. "Sappho and Diomedes." *Museum Philologum Londiniense* 1: 37–49.

Turyn, A. 1942. "The Sapphic Ostracon." *Transactions of the American Philological Association* 73: 308–18.

West, M.L. 1970. "Burning Sappho." *Maia* 22: 307–30.

Wills, G. 1967. "The Sapphic 'Umwertung aller Werte.' " *American Journal of Philology,* 88: 434–42.

Winkler, John J. 1990. *The Constraints of Desire: The Anthropology of Sex and Gender in Ancient Greece* (New York).

38

De-constructing the Lesbian Body:
Cherríe Moraga's Loving in the War Years

YVONNE YARBRO-BEJARANO

Yvonne Yarbro-Bejarano is Associate Professor of Romance Languages and Comparative Literature at the University of Washington. She is currently completing a feminist analysis of Lope de Vega's honor plays, and is working on a book on Chicana lesbian writers for The University of Texas Press. In this essay, reprinted from Chicana Lesbians: The Girls Our Mothers Warned Us About *(1991), she argues that Moraga's poetry continually dismantles and recomposes the body in order to make visible the intersecting identities—those of race, class, gender, and culture, as well as sexuality—through which the Chicana subject speaks. Recognizing that the female body has been appropriated, Moraga's poetic construction, deconstruction, and reconstruction of the body seeks to reclaim it from what she takes to be the mind/body dualism of Western culture; and, just as her poetry struggles with external racism and homophobia, so must it resist the oppressive sexual codes that she has internalized.*

In her writing, Cherríe Moraga enacts an impossible scenario: to give voice and visibility to that which has been erased and silenced. Constructed as radically other by the tradition that defines literary authority as white, male, privileged, heterosexual, and culturally dominant, Moraga opens up a space in her writing for a subjectivity that is shaped across and through a multiplicity of discourses in relation to the unified female subject of much white feminist theory.[1] As Norma Alarcón points out, many of the positions from which the Chicana subject speaks are occupied in relation to racial, class, and cultural conflicts and divisions, as well as gender ones. As we renew the emphasis on race, culture, and class as categories of subject formation and oppression, it is crucial to remember that these categories are themselves inflected by constructions of dominant and subordinate sexuality. The mapping of subjectivity and oppression in Moraga's writing is the cartography of lesbian desire, the unspeakable speaking and unrepresentable desire of the lesbian subject *of color,* the Chicana *lesbian.*

The sexual specificity of Moraga's concerns is pre-texted in the title of her book, *Loving in the War Years.*[2] The Chicana lesbian is embattled not only on the streets but also on the field of representation. The attempt to make visible what has always been invisible and to say what has never been said (*lo que nunca pasó por sus labios*) involves the textual construction of the lesbian body and lesbian desire as well as the destruction of conventional codes that govern the representation of female desire and the female body, for example, as object of male heterosexual desire.

But heterosexism and homophobia are not just "out there"; the Chicana lesbian is besieged from within as well as from without. She struggles with the internalization of oppressive attitudes and representational codes in the area of sexuality as well as in those of race, culture, and class. The Chicana lesbian writing subject cannot inhabit a "pure" place of opposition or rejection from which she can construct or destroy the representation of female desire and the female body. Instead, lesbian desire and the lesbian body themselves become the field of negotiation and (de)construction, Gloria Anzaldúa's "borderland," the "third space" of flux and translation.[3]

While *Loving in the War Years* engages the contradictory and complex multiplicity of a Chicana lesbian subject in many different ways, I would like to focus on the representation of the body as site of the struggle to represent a Chicana lesbian desire. In this sense Moraga's writing embodies a "sexual/textual" project that disrupts the dualisms between mind and body, writing and desire. This concern is not limited to *Loving in the War Years,* but runs through all her writing, for example, in the preface to *This Bridge Called My Back,* in which she develops the image of the title: "How can we—this time—not use our bodies to be thrown over a river of tormented history to bridge the gap?"[4]

This bridge-body is rarely recuperated in its entirety in the poems of *Loving in the War Years,* but rather in fragments. Virtually every poem in the collection hinges on some part of the body: "the part of the eye/that is not eye at all/but hole" in "Fear, a Love Poem" (p. 33), "the very old wound in me/between my legs" in "Passage" (p. 44). Moraga's poetry constantly constructs, destructs, and re-constructs the entire female body in the recognition of how it has been appropriated and in the attempt to reclaim it. In "The Voices of the Fallers," Moraga uses the metaphor of falling to explore the potentially fatal perils of lesbian existence.

> I was born queer with the dream
> of falling
> the small sack of my body
> dropping
> off a ledge
> suddenly.

One by one, the parts of the body fragment from the whole and fall through space, to re-assemble only in "dead/silent/collision/with the sand":

> *Listen.*
> Can you hear my mouth crack
> open   the sound
> of my lips bending
> back against the force
> of the fall?

> *Listen.*
> Put your ear deep
> down
> through   the opening
> of my throat and
> *listen.*

her   shoulder first
tumbling
off
the cliff   the legs

following
over
her head....

her body's
dead

silent

collision
with the sand. (pp. 1–3)

The need to speak the unspoken ("trying to make it *be* said, to come out of your mouth")
lends special weight to images of the mouth, tongue, lips, and throat.[5] In her interview
with Moraga, Mirtha Quintanales connects the fundamental importance of this task
with the pervasive imagery of mouths, lips, and throats in Moraga's writing, especially
her poetry. The mouth plays a crucial role in Moraga's sexual/textual project, fusing
two taboo activities, female speaking and lesbian sexuality. The mouth and the cunt
merge, both represented as organs of speech and sex. In this context of speech/sex, the
lesbian body is "whole":

Stretching my legs and imagination so open
to feel my whole body cradled
by the movement of her mouth, the mouth
of her thighs rising and falling, her arms
her kiss, all the parts of her open
like lips moving, talking me into loving. (p. 140)

Moraga develops this connection further at the end of the essay "A Long Line of
Vendidas":

In recent months, I have had a recurring dream that my mouth is too big
to close; that is, the *outside* of my mouth, my lips, cannot contain the
inside—teeth, tongue, gums, throat. I am coming out of my mouth, so to
speak. . . .

I say to my friends as I drive down 91 South, "The Mouth is like a cunt."

La boca spreads its legs open to talk, open to attack. "I am a lesbian. And
I am a Chicana," I say to the men and women at the conference. I watch
their faces twist up on me. "These are two inseparable facts of my life. I
can't talk or write about one without the other."

My mouth cannot be controlled. It will flap in the wind like legs in sex,
not driven by the mind. It's as if la boca were centered on el centro del
corazón, not in the head at all. The same place where the cunt beats.

And there is a woman coming out of her mouth.

Hay una mujer que viene de la boca. (p. 142)

This remarkable passage re-constructs the lesbian body and redistributes her anatomy, decentering the mind and the head and locating "la boca" (newly defined as "mouth/cunt") in the heart. The process reveals the constructedness not only of our attitudes about our bodies, but of our very bodies themselves.

In "Anatomy Lesson," the heart is associated with the dangers of "loving in the war years," as expressed in the title poem: "maintaining/this war time morality/where being queer/and female is as rude/as we can get" (p. 30). The heart is a detachable piece of the anatomy that must be placed in the back pocket "when entering a room full of soldiers who fear hearts" (p. 68). The power of the absent heart makes the soldiers beg to see "what it is they fear they fear." But the poetic voice warns against seduction, underwriting the strategy of self-protection as long as those who fear also wear guns:

> Hang onto your heart.
> Ask them first what they'll give up to see it.
> Tell them that they can begin with their arms.
>
> Only then will *you* begin to negotiate. (p. 68)

The displacing of the head in favor of the heart as center and throne of speech/sexuality operates within the mind/body duality that permeates Western culture. Besides the project of reconstruction and recuperation of the female body, the representation of the body in pieces in Moraga's writing also comments on the ways women are trained to separate from their bodies, site of base impulses and decay in patriarchal discourses.

The opening image of Moraga's second play *The Shadow of a Man,* is the young girl Lupe's disembodied head illuminated by a candle in the shadow of the cross. This image reveals the role of religion in the inculcation of this kind of sublimation and anticipates the bodyless character of Cerecita in the first draft of Moraga's third play *Heroes and Saints.* The female subject of the action is a young Chicana who has no body, only a head.[6] The political aspect of Moraga's dramaturgy comes most to the foreground in this text, since the historical referent of the bodyless female subject is a limbless child born to farmworkers exposed to pesticides in McLaughlin, California, depicted in the United Farmworkers' film *The Wrath of Grapes.* In a reversal of the usual scenario, in which women desperately try to rid themselves of the body, Cerecita is only a head that desperately seeks a body. She delights in her tongue and its multiple possibilities, linguistic, sexual, and visionary: "the power of communication through speech . . . to give tongue . . . to speak in tongues." Frustrated in her attempt to construct herself a body through her sexuality, Cerecita renounces her mouth as sexual organ and sublimates her sexual energy into a visionary "speaking in tongues" to become the saint of the title at the end of the play.

In the poem "For the Color of My Mother," the materiality of the mother's head works against its association with mind and sublimated sexual energy. In its marked *mestiza* physiognomy ("the unnamed part of the mouth/the wide-arched muzzle of brown women"), the head signifies the possible "bridge" among women of color:

> as it should be,
> dark women come to me
> > sitting in circles

I pass thru their hands
the head of my mother
painted in clay colors

touching each carved feature swollen eyes and mouth

they understand the explosion, the splitting
open   contained within the fixed expression

they cradle her silence

nodding to me (p. 61)

Like the shifting meanings of the head, the images of amputation in Moraga's writing do not always signify loss of (parts of) the body that is there and not there at the same time. In *Heroes and Saints,* the bodyless Cerecita possesses one through the force of her dreams and her desire, while the gay priest longs to enter her mind to escape his body. One scene culminates in the ritual of communion, which the priest calls the commingling of their amputated parts, since both are cut off in different ways from their bodies. In "You Call It, *Amputation,*" the body registers the loss yet continues to possess the absent part:

You call it
am pu tation
but even after the cut
they say the toes still itch
the body remembers the knee,
gracefully bending
she reaches down to find her leg gone
the shape under the blanket dropping off
suddenly, irregularly

...

still, I feel
the mutilated body
swimming in side stroke
pumping twice as hard
for the lack
of body, pushing
through your words
which hold no water
for me. (p. 82)

In other texts in *Loving in the War Years,* the pain of the body in pieces is associated with the conflicted relationship between the writing subject and her culture, particularly with the faith of the women in her culture and her family. In a dream, her grandmother appears to her

> ... *outside la iglesia. Standing in front as she used to do after la misa. ... She shows me her leg which has been operated on. The wound is like a huge crater in her calf—crusted, open, a gaping wound.* (pp. iii–iv)

In the Introduction, the writing subject describes how the women who have come to see the image of La Virgen de Guadalupe in Mexico cling to the handrailing of the moving sidewalk:

> . . . their hips banging up against the railing over and over again as it tried to force them off and away. They stayed. In spite of the machine. They had come to spend their time with La Virgen. I left the church in tears, knowing how for so many years I had closed my heart to the passionate pull of such faith that promised no end to the pain. I grew white. Fought to free myself from my culture's claim on me. (p. ii)

Moraga's work is steeped in Catholicism, but as she says in the Preface to Bridge, she does not embrace the resigned faith of institutionalized religion, but the "faith of activists" that "we have the power to . . . change our lives." (p. xviii) At the same time, "faith" is translated to act as a counterbalance to the fear of betrayal by women; faith can mean the desire to believe in the possibility of faithfulness to one another as women, as Chicanas. In "The Pilgrimage," the poetic voice makes the connection between the mother's faith and the daughter's faith in a vision of women bonding. This translation of the concept of faith from one context to another is accomplished through the oral tradition, the mother('s) tongue ("hay una mujer que viene de la boca"), and the act of appropriation of the bleeding and "brown knotted knees" through writing itself which is at the same time a "dreaming":

> She saw women
> maybe the first time
> when they had streamed in long broken
> single file
> out from her mother's tongue—
>
>> "En México, las mujeres crawl
>> on their hands and knees
>> to the basílica door.
>> This proves their faith."
>
> The brown knotted knees were hers
> in her dreaming, she wondered
> where in the journey
> would the dusty knees begin
> to crack,
> would the red blood of the women
> stain the grey bone of the road. (p. 18)

In "Raw Experience" the poetic voice observes her body fragment into "hands," "face," and "mouth":

> I watch myself for clues,
> trying to catch up
> inhabit my body
> again. (p. 49)

Here, as in the description of the women whose hips bang against the railing at the basílica, what separates her from her body and the bodies of the women of her culture is her "whiteness." As a woman of mixed race, Moraga writes an account of a reconnection with "brownness," her own, her mother's, that of *mestizas* and women of color. As is characteristic of the handling of other body parts, the meaning of "skin" is not fixed, but slides between that of badge of difference and that of porous boundary through which connections can be made. In "It Got Her Over," her skin

> had turned on her
> ...
> In the light of Black
> women and children
> beaten/hanged/raped/
>
> ...
>
> Her skin had turned
> in the light of these things.
> Stuck to her now
> like a flat immovable paste
> spread grey over a life.
>
> Still,
> > *it got her over.* (pp. 69–70)

Even though white-skin privilege has helped her survive "in the war years," it cannot help her "get over" her shame at "guilt by association/complicity to the crime":

> recently taken to blushing
> > as if the blood wanted
> to swallow
> > the flesh.
> > ...
> *See this face?*
> > > Wearing it like an accident
> of birth.
> > It was
> a scar sealing up
> a woman, now darkened
> by desire. (pp. 70–71)

In "La Güera," "looking white" both afforded privilege and separated her from her mother, until the oppression she experienced by acknowledging her lesbianism connected her with her mother's own silence and oppression (p. 52).

By representing skin color as something she has or becomes rather than as an essence, by detaching "skin" and "face" from the body or calling it a scar or an accident, Moraga displays the constructedness of "race" in much the same way as her representation of the body undermines an essentialist reading. This is what allows her to write "My brother's sex was white. Mine, brown" (p. 90). If she "grew white" she can also "go brown," as in "For the Color of My Mother": "*I am a white girl gone brown to the blood color of my mother/speaking for her*" (p. 60). Skin can establish boundaries and separation:

> I want to feel
> your touch *outside*
> my body, on the *surface*
> of my skin.

I want to know, *for sure,*
where you leave off
and I begin. (p. 35)

But it is also a "boundary" in Gloria Anzaldúa's sense of a place where two edges meet
and mingle:

seeing yourself for the first time
in the body of this sister

...

like you whom
you've taken in
under your bruised wing

...

taking all this under your wing
letting it wrestle there
into your skin
        changing you. (pp. 27–28)

In "Winter of Oppression, 1982," the *whiteness* of the bodies of the Jewish victims of
the Holocaust provides the shock that loosens the moorage of the concepts "dark" and
"white" and permits the perception of "a colored kind of white people." The writing
subject realizes the impossibility of either choosing or forgetting, of simply falling back
"upon rehearsed racial memory" (pp. 74–75). While retaining a sense of the specificity
of her own oppression as a Chicana lesbian, the writing subject struggles to make the
connections with other kinds of oppression:

I work to remember
what I never dreamed possible
what my consciousness could never
contrive.

Whoever I am

I must believe
I am not
and will never be
the only
one
who suffers. (pp. 75–76)

The dismantling and recomposition of the lesbian body in Moraga's writing is part of
a process of making sense out of the rifts and splits of what Anzaldúa calls "our shifting
and multiple identity."[7] I stress the "process of making sense" rather than the production
of a fixed meaning, for it is the multiplicity of the meanings that attach to the parts
and the whole of the lesbian body/text that allows for diverse de-connections and connections to be made, from "a colored kind of white people" to the cluster of alliances
particularly significant to this process: the tongue that both speaks and caresses, that

connotes the association with the mother('s) tongue and the possibility that something may not be said but still be heard, just as the mouth muzzled in sex still speaks:

la lengua que necesito
para hablar
es la misma que uso
para acariciar

tú sabes.
you know the feel of woman
lost en su boca
    amordazada

it has always been like this.

profundo y sencillo
lo que nunca
pasó
por sus labios

but was
   utterly
   utterly
   heard. (p. 149)

Notes

1. Norma Alarcón, "The Theoretical Subject(s) of *This Bridge Called My Back* and Anglo-American Feminism," in *Making Face, Making Soul: Haciendo Caras,* ed. Gloria Anzaldúa (San Francisco: Aunt Lute, 1990), 356–69.

2. Cherríe Moraga, *Loving in the War Years: Lo que nunca pasó por sus labios* (Boston: South End Press, 1983). Further references will be cited in the text.

3. Gloria Anzaldúa, *Borderlands/La Frontera: The New Mestiza* (San Francisco: Spinsters/Aunt Lute, 1987).

4. Cherríe Moraga and Gloria Anzaldúa, eds., *This Bridge Called My Back: Writings by Radical Women of Color* (Watertown, Mass.: Persephone Press, 1981; 2d ed. New York: Kitchen Table Press, 1983), p. xv. Further references will be cited in the text.

5. Mirtha N. Quintanales, "Loving in the War Years: An Interview with Cherríe Moraga," *off our backs* (January 1985): 12–13.

6. On one hand, this character functions intertextually to place Moraga's play within a specifically Chicano theatrical tradition—namely in relation to Luis Valdéz's *The Shrunken Head of Pancho Villa.* In Valdéz's play, one of the sons of a Chicano family is a head, a reference to the legend that Pancho Villa's body was dug up and decapitated, but the head was never found. During the course of the play, another of the sons is politicized and sent to jail for being a kind of barrio Robin Hood. He returns from the brain-washing experience of incarceration as a body with no head. Implied is the possibility of political movement if the "body" of barrio youth could somehow be joined to the spirit of the Mexican revolution symbolized by the head of Pancho Villa. Moraga recognizes her indebtedness to the political and esthetic dimensions of this play, while at the same time appropriating and transforming the image within a feminist context of concern with questions of the body and sexuality.

7. Preface, *Borderlands/La Frontera,* n.p.

39

When Jack Blinks:
Si(gh)ting Gay Desire in
Ann Bannon's Beebo Brinker

MICHÈLE AINA BARALE

Michèle Aina Barale is Assistant Professor in the Department of English and the Department of Women's and Gender Studies at Amherst College. A co-editor of this volume, she has written on The Well of Loneliness *(in* Inside/Out *ed. Diana Fuss, 1991), on the British author, Mary Webb, in* Daughters and Lovers *(1986), and is completing a book on lesbian writers,* Below the Belt: Essays in Queer Reading *(Routledge). Analyzing here the rhetorical strategies that allowed* Beebo Brinker *to be a cross-over text—a novel originally enjoyed by a heterosexual male audience before finding a lesbian readership—she suggests that those same strategies also disrupt established understandings of gender and refute definitions of desire as the product of a biologically constituted gender. Barale argues that the dominant culture's appropriation of gay texts can be understood therefore as dependent upon the way those texts offer heterosexual readers the covert enjoyment of cross-sexual and cross-gender identification. By pulling together both the heterosexual audience as well as the specifically lesbian author, the essay demonstrates that it is sexuality itself, and not just gayness, that constitutes the focus of gay studies.*

Lesbian narratives do more than re-focus their perspective from dominant cultural figures to those of the subculture, although that is certainly part of their force and their appeal. They also appropriate the dominant culture's own understandings of gender and sexuality, and they do so in order to subvert those understandings for their own sub-cultural purposes. Such narrational strategies serve to cast doubt upon the presumed "naturalness" of gender and sexuality, and call into question common assumptions about the strict oppositions that "gender" and "sexuality" are supposed to encompass: masculinity and femininity in the one case, and hetero- and homosexuality in the other. In addition, these subversive narratives also work to pry gender apart from sexuality—making each distinct from the other, rather than allowing them to function as (con)fused categories of meaning and even interchangeable predictors of what can be expected. By rupturing their assumed unity, gender is refused its culturally presumptive role as sexuality's explicator: neither sexual practice nor preference can be predicated upon the basis of gender. To put it in more colloquial and even personal terms, what I do in bed and who I do it with cannot be accounted for by my gender. Nor, to turn it around, is my gender explained by noting either who or what I sexually find appealing.

One of the benefits of these uses, or shall we better say *mis*uses, of gender and sexuality is the production of narratives which, even when *appearing* to represent lesbians and lesbian desire in heterosexually familiar ways, serve to signify something quite different to the lesbian reader in particular, but also the subcultural reader in general. I want to examine in this essay how a lesbian author, Ann Bannon, can manipulate the telling of an overtly lesbian story, *Beebo Brinker,* in such a way that the heterosexual male reader is, first, invited into the text, then alternately threatened and titillated, and finally implicated in desires that are both lesbian and gay. Ultimately, I will argue that Bannon's novel offers her heterosexual male reader safe entry into gay textual territory, calming his panic by controlling his gaze, repeatedly permitting him to "think hetero" even when he's watching gayness. She does this, I will argue, not to educate him, not to make him more sensitive to or aware of homosexuality's moral rightness; the instructional uses of *Beebo Brinker* are decidedly lesbian. Rather Bannon does this to blur distinctions between something called heterosexuality and some other thing called homosexuality.

I want to suggest that among the pleasures—and the dangers—offered the heterosexual male reader of this novel is the opportunity to engage in non-heterosexual imaginings. Moreover, it is the opportunity to encounter them not as the distant observer of Other Folks rituals of romance, but as participant. To put it simply, *Beebo Brinker* invites the straight male reader to leave his homosexual panic behind. It shows him how folks who might look straight—folks like himself, for instance—do indeed have dreams and desires of a gayer sort. It invites him to come in out of the cold and take part in Close Encounters of the Queer Kind.

Ann Bannon's 1962 novel, *Beebo Brinker,* serves as a particularly handy text with which to demonstrate subcultural appropriation and subversion since it is an example of the cross-over novel in reverse: a text whose initial audience was presumed by Fawcett/ Gold Medal to be primarily male heterosexual but which found and, over two decades maintained, enough of a place within a lesbian readership that The Naiad Press reprinted it in 1983 and again in 1986.[1] My belief that *Beebo*'s marketing was initially targeted at a non-gay male audience is based upon a number of extra-textual factors, including its cover and copy[2] as well as upon the more general evidence offered by the history of the growth of the modern paperback industry itself. That industry's enormous expansion at the end of World War II can be explained, at least in part, by the return of the demobilized forces that had learned the pleasures of the small, inexpensive, and even disposable book through the ubiquitous presence of the Armed Services Editions of literary reprints.[3] In addition, by 1962, Fawcett had already associated itself with the production of sexually daring novels by its publication of Teresa Torres's 1950 bestseller, *Women's Barracks,* whose sales were undoubtedly encouraged by its cover—as four women remove their uniforms, a fully clothed, cigarette smoking WAC observes them ("The frank autobiography of a French girl soldier" reads the cover blurb in bright red)—and by that novel's status as a prime exhibit for the 1952 U.S. House of Representatives Committee on Current Pornographic Materials.[4]

There was probably a gay and lesbian audience for novels such as Torres's since the cover clearly implies the possibility of lesbian activity—at least in the form of spectatorship. Moreover, Fawcett had already published four Bannon novels and seemed able to presuppose the existence of an eager audience for this novel since it used the cover to identify her as the author of *I Am A Woman* (1959) and *Odd Girl Out* (1957), earlier novels in which Beebo Brinker figures.[5] In addition, Barbara Grier's 1970 review for *The Ladder* asserts that Bannon's "almost classic series" of lesbian novels had become hard-to-find "collector's items," a fact that suggests the presence of a loyal audience who is more likely gay than not.[6] But neither the lesbian implications of the Torres cover, nor Fawcett's self-serving advertisement of Bannon's earlier novels, should be understood as evidence that the sought-after audience for the original publication of *Beebo Brinker* was anything other than the heterosexual reader, most broadly, and the male consumer, most specifically. The publication of novels with overt lesbian content is like the use of covers promising a peek into the mysteries of women's barracks: both offered the heterosexual male reader entry into territory usually forbidden him, and both therefore embellished upon culture-wide fantasies that associate the libidinous with women's secret domains.

I am suggesting, therefore, that *Beebo Brinker* was originally perceived by its publisher as being of interest to the dominant culture, that the non-heterosexuality of its eponymous hero presented no impediment to the heterosexual appropriation of its narrative. But I want to go even further, and argue that the very factors in its narrative that enabled the novel to be enjoyed by heterosexuals are the same ones that, from a gay perspective, provoke a subversive reading of the text. What I will contend is that the novel *appears* to substantiate an understanding of gender as monadic, as singly and solely male, with women constituting a category whose meaning is not only male-constructed but male-referenced.[7] However, the novel, in fact, can be demonstrated as undoing, as destabilizing, such a mono-gender system in order to reconstruct a system of lesbian desire and gay subjectivity. The novel inscribes the male upon its narrative and privileges him as the proper and entitled gazer upon the world, but it calls into question the meaning of male. And although the novel identifies its lesbian hero as butch, as "different" from other "girls," as unable to name herself before the acquisition of a male's language, and as caught up in the ideology of romance as any heterosexual woman, Bannon begins to construct representations of a desire that are specifically lesbian.

By destabilizing the coherency of "male" as a meaningful term, and by reconstructing lesbian sexuality as something that can be recognized by a male gazer, inflected by a male diction, and as something that, at times, even seems to *resemble* male sexuality in appearance and behavior, *Beebo Brinker* makes use of a dominant heterosexual ideology in order to subvert it for its gay characters' and its gay readers' pleasures. The novel's representation of gay desire and agency is not only *un*like the non-gay version, but is most recognizable only to those who can share in it. Lesbian representation is thereby achieved, but is perceptible only by those who can read its meaning through their own experience. Such experience is certainly most commonly gained sexually. But that is not its sole means of access.

It takes just a little more than the very first page (35 lines plus two more lines on the next page) for Bannon to suitably name and privilege a man as the world's surveyor—and then un-make him. Thus, it is through a male perspective that the reader is enabled to enter the textual world of the novel whose title, a name of ambiguous gender, calls for some kind of identification, a clarity we are allowed to expect will come from the male gazer. First, however, Bannon names him so as to designate this male as the generic representative of all men and, in the same breath cites the educated shrewdness of his gaze: "Jack Mann had seen enough in his life to swear off surprise forever." As his first name implies, Jack is a most average fellow. After having served as a medic aboard a Navy hospital ship stationed in the Pacific during World War II, Jack did not carry out his fantasies of attending medical school. Instead, he completed the engineering degree he had begun before his military service. Like any number of young men of his generation, when the novel begins, Jack is settled in a stable job as head of drafting for a well-paying firm in New York. But the ordinariness of his life is redeemed by his surname and elevated to the position of a universal. He may be "every man Jack," but he is also Man, *der Mann,* representative of not only the entire category male, but, as male, representative of the category human. As both the most pedestrian and most constitutive of males, Jack Mann is doubly entitled to watch the world go by.[8] Besides, he is an unusually experienced observer, having seen not only the torn and often irreparable bodies of soldiers, but the "sensuous Melanesian girls" and "bronze bare-chested surfers" of Hawaii, as well as the "sly stinking misery of the caves of Iwo Jima" (7). The education of his gaze is emphasized by his terrible vision of male bodies endangered and broken, while his gaze's privilege is underscored by the racial otherness of the female bodies it has focused upon. He has seen both the worst of the world, and the "different" in the world.[9] He is a common man of uncommon vision, unneedful of any further optical education. Unlike his medieval allegorical counterpart, this Jack is an Everyman who does not need his eyes opened to the ways of the world.

What Bannon has done here, of course, is provide the expected male vantage point for her narrative. And she has inscribed her male character with attributes just enough average yet just enough superior to make him a perfect icon for a male reader. Jack may look like a typical guy, but even though he's a middle-aged, bespectacled engineer, he has knowledge of the atypical and thus can fulfill the male reader's wish to conceive of himself as also capable of far more than his appearance might suggest. Having established Jack as a site of narrative access, Bannon now uses the next three paragraphs of the first page to complicate his inscription as male.

Jack fell in love and had a disastrous affair, one both "unhappy and violent" while aboard the hospital ship (7). Yet, "lousy" as that affair was, it was also "peculiarly good now and then" (7). Thus, rather than sour on love, Jack is sold on it, so much so that he has "organized his life around" it and uses his considerable paycheck to "pamper whatever passion came his way" as well as to help "stray people out of trouble, the way others help stray cats" (7). This generosity has meant that he has been taken advantage of more than once, and he has consequently "turned cynic" (7). Yet, "buttoned . . . down under skepticism" there is still hope (7). And the first page's final line indicates the nature of that hope: Jack wants "to stabilize his life, settle down with one person . . ." (7).[10]

The addition of love as his organizing principle, and the suggestion that his cynicism is only camouflage for an ever-hopeful heart, inscribe Jack with what might be considered an almost feminine sensibility. Beneath his common but untrusting exterior, Jack is something of a pretty tender fellow. Although such a depiction does indeed allow the straight male reader a place in which to be the love-struck, even wounded fellow that he has sometimes felt himself to be, and while Jack's quasi-heroic qualities are not utterly undermined by this information, some reevaluation is called for since the text implies that Jack is a fool for love. The heterosexual male who can initially identify with Jack Mann now must adjust his self-siting so as to encompass Jack's longing for love and/or love's misuse of him. Thus Jack's original appositives, engineer and vet, are joined by a third, lover. But the new term does not denote male prowess or derring-do. Instead, it undercuts the usual gendered meaning of that title as it is typically applied to men. However, the next, and *last,* line of the first page mitigates this picture of Jack as a man helplessly paying a high price for love: Jack wants stability and monogamy, we are told, and it is hardly wimpish to make mistakes, or even to sow one's wild oats while searching for the right person with whom to settle down. It's human. Moreover, it's the suitably noble purpose that sanctifies love's more humiliating experiences. It's even the stuff of fond reminiscence and affectionate teasing after the Right One has come along because—turn the first page—it is a search that enables one to "live out a long rewarding love" (8). Jack, it seems, is a family man. The only hitch, as the next line and a half inform us, is that "Jack Mann could only love other men: boys, to be exact" (8).

This turn of events, I will argue, serves to reposition Jack for the male heterosexual reader who now must learn to read from a gay male's point of view or close the book. In the terms of dominant culture, Jack is un-manned. It was a sailor and not a WAVES nurse who occasioned that first disastrous affair, and it is men whom Jack has pampered and for whom he now keeps his eyes open. And not just any men, either, but young men: Jack is a gay male who prefers boys and who pays their way. If Jack as a Lover necessitated some reevaluation of the first three paragraphs that inscribe him as the typical and universal male gazer, Jack as boy-lover completely undoes his surname's honorific. Bannon has used Jack as a lure, his privileged position as male observer as bait, not only to catch an innocent reader of the dominant culture but in order to hook— and then fillet—ideologies of masculinity. And now, having unmade Jack as the conventional, adventuring male, Bannon states that the source of his visual acuity is his very gayness—"His emotional differentness had given Jack a good eye for people, a knack for sizing them up fast" (8).

Thus, Bannon makes use of the male's franchise on gazing, she makes his stare one of experienced probity, but she locates Jack's particular aptitude for such activity in the fact that Jack is bored and restless because he is between boys. Jack is, in fact, looking for the right guy in Greenwich Village streets when he spies "a handsome girl" carrying a wicker suitcase. Jack, the potential lover of boys, provides the reader with the first sight of Beebo.

I am going to assume that at this crisis-laden moment in the novel, some 91 lines into its text, the non-gay male reader keeps on reading. Moreover, I am going to suggest that he is encouraged to continue reading because of the appearance of Beebo Brinker— her appearance narratively at this point in the text and descriptively as well—and because he is being given the opportunity to apprehend her through the eyes of someone who seems to promise an "insider's view." Had Bannon continued to flesh out Jack in these initial pages, the heterosexual reader might become homophobically anxious enough to be forced to disengage from the character. Instead, Bannon controls the level of discomfort, first bonding the reader to Jack, then complicating the nature of that bond, then betraying it, and finally giving the reader good cause to continue to read with Jack nonetheless. For, just when the heterosexual male reader might be faced with the possibility of experiencing his identification with a gay male, Bannon redirects the reader's narrative engagement by introducing a woman upon whom the male reader's gaze can be legitimately focused.

It is quite interesting, of course, that Jack's replacement is not only female but "handsome." The attractive irony in this initial description of Beebo implies her physical connection with male attractiveness and thus makes her a fitting substitute for Jack's appeal; it also suggests that Beebo is not typically feminine and hence that she is possibly a lesbian.[11] Jack now follows her through the crowded Greenwich Village streets, an activity that leads to one further assumption: I will suggest that having mercifully had his narrative interest in Jack deflected to the object of Jack's gaze, the non-gay male gazer can now indulge his curiosity about not only "handsome girls" but also about what men who like boys do with such girls. He can read on to find out what a man, whose sexual preference is for his own sex, might find attractive in a woman whose appearance suggests that she is not typical of her own sex. To put it another way, the male reader is allowed to entertain the notion that heterosexual attraction is still possible in men who prefer men. Or, to state it bluntly, the reader is given the opportunity to redeem himself from *his* initial interest in Jack by being allowed to imagine that Jack is experiencing an erotic pull towards this woman. If Jack was un-manned by his gayness, his gayness can now, in turn, be re-manned with the appearance of Beebo. Just as Jack's masculinity can be restored by the addition of a woman, so too can be the reader's, and the fears of the homophobic reader can be safely put to bed.

In fact, to further the text's heterosexual inscription, Jack's initial encounter with Beebo, followed by their first evening together in Jack's apartment, is similarly filled with erotic potential. On the one hand, their meeting hints of violence (Jack quite literally stalks Beebo through New York streets) and of possible rape (Jack gets Beebo drunk after dinner and begins to undress her). On the other hand, we are offered as well the strong possibility that a mutually-agreed-upon sexual experience is about to be had, since at the evening's conclusion Beebo tipsily climbs into Jack's bed, her earlier wariness having been undone by peppermint schnapps and Jack's kindness. Jack the Mann and the handsome girl seem likely to embark upon activities of the so-called heterosexual sort, precisely because Bannon has employed conventions of behavior—the pick-up, dinner, liquor, and lengthy, intimate conversation—associated with male-female erotic adventures, conventions that offer the titillating potential for both forced and desired sex.

But before we look more closely at Jack and Beebo's meeting and their subsequent night together, Beebo herself needs attending to, since she is the necessary female whose presence initially permits her straight male reader's heterosexual safety.[12] Bannon's creation of a "handsome girl" is intriguingly oxymoronic; that is, the two terms are conceptually exclusionary: they are connotatively at odds with one another (one might even say perverse). Bannon has made Beebo visually ascertainable as female (though not as woman, interestingly enough), as well as visually associated with the male, but not with just any male as the term "mannish" would have done. Beebo resembles an attractive male. Thus, Jack's interest in "tailing" a handsome girl becomes, for the reader, both more clear and more ambiguous at the same time. Is he following her as a *gay* male, fascinated by her boyish appearance, or is he following her as a gay *male,* suddenly attracted by her girlish appeal? Is Jack momentarily heterosexual in his desire, or is he overwhelmingly gay, drawn towards all maleness, even when that maleness resides in a female? However, if the heterosexual male reader finds some slim comfort in Jack's sudden interest in a girl, the reader, unlike Jack, is presented with a stumbling block in the form of that handsome adjective.

Girls who can be described as attractive men are not considered to *be* men. They are presumed to be lesbians, butches, dykes. Beebo the girl, who is also Beebo the boy, is thus also Beebo the lesbian, who must be therefore Beebo the female. The confused status of a re-manned Jack is mirrored in Beebo's confusing amalgam of gender and sexuality. Our confusion is only increased as Bannon multiplies the contradictions of Beebo's appearance. She has "a strong face and bewildered eyes. . . . Irish coloring, but not an Irish face. She walked with firm strides, yet clearly did not know where she was. . . . Jack was amused at the girl's odd air of authority, the set of her chin, the strong rhythm of her walking. . . . Her face . . . was a map of confusion" (9). Beebo is, as well, a walking contradiction. This representation of the female as a composition of opposing signs is one that is textually useful here because it makes Beebo a site of perplexity that is eminently in need of interpretation. It is the gazer/reader who must provide Beebo with coherent meaning; he must posit her intentions amid all these contradictory signals, just as he must read the codes of gender in specific ways if he is to read her solely as a "girl." Beebo's mixture of authority and bewilderment permits the male heterosexual reader some respite from the possible threat of that "handsome" designation, with its overtones of a fine, but masculine, form. Instead, this handsome figure is girlishly confused as to her whereabouts. Also, as we will learn, she is gayly confused as to her sexuality. Jack will, over time, remedy both situations.

When Beebo stops walking, Jack waits "discreetly behind her, leaning against a railing and lighting a cigarette" as he continues to observe her. At this moment, for the space of some thirteen words, our own reading gaze is shifted from Jack's gaze to Beebo's interior: *"She searched . . . for a cigarette in her pocket, but found only tobacco crumbs"* [italics mine] (9–10). For this brief moment of a sentence we lose our perspective on Beebo from Jack's point of view. Let us say that Jack blinks. In that instant we are given information about what Beebo wants and what it is that she finds when she searches. We enter, in that blink of Jack's eye, not only into Beebo's desire, but into her pocket, where she finds the residue of its past contents. When *his* eye is shuttered, *her* interior, the handsome girl's pocket, is perceivable. When *his* gaze is obscured, *her* desire and its satisfactions can emerge.

Beebo's willingness to smoke on city streets may indeed be evidence that she's "come a long way, baby" as a cigarette ad assures its consumers. However nice girls, which is also to say "real women" don't light-up on the street. That Beebo does so may well be evidence of the liberty she now feels free to indulge in this new environment. And it may also be an activity that faintly tinges the air around her with the scent of her difference, her deviation from feminine norms of polite public behavior.[13] But there's more here. Even in the tobacco-espousing era of this novel, cigarette smoking was understood to be a habit, was viewed as an activity the smoker was forced to by cravings beyond control. At this moment in the text, fresh from the farm and at-large in New York, Beebo is impelled to lay aside the rules of feminine decorum in order to satisfy her inner need, her desire.[14]

But if this is a moment when, à la Freud, a cigar isn't only that, it is also an instance when a pocket is more than a pocket. Rather, Beebo's pocket, like the cigarettes Jack is about to offer her, represents the existence of a sexual identity, signifies its experiential presence or potential, but does not precisely locate it within the body. Both pocket and pack are, in fact, artifacts, productions of material culture and economy. And at the moment, one is filled and the other is not, but that emptiness nonetheless offers telltale evidence of what might satisfy Beebo's needs.

Because Jack cannot see into her pocket, Beebo alone knows what might be there. Both entry and touch are acts that are decidedly sexual, in this instance auto-erotic acts. Since this is a lesbian, however, that entry and touch can be seen to represent not only lesbian sexual practice, but to signify as well the lack of gender differentiation that characterizes lesbian desire. She alone knows what might be in her pocket, although another smoker, like a fellow homosexual, might well recognize the meaning of her hand-to-pocket gesture and correctly surmise that she, too, is a smoker searching for her pleasure. Even though her hopes are thwarted and her hand cannot provide for her, both her pocket and her hand have routinely done so in the past, and presumably can do so in the future. Her pocket exists as a space apart from the male gaze's acquisition, yet as a site that can be presumed *if,* like Jack, the reader can recognize the existence of a shared sexuality. For that to happen, however, the reader must cease the homophobic distancing of a heterophilic gaze. The text, here, will not help with this.

Having been disappointed in her quest, Beebo now turns *her* gaze on Jack, looking "square at him" only quickly to drop her eyes (10). For this moment, the perspective of the gaze is reversed. The lesbian has been backgrounded so that it is the endangered female who comes forth. Jack correctly reads her brief stare as the reaction of a lost girl to a strange man's interest. He properly estimates that she is too broke to spend money on cigarettes and so he approaches her, pulls a pack from his pocket, and extends it "with one cigarette bounced forward for her to take." She looks up, startled, then shakes her head and looks away, afraid of him. Jack kids her to reassure her: " 'You'd take it if I were somebody's grandmother. . . . Don't hold it against me that I'm a man' " (10).

In this moment of smoking recognition, Jack offers to share with Beebo the object of their mutual pleasure. One cigarette visibly protrudes for her taking; the rest remain hidden in the pack—a pack that Jack will, in just a few minutes, tuck into her pocket as a "loan." In Jack's proffering of the cigarette and in its phallic protrusion from the pack, Bannon seems to be creating further male and even heterosexual signals for the reader: Jack Mann has in his pack the very thing that Beebo's pocket lacks. Moreover, Beebo's need provides the means for Jack's engagement with her. It also enables him, a moment later, under the rubric of generosity, to place his pack in the very pocket that has been found wanting. A *straight*-forward reading of his gestures could certainly suggest merely Jack's kindness to strangers or, conversely, his ability to take advantage of a propitious circumstance in order to meet a girl. The lesbianism of Beebo's pocket and Jack's own wish that Beebo think of his actions as those of a grandmother, however, undo such a reading. Just when Jack is coming-on manly, he comes on maternally. Having been re-manned with Beebo's entrance, he is unmanned with his own words.

What does it mean when a gay male's property resides on loan in the locus of lesbian desire? Certainly we have parody here, but there is something more, too. Jack's gesture can be seen as the loan of his sexual self-knowledge to someone who has yet to realize that the site of her pleasure lies in other pockets rather than packs, and who has yet to learn that her satisfaction will be those of borrowed "fags" until such time as she can acquire her own brand of choice. The apparent heterosexuality of a male's entry into a female is thus homosexually revised. Bannon reverses the more usual heterosexualizing of potentially homosexual moments. It is a heterosexualizing we have so come to expect that it is nearly invisible in narratives and films. When, for instance, a film depicts the pleasures of intimate male buddyhood, the erotic possibilities of such bonding necessitate both the assurance of virility by the presence of violence and the certainty of heterosexuality by the presence of one or more female love/lust objects. But such narrational hedgings are only the more obvious examples of heterosexual salvagings; visual association of the heterosexual with the homosexual can also work protectively, gracefully superimposing not simply our comforts with the "right" sexuality but gently guiding our understanding of the "other" sexuality so that its threatening significance can be ignored. For example, during the final film credits of *Victor/Victoria,* (Blake Edwards, 1982), the camera lingers almost lovingly upon the at-long-last *properly* paired James Garner and Julie Andrews and then moves to show us the gay couple of Robert Preston and Alex Karras. As it moves, the camera carries with it an image of heterosexuality that it gently places upon the two men: these are no threat, the camera suggests; don't be frightened; just think of them as . . . another happy/heterosexual couple.

Bannon's strategic subversion of the heterosexual potential lurking in Jack and Beebo's cigarette exchange undermines a non-gay reader's hope that this moment or this couple might be recuperated, salvaged for heterosexuality. It's rather like the concluding scene of *Cage aux Folles* (Edouard Molinaro, 1979) when the son's marriage is *not* permitted to inscribe heterosexuality entirely upon the gay couple; instead, as the ceremony proceeds, ZaZa begins to complain loudly to Albin, her queenly querulous voice rising and completely drowning out the priest's words.

Once the homosexual subtext of the cigarette exchange emerges, the scene's heterosexual suggestiveness is completely undermined. Bannon revises the significance of both phallic protrusions and the system of male-owned commodities, in which the female obtains use of *his* wealth in exchange for her sexual and reproductive services. Instead,

Jack's loan is for the purpose of Beebo's self-knowledge and self-satisfaction, both of which will come about quite apart from his own sexual pleasure. His entry into her interior originates in his grandmotherly self-identity and, like the loan, is intended to enable her to learn, not the joys of male protrusions but the pleasures of female pockets.

The third and final scene I want to examine takes place in Jack's apartment approximately ten pages later. It is possible, of course, that some slow-learning reader is still hoping for a redemptive vision of Jack in the sack, although I suspect that, by this point, most heterosexual readers have gotten wise to Bannon's ways with Jack and are continuing to read simply out of interest. With the scene's final image of Jack and Beebo in bed together, Bannon calls into question the presumed heterosexuality of all such male-female embeddings, and she does so by continuing to make use of behaviors and tropes generally coded heterosexual.

During the course of the evening, Beebo drinks a great deal of schnapps. Although in other novels in the series she is an alcoholic, in this we learn she is a virgin drinker and she becomes, at first, quite garrulous and then quite woozy. When, with Jack's help, she stumbles in to the bedroom and throws herself "spread-eagled" upon the double bed, Jack undresses her. Bannon allows the erotic possibilities to become conscious here; she allows Beebo to become suddenly alert as she feels Jack yank off her socks, and gives Beebo the angry protest: "Why, you lousy man" (22). However, Jack then calms Beebo's fears by dramatically sniffing her socks, grimacing, and responding: "God, what an exciting creature you are," while surveying her "with all the ardor of an old hen," a repetition of the grandmother motif (22).

Having quelled that momentary heterosexual eruption, Bannon then has Jack give Beebo one of his nightshirts—a garish scarlet and orange cotton flannel (is Bannon putting to rest stereotypes of the gay male's sartorial good taste?) as he explains: "I like flashy sleepers" (22). This could be a *Pajama Game* (1957) moment, in which a female's femininity is exaggerated by her diminutive appearance in the top half of the larger male's apparel. (She cannot, of course, wear the bottom half as well, because not only is it important that her legs be visible, but it is also necessary that the site of *his* manhood be visibly located beneath the waist while modestly covered by the pajama trousers.) But, this isn't *Pajama Game,* if for no other reason than that Bannon has already informed us that Beebo has four inches on Jack (10)—he's not so much short as she is tall—and that her body is "all muscular angles," while her posture, like her voice is adamantly and permanently boyish (22). The nightshirt, thus, has no femininity to underscore for Beebo; moreover it is a less than graceful fit. Beebo's gawky appearance in Jack's garment makes the heterosexuality of all *Pajama Games* suspect. In his nightshirt she appears hopelessly un-girlish and, furthermore, Jack's words suggest that this is an article of clothing others of his sleepers have worn for his *aesthetic* pleasures, if nothing else. Beebo is, therefore, garbed in the apparel of Jack's male lovers and that fact then serves to confuse the scene's resemblance to *Pajama Game*'s heterosexuality still further. As with Jack's earlier interest in tailing Beebo, one might wonder here about the exact nature of the attraction that is found in the demi-dressed female. Is this attraction based upon the semi-visibility of her femininity? Or does it derive from the male inscription her borrowed costume provides? Does the half-male-pajamaed woman provoke both male and female heterosexual interest precisely because, for each, she can signify the male? Do heterosexual women in the audience use the half-male-clad female figure as a pedagogical device whereby they can learn a clothing code attractive to male heterosexuals who find the figure alluring precisely because it *is* coded male?

At any rate, Beebo dons the nightshirt, a garment which precludes the possibility that Jack can wear its bottom half, is helped into the bathroom where she throws up her schnapps, is given mouthwash, has her hands and face washed for her, and is guided back to bed, where she promptly falls asleep. Just before he turns out the light, Jack gazes at the unconscious Beebo in his bed, smoothing the hair off her forehead, "admiring her features and flawless skin, an admiration without the least taint of physicality" (23)— and he scoffs at himself "for wishing she were the boy she so resembled at that moment" (23). He then lies down next to her and goes to sleep.

In that darkness, the sleeping couple look hopelessly heterosexual. But as we now know, there is a grandmother in that bed who wishes that the body next to his were a boy who looks just like the girl who is there, and the girl who is there looks just like the boy she fears she is and fears she isn't. We have come to know Jack's wishes and to infer Beebo's desire; the content of their dreams we can begin to guess. This sleeping couple has become a textual site where the appearance of heterosexual pairing provides the very bed for gay fantasies and lesbian desires to unfold in the comfortably shared dark. Gay readers have been offered a place in which to dream; they have been invited to understand that even the most sanctified sites of heterosexuality are spaces in which homosexuality can and does live. And the straight male reader now knows this too. The heterosexuality of his bed, his partners, and himself has just been called into question. Might that heterosexuality, too, be only an appearance beneath which reside unspoken wishes and unarticulated dreams whose telling would unmake the very bed of his identity? Only a mistaken gazer, one uneducated by these first few pages' lessons, can see this sleeping couple and believe that their anatomical differences and their intimate nestling can offer any proof of their heterosexuality.

NOTES

1. Ann Bannon, *Beebo Brinker* (Greenwich, CT: Gold Medal/Fawcett, 1962); reprinted (Tallahassee, FL: Naiad, 1983). All references are to the Naiad edition; citations appear in parentheses in the text.

2. In an earlier essay, I argued that the same sort of relationship between cover and audience can be seen in the covers of the last three decades of reprints of *The Well of Loneliness*. See my "Below the Belt: Uncovering *The Well of Loneliness*," in *Inside/Out: Lesbian Theories, Gay Theories*, ed. Diana Fuss (New York: Routledge, 1991) 235–258.

3. See Thomas L. Bonn, *Under Cover: An Illustrated History Of American Mass Market Paperbacks* (Middlesex; New York; Victoria; Ontario: Penguin, 1982) 47–48.

4. See Bonn, *Under Cover*, p. 70 and Kate Adams, "Making the World Safe for the Missionary Position: Images of the Lesbian in post-World War II America," in *Lesbian Texts and Contexts: Radical Revisions*, eds. Karla Jay and Joanne Glasgow (New York and London: New York University Press, 1990) 255–274.

5. Bannon's four previous novels, *Odd Girl Out* (1957), *I Am A Woman* (1959), *Woman In The Shadows* (1959), and *Journey To A Woman* (1960) were all Fawcett Gold Medal originals. All four novels depict the romantic adventures of a set of interrelated characters and although they precede *Beebo Brinker* in publication, *Beebo Brinker* chronologically begins the series. All of these novels have been reprinted by Naiad Press.

6. Barbara Grier [pseud. Gene Damon], *Lesbiana: "Book Reviews" from The Ladder, 1966–1972* (Tallahassee, FL: Naiad, 1976) 203.

7. My understanding of a mono-gender system relies heavily upon Teresa de Lauretis's essay, "Sexual Indifference and Lesbian Representation," *Theatre Journal* 40:2 (May, 1988) 155–177 (reprinted in this volume), and, I hope, does not misrepresent her. Dean MacCannell and Juliet Flower MacCannell's essay, "The Female Beauty System," in *The Ideology of Conduct: Essays in Literature and the History of Sexuality*, eds. Nancy Armstrong and Leonard Tennenhouse (New York and London: Methuen, 1987) 206–238, although quite differently focused, dovetails usefully with de Lauretis. Both articles are concerned with the meaning of woman as a gender given her historical

male construction, although de Lauretis, as her title indicates, is particularly interested in problems of lesbian representation in light of the appropriation of female sexuality by heterosexual males. I am making considerable conceptual use, as well, of Eve Kosofsky Sedgwick's "Across Gender, Across Sexuality: Willa Cather and Others," *South Atlantic Quarterly* 88:1 (Winter, 1989) 53–72 where she, like de Lauretis, and like Gayle Rubin ("Thinking Sex: Notes for a Radical Theory of the Politics of Sexuality" in *Pleasure And Danger: Exploring Female Sexuality,* ed. Carole S. Vance [Boston: Routledge, 1984] 267–319; reprinted, with revisions, in this volume) of whom she makes most interesting use, begins to disentangle sexuality from gender:

> Let's hypothesize, with Gayle Rubin, that the question of gender and the question of sexuality, inextricable from each other though they are in that each can be expressed only in the terms of the other, are nonetheless not the same question, that gender and sexuality represent two analytic axes that may productively be imagined as being as distinct from each other as, say, gender and class, or class and race.

8. MacCannell and MacCannell: "The main expression of masculine orientation toward women in our society is a non-reciprocal license to study, stare, examine . . ." ("Female Beauty," 207).

9. I am grateful to the unnamed *Feminist Studies* reviewer who pointed out to me that Jack's knowledge of racial difference might sensitize him to gender and sexual differences.

10. Although Bannon had no control over how much text would make up any page, she is, obviously, in control of the content in and ordering of her paragraphs. It is a matter of chance that the novel's first page ends where it does, but it is not at all chance that the first three paragraphs function in one way, that the next three function in another, and that the seventh, concluding on page seven's verso, destabilizes both previous sets.

11. My suggestion that Beebo's heterosexuality can be considered questionable by the presence of nothing more than the dictional designation "handsome" is based upon early feminism's premise that a woman can never prove she is not lesbian. The gender system is so tightly tied to heterosexuality that the slightest deviation from its conventions is sufficient to call into question sexual orientation. Because Bannon inscribes Beebo with more than one such non-conforming sign, I think it is fair to assume that she has chosen the word "handsome" knowledgeably, and rejected its possible alternatives—"pretty," "cute," "beautiful," "lovely," "attractive," "striking," and so forth—purposefully. Bannon, in other words, intended the term's "masculine" connotation.

12. Eve Kosofsky Sedgwick, of course, posits this male-male-female triangle as the basic cultural unit by which gender oppression and, frequently, homophobia are maintained. See *Between Men: English Literature and Male Homosocial Desire* (New York: Columbia University Press, 1985) 21–27. I will push just a little further regarding this scene in the novel, and allow myself to be tempted to the extreme by Sedgwick's own daring: it seems to be very plausible that the heterosexual male reader understands quite well his attraction to other men. What confuses him is his attraction to women. If nothing else, Jack's seeming erotic interest in a woman—an interest designated by his following her—holds out the possibility that some light will be shed on the nature of heterosexual erotic attraction. But the fact that Jack stalks her though crowded city streets, aware that she seems lost, also suggests the possibility that there is a kind of voyeuristic violence attached to men's attraction to women. Also, Beebo's physical description, with its hint of masculinity, serves to associate such violent interest with both female and male objects of desire.

13. I am grateful to Martha Vicinus for reminding me of what nice girls didn't do in the early 1960s.

14. I am grateful to Eve Sedgwick and Andrew Parker for their insights into the ways in which homosexuality and addiction are entwined in the cultural imagination. One may, of course, want simply to name tobacco as another form of drug and thus understand homosexuals as having kinship with other self-abusers and self-deluders—those members of the so-called drug subculture. But if, instead, we think of the desire for tobacco as a craving we are helpless to deny, the need to control the body's incessant demand to smoke begins to seem analogous to the need to control the feared emergence of homosexual fantasies in the heterosexual (the "non-smoker," as it were). From deep within the body, bypassing the mind's knowledge of danger and the will's ability to deny satisfaction, an urge forces its way into consciousness. I cannot help but wonder if some

complicated part of contemporary anti-smoking rhetoric isn't only about health but also reflects a deep-seated homosexual panic; isn't there some way in which one group's desire to satisfy its smokey yearnings might not somehow call to mind the way a very different set of longings keep arising—past all the censors and all volition—in the imagination of another group? Our national concern with all addiction, and our attempt to name a wildly broad group of behaviors "addictive," seems invested in more than pink lungs and soaring medical costs.

40

"It's Not Safe. Not Safe at All":
Sexuality in Nella Larsen's Passing

DEBORAH E. MCDOWELL

Deborah E. McDowell, Professor of English at the University of Virginia, is the author of " 'The Changing Same': Studies in Fiction by African American Women," editor of the Beacon Black Women Writers series, and co-editor with Arnold Rampersad of Slavery and the Literary Imagination *(1989). This essay is excerpted from her Introduction to the 1986 single volume edition of* Quicksand and Passing. *Even in the Freudian 1920s of Nella Larsen's day, entrenched myths of Black women's hypersexuality led Black women novelists to handle sexuality cautiously. McDowell suggests that for Larsen discretion involved finding a way to depict Black female sexuality while still establishing Black women as respectable in the eyes of the Black middle class. Although Larsen risks suggesting the existence of lesbian desire in* Passing, *she also misdirects her readers chiefly by submerging that dangerous sexual story in the safer plot of racial passing. By such narrative disguise and self-contradiction, says McDowell, Larsen performs the very act—passing—that the novel has worked so hard to expose.*

Until the early 1970s when previously "lost" work by women writers began to be recovered and reprinted, Nella Larsen was one of several women writers of the Harlem Renaissance relegated to the back pages of that movement's literary history, a curious fate since her career had such an auspicious beginning. Touted as a promising writer by blacks and whites alike, Larsen was encouraged by some of the most influential names on the 1920s arts scene. Walter White, onetime director of the NAACP, read drafts of *Quicksand* and urged Larsen along to its completion. Carl Van Vechten, popularly credited with promoting many Harlem Renaissance writers, introduced the novel to his publisher, Knopf. These efforts paid off. Larsen won second prize in literature in 1928 for *Quicksand* from the Harmon Foundation which awarded outstanding achievement by Negroes. *Quicksand* was also well received by the critics. In his review of the novel W.E.B. Du Bois, for example, praised it as the "best piece of fiction that Negro America has produced since the heyday of Chesnutt."[1] *Passing* was equally well received. One reviewer gave the novel high marks for capturing, as did no other novel of the genre, the psychology of racial passing with "consummate art."[2] Due largely to the success of these first two novels, Larsen won a Guggenheim in 1930—the first black female creative writer to be so honored—to do research on a third novel in Spain and France. That novel was never published.

After the publication of *Passing*, Larsen published her last piece, a story entitled "Sanctuary." The subject of much controversy, many speculate that the scandal it created helped to send Larsen into obscurity. Following the publication of the story in 1930

616

Larsen was accused of plagiarism. One reader wrote to the editor of the magazine about the striking resemblance of Larsen's story to one by Sheila Kaye-Smith, entitled, "Mrs. Adis," published in the January 1922 issue of *Century* magazine. The editor of the *Forum* conducted an investigation and was finally convinced that the resemblance between the stories was an extraordinary coincidence. In compliance with the editor's request, Larsen wrote a detailed explanation of the way in which she came by the germ for her story, trying to vindicate herself. Despite her editor's support, Larsen never recovered from the shock of the charge.[3] She disappeared from the literary scene and returned to nursing at Bethel Hospital in Brooklyn where she remained until her retirement. She died in Brooklyn in 1963, practically in obscurity.

Since the very beginning of their history running over roughly 130 years, black women novelists have treated sexuality with caution and reticence, a pattern clearly linked to the network of social and literary myths perpetuated throughout history about black women's libidinousness. It is well known that during slavery the white slave master constructed an image of black female sexuality which shifted responsibility for his own sexual passions onto his female slaves. They, not he, had wanton, insatiable desires that he was powerless to resist. The image did not end with emancipation. So persistent was it that black club women devoted part of their first national conference in July 1895 to addressing it.[4] Though myths about black women's lasciviousness were not new to the era, a letter from one J.W. Jacks, a white male editor of a Missouri newspaper, made them a matter of urgent concern to black club women. Forwarded to Josephine S. Pierre Ruffin, editor of the *Woman's Era*,[5] the letter attacked black women's virtue, supplying "evidence" from other black women. According to Jacks, when a certain Negro woman was asked to identify a newcomer to the community, she responded, "the negroes will have nothing to do with 'dat nigger,' she won't let any man, except her husband sleep with her, and we don't 'sociate with her."[6] Mrs. Ruffin circulated the letter widely to prominent black women and to heads of other women's clubs around the country, calling for a conference to discuss this and other social concerns of black women.

Given this context, it is not surprising that a pattern of reticence about black female sexuality dominated novels by black women in the nineteenth and early twentieth centuries. They responded to the myth of the black woman's sexual licentiousness by insisting fiercely on her chastity. Fighting to overcome their heritage of rape and concubinage, and following the movement by black club women of the era, they imitated the "purity," the sexual morality of the Victorian bourgeoisie. In such works as Emma Dunham Kelley's *Megda* (1891), Frances E.W. Harper's *Iola Leroy* (1892), and Pauline Hopkins's *Contending Forces* (1900),[7] black heroines struggle to defend and preserve the priceless gem of virginity.

Even in Larsen's day, the Freudian 1920s, the Jazz Age of sexual abandon and "free love"—when female sexuality, in general, was acknowledged and commercialized in the advertising, beauty, and fashion industries—black women's novels preserve their reticence about sexuality. Larsen and Jessie Fauset, among the most prolific novelists of the decade, lacked the daring of their contemporaries, the black female blues singers such as Bessie, Mamie, and Clara Smith (all unrelated), Gertrude "Ma" Rainey, and Victoria Spivey. These women sang openly and seductively about sex and celebrated the female body and female desire as seen, for example, in a stanza from Ma Rainey's, "It's Tight like That": "See that spider crawling up the wall . . . going to get his ashes hauled./Oh it's tight like that." Or Clara Smith's "Whip It to a Jelly": "There's a new game, that can't be beat/You move most everything 'cept your feet/Called whip it to a jelly, stir it in a bowl/You just whip it to a jelly, if you like good jelly roll."[8]

Jessie Fauset and Nella Larsen could only hint at the idea of black women as sexual subjects behind the safe and protective covers of traditional narrative subjects and conventions. Though their heroines are not the paragons of chastity that their nineteenth-century predecessors created, we cannot imagine them singing a Bessie Smith lyric such as "I'm wild about that thing" or "You've got to get it, bring it, and put it right here." Rather, they strain to honor the same ethics of sexual conduct called for by a respondent to a 1920s symposium titled "Negro Womanhood's Greatest Needs." Conducted by some of the same leading Negro club women who had organized around Jacks's libelous attack on black women's virtue, the symposium ran for several issues in the *Messenger,* one of the black "little magazines" of the period. The writer lamented what she called the "speed and disgust" of the Jazz Age which created women "less discreet and less cautious than [their] sisters in years gone by." These "new" women, she continued, were "rebelling against the laws of God and man." Thus, she concluded that the greatest need of Negro womanhood was to return to the "timidity and modesty peculiar to pure womanhood of yesterday."[9]

The blues lyrics and the club women's symposium capture, respectively, the dialectic of desire and fear, pleasure and danger that defines women's sexual experiences in male-dominated societies. As Carole Vance maintains, "Sexuality is simultaneously a domain of restriction, repression, and danger as well as a domain of exploration, pleasure, and agency."[10] For women, and especially for black women, sexual pleasure leads to the dangers of domination in marriage, repeated pregnancy, or exploitation and loss of status.

Both *Quicksand* and *Passing* wrestle simultaneously with this dialectic between pleasure and danger. In their reticence about sexuality, they look back to their nineteenth-century predecessors, but in their simultaneous flirtation with female sexual desire, they are solidly grounded in the liberation of the 1920s. Their ideological ambivalences are rooted in the artistic politics of the Harlem Renaissance, regarding the representation of black sexuality, especially black female sexuality.

The issue of representing black sexuality was highly controversial during the movement. As many have argued, Carl Van Vechten's novel *Nigger Heaven* (1926) set the pattern that would dominate the literary treatment of black sexuality in the decade. Amritjit Singh suggests, for example, that the novel "had a crippling effect on the self-expression of many black writers by either making it easier to gain success riding the bandwagon of primitivism, or by making it difficult to publish novels that did not fit the profile of the commercial success formula adopted by most publishers for black writers."[11]

Such novels as Claude McKay's infamous *Home to Harlem* (1928) and Arna Bontemps's *God Sends Sunday* (1931) are said to follow the Van Vechten script. In them black women are mainly "primitive exotic" sex objects, many of them prostitutes, an image which Nathan Huggins correctly identifies as a "male fantasy." It is difficult, he adds rightly, "to draw sympathetic females whose whole existence is their bodies and instinct." Besides, he concludes, "Perhaps women, whose freedom has natural limitations—they have babies—are essentially conservative."[12] Helga Crane's outcome poignantly demonstrates this connection between sexuality and reproduction.

There were those—Jessie Fauset, Nella Larsen, W.E.B. Du Bois, among them—who found the primitive/exotic stereotype associated with Van Vechten limited, at best. Du Bois voiced his objections vehemently on the pages of the *Crisis,* virtually waging a one man, morality-minded campaign against the "nastiness" he saw embodied in novels that seemed to follow the Van Vechten lead. Du Bois was committed to the struggle of "racial uplift" and social equality, a struggle best waged, in his opinion, by the "talented tenth," the elite group of black intellectuals and artists. In that struggle, art had a vital, and necessarily propagandistic role to play.[13]

Du Bois reviewed Claude McKay's *Home to Harlem* and Larsen's *Quicksand* together for the *Crisis,* praising Larsen's novel as "a fine, thoughtful and courageous piece of work," while criticizing McKay's as so "nauseating" in its emphasis on "drunkenness, fighting, and sexual promiscuity" that it made him "feel . . . like taking a bath."[14]

In this context, Larsen was indeed caught between the proverbial rock and hard place. On the one side, Carl Van Vechten, roundly excoriated along with his "followers" by many members of the black middle-class intelligentsia, was her friend. He was responsible for introducing *Quicksand* to Knopf, and perhaps Larsen showed her gratitude by dedicating *Passing* to him and his wife Fania Marinoff. On the other side, Larsen was a member of the black intelligentsia whose attitudes about art Van Vechten had criticized in *Nigger Heaven,* using Russett Durwood as mouthpiece. Durwood advises Byron Kasson, the would-be black writer, to abandon the old cliches and formulas and write about what he knows—black life in the raw. Harlem is "overrun with fresh, unused material," he tells Kasson. "Nobody has yet written a good gambling story; nobody has touched the outskirts of cabaret life; nobody has gone into the curious subject of the diverse tribes of the region." He concludes with the prediction that if the "young Negro intellectuals don't get busy, a new crop of Nordics is going to spring up . . . and . . . exploit this material before the Negro gets around to it."[15] Van Vechten was one such Nordic.

In her criticism of such black bourgeois intellectuals as Robert Anderson and James Vayle in *Quicksand,* Larsen would seem to share some of Van Vechten's opinions of that class. But as much as she could poke fun at their devotion to "racial uplift," she belonged, blood and breath, to that class, and must have found it extremely difficult to cut her ties with it.

To be writing about black female sexuality within this conflicted context, then, posed peculiar problems for Larsen. The questions confronting her might well be formulated: How to write about black female sexuality in a literary era that often sensationalized it and pandered to the stereotype of the primitive exotic? How to give a black female character the right to healthy sexual expression and pleasure without offending the proprieties established by the spokespersons of the black middle class? The answers to these questions for Larsen lay in attempting to hold these two virtually contradictory impulses in the same novel. We might say that Larsen wanted to tell the story of the black woman with sexual desires, but was constrained by a competing desire to establish black women as respectable in black middle-class terms. The latter desire committed her to exploring black female sexuality obliquely and, inevitably, to permitting it only within the context of marriage, despite the strangling effects of that choice both on her characters and on her narratives.

Irene . . . was trying to understand the look on Clare's face as she had said goodbye. Partly mocking, it had seemed, and partly menacing. *And something else for which she could find no name.* [Emphasis added]
      —*Passing*

She wished to find out about this hazardous business of "passing," this breaking away from all that was familiar and friendly to take one's chance in another environment.
      —*Passing*

While in *Quicksand* Larsen explores the question of female sexuality within the "safe" and "legitimate" parameters of marriage, in *Passing,* she takes many more risks. Although Clare and Irene—the novel's dual protagonists—are married, theirs are sexless marriages. In Clare's case, the case of a woman who is "passing," the frequent travels of her financier husband and her fear of producing a dark child, explain this situation. In Irene's case, the narrative strongly indicates, her own sexual repression is at fault. It is significant that Irene and her husband sleep in separate bedrooms (he considers sex a joke) and that she tries to protect her sons from schoolyard discussions about sex. Having established the absence of sex from the marriages of these two women, Larsen can flirt, if only by suggestion, with the idea of a lesbian relationship between them.

It is no accident that critics have failed to take into account the novel's flirtation with this idea, for many are misled, as with *Quicksand,* by the epigraph.[16] Focusing on racial identity or racial ambiguity and cultural history, the book invites the reader to place race at the center of any critical interpretation. Interestingly, Larsen uses the almost romantic refrain of Countée Cullen's poem "Heritage" as the novel's epigraph—"One three centuries removed/From the scenes his fathers loved,/Spicy grove, cinnamon tree,/What is Africa to me?"—foregoing the more dramatic and more appropriate possibilities of the poem's ending:

> All day long and all night through,
> One thing only must I do:
> Quench my pride and cool my blood,
> Lest I perish in the flood.
> Lest a hidden ember set
> Timber that I thought was wet
> Burning like the dryest flax,
> Melting like the merest wax,
> Lest the grave restore its dead.

Not only does the epigraph mislead the reader, but Irene, the central consciousness of the narrative, does as well. It is largely through her eyes, described appropriately as "unseeing," that most of the narrative's events are filtered, significantly, in retrospect and necessarily blurred. The classic unreliable narrator, Irene is confused and deluded about herself, her motivations, and much that she experiences. It is important, therefore, to see the duplicity at the heart of her story. As Beatrice Royster rightly observes,

> Irene is an ideal choice as narrator of a tale with double meanings. She tells the story as the injured wife, betrayed by friend and husband; she tells it as a confession to clear her conscience of any guilt in Clare's death.[17]

Irene paints herself as the perfect, nurturing, self-sacrificing wife and mother, the altruistic "race woman," and Clare as her diametrical opposite. In Clare, there was "nothing sacrificial." She had "no allegiance beyond her own immediate desire. She was selfish, and cold and hard," Irene reports. Clare had the "ability to secure the thing that she wanted in the face of any opposition, and in utter disregard of the convenience and desires of others. About her there was some quality, hard and persistent, with the strength and endurance of rock, that would not be beaten or ignored." Irene describes Clare as "catlike," suggesting that she is given to deception, to furtive, clandestine activity. On the basis of her observations of Clare, Irene concludes, with an attitude of smug self-satisfaction, that she and Clare are not only "strangers . . . in their racial consciousness," but also "strangers in their ways and means of living. Strangers in their desires and ambitions."

As is often typical of an unreliable narrator, Irene is, by turns, hypocritical and obtuse, not always fully aware of the import of what she reveals to the reader. Ironically, detail for detail, she manifests the same faults of which she so harshly accuses Clare. Despite her protestations to the contrary, Irene, with a cold, hard, exploitative, and manipulative determination, tries to protect her most cherished attainment: security, which she equates with marriage to a man in a prestigious profession, the accoutrements of middle-class existence—children, material comfort, and social respectability. Moreover, Irene resorts to wily and feline tactics to insure that illusion of security. After persuading her husband to abandon his dream of leaving racist Harlem to practice medicine in Brazil, Irene rationalizes that she had done this, "not for her—she had never really considered herself—but for him and the boys."

Even Irene's work with racial uplift programs, such as the Negro Welfare League, reveal her true value orientation. Although she deludes herself that this work is a barometer of her racial consciousness, it is actually self-serving, not undertaken for the good of the race. The social functions that Irene arranges, supposedly designed to aid the unfortunate black masses and to give them a sense of belonging, are so heavily attended by prominent whites that her husband, Brian, fears, " 'Pretty soon the colored people won't be allowed in at all, or will have to sit in Jim Crowed sections.' " Thus, the narrative betrays Irene at every turn, as she comes to evince all that she abominates in Clare.

Not only does Larsen undercut Irene's credibility as narrator, but she also satirizes and parodies the manners and morals of the black middle class that Irene so faithfully represents. That parody comes through in the density of specificity in the novel, as seen in the description of a typically run morning in Irene's household:

> They went into the dining-room. [Brian] drew back her chair and she sat down behind the fat-bellied German coffeepot, which sent out its morning fragrance mingled with the smell of crisp toast and savoury bacon, in the distance. With his long, nervous fingers he picked up the morning paper from his own chair and sat.
> Zulena, a small mahogany-coloured creature, brought in the grapefruit.
> They took up their spoons.

The descriptions of the endless tea and cocktail parties and charity balls capture the sterility and banality of the bourgeoisie, likewise emphasizing Larsen's satire.

> There were the familiar little tinkling sounds of spoons striking against frail cups, the soft running sounds of inconsequential talk, punctuated now and then with laughter. In irregular small groups, disintegrating, coalescing, striking just the right note of disharmony, disorder in the big room, which Irene had furnished with a sparingness that was almost chaste, moved the guests with that slight familiarity that makes a party a success.

Although Irene is clearly deluded about her motives, her racial loyalty, her class, and her distinctness from Clare, the narrative suggests that her most glaring delusion concerns her feelings for Clare. Though, superficially, Irene's is an account of Clare's passing for white and related issues of racial identity and loyalty, underneath the safety of that surface is the more dangerous story—though not named explicitly—of Irene's awakening sexual desire for Clare. The narrative traces this developing eroticism in spatial terms. It begins on the roof of the Drayton Hotel (with all the suggestions of the sexually illicit), intensifies at Clare's tea party, and, getting proverbially "close to home," explodes in Irene's own bedroom. Preoccupied with appearances, social respectability, and safety, however, Irene tries to force these emerging feelings underground. The narrative dramatizes that repression effectively in images of concealment and burial.

Significantly, the novel's opening image is an envelope (a metaphoric vagina) which Irene hesitates to open, fearing its "contents would reveal" an "attitude toward danger." Irene's fears are well founded, given the sexual overtones of Clare's letter:

> "for I am lonely, so lonely . . . cannot help longing to be with you again, as I have never longed for anything before; and I have wanted many things in my life. . . . It's like an ache, a pain that never ceases . . . and it's your fault, 'Rene dear. At least partly. For I wouldn't now, perhaps, have this terrible, this wild desire if I hadn't seen you that time in Chicago."

Irene tries to preserve "a hardness from feeling" about the letter, though "brilliant red patches flamed" in her cheeks. Unable to explain her feelings for Clare, "for which she could find no name," Irene dismisses them as "Just somebody walking over [her] grave." The narrative suggests pointedly that Clare is the body walking over the grave of Irene's buried sexual feelings.

Lest the reader miss this eroticism, Larsen employs fire imagery—the conventional representation of sexual desire—introducing and instituting this imagery in the novel's opening pages. Irene begins her retrospective account of her reunion with Clare, remembering that the day was "hot," the sun "brutal" and "staring," its rays "like molten rain." Significantly, Irene, feeling "sticky and soiled from contact with so many sweating bodies," escapes to the roof of the Drayton Hotel where she is reunited with Clare, after a lapse of many years. (Irene is, ironically, "escaping" to the very thing she wants to avoid.)

From the very beginning of their reencounter, Irene is drawn to Clare like a moth to a flame. (Suggestively, Clare is frequently dressed in red). The "lovely creature" "had for her a fascination, strange and compelling." Because so many critics have missed the significance of the erotic attraction between Irene and Clare, it is useful to trace this theme by quoting from the novel in substantial detail.

When the two are reunited, Irene first notices Clare's "tempting mouth"; her lips, "painted a brilliant geranium-red, were sweet and sensitive and a little obstinate." Into Clare's "arresting eyes" "there came a smile and over Irene the sense of being petted and caressed." At the end of this chance encounter, "standing there under the appeal, the caress, of [Clare's] eyes, Irene had the desire, the hope, that this parting wouldn't be the last."

When Irene has tea at Clare's house, she notices that Clare "turned on . . . her seductive caressing smile." Afterwards, a "slight shiver [runs] over [Irene]" when she remembers the mysterious look on Clare's "incredibly beautiful face." "She couldn't, however, come to any conclusion about its meaning. . . . It was unfathomable, utterly beyond any experience or comprehension of hers."

The awakening of Irene's erotic feelings for Clare coincides with Irene's imagination of an affair between Clare and Brian. Given her tendency to project her disowned traits, motives, and desires onto others, it is reasonable to argue that Irene is projecting her own developing passion for Clare onto Brian, although in "all their married life she had had no slightest cause to suspect [him] of any infidelity, of any serious flirtation even." The more the feelings develop, the more she fights them, for they threaten the placid surface of her middle-class existence as a doctor's wife. "Safety and security," Irene's watchwords, crop up repeatedly in the novel, after Clare arrives, and explain Irene's struggle to avoid her.

Not deterred, however, Clare visits Irene's house unannounced, coming first to the bedroom where she "drop[s] a kiss on [Irene's] dark curls," arousing in Irene "a sudden inexplicable onrush of affectionate feeling. Reaching out, she grasped Clare's two hands in her own and cried with something like awe in her voice: 'Dear God! But aren't you lovely, Clare!' " Their conversation in this scene has a sexual double edge, heightened by Irene's habitual gesture of lighting cigarettes.

Clare scolds Irene for not responding to her letter, describing her repeated trips to the post office. "I'm sure they were all beginning to think that I'd been carrying on an illicit love-affair and that the man had thrown me over." Irene assures Clare that she is concerned simply about the dangers of Clare's passing for white in Harlem, the risks she runs of being discovered by "knowing Negroes." Clare's immediate response is "You mean you don't want me, 'Rene?" Irene replies, "It's terribly foolish, and not just the right thing." It's "dangerous," she continues, "to run such silly risks." "It's not safe. Not safe at all." But "as if in contrition for that flashing thought," "Irene touched [Clare's] arm caressingly."

Irene's protestations about race are noticeably extreme and disproportionate to the situation, especially since she passes occasionally herself. Further, they function in the same way that Helga's response to Axel Olsen functions: as a mask for the deeper, more unsettling issues of sexuality. Irene tries to defuse the feelings by absorbing herself in the ritual of empty tea parties, but "It was as if in a house long dim, a match had been struck, showing ghastly shapes where had been only blurred shadows."

At one such party, near the narrative's end, Clare is, in typical fashion, an intruding presence, both at the party and in Irene's thoughts. "Irene couldn't remember ever having seen [Clare] look better." Watching "the fire roar" in the room, Irene thinks of Clare's "beautiful and caressing" face.

In the final section of the novel, Clare comes to Irene's house before they go to the fateful Christmas party. Coming again into Irene's room, "Clare kisse[s] her bare shoulder, seeming not to notice a slight shrinking." As they walk to the party, Clare at Brian's side, Irene describes a "live thing pressing against her." That "live thing," represented clearly as full-blown sexual desire, must be contained, and it takes Clare's death to contain it. Significantly, in Irene's description of the death, all of the erotic images used to describe Clare throughout the novel converge.

> Gone! The soft white face, the bright hair, the disturbing scarlet mouth, the dreaming eyes, the caressing smile, the whole tortured loveliness that had been Clare Kendry. That beauty that had torn at Irene's placid life. Gone! The mocking daring, the gallantry of her pose, the ringing bells of her laughter.

Although the ending is ambiguous and the evidence circumstantial, I agree with Cheryl Wall that, "Larsen strongly implies that Irene pushes Clare through the window," and, in effect, becomes "a psychological suicide, if not a murderer."[18] To suggest the extent to which Clare's death represents the death of Irene's sexual feelings for Clare, Larsen uses a clever objective correlative: Irene's pattern of lighting cigarettes and snuffing them out. Minutes before Clare falls from the window to her death, "Irene finished her cigarette and threw it out, watching the tiny spark drop slowly down to the white ground below." Clearly attempting a symbolic parallel, Clare is described as "a vital glowing thing, like a flame of red and gold" who falls from (or is thrown out of) the window as well. Because Clare is a reminder of that repressed and disowned part of Irene's self, Clare must be banished, for, more unacceptable than the feelings themselves is the fact that they find an object of expression in Clare. In other words, Clare is both the embodiment and the object of the sexual feelings that Irene banishes.

Larsen's becomes, in effect, a banishing act as well. Or put another way, the idea of bringing a sexual attraction between two women to full narrative expression is, likewise, too dangerous a move, which helps to explain why critics have missed this aspect of the novel. Larsen's clever narrative strategies almost conceal it. In *Passing* she uses a technique found commonly in narratives by Afro-American and women novelists with a "dangerous" story to tell: "safe" themes, plots, and conventions are used as the protective cover underneath which lie more dangerous subplots. Larsen envelops the subplot of Irene's developing if unnamed and unacknowledged desire for Clare in the safe and familiar plot of racial passing.[19] Put another way, the novel's clever strategy derives from its surface theme and central metaphor—passing. It takes the form of the act it describes. Implying false, forged, and mistaken identities, the title functions on multiple levels: thematically, in terms of the racial and sexual plots; and strategically, in terms of the narrative's disguise.

The structure of the novel complements and reinforces this disguise. Neat and symmetrical, *Passing* is composed of three sections, with four chapters each. The order and control which that tight organization suggests are a clever cover for the unconventional subplot in the novel's hiding places.

The novel performs a double burial: the erotic subplot is hidden beneath its safe and orderly cover and the radical implications of that plot are put away by the disposal of Clare. Although she is the novel's center of vitality and passion, that vitality and passion, which the narrative seems to affirm, are significantly contained by the narrative's end. And Clare becomes a kind of sacrificial lamb on the altar of social and literary convention.

Clare suffers the fate that many a female character has suffered when she has what Rachel Blau DuPlessis terms, "an appropriate relationship to the 'social script.'" Death results, she continues, when "energies of selfhood, often represented by sexuality . . . are expended outside the 'couvert' of marriage or valid [generally spelled heterosexual] romance."[20] While Larsen criticizes the cover of marriage, as well as other social scripts for women, she is unable in the end to extend that critique to its furthest reaches.

In ending the novel with Clare's death, Larsen repeats the narrative choice which *Quicksand* makes: to punish the very values the novel implicitly affirms, to honor the very value system the text implicitly satirizes. The ending, when hidden racial identities are disclosed, functions on the ideological as well as the narrative level. Larsen performs an act of narrative "dis"-closure, undoing or doing the opposite of what she has promised. Or, to borrow from *Quicksand,* Larsen closes *Passing* "without exploring to the end that unfamiliar path into which she had strayed."

NOTES

1. W.E.B. Du Bois, *Voices of a Black Nation: Political Journalism in the Harlem Renaissance,* ed. Theodore G. Vincent, reviews of *Home to Harlem,* and *Quicksand* (San Francisco: Ramparts, 1973), p. 359.

2. "The Browsing Reader," the *Crisis* 36 (July 1929): 234. Nella Larsen, *Passing,* was first published by Knopf, London and New York, 1929.

3. For the full accusation and the explanations that Larsen and her editor provided, see "Our Rostrum," in the *Forum* 83 (1930): 41.

4. During the nineteenth century, black women formed a network of clubs throughout the country, in which politically minded black women were committed to racial uplift (or Negro improvement). The clubs were largely unaffiliated until they convened in Boston in 1895 for their first national conference and became the National Association of Colored Women (NACW) in 1896. Predating both the NAACP and the Urban League, the NACW was the first national black organization with a commitment to racial struggles. For a detailed description of the activities of the organization see "Black Feminism versus Peasant Values," in Wilson J. Moses, *The Golden Age of Black Nationalism* (Hamden, Conn.: Archon Books, 1978), pp. 103–31.

5. Founded and edited by Mrs. Ruffin, a social activist, the *Woman's Era* was the first magazine in the United States to be owned, published, and managed exclusively by black women.

6. Quoted in Moses, *Golden Age,* p. 115.

7. Though Harriet Wilson's recently discovered novel, *Our Nig* (1859), predates these novels influenced by the efforts of the club movement, the emphasis on the priceless gem of virginity is still strong. See the Vintage edition of the novel edited and with an introduction by Henry Louis Gates, Jr., New York, 1983.

8. For a discussion of black women blues singers see Michele Russel's "Slave Codes and Liner Notes," in *But Some of Us Are Brave,* ed. Gloria Hull, Patricia Bell Scott, and Barbara Smith (Old Westbury: The Feminist Press, 1982), pp. 129–40.

9. The *Messenger,* 9 (September 1927): 150.

10. Carole Vance, "Pleasure and Danger: Toward a Politics of Sexuality," in *Pleasure and Danger: Exploring Female Sexuality,* ed. Carole S. Vance (Boston: Routledge and Kegan Paul, 1984), p. 1. For an excellent discussion in Vance's anthology, of the sexuality of black women, see Hortense Spillers, "Interstices: A Small Drama of Words," pp. 73–100. See also Rennie Simson, "The Afro-American Female: The Historical Context of the Construction of Sexual Identity," and Barbara Omolade, "Hearts of Darkness," both in *Powers of Desire: The Politics of Sexuality,* ed. Ann Snitow *et al.* (New York: Monthly Review Press, 1983).

11. Amritjit Singh, *The Novels of the Harlem Renaissance* (University Park and London: Pennsylvania State University Press, 1976), p. 25.

12. Nathan Huggins, *Harlem Renaissance* (New York: Oxford University Press, 1971), pp. 188–89.

13. In a statement well known to students of the Harlem Renaissance, Du Bois argued, "All art is propaganda and ever must be, despite the wailing of the purists." ("Criteria of Negro Art," in *W.E.B. Du Bois: The Crisis Writings,* ed. Daniel Walden [Greenwich, Conn.: Fawcett, 1972], p. 288). In a section of this essay which has interesting implications for Larsen's treatment of black female sexuality, Du Bois describes two plays, "White Cargo" and "Congo." In the first, "there is a fallen woman. She is black. In 'Congo' the fallen woman is white. In 'White Cargo' the black woman goes down further and further and in 'Congo' the white woman begins with degradation but in the end is one of the angels of the Lord" (p. 288).

14. Reviews of *Home to Harlem* and *Quicksand* in *Voices of a Black Nation,* p. 359.

15. Carl Van Vechten, *Nigger Heaven* (New York: Knopf, 1926), pp. 222–23.

16. See, for example, Hugh Gloster, *Negro Voices in American Fiction* (New York: Russell and Russell, 1948); J. Sauners Redding, *To Make a Poet Black* (Chapel Hill: University of North Carolina Press, 1945); Hiroko Sato, "Under the Harlem Shadows: A study of Jessie Fauset and Nella Larsen," in *The Harlem Renaissance Remembered,* ed. Arna Bontemps (New York: Dodd, Mead, 1972); and Robert Bone, *The Negro Novel in America* (New Haven: Yale University Press, 1972).

17. Beatrice Royster, "The Ironic Vision of Four Black Women Novelists: A Study of the Novels of Jessie Fauset, Nella Larsen, Zora Neale Hurston, and Ann Petry," Ph.D. dissertation, Emory University, 1975, p. 86.

18. Cheryl Wall, "Passing for What? Aspects of Identity in Nella Larsen's Novels," *Black American Literature Forum* 20: 1–2, 1986, 97–112.

19. In her novel *Plum Bun,* published the same year as *Passing,* Jessie Fauset, another black female novelist of the period, used fairy tale conventions to deflect her critique of the romance and the role its underlying ideology plays in disempowering women. See the edition of Fauset's novel, with an introduction by Deborah E. McDowell (London: Routledge and Kegan Paul, 1985).

20. Rachel Blau DuPlessis, *Writing beyond the Ending: Narrative Strategies of Twentieth-Century Women Writers* (Bloomington: Indiana University Press, 1985), p. 15.

41

Different Desires:
Subjectivity and Transgression
in Wilde and Gide

Jonathan Dollimore

Jonathan Dollimore, who serves as Reader in English and American Studies at the University of Sussex, is a literary and cultural critic. In this essay he compares two homosexual authors who were contemporaries about a century ago—André Gide and Oscar Wilde. Dollimore argues that there were crucial and, for us today, instructive differences between them. As Gide understood his own life-story, his transgressive breakthrough into homosexual behavior was a liberation of his authentic, inner self. But in Wilde's view all desire was socially produced, and there was no such thing as an inner self waiting to be freed. If Gide was a humanist, Wilde was a socialist, committed not to individual self-discovery but rather to struggle for the transformation of those social conditions which produce misery. Wilde thought that his transgressive homosexual behavior could be a part of that struggle. As an inversion of the normal, homosexuality was in many ways potentially a subversion as well. What Dollimore ultimately suggests is that for us Wilde should be more exemplary than Gide. Jonathan Dollimore is the author of Radical Tragedy: Religion, Power, and Ideology in the Drama of Shakespeare and His Contemporaries *(1984), and of* Sexual Dissidence: Augustine to Wilde, Freud to Foucault *(1991).*

In Blidah, Algeria, in January 1895 André Gide is in the hall of a hotel, about to leave. His glance falls on the slate which announces the names of new guests: "suddenly my heart gave a leap; the two last names . . . were those of Oscar Wilde and Lord Alfred Douglas."[1] Acting on his first impulse, Gide "erases" his own name from the slate and leaves for the station. Twice thereafter Gide writes about the incident, unsure why he left so abruptly; first in his *Oscar Wilde* (1901), then in *Si le grain ne meurt (If It Die,* 1920, 1926). It may, he reflects, have been a feeling of *mauvaise honte* or of embarrassment: Wilde was becoming notorious and his company compromising. But also he was severely depressed, and at such times "I feel ashamed of myself, disown, repudiate myself."[2] Whatever the case, on his way to the station he decides that his leaving was cowardly and so returns. The consequent meeting with Wilde was to precipitate a transformation in Gide's life and subsequent writing.

Gide's reluctance to meet Wilde certainly had something to do with previous meetings in Paris four years earlier in 1891; they had seen a great deal of each other across several occasions, and biographers agree that this was one of the most important events in Gide's life. But these meetings had left Gide feeling ambivalent toward the older man, and it is interesting that not only does Gide say nothing in *If It Die* about Wilde's obvious and deep influence upon him in Paris in 1891, but, according to Jean Delay, in the manuscript of Gide's journal the pages corresponding to that period—November to December 1891—are torn out.[3]

Undoubtedly Gide was deeply disturbed by Wilde, and not surprisingly, since Gide's remarks in his letters of that time suggest that Wilde was intent on undermining the younger man's self-identity, rooted as it was in a Protestant ethic and high bourgeois moral rigor and repression that generated a kind of conformity to which Wilde was, notoriously, opposed. Wilde wanted to encourage Gide to transgress. It may be that he wanted to reenact in Gide the creative liberation—which included strong criminal identification—which his own exploration of transgressive desire had produced nine years earlier. (Wilde's major writing, including that which constitutes his transgressive aesthetic, dates from 1886, when, according to Robert Ross, he first practiced homosexuality.)[4] But first Wilde had to undermine that lawful sense of self which kept Gide transfixed within the law. So Wilde tried to decenter or demoralize Gide—"demoralize" in the sense of liberate from moral constraint rather than to dispirit; or, rather, to dispirit precisely in the sense of to liberate from a morality anchored in the very notion of spirit. ("Demoralize" was a term Gide remembers Wilde using in just this sense, one which, for Gide, recalled Flaubert.) Hence, perhaps, those most revealing of remarks by Gide to Valéry at this time (December 4, 1891): "Wilde is religiously contriving to kill what remains of my soul, because he says that in order to know an essence, one must eliminate it: he wants me to miss my soul. The measure of a thing is the effort made to destroy it. Each thing is made up only of its emptiness." And in another letter of the same month: "Please forgive my silence: since Wilde, I hardly exist anymore."[5] And in unpublished notes for this time he declares that Wilde was "always trying to instil into you *a sanction for evil.*"[6] So, despite his intentions to the contrary, Wilde at that time seems indeed to have dispirited Gide in the conventional sense. Yet perhaps the contrary intention was partly successful; on January 1, 1892 Gide writes: "Wilde, I think, did me nothing but harm. In his company I had lost the habit of thinking. I had more varied emotions, but had forgotten how to bring order into them."[7] In fact, Gide reacted, says Delay, in accordance with his Protestant instincts, reaffirming a moral conviction inseparable from an essentialist conception of self (cf. *Journal,* December 29, 1891: "O Lord keep me from evil. May my soul again be proud"). Even so, this meeting with Wilde is to be counted as one of the most important events in Gide's life: "for the first time he found himself confronted with a man who was able to bring about, within him, a transmutation of all values—in other words, a revolution."[8] Richard Ellmann concurs with this judgment and suggests further that Wilde's attempt to "authorize evil" in Gide supplies much of the subject of *The Immoralist* and *The Counterfeiters,* the former work containing a character, Ménalque, who is based upon Wilde.[9]

It is against the background and the importance of that earlier meeting, together with the ambivalence toward Wilde which it generated in Gide, that we return to that further encounter in Algeria four years later. If anything, the ambivalence seems even stronger; in a letter to his mother Gide describes Wilde as a terrifying man, a "most dangerous product of modern civilization" who had already depraved Douglas *"right down to the marrow."*[10] A few days later Gide meets them again in Algiers, a city which Wilde declares his intention to demoralize.[11] It is here that there occurs the event which was to change Gide's life and radically influence his subsequent work, an event for which the entire narrative of *If It Die* seems to have been preparing. He is taken by Wilde to a café. It is there that "in the half-open doorway, there suddenly appeared a marvelous youth. He stood there for a time, leaning with his raised elbow against the door-jamb, and outlined on the dark background of the night." The youth joins them; his name is Mohammed; he is a musician; he plays the flute. Listening to that music, "you forgot the time and place, and who you were."[12] This is not the first time Gide has experienced this sensation of forgetting. Africa increasingly attracts him in this respect;[13] there he feels liberated and the burden of an oppressive sense of self is dissolved: "I laid aside anxieties, constraints, solicitudes, and as my will evaporated, I felt myself becoming porous as a beehive."[14] Now, as they leave the café, Wilde turns to Gide and asks him if he desires the musician. Gide writes: "how dark the alley was! I thought my heart would fail me; and what a dreadful effort of courage it needed to answer: 'yes,' and with what a choking voice!" (Delay points out that the word "courage" is here transvalued by Gide; earlier he had felt courage was needed for self-discipline, whereas now it is the strength to transgress.)[15]

Wilde arranges something with their guide, rejoins Gide, and then begins laughing: "a resounding laugh, more of triumph than of pleasure, an interminable, uncontrollable, insolent laugh . . . it was the amusement of a child and a devil." Gide spends the night with Mohammed: "my joy was unbounded, and I cannot imagine it greater, even if love had been added." Though not his first homosexual experience, it confirmed his (homo)sexual "nature," what, he says, was "normal" for him. Even more defiantly Gide declares that, although he had achieved "the summit of pleasure five times" with Mohammed, "I revived my ecstasy many more times, and back in my hotel room I relived its echoes until morning"[16] (this passage was one of those omitted from some English editions). At this suitably climactic moment we postpone further consideration of Gide and turn to the antiessentialist, transgressive aesthetic which Wilde was advocating and which played so important a part in Gide's liberation or corruption, depending on one's point of view. And I want to begin with an indispensable dimension of that aesthetic: one for which Wilde is yet hardly remembered, or, for some of his admirers, one which is actively forgotten; namely, his advocacy of socialism.

Wilde begins his *The Soul of Man under Socialism* (1891) by asserting that a socialism based on sympathy alone is useless; what is needed is to "*try and reconstruct society on such a basis that poverty will be impossible.*" It is precisely because Christ made no attempt to reconstruct society that he had to resort to pain and suffering as the exemplary mode of self-realization. The alternative is the socialist commitment to transforming the material conditions which create and perpetuate suffering. One might add that, if the notion of redemption through suffering has been a familiar theme within English studies, this only goes to remind us of the extent to which, in the twentieth century, criticism has worked in effect as a displaced theology or as a vehicle for an acquiescent quasi-religious humanism. So Wilde's terse assertion in 1891 that "pain is not the ultimate mode of perfection. It is merely provisional and a protest"[17] may still be an appropriate response to those who fetishize suffering in the name, not of Christ, but of the tragic vision and the human condition (sainthood without God, as Camus once put it).

Wilde also dismisses the related pieties, that humankind learns wisdom through suffering, and that suffering humanizes. On the contrary, "misery and poverty are so absolutely degrading, and exercise such a paralyzing effect over the nature of men, that no class is ever really conscious of its suffering. They have to be told of it by other people, and they often entirely disbelieve them." Against those who were beginning to talk of the dignity of manual labor, Wilde insists that most of that too is absolutely degrading. Each of these repudiations suggests that Wilde was fully aware of how exploitation is crucially a question of ideological mystification as well as of outright coercion: "to the thinker, the most tragic fact in the whole of the French Revolution is not that Marie Antoinette was killed for being a queen, but that the starved peasant of the Vendée voluntarily went out to die for the hideous cause of feudalism." Ideology reaches into experience and identity, reemerging as "voluntary" self-oppression. But it is also the ruling ideology which prevents the rulers themselves from seeing that it is not sin that produces crime but starvation, and that the punishment of the criminal escalates rather than diminishes crime and also brutalizes the society which administers it even more than the criminal who receives it.[18]

There is much more in this essay, but I have summarized enough to show that it exemplifies a tough materialism; in modern parlance one might call it antihumanist, not least because for Wilde a radical socialist program is inseparable from a critique of those ideologies of subjectivity which seek redemption in and through the individual. A case in point would be Dickens's treatment of Stephen Blackpool in *Hard Times* (Wilde made a point of disliking Dickens); another might be Arnold's assertion in *Culture and Anarchy*: "Religion says: 'The Kingdom of God is within you'"; and culture, in like manner, places human perfection in an internal condition, in the growth and predominance of our humanity proper."[19] But isn't a category like antihumanism entirely inappropriate, given Wilde's celebration of individualism? The term itself, antihumanism, is not worth fighting over; I have introduced it only as a preliminary indication of just how different is Wilde's concept of the individual from that which has prevailed in idealist culture generally and English studies in particular. It is this difference which the next section considers.

Individualism

In Wilde's writing, individualism is less to do with a human essence, Arnold's inner condition, than a dynamic social potential, one which implies a radical possibility of freedom "latent and potential in mankind generally." Thus individualism as Wilde conceives it generates a "disobedience [which] in the eyes of anyone who has read history, is man's original virtue. It is through disobedience that progress has been made, through disobedience and through rebellion."[20] Under certain conditions there comes to be a close relationship between crime and individualism, the one generating the other.[21] Already, then, Wilde's notion of individualism is inseparable from transgressive desire and a transgressive aesthetic. Hence, of course, his attack on public opinion, mediocrity, and conventional morality, all of which forbid both the desire and the aesthetic.[22]

The public which Wilde scorns is that which seeks to police culture; which is against cultural difference; which reacts to the aesthetically unconventional by charging it with being either grossly unintelligible or grossly immoral. Far from reflecting or prescribing for the true nature or essence of man, individualism will generate the cultural difference and diversity which conventional morality, orthodox opinion, and essentialist ideology disavow. Wilde affirms the principle of differentiation to which all life grows and insists that selfishness is not living as one wishes to live, but asking others to live as one wishes to live, trying to create "an absolute uniformity of type." And unselfishness not only recognizes cultural diversity and difference but enjoys them. Individualism as an affirmation of cultural as well as personal difference is therefore fundamentally opposed to that "immoral ideal of uniformity of type and conformity to rule which is so prevalent everywhere, and is perhaps most obnoxious in England."[23]

Uniformity of type and conformity to rule: Wilde despises these imperatives not only in individuals but as attributes of class and ruling ideologies. Wilde's Irish identity is a crucial factor in his oppositional stances, and it is instructive to consider in this connection a piece written two years earlier, in 1889, where he addresses England's exploitation and repression of Ireland. "Mr Froude's Blue Book" is a review of J.A.

Froude's novel, *The Two Chiefs of Dunboy*. In the eighteenth century, says Wilde, England tried to rule Ireland "with an insolence that was intensified by race-hatred and religious prejudice"; in the nineteenth, with "a stupidity . . . aggravated by good intentions." Froude's picture of Ireland belongs to the earlier period, and yet to read Wilde's review now makes one wonder what if anything has changed in Tory "thinking" except that possibly now the one vision holds for both Ireland and the mainland:

> Resolute government, that shallow shibboleth of those who do not understand how complex a thing the art of government is, is [Froude's] posthumous panacea for past evils. His hero, Colonel Goring, has the words Law and Order ever on his lips, meaning by the one the enforcement of unjust legislation, and implying by the other the suppression of every fine natural aspiration. That the government should enforce iniquity, and the governed submit to it, seems to be to Mr Froude, as it certainly is to many others, the true ideal of political science. . . . Colonel Goring . . . Mr Froude's cure for Ireland . . . is a "*Police at any price*" man.[24]

Individualism joins with socialism to abolish other kinds of conformity, including, says Wilde, family life and marriage, each being unacceptable because rooted in and perpetuating the ideology of property.[25] Individualism is both desire for a radical personal freedom and a desire for society itself to be radically different, the first being inseparable from the second. So Wilde's concept of the individual is crucially different from that sense of the concept which signifies the private, experientially self-sufficient, autonomous, bourgeois subject; indeed, for Wilde, "Personal experience is a most vicious and limited circle" and "to know anything about oneself one must know all about others."[26] Typically, within idealist culture, the experience of an essential subjectivity is inseparable from knowledge of that notorious transhistorical category, human nature. This is Wilde on human nature: "the only thing that one really knows about human nature is that it changes. Change is the one quality we can predicate of it."[27] To those who then say that socialism is incompatible with human nature and therefore impractical, Wilde replies by rejecting practicality itself as presupposing and endorsing both the existing social conditions and the concept of human nature as fixed, each of which suppositions socialism would contest: "it is exactly the existing conditions that one objects to . . . [they] will be done away with, and human nature will change."[28] Elsewhere Wilde accepts that there is *something* like human nature, but, far from being the source of our most profound being, it is actually ordinary and boring, the least interesting thing about us. It is where we differ from each other that is of definitive value.[29]

Art versus Life

The key concepts in Wilde's aesthetic are protean and shifting, not least because they are paradoxically and facetiously deployed. When, for example, he speaks of life—"poor, probable, uninteresting human life"[30]—or reality as that to which art is opposed, he means different things at different times. One of the most interesting and significant referents of concepts like life and reality, as Wilde uses them, is the prevailing social order. Even nature, conceived as the opposite of culture and art, retains a social dimension,[31] especially when it signifies ideological mystification of the social. That is why Wilde calls being natural a "pose," and an objectionable one at that, precisely because it seeks to mystify the social as natural.[32]

Nature and reality signify a prevailing order which art ignores and which the critic negates, subverts, and transgresses. Thus, for example, the person of culture is concerned to give "an accurate description of what has never occurred," while the critic sees "the object as in itself it really is not"[33] (Wilde is here inverting the proposition which opens Arnold's famous essay, "The function of criticism at the present time"). Not surprisingly, then, criticism and art are aligned with individualism against a prevailing social order; a passage which indicates this is also important in indicating the basis of Wilde's aesthetic of transgressive desire: "Art is Individualism and Individualism is a *disturbing and disintegrating force.* There lies its immense value. For what it seeks to disturb is monotony of type, slavery of custom, tyranny of habit."[34] Art is also self-conscious and critical; in fact, "self-consciousness and the critical spirit are one."[35] And art, like individualism, is oriented toward the realm of transgressive desire: "What is abnormal in Life stands in normal relations to Art. It is the only thing in Life that stands in normal relations to Art."[36] One who inhabits that realm, "the cultured and fascinating liar," is both an object and source of desire.[37] The liar is important because he or she contradicts not just conventional morality, but its sustaining origin, "truth." So art runs to meet the liar, kissing his "false beautiful lips, knowing that he alone is in possession of the great secret of all her manifestations, the secret that Truth is entirely and absolutely a matter of style." Truth, the epistemological legitimation of the real, is rhetorically subordinated to its antitheses—appearance, style, the lie—and thereby simultaneously both appropriated and devalued. Reality, also necessarily devalued and demystified by the loss of truth, must imitate art, while life must meekly follow the liar.[38]

Further, life is at best an energy which can only find expression through the forms that art offers it. But form is another slippery and protean category in Wilde's aesthetic. In one sense Wilde is a proto-structuralist: "Form is the beginning of things.... The Creeds are believed, not because they are rational, but because they are repeated.... Form is everything.... Do you wish to love? Use Love's Litany, and the words will create the yearning from which the world fancies that they spring."[39] Here form is virtually synonymous with culture. Moreover, it is a passage in which Wilde recognizes the priority of the social and the cultural in determining meaning, even in determining desire. So for Wilde, although desire is deeply at odds with society in its existing forms, it does not exist as a presocial authenticity; it is within and in-formed by the very culture which it also transgresses.

Transgression and the Sense of Self

Returning now to Gide, we are in a position to contrast his essentialism with Wilde's antiessentialism, a contrast which epitomizes one of the most important differences within the modern history of transgression. In a way that perhaps corresponds to his ambivalence toward Wilde, Gide had both submitted to and resisted the latter's attempts to undermine his sense of self. Both the submission and the resistance are crucial for Gide's subsequent development as a writer and, through Gide's influence, for modern literature. The submission is apparent enough in the confirmation of his homosexual desire and the way this alters his life and work. In 1924 he published *Corydon*, a courageous defense of homosexuality which he later declared to be his most important book (*Journal,* October 19, 1942). In *Corydon* he did not just demand tolerance for homosexuality but also insisted that it was not contrary to nature but intrinsically natural; that heterosexuality prevails merely because of convention; that historically homosexuality is associated with great artistic and intellectual achievement, while heterosexuality is indicative of decadence. About these provocative and suspect claims I have only the space to observe that the fury they generated in the majority of commentators is as significant as Gide's reasons for making them in the first place. Two years later Gide published the equally controversial commercial edition of *If It Die,* which, as already indicated, contained, for that time, astonishingly explicit accounts of his homosexuality, and for which, predictably, Gide was savagely castigated. Much later still, Gide was to write to Ramon Fernandez, confirming that "sexual non-conformity is the first key to my works"; the experience of his own deviant desire leads him first to attack sexual conformity and then "all other sphinxes of conformity," suspecting them to be "the brothers and cousins of the first."[40]

But Gide—having with Wilde both allowed and encouraged the subversion of an identity which had hitherto successfully, albeit precariously, repressed desire—does not then substitute for it the decentered subjectivity which animates Wilde's aesthetic; on the contrary, he reconstitutes himself as an essentially new self. Michel in *The Immoralist* (1902) corresponds in some measure to Gide in Algiers (while, as earlier remarked, another character in that novel, Ménalque, is probably based on Wilde). For Michel, as for Gide, transgression does not lead to a relinquishing of self but to a totally new sense of self. Michel throws off the culture and learning which up to that point had been his whole life in order to find himself: that "authentic creature that had lain hidden beneath . . . whom the Gospel had repudiated, whom everything about me—books, masters, parents, and I myself had begun by attempting to suppress. . . . Thenceforward I despised the secondary creature, the creature who was due to teaching, whom education had painted on the surface." He composes a new series of lectures in which he shows "culture, born of life, as the destroyer of life." The true value of life is bound up with individual uniqueness: "the part in each of us that we feel is different from other people is the part that is rare, the part that makes our special value."[41]

Whereas for Wilde transgressive desire leads to a relinquishing of the essential self, for Gide it leads to a discovery of the authentic self. As he writes in *If It Die,* it was at that time in Algiers that "I was beginning to discover myself—and in myself the tables of a new law."[42] And he writes to his mother on February 2, 1895: "I'm unable to write a line or a sentence so long as I'm not in *complete possession* (that is, WITH FULL KNOWLEDGE) of myself. I should like very submissively to follow nature— the unconscious, which is within myself and must be *true.*"[43] Here again there is the indirect yet passionate insistence on the naturalness, the authenticity of his deviant desire. With that willful integrity—itself a kind of perversity?—rooted in Protestantism, Gide not only appropriates dominant concepts (the normal, the natural) to legitimate his own deviation but goes so far as to claim a sanction for deviation in the teachings of Christ.[44] (In his journal for 1893 [detached pages] he wrote: "Christ's saying is just as true in art: 'Whoever will save his life [his personality] shall lose it.' " He later declared, after reading Nietzsche's *Thus Spake Zarathustra,* that it was to this that Protestantism led, "to the greatest liberation.")[45] Delay contends, plausibly, that some of the great Gidean themes, especially those entailing transgression, can be found in the rebellious letters that he wrote to his mother in March 1895, letters inspired by his self-affirmation as a homosexual.[46]

It would be difficult to overestimate the importance, in the recent history of Western culture, of transgression in the name of an essential self which is the origin and arbiter of the true, the real, and the moral; that is, the three main domains of knowledge in Western culture: the epistemological, the ontological, and the ethical. Its importance within the domain of sexuality and within discourses which intersect with sexuality is becoming increasingly apparent, but it has been central also in liberation movements which have not primarily been identified with either of these. This, finally, is Gide in 1921:

> The borrowed truths are the ones to which one clings most tenaciously, and all the more so since they remain foreign to our intimate self. It takes much more precaution

to deliver one's own message, much more boldness and prudence, than to sign up with and add one's voice to an already existing party. . . . I believed that it is above all to oneself that it is important to remain faithful.[47]

Paradox and Perversity

The contrast between Gide and Wilde is striking: not only are Wilde's conceptions of subjectivity and desire antiessentialist but so too—and consequently—is his advocacy of transgression. Deviant desire reacts against, disrupts, and displaces from within; rather than seeking to escape the repressive ordering of sexuality, Wilde reinscribes himself within and relentlessly inverts the binaries upon which that ordering depends. Inversion, rather than Gide's escape into a pre- or trans-social reality, defines Wilde's transgressive aesthetic. In Gide, transgression is in the name of a desire and identity rooted in the natural, the sincere, and the authentic; Wilde's transgressive aesthetic is the reverse: *in*sincerity, *in*authenticity, and *un*naturalness become the liberating attributes of decentered identity and desire, and inversion becomes central to Wilde's expression of this aesthetic, as can be seen from a selection of his *Phrases and Philosophies for the Use of the Young* (1894):

If one tells the truth, one is sure, sooner or later, to be found out.
Only the shallow know themselves.
To be premature is to be perfect.
It is only the superficial qualities that last. Man's deeper nature is soon found out.
To love oneself is the beginning of a lifelong romance.[48]

In Wilde's writings a noncentered or dispersed desire is both the impetus for a subversive inversion *and* what is released by it. Perhaps the most general inversion operating in his work reverses that most dominating of binaries, nature/culture; more specifically, the attributes on the left are substituted for those on the right:

X for	Y
surface	depth
lying	truth
change	stasis
difference	essence
persona/role	essential self
abnormal	normal
insincerity	sincerity
style/artifice	authenticity
facetious	serious
narcissism	maturity

For Michel in *The Immoralist* and to an extent for Gide himself, desire may be proscribed, but this does not affect its authenticity; if anything, it confirms it. In a sense, then, deviant desire is legitimated in terms of culture's opposite, nature, or, in a different but related move, in terms of something which is precultural or *always more than* cultural. Gide shares with the dominant culture an investment in the Y column above; he appropriates its categories *from* the dominant *for* the subordinate. In contrast, for Wilde transgressive desire is both rooted in culture and the impetus for affirming different/alternative kinds of culture. So what in Gide's conception of transgression might seem a limitation or even a confusion—namely, that the desire which culture outlaws is itself thoroughly cultural—in fact facilitates one of the most disturbing of all forms of transgression: the outlaw turns up as inlaw; more specifically, that which society forbids

Wilde reinstates through and within some of its most cherished and central cultural categories—art, the aesthetic, art criticism, individualism. At the same time as he appropriates those categories he also transvalues them through inversion, thus making them now signify those binary exclusions (the X column) by which the dominant culture knows itself (thus abnormality is not just the opposite, but *the necessarily always present* antithesis of normality). It is an uncompromising inversion, this being the (perversely) appropriate strategy for a transgressive desire which is of its "nature," according to this culture, an inversion.

But inversion has a specific as well as a general target: as can be seen from the *Phrases and Philosophies* just quoted, Wilde seeks to subvert those dominant categories which signify *subjective depth*. Such categories (the Y column) are precisely those which ideologically identify (interpellate?) the mature adult individual, which confer or ideologically coerce identity. And they too operate in terms of binary contrast: the individual knows what he—I choose the masculine pronoun deliberately[49]—is in contrast to what he definitely is not or should not be. In Wilde's inversions, the excluded inferior term returns as the *now superior* term of a related series of binaries. Some further examples of Wilde's subversion of subjective depth are:

> A little sincerity is a dangerous thing, and a great deal is absolutely fatal.[50]
> All bad poetry springs from genuine feeling.[51]
> In matters of grave importance, style, not sincerity, is the *vital* thing.[52]
> Only shallow people . . . do not judge by appearances.[53]
> Insincerity . . . is merely a method by which we can multiply our personalities.
>   Such . . . was Dorian Gray's opinion. He used to wonder at the shallow
>   psychology of those who conceived the Ego in man as a thing simple,
>   permanent, reliable, and of one essence. To him man was a being with myriad
>   lives and myriad sensations, a complex, multiform creature.[54]

At work here is a transgressive desire which makes its opposition felt as a disruptive reaction upon, and inversion of, the categories of subjective depth which hold in place the dominant order which proscribes that desire.

The Decentered Subject and the Question of the Postmodern

Wilde's transgressive aesthetic relates to at least three aspects of contemporary theoretical debates: first, the dispute about whether the inversion of binary opposites subverts or, on the contrary, reinforces the order which those binaries uphold; second, the political importance—or irrelevance—of decentering the subject; third, postmodernism and one of its more controversial criteria: the so-called disappearance of the depth model, especially the model of a deep human subjectivity. Since the three issues closely relate to each other, I shall take them together.

It might be said that Wildean inversion disturbed nothing; by merely reversing the terms of the binary, inversion remains within its limiting framework: the world turned upside down can only be righted, not changed. Moreover, the argument might continue, Wilde's paradoxes are superficial in the pejorative sense of being inconsequential, of making no difference. But we should remember that in the first of the three trials involving Wilde in 1895 he was cross-examined on his *Phrases and Philosophies,* the implication of opposing counsel being that they, along with *Dorian Gray,* were "calculated to subvert morality and encourage unnatural vice."[55] There is a sense in which evidence cannot get more material than this, and it remains so whatever our retrospective judgment about the crassness of the thinking behind such a view.

One of the many reasons why people thought as they did was to do with the perceived connections between Wilde's aesthetic transgression and his sexual transgression. It is not only that at this time the word "inversion" was being used for the first time to define a specific kind of deviant sexuality and deviant person (the two things now being indissociable), but also that, in producing the homosexual as a species of being rather than, as before, seeing sodomy as an aberration of behavior,[56] society now regarded homosexuality as rooted in a person's identity; this sin might pervade all aspects of an individual's being, and its expression might become correspondingly the more insidious and subversive. Hence in part the animosity and hysteria directed at Wilde during and after his trial.

After he had been found guilty of homosexual offenses and sentenced to two years' imprisonment with hard labor, the editorial of the London *Evening News* subjected him to a vicious and revealing homophobic attack. He had, it claimed, tried to subvert the "wholesome, manly, simple ideals of English life"; moreover, his "abominable vices . . . were the natural outcome of his diseased intellectual condition." The editorial also saw Wilde as the leader of a likeminded but younger subculture in London.[57] The view expressed here was, and indeed remains, for some, a commonplace: sexual deviation is symptomatic of a much wider cultural deterioration and/or subversion. There is an important sense in which Wilde confirmed and exploited this connection between discursive and sexual perversion: "What the paradox was to me in the sphere of thought, perversity became to me in the sphere of passion."[58] This feared crossover between discursive and sexual perversion has sanctioned terrible brutalities against homosexuals; at the same time, at least in this period, it was also becoming the medium for what Foucault calls a reverse or counter-discourse,[59] giving rise to what is being explored here in relation to Wilde—what might be called the politics of inversion/perversion (again crossing over and between the different senses of these words). Derrida has argued persuasively for binary inversion as a politically indispensable stage toward the eventual displacement of the binary itself.[60] The case of Wilde indicates, I think, that in actual historical instances of inversion—that is, inversion as a strategy of cultural struggle—it already constitutes a displacement, if not of the binary itself, then certainly of the moral and political norms which cluster dependently around its dominant pole.

We begin to see, then, why Wilde was hated with such an intensity, even though he rarely advocated in his published writings any explicitly immoral practice. What held those "wholesome, manly, simple ideals of English life" in place were traditional and conservative ideas of what constituted human nature and human subjectivity, and it was *these* that Wilde attacked: not so much conventional morality itself as the ideological anchor points for that morality; namely, notions of identity as subjective depth whose criteria appear in the Y column above. And so it might be said that here, generally, as he did with Gide more specifically, Wilde subverts the dominant categories of subjectivity which keep desire in subjection and subverts the essentialist categories of identity which keep morality in place. Even though there may now be a temptation to patronize and indeed dismiss both the Victorians' "wholesome, manly, simple ideals of English life" and Wilde's inversion of them, the fact remains that, in successively reconstituted forms, those ideals, *together with* the subject positions which instantiate them, come to form the moral and ethical base of English studies in our own century and, indeed, remain culturally central today.

I am thinking here not just of the organicist ideology so characteristic of an earlier phase of English studies, one that led, for example, to the celebration of Shakespeare's alleged "national culture, rooted in the soil and appealing to a multi-class audience," but more specifically and importantly of what Chris Baldick in his excellent study goes on to call its "subjective correlative"; namely, the *"maintenance of the doctrine of psychic wholeness in and through literature as an analogue for a projected harmony and order in society."*[61] For I.A. Richards, all human problems (continues Baldick) become problems of mental health, with art as the cure, and literary criticism becomes "a question of attaining the right state of mind to judge other minds, according to their degree of immaturity, inhibition, or perversion." As Richards himself puts it, sincerity "is the quality we most insistently require in poetry. It is also the quality we most need as critics."[62] As a conception of both art and criticism, this is the reverse of Wilde's. Similarly with the Leavises, whose imperative concept was the related one of "maturity," one unhappy consequence of which was their promotion of the "fecund" D.H. Lawrence against the perverse W.H. Auden. As Baldick goes on to observe, "this line of critics is not only judicial in tone but positively inquisitorial, indulging in a kind of perversion-hunting" which is itself rooted in "a simple model of [pre- or anti-Freudian] normality and mental consistency."[63]

This tradition has, of course, been subjected to devastating critiques in recent years; in particular, its notions of subjective integration and psychic wholeness have been attacked by virtually all the major movements within contemporary critical theory, including Marxism, structuralism, poststructuralism, and psychoanalysis. Yet Wilde's subversion of these notions is still excluded from consideration, even though we now think we have passed beyond that heady and in many ways justified moment when it seemed that only Continental theory had the necessary force to displace the complacencies of our own tradition. The irony, of course, is that while looking to the Continent we failed to notice that Wilde has been and remains a very significant figure there. (And not only there: while the *Spectator* [February 1891] thought *The Soul of Man under Socialism* was a joke in bad taste, the essay soon became extremely successful in Russia, appearing in many successive editions across the next twenty years.) Perhaps, then, there exists or has existed a kind of "muscular theory," which shares with the critical movements it has displaced a significant blindness with regard to Wilde and what he represented. This almost certainly has something to do with the persistence of an earlier attempt to rid English studies of a perceived "feminized" identity.[64]

Recent critics of postmodernism, including Fredric Jameson, Ihab Hassan, Dan Latimer, and Terry Eagleton,[65] have written intriguingly on one of its defining criteria: the disappearance of the depth model. In a recent essay, Eagleton offers an important and provocative critique of postmodernism: "confidently post-metaphysical [it] has outlived all that fantasy of interiority, that pathological itch to scratch surfaces for concealed depths." With the postmodern there is no longer any subject to be alienated and nothing to be alienated from, "authenticity having been less rejected than merely forgotten." The subject of postmodernist culture is "a dispersed, decentered network of libidinal attachments, emptied of ethical substance and psychical interiority, the ephemeral function of this or that act of consumption, media experience, sexual relationship, trend, or fashion." Modernism, by contrast, is (or was) still preoccupied with the experience of alienation, with metaphysical depth and/or the psychic fragmentation and social wretchedness consequent upon the realization that there is no metaphysical depth or (this being its spiritual instantiation) authentic unified subject. As such, modernism is "embarrassingly enmortgaged to the very bourgeois humanism it otherwise seeks to subvert"; it is "a deviation still enthralled to a norm, parasitic on what it sets out to deconstruct." But, concludes Eagleton, the subject of late capitalism is actually neither the "self-regulating synthetic agent posited by classical humanist ideology, nor merely a decentered network of desire [as posited by postmodernism], but a contradictory amalgam of the two." If in one respect the decentered, dispersed subject of postmodernism is suspiciously convenient to our own phase of late capitalism, it follows that those poststructuralist theorists who stake all on the assumption that the unified subject is still integral to contemporary bourgeois ideology, and that it is always a politically radical act to decenter and deconstruct that subject, need to think again.[66]

Eagleton's argument can be endorsed with yet further important distinctions. First, even though the unified subject was indeed an integral part of an earlier phase of bourgeois ideology, the instance of Gide and the tradition he represents must indicate that it was never even then exclusively in the service of dominant ideologies. Indeed, to the extent that Gide's essentialist legitimation of homosexual desire was primarily an affirmation of his own nature as pederast or paedophile, some critics might usefully rethink their own assumption that essentialism is fundamentally and always a conservative philosophy. In Gide we find essentialism in the service of a radical sexual nonconformity which was and remains incompatible with conventional and dominant sexual ideologies, bourgeois and otherwise. Even a glance at the complex and often contradictory histories of sexual liberation movements in our own time shows that they have, as does Eagleton's contradictory subject of late capitalism, sometimes and necessarily embraced a radical essentialism with regard to their own identity, while simultaneously offering an equally radical antiessentialist critique of the essentializing sexual ideologies responsible for their oppression.

This is important: the implication of Eagleton's argument is not just that we need to make our theories of subjectivity a little more sophisticated, but rather that we need to be more historical in our practice of theory. Only then can we see the dialectical complexities of social process and social struggle. We may see, for example, how the very centrality of an essentialist concept to the dominant ideology has made its appropriation by a subordinate culture seem indispensable in that culture's struggle for legitimacy; roughly speaking, this corresponds to Gide's position as I am representing it here. The kind of challenge represented by Gide—liberation in the name of authenticity—has been more or less central to many progressive cultural struggles since, though it has not, of course, guaranteed their success.[67] Conversely, we may also see how other subordinate cultures and voices seek not to appropriate dominant concepts and values so much as to sabotage and displace them. This is something we can observe in Wilde.

Whether the decentered subject of contemporary poststructuralism and postmodernism is subversive of, alternative to, or actually produced by late capitalism, there is no doubt that Wilde's exploration of decentered desire and identity scandalized bourgeois culture in the 1890s and in a sense cost him his life. The case of Wilde might lead us to rethink the antecedents of postmodernism and, indeed, of modernism as they figure in the current debate which Eagleton addresses. Wilde prefigures elements of each, while remaining importantly different from—and not just obviously prior to—both. If his transgressive aesthetic anticipates postmodernism to the extent that it suggests a culture of the surface and of difference, it also anticipates modernism in being not just hostile to but intently concerned with its opposite, the culture of depth and exclusive integration. Yet Wilde's transgressive aesthetic differs from some versions of the postmodern in that it includes an acute political awareness and often an uncompromising political commitment; and his critique of the depth model differs from the modernist in that it is accompanied not by *Angst* but by something utterly different, something reminiscent of Barthes's *jouissance,* or what Borges has perceptively called Wilde's "negligent glee . . . the fundamental spirit of his work [being] joy."[68]

An antiessentialist theory of subjectivity can in no way guarantee, *a priori,* any effect, radical or otherwise; nor, more generally, can any transgressive practice carry such a guarantee. But there is much to be learned retrospectively both from the effects of antiessentialism and the practice of transgression, especially in the light of the currently felt need to develop new strategies and conceptions of resistance. Orthodox accounts of resistance have proved wanting, not least essentialist ideas of resistance in the name of the authentic self, and—in some ways the opposite—resistance in terms of and on behalf of mass movements working from outside and against the dominant powers. And so we have become acutely aware of the unavoidability of working from within the institutions that exist, adopting different strategies depending on where and who we are, or, in the case of the same individual, which subject positions he or she is occupying. But is this the new radicalism, or incorporation by another name?

It is in just these respects, and in relation to such pressing questions, that, far from finding them irrelevant—the one a *passé* wit and the other a *passé* moralist/essentialist—I remain intrigued with Wilde and Gide. In different ways their work explores what we are now beginning to attend to again: the complexities, the potential, and the dangers of what it is to transgress, invert, and displace *from within;*[69] the paradox of a marginality which is always interior to, or at least intimate with, the center.

I began with their encounter in Algiers in 1895. Gide, dispirited in the sense of being depressed and unsure of himself, sees the names of Wilde and Douglas and erases his own name as a result, preempting perhaps the threat to his own identity, social and psychic, posed by Wilde's determination to demystify the normative ideologies regulating subjectivity, desire, and the aesthetic. Nevertheless the meeting does occur, and Gide does indeed suffer an erasure of self, a decentering which is also the precondition for admitting transgressive desire, a depersonalization which is therefore also a liberation. Yet, for Gide, transgression is embraced with that same stubborn integrity which was to become the basis of his transgressive aesthetic, an aesthetic obviously indebted, yet also formed in reaction to, Wilde's own. Thus liberation from the self into desire is also to realize a new and deeper self, belief in which supports an oppositional stand not just on the question of deviant sexual desire, but on a whole range of other issues as well, cultural and political. Integrity here becomes an ethical sense inextricably bound up with and also binding up the (integral) unified self.[70] So the very categories of identity which, through transgression, Wilde subjects to inversion and displacement are reconstituted by Gide for a different transgressive aesthetic, or, as it might now more suitably be called in contradistinction to Wilde, a transgressive ethic: one which becomes central to the unorthodoxy which characterizes his life's work. In 1952, the year after his death, his entire works were entered in the Roman Catholic Index of Forbidden Books; six years earlier he had been awarded the Nobel Prize for Literature.

Wilde's fate was very different. Within weeks of returning from Algiers to London he was embroiled in the litigation against Queensberry which was to lead to his own imprisonment. He died in Paris in 1900, three years after his release. So, whereas Gide lived for fifty-seven years after that 1895 encounter, Wilde survived for only six. And yet it was also Wilde's fate to become a legend. Like many legendary figures, he needs to be rescued from most of his admirers and radically rethought by some, at least, of his critics.

NOTES

Thanks to Joseph Bristow for his comments on an earlier draft of this paper.

1. André Gide, *If It Die* (1920; private edition 1926), trans. Dorothy Bussy (Harmondsworth: Penguin, 1977), p. 271.

2. Ibid., pp. 271, 273.

3. Jean Delay, *The Youth of André Gide,* abridged and trans. J. Guicharnaud (Chicago and London: University of Chicago Press, 1956–57), p. 290.

4. Richard Ellmann, ed., *The Artist as Critic: Critical Writings of Oscar Wilde* (1968; London: W.H. Allen, 1970), p. xviii. Those aspects of Wilde's transgressive aesthetic which concern me derive mainly from work published across a relatively short period of time, the years 1889 to 1891. My exploration of this aesthetic rests on a reading of Wilde which is avowedly partial, concentrating on what has hitherto been excluded. Too often supposedly impartial readings of Wilde merely re-present a certain consensus—hence presumably his continued exclusion from certain "impartial" versions of "English" studies. More important is his exclusion from cultural criticism and literary theory: Wilde has considerable significance for contemporary debates yet does not as yet figure within them. What Richard Ellmann said of Wilde nearly twenty years ago is still true today: he "laid the basis for many critical positions which are still debated in much the same terms, and which we like to attribute to more ponderous names" (ibid., p. x). Thomas Mann compared Wilde with Nietzsche; Ellmann in 1968 adds the name of Roland Barthes. In 1987 we could add several more, especially in relation to the renewed interest in Wilde as the result of Ellmann's major biography. And it is in relation to that interest that I want to acknowledge that there is of course more—much more—to be said: about those of Wilde's works discussed here; about other works not discussed; about Wilde himself; and especially about other ideas of his which intersect with and contradict the transgressive aesthetic explored here.

5. J. Guicharnaud, trans., *Correspondence 1890–1942, André Gide–Paul Valéry* (1955), cited here from the abridged version, *Self-Portraits: The Gide/Valéry Letters* (Chicago and London: University of Chicago Press, 1966), pp. 90, 92.

6. Delay, *Youth*, p. 291.

7. André Gide, *Journals*, 4 vols. (New York: Alfred A. Knopf, 1947–51).

8. Delay, *Youth*, pp. 289, 290, 291, 295.

9. Richard Ellmann, ed., *Oscar Wilde: A Collection of Critical Essays* (Englewood Cliffs, N.J.: Prentice-Hall, 1969), p. 4.

10. Quoted from Delay, *Youth*, p. 391 (my italics).

11. André Gide, *Oscar Wilde*, trans. Bernard Frechtman (New York: Philosophical Library, 1949).

12. Gide, *If It Die*, pp. 280, 281.

13. Ibid., pp. 236–37, 247–49, 251, 252, 255, 258–59.

14. Ibid., p. 264.

15. Delay, *Youth*, p. 394.

16. Gide, *If It Die*, pp. 282, 284–85.

17. Oscar Wilde, *The Soul of Man under Socialism* (1891), reprinted in Ellmann, ed., *The Artist as Critic*, pp. 256 (his italics), 286–88, 288.

18. Ibid., pp. 259, 268, 260, 267.

19. Matthew Arnold, *Culture and Anarchy* (1869; London: Smith Elder, 1891), p. 8.

20. Wilde, *The Soul of Man under Socialism*, pp. 261, 258.

21. Wilde reiterates this elsewhere: see Oscar Wilde, "Pen, Pencil and Poison" (1889), in Ellmann, ed., *The Artist as Critic*, p. 338; "The Critic as Artist" (1890), in ibid., p. 360. Cf. Ellmann's formulation of Wilde's position: "since the established social structure confines the individual, the artist must of necessity ally himself with the criminal classes" (ibid., p. 3).

22. See also Wilde, "The Critic as Artist," p. 341; Wilde, *The Soul of Man under Socialism*, pp. 271–74.

23. Wilde, *The Soul of Man under Socialism*, pp. 273, 284–85, 286.

24. Oscar Wilde, "Mr Froude's Blue Book" (1889), in Ellmann, ed., *The Artist as Critic*, pp. 136–37.

25. Wilde, *The Soul of Man under Socialism*, p. 265.

26. Oscar Wilde, "The Decay of Lying" (1889), in Ellmann, ed., *The Artist as Critic*, p. 310, and "The Critic as Artist," p. 382.

27. Wilde, *The Soul of Man under Socialism*, p. 284.

28. Ibid., p. 284.

29. Wilde, "The Decay of Lying," p. 297.

30. Ibid., p. 305.

31. For example, Wilde, "The Critic As Artist," pp. 394, 399.

32. Oscar Wilde, *The Picture of Dorian Gray* (1890–91; Harmondsworth: Penguin, 1949), p. 10.

33. Wilde, "The Critic as Artist," pp. 343, 368.

34. Wilde, *The Soul of Man under Socialism,* p. 272 (my italics).

35. Wilde, "The Critic as Artist," p. 356.

36. Oscar Wilde, "A Few Maxims for the Instruction of the Overeducated," *The Complete Works,* with introduction by Vyvyan Holland (London and Glasgow: Collins, 1948), p. 1203.

37. Wilde, "The Decay of Lying," pp. 292, 305.

38. Ibid., p. 305.

39. Wilde, "The Critic as Artist," p. 399.

40. Delay, *Youth,* p. 438.

41. André Gide, *The Immoralist* (1902; Harmondsworth: Penguin, 1960), pp. 51, 90, 100.

42. Gide, *If It Die,* p. 298.

43. Delay, *Youth,* p. 396.

44. Gide, *If It Die,* p. 299.

45. Delay, *Youth,* p. 467.

46. Ibid., p. 407.

47. Gide, *Journals,* p. 338. Cf. ibid., pp. 371–76.

48. Oscar Wilde, *Phrases and Philosophies for the Use of the Young* (1894), in Ellmann, ed., *The Artist as Critic,* pp. 433–34.

49. The attacks on Wilde after his trial frequently reveal that it is masculinity which felt most under threat from him and which demanded revenge.

50. Wilde, "The Critic as Artist," p. 393.

51. Ibid., p. 398.

52. Oscar Wilde, *The Importance of Being Earnest* (1894–99), ed. R. Jackson (London: Ernest Benn, 1980), p. 83 (my italics).

53. Wilde, *The Picture of Dorian Gray,* p. 29.

54. Ibid., pp. 158–59.

55. H.M. Hyde, *Oscar Wilde: A Biography* (1976; London: Methuen, 1982), p. 271.

56. Michel Foucault, *The History of Sexuality,* vol. 1: *An Introduction* (1978; New York: Vintage Books, 1980), p. 43.

57. H.M. Hyde, *The Trials of Oscar Wilde* (London: William Hodge, 1948), p. 12.

58. Oscar Wilde, *De Profundis* (1897), in *The Letters of Oscar Wilde* (London: Rupert Hart-Davis, 1962); cited from the abridged edition, *Selected Letters* (London: Oxford University Press, 1979), p. 194. In certain important respects, *De Profundis* is a conscious renunciation by Wilde of his transgressive aesthetic. This is a work which registers many things, not least Wilde's courage and his despair during imprisonment. It also shows how he endured the intolerable by investing suffering with meaning, and this within a confessional narrative whose aim is a deepened self-awareness: "I could not bear [my sufferings] to be without meaning. Now I find hidden somewhere away in my nature something that tells me that nothing in the whole world is meaningless . . . that something . . . is Humility." Such knowledge and such humility, for Wilde (and still, for us now), is bought at the cost of fundamentally—deeply—renouncing difference and transgression and the challenge they present. In effect, Wilde repositions himself as the authentic, sincere subject which before he had subverted: "The supreme vice is shallowness," he says in his work, and he says it more than once. And later: "The moment of repentance is the moment of initiation" (ibid., pp. 195, 154, 215). This may be seen as that suffering into truth, that redemptive knowledge which points beyond the social to the transcendent realization of self, so cherished within idealist culture; those who see *De Profundis* as Wilde's most mature work often interpret it thus. I see it differently—as tragic, certainly, but tragic in the materialist sense of the word: a kind of defeat of the marginal and the oppositional which only ideological domination can effect; a renunciation which is experienced as voluntary and self-confirming but which is in truth a self-defeat and a self-denial massively coerced through the imposition, by the dominant, of incarceration and suffering and their "natural" medium, confession. What Wilde says here of the law is true also of the dominant ideologies he transgressed: "I . . . found myself constrained to appeal to the very things against which I had always protested" (ibid., p. 221).

59. Foucault, *History,* p. 101.

60. Jacques Derrida, *Positions* (London: 1981), pp. 41–42.

61. C. Baldick, *The Social Mission of English Criticism 1848–1932* (Oxford: Clarendon, 1983), pp. 213–18 (my italics).

62. I.A. Richards, quoted in ibid., p. 215.

63. Ibid., p. 217.

64. B. Doyle, "The Hidden History of English Studies," in Peter Widdowson, ed., *Re-Reading English* (London: Methuen, 1982); Terry Eagleton, *Literary Theory: An Introduction* (Oxford: Blackwell, 1983); Baldick, *Social Mission.* On Wilde in Germany, see Manfred Pfister, ed., Oscar Wilde, *The Picture of Dorian Gray* (Munich: Wilhelm Fink, 1986).

65. Fredric Jameson, "Postmodernism and Consumer Society," in H. Foster, ed., *The Anti-Aesthetic: Essays on Postmodern Culture* (Washington, D.C.: Bay Press, 1983); Fredric Jameson, "Postmodernism, or the Cultural Logic of Late Capitalism," *New Left Review* 146 (1984); Ihab Hassan, "Pluralism in Postmodern Perspective," *Critical Inquiry* 12, no. 3 (1986): 503–20; Dan Latimer, "Jameson and Postmodernism," *New Left Review* 148 (1984): 116–28; Terry Eagleton, "Capitalism, Modernism and Postmodernism," in *Against the Grain* (London: Verso, 1986), pp. 131–47.

66. Eagleton, "Capitalism, Modernism and Postmodernism," pp. 143, 132, 145, 143–45.

67. M. Berman, *The Politics of Authenticity: Radical Individualism and the Emergence of Modern Society* (London: Allen & Unwin, 1971).

68. Ellmann, ed., *Oscar Wilde,* p. 174.

69. See Jacques Derrida, *Of Grammatology* (1967), trans. Gayatri Spivak (Baltimore, Md., and London: The Johns Hopkins University Press, 1976), pp. lxxvi–lxxviii; Derrida, *Positions,* pp. 41–42; R. Terdiman, *Discourse/Counter Discourse: Theory and Practice of Symbolic Resistance in Nineteenth-Century France* (Ithaca, N.Y.: Cornell University Press, 1985), esp. Introduction. Some of the most informative work addressing inversion and transgression is historically grounded; I have in mind especially recent work on early modern England. See, for example, D. Kunzle, "World Turned Upside-Down: The Iconography of a European Broadsheet Type," in Barbara Babcock, ed., *The Reversible World: Symbolic Inversion in Art and Society* (Ithaca, N.Y., and London: Cornell University Press, 1978); Christopher Hill, *The World Turned Upside Down: Radical Ideas during the English Revolution* (Harmondsworth: Penguin, 1975); P. Stallybrass and A. White, *The Politics and Poetics of Transgression* (London: Methuen, 1986); S. Clark, "Inversion, Misrule and the Meaning of Witchcraft," *Past and Present* 87 (1980): 98–127. Kunzle, discussing the iconography of the world turned upside-down broadsheets, offers a conclusion which registers the complex potential of inversion and is, quite incidentally, nicely suggestive for understanding Wilde: "Revolution appears disarmed by playfulness, the playful bears the seed of revolution. 'Pure' formal fantasy and subversive desire, far from being mutually exclusive, are two sides of the same coin" ("World Turned Upside-Down," p. 89). This is the appropriate point at which to note that the fuller study to which this article is a contribution necessarily addresses other considerations in relation to transgression in Wilde and Gide, most especially those of class, race, and colonialism. A crucial text for the latter is Gide's *Travels in the Congo* (1927–28), trans. D. Bussy (Harmondsworth: Penguin, 1986). But see also Jean-Paul Sartre, *What Is Literature?* (1948; London: Methuen, 1967), esp. pp. 52, 98–99, 133.

70. It is instructive to see in Gide's writing how complex, vital, and unconventional the existential and humanist commitment to sincerity of self could be, especially when contrasted with its facile counterpart in English studies, or indeed (a counter-image) the reductive ways in which it is sometimes represented in literary theory. See especially the following entries in Gide's *Journals:* December 21 and detached/recovered pages for 1923; January 1925; October 7 and November 25, 1927; February 10 (especially) and December 8, 1929; August 5 and September 1931; June 27, 1937.

42

The Somagrams of Gertrude Stein*

CATHARINE R. STIMPSON

Catharine R. Stimpson is a literary critic, a past-President of the Modern Language Association, and a prominent United States spokeswoman for higher education. As a critic Stimpson has focused on modernism, particularly on the life and writings of one of the greatest of the modernists, Gertrude Stein. Stimpson has sought to determine how Stein's violations of the code of "the well-spoken Christian lady" helped to produce both her innovative literary accomplishments and her readers' response to them. In this essay Stimpson considers a series of representations of the female body—some by Stein herself, others about Stein's body by her friends, enemies, and interpreters. Of the representations by others Stimpson shows that some emphasize fatness, partly to register monstrousness, partly to de-eroticize Stein so as to deflect attention from her lesbianism; some situate her in the home so as to tame her; some figure her as an ancient Roman so as to cast her out of the present world. But Stein's own representations reveal a growing capacity to relinquish her early secrecy about her lesbianism and to figure the female body as a site of pleasure. Catharine R. Stimpson, University Professor at Rutgers University, is the author of Where the Meanings Are: Feminism and Cultural Spaces *(1988).*

"Behind thoughts and feelings, my brother," wrote Nietzsche in "The Despisers of the Body" in *Thus Spake Zarathustra,* "there is a mighty lord, an unknown sage—it is called Self; it dwelleth in thy body, it is thy body." But when we represent the body, we must transmute our dwelling into a ghost-ridden, ghost-written language. Soma must become a somagram.

The somagrams of Gertrude Stein—hers and ours about her—illustrate this well-worn axiom. They reveal something else as well: attempts—hers and ours—to fix monstrous qualities of the female body. Like all monstrosities, we despise them, and thus we seek to fix, to repair them. However, like all monstrosities, we also need them, and thus we seek to fix, to stabilize them. We often toil in vain.

For those who would represent her, Stein's body presents an alarming, but irresistible, opportunity. For her body—the size of it, the eyes, nose, sweat, hair, laugh, cheekbones—was at once strange, an unusual presence, and special, an invigorating one. Increasingly indifferent to "feminine" norms of dress, style, and action, Stein herself appeared to behave as if that strangeness—like her writing itself—was more special than strange, at once original and right.

Mixing attraction and repulsion, those who represented her often choose to stress Stein's size. Clearly, she was fat, but her fatness is also a signifier valuable because

*For permission to photocopy this selection please contact Harvard University Press. Reprinted by permission of the publishers from *The Female Body in Western Culture,* edited by Susan Suleiman, Cambridge, Mass.: Harvard University Press, Copyright © 1985, 1986 by the President and Fellows of Harvard College.

capacious enough to absorb contradictory attitudes towards the female body. In a complementary act, Stein's representors also note how thin Alice B. Toklas was. They make the women, partners in life, counterparts in proportion. So doing, they sharpen divisions within Stein's domestic union.

For Stein's admirers, weight is a sign of life. She is, in all ways, outsized. Poignantly, in some photographs of her when she was tired and dying, she is much thinner. For Mabel Dodge Luhan, Stein's body is attractively exceptional rather than ludicrously freakish:

> Gertrude Stein was prodigious. Pounds and pounds and pounds piled up on her skeleton—not the billowing kind, but massive, heavy fat. She wore some covering of corduroy or velvet and her crinkly hair was brushed back and twisted up high behind her jolly, intelligent face. She intellectualized her fat, and her body seemed to be the large machine that her large nature required to carry it.
> Gertrude was hearty. She used to roar with laughter, out loud. She had a laugh like a beefsteak. She loved beef. . . . (Luhan 1935:324)

Picasso, in his 1906 portrait, the most famous visual representation of Stein's body, drapes immense breasts, buttocks, hips, and thighs in dark cloth. However, the face and body are powerful. Because the browns and oranges of the sitter's clothing blend with the browns and oranges and dark blues of the background, the body seems at home, in place.

For more ambivalent admirers, Stein's fatness is a fact that they, and she, must transcend. Saying that Stein weighed two hundred pounds, less impartially judging that ugly, and then equating beauty and erotic love, Alfred Kazin states: "Stein and Toklas were certainly not beautiful, so their physical love for each other is all the more impressive" (Kazin 1977:33). A chatty biography for children begins with an unhappy adolescent Gertrude wishing that she "weren't so large," and gazing enviously at the "slender grace" of her more flirtatious, and feminine, friends. However, this Gertrude consoles herself by being "different in more important ways" as well. Splitting lively mind from lumpy body, Gertrude reminds herself that her mind is "quicker" than that of those friends (Wilson 1973:1).

Stein's detractors reverse the response of her genuine admirers. To them, her physical fatness is nothing less than proof of a hideous cultural and psychological overrun. She is nothing less than ". . . [a] . . . ten-ton granite American expatriate" (Corke 1961:370). At their most hostile, such detractors—men and women alike—go on to comment on Stein's Jewishness. Katherine Anne Porter, whose stiletto persistently flicked out at Stein, sneered at her as ". . . a handsome old Jewish patriarch who had backslid and shaved off his beard" (Porter 1952:43). Inevitably, detractors of Stein's body conflate her mind and body. They then disdain and fear her work. They seek to neutralize the threat to a dominant ideology of the well-spoken Christian lady that her potent combination of nature and culture offers: the body that she lived in; the family religion she more or less abandoned; the writing she never abandoned.

In a subtle maneuver, to picture Stein as fat also deflected the need to inscribe her lesbianism fully and publically. One could offer a body, but not an overtly erotic one. One could show some monstrosity, but not too much. Although people referred to such "mannish" characteristics of Stein's as her sensible shoes, no one spoke openly of her lesbianism until after her death in 1946. Her friends protected her desire for privacy. Her detractors evidently found the taboo against mentioning lesbianism stronger than their desire to attack. Moreover, a popular icon of the lesbian, which *The Well of Loneliness* codified—that of a slim, breastless creature who cropped her hair and wore sleek, mannish clothes—did little to reinforce an association between the ample Stein and deviancy. She may have cropped her hair, with Toklas as her barber, but she wore flowing caftans, brocaded vests, and woolen skirts.

After her death, Stein's lesbianism became more than a pronounceable, permissible subject for investigation. In the 1960s, in the women's movement and the gay movement, it stimulated celebration. In popular culture, her lesbianism evoked crass, but affectionate jokes, as if it were odd but fun. In the *National Lampoon,* for example, "Gertrude Steinbrenner," a "Lesbo Boss," who looks like a hybrid of George Steinbrenner and Picasso's Gertrude Stein, buys the New York Yankees and feistily brings her team into the modernist movement. Her cubist field has eight bases; Diaghilev inspires her uniforms (Barrett 1982).[1] Significantly, in the same period, critics begin to reinterpret her Jewishness. It no longer deforms her, but rather, like her sexuality, gives her the subversive perspectives of marginality.

Stein was, of course, far more than the fat lady of a Bohemian circus. She was a serious modernist, whose formal experiments were as radical, if not more so, as those of any other modern writer. The fact that her work provokes so much ridicule and anxiety—which oftens masks itself as ridicule—is one mark of her radicalism. Not even Stein's most ardent detractors can dismiss her, try though they might. Confronting such an alliance of body and literary activity, people, whether supporters or detractors, drew on two mutually contradictory sets of metaphors to depict her. The incompatibility of these sets itself reflects the difficulty, which Stein ultimately transcended, of having such a body devoted to such a cultural task.

The first set of metaphors domesticates Stein. Meant to praise, and to honor the monstrous lesbian as crafter, they also replace her securely within the woman's traditional domain of the home. Because Stein's fatness also evokes the association of the fleshy female body with fertility, a Venus von Willendorf, this taming language has an added resonance. In 1922, Sherwood Anderson, one of her most loyal friends, wrote effusively of meeting her in Paris the year before:

> In the great kitchen of my fanciful world in which I have, ever since that morning, seen Miss Stein standing, there is a most sweet and gracious aroma. Along the walls are many shining pots and pans, and there are innumerable jars of fruits, jellies, and preserves. Something is going on in the great room, for Miss Stein is a worker in words with the same loving touch in her strong fingers that was characteristic of the women in the kitchen of the brick houses in the town of my boyhood. She is an American woman of the old sort . . . who cares for the handmade goodies. (White 1972:24)

In the same year, Man Ray took his famous photograph of Stein and Toklas at 27 rue de Fleurus. Toklas, in a low chair, and Stein, in an easy chair, sit on either side of the fireplace. Between them is wooden table, above them paintings. Toklas wears a dress with ruffled collar and sleeves. The vaster Stein is clad in habitual items from her wardrobe: woolly socks, sandals, a blouse with a broach at the throat, a flowered jacket.[2] Indeed, several of the most widely circulated photographs of Stein frame her at home—in Paris or in the country.

The second set of metaphors inverts such cozy portraits of Stein at home by the range. In them, she is beyond society and social control, beyond ordinary sexuality, and therefore, beyond the need for sexual control. If the first set of metaphors drains monstrosity of its threat by enclosing it, the second does so by casting it out and away from daily history. In part, these metaphors transmogrify Stein into a sacred monster—to be sought after by some, cursed by others. Describing Stein after a walk in the Tuscan hills, Mabel Dodge Luhan oracularizes her:

... when she sat down, fanning herself with her broad-brimmed hat with its wilted, dark brown ribbon, she exhaled a *vivid steam around her.* (italics mine, Luhan 1935:327)

In 1920, a head of Stein that Jacques Lipchitz sculpted—with a topknot of hair, high cheekbones, narrow oval eyes—helped to create a linkage between Stein and Buddha. Sinclair Lewis, as an insult, called her "Mother Superior." Moving between polarities, Sherwood Anderson,

... was the first of several hundred people to liken her to a monk. Some religious quality about her unadorned habiliments brought to mind not so much a nun as a monk. There was something sexless about her, too, a kind of dynamic neuter. She was a robe surmounted by a head, no more carnal than a portly abbot. (Rogers 1948:39)

Such distancing metaphors also eject Stein back into time past. With suspicious frequency, her viewers compare her to a Roman emperor or well-born citizen. In Picabia's portrait of 1933, she stands—in a striped, toga-like robe. Two years later, an interviewer wrote:

The hair is close-cropped, gray, brushed forward or not brushed at all but growing forward in curls, like the hair of Roman emperors. (Preston 1935:187)

Physically, her strong bones, and that hair, made such an identification plausible. Psychologically, she seemed Roman in the persistence and case of her will—especially, in a conjunction of metaphors, when she was at home. As Roman, Stein could also be "mannish," without any direct declaration of lesbianism.

Hemingway's is the saddest engagement with the Roman metaphor. In his memoirs the now-alienated man, who was once surrogate son and brother, took revenge on Stein. He first remembers being responsive to her body. Describing it, he performs one of his standard rhetorical moves: rummaging through a number of non-Anglo-Saxon cultures for tropes to express pleasure. Stein has beautiful eyes, a "German-Jewish" face, "immigrant hair," and the face of an Italian peasant woman (Hemingway 1964:14). Centering his erotic recall on his relationship with Stein, Hemingway refers to Toklas only as "the friend." However, Hemingway centers his bitterness on that friend. For, he tells us, the relationship with Stein ended, although not formally, when he once went unexpectedly to 27 rue de Fleurus. He overheard Toklas speaking to Stein "as I had never heard one person speak to another; never, anywhere, ever" (p. 118). Given Hemingway's experience, his adverbial stresses seem disingenuous. Despite this, he goes on to tell of hearing Stein beg "Pussy" for mercy. In his shock, he strips both women of their bodies and reduces them to invisible, but scarring voices. His final word for Stein tries to restore the power of which the scene has denuded her: she is again "Roman" (p. 119).

Stein's somagrams of her body partially resemble and reinforce the patterns of representation I have outlined. For example, in the erotic celebrations of her relationship with Toklas, she famously and notoriously acts out the part of "Caesar."[3] Whether they resemble others' representations of her or not, her somagrams are never radically visceral or visual. She is no physiological blueprinter. In her salon, she also "... frowned on anything that smacked of vulgarity" (Mellow 1974:324). She might voyeuristically provoke gossip and displays, but she believed in discretion. To measure her reticence one might compare her to Apollinaire in 1909. She was writing "Ada," the lyrical portrait about her growing relationship with Toklas, and "Miss Furr and Miss Skeene," a witty short story about a disintegrating relationship between two other women. Neither has any explicit sexual detail whatsoever. Meanwhile, Apollinaire was publishing and endorsing the first anthology of the works of Sade.

Nevertheless, during her career, Stein's somagrams became freer and more flexible, as she became less monstrous to herself. Her happiness with Toklas diluted the guilts and stains of a homosexuality that violated the "decent" norms of the heterosexual bourgeois family to which Stein had once been committed. She was increasingly confident of herself as a writer, even boisterously so. So doing, she became more sympathetic to women's aspirations and talent (DeKoven 1983:137). Though Stein was never a public feminist, during the 1920s she began to cut the cord she and Western culture had tied between masculinity and towering creativity.

Her body also enlivens her writings, be they somagrams or not, be they lyrics, meditations, or diary-like notations. For her texts read as if her voice were in them, as if she were speaking and dictating as much as writing. Unlike a Charles Olson, Stein lacks a theory about the relationship of the poetic line to the human breath. Nevertheless, she illustrates that "The best writing is energized by speech, and the best speech surges forward like a wave . . . In poetry, writing is not the same as speech, but is transformed by speech . . ." (Vernon 1979:40). Once, when Stein was objectifying mutton in *Tender Buttons,* written in 1911 but not published until 1914, she mused and teased, "A sign is the specimen spoken" (Stein 1971:182). Stein's work is liveliest when read and heard; when our own o/aural talents lift her words from the page and animate them in an informal or formal, private or public, theatrical environment.

Stein's somagrams became freer and more flexible in at least two entwined ways, which in turn entwine psychology and rhetoric. Firstly, she modified her motives for being discreet when she wrote about the female body. In the first decade of the twentieth century, she was fearful of what she might say, of what she might confess—to herself and others. She disguised her own lesbian experiences by projecting them onto others or by devising what William Gass, one of her most scrupulous and sensitive critics, has called her "protective language":

> . . . a kind of neutralizing middle tongue, one that is neither abstractly and impersonally scientific nor directly confronting and dramatic, but one that lies in that gray limbo in between. . . . (Gass 1972:89)

Perhaps her fear was never wholly to disappear. Still, Stein was later to see the body as but one element in a larger physical, emotional, social, linguistic, and metaphysical universe.[4] Even in Q.E.D. (1903), Stein wrote about women's bodies as signifiers of psychic and national types: the body of Helen Thomas demonstrates the American version of an "English handsome girl"; that of Mabel Neathe the American version of an older, decadent Italian aristocracy; that of Adele (based on Stein herself) the values of a young, hearty, middle-class woman. In Q.E.D. too, the lesbian triangle of Helen, Mabel, and Adele is less an erotic intrigue, though Adele's introduction to erotic experience matters, than an arena of power plays. For Stein, I believe, too great a preoccupation with the body would grossly swell its importance. Though some inhabitants of the twentieth century might be skeptical, such a belief is legitimate, not a prude's rationalization of sexual repression. Stein once said that sex, like violence, was the root of much emotion. Nevertheless, it was but part of a whole; sexual passion was less than passion conceived as "the whole force of man."[5]

> Literature—creative literature—unconnected with sex is inconceivable. But not literary sex, because sex is a part of something of which the other parts are not sex at all. (Preston 1935:191)

Throughout her writing, Stein so places the female body that it merges with, and gives way to, other activities. For example, in 1940, in *Ida,* Stein has a passage about

Ida's adolescence. She simultaneously alludes to menstruation and slides away. The double process of allusion and slippage both evokes the body and dissipates its presence:

> And so Ida went on growing older and then she was almost sixteen and a great many funny things happened to her. Her great-aunt went away so she lost her great-aunt who never really felt content since the orange blossoms had come to visit her. And now Ida lived with her grandfather. She had a dog, he was almost blind not from age but from having been born so and Ida called him Love, she liked to call him naturally she and he liked to come even without her calling him. (Stein 1971:340)

In her blurring, the boundaries of gender identity themselves decompose. Female and male become fe/male. "Arthur angelic angelica did spend the time," Stein gossips (Stein 1975:39). As she wipes out punctuation marks, she makes it equally possible that someone is telling Arthur about Angelica; that angelic Arthur is spending time with Angelica; that angelic Angelica is spending time with Arthur; that two angels are spending time together; or that Arthur and Angelica are one heavenly creature.

Invariably, inevitably, the body fuses with writing itself. Stein merges herself with her work, and that unity with the world. Look at "Sacred Emily," a 1913 piece in which Stein first said, "Rose is a rose is a rose." Its first line is "Compose compose beds" (Stein 1968:188). Multiply punning, the line refers to gardens and to flowering beds; to making beds, that site of sleep and sex; to making beds musical, and to making beds a language game. Even in "Lifting Belly," Stein's most ebullient record of her life with Toklas, sexual tension, foreplay, and climax interweave with other, fragmenting sensations and phenomena to create "... a tense we might call 'present sensual...'" (Retallack 1983:251). The phrase "Lifting belly" becomes both a repetitive synecdoche for a repeated, repeatable sexual act and a generalized metonymy for Stein's life at large. Because the poem has such a successful de-centering device, almost any group of lines, pulled out at random, inflects the 'present sensual' tense:

> Lifting belly is a credit. Do you care about poetry?
> Lifting belly in spots.
> Do you like ink.
> Better than butter.
> Better than anything.
> Any letter is an alphabet.
> When this you see you will kiss me.
> Lifting belly is so generous.
> Shoes. (Stein 1980:48).[6]

Indeed, in Stein's more abstract writing, the body disappears into language utterly, or becomes an example of a linguistic category. Kisses may illustrate, not the body in action, but a problematic grammatical class: the noun.

Stein's second demonstration of a freer, more freeing, more flexible sense of women's bodies is her growing ability to represent the body as a site of pleasure. In her work in the first part of the twentieth century, the experience of eros, for heterosexual and homosexual women alike, breeds frustration, anxiety, and guilt—particularly for more vulnerable and powerless women. For heterosexual women, eros is inseparable from a fated, dutiful maternity. No matter what their sexuality, women's bodies are mortal. In *Three Lives,* Good Anna dies after an operation, Melanctha dies in a home for poor consumptives, Gentle Lena dies, worn out after three pregnancies, giving birth to a fourth child, itself still-born.

Then, in 1909, Stein began to write of sexuality with pleasure (Schmitz 1983: 194–196). To be sure, she continued to remember sexual trauma and unhappiness. In *How To Write,* published about thirty years after Stein's wretched entanglement with May Bookstaver, she has a long, broody paragraph about Mabel Haynes, Stein's rival for May's allegiance, and about Mabel's subsequent career as wife and mother (Stein 1975:222). Stein could also write ambivalently about sexuality. In *Tender Buttons,* she ends her first section "Objects," with "This Is The Dress, Aider." "Aider" puns on "To aid" and "Ada," that surrogate name for Toklas. Only two lines long, the meditation replicates the rhythms of an act that seems at once richly pleasurable and violent. Stein, in *Tender Buttons* and elsewhere, was to become more and more skillful in imitating the rhythms of an act in order to name it without resorting to, and consorting with, jaded old nouns. "This Is The Dress" ends: "A jack in kill her, a jack in, makes a meadowed king, makes a to let" (Stein 1971:176). The act seems to be sexual, but it may, of course, also be anything that follows a pattern of building and releasing tension. The last three words, for example, may allude to "a toilet," which, in turn, may be the process of getting dressed, or of going to the bathroom, or of both.

To be sure, too, Stein never lost her sense of the body's fragility. In the 1930s, she was, as if it were a minor obsession, to work and rework the stories of two mysterious, sinister deaths near her country home. In one, Madame Pernollet, a hard-toiling hotel-keeper's wife in Belley, has died—five days after falling onto a cement courtyard. In the second, a Madame Caeser (that Roman word again) had been living with a Madame Steiner (another extension of Stein's own name). However, an Englishwoman has interrupted their idyll. After some complications, she is found dead. Despite the fact that she has two bullets in her head, she is declared a suicide. As if to compensate for such a sense of fragility, and to declare her own power over the body, Stein, in the 1930s, was to give the author herself the power to destroy. In *Everybody's Autobiography* she notes, with aplomb:

> . . . Give me new faces new faces new faces I have seen the old ones . . . Having written all about them they ceased to exist. That is very funny if you write all about any one they do not exist any more, for you, and so why see them again. Anyway that is the way I am. (Stein 1973:118)

In spite of such strong residual memories and perceptions, Stein's eventual delight in the female body spins and rushes through her work, inseparable from her pleasure in food, or a dog, or the landscape, or a French hat. "It is very pretty," she writes, "to love a pretty person and to think of her when she is sleeping very pretty" (Stein 1975:359). Because she is happy as both carnal participant and observer, as both actor and audience, she sites/cites her body, and that of her partner/s, in a "magic theater" (Fifer 1979:473). However, the celebration of the body is more than a performance. Inverting the puritanism that Stein never fully escaped, the celebration of the body can be ethically charged as well. For it becomes ". . . at its climax a celebration of the capacity we have for emotion, for 'care,' the tenderest mode of human feeling and behavior" (Secor 1982:304).

Given this, Stein's coding of sexual activities ceases to be a suspect evasion and becomes, instead, a privileged, and a distinguished, "anti-language." The sociolinguist, M.A.K. Halliday, writes of anti-languages as the speech of anti-societies, "set up within another society as a conscious alternative to it" (Halliday 1976:570). The anti-language has several purposes: to display a speaker's abilities; to preserve secrecy; to act out a "distinct social structure" (p. 572); to socialize people into that structure. In brief, the monsters speak up within, and for, their lair. Halliday writes, not of homosexual anti-societies, but of criminal underworlds, prisons, and vaudeville. Nevertheless, Stein and Toklas, in their own home and in the social circles they inhabited, were citizens of a homosexual anti-society. For that home, and for those circles, Stein, as part of her vast experiments, uttered an anti-speech that has become more public as the dominant society has become less hostile to her subjects.

Whether or not her anti-language is "female" as well is a far more perplexing matter. In 1976, Ellen Moers rightly suggested that Stein deploys landscape to project and to represent female sexuality. In so doing, she extends a female literary tradition (Moers, p. 254). Stein does often resort to nature to emblemize female sexuality, female being, and her own creativity. In one of her later presentations of self-as-writer, Stein brought together two complementary quasi-natural metaphors: the fountain—traditionally masculine, and the womb—invariably feminine.

> Technique is not so much a thing of form or style as the way that form or style came and how it can come again. Freeze your fountain and you will always have the frozen water shooting into the air and falling and it will be there to see—oh, no doubt about that—but there will be no more coming . . . You cannot go into the womb to form the child; it is there and makes itself and comes forth whole—and there it is and you have made it and have felt it, but it has come itself. . . . (Preston 1935:188)

Stein also belongs to the history of women writers as women writers for reasons other than her landscape imagery. They include her cultural marginality, her interest in domesticity, and her teasing of patriarchs and of gender relations. Moreover, her lesbianism—the sexual deposition of her body, her choice of a woman as lover/companion—helped to give her the distance she needed to reform English literature and the homely security she needed if she were to be such an intrepid pioneer.[7]

The question of a women's tradition provokes yet another query: that of its causes. Clearly, a common history and culture, not a common psychobiology, can determine a women's tradition. When Stein adapted George Eliot's landscape metaphors, even as she devised her own, she could have done so because she had read, and admired, Eliot as a precursor; because she had read, and admired Eliot's texts as texts that were, in part, *about* women's experiences. However, since Moers's work in the mid-1970s, attempts to adjectify Stein's work as "female" have entangled that work far more deeply with Stein's femaleness as femaleness, as an elemental condition, inseparable from the body.

Some of these efforts derive from critics who owe a strong theoretical allegiance to United States radical feminism. As they construct the world, they profoundly genderize it. Knowing, thinking, writing—all are dualistic, male or female. Two such critics claim:

> Patriarchal expressive modes reflect an epistemology that perceives the world in terms of categories, dichotomies, roles, stasis, and causation, while female expressive modes reflect an epistemology that perceives the world in terms of ambiguities, pluralities, processes, continuities . . . complex relationships. (Penelope and Wolfe 1983: 126)

For them, Stein, a woman deep within the process of creation, is a prophet of a female expressive mode emerging fully in the late twentieth century.

Other critics genderize the world less radically. They reflect the influence of a liberal United States feminism that fears casting "femaleness" and "maleness" in the eternal bronze of an essential. Nevertheless, they, too, deploy contemporary theories of the female to place Stein as a writer. Subtle, supple, finely intelligent, Marianne DeKoven adapts the theories of Kristeva and Derrida to distinguish between two languages: our conventional, patriarchal speech, and an experimental, anti-patriarchal speech. The former celebrates the triumph of the male over the female; the post-Oedipal over the pre-Oedipal; the father's dictionary over the mother's body; meaning over things; the linear over the pluridimensional—in brief, the signified over the signifier. For DeKoven, Stein is the great, subversive experimental writer in English. Rejecting the repressions of patriarchal language, locating herself in the psychosocial position of women, loving the play of the signifier, Stein necessarily reclaims the mother's body as well (DeKoven 1983).

I admire such ideas, and resist them. Elsewhere I have tangled with my general ambivalence about "female" writing.[8] Let me now think more particularly of Stein. To begin, she was a fresh, brilliant, thoughtful literary theoretician. To be sure, in her theory and practice, she praised the spontaneous, the immediate "flow" of language from writer to page. Nevertheless, banks of theory line that flow, rocks of theory interrupt it, bridges of theory cross it. For better or worse, Stein is utterly impure: linear as well as pluridimensional, "male" as well as "female," the fountain as well as the womb.

Given this, one might argue that Stein clinches the case for Kristeva (Kristeva 1980). First, like male avant-garde writers, Stein reaches back and down into pre-Oedipal speech. Next, she shows how pre- and post-Oedipal mix; how the semiotic and the symbolic play off and against each other. However, studies of the ways in which children actually acquire language render suspect the terms "pre-Oedipal" and "post-Oedipal," as well as a picture of childhood that transforms children into boys and girls whose primary schooling in language is first with the mother's body and then with the father's rule. Of course, the sex of the parent still matters to the child. A mother's voice, for example, has a different frequency than that of a father. Nevertheless, in the acquisition of language, infants may share a mentality and competence that transcends sex and gender—be it their own, or that of the parents.

A characteristic of that mentality and competence is the surprisingly early age at which they adopt, and adapt, rules. First, at ten to twelve months, children demonstrate a "holophrastic speech," single word utterances used to express complex ideas about their environment (Dale 1972). Next, at about eighteen to twenty months, they progress to two-word utterances: a "pivot word" that appears in the same position in every phrase, an "open word" that changes. Next, children do more word combinations, formulate noun phrases, and differentiate classes of modifying words. Even as infants, children are regulatory, rule-making, rule-analyzing creatures who seek to combine creativity with patterns, self with laws, needs with necessities. As a leading linguist writes:

> It is striking how little difficulty a child has with any of the general mechanisms of language: the notion of a sentence, the establishment of word classes and rules for combining them, the concept of inflections, the expression of a wide variety of meanings, and more. All are present from a very early age . . . As impressive as the complexity of child language is, it appears to be outstripped by the uses to which a child wants to put it . . . the child is above all attempting to express his own ideas, emotions, and actions through whatever system he has thus far constructed. . . . (Dale 1972:50)

In brief, when Gertrude and her brother Leo were little, they grasped, grappled with, and broke the rules of language *as children,* each with his or her individual being. As they grew up, they entered an adult world. As Stein knew, it gave men more power than women—including greater power over and within the female body. Because of this, we can legitimately call this world "post-Oedipal." Stein's sense of her own monstrosity in this world—as a sexual being, as a marginal cultural citizen—influenced her writing, and her somagrams. However, laboring with language in this world, Stein came to believe that women were in many ways more capable than men. Women could assume power over and within language, over and within their bodies. Resiliently, she transformed the monstrous into pleasure and into art. Because of this, we can call her a visionary of the "post-post-Oedipal."

If we do so, however, we must limit our Oedipal vocabulary to a way of talking about historical experience and various social uses of language. Stein's texts, including her somagrams, warn us against going on to genderize grammar itself. Her literary language was neither "female," nor an unmediated return to signifiers freely wheeling in maternal space. It was instead an American English, with some French twists and a deep structure as genderless as an atom of platinum. It could bend to patriarchal pressures, or lash against them. It could label and curse monsters, or, finally, respond to a monster's stubborn and transforming will.

NOTES

1. See, too, the cartoon strips of T. Hachtman, first in the *Soho News* and then gathered in Hachtman (1980). My thanks to Albert Sonnenfeld for bringing the Barrett piece to my attention.
2. The best collection of reproductions of paintings, photos, and sculptures of Stein is in Hobhouse (1975).
3. The translation of Stein's private sexual language begins with Bridgman (1970). It continues with Simon (1977); Stimpson (1977); Fifer (1979); Stimpson (forthcoming), with further references.
4. My position modifies that of Wilson (1952). He believes that Stein's denial of her sexuality was greatly responsible for much of the opacity of her prose. See too Phelps (1956).
5. To adopt Stein's terms, the body may belong to the realm of "identity," not to the more significant realm of "entity."
6. Note that "shoes" puns on "choose" and "chews."
7. Secor (1982), DeKoven (1983), and Schmitz (1983) persuasively analyze Stein as an anti-patriarchal writer. I am writing a longer work on Stein that will treat her as an anti-patriarchal writer, with strong moorings to the patriarchy.
8. For more comment, see Jardine (1981) and Stimpson (1983).

REFERENCES

Barrett, Ron, 1982. "A Portrait of Gertrude Steinbrenner," *National Lampoon* July, 70–73.
Bridgman, Richard, 1970. *Gertrude Stein In Pieces* (New York: Oxford University Press).
Corke, Hilary, 1961. "Reflections on a Great Stone Face," *Kenyon Review* XXIII:3 (Summer), 367–389.
Dale, Philip S., 1972. *Language Development: Structure and Function* (Hinsdale, Illinois: Dryden Press).
DeKoven, Marianne, 1983. *A Different Language: Gertrude Stein's Experimental Writing* (Madison: University of Wisconsin Press).
Fifer, Elizabeth, 1979. "Is Flesh Advisable? The Interior Theater of Gertrude Stein," *Signs: Journal Of Women in Culture and Society* 4:3 (Spring), 472–483.
Gass, William, 1972. "Gertrude Stein: Her Escape from Protective Language," in *Fiction and the Figures of Life* (New York: Vintage Books), 79–96.
Hachtman, T., 1980. *Gertrude's Follies* (New York: St. Martin's).
Halliday, M.A.K., 1976. "Anti-Languages," *American Anthropologist* 78:3 (September), 570–584.
Hemingway, Ernest, 1964. *A Moveable Feast* (New York: Charles Scribner's Sons).
Hobhouse, Janet, 1975. *Everybody Who Was Anybody: A Biography of Gertrude Stein* (New York: G.P. Putnam's Sons).
Jardine, Alice, 1981. "Pre-Texts for the Transatlantic Feminist," *Yale French Studies* 62, 220–236.
Kazin, Alfred, 1977. "Gay Genius and the Gay Mob," *Esquire* 88:6 (December), 33–34, 38.

Kristeva, Julia, 1980. *Desire in Language: A Semiotic Approach to Literature and Art,* ed. Leon S. Roudiez (New York: Columbia University Press).

Luhan, Mabel Dodge, 1935. *European Experiences,* Vol. II of *Intimate Memories* (New York: Harcourt, Brace and Co.).

Mellow, James R., 1974. *Charmed Circle: Gertrude Stein and Company* (New York: Praeger Publishers).

Moers, Ellen, 1976. *Literary Women: The Great Figures* (Garden City, New York: Doubleday and Co.).

Penelope, Julia and Susan J. Wolfe, 1983. "Consciousness as Style: Style as Aesthetic," in Barrie Thorne, Cheris Kramarae, and Nancy Henley, eds., *Language, Gender and Society* (Rowley, Mass.: Newbury House Publishers, Inc.), 125–139.

Phelps, Robert, 1956. "The Uses of Gertrude Stein," *Yale Review* XLV:4 (June), 603.

Porter, Katherine Anne, 1952. *The Days Before* (New York: Harcourt, Brace and Co.).

Preston, John Hyde, 1935. "A Conversation," *Atlantic Monthly* CLVI (August), 187–194.

Retallack, Joan, 1983. "High Adventures of Indeterminacy," *Parnassus* 11:1 (Spring/Summer), 231–262.

Rogers, W.G., 1973 (1948). *When This You See Remember Me: Gertrude Stein In Person* (New York: Avon Books).

Schmitz, Neil, 1983. *Of Huck and Alice: Humorous Writing in American Literature* (Minneapolis: University of Minnesota Press).

Secor, Cynthia, 1982. "Gertrude Stein: The Complex Force of Her Femininity," in Kenneth W. Wheeler and Virginia Lee Lussier, eds., *Women, The Arts, and the 1920s In Paris and New York* (New Brunswick: Transaction Books), 27–35.

Simon, Linda, 1977. *The Biography of Alice B. Toklas* (Garden City, New York: Doubleday and Co.).

Stein, Gertrude, 1968 (1922). *Geography and Plays,* with a Foreword by Sherwood Anderson (New York: Something Else Press, Inc.).

——— 1971. *Writings and Lectures 1909–1945,* ed. Patricia Meyerowitz (Baltimore: Penguin Books).

——— 1973 (1937). *Everybody's Autobiography* (New York: Vintage Books).

——— 1975 (1931). *How To Write,* with a New Preface and Introduction by Patricia Meyerowitz (New York: Dover Publications).

——— 1980. *The Yale Gertrude Stein,* ed. Richard Kostelanetz (New Haven and London: Yale University Press).

Stimpson, Catharine R., 1977. "The Mind, the Body, and Gertrude Stein," *Critical Inquiry* 3:3 (Spring), 489–506.

——— 1983. "Feminism and Feminist Criticism," *Massachusetts Review* XXIV:2 (Summer), 272–278.

——— forthcoming. "Gertrice/Altrude," in Ruth Perry, ed., *Mothering the Mind* (New York: Holmes and Meier).

Vernon, John, 1979. *Poetry and The Body* (Urbana: University of Illinois Press).

White, Ray Lewis, ed., 1972. *Sherwood Anderson/Gertrude Stein, Correspondence and Personal Essays* (Chapel Hill: University of North Carolina Press).

Wilson, Edmund, 1952. *Shores of Light* (New York: Farrar, Straus and Young).

Wilson, Ellen, 1973. *They Named Me Gertrude Stein* (New York: Farrar, Straus and Giroux).

Suggestions for Further Reading

These suggestions for further reading provide some guidance to relatively recent, and mostly English-language, publications in lesbian/gay studies. It need hardly be said, but perhaps we should say it anyway: These suggestions do not constitute a *full* bibliography even of recent English-language publications. Such a bibliography, if it could be compiled, might easily be ten times as long as this one is! And the space available to us is limited. If you seek more suggestions than we can provide here, you may want to consult these reference works: Dolores Maggiore, *Lesbianism: An Annotated Bibliography and Guide to the Literature, 1976–1986* (1988), Wayne R. Dynes, *Homosexuality: A Research Guide* (1987), Cal Gough and Ellen Greenblatt, eds., *Gay and Lesbian Library Service* (1990), and Simon Stern, "Lesbian and Gay Studies: A Selective Bibliography," *Yale Journal of Criticism*, 3 (1989). In addition, some of the books listed below include extended bibliographies (the titles of these books are asterisked).

I. Journals, periodicals. *GLQ: A Journal of Lesbian and Gay Studies* provides wide coverage of the field. *The Journal of Homosexuality* is especially strong in the quantitative social sciences, though it also carries articles in other areas including literary criticism. *Journal of the History of Sexuality* publishes regularly in lesbian/gay history. *differences: A Journal of Feminist Cultural Studies* is another periodical well worth following; it is home to much work in queer theory. *Genders* carries a wide range of lesbian/gay studies articles—in history, literary criticism, cultural studies, and art history. *Hypatia* and *Lesbian Ethics* carry philosophy. *Signs, Feminist Review*, and *Feminist Studies* all include current scholarship on lesbianisms, done from many different disciplinary perspectives. *Radical America, Socialist Review, Radical History Review, Radical Teacher*, and *Social Text* all carry some lesbian/gay studies work, particularly work that is politically inflected. *Camera Obscura, Discourse*, and *Jump Cut* carry some lesbian/gay studies work on film and popular culture, while *Raritan, ELH: A Journal of English Literary History, Representations, Critical Inquiry*, and *Yale Journal of Criticism* carry some in literary criticism. The *Lesbian and Gay Studies Newsletter* provides networking news for students and teachers, and reviews of books. It also provides, in every issue, a list of the various discipline-specific bulletins in lesbian/gay studies (such as the *Association of Lesbian/Gay Psychologists Newsletter* and *G&L Caucus News of the College Art Association*), and of the bulletins produced by specific centers for lesbian/gay studies (such as *Centre/Fold: Toronto Centre for Lesbian & Gay Studies Newsletter* and *Homologie Documentatiecentrum Homostudies*, University of Amsterdam), along with information on how to subscribe to them.

There are other periodicals which are relatively less academic and professional, relatively more community-based and popular. These include the women's journals *Conditions, Sinister Wisdom, Heresies, Frontiers, Off Our Backs, On Our Backs*, and *Sojourner;* the black gay journal *Other Countries;* and *Out/Look, Christopher Street, The Guide, Magnus, QW*, and *The Advocate*. All make contributions to lesbian/gay studies. So do community newspapers, such as *Angles* (Vancouver), The *Bay Area Reporter* (San Francisco), *Capital*

Gay (London), *The Blade* (Washington, D.C.), *Gai Pied Hebdo* (Paris), *Bay Windows* (Boston), *Rites* (Toronto), and *Windy City Times* (Chicago).

II. The AIDS crisis. Since the beginnings of the AIDS crisis, we have given much of our energy, intellectual energy included, to fighting AIDS. This fight is now as central to lesbian/gay studies as to everyday life. Diane Richardson, *Women and AIDS* (1988), and *Women, AIDS, and Activism,* by the ACT-UP/New York Women and AIDS Book Group (1990), are both valuable. Along with the Patton essay on Africa reprinted in this volume, see also Paula Treichler, "AIDS, Africa, and Cultural Theory," *Transition,* 51 (1991), and Simon Watney, "Missionary Positions," *Critical Quarterly,* 30 (1989). "Central Americans Tackle AIDS," *Outweek,* Oct. 10, 1990, is an informative newsstory in a magazine that is now defunct. Douglas Crimp with Adam Rolston, *AIDS Demo Graphics* (1990), is good on activism in the United States, while Douglas Crimp, ed., *AIDS: Cultural Analysis/Cultural Activism* (1988) has much to say about the social construction of AIDS. Cindy Patton, *Inventing AIDS** (1991), is important on the AIDS service industry worldwide, and Simon Watney, *Policing Desire: Aids, Pornography, and the Media* (1987), discusses how and why AIDS is misrepresented in the popular media, especially in English-speaking countries. Also useful are Elizabeth Fee and Daniel M. Fox, eds., *AIDS: The Burdens of History* (1988), and *AIDS: The Making of a Chronic Disease* (1992), Erica Carter and Simon Watney, eds., *Taking Liberties: AIDS and Cultural Politics** (1989), Emmanuel S. Nelson, ed., *AIDS: The Literary Response* (1992), James Meyer, "AIDS and Postmodernism," *Arts Magazine,* 66 (1992), and Tessa Boffin and Sunil Gupta, eds., *Ecstatic Antibodies* (1990). Michael Callen, *Surviving AIDS* (1990), collects some compelling statements by P.W.A.'s. See also the wonderful Oakland zine *DPN:Diseased Pariah News.* Donna J. Haraway, *Simians, Cyborgs, and Women: The Reinvention of Nature* (1991), includes on pp. 203–230 a thoughtful discussion of the ways in which immunological writing, usually regarded as just plain science, can be political.

III. Contemporary testimony and memoirs. In recent years the genre of memoir or testimony has, perhaps especially in the United States, become important as a means of explaining and illustrating differences in lesbian, bisexual, queer, and gay identities, differences inflected by race, class, ethnicity, religion, and sexual practice. Among the notable collections are: Cherríe Moraga and Gloria Anzaldúa, eds., *This Bridge Called My Back: Writings By Radical Women of Color* (1981), Gloria Anzaldúa, ed., *Borderlands/ La Frontera: The New Mestiza* (1987), Juanita Ramos, ed., *Compañeras: Latina Lesbians* (1987), Will Roscoe, ed., *Living the Spirit: A Gay American Indian Anthology* (1988), Frances Rooney, ed., *Our Lives: Lesbian Personal Writings* (1991), Michael J. Smith, ed., *Black Men/White Men: A Gay Anthology* (1983), Joseph Beam, ed., *In The Life: A Black Gay Anthology* (1986), Essex Hemphill, ed., *Brother to Brother: New Writings by Black Gay Men* (1991), Loraine Hutchins and Lani Kaahumani, eds., *Bi Any Other Name: Bisexual People Speak Out* (1991), Julia Penelope and Susan J. Wolfe, eds., *The Original Coming Out Stories* (rev. ed., 1989), Evelyn Torton Beck, ed., *Nice Jewish Girls: A Lesbian Anthology* (1982), Christie Balka and Andy Rose, eds., *Twice Blessed: On Being Lesbian or Gay and Jewish* (1989), and *Coming to Power: Writings and Graphics on Lesbian S/M,* by SAMOIS (1981). Three contributions from England are *Inventing Ourselves: Lesbian Life Stories,* by the Hall Carpenter Archives Lesbian Oral History Group (1989), *Walking After Midnight: Gay Men's Life Stories,* by the Hall Carpenter Archives Gay Men's Oral History Group, and Kevin Porter and Jeffrey Weeks, eds., *Between the Acts: Lives of Homosexual Men, 1885–1967* (1991). Garry Wotherspoon, ed., *Being Different* (1986), offers accounts by nine Australian gay men.

Notable works by individual authors include: Samuel R. Delany, *The Motion of Light in Water: Sex and Science Fiction Writing in the East Village, 1957–1965* (1988), Elsa Gidlow, *Elsa, I Came With My Songs: The Autobiography of Elsa Gidlow* (1986), Donald Vining, *A Gay Diary* (1979), Audre Lorde, *Zami: A New Spelling of My Name* (1983), Paul Goodman, *Five Years* (1966), Judy Grahn, *A Woman is Talking to Death* (1977), Cherríe Moraga, *Loving in the War Years* (1983), Anita Cornwall, *Black Lesbian in White America* (1983), Eve Kosofsky Sedgwick, "A Poem is Being Written," *Representations,* #17 (1987), Martin Duberman, *Cures: A Gay Man's Odyssey* (1991), Minnie Bruce Pratt, *Crime Against Nature* (1990), Jackie Goldsby, "What It Means To Be Colored Me," *Out/Look,* Summer (1990), Kitty Tsui, *The Words of a Woman Who Breathes Fire* (1983), Mab Segrest, *My Mama's Dead Squirrel: Lesbian Essays on Southern Culture* (1985), and David Wojnarowicz, *Close to the Knives: A Memoir of Disintegration* (1991).

IV. Collections of source materials. For students who would like to do historically oriented research, there is now a range of easily accessible printed collections of source materials. For the United States, Jonathan Ned Katz, *Gay American History** (1976; rev., with a new bibliographical essay, 1992), a one-volume work, is a handy beginning. Katz also provides a series of more than fifty volumes of reprinted American and modern Western European sources, titled *Homosexuality: Lesbians and Gay Men in Society, History, and Literature* (1975). Randolph Trumbach provides three volumes of documents on sodomy from early modern England: the 1742 version of *Select Trials at the Sessions-House in the Old-Bailey,* 2 vols. (1985), and *Sodomy Trials: Seven Documents* (1986). Lillian Faderman and Brigitte Eriksson, *Lesbian-Feminism in Turn-of-the-Century Germany* (1980), offers documents, in English translation, for the period from about 1895 to about 1921. For key documents of lesbian/gay history from modern Great Britain, see Bob Cant and Susan Hemmings, eds., *Radical Records: Thirty Years of Lesbian and Gay History, 1957–1987* (1988). Winston Leyland, ed., *Gay Roots: Twenty Years of "Gay Sunshine"* (1991), reprints key pieces from a journal which was influential among United States gay men in the 1970s. Ed Jackson and Stan Persky, eds., *Flaunting It: A Decade of Gay Journalism from "The Body Politic"* (1982), similarly reprints key pieces from a Toronto-based journal which was internationally popular among the gay male left during the same period. *"Sinister Wisdom" #43/44: The 15th Anniversary Retrospective* (1991), includes many significant articles, especially of the 1980s, from this journal, which was then, and continues to be, widely read among United States lesbians. Allen Young and Karla Jay, eds., *Out of the Closets: Voices of Gay Liberation, the Twentieth Anniversary Edition* (1992), is a reprint, with a historical introduction by John D'Emilio, of a landmark 1972 collection of articles and credos by United States lesbian/gay liberationists of the Stonewall era.

V. Collections of academic articles by various authors. Martin Bauml Duberman, Martha Vicinus, and George Chauncey, Jr., eds., *Hidden from History: Reclaiming the Gay and Lesbian Past* (1989), is a very useful collection of historical articles, a collection which includes some coverage of South Africa, Japan, China, Russia, and Cuba, as well as Western Europe and the United States. Karla Jay and Joanne Glasgow, eds., *Lesbian Texts and Contexts: Radical Revisions* (1990), is mostly about lesbian literature. Two older anthologies have made, and continue to make, a major impact on contemporary discussions of sexual politics. They are Carole Vance, ed., *Pleasure and Danger: Exploring Female Sexuality* (1984), and Ann Snitow, Christine Stansell, and Sharon Thompson, eds., *Powers of Desire: The Politics of Sexuality* (1983). Robert Boyers and George Steiner, eds., *Homosexuality: Sacrilege, Vision, Politics* (1982), is a reprint of a special issue of the journal *Salmagundi,* an issue devoted to lesbian/gay topics. Estelle B. Freedman, Barbara

C. Gelpi, Susan L. Johnson, and Kathleen M. Weston, eds., *The Lesbian Issue: Essays from "Signs"* (1982), is a diverse grouping, perhaps especially strong in the social sciences. Ronald Butters, John M. Clum, and Michael Moon, eds., *Displacing Homophobia: Gay Male Perspectives in Literature and Culture* (1989), has valuable articles on theory and on several authors of the gay male canon, including Wilde, Whitman, and Shakespeare. For a collection which is especially strong in theory and cultural studies, see Diana Fuss, ed., *Inside/Out: Lesbian Theories, Gay Theories** (1991). The Summer 1991 issue of the periodical *differences* is guest-edited by Teresa de Lauretis and titled *Queer Theory: Lesbian and Gay Sexualities.* It includes articles on lesbian s/m and Robert Glück's fiction, among other topics. Dennis Altman, Carole Vance, Martha Vicinus, and Jeffrey Weeks, eds., *Homosexuality, Which Homosexuality?* (1989), is important on history and theory. Jeffner Allen, ed., *Lesbian Philosophies and Cultures* (1990), is largely, as the title indicates, about lesbian philosophy. Simon Shepard and Mick Wallis, eds., *Coming on Strong: Gay Politics and Culture* (1989), is perhaps especially interesting on contemporary gay male cultural politics. *How Do I Look? Queer Film and Video,* by Bad Object Choices (1991), is important on the visual media. Kathy Peiss and Christina Simmons with Robert Padgug, eds., *Passion and Power: Sexuality and History* (1989), is strong on United States lesbian/gay history.

VI. History. The Duberman, Vicinus, and Chauncey collection, cited earlier in Section V, is a good place to begin. For early efforts to think through some of the conceptual issues in lesbian/gay history, see the various articles gathered in *Radical History Review,* 20 (1979). For more recent work on these conceptual issues, see—along with the D'Emilio, Halperin, Scott, and Vicinus essays included in this book, and the Altman, Vance, Vicinus, and Weeks anthology cited earlier in Section V—Lisa Duggan, "History's Gay Ghetto: The Contradictions of Growth in Lesbian and Gay History," in Susan Porter Benson, Steve Brier, and Roy Rosenzweig, eds., *Presenting the Past: Essays on History and the Public* (1986), pp. 281–290.

For male homosexualities in China, see Bret Hinsch, *Passions of the Cut Sleeve: The Male Homosexual Tradition in China* (1990). On Japan see Paul Schalow, tr. and ed., Ihara Saikaku, *The Great Mirror of Male Love* (1990), Gregory M. Pflugfelder, "Strange Fates: Sex, Gender, and Sexuality in *Torikaebaya Monogatari*" in *Monumenta Nipponica,* 47 (1992), and Tsuneo Watanabe and Jun'ichi Iwata, *Love of the Samurai: A Thousand Years of Japanese Homosexuality* (1989). On Russia, see Laura Engelstein, "Lesbian Vignettes: A Russian Triptych from the 1890's," *Signs,* 15 (1990). For Australia, see Robert Aldrich and Garry Wotherspoon, eds., *Gay Perspectives: Essays in Australian Gay Culture* (1992). There is also a helpful account of Sydney: Garry Wotherspoon, *"City of the Plain": A History of a Gay Subculture* (1991). India and Africa are presently better served by anthropological than historical scholarship. For some suggested titles, see Section VII. For Mexico, see Ian Lumsden, *Homosexuality, Society, and the State in Mexico* (1991). For Brazil, see João Trevisan, *Perverts in Paradise* (tr. Foreman, 1986). For Latin America generally during the colonial era, see Asuncion Lavrin, *Sexuality and Marriage in Colonial Latin America* (1989). For early modern Spain, see Rafael Carrasco, *Inquisicion y repression sexual en Valencia: Historia de los sodomitas, 1565–1785* (1985), and for the modern, post-Franco period, Antoni Mirabet i Mullol, *Homosexualidad Hoy* (1985). Winston Leyland, ed., Ahmad al-Tifashi, *The Delight of Hearts* (tr. Lacey, 1988), provides some guidance on medieval Islamic history and culture. For male homosexualities in the contemporary Islamic world, see Arno Schmitt and Jehoeda Sofer, eds., *Sexuality and Eroticism among Males in Moslem Societies* (1992).

On medieval France, and indeed on Christian medieval Europe as a whole, see John Boswell, *Christianity, Social Tolerance, and Homosexuality: Gay People in Western Europe from the Beginning of the Christian Era to the Fourteenth Century* (1980). Philippe Ariès and André Béjin, eds., *Western Sexuality: Practice and Precept in Past and Present Times* (1985), includes essays on topics, mostly European, from antiquity to the twentieth century. D.A. Coward, "Attitudes to Homosexuality in Eighteenth-Century France," *Journal of European Studies,* 10 (1980), has some materials on the French Enlightenment, as do Robert Maccubbin, ed., *'Tis Nature's Fault: Unauthorized Sexual Behavior During the Enlightenment* (1987), and Roy Porter and G.S. Rousseau, eds., *Sexual Underworlds of the Enlightenment* (1988). Michel Foucault, *The History of Sexuality: An Introduction, Vol. I* (tr. Hurley, 1978), is related perhaps centrally to early modern France, but it is also important as a contribution to theory; and it has decisively influenced recent writing concerned with many different topics and periods. On the era following World War II in France, see Jacques Girard, *Le mouvement homosexuel en France, 1945–1980* (1981). For an account of the rise of the movement in French-speaking Canada, see Paul François Sylvestre, *Les homosexuels s'organisent* (1979).

On modern German history there are three valuable general works: Hans-Georg Stumke and Rudi Finkler, *Rosa Winkel, Rosa Listen* (1981), *Eldorado,* by the Berlin Museum (1984), a finely illustrated book based on an exhibition, sponsored by this museum, on German lesbian/gay life from about 1850 to about 1950, and Hans-Georg Stumke, *Homosexuelle in Deutschland: Eine politische Geschichte* (1989). See also John Lauritsen and David Thorstad, *The Early Homosexual Rights Movement, 1864–1935* (1974), James Steakley, *The Homosexual Emancipation Movement in Germany* (2nd ed., 1982), Isabel Hull, *The Entourage of Kaiser Wilhelm II, 1888–1918* (1982), John Fout, "Sexual Politics in Wilhelmine Germany: The Male Gender Crisis, Moral Purity, and Homophobia," *Journal of the History of Sexuality,* 2 (1992), Hubert Kennedy, *Ulrichs: The Life and Works of Karl Heinrich Ulrichs, Pioneer of the Modern Gay Movement* (1988), George Mosse, *Nationalism and Sexuality: Middle-Class Morality and Sexual Norms in Modern Europe* (1985), Heinz Heger, *The Men with the Pink Triangle* (tr. Fernbach, 1980), Richard Plant, *The Pink Triangle: The Nazi War Against Homosexuality* (1986), and, on the lesbian movement of the early 1970s, Ilse Kokula, *Der Kampf gegen Unterdrückung* (1975). On Italy, see Judith Brown, *Immodest Acts: The Life of a Lesbian Nun in Renaissance Italy* (1986), James M. Saslow, *Ganymede in the Renaissance: Homosexuality in Art and Society* (1986), and Guido Ruggiero, *The Boundaries of Eros: Sex, Crime, and Sexuality in Renaissance Venice* (1985). Kent Gerard and Gert Hekma, eds., *The Pursuit of Sodomy: Male Homosexuality in Renaissance and Enlightenment Europe* (1988), includes articles on the Netherlands and on many other European societies as well.

Alan Bray is the author of two important publications on early modern Great Britain: *Homosexuality in Renaissance England* (1982), and "Homosexuality and the Signs of Male Friendship in Elizabethan England," *History Workshop Journal,* #29 (1990). Mary McIntosh's "The Homosexual Role," *Social Problems,* 16 (1968), is a wide-ranging essay in historical sociology, an essay which has been very influential, particularly on historical writing in England and the United States. G.S. Rousseau, *Perilous Enlightenment* (1991), collects this author's diverse essays on sex in eighteenth-century England. Henry Abelove, *The Evangelist of Desire: John Wesley and the Methodists* (1990), discusses the construction of sex in an eighteenth-century religious community. For an effort to account for the beginnings of heterosexuality, see Abelove's essay "Towards a History of Sexual Intercourse During the Long Eighteenth Century in England," in Andrew Parker, Mary Russo, Doris Sommer, and Patricia Yaeger, eds., *Nationalisms and Sexualities* (1991), pp. 335–342. Jeffrey Weeks, *Sex, Politics, and Society: The Regulation of Sexuality Since 1800*

(1981), is valuable, as is also the same author's history of the development of the lesbian/gay liberation movement in England, *Coming Out: Homosexual Politics in Britain, from the Nineteenth Century to the Present* (1977). Lillian Faderman, *Surpassing the Love of Men: Romantic Friendship and Love between Women from the Renaissance to the Present* (1981), includes materials on Great Britain and on other societies, too. For more on Great Britain, see Martha Vicinus, *Independent Women: Work and Community for Single Women, 1850–1920* (1985), Frank Mort, *Dangerous Sexualities: Medico-moral Politics in England Since 1830* (1987), Andrew Hodges, *Alan Turing: The Enigma* (1983), and Kobena Mercer, "Welcome to the Jungle: Identity and Diversity in Postmodern Politics," in Jonathan Rutherford, ed., *Identity: Community, Culture, Difference* (1990), pp. 43–71.

John D'Emilio and Estelle B. Freedman, *Intimate Matters: A History of Sexuality in America** (1988), is an interpretive overview which includes much material on United States lesbian/gay history. So, too, does the Peiss, Simmons, and Padgug anthology cited earlier in Section V. On the colonial period in the Southwest, see Ramón A. Gutiérrez, *When Jesus Came, the Corn Mothers Went Away: Marriage, Sexuality, and Power in New Mexico, 1500–1846* (1990).

Carroll Smith-Rosenberg, *Disorderly Conduct: Visions of Gender in Victorian America* (1985), is a collection of essays by this pioneering author. Martin Duberman's essays are collected in *About Time: Exploring the Gay Past* (2nd ed., 1991), and John D'Emilio's in *Making Trouble: Essays on History, Politics, and the University* (1992). D'Emilio is also the author of an account of the rise of the United States lesbian/gay movement: *Sexual Politics, Sexual Communities: The Making of a Homosexual Minority in the United States, 1940–1970* (1983). For more on United States history, see Lillian Faderman, *Odd Girls and Twilight Lovers: A History of Lesbian Life in Twentieth-Century America* (1991), Allan Bérubé, *Coming Out Under Fire: Gay Men and Women During World War II* (1990), George Chauncey, Jr., "The Policed: Gay Men's Strategies of Everyday Resistance," in William R. Taylor, ed., *Inventing Times Square: Commerce and Culture at the Crossroads of the World* (1991), pp. 315–328, Blanche Wiesen Cook, *Eleanor Roosevelt* (1992), Katie King, "The Situation of Lesbianism as Feminism's Magical Sign: Contests for Meaning and the U.S. Women's Movement, 1968–1972," *Communication,* 9 (1986), Alice Echols, *Daring To Be Bad: Radical Feminism in America, 1967–1975* (1989), Donn Teal, *The Gay Militants* (1971), Stuart Timmons, *The Trouble with Harry Hay: Founder of the Modern Gay Movement* (1990), Dennis Altman, *The Homosexualization of America* (1982), John Mitzel, *The Boston Sex Scandal* (1980), and Jonathan Ned Katz, "the Invention of Heterosexuality," *Socialist Review,* 21 (1990). Salvatore Licata and Robert P. Peterson, eds., *The Gay Past: A Collection of Historical Essays* (1985), includes materials on the United States and other societies as well. For a contribution to contemporary intellectual history, see Lawrence Mass, *Dialogues of the Sexual Revolution,* 2 vols. (1990), which includes interviews with some lesbian/gay studies scholars.

VII. Anthropology. Along with the Whitehead article in this book, see also, on the Native American berdache, Walter Williams, *The Spirit and the Flesh: Sexual Diversity in American Indian Culture* (1986), Ramón A. Gutiérrez, "Must We Deracinate Indians to Find Gay Roots?," *Out/Look,* Winter (1989), Will Roscoe, *The Zuni Man-Woman* (1991), and Jonathan Goldberg, "Sodomy in the New World: Anthropologies Old and New," *Social Text,* 9 (1991). For more on the anthropology of North America, see Esther Newton, *Mother Camp: Female Impersonators in America* (2nd ed., 1979), Kenneth Read, *Other Voices: The Style of a Male Homosexual Tavern* (1980), which focuses on a North-western United States city, and Gayle S. Rubin, "The Catacombs: A Temple of the

Butthole," in Mark Thompson, ed., *Leatherfolk: Radical Sex, People, Politics, and Practice* (1991), pp. 119–141, an account of a San Francisco fist-fucking club.

For two contributions to the anthropology of Africa, see Gill Shepherd, "Rank, Gender, and Homosexuality: Mombasa as a Key to Understanding Sexual Options," in Pat Caplan, ed., *The Cultural Construction of Sexuality* (1987), pp. 240–270, and Malek Chebel, *L'esprit de sérail: perversions et marginalités sexuelles au Maghreb* (1988). On India, see Serena Nanda, *Neither Man Nor Woman: The Hijras of India* (1988)—from which an excerpt appears in this book, Owen M. Lynch, ed., *Divine Passions: The Social Construction of Emotions in India* (1990), and Suddhir Kakar, *Intimate Relations: Exploring Indian Sexuality*. On Melanesia, see Gilbert Herdt, ed., *Ritualized Homosexuality in Melanesia* (1984), *The Sambia: Ritual and Gender in New Guinea* (1987), and *Guardians of the Flutes: Idioms of Masculinity* (1981). On Japan, see Jennifer Robertson, "Gender-Bending in Paradise: Doing 'Female' and 'Male' in Japan," *Genders*, #5 (1989). For a study on Brazil, see Richard Parker, *Bodies, Pleasures, and Passions: Sexual Culture in Contemporary Brazil* (1991). Roger N. Lancaster's essay on Nicaragua, "Subject Honor and Object Shame: The Construction of Male Homosexuality and Stigma in Nicaragua," *Ethnology*, 27 (1988), is often cited. Jürgen Lemke provides a study of contemporary gay men in what was until recently East Germany: *Gay Voices from East Germany* (ed. Borneman, 1991). For a comparative approach, see Frederic L. Whitam and Robin M. Mathy, *Male Homosexuality in Four Societies: Brazil, Guatemala, the Philippines, and the United States* (1986). Sherry Ortner and Harriet Whitehead, eds., *Sexual Meanings: The Cultural Construction of Gender and Sexuality* (1981), includes valuable pieces on several different cultures, as does also Evelyn Blackwood, ed., *Anthropology and Homosexual Behavior* (paperback ed., 1986).

Gilbert Herdt and Robert J. Stoller, *Intimate Communications: Erotics and the Study of Culture** (1990), is general and theoretical. So, too, are Herdt's "Representations of Homosexuality: An Essay on Cultural Ontology and Historical Comparison, Parts I and II," *Journal of the History of Sexuality*, I (1991), and Gayle S. Rubin's deservedly famous essay, "The Traffic in Women: Notes on the 'Political Economy' of Sex," in Rayna Rapp, ed., *Toward an Anthropology of Women* (1975), pp. 157–210.

VIII. Sociology, Psychology. Four early and general sociological studies are Erving Goffman, *Stigma: Notes on the Management of Spoiled Identity* (1963), John H. Gagnon and William Simon, *Sexual Conduct: The Social Sources of Human Sexuality* (1973), Barry D. Adam, *The Survival of Domination: Inferiorization and Everyday Life* (1978), and Kenneth Plummer, ed., *The Making of the Modern Homosexual* (1981). Some more recent general studies include Jeffrey Weeks, *Sexuality and Its Discontents* (1985), David F. Greenberg, *The Construction of Homosexuality** (1988), John DeCecco, ed., *Gay Relationships* (1988), Warren J. Blumenfeld and Diane Raymond, *Looking at Gay and Lesbian Life* (1988), Frederick W. Bozett and Marvin B. Sussman, eds., *Homosexuality and Family Relationships* (1989), and Gilbert Herdt, ed., *Gay and Lesbian Youth* (1989). For studies on the United States, see the early but still useful Laud Humphreys, *Tearoom Trade: Impersonal Sex in Public Places* (2nd ed., 1974), Susan Krieger, *Mirror Dance: Identity in a Women's Community* (1983), Joseph Goodwin, *More Than You'll Ever Be: Gay Folklore and Acculturation in Middle America* (1987), Kath Weston, *Families We Choose: Lesbians, Gays, and Kinship* (1991), Dolores J. Maggiore, ed., *Lesbians and Child Custody: A Casebook* (1992), and Gary David Comstock, *Violence Against Lesbians and Gay Men* (1991). For an essay on Canada, see Barry D. Adam, "The Construction of a Sociological 'Homosexual' in Canadian Textbooks," *Canadian Review of Sociology and Anthropology*, 23 (1986), and for a recent study on South Africa, see Gordon Isaacs and Brian McKendrick, *Male Homosexuality in South Africa: Identity Formation, Culture, and Crisis* (1992).

On psychology a good place to begin is Gregory M. Herek, "The Social Psychology of Homophobia: Toward a Practical Theory," *New York University Review of Law and Social Change*, 14 (1986). See also Suzanne Pharr, *Homophobia: A Weapon of Sexism* (1988), and Warren Blumenfeld, ed., *Homophobia: How We All Pay the Price* (1992). For various perspectives on the psychosocial development of lesbians, see *Lesbian Psychologies*, by the Boston Lesbian Psychologies Collective (1987). For a perspective on the psychosocial development of gay men, see Richard Isay, *Being Homosexual: Gay Men and Their Development* (1989). An early study that may be still useful is Barry Dank, "Coming Out in the Gay World," *Psychiatry*, 34 (1971). On issues in the psychology of education, see Karen Harbeck, ed., *Coming Out of the Classroom Closet: Gay and Lesbian Students, Teachers, and Curricula* (1992), Michèle Aina Barale, "The Lesbian Academic: Negotiating New Boundaries," *Women and Therapy*, 8 (1988), Eve Kosofsky Sedgwick, "Pedagogy in the Context of an Antihomophobic Project," *South Atlantic Quarterly*, 89 (1990), and Michael Lynch, "Last Onsets: Teaching with AIDS," *Profession 90* (1990).

On the ways in which psychologists, physicians, anatomists, psychiatrists, psychoanalysts, and sexologists have over the years viewed and treated us, see, along with the Abelove essay included in this volume, Bert Hansen, "American Physicians' Earliest Writings about Homosexuals, 1880–1900," *Milbank Quarterly*, 67 (1989), Katharine Park and Lorraine J. Daston, "Hermaphrodites in Renaissance France," *Critical Matrix*, 1 (1985), Jennifer Terry, "Lesbians Under the Medical Gaze: Scientists Search for Remarkable Differences," *Journal of Sex Research*, 27 (1990), Ronald Bayer, *Homosexuality and American Psychiatry* (2nd ed., 1987), Arnold I. Davidson, "Closing Up the Corpses: Diseases of Sexuality and the Emergence of the Psychiatric Style of Reasoning," in George Boolos, ed., *Meaning and Method: Essays in Honor of Hilary Putnam* (1990), pp. 295–324, Kenneth Lewes, *The Psychoanalytic Theory of Male Homosexuality* (1988), and Janice Irvine, *Disorders of Desire: Sex and Gender in Modern American Sexology* (1990).

IX. Classics. K.J. Dover, *Greek Homosexuality* (1978), is a pioneering work. Two valuable, more recent works are David M. Halperin, *One Hundred Years of Homosexuality and Other Essays on Greek Love* (1990), and John J. Winkler, *The Constraints of Desire: The Anthropology of Sex and Gender in Ancient Greece* (1990). David M. Halperin, John J. Winkler, and Froma I. Zeitlin, eds., *Before Sexuality: The Construction of Erotic Experience in the Ancient Greek World* (1990), is a collection of key essays. Along with the Winkler essay on Sappho included in this book, see also Eva Stehle Stigers, "Sappho's Private World," in Helene P. Foley, ed., *Reflections of Women in Antiquity* (1981), pp. 45–61. Michel Foucault's two books on antiquity have been, and continue to be, influential: *The Use of Pleasure, The History of Sexuality, Vol. II* (tr. Hurley, 1985), and *The Care of the Self, The History of Sexuality, Vol. III* (tr. Hurley, 1986). Eva Cantarella, *Secondo Natura: La Bissesualità nel Mondo Antico* (1988), is valuable. For more on Greece, see Martin Kilmer, *Greek Erotica on Attic Red-Figure Vases* (1991), Bernard Sergent, *Homosexuality in Greek Myth* (tr. Goldhammer, 1986), Felix Buffière, *Eros Adolescent: la Pédérastie dans la Grèce Antique* (1980), and Mark Golden, *Children and Childhood in Classical Athens* (1990). On ancient Roman culture, see Judith P. Hallett, "Female Homoeroticism and the Denial of Roman Reality in Latin Literature," *Yale Journal of Criticism*, 3 (1989), Saara Lilja, *Homosexuality in Republican and Augustan Rome* (1983), and John R. Clarke, "The Decor of the House of Jupiter and Ganymede at Ostia Antica: Private Residence Turned Gay Hotel?," in Elaine Z. Gazda, ed., *Roman Art in the Private Sphere* (1991), pp. 89–104. On early Christian culture, see Boswell, cited earlier in Section VI, Peter

Brown, *The Body and Society: Men, Women, and Sexual Renunciation in Early Christianity* (1988), and Bernadette J. Brooten, "Paul's Views on the Nature of Women and Female Homoeroticism," in Clarissa W. Atkinson, Constance H. Buchanan, and Margaret Ruth Miles, eds., *Immaculate and Powerful: The Female in Sacred Image and Social Reality* (1985), pp. 51–87.

X. Philosophy. The Allen anthology, cited in Section V, is a good place to begin. Also notable are Marilyn Frye, *The Politics of Reality: Essays in Feminist Theory* (1983), Monique Wittig, *The Lesbian Body* (tr. LeVay, 1975), and *The Straight Mind and Other Essays* (1992)—an excerpt from which appears in this book—and Carol Anne Douglas, *Love and Politics: Radical Feminism and Lesbian Theories* (1990). Judith Butler, *Gender Trouble: Feminism and the Subversion of Identity* (1990), is important as a contribution to many different current discussions in philosophy and theory. Edward Stein, ed., *Forms of Desire: Sexual Orientation and the Social Constructionist Controversy* (paperback ed., 1992), reprints some of the key essays in the dispute—largely historiographic—between the parties usually called essentialists and constructionists. Stein also provides a philosophical introduction. On this dispute, see also Halperin, cited earlier in Section IX, and Diana Fuss, *Essentially Speaking: Feminism, Nature, & Difference* (1989). Richard Mohr, *Gays/Justice: A Study of Ethics, Society, and Law* (1989), is a pioneering contribution to political philosophy. See also Sarah Hoagland, *Lesbian Ethics: Towards New Value* (1988), Joyce Trebilcot, *In Process: Lesbian Radical Essays* (1989), and Claudia Card, "Lesbian Attitudes and 'The Second Sex,' " *Women's Studies International Forum*, 8 (1985), and *Feminist Ethics* (1991), and Annamarie Jagose, "Irigaray and the Lesbian Body: Remedy and Poison," *Genders*, 13 (1992).

XI. Politics, Law. Three early studies are *Homosexuality: Power and Politics*, by the Gay Left Collective (1980), Paul Goodman's 1969 essay, "The Politics of Being Queer," in Taylor Stoehr, ed., *Nature Heals: The Psychological Essays of Paul Goodman* (1977), pp. 216–225, and Toby Marotta, *The Politics of Homosexuality* (1981). Two more recent studies are Shane Phelan, *Identity Politics: Lesbian Feminism and the Limits of Community* (1989), and Margaret Cruikshank, *The Gay and Lesbian Liberation Movement* (1992). Also useful is Charlotte Bunch, *Passionate Politics: Feminist Theory in Action* (1987). Judith Butler and Joan W. Scott, eds., *Feminists Theorize the Political* (1992), is an important collection.

On lesbian/gay political activism worldwide, see Barry D. Adam, *The Rise of a Gay and Lesbian Movement** (1987) and Stephan Likosky, ed., *Coming Out: An Anthology of International Gay and Lesbian Writings* (1992). Randy Shilts, *The Mayor of Castro Street* (1982), treats organizational and electoral politics in San Francisco. Lawrence Murphy, *Perverts By Official Order: The Campaign Against Homosexuals by the United States Navy* (1988), Mary Ann Humphrey, *My Country, My Right to Serve* (1990), and Kate Dyer, ed., *Gays in Uniform: The Pentagon's Secret Reports* (1990), describe the discrimination against lesbians and gay men, and the contemporary struggle to end it, in the United States armed services. On another kind of contemporary political struggle in the United States, see Weston, cited earlier in Section VIII. For an account of the emerging forms of queer politics, see Lisa Duggan, "Making It Perfectly Queer," *Socialist Review*, 22 (1992). Simon Nkoli, "When Mandela Becomes Prime Minister . . . ," *Radical America*, 22 (1991), is a report from South Africa. Gary Indiana, "The Boys in the Baltic: Gay 'Liberation' Comes to the Soviet Union," *Village Voice*, June 26, 1990, is a preliminary journalistic account of a situation which is changing rapidly. Nicholas D. Kristof, "China

Using Electrodes to 'Cure' Homosexuals," *New York Times,* January 29, 1990, provides some information about China. On the AIDS crisis, see Section II.

On sexual politics, see the Rubin essay included in this book, the Vance anthology, and the Snitow, Stansell, and Thompson anthology, both cited earlier in Section V. Other titles include Varda Burstyn, ed., *Women Against Censorship* (1985), *Caught Looking: Feminism, Pornography, and Censorship,* by Caught Looking, Inc. (1988), Carole Vance, "Misunderstanding Obscenity," *Art in America,* May (1990), Janice G. Raymond, *The Sexual Liberals and the Attack on Feminism* (1990), Dennis Cooper, "Square One," in *Wrong* (1992), pp. 81–92, Catherine A. MacKinnon, *Feminism Unmodified: Discourses on Life and Law* (1987), Joan Nestle, ed., *The Persistent Desire: A Femme-Butch Reader* (1992), and *A Restricted Country* (1987), Sheila Jeffreys, *Anti-Climax* (1990), Mario Mieli, *Homosexuality and Liberation: Elements of a Gay Critique* (tr. Fernbach, 1980), the SAMOIS anthology cited earlier in Section III, Robin Linden, Diana E.H. Russell, and Susan Leigh Star, eds., *Against Sadomasochism: A Radical Feminist Analysis* (1983), Geoffrey Mains, *Urban Aboriginals: A Celebration of Leathersexuality* (1991), Guy Hocquenghem, *Homosexual Desire* (1978), Sarah Lucia Hoagland and Julia Penelope, eds., *For Lesbians Only: A Separatist Anthology* (1988), Roland Barthes, *A Lover's Discourse: Fragments* (tr. Howard, 1978), Susie Bright, *Susie Sexpert's Lesbian Sex World* (1990), and *Susie Bright's Sexual Reality: A Virtual Sex World Reader* (1992), Thomas Geller, ed., *Bisexuality: a Reader and a Sourcebook* (1990), John Stoltenberg, *Refusing to Be a Man: Essays on Sex and Justice* (1989), Scott Tucker, "Gender, Fucking, and Utopia: An Essay in Response to John Stoltenberg's 'Refusing to Be a Man,' " *Social Text,* 27 (1990), Gillian E. Hanscombe and Martin Humphries, eds., *Heterosexuality* (1987), Kobena Mercer and Isaac Julien, "Race, Sexual Politics, and Black Masculinity: A Dossier," in Rowena Chapman and Jonathan Rutherford, eds., *Male Order: Unwrapping Masculinity* (1988), pp. 97–164.

Additional titles on sexual politics include Craig Owens, "Outlaws: Gay Men in Feminism," in Alice Jardine and Paul Smith, eds., *Men in Feminism* (1987), pp. 219–232, Ed Cohen, "Foucauldian Necrologies: 'gay' 'politics'? politically gay?," *Textual Practice,* 2 (1988), Daniel Tsang, ed., *The Age Taboo* (1981), Theo Sandfort, Edward Brongersma, and Alex van Naerssen, eds., *Male Intergenerational Intimacy* (1992), Anne Bolin, *In Search of Eve: Transsexual Rites of Passage* (1988), Rudolf M. Dekker and Lotte C. van de Pol, *The Female of Female Transvestism* (1989), and Marjorie Garber, *Vested Interests: Cross-Dressing and Cultural Anxiety* (1992). For an exemplary instance of applied sexual politics, see Pat Califia, *The Advocate Adviser* (1991), a collection of this author's advice columns from *The Advocate.*

On law in the United States, there are two important pieces by Janet E. Halley: "The Politics of the Closet: Towards Equal Protection for Gay, Lesbian, and Bisexual Identity," *UCLA Law Review,* 36 (1989), and "Misreading Sodomy: A Critique of the Classification of 'Homosexuals' in Federal Equal Protection Law," in Julia Epstein and Kristina Straub, eds., *Body Guards: The Cultural Politics of Gender Ambiguity* (1991), pp. 351–377. See also Mohr, cited earlier in Section X, Cass R. Sunstein, "Sexual Orientation and the Constitution: A Note on the Relationship Between Due Process and Equal Protection," *University of Chicago Law Review,* 55 (1988), and *Sexual Orientation and the Law,* by the editors of the *Harvard Law Review* (1990). For law in Canada, see the thoughtful study by Gary Kinsman, *The Regulation of Desire: Sexuality in Canada* (1987). Finally, for up-to-date and ongoing information and analysis on all the political and legal issues touched on in this bibliography, see the community newspapers and periodicals listed in Section I.

XII. Literary Studies. Jeannette Foster, *Sex Variant Women in Literature* (1956), is a foundational work of comprehensive scope. Jonathan Dollimore, *Sexual Dissidence:*

Augustine to Wilde, Freud to Foucault (1991), provides extended coverage of the gay male canon. Five general and theoretical works are Marylin R. Farwell, "Toward a Definition of the Lesbian Literary Imagination," *Signs,* 14 (1988), Harold Beaver, "Homosexual Signs (In Memory of Roland Barthes)," *Critical Inquiry,* 8 (1981–82), Lee Edelman, "Homographesis," *Yale Journal of Criticism,* 3 (1989), Judith Roof, *A Lure of Knowledge: Lesbian Sexuality and Theory* (1991), and Jean E. Kennard, "Ourself Behind Ourself: A Theory for Lesbian Readers," in Elizabeth A. Flynn and Patrocinio Schweickart, eds., *Gender and Reading: Essays on Readers, Texts, and Contexts* (1985), pp. 63–80. There are also six general and diverse collections: the Jay and Glasgow anthology and the Butters, Clum, and Moon anthology, both cited earlier in Section V, Monika Kehoe, ed., *Historical, Literary, and Erotic Aspects of Lesbianism* (1986), Stuart Kellogg, ed., *Literary Visions of Homosexuality* (1983), Joseph Boone and Michael Cadden, eds., *Engendering Men: The Question of Male Feminist Criticism* (1990), and Mark Lilly, ed., *Lesbian and Gay Writing: An Anthology of Critical Essays* (1990). For a collection of some women's accounts of their experiences as writers, see Betsy Warland, ed., *InVersions: Writing by Dykes, Queers, and Lesbians* (1991). In a similar vein, see also Adrienne Rich, *On Lies, Secrets, and Silences: Selected Prose, 1966–1978* (1979).

On Spanish-language literatures, see Paul Julian Smith, *The Body Hispanic: Gender and Sexuality in Spanish and Spanish-American Literature* (1989), Brianda Domecq, *Acechando al unicornio: La virginidad en la literature mexicana* (1988), Sergio Ortega, *De la santidad a la perversion, o de porque no se cumplia la ley de Dios en la sociedad novohispana* (1986), David William Foster, *Gay and Lesbian Themes in Latin American Writing* (1991), and Sylvia Molloy, "Too Wilde for Comfort: Desire and Ideology in Fin-de-Siècle Spanish America," *Social Text,* 10 (1992). For a contribution on African literatures, see Chris Dunton, " 'Wheyting Be Dat?' The Treatment of Homosexuality in African Literature," *Research in African Literature,* 20 (1989). For a contribution on Japanese literature, see Earl Jackson, "Kabuki Narratives of Male Homoerotic Desire in Saikaku and Mishima," *Theatre Journal,* 41 (1989). On German literature, see Tomas Vollhaber, *Das Nichts, Die Angst, Die Erfahrung: Untersuchung zur zeitgenössischen schwulen Literatur* (1987), Marita Keilson-Lauritz, *Von der Liebe die Freundschaft heisst: zur Homoerotik im Werk Stefan Georges* (1987), Paul Derks, *Die Schande der Heiligen Päderastie: Homosexualität und Hoffentlichkeit in der deutschen Literatur 1750–1850* (1990), and James W. Jones, *"We of the Third Sex"—Literary Representations of Homosexuality in Wilhelmine Germany* (1990).

On early and early modern British literature, see Carolyn Dinshaw, *Chaucer's Sexual Poetics* (1989), Leonard Barkan, *Transuming Passion: Ganymede and the Erotics of Humanism* (1991), Joseph Pequiney, *Such is My Love: A Study of Shakespeare's Sonnets* (1987), Bruce R. Smith, *Homosexual Desire in Shakespeare's England: A Cultural Poetics* (1991), Gregory W. Bredbeck, *Sodomy and Interpretation: Marlowe to Milton* (1991), Jonathan Goldberg, "Bradford's Ancient Members and a Case of Buggery . . . Amongst Them," pp. 60–76 in the Parker, Russo, Sommer, and Yaeger anthology cited earlier in Section VI, Valerie Traub, *Desire and Anxiety: Circulations of Sexuality in Shakespearean Drama* (1992), Jonathan Dollimore, "Subjectivity, Sexuality, and Transgression: The Jacobean Connection," in *Renaissance Drama,* 17 (1986), and James Holstun, " 'Will You Rend Our Ancient Love Asunder?': Lesbian Elegy in Donne, Marvell, and Milton," *ELH,* 54 (1987). On the Restoration and eighteenth century, see Laurence Senelick, "Mollies or Men of Mode? Sodomy and the Eighteenth-Century London Stage," *Journal of the History of Sexuality,* 17 (1990), Claude J. Summers, ed., *Homosexuality in Renaissance and Enlightenment England: Literary Representations in Historical Context* (1992), Michael Kimmel, ed., *Love Letters Between a Certain Late Nobleman and the Famous Mr. Wilson* (1990), Kristina Straub, *Sexual Subjects: Eighteenth-Century Players and Sexual Ideology* (1992), and George

E. Haggerty, "Literature and Homosexuality in the Late Eighteenth Century: Walpole, Beckford, and Lewis," *Studies in the Novel,* 18 (1987). On Byron, see Louis Crompton, *Byron and Greek Love: Homophobia in Nineteenth-Century England* (1985), Jerome Christensen, "Setting Byron Straight: Class, Sexuality, and the Poet," in Elaine Scarry, ed., *Literature and the Body* (1988), pp. 125–159, and Susan J. Wolfson, " 'Their She Condition': Cross-Dressing and the Politics of Gender in *Don Juan,*" *ELH,* 54 (1987). See also D.A. Miller, "The Late Jane Austen," *Raritan,* 10 (1990).

Two books by Eve Kosofsky Sedgwick have been, and continue to be, deservedly influential. *Between Men: English Literature and Male Homosocial Desire* (1985), begins with Shakespeare and ends with the twentieth century, but it is perhaps best known for its contribution to theory and for its treatment of nineteenth-century English fiction. *Epistemology of the Closet* (1990), which is excerpted in this book, is also important as a contribution to theory. In addition *Epistemology* provides readings of James, Melville, Nietzsche, and Proust, among others. For more on the British nineteenth century, see Richard Dellamora, *Masculine Desire: The Sexual Politics of Victorian Aestheticism* (1990), Wayne Koestenbaum, *Double Talk: The Erotics of Male Literary Collaboration* (1989), Christopher Craft, " 'Descend, and Touch, and Enter': Tennyson's Strange Manner of Address," *Genders,* 1 (1988), Terry Castle, "Marie Antoinette Obsession," *Representations,* #38 (1992), Joseph Litvak, *Caught in the Act: Theatricality in the Nineteenth-Century English Novel* (1992), Jeff Nunokawa, "*In Memoriam* and the Extinction of the Homosexual," *ELH,* 58 (1991), Linda Dowling, "Ruskin's Pied Beauty and the Constitution of a 'Homosexual' Code," *Victorian Newsletter,* 75 (1989), Timothy D'Arch Smith, *Love in Earnest: Some Notes on the Lives and Writings of English 'Uranian' Poets from 1889 to 1930* (1970), and D.A. Miller, *The Novel and the Police* (1988). For some valuable works on Wilde, see Ed Cohen, "Writing Gone Wilde: Homoerotic Desire in the Closet of Representation," *P.M.L.A.,* 102 (1987), Kevin Kopelson, "Wilde, Barthes, and the Orgasmics of Truth," *Genders,* 7 (1990), and Neil Bartlett, *Who Was That Man? A Present for Mr. Oscar Wilde* (1989). On Virginia Woolf, see Sherron E. Knopp, " 'If I Saw You Would You Kiss Me': Sapphism and the Subversiveness of Virginia Woolf's *Orlando,*" *P.M.L.A.,* 103 (1988), and Jane Marcus, *Virginia Woolf and the Languages of Patriarchy* (1987). On Radclyffe Hall, see Michael Baker, *Our Three Selves: The Life of Radclyffe Hall* (1985), and Jean Radford, "An Inverted Romance: *The Well of Loneliness* and Sexual Ideology," in Jean Radford, ed., *The Politics of Popular Fiction* (1986), pp. 97–111. See also Jan Hokenson, "The Pronouns of Gomorrah: A Lesbian Prose Tradition," *Frontiers,* 10 (1988), Martin Taylor, *Lads: Love Poetry of the Trenches* (1989), P.N. Furbank, *E.M. Forster: A Life,* 2 vols. (1977, 1978), Sara Suleri, *The Rhetoric of English India* (1992), Sally Munt, ed., *New Lesbian Criticism: Literary and Cultural Readings* (1992), and Gregory Woods, *Articulate Flesh: Male Homo-eroticism and Modern Poetry* (1987). For an account of the gay male stage in twentieth-century Great Britain and the United States as well, see John M. Clum, *Acting Gay: Male Homosexuality in Modern Drama* (1992). For some recent developments in Great Britain, see Alan Sinfield, "Closet Dramas: Homosexual Representation and Class in Postwar British Theater," *Genders,* 9 (1990).

On United States fiction, see Bonnie Zimmerman, *The Safe Sea of Women: Lesbian Fiction, 1969–1989* (1990), Juan Bruce-Novoa, "Homosexuality and the Chicano Novel," *Confluencia,* 2 (1986), Roger Austen, *Playing the Game: The Homosexual Novel in America* (1977), Joseph Boone, *Tradition Counter Tradition: Love and the Form of Fiction* (1987), Sharon O'Brien, *Willa Cather: The Emerging Voice* (1987), Robert K. Martin, *Hero, Captain, and Stranger: Male Friendship, Social Critique, and Literary Form in the Sea Novels of Herman Melville* (1986), Michael Moon, " 'The Gentle Boy from the Dangerous Classes': Pederasty, Domesticity, and Capitalism in Horatio Alger," *Representations,* #19,

(1987), Claude J. Summers, *Gay Fictions, Wilde to Stonewall: Studies in a Male Homosexual Literary Tradition* (1990), Barbara Smith, "The Truth That Never Hurts: Black Lesbians in Fiction in the 1980's," in Joanne M. Braxton and Andree Nicola McLaughlin, eds., *Wild Women in the Whirlwind: Afra-American Culture and the Contemporary Literary Renaissance* (1990), pp. 213–245, David Bergman, *Gaiety Transfigured: Gay Self-Representation in American Literature* (1991), and Catharine R. Stimpson, *Where the Meanings Are: Feminism and Cultural Spaces* (1988). On Thoreau, see Michael Warner, "Walden's Erotic Economy," in Hortense Spillers, ed., *Comparative American Identities: Race, Sex, and Nationality in the Modern Text* (1991), pp. 157–174; on Djuna Barnes, Mary Lynn Broe, ed., *Silence and Power: A Reevaluation of Djuna Barnes* (1991); and on Charles Warren Stoddard, Roger Austen, *Genteel Pagan: The Double Life of Charles Warren Stoddard* (1991).

On United States poets and poetry, see Gloria T. Hull, *Color, Sex, and Poetry: Three Women Writers of the Harlem Renaissance* (1987), from which an excerpt appears in this book; Hull's essay, "Living on the Line: Audre Lorde and 'Our Dead Behind Us,' " in Cheryl A. Wall, ed., *Changing Our Own Words: Essays on Criticism, Theory, and Writing by Black Women* (1989), pp. 150–172; and the Yarbro-Bejarano piece included in this book. See also Robert K. Martin, ed., *The Continuing Presence of Walt Whitman: The Life after the Life* (1992), and *The Homosexual Tradition in American Poetry* (1979), Paula Bennett, *Emily Dickinson: Woman Poet* (1990), Michael Moon, *Disseminating Whitman: Revision and Corporeality in* Leaves of Grass (1991), Michael Lynch, " 'Here is Adhesiveness': From Friendship to Homosexuality," *Victorian Studies,* 29 (1985), Charles Shively, *Drum Beats: Walt Whitman's Civil War Boy Lovers* (1989), Judy Grahn, *The Highest Apple: Sappho and the Lesbian Poetic Tradition* (1985), and Thomas E. Yingling, *Hart Crane and the Homosexual Text: New Thresholds, New Anatomies* (1990).

On French literature, see the early collection by George Stambolian and Elaine Marks, eds., *Homosexualities and French Literature* (1979), Joan DeJean, *Fictions of Sappho, 1546–1937* (1989), Emily S. Apter, *André Gide and the Codes of Homotextuality* (1987), Michael Lucey, "The Consequence of Being Explicit: Watching Sex in Gide's *Si le grain ne meurt,*" *Yale Journal of Criticism,* 4 (1990), Karla Jay, *The Amazon and the Page: Natalie Clifford Barney and Renée Vivien* (1988), Gayle S. Rubin's "Introduction" to Renée Vivien, *A Woman Appeared to Me* (tr. Foster, 1976), pp. iii–xix, Shari Benstock, *Women of the Left Bank: Paris, 1900–1940* (1986), Michael Wilson, " 'Sans les femmes, qu'est-ce qui nous resterait?' Gender and Transgression in Bohemian Montmartre," pp. 195–222 in Epstein and Straub, cited earlier in Section XI, and D.A. Miller, *Bringing Out Roland Barthes* (1992), and "Body Bildung and Textual Liberation," in Denis Hollier, ed., *A New History of French Literature* (1989), pp. 681–687. For Proust, compare J.E. Rivers, *Proust and the Art of Love: The Aesthetics of Sexuality in the Life, Times, and Art of Marcel Proust* (1980), and Sedgwick's *Epistemology,* cited earlier in this section. See also Leo Bersani, *The Culture of Redemption* (1990), and Kaja Silverman, *Male Subjectivity at the Margins* (1992). On French Canadian fiction, see Robert Schwartzwald, "Fear of Federasty: Quebec's Inverted Fictions," pp. 175–195 in Spillers, cited earlier in this section.

XIII. Cultural Studies. A good place to begin is the Fuss anthology, cited earlier in Section III. On film there are now several valuable studies: Vito Russo, *The Celluloid Closet: Homosexuality in the Movies* (rev. ed., 1987), Teresa de Lauretis, *Technologies of Gender: Essays in Theory, Film, and Fiction* (1987), Michael Moon, "Flaming Closets," *October,* 51 (1989), Richard Dyer, *Heavenly Bodies: Film Stars and Society* (1986) and *Now You See It: Studies in Lesbian and Gay Film* (1990), Peter Steven, ed., *Jump Cut: Hollywood, Politics, and Counter Cinema* (1985), *Camera Obscura,* #25–26 (1991), and the Bad Object Choices anthology, cited earlier in Section V. On opera, see Wayne Koestenbaum, "Opera and Homosexuality: Seven Arias," *Yale Journal of Criticism,* 5 (1991). On television, see, along with the Torres article included in this book, Larry Gross, "Sexual Minorities and the Mass Media," in Ellen Seiter, Hans Borchers, Gabrielle Kreutzner, and Eve-Maria Worth, eds., *Remote Control: Television, Audiences, and Cultural Power* (1990), pp. 130–149.

On performance, see Sue-Ellen Case, ed., *Performing Feminisms: Feminist Critical Theory and Theater* (1990), from which the de Lauretis essay included in this volume is reprinted. See also Sue-Ellen Case, *Feminism and Theater* (1988), Jill Dolan, *The Feminist as Spectator* (1988), and "Breaking the Code: Musings on Lesbian Sexuality and the Performer," *Modern Drama,* 32 (1989), Lynda Hart, ed., *Making a Spectacle: Feminist Essays on Contemporary Women's Theater* (1988), and Kate Davy, "Constructing the Spectator: Reception, Context, and Address in Lesbian Performance," *Performing Arts Journal,* 10 (1986). On sport, there are two useful books: Helen Lenskyj, *Out of Bounds: Women, Sport, and Sexuality* (1986), and Brian Pronger, *The Arena of Masculinity: Sports, Homosexuality, and the Meaning of Sex* (1990). On dance music, see Anthony Thomas: "The Gay Black Imprint on American Dance Music," *Out/Look,* Summer (1989). On pulp fiction, see, along with the Barale piece included in this volume, Suzanna Danuta Walters, "As Her Hand Crept Slowly Up Her Thigh: Ann Bannon and the Politics of Pulp," *Social Text,* 8 (1989), and Susannah Radstone, ed., *Sweet Dreams: Sexuality, Gender, and Popular Fiction* (1988). On the illustrator Charles Demuth, see Jonathan Weinberg, "Demuth and Difference," *Art in America,* 76 (1988). On camp, see Philip Core, *Camp: The Lie That Tells the Truth* (1984). On lesbian/gay sensibility, compare Judy Grahn, *Another Mother Tongue: Gay Words, Gay Worlds* (1984), and Michael Bronski, *Culture Clash: The Making of Gay Sensibility* (1984).

On photography, there are two general studies: Tessa Boffin and Jean Fraser, eds., *Stolen Glances: Lesbians Take Photographs* (1991), and Peter Weiermair, *The Hidden Image: Photographs of the Male Nude in the Nineteenth and Twentieth Centuries* (1988). See also, along with the Crimp, Mercer, and Meyer pieces reprinted in this book, Judith Butler, "The Force of Fantasy: Feminism, Mapplethorpe, and Discursive Excess," *differences,* 2 (1990), and Paul Morrison, "Coffee Table Sex: Robert Mapplethorpe and the Sadomasochism of Everyday Life," *Genders,* 11 (1991). On painting and sculpture, see Emmanuel Cooper, *The Sexual Perspective: Homosexuality and Art in the Last One Hundred Years in the West* (1986).

Postcript: This bibliographical essay was completed in August 1992. It surveys only those books and articles which had then been published. Much, much more work in lesbian/gay studies is about to appear.